THE BEGUINES AND BEGHARDS
IN MEDIEVAL CULTURE

The BEGUINES and BEGHARDS
IN MEDIEVAL CULTURE

With special emphasis on the
Belgian scene

Ernest W. McDonnell

1969
OCTAGON BOOKS
New York

Originally published in 1954

Reprinted 1969
by special arrangement with Rutgers University Press

OCTAGON BOOKS
A DIVISION OF FARRAR, STRAUS & GIROUX, INC.
19 Union Square West
New York, N. Y. 10003

AM

LIBRARY OF CONGRESS CATALOG CARD NUMBER: 72-96187

Printed in U.S.A. by
TAYLOR PUBLISHING COMPANY
DALLAS, TEXAS

To My Mother

Preface

In the wake of Gregorian Reform Western Europe was subjected to continuous waves of religious excitement, sometimes assuming substantial proportions, sometimes of merely local significance. It aimed at the renewal of original monastic ideals or, responding to the spiritual needs of urban centers, demanded within the world a recovery of the primitive church and emulation of the apostolic life. But the reform movement early became bifurcated: those who preached submission to the hierarchy and acceptance of the sacraments of the Church were challenged by others who openly revolted against the established ecclesiastical order. Shortcomings of the *ordo* convinced many a layman that he might better find assurance of salvation by nonecclesiastical paths. Thus older monachism and parochial authority alike met increasing competition from semireligious or extraregulars who ran the gamut from undivided obedience to canonical prescriptions to public flouting of their validity. Lay spirituality often testifies to lively religious sensibilities injured by current abuses.

Semireligious activity assumed a variety of forms, and motives are complex. Aims and methods, although bearing a similarity due to identical environment, are sufficiently individual to warrant a careful examination of each movement or confraternity. Whereas these manifestations of popular piety in southern Europe are well known in the English-speaking world, the beguines have received but one monographic treatment, this at the hands of Professor Dayton Philips. French, German, and Dutch-Flemish students have produced a truly voluminous literature which unfortunately has awakened little response outside the Continent. As the masculine counterpart, the beghards, on the contrary, have nowhere been awarded the same attention.

These brotherhoods and sisterhoods have evoked manifold interpretation in contemporary record as well as in modern scholarship. Nor was it by any means peculiar to the Clementine era that the terms *beguine* and *beghard* should be applied generically, often with the slightest appreciation of a particular kind of extraregular discipline or social organism. For some historians they have loomed large in the history of lay piety, a chapter in sectarianism adumbrating the Protestant Reformation. For others they acted, particularly in the diocese of

Liége, as a counterpoise to heretical currents. For some their origins and organization are to be sought primarily in socioeconomic motivation, an essay in corporate life answering the needs of the poor or the maladjusted. Still others have treated them with purely devotional considerations, an object lesson in moral-didactic values. It is a theme that has appealed alike to the moralist who wishes to instruct even as the hagiographer did and to the sentimentalist who is motivated by religious, patriotic, or antiquarian interests. But sentiment and didacticism are poor masters of discrimination. While German scholarship, despite occasional narrow interpretation, has been uniformly sound, consistent with the best historical canons, Belgian contributions include, alongside certain fundamental works, much literature dictated by such devotional-didactic and provincial interests. It is precisely this type of treatment which nourishes the conviction among the uninformed that this is an esoteric subject, a mere curiosity of the past.

The purpose of this study is twofold: first, to present to the English reader the beguine-beghard movement broadly conceived as a cultural force, and secondly, to examine immediately, with the desirability of a synthetic treatment in mind, the three types of sources: 1) hagiographical and literary references; 2) the Roman bullarium, conciliar legislation, and chronicles; and 3) testaments, property deeds, and town ordinances. Each category poses peculiar problems; each sheds light on a particular facet of the subject. While the multiplication of beguine houses in north European towns and the high frequency and rich diversity of comment from all sections of medieval society testify to a vigorous, ample movement, the multifarious application of the terms, with numerous synonyms and corruptions, readily confirms its heterogeneous and complex character. To regard it merely as a study in charity and the poor problem, specifically with reference to the *Frauenfrage* of the Middle Ages, or to present it simply as an exercise in moral instruction does a grave injustice to a phenomenon manifesting itself in industry, canon law, parochial organization, learning and literacy, politics, and spirituality of the Cistercian, Dominican, or Franciscan variety or the nonconformist. For invaluable guidance and penetrating insight the author is deeply indebted in particular to the Europeanwide perspective of Herbert Grundmann and, more recently, Alcantara Mens, the institutional analysis of L. J. M. Philippen, the pregnant research of Joseph Greven, together with the fresh re-examination of the Nivelles question by R. Hanon de Louvet, and the illuminating interpretation of Cistercian hagiography and spirituality by Simone Roisin.

It has not been the intention of the author to pursue the movement farther than 1500, with 1400 serving more or less as the terminus. Even though the beguinage continued to flourish in Belgian cities until the

French Revolution, and in some places even to the present, the first
two hundred years after Mary of Oignies had already witnessed the
transformation of spontaneity, which likened the movement so closely
to the enthusiasm, even joyousness, of the Franciscan, to institutionalization. Such crystallizing was dictated partly by persecution which
compelled justification and defense, partly by a gradual development
into refuges for the socially dispossessed and infirm, and of course in
no small measure by the inability of original zeal to perpetuate itself.

The terms *Belgium* and *Belgians* are utilized here only for the sake
of convenience. They could be little else in an age which recognized
ill-defined boundaries, overlapping jurisdictions, competition between
the authority of the universal Church and more modest political units,
and overlordship from Empire and Kingdom. Furthermore, the author
has sometimes seen fit to discuss certain towns or areas in the light of
contemporary political experience. Breda and Bois-le-Duc, just inside
the present Dutch frontier, lay then within the jurisdiction of the
bishop of Liége. Valenciennes, once the capital of Hainault, Lille, St.
Omer, Cambrai, and Douai were originally within the competence of
the counts of Flanders and Hainault.

In addition to the written word, those scholars and friends who have
made this study possible by personal counsel and encouragement are
too numerous to acknowledge in completeness. However, special gratitude must be expressed to Professor Henry S. Lucas, of the University of Washington, to whom the author owes his first introduction
to medieval culture and the exactions of historical scholarship. Indeed,
the possibilities of this study were first glimpsed under his tutelage
before the war. It was Professor R. L. Reynolds, of the University of
Wisconsin, who continued the process of formation. Others who have
been generous in time and counsel are Professors François Ganshof
of the University of Ghent and Paul Bonenfant of the University of
Brussels. Professor Peter Charanis, with whom it has been the author's
good fortune to be associated as an office-mate at Rutgers University,
has been a source of constant encouragement and unstinting help-
fulness.

The author feels a peculiar indebtedness to the Belgian-American
Educational Foundation for making available a most rewarding year
of research and field work in Belgium during the academic year 1950–
1951. Not only did the Research Council of Rutgers University provide a grant to tap materials in the New York and Princeton areas
but, together with the Calm Foundation at Rutgers, it has largely
met the cost of publication. Important assistance was rendered by Dr.
Mason W. Gross, provost of the University.

Full cooperation has always been extended by the staffs of the
libraries of the Universities of Washington (Seattle), Brussels, Wiscon-

sin, Rutgers, Columbia, and Princeton, as well as Union Theological
Seminary, Princeton Theological Seminary, the Bollandists in Brussels,
the New York Public library, and above all, Gardner A. Sage library
in New Brunswick, N. J. For the Belgian scene the Bibliothèque
Royale de Belgique at Brussels offered an unparalleled fund of both
published and unpublished materials. The staff of the Archives Générales du Royaume de Belgique and Mme. Bonenfant, director of the
Archives de l'Assistance Publique de Bruxelles, lent ready assistance
in the project. To Mrs. Eleanor Vuoncino I express gratitude for
clerical assistance.

Alongside such acknowledgment, however, it is necessary promptly
to admit that the conclusions are the author's. For errors in judgment
or mistaken facts he must assume full responsibility.

Rutgers University
New Brunswick, N. J.

                                              ERNEST W. McDONNELL

Abbreviations

AA. SS.	*Acta Sanctorum.*
AAAB.	*Annales de l'académie royale d'archéologie de Belgique.*
AAPB.	*Archives de l'Assistance Publique, Brussels.*
AB.	*Analecta Bollandiana.* Paris-Brussels, 1882ff.
AFH.	*Archivum Franciscanum Historicum.* Florence, 1908ff.
AGR.	*Archives Générales du Royaume, Brussels.*
AHEB.	*Analectes pour servir à l'histoire ecclésiastique de la Belgique.* Louvain, 1864-1913.
AHVN.	*Annalen des historischen Vereins für den Niederrhein, insbesondere die alte Erzdiözese Köln.* Cologne, 1855ff.
ALKM.	*Archiv für Literatur- und Kirchengeschichte des Mittelalters,* ed. H. Denifle and Fr. Ehrle, Berlin, 1885ff.
Alemannia.	*Alemannia. Zeitschrift für Sprache, Literatur und Volkskunde des Elsasses und Oberrheins und Schwabens.* Bonn, 1873-1914.
Anal. Praem.	*Analecta Praemonstratensia.* Tongerloo, 1925ff
ASEB.	*Annales de la société d'émulation de Bruges.*
Ann. cercle arch. Mons.	*Annales du cercle archéologique de Mons.* Mons, 1857ff.
ASAN.	*Annales de la société d'archéologie de Namur.*
BARB.	*Bulletin de l'académie royale de Belgique.*
BCRH.	*Bulletin de la commission royale d'histoire de Belgique.* Brussels, 1834ff.
Belfried.	*Der Belfried. Eine Monatsschrift für Geschichte und Gegenwart der belgischen Lande.* Leipzig, 1917ff.
Berlière, *MB.*	Berlière *Monasticon belge.*
BF.	Sbaralea, *Bullarium Franciscanum.*
BIAL.	*Bulletin de l'institut archéologique liégeois.*
Bibl. Max. Vet. Pat.	*Bibliotheca Maxima Veterum Patrum,* XXIV-XXV. Lugdunum, 1677.
BNB.	*Biographie nationale de Belgique.* Brussels, 1866ff.
Böhmer-Ficker.	Böhmer, *Regesta imperii inde ab a. 1198-1254.*
BOP.	Ripoll,*Bullarium Ordinis Praedicatorum.*
Bouquet.	Bouquet, *Recueil des historiens des Gaules et de la France.*
BSAHL.	*Bulletin de la société d'archéologie et d'histoire de Liége.*
BSSLL.	*Bulletin de la société scientifique et littéraire de Limbourg.*
BG.	*Bijdragen tot de Geschiedenis bijzonderlijk van het aloude Hertogdom Brabant.* Antwerp, 1902ff.
CCHB.	*Catalogus codicum hagiographicorum bibliothecae regiae Bruxellensis.*

CESL.	Cartulaire de l'église Saint-Lambert de Liége.
CHD.	Caesarius of Heisterbach, Dialogus Miraculorum.
CUP.	Denifle and Chatelain. Chartularium Universitatis Parisiensis.
DDC.	Dictionnaire du droit canonique, ed. R. Naz, Paris, 1935ff.
DHGE.	Dictionnaire d'histoire et de géographie ecclésiastiques, ed. A. Baudrillart, A. De Meyer and E. Van Cauwenbergh, Paris, 1912ff.
DTC.	Dictionnaire de théologie catholique, ed. E. Vacant, E. Mangenot, et al. Paris, 1903ff.
D. War. Belf.	Dietsche Warande en Belfort. Antwerp, 1901ff.
Friedberg.	Richter and Friedberg. Corpus iuris canonici.
GC.	Gallia Christiana.
Hefele-Leclercq.	Hefele-Leclercq, Histoire des conciles.
HJ.	Historisches Jahrbuch. Munich, 1880ff.
HLF.	Histoire de la littérature de la France.
Inv. Lille.	Inventaire ... des archives de la chambre des comptes à Lille.
Leodium.	Leodium, chronique mensuelle de la société d'art et d'histoire du diocèse de Liége. Liége, 1902ff.
MDAC.	Martene and Durand, Amplissima Collectio.
MDT.	——Thesaurus novus anecdotorum.
Messager.	Messager des sciences historiques et archives des arts de Belgique.
MF.	Miraeus and Foppens, Opera diplomatica et historica.
MGH. SS.	Monumenta Germaniae Historica, Scriptores.
MOPH.	Monumenta Ordinis Praedicatorum Historica.
NAK.	Nederlandsch Archief voor Kerkgeschiedenis. Leiden-Schiedam, 1829ff.
OGE.	Ons Geestelijk Erf. Antwerp, 1927ff.
P.	Potthast, Regesta Pontificum Romanorum.
PG.	Patrologia Graeca, ed. J. P. Migne.
PL.	Patrologia Latina, ed. Migne.
Quétif-Echard.	Quétif and Echard, Scriptores Ordinis Praedicatorum.
QF.	Quellen und Forschungen zur Geschichte des Dominikanerordens in Deutschland.
RB.	Revue Bénédictine. Maredsous, 1884ff.
RHE.	Revue d'histoire ecclésiastique. Louvain, 1900ff.
RQ.	Römische Quartalschrift für christliche Alterthumskunde und für Kirchengeschichte.
RR.	Roman de la Rose.
SATF.	Société des anciens textes français.
Stud. euch.	Studia eucharistica.
VKMVA.	Verslagen en Mededeelingen der Koninklijke Vlaamse Academie voor Taal en Letterkunde. Ghent.
V. Ab.	Vita Abundi (see Gosuin de Bossut and Bibl. roy. de Belg.).
V. Al. Scar.	Vita Aleydis Scarembecanae.
V. Arn. Villar.	Vita Arnulfi Villariensis (see Gosuin de Bossut).
V. Beat.	Vita Beatricis.
V. Bonif.	Vita Bonifacii.
V. Cath.	Vita Catherinae.
V. Chr. Mir.	Vita Christinae Mirabilis (see Thomas of Cantimpré).

V. Chr. Stumb.	*Vita Christinae Stumbelensis.*
V. Col.	*Vita Coletae.*
V. Gert.	*Vita Gertrudis ab Oosten.*
V. Gob.	*Vita Goberti Asperimontis.*
V. God. Pach.	*Vita Godefridi Pachomii.*
V. God. Sacr.	*Vita Godefridi Sacristae.*
V. Guil.	*Vita Guillelmi.*
V. Id. Lew.	*Vita Idae Lewensis.*
V. Id. Lov.	*Vita Idae Lovaniensis.*
V. Id. Niv.	*Vita Idae Nivellensis.*
V. Isab.	*Vita Elisabethae seu Isabellae* (see Agnes d'Harcourt).
V. Jul. Cornel.	*Vita Julianae Cornelensis.*
V. Juetta.	*Vita Juettae reclusae Huyi* (see Hugh of Floreffe).
V. Lutg.	*Vita Lutgardis* (see Thomas of Cantimpré).
VMO.	*Vita Mariae Oigniacensis* (see Jacques de Vitry).
VMO. Suppl.	*Supplementum* (see Thomas of Cantimpré).
V. Od.	*Vita Odiliae.*
V. Sim.	*Vita Simonis.*
V. Yol.	*Vita Venerabilis Yolandae,* (see Wiltheim).
Wauters, *TC.*	Wauters, *Table chronologique des chartes et des diplômes.*
ZKG.	*Zeitschrift für Kirchengeschichte.* Gotha, 1877ff.

Contents

Preface vii
Abbreviations xi

Part One: A CASE STUDY IN THE *VITA APOS-
TOLICA*

   I INTRODUCTION 3
  II OIGNIES-SUR-SAMBRE 8
 III THE EDUCATION OF JACQUES DE VITRY IN BELGIUM . . . 20
 IV THE CURE OF OIGNIES AND NIVELLES 40

      John of Nivelles 40
      Lesser Luminaries 45
      William, Founder of L'Olive 47
      Mary and the Lay World 50
      Theodore of Celles 53

   V THE SEMIRELIGIOUS UNDER DISCIPLINE 59

      The Beguinage of Oignies 59
      The Beguinages of Nivelles 62
      Namur 69

  VI THE PURITAN ETHIC IN LIEGE 71

Part Two: THE EXTRAREGULAR IN STATE AND
SOCIETY

    I SOCIAL ORIGINS: THE *Frauenfrage* 81
   II OLDER MONACHISM AND THE *Cura Monialium* 101
  III THE *Via Media* 120
  IV APOSTOLIC POVERTY 141
   V PROTECTION BY THE HIERARCHY 154
  VI MASTER RENIER OF TONGRES 165
 VII BEGUINE PAROCHIAL ORGANIZATION UNDER CISTERCIAN . .
      AUSPICES 170
VIII "MURO INEXPUGNABILI BELLATORUM" 187

IX COMITAL PATRONAGE IN FLANDERS 205
X RELATIONS WITH LAY AUTHORITIES IN BRABANT AND HOLLAND 218
XI ROYAL PATRONAGE IN FRANCE 224
XII THE BEGUINAGES AND INDULGENCES 234
XIII THE BEGUINAGES AND THE INTERDICT 241
XIV THE BEGHARDS 246
XV THE CELLITES 266
XVI THE EXTRAREGULAR IN INDUSTRY 270

Part Three: SPIRITUAL CURRENTS IN BELGIUM
             AND RHINELAND

I HILDEGARDE OF BINGEN AND BELGIAN MYSTICISM 281
II JULIANA OF CORNILLON: DEVOTION TO THE EUCHARIST . . 299
    The Search for Security 301
    Institution of the Feast 305
    Roots of the Cult 310
III CITEAUX AND BEGUINE SPIRITUALITY 320
IV THE PREACHERS AND BEGUINE SPIRITUALITY 341
    The Pulpit 341
    "Virgo Devota Ordinis Praedicatorum" 344
    Meister Eckhart's Pastoral Care 355

Part Four: POPULAR DEVOTIONAL LITERATURE

I LITERACY IN CISTERCIAN AND BEGUINE CIRCLES 365
II LETTERS AND THE BEGUINAGE 388
    Lambert le Bègue 388
    French Materials 391
    Creation of Flemish Prose 392
    A Dialogue with the Bridegroom 396
    Beguine Spirituality in Delft 397
    Dominican Leadership 399

Part Five: POSITIVE AND NEGATIVE EVIDENCE

I "HORTUS DELICIARUM" 409
    The Closed Circle 409
    The Well-Tended Vineyard 413
    Sheep or Wolves 417
    An Oasis in Egypt 421
    Gilles li Muisis 424

II Etymology and Heresy 430

III The Crucible of Criticism 439

IV The Hierarchy Undiminished 456

V The Protest of Rutebeuf 465

Part Six: THE EXTRAREGULAR AND THE
INQUISITION

I "Institutum Beghinarum est Belgio Proprium" 477

II Tares in the Vineyard 488

    William Cornelius 488

    The "beguine clergeresse" 490

    Bloemardinne of Brussels 492

    Freedom of the Spirit 496

    John of Brünn 498

    The Turlupins 500

    "Homines Intelligentiae" 502

III Suspicion in Thirteenth-Century Synodal Legislation   505

IV Henry ii of Virnebourg 516

V The Clementine Decrees 521

VI Rehabilitation of the Beguinage 539

    Belgium 539

    France 546

    The Netherlands 548

VII Charles iv and the Second Crisis 557

Bibliography 575

Index 613

Part One

A CASE STUDY IN *the Vita Apostolica*

> *"Quid sine zelo Dei dispensator verbi Dei et minister? quod sine armis miles, sine stivo agricola, sine temone currus, sine malo navis, sine anima homo."*—Ryckel, *Vita S. Beggae,* p. 293.

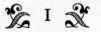

Introduction

The diocese of Liége during the reign of Hugh of Pierrepont (1200-1229) was swept by a wave of popular religious excitement and mysticism which regarded renunciation, combined with *labor manuum,* as the basis of reform, the salvation of souls on the home front and far afield as the objective, and close observance of chastity or continence as a prerequisite for personal perfection. Alongside the phenomenal multiplication of Premonstratensian and especially Cistercian houses, extraregular and semireligious communities, leper-houses, and other charitable foundations sprang up in great number, not to mention the appearance of recluses and the stigmatized whose life was basically contemplative. However much leavened by Bernardine spirituality and compliant with Cistercian guidance, the Belgian feminine religious movement, as an expression of native piety, offers in both purpose and method as well as in antiquity a remarkable parallel to the Franciscan way of life. It was a similarity which did not escape the keen eye of Jacques de Vitry, who first discerned the historical significance of the *mulieres religiosae, virgines continentes,* or *dilectae Deo filiae.*

These sisterhoods, like the corresponding brotherhoods, owed their existence to a plethora of socioeconomic forces and penitential yearnings, principally among townsmen, for which adequate solution no longer could be found in older branches of monachism. But beguinal life was more than just an answer to the medieval *Frauenfrage.* Drawn, at least in part, at the outset from noble and patrician stock, the beguines represented something in addition to democratic-urban or antiabbatial tendencies. Nor can their convents be regarded simply as a charitable establishment or the defense of individual work against guilds. Only from the end of the thirteenth century on did the reaction of towns to a feudal-monastic world find real expression in the beguinage. Similarly, to dwell exclusively on sectarian significance is to overlook a way of life which was at all times bifurcated. Moreover the heterodox beguine was exceptional in the Low Countries; few withdrew from the priesthood in search of a freer and more personal religious life.

To Foulques of Toulouse and the bishop of Acre the *mulieres religiosae* of the Mary of Oignies stamp formed an impenetrable bulwark to the multiple threat of infidel and heretic. True, absence of congregational organism, hardened by uniform rule and directed by a single head, sometimes left the way wide open to deviations of piety. Nevertheless intense veneration of the eucharist in the diocese of Liége, culminating in recognition of the Juliana-sponsored feast of the sacrament, acted as an invincible challenge to Gnostic-Manichaean criticism. By the same token, beguine parochial organization offered an effective deterrent to moral turpitude and spiritual defection. The Cistercian *vitae* are as much instinct with antiheretical fervor, with particular reference to the Albigensians, as the biased chroniclers of the campaigns. In short, hagiographic sources for the beguine movement illustrate conclusively that crusade fervor and the *vita apostolica* were essentially two aspects of the same program. The sociological explanation of this phenomenon, cogent as its argument is, must therefore be tempered by a consideration of religious motivation which dictated the peculiar choice the *mulieres religiosae* made. The beguinage started out as a socioreligious institution, supplementing nunneries which were no longer able to contain the influx of pious women.

The spiritual interests of *mulieres religiosae* could be met either by traditional monasticism or by two other forms: the already ancient *reclusorium* or *inclusorium*[1] and the new semireligious or extraregular institution of the beguinage. In spite of overlappings, these two forms should not be confused.[2] The recluse (*reclusus/a* or *inclusus/a*) was a man or, more commonly, a woman who found the desired solitude in a cell in the shadow of a church or chapel instead of in common life. The beguines, on the contrary, did not withdraw from the world. In the period of full development they generally belonged to a community to which was sometimes applied the term *conventus*, always employed for abbeys.[3] But this common life was pursued halfway between the rules of religious orders and the freedom of laymen. The beguine, like the recluse, submitted to spiritual direction of curés and chaplains; yet she resided, according to her fortune and social status,

---

[1] Doerr, *Das Institut der Inclusen in Süddeutschland;* Mens, *Oorsprong,* pp. 323ff; Arnim Basedow, *Die Inclusen in Deutschland, vornehmlich in der Gegend des Niederrheins um die Wende des 12. und 13. Jahrhunderts, unter besonderer Berücksichtigung des Dialogus Miraculorum des Caesarius von Heisterbach* (Heidelberg, 1895).

[2] E.g., Mens, *Oorsprong,* pp. 354ff; cf. De Louvet, *L'Origine nivelloise,* pp. 7-10, 24-30.

[3] For a modern distinction between *convent* and *couvent* consult J. Deshusses in *DDC.,* IV (1949), 755-756; id., "Conventualité," *ibid.,* 556-558.

in a common house or her own dwelling, which she eventually willed to the community.

Whereas most German cities witnessed the multiplication of small beguine convents, Belgium was noted for the large establishment known as the beguinage or begijnhof—the creation of the beguine parish. Philippen's four stages of evolution have become classic.

[I.] The first stage[4] was marked by individual initiative, with beguines, or rather their prototypes, the ecstatic women, residing scattered about a city or under the parental roof. Preferring to abide by evangelical counsel without divorcing themselves from the world, the *conversae a saeculo* identified themselves with a monastery either by voluntary services or by handing over a part of their property. Contemporaries speak of this first phase as *beguinae singulariter in saeculo manentes*. It was a spontaneous movement which recognized no one as a single founder or legislator. The beguines were not bound by the triple vows, for they abandoned neither house nor trade; nor did they renounce altogether the possibility of marriage. Jacques de Vitry, in depicting Mary of Oignies as a *conversa* of the Augustinian priory, praises what the chronicles call the *religio beguinarum* whom he is content to call *mulieres sanctae*.

[II.] Under the guidance of the clergy, their separation from the *boni christiani* with their heterodox overtones was complete at the beginning of the thirteenth century, the beguinal state assuming more and more the character of religious associations of disciplined women (*congregationes beguinarum disciplinatarum*) for common spiritual experience.[5] Not until the latter half of the thirteenth century would qualifications be dropped from the early formulas, *mulieres vulgariter dictae beguinae* and *mulieres quae beguinae dicuntur,* which once suggested disparagement. The women submitted to a grand mistress, aided by a council of other mistresses, each with a specific function. In organization and daily practices they often emulated the nunnery. They held meetings, followed common exercises, performed acts of charity, and recommended compulsory prayers. But ordinary religious practices remained parochial as before. To foster piety, practical or contemplative, to hold aloof from the dangers of the world without stopping ordinary work, such was the aim. Since their avowed purpose was the recovery of the simplicity of the primitive church, they sometimes adopted methods considered reprehensible by civil and church authorities. While the Cistercians defined the admission or affiliation of women to be approved, others were obliged to seek authorization to form new communities which would allow freedom necessary for work. This stage found a spokesman in the bishop-elect of Acre who

[4] Philippen, *Begijnhoven,* pp. 40-57.
[5] *Ibid.,* pp. 58-68.

pleaded the cause of the *beguinae disciplinatae* at the papal curia in 1216. Their situation was delicate, since the Fourth Lateran Council had just voiced disapproval of *religiones novae.* Jacques de Vitry argued that a valid vocation, for want of dowry or material resources, might not meet the requirements of an approved order. In place of condemning these persons to remain in the world, it would therefore be better to allow them to form free communities with severe restraint. With papal consent they achieved legal existence.

[III.]   Hence the *beguinae clausae*[6] made their appearance with the erection of an infirmary. The *curtis* of the beguines, responding to the demands of the Church, awakened lively sympathies, thus persuading certain bishops to regard it as an order indirectly recognized by the papal curia. The bull *Gloriam virginalem*, promulgated by Gregory IX in June, 1233, was interpreted in this sense and consequently contributed much to the maturing of the beguinages. The rule which a canon of the chapter of St. Lambert, Jacques Pantaleon, drew up for the direction of the *beguinae clausae* and which received confirmation from Bishop Robert de Thourote did not imply approbation of the *religio beguinarum* as an independent order, but it constituted a favorable interpretation of the Lateran decree. Such organizations were designed to aid widows and unmarried women who were unable to join monastic congregations; episcopal injunction and civil intervention prevented the disturbance of those who wished to dedicate themselves to the service of God.

[IV.]   The final stage was marked by parochial organization.[7] Ecclesiastical authorities did not hesitate to erect *curtes* into autonomous parishes, thus endowing them with a civil and religious personality. In Flanders and Walloon Belgium, when the *curtis* was large enough to contain the extraregular population, the bishops detached its territory from the original parish. If of insufficient size, a more favorable location was provided, generally granted with full title by a seignorial lord or by abbeys. The secular arm cooperated by conferring *privilegia beguinalia* including exemption from taxes and, in the case of beghards, military service.

In drawing this distinction between *beguinae clausae* and *beguinae singulariter in saeculo degentes* one must remember that the latter did not disappear with the establishment of beguine convents. Certain beguines continued to live isolated in the world, scattered about the city. It is they above all who by their mendicancy, vagabondage, doctrinal errors, and moral aberration caused the most trouble for the *beguinae clausae,* at times discrediting the whole movement. The distinction was made more difficult for the contemporary mind inasmuch as the

[6] *Ibid.,* pp. 69-88.
[7] *Ibid.,* pp. 89-126.

beguinae clausae were not religious in the medieval sense. Robert de Thourote warned the "holy persons" in his diocese not to "live in the manner of beguines outside beguine enclosures," declaring that they had usurped the name of beguines. Those who preferred an isolated existence must forfeit beguinal privileges.[8]

This first part localizes these semireligious currents in the Nivelles-Oignies area[9] with some attention also being paid to Namur and Liége; at the same time it is a case study of the *vita apostolica* as a program and an ideal. Although Mary of Oignies, the finest example of the early *mulier sancta,* has usually been regarded as a prototype of the beguine of the succeeding generation, this treatment, despite certain documentary evidence, should not be construed as a brief for the seniority of Nivelles over Liége—although this view has pretty well prevailed since Greven's investigation—or the priority of Master John over Lambert le Bègue. Such questions, after all, are quite academic. The phrase „circle of Mary of Oignies at Nivelles" which De Louvet has recently challenged as a myth when applied to future beguines[10] nevertheless accurately describes the group of priests, canons, laymen, and ecstatic women who were in large measure molded by her apostolic zeal and were ready to execute her will.[11]

The Belgian extraregular was but one manifestation of a European-wide movement during the medieval reform; the Rhineland experienced the same sort of religious excitement which led equally early to beguine organization.[12] As ascesis developed into mysticism, we find that Franciscans and Dominicans, together with their numerous affiliations, Waldensians, Humiliati, the beguinages, and *sorores pauperes,* as well as innumerable penitential bands, all had roots in much the same soil. Towns were the matrix from which the new forms sprang; the burghers and craftsmen demanded a new criterion for judging the worth of existing religious practices. Extraregulars and semireligious associations could provide an answer within canonical prescriptions; or they could become a competing force.

---

[8] See below pp. 127, 163.

[9] Nivelles, which today is in the diocese of Malines, then belonged to the diocese of Liége.

[10] De Louvet, *op. cit.,* pp. 10f, 14.

[11] De Louvet does admit, but without amplification, that Mary's life betrayed traits which would not be found in the ordinary recluse. Her experience represents a mingling of the practical with the contemplative.

[12] Grundmann, "Zur Geschichte der Beginen im 13. Jahrhundert," *Arch. f. Kulturgeschichte,* XXI (1931), 296-320.

II

Oignies-sur-Sambre

Like many another canonical community established or reformed during the twelfth century within the prescriptions of the Augustinian rule,[1] the priory on the left bank of the Sambre at Oignies,[2] with its chapel dedicated to St. Nicholas,[3] had been modestly founded by the priest, Gilles of Walcourt (d. 1233), formerly chaplain for Wéry III, lord of Walcourt (1165-1206),[4] and two of his brothers, John and Robert, shortly before the close of the twelfth century,[5] with proceeds

[1] Mandonnet, *Saint Dominique*, II, 167ff; Dickinson, *The Origins of the Austin Canons*, pp. 7-90; De Moreau, *Histoire de l'église en Belgique*, III, 423-438, 454-455; Axters, *Geschiedenis van de Vroomheid*, I, 238-293.

[2] Thomas of Cantimpré, *VMO. Suppl.*, 575 E, no. 9.

[3] Poncelet "Chartes du prieuré d'Oignies de l'Ordre de Saint-Augustin," *ASAN.*, XXXI (1912), 1-300; XXXII (1913), 1-168.

[4] *MDAC.*, VI, 328. For Wéry III, consult Lahaye, *Cartulaire de Walcourt*, pp. xvi-xxi; Roland, "Les seigneurs et comtes de Rochefort," *ASAN.*, XX (1893), 338-345; Toussaint, *Histoire de Walcourt*, pp. 26-54; id., *Histoire d'Oignies*, pp. 5off. Toussaint not only relies heavily on Moschus but offers an account that is uncritical and panegyric in character (*e.g.*, his treatment of Baldwin of Barbençon, *Histoire d'Oignies*, pp. 53ff). According to the chronicle *MDAC.*, VI, 328; reproduced in *AHEB.*, X (1873), 102), jealous courtiers accused Gilles, whose piety sometimes made him remiss in the performance of his chaplain duties, of unfaithfulness to his master, claiming that he had secretly hidden in a coffer in the chapel a treasure that represented the fruits of malfeasance. Opening of the strong-box, however, confirmed Gilles' devotion for in it were only a hair shirt, other accessories of the penitential life, and altar ornaments. So moved was he by the suspicion cast on his intentions that he decided to abandon the world.

[5] The date 1192 once erroneously assigned to the Fosses document of 1198 (*ASAN.*, XXXI (1912), 2-3, no. 2; MF., II, 1193; *MDAC.*, I, 999) led Berlière (*MB.*, I, 451), among others, to choose it as the critical year for the foundation; cf. Wauters, *TC.*, III, 22; Hauck, IV, 1005; both the seventeenth century MSS. on Oignies in *Documents relatifs au comté de Namur* (Bibl. roy. de Belgique, cod. 6594-6639, f. 155) and the *Initium prioratus Oegniacensis in Sacra dioecesis Namurcensis chronologia* (Bibl. roy. de Belgique, cod. 19668, f. 190v), which followed Miraeus (*ibid.*, f. 192r), accepted 1192 as the foundation year when they assigned to Gilles a forty-one-year priorate and put his death in 1233. The apocryphal account of Gilles d'Orval (*Gesta episc. Leod., MGH. SS., XXV, 118*) makes Mary of Oignies responsible for the "conversion" of these brothers. Poncelet (*ASAN.*, XXXI, pp. v-vi) maintained, without depreciating the contents, that the Fosses document must have originated in 1198, especially since it contains the clause, "approbante .. et confirmante domino Alberto de Cuc Leodiensi episcopo," the bishop who was elected in November, 1194, but was not consecrated as such by the archbishop of Cologne until January, 1196. Moreover,

from the sale of their paternal estate.[6] A fourth brother, who usually goes under the name of Hugh of Oignies, achieved distinction as a goldsmith.[7] Although he lived in common with his brothers,[8] he did not become a cleric. The artist who inscribed on one of his creations the epigraph which would seem to befit a *conversus* in an Augustinian house: "Liber: scriptus: intus: et: foris: Hugo: scripsit: intus: quaestu: foris: manu. Orate pro eo ore: *canunt: alii: cristum: canit: arte: fabrili:* Hugo: sui: quaestu: scripta: laboris: arans",[9] reaped considerable renown from his work, as the chronicle further confirms: "In arte aurifabricae operator famosissimus."[10]

This coenobium, founded by secular priests for "apostolic perfection,"[11] was not affiliated with any congregation; but it followed from the earliest period the rule of St. Augustine[12] under the direction of a prior, freely elected by the brethren, then presented to the chapter of Fosses, and finally confirmed by the bishop of Liége. On the autho-

the witnesses of this document are pretty much the same as the ones who signed Bishop Albert's confirmation in 1198 (*ASAN.,* XXXI, 1-2, no. 1). For the foundation, see *Historia fundationis venerabilis ecclesiae beati Nicolae Oigniacensis in MDAC.,* VI, 327-330; Reusens reproduced it in *AHEB.,* X (1873), 101-107. Funk (*Jakob von Vitry,* p. 9) casts aspersions upon the *Historia fundationis* as a rather late production (fourteenth century). The chronicle certainly belongs after 1243, for the author uses an act of Prior Siger (Berlière, *MB.,* I, 453f), and even after 1289, because in it appear expressions of a document of Bishop Guillaume of Cambrai (1286-1296). Nevertheless this single source for the existence of the priory before the earliest donation charters finds agreement, at least in broad outline, in other fragmentary evidence (Poncelet, in *ASAN.,* XXXI, pp. ii-iii).

[6] The father, John, is described in the chronicle as "divitiis temporalibus et spiritualibus sufficienter abundans" (*MDAC.,* VI, 327 D); cf. Moschus, *Coenob. mon. Ogniac.,* p. 8. A document in the Walcourt cartulary (Lahaye, *Cartulaire de Walcourt,* p. 9), dated December, 1232, states that Thierry III, lord of Walcourt, gave to the abbey of Jardinet various pieces of property at Walcourt, including the "pratum quod fuit prioris de Ognas et ejus partionariorum." This substantiates the passage in the chronicle: "de fratrum suorum consilio ... venditis enim omnibus jure sibi hereditario competentibus in Walecuria et circa partes illas ..." De Ram (*Hag. nat.,* I, 57f) distinguished Gilles the founder from the Gilles who retired to St. Nicholas with his brothers. Cf. the treatment given to Gilles of Walcourt in *Sacra dioecesis Namurcensis chronologia* (Bibl. roy. de Belgique, cod. 19668, f. 190v).

[7] Helbig, *La sculpture et les arts plastiques,* pp. 77-89; Emile Van Arenbergh, in *BNB.,* IX (1886-1887), 633-635; Poncelet, in *ASAN.,* XXXI, pp. lxviiif; Toussaint, *Histoire d'Oignies,* pp. 42-52; id., *Histoire de Walcourt,* pp. 38ff. Among his creations was a reliquary with the face of St. Feuillen which he made for the chapter of Fosses, the superior of the priory. Besides, the saint's body only recently had been discovered (*Annales Fossenses, MGH. SS.,* IV, 31: "1176. Hoc anno revelatum est Fossis corpus, Beati Foillani, in medio castro, sub Raufo Leodiensi episcopo"). Cf. Paul Rops, "Une œuvre inédité de frère Hugo," *ASAN.,* XXIV (1900), 349-360.

[8] *AHEB.,* X (1873), 100; cf. Gilles d'Orval, *Gesta Episc. Leod., MGH. SS.,* XXV, 118.

[9] Poncelet, *ASAN.,* XXXI, p. lxviii.

[10] *AHEB.,* X, 100; cf. Moschus, *Coenob. mon. Ogniac.,* p. 8: "Hugo aurifaber celebris, nullique id temporis in ea arte secundus."

[11] *Ibid.,* p. 8.

[12] See the document of Duke Henry of 1214 (*ASAN.,* XXXI, 19, no. 19: "sub regula beati Augustini Domino in perpetuum serviant"). Cf. the brief of Guillaume d'Avesnes, bishop of Cambrai, of 1289 (*MDAC.,* I, 1386 D).

rity of Moschus[13] the priorate of Oignies was limited after 1242 to twelve years, a practice which continued until the fourteenth century when Jean de Hévillers prolonged his tenure to almost twenty-seven years.[14] The diocesan head remained in spiritual matters the immediate superior of the prior to the exclusion of visitors or the general of a regular order. To the nominal number of canons inhabiting the house[15] must be added *conversi*.[16] Mary of Oignies herself appears to have resided there as a lay sister—a *conversa*. The canons regular who accepted Augustinian regulations followed the "royal middle path";[17] theirs was an institute which in the example of the Apostles had the power of binding and loosing.[18] Simple in food and dress without intolerable harshness, they combined contemplation with intensive pastoral care.[19] As an example of the *vita apostolica*—the missionary zeal of the primitive church predicated on simplicity and renunciation—the Oignies ordinances of 1251 emphasize the necessity of emulating the "poverty of Christ."[20] Among such communities which fascinated Jacques de Vitry because of "the purity of their religion and fervor in charity"[21] were St. Jean-des-Vignes at Soissons,[22] St. Aubert in Cambrai,[23] St. Mary at Blois,[24] as well as St. Nicholas of Oignies.

So humble and inconsequential was the name of this Augustinian

[13] Moschus, *Coenob. mon. Ogniac.*, p. 18. Yet no trace of this regulation is to be found in the statutes of May 6, 1243, and November 13, 1250, or in the special *consuetudines* drawn up before June 24, 1251, which foresaw only the possibility of an election "obeunte priore" (for the 1251 provision, see *ASAN.*, XXXI, 131-133; cf. Poncelet, *ibid.*, p. xvi).

[14] During his priorate of twenty-six years and ten months Jean de Hévillers maintained the rights of his community against the demands of the count of Namur and the knight, Brant d'Aiseau, but he exhausted the resources of the monastery by constructing for himself magnificent quarters (Moschus, *Coenob. mon. Ogniac.*, pp. 55-57; cf. Berlière, *M.B.*, I, 455).

[15] The number of canons rose to twelve, in the fifteenth century to twenty, and in 1788 to twenty-three (Poncelet, in *ASAN.*, XXXI, p. ix).

[16] For the *conversi*, see *VMO., Suppl.*, 575 F: "Andreas frater conversus in monasterio de Oignies, homo utique etsi laicus, tamen religione probatus." The *consuetudines* of 1251 contain an article on *"laici fratres scilicet conversi inter canonicos regulares sine proprio viventes"* (*ASAN.*, XXXI, 143).

[17] Jacques de Vitry, *Hist. Occid.*, p. 319; *Sermo XXX ad canonicos regulares* (Pitra, *Anal. nov.*, II, 387).

[18] Thus Stephen of Grammont put it (*V. Steph., AA. SS.*, V (February 8, ii), 207 E, no. 29): "Canonicorum institutio habet potestatem exemplo Apostolorum ligandi atque solvendi." Cf. Dickinson, *Origins*, pp. 220-222.

[19] "Sub unius abbatis vel prioris obedientia continenter vivunt, proprium autem eis habere non licet: animarum curas licitum est eis suscipere, et ecclesias parochiales regere" (Jacques de Vitry, *Hist. Occid.*, pp. 319-320; for the Premonstratensians, p. 322: "Parochiales ecclesias, et animarum Saecularium curas in propriis personis suscipiunt"; cf. Schreiber, *Gemeinschaften*, pp. 360-1).

[20] *ASAN.*, XXXI, 136; cf. 137.

[21] Jacques de Vitry, *Hist. Occid.*, p. 321.

[22] *GC.*, IX, 456; Cottineau, II, 3051.

[23] *GC.*, III, 53; Cottineau, II, 2599.

[24] Thomas of Cantimpré, *BUA.*, I, 16, 2 (p. 57).

house,[25] even in nearby Nivelles, during the first few years of its existence that Mary of Oignies' husband, John, and his brother, Master Guido, were surprised at her proposal to retire there. But she could no longer endure the press of her admirers who came to Willambroux with its leper-house.[26] From her husband she therefore received permission to visit for the first time the priory and, if she desired, to remain there.[27] Within a generation its condition was to be radically altered. Mary's personality and relics, Jacques de Vitry's undiminished zeal and solicitude, Hugh's works of art, numerous papal and episcopal privileges and indulgences, donations from the local nobility, and burial of important persons in the church[28] all account for its renown to which Bishop Guillaume of Cambrai made allusion in his letter of 1289.[29]

At the close of the twelfth century (1198) the foundation of St. Nicholas had as its first benefactor the Brabançon noble, Baldwin of Loupoigne (or *Lopon*), lord of Aiseau,[30] who had already been generous to Villers.[31] He and his wife, Oda, with the consent of their sons and other relatives[32] and the approval of Bishop Albert of Cuyck, granted to the canons the tithe of Roux, a piece of land known as Couturelle (*Culturiola*), the tithe of hay of Oignies, patronage of the church of Moignelée, and permission to acquire around the monastery a bonnier of land.[33] In the second document, dated 1198, the Premonstratensian chapter of Fosses, through Henry, its provost, and R., the deacon,

[25] *VMO.*, 568 D: "De quo etiam, pro novitate et paupertate domus, vix inter homines aliqua mentio tunc erat."

[26] "Frequentiam hominum ad eam ex devotione concurrentium" *(idem)*; see below, p. 51.

[27] Hucq, in *ASAN.*, XXXVIII (1927), 234ff; for relics besides Mary's, see *VMO.*, 567 F (91).

[28] Among the persons who were buried at Oignies were John of Dinant (*VMO.*, 557), Jacques de Vitry (see below, p. 39), Gertrude de Marlemont (d. March 3, 1228), Gerard de Marbais, knight and castellan of Brussels, Henry de Ham, and a number of the family of Chenois, owners of a part of the seigniory of Tamines (Poncelet, in *ASAN.*, XXXI, p. viii, note 2).

[29] MDAC., I, 1386. The bishop attributes the prestige of the priory primarily to Mary of Oignies and Jacques de Vitry.

[30] Oignies was one of four villages that made up the seigniory of Aiseau which, in turn, contained Moignelée and Le Roux and, although having contact with both Liége and Namur, belonged to the duchy of Brabant. Duke Henry, in taking the church under his protection in September, 1210, declared that it was "in nostro sita dominio ac potestate", (*ASAN.*, XXXI, 7, no. 6), an assertion that he renewed in October, 1216 (*ibid.*, 23f, no. 25). Cf. De Seyn, *Dictionnaire*, s.v. Aiseau; Tarlier and Wauters, *Géog. et hist. des communes belges. Prov. de Brabant. Canton de Genappe* 1859), p. 45.

[31] On May 4, 1197, Henry I of Brabant confirmed the property of Villers including Baldwin's donation of a wood (De Moreau, *L'abbaye de Villers*, p. 77); cf. Tarlier and Wauters, *l.c.*

[32] From the document of 1197 mentioned in the foregoing note we may conclude that these relatives were Baldwin's brothers, John and Arnulf.

[33] In 1198 Bishop Albert of Liége confirmed the donation of the property of Couturelle and the tithe of Roux lez-Fosses (*ASAN.*, XXXI, 1-2, no. 1; published

recognized the new house and its carefully enumerated holdings with the stipulation of an annual rent of one gold denier to be paid to the church of St. Feuillen and the right to confirm the prior who had been elected by the canons.[34] The role of Fosses in the founding of the monastery is explained either by the possession of certain spiritual rights in the region or simply by the desire of Baldwin of Loupoigne to entrust to an ancient collegiate church superintendence of the new house. In place of making his donations direct to the canons, he thus handed them over for their benefit "super altare beati Foillani Fossensis."[35] In addition to Albert of Cuyck's approval, Baldwin's donations received the confirmation of the successor, Hugh of Pierrepont (1200-1229) who came on July 24, 1204 to dedicate the new church which Gilles, the founder and first prior, had just completed.[36] Some twenty years later, however, its steady growth dictated a new building program, begun about 1220, and culminating in the dedication of the new church with its five altars by Jacques de Vitry in January, 1228 or 1229.[37] To promote the construction of larger conventual quarters Gregory IX issued a bull on April 19, 1234, granting a forty-day indulgence to the faithful of the provinces of Rheims, Cologne, and Trèves who would lend their support.[38]

The priory obtained from the papal curia a great number of bulls and indults, protection and confirmation briefs, privileges, and indulgences. One such document came from Innocent III,[39] three from Honorius III,[40] seven, besides the one already cited, from Gregory IX,[41] five from Innocent IV,[42] one from Clement IV,[43] one from Gregory X,[44] one from Nicholas IV,[45] and one from Boniface IX,[46] More immediately, the monastery was granted important privileges from the bishops of Liége[47] and Cambrai.[48] Although it was not until Septem-

under the date 1196 by FM., II, 1199). For the rights over Moignelée, see Poncelet in ASAN., XXXI, p. xxxv.

[34] Ibid., 2-3, no. 2; MF., II, 1193; MDAC., I, 999.

[35] ASAN., XXXI, 2.

[36] Ibid., 4-5, no. 3; MF., II, 1208.

[37] VMO. Suppl., 579 C.

[38] ASAN., XXXI, 69f, no. 75.

[39] July 17, 1207, ibid., 5-6, no. 4.

[40] March 27, 1219, ibid., 31f, no. 33; cf. bulls of July 18, 1223-July 17, 1224, ibid., XXXII, 130, nos. 382-383.

[41] August 4, 1227 (ibid., XXXI, 49-52, no. 56); May 9, 1228 (56, no. 58); June 19, 1235 (71, no. 77); July 23, 1235 (72, no. 78); January 7, 1239 (86, no. 98); January 15, 1239 (87, no. 99); March 18, 1239 (87f, no. 100).

[42] June 25, 1243-June 24, 1244 (ibid., 100f, no. 112, 113); January 11, 1249 (117f, no. 131); January 11, 1249 (117, no. 130); January 11, 1249 (118) no. 132).

[43] May 11, 1266 (ibid., 173, no. 175).

[44] October 20, 1271 (ibid., 185, no. 189).

[45] September 18, 1291 (ibid., 283f, no. 273).

[46] February 16, 1397 (ibid., XXXII, 89, no. 369).

[47] Besides episcopal acts already cited, see 1219 (ibid., XXXI, 35, no. 37); 1229 (59, no. 61); 1231 (59, no. 62; Quinaux, Notice historique sur ... Leffe, p. 139);

ber, 1210, that Duke Henry I of Brabant took under his protection
the church of St. Nicholas and all its possessions,[49] he must already
have shown interest in this foundation "in nostro sita dominio ac
potestate." The marquis of Namur[50] and the counts of Flanders[51] in
like fashion extended privileges and rights to the community.

Alongside purchases,[52] successive donations of lands and tithes provided a greater measure of material well-being to an establishment
that was already benefiting from Jacques de Vitry's patronage and
papal concessions. The bulk of these possessions belong to the first
fifty years, for after the middle of the century Oignies was afflicted
with the same economic troubles that beset all monastic institutions
and churches generally.[53] Following Baldwin's example, Elizabeth de
Merbes[54] and one Godfrey[55] left to the canons their share of the tithe
of Vogenée, with reservations for the leper-house.[56] The priory also
received the tithes of Brugelette,[57] Doumont,[58] Solre-sur-Sambre,[59]
Wanfercée,[60] Rhisnes,[61] and the properties of Vichenet,[62] Mévergnies,[63]

December 18, 1233 (ASAN., XXXI, 68, no. 73); April, 1236 (76, no. 84); March, 1236
(AHEB., VII, 365-367; ASAN., XXXI, 76, no. 83); January 26, 1237 (79, no. 87);
cf. March 19, 1237 (80, no. 88); on May 6, 1243 Robert de Thourote approved the
reform statutes (94-96; MDAC., I, 1276); April 10, 1245 (ASAN., XXXI, 105f; Schoolmeesters, Regestes de Robert de Thourote, in BSAHL., XV, 116); June 2, 1245
(ASAN., XXXI, 106, no. 117; Schoolmeesters, op. cit., 119); March 31, 1246 (ASAN.,
XXXI, 109f, no. 121; Schoolmeesters, op. cit., 124); February 18, 1264 (ASAN., XXXI,
168, no. 168; Delescluse and Brouwers, Catalogue des actes de Henri de Gueldre,
p. 361.
   48 May 13, 1215 (ASAN., XXXI, 21, no. 22); April 21, 1219 (ibid., 32f, no. 34);
1289 (MDAC., I, 1386f).
   49 ASAN., XXXI, 7, no. 6; MF., II, 1210; Wauters, TC., III, 330.
   50 July, 1233 (ASAN., XXXI, 64f, no. 70); cf. February, 1235/6 (ibid., 74f, no. 81).
   51 In August, 1238 Thomas and Jeanne donated to the church 12 bonniers of
land at Waudrez (ibid., 84, no. 95; cf. 83, no. 94), an act afterwards confirmed by
John d'Avesnes (April, 1289, ibid., 261f, no. 256). In June, 1247, Prior Siger rented
to Lambert de Tournai, a burgher of Binche, land near the bridge at Waudrez
which Countess Jeanne had once given to the priory (ibid., 114f, no. 126).
   52 Ibid., 16f, no. 16; 18f, no. 18; January, 1216 (ibid., 22f, no. 24; 37f, no. 39).
   53 Poncelet, in ASAN., XXXI, p. xliii.
   54 1210 (ibid., 8, no. 7; cf. 13, no. 12); 1209 (ibid., 14, no. 13); October 30, 1259
(ibid., 159, no. 156); cf. act of May 14, 1255 (ibid., 147f, no. 145).
   55 1216 (ibid., 24f, no. 26).
   56 1208 (ibid., 6, no. 5); May 14, 1255 (ibid., 147f, no. 145).
   57 January 1210/1-1215 (ibid., 9, no. 8; 10, no. 9); cf. February, 1210/1 (ibid., 11,
no. 10); before May 13, 1215 (ibid., 20, no. 20; 20f, no. 21); May 13, 1215 (ibid., 21f,
nos. 22-23); April 11, 1217 (ibid., 25f, no. 27); February, 1218/9 (ibid., 30f, no. 32);
April 21, 1219 (ibid., 32f, no. 34).
   58 July 24, 1239 (ibid., 88f, no. 101).
   59 April 20, 1211 (ibid., 12, no. 11); March, 1211/2 (ibid., 16, no. 15).
   60 1213 (ibid., 17f, no. 17); August 2, 1238 (ibid., 82f, no. 93; cf. February, 1244/5,
(ibid., 104f, no. 115); April 10, 1245 (ibid., 105f, no. 116; Schoolmeesters, "Regestes
de Robert de Thourote," BSAHL., XV, 116); cf. ASAN., XXXI, 106, no. 117 and
BSAHL., XV, 119 (June 2, 1245); July, 1245 (ASAN., XXXI, 107f, no. 118); 1245
(ibid., 109, no. 120); December, 1249 (ibid., 119-121, no. 134).
   61 December, 1228 (ibid., 58, no. 60); confirmation by Hugh of Pierrepont, 1229

Roselies,[64] and Erbault. Pilgrims, charmed by the relics of Mary of
Oignies and confident with papal indults, contributed to the expansion of the church. Nor were the brethren forgotten by priests and
laymen in their wills.

The demand of the community for immunity from secular jurisdiction, with specific reference to the lords of Aiseau, was answered by
Gregory IX in the great charter of August 4, 1227, and ratified on
different occasions thereafter by competent authorities. The bishops
of Liége, in their capacity as heads of the diocese, were the guardians
and defenders of the privileges of Oignies against usurpation. Engelbert de la Marck in 1359 (September) and Jean d'Arkel in 1372 (July
15) seem to have considered as detrimental to their own authority
the abuse of power by the seigniors of Aiseau within the monastery
and against the persons dependent on it. Consequently they demanded
reparation for violence to themselves and the priory.

Religious integrity did not remain commensurate with material
prosperity. By 1227 there is a strong hint that even before Gilles'
death the convent must have entered a period of decay, for the pope
in his charter forbade separation from the community without the
prior's consent, "nisi arctioris religionis obtentu."[65] Enjoying fully
for a generation the reputation of its devout men and women, St.
Nicholas had steadily extended its spiritual functions[66] while waxing
strong in temporal possessions. What suggests even more sharply the
presence of decay, which usually attends material well-being, is the
hardening of institutional forms—in this case recommended by Dominican visitors in 1243 under episcopal auspices—and increasing econo-

(ibid., 59, no. 61; Poncelet, *Hugues de Pierrepont*, p. 259, no. 279); cf. September,
1234 (*ASAN.*, XXXI, 70f, no. 76); February, 1236 (*ibid.*, 74f, no. 81); October 5, 1236
(*ibid.*, 77, no. 85).

[62] For the properties of Vichenet, see Poncelet, in *ibid.*, pp. xxxii-xxxiii. In 1211
Baldwin de Merlemont, canon of Moustier-sur-Sambre, donated with the approval
of Abbess Margaret and the monastery his property at Vichenet to the chapel of
Saint-Remi with the intention of making this priory a dependent of Oignies (*ibid.*,
14f, no. 14); 1214 (*ibid.*, 19, no. 19); October, 1216 (*ibid.*, 23f, no. 25); 1219 (*ibid.*, 35,
no. 37); 1223 (*ibid.*, 41, no. 44).

[63] October, 1218 (*ibid.*, 29, no. 31).

[64] Before July 3, 1217 (*ibid.*, 26, no. 28); July 3, 1217 (*ibid.*, 27, no. 29); July 3-
November 1, 1217 (*ibid.*, 28f, no. 30).

[65] *Ibid.*, 49.

[66] Completing the patronage enjoyed by St. Nicholas over the Moignelée church
since Baldwin of Loupoigne's donation in 1198 (*ASAN.*, XXXI, 2) and confirmed
by Hugh of Pierrepont in 1204 (*ibid.*, 5), the parish of Moignelée was transferred
to the spiritual jurisdiction of Oignies with the approval of Jean d'Eppes on
December 18, 1233 (*ibid.*, 68, no. 73) and Henry de Beaumont, archdeacon of Liége,
in August, 1235 (*ibid.*, 72-73, no. 79). A canon from Oignies was appointed rector
of the parish (cf. Poncelet, in *ibid.*, pp. xxxv, xxxix). In addition to Moignelée and
Oignies, Aiseau, Le Roux, Wanfercée, and Rhisnes were served by priests named
by the prior and invested by the bishop.

mic concern, the latter being expressed in the *Fundatio Pitantiarum Vini Religiosorum Oigniacensium*.[67]

Baldwin de Barbençon, the second prior[68] and Gilles' nephew, died in 1242.[69] Although former chaplain for several years at Aywières,[70] arbiter and witness in numerous documents for a quarter of a century,[71] and respected at Oignies as a sound preacher,[72] he unfortunately "became involved in a less worthy fashion in temporal affairs

---

[67] *Ibid.*, 101-103, no. 114; *MDAC.*, I, 1278-1280; *MF.*, 207-8.

[68] Gilles was still alive in June, 1233 (*ASAN.*, XXXI, 63, no. 68; *CSEL.*, I, 313).

[69] Berlière, *MB.*, I, 453; Moschus (*Coenob, mon. Ogniac.*, p. 13) not only points out that Baldwin died shortly after John of Nivelles, but that his mother was Gilles' sister. Baldwin's name is noted under February 23 in the Floreffe necrology (*AHEB.*, XIII, 41).

[70] Berlière, in *RB.*, XXV (1908, 192f, P.J. IV (December 26, 1234); cf. *ZKG.*, XVI (1896), 114. His chaplaincy would seem to go back at least to 1215.

[71] During his association with the Cistercian nunnery Baldwin was witness in documents of 1215 (*Cartulaire de l'abbaye d'Aywières*, AGR., arch. eccl., 5338, f. 53v), 1219 (f. 59v), and March 25, 1231 (f. 71v). During the summer of 1231 Baldwin, priest of Aywières, and Henry de Beaumont, archdeacon of Liége, arbitrated the dispute arising from the priest Ivan's refusal to accept the division of his charge in Nivelles into multiple parishes (Balau, "L'organisation paroissiale de la ville de Nivelles au XIIIe siècle." *BSAHL.*, XIII (1902), 59-88; Tarlier and Wauters, *Géog. et des communes belges. Province de Brabant. Ville de Nivelles* (1862), 107-108). Their decision was dated July in the documents (Balau, in *BSAHL.*, XIII, 77-78, P.J. II), but they had already passed judgment for as early as June 29 their verdict was upheld by Jean d'Eppes, acting as deputy of the Holy See, and his two colleagues, Jean de Huy, abbot of Floreffe, and Hugh de Celles, scholasticus of St. Paul in Liége (*ibid.*, 79, P.J. III); the same day Jean d'Eppes voiced his approval in his episcopal capacity, declaring that Ivan had promised in his presence not to challenge the decision (*ibid.*, 79-80, P.J. IV). In July Ivan (*ibid.*, 80-81, P.J. V) as well as Oda of Looz, abbess of Nivelles, the provost, dean, and the whole chapter (*ibid.*, 82-83, P.J. VI) accepted the judgment. In another July document (*ibid.*, 83-86, P.J. VII) the provost of Nivelles, the dean, and Baldwin de Barbençon, empowered by the deputies of the apostolic legate, proceeded to apportion the properties among the new parishes and to determine the share to be left to former titularies of Notre-Dame. On February 27, 1233, Baldwin, as *penitenciarius* of the bishop of Liége, agreed to mediate the difference between the priory on the one hand and Jean and Matthew de Tamines on the other over fishing rights (*ASAN.*, XXXI, 61-62, no. 66); his decision was rendered the following May 14 (*ibid.*, 62-63, no. 67). First cited as prior in a document of January 22, 1234 (*ibid.*, 69, no. 74; (*Cartulaire de Floreffe*, f. 83, Archives de l'Etat at Namur; Barbier, *Histoire de l'abbaye de Floreffe*, II, 86), he continued to act as arbiter: on December 26, 1234 (*Cartul. d'Aywières*, f. 79v); March 1-29, 1236, n.s., Baldwin granted to Floreffe patronage of the chapel which the clerk, Richard, his relative, had built and endowed in the hospital of Beaumont (*AHEB.*, VII, 1870, 365; *ASAN.*, XXXI, 76, no. 83); this cession was confirmed by Jean d'Eppes in March, 1226 and by Henry de Beaumont on March 29 (*AHEB.*, VII, 366-367). On July 17, 1238, Baldwin and his convent on the one hand, and Th., provost, J., dean, and the chapter of St. Aubain of Namur, on the other hand, appointed respectively Thierry of Dinant, a canon of Oignies, and Thomas, cantor of St. Aubain, to settle differences pertaining to the Rhisnes church (*AHEB.*, VI, 123); the differences were composed on July 26 (*ibid.*, XI, 106; *ASAN.*, XXXI, 82, no. 92). In March, 1240, Baldwin and the priory granted to Mary of Fosses an anniversary in their church (*ibid.*, 90f, no. 103). For other documents where he is not mentioned by name, see *ibid.*, 87, no. 99 (January 15, 1239); 87f, no. 100 (March 18, 1239).

[72] *V. Lutg.*, 205 F (III, 8).

against the advice of his friends."[73] During his rule of eight years discipline was relaxed; obedience to superiors became defective. The precarious condition in which the house now found itself compelled Bishop Robert de Thourote during the priorate of Siger[74] to deputize for a canonical visitation two Dominicans of Liége, Gerard of Rheims[75] and Gossuin with the purpose of restoring order. At their recommendation the customs of the priory, beyond the Augustinian rule ("certas institutiones preter regulam"), were for the first time to be codified by the prior, subprior and two *probi viri* chosen either from the brethren themselves or from the outside; the recommendations were given episcopal approval on May 6, 1243,[76] with the stipulation that the rule should be completed before the Nativity of John the Baptist (June 24). It was a far cry from the fervor and spontaneity of personal religion which Mary of Oignies had known and had best exemplified in her own daily life, for discipline and religious exercises must henceforth be precisely defined and regularized. No canon was to hear the confessions of the beguines or others unless the prior prescribed it. In the town of Oignies no one, with the exception of the prior, subprior, and village priest, was allowed to hear the confessions of laymen or beguines save in cases of necessity. Nor was anyone even expected to ask permission to hear these confessions.[77] In the interests of uniformity an ordinary of church services was to be prepared "because of the weakness of memory." Just as the appearance of laymen in the refectory was discouraged, so canons must not leave the convent to go into Oignies or the parishes without a companion. Finally, the visitors insisted that the money bequeathed by Jacques de Vitry should be used for the purposes for which it was intended.

This institutionalization went apace with and was in large measure the result of increased wealth. The *Fundatio Pitantiarum*, composed about 1244 by the prior, Siger, and sealed by Bishop Robert of Liége, assigns to Jacques de Vitry major credit for promoting the temporal and spiritual interests of the community. It corroborates the statement in the Rouge-Cloître MS.[78] and the *Supplementum*[79] that although called by the curia to a bishopric and cardinalate he never forgot the "pauper schola" that he left behind in Belgium. On the contrary, taking pains to fill its needs with Roman resources, he sent much gold from the city so that the brethren and guests were never without a supply of wine. What Oignies and, indeed, the whole diocese of Liége

[73] *Idem.*
[74] Berlière, *MB.*, I, 453f; Moschus, *Coenob. mon. Ogniac.*, pp. 17-19.
[75] Gerard of Rheims achieved some distinction for his sermons towards the middle of the century (Quétif-Echard, I, 479f).
[76] *ASAN.*, XXXI, 94-96, no. 108; MDAC., I, 1276-1278.
[77] *ASAN.*, XXXI, 95; MDAC., I, 1277 B.
[78] *AA. SS.*, XXV (June 23, v), 582 B (4).
[79] *VMO.* Suppl., 572ff.

meant to this eminent churchman will be described later in greater detail. Suffice it to say here that the *Fundatio* begins by commending the cardinal's scorn of riches when he first joined the canons regular as a humble priest and espoused the *vita apostolica* completely under the influence of Mary of Oignies. Yet eagerness to save souls and to promote the claims of the "primitive church" was commingled with a willingness to adapt himself to official duties which eventually led him through the hierarchy to a cardinal's hat. When he embarked at Genoa in the autumn of 1216 for the East[80] he took pains, as a newly appointed bishop, to assure ample quarters and supplies for himself and his servants.[81] As his position grew in importance with promotion by the Roman curia, Jacques de Vitry desired to provide his favorite sanctuary with silken vestments, relics of saints, other church ornaments and "innumerable" books,[82] as well as to fortify the house with "not a few privileges from the apostolic see." In March, 1220 he informed his Belgian friends, the abbess of Aywières and Master John of Nivelles, in a period of depression and infirmity that for the peace of his soul he was forwarding oriental silks taken by the crusaders at Damietta.[83] Again, we have it on Thomas of Cantimpré's authority that when the vestments and relics were destroyed by an accidental fire, it was Jacques de Vitry, still bishop of Acre (1216-1227), who replaced "within ten years" the lost objects from the East.[84] Among the oriental objects may very well have been an episcopal miter which eventually found its way into the Convent of the Sisters of Notre-Dame at Namur.[85] Besides, the bishop donated much money for the purpose of acquiring property, thereby lightening the poverty of St. Nicholas.

"Realizing that the absence of wine would dissuade educated and 'mature' persons from submitting there to the yoke of the order and fearing that, for want of counsel and the dearth of distinguished persons, the religion of the place would become lukewarm and the church would be less frequented by substantial people (*a bonis*)," the cardinal on his death bequeathed 1500 *l.* to acquire vineyards or at least land on which viticulture could be practiced. From the produce of this property the convent, the infirm, and guests would, it

[80] The bishop landed at Acre on November 4, 1216 ("*sexta ... feria post festum Omnium Sanctorum*"), Ep. 2 (end of March, 1217), ZKG., XIV, 109.

[81] Ep. I (October, 1216), *ibid.*, 105.

[82] *ASAN.*, XXXI, 102; MDAC., I, 1278 E. Cf. Greven, *Exempla*, p. x. For the library of St. Nicholas, see Poncelet in *ASAN.*, XXXI, pp. xxii-xxiii.

[83] Ep. VI, ZKG., XVI, 83, cf. 78.

[84] *VMO.* Suppl., 576 (13). Cf. fragment assigned by Poncelet to ca. 1224 (*ASAN.*, XXXI, 43, no. 47).

[85] Jos. Braun ("Die Paramente im Schatz der Schwestern U. L. Frau zu Namur," *Zeitschr. f. christliche Kunst*, 1906, coll. 289-304) was inclined to credit the two miters to the goldsmith of Oignies; Greven ("Die Mitra des Jakob von Vitry und ihre Herkunft," *ibid.*, 1907, coll. 217-222) was convinced that one, and possibly both, were of oriental origin, presumably sent by Jacques de Vitry.

was hoped, be well enough provided with wine, since the faculties of the church had not heretofore been adequate. We have seen that the earliest statutes, dating from the same decade as Jacques' death, took precautions to prevent the abuse of hospitality and the consequent neglect of study and meditation. But Mary's biographers leave no doubt that outsiders from all classes had been eagerly welcomed from the beginning.[86] Finally, the prior established, in consequence of the cardinal's generosity, a pittance of wine and instituted a solemn mass which was to be celebrated daily before the donor's tomb.[87] In this document we have a splendid example of a convent admitting its compromise with the world, brought about by a well-intentioned, but practical-minded patron, which might seriously obstruct, if not thoroughly vitiate, the original aims, conceived in humility and poverty. At the same time it is a good commentary on the basic realism of the cardinal's nature—minutiae as well as big issues deserved meticulous care.

Episcopal orders notwithstanding, codification of the statutes was not yet complete. Seven years later (1250) Peter of Albano, apostolic legate then passing through Belgium, was obliged to order a new inspection of the community, entrusting it to his chaplain, Stephen, as well as the two Dominicans from Liége.[88] The compilation of customs was to be finished before the feast of John the Baptist, on pain of complete deprivation of wine until the legatine decree had been executed. This time the canons obeyed, the register of statutes appearing before June 24, 1251.[89] In the interests of uniform religious practices the legate expressed again the need for an ordinary of prayers and hymns to be read and sung in services and ceremonies day and night. Like contemporary conciliar legislation, the statutes forbade law cases to be held in the monastery or the admission of laymen, especially during periods of silence and lection.[90] Ornaments, chalices, and all books must be registered and the sacristan was expected to render an annual account.[91] With Baldwin's apparent malfeasance still fresh in mind, both the 1250 statutes and the 1251 ordinances prescribed close supervision of the prior's business transactions. Of special interest for this

[86] In spite of subsequent restrictions (statutes of September 10, 1405, published by John of Bavaria, bishop of Liége, *ASAN*, XXXII, 98 and constitution granted by Engelbert Desbois, bishop of Namur, on June 4, 1650, *ibid.*, 106-108) it is evident from the provisions made in the accounts for lodging and food for *"hostes et sourvenants"* that the practice never completely degenerated (cf. Poncelet, in *ASAN.*, XXXI, pp. xi-xii).

[87] *Ibid.*, 103; MDAC., I, 1278f.

[88] *ASAN.*, XXXI, 123-128, no. 137; Martène, *De antiquis ecclesiasticis ritibus*, III, 345f.

[89] *ASAN.*, XXXI, 131-144, no. 141. The cardinal-legate confirmed the statutes on November 13, 1250, at Floreffe whose church he dedicated on that day.

[90] *Ibid.*, 126.

[91] *Ibid.*, 127.

study was the continued hostility to the *cura beguinarum*[92] which already had been reflected in the 1243 constitution. An amplification of most of these provisions was contained in the register: the election, installation, and conduct of the prior, no alienation of property without the consent of the chapter, with 20 *l.* of Louvain being the critical amount;[93] election, office, and dismissal of the subprior.[94]

[92] See below, p. 60.

[93] 1251 ordinances: "Ne possessiones alienentur vel commutentur nisi per consilium totius capituli" (*ASAN.*, XXXI, 134; cf. 140: "De negociis que prior non sine consilio fratrum debeat tractare"); 1250 statutes, *ibid.*, 128.

[94] Subsequent reforms of the monastery included that of September 10, 1405, undertaken by the bishop of Liége at the end of a canonical visitation by Gilles Bofis, a lawyer, and Gerard de Momalle, canon of St. Denis at Liége (*ibid.*, XXXII, 95-101, no. 376; Martène, *De antiquis eccl. ritibus*, III, 347f); that the prior Jaspar Offus in 1499 in the wake of relaxed discipline (*ASAN.*, XXXI, p. xviii, text not given by Poncelet); the constitution promulgated by Engelbert Desbois, bishop of Namur, in 1650 (*ibid.*, XXXII, 104-118, no. 378).

⚜ III ⚜

The Education of Jacques de Vitry
in Belgium

No person was more closely identified with the early beguine movement and the Cistercian world as it came to grips with the acute *Frauenfrage* in the north than Jacques de Vitry.[1] He, more accurately than anyone else, justly appraised and vividly described, with a European-wide perspective, the aims and problems, while suggesting their solution, of the semireligious communities which were beginning to assume huge proportions in Belgium, and more specifically in the diocese of Liége, to which he most properly belonged by religious profession at Oignies, apostolic work, and auxiliary duties for the episcopal curia. He made himself patron and spokesman of the extraregular at the papal court.[2] At the same time his enthusiasm was tempered by a consideration of the dangers that lurked in secret conventicles and extraregular associations unless they were completely incorporated into the ecclesiastical structure and remained obedient to its doctrine and laws. As an active intermediary between Cistercian and beguine, Jacques lent his support to the establishment of nunneries and corresponded from the East not only with Master John of Nivelles and his brethren at Oignies, but with Walter, abbot of Villers,[3] and Lutgard of St. Trond and the convent of Aywières.[4] Similarly, he has been represented as the bridge between the popular religious excitement in Umbria and Tuscany which was concentrated in St. Francis of Assisi and the feminine religious movement in the diocese of Liége.[5]

Jacques de Vitry was an eyewitness and chronicler of the siege of

---

[1] For the life and writings of Jacques de Vitry see Funk, *Jakob von Vitry;* Matzner, *De Jacobi Vitriacensis vita;* Daunou, in *HLF.*, XVIII (1835), 209-246; Greven, *Anfänge,* pp. 56-59, 119-121.

[2] See below, p. 156.

[3] Ep. VI (March, 1220), ed. Röhricht, *ZKG.*, XVI (1896), 72-84; Ep. VII (April 18, 1221), *ibid.*, 84-113.

[4] Ep. I (October, 1216), *ibid.*, XIV (1894), 101-106; Ep. II (March, 1217), *ibid.*, 106-118; Ep. VI (*l.c.*).

[5] See below, pp. 313f.

Damietta, canon regular and pastor in Brabant and Liége attuned to
the demands of the *vita apostolica*, fashioner and purveyor of *exempla*,
compelling crusade-preacher, bishop of Acre, auxiliary bishop of Liége,[6]
and cardinal-legate at the court of his friend, Pope Gregory IX. His
academic interests and spiritual objectives[7] were encouraged, broadened, and channelled by personal association with Mary of Oignies as
well as communication with Aywières, even as ubiquitous travel informed his understanding. Despite indefatigable labors as a crusade
preacher[8] and official duties which consumed the years following his
elevation to the episcopate in 1216, Belgium remained the lodestone
which drew him consciously northward. Jacques was French, belonging to a noble family in Rheims[9] and enjoying prebends to pursue his
studies at Paris. But, however notable his success as preacher in France
or his renown in the Levant, he never forgot the solitude of St. Nicholas or the directness and simplicity of Mary. The awakening which
this new devotion caused in him was the big event of his life. Nivelles,
Aywières, Oignies, and Liége — all had a compulsion which he was
powerless to resist. From his donations and legacies, by his protection
and indults, Belgian religious houses obtained material support. The
fact that the manuscripts of the *Sermones feriales et communes*, which
belong to the period of his cardinalate (1229–1240), occur only in
Belgium and that originally three of them lay in monasteries of that

[6] Berlière, "Les évêques auxiliaires de Liége," *RB.*, XXIX (1912), 69-73; Ernst,
Tableau historique, pp. 64-76; Hugo, Ann. Praem., 1, 889; Van Gestel, *Hist. sacr.
Mechl.*, p. 232. cf. Matthew Paris, *Chron. maj.*, ed. Luard, III, 236 (an. 1232).

[7] For limitations of learning see *Sermo XV, Quod in Gazophylacio Scripturarum
refici deberemus, antequam alias reficiamus* (Pitra, *Anal. Nov.*, II, 359-364); *Sermo
XVI, Ad scholares (ibid.,* 365-372).

[8] By 1211 William, archdeacon of Paris, and Master Jacques de Vitry, under
commission of the papal legate, Bishop Raymond of Usèz, assumed the office of
preaching in France and Germany, winning *ad Christi miliciam* during the winter
"an unbelievable multitude of the faithful" who began to arrive the following spring
in the county of Toulouse (Pierre de Vaux-Cernay, *Historia Simonis Comitis de
Monte-Forti, MGH. SS.*, XXVI, 399, cap. 58, 62; for the date, see Berlière in *RB.*,
XXIX (1912), 70; Funk, *Jakob von Vitry,* pp. 33-35). For the very late date 1217
Guillaume de Puy-Laurens, no longer an eyewitness (*Historia Albigensium, MGH.
SS.*, XXVI, 597, cap. 30), reports that Foulques of Toulouse, together with Jacques,
was sent to preach the cross in France. Cf. *MDAC.*, VI, 327-330; Vincent of Beauvais,
Spec. Hist. (XXX, 10), *MGH. SS.*, XXIV, 165-166; John of Colonna, *Mare historia-
rum, ibid.*, 281; Matthew Paris, *Vita Stephani Archiepiscopi Cantuariensis, ibid.*,
XXVIII, 443; Thomas of Cantimpré, *BUA.*, I, 22, 2 (pp. 89f); II, 18, 2 (pp. 22ff);
for Jacques' own evidence, *VMO.*, 569 (96); *Exempla*, ed. Crane, nos. 26, 121; Greven,
Exempla aus den Sermones feriales, p. 58, no. 98 (cf. Frenken, *Exempla*, pp. 143f,
no. 95). Cf. Greven, "Frankreich und der fünfte Kreuzzug," *HJ.*, XLIII (1923), 15-52;
for Jacques and indulgences see Paulus, *Geschichte des Ablasses*, I, 241f; II, 53f,
137f, 194f.

[9] The question of Jacques de Vitry's birthplace (Funk, *Jakob von Vitry*, pp. 4-7;
Berlière in *RB.*, XXIX (1912), 69; Frenken, *Exempla*, pp. 19-22) may be resolved by
an *exemplum* from the *Sermones feriales* where he refers to himself as "Magistrum
Jacobum, Remensem nacione, canonicum Cameracensem" (Greven, *Exempla*, p. 7
and note 2; id., in *HJ.*, XLIII (1923), 21, note 21).

country leads to the conclusion that Jacques de Vitry transmitted this collection of sermons to his Belgian friends without caring for further dissemination.[10] Besides, many an *exemplum* was the fruit of preaching, study, and observation in that country[11] as well as in northern France, especially Paris.[12]

Thomas of Cantimpré brings out clearly in the *Supplementum,* written shortly after Gregory IX's election to the Holy See in 1227, that what took his friend to Oignies was Mary's renown and the desire to identify himself with her work.[13] However much Funk[14] challenged this presentation — the departure from Paris where he had pursued his theological studies with immoderate fervor[15] and the visit to Oignies (on account of Mary), affiliation with the canons regular (at Mary's behest), preaching activity (under Mary's guidance), and ordination (at Mary's insistence) — as a tissue of hagiographical devices, it nevertheless is plausible, if judged in the light of the *Vita Mariae Oigniacensis* itself. It is an account which richly deserves attention even if it came from the "great story-teller before the Lord."[16] Jacques de Vitry, after all, was no different from many a devout person of his day who eagerly gathered news of women mystics and established communication with them in person or by correspondence. In the Augustinian priory Mary's personality and the ascetic atmosphere of which it remained the center worked a profound change in a man who was always earnestly religious, but till then only in an institutional and theological sense.[17] Zealous for the salvation of souls, she asked him to settle in the community and to dedicate himself to the apostolic mission. But first he ought to return to Paris to complete his studies. Soon after his ordination in 1210 by Bishop Pierre de Nemours (1208–1219)[18] Jacques was back in Brabant, for the following year he affixed his signature with the title of *magister* to a ducal document on behalf of the abbey of Aywières.[19] He now affiliated himself with the priory and, with the encouragement

---

[10] Greven, *Exempla*, p. x. J. Coenen (*Annales du cercle hutoise des sciences et beaux-arts*, XX (1926), 141), without citing his source, reports that after reading one of Jacques' works where it was a question of Peter the Hermit a canon Maurice developed an admiration for the founder of his convent of Neufmoustier.

[11] Crane, *Exempla*, no. 35; Greven, *Exempla*, nos. 4, 44, 45.

[12] Crane, *Exempla*, nos. 23, 31, 103, 115, 208; Greven, *Exempla*, nos. 6, 16, 17, 18, 35, 36, 37, 40, 46, 61, 84, 86, 97, 101, 104, 105.

[13] *VMO., Suppl.*, 573.

[14] Funk (*Jakob von Vitry*, pp. 18ff) was particularly severe in his refutation of the historicity of Thomas of Cantimpré's account. Cf. Greven's criticism (*Anfänge*, pp. 104f, note 1).

[15] *VMO. Suppl.*, 573 D.

[16] Berlière, in *Arch. belg.*, I (1899), 98.

[17] Funk, *Jakob von Vitry*, p. 69: "Jakob ist ein durchaus religiöser Mensch, aber … seine Religiosität ist voll und ganz kirchlich-traditionell und … scholastisch-wissenschaftlich orientiert."

[18] *VMO. Suppl.*, 573 E; cf. *VMO.*, 566 (86).

[19] Berlière in *RB.*, XXV (1908), 185.

of Mary and other colleagues, assumed pastoral duties.[20] He celebrated his first mass in this church in her presence.[21] Under her tutelage he developed into a worthy successor to the evangelical preacher of the previous century and a prefiguration of the friars. One pain lingered, troubling him incessantly: "Periculum ... animarum regiminis, dum defectus meos considero multiplices, et qualem oporteat esse episcopum ex apostoli verbis animadverto" (cf. I Tim. III, 2–7).[22] It is not altogether rhetoric or polemic to add with the Dominican that "Jacques deserted for the love of the handmaiden of Christ, country, kinsmen, and the mother of all arts at Paris." That the contribution was far from unilateral, however, may be concluded from the greeting she tendered him on his return.[23]

Mary's early desire to withdraw from the world was to yield in mature years to an all-consuming passion for the cure of souls. Thus she preferred to surround herself with preachers and men intensely concerned with spiritual ministration.[24] Her knowledge of Scripture was fostered by their sermons.[25] For his own external activity, namely preaching in the field, Jacques readily attributed to her major assistance through her enthusiasm and freshness of approach. He was merely her instrument, he tells us, providentially sent so that he might preach what she inspired in him through her prayers. Unable to perform this task herself, she chose to accomplish this mission through a deputy.[26] She even obtained for him special favors in delivering his sermons.[27].

Not only did Mary incite Jacques de Vitry to become a "preacher to peoples" and to recover souls,[28] but she served as a conscience and a seeress. Approaching death, she singled out for special prayer "her preacher" whose sins she knew "as if she had seen them written before her in a book."[29] She also prophesied repeatedly his future career, especially with reference to the Albigensian crusade[30] and the then improbable appointment to the bishopric of Acre.[31] This prerogative,

---

[20] VMO. Suppl. 573 (2); cf. 581 D; Vincent of Beauvais, Spec. Hist. (XXX, 10), MGH. SS., XXIV, 165; Gilles d'Orval, Gesta Episcoporum Leodiensium (III, 77), ibid., XXV, 118; cf. Funk, Jakob von Vitry, pp. 15-21.
[21] VMO., 566 D (86).
[22] Ep. I (October, 1216), ZKG., XIV (1894), 101.
[23] VMO. Suppl., 573 E (2).
[24] VMO., 562 F (68).
[25] Idem; 563 (71).
[26] Ibid., 562-563 (69).
[27] Rouge-Cloître MS., AA. SS., XXV (June 23, 'v), 581 D; cf. VMO. Suppl., 573 (1); Vincent of Beauvais, Memoriale omnium Temporum, MGH. SS., XXIV, 160; Spec. Hist., ibid., 165.
[28] VMO. Suppl., 573 D (2).
[29] VMO., 570 (101).
[30] Ibid., 565 E (82).
[31] VMO., Suppl., 573 (3). Thomas of Cantimpré claims that the prophecy took place four years before the election and consecration, hence in 1211 or 1212.

however, had to be shared with another mystic, Lutgard of Aywières, who shortly before his election to the bishopric intervened when he was showing to a languishing *mulier religiosa* "too human a love" to the detriment of his preaching.[32]

Long after her death Mary continued to come back to Jacques in visions, bolstering him in crises and acting as a mentor. Until his death in 1240 he remained the constant sponsor of her name. When invited to consecrate the new church at Oignies about 1226, he translated for the first time "her bones some of which he deposited in small boxes, consecrated by himself, together with other saints' relics; he then granted indulgences to all men and women who, visited her tomb and contributed to the building of the church."[33] Yet she was more than a patron saint, for he had worked with her. In 1227 when he consecrated at the instance of Prior Gilles five altars — four to saints and one to the Trinity — he was obeying a vision in which she had appeared to him and ordered him to perform this ceremony.[34] Before dying she left him her girdle and the linen which she used to wipe her tears as well as other small things "dearer to me than gold and silver."[35] He carried with him on his first journey to Rome one of her fingers, and the successful riding of the misfortunes which befell him in crossing a river in Lombardy was convincing proof that the efficacy of these relics must not be questioned.[36] On another journey, this time from Acre to Rome (1226), he came near shipwreck but was spared by the intercession of his saint and by her relics "which he always wore around his neck."[37] Similarly, the tone and content of the *Vita Mariae Oigniacensis* indicate that it was written on the spot when memories were still lively and compelling. In her prophecies and revelations he generally placed undiminished confidence. Nevertheless, when called upon to decide whether to remain faithful to modest apostolic work in Belgium or to enter the more lucrative but precarious curial circles, he was not dissuaded from his choice by her alleged reproaches.[38] For Thomas of Cantimpré and the canons of Oignies this was the crucial decision of his life. Utilizing hagiographical devices as well as argument premised on the *vita apostolica,* the Dominican set out in the *Supplementum* primarily to prove that his master had committed a serious error. Thus he underscored Mary's pivotal role in Jacques de Vitry's

[32] *V. Lutg.,* 196-197 (II, 3). At his death in 1240 Lutgard, although in Brabant, was said to have seen Jacques' soul ascending to heaven *(ibid.,* 205, III, 5).

[33] *Comm. praev., VMO.,* 542 (1); cf. Eugene Hucq, "Le sarcophage présumé de la bienheureuse Marie d'Oignies," *ASAN.,* XXXVIII (1927), 231-244; Poncelet, in *ASAN.,* XXXI (1912), p. lxv.

[34] *VMO. Suppl.,* 579 (21).

[35] *VMO.,* 569 B (96).

[36] Ep. I, *ZKG.,* XIV (1894), 102.

[37] *VMO. Suppl.,* 578 (20).

[38] *Ibid.,* 579 (23).

career to demonstrate that his rightful place was back at Oignies.

In spite of this one significant deviation from her precept, as Thomas presents it, the confessor never forgot his protectress and even transferred her merits to his friends. Cardinal Ugolino, the future Pope Gregory IX, deeply disturbed by corruption and defection from the faith, was often on the point of despair; fearing that he might succumb under these assaults and even become guilty of apostasy,[39] he confided his lack of security and assurance to Jacques de Vitry in an intimate conversation and asked his advice and prayers. Jacques did what he could to console his friend "who had long wanted to see him" and concluded by suggesting that he read the biography of Mary of Oignies and even proffered to him one of her fingers in a silver case which he asserted had preserved him from danger on land and sea.[40]

By training Jacques de Vitry was a theologian, by calling, another priest in the hierarchy; by temperament he was a churchman to the core. So true is this that he does not write as a historian, penetrating as his observations could be, but as a prelate and an apostle, keenly conscious of his mission.[41] Knowledge must be purposeful, the end being an increase in the understanding of Christ.[42] His writings are all heavily freighted with scriptural quotations and allusions. They even augment the narrative of contemporary events. He sees the world with a religious eye and judges it with the conviction of a moralist. Everything is described in white and black, as sanctity or sin. But let him voice his own confidence: "Jews combat the incarnation of Christ, heretics the truth of Scripture, both thereby attacking the Christian faith; schismatics the obedience and unity of the Church, Saracens and pagans ecclesiastical peace, tyrants and wicked Christians the freedom of the Church, false brethren charity. Against Jews and heretics are raised the holy doctors, opening to them the means of knowing Scripture; against the schismatics communion of the saints, the rule of prelates, and obedience of subjects; against the violence of pagans and Saracens the temporal sword; against tyrants and false brethren the spiritual sword which is used against both heretics and schismatics to compel them to return to the Church."[43] Before Damietta, he complains, martyrdom was not intended for him. He had gone forth without arms in the company of the legate and patriarch who bore a cross, but "it did not please God to call me, unworthy and miserable,

[39] *VMO. Suppl.*, 577 (15).

[40] *Ibid.*, 578 (16-17); cf. *V. Lutg.*, 209 A (III, 19).

[41] Funk, *Jakob von Vitry*, pp. 184f; Crane, *Exempla*, nos. 86, 87, 89, 90, 122, 124.

[42] "Omnis quidem scientia debet referri ad cognitionem Christi..." (Pitra, *Anal. Nov.*, II, 360; cf. 368). For an indictment against false values pursued by scholars see *ibid.*, 359, 366f.

[43] *Sermo XXXVII ad fratres ordinis militaris, insignitos charactere Militiae Christi, ibid.*, 405.

to his martyrs; he wanted to preserve me for labor and sorrow."[44] Yet moral earnestness was tempered by a shrewd, practical sense. Just as he knew how to enliven his sermons with humor,[45] so he withheld approval from demonstrations of immoderate or misguided zeal.[46]

Jacques de Vitry must have made his first acquaintance with the apostolic calling while still a student at Paris. Here he had found "true preachers" who, like John of Nivelles and John de Liro, were intent on redemption of souls and faithful discharge of duties.[47] Yet theirs was merely a continuation of recent reform efforts sponsored by the "building" bishop of Paris, Maurice of Sully (1160—1196),[48] who directed the pastors of the diocese to preach daily and, to aid them in their work, prepared a manual of homilies.[49] Of more immediate importance was the popular preacher, in apostolic style, Foulques de Neuilly (d. 1202)[50] whose rugged enthusiasm was not sufficient, however, to overcome charges of illiteracy and the indifference of the public.[51] In Paris he proved to be a forceful penitential preacher in the open square and, like the canon Rudolf in the archbishopric of Mainz[52] and Master William of Auvergne, a theologian at the university,[53] both in the next generation, he converted numerous prostitutes, urging them to cut their hair and to submit to monastic discipline.[54] Although once pursuing a worldly life and full of animal spirits,[55] Foulques had studied in Paris under Master Peter Cantor (d. 1197)[56] in the cathedral of Notre-Dame.[57] Jacques de Vitry dwells with particular fondness on Foulques' direct but untutored approach[58]

[44] Ep. VI (March, 1220), ZKG., XVI (1896), 81f.

[45] E.g., Crane, Exempla, nos. 220, 277.

[46] Ibid., nos. 55 (for a possible reference to Guillaume de l'Olive see below p. 49, n. 81), 85.

[47] Hist. Occid., cap. ix, pp. 289f.

[48] Lecoy de la Marche, pp. 42ff; HLF., XV (1869), 149-158.

[49] Lecoy de la Marche, p. 46; C. A. Robson, Maurice of Sully and the Medieval Vernacular Homily with the Text of Maurice's French Homilies from a Sens Cathedral Chapter MS. (Oxford, 1952).

[50] Hist. Occid., cap. vi, pp. 275-277; cf.Milton R. Gutsch, " A Twelfth Century Preacher—Fulk of Neuilly," in The Crusades and Other Historical Essays, pp. 183-206; Simon, pp. 3-5.

[51] Gutsch, op. cit., p. 185.

[52] De Rebus Alsaticis ineuntis saeculi XIII, MGH. SS., XVII, 234f; see below, p. 161.

[53] These were Filles-Dieu (Alberic de Trois-Fontaines, Chron., MGH. SS., XXIII, 917, an. 1225).

[54] Bouquet, XIX, 245; Hist. Occid., p. 276.

[55] "Tanquam animalis, et non intelligens, quae Dei sunt, saeculariter prius valde vixerat" (idem).

[56] Ibid., pp. 280-289 (cap. 8); Gutjahr, Petrus Cantor Parisiensis, p. 17.

[57] PL., CCV, 12-14; Gutjahr, op. cit., passim; Grabmann, Geschichte der scholastischen Methode, II, 478-501.

[58] "Sacerdos ruralis, simplicis valde et illiterati" (Hist. Occid., p. 275); "erubescens ... quod idiota et illiteratus esset, et divinas scripturas ignoraret ..." (ibid., p. 277).

as he broke his bread with children. Such simplicity could not be expected from educated priests who were intent on vain disputations and word battles in Paris lecture halls.[59] The preacher was intensely practical; he knew how to employ various expedients to collect an audience[60] and, on occasion, to move "multitudes" to take the cross against infidels.[61] Similarly, the authority of the precentor, often called to higher dignities, grew so great that even masters and students left their tablets and schedules to report his sermons.[62] Judging from the warm praise he bestowed on him, Jacques may very well have been one of his pupils.[63]

Such men had thus helped to mold the character of Jacques de Vitry, but without the forcefulness of the Oignies experience. Since it is "hard to stand in fire without burning," he once wrote, and there is nothing more hostile to piety and peace of mind than the tumult of men and association with the wicked, many have renounced the world in order more safely to flee the threatening dangers and its blandishments and have sought a harbor in regular life.[64] That is why he left Paris, whose worldly and sterile academic life were matched only by its moral turpitude, in order to seek out the sanctuary of St. Nicholas.[65] Such a decayed atmosphere and the pursuit of ulterior motives were incompatible with apostolic aims, at least until one was sure of himself. Some sixty years later the Dominican, Peter of Dacia, reacted somewhat differently to a city where he found the "most devout novices, the most learned students, the most religious monks, and the kindest prelates; among whom, as stones of fire, superb men, I myself converse as the shame of men and the outcast of the people..." But arid in the midst of such great devotion of so many men, cold among so many fervent men, remiss in their so strenuous conversation, and lax beside their strict religion, he longed to be back in the company of the beguine Christine of Stommeln in whom he too had discovered a mentor. At least through her intercession may he be awakened "from this torpor of insensibility, this lukewarmness of negligence, this loitering drowsiness of mine."[66]

---

[59] "Litterati ... circa disputationes vanitatis et pugnas verborum intenti" (ibid., p. 276).

[60] Jacques de Vitry, Exempla, ed. Greven, pp. 35f, no. 52.

[61] Guillaume de Nangis, Chronicon, an. 1202, Bouquet, XX, 750.

[62] Hist. Occid., pp. 287f.

[63] Cf. Funk, Jakob von Vitry, pp. 11, 69. Peter taught at Paris from 1170 to 1197 (CUP., I, 14, no. 3). The Historia Fundationis (MDAC., VI, 327-330) indicates that Jacques studied there as early as 1187; hence Funk (pp. 8-10) concludes that he was born during the decade 1160-1170. Cf. Thomas of Cantimpré, BUA., II, 1, 19 (p. 121f); II, 30, 12 (p. 326); CHD., XII, 48.

[64] Hist. Occid., p. 295.

[65] Ibid., cap. 7, pp. 277ff; cap. 11, pp. 295f; cf. Speculum Exemplorum, Sermo LXIV (Pitra, Anal. Nov., II, 456).

[66] Acta Chr. Stum., 267 (II, 41).

As a crusade preacher against the Albigensians, Jacques de Vitry had a majestic bearing that compelled respect.[67] He always came as the deputy of the pope, as a prince with a band of co-workers drawn from older monastic orders[68] and, as bishop-elect to Acre, he arrived in Italy with a retinue of servants, horses, and beasts of burden.[69] At the same time his sermons, geared to the needs and ability of his audience[70] and informed with the familiar, did not fit into the frame-work of the usual service; the congregations' grew so large that they had to be held outside. Thomas of Cantimpré, as a lad not yet fifteen years old, had been much impressed by his preaching in Brabant and Liége.[71] Nor did Jacques himself neglect to remind his friends of the effectiveness of his exhortation to confess, to embrace the Christian life, or to take the cross.[72] The French Dominican, Stephen of Bour-bon, in his *Septem Dona Spiritus Sancti*[73] affirms that his preaching in the kingdom and the use of *exempla* stirred France as never, in the memory of man, a preacher had moved it.[74] This judgment received the support of Jacques' successor to the see of Tusculum, Odo of Châteauroux, with emphasis on his appeal to women.[75]

Although not an innovator of examples, it was Jacques who gave currency to a practice that scarcely is earlier than 1200 and made it a device which Dominicans, among others, were soon to turn to such good advantage.[76] The beguines of Léau to whom Beatrice of Nazareth

[67] Rouge-Cloitre MS., *AA. SS.*, XXV (June 23, v), 581 D.

[68] Greven, in *HJ.*, XLIII (1923), 21f.

[69] Ep. I, *ZKG.*, XIV, 101.

[70] See the homely example of sewing given to the Black Nuns in Sermo XXVII (Pitra, *Anal. Nov.*, II, p. xx, note 3).

[71] *VMO. Suppl.*, 581 (27). See the tradition as perpetuated by Vincent of Beauvais: "...Melliflua sua predicatione multos de Francie regno contra Albigenses dato signo crucis transmisit" (*Memor. omn. Temp.*, *MGH. SS.*, XXIV, 160); and, with reference to his preaching against the Albigensians in France: "eloquii suavitate atque dul-cedine multos atque innumerabiles ad signum crucis accipiendum provocavit" (*Spec. Hist.*, cap. 30, *ibid.*, 166); Guillaume de Puy-Laurens: "Magister Iacobus de Vitriaco. vir magne honestatis, litteraturae et eloquentie" (*Hist. Albig.*, *ibid.*, XXVI, 597); cf. Trithemius: "Vir in divinis scripturis eruditus et secularium non ignarus, mori-bus et vita spectabilis, in declamandis sermonibus ad populum excellentis ingenii fuit, et crucem contra Albienses (sic) haereticos gloriose praedicans, multos fideles in eos Apostolica authoritate signavit" (*De Scriptoribus ecclesiasticis*, cap. 432, in Fabricius, *Bibliotheca eccl.*).

[72] Ep. II, *ZKG.*, XIV, 108-110, 112; cf. Crane, *Exempla*, pp. 63f.

[73] The full title is *Tractatus de diversis materiis praedicabilibus, ordinatis et distinctis in septem partes secundum septem dona Spiritus Sancti* (Lecoy de la Marche, pp. 106, 109ff; De Vooys, *Middelnederlandse Legenden*, p. 44). The preface to the tract is published partly in Latin but mostly in translation in *HLF.*, XIX (1838), 31-36.

[74] "Praedicando per regnum Franciae et utens exemplis in sermonibus suis, adeo totam commovit Franciam, quod non patet memoria aliquem ante vel post sic movisse" (*HLF.*, XVIII, 1835, p. 213; Pitra, *Anal. Nov.*, p. xx, note 3).

[75] Pitra, *Anal. Nov.*, II, 297f, 331; Welter, p. 245, n. 55; Glorieux, I, 304-311.

[76] Thomas of Cantimpré and Stephen of Bourbon are cases in point. For a history of examples consult the introductions of Crane and Frenken. Cf. Charles H. Haskins,

was entrusted by her father employed the technique for edification.[77] The prerequisite for successful preaching had been posited in the preface to the *Vita Mariae Oigniacensis:* "Multis enim incitantur exemplis, qui non moventur praeceptis."[78] In examining the potential of the sermon and the new orientation it was receiving, Jacques defined this corollary further in the introduction to the *Sermones Vulgares* whose very fabric consists of "anecdotes" and Biblical texts. Rough preaching converts more laymen than the elaborate sword of a subtle sermon. Leaving behind affected and polished speech, one ought to turn his mind to the edification of rude men and the education of peasants to whom he must present again and again the tangible and concrete which they know from experience. For they are moved more by strange illustrations than by authorities or profound observations. Examples should at all times be edifying; purposeless tales, affected poems, and "pagan" fables must be omitted. Those conclusions of philosophers which are useful may be interspersed too. In practice examples were introduced not merely for edification, although a moral is generally deduced, but to excite attention. "Believe me, I speak from experience: once when I had preached a little too long and observed how the people fidgeted and fought sleep, then with one word I woke them all up and made them attentive. I remember saying that he who sleeps or dozes will not disclose my secrets or advice. Everyone . . . opened his eyes and, after making a noise, listened attentively in silence to my useful and serious words."[79] Jacques mastered the technique of showmanship and was an accomplished raconteur. He recognized the value of direct over indirect discourse for dramatic effect. He knew how to cajole as well as to exhort and upbraid an audience.[80] To make his sermons palatable he related personal experiences, tapped folk lore and beast fables, and gleaned pious legends from patristic sources.

However anxious to utilize the new sources of spiritual energy to rejuvenate a decadent society and arrest defection from orthodoxy, Jacques de Vitry never once considered a solution outside the ecclesiastical fabric or prescribed doctrine. At heart he was a traditionalist who did not question for a moment the intrinsic worth of the institution he had set out to defend. The rigidity of his teaching, within the scope defined by the Fourth Lateran Council, must be explained in large measure by the menace of the Albigensians. He was at one

"The University of Paris in the Sermons of the Thirteenth Century." *American Historical Review*, x (1904), 1-27; revised in *Studies in Mediaeval Culture* (Oxford Press, 1929), pp. 36-71; Welter, pp. 66-69, 118-124, 137ff.

[77] *V. Beat.*, ed. Henriquez, p. 10. Cf. Humbert de Romans, *De modo prompte cudendi sermones, Bibl. Max. Vet. Pat.*, XXV, 433 F.

[78] *VMO.*, 547 D.

[79] Pitra, *Anal. Nov.*, II, 193.

[80] Crane, *Exempla*, p. 59, no. 129.

with the Flemish moralist for whom any probing of the mystery of
the Trinity was cause for alarm:

> Beeste es die mensche, die wille roeken
> Te naeuwe omme die Godheit loeken;
> Hets recht dat hijt beweent.[81]

For those beguines who were condemned at the Council of Vienne
for disputing doctrine and discussing the nature of the Trinity the
bishop would have shown no more sympathy than he did for a simple
uneducated townsman.[82] Refusal to receive the sacraments from unworthy hands signifies "excessive simplicity."[83] The axiom with which
he introduced one of his beast fables summarizes his position: "Quanto
magis nos Deo patri nostro et matri nostre ecclesie obedire debetis, et
florem juventutis Domino consecrare."[84] Even the Franciscans though
imitating the primitive church and informed with evangelical fervor,
seemed to him on one occasion dangerous, for instead of submitting
to the test and discipline of conventual life, the young and imperfect,
setting out in pairs, were attracted by a world-wide mission free from
diocesan controls.[85] Yet this criticism, however easily understandable,
did not belie his undiminished admiration for their way of life. A few
months later (September 22, 1220) Honorius III forbade St. Francis
and his priors and *custodes* to admit anyone to the profession of the
order unless he had undergone a year of probation.[86] Lest the recruits
"wander outside obedience and corrupt the purity of their poverty,"
this decree was designed not only to restrict membership to worthy candidates but to prevent easy separation. Thus was removed the one
obstacle to Jacques de Vitry's whole-hearted acceptance of the Franciscan program. In like fashion he labored to secure for the beguines
papal recognition, thereby anticipating the charge from their foes that
as a new unauthorized society they were incompatible with Lateran
decisions.

Although much too human to be a saint, Jacques identified himself
with the reform currents, while deploring decay inside and outside the
Church. During his first sojourn in Rome curial intrigue and ambition
repelled him even as Thomas of Cantimpré afterwards assailed the
papal court.[87] "I found much that was contrary to my spirit," he com-

---

[81] Jacob van Maerlant, *Van der Drievoudecheide* (ed. Verdam and Leendertz,
Strophische Gedichten, p. 68, vss. 43-45).

[82] "De quodam simplici layco [in Huy] valde fervente et sine sciencie zelum
nimium habente" (Greven, *Exempla*, p. 31, no. 44); De Vooys, *Middelnederlandse
Legenden*, p. 130.

[83] Crane, *Exempla*, p. 68, no. 155.

[84] *Ibid.*, p. 122, no. 290.

[85] Ep. VI (March, 1220), *ZKG.*, XVI (1896), 83.

[86] P. 6361, 7123, 7373, 7903, 10501, 10548, 11416, 11417, 11424.

[87] Thomas of Cantimpré (*VMO. Suppl.*, 577 E, no. 15) relates that when his friend
sent to Ugolino a heavy silver cup, finely wrought and beautiful to behold, full of

plained.[88] So engrossed were the officials with secular and temporal affairs, kings and kingdoms, disputes and suits, that scarcely any time remained for spiritual affairs.[89] But, he hastens to add, there is one solace in these decayed circles: many wealthy laymen of both sexes have abandoned their personal possessions for Christ and fled the world. These are the Friars Minor who enjoy the patronage of pope and cardinals. Instead of being preoccupied with secular matters, they work strenuously and eagerly every day to draw souls, which are dying, away from the vanities of the world. If prelates are like dumb dogs unable to bark, it is these simple, poor men who hold out the promise of salvation.[90] Corruption thus calls forth life. Everywhere Jacques saw forces at work combatting evil. The sinful Christians who followed the path of the crusaders and besmirched the Holy Land may well give rise to despair.[91] But to offset them there are many who look upon the expedition as "conversion" and a path to salvation.[92] Joyfully he announces in his sermon to the crusaders that "through this pilgrimage many have been saved who would otherwise have remained in their sins."[93] In short, the greatest good to come from crusading lies in the fact that after taking the cross men hasten to confession in order not to lose the advantage of their labor and promise to refrain from sin in the future in order not to lose so much good.[94] Alongside conscientious preachers like Foulques de Neuilly, Stephen Langton, archbishop of Canterbury, Master Walter of London, Master Robert de Courçon, afterwards cardinal,[95] Alberic of Laon, later archbishop of Rheims, Master John de Liro and John of Nivelles are numerous false prophets — the "cautones Satanae" — who feverishly seek offices and prebends, hawk fake relics to the laymen, deceive in divers ways the simple and naive, and extort sums under false pretenses by shaking their little

nutmeg, the bishop, "a consistent spurner of wealth," sent the cup back but kept the nutmeg, adding that it was from the East whereas the cup was the fruit of Rome. For the reaction of Jacques as well as Robert de Courçon, Peter Cantor, and Bishop Guy of Cambrai to pluralism see BUA., I, 19, 8 (pp. 73f).

[88] Hist. or., cap. 15, pp. 45f; cf. cap. 71, pp. 129f. For criticism of the regular and secular clergy in Sermones Vulgares see Crane, Exempla, nos. 1, 2, 3, 5, 6, 7, 10, 11, 12, 14, 16, 17, 19, 20 bis, 21, 22, 23, 43, 46, 48, 49, 50, 51, 58, 59, 60, 63, 67, 69, 70, 71, 84, 92, 117, 130, 140, 197, 210, 231, 233, 240, 241, 247, 264, 299.

[89] Ep. I, ZKG., XIV (1894), 103.

[90] Ibid., 103f; cf. 105.

[91] Hist. or., cap. 1 (pp. 1f); 68 (pp. 124f); 70 (pp. 127-129); 72 (pp. 130-132); 73 (pp. 133-136); 74 (p. 136).

[92] Sermo XLVIII, Ad cruce signatos vel cruce signandos (Pitra, Anal. Nov., II, 427).

[93] Ibid., 429. Cf. Odo de Châteauroux, Sermo XII, De invitatione ad crucem, ibid., 331f.

[94] Ibid., 429.

[95] Cf. Silvere Hanssens, "De legatiereis van Robert van Courson in Vlaanderen en Henegouwen," Misc. hist .... Alberti de Meyer, I, 528-538; Ch. Dickson, „Le cardinal Robert de Courson, sa vie," Archives d'histoire doctrinale et littéraire du moyen âge, IX (1934), 53-142.

bells. They inspire security in sin provided they are given alms, and this ill-gotten wealth they spend for bad ends. But the prelates who give them letters will be held accountable.[96]

Put simply, Jacques de Vitry's lifework was basically twofold: first to attack by sermon and crusade the opponents of the Church, both within and outside the pale, and then, in the interests of internal reform, to identify himself with and defend constructive religious communities. From these two closely related major aims flowed all the manifold subordinate interests, in the realm of both action and intellect. An incident is related which illustrates his sense of mission. Foulques of Ghent, a member of the patrician family Uutenhove and brother of Ermentrude (d. 1243) who founded beside St. Michael's the famous hospital of La Biloke,[97] had embraced the religious life, belonging in 1206 to the chapter of St. Pierre at Lille.[98] His virtue and knowledge had been attracting much attention when Jacques de Vitry arrived in that city to preach the crusade against the Albigensians. The papal deputy solicited aid from Foulques, but possibly for reasons of health he refused to answer the summons. Jacques thereupon became so incensed that he wished to have the canon rendered useless for all activity. According to Thomas of Cantimpré[99] the curse bore fruit, for he was afflicted for the rest of his life with continuous fevers and general infirmity. More prosaic sources, however, record his frequent endowment of the hospital.[100]

For the raptures of the *mulieres religiosae*, their body-destroying austerities, their inexhaustible flood of tears, the sense-experiences of their faith, their mystical marriage with the heavenly Bridegroom, and the excruciating reliving of the passion, Jacques shared fully the predilection—and credulity—of his age. Whether contemplating the awful experiences of Mary or the virtues of a relic, his mind suffered from the limitations which the naivite and coarse eschatology of the high middle ages could impose. But he was made of firmer stuff than his Dominican admirer. His vision remained clear; he was not likely to be

[96] *Hist. Occid.*, p. 291.

[97] Walters, *Geschiedenis der Zusters der Bijloke te Gent*, I, 48-54; MF., II, 99; GC., V, 219f; Paul Bergman in BNB., XXV (1930-1932), 986-988 ((based chiefly on Walters).

[98] Hautcoeur, *Histoire de Saint-Pierre*, I, 92f. His name occurs frequently in cartularies (*Cartul. de S. Pierre*, I, 85-86, no. 82 (1206); 1209, *ibid.*, 91-92, no. 89; July 3, 1210, *ibid.*, 93-94, no. 92; 1215, *ibid.*, I, 110-111, no. 112; 1221, *ibid.*, 157-158, no. 163). Walters too publishes several documents (*op. cit.*, II-III, 223, no. 2 (August, 1208); 224-225, no. 3; 228-230, no. 5 (May 13-20, 1212); 230-231, no. 6 (May 18, 1212); 231, no. 7 (1212); 234-235, no. 11 (March, 1218); 236-237, no. 13 (June, 1219), etc.).

[99] BUA., I, 22, 2 (pp. 89f).

[100] Cf. Walters, *op cit.*, I, 49ff; Foulques appears in several other documents: *Cartul. de S. Pierre*, I, 123-124, no. 127; 124-128, no. 128; 128-129, no. 129; 130, no. 131; 131-132, no. 133; 137-140, no. 142; 141-142, no. 145; 155, no. 155. Care must be exercised not to confuse him with another Foulques of Ghent (*ibid.*, I, 219, 243, 245, 246, 255, 263, 270, 297; cf. Hautcoeur, *Hist.*, p. 92, note 4).

more gullible than commonly accepted practices demanded. Earthly values must be measured in relation to eternity, but still they take the form of harsh fact. The academic world of Paris had failed to satisfy him because sophistication was incompatible with moral earnestness. That he could, on the contrary, be intensely practical and hardheaded is amply demonstrated by his provision for the material wellbeing of St. Nicholas. He likewise recognized clearly the strategic advantage to be obtained from an attack upon the Saracens in Egypt.[101] Nor was he one to slight possible promotion. On the other hand, his was the career of a man of action who finds strength in cultivating the interior life. Books were his weapons,[102] and the convent a retreat. Writing to his Belgian friends, he bemoaned the lack of time for prayer and study.[103] Returning to Oignies and Liége after his resignation of the bishopric of Acre he found himself once again for a short time in his true element—in contemplation and pastoral care—before being summoned to Rome to receive the cardinalate.[104] During prolonged absence correspondence was the product of strong friendship which alone sustained him in time of peril.[105]

Even as the *Historia Orientalis* and the letters are largely, but not exclusively, concerned with events and deeds, so they find their complement in the *Historia Occidentalis* and the biography of Mary of Oignies, both of which concentrate on manifestations of interior experience and the unfolding of fruitful spirituality. Chronicle is then supplemented by exhortation of sermon and by illustration of *exemplum*. The one is a composite picture of the moral conditions of western Europe together with a passionate justification of the apostolic life within the ecclesiastical pattern; the other is a case study of a personality which, fired by evangelical precept, illuminates a darkened society. In either case Jacques de Vitry's survey of world conditions comprehends the religious element only; the demands of apostolic life make him ready to condemn or sanctify. No contemporary was more sensitive to the shortcomings and potentialities of the extraregular as well as monastic world. He explored and understood the program of the Cistercians,[106] the military orders,[107] the Benedicti-

---

[101] Ep. IV (September 22, 1218), *ZKG.*, XV (1895), 570ff.

[102] Ep. I, *ibid.*, XIV, 103; cf. 105.

[103] Ep. VI, *ibid.*, XVI, 83: "Ego autem jam debilis et confractus corde in pace et tranquillitate vitam eam finire desidero." Cf. Ep. II, *ibid.*, XIV, 113.

[104] Alberic de Trois-Fontaines, *Chronica, MGH. SS.*, XXIII, 923.

[105] Ep. I, *ZKG.*, XIV, 101, 106. To Mary and Lutgard Jacques could add as a friend Christine Mirabilis (*VMO.*, prol., 549 A; for identification see *V. Lutg.*, 195 C (II, 22) and a host of lesser *mulieres sanctae*.

[106] *Sermo XXVIII, Ad monachas albas Cisterciensis ordinis et grisias et alias* (Pitra, *Anal. Nov.*, II, 376-382; *Hist. Occid.*, caps. 14, pp. 299-304; 15, pp. 304-307).

[107] Knights of the Hospital (*Hist. or.*, cap. 64, pp. 111-115; Sermones XXXIX-XL, Pitra, *Anal. Nov.*, II, 345); the Temple (*Hist. or.*, cap. 65, pp. 115-120; cf. pp. 108f); Teutonic knights (*ibid.*, cap. 66, pp. 120-123).

nes,[108] and the manifold bodies of Augustinian canons[109] who follow the "royal middle path." These congregations, having the same rule but different institutes, are seven in number: Prémontré,[110] Grammont,[111] St. Victor,[112] Arrouaise,[113] Vaul-les-Choux,[114] Val-des-Ecoliers, and the Friars Preachers.[115] In the midst of the desert, which was Paris, stood "the spiritual oasis of St. Victor which administered pure waters to the students in the city and diverse peoples coming from everywhere."[116] Judging from the enthusiasm with which Jacques praises this "port of tranquillity for students,"[117] it is possible that he himself retired to this house for a serenity that could not be found in the turbulence of the streets. Elsewhere he voiced his personal dependence on and gratitude to the Victorines, especially when he speaks of the great theologians of the school.[118] His own theology was conceivably influenced by Hugh,[119] "second after Augustine in learning."[120]

Jacques observed the early Franciscan women in northern Italy. Their residence in hospitals near cities and pursuit of voluntary poverty mitigated by manual work[121] must have reminded him of Mary and

[108] *Ibid.*, cap. 20, pp. 316-319; *Sermo XXII, Ad monachos nigros* (Pitra, *Anal. Nov.*, II, 372-375); *Sermo XXVII, Ad moniales nigras* (*ibid.*, 375-376); cf. Sermones XXIII, XXVI (*ibid.*, 345).

[109] *Hist. Occid.*, cap. 21, pp. 319-321; *Sermo XXX, Ad canonicos regulares* (Pitra, *Anal. Nov.*, II, 385-390). In the fifteenth century John Gielemans (*Anecdota*, p. 150) drew a distinction between the older canons—namely the branches described by Jacques de Vitry—and the new communities of his own day. On his deathbed in 1384 Gerard Groote recommended that his followers join the Augustinian order "for their rules are not so harsh as those of the Carthusians and Cistercians (Hyma, pp. 46f).

[110] *Hist. Occid.*, cap. 22, pp. 321-325.

[111] *Ibid.*, cap. 15, pp. 311-315.

[112] *Ibid.*, cap. 24, pp. 327-329; cf. Bonnard, *Histoire de St. Victor de Paris.*

[113] *Hist. Occid.*, cap. 23, pp. 325-326; cf. *Vita B. Heldemari Eremitae, fundatoris Aroasiae in Belgio, AA. SS.*, II (January 13, ii), 113-116.

[114] *Hist. Occid.*, cap. 17, pp. 307-309.

[115] Pitra, *Anal. Nov.*, II, 387, 389; see below.

[116] *Hist. Occid.*, p. 327. For this order alone did Rutebeuf find praise (*La Voie de Paradis*, Jubinal, II, 197, vss. 726ff; cf. *Vie du monde, ibid.*, II, 39, vss. 122-125; see below, p. 470.

[117] "Portus tranquillissimus scholarium" (*Hist. Occid.*, p. 327); cf. Bonnard, *op. cit.*, I, 194; CHD., II, 10 (ed. Strange, I, 75).

[118] *Hist. Occid.*, pp. 327-329. In his own day St. Victor had suffered a declension from Hugh's doctrinal unity and Richard's solid method (Bonnard, *op cit.*, I, 277f).

[119] Funk, *Jakob von Vitry*, pp. 11, 69, 154; Matzner, *De Jac. Vitriac.*, pp. 4f.

[120] Thomas of Cantimpré, *BUA.*, II, 16, 5 (p. 215). A small band of impoverished clerics from Aire in the diocese of Terouanne, who obtained from Robert de Cresch in 1202 a little church of St. Andrew, adopted the rule of St. Victor and eventually received from Gregory IX a bull of protection dated August 4, 1227. Bonnard reports, without citing his authority (*op. cit.*, I, 178; the bull is in neither Auvray nor Potthast), that Jacques de Vitry secured for them the favor of Matilda, widow of Count Philip of Flanders.

[121] "Mulieres vero iuxta civitates in diversis hospiciis simul commorantur, nichil accipiunt, sed de labore manuum vivunt" (Ep. I, *ZKG.*, XIV, 104). It is not clear from the context whether these are Clarisses or tertiaries. Jacques de Vitry presents the *fratres minores* and *mulieres* as separate in 1216, both having an organization con-

her coterie in Belgium. They were much distressed because they received from clergy and laity more respect than they desired. In like fashion he evaluated properly and with profound sympathy the significance of the Humiliati, in the light of Innocent III's favorable policy, as an effective answer to heresy in Milan.[122] In this "fovea hereticorum" they "abandon everything for Christ, form congregations, live by the labor of their hands, preach frequently and listen with eagerness to the word of God"; in short, they are firm in the faith and perform good works.[123] This *religio* had multiplied in the diocese to such an extent that one hundred fifty congregations of men and women had been organized, not to mention those who remained in their own homes. The Humiliati of Lombardy and the *mulieres religiosae* in Belgium alike faced criticism from "maliciosis et secularibus hominibus."[124] Both served as a bulwark against further defection. Jacques' emphasis on preaching, voluntary poverty, manual work, informal organization, and particularly the presence of "tertiaries"—"qui in domibus propriis remanserunt"—offers a cogent argument that these semireligious communities, owing their existence to the spiritual yearnings of townsmen, are all manifestations of a common phenomenon.

It is precisely the way of life pursued by Franciscan, Humiliati, and beguine which constitutes the consolation and hope of a Church beset with internal decay and rent by sectarianism. Jacques de Vitry was not at a loss to explain why Francis had set in motion the popular reform movement of the Middle Ages. A total disregard for class lines, complete renunciation of earthly goods, undivided dedication to gospel preaching, uninhibited social service accompanied by unbounded zeal, and a freshness of approach provide the answer.[125] To implement their aims the immediate disciples could follow the example or Testament of the Poverello whose humility and joyousness were irresistible in the early days of the movement.[126] That the feminine religious movement, although much broader and with a somewhat different

sistent with the primitive church. After caring for souls in the towns during the day, the brethren would return for the night to hermitages and solitary places outside the walls where they devoted themselves to meditation. The women lived in common in hospitals, depending on their hands for a livelihood. Cf. Goetz in *Hist. Vierteljahrschrift*, VI (1903), 28f; Lemmens' objections in *RQ.*, XVI, 98.

[122] Ep. I, *ZKG.*, XIV, 102; *Hist. Occid.*, cap. 28, pp. 334-337. Jacques de Vitry commended the order of St. Antony as well as the Brethren of the Holy Ghost, whereas he contemned the other hospital orders for abuse which sprang from their desire to equip themselves with indulgence-letters (*ibid.*, p. 341). For a similar description of Milan, see Matthew Paris, *Chron. Maiora* (an. 1236), *MGH. SS.*, XXVIII, 133 ("nutrix ac tutrix fuit hereticorum et toti imperio rebellium"); 134 ("civitas illa omnium hereticorum, Paterinorum, Luciferanorum, Publicanorum, Albigensium").

[123] Ep. I, *ZKG.*, XIV, 102: "In fide perfecti et stabiles, in operibus efficaces."

[124] See below, p. 442. Cf. Zanoni, *Gli Umiliati*, p. 260; Greven, *Anfänge,* pp. 76f.

[125] See, for example, the picture of Francis in the Saracen camp (Ep. VI, *ZKG.*, XVI, 83; *Hist. Occid.*, p. 353).

[126] Ep. I, *ZKG.*, XIV, 104.

emphasis in northern Europe, still waxed strong in Italy is further proven by the *mulieres sanctae* in Genoa. Religious excitement, penitential in character, prevailed in this port, for "a great number of wealthy and noble women took the cross." "The citizens who were about to attack a castle," Jacques continues, "took away my horses ... as was the custom of the city in time of war ... and I enrolled their wives under the cross. They were so fervent and pious that they hardly allowed me to rest from early morning until night, so anxious were they either to hear some edifying word from me or to make their confessions." [127] After the men came back from the army they returned the horses and, learning that their wives and sons had taken the cross, they too heeded the preacher's exhortation.

If Jacques de Vitry regarded the appearance of the Franciscans and beguines as the most comforting happening of his day, he did not devote the same attention to the Order of Preachers. The "nova religio et praedicatio Boneniensium canonicorum" which occupies a chapter of the *Historia Occidentalis*[128] does not concern Dominicans, close resemblance in aims and methods notwithstanding. These canons depend on alms for a life geared to strict necessity, gather recruits from students of Bologna, zealously read Scripture or listen to lectures on it, and then proclaim what they have heard in Sunday sermons. Funk,[129] following the evidence marshalled by Denifle,[130] maintained that this community was identical with the *Canonici S. Salvatoris* who had separated from the chapter in Bologna and had taken residence outside the city in S. Maria in Reno. To be sure, the *Sermo ad canonicos regulares* numbers the Friars Preachers among the Augustinian congregations. These, having cast off the burden of temporal possessions, proceed to battle, awaiting the cares, difficulties, and other obstacles which come from riches and worldly goods; naked, they follow the Naked, joyfully embracing poverty.[131]

To this evidence must be added the observation, applicable to the Belgian-Rhenish area, which an *exemplum* in the *Sermones vulgares* contains: "I knew some of the Preachers who were called religious and seemed to have zeal, but not according to knowledge. When they came to those regions in which *religio* flourished before other places, especially among nuns and other virgins living together in

[127] *Ibid.*, 105.
[128] *Hist. Occid.*, cap. 27, pp. 333-334.
[129] *Jakob von Vitry*, pp. 156f.
[130] Denifle, "Die Constitutionen des Prediger-Ordens vom Jahre 1228," *ALKM.*, I (1885), 171; Goetz, in *Hist. Vierteljahrschrift*, VI (1903), 30, note 1. Mandonnet in his essay, "Les chanoines-prêcheurs de Bologne d'après Jacques de Vitry" (*Pages d'histoire dédiées à la société d'histoire suisse*, Fribourg, 1903, pp. 69f, reprinted in *Saint Dominique*, I, 231-247) and Felder (*Geschichte der wissenschaftlichen Studien im Franziskanerorden*, p. 138) believed that this was a reference to the Dominicans.
[131] Pitra, *Anal. Nov.*, II, 389; cf. 387.

various communities, they began to preach and to hear confessions."[132]

It appears that after his elevation to the episcopate Jacques de Vitry was absent from Belgium for ten years. During much of this time he was in the Levant. On his second journey to Rome he was authorized to abandon his bishopric and return to Oignies. In 1226, after being present on September 20 at the installing of Henry of Mulnarken as archbishop of Cologne,[133] he dedicated the chapel at the abbey of St. Gerard of Brogne (October 4).[134] Throughout this period he was closely associated with Hugh of Pierrepont, not only as suffragan bishop but on a personal plane, whether·accompanying him back in 1215 to the Fourth Lateran Council[135] or assisting him in the latter's dying moments. Before February 5, 1227, he was commissioned by the bishop to make known his refusal of the aichbishopric of Rheims to which he had been elected.[136] The admiration which Hugh won from the Liégeois after the battle of Steppes (1213) is emphasized by the chronicler on this occasion.[137] On March 27 Jacques de Vitry's name appears between those of Hugh of Liége and Milo of Beauvais as a witness at Aix-la-Chapelle in a charter of King Henry on behalf of the Teutonic Order.[138] But he was soon on his way to Rome whither Gregory IX, who was elected on March, 19, 1227, called him.[139] Although he was instructed to preach a crusade against the Albigensians,[140] it was not long before he was back in Belgium, for he dedicated in the same year the church of Liedekerke, dependent on the abbey of Ninove[141] and, at the request of the prior, Gilles, the altars

[132] Crane, *Exempla*, p. 36, no. 80. For relevance to the *cura monialium* and *beghinarum*, above all in the north, see below, pp. 189ff, 341ff.

[133] *Annal. Colonien. Max.*, *MGH. SS.*, XVII, 840; *Catalog. Archiep. Colonien.*, ibid., XXIV, 355.

[134] *AHEB.*, XVIII, 345, note 3; cf. Berlière, *MB.*, I, 33.

[135] The bishop journeyed to Rome in the company of Renier, monk of St. Jacques, Abbot Otto of St. Laurent (*ibid.*, II, 41), Abbot Chrétien of St. Trond, Jacques de Vitry, and Abbot Robert of Lobbes (Daris, *Histoire*, pp. 36f; Nimal, *Vie et œuvres*, pp. 15f).

[136] Alberic de Trois-Fontaines, *Chron.*, *MGH. SS.*, XXIII, 919; Renier, *Annales MGH. SS.*, XVI, 680; Berlière, *Les évêques auxiliaires de Liége*, p. 12; Poncelet, *Hugues de Pierrepont*, p. xi. The archbishop, Guillaume de Joinville, died on November 6, 1226; after Hugh's refusal, Henry de Dreux was named successor on April 18, 1227 (Eubel, *HC.*, I, 440).

[137] Renier, *Annales, MGH. SS.*, XVI, 680.

[138] Berlière, in *RB.*, XXIX (1912), 71; Böhmer-Ficker, no. 4038.

[139] Alberic de Trois-Fontaines, *Chron., MGH. SS.*, XXIII, 919 (speaks of journey to Holy Land), 923. Jacques de Vitry is met for the first time as cardinal on July 29, 1229 (P. 8441).

[140] Philip Mousket, *Historia Regum Francorum, MGH. SS.*, XXVI, 795. According to Thomas of Cantimpré (*VMO. Suppl.*, 579 C, (21), whose sense of chronology, however, is defective, Jacques carried on zealous preaching from Oignies to the neighbouring parts of Lotharingia. For a role in the entourage of Frederick II during this summer and a possible journey to the Holy Land, see Berlière, in *RB.*, XXIX (1912), 71. Funk (*Jakob von Vitry*, pp. 58f) did not think that Jacques made another trip to the East.

[141] Baldwin of Ninove, *Chronicon, MGH. SS.*, XXV, 540.

of the Oignies church.[142] At the same time he consecrated Mary's bones, placed her relics in a shrine, and granted an indulgence to all who came to revere them.[143] Whereas he dedicated on March 26, 1228, the church of the monastery of St. Gertrude at Louvain[144] and the abbey church of the Parc near the same city a week later (April 2),[145] the following spring (March 25, 1229) he dedicated the altar and cemetery of the Premonstratensian monastery of Ile-Duc at Gempe.[146]

Continuing the favorable curial policy towards the Friars Preachers created by Innocent III and Honorius III, Gregory IX issued a bull on May 13, 1227, calling upon the episcopate to invite Dominicans to the respective dioceses and authorize their ministry.[147] It was in accordance with this policy that Hugh of Liége, then suffering from a fatal sickness which had confined him at Huy during Lent, allowed the friars on April 11, 1229, to settle in Liége, and there to lecture on theology, hear confessions, and give absolution.[148] As witnesses of his action he named Jacques de Vitry and his nephew, Jean d'Eppes, who as his successor (1229–1238) proceeded to execute the order.[149] Two years earlier (1227) the bishop had made his will the text of which is no longer extant. However, it is known by other acts and contemporary annalists that he designated as executors Jacques de Vitry, bishop of Acre, the abbots of Foigny, Vaucelles, and Floreffe, and with them, Baldwin de Barbençon, the renowned preacher. It was his wish that they remit 32,000 marks with the purpose of restoring what he had acquired "non juste" and to distribute the remainder in alms to monasteries, churches, the poor, widows, orphans, religious, and lepers.[150]

On April 11 Jacques de Vitry consecrated the oil in the church of Neufmoustier.[151] When the bishop died the following day in the castle at Huy his friend was at his side. On Good Friday, April 13, he accom-

---

[142] VMO. Suppl., 579 C (21).

[143] Comm. praev., VMO., 542 (1); the date here is 1226. Ernst (Suffragans, p. 71) called him at this point legate of Honorius.

[144] Molanus, I, 233; cf. Berlière, in RB., XXIX (1912), 71.

[145] Sanderus, Chorog. sac. Brab., I, 176 (here the date is given as 1228); Ernst (Suffragans, p. 72) places the event in 1229. Cf. Raymaekers, Geschiedkundige Navorschingen over de aloude Abdij van 't Park (trans. Jansen), p. 29.

[146] Hugo, Annal. Praem., I, 889.

[147] P. 7901.

[148] Poncelet, Hugues de Pierrepont, p. 250, no. 267; Chapotin, Histoire des Dominicains, p. 129, note; BCRH., I ser., IX (1844), 35f; cf. Gregory's instructions to the duke of Brabant, February 5, 1231 (ibid., 36; cf. 37-39).

[149] August 10, 1229, Chapotin, op. cit., p. 130, note 1.

[150] Renier, Annales, MGH. SS., XVI, 680; cf. Poncelet, Hugues de Pierrepont, pp. xi-xii. In the presence of the dean of St. Jean, Cistercian abbots, and his friend Jacques de Vitry, the bishop recognized shortly before his death the rights of the chapter of St. Lambert "ex antiqua consuetudine" (CESL., I, 252; Poncelet, Hugues de Pierrepont, p. xxxvi).

[151] Alberic de Trois-Fontaines, Chron., MGH. SS., XXIII, 923, 924.

panied the body as it was transferred by water to the cathedral of St. Lambert where it was buried in spite of Hugh's preference for burial in the church of the Cistercian monastery of Val-Saint-Lambert.[152] It is possible that during this visit to Huy Jacques heard about a case of stigmatization which occurred on Good Friday.[153] It was perhaps during the same month that the cardinal gave his blessing to Thierry, abbot of St. Jacques in Liége.[154] Thomas of Cantimpré speaks of an interim rule of the diocese by Jacques de Vitry[155] which possibly took place during Hugh's sickness and following his death. But Jean d' Eppes was elected promptly on April 17.[156] Funk, exhibiting characteristic hostility to the Dominican's evidence in the *Supplementum,* put little stock in the account.[157]

From then until his death at Rome eleven years later, on the vigil of St. Philip and St. James (April 30, 1240),[158] Jacques de Vitry's life no longer was so intimately bound up with Belgium. Yet elevation to the cardinalate did not cause him to forget completely his friends in the north: on December 26, 1234, he left to Aywières, while still reserving for himself the usufruct, the property which the prior of Oignies had acquired for him in the monastery.[159] In accordance with his wishes his body was transferred to Oignies and buried in the church which he himself had consecrated.[160]

[152] Renier, *Annales, MGH. SS.,* XVI, 680; *Annal. S. Jacobi Leod., ibid.,* 642; *V. Od.,* 258-261; Gilles d'Orval, *Gesta Episcoporum Leod., MGH. SS.,* XXV, 122; cf. De Theux, *Le chapitre de Saint Lambert,* I, 198f; Alphonse Le Roy, in *BNB.,* IX (1886-1887), col. 675.

[153] Greven, *Exempla,* pp. 31f, no. 44, and note 5.

[154] Renier, *Annales, MGH. SS.,* XVI, 680; MDAC., V, 66. Berlière (*MB.,* II, 14) assigns the act to May.

[155] VMO. *Suppl.,* 580 D (26): "Cum totius episcopii Leodiensis cura quasi mitra potestatis et administrationis tibi fuerit plene commisa."

[156] Eubel, *HC.,* I, 314.

[157] Funk, *Jakob von Vitry,* p. 60.

[158] Alberic de Trois-Fontaines, *Chron., MGH. SS.,* XXIII, 948, 950; Thomas of Cantimpré held that Jacques was first buried in the Dominican house at Rome (*VMO. Suppl.,* 582 (4); *V. Lutg.,* 205 D (III, 5). The cardinal is mentioned in the Floreffe necrology (*AHEB.,* XIII, 190).

[159] Berlière, in *RB.,* XXV (1908), 192f, P.J. IV.

[160] *VMO. Suppl.,* 582 (4); Vincent of Beauvais, *Spec. Hist., MGH. SS.,* XXIV, 166.

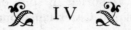

IV

The Cure of Oignies and Nivelles

JOHN OF NIVELLES

To be singled out for special comment, aside from Jacques de Vitry, is another friend and pastor of Mary of Oignies, Master John of Nivelles. Not only does he appear as witness and arbiter for over thirty years in numerous monastic documents but to him is also assigned a brief but usually critical role in no less than five hagiographic accounts, all informed with Cistercian piety and apostolic fervor.[1] Thomas of Cantimpré heard much good concerning him; but more important, personal acquaintance with John made Mary's work vivid for the Dominican.[2] John's name indicates that he came from the town which Mary claimed as her birthplace and which Thomas regarded as the point of origin of the beguine movement.[3] Whether John was actually the founder of the *novella plantatio* of beguines in Liége is a moot question, but it is abundantly evident that through personal solicitude as well as through friends he was vitally concerned with the *Frauenfrage* in the diocese and sought its solution both in the promotion of Cistercian nunneries and through guidance of extraregular communities.

Like John de Liro, with whose name his is often linked in cartularies, John of Nivelles became, towards the close of the twelfth century, a

[1] *VMO.*, 560 (57); *V. Ab.*, f. 19r (cap. xv); *V. Sim. Aln.*, f. 215v; *V. Guil.*, 497-498 (13); *V. Arn. Villar.*, 573 E (38).

[2] *BUA.*, II, 31, 3 (pp. 362f); 54, 18 (p. 529). See below, p. 156.

[3] Greven (*Anfänge*, pp. 84-88) and more so Van Mierlo (*VMKVA.*, 1926, pp. 624, 648, 651-655; *ibid.*, 1925, pp. 419-421) built up John of Nivelles on the strength of the Dominican's evidence in order further to eclipse Lambert le Bègue as the founder of the first beguinage (see below, pp. 71f). In answer to Greven's thesis, Kurth (*BARB.*, 1919, 140f) challenged the contention that John came from the Nivelles in Brabant. The champion of Liége priority suggested a hamlet in the commune of Lixhe, a short distance north of Liége, in the valley of the Meuse; from this he concluded that John passed his entire career at Liége. Clinging to the evidence of the *V. Od.* ("*nova plantatio*") in 1212, *AB.*, XIII, 219; cf. Greven, in *HJ.*, XXXV, 1914, 33f), Van Mierlo pronounced his verdict on Kurth's objections (*VMKVA.*, 1925, 419): "De vorming van de Begijnen te Luik is uitgegaan van den kring der vromen te Nijvel, waartoe die Joannes ontegesprekelijk behoorde."

magister[4] at Paris but, under the influence of such popular preachers as Foulques de Neuilly and Peter Cantor, he turned to the care of souls.[5] He first appears in 1199 as witness in an act whereby the abbot of St. Laurent placed the hospital of St. Christopher under the Augustinian rule.[6] He must have left Paris shortly before Foulques' death, for by 1202 he is mentioned as canon of St. Jean's in Liége.[7] He afterwards became dean of St. Lambert,[8] where he discharged pastoral duties among the *mulieres sanctae*. Probably following Mary's death (June 23, 1213)[9] and certainly after the plundering of Liége in 1212, for the *Vita Mariae Oigniacensis* relates on this occasion one of his visits to the priory,[10] but before July 27, 1219, the date of the death of the bishop of Cambrai, John of Béthune, who, as we shall see below, ordained the hermit-priest William, John of Nivelles was himself persuaded by a deepening sense of the value of evangelical poverty and the worthlessness of worldly fame[11] to enter the Augustinian house. Here he died on March 16, 1233. Had attention been paid to the reference to him in the *Vita Abundi* it would have helped to date the monk's death.[12] On March 29, 1219, John received from Honorius III the mission to collect crusade-taxes in the diocese with the canons of the cathedral.[13] But already earlier he had attracted the attention of the curia for this purpose. On January 8, 1216, Innocent III, in exhorting the crusaders in the province of Cologne to leave for the Holy Land, designated as their directors, to preach the cross and collect funds, Master Oliver, *scolasticus* of Cologne, and John of Xanten, Herman, deacon of Bonn, Master John of Nivelles, canon of the diocese of Liége, and Master Arnold, priest of Münster.[14] From

[4] It seems to be a question of a law degree, for in 1212 John hung his seal (*sigillum Johannis de Nivella, jurisperiti et boni viri*) to a decision by Liége canon lawyers on a matter raised by the abbot of St. Hubert (Kurth, *Les chartes de l'abbaye de Saint-Hubert*, p. 212; *BARB.*, 1919, 139).

[5] Jacques de Vitry, *Hist. Occid.*, pp. 289-290.

[6] Berlière, *MB.*, II, 41; Ernst, *Suffragans*, p. 216; Jean d'Outremeuse, *Ly Myreur des Histors*, IV (ed. Bormans), 563f.

[7] *Cartul. de l'abbaye d'Aywières*, f. 9. A John of Nivelles is mentioned as a witness in a document dated at Liége after March 5, 1200 (*CESL.*, I, 123).

[8] Thomas of Cantimpré, *BUA.*, II, 31, 3 (p. 362: "Magister Ioannes de Nivella, Leodiensis ecclesiae decanus"); 54, 18 (p. 529: "quondam Leodiensi decano"); MF. III, 393; GC. III, 927; cf. Greven, in *HJ.*, XXXV (1914), 30, 49f; Berlière, *MB.*, I, 451, note 1. De Theux (*Le chapitre de Saint Lambert à Liége*, I, 200) doubted that John was dean; but then, he assigns the date of his death to March 10, ca. 1216.

[9] It must have been in or after 1213, for John was still mentioned as canon of St. Jean (*Cartul. d'Aulne*, f. 225; Devillers, I, 156).

[10] *VMO.*, 561.

[11] Thomas of Cantimpré, *BUA.*, II, 31, 3 (p. 362); cf. 31, 5 (p. 365: "quidam magister Ioannes . . . in monasterio de Oignies").

[12] Balau (*Sources*, p. 437) accepted De Reiffenberg's date of 1228.

[13] Pressutti, *Regest. Hon.* III, I, 326, no. 1972; *AHEB.*, XXV, 167.

[14] Ennen-Eckertz, *Quellen*, II (1863), 58-61, no. 50; Wauters, *TC.*, III, 441; not in Potthast. See the account of this commission to Oliver and Herman, but without mention of John of Nivelles, in Renier, *Annales, MGH. SS.*, XVI, 671.

such commissions, as well as Thomas of Cantimpré's evidence,[15] we may thus conclude that John, no less than Jacques de Vitry, owed his dedication to the *vita apostolica* and his unfagging zeal to save souls, whether by crusade preaching or a home mission, primarily to Mary of Oignies. The *Vita Guillelmi* makes it clear that his approach was a constructive one. Just as the Oignies canons worked in the neighborhood, preaching and administering the sacraments, so John refused to countenance eremitical life that eschewed social responsibility. By converting Guillaume to a broad program which led eventually to the priesthood and the founding of the Cistercian nunnery of l'Olive, John was promoting the work to which he dedicated his own life and which Jacques de Vitry so eloquently describes.

After 1199 John of Nivelles' name occurs frequently in documents. He acted as witness in 1202 when Hugh of Pierrepont granted to women wishing to live under the Benedictine rule the church of St. Stephen at Aywières, its patronage and adjacent land.[16] He was probably canon of St. Jean's in documents dated December, 1203,[17] and in 1205.[18] It was in this capacity that in 1208 (July 14–August 15), on the occasion of the transformation of Neufmoustier into an abbey and the resignation of the prior René, John of Nivelles, together with John de Liro and Peter Scholasticus, presided over the election of Alexander as the first abbot at the instance of the bishop.[19] John was present when Hugh made known in 1211 the agreement concluded between the abbey of Val-Saint-Lambert on the one hand, and the brethren of the new hospital of Liége and the chapter of St. Gilles, on the other, on the matter of one fourth of the tithe of Nandrin and a *rente* at Goreaux.[20] The following year he witnessed, without his capacity being designated, the document whereby Arnold de Lowaige, a knight, and his relatives donated to the new hospital at Liége the

[15] *BUA.*, II, 31, 3 (pp. 362f); cf. Thomas' eloquence on this care of the poor; Van Rooijen, *Theodorus van Celles*, pp. 93f. In his *Sermones de Tempore et Sanctis* Eudes or Odo of Châteauroux admits indebtedness to a John of Nivelles who may be the one in question: I, 31, 35, 48, 70 (Pitra, *Anal. Nov.*, II, 195, 196, 198); II, 24, 145, 146, 171 (pp. 221, 225, 226); III, 10, 11, 37, 78, 79 (pp. 238, 239, 241); IV, 24, 56, 64, 87, 91, 94, 102 (pp. 257-260); VI, 7, 10, 16, 17, 65, 106, 125 (pp. 324-328).

[16] *Cartul. de l'abbaye d'Aywières*, f. 8r; Poncelet, *Hugues de Pierrepont*, pp. 5f, no. 6; E. Poswick, "Documents inédits sur la haute avouerie de Hesbaye," *BIAL.*, XI, 199.

[17] *CESL.*, I, 138.

[18] Berlière, *MB.*, I, 451, note 1.

[19] Poncelet, *Hugues de Pierrepont*, p. 264, no. 8; Kurth, "Documents historiques sur l'abbaye de Neufmoustier près de Huy," *BCRB.*, ser. 5, II (1892), 61f; Alberic de Trois-Fontaines, *Chron.*, *MGH. SS.*, XXIII, 888f; cf. J. Brassine, "L'oeuvre de Maurice de Neufmoustier," *BSAHL.*, XII, 139. In referring to this assignment, Jean d'Outremeuse, who often transmits details in error, wrongly calls John cantor (*Chronique*, ed. Borgnet, V, 4: "Johans de Nyvelle cantre et Johans de Liroul I docteur").

[20] Poncelet, *Hugues de Pierrepont*, p. 92, no. 86; Schoonbroodt, *Val St. Lambert.* p. 18, no. 42.

tithe they possessed at Glons.[21] In 1213 John of Nivelles, canon of St. Jean's, is mentioned, among others, as a papal arbiter to settle a point of dispute between Aulne and the knight Lithold of Noville.[22] Six years later (1219) he and the prior of St. Severin were called upon the arbitrate a dispute between the abbey of Val-Saint-Lambert and Liebert l'Ardenais, a knight, with regard to the tithe of Nandrin.[23] In February, 1225, John, as a brother of Oignies, together with A., canon of Nivelles, and G., chaplain of St. Sepulchre, settled a dispute between Aywières and Orval over property at Monstreux which had been left by Walter of St. Cyr, a monk of Orval.[24] In an undated document (1209—1229)[25] Wazelin, abbot of St. Jacques at Liége, Master John of Nivelles, canon of St. Jean's, and Master Walter Magnus or le Grand arbitrated a dispute between the abbey of Floreffe and Roger, canon of St. Croix at Liége, over the allod of Thiméon. His name occurs in an act of the Val-des-Ecoliers at Liége in October, 1231.[26] The necrology of Floreffe places his death on the fifteenth of March: "Sancte recordationis magistri Johannis de Nivella, canonici de Oengnies et fratris nostri."[27] Before February, 1212, John is listed among the witnesses of a document in which Liége lawyers answered a question of Abbot Guillaume of St. Hubert with respect to the validity of the sale of Baisy.[28]

So great was the favor that John of Nivelles won, by sermon and example, in his pastoral activity among the *mulieres religiosae* who safeguarded their chastity, particularly during the plundering of Liege (May 3-7, 1212),[29] by the soldiers of Henry I of Brabant, that he was called by his friend, Jacques de Vitry, "the light, teacher, and father of the entire diocese."[30] Caring naught for loss of property, but grieving bitterly over violation of churches and destruction of souls, the "pater filios plorabat, patronus ecclesias, amicus Sponsi Virgines, quas casto

---

21 Poncelet, *Hugues de Pierrepont*, p. 109, no. 105.

22 Devillers, *Description*, V, 7, no. 7.

23 Schoonbroodt, *Val St. Lambert*, p. 23, no. 58; *BCRB.*, ser. 5, IV (1894), 178-180.

24 *Ibid.*, II (1892), 573; *Cartul. de l'abbaye d'Aywières*, f. 76r.

25 Poncelet, *Inv. anal. de S. Croix*, I. (1911), 27, no. 49; *AHEB.*, IX, 265. Wazelin, monk of Florennes, became abbot of Saint Jacques in 1209; he resigned his post in 1229 in order to enter the Cistercian abbey of Val-Saint-Lambert as a monk.

26 MF. III, 393, cap. 110; cf. Ernst, *Suffragans*, p. 312.

27 *AHEB.*, XIII, 50.

28 Kurth, *Chartes de l'abbaye de S. Hubert*, I, 212f, no. 162.

29 *VMO.*, 560 (57): "Qui cum rumores pessimos percepisset, mente consternatus, incomparabiliter doluit, et maxime quia de sanctis virginibus, quas ipse per praedicationem et exemplum Domino acquisiverat." Cf. *Triumphus Sancti Lamberti in Steppes, MGH. SS.*, XXV, 175-177; *Gesta, MGH. SS.*, XXV, 225; Renier, *Annales, MGH. SS.*, XVI, 664. For the events, see Kurth, *La Cité de Liége*, I, 117ff; Greven, in *H.J.*, XXXV (1914), 30, note 3. The ideal of chastity as Liége women understood it is well brought out in *V. Od.*, 231, 283.

30 "Totius episcopatus lucerna, doctor et pater spiritualis" (*VMO.*, 560; cf. *Hist. Occid.*, cap. 9, p. 290; *MDAC.*, VI, 329; *V. Guil.*, 497f). For a similar tribute to Peter Cantor, see *Hist. Occid.*, p. 289.

Sponso castas exhibere desponderat."[31] It seemed logical to Van Mierlo to conclude that John's solicitude for the feminine religious movement in Liége had been awakened by Mary of Oignies and the Nivelles community.[32] A document of 1224 mentions *sorores* who lived near the hospital of St. Christopher.[33] These *sorores* are later known as beguines.[34] In this document the cardinal-legate, Conrad, bishop of Porto, determined that the *mulieres religiosae* living about St. Christopher, should pay an annual rent of 5 tenths instead of the 4 tenths which the archdeacon of Condroz, Thomas of Hemricourt (1207—1220), had fixed previously. Thus the existence of beguines at St. Christopher before 1220 finds confirmation; this would also carry one back to about 1210 when the *Vita Odiliae* speaks of the *novella plantatio religionis* and John de Liro.[35] It has also been suggested, but without conclusiveness, that John of Nivelles and the Jehans li Beguins of Liége who is mentioned as the founder of the beguinage in the French beguine rule from the Rheims area under the name of *Règle des Fins Amans* (1300) were one and the same person. Humility, poverty, and purety induced *gens beguins* and *beguines* to follow him.[36] The question still remains whether these Liége women had organized themselves into a community before his activity among them or whether this institution was the fruit of his own work after the example of the beguines around Mary.[37] Although documentary evidence does not confirm the appearance of bona fide Liége beguines until 1240,[38] there was thus a strong tradition that linked a zealous priest like John, as well as Lambert le Bègue, with the early beguinage.

John's interest in the feminine religious movement was equally demonstrated in his promotion of Cistercian nunneries. In February, 1229, Gilles de Rochefort exchanged with the abbey of St. Hubert patronage of the church of Marcourt for that of St. Remy, where he

[31] *VMO.*, 560 (57). For Van Mierlo (*VMKVA.*, 1926, p. 622) this sentence proved further that John founded the first beguinage in Liége. It agrees with *V.* Od. (219) that after 1200 such a community was still a *"novella plantatio"*.

[32] *VMKVA.*, 1926, p. 652.

[33] Schoolmeesters, "Lambert le Bègue et l'origine des béguines," *Leodium,* XI (1912), 130.

[34] Van Mierlo, in *VMKVA.*, 1926, p. 624.

[35] See below, pp. 162, 432; cf. Daris, *Notices,* XI, 133.

[36] *Christ, La règle des Fins Amans, p. 197, lines 15off:* "Savés, pour quoi eles sont appelées beguines? Piech 'a que devers Liége avoit .j. home, Jehans li beguins avoit a nom; qui atroit touz a sa maniere pour servir en humilité, en povreté et neté. Celes qui le sivroient et le creoient appelerent les gens beguins pour le nom leur pere, et ausi de beguine vint beguinsies. Leur droit noms est religieuses de leur seigneur qui morut seur le rain de la crois en chantant: oci le vilain! ... Et pour chou je appele les beguines religieuses"; cf. *ibid.,* pp. 183, 188f; Axters, *Geschiedenis van de Vroomheid,* I, 314.

[37] *Greven, Anfänge,* pp. 68f, 87, 189. Ryckel (p. 290) speaking of Elizabeth de Gravio on the basis of Thomas of Cantimpré's testimony, was uncertain whether they were even then in a single group or still scattered.

[38] Philippen, *Begijnhoven,* p. 210.

intended to establish a Cistercian nunnery—the Secours-Notre-Dame.[39] This transaction was made known by Thierry of St. Hubert to Master John of Nivelles and Margaret de Glimes who was invited to come with her companions from some undesignated place to establish the new community.[40] The projected foundation was not long in taking shape, for on June 13, 1230, Gilles informed the bishop of Liége that he had relinquished his allod of St. Remy to the abbey "recently founded" "domum quam nuper fundavimus").[41] If John of Nivelles' role is incidental here, it appears that he was more active in establishing Jardinet near Walcourt for Thierry II of Walcourt or Rochefort (1192—1234) and his wife Gertrude in December, 1232.[42]

Of the esteem which Jacques de Vitry expressed for John in the *Historia Occidentalis* the correspondence offers further proof.[43] The ties between these two champions of the *vita apostolica* were rendered all the closer through mutual friends and common interests.

LESSER LUMINARIES

Among the other ministrants of Nivelles and Oignies were the elderly and infirm John of Dinant, known as "the Gardener" (*Hortulanus*), who by his warnings and an example of renunciation had won many souls, and his friend, Richard of Manechan-Capella (fl. 1195),[44] both of whom died before Mary;[45] a cleric Lambert and a priest of Nivelles, named Werric (*Guerricus*), who, among others, were reported to have been cured by Mary of a severe illness.[46] The ascetic Master

[39] Kurth, *Chartes de l'abbaye de Saint-Hubert en Andenne*, I, 251f, no. 198; Berlière, in *RB.*, IX (1892), 423f; id., *MB.*, I, 87f; Roland, "Les seigneurs et comtes de Rochefort," *ASAN.*, XX (1893), 363-366; Toussaint, *Histoire de Walcourt*, pp. 65-69.

[40] Berlière, in *RB.*, IX (1892), 423f. Roland suggests that they came from Aywières (*ASAN.*, XX, 365).

[41] *GC.* III, instr., 171; *ASAN.*, III, 298. In 1234 Gilles completed the endowment of the monastery by the donation of Falemby (*ibid.*, III, 300).

[42] "Coenobium de Jardinio beatae Mariae, juxta Walcuriam situm, uxore mea domina Gertrude consentiente, super altare praedicti loci, in manus magistri Joannis de Ogniaco, ad opus monialium Cisterciensis ordinis resignavi..." (MF. IV, 544; Toussaint, *Histoire de Walcourt*, p. 257; Lahaye, *Cartulaire de Walcourt*). For Jardinet, consult Berlière, *MB.* I, 77-81; Gaillot, *Histoire de Namur*, IV, 219-225; Toussaint, *op. cit.*, pp. 187-243; id., *Histoire d'Oignies*, p. 13. For Thierry II of Walcourt see Roland, in *ASAN.*, XX, 346-359; XXIV (1900), 361-367.

[43] Ep. VI (March, 1220), *ZKG.*, XVI, 72; on April 18, 1221 another letter was sent to Walter, abbot of Villers, Master John of Nivelles and his brethren at Oignies (Ep. VII, *ibid.*, 86). It is possible that he was among the *carissimis* to whom Ep. I (October, 1216) was addressed (*ibid.*, XIV, 101).

[44] *VMO.*, 559 (53). In a variant of his letter of March, 1220, to John of Nivelles and the abbess of Aywières, Jacques de Vitry addressed another John of Dinant (*ZKG.*, XVI, 83). The *vita* presents Richard in a hagiographical device.

[45] *VMO.*, 559 (53); 570 F (104).

[46] *Ibid.*, 559 F (55). Jacques de Vitry received the account from the priest's own lips. Master Guido, too, experienced such a cure (*ibid.*, 560 A).

Guido (d. September 8, 1227),[47] "priest of the beguines at Nivelles,"[48] often appears in the *Vita Mariae Oigniacensis*, after lengthy service as chaplain of the church at nearby Willambroux, as the director and spiritual father of his sister-in-law.[49] It may have been he who hastened the couple's decision to adopt a new life, Guido lodging with his brother John while Mary retired to her cell.[50] Helwide, who, as possibly the first recluse of Willambroux, enjoyed Mary's friendship for almost twelve years,[51] was also the recipient of Guido's consolation.[52] The chapel of the hospital of Saint-Sepulchre in Nivelles was afterwards entrusted to him; he must have left the leper-house not long after his sister-in-law's departure in 1207.[53] The *Planctus Virginum super mortem Guidonis Sacerdotis S. Sepulchri in Nivella*, a eulogy composed by the local beguines, calls Guido the "sanctae virginitatis hortulanus," adding that "countless numbers" of ecstatic women from Germany, Champagne, Flanders, and France put themselves under his direction at Nivelles.[54] In other words, he was no less successful than John of Nivelles in adapting his apostolic mission to women who came from distant as well as adjacent lands to receive instruction in beguinal life. Some of them swelled the Nivelles community, thereby contributing to the demand for the erection of ten new parishes in May, 1231, as well as documenting Thomas of Cantimpré's subsequent description. Others who returned to their homes popularized this mode of existence, with encouragement and protection from pope and bishop. This coterie also included another Guido, a former precentor in the cathedral at Cambrai, who visited Mary in her cell.[55]

John of Nivelles' companion and fellow-pastor, Master John *de Liro*

[47] *Ibid.*, 565 B. Cf. Greven, *Anfänge*, pp. 84-86; Ryckel, pp. 291-294.

[48] Thomas of Cantimpré: "Vidi sanctum virum magistrum Guidonem, presbiterum beghinarum in Nivella" who as a young man had supervised the schools of Soignies in Hainault (*BUA.*, II, 30, 31, p. 338); cf. Mosheim, p. 127; Wauters, *TC.*, III, 519 (October, 1219). As the prototype of the "rector beghinarum" see Philippen, *Begijnhoven*, p. 247.

[49] *VMO.*, 560 A (55); 565 B (80); 568 D (93). Cf. Greven, *Anfänge*, pp. 49f.

[50] ".. In cella sua, juxta ecclesiam apud Oignies ... altera die cum esset in cellula sua" (VMO., 553 (27); 56 (72). See Hanon de Louvet (*Origine Nivelloise*, pp. 11f) for an interpretation of this detail.

[51] *Ibid.*, pp. 12-13, notes 33, 40.

[52] *VMO.*, 56 (80). A priest Gerard who had served as chaplain of the church of St. Sixtum in Nivelles first sought the intercession of his close friend Arnulf of Villers on behalf of his ailing mother Cecilia (*V. Arn. Villar.*, 572 (35). Afterwards, as his mother approached death, he solicited the aid of Master Guido of Nivelles and nine other priests (36).

[53] For a summary of documentary evidence for Guido's later life consult Hanon de Louvet, *op cit.*, p. 20 and notes 69-70.

[54] For the text see Ryckel, p. 294; Greven, *Anfänge*, p. 85 (text), 85f (criticism); cf. Philippen, *Begijnhoven*, pp. 63f; Hanon de Louvet, *op. cit.*, pp. 21f, 41f. The last named (p. 22, note 74) rejects a translation of *Campina* as Champagne (cf. Van Mierlo, in *DHGE.*, VII, 465; Mens, *Oorsprong*, p. 264 note).

[55] *VMO.*, 556 B.

or *Lirot*, generally said to be of Lierre,[56] was, according to Jacques de Vitry, a talented preacher, one more product of the Paris reformers.[57] He, together with Christine Mirabilis, persuaded Lutgard, despite language difficulties,[58] to transfer in 1206, when she was twenty-four, from the Benedictine convent of St. Catherine at St. Trond to the Cistercian nunnery at Aywières.[59] As further evidence of friendship between John and Lutgard, Thomas of Cantimpré relates that they entered into a pact in accordance with which whoever died first should appear before the other. After his death John returned to his friend in a vision, clad in a parti-colored robe of glory. The white signified chastity, the red his labors and trials, while the blue, the perfection of spiritual life.[60] Among John de Liro, Gilbert of Mont Cornillon, and other "heralds of Christ," an enemy of Odilia sowed suspicion against the "servant of Christ." Some vouched for the widow's integrity, others believed that she had seduced them. Odilia, seeing herself scorned and desiring to placate one of them who had been disturbed, sought out John. He was favorably moved by her pleas.[61] Shortly before Jacques de Vitry's mission to the papal curia in 1216 to secure official recognition of the feminine religious movement in the Liége-Nivelles area,[62] John de Liro had set out for Rome for much the same purpose, only to perish in the Alps.[63]

WILLIAM, FOUNDER OF L'OLIVE

The hermit-priest William, who is primarily identified with the beginnings of the Cistercian nunnery of l'Olive in Hainault, also deserves to be mentioned as one who shared the confidence of Mary of Oignies. From his biography,[64] presumably written by the chaplain

[56] Although *de Liro* has usually been translated "de Lierre" or "van Lier," Van Roy (*Lutgardis*, p. 58) notes that nowhere does one find the word *Lirum* to designate the town of Lierre (Lira, 1188-99; Liéra, 1212). The priest is presumably identical with the Jean de Lirot mentioned by Lecoy de la Marche (pp. 70, 476).
[57] *Hist. Occid.*, pp. 289f; cf. *V. Lutg.*, 195 C; *Gesta Trud.*, MGH. SS., X, 391.
[58] See below p. 383.
[59] *V. Lutg.*, 195 C, 197 F.
[60] *Ibid.*, 197f (II, 8).
[61] *V. Od.*, 219; cf. 218.
[62] See below p. 156.
[63] "Curiam ergo Romanam idem Joannes pro negotiis adiens religiosarum mulierum, quae per Brabantiam ab gemulis turbabantur; veniens circa montes Alpium, est defunctus" (*V. Lutg.*, 197 F [II, 8]; cf. Greven, *Anfänge*, pp. 54, 133f).
[64] *V. Guilielmi Presbyteri Eremitae, AA. SS.*, V (February 10, ii), 495-500. The life as Jacques de Guise gives it in the *Chronica Hanoniae* (MGH. SS., XXX, 1, 277f; here caps. 51-59 are omitted) is abbreviated from the Bollandist edition from caps. 54-56; from cap. 57 on it is more extended. A French translation was prepared in 1446 by order of Philip the Good (*Comm. praev. V. Guil.*, 495 (11); cf. *Annales de Hainaut*, part III, vol. IV, bk. 20, caps. 54-68, contained in *Histoire de Hainaut*, XIV (Paris-Brussels, 1832), 224-285). For William see also Wauters, in *BNB.*, VIII (1884-1885), 443-444.

monk of the convent, dedicated to the superior Catherine,[65] and communicated by Henriquez to the Bollandists,[66] we have no evidence that she played a decisive role in the unfolding of his interior life; nevertheless the biographer assigns to John of Nivelles responsibility for drawing him from unproductive penitential exercises to zealous proselytism. On the other hand, there is no doubt that Mary too acted as leaven on his spiritual growth. Through these two members of the Oignies circle he was fired with its austerity, voluntary poverty, and passion for the salvation of souls which prompted him in the latter part of his life to direct one segment of the feminine religious movement.

William was born in the latter part of the twelfth century[67] in that part of Brabant where Flemish predominated. Belonging to the middle class of society, being neither rich nor poor,[68] he was destined by his parents to be a baker.[69] Given over to pleasures with a lightness of mind, he travelled to nearby lands[70] and finally came into the French-speaking area where he decided that he could further his business only by learning that tongue. He spent some time in the Premonstratensian monastery of Thenailles (Tenoille),[71] near Vervins in the diocese of Laon, where he plied his trade without binding himself to the order[72] and where he enjoyed tranquillity although he was not yet properly fortified against temptations. Having finally left this retreat to give himself over again to the pleasures of the world,[73] he had, it was said, a vision as a result of which he changed completely his way of life.[74] Filled with poignant remorse, he settled on the borders of the duchy of Brabant and the county of Hainault near Morlanwelz in a place called Champ-du-potier (Ager figuli) which belonged to Eustache III, lord of Le Roeulx (1190—1210).[75] It lay in the midst of a luxuriant green forest and was watered by a health-giving spring. But to the penitent it offered only the roughest kind of

[65] V. Guil., prol. 495-496; cf. Berlière, MB., I, 375.

[66] Comm. praev., V. Guil., 495 (13); cf. no. 12.

[67] William died on February 10, 1240/41 at the age of sixty-six (Wauters, l.c.; Le Jeune, in Monographies, II, 202 and Annal. cercle arch. Mons, I (1857), 299; V. Guil., 500 (33), or, according to Arnold Rayssius (Hierogazophylacium Belgicum, sive Thesaurus sacrarum reliquiarum Belgii (Duaci, 1628), p. 46), at forty-six. The vita describes him as belonging to the age of John de Béthune, bishop of Cambrai (1200-1219), and Jeanne of Constantinople (V. Guil., 496 (2); cf. 499 (24).

[68] Ibid., 496 (1); "Et licet nobilibus non esset ortus natalibus, non infimis tamen sumpsit originem."

[69] Ibid., 496 (4).

[70] Ibid., 496 (4-5).

[71] Cottineau, II, 3143, s.v. Thenailles.

[72] The French version of Jacques de Guise (l.c., p. 227) translated "in arte pistoria" as "au métier de pêcheur," confusing piscor and pistor. Le Jeune followed the same reading (Monographies, II, 200).

[73] V. Guil., 496 E (6).

[74] Ibid., 496 E-F (7).

[75] Ibid., 497 A; Le Jeune, Monographies, VI, 108-110.

existence. Having given animal spirits free rein in the world, he now chose in abject contrition to follow the ways of beasts by walking on hands and feet and fixing his eyes on the ground as a steady reminder that he was of the dust and would return to it. Even the three loaves of bread which he had brought from town must yield to a subsistence on vegetables and herbs.[76] His strange behavior was soon being bruited by shepherds, and neighbors goodnaturedly proceeded to build a hut for him.[77] Furthermore William sought the permission of the parish priest to remain on the domain of Eustache.[78] At the same time the *vita* is not wanting in the usual temptations and assaults of demons which precipitated the crisis in his life.[79] Favored by more extensive land donated by Bertha or Beatrice, the widow of Eustache,[80] and encouraged by the exhortations of the apostolic-minded John of Nivelles to abandon his bestial habits,[81] William began to study and to understand better his social obligations. So great was his zeal for knowledge, "which rose in him like a bubbling fountain," that while he held in one hand a bush-hook to clear away the brush or an axe to fell trees he carried in the other a psalter or whatever book he could get. If he wished to speed up his work, he would put his book on the trunk or in the branches of a tree; in this way he could work more quickly with both hands and at the same time read easily.[82] Thus while the exterior man worked to keep alive, the interior man was strengthened and refreshed by learning.

Informed of the perfection of this hermit, John of Béthune, bishop of Cambrai (1200—1219), advanced him through the ranks leading to the priesthood.[83] Following his ordination, William proceeded to replace his first oratory with a stone church with the alms of the faithful.[84] In describing reaction to his work, the *vita* follows the usual

---

[76] *V. Guil.*, 497 (10).

[77] *Ibid.*, 497 (12).

[78] *Ibid.*, 497 (9).

[79] *Ibid.*, 496 (6); 498f (19-21).

[80] *Ibid.*, 498 (14, 17); for the son, Eustache IV (1210-1221), see Le Jeune, *Monographies*, VI, 110-113. Eustache IV exhibited considerable interest in furthering monastic life: in 1216 he made a donation to the abbot of Bonne Esperance to establish an anniversary (*ibid.*, VI, 111), and in 1217 a donation to Epinlieu at Mons (Devillers, *Description*, III, 7); in 1221 he ratified a donation made by his grandfather to Aulne in 1189 (*ibid.*, I, 104). For Eustache's interest in the Brugelette tithe which had been yielded to Oignies, see *ASAN.*, XXXI, 9f, no. 8 (January, 1211 n.s.-1215); 10, no. 9 (February, 1211); 20, no. 20 (before May 13, 1215); before May 13, 1215 he confirmed as suzerain the donation by Baldwin of Brugelette to the church of Oignies of the tithe that he had at Brugelette, held in fee from the knight Jacques (*ibid.*, 20f, no. 21).

[81] *V. Guil.*, 497-498 (13). Jacques de Vitry relates such an act of penance in an *exemplum* to demonstrate how indiscretion may lead to presumption (ed. Crane, pp. 21f, no. 55). Was he referring here to William's aberration?

[82] *V. Guil.*, 498 (18; cf. 15).

[83] *Ibid.*, 499 E (24).

[84] *Ibid.*, 499 (25).

pattern. Some, desiring to imitate him, attached themselves to the
hermit. Others, considering this austerity to be folly, ridiculed him
and shunned his company, for "they preferred to eat the viands and
garlic of Egypt than to be refreshed by spiritual manna in the desert."[85]
Some of the brethren who associated with him under pretense of piety
proved to be false. Among those who desired to join his community
were Augustinians, but they received from him such a feeble welcome
that they retired in confusion.[86] He had vowed, the *vita* explains, to
establish the Cistercian rule there. With this purpose in mind he
arrived at the nunnery of Fontenelles, where the piety and austerity
of the inhabitants persuaded him to request permission from the
abbess to take some of them back with him. This colony lived "for some
time" in solitude and utmost poverty; but finally, oppressed by such
great want and hardship, they returned to their own monastery.[87] It
was then that he turned to Moustier-sur-Sambre which contained
noble women who had abandoned wealth and marriage;[88] about 1218
he induced seven of them to form a community in the forest of Marie-
mont, at Morlanwelz, on the domain belonging to the lords of Le
Roeulx. They served as the nucleus for N.-D. de l'Olive,[89] an affiliate
of Clairvaux. Following a dispute with the Premonstratensians of
Bonne-Esperance,[90] l'Olive was accorded by Innocent IV in 1245
(February 9)[91] papal protection of person and property.

Without regard for chronology, the biographer draws his account
of the hermit-priest to a close by describing his close friendship for
Mary of Oignies.[92] He "knew her well." When she was near death, he
hastened to Oignies but was not allowed to approach her side until
she intervened. He died in 1240 at the age of sixty-six.[93]

MARY AND THE LAY WORLD

Jacques de Vitry is but the most notable example of recreation in
Mary's hands. Yet her mission started at home, for her two brothers,
formerly given over to the world, were eventually persuaded to abandon
all for the Cistercian order.[94] Friends and the curious alike, coming

[85] *Ibid.*, 498 (16).
[86] *Ibid.*, 500 (26); Jacques de Guise, *Chron. Han.*, MGH. SS., XXX, 1, 277 (XX, 61).
[87] *V. Guil.*, 500 (26); Jacques de Guise, *Chron. Han.*, MGH. SS., XXX, 1, 278
(XX, 61-62).
[88] *V. Guil.*, 500 (27).
[89] *Ibid.*, 500 (28): "Ita ut multae nobiles virgines, quae multis affluebant divitiis,
contemnentes terrenas nuptias, sponso coelesti, harum religiosarum exemplo com-
motae, adhaeserunt." Cf. Le Jeune, "L'ancienne abbaye de l'Olive," *Annal. cercle
arch. Mons,* I (1857), 295-306.
[90] Berliere, *MB.*, I, 373; Le Jeune, *Monographies*, II, 203.
[91] *V. Guil.*, 494 (2-4).
[92] *Ibid.*, 500 (29).
[93] *Ibid.*, 500 (33).
[94] *VMO.*, 562 A (64).

even from "distant parts" to see her,[95] had once obliged her to move
from Willambroux to Oignies.[96] Although Mary diverted sinners from
the path of destruction through her ministration, she could be repelled
by the corruption of the laity as she passed through Nivelles on her
way to Willambroux to visit friends.[97] The hold which she had over
laymen can well be illustrated by the conversion of a rich merchant
of Nivelles who came with other citizens to Willambroux to visit
her.[98] But better still is the spiritual awakening of the Brabançon
knight, Ivan de Rèves,[99] who was related to her.[100] Indeed, his early
secular interests, his conversion, and ridicule that was heaped on him
by erstwhile friends and relatives because of his acceptance of voluntary poverty are all reminiscent of the experiences of his contemporary, Francis of Assisi. Mary of Oignies played as vital a part in
causing his change of heart as she did in recreating Jacques de Vitry.
Ivan belonged to a noble family in Rèves, located southeast of Nivelles, with extensive holdings in Lillois.[101] From 1198, when he is mentioned with his brother Walter as a witness in a document,[102] until
about 1241, presumably the date of his death, his name may be detected in a number of isolated sources.[103] As a "nobilis vir" his name
appears in a document of 1210 which describes his donation of property to the nuns of Aywières, enabling them to move to Lillois near
Nivelles.[104] In 1213, the year of Mary's death, he is mentioned for the
first time as "Iwanus clericus de Roavia,"[105] and a year later (1214) as
priest.[106] In June, 1219, he is referred to as priest and canon at Laon
("Domino Ywano de Roavia, sacerdoti et canonico Laudunensi") and
as witness, "Dominus Ywanus de Roavia," in 1224. In 1231 he is again
referred to as "plebanus Nivellensis," and in July, 1233, as "quondam
plebanus." On August 14, 1234, and again on June 23, 1235, he was
the "prepositus Nivellensis."[107]

It was presumably between 1210 and 1213 that the events described

[95] *Ibid.*, 562 (65); 568 (93); 569 (98); 571 (106).
[96] See above, p. 11.
[97] *VMO.*, 562 (67). Cf. Jacques de Guise, *Ann. Han.*, MGH. SS., XXX, 1, 28of
(XX, 65).
[98] *VMO., Suppl.*, 574 (4).
[99] *VMO.*, 56of (58-60). Cf. Greven, *Anfänge*, pp. 91ff.
[100] *VMO.*, 560 D.
[101] Tarlier and Wauters, *Géog. et hist. des communes belges. Prov. de Brabant.*
Canton de Nivelles (1860), 64.
[102] Duvivier, *Actes et documents, nouvelle série*, p. 252.
[103] For a summary see Greven (*Anfänge*, pp. 109-110).
[104] Berlière, "Notice sur d'anciennes archives de l'abbaye d'Aywières," *BCRH.*,
5th ser., II (1892), 573; Tarlier and Wauters, *Géog. et hist. des communes belges.*
Province de Brabant .Canton de Nivelles, p. 64.
[105] Berlière, in *RB.*, XXV (1908), 190-191. *V. Lutg.* (197, II, 5) mentions a Maria
de Roavia, Marie de Rèves.
[106] Greven, *Anfänge*, p. 110.
[107] *Idem.*

in the *Vita Mariae Oigniacensis* took place.[108] A desire for ostentation and worldly splendor had induced the impecunious knight to borrow from a wealthy burgher in Nivelles who was himself eager to court the friendship and ape the manners of the petty nobility. These superfluous expenses which, the moralist Jacques de Vitry adds without probing further economic difficulties, are customary among knights, made it increasingly difficult to break away from his creditor. It was from this glittering circle that Mary of Oignies made an effort through counsel and prayer to draw him to a life of renunciation. But the world was still too enticing for Ivan; he was soon frequenting the merchant's table again. Not until Mary's messenger appeared at the door and ordered him to hasten to her, then residing outside Nivelles, did he tear himself loose. The hagiographer now employs the devices current in thirteenth century literature and art under the influence of Citeaux and Bernard. Ivan found her in tears, clasping the feet of the Crucified, and learned that his vacillation and hesitation were responsible for Mary's grief. Only then did his "conversion" become complete.

Among the laymen whose patronage of semireligious associations warrants attention at this stage, even though the circle of Oignies is not directly concerned, was the knight of "rare piety," Philip de Montmirail, who admired much the religious men and women in Greece, Lombardy, Burgundy, Provence, France, Flanders, and Brabant.[109] Inadequate though his paternal property might be, records the enthusiastic Dominican chronicler as he describes the religious fervor that had earlier excited Jacques de Vitry, the knight was reputed to be the founder of no less than eight Cistercian monasteries, not to mention the beguinages to which he made donation.[110] Immediately after corroborating Philip's interest in establishing monasteries for white nuns in France, Stephen of Bourbon[111] describes the mysticism of a beguine.

[108] *Ibid.*, p. 113.
[109] Thomas of Cantimpré, *BUA.*, I, 1, 4 (p. 5); II, 38, 2 (pp. 391-7): "Vidimus et valde dilectum ac familiarem habuimus nobilem Philippum militem de Monmiral vitae perfectissimae virum ... Noverat enim multos valde religiosae vitae viros ac feminas, quos in Graeciae, Longobardiae, Burgundiae, Provinciae, Galliae, Flandriae atque Brabantiae partibus quaerendo lustraverat: quorum virtutes, mores, et verba miro cum fervore et desiderio referebat, et ad meliora per hoc mentes audientium excitabat ... Vix enim habuit de omnibus paternis bonis necessarium vitae victum, et tamen octo monasteriorum Cisterciensis ordinis fundator extitit indefessus, exceptis congregationibus beghinarum, quas usque ad quinque milia, et eo amplius in diversis, locis, in Christi servitio mancipavit." Cf. Mosheim, pp. 131ff; Ryckel, pp. 474-475. Existence of the eastern branches is corroborated by Jacques de Vitry who knew whereof he spoke: Cistercian houses for women had been rising in Constantinople, Cyprus, Antioch, Tripoli, and Acre (*Hist. Occid.*, pp. 306-307).
[110] See below, pp. 107f, 110.
[111] Stephen of Bourbon, *Anec. hist.*, pp. 20-21, no. 11.

THEODORE OF CELLES

Theodore of Celles (ca. 1166–1236),[112] too, is supposed to have entered into intimate association with this religious circle at Oignies, and notably with Mary, but it is as the reputed founder of the Brethren of the Cross, which order may best be regarded as a fusion in the diocese of Liége of the ideals of the *vita apostolica* and evangelical poverty with crusading fervor, that he deserves special attention. Half contemplative, half active, the brethren, in addition to pursuing like other canons regular the *vita communis* built upon canonical hours and other liturgical practices, preached the cross and assumed ordinary pastoral duties. The statutes of 1245 underlined, alongside canonical prayer, the necessity of fostering study and preaching and even mentioned "scriptores" who busied themselves with the copying and expounding of books.[113] Since sermon and confession were represented in this earliest constitution,[114] and in the work of Theodore himself, as normal activity, it is not altogether correct to claim with Ramaekers[115] that a new era opened for the order in 1318 (March 29) when Pope John XXII formally empowered the brethren to perform these functions.

Theodore's biography possesses the peculiarity of not having come down, even piecemeal, in a contemporary form, but entirely in the late and, in certain respects, apocryphal record which Henry Russelius, a member of the order, concocted from abundant reading during the first half of the seventeenth century[116] in an effort to offset the dearth

[112] Van Rooijen, *Theodorus van Celles;* De Moreau, *Histoire de l'église en Belgique,* III, 462-471; De Theux, *Le chapitre de Saint-Lambert à Liège,* I, 190-191; Helyot, *Histoire des ordres monastiques,* II (Paris, 1792), 227-234; Berlière's article in *BNB.,* XXIV 1926-27), col. 755; Willem Sangers' „De Mariakroniek in de orde van 't H. Kruis I. Vader Theodorus van Celles," *De Zegepraal des Kruises,* XX (Diest, 1941), 179-189 is a pious treatment. Eug. del Marmol sheds no light on Theodore in his article ("Celles—son vieux château, ses seigneurs, sa seigneurie," *ASAN.,* XIII [1875], 277-302). For a valuable summary of the history of the order see Ramaekers, *Privileges;* P. A. Ceyssens, "Croisiers," *DDC.,* IV (1949), 800-814.

[113] Dist. I, cap. 1, *De officio Ecclesiae* (ed. Hermans, Annales, II, 32); dist. I, cap. 16, *De levi culpa* (*ibid.,* II, 43-45); dist. II, cap. 8-9 (*ibid.,* II, 57-58). For the whole constitution dating from June-July, 1245, see *ibid.,* II, 30-59.

[114] For the pastoral privileges of the order, see Ramaekers, *Privileges,* pp. 45-55.

[115] In addition to constitutional provisions there is evidence that before 1318 the brethren were occasionally empowered by episcopal offices to hear confession and to preach (cf. Van Rooijen, *Theodorus van Celles,* p. 241 on the concession of the bishop of Paris in 1259). Nevertheless Ramaekers concludes (*Privileges,* p. 49) that "*vanaf 1318 de zielzorg der Kruisheeren een aanvang neemt.*" Again he maintains (p. 17) that although after the crusades the order became more contemplative, it added to its pastoral tasks education of the young and care of the sick.

[116] See Balau's note on Russelius (d. December 9, 1648) (*BNB.,* XX, 1908-1910, col. 459) who was a member of the order, having made his profession at the convent at Huy under the general of the order, Herman Hasius (1602-1618). As prior of the convent of Suxy, near Chiny, he published at Cologne in 1635 the rare chronicle of the Brethren, extending to the election of General Augustin Neerius (1619). This *Chronicon cruciferorum, sive synopsis mirabilium sacri et canonici ordinis sanctae*

of archival materials prior to 1248. Not the slightest reference to Theodore can be detected in either the *vitae* or thirteenth century documents to augment the historical value of this work. Although resting
exclusively on oral tradition [117] and consequently suspicious in character,[118] it nevertheless is constructed entirely in the spirit of the
medieval reformation, based on emulation of the primitive church
and aiming at the salvation of souls. Even as the world depicted by
Jacques de Vitry and Thomas of Cantimpré in their biographies was
militantly antiheretical, so Russelius' account of his order, no less than
the Cistercian *vitae,* is cast in the same heroic mold, with the Albigensians as the foe to be overcome.[119]

Coming from old noble stock at Celles in the present province of
Namur and arrondissement and canton of Dinant, so runs Russelius'
account, Theodore accompanied Rudolph of Zähringen, bishop of
Liége (1167—1191), in 1189 on Frederick Barbarossa's expedition to the
Holy Land. On a visit to Jerusalem after the fall of St. John of Acre
(July 12, 1191), he was so impressed by the "canonici ecclesiae Golgo-
tanae, atque sepulchri Dominici," who followed the Augustinian
rule,[120] that, back in Liége, he was himself later to found an order
similar in organization and spirit. The chronicler makes much of his
veneration of the Virgin [121] who was invoked at Celles under the name
of Notre Dame de Foi.[122] Holding a canonicate given to him by Rudolph (d. August 5, 1191) until 1210, he exhibited lively interest in the
vita communis, urged in vain about 1203 by the papal legate Guy of
Preneste in the cathedral and collegiate churches of Liége.[123] Desiring to possess nothing of his own, Theodore was determined to
belong to what Wazo, as dean of St. Lambert, then bishop (d. July 8,
1048), had once called the "poor men of Christ."[124] The property that

crucis was edited by Hermans (*Annales,* I, part 1 (1200-1500) pp. 27-200; part II
(1500-1635), 1-29. On Russelius, see also Van Rooijen, *Theodorus van Celles,* pp. 5-6,
203. Cf. Haass, *Die Kreuzherren in den Rheinlanden,* pp. 1-10; id., in *Rheinische
Vierteljahrsblätter,* III (1933), 124-129. In his dedicatory letter to the general of the
order Russelius admits that he read for about twenty years more than three hundred
authors and exhausted the archives of Huy (Hermans, *Annales,* I, 28). Cf. A. Van
Asseldonk, "Handschriften van Kruisheren uit de XVe en XVIe eeuw over het ontstaan der Orde van het H. Kruis," *Clairlieu,* I (Diest, 1943), 83-102.
[117] In reporting Rudolph's death Russelius followed Gilles d'Orval (*Gesta episc.
Leod.,* MGH. SS., XXV, 113); the account of the war against Brabant (1212-1213)
(Hermans, *Annales,* I, 35) was borrowed from the *V. Od.* (contained in the *Triumphus S. Lamberti in Steppes, MGH. SS.,* XV, 181).
[118] Cf. De Moreau's judgment (*Histoire de l'église en Belgique,* III, 463, 466-468).
[119] Hermans, *Annales,* I, 30, 33-35.
[120] *Ibid.,* I, 31; cf. II, 73.
[121] *Ibid.,* I, 31; cf. Sangers' article in *De Zegepraal des Kruises,* XX (1941), 179ff:
L. Emond ("De Mariakultus in de Orde van het H. Kruis," *OGE.,* I (1927), 49-55)
is concerned with the modern period.
[122] Hermans, *Annales,* I, 9.
[123] *Ibid.,* I, 32; *CESL.,* I, 132-135.
[124] Anselm, *Gesta Episc. Leod., MGH. SS., VII, 212:* "Hactenus eramus pauperes

was made available to him he regarded as primarily intended for the poor. That was the original way of looking at church property; it was the "patrimonium pauperum" or, as Russelius puts it: "Theodorus igitur, non ut Dominus, sed ut fidelis Domini sui dispensator, annonam suam coepit egentibus communicare et sanctissimarum quarumcunque personarum ambire familiaritatem."[125] This desire for apostolic poverty would appear, therefore, to have led him to associate with "very holy persons" who, in turn, confirmed his decision. Thus it was about 1209 that he first made the acquaintance of Mary of Oignies, "who predicted for him many things that afterwards happened."[126] His early zeal for the salvation of souls, undoubtedly now sharpened by her encouragement, induced him to heed Innocent's call for the preaching of a crusade in Belgium and France against the Albigensians. In Provence he met Dominic and Foulques of Toulouse, both of whom he admired greatly. When the apostolic legate commissioned Theodore in 1210 to preach the cross, recruit forces for this apostolate, and collect funds,[127] the latter commended himself to the prayers of Mary before returning to Liége.[128] Thus imbued with evangelical fervor, he shortly after abandoned to Hugh of Pierrepont his canonicate as a part of his renunciation of the world and settled at Clairlieu near the chapel of St. Theobald, located from the days of Theoduin (1048–1075) at the gates of Huy, which the bishop now gave him. Here he was to lay the foundations of the Brethren of the Cross (fratres Sanctae Crucis) in the Low Countries.[129]

Four clerici joined him in preaching the cross in the surrounding region "against heretics and afterwards for the relief of the Holy Land." Their objective was "juxta Cruciferorum Hierosolymitanorum vivendi normam, sub regula Beati Patris Augustini Deo militare."[130] In 1214 they turned to Cardinal Ugolino, then acting as papal legate in Germany, for official recognition. At his advice Theodore and his

Christi, matris ecclesiae canonici; reliquum est tibi famulemur servi empticii." Cf. Van Rooijen, op. cit., pp. 82, 223.

[125] Hermans, Annales, I, 33; cf. Van Rooijen, op. cit., p. 87.

[126] Hermans, Annales, I, 33: "Unde factum est, ut successu temporis, Mariae quoque Ogniacensis faeminae propter vitae sanctimoniam nominatissimae, notitiam pariter iniret et amicitiam, quae et ei multa praedixit, quae postmodum probavit eventus."

[127] Ibid., I, 34, cf. 35; cf. Van Rooijen, op. cit., pp. 110-111, 128-129; Ramaekers, Privileges, pp. 14, 48.

[128] Hermans, Annales, I, 34: "Theodorus obedientiae filius, ubi Ogniacum cum Episcopo venit, Mariae se precibus commendat."

[129] In 1532 Johannes Stochemius, one of the chroniclers of the Brethren of the Cross in the Low Countries, gave as the date "circa annum Domini 1210," but expressly notes that neither a copy nor a vidimus of the foundation document could be found (Hermans, Annales, II, 63). Haass (Die Kreuzherren in den Rheinlanden, pp. 3-4) discusses the date of foundation. Ramaekers (Privileges, p. 14) accepts the year 1211. Historical ground, however, is not reached until 1248.

[130] Hermans, Annales, I, 35.

56 THE BEGUINES AND BEGHARDS

companions, like others instituting or sponsoring new forms of regular and extraregular life, attended the Fourth Lateran Council to solicit curial attention, but papal approval was not forthcoming until May 3, 1216.[131] Even then the Belgian group was not recognized as an independent organism, but as one segment of Christian knighthood, embracing equally Italy, Crete, and Cyprus.[132] Subsequently Theodore labored among the Brethren of the Cross in Italy where they maintained hospitals to aid sick pilgrims and crusaders. After Honorius III's death (1227) Theodore travelled with Jacques de Vitry to Rome to visit their mutual friend Ugolino, now elevated to the Holy See.[133]

Although it is perhaps too much to say that the brethren of Clairlieu depended on alms at the beginning, there is no doubt that poverty was cherished by them and that the order was instinct with the spirit of the *vita apostolica*. We have seen how those connected with the priory of Oignies were deeply moved to proclaim the divine word and to support crusade preaching with the aim of saving souls; but this objective owed its success to close imitation of apostolic simplicity in accordance with the Augustinian rule—to fulfil literally Christ's injunction to the apostles to dispense with all unessentials on their missions. This was the *vita primitivae ecclesiae* which Jacques de Vitry, among others, advocated.[134] That Oignies and Clairlieu both abided by canonical tradition, prescribed by Augustinian regulations, is fact;[135] to speak of actual connection between them, similar as their aims and methods were, is mere conjecture. It is possible that Peter of Walcourt, Theodore's successor, brought some of the spirit of Oignies with him. In any case, one may assume that it was the evangelical aims of Mary that enriched and gave direction to the work of Oignies and Clairlieu alike. She was for both the representative personality of Oignies, Jacques de Vitry, and for the founder of Clairlieu, Theodore of Celles, the spiritual mother who drove them to a zealous pursuit of the apostolic life.[136]

Although this conclusion rests on the doubtful premise that Russelius employed materials which are no longer extant, the chronicle offers nothing that to one, fully conversant with the literature of Jacques de Vitry and Thomas of Cantimpré, appears improbable out-

[131] Haass, *Die Kreuzherren in den Rheinlanden*, p. 2; the events of 1216, centering around curial recognition, are clothed in legend and presented with hagiographical devices (Hermans, *Annales*, I, 36-37). Cf. De Moreau, *Histoire de l'église en Belgique*, III, 465.
[132] Hermans, *Annales*, I, 36.
[133] Haass, *Die Kreuzherren in den Rheinlanden*, pp. 2-3; Hermans, *Annales*, I, 38.
[134] Funk, *Jakob von Vitry*, p. 129.
[135] For the application of the Augustinian rule both at Clairlieu and Oignies, see Van Rooijen, *op. cit.*, pp. 135-145; for Clairlieu, see *ibid.*, pp. 123-134.
[136] *Ibid.*, p. 144.

side of defective chronology. Firmly anchored on the spirituality of
Oignies and Nivelles in the first third of the thirteenth century, it
places that religious experience in a perspective that agrees well with
contemporary hagiographical accounts, recast and corrected by modern
scholarship. The beginnings of the order nevertheless remain obscure.
For the alleged role of Innocent III and Ugolino, or Gregory IX, there
is not a particle of evidence. Even after Theodore's death tradition
continued to envelop this small, informal organization. The only
modus vivendi was the rule of Augustine, supplemented with usages
of the *canonici* and the example of the founder. The habit was still
that of *clerici*. Historical ground is not reached until the promulgation of the constitution by Peter Walcourt at Lyons in 1245[137] and
the privileges of 1248. On January 26 of this last year the bishop-elect,
Henry of Guelders, authorized the erection of a church in the vicinity
of Huy;[138] the following October 1, Innocent IV in two bulls approved
the foundation of the community as an *ordo canonicus*. Besides a
special protection brief for the Huy community which is couched in
general terms,[139] the pope promulgated on this date a second bull,
Religiosam vitam eligentibus,[140] the "privilegium commune" of the
Augustinian order which contains the various ingredients of the protection privilege.[141] In answer to the request made at the council of
Lyons,[142] the curia took the property and possessions of the mother
house of Huy under its protection, granted the brethren a series of
privileges, including the right to bury whoever desired it in their
churches or cemeteries, to hear divine offices during interdict, and
exemption from the levies of spiritual and temporal lords, and at the
same time confirmed the statutes in two *distinctiones* for which Thomas' successor, Peter of Walcourt (d. December 30, 1249),[143] was responsible. Informed with Augustinian prescriptions, he abided essentially
by the Dominican rule of Raymond of Pennafort.[144] It was also agreed

---

[137] Hermans, *Annales*, II, 30ff, no. 2.

[138] *Ibid.*, II, 63-64; Delescluse and Brouwers, *Catalogue de Henri de Gueldre*,
p. 6; Sangers, "De oudste constituties der Kruisherenorde," *Miscellanea historica in
honorem Leonis Vander Essen*, I (Paris-Brussels, 1947), 315-327; cf. P. Hofmeister,
"Die Verfassung des holländischen Kreuzherrenordens," in *Festschrift U. Stutz,
Kirchenrechtliche Abhandlungen*, Heft 117-118 (Stuttgart, 1938), 189-223. All pertinent documents have been studied by Ramaeker's oft-cited essay.

[139] Bull, *Sacrosancta Romana ecclesia* (Hermans, *Annales*, I, 529, no. 157b;
P. 13037).

[140] Russelius, 56; Hermans, *Annales*, II, 64-68, no. 4; P. 13036.

[141] For the formula of this *privilegium commune*, see Tangl, *Die päpstlichen
Kanzleiordnungen*, p. 233.

[142] Russelius, in Hermans, *Annales*, I, 47-48.

[143] For Peter, see Russelius' account in Hermans, *Annales*, I, 46-49.

[144] Denifle, "Die Constitutionen des Predigerordens in der Redaction Raimunds
von Penafort," *ALKM.*, V (1889), 530-564; id., "Die Constitution des Predigerordens,"
ALKM., I (1885), 165-227; II (1886), 540-564. For a comparison of the early statutes
of the Brethren of the Cross with those of the Dominicans, see Hermans, *Annales*,
II, 31-59; Haass, *Die Kreuzherren in den Rheinlanden*, pp. 5-7.

that the brethren who had previously worn the habit of the **secular**
clergy *(habitus clericalis)* should don the monastic habit *(habitus
monachalis)*.[145] On October 23 a new papal brief was despatched to
the bishop of Liége, communicating to him approval of the statutes
rooted in Dominican constitutional experience as well as the new
habit and urging episcopal confirmation. The letter also mentions the
right of the brethren to acquire property.[146] At the end of the year
(December 31) the bishop approved the papal directives.[147] From then
on, additional privileges were extended to the Huy community[148] and
secondary houses[149] with regularity.

---

[145] Cf. Axters, *Geschiedenis van de Vroomheid*, I, 290-293; Haass, *Die Kreuzherren in den Rheinlanden*, p. 5.

[146] Hermans, *Annales*, II, 68-69, no. 5; *BOP.*, VII, 21; MF., IV, 38; Ernst, *Suffragans*, p. 80; Wauters, *TC.*, IV, 540; Delescluse and Brouwers, *Catalogue de Henri de
Guelders*, pp. 12.

[147] Hermans, *Annales*, II, 69-71, no. 6; *BOP.*, VII, 21; MF., IV, 38; Wauters, *TC.*,
IV, 546; Delescluse and Brouwers, *Catalogue de Henri de Guelders*, pp. 14-15. The
brief is addressed to the "priori et fratribus S. Crucis extra muros oppidi Huyensis."

[148] On January 4, 1249 Peter, cardinal legate of St. George *ad velum aureum*,
authorized them to ring bells and hold offices in churches and chapels not yet dedicated (Hermans, *Annales*, II, 71-72, no. 7). On March 12, 1250, the bishop-elect
granted them a cemetery (*ibid.*, II, 72, no. 8; MF., IV, 39; Delescluse and Brouwers,
Catalogue de Henri de Guelders, p. 22; Wauters, *TC.*, IV, 583; Galliot, *Histoire de
Namur*, III, 225. In 1254 Huy received confirmation of its privilege to hold religious
services during interdict (Hermans, *Annales*, II, 81; P. 15445). Then followed on
April 13, 1277 (Hermans, *Annales*, II, 83, no. 13) and October 11, 1284 (*ibid.*, II,
84, no. 14; P. 22179) occurred further privileges.

[149] The Namur house received on July 1, 1254, from Innocent IV the same protection brief and privileges as conferred on Huy while the bishop of Liége allowed
it to have a cemetery (March 12, 1250) (Hermans, II, 77-81, no. 10 and p. 72; P. 15439;
MF., IV, 40). A protection letter was granted to the Cologne house in 1311 (Hermans, II, 100; Sauerland, IV, no. 836), St. Agatha in 1433 (Hermans, II, 236), and
Beyenburg (1318) (Haass, *op. cit.*, p. 45).

V

The Semireligious under Discipline

THE BEGUINAGE OF OIGNIES

Alongside the canons regular of St. Nicholas, women and girls, following the example of the mother[1] and sister[2] of the founders, took up residence at Oignies,[3] even as San Damiano became a companion house to the Porziuncula.[4] Mary of Oignies possessed a personality that quickly left a deep imprint on the canons and *mulieres religiosae* who associated with her; the community was literally informed with her asceticism but ever submissive to ecclesiastical law and restrained in the bounds laid down by institutional religion. Although these "sorores" whom Jacques de Vitry brings to life may be said to have formed a kind of beguinage, it is significant that the organizational work by the priests cited above was for the most part concerned only with limited areas. Despite John de Liro's intentions and Jacques de Vitry's appearance at the papal curia, these men contributed little to secure a common rule or to obtain recognition as an independent order. The beguine movement at all times remained a poorly organized, almost amorphous movement with each community possessing its own statutes and regulations which, although similar in aim and content, never transcended diocesan lines at best. Nor is it possible to discern in these canons any anticipation of the beghards. These unorganized groups of ecstatic women who were originally called *mulieres religiosae* nevertheless adopted under the guidance of a priest or confessor the new type of *conversio* free from monastic dependence. By personal choice they conformed to evangelical precepts and carried on works of charity.

A document, dated July 24, 1239, reveals the existence of several

---

[1] Jacques de Vitry speaks of her on the death-bed as "mater fratrum de Oignies" (*VMO.*, 559 E); Thomas of Cantimpré later referred to her as "mater prioris" (*VMO., Suppl.*, 576 A). Poncelet regarded her (*ASAN.*, XXXI, p. ix) as the first beguine in the community at the gates of the monastery.

[2] A blood sister lived "*in quarto milliario a monasterio*" (*VMO., Suppl.*, 576 A, no. 10; cf. 558 F, no. 50).

[3] *MDAC.*, VI, 328; *VMO.*, 550-551.

[4] Cuthbert, *Life of St. Francis of Assisi*, p. 141.

beguines and recluses in this area. It is a will of a priest of Walcourt, named Robert, who made small bequests, among others, to "recluse de Ivia (Yves), illi de Barbeçon (Barbençon), illi de Gozées, recluse de Nalines, illi de Meting (Mettet) et nepti sue, beginis de Ivia, illi de Walcuria, illis de Nivella, capitulo de Ognies, beguinis de Ognies."[5] The cottages of the Oignies beguines were built on a piece of ground belonging to the monastery and located between it and the Sambre. This proximity at first presented no problem; the first inhabitants were close relatives of the canons and all were imbued with the same spirit of asceticism. Some thirty years later, however, the beguines had become not only a burden but a source of distraction for the priory in which, after all, discipline had been measurably relaxed. Therefore, in the statutes of May 6, 1243, the bishop of Liége determined that only the prior, subprior, and village priest could hear the confessions of the beguines.[6] Furthermore the statutes issued on November 13, 1250, by the cardinal legate, Peter, bishop of Albano, formally prescribed the demolition of the beguine houses between the monastery and the river as their occupants died; no others were to be built there "since the beguines cannot be seen from or look through the windows and doorway of the convent from such close range without great danger."[7] A concession was also made to permit the sale of wine at a nominal price to neighboring beguines and other poor persons who were unable to procure such necessities at more distant places without expense.[8]

The beguinage moved to another part of the town. Legacies and donations provided small permanent lodgings[9] while business trans-

---

[5] C. Roland, in *ASAN.*, XX (1893), 354, note 2.

[6] *ASAN.*, XXXI (1912), 95; *MDAC.* I, 1277 B; see above, p. 16.

[7] *ASAN.*, XXXI, 127: "Item, statuimus quod domus beghinarum que inter monasterium et Sambriam sunt locate, post decessum earum que ad presens in eisdem commorantur sine mora destruantur, nec liceat aliis in posterum edificare ibidem, cum non sine periculo ipse beghine per fenestras et ostia ipsius monasterii nimis e vicino videre valeant et videri."

[8] Idem: "Prohibemus autem ne publica taberna sustineatur in domo cervisie sive vini. Permittimus tamen quod beghinis vicinis honestis quibus sine scandalo denegari non posset, ceteris etiam vicinis pauperibus qui sine dispendio ad remotiora loca pro hujusmodi necessariis mittere nequeunt, hec moderato precio vendantur."

[9] J., priest of Houtain-le-Val, provided in his will dated December, 1249 *(ibid.,* XXXI 120) that the priory of Oignies should pay his niece Mary, a beguine and daughter of Ralph Folart de Baling, annually 5 hogsheads of wheat and 1 hogshead of grain just as they were due to him. Michael, priest of Walcourt, and Jacques, his brother and priest of Nalinnes, left 60 s. to the "povres beguines" (before 1276, *ibid.,* 203); see the provision made by Catherine, widow of Lambert Borkenon de Châtelet, November, 1315 *(ASAN.,* XXXII, 1913, 47-48, no. 329); on July 2, 1288, the guardian of the Friars Minor at Nivelles and Peter, priest of St. Sepulchre in the same town, made known that demoiselle Oude de Trazegnies, a beguine, had donated to the priory of Oignies two bonniers of land at Brugelette and that she could retire to the common beguinage of Oignies *(ASAN.,* XXXI, 258-260, no. 254).

actions by the beguines indicate some financial independence.[10] The counts of Namur granted the community various privileges and immunities. According to the enumeration of income in the county, drawn up in 1289, only 6 deniers were collected at Oignies "de chascun feu de beghinage" instead of 12.[11] As for formorture and mortmain, the countess, probably Isabella of Luxembourg, the second wife of Guy of Dampierre, temporarily exempted the beguines of Oignies from them.[12] This exemption was made final by the action of John of Flanders, count of Namur, in 1327 (October 14).[13]

The priory of Oignies had surveillance of the beguinage and retained the right of collation of vacant houses.[14] Older members, as elsewhere, were entrusted with internal affairs. The sisters, although each occupied her own cottage, spent most of the time in common[15] and took their meals together. From the beginning the prior's mother, as the oldest, had ordered her companions to take their places at the common table. While Jacques de Vitry described the inhabitants as living near the priory in mutual assistance and consoling one another in afflictions,[16] Thomas of Cantimpré has left a picture of daily life inside the beguinage that was far from being unruffled.[17]

On Trinity day (ca. 1210) Gilles had gone for the evening to visit his sister suffering from a severe malady. The other canon priests were out in the different parishes in accordance with episcopal injunction. Mary,

[10] On August 2, 1284 Gilles de Tournai, canon of St. Barthélémy, made it known that Marie of Walcourt, beguine of Huy, had given all her property to the priory at Oignies (*ibid.*, 239-240, no. 237). On August 10, 1315, Martin de Menonry sold to Marie d'Ohain dite Rocette, a beguine at Oignies, two hogsheads of spelt in rent (*ASAN.*, XXXII, 45-46, no. 327); Maheau de Velaine, living in the beguinage of Oignies, bought on February 16, 1318 from Pieret son of Coulon de Menonry five hogsheads of spelt in income secured at Aiseau (*ibid.*, 52, no. 332); on February 17, 1308, the prior and convent of Oignies authorized Brother Baldwin living at Vichenet to sell a journal of land willed by Marie de Corroy, formerly a beguine at Oignies (*ibid.*, 38, no. 318).

[11] Brouwers, *L'administration du comité de Namur*, II, 2, 416: "Si a li cuens talle c'on prent ale Saint Remi, dou cheruier à 2 chevas u plus 2 s., de home à 1 cheval 18 d., de home sens cheval 12 d., de chascun feu de beghinage 6 d., et de feme nient beghine sens mambour 6 d.; se vaut par an 38 s., et croist et abaisse." Elsewhere much the same statement is found for Oignies, except it reads "*de feme veve 6 d.*" in place of beguine. For further comital relations with these extraregulars, see *ibid.*, II 2, 34, 38 (Maroie li Beguine); 132, 138; 216 (Beatrice li Beguine); 122, 124, 130 (Pierars li fis le Beguine).

[12] *Ibid.*, II, 2, 417: "Encor i a li cuens le mortemain et le formorture fors k'à beghines, et des beghines l'a medame li contesse mis en respit a se volenteit."

[13] *ASAN.*, XXXII, 53f, no. 334; Galliot, *Histoire de Namur*, I, 427.

[14] In October, 1283 the priory granted for life to Emma d'Aiseau the beguine house which had successively belonged to Hawide de Charnoit and Hawide le Gehotte, provided she neither married nor received suspected persons (*ASAN.*, XXXI, 237f, no. 235). In return she was to pay 1 hogshead of spelt in the measure of Fosses to the provisors on the feast of St. Andrew (November 30). The term *beguine* is not applied to Emma.

[15] *VMO. Suppl.*, 576 A.

[16] *VMO.*, 547 (3).

[17] *VMO. Suppl.*, 576 B (10).

seeing the church without a priest, feared to be deprived of mass on a day of solemn festival. Noon approached; the mother of the prior, "almost one hundred years old," and the other beguines (*aliae religiosae mulieres quae inibi Domino serviebant*) were preparing for dinner. Mary, in whom many of her companions recognized the gift of prophecy, came to them saying: "Don't sit down to the table, the prior will soon come to hold service." The old woman, dumbfounded, answered: "Sit down and let us eat. Do you think for a moment that my son, tired from travelling, will, if he comes back, hold mass at such an hour." When the *sorores mulieres* hesitated, saying that Mary was not capable of lies, the superior replied impatiently: „The idea! Your Mary has never lied? Sit down and eat." Mary however re-entered the church, rang the bell for service, the prior arrived and without saying a word, mounted the altar. The old woman, confused, left the table and after mass, begged Mary to forgive her for her haste.

Those members with some substance were assured their livelihood in the beguinage by means of an annual income of four or five hogsheads of spelt; the upkeep of poorer members was assured by legacies, foundations or the charity of the faithful. The necrology of Floreffe, second daughter of Prémontré, lists the names of several beguines and recluses, including a few from Oignies, for whom anniversaries had been founded. The majority presumably belong to the thirteenth century.[18] The last documentary mention of the beguinage at Oignies is contained in an act, dated November 20, 1352, in which the echevins of the two courts of Velaine report that Maroie de Velaine, a beguine at Oignies, bought from Maroie, daughter of Louis de Jemeppe, four hogsheads of spelt.[19]

THE BEGUINAGES OF NIVELLES

According to Thomas of Cantimpré,[20] who cites witnesses still living in his own day, and before him Caesarius of Heisterbach,[21] the beguine movement started in Nivelles. The *Vita Idae Nivellensis* which recounts Ida's (March, 1199—December 11, 1231) temporary withdrawal at the age of nine, after her father's death, to a group of seven pious women near the church of St. Sépulchre and her espou-

---

[18] Barbier "Nécrologe de l'abbaye de Floreffe, de l'ordre de Prémontré, au diocèse de Namur," *AHEB.*, XIII (1876), 5-70, 190-286. Among the beguines from Oignies are a Marie who is not to be confused with Jacques de Vitry's patron (Barbier regards her merely as a benefactress of the abbey, *ibid.*, 53, note 4) (March 22, p. 53); Bertha (April 14, 1337, p. 64); Ivette who gave the abbey a hogshead of spelt (July 16, p. 224). A number of beguines lack place names (January 10, p. 20; July 6, 219).

[19] *ASAN.*, XXXII, 71, no. 358. The necrology of Floreffe lists under September 15 a Margarete de Velaines, beguine, for whom the abbey held 2 hogsheads of spelt (*AHEB.*, XIII, 250).

[20] "In hac urbe (i.e. Nivelles), ut pluribus adhuc viventibus notum est, mulierum devotarum, que beghine dicuntur, nunc late diffusa per orbem religiositas inchoavit" (*BUA.*, II, 51, 12 (p. 478); cf. Greven, *Anfänge,* pp. 47f). Philippen (*Begijnhoven,* p. 64, note 4) read *urbem* in place of *orbem*.

[21] See below p. 329.

sal of the Cistercian rule at sixteen corroborates this evidence of early religious excitement in this area, *quidam paradisus deliciarum.* Observing continence and poverty, moved by the same spirit of devotion and peace, and residing in common *(consodales)*, these women betray certain characteristics of beguines somewhat before the term was applied. One of them, named Mary, afterwards left this community to live as a recluse at Willambroux. From her the biographer, presumably Gosuin de Bossut, gathered his information on Ida's sojourn in the house from 1208 to 1212.[22]

To maintain with older commentators that the canonesses and beguines were identical even though failure to profess irrevocable monastic vows gave both semireligious status[23] would overlook the fact that the communities claiming Gertrude and Begga as founders remained essentially aristocratic whereas the beguines came principally from the middle and lower classes.[24] The first belonged to the feudal era, the second to an urban civilization. The one was an appanage of the nobility, sometimes more distinguished by family connections than religious fervor, the other eventually absorbed the poor. Jacques de Vitry deplored that in Hainault, Brabant, and certain German provinces religious communities "no longer accepted but daughters of knights and nobles, preferring the nobility of the world to that of religion and conduct." Those women who do not wish to be called "nuns" in place of "canonicas saeculares seu domicellas" merit censure.[25] No document exists to prove that St. Gertrude forbade admission to non-noble women, but as at Mons, Moustier-sur-Sambre,[26] Maubeuge, Namur,[27] Andenne,[28] Maseyck or Thorn,[29] so at Nivelles commoners were excluded.[30] The rule of March 18, 1462, after confirming to the abbess the right to fill prebends, asserted that collation should take place within six months. The candidate had to meet the basic qualification of noble birth within four degrees on both sides

[22] *V. Id. Niv.*, 201f; cf. Roisin, *Hag. cist.*, p. 54; De Louvet, *L'Origine nivelloise*, pp. 22, 15-16, notes 49-50; Greven, in *HJ.*, XXXV (1914), 58.

[23] Van Espen, *Jus eccl. univ.*, I, 355-358 (I, tit. xxxii, de *quasi-regularibus*, cap. ii); Zypaeus, *Iur. pontif. novi*, lib. III, *de Regul.*, pp. 302-306.

[24] Tarlier and Wauters, *Géog. et hist. des communes belges. Prov. de Brab. Ville de Nivelles*, p. 90; for the abbey of St. Gertrude, consult Delanne, *Histoire de Nivelles*, pp. 158-212. Cf. Humbert de Romans, *De Modo prompte cudendi Sermones*, II, 44: *Ad mulieres religiosas quascunque, Bibl. max. vet. pat.*, XXV, 478 D-G.

[25] *Hist. Occid.*, p. 347, cap. xxxi.

[26] "In quo domicelle nobiles sub dominio abbatisse sue conversantur, licite secundum suas antiquas tradiciones propriis utentes bonis, bona sua per se quelibet habent divisa" (Jacques de Guise, *Ann. Han., MGH. SS.*, XXX, 1, 278).

[27] Cf. Wilmet, in *ASAN.*, VI (1859—1860), 56.

[28] In August, 1207 Philip, marquis of Namur, limited admission to the monastery at Andenne to women of noble lineage (MF., I, 196); Galliot, *Histoire de Namur*, V, 360f, cf. 178—181; Wauters, *TC.*, III, 275.

[29] Wauters, *TC.*, VI, p. xv.

[30] Tarlier and Wauters, *Géog. et hist. des communes belges. Province de Brabant. Ville de Nivelles* (1862), pp. 90, 150.

of the house. After six months right of appointment devolved to the provost and the canonesses.[31] Moreover Berlière was none too certain about the existence of secular canonesses at Nivelles; they resembled rather nuns, bound by the vow of perpetual chastity and observing *regularis vitae disciplinam* under the Benedictine rule.[32]

Towards the middle of the thirteenth century the Nivelles community of beguines had grown to sizable proportions, even two thousand, if one wishes to believe the doubtful testimony of the Dominican hagiographer.[33] But an act dated February 21, 1284,[34] which made official the nomination of Jehan le Sermonneur as a kind of almoner, indicates that the beguinage of Saint-Syr had fifty-one beguines; that number must have been considerable, for the document had previously referred to the very large number of beguines in this parish (*multitudo permaxima beghinarum*). Again, the testament of Margaret de Lens (December 17, 1248) suggests that Nivelles then had more beguines than such places as St. Quentin and Binche.[35] Some have erroneously made Elizabeth de Gravio (de Grez?) the "mistress" of the Nivelles community.[36] Arnold Raissius in the *Auctarium,* on the other hand, identified Hadewijch with her *socia,* equating this in turn with *magistra*.[37] Yet according to Thomas, Elizabeth lived in Nivelles simply as a pious young girl and had a companion at the time of the recorded walk from Nivelles to Lillois. Elizabeth was dead when the Dominican composed his work: he gives her name but is silent about that of her companion who had become mistress of the beguines (*magistram nunc*).[38] However unreliable the number and uncertain the Nivelles origin of the beguinage, the town was the center of a lively "religiositas," above all in feminine circles. The necrology of Floreffe lists at least two beguines without dates from this area: Hawidis who left a psalter to found an anniversary for herself,[39]

[31] Barbier, "Un document concernant le chapitre noble de Moustier-sur-Sambre (July 7, 1380)," *AHEB.*, XXXII (1906), 67-69; cf. Honorius IV's prohibition of discrimination at Andenne (October 8, 1285), *BCRH.*, ser. 4, II, 113.

[32] Berlière, *MB.*, I, 61-63.

[33] "Elisabeth de Gravio apud Nivellam in Brabantia virgo devotissima fuit. Haec cum socia devota et bona quam viventem adhuc et magistram nunc duorum millium beghinarum, prodere noluimus de Nivella in Lenlos and duo fere millia properabat." (Thomas of Cantimpré, *BUA.*, II, 54, 10 (p. 522); Mosheim, p. 127). For a criticism of this estimate see De Louvet, *op. cit.*, p. 54.

[34] *Ibid.*, pp. 68f, P. J. 15; cf. p. 55.

[35] *Ibid.*, p. 23, and note 78.

[36] This error goes back to Ryckel (p. 290) and was perpetuated by Nimal, *Beguinages*, p. 16; cf. De Louvet, *op. cit.*, p. 54, note 217. De Gravio seems to be the Latin form for the family of Grez or Greis (Van Mierlo, in *D. War. en Belf.*, XXI (1921), 634, note 1).

[37] *Ibid.*, p. 623.

[38] De Louvet (*op. cit.*, p. 54) finds nothing in the account that localizes the beguines in Nivelles rather than in a great center like Cologne.

[39] April 22, *AHEB.*, XIII (1876), 67.

and Gertrude who donated half a hogshead of spelt.[40] By 1231 the growth of population had warranted the establishment of ten new parishes.[41]

If the biographer of Ida of Nivelles describes the interpenetration of the two principal hearths of mysticism in Walloon Brabant—the beguinages and Cistercian nunneries—Caesarius of Heisterbach, Thomas of Cantimpré as well as the chronicler of Villers and its monks have drawn from obscurity a few names famous for austerity but not necessarily to be confused with the beguines. Maria de Gravio, probably a relative of Elizabeth, was interred at Villers.[42] Diedela or Tiedela was also associated with the Cistercian monastery.[43] Godfrey Pachomius, shortly before his death, secured permission from his abbot to visit the *sanctas animas* at Nivelles, especially a *beata anima semper languens*[44] The *Vita Goberti Asperimontis* assigns to the beguine Emmeloth or Grimelothe a decisive role in the spiritual unfolding of its hero.[45]

The renown as well as the nature of Nivelles spirituality may well be judged through the appeal made by Philip III to a beguine to ascertain the innocence of his second wife. This clearly demonstrates that the interest of the French court was not merely charitable. It was as much attuned to the peculiar type of spirituality found among Belgian beguines as were the monks of Villers.[46]

Not until the second half of the thirteenth century is there evidence of official recognition together with endowment and enlargement. In 1267 Renier, scholasticus of Tongres, left to the beguines at Nivelles in his will one mark.[47] Shortly before (June 13, 1262) Urban IV had issued a bull at Viterbo extending to the community in ordinary terms papal protection.[48] Ten years later (July 11, 1272) Gregory X, in

[40] April 27, *ibid.*, 69.
[41] Balau, "L'organisation paroissiale de la ville de Nivelles au XIIIe siècle," *BSAHL.*, XIII (1902), 59-88.
[42] See below p. 334.
[43] See below p. 329.
[44] *V. God. Pach.*, c. 26, *AB.*, XIV, 267.
[45] See below p. 321.
[46] See below p. 331. De Louvet identifies her with a seeress at Spalbeek, northeast of Hasselt in Limbourg (*op. cit.*, pp. 49ff).
[47] Paquay, *Regesta de Renier*, p. 74; see below pp. 165-169.
[48] De Louvet, *op. cit.*, p. 58, P. J. 2. This was a part of general papal policy with respect to beguines and recluses during the summer of 1262 when four bulls were issued for the diocese of Liége whereby Urban IV took under his protection their persons and goods (July 7) (MF., I, 429; Wauters, *TC.*, V, 273), entrusted to the dean of Liége their defense, above all against violators (July 11) (MF., I, 430; Wauters, *TC.*, V, 273), authorized them during interdict to have divine offices celebrated (July 7), and finally declared them exempt from tailles, tonlieux, and other imposts (July 7) (De Louvet, *op. cit.*, p. 31). However, the simultaneous promulgation of these four acts did not occur until six months later (December 29). Renier was chosen by the bishop of Liége Henry of Guelders, to publish them (*ibid.*, p. 59) P. J. 3).

response to a petition, authorized the beguins and beguines, as well as recluses in the parishes of Gouthal, Saint Sépulchre, Saint Jacques, Saint Syr, and Willambroux, to have divine offices celebrated and sacraments administered during interdict, with the usual restrictions.[49] It is evident from this bull that beguine parishes were absent in Nivelles (in parrochiis ecclesiarum de Nivella ubi degitis). In line with the rehabilitation proceedings Bishop Adolph de la Marck in 1330 (December 9) attested to the worthiness of the Nivelles community, instructing the local pastors not to compromise their privileges.[50]

In the parish of Saint-Sépulchre (de Sepulcro) there resided in one house a group of maidens, animated with beguinal fervor and living in common. Here Ida of Nivelles had dwelled from 1208 to 1211. Master Guido became their spiritual director until his death (1227). The existence of the beguinage of Saint-Sépulchre is confirmed by two testaments of 1282, the first (April 24) from Gerard de Huldenberg, canon of Nivelles, and the other (August 9) from Agnes du Vivier, beguine of St. Syr.[51]

The earliest mention of a beguinage in the parish of Gouthal or Goutalle (de Gotallo) occurs in the oldest known will of a Nivelles beguine, drawn up in May, 1273, for Beatrice de Hémelette, an inmate in the local beguinage.[52] It indicates that connected with the beguine house was a hospital, located in a place called Goutisiau, also mentioned in the Polyptique of Villers (1272).[53] Within two years many other favors were being extended in other testaments.[54]

Although a long line of recluses, beginning with Helwide in 1195, may be traced at Willambroux long before it was erected into the parish of Saint Jacques (de Sancto Jacobo... de Awillombruuc) (1231), no beguinage is detected until 1282, in the will of the canon Gerard. De Louvet regards is as a natural development of the reclusorium, which should not be confused with the leper-house. Ten years later (January 21, 1292) this beguinage evidently had only four inmates, to judge from the donation of Béatris Oulhyette.[55]

The beguinage of La Reine or La Royauté owed its origins, according to well-established tradition, to Mary of Brabant, sister of Duke John I and queen of France through her marriage with Philip III, in gratitude for the testimony delivered on her behalf by a Nivelles be-

---

49 Ibid., pp. 59f, P. J. 4; cf. pp. 31f. 49.

50 Tarlier and Wauters, Géog. et hist. des communes belges. I. Arrondissement de Nivelles. Prov. de Brab. Ville de Nivelles, p. 150.

51 De Louvet, op. cit., pp. 66-67, P. J. 13; cf. p. 33 and note 116.

52 Ibid., p. 60, P. J. 5; cf. pp. 33f.

53 See below p. 336.

54 De Louvet, op. cit., pp. 35f.

55 Ibid., pp. 36f.

guine to whom was attributed the gift of prophecy.[56] Actually, a house in the parish Saint-Syr, called La Reine or La Royauté was occupied by beguines well before 1261. This beguinage is mentioned in no less than three documents prior to June 24, 1275, the date of Mary's coronation.[57] It was located on the estate of Renier Bouchial, citizen of Nivelles, who in 1261 renewed before the echevins and the curé of Saint Syr the donation he had made to the abbot of Villers provided the beguines continued to reside there.[58] The antiquity of the house, De Louvet maintains, makes it clear that its royal origins must go back either to Louis IX's mother, Blanche of Castille (d. December, 1252,) or his wife Margaret of Provence (d. 1295), queen from 1234 to 1270, with preference being expressed for Blanche while she was regent (1226—1236).[59] The beguine Agnes listed in the Polyptique of Villers (1272) is the earliest in Saint Syr who is known by name and to whom Villers paid a life pension of one half hogshead of wheat, guaranteed by the grange of Stoisy (lez-Nivelles). The fact that she was called prioress, a term equivalent to mistress, suggests that this beguine convent sheltered a group of pious women.[60]

About 1280 the growing beguinage in the parish of Saint Syr required a hospital for the poor and infirm inmates.[61] Therefore, on May 23, 1281, Jean d'Enghien, bishop of Liége, authorized the construction of a hospital connected with La Reine. To encourage its erection he agreed that divine offices could be held in low voice two or three times a week without reference to holy days. At the same time the rights of the curé and the parish church of Saint Syr were safeguarded.[62] Approval came on May 28 from Elizabeth (Isabelle) de Bierbais, abbess of Nivelles, who, however, insisted as "guardian and protector of the beguinage of La Reine" on retaining "le souverainetet et le warde" of the hospital.[63] The next day the parish priest expressed on behalf of the poor and infirm beguines his sympathy for the erection of a hospital conforming to the conditions stipulated by the letter of May 23 which safeguarded the rights of his church.[64] Its construction was

---

[56] Tarlier and Wauters, op. cit., p. 33; Wauters, Duc Jean I, pp. 55-58; for other evidence, see De Louvet, op. cit., pp. 37-39. The ducal letters of July 25, 1292 (ibid., pp. 74f, P. J. 22) and June 15, 1296, attribute the foundation of the hospital to the queen. Consult De Louvet's interpretation, pp. 48f.

[57] February, 1261 (ibid., p. 58, P. J. 1); December 17, 1274 (ibid., p. 61, P. J. 6); 1272 (Polyptique of Villers, AHEB., XXXIII, 160).

[58] De Louvet, op. cit., pp. 57f, P. J. 1; p. 61, P. J. 6 (December 17, 1274), cf. pp. 40f.

[59] Ibid., pp. 40-41.

[60] AHEB., XXXII, 354; cf. De Louvet, op. cit., pp. 42f.

[61] See the evidence of the February 21, 1284, document (ibid., pp. 68f, P. J. 15). For the beguines of the hospital see ibid., pp. 61f, P. J. 7 (February 21 and March, 1281); pp. 63f, P. J. 8 (March 5, 1281).

[62] Ibid., pp. 64f, P. J. 9.

[63] Ibid., p. 65, P. J. 10.

[64] Ibid., pp. 65f, P. J. 11.

slow, for on March 17, 1282, Jehan Le Petit of Glabais sold various goods for the benefit of this new hospital and its poor beguines unless the hospital was not undertaken for certain.[65] Agnes du Vivier, beguine of Saint Syr, reserved in her testament of the following August 9[66] a bonnier of land for the hospital, but in her legacies made to the hospitals of Nivelles only the beguine infirmary of Goutisiau (parish of Gouthal) is named, while the "poor" beguines of Saint Syr received a hogshead of wheat. On January 5, 1285, the new bishop of Liege, Jean de Flandre, authorized the celebration of daily mass in the new hospital of the beguines and granted thirty days of indulgences to all its benefactors. Like his predecessor, he carefully safeguarded the right of the curé by forbidding the ringing of a bell.[67]

This is the period in which Mary of Brabant resolved to finish the hospital.[68] A few months later (August, 1284) a new appeal for charity was made to the faithful by Abbot Jean of Citeaux in order to hasten its completion. The work had proved far more costly than the beguinage could stand.[69] Jehan "le Sermonneur" was entrusted with the task of raising funds and extending indulgences. By 1286 results were being achieved.[70] Furthermore, on July 16 of that year the bishop allowed priests to celebrate not only low mass, as in 1281, but high mass without prejudice, as previously, to the parish church. He took under his protection the hospital and granted a thirty-day indulgence to its benefactors.[71] In 1288 (November 16) the mambours of the hospital were authorized by the bishop to hang a bell in the chapel of the hospital.[72]

Nor did Duke John I of Brabant neglect this foundation; on July 22, 1292, the mambours were permitted to acquire property and rents in his domain up to 100 *livres* of Louvain, notwithstanding a general edict to the contrary.[73] John II renewed the privilege in spite of an inveterate dislike of acquisitions by the religious (July 15, 1296).[74]

[65] *Ibid.*, p. 66, P. J. 12.
[66] *Ibid.*, pp. 66f, P. J. 13.
[67] *Ibid.*, pp. 67f, P. J. 14.
[68] The earliest mention of this appears on February 21, 1284 (*ibid.*, pp. 68f, P. J. 15); cf. De Louvet, pp. 45f.
[69] Such is De Louvet's interpretation of *opere sumptuoso* (*op. cit.*, p. 46, note 175), whereas Wauters held that although the queen had the best intentions in founding the community in *luxury* and endowing it with some income, the latter soon proved insufficient, obliging the poor and sick beguines to turn to the faithful for maintenance (Tarlier and Wauters, *op. cit.*, p. 150; Wauters, *Duc Jean I*, p. 61).
[70] For examples of donations see De Louvet, *op. cit.*, pp. 46f.
[71] *Ibid.*, pp. 71f. P. J. 19.
[72] *Ibid.*, p. 74, P. J. 21.
[73] *Ibid.*, pp. 74f, P. J. 22.
[74] "Jay soit chose ke nos aiens commandeit ke on ne laist entreir de religion gens pour acquere en nostre terre" (this letter is identical with the earlier act, *ibid.*, p. 48; Tarlier and Wauters, *op. cit.*, p. 150).

NAMUR

By the fifteenth century Namur had witnessed the rise of no less than five beguine establishments, thus testifying to lively activity among the semireligious there.[75] The first foundation, known variously as the Great Beguinage, the beguinage of St. Aubain or of Géronsart, or, more commonly, the beguinage Hors-postil ("extra-posticum"), a name derived from the false gate, owed its beginnings to a widow Eve, who in 1235 donated three houses which she owned *in fraterno vico* near St. Aubain to the "mulieres religiosae conversationis, quae vulgo beghinae nuncupantur". To this were added four bonniers of land in the region of Bouges and a fourth house, then occupied by Gile of Emines and her mother, which would belong to the community after their death. The prior of Géronsart and the dean of the chapter were designated as mambours. Sibyl, who was appointed superior, was assigned an annual income of half a hogshead of grain while the community was to enjoy the produce of the land. The mambours were given full control over the admission and expulsion of beguines.[76] This donation act, no more than elsewhere, did not create the beguinage, for the donor speaks of them as already being well known. Besides those who resided in their own homes, there was also a *curia* at Jambes, below the church of St. Symphorien, near the hospital of St. Calixtus.[77] From the abbey of Moulins comes a will drawn up in 1268 by Marie Bernarde, beguine of St. Symphorien, in the presence of Master Henry, pastor of the church, and Gerard, the chaplain, whereby she left a hogshead of spelt to her sister Isabella for life, and after her, to the Table of the Poor.[78] Thus at Jambes in the thirteenth century there were beguines who had free exercise of property.

The *Vita Julianae Corneliensis* offers a brief glimpse of the "pauperes beghinae" at Namur who provided refuge for the exiles from Liége about 1250. The archdeacon, who was solicitous for their well-being, built for the indigent and infirm beguines a hospital near St. Symphorien.[79]

The pastor who witnessed the above-mentioned will was the same "Magister Henricus investitus"[80] whose investiture is recorded in the cartulary of Notre Dame in an act prepared by the abbot of Villers in 1231.[81] Thus he was curé for more than forty years while his jurisdiction over the beguines was one of the clauses in the foundation. The hospital or beguinage of Jambes, located outside the city, does not

[75] Wilmet, "Histoire des béguinages de Namur," *ASAN.*, VI (1859—1860), 43-90; Borgnet and Bormans, *Cartulaire de la commune de Namur*, I, pp. xxxiiifff.
[76] *Ibid.*, I, 25-27, no. 10 (French transl., 27-30, no. 11); Wilmet, in *ASAN.*, VI, 47f.
[77] *Ibid.*, 48, 55.
[78] *Ibid.*, 49.
[79] *V. Jul. Cornel.*, 468 D-E; see below pp. 304f.
[80] *ASAN.*, V, 70.
[81] Wilmet, *op., cit.*, p. 50, note 2.

seem to have received many gifts from the Namurois. Not until 1367 do the fragmentary documents indicate that a chaplain of Notre Dame, Jean de Gossignées, left to it *deux moyens ecus* on condition that a lamp be kept burning night and day before the altar of St. Agnes; to Sibille, beguine of St. Symphorien, he also gave the arrears of his pension from Huy.[82]

A second community, known as the beguinage *delle Tour* from its proximity to the walls, was already fully established in the fourteenth century. Like the Great Beguinage it depended on the chapter of St. Aubain.[83] A third foundation was made by Jean Wiart, a parishioner of St. John the Evangelist, when, on March 30, 1350, he donated his house to "poor respectable beguines." The *jus patronatus* was entrusted to the local priest who continued to exercise this right until 1493 (October 21). A still larger addition to the Great Beguinage was made possible by Denys de Vedrin who was cited because of his liberality as the "founder of the hospital of the beguines Hors-postil."[84]

While the beguinage of Thomas le Coq goes back to the early fourteenth century, the beguinage of Rhynes is mentioned in 1420.[85] Inasmuch as these convents were unable to accommodate all the candidates, Gertrude Dupont founded on November 19, 1398, not far from the Friars Minor a beguinage for seven poor "demoiselles" of the third order of St. Francis.[86] Since Jean de Heinsberg, bishop of Liége, indicates that the founder's intention was carried out after her death, the year 1427 in which the chapel was dedicated has sometimes been regarded as the date of foundation.[87] This document also makes it clear that the community was designed for poor beguines.

Thus the beguinage Dupont, together with those of Rhynes, du Coq, delle Tour, and Hors-postil, brought to five the number of beguine communities in the city in the fifteenth century. There was no other retreat to receive these women: Salzinnes was not open to the public, and the chapters of Moustiers and Andenne admitted only the nobility.

[82] *Ibid.*, 51; cf. the legacy of Jean Willame de Selh, canon of Notre-Dame, in 1378. In her will, dated October, 1281, Elise, the second wife of Wauthier al Scathe (or al Scace), echevin at Namur in 1262, left, in addition to numerous legacies for Cistercians and the friars, to the beguines of St Aubain 2 hogsheads of rye and a similar amount to those of St. Symphorien (Barbier, in *AHEB.*, XXXVI [1910], 90; for the whole will, 87-98). 40 s. were earmarked for the hospital of St. Symphorien (*ibid.*, 92). This hospital, founded by Henry of Guelders in 1252, should not be confused with the hospital of the same name. Cf. *ASAN.*, XXVI, 189-204.

[83] Wilmet, *op. cit*, p. 51.

[84] *Ibid.*, 52.

[85] *Ibid.*, 53.

[86] *Chron. de Boneffe*, in *ibid.*, 54. Nicholas Dupont, also called Colar or Colin Dupont, together with his wife Gertrude, had founded a benefice on March 2, 1388, Gertrude's subsequent endowment followed her husband's death.

[87] "Beghinasium Namurci instituitur anno 1427" (in accepting 1398 as the date of foundation, Wilmet subjected the year 1427 to severe criticism, *ibid.*, 54-55).

[88] *Ibid.*, 56.

VI

The Puritan Ethic in Liège

Contemporaneous with Peter Waldo's activity in Lyons and briefly antedating the apostolic mission of Foulques de Neuilly in northern France, Lambert le Bègue (d. 1177)[1] urged clerical reform in Liége and translated portions of the Bible and hagiographical records, not, however, as in the case of Waldo, to serve as manuals for himself and preachers, but for the edification of laymen.[2] The son of a smith, Lambert proudly numbered himself among the working classes[3] and therefore, in the face of criticism, addressed his mission to weavers and furriers instead of princes.[4] The priest of St. Christopher was an apostolic preacher, but he was more. He became the center of a tradition the very reasonableness of which has made it die hard. Around his church in Liége, runs a late account, he allowed *mulieres sanctae*— among them daughters of barons, knights, nobles, burghers—to settle in what was eventually regarded as the first beguinage.[5] Not only

---

[1] Greven, *Anfänge*, pp. 158-191; Kurth, *La Cité de Liége*, I, 88-90; II, 220, 255, 270, 287-289; id., "De l'origine liégeoise des béguines," *BARB.*, 1912, pp. 437-462; cf. Greven's repudiation of this essay, "Der Ursprung des Beginenwesens, eine Auseinandersetzung mit Godefroid Kurth," *HJ.*, XXXV (1914), 26-58, 291-318; Van Mierlo, too has busied himself with minimizing Lambert's role: "De bijnaam van Lambertus le Beges en de vroegste beteekenis van het woord begijn," *VMKVA.*, 1925, 405-447; "Les béguines et Lambert li Beges," *RHE.*, XXIII (1927), 785-801; "Lambert le Beges in verbond met den oorsprong der begijnen," *VMKVA.*, 1926, 612-660; cf. Callaey's middle position, "Lambert le Beges et les béguines," *RHE.*, XXIII (1927), 254-259; Mens, *Oorsprong*, pp. 409-427 (a bibliography of the Lambert question appears on pp. 426-427); Balau, *Sources*, pp. 328-332; Mandonnet, *Saint Dominique*, II, 37-39; Philippen, *Begijnhoven*, pp. 59-62.

[2] Grundmann, *Religiöse Bewegungen*, pp. 452ff.

[3] "...Recolo quod de humiliori plebe et stolidis... parentibus natus essem" (Fredericq. *Corpus*. II, 26; Fayen, in *BCRH.*, ser. 5, vol. IX (1899), 343); *"quod de humiliori plebe oriundus sim"* was a charge hurled against him by his foes. While Alberic de Trois-Fontaines called the Liége priest *magister (Chron., MGH. SS.,* XXIII, 855), the author of *V. Od.* was content to refer to him as a *vir rusticus* (*AB.*, XIII, 206).

[4] Fredericq, *Corpus*, II, 26; Fayen, p. 343.

[5] The roots of this tradition are to be found in *V. Od.* (I, 4), 206 and Gilles d'Orval (*Gesta Pontif. Leod., MGH. SS.,* XXV, 110): "...Qui Lambertus li Beges, puia balbus erat, de Sancto Christoforo dicebatur, a cuius cognomine mulieres et puelle que caste vivere proponunt Beguines Gallice cognominantur, quia ipse primus extitit, qui eis premium castitatis verbo et exemplo predicavit." These

was Lambert credited with initiating direction of the feminine religious movement in Belgium and enjoining chastity as its raison d'être,
but the word *beguine* has often been considered a derivative of *le
Bègue*. It is less easy to regard him as the founder or legislator of
beguinages—for no one can really claim that distinction—than to
study him as an apostle of a popular religious movement which
ultimately aimed at organizing *mulieres sanctae* in *curtes* and beguine
parishes. For a question which has provoked so much disagreement
Callaey's conclusion seems sane: "Before Mary of Oignies and John of
Nivelles Lambert, as much by his preaching as by his Life of St. Agnes
and written exhortations, established a model and line of conduct for
persons directed by him and anxious to live in chastity. By his commentary on the Acts of the Apostles he put those of his audience who
were craving evangelical perfection in contact with the example of
the primitive Christian community from which the beguinages drew
inspiration. His apostolate prepared the ground for those who came
after him to take charge of religious education at Liége, like Jean,
Odilia's son, or the organizer of beguines in regular communities like
John of Nivelles."[6]

All the documents we have relating to this popular preacher come
from the same source and present only one side of his activity. That
is the side by which he wished to be known. The letters to Calixtus
III[7] are all a vindication of his work and a retort to his foes. On the
other hand, to picture him as an immoderate and imprudent agitator,
confounding indiscriminately in his vilification the whole clergy[8] is
to do him a grave injustice. Nor did he incur ecclesiastical displeasure
solely because of his audacity to translate scripture or to preach
without license. By attributing to himself and a few partisans the
merit of reflecting in their virtue the image of Christ,[9] and by casting
aspersions on the sacraments of baptism and the eucharist,[10] fasting,[11]
and the competence of ecclesiastical jurisdiction,[12] he was laying

sources, as well as Alberic's chronicle, are all late—when Lambert was becoming
a legendary personage (cf. Van Mierlo, in *VMKVA.*, 1926, 637-640). Cf. Jean des
Preis dit d'Outremeuse (d. 1400), *Ly Myreur des Histors* (ed. Bormans, IV, 462);
P. Meyer, in *Romania*, XXIX, 532.

[6] Callaey, in *RHE.*, XXIII (1927), 259.

[7] The six letters have been edited twice: Fayen, in *BCRH.*, 5 ser., vol. IX
LXVIII (1899), 323ff, and Fredericq, *Corpus*, II, 9ff: no. 1, Fayen, 323-326; Fredericq, 9-11, no. 11; no. 2, Fayen, 326-328 and Fredericq, 12-13, no. 12; no. 3, Fayen,
328-330 and Fredericq, 13-14, no. 13; no. 4, Fayen, 330-337 and Fredericq, 19-23, no.
15; no. 5, Fayen, 338-343 and Fredericq, 15-17, no. 14; no. 6, Fayen, 343-356 and
Fredericq, 26-32, no. 16.

[8] *E.g., Antigraphum Petri* (ed. Fayen), *passim*, esp. 272-274.

[9] Fredericq, *Corpus*, II, 30; Fayen, 351.

[10] Fayen, 324f, 353f.

[11] *Ibid.*, 290.

[12] *Ibid.*, 287, 295f.

himself open to the charge of heterodoxy.[13] According to Lambert, his enemies claimed that his "sectarians" neither attended church nor received the body of Christ. Although disclaiming any such intention, he did not deny, in a disarming fashion, that "there are some—poor clerics, many laymen—who, seeing in me humble attire, simple food, contempt of fame and riches, greater concern and care for divine worship, desire to emulate divine law through me."[14]

Yet his was at once a counterpoise to clerical delinquency under Bishop Rudolph of Zähringen (1167—1191) and a response to lay needs, although tradition may have been too generous with the man who "moved the entire city" in the face of priestly error.[15] Alberic de Trois-Fontaines was not far wrong, certainly not in spirit if not completely in fact, when he spoke of Lambert as "a fervent preacher of the new religion which filled Liége and the neighboring regions."[16] Notwithstanding the specific meaning of religio, the passage suggests the role later assigned to Gerard Groote—"the source and origin of the New Devotion."[17]

Lambert was admitted to the priesthood by illegitimate means, as he himself confesses without adding details.[18] Yet following his ordination by Bishop Henry II of Leyen (1145—1164) against whom he afterwards lodged protests, he endeavored to relive the vita apostolica as an example for fellow prelates who were tainted with simony and concubinage. The vices of the age are depicted by contemporary moralists in ugly colors. To cope with the prevalence of simoniacs in the diocese intervention by the legate Henry of Albano at the synod of 1188 is mentioned by Gislebert de Mons[19] and Alberic de Trois-Fontaines,[20] but while Alberic relates that sixty-six clerics resigned their benefices, the former makes it four hundred. However, the canon of St. Lambert who wrote the Vita Odiliae during the 1240's[21]

---

[13] Cf. Greven, Anfänge, pp. 174-176.

[14] Fredericq, Corpus, II, 30; Fayen, 351.

[15] Gilles d'Orval, MGH. SS., XXV, 110.

[16] Chron., MGH. SS., XXIII, 855: "Nove religionis que fervet in Leodio et circa partes illas ferventissimus predicator." In a fourteenth—cytury Ms. in the Bibl. nat. at Paris (4896 A) the word religionis is followed by the clause, "que vocatur religio beguinarum" (Van Mierlo, in VMKVA., 1926, 637, note 1). Cf. Greven, Anfänge, pp. 165f and note 1.

[17] Sharing the opinion of John Vos of Heusden, prior of Windesheim, and J. Busch who helped to reform monasteries in central Germany, Pomerius in his biography of Ruysbroeck (II, 8) calls Gerard Groote "fons et origo modernae devotionis in Bassa Almania inter canonicos regulares" (AB., IV (1855), 288). Cf. Hyma, pp. 38-40.

[18] Fredericq, Corpus, II, 27; Fayen, 343-345.

[19] Chronique, ed. Vanderkindere, p. 205; MGH. SS., XXI, 555.

[20] Chron., MGH. SS., XXIII, 861. Alberic borrowed this passage from the Chronicon Clarevallense ad a. 1187, in PL., CLXXXV, 1251.

[21] Daris, "Examen critique de la vie d'Odile et de Jean, son fils," BIAL., XI, 153-188.

goes farther by describing the sale of benefices on the market through
the offices of a butcher named Udelinus.[22] Caesarius of Heisterbach,
too, relates in retrospect that Rudolph took so much pride in simony
that once, when he had sold a prebend of one of his churches, he
clasped the money to his breast and exclaimed in the presence of
many bystanders: "I have greatly enriched the church of Liége and
have increased its revenues. For the prebend which my predecessors
sold for ten marks, I have brought up to forty."[23] Venality is common
to all indictments. For the author of the life of Odilia the bishop
may not have been "the worst as the century went, but he was
nevertheless incensed with avarice";[24] he then proceeds to add details
not warranted by sober documentation: not only do clerics marry
in public, but a concubine is presented, transformed into a goddess,
to receive the homage of clergy and people. The fire of 1185 was too
good a theme for the author to refrain from developing. While Lambert le Petit relates a natural accident without adding reflection,[25]
the hagiographer depicts a catastrophe foreseen and announced in
advance by Lambert le Bègue as punishment for the disorders of the
clergy.[26] That moral decay was not arrested may be concluded from
the statutes issued by the legate Guy de Preneste for the chapter of St.
Lambert (1203). Absenteeism, failure of the canons to secure ordination, concubinage, abandonment of ecclesiastical attire and tonsure
were all singled out for stricture.[27]

Thirteen years before Lambert's communication with Calixtus III
(1175—1177) the canons of St. Paul allowed him the use of a small
church for his preaching.[28] Within three years he had succeeded in
rehabilitating it. The ceiling was vaulted, windows cut, cracks in the
walls repaired, illumination increased, and steps taken to improve
the service. But as the congregation grew the canons demanded
higher rent. When the priest balked, he was obliged to leave. It is
doubtful what his next appointment was; presumably he was assigned
to a small benefice in the country.[29] His first attempt to reform the
Liége clergy occurred at the diocesan synod called on March 13, 1166,
by Alexander II of Oeren (1165—1167), Rudolph's immediate predecessor. Lambert protested how, contrary to the decisions of the canons
and regulations imposed by Henry II of Leyen at the synod of 1145

---

[22] *AB.*, XIII, 206.

[23] *CHD.*, VI, 5. (ed. Strange, I, 354).

[24] AB., XIII, 206: "...Rudulphus, vir secundum saeculi dignitatem non infimus,
avaritiae tamen facibus succensus, episcopalem adeptus est dignitatem."

[25] Cf. Balau, *Sources*, p. 426.

[26] *AB.*, XIII, 207.

[27] *CESL.*, I, 132f.

[28] Fredericq, *Corpus*, II, 27; Fayen, 345.

[29] Fredericq, *Corpus*, II, 27; Greven, *Anfänge*, pp. 175, 181f; AB., XIII, 206.

for the purpose of tightening clerical discipline, sons of priests were being admitted to clerical status; again, in violation of legislation promulgated by Eugenius III at the council of Rheims (March, 1148),[30] the clergy were wearing superfluous and luxurious attire. Priests were charging excessive fees for administering baptism, extreme unction, and burial. Mass was accompanied with superstitious practices. If Lambert was harsh on clerical delinquency, falling back on the excommunication of married priests demanded in the synod of Liége of 1131,[31] he was also accused of aiming at the abolition of overseas pilgrimages and visitation of shrines. But again he disclaimed any intention of doing more than reform.[32]

The *Antigraphum* is the only work of Lambert, besides the *epistolarium*, that has survived.[33] As he himself acknowledges in one of his letters, it was presented for examination during his contest with the bishop to the antipope, Calixtus III, then recognized in the diocese as legitimate. Although heavily freighted with scriptural citation, it contains many virulent references to current abuses. The preface explains the origin of the work.[34] Lambert had addressed to a friend named Peter a letter in which he reproaches himself for his opposition to the Liége clergy, provoked by his reform program. He has handled the matter wrongly and Peter has been obliged to caution him about his procedure. The letter is intended to bring from a friend an answer that follows under the address "Lamberto presbitero de Tectis." In it is brought together everything that can justify Lambert's position. Its strongly polemical character appears not only in the defense of the position previously taken, but also in the new charges against his colleagues.

It is significant that among the most bitter opponents should be two abbots of an order noted for a militant antiheretical stand. Even before colliding with episcopal authority Lambert had not been on the best footing with the regular clergy. He had fallen out with the canons of St. Paul, and when he preached in the Augustinian church at Liége, the canon Gislebert challenged his views on the real presence. But before the episcopal tribunal the most outspoken plaintiffs besides Heverlin de Fooz, abbot of St. Lawrence (1161-1183), were the abbots of the Premonstratensian abbeys of Floreffe[35] and Mont Cornillon.[36]

[30] Mansi, XXI, 714, can. 2.
[31] Fayen, 272f and note 1; *Annales Rodenses, MGH. SS.*, XVI 709; Anselm of Gembloux, *Cont. Sigeb. Chron. ibid.*, XI, 383.
[32] Fredericq, *Corpus*, II, 28.
[33] See below, pp. 389f.
[34] Fayen, 266f.
[35] For Abbot Herman (1173-1194) see Berlière, *MB.*, 114. On April 4, 1184 he was present at the dedication of the church at Herlaimont by Rudolph of Liége (*AHEB.*, VII, 371).
[36] Fredericq, *Corpus*, II, 16.

The head of the latter house, Lucas (1138–1178), had already entered the lists against heresy.[37] How disturbed the order was at the Apostolici is suggested by the letter which Everwinus of Helffenstein, the first prior of Steinfeld, sent to St. Bernard of Clairvaux in 1146 in quest of assistance in exterminating heresy.[38] The character which the Cistercian abbot assigns to this sect betrays a striking similarity to the practices of Lambert and his followers: frequent church attendance and a disciplined life. Of particular importance are the sentences: "Mulieres relictis viris, et item viri dimissis uxoribus ad istos se conferunt. Clerici et sacerdotes populis ecclesiisque relictis intonsi et barbati apud eos inter textores et textrices plerumque inventi sunt."[39]

In spite of an appeal to the Holy See in the face of condemnation at the synod, Rudolph had Lambert imprisoned in the castle of Rivogne. After sixty-three days of imprisonment, he escaped and took refuge at Troyes. From there he departed for Rome where his brother Peter, who had gone ahead, had just died. Calixtus III received Lambert's appeal from partisans who had been summoned to the synod to vouch for the doctrinal errors of their leader. The antipope thereupon instructed on September 2, 1175–77, the bishop, the provost, Henry de Jauche, the archdeacons, and the clergy of Liége to release the preacher and to allow him to proceed to the Roman curia. After all, "he had not been convicted, had not confessed, and had appealed to the papacy." Rudolph must also reinstate five other priests who had also turned to Rome.[40] Shortly afterwards Lambert is lost to sight.

Lambert's lengthy letter to Calixtus III contains an exhortation to Sunday worship. Setting himself to the task of counteracting by example and sermon the secular side of bourgeois culture in Liége, the priest of St. Christopher instituted a veritable puritanical regime the nucleus of which were small Bible-reading societies of devout laymen. Dismayed at the "infinite number of men and women who use Sunday not to atone for their delinquencies but to multiply their sins," he exhorts them to observe the Sabbath instead of profaning it. They have violated the day not so much by manual work—in fact, he will make concessions to the agricultural laborer on this score—as by indulging in the "vices of the modern age" in excess of those misdeeds amassed during the week:[41] they hasten to mimes, acrobats, and actors, give themselves over to drunkenness and dice, lead or watch seductive dances of women, and engage in obscene songs and shameful acts in front of churches or over the graves of parents and

---

[37] Hugo, *Ann. Praem.*, I, 315.

[38] *Ibid.*, II, 851-853; *PL.*, CLXXXII, 676ff.

[39] *PL.*, CLXXXIII, 1135.

[40] Fredericq, *Corpus*, II, 13-14; Fayen, 328-329.

[41] For a contemporary description of these peccadilloes see Hoffmann von Fallersleben, in *Horae Belgicae*, VI, 1-2; cf. notes on pp. 213-215.

kinsmen.[42] Elsewhere a similar indictment is hurled against prelates.[43]

This exhortation received a sympathetic response in subsequent moral—didactic literature as well as in conciliar legislation. Far better would it be, wrote Jan Weert of Ypres in the fourteenth century,[44] if weavers and fullers worked even on Sundays instead of frequenting the tavern and drinking so much that they lose their heads. There they indulge in vain boasting, cursing, buying and selling, and gambling.[45] Just as diocesan and provincial assemblies did, popular preachers like the Franciscan Berthold of Regensburg voiced disapproval at such profaning of the Sabbath. "Thou shalt not dance on the day of rest, nor play nor dice, for want of something to do." When the congregation protested that this narrow path left no means of passing the day, Berthold suggested church services, good works, almsgiving, and the earning of indulgences. He clinched his moral precepts with a quotation from Augustine: "It is better even to do field work on holy-day than to dance." "Except at weddings," the friar adds. "There, folk may dance without mortal sin. On the other hand, you may so dance as to commit mortal sin. He who goes to field work and he who dances, alike sin mortally; but field work is of some use; dancing profits no man."[46]

So strong was the appeal of the flagellants' austerity in Tournai— the like of which Gilles li Muisis had never seen before[47]—that men and women laid aside their fine clothes and ornaments: women changed their hair style, removing the horns which provoked the wrath of many a preacher and didactic poet; gambling, dancing, immoral songs and other frivolities ceased; they even put an end to illicit sex relations.[48]

Ample precedents for the moral rigorism of Calvin and the Puritans are thus furnished by orthodox teachers as well as by the semireligious in the Middle Ages. Indeed it is more correct to derive modern English Sabbatarianism, for example, not from Reformed or Calvinistic origins but from medieval doctrine, which survived in Anglican teaching and legislation, that the day must be devoted wholly to religious ends.[49]

[42] Fredericq, Corpus, II, 29; Fayen, 350.

[43] Antigraphum Petri, ed. Fayen, 316.

[44] Jan Weert wrote Die Niwe Doctrinael (ed. Blommaert, Oudvlaemsche Gedichten, III, 75-105) which he also called Spieghel der Sonden (vss. 68-69) to distinguish it from Boendale's Dietsche Doctrinael. For the poet see J. Stecher, in BNB., V (1876), 905-907, who stresses his lay character.

[45] Niwe Doct., 1709-1724; cf. 192ff. For further attacks on tavern and alehouse which established themselves as deadly rivals to church ordinances, see Owst, Literature and Pulpit, pp. 434-436; id., Preaching in Medieval England, pp. 178f.

[46] Predigten, ed. Pfeiffer, I, 268. For condemnation of dancing, see Coulton, Five Centuries, I, 531-538.

[47] Fredericq, Corpus, II, 109; for the flagellants see below, pp. 370-72.

[48] Fredericq, Corpus, II, 104.

[49] M. M. Knappen, Tudor Puritanism (University of Chicago, 1939), p. 447.

Part Two

THE EXTRAREGULAR IN STATE AND SOCIETY

"Virgines et aliae mulieres, quibus secundum instabilitatem prosperitatis mundanae prosperum statum in seculo sua videtur nobilitas polliceri." Bull of Honorius III to Cardinal Ugolino of August 27, 1218, *BF.*, I, 1; cf. Potthast, 5896.

I

Social Origins: The *Frauenfrage*

Herbert Grundmann[1] marshalled a persuasive array of evidence from the early history of the Humiliati, Waldensians, and Franciscans to refute the easily generalized sociological views widely prevalent after 1880, especially in certain German circles, that the religious cult of poverty, with its frequent anticlerical strain, was born in the lowest social strata—among impoverished workers or the urban "proletariat." Essentially democratic in nature, it was regarded as a reaction of urban civilization to feudal society from which monachism drew its sustenance. This socioeconomic interpretation rested on the conclusion that the widely diversified semireligious or extraregular groups primarily constituted a body of social protest, springing from economic need on the part of the *minores* and directed against the *majores*.[2] Such an interpretation was assumed to be especially true for

[1] Grundmann, *Religiöse Bewegungen*, pp. 157-169; cf. *ibid.*, pp. 188ff on the beguines and pp. 29ff on the Cathari; cf. Mens." Innerlijke drijfveeren en herkomst der kettersche bewegingen in de Middeleeuwen. Religieus ofwel sociaal oogmerk?" *Miscellanea historica in honorem Leonis Van der Essen*, I, 299-313; Van Mierlo, in *RHE.*, XXVIII (1932), 379f.

[2] Troeltsch, *Grundlagen der christlichen Kirchen*, p. 362: "...Haben umgekehrt die Sekten die Beziehungen zu den Unterschichten oder doch zu den gegen Staat und Gesellschaft im Gegensatz befindlichen Elementen der Gesellschaft, arbeiten sie von unten herauf und nicht von oben herunter." Cf. *ibid.*, pp. 349, 352; Wigger, in *Jahrbücher des Vereins für Mecklenburgische Geschichte und Alterthumskunde*, XLVII (1882), 3: "Sie gingen vorzugsweise aus den unbemittelten Ständen hervor und lebten vielfach in Dürftigkeit von ihrer Hände Arbeit..." Emphasizing the term "Willigen Armen" which frequently appears in Lübeck wills as elsewhere, Brehmer (in *Zeitschrift des Vereins für Lübeckische Geschichte und Altertumskunde*, IV [1884], 87), although admitting that some recruits came from families of substance, assigns the majority to the servant class ("Sie gehörten zumeist den unteren Ständen an, vornehmlich zogen sich die alten Dienstfrauen der Patricierfamilien dorthin zurück, doch fanden sich unter ihnen bisweilen auch Frauen aus den angesehenen Familien der Stadt"). Hartwig (in *Hansische Geschichtsblätter*, XIV, 1908, p. 82), too, acknowledged that alongside poor woman, especially old servants of patrician families, well-to-do women occasionally received care in the Lübeck beguine convent. Such distinctions were disregarded by Norrenberg (*Frauen-arbeit und -arbeiterinnen*, pp. 50-55) and Woikowsky-Biedau (*Das Armenwesen*, pp. 31-37, 54-59, 85-90) who were among the strongest proponents of the socioeconomic interpretation. While Hauck (V 1, 382) speaks thus of the ecstatic women at the beginning of the thirteenth century in the Rhineland:

the Humiliati who worked in the Lombard wool industry. Actually their role was similar to that of the Quakers of a later date: by forming religious-economic associations they not only guarded themselves against exploitation but also became economically powerful and. eventually, capitalists.[3] Even the Spiritual Franciscans, who appealed broadly to the working classes and accepted recruits from the dregs of society, sometimes cut across class lines.[4]

Many German scholars have been reluctant to accept such generalizations without qualification. In Frankfurt[5] and Cologne[6] as well as in Strasbourg[7] during the thirteenth and fourteenth centuries women from all classes, and not least from patrician families, dedicated their lives as beguines to divine service.[8] But this does not invalidate the basic premise that as a product of urban civilization and as an expression of lay spirituality, the foundations were often, especially after the first generation of spontaneity, intended for the poor.[9] When voluntary poverty lost its appeal, more and more women, instead of submitting willingly to its yoke, were driven by necessity to seek refuge from misery and want. By the fourteenth century beguinages were often assuming the character of poor houses where girls and widows could receive lodging and sometimes money, bread, light, and fuel. At the same time many houses were beginning to play another socioeconomic role through industrial activity, with the resultant overlapping of guild organization.

Motives are at best obscure and elusive. By examining the hagiographer and moralist uncritically one would conclude that spiritual

"Sie gehörten den mittleren und niederen Schichten der Bevölkerungen," he also indicates (IV, 902-903) how the Waldensians cut through all classes. Cf. Phillips, *Beguines in Medieval Strasburg*, p. 149; Volpe, *Movimenti religiosi*, pp. 113ff; Tarlier and Wauters, *Géog. et hist. des communes belges. I. Arrondissement de Nivelles. Prov. de Brab. Ville de Nivelles*, p. 150; Zanoni, *Gli Umiliati*, pp. 19-26; Uhlhorn, *Liebesthätigkeit*, II, 376-377; Liebe, in *Archiv f. Kulturgeschichte*, I (1903), 35-49; Hauber, *ibid.*, XIV, 286; Rücklin, p. 137 and p. 231.

[3] Zanoni, *Gli Umiliati*, p. 157; Volpe, *Movimenti religiosi*, pp. 113f.

[4] Emery, *Heresy and Inquisition in Narbonne*, pp. 145, 167 (App. iv, no. 4): e.g., the case of Blasius Boerii, a tailor, who became a consul and councillor repeatedly.

[5] Kriegk, *Deutsches Bürgerthum*, II, 102.

[6] Asen, in *AHVN.*, CXI (1927), 92.

[7] Schmidt, in *Alsatia*, VII (1858-1860), 152: the appearance of *adeligen oder reicheren Bürgerinnen;* cf. 187ff; he accurately classified the Strasbourg beguines in three groups: houses for the poor (pp. 150-187), houses for the well-to-do (pp. 187-196), and converted penitents (pp. 196-206). Cf. Phillips, *Beguines in Medieval Strasburg*, p. 149.

[8] Greving, in *AHVN.*, LXXIII (1902), 26-27; Schroeder, in *ibid.*, LXXV (1903), 1ff; Zuhorn, in *Westf. Zeitschr. f. vaterl. Gesch. u. Altertumskunde*, XCI (1935), 1ff; Uhlhorn, *Liebesthätigkeit*, II, 377-378: "Durchweg sind die Beginen arm und gelten als solche, die man als Arme unterstützt. Die Beginenhäuser werden gestiftet und mit Legaten bedacht, um armen Witwen und Jungfrauen eine Hülfe zu ihrem Unterhalt zu bieten." Hence the name *die arme Kinder* is derived from hard necessity. Cf. Uhlhorn's conclusions on pp. 381-382.

[9] Greving, in *AHVN.*, LXXIII (1902), 26-27; Woikowsky-Biedau, *op. cit.*, pp. 31-32, 85-90.

forces were of paramount importance, whereas socioeconomic causation can be discerned in these sources only by reading between the lines, if at all. Statutes and cartularies reveal more faithfully the complexity of the problem. The Ghent memorial of 1328, drawn up at the instance of the bishop of Tournai to rehabilitate the local beguines, demonstrates that contemporaries were fully cognizant of impersonal forces.[10]

> Jeanne and her sister Margaret, successive countesses of Flanders and Hainault, had observed (a hundred years before) that these counties teemed with women who were denied suitable marriage because of their own situation or that of their friends, and that daughters of respectable men, of noble and ignoble birth, desired to live in chastity but on account of numbers or the poverty of their parents were unable to do so easily. Furthermore respectable demoiselles and impoverished noble women must beg or pursue a life embarrassing to themselves and their kin unless a proper remedy was provided. Under divine inspiration, as is piously believed, they founded in various parts of Flanders, having first sought the counsel and approval of diocesan and other worthy authorities, spacious places called beguinages (curie beghinarum). Here, by living in common, these women, girls or demoiselles, were received to preserve their chastity by vow or without vow and to provide themselves with food and clothing without embarrassment to themselves or the convenient conniving of their friends.[11]

Eileen Power has indicated some of the factors which governed the embracing of monastic status: career and vocation for girls,[12] a "dumping ground" for political prisoners,[13] acceptance of the illegitimate, deformed or half-witted,[14] coercion by relatives,[15] and refuge for maladjusted widows and wives.[16]

It was Carl Bücher[17] who brought into sharp focus the Frauenfrage of the Middle Ages on which much of German scholarship concerning the regular and extraregular concentrated for a generation prior to Greven's fresh perspective. The question concerns primarily material provision for those women who were prevented from fulfilling their "natural calling." It grew in part out of the disappearance of a suitable ratio between the number of marriageable males and females. This disproportion may be explained by the higher mortality rate among men, partly for natural, partly for social reasons.[18] Among the factors responsible for this disproportion were wars, crusades, and

---

[10] For an introduction to the schools of interpretation consult Greven, Anfänge, pp. 1-27; Philippen, Begijnhoven, pp. 1-15.

[11] Béthune, Cartulaire, p. 74; Fredericq, Corpus, I, 176.

[12] Power, Medieval English Nunneries, pp. 25-29.

[13] Ibid., pp. 29-30.

[14] Ibid., pp. 30-33; cf. Berlière, Le recrutement, pp. 26-31.

[15] Power, Medieval English Nunneries, pp. 33-38.

[16] Ibid., pp. 38-41.

[17] Bücher, Die Frauenfrage im Mittelalter (Tübingen, 1882); cf. Finke, Die Frau im Mittelalter, pp. 98ff; Woikowsky-Biedau, op. cit., p. 33; Uhlhorn, Liebesthätigkeit, II, 378ff.

[18] Bücher (Die Frauenfrage, p. 6) established the ratio of men and women in

the natural longevity of women. In addition one must mention celibacy: the partly necessary, partly voluntary withdrawal from marriage of a number of the marriageable men, dictated to some extent by monastic requirements.[19] But it was by no means canonical prescription alone which demanded nonmarital status: the craft organization of industry as well worked to the disadvantage of marriage for certain elements of the male population. Marriage of the artisan depended on admission to masterhood, and this in turn depended on conditions which favored the masters of the guild.[20] Guild regulations prohibited admission of married apprentices.[21] Due to the closing of many guilds and the limitation of work the fourteenth and fifteenth centuries witnessed the emergence of a class which did not enjoy the prospect of independence and the founding of families.

Bücher's thesis conducted directly to emphasis on socioeconomic motivation, even to the exclusion of religious interests. For Norrenberg the beguine house sprang up alongside the guilds. When female labor was forbidden in the latter, beguine life offered independent livelihood and work in the towns.[22] For Woikowsky-Biedau[23] the beguinage was a poor house rather than a religious institution; social and economic causes, not religious yearnings, led to its foundation. Bücher himself regarded beguine houses as charitable foundations, designed to aid the indigent and unmarried. The only student who has contributed to the beguine problem in English also subscribes to this school of interpretation. There is "no indication," writes Phillips, "that an associated religious life had essential significance for beguines. Indeed, if the exact nature of the beguine life had been more accurately interpreted, the beguinehouse would never have been considered a religious association."[24] While "religious factors worked to give groups of women within the beguinehouses a corporative character..., the religious forces involved were far less important than were economic considerations..."[25] That the Frauenfrage was essentially socioeconomic cannot be contested. But it also involved a religious question, the pastoral care of women. This in turn was

385 for Frankfurt a. M. at 1,000 : 1,100; in Nürnberg at 1,000 : 1,168 in 1449, in Basel at 1,000 : 1246 in 1454. In Nürnberg the excess of women was felt not only in burgher families, but also among the working classes.

19 Bücher (Die Bevölkerung von Frankfurt, I, 507ff; Die Frauenfrage, p. 9) estimated that in Frankfurt a. M. for the fourteenth and fifteenth centuries the clergy numbered 200-250 persons for a population of 8,000-10,000. For Lübeck one may assume for the same period 250-300 clergymen and about 100 monks (Hartwig, in Hansische Geschichtsblätter, XIV, 1908, pp. 39ff).

20 Ibid., pp. 57ff.

21 Bücher, Die Frauenfrage, p. 10.

22 Norrenberg, Frauen-arbeit und -arbeiterinnen, p. 50f.

23 Woikowsky-Biedau, Das Armenwesen, p. 31.

24 Phillips, Beguines in Medieval Strasburg, p. 152.

25 Ibid., p. 156; cf. 27-30.

reflected in the extraordinary influx to nunneries, the growth of semi-religious life, and the lively controversy within new and old monachism over the *cura mulierum*.

One factor which persuaded women of gentle birth to embrace a rule or adopt the penitential life was the very narrowness of the sphere to which they were confined. An honest occupation was not an honorable occupation. By working in the fields or spinning, baking, and brewing with the wife at home the daughter in a humble family could earn a supplementary if not a living wage. If an artisan was too poor to provide his daughter with a sufficient dowry he could, and often did, apprentice her to a trade.[26] The number of industries carried on by women in the Middle Ages shows that for the bourgeoisie and lower classes there were other outlets besides marriage. From 1320 to 1500 in Frankfurt sixty-five lines of work are listed in which only women workers appeared, seventeen in which they predominated, thirty-eight in which men and women were equal, and eighty-one in which men dominated. In other words, there were no fewer than 201 occupations in which women were engaged.[27] In Cologne three crafts appealed primarily to women: spinners, gold spinners who were often associated with gold beaters, and silk weavers.[28] Nowhere is female labor better illustrated than in the Flemish cloth industry where the beguinage and beghard convents alike were interlaced in the fourteenth century with guild organization as well as incorporated into the ecclesiastical structure through adoption of the third rule. Domestic service also provided a valuable outlet for the frustrated girl. The knight or country gentleman, on the contrary, was not able to apprentice his superfluous daughters to weavers. Thus for them it was either marriage or a convent where they might go with a smaller dowry than a husband of their own rank would demand. The convent was thus the natural and obvious alternative to marriage.[29] The anxiety of the upper classes to secure a place for their children in nunneries led to overcrowding. The logical consequence was the strong connection that was frequently established between the nunnery and certain families from which, in each generation, it received the daughters or a niece or her dower. Thus a close link bound each nunnery to the family of the patron. Since admission fees were prohibitive, a *medium vitae genus inter monasticum et saeculare* offered another solution. If a girl was unable to make a rich marriage, runs one Lübeck source, she became a beguine.[30]

[26] Power, *Medieval English Nunneries*, p. 4.

[27] Norrenberg, pp. 46, 50.

[28] Behaghel, *Die gewerbliche Stellung der Frau*, pp. 3, 84-89.

[29] See the case of Osilia of Liége, who was disappointed in marriage and was twice widowed (*CHD.*, [XI, 29], ed. Strange, II, 263).

[30] Schroeder, in *AHVN.*, LXXV (1903), 2.

In short, girls and widows to whom marriage, for one reason or another, was unacceptable could be provided for in one of three ways: work in the home, employment in a craft, or support in a monastery or convent, in either regular or extraregular capacity.

Competent scholarship must recognize the socioeconomic factors summed up in the concept *Frauenfrage* but at the same time will acknowledge the potentiality of religious motivation for decision. To approach the cult of chastity cynically, without reservation for a measure of sincerity, and to disregard the compulsion of voluntary poverty is to distort two basic religious concepts of the age of Mary of Oignies. Identification of the well-to-do with a beguine society and the *vita apostolica* proves that something more than economic necessity motivated them.[31] The statutes uniformly prescribe that a part of each day should be set aside for prayer and religious exercises; the beguine on admission vowed to remain pious and chaste during residence and to abide by the orders of the mistress and the organization; adequate provision is made for supervision by monks, priests, and friars with adoption of the third rule or Augustinian regulations being often recommended. Securing a prebend and habit was contingent on the acceptance and continuous observance of such prescriptions.

Genuineness and depth of this religious motivation may be measured by social-caritative activity. To balance the materialistic interpretation which sees in the beguine either an industrial worker or a burden for society, one must be ready to admit the validity of spiritual forces which engaged the attention of many contemporary observers. If there was in 1245 a *multitudo beghinarum cupiens tumultus saecularium declinare,*[32] not all the *mulieres sanctae* were employed in useful work, charitable or otherwise. Jacques de Vitry describes some addicted to transports, suspended consciousness, and other abnormal experiences.[33] But these were not numerous. The oldest rule for the Bruges beguinage (ca. 1300), in which externals are singularly dwarfed by meticulous definition of religious exercises, persuaded Hoornaert that "here was a foundation with a purely contemplative purpose."[34] For Zuhorn[35] and Hauck[36] also religious enthusiasm was decisive.

The youth of many girls who took the veil is proof that anything like a vocation of free choice of livelihood was seldom possible.[37] The

[31] Cf. Uhlhorn, *Liebesthätigkeit,* II, 377.

[32] Walter de Marvis, bishop of Tournai, see *ASEB.,* 1904, pp. 286f.

[33] *VMO.,* 548 E-F.

[34] Hoornaert, in *ASEB.,* LXXII (1929), 5.

[35] Zuhorn, in *Westf. Zeitschr. f. vaterl. Gesch. u. Altertumskunde,* XCI (1935), 5.

[36] Hauck, IV, 933: "...Das religiöse Element war doch zuletzt das entscheidende." Cf. IV, 422-423.

[37] Power, *Medieval English Nunneries,* pp. 25-29.

age of profession was sixteen; often younger girls were received as novices and prepared for the veil. The reception of children at a tender age was rather encouraged than otherwise by the church. Similarly, the beguinage which in Belgium approached the discipline demanded by claustration might not always set definite age limits, but young girls and women under thirty were required at Paris to submit to special supervision of their conduct.[38] On the other hand, it is difficult to claim that children who professed at such an early age could have had no consciousness of vocation for the religious life; the history of medieval women saints would seem to disprove this. That collector par excellence of edifying anecdotes, Caesarius of Heisterbach, tells of many youthful enthusiasts in the *Dialogus Miraculorum* which he wrote between 1220 and 1235 for the instruction of novices in his own Cistercian house. At Lutzerath, in the diocese of Trèves, for example, no girl was received by ancient custom but at the age of seven or less.[39] Another child, destined for a worldly match, protested daily that she would wed Christ only, and when forced to wear rich garments, asserted that "even if you turn me to gold you cannot make me change my mind," until the exhausted parents allowed her to enter a nunnery where, though very young, she was soon chosen abbess. Her sister, given to marriage while yet a child, was widowed and "still young" entered the same house.[40] Still another, fired by their example, escaped to the nunnery in man's clothes; her sister, trying to follow, was caught by her parents and married. "But I hope," adds Caesarius with proper appreciation, "that God may not leave unrewarded so fervent a desire to enter religion."[41] Mary of Oignies herself was credited with religious precocity as she followed in the footsteps of Cistercian monks.[42] The beguine Christine of Stommeln said of herself: "So far back as my memory can reach, from the earliest dawn of my childhood, whensoever I heard the lives and manners, the passion and the death of the saints and especially of our Lord Christ and His glorious Mother, then in such hearing I was delighted to the very marrow."[43] At the age of ten she, like Catherine of Siena,[44] contracted a mystical marriage with the heavenly Bridegroom, and at the age of thirteen her spiritual yearnings caused her to flee, against the wishes of her parents, to Cologne where she

[38] Le Grand, *Les béguines de Paris*, art. 9 (p. 54), art. 17 (p. 56), art. 11 (p. 54): "Nulle jueune fame ne soit souveraine en chambre, se elle ne passe trente ans"; cf. *ibid.*, p. 38.

[39] *CHD.* (VI, 37), ed. Strange, I, 450-451.

[40] *Ibid.*, (I, 42), ed. Strange, I, 53.

[41] *Ibid.*, ed. Strange, I, 53-54. For some understanding of social causes, see *ibid.*, (I, 28), ed. Strange, I, 34.

[42] *VMO.*, 550 B, no. 1.

[43] *V. Chr. Stumb.*, 236-237.

[44] *V. Cath. Sen.*, *AA. SS.*, XII (April 30, iii), 871 (36); 872 (38).

associated with beguines as early as 1265.[45] Mechtild of Magdeburg likewise claimed to have been visited by the Holy Spirit from the age of twelve on.[46] Birlinger, in his studies of German Dominican nuns in the Middle Ages, cites many examples attesting to such religious precocity.[47]

The beguinage of Belgium and the convent of Germany presented a twofold aspect: they were charitable houses for unmarried and widowed women, but they were also retreats for the contemplative. It is not enough to represent the houses as a fusion of monastic and secular elements; their origins must be assigned to a complex of socioeconomic and religious motivation. Kriegk has summarized the problem well: the beguines were for the most part poor girls or widows who could live more easily by associating with others of their kind than separately. But this was not the primary purpose of the convents, for in Frankfurt distinguished and wealthy individuals made their appearance as beguines in the thirteenth century; only later did the socioeconomic factor predominate. Yet even in the fourteenth and fifteenth centuries, when the houses were often being founded for "poor" beguines and were therefore called domus pauperum, the religious motive was never entirely absent.[48]

Grundmann argues the point cogently: this popular religious movement did not constitute a protest of the poor and downtrodden against economic well- being, the accumulation of wealth and luxury, or the beginnings of capitalism, for this mystical excitement was particularly strong in precisely those circles which could have benefited the most from material things. No more than Peter Waldo, the Humiliati, or the Franciscans did the early beguines protest against the abundance of others; they voluntarily withdrew from their patrimony for the sake of the evangelical ideal, the renunciation of the goods of the world, and in search of voluntary poverty.[49] The career of Mary at Oignies and Willambroux followed a pattern imitated then in many parts of western Europe. In the convent of St. Gertrude at Nivelles lived a girl, Clementia by name, of gentle birth who attempted to expiate an error by devoting herself to charitable activity and, to the point of destitution, lavishing her wealth on the needy. A pilgrim gave 5 s. to aid her.[50]

The proportion of women who became nuns was very small in

[45] V. Chr. Stumb., 236-237.
[46] Preger, Geschichte der deutschen Mystik, I, 91-92.
[47] Birlinger, "Leben heiliger alemannischer Frauen des XIV, XV Jahrhunderts. IV. Die Nonnen von Kirchberg bei Haigerloch," Alemannia, XI (1883), 1-20. Mechtild von Waldeck was eight when she entered a convent (ibid., p. 10), Werntrudis von Bürn about nine (ibid., p. 1).
[48] Kriegk, Deutsches Bürgerthum, I, 102.
[49] Grundmann, Religiöse Bewegungen, p. 196.
[50] CHD. (XI, 28), ed. Strange, II, 262-263.

comparison with the total female population. Medieval nunneries admitted only the titled and women of property[51]—they were aristocratic institutions, a refuge for helpless or superfluous daughters of noble families and the country gentry, as well as widows who found in a complete withdrawal from the world either the tranquillity conducive to devotional exercises or less desirably an escape from unfavorable external circumstances. Ever since the days of Paula and Melania, who left Rome in the fourth century to found sisterhoods, it had been a not uncommon sight in the West to see highborn ladies, brought up on every luxury, voluntarily abandon all worldly goods, sever the usual bonds with society, and surrender themselves to lives of hardship and devotional practices. Such was the purpose of the Cistercian nunnery of Helfta founded in 1229 by Count Burchard of Mansfeld and his wife Elizabeth, countess of Schwarzburg, who was herself eventually to join this circle made up of daughters of the Thuringian nobility.[52]

The free and imperial abbeys came to belong exclusively to the high nobility, and when this class had been decimated by war and, accompanied with straitened financial conditions, was in danger of disappearing, they opened their doors to the sons and daughters of the *ministeriales*.[53] In Belgium it was rather the small nobility and the bourgeois families that provided recruits for the monasteries, but a certain number of Benedictine and Cistercian nunneries, together with secular chapters, were still reserved for daughters of the nobility.[54] In the diocese of Liége such chapters as Nivelles, Andenne, Moustier-sur-Sambre, Namur, Maseyck or Thorn, provided for members of the lower classes neither a stronghold for chastity nor a retreat in the face of misfortune. In 1285 (October 8) Honorius IV, disturbed by this practice, branded, in the wake of an investigation by the Dominican prior at Valenciennes and the Franciscan guardian at Cam-

[51] Power, *Medieval English Nunneries*, pp. 4-6; Berlière, *Le recrutement*, pp. 14-26; Johannes Ramackers, "Adlige Praemonstratenserstifte in Westfalen und am Niederrhein," *Anal. Praem.*, V (1929), 200-238, 320-343; VI (1930), 281-332; Aloys Schulte, *Der Adel und die deutsche Kirche im Mittelalter (Kirchenrechtliche Abhandlungen*, hrsg. v. U. Stutz, Hft. 63-64, 2. Aufl., Stuttgart, 1922). Working on cathedral chapters, Benedictine monasticism, and colleges of canonesses, Schulte arrived at the conclusion that in the German church of the Middle Ages there were, alongside convents which were recruited from the various classes of nobility, a considerable number of those which were even more exclusive since they admitted only the highborn, the lower nobility being excluded. The Dominicans and Franciscans, on the contrary, did not close the door to any class: "Wir finden," writes Kothe *(Kirchliche Zustände Strassburgs*, p. 42) with respect to this Rhenish city, "Söhne von städtischen Adelsfamilien, Handwerkern, auswärtigen Rittern und sonstigen Fremden bunt durcheinander." The friar made no distinction in class or birth in recruiting (Ramackers, *op. cit.*, p. 205).
[52] Preger, *Geschichte der deutschen Mystik*, I, 113.
[53] Berlière, *Le recrutement*, p. 15, note 2; Hauck, IV, 326-327.
[54] Berlière, *Le recrutement*, p. 15, note 2. Cf. *Collectio de Scandalis Ecclesiae*, ed. Döllinger, *Beiträge zur Culturgeschichte, III*, 197.

brai, such discrimination against non-nobles as irreligious.[55] Similarly, many monasteries had developed into apanages of noblemen's sons, for exclusivism was a policy no longer confined to families of the founders but exploited by the noble estate whether the monastery was of noble origin or had only later fallen into the hands of that class.[56] Notwithstanding their wider appeal, even the mendicant orders drew upon the upper classes for recruits. In 1263 the pope spoke of the daughters of kings and dukes who embraced the order of St. Clara.[57] The seven Dominican nunneries at Strasbourg betrayed the same social structure,[58] whereas St. Gertrude at Cologne was drawn principally from the local patriciate.[59]

Jacques de Vitry clearly recognized that rich endowments corrupt monachism; monastic discipline seldom flourishes without perpetual voluntary poverty.[60] While the Dominicans, for example, carefully guarded their recruiting to keep the membership strong and well trained, the Benedictine monasteries were often yielding to external forces, with a willingness to compromise with the world—admitting small children, the illegitimate, and deserters from other orders.[61] There is no doubt that defective recruiting, accompanied with relaxation of the rule, contributed to the deterioration of the Benedictine order from the thirteenth century on. Yet it was the very elasticity in that organism—absence of a general and efficient visitation system notwithstanding— which enabled some houses in Belgium, northern France, Bavaria, and England to retain their spiritual and intellectual ideals.[62] But frequently its monks and nuns went over to Citeaux; the seven nuns of Moustier-sur-Sambre and Lutgard sought at the advice of John de Liro a more literal observance of the rule in the new Cistercian convents of l'Olive and Aywières.[63] It was probably the desire for a stricter rule that persuaded gentle-born Sybille de Gages to leave

---

[55] BCRH., 4 th ser., II, 113; cf. Wauters, TC. VI, p. xv. See above, pp. 64n.

[56] Berlière, Le recrutement, pp. 16-18 (for Germany); 19 (for Belgium and Holland).

[57] "Flectitur nobilitatis apex ad eius sectanda vestigia et a superbi sanguinis genere sancta humilitate degenerat; nonnullae ducum ac regum matrimonio dignae Clarae invitante preconio arctam penitentiam faciunt, et quae potentibus nupserant, Claram suo modulo imitantur" (AFH., III, 652; cf. Grundmann, Religiöse Bewegungen, p. 194).

[58] Kothe, Kirchliche Zustände Strassburgs, p. 46.

[59] Löhr, in AHVN., CX (1927), 87f, 91f, 96ff.

[60] Cf. Coulton, Five Centuries of Religion, II, 102.

[61] Berlière, Le recrutement, pp. 26-31; Oliger, "De pueris oblatis in ordine Minorum (cum textu hucusque inedito Fr. Iohannis Pecham)," AFH., VIII (1915), 389-447; X (1917), 271-288. Since several monks at St. Trond in the days of Abbot Guillaume de Ryckel were illegitimate sons of nobles, admission had to be restricted (Gesta Abb. Trud., Cont. Tertia, Pars II, MGH. SS., X, 402).

[62] Berlière, Le recrutement, p. 65.

[63] V. Lutg., 195; cf. Berlière, in RHE., I (1900), 460-464.

Nivelles for Aywières.[64] Yolende, of Benedictine profession, inured by noble birth to the pleasures of the world, turned to the same retreat at Lutgard's behest.[65] More notable was the dissatisfaction of the nun Gisele who, possessed *artioris vite desiderio ad ordinem Cisterciensem ascendere*, proceeded to found La Cambre near Brussels.[66] From the second half of the twelfth century Benedictines, Premonstratensians, and Camaldulensians were authorized to enter an *arctior religio*, whose requirements were better met by the Cistercians[67] and Carthusians.[68] The last named, in particular, were singled out for strictness; from them one could not pass to an *ordo laxior*.[69] To canons regular of Eaucourt who protested that some were going over to Clairvaux, St. Bernard made answer "ea videlicet intentione, ut ob tenorem arctioris vitae, ab institutionibus beati Augustini ad observantias sancti Benedicti Dei adjutorio sic transeant."[70] Conversely, in cases of necessity the pope would give a novice dispensation to exchange to a less severe order, but even he was not supposed to permit a return to secular life.[71] The general chapter of Cîteaux in 1251 expressed alarm at the transfer of Cistercians to the Black Monks or other orders.[72] In 1274, when the Second Council of Lyons was registering disapproval at the itinerant clergy,[73] the general chapter again agreed to refuse admission to Carmelites.[74]

Thirteenth-century conciliar legislation demonstrates indirectly but conclusively the economic straits through which monastic establishments were passing and which sometimes created acute recruiting problems. Even as the synod of Paris (1212—1213) voiced grave concern at any decrease in the number of monks of an abbey as long as its revenues sufficed,[75] so the synod of Pont-Audemer (prov. Rouen) urged in 1279 the re-establishment of the number of monks originally fixed in monasteries and priories whose income had not diminished.[76] In

---

[64] *V. Lutg.*, 205 E (III, 6); Mahy, in *Annales du cercle arch. d'Ath et de la région*, I (1912), 26.

[65] *V. Lutg.*, 198 E, (I, 12).

[66] *Gesta Sanctorum Villariensium, MGH. SS.*, XXV, 230; Manrique, *Annal. Cist.*, III, 379; GC., V, instrum. 298; MF., I, 400; Wauters, *TC.*, III, 161. For further examples of Benedictines becoming Cistercians, see CHD. (I, 25), ed. Strange, I, 30-31; cf. *ibid.*, (IV, 46), ed. Strange, I, 213.

[67] Jacques de Guise, *Ann. Han., MGH. SS.*, XXX, 1, 279 (XX, 64).

[68] P., 2763 (April 29, 1206).

[69] *Ibid.*, 3236 (December 3, 1207), 3503 (September 22, 1208).

[70] Ep. iii (an. 1120), *PL.*, CLXXXII, 88.

[71] CHD (I, 15), ed. Strange, I, 21-22.

[72] Canivez, *Statuta*, II, 361, no. 5.

[73] See below, p. 514.

[74] Canivez, *Statuta*, III, 127, no. 3; cf. *ibid.*, III, 140-141, no. 8 (an. 1275).

[75] II, can. 22, Mansi, XXII, 832.

[76] Can. 12, Mansi, XXIV, 223; cf. council of Nantes (1264), can. 2, Mansi, XXIII, 1119; Council of Rheims (1271), Hefele-Leclercq, VI, 1, 151; council of London (1268), can. 50, Mansi, XXIII, 1255; synod of Rouen (1231), can. 6, Mansi, XXIII, 215; synod of Langeais (prov. Tours) (1278), can. 12, Mansi, XXIV, 215, forbade

1231 the council of Rouen had recommended that all monks who lived apart be recalled by the abbots of the respective houses if the priory could sustain at least two monks.[77] Again, abbots and conventual priors should have in their churches, if revenue permitted, the accustomed number of *deservientes* from whom they might demand only those dues and obligations bearing episcopal sanction.[78] The synod of Montpellier (1215) recommended that whenever income proved insufficient, two churches should be united to made possible the *vita canonica* which demanded the presence of at least three persons.[79] In May, 1243, Countess Jeanne requested from the abbot of Clairvaux permission to raise the number of inmates of a La Biloke at Ghent from twenty-five to forty.[80]

But this body of evidence must be counterbalanced by the more persistent complaints from many quarters about overpopulation which taxed the resources of the house. The admonition voiced at Constance in 1270, "Cavetur, ne plures in monasteriis recipiantur persone, quam facultatibus suis possint sustentari,"[81] found increasing justification in a period of declining revenue. On July 5, 1245, Innocent IV authorized the nuns of Val-Benoît to admit only those who would not become a burden, since "the number of sisters... has grown so much that they can hardly maintain themselves..."[82] Ten days later he imposed heavy penalties on those who sequestrated the property of the abbey or laid claims to its *novales*.[83] Distressed at the strain being put on nunneries by the steady influx of *mulieres religiosae,* Humbert de Romans, minister-general of the Order of Preachers, declared in a brief from the general chapter at Strasbourg in 1260 that since abuses accompany overpopulation he forbade admissions beyond the normal number.[84] Yet the provincial minister Hermann von Minden (1286–1290) confessed that in his day the established number was still being exceeded. He set the maximum number of inmates for the newly incorporated nunnery of St. Agnes in Freiburg i. Br. at forty.[85] Pope Clement IV on March 21, 1267 determined the population of Cister-

a monastery to receive more monks or nuns than it could support; cf. Tangl. *Die päpstlichen Kanzlei-ordnungen*, 316, no. 119; 315-316, no. 117.

[77] Can. 37, Mansi, XXIII, 218.

[78] Council of Paris (1248), can. 5, Mansi, XXIII, 765. Steps should also be taken, income permitting, to hand over the care of divine service in older priories to monks or canons regular (can. 4, *idem*).

[79] Can. 31, Mansi, XXII, 946; cf. can. 30, *idem;* council of Narbonne (1227), can. 10, Mansi, XXIII, 24. Cf. Canivez, *Statuta*, II, 210, no. 36 (an. 1239).

[80] MF., III, 593; *GC.*, V, 333; Wauters, *TC.*, IV, 394.

[81] Mone, in *Zeitsch. f. Gesch. d. Oberrh.*, XII (1861), 44.

[82] Cuvelier, *Cartulaire du Val-Benoit*, p. 110, no. 88.

[83] *Ibid.*, pp. 111-112, no. 89 (July 15, 1245); cf. pp. 112-113, no. 90 (July 27, 1245); pp. 113-118, no. 91 (August 12, 1245).

[84] Löhr, in *AHVN.*, CX (1927), 85-86.

[85] *RQ.*, 1926, 161. The provincial Egeno von Stoffen in 1307 set the maximum at 52 for Himmelskron near Worms and 60 for Ötenbach (1310).

cian nunneries "lest the multitude should create confusion or because of too close restriction divine service should suffer."[86] The cartularies offer numerous examples of relatives establishing for members of an abbey an annual pension to assure to them an adequate livelihood. Although the monastery was supposed to be responsible for maintaining its inmates, the overloading and diminishing revenue made it increasingly desirable for the inhabitants to receive such outside assistance.[87] Otherwise the monastery would degenerate into a poorhouse, thus leading to corruption.[88] In order to provide a better existence for the abbess and the eighty nuns in the Cistercian nunnery of Lichtenthal (Lucidevallis), in the diocese of Speier, many of whom came from comital and other noble families, and to relieve them from pressing need,[89] Clement VI in 1345 (November 21) incorporated the parish church at Malsch, whose *ius patronatus* belonged to the abbey, with all income and appurtenances.[90] Twenty years later (July 8, 1366) Abbess Adelheid and the convent, at the advice of their visitor, Abbot Gottfried of Neuburg, set the number of inhabitants at sixty, to wit, 51 who had taken the veil and 9 servants. Only for members of princely families would exception be made.[91] Such examples quickly multiply for Germany,[92] all illustrating how Alexander IV's prescription for a maximum of forty[93] remained a dead letter. The general chapters of Citeaux attempted legislation for the same end.[94]

After a house was established in Cologne in 1227 for the White Women (*Albae Dominae*), the pressure continued so strong that Arch-

[86] Hautcoeur, *Histoire de Flines*, p. 49. Cf. id., *Cartulaire de Flines*, p. 184 (June 18, 1270).

[87] Mone, in *Zeitsch. f. Gesch. d. Oberrh.*, XII (1861), 43, 44; XIII (1861), 62 note.

[88] *Chron. Nicalai de Siegen* (an. 1457), cited by Mone, *ibid.*, XIII, 62: "Salubre et multum conveniens esset, videlicet quod filiae sive puellae nobilium et divitum ad monasteria monialium non admitterentur neque susciperentur, nisi puellae affectarent et inibi permanere intenderent: nam si puellae non affectant, sed parentum rogatu ibidem aut inibi colliguntur, tunc saepius cedit in dampnum monasterii, et quod ego magis pondero, in animarum periculum et monasticae disciplinae ruinam."

[89] *Ibid.*, XIII, 77: "Et per hospitalitates cotidianas et inevitabiles eedem abbatissa et moniales multipliciter aggravantur et multis aliis variis et diversis necessitatibus constringuntur."

[90] *Ibid.*, VIII, 77-78.

[91] *Ibid.*, XIII, 344-346.

[92] In 1231 the maximum at Wächterswinkel was fixed at 100 (*ibid.*, VIII, 44); Archbishop Peter of Mainz (1306-1321) limited on pain of excommunication the number of nuns at Schmerlenback at 32 and the monks at Nordheim at 24 (1312), *ibid.*, VIII, 44. The Cistercian abbots of Bellevaux and Lützel limited the number of nuns at Marienau for want of means (1283) (*ibid.*, XIII, 50-51); for Lixheim, June 29, 1265 (*ibid.*, XIII, 62); St. Agnes at Mainz in 1290 (Baur, *Hessische Urkunden*, I, 441); St. Jakob in the same city, 1282 (*ibid.*, I, 336). Cf. Bebenhausen, Mone in *Zschr. f. Gesch. Oberrh.*, XX (1867), 236-237.

[93] *Ibid.*, VIII, 77.

[94] Canivez, *Statuta*, II, 248, no. 15 (an. 1242); II, 260, no. 7 (an. 1243); III, 71, no. 15 (an. 1269).

bishop Sifrid agreed in 1294 that the number should be kept at 30.[95] In 1217 the abbey of Meer was obliged to restrict its inmates to 40 with the approval of Honorius III (August 31, 1217).[96] When Archbishop Henry of Cologne allowed a citizen of Duisberg, named Alexander, to erect on his allod at Düssern a church for nuns, provision was made for thirteen Cistercians;[97] three years later the population had risen to twenty-five.[98] The nunnery established at Oberwesseling about 1238 by Countess Mechtild von Sayn was so popular that Innocent IV limited the number to 50 in his confirmation bull.[99] On October 18, 1291, the magistracy of Wesel decreed that the population of the two nunneries established there about the middle of the century was not to exceed 40 without special permission.[100]

To maintain the same number of beguines in a convent the deceased was to be promptly replaced. On October 13, 1294, Kunigunde, widow of the knight Götz von Hohenloch, and her daughter Junta gave to the St. Clara convent in Strasbourg their house *zur Kugel* in which sixteen *paupercule begine* might reside. If the community did not find a replacement within a fortnight, the guardian of the Friars Minor was to choose the successor.[101] On August 1, 1296, Burga, widow of Conrad Metzer von Hagenau, gave to the St. Clara convent a house in the Stadelgasse for twenty poor beguines under the same conditions.[102]

The council of Cologne (1310), echoing earlier legislation against the trend to convert monasteries and nunneries into appanages for families of title and substance,[103] opposed the payment of admission fees.[104] Since monastic life was considered a respectable career and was dominated by the nobility, it was common to introduce children at an early age.[105] Just as Peter the Venerable had recognized in his Statutes[106] the dangers that attended the admission of children into religious houses, so Robert de Courçon's council at Paris (1212–1213) decreed that no one might enter before he was eighteen.[107] Monks who had not yet attained their fifteenth year were to be placed

[95] Lacomblet, II, p. xv.
[96] *Ibid.*, II, 35-36, no. 65; P., 5599.
[97] Lacomblet, II, 103, no. 195.
[98] *Ibid.*, II, p. xv.
[99] *Ibid.*, II, 160, no. 307; cf. p. xv, 160, note 2; for *albae dominae* at Cologne, *ibid.*, p. 84, note 1.
[100] *Ibid.*, II, 545, no. 917.
[101] *Strasb. UB.*, III, 101, no. 323; cf. *ibid.*, III, 102-103, no. 327 (January 11, 1295); Schmidt, in *Alsatia*, 1858-1860, p. 183.
[102] *Ibid.*, p. 165.
[103] E.g., Council of Paris (1212-1213), II, can. 27, Mansi, XXII, 833.
[104] Can. 28, Mansi, XXV, 240; cf. Boehmer, *UB. Frankfurt*, I, 265 (May 25, 1292); cf. 342-344, 367f, 382f.
[105] Canivez, *Statuta*, III, 239, no. 10 (an. 1287), cf. Berlière, *Le recrutement* pp. 8-9.
[106] Statute 36, *PL.*, CLXXXIX, 1036.
[107] II, can. 2, Mansi, XXII, 826; Rouen (1231), can. 48, Mansi, XXIII, 229.

in conventual priories which observed the *vita communis*.[108] Enlarging
on this principle the Council of Bourges in 1286 forbade the sending
of monks who were not yet twenty to distant priories where common
life did not obtain.[109] The national German council held at Würzburg
in March, 1287, recommended that a nun who had passed a year in
probation should take the veil and have her hair cut as soon as she
had passed her fifteenth year.[110]

Thirteenth century conciliar legislation frequently reflected the
growing concern of ecclesiastical authorities over the multiplication of
extraregular communities and the consequent relaxation of the triple
vows. The council of Canterbury (1236) ordained that no married
person could embrace monastic status (*ad religionem*) without episcopal permission.[111] Again, a woman must not take vows without the
consent of her husband and the advice of a priest.[112] Similarly, the
synod of Lambeth (1330) sought to control recluses by requiring
episcopal approval.[113] The council of Paris (1212-1213) recognized the
socioeconomic conditions at the basis of this type of piety by pointing
out that in certain monasteries nuns were being allotted an insufficient
sum of money for their upkeep, thus obliging them to look elsewhere
for a livelihood. Monasteries ought to provide from common goods
for all the needs of their inhabitants; if the income is insufficient, let
the bishop reduce the number of nuns.[114]

Since married women were reported to be living in certain nunneries and inasmuch as *hoc sit contra Ordinis honestatem*, the Cistercian
general chapter in 1275 instructed abbesses to discourage henceforth
such a practice.[115] On the other hand, women who take private vows
of chastity without entering a convent must live in their homes
under the direction of the pastor.[116] The council of Tarragona (1317)
refused to countenance a vow of chastity from a girl unless it was
taken strictly in accordance with canon law.[117] The council of Mainz
(1261), with the beguines specifically in mind, expressed its disapproval at the instability of women who take the vow of chastity and
adopt a peculiar habit without entering a convent. Since young

[108] Synod of Château Gontier (1231), can. 25, Mansi, XXIII, 238.
[109] Can. 23, Mansi, XXIV, 637f.
[110] Can. 19, Mansi, XXIV, 857.
[111] Can. 31, Mansi, XXIII, 425.
[112] Can. 32, Mansi, XXIII, 425.
[113] Can. 9, Mansi, XXV, 896: "Ad haec, districtius inhibemus, ne inclusi, vel
inclusae, constituantur alicubi sine nostra licentia speciali, pensatis sociis, moribus,
et qualitate personae, et unde debeat sustentari. In domibus eorum, personae
saeculares nullatenus hospitentur, sine causa honesta, et manifesta."
[114] III, can. 6, Mansi, XXII, 835.
[115] Canivez, *Statuta*, III, 142, no. 15.
[116] Council of Mainz (1233), can. 45, Hefele-Leclercq, V, 2, 1549.
[117] Can. 4, Mansi, XXV, 629.

beguines too often have caused scandal, the age of forty must be considered critical for admission to a beguinage. No cleric or monk may enter a beguine house. If he speaks to one of the inmates, it must be done in church and before witnesses.[118] This last clause contains a prohibition which remains uniform in all beguine rules. In the same year the synod of Magdeburg required beguines, like other parishioners, to obey their priests.[119]

Contemporary evidence, whether hagiographical or archival, points conclusively to the patrician and bourgeois extraction of the beguines and their forerunners, the *mulieres sanctae,* at least until the middle and even to the close of the thirteenth century. It was women of gentle birth in Liége whom Lambert le Bègue is supposed to have supervised and organized into the first beguinage.[120] Back of tradition must be a germ of fact. As in the case of Ottonian hagiography, they sprang from well-to-do stock—parents who were not always sympathetic to the religious precocity of their children but nonetheless Godfearing. Thus the biographer consistently underlines the noble origins of the saints, but often with the use of such nondescript adjectives as *honestus* and *nobilis.*[121] But the sometimes inadvertent intrusion of details and more precise description lend individuality to an otherwise often stereotyped pattern. In the instructions to Master Henry Braem, canon of Tournai and professor of laws, of June 12, 1319, the count of Flanders, Robert, seeking to regularize the status of the *religiose mulieres, que beghine nuncupate fuerant* in the midst of Europeanwide persecution, recommended that only women "of condition" be received or allowed to reside in beguinages.[122] Here "of condition" has a two-fold meaning: first, like *honestus, nobilis,* or *probus,* the phrase may signify "respectable," the possession of sound moral character; and secondly, sufficient material worth and proper family connection to forestall the deviations of piety and moral turpitude associated with recruits of lower station. Just as in public affairs substance is equated with respectability and property with moral worth, so the two concepts are fused in the mind of the hagiographer. Jacques de Vitry leaves no doubt as to the meaning when he discusses secular canonesses who are unwilling to accept any but daugh-

---

[118] Can. 23, Mansi, XXIII, 1089. Gerhard, archbishop of Mainz, authorized Magister Dithmar, priest in Frankfurt, to receive girls and women *ad ordinem begginarum* who were not yet forty years old (Boehmer, *UB. Frankfurt,* I, 262, November 22, 1291). The Cistercian order went on record as opposing the election of nuns to the abbacy unless they had reached their thirtieth year (Canivez, *Statuta,* II, 361, no. 6, an. 1251).

[119] Can. 18, Hartzheim, III, 80; Hefele-Leclercq, VI, 1, 110.

[120] Jean d'Outremeuse, *Ly Mireurs des Histors,* ed. Bormans, IV (Brussels, 1877), 462.

[121] Zoepf, *Das Heiligen-Leben im 10. Jahrhundert,* pp. 53-54.

[122] Béthune, *Cartulaire,* p. 67.

ters of knights and nobles, *religioni et morum nobilitati saeculi nobilitatem praeferentes*.[123]

The *mulieres religiosae* in the Nivelles-Liége area are described by Jacques de Vitry in the preface to the *vita* of Mary of Oignies as coming from families of substance and affluence to pursue a scanty livelihood by manual work[124] or in imitation of apostolic poverty. Actually the women in *curtes* did not customarily beg, but contributed to the support of the beguinage to which they belonged. When Jacques was journeying through Italy on his way to the Roman curia in the summer of 1216, he carried with him fresh memories of the Belgian feminine movement; the initial phase in the development of the Clarisses which he then witnessed struck a familiar chord in a man who had known so well the Mary of Oignies type.[125] Among the *mulieres sanctae* of noble or upper bourgeois extraction were included all the leading luminaries. Born of wealthy parents[126] in the second half of 1177 or at the beginning of 1178, Mary of Oignies, just as Francis of Assisi was doing in Umbria, gave her worldly goods to the poor and dedicated herself to the cult of property.[127] Voluntary espousal of poverty is much more common in the sources than adaptation to it as the original state. The mother of Lutgard of Tongres belonged to a noble family, while her father appears to have been a successful burgher who, desiring to see his daughter comfortably endowed, entrusted to a merchant twenty silver marks on her behalf.[128] These rich prospects she rejected with the sympathy of her mother. While the parents of the beguine Mary of Lille from Diest were *honesti et divites*,[129] the father of another beguine in Malines sold wine in the fish market.[130] The writings of the former beguine, Mechtild of Magdeburg, instinct with chivalric and court conventions, suggest broadly that she must have belonged to that social bracket which not only could rear her in these graces but also give her the education necessary to fashion them in her own words.[131] Ida of Louvain, an inhabitant of a Cistercian nunnery near Malines,[132] and

[123] *Hist. Occid.*, p. 347; cf. the explanation of Agnes d'Harcourt in her life of Isabella: "licet prosapia esset tam nobilis, nobilior etiam erat moribus atque illustrior. Noverat probe hanc solam esse veram nobilitatem" (*V. Isab.*, 798 E, (2). Thomas of Cantimpré (*BUA.*, I, 11, 3, p. 42) on the abbess of Florival: "haec nobilis genere, sed nobilior virtute."
[124] *VMO.*, 547 F: "licet parentes earum multis divitiis abundarent."
[125] Ep. I, *ZKG.*, XIV, 104: "Mulieres vero juxta civitates in diversis hospitiis simul commorantur, nihil accipiunt, sed de labore manuum vivunt."
[126] *VMO.*, 550 A: "quae (non) mediocribus orta parentibus..."
[127] *Ibid.*, 550 B, 558 A.
[128] *V. Lutg.*, 191 E: "Pia Lutgardis Virgo, ex illa quondam famosissima civitate Tungrensi, matre nobili, patre cive, originem duxit."
[129] Gielemans, *Ex novali sanctorum*, in *Anecdota*, p. 419 (III, 22).
[130] *Ibid.*, p. 431, no. 91.
[131] Preger, *Geschichte der deutschen Mystik*, I, 91-92.
[132] *V. Id. Lov.*, 158 F-159 A, (1, 4): "locupletibus et honestis exorta parentibus."

Juliana of Cornillon at Liége (d. 1258)[133] likewise came from the
same stratum of society. Margaret of Ypres had "respectable" parents,[134]
while ida of Nivelles[135] and Beatrice of Nazareth[136] were both daughters of rich merchants. Ida of Nivelles fled through the window to join
the *pauperes virgines* living near the church of Saint-Sepulchre, but
almost immediately one of her relatives took interest in her fortune.[137]
While preaching in Brabant, Jacques de Vitry encountered a *religiosa
virgo* who had abandoned all for Christ and led a life of poverty.[138]
Ida of Léau perhaps was less fortunate; at least the hagiographer
deems it necessary to explain that Providence intended moderate
circumstances for her so that her spiritual life would not be upset by
preoccupation with too great poverty or by the vanity which attends
good birth or great riches.[139] The maternal grandparents of Clarissa
Leonard, a beguine of Malines, acting as money-changers and rag-
dealers had become well-to-do *(quaestuosos)*. For such employment,
however, she herself betrayed no aptitude.[140] Following her mother's
death, the nineteen-year-old girl distributed her inheritance in alms,
keeping for herself a single *livre antiquorum grossorum*. As she approached fifty she began to worry about subsistence in old age, especially since her *livre*, which had once been worth twelve French crowns,
now brought only ten.[141] Elizabeth of Spalbeek spent her youth with
modest means.[142]

In Germany, too, where the beguine movement is too often depicted
as basically poor in origins, the facts demolish many current views. In
his examination of 1700 references from 1223 to 1450 in which the beguines have family names Asen discovered that almost all well-known
patrician families of Cologne are represented.[143] Here, no less than
in Belgium, members came from the middle class: the first well-known
beguine is Sophia, daughter of Hermann de Cervo.[144] The parents
of the beguine Christine of Stommeln were reduced to poverty because
her father Henry Bruso lost everything by reason of his standing surety

---

133 *V. Jul. Cornel.*, 443 C; cf. Alph. Le Roy, "Sainte Julienne," *BNB.*, X (1889),
610-617.
134 *V. Marg. Ypr.*, p. 146: "honestis parentibus oriunda."
135 *V. Id., Niv.*, ed. *Henriquez*, p. 212.
136 *V. Beat.*, ed. Henriquez, pp. 1-3: "parentibus mediocribus" (p. 1).
137 *V. Id. Niv.*, 201-202.
138 Greven, *Exempla*, p. 32, no. 45.
139 *V. Id. Lew.*, 109, (5-6): Ida's father Gilbert is described as "honestus, prudens,
hilaris, multaque valetudine temporali sufficienter praeditus" (D) and "rerumque
temporalium affluentia dapsili non mediocriter abundantes" (E).
140 Gielemans, *Anecdota*, p. 436.
141 *Ibid.*, p. 437.
142 *V. El. Spal., CCHB.*, I, 378 (29).
143 Asen, in *AHVN.*, CXI (1927), 92f, 96. Just as the first known beguines were
patrician, Asen concludes, so the oldest convent was founded by a patrician. See
the list of other patrician families which became founders of convents (96).
144 *Ibid.*, 93.

between Jews and Christians; whereupon he was obliged to leave the village and move to Cologne. When the daughter returned she found the farm and house deserted.[145] On the other hand, the band of beguines from which the Dominican convent Engeltal eventually developed possessed no property with which to establish a nunnery.[146]

For France even Jean de Meung lists "sleek beguines" with rich abbesses, the wives of baillis, knights, and burghers, and nuns of noble stock as profitable penitents.[147] The beguinage at Rheims, founded in 1249, had noble-rich inmates like Beatrice of Vandreuil, daughter of a knight;[148] demoiselle Widle,[149] and demoiselle Isaberon;[150] or by beguines of bourgeois extraction who donated, sold, and willed their property: Alis la Baconnelle,[151] Rose la Picavette,[152] and Sebilla de Donchery who donated 220 *livres parisis* on December 2, 1322, to the hospital in the city.[153] Although alms were distributed from the beginning to indigent inmates, a century later, in 1364, the statutes forbade admission to needy beguines or those who were obliged to earn a livelihood.[154] This, of course, does not rule out the presence of some charges. Just as candidates for the nunnery and beguinage alike were often described as *domicella* or *damoysele*, so documents refer to *domine, que beggine nominantur*, the term *domina* being used because the inhabitants of the convents presumably belonged to the upper classes. From the fact that the term *beguine* was used conjointly with *domina*, it may be concluded on the basis of the Cologne records that the name was not always, even in the earliest days, a label of contempt to signify a heretic.

In conclusion, hagiographical materials which generally underscore noble or bourgeois origins find some support in the archives. Nevertheless, it has been rightfully said that "in the thirteenth century the institutions of oblates, *donati, conversi*, and the feminine religious movement itself cannot be understood without their substratum of temporal conditions. Faced with the impossibility of living in impoverished families, in the midst of dire social circumstances, laymen, women, children, gave themselves or were given to organisms of common life, better armed to defend them."[155] If "this category of

---

[145] *Acta Chr. Stumb.*, 274 A (II, 64).
[146] *Deutsches Nonnenleben*, p. 264. For further evidence of indigence as a determining factor, see below, pp. 477-78.
[147] *RR.*, vss. 12238-12246.
[148] Robert, *Les Béguines de Reims*, pp. 36f, P. J. vi (February 24, 1308).
[149] *Ibid.*, pp. 29-34, P. J. iv (February 26, 1275).
[150] *Ibid.*, p. 20.
[151] *Ibid.*, pp. 34-36, P. J. v (December 27, 1278).
[152] *Ibid.*, pp. 37-39, P. J. vii (August 23, 1314).
[153] *Ibid.*, pp. 39-41, P. J. viii.
[154] *Ibid.*, p. 49: "Des lors et avant aucune ne soit recepue qui par defaute de ces necessiteis avoir il li conveingne aler ouvrer devant aultruy a journees."
[155] Mandonnet, *Saint Dominique*, I, 102f.

half-religious, half-secular workers (i.e., *conversi*) is entirely characteristic of the feudal era."[156] the beguines and beghard represented
an extension of the principle during urban growth when occasional
heretical tendencies posed a new set of problems to the canonists.

[156] J. Bonduelle, in *DDC.*, IV (1949), 575.

❧ II ❧

Older Monachism and the *Cura Monialium*

The Premonstratensians whose work, through regularization of contemporary spiritual ministration and in anticipation of the friars a century later, primarily concerned combatting heresy and the salvation of souls, brought many of the twelfth-century ecstatic-pious women together in nunneries or double monasteries.[1] Norbert's canons were clerics who embraced the rule of St. Augustine in order to lead in common a strongly ascetic life. Unlike older forms of monachism he made preaching and intensive local cure of souls the significant tasks of his order, thus stimulating direct interest in the spiritual well-being of *mulieres religiosae*. As the feminine religious movement expanded with the order, the Premonstratensians acknowledged a solution of the *Frauenfrage* as one of their duties,[2] for after setting out to reform chapters of canons where daily life and zeal left much to be desired, he turned to the nuns subject to these chapters and offered them solitude and peace in his cloisters.[3] But unlike Fontevrault (dioc. Poitiers) where women comprised the dominant part of the monastic society, they lived in the Premonstratensian houses for men as "inclusae" or "conversae" in strict claustration,[4] were under the direction of the abbot, cared for the household tasks of the brethren, and originally did not participate in services.[5]

In *De Miraculis Sanctae Mariae Laudanensis*, written in 1149 or 1150, Herman of Tournai describes vividly the influx of these women

[1] Greven, *Anfänge*, pp. 113, 198ff; Erens, "Les soeurs de l'Ordre de Prémontré," *Anal. Praem.*, V (1929), 5-26; id., in *DTC.*, XIII, 1 (1936), col. 8; Grundmann, *Religiöse Bewegungen*, pp. 47-50, 175-177; Colvin, *The White Canons in England*, pp. 327-336; Berlière, *Monastères doubles*, pp. 3ff.

[2] Greven, *Anfänge*, pp. 198ff; Decker, pp. 19-21.

[3] Hilpisch, *Doppelklöster*, pp. 60, 69.

[4] "... Ut etiam artiorem et districtiorem in eius (i.e., Norberti) monasteriis videamus esse conversationem feminarum quam virorum" (Herman of Tournai, *De Miraculis Sanctae Mariae Laudanensis*, MGH. SS., XII, 659 (II, 7).

[5] Lamy, *L'abbaye de Tongerloo*, pp. 92ff; Erens, in *Anal. Praem.*, V, 14-15. Since their tasks consisted principally of stitching, sewing, weaving, and washing for the brethren (*Comm. praev. ad Vitam S. Norbertini*, AA. SS., XXI [June 6, i], 806, no. 31), there was at first little opportunity to establish a *Xenodochium* (cf. Madelaine, *Histoire de Saint Norbert*, I, 167).

without social distinction to Norbertine convents: "Although recluses are known to lead in silence an ascetic and humble life—the power of Christ working in wondrous fashion—we daily see women, not only farmers' daughters or the poor, but even rich and noble widows and young girls, who after scorning the pleasures of the world hasten to these monasteries for the sake of conversion as if to mortify their tender flesh, so that we think that today there are more than ten thousand women in them."[6] Adding again that there were more than one thousand *conversae* in the diocese of Laon alone, the chronicler emphasizes, in contrast to the aloofness of Cîteaux, Norbert's pride in accepting women as well as men.[7] These are, of course, round numbers common in medieval sources; their exaggeration becomes the more obvious when the early statutes speak of one or two sisters engaged in table service and when in 1240 the number of inmates at Bonoeil was fixed at twenty.[8] On the other hand, the numerous foundations of Premonstratensian nunneries in northeastern France and Germany until the middle of the thirteenth century[9] offer conclusive evidence that the Norbertine program filled a need which in the Latin countries was answered not so much by religious order as by heresy.

Premonstratensian nunneries spread. At Fontenelles, the bishop of Laon, Barthélemy de Jura, built a new, well-endowed convent[10] for the community over which Rycwera (d. 1136), "the first woman to take the Premonstratensian habit from St. Norbert," had been head.[11] From Fontenelles it was transferred to Rosières and finally to Bonoeil in Picardy.[12]

Remaining apart from the men, runs Jacques de Vitry's commentary,[13] the early sisters did not sing in the choir or church but engaged

---

[6] *MGH. SS.*, XII, 659: "Et cum in tanta districtione et vilitate cum silentio sciantur esse reclusae, miro tamen modo Christi operante virtute, cotidie videmus feminas non modo rusticas vel pauperes, sed potius nobilissimas et ditissimas, tam viduas juvenculas quam etiam puellulas, ita conversionis gratia spretis mundi voluptatibus ad illius institutionis monasteria festinantes, et quasi ad mortificandam teneram carnem currentes, ut plus quam decem millia feminarum in eis hodie credamus contineri." For noble women at Tongerloo, see Lamy, *L'abbaye de Tongerloo*, p. 100; for further evidence consult Grundmann, *Religiöse Bewegungen*, p. 49, note 82. Cf. Jacques de Vitry, *Hist. Occid.*, p. 323; letter of Abbot Philip of Parc at Louvain to Hildegarde of Bingen, *PL.*, CXCVII, 277.

[7] "In Cistellensi coenobio soli viri suscipiuntur, domnus vero Norbertus cum sexu virili etiam femineum ad conversionem suscipi constituit" (Herman of Tournai, *De Mirac. S. Mariae Laud.*, *MGH. SS.*, XII, 659; cf. 657; see Heinsberg in Lacomblet, II, p. xv, 2).

[8] Hugo, *Annal.*, I, col. 392.

[9] Lamy, *L'abbaye de Tongerloo*, pp. 92ff; Greven, *Anfänge*, pp. 112ff; Grundmann, in *Archiv f. Kulturgeschichte*, XXI, 315ff.

[10] Hugo, *Annal.*, I, *Probationes*, col. cccviii.

[11] *Comm. praev. de B. Rycwera*, *AA. SS.*, LXI (October 29, xiii), 53 D, no. 7; cf. 51-53.

[12] Hugo, *Annal.*, I, 389ff; pr. 318-321; Cottineau, I, 427.

[13] *Hist. Occid.*, pp. 323-324. When the sisters formed separate convents they

in silent prayer, reading their psalter and canonical hours, or invoking the Virgin. Priests and clerics heard their confessions through windows and instructed them at fixed times in the divine word. But in time these narrow windows, which had once afforded communication between monk and nun, were enlarged into ample bays; after the first fervor had cooled off, unexpected security began to produce negligence and sluggishness. Since proximity of the sexes caused irregularities, the plenary session of abbots which is usually put about 1141, during the generalate of Hugh of Fosses, suppressed double monasteries.[14] Women's convents must be established as separate monasteries, two leagues distant. In spite of physical separation, full autonomy was, however, not yet achieved, for the sisterhood drew its sustenance from the parent-abbey.[15] This early change in Premonstratensian policy also may be assigned in part to a deviation from the original Norbertine program, with the resultant approximation to older forms of monachism. As spiritual ministration yielded to monastic duties, the canons lost those characteristics which they had inherited from the "wandering preachers."

The burden of *cura monialium*, however, brought increasing insistence in chapter legislation to bar the admission of women either as canonesses or lay sisters.[16] Suppression of double monasteries must be supplemented by prohibiting the incorporation of new nunneries. On May 13, 1198, the privilege *De non recipiendis sororibus*, granted by Innocent III,[17] in accordance with this chapter legislation,[18] con-

became contemplative, subject to the law of enclosure. They acted as *sorores cantantes*, attached to the service of the choir, or *sorores non cantantes*, attentive only to menial tasks. Cf. Erens, in *DTC.*, XIII, 1 (1936), 8.

[14] Lamy, *L'abbaye de Tongerloo*, pp. 96f. In the twelfth century sisters were to be found near Afflighem, St. Martin at Tournai, and Gorze (Greven, *Anfänge*, pp. 112f); in Belgium the abbeys of Parc, Tongerloo, Bonne-Esperance, and Floreffe were double monasteries (cf. MF., III, 59-60). The Floreffe convent was located near St. Martin's in a place still called in modern times the Beguinage (*Chronic. Abbat. Floreff.*, in *AHEB.*, VIII [1871], 419; Berlière, *MB.*, I, 130). On land at Brouffe or Vérofle donated to Floreffe by Matilda, wife of Wichard, with the approval of Bishop Alexander of Liége in 1134, the abbot built a house for Norbertine nuns (*Annal. de Floreffe*, by Christophe de Heest in Galliot, IV, 260). For further donations to them see *AHEB.*, XIII (1876), 31 and note 3; Berlière, *MB.*, I, 130f (ca. 1175 or 1178); *AHEB.*, VIII (1871), 366 (1188). Under Abbot Walter they were replaced by canons, the superior taking the title of *magister*.

[15] Berlière, *Doubles monastères*, p. 23.

[16] See the codification of this legislation at the end of the twelfth century in Martène, *De antiquis ecclesiae ritibus*, III, 894-926. The decree is recalled in a supplement to these statutes: "Quoniam instant tempora periculosa et Ecclesia supra modum gravatur, communi consilio capituli statuimus ut amodo nullam sororem recipiamus. Si quis autem hujus statuti transgressor exstiterit, abbatia sua sine misericordia privetur" (*ibid.*, 925). Erens (*Anal. Praem.*, V, 10, note 16) regards these addenda as scattered decrees from general chapters.

[17] Ep. I, 198, *PL.*, CCXIV, 173-174; P. 168: "Olim in communi capitulo statuistis et postmodum sub interminatione gravis pene sepius innovastis, ut nullam de cetero in sororem recipere teneamini vel conversam, presertim cum ex hoc aliquando incommoda fueritis multa perpessi."

demned the feminine branch of the order to gradual extinction.[19]
After Innocent's death Abbot Gervasius of Prémontré solicited from
the new papal curia confirmation of renewed interest of the chapter
in exclusion of women.[20] Such inveterate hostility finds an echo in
Jacques de Vitry, but unfortunately he contributes nothing to the
dating of the chapter decision.[21] The measure, moreover, appears to
have been received reluctantly, for a general chapter at the beginning
of the thirteenth century proposed to receive women again at Bonoeil.
Hugh III, accordingly, prescribed their mode of life: the new candidate
was to be admitted with the consent of the father-abbot, prior, subprior,
and elders of the abbey; a maximum population was established;
nuns must conform to the statutes of the order; and the nun whom the
father-abbot placed over the community was no longer to be called
prioress but *magistra*, "for she had no jurisdiction."[22] But the final
blow was not delivered until 1270 when, at the proposal of the abbot
of Floreffe, Walter d'Obaix (1268-1280), the general chapter decided
categorically to receive no more nuns and to permit the existing
members to enter other orders.[23]

Had Norbert done nothing else but introduce "so many" women to
divine service by his preaching, the chronicler adds, he would have
been worthy of the highest praise.[24] Through affiliation with the Premonstratensian order and observance of the Augustinian rule, together
with the Customs of Prémontré, the opportunity was thus opened for
the first time to religious women of all classes to achieve in strict
claustration, in an unconditional obligation to continence, and a
contemplative life predicated on poverty and humility an existence
instinct with a spirituality then widely prevalent. When the order

[18] Nunneries sometimes rose in isolated places without being directly dependent
on the convents of men. This is the meaning of the statute: "... Non recipere altaria
ad que cura animarum pertinet, nisi possit esse abbatia. Unum tamen licebit haberi
unicuique ecclesie, ubi sororum claustrum edificetur." R. Van Waefelghem, "Les
premiers statuts de l'ordre de Prémontré," in *Analectes de l'Ordre de Prémontré*
(Louvain, 1913), p. 45; cited by Erens, in *Anal. Praem.*, V, 7, note 3.
[19] Berlière, *Doubles monastères*, pp. 24f.
[20] Hugo, *Sacrae antiquitatis monumenta*, pp. 96f; Berlière, *Doubles monastères*,
p. 24.
[21] *Hist. Occid.*, pp. 324f: "Prudenter igitur licet sero in generali capitulo Prae-
monstratenses unanimiter firmaverunt, quod feminas de cetero in ordine suo non
essent recepturi."
[22] Hugo, *Annal.*, I, *Probationes*, col. cccxx. This decree was approved by Innocent IV in the bull *Licet sicut vestra* of December 11, 1247 (*idem*; P. 12786). Cf.
Erens, in *Anal. Praem.*, V, 11-12.
[23] Greven, *Anfänge*, pp. 116f; Berlière, *MB.*, I, 117, 130-131. In Lefèvre's edition
of the Statutes of Prémontré, revised by order of Gregory IX and Innocent IV, Dist.
IV, cap. II (*De receptis Sororibus*, pp. 112-114) cautioned against possession of property, regulated the habit, and prescribed close discipline (cf. cap. 13). Cap. 12 (pp.
114f) forbade further admission of women — even for the boarding and lodging of a
secularis puella—except when *cantantes sorores* were provided for "ab antiquo".
[24] Herman of Tournai, in *MGH. SS.*, XII, 659.

no longer founded such societies and even refused admission to women, only then did it become apparent that these nunneries had not
been merely the consequence of Norbertine propaganda, but the
expression of a vigorous feminine religious movement which, far from
losing momentum in the face of Premonstratensian rejection, simply
assumed new forms.[25]

When the chief competing order, the Premonstratensians, refused to
admit women henceforth into their ranks, then, wrote Jacques de Vitry
with characteristic enthusiasm, "Cistercian nunneries multiplied like
the stars in the sky..."[26] Even allowing for exaggeration and partia-
lity when he recounts the growth of semireligious communities, the
building of monasteries, and above all the haste with which maidens,
widows, and married women, with the consent of their husbands,
sought to enter the cloister,[27] thereby opposing mystical to carnal
marriage, De Vitry nevertheless captured the mood that must have
prevailed among the *mulieres sanctae* for whom the closer regimen
of Citeaux acquired greater importance in proportion to the corruption of other congregations. Nuns abandoned their convents, changed
their habit, and eagerly sought the fruits of the stricter life[28]—*ut
arciori paupertate arcerentur*.[29] Similarly, noble women forsook their
patrimony in deference to a retreat in the nunneries of this order. But
let the chronicler present his own picture: In the early days of Citeaux
women could not hope to meet its strict prescriptions or attain its
height of ascetic perfection, for even strong men found close observance of a revitalized Benedictine rule an almost unbearable burden.
Later, however, *Deo devotae virgines et sanctae mulieres,* whose zeal
and longing for the "Holy Spirit" conquered feminine weakness,
betook themselves to the quiet harbor of the order and adopted its
habit to escape the shipwreck of the world. They dared not trust
themselves to other congregations because of widespread dissolute life.
Corruption and moral decay were so far advanced among most nuns
that no certain refuge could be expected in their midst. Anyone who
is acquainted with the thousandfold arts and tricks of these women
knows how difficult it is to preserve chastity among the unchaste.[30]

The strongly ascetic tenth abbot of Villers, Walter of Utrecht
(1214—1221), "burning with divine love and completely absorbed in

---

[25] Grundmann, *Religiöse Bewegungen,* p. 176.

[26] *Hist. Occid.,* p. 305.

[27] *Ibid.,* pp. 305-306; cf. *Sermo ad monachas albas Cisterciensis ordinis et grisias
et alias* (Pitra, *Anal. Nov.,* II, 376). Thomas of Cantimpré, *BUA.,* II, 29, 39 (p. 317):
"Vidimus enim plures filias comitum et baronum, quae spretis nuptiis, in monasteriis vel congregationibus virginum vitam caelibem delegerunt."

[28] *Hist. Occid.,* p. 306; cf. *VMO.,* prol., 54.

[29] Jacques de Guise, *Ann. Hanon., MGH. SS.,* XXX, 1, 279.

[30] *Hist. Occid.,* pp. 304f.

God,"[31] desired nothing so much as to draw men to the monastic
way of life and to found convents of women.[32] It is probable that in
such preoccupation with feminine spiritual needs he was merely following the example of his predecessors, but obscurity envelops the beginnings of Cistercian nunneries.[33] Even Angelo Manrique, the official
historian of the order,[34] who waxes so eloquent over the masculine
movement in the twelfth century, offered but fragmentary information
concerning convents of women during the same period. Following the
establishment by Stephen Harding, shortly before his death in 1133, of
what has generally been regarded as the first Cistercian nunnery—the result of the removal of Benedictine nuns from Jully-les-Nonnains to Tart
near Dijon[35]—only scattered references can be gleaned with respect to
the origins of other houses. Cultivation of monastic virtues and absorption with personal salvation offer a partial explanation for the neglect
of pastoral ministration afield. Manrique notes the appearance of nunneries in Swabia near Ulm[36] and in Spain[37] in the year 1145. He not
only mentions a convent in England as early as 1163[38] but adds, in anticipation of Jacques de Vitry's testimony some fifty years later, that
women as well as men were running to the order at this time. In
Belgium, according to Canivez,[39] the earliest nunnery did not appear
before 1180. On the authority of Caesarius of Heisterbach, they must
have been well established in Brabant by the end of the twelfth
century and even mingled with the beguine movement.[40] Whereas
Bishop Barthélemy of Laon (1113-1150) is supposed to have founded the nunnery of Montreuil-les-Dames in 1136,[41] Abbot Stephen of
Obazine established seven years later the convent of Coyroux or Coiroux (dioc. Limoges) where he introduced the practice of strict clau-

[31] Cron. Villar. mon., MGH. SS., XXV, 199.
[32] Idem. Examples of Walter's interest in the mulieres sanctae may be found in
CHD., II, 19 (ed. Strange, I, 88-89); II, 20 (I, 89-90).
[33] Vacandard, Vie de Saint Bernard, II, 557; Winter, Die Cistercienser des nordöstlichen Deutschlands, II, 1f concluded that early nunneries designated as Cistercian were not officially recognized as members of the order, nor were their affairs
supervised by the general chapter (cf. Boyd, A Cistercian Nunnery in Medieval Italy,
pp. 8of). For the foundation and direction of nunneries by Villers consult De
Moreau, L'abbaye de Villers, pp. 110-114; Roisin, in RHE., XXXIX (1943), 354ff.
[34] Manrique, Cisterciensium Annalium (4 vols, in 2, Lugduni, 1642-1659).
[35] De Illustri Genere S. Bernardi, PL., CLXXXV, 2, 1387-1388; cf. Boyd, op. cit.,
p. 76; Cottineau, II, 3122.
[36] Manrique, Cist. Annal., II, 22, no. 11.
[37] Ibid., II, 22-23, nos. 12-13.
[38] Ibid., II, 376-377, nos. 6-7.
[39] Canivez refers (L'ordre de Citeaux, p. 124) to the abbey of Herckenrode at
Curange, near Hasselt (1182); cf. GC., III, 1032; instrum; col. 171. For documents
see Daris, "Le cartulaire de l'abbaye de Herkenrode," BIAL., X (1870), 461-506; XI
(1871), 19-106; id., Notices, IV (1871), 1-138; V (1872), 207; XVI (1885), 261; XVII
(1886), 36; id., "Notice sur Herckenrode," AHEB., XVI (1879), 221-313; VI (1869), 137.
[40] See below, p. 329.
[41] Herman of Tournai, in MGH. SS., XII, 659; PL., CLVI, 1001-1002.

stration and which he kept under his immediate supervision.[42] Manrique was unable to detect any trace of these nunneries in Italy before 1212.[43]

Although Herman's account of Barthélemy's foundation contains an apocryphal element,[44] his description of the feminine branch under Cîteaux compels credence by virtue of its vividness. These nuns, or perhaps *conversae*, took literally the words of Matthew: "The kingdom of Heaven suffereth violence and the violent take it by force" (XI, 12). "Striving to conquer not only the world but their own sex as well, of their own free will they embraced violently, nay joyfully, the order of Cîteaux, which many robust men and youths fear to enter. Laying aside all linen garments and furs, they wore only woolen tunics. They did not only womens' work such as spinning and weaving, but they went out and worked in the fields, digging, cutting down and uprooting the forest with axe and mattock, tearing up thorns and briers, laboring assiduously with their hands and in silence seeking their food. Imitating in all things the monks of Clairvaux, they proved the truth of the Lord's saying, that to the believer all things are possible."[45] Thus early Cistercian nuns imitated the *conversi* by performing agricultural tasks in the fields. By omitting reference to intervention of bishop or order in this espousal of the Cistercian rule, Herman underlines the spontaneous character of the movement.

In his own day Jacques de Vitry, writing about 1220, witnessed the foundation or affiliation of seven Cistercian convents within a short time in the single diocese of Liége—presumably the abbeys[46] of Aywières,[47] La Ramée,[48] Parc-les-Dames,[49] Salzinnes,[50] Robermont,[51]

[42] Manrique, *Cist. Annal.*, I, 430.

[43] *Ibid.*, III, 572f.

[44] After establishing three Cistercian monasteries and five Premonstratensian houses, the bishop wished to fill the complement of the nine angelic virtues. Therefore he founded near Clairfontaines a nunnery over which he placed Guiburg. By the possession of this one abbey alone, wrote the enthusiastic Herman, the church of Laon would deserve to rank before all others.

[45] *De Mirac. S. Mariae Laudun.*, PL., CLVI, 1001-1002.

[46] *Hist. Occid.*, p. 306. For identification of the abbeys see Greven, *Anfänge*, pp. 121, note 2, 151ff; the Bollandist substitutes Herckenrode, Hocht, and Oplinter for Salzinnes, Robermont, and Val-Notre-Dame (*AA. SS.*, LXI [October 29, xiii], 101 E, no. 6).

[47] Aywières was a community founded in 1202 at Awirs, a village between Huy and Liége, was transferred to Lillois (N. of Nivelles) at least by 1210 and was permanently established at Couture-Saint-Germain (NE. of Nivelles) between 1214-1217. It was incorporated in the Cistercian order and placed under the spiritual direction of the abbot of Aulne. Cf. Roisin, in *RHE.*, XXXIX (1943), 356, 358; Canivez, *L'ordre de Cîteaux*, pp. 172-186; id., in *DHGE.*, V (1931), 1326-1328; Tarlier and Wauters, *Géog. et hist. des communes belges.* I, *Canton de Wavre*, pp. 106-109.

[48] Probably in the beginning a Benedictine house, noted in 1214 at Kerkom (NE. of Tirlemont), and in 1216 at Jauchelette (SE. of Jodoigne). They embraced the Cistercian rule about 1214. *Comm. praev. V. Id. Lew.*, 102-103; Tarlier and Wauters, *Géog. et hist. des communes belges.* II. *Canton de Jodoigne*, pp. 67-73;

Val-Notre-Dame,[52] and Florival—and even personally took a hand in the establishment of certain nunneries. In 1214 or 1215 he appears to have been entrusted by Countess Jeanne of Flanders, in a communication to Abbot Adam of Citeaux, with the completion of the convent of Epinlieu begun near Mons, in the county of Hainault and diocese of Cambrai, under her parents with the donation of Beatrice of Lens.[53] However, the cartulary contains a document whereby she gave 6 bonniers of land at Epinlieu to erect a Cistercian nunnery a couple of years later (November 25, 1217).[54] From then on it was the object of frequent comital attention.[55] In the abbey of Aywières Jacques de Vitry exhibited a lively and persistent interest, even when in the East, as the letter written from Acre at the end of March, 1217, to the abbess, Lutgard of St. Trond, and the convent reveals. As early as 1211 "Magister Jacobus de Vitriaco" appeared as a witness to a document whereby Henry of Brabant confirmed to the nuns of Aywières the tithe at Rèves which Wautier de Rèves had handed over to them.[56] In his capacity of apostolic sublegate (sedis apostolicae legati vices agens) Jacques de Vitry approved after 1213 the tithe at Braine for the convent.[57] About the same time (1213) he intervened between Aywières and Iwan de Rèves.[58] The Inventaire et repertoire des

Canivez, L'ordre de Cîteaux, pp. 187-193; GC., III, 604; cf. Wauters, TC., III, 453 (May, 1216).

[49] Parc-les-Dames between Aerschot and Louvain, originally an Augustinian house, embraced the Cistercian rule about 1215 (GC., V, 74; Canivez, L'ordre de Cîteaux, pp. 212-214).

[50] The origins of Salzinnes in Namur are obscure. The inhabitants were first mentioned as religiosa puellarum congregatio in 1202 (GC., III, 601; AHEB., III, 1866, 188; X, 447; XVI, 328-329; Berlière, MB., I, 101-110; Canivez, L'ordre de Cîteaux, pp. 317-323) and again in the same year as sorores ecclesie beati Georgii prope Namurcum (AHEB., III, 480). In June, 1203 they were called dominae sancti Georgii Namurcensis mulieres religiosae (AHEB., III, 189) and in 1211 dominae sancti Georgii (MF., II, 1211). On August 30, 1218 the house was referred to as abbatis Vallis sancti Georgii Cisterciensis Ordinis (AHEB., III, 481).

[51] Robermont was founded about 1197 for Augustinian nuns who in 1215 took the Cistercian rule and in 1231 moved to Val-Benoit in Liége (Berlière, MB., II, 180, 194; Canivez, L'ordre de Cîteaux, pp. 270-275).

[52] Val-Notre-Dame at Huy was first a hospital; by 1210 it had become a Cistercian nunnery (AHEB., XIV, 74; XVII, 43). Cf. Canivez, L'ordre de Cîteaux, pp. 280-284; Berlière, MB., II, 204-211.

[53] Jacques de Guise, Annal. Hanon. (XX, 49), MGH. SS., XXX, 1, 276f; Berlière, in RB., IX (1892), 381-383.

[54] GC., III, instrum., col. 38; Devillers, Description, III, 65; MF., III, 380; AHEB., XV (1878), 178-179. The preceding June Jeanne had granted the house an income of 20 l. albas (ibid., XV, 179).

[55] E.g., July, 1226 (Devillers, Description, III, 65; Wauters, TC., IV, 13); May, 1228 (ibid., IV, 61-62); May, 1229 (ibid., IV, 80). For a summary of Jeanne's concern for Cistercian nuns consult Luykx, in OGE., XVII (1943), 10-19; id., Johanna, pp. 311-331, 348-351.

[56] AGR., arch. eccl., Cart. d'Aywières, 5338, f. 21v.

[57] Ibid., f. 6ov; ZKG., XVI (1896), 114.

[58] Berlière, in RB., XXV, 190-191, PJ. I; 191-192, PJ. 2. This cleric, who belonged to the important family of Rèves and was attached to the church at Nivelles (prae-

lettriages et documents du monastère, composed in 1640 by Antoine
Cornoz, a monk at Aulne, contained the analysis of one of Jacques'
letters which enumerates a donation he made to Aywières.[59] While the
Jean de Cambrai mentioned in this brief was acting in 1217 as chaplain to the bishop of Acre, the latter recommended him to the prayers
of Aywières.[60] As for the incorporation of the monastery of Doorezeele
to Cîteaux, Berlière concluded[61] that this was not the work of Jacques
de Vitry but rather of his successor.

The Franciscan Jacques de Guise (d. February 6, 1399) has left in
the *Annales Historiae Illustrium Principum Hanoniae*[62] an illuminating episode concerning the feminine religious movement in the
days of Mary of Oignies. It is not merely as the record of the foundation
of Fontenelles (*de Fonte Beatae Mariae*) near Valenciennes (diocese of
Cambrai) that the account gains significance. It also offers further evidence, late is it is, of solicitation by other churchmen than John de Liro
and Jacques de Vitry for official recognition of extraregulars and eventual affiliation with a recognized order. The anachronistic use of the
word *beguine,* derived from tradition or attached to *mulieres sanctae*
for convenience, does not detract from its value. The chronicler himself
admits reliance on a popular account or tradition within the
nunnery.[63]

The monastery traced its origins back to two beguines, Jeanne and
Agnes, daughters of the knight Hellin of Launoy (de Alneto),[64] who
founded an oratory in honor of the Virgin on the banks of the Scheldt
about 1212 to serve as a retreat. It was not at first a monastic foundation but a free assembly of girls and widows. These "Christi discipule" were not bound by rule or statutes; nor did they adopt an
approved habit and observe regular ceremonies. They lived only in
accordance with divine precepts and evangelical counsel.[65] So fired

positus Nivellensis) (Cart. d'Aywieres, f. 22ᵛ-23ʳ), had made a donation in 1210 (*ibid.,*
f. 12ʳ-12ᵛ; Poncelet, *Hugues de Pierrepont,* p. 86, no. 78). The bishop of Liege made
it known that Iwan de Rèves, a *nobilis vir,* had donated to the nuns all his possessions at Lillois. Iwan's name occurs frequently in the Aywières cartulary; 1211
(f. 21ᵛ); 1211 (f. 22ʳ); 1212 (f. 12ᵛ; Poncelet, *Hugues de Pierrepont,* p. 108, no. 104);
1214 (f. 24ʳ-24ᵛ; 53ᵛ-54ʳ); 1224 (f. 29ʳ-29ᵛ); 1234 (f. 23ʳ); 1235 (f. 59ʳ) perhaps on behalf of his sister or relative, Marie de Rèves, which made possible the transfer to
Lillois.

[59] *ZKG.,* XVI (1896), 113-114; Berlière (*RB.,* XXV, 185-186) concluded that the
document was dated 1210-1216.

[60] *ZKG.,* XIV (1894), 118.

[61] *RB.,* XXV, 187-190; cf. Canivez, *L'ordre de Cîteaux,* pp. 478-480.

[62] (XX, 13), *MGH. SS.,* XXX, 1, 264-265; (XX, 14), 265.

[63] *Ibid.,* 264.

[64] *GC.,* III, 184; cf. Luykx, *Johanna,* pp. 301, 338, 456.

[65] "Hee siquidem tunc temporis Christi discipule nec regula speciali aut statutis
obediencialibus, habitu approbato aut cerimoniis regularibus minime vinciebantur,
sed solum divinis preceptis et consiliis ewangelicis, et iuxta collationes in Vitis
patrum contentas, observaciones grosso et rudi modo, prout melius poterant, innite-
bantur obnixe" (*MGH. SS.,* XXX, 1, 264).

with enthusiasm were they and so wide their renown that from neighboring cities noble women and daughters of well-to-do families hastened to partake of this hope of perfection, devotion, and contemplation. The site soon became inadequate for the "three hundred"[66] *Christi discipulae,* necessitating, with the assistance of Amatildo, lord of Pons, a transfer to larger quarters. But refusal of the church of Crespin to allow encroachment on its parochial prerogatives temporarily hampered removal. In 1215, when the cardinal-legate, Robert de Courçon, arrived in Cambrai, he was approached by Hellin and Amatildo of Pons, who secured approval for this discipline.[67] The following year the church of Crespin agreed to a settlement which was deemed not prejudicious to its interests.[68] A new chapel was established for the *mulieres religiosae* from the alms of the faithful.[69] At the same time their growth dictated the acceptance of an approved order, a humble habit, and obedience.[70] The decision was overhelmingly for affiliation with the Cistercians. Thus in December, 1216, Abbot Adam of Citeaux, moved by the devotion of the *dilectae in Christo sorores de domo Sancte Marie de Fonte,* allowed incorporation, subjecting them to the authority of the abbot of Clairvaux.[71] In June, 1218, Abbess Hawidis and the nuns of Fontenelles were recognized as its daughter by the general chapter.[72]

We have already had occasion to examine the contribution of several laymen and clergymen in establishing Cistercian houses: William de l'Olive, John of Nivelles, and Philip of Montmirail. To the list must be added the wealthy burgher of Tirlemont, Barthélemy de Vleeschouwer, father of Beatrice of Nazareth.[73] After the death of his wife Gertrude he devoted himself to the feminine religious movement. With his younger son Wicbert he is credited by the *Vita Beatricis* with the founding of Florival,[74] Val-des-Vierges,[75] and in 1235 Notre-

---

[66] *Ibid.,* 264.

[67] *Ibid.,* 265: "ad quem accesserunt dictus Hellinus et Amatildus de Pons, qui pro Christi discipularum et earum ritu approbacionis graciam impetrarunt."

[68] (XX, 14), *ibid.,* 265; Wauters, *TC.,* III, 466.

[69] *MGH. SS.,* XXX, 1, 264.

[70] *Ibid.,* 265: "ut sub certa religione approbata et habitu humili deinceps et sub obediencia vivere possent."

[71] *Idem;* Wauters, *TC.,* III, 461.

[72] *MGH. SS.,* XXX, 1, 266.

[73] Christopher Butkens, author of the *Trophées du Brabant,* was responsible for circulating a number of false chronicles in which, for example, Bartholomew was a descendant of the castellans of Brussels, the de Aa. Until about 1650 he was known only under the name of Bartholomaeus. Cf. Van Mierlo, "Barthélémy de Tirlemont," in *DHGE.,* VI, 972-973; id., "Een reeks valsche kronieken van Christophorus Butkens," *Anal. Praem.* II (1926), 60-81, 113-138; Bets, *Geschiedenis der gemeenten Oplinter, Bunsbeek en Hauthem alsook der abdij van Oplinter,* (Louvain, 1870).

[74] Florival is located at Archennes-sur-Dyle, between Louvain and Wavre, where it appears that about 1190 a group of nuns, professing the Benedictine rule and dependent on the abbey of Afflighem, settled. Early in the thirteenth century (ca. 1218) it adopted the rule of Citeaux and passed under the jurisdiction of the abbot

Dame of Nazareth near Lierre.[76] Both took up residence in the Cistercian circles as *conversi*.[77] The whole family, in fact, was imbued with asceticism. Like Beatrice, her three sisters became Cistercian nuns. The older brother became a Premonstratensian canon at Averbode.

Among the princes and feudal lords who promoted Cistercian growth were Henry II of Brabant, who founded Val-Duc (Hertogendael);[78] Baldwin II of Courtenay, count of Namur, Moulins (1233);[79] Gerard, count of Looz, Herckenrode;[80] Margaret de Guines, castellan of Courtrai, Mont-d'Or at Wevelghem;[81] Count Albert of Moha, Val- Notre-Dame at Antheit near Huy;[82] Beatrice of Courtrai (d. 1288), Groeninghe-lez-Courtrai;[83] Alice de Boulaere, or Boulers, Beaupré;[84] Countess Ermesinde, widow of Thibaud de Bar, Clairefontaine, southeast of Arlon;[85] the knight Arnold de Corswarem, Paix-Dieu at Huy (1231);[86] Guillaume de Harenton, Argenton.[87] Just as the counts of Looz took an interest in the nunnery of Orienten at Rummen,[88] so Solières was associated with the lords of Beaufort.[89]

Yet none was more generous than the two countesses of Flanders. In addition to what has already been said, Jeanne not only served as protector of about fifteen nunneries,[90] but established three: Marquette at Lille which both she and her first husband Ferrand cherished above all the rest;[91] La Biloke at Ghent;[92] and Maegdendael at

of Villers. *GC.*, V, 64-68; *AHEB.*, XVIII, 119; Canivez, *L'ordre de Cîteaux*, pp. 194-198; Tarlier and Wauters, *Géog. et hist. des communes belges, Canton de Wavre*, pp. 195-197.

[75] Founded about 1221-1223, at Oplinter (NE. of Tirlemont). *GC.*, V, 76-78; Tarlier and Wauters, *Géog. et hist. des communes belges, Canton de Tirlemont*, pp. 32f; Canivez, *L'ordre de Cîteaux*, pp. 202-204.

[76] *GC.*, V, 151-153; Canivez, *L'ordre de Cîteaux*, pp. 236-238.

[77] *V. Beat.*, ed. Henriquez, pp. 2-3.

[78] *GC.*, V, 83; Canivez, *L'ordre de Cîteaux*, pp. 198-202. For another example see *GC.*, V, *instrum.*, 309, no. 3.

[79] Berlière, *MB.*, I, 82-86; 174-176; *AHEB.*, V (1868), 375f; cf. VIII (1871), 1-18; for Jean d'Eppes' approval, MF., II, 1222; cf. Canivez, *L'ordre de Cîteaux*, pp. 325-331.

[80] See above, p. 106n.

[81] *GC.*, III, 309-313; Canivez, *L'ordre de Cîteaux*, pp. 423-429.

[82] See above, p. 108n.

[83] Canivez, *L'ordre de Cîteaux*, pp. 413-423; for Beatrice see Saint-Genois in BNB., II (1868), 26-28; cf. *Messager*, 1843, 222-223.

[84] 1228, *GC.*, V, *instrum.*, coll. 299-300; cf. 78-79; Canivez, *L'ordre de Cîteaux*, pp. 445-448; id., "Beaupré de Grammont", *DHGE.*, VII (1934), 233f.

[85] Canivez, *L'ordre de Cîteaux*, pp. 296-303.

[86] Berlière, *MB.*, II, 174-178; Canivez, *L'ordre de Cîteaux*, pp. 279-280.

[87] Gaillot, *Histoire de Namur*, IV, 297-302; V, 394ff (PJ.); Canivez, *L'ordre de Cîteaux*, pp. 339-345; Berlière, "Argenton", *DHGE.*, IV (1930), 65f.

[88] Tarlier and Wauters, *Géog. et hist. des communes belges, Canton de Léau*, pp. 200-203; Canivez, *L'ordre de Cîteaux*, pp. 204-209.

[89] Gaillot, *Histoire de Namur*, IV, 309-313; Canivez, *L'ordre de Cîteaux*, pp. 284-291.

[90] E.g., Spermaille at Bruges (1235), *GC.*, V, 295-298; Canivez, *L'ordre de Cîteaux*, 291; pp. 430-433.

[91] Jacques de Guise, *Ann. Han.*, (XX, 49), *MGH. SS.*, XXX 1, 275; Luykx, in *OGE.*, XVII (1943), 12-14; id., *Johanna*, pp. 180f, 190, 423-425, etc.

Audenarde on the left bank of the Scheldt.[93] Her sister was responsible
for Flines[94] and, with the assistance of Walter, lord of Axel, Ter-
Hagen (1230).[95] Both endowed Oost-Eeckloo (1228), two miles from
Ghent.[96]

The dichotomy of function, characteristic of several Villers abbots,[97]
is well illustrated by William of Brussels (1221-1237) whose concern
for material well-being, says the chronicler, however, was farthest
from him.[98] Donations of land, tithes, rents, and *jura patronatus*
were numerous, especially in the centers of Mellemont, Velp, Dhuy,
the Neuve-Cour, Schooten, and Diepenbeek.[99] Far from being diminished, William's eagerness to promote the building of women's
convents in the days of Jacques de Vitry and to affiliate already-
established monasteries marks the acme of Villers' prestige in this
work.[100] He even secured the nomination of the pastor of the Great
Beguinage at Louvain.[101] In the absence of prior and prelate, Honorius III made him veritable abbot of the leper-house of Terbank, a
few years after its foundation by Henry I of Brabant,[102] ordering him
to supervise and control the spiritual and temporal interests of this
establishment (January 12, 1224), even though as a double monas-

[92] GC., V, 219-220, *instrum.*, 328f, 333; Luykx, in *OGE.*, XVII (1943), 14-16; id., *Johanna*, pp. 311, 315, 317, 352f, 599-601, etc.; Walters, *Gesch. van de zusters der Bijloke te Gent.*

[93] Canivez, *L'ordre de Cîteaux*, pp. 441-445; Luykx, in *OGE.*, XVII (1943), 16-19.

[94] Hautcoeur, *Cartulaire de Flines*, I, 10 (foundation charter, October 9, 1234); id., *Histoire de Flines*, pp. 16-19, 31ff.

[95] Canivez, *L'ordre de Cîteaux*, pp. 480-487. Margaret issued a charter to the Cistercian convent at Ath in June, 1258 (Jacques de Guise, *Ann. Han., MGH. SS.*, XXX, 1, 303; cf. Wauters, *TC.*, V, 183).

[96] CC., V, 227; Canivez, *L'ordre de Cîteaux*, pp. 488-493.

[97] The chronicle brings this out repeatedly (e.g., *MGH. SS.*, XXV, 198).

[98] "De temporalibus ei cura extrema erat" (*ibid.*, XXV, 200). He acquired the property of Thielt and Beauvechain; under him the house began "to be enriched with income and possessions" (*idem*). Yet the administration was frugal. See De Moreau, *L'abbaye de Villers*, pp. 57-62.

[99] *Ibid.*, p. 58.

[100] In the course of time certain nunneries were detached from Villers to pass under the jurisdiction of Aulne or St. Sauveur in Antwerp. Yet under the abbacy of Robert of Namur (1647-1652) Villers still directed the following nunneries: in the southern provinces, Argenton near Gembloux, Florival near Wavre, l'Olive near Morlanwelz, Wautier-Braine near Braine-l'Alleud; in the northern provinces, Mag-dendael at Oplinter, Nazareth near Lierre, Muysen which transferred to Malines, Val-Duc at Hamme-Mille, Parc-les-Dames at Wesemael, Rothem near Diest, Terbeek near St. Trond, Val-des-Roses at Wavre-Sainte Catherine, La Vignette (*Vinea Nostrae Dominae*) at Terbanck at the gates of Louvain. Cf. Canivez, *L'ordre de Cîteaux*, pp. 90f.

[101] See below, pp. 170-72.

[102] Bets, "Notice sur la ladrérie de Ter Banck," *AHEB.*, VII (1870), 307-328; VIII (1871), 59-69; Canivez, *L'ordre de Cîteaux*, pp. 221-223. Molanus (I, 327-328) suggests that it existed some time before 1203. The cardinal-legate Guy mentioned during his tour of duty in Germany in 1203 "domum leprosorum religiose viventium, noviter plantatam" (*ibid.*, I, 330).

tery[103] it followed the rule of St. Augustine.[104] About the same time (1222) Arnulf, a lay brother of Villers, advised Countess Blanche of Champagne, hardpressed by the campaigns of Erald de Rammery, to found the Cistercian nunnery of Argensolles between Epernay and Vertus (diocese of Soissons), as a condition for peace.[105] According to Gosuin de Bossut, Arnulf was equally effective in determining Gilles Berthout to found the Cistercian nunnery of Val-des-Roses near Malines. So pressed had the knight been by difficulties that he was on the point of abandoning his undertaking; it was William of Villers who advised him to seek the counsel and encouragement of the *conversus*.[106]

Not merely content with promoting the foundation or incorporation of women's convents, the abbots of Villers eagerly accepted their direction. The *Vita Godefridi Sacristae*[107] describes the origins of La Cambre on the southern outskirts of Brussels in 1201 under Villers auspices. The Benedictine nun, Gisele of Brussels, who went over to Citeaux in her desire to embrace a stricter life,[108] found a patron in Abbot Charles and became its founder.[109] Boniface, bishop of Lausanne, after being persecuted by Frederick II, took refuge in this convent, became its chaplain, and died here in 1260.[110] The chronicle informs us that William of Brussels, after becoming abbot of Clairvaux, visited it "with the permission"[111] of the abbot of Villers, its immediate father. This set a precedent that created a position in fact which became a legal right and Villers thus lost, to the advantage of Clairvaux, supervision of the Brussels nunnery.[112] In 1233 William

[103] At first, says Molanus (I, 327), "it was a convent of brethren and sisters lepers under the rule of St. Augustine."
[104] When the men and women lepers were no longer considered fit to maintain discipline in the monastery, a convent of sisters of the Order of St. Augustine was established there under the abbot of Villers (*ibid.*, I, 327).
[105] *V. Arn. Villar.*, 571-572, nos. 30-32; *GC.*, X, instrum., col. 130; IX, 478-480; cf. Canivez, *Statuta*, II, 33-34, no. 20 (an. 1224); II, 36-37, no. 8 (an. 1225). The general chapter paid its respects to Blanche in 1228 (*ibid.*, II, 66, no. 7) and 1229 (*ibid.*, II, 77, no. 11). Cf. Arthur Prévost, "Argensolles," *DHGE.*, IV (1930), 16-19; cf. Alberic de Trois-Fontaines, *Chron.*, *MGH. SS.*, XXIII, 912.
[106] *V. Arn. Villar.*, 576, no. 54.
[107] *Gesta, MGH. SS.*, XXV, 230; cf. Canivez, in *DHGE.*, XI (1949), 565-567; id., *L'ordre de Cîteaux*, pp. 149-156.
[108] "Arctioris vitae desiderio" (*Gesta, MGH. SS.*, XXV, 230; *Comm. praev. (V. Gob. Asper.*, 373, A-B).
[109] *Cron. Villar. mon., MGH. SS.*, XXV, 197; Sanderus, *Chorog. Sac. Brab.*, I, 562-563.
[110] *V. Bon.*, 151ff, 156 (10); 159 (12); Henne-Wauters, *Histoire de Bruxelles*, III, 613; Canivez, in *DHGE.*, IX (1937), 955f.
[111] *Cron. Villar. mon., MGH. SS.*, XXV, 202, cap. 17.
[112] *Idem.* In the statutes of the general chapter of 1232 there is a decision that seems to have entrusted at least for a time the paternity of La Cambre to the abbey of Aulne and suggests that the incorporation of the nunnery to the order of Citeaux had been brought into question (Canivez, *Statuta*, II, 107, no. 37: "Ad mandatum domini Papae conceditur ut abbatia Camerae Sanctae Mariae Ordini societur et per abbatem de Alna visitetur").

took charge of Val-Duc which Duke Henry had founded near Louvain for his daughter Margaret.[113] He also worked for the affiliation of the Augustinian nunnery of Solières to the Cistercian order (1232),[114] while Salzinnes[115] and La Ramée[116] entrusted to him supervision of their temporal affairs. After being associated with Villers for a considerable time, Aywières was probably one of the abbeys whose direction Walter relinquished.[117] When the empress Marie (d. 1260), sister of Duke Henry II of Brabant and widow of Otto IV, founded in 1231 the monastery of Binderen at Helmont in northern Brabant, Innocent IV entrusted it to Abbot Arnulf of Louvain in 1246.[118] Wauthier-Braine,[119] Florival,[120] Parc-les-Dames,[121] and without doubt a good number of nunneries in Brabant and elsewhere[122] also depended on Villers.

The statutes of the general chapters mention the intervention of William of Brussels in the inquests on the material condition preparatory to the affiliation of several abbeys:[123] l'Olive (1234),[124] Jardinet (1234),[125] Nazareth, Soleilmont, and Val-Saint-Bernard, all in 1236,[126] and Terbeek (1237).[127]

[113] Thomas of Cantimpré, *BUA.*, II, 10; 8 (p. 163); *Cron. Villar. mon., MGH. SS.*, XXV, 202, cap. 17; *GC.*, V, 83 where the date is given as 1232; Hauck (IV, 1005) places it in 1235.

[114] Gilles d'Orval, *Gesta Episc. Leod., MGH. SS.*, XXV, 125; MF., III, 401f; Berlière, *MB.*, II, 188.

[115] In January, 1226 the abbess of Val-Saint-Georges near Namur completed a sale of property to the chapter of Saint-Lambert with William's consent (*CESL.*, I, 215-216, no. 152).

[116] About 1230 William approved a payment made by the nunnery to the chapter of St. Lambert (*ibid.*, I, 271, no. 207).

[117] *Cron. Villar. mon., MGH. SS.*, XXV, 199; GC., II, 603. Walter of Utrecht granted the abbess and her community permission to transfer their monastery to a more favorable place (De Moreau, *L'abbaye de Villers*, p. 112).

[118] *Cron. Villar. mon., MGH. SS.*, XXV, 409; *GC.*, V, 409. It was at first decreed that although inspected by the abbots of Villers and Lieu Saint Bernard the foundation would be a daughter of Citeaux, as a decision of the general chapter of 1237 testifies (Canivez, *Statuta*, II, 174, no. 31). The general chapter of 1246, however, placed the nunnery under the authority of Villers, but allowed the abbots of Aulne and Lieu Saint Bernard to install the abbess and incorporate the convent in the order (*ibid.*, II, 312, no. 56). cf. Canivez, in *DHGE.*, VIII (1935), 1500f.

[119] 1232, Canivez, *Statuta*, II, 107, no. 34; *GC.*, III, 606. In the course of a canonical visit to the house Abbot Walter de Jodoigne died (*Cron. Villar. mon., Cont. I a, MGH. SS.*, XXV, 209, cap. 1).

[120] *GC.*, V, 64-68.

[121] Canivez, *L'ordre de Cîteaux*, p. 213.

[122] A necrology of Villers, covering the years 1574 of 1792, cites several abbeys of Cistercian nuns where the monks of Villers heard confessions: Val-des-Vierges at Oplinter, Nazareth, Terbeek, La Vignette at Louvain, Rothem, Muysen, l'Olive, Parc-les-Dames, and Differdange (*AHEB.*, IX [1872], 51-90).

[123] For a statement of policy on this matter, see Canivez, *Statuta*, II, 74, no. 42 (an. 1229).

[124] *Ibid.*, II, 135, no. 42.

[125] *Ibid.*, II, 129, no. 18.

[126] Inspection of these three nunneries was shared by the abbots of Villers, Val-Saint-Lambert, and Grand-Pré preparatory to incorporation (*ibid.*, II, 168, no. 66).

Aulne (dioc. Tournai), although less well known, was often concerned with the incorporation of pious women into the order.[128] Its abbot, together with the abbot of Cambron, was charged by the general chapter, at the request of Henry, archdeacon of Liége, with preliminary investigations for the affiliation of Wauthier-Braine (1233),[129] the "Palace of the Blessed Virgin" (*Aula Beatae Virginis*) (1237),[130] Paix-Dieu (1241),[131] Helmont (1246).[132] Its abbot seems to have received the right to visit La Cambre at least temporarily.[133] To it was entrusted the paternity of the abbeys of l'Olive,[134] Jardinet,[135] Soleilmont,[136] Val-des-Vierges,[137] and in 1239 that of Aywières, one of the numerous communities whose direction Walter of Villers had first assumed.[138]

The abbots of Cambron and Loos (dioc. Cambrai) were enjoined to regularize the life of Fontenelle.[139] But such examples, as the *Statuta* testify so abundantly, are legion—wherever the order struck root. The periods of most pronounced growth of nunneries are 1214–1219 and especially 1227–1238. After 1247 foundations suddenly stop in Belgium.

Examples of voluntary contraction of the *cura monialium* notwithstanding, it may thus be said without exaggeration that outside of the hours of prayer Villers abbots and monks during the first half of the thirteenth century often went about spreading edifying stories, espe-

---

[127] *Ibid.*, II, 180-181, no. 63.
[128] Berlière, *MB.*, I, 329-342; Canivez, "Aulne", *DHGE.*, V (1931), 667-669.
[129] Canivez, *Statuta*, II, 116, no. 27.
[130] The abbot had the assistance of the head of Val-Dieu in handling this daughter of Clairvaux (*ibid.*, II, 181, no. 64).
[131] With the cooperation of the abbot of Villers (*ibid.*, II, 237, no. 36).
[132] *Ibid.*, II, 174, no. 30.
[133] *Ibid.*, II, 107, no. 37.
[134] *Ibid.*, II, 135, no. 42.
[135] *Ibid.*, II, 129, no. 18 (an. 1234).
[136] *Ibid.*, II, 168, no. 66; Devillers, in *Ann. cercle arch. Mons*, IV, 249, no. 57; cf. *MF.*, III, 401-2; Gaillot, *Histoire de Namur*, V, 412.
[137] Canivez, *Statuta*, II, 179-180, no. 59 (an. 1237).
[138] A conflict developed between Clairvaux and Aulne over the paternity of Aywières (De Moreau, *L'abbaye de Villers*, p. 112). The author gives the date of 1238 but the cartulary of Aulne (Devillers, *Description*, I, 35, nos. 55-56; *Ann. cercle arch. Mons*, IV, 249) assigns the date 1239 to two documents treating this conflict. It was a question of the arbitration of the abbots Jean d'Orval and Guillaume de Valloires (in Picardy, dioc. of Amiens) which took place in April, 1239 (cf. Tarlier and Wauters, *Géog. et hist. des communes belges. Canton de Wavre*, p. 106). Echoes are found in the statutes of the chapters from 1235 to 1238 (Canivez, *Statuta*, II, 146, no. 32, here the difficulty was submitted to the abbots of Preuilly, Trois-Fontaines. and Ter Doest); *ibid.*, II, 196, no. 58, an. 1238, here it was the abbots of Orval and Valloires who were concerned). The abbot of Aulne was with others charged to visit the nunnery in 1239 and to reform certain abuses introduced by the abbess (*ibid.*, II, 207, no. 23). Cf. Roisin, in *RHE.*, XXXIX, 355, note.
[139] Canivez, *Statuta*, II, 106-107, no. 34 (an. 1232); *GC.*, III, 184. For Cambron and Le Saulchoir, Canivez, *Statuta*, II, 117, no. 32 (an. 1233); cf. *ibid.*, II, 131, no. 25 (an. 1234).

cially in nunneries and before novices, in the fashion of Caesarius of Heisterbach, and kindling the desire of neighboring lords to increase the abbatial domain.[140] "Our Fathers," relates the first edition of the *Gesta Sanctorum Villariensium*, compiled at the beginning of the fourteenth century,[141] "have told us that formerly religious feeling was intense at Villers." The leadership of the abbey in things of the spirit in Brabant was earlier corroborated by the Dominican Thomas of Cantimpré.[142] Such partial judgment finds no clearer proof than in this keen interest in Cistercian nunneries and beguinal societies.

Although under Abbot Walter's direction at Villers several nunneries sprang up in the diocese of Liége, he nevertheless considered that the pressing *cura monialium* would increase the burden of governing his own monastery properly. He was fearful that if the older monks, who fired the order with their zeal and whose exemplary conduct endowed it with a luster, were dispersed in these convents to hear confessions, the young would be less excited to fervor and discipline would be relaxed.[143] Such considerations therefore induced him to hand over to the abbot of Citeaux direction of eight communities; he then concentrated his own energy on the immediate charges and extension of the domain of his monastery.[144] His distaste for the care of nuns was symptomatic of the sentiment which was then widely prevalent in certain quarters in the order and which shortly inspired in the general chapters official repudiation of this *taedium et gravamen*.[145]

Chapter legislation reveals an obvious contradiction in policy. On the one hand, the Cistercian monks often exhibited in action and legislation the same reluctance to assume the *cura monialium* that the mendicant orders afterwards demonstrated. At the same time we have witnessed the willingness of monasteries to incorporate nunneries and to take charge of their material well-being. The 1228 canon, far from retarding assimilation, actually seems to have fostered it. Fragmentary as the evidence is concerning the beginning of women's convents, it is apparent that from the early twelfth century the *Frauenfrage* was obtruding itself here too. The enthusiastic passage cited above in which Herman of Tournai underlines a predilection for austerity is matched by equally grave misgivings with regard to association with nuns or *conversae*. Monastic disciplinarians were ever anxious to ex-

---

140 De Moreau, *Le Polyptique*, pp. 372-373.

141 *MGH. SS.*, XXV, 234-235; for the date see De Moreau, *L'abbaye de Villers*, pp. xviii-xxiv; cf. Roisin, *Hag. cist.*, pp. 24f.

142 Thomas of Cantimpré, *BUA.*, I, 9, 2-3 (p. 37); II, 25, 5 (p. 246).

143 *Cron. Villar. mon.*, *MGH. SS.*, XXV, 199.

144 *Cron. Villar. mon.*, *MGH. SS.*, XXV, 199; De Moreau, *L'abbaye de Villers*, pp. 54f.

145 Canivez, *Statuta*, II, 68-69, no. 17 (an. 1228).

clude women from the precincts of their abbeys and to make them feel out of place in religious processions.[146] Their intrusion, the dangers of cohabitation and familiarity, of course, are all dutifully stressed,[147] but this represents no departure from the medieval attitude. That does not involve necessarily the labors of pastoral care.

The *Liber Usuum Conversorum* extended the prohibition upon the entrance of women to the Cistercian granges where the lay-brothers of the order carried on their agricultural work.[148] Enforcement of the rule entailed a denial of ordinary monastic hospitality to women[149] and even to male escorts. Food was dispensed at the door of the monastery to women of the neighborhood only in times of famine, while men who came with women to the monastery had to remain outside and receive their food there. Eventually the larger monasteries built small lodges outside their gates where women could be received. In 1157 they were permitted to enter Cistercian churches during nine days following dedication.[150] At other times religious services could not be held in the abbey as long as it was profaned by the presence of women. Severe penalties were imposed on the abbot who transgressed the ordinances; even if a woman entered the monastery without his knowledge, he was penalized, while the abbot who consented to entrance of a woman might be deposed.[151]

The earliest extant legislation of the general chapter on the subject of nunneries is a statute of 1213 which not only presupposes the existence of numerous Cistercian convents but also discloses the plan of their organization. Inmates of nunneries belonging to the order should not set foot outside the convent walls without permission from their father-abbots; houses which desired admission to the order must first meet the requirements of strict enclosure.[152] In 1218 the chapter defined more closely the requirement of claustration: the abbess, accompanied by two nuns, might leave the convent in cases of necessity in order to transact the business of the cloister; yet the consent of the father-abbot should even then be secured if possible.[153] The rule of enclosure was accompanied by other restrictive legislation. In 1216 the chapter ordained that nunneries must be at a distance of at least six leagues from any Cistercian monastery for men and at least ten leagues from another Cistercian nunnery.[154] Nuns

---

[146] *De Miraculis, PL.,* CLXXXV, 1298 C.
[147] Canivez, *Statuta,* I, 14, no. 7; 224, no. 4 (1198); 257, no. 46 (1200); II, 19, no. 30 (1222); 48, no. 3 (1226); 92, no. 6 (1231); 140, no. 10 (1235).
[148] *Ibid.,* I, 14, no. 7.
[149] Cf. *ibid.,* II, 140, no. 10 (1235).
[150] *Ibid.,* I, 61, no. 10.
[151] *Ibid.,* I, 211, no. 6; cf. 156, no. 50; 157, no. 55.
[152] *Ibid.,* I, 405, no. 3.
[153] *Ibid.,* I, 502, no. 84.
[154] *Ibid.,* I 485, no. 4. Already in 1212 a complaint had been lodged at the prox-

could own no property of their own; the number of inmates in any
convent was to be determined by the father-abbot.[155] The still excessive population in cloisters necessitated the establishment of a maximum number of nuns in each house.[156] Departure from a cloister for
the purpose of founding branches is permitted only in earlier
canons.[157] Since abbesses were not allowed to hear confessions,[158]
abbots who exercised visitatorial power were to delegate *viros honestos
et prudentes* for this purpose.[159]

The frequency of such legislation testifies to its inadequacy, for
nunneries continued to be incorporated without observing the rule
of strict enclosure. In 1220 the chapter forbade the affiliation of existing nunneries.[160] But this decree was completely disregarded by secular and ecclesiastical authorities; sometimes it was deliberately evaded
by Cistercian abbots.[161] Admitting failure to enforce this legislation
governing incorporation, the chapter of 1225 decreed that nunneries
henceforth should not be affiliated unless their endowments were
sufficiently large to make strict segregation of the nuns possible;
nunneries which had joined the order within the preceding four years
were to be subject to enclosure or to be severed from the congregation.[162] If nuns are excommunicated, they can be absolved by the
father-abbot.[163] In 1228 the general chapter formulated new and
drastic legislation concerning nunneries. Not only were existing convents
no longer to be admitted to the order, but henceforth no new nunnery could be built under its name or jurisdiction. It was still possible,
however, for a nunnery to follow the Cistercian rule without being
affiliated with the order and sharing its privileges; the chapter conce-
ded that it would place no obstacle in the way of nunneries desiring to
pursue such a course, but it would not undertake their supervision
or be responsible for spiritual direction.[164] The following canon is

imity to monasteries for men (*ibid.*, I, 403, no. 62).

[155] *Ibid.*, I, 505, no. 12 (1219); cf. *ibid.*, I, 502, no. 84 (1218).

[156] *Ibid.*, I, 505, no. 12 (1219); II, 36, no. 7 (1225); II, 248, no. 15 (1242).

[157] *Ibid.*, I, 405, no. 3 (1213); the rule of claustration was tightened: *ibid.*, I, 505.
no. 12 (1219); II, 36, no. 7 (1225); II, 67, no. 13 (1228); II, 76, no. 5 (1229).

[158] *Ibid.*, II, 68, no. 15 (1228).

[159] *Ibid.*, II, 113, no. 12 (1233); II, 169, no. 7 (1237).

[160] *Ibid.*, I, 517, no. 4.

[161] *Ibid.*, II, 17, no. 23 (1222).

[162] *Ibid.*, II, 36, no. 7 (1225).

[163] *Ibid.*, II, 56, no. 2 (1227).

[164] *Ibid.*, II, 68, no. 16: "Nulla monasteria monialium de cetero sub nomine aut
sub iurisdictione Ordinis nostri construantur, vel Ordini socientur. Si quod vero
monasterium monialium nondum Ordini sociatum vel etiam construendum, nostras
institutiones voluerit aemulari, non prohibemus; sed curam animarum earum non
recipiemus, nec visitationis officium eis impendemus. Qui vero super hoc faciendo
petitionem ad Capitulum deportaverit, vel aliquid scienter procuraverit, per quod
possit institutio tam utilis enervari; si monachus fuerit, vel conversus, a domo propria emittatur, non reversurus, nisi per Capitulum generale; si abbas fuerit, sit in

equally illuminating: „De his quae sunt iam Ordini sociatae a septem annis et infra, antiqua sententia teneatur, videlicet ut penitus infra triennium includantur; et quae includi noluerint, ubicumque fuerint, a custodia Ordinis se noverint separatas. Huic etiam sententiae additur, ut abbas, qui post triennium visitaverit non inclusas, irrefragabiliter deponatur. Ut autem removeatur a Capitulo generali earumdem taedium et gravamen, diffinitores in posterum omni anno ipsis diffinitoribus ad decidendum causas earum, tres constituant auditores."[165] From this time on there existed two classes of Cistercian nunneries: those which belonged to the order and shared its privileges and those which followed the rule without belonging to the order.[166]

No matter how frequent the foundation of nunneries, Jacques de Vitry complained that in the Liége area alone there were so many pious women that three times as many Cistercian convents would be needed to take care of them.[167] It was this breach that the beguinage and, to a lesser degree, the various bands of penitents[168] were intended to fill.

pane et aqua, extra stallum abbatis usque ad sequens Capitulum generale, in ipso Capitulo veniam petiturus."
[165] *Ibid.*, II, 68-69, no. 17.
[166] Winter, *Die Cistercienser*, II, 14.
[167] *Hist. Occid.*, p. 306.
[168] Lacomblet, II, p. xv, cf. 84, note 1.

III

The *Via Media*

We have already examined as the basis of beguine life socioeconomic causation in competition with, or better still, in cooperation with religious motivation. Since Joseph Greven's exhaustive exploration of the early stages of the movement as a spontaneous reaction to Norbertine reluctance to accept the *cura monialium* and as an answer to the paucity of Cistercian convents, the *VMO.,* together with the *Supplementum,* and the Nivelles-Oignies circle depicted therein have often been taken as the starting point for a study of these extraregulars. But it was a spontaneous and popular movement, an embodiment of the *vita apostolica* with deep roots in Gregorian Reform. References to beguine societies always imply previous existence.[1] Consequently it is futile to seek a single founder of a movement which, after long remaining anonymous and ill-defined, never developed into a congregation or accepted a uniform rule. Lambert le Bègue in Liège, the pastors of Nivelles and the Rhineland, all played a role in channelling and directing a new way of penitential life, the very essence of which remained its voluntary, temporary, and informal character.

The piety of the first inhabitants of Oignies had given the convent a small name. But John of Nivelles, John of Dinant, and John de Liro were never really impressive outside their immediate circles. It took the zeal and spiritual career of Mary of Oignies, born in 1176 at Nivelles, to endow Willambroux[2] over a period of fifteen years and then, after 1207, St. Nicholas and, indeed, the entire Nivelles-Oignies area, with a reputation as the center of practical lay piety that carried beyond the confines of the diocese of Liège.[3] Her ecstatic experiences, accompanied with mortification of the flesh, renunciation of an early marriage and dedication to chastity, undivided and undiminished devotion to the eucharist, ardent and spontaneous pursuit of apostolic poverty in a manner reminiscent of Francis of Assisi, and complete

---

[1] Kurth, in *BARB.,* 1912, p. 456.
[2] Tarlier and Wauters, *Géog. et hist. des communes belges.* I. *Arrond. de Nivelles. Ville de Nivelles,* pp. 150-151.
[3] *V. Gob.,* 384 E.

and self-effacing humility, together with a lively interest in the neighboring leper-house, are all symptomatic of the more ascetic side of beguine life. Just as such asceticism, however, must not be considered the norm for the "religiositas beguinarum" as depicted in later rules, so it must be remembered that the *vita* is absorbed with interpretation on a spiritual plane. To male associates Mary offered a practical example of the *vita apostolica*. To girls and widows she became the prototype of the beguine; they too wanted to preserve their chastity and to share the name of "paupercula Christi." We have seen on the authority of Thomas of Cantimpré that her renown even penetrated to Paris where it whetted Jacques de Vitry's interest in popular devotion.[4] If after her death she continued to act as a patron saint in whom he could take refuge, she too was fortunate in having for a biographer one of the most prominent churchmen of the day close to curial circles. For him she shone among the other *mulieres sanctae* as the sun among the stars.[5] In turn, his prestige and energetic defense of her and the beguine movement focused favorable attention on this mode of existence and helped to assure its success as a counterpoise to heresy.

Through the first quarter of the thirteenth century ecstatic women and recluses, either as individuals or in loosely knit groups, not directly affiliated with any monastic order, were called *mulieres religiosae, virgines continentes*. Mary was the first of these to be explicitly linked in retrospect with a small community of "beguinae."[6] Under the guidance of a spiritual director or confessor, at first usually a Cistercian, later Dominicans and Franciscans, they pursued their "conversion" as extraregulars, since they did not take irrevocable vows. In the Rhineland as well as in Belgium they represent essentially a type of *conversae*.

These Belgian *mulieres religiosae*, although living among laymen, were often considered by the contemporary mind superior in charity to those who professed the triple monastic vows. John Malderus (1563–1633), bishop of Antwerp and founder of the college of theology connected with the University of Louvain, summarized the problem well: The institute of beguines, although not of religious status, is nevertheless religious and a training ground of that more perfect status in which, according to the temperament and customs of the Belgian people, women lived, devoted to God. Granted that it is of greater

---

[4] *VMO., Suppl.*, 573 D. Only in this light can the sentence in the *Historia fundationis* be said to contain more than rhetoric: "De diversis mundi partibus, in quas religionis eorum fama diffundebatur, multi ad eos magnates et personae graves renuntiantes saeculo devenerunt" *(MDAC.*, VI, 329). Cf. Funk, *Jakob von Vitry*, p. 17.

[5] *VMO.*, 549.

[6] *VMO., Suppl.*, 580: "...In humili loco de Oignies inter oves beghinarum, quas abominantur Aegyptii."

merit to bind oneself by the solemn vows of chastity, obedience, and poverty, nevertheless it was a common capacity of many pious women in Belgium to rejoice in excellence rather than to promise it. They preferred to remain chaste perpetually than to vow perpetual chastity. Likewise they were more eager to obey than to vow obedience, to cultivate poverty by frugal use of their fortunes than to abandon everything at once: they might be kinder to the poor if something were left. They preferred to submit daily, as it were, to obedience within the enclosure than to be confined once and for all. In constant spontaneity they found compensation for perpetual claustration.[7] Malderus thus emphasized not only the voluntary character of beguine life, but the personal nature of the vow itself. For indelible monastic status was now substituted voluntary agreement to the triple vows. Obedience was exacted only so long as the beguine abided by the prescriptions of the several beguinages: or it could generally be terminated whenever this peculiar spiritual refreshment or social pressures were no longer compelling. A future compromise with the world was thus possible. Sincerity was less likely to be sacrificed to hypocrisy.

Caesarius of Heisterbach's conclusion sounds the keynote of the beguine world: "Licet enim huiusmodi mulieres, quales in dyocesi Leodiensi plurimas esse novimus, in habitu seculari secularibus cohabitent, multis tamen claustralibus caritate superiores sunt: inter seculares spirituales, inter luxuriosos celibes, in medio turbarum vitam ducunt heremiticam."[8] The Franciscan Gilbert of Tournai, the probable author of the tract *Collectio de Scandalis Ecclesiae* in anticipation of the Second Council of Lyons (1274), ended his discussion of conditions among Cistercian nuns with a similar observation concerning the beguines: "Et apud nos mulieres aliae, de quibus nescimus, utrum debeamus eas vel saeculares vel moniales appellare, partim enim utuntur ritu saeculari, partim etiam regulari."[9] Broadening

---

[7] Ryckel, p. 731: "Institutum Begginariorum, quamvis non sit religiosus status, est tamen religiosum, et perfectioris illius status quoddam tyrocinium, in quo secundum temperamentum et morum suorum Belgicae gentis devotus Deo faemineus sexus apte satis et quasi connaturaliter sibi vivit. ... Itaque licet majoris sit meriti se Deo obligare per solemnia vota castitatis, obedientiae et paupertatis; commune tamen in Belgio multarum tale ingenium est piarum faeminarum, ut praestare magis gaudeant quam polliceri audeant; castae esse perpetuo, quam castitatem perpetuam promittere malint; item obedire, quam obedientiam vovere, et in frugali usu suarum fortunarum paupertati studere, quam omnino simul omnia relinquere ea, quibus Christi pauperibus, si quid supersit, benigniores sint; denique libera sese quasi quotidie servitute intra claustrum obedientiae concludere, quam simul et semel includi, ut repetita spontaneitate, pretium perpetuae clausurae aliquousque compensent." For Malderus, see Ch. Piot in *BNB.*, XIII (1894-1895), coll. 223-226.

[8] Hilka, *Wundergeschichten*, III, 26-27; Kaufmann, *Caesarius von Heisterbach*, p. 177.

[9] Döllinger, *Beiträge zur politischen, kirchlichen und Kulturgeschichte der letzten sechs Jahrhunderte*, III (Vienna, 1882), 197.

this basic definition to encompass kindred masculine communities, Matthew Paris, too, was impressed by the informal character of semi-religious life: "Eisdem temporibus (i.e. 1243) quidam, in Alemannia precipue, se asserentes religiosos, in utroque sexu, set maxime in muliebri, habitum religionis set levem susceperunt, continentiam et vite simplicitatem private voto profitentes, sub nullius tamen sancti regula coarctati, nec adhuc ullo claustro contenti."[10] The protest which Robert de Béthune lodged on June 20, 1311, with respect to the encroachment of the bishop of Tournai against the beguinage at Ghent indicates that comital understanding of the movement, however congenial it consistently was, ended with the same conclusion: "cum persone sint seculares non ecclesiastice." To the count therefore devolved temporal jurisdiction of the community and, from "ancient" custom, the right to install, depose, or supervise the mistress.[11] An ordinance passed at Cologne in 1407 did not list beguine convents among the "collegien ind geystlichen luden bynnen Coelne ind die orden".[12] It was precisely this absence of regular condition together with the intrusion of suspicious novelties that provoked the wrath of Guillaume de Saint-Amour, that ardent champion of the hierarchy inviolate.[13] Back of his charges of hypocrisy may be discerned hostility to competition with established prerogative.

Like the third orders the beguinage was thus, in the eyes of contemporaries, half-religious, half-secular. The beguine, although not a nun, was nevertheless through the leavening of everyday life by devotional exercises more than a lay person. Hers was the middle path; in Belgium, however, she submitted to close ecclesiastical supervision and secular sponsorship a religious individualism which could otherwise easily lead to disorders and heterodox thought, thereby justifying the canonist's use of the term *secta*. During persecution it was not *ordo* or *religio* but *status* that was prohibited: "Statum ipsarum prohibendum duxit perpetuo et a Dei ecclesia penitus abolendum."[14] Thus the

[10] Matthew Paris, *Chron. majora*, MGH. SS., XXVIII, 234; cf. 417, 430.
[11] Béthune, *Cartulaire*, p. 61.
[12] Ennen, *Geschichte der Stadt Köln*, III, 827. In the Rhineland the secular character of the beguines is constantly underlined: "Constat, quod haec bagutta sicut et ceterae baguttae sunt et erant personae saeculares" (*ibid.*, III, 827, note 3). On the other hand, Christine of Stommeln who associated with the beguines of Cologne (*V. Chr. Stumb.*, 372 A, no. 23; *V. Chr.*, 269 F, II, 49) is reported by the hagiographer to have been tempted by the devil to abandon chastity and resume a normal lay life: "Si velles vivere ut seculares, vel saltem sicut alii religiosi; et abrenuntiares huic vitae quam assumpsisti, vellem te facere praedivitem." To her protest comes the reply: "Clerici et religiosi et omnes continentes decepti sunt quia haeresis est sic vivere: Deus enim a principio sic ordinavit ut omnes viverent in matrimonio, et tu fac similiter" (*ibid.*, 372 B-C, no. 24; 269 F, II, 49).
[13] "Qui licet non sint regulares proprie" (Mosheim, p. 33); "cum nullius sint religionis per sedem Apostolicam approbatae" (*ibid.*, p. 27), an echo of can. 13 of the Fourth Lateran Council.
[14] John XXII's bull to the bishop of Tournai, December 30, 1320 (Béthune,

continuer of the *Gesta Abbatum Trudonensium,* too, attributed the beginnings of the *status beginarum* to the episcopate of Robert de Thourote.[15] Clement V protested in his decree *Cum de quibusdam* (1311) that the beguines owed no obedience, refused to renounce their property, and embraced no approved rule: in short, they did not live "religiose" although they wore a habit which was of the beguines and cleaved to some religious.[16] In light of these considerations the reservations entertained by John XXII and afterwards Benedict XII with respect to their "status" become more cogent.[17] If the phrase *ad ordinem begginarum* occurs under Archbishop Gerhard of Mainz (1291), it is only application by analogy, without precise meaning.[18] On the other hand, statutes and rules prescribed a carefully circumscribed existence which more closely befitted a *clausura*[19] than opponents were willing to acknowledge. "Although Belgian beguines are not bound by vows, they nevertheless remain fixed in one place where they settle voluntarily, not by necessity."[20] By thus assigning to these extraregulars *stabilitas,* an unwillingness to shift from one house to another, Ryckel passes a judgment as correct for the thirteenth century as for the seventeenth. Beguine life has been described as one result of the "democratization" of the mystical reform movement set in motion during the Investiture Wars.[21] The beguinage answered the needs of the ecstatic elements of the urban population in an age when the bourgeoisie was growing increasingly impatient with the mixing of monachism in its religious affairs.[22] *Conversi,* while being attached

Cartulaire, p. 69); Clement V's decretal, *Cum de quibusdam mulieribus* (Fredericq, *Corpus,* I, 167-168; cf. the communication of Count Robert of Flanders on June 12, 1319: "Statusque... Beghinarum de novo sit prohibitus et a Dei ecclesia penitus abolendus," Bethune, *Cartulaire,* p. 67; cf. p. 72, no. 104); see further, Fredericq, *Corpus,* I, 171, 174, 176, 179; II, 73, 75, 78, 80, 86, 87, 95; Ennen-Eckertz, *Quellen.* II. 445, no. 428.

[15] 1241-1245, *Gesta Abb. Trud., Cont.Tertia, Pars II, MGH.SS.,* X, 395.

[16] Fredericq, *Corpus,* I, 167.

[17] Bull, "Racio recta non patitur" (August 13, 1318), *ibid.,* II, 74; cf. II, 93.

[18] Boehmer, *UB. Frankfurt,* I, 262. *Ordo* is defined in Codex Juris Canonici (can. 488, § 2) as a religious organization in which solemn vows are taken (*religio in qua vota sollemnia nuncupantur*) whereas a *congregation* is defined as a religious body whose members make only simple vows (for the distinction of vows see below note 26) While a religious house (*domus religiosa*) is the residence of a religious organization (*domus alicuius religionis in genere*), a house of regulars (*domus regularis*) is the house of an Order (*domus Ordinis*) (§ 5). Alongside the early use of *ordo* which merely signified monastic status or the whole body of regulars developed this more precise meaning, indicating a unified congregation, a distinctive order wherein unity was assured by hierarchy and government as well as by identical observances (Ph. Schmitz, in *DHGE.,* VII [1934], 1060; Ducange, *Glossarium,* IV, 728-730).

[19] E.g., December 8, 1323, AAPB., Carton H. 262; Fredericq, *Corpus,* II, 82.

[20] Ryckel, p. 200: "... Licet nulla vota ligent, tamen immobiliter inhaerent uni loco, in quo sese sponte stabiliunt, non necessitate."

[21] Philippen, in *AAAB.,* LXXIII, ser. 7, vol. III (1926), 239.

[22] Pirenne, *Histoire de Belgique,* I (1929), 365.

to a church domain as serfs, with privileges inherent in this condition, were not obligated by the triple vows, but only by that of obedience, or by a promise of fidelity and stability. Penitence could dictate their choice.[23] Just as Mary of Oignies may be regarded as a *conversa* in the Augustinian priory, so chroniclers sometimes treated the term as synonymous with *beguine,* or at least paired them in the age of the friars.[24]

Nor does the use of the phrases "religio beguinarum" or "mulieres religiosae" elucidate further contemporary understanding of beguinal status.[25] The term *religio* in medieval literature in the main denotes monastic life, a religious order, a dedication confirmed by the triple vow.[26] Just as heretics and pseudo-preachers might be said to hide under the appearance of the Catholic religion and the habit of spi-

---

[23] J. Bonduelle, "Convers," *DDC.,* IV, 562-588.

[24] With respect to Franciscan concern: "Fratres conversos et conversas seu beginas, servos et ancillas multas habebant, que agros et vineas colebant et in aliis servie-bant" (*De Rebus Alsaticis, MGH. SS.,* XVII, 235, no. 8). The chronicler had just made a similar reference to the Dominicans who "censum per fratres suos conversos et beginas et servos et ancillas annis singulis collegerunt" (*ibid.,* 234). Cf. Council of Trèves (1277), can. 8: "Begardos vel conversos seu alios" (*MDAC.,* VII, 115; Fredericq, *Corpus,* I, 142).

[25] See, for example, reference by Count Robert de Béthune on June 12, 1319 to the abolition of the status of *religiosae mulieres* of St. Elizabeth at Ghent (Béthune, *Cartulaire,* p. 67, no. 94). For a case of *moniales* and *virgines religiose* in juxta-position, see Crane, *Exempla,* p. 27, no. 65.

[26] Ducange, *Glossarium,* V, 688f, *s. v. religio.* Unlike *ordo,* however, *religio* is generic in the *Codex Juris Canonici.* "Status religiosus seu stabilis" is a way of common life whereby the faithful undertake through the triple vows (but without closer definition) to observe evangelical counsels (can. 487). *Religio* is a society, approved by legitimate ecclesiastical authority, whose members, in accordance with the special laws of that society, make public vows, either perpetual or temporary, the latter to be renewed when the time expires ("vota publica, perpetua vel tempo-raria, elapso tamen tempore renovanda" [can. 488, § 1], for temporary vows consult Bachofen, *Commentary,* III, 55f). Vows are public if accepted with the intervention of the Church (*ibid.,* 55). Again, can. 488, § 2 speaks, with respect to a *religio exempta,* of a "religio sive votorum sollemnium sive simplicium" or, with regard to a *congregatio religiosa,* a "religio in qua vota dumtaxat simplicia sive perpetua sive temporaria emittuntur." (For the elasticity of this term see can. 488, § 5 cited above in note 18). The distinction between solemn and simple vows engaged the attention of canonists and theologians (Bachofen, *Commentary,* III, 56ff). Boniface VIII (*Sexti Decret.* II, tit. XV, *De voto et voti redemptione;* Friedberg, II, 1053) declared that a vow "solennisatum fuerit per susceptionem sacri ordinis, aut per profes-sionem expressam vel tacitam, factam alicui de religionibus per sedem apostolicam approbatis." Can. 673, § 1 (II, *de personis,* tit. XVII, *De societatibus sive virorum sive mulierum in communi viventium sive votis*) defines the problem further with respect to the extraregular: A society of men or women whose members imitate the way of life of religious by living in common under the direction of superiors according to approved constitutions, but without being bound by the usual three public vows, is not properly *religio;* nor are its members properly designated religious (*religiosi*). Such a society is clerical or lay and must be acknowledged either by the Holy See or by the Ordinary (can. 673, § 2; cf. can. 488, §§ 3, 4). While *religio* is historically tantamount to monastic life, it also signifies an order. Such

ritual life ("*sub specie religionis Catholicae et habitu spiritualis vitae*"),[27] so the beguines flourished under the teaching of the Dominicans "specie religionis."[28] Nevertheless, if Lambert le Bègue was identified with the new "religio" which pervaded Liége and its environs, a peculiar habit, observance of chastity, and recommendation by lay and ecclesiastical authority all argued for an elastic application of the term. But such usage adds nothing to canonical interpretation of *status*. Recommending a way of life consistent with ethical rather than institutional religion, with personal experience in place of external forms, Gerard Groote, in examining the question whether the purchase of a prebend in a beguinage is simony, was repelled by the usual interpretation of *religio*. For "if devout women separate themselves from the world, and try to serve God in the privacy of their homes, without taking monastic vows, they are just as religious as the nuns in their convents. To love God and worship him is religion, not the taking of special vows. For the cause and purpose of things give them their names and forms. If it is, therefore, one's aim to live a religious life, his way of living becomes religious in God's opinion, and according to the judgment of our consciences."[29] Obligation springs from within the individual and finds sanction before his conscience; confronted with such compulsion, a beguine may not return to the world in good conscience.[29a]. Although acknowledging that a new religious order may not be founded without papal permission, Gerard saw nothing wrong for two or more persons to live together observing certain established rules or the Gospel, the rule of all rules. "The mere name *religio* signifies but little; it is not the name which determines the nature of a thing... There are many who are not protected by the name *religio*, and yet they may be more religious than those whom the Church calls

dual meaning appears in the Fourth Lateran Council (can. 13: "religionum diversitas... ad religionem converti" but "de religionibus approbatis," Hefele-Leclercq, V, 2, 1344). Elaboration of this canon by the Second Council of Lyons (1274) (can. 23, *ibid.*, VI, 1, 201-202) equates *ordo* and *religio* ("ne aliquis de cetero novum ordinem aut religionem inveniat, vel habitum novae religionis assumat") with *ordines* being employed more often for the mendicant organisms. Again, if the *Codex* (can. 488, § 2) calls a *congregatio monastica* a "union of several autonomous monasteries under the same superior" (cf. *DDC.*, IV [1949], 177), the "congregatio pauperum beghinarum" at Brussels (April, 1251, orig. AAPB. H. 263; AGR., 13403, f. 41r, no. 2) hardly fulfills this definition. It fits rather the definition of *congregatio religiosa* or *congregatio*. Similarly, *sorores* are women who have taken simple vows while *moniales*, or nuns, are religious women with solemn vows, or whose vows are normally solemn, but which, by a disposition of the Holy See, are simple in certain regions (can. 488, § 7: "sororum, religiosae votorum simplicium; monialium, religiosae votorum sollemnium aut... religiosae quarum vota ex instituto sunt sollemnia, sed pro aliquibus locis ex Apostolicae Sedis praescripto sunt simplicia").

27 *Ann. Rod.*, an. 1135, *MGH. SS.*, XVI, 711.

28 See below p. 201. Cf. objections of the Council of Trèves (1310) to beghards, can. 51 (Fredericq, *Corpus*, I, 155).

29 *De Simonia ad Beguttas* (ed. De Vreese, p. 3); quotation from Hyma, p. 25.

29a *De Simonia* (ed. De Vreese), pp. 2f.

religious." The beguine movement may be compared to the third order which, although not a full-fledged *religio*, nevertheless is a way of life that has something in common with monastic orders. Hence it merited ecclesiastical approval.[29b]

Bishop Robert de Thourote's willingness to sponsor semireligious status grew out of concern over inadequate existing orders and conviction in the intrinsic worth of "disciplined" beguines. "Those who do not reside within the enclosure of a beguinage, but live outside although they call themselves beguines and dwell among women in the manner of beguines, attired like them in a modest habit, we do not wish to favor with extraordinary privileges... Just as merchants, cloth manufacturers, bakers, brewers, fullers, weavers, and other crafts of all kinds ought to choose and establish masters, captains, or heads for their corporations, so for three beguines or more who live together in one house, there shall be a mistress."[30]

Although a formal "professio religiosa" might be avoided, some of the stricter sisterhoods approximated religious status, even with the appearance of simple vows. One hears that *"puelle votum fecerunt et se obtulerunt domino Jesu Christo"* (1272) or a beguine *"religiose vivere vult"* as long as she served God (1287).[31]

On January 7, 1421, Martin V expressed to the archbishop of Cologne his concern over conventicles of men and women who claimed to be religious but without abiding by a definite rule.[32] Although congregations are not specified, there is no doubt that this communication constitutes a criticism of the extraregulars in general. Under their pretense of piety, sectarianism and heresy germinate freely. This, of course, is merely a reiteration of fourteenth-century papal reaction. One can imagine the satisfaction with which Innocent VIII, towards the close of the fifteenth century (August 17, 1485), confirmed the profession made by the *sorores beguinae* at Mons of the Order of St. Augustine.[33] Hereby they were submitting to the "jugo religionis." Nevertheless, the dean of Christianity, delegated by Henry of Berghes, bishop of Cambrai, was to receive their vows in the face of lively opposition from the chapter of St. Waudru.[34]

[29b] *Ibid.*, pp. 29f; quotation from Hyma, pp. 25f.

[30] Philippen, *Begijnhoven*, p. 304; Nimal, *Béguinages*, p. 44.

[31] Asen, in *AHVN.*, CXI (1927), 89. See Provincial Herman von Minden's advice to Countess Bia von Regenstein in 1289 that "sive... religiosam vitam profiteamini sive foris sine obligatione qualibet maneatis" she may enjoy the benefits of the Dominican order (Finke, p. 145).

[32] Lacomblet, IV, 154, no. 132.

[33] Devillers, *Description*, II, 220-222, no. 54.

[34] On May 9, 1484, the four canonesses, accompanied by Gilles Drulin, their bailli, and other officials, tried to seize the beguinage (*ibid.*, II, 128 and note 2). Through the mediation of the duchess of Burgundy among others an agreement was reached on March 8, 1497 (*ibid.*, II, 223-225, no. 56), whereby the Black

While the beguine might be directed by or affiliated with a recognized order—particularly in accordance with the third rule—in order to meet ecclesiastical objections, and even though the beguine parish became normal as the final stage of development,[35] irrevocable vows were not prescribed. Unlike monastic status, the mode of beguinal life tended to remain informal, with individual wishes being considered. This John XXII recognized in the bull, *Racio recta non patitur*, as he sought to forestall blanket condemnation of the movement: "In multis mundi partibus sunt plurime mulieres, que similiter beghine vulgo vocate segregatim quoque in parentum hospiciis vel in suis, interdum vere in aliis aut conductis sibi communibus domibus insimul habitantes."[36] A distinctive habit evolved slowly, but uniformity was at first not its characteristic.[37] The 1323 rule of the Antwerp beguinage contains the suggestion of conformity by recommending that its members should wear modest clothes as in other Brabançon houses, in Louvain, Brussels, and Malines.[38] Attempts have also been made to derive the word *beguine* from the gray-brown color of the penitent rope of undyed wool worn by these women.[39] Description of habit is often negative: beguines are ordinarily advised what they should not wear. More simple in form and devoid of ornamentation as well as eschewing bright and mixed colors—in short, *curioso habitu et pomposo*—the early *vestis beghinalis* resembled in other respects the attire of townswomen.[40] Similarly, membership in hospital brotherhoods

Sisters retired from the beguinage and settled in a house on Rue des Juifs which came to be known as Rue des Soeurs-Noires.

[35] Philippen, *Begijnhoven*, pp. 89-126.

[36] Fredericq, *Corpus*, II, 73.

[37] For a summary of the problem consult Philippen, *Begijnhoven*, pp. 178-180; id., *Onze Begijntjes*, pp. 76-77; cf. Phillips, *Beguines in Medieval Strasburg*, p. 157. In a document of March, 1251 concerning the *curtis beghinarum* at Diest, Arnold, seigneur of Diest, concluded: "Ut quecunque religiosarum, alibi in opido nostro de Dist commorantium, supradicto tali magistro seu procuratori suo obedire noluerit, per memoratum scolthetum nostrum simili mode vestes religionis quas gesserint exuere et seculariter vivere compellantur" (cited by Philippen, in *OGE.*, III [1929], 167, note 1).

[38] Philippen, *Begijnhoven*, p. 336; statutes of Ypres (MF., IV, 254: "se elles y (i.e., Ypres) demorent que elles soient en humele habit si comme autres Beghines."

[39] Phillips, *Beguines in Medieval Strasburg*, p. 2; Philippen, *Onze Begijntjes*, pp. 76-77.

[40] Statutes of Lierre (1401), Philippen, *Begijnhoven*, p. 340, Bijl. V: "Item wat vrouwen ofts joffrouwe die opt hof comt wonen ende beghine wil sijn ende die werlec cledre daer brengd, die en sal die werlec cledre niet langer dragen dan dierste jaer bedectelec ende darenboven beghinen cledre ghecrige ende die werlec cledre vercopen of veranderen van verwen oft van maecsele." Cf. St. Trond statutes, ibid., p. 310; for Ghent, Béthune, *Cartulaire*, p. 21. The *Règle des Fins Amans* (Christ, *op. cit.*, p. 200, lines 274ff) underscored the necessity of humility and charity which should dictate "li abis communs et l'ame ordenée des religieuses." Among the women who attracted the attention of the Dominicans in the Rhineland were "pauperes sorores, hoc est mulierculas aliquas, que aliqualem habitum religionis deferebant..." The chronicler had just referred to the founding of the Penitents of Mary Magdelena. But here too is a reference to the extra-regular of beguine type

was reflected in adoption of prescribed habit, usually of plain color.[41] Robert de Thourote's rule of 1246 recommended that the superior's approval of dress should be solicited when a new recruit sought admission to the community.[42] Repressive legislation[43] and hostile public opinion[44] regarded this beguine habit as further evidence of encroachment on monastic preserves without compensation from discipline and renunciation. A beguine in the Cologne area in 1274 confessed that she wished to dedicate herself to divine service "sub veste et habitu beckinali."[45] Such dedication together with the obligation to wear a distinctive habit was thus said to be after the manner of the religious ("ut moris est religiosorum").[46] Women inmates of the hospital at Soest were instructed to dress "more begginarum."[47] To complicate inquisitorial processes in the wake of Clementine legislation was the tendency to confuse beguines with sisters of the Franciscan third order "in statu et habitu."[48] Conversely, John Gielemans, in observing that the beguines at Lens-Saint-Remy in Brabant had "recently" embraced the Augustinian rule and thus adopted regular vestment underlined the efficacy of religious habit in general as a safeguard against external dangers.[49]

Alongside monastic and mendicant orders sprang up bands of the faithful who observed chastity, poverty, and obedience and were recognized as brotherhoods or sisterhoods by the Holy See without, however, their profession producing the effects of solemn vows. Whereas the Humiliati passed from a simple confraternity to a religious order, the beguines were "rather the ancestors of societies without vows than religious congregations."[50] The real difference be-

---

(Res Alsat., MGH. SS., XVII, 234). In 1282 a beguine at Basel is reported to have worn a religious habit for thirty years (Ann. Colm. Mai., ibid., 209). About 1289 Hermann von Minden allowed Countess Bia von Regenstein to remain with Dominican nuns "in habitu viduali vel etiam in habitu beginarum cum tunica et scapulari" (Finke, p. 145). Cf. Ryckel on the Anderlecht beguines (p. 200); Tirlemont statutes (late XV C.), in Arch. f. Kulturgesch., XIV (1919), 282-284. Lady Benigna, sister of the priest of Stommeln, is described as a "habitu et actu Begina" (Acta Chr. Stumb., 279 B, (III, 14).

[41] Reicke, II, 38 and note 9 for examples from Hildesheim and Lübeck.

[42] Nimal, Béguinages, p. 53. Cf. Diest statutes (1361), Philippen, in BG. IV (1905), 337.

[43] Decree Cum de quibusdam mulieribus (1311): "...Religiose nequaquam existunt, quamquam habitum, qui Beguinarum dicitur, deferant" (Fredericq, Corpus I, 167).

[44] See below, pp. 463, 471.

[45] Asen, in AHVN. CXI (1927), 89.

[46] Ibid., 90. Compare the "puelle deo dedite et oblate" (i.e., beguines) here with the equation: "a deodata ancilla Dei"—"religiosa" in Gregory I (Ducange, Glossarium, V, 689, s.v. religiosa).

[47] Reicke, I, 288.

[48] Letter of Frederick II of Siereck, October 6, 1318 (Fredericq, Corpus, II, 75).

[49] Gielemans, Ex Novali Sanctorum (III, 6), Anec., pp. 151f.

[50] J. Creusen, "Congrégation religieuse," DDC. IV, 181-194.

tween monastic and beguinal status lay in the conception of the vows. The latter acknowledged the validity of the two precepts, chastity and obedience, but not voluntary poverty. But the beguine's obligation was ordinarily considered only temporary in nature. Observance of these two vows was conditioned by personal desire and contingent on residence. There was in the main no compulsion to abide by them except during identification with the community. According to the oldest beguine statutes of St. Trond the beguine must promise "by hare kerstelycker trouwen in stat van eede."[51] At first profession seems to have consisted only of close observance of the statutes of the beguinage during residence. But vows of temporary avoidance of marriage and simplicity of life were taken privately from the confessor or spiritual director. Both vows moreover were implicit in the promise of temporary obedience to the statutes. In any case, with voluntary or compulsory separation validity of profession disappeared.

Simple vows made without witnesses were distinguished from public profession of chastity. The hierarchy early intervened to consecrate with its authority the status of maidens and widows. As soon as religious life began to organize, admission to the cloister was accompanied by donning a habit which signified definitive consecration to God. Thus gradually developed the distinction between private and public vows—those received in the name of the church and recognized by it. To the question of validity of marriage contracted by a person who flouted the vow of virginity or chaste widowhood, popes and councils declared that the simple promise of continence did not undermine the validity of such a union. On the contrary, a vow exacted for admission to an order or confirmed by solemn consecration absolutely prohibited marriage. "Solemn profession" thus assumed a peculiar juridical meaning as opposed to the "simple vow."[52]

Although among beguines chastity sometimes took on the aspects of a cult[53] and, with the recommendation of perpetuity, consequently

---

[51] Philippen, Begijnhoven, p. 309.

[52] Creusen, in DDC. IV, 182; cf. 183. Can. 488, § 7 of Codex Juris Canonici distinguishes sorores ("religiosae votorum simplicium") and moniales ("religiosae votorum sollemnium"). See Jacques de Vitry's distinction: "Istud attendere debent moniales et virgines religiose ut malis et discolis patienciam exhibeant" (Crane, Exempla, p. 27). For the profession of Marseilles beguines, see Albanès, 257.

[53] The hagiographer delighted in the successful defense of chastity during the severe test of the sack of Liége in 1212. When maidens were unable to find refuge in the local churches, they threw themselves into the Meuse or sewers, preferring death to violation (such is Jacques de Vitry's interpretation, VMO., 548 [5]; see above, p. 43; cf. Triumphus Sancti Lamberti in Steppes, MGH. SS., XXV, 176f). The Gesta Sanctorum Villariensium (ibid., 225) omits that the honor of women was endangered by Brabançon soldiers. For the cult as Mary of Oignies envisaged it, see the extract of Vincent of Beauvais in Gesta Abb. Trud., MGH. SS., X, 392, an. 1212. Phillips (Beguines in Medieval Strasburg, p. 214) categorically denies that married women or widows were ever directly called beguines. Yet in the light of the whole Belgian evidence such a conclusion is difficult to maintain.

of a vow,[54] beguinal status did not entail unequivocable renunciation
of family life. The Bocholt beguines, whose fidelity measured up to
Johannine standards, desired to do peance "promissa continentia
vel etiam non promissa," for "in castimonia perpetua elegerimus
conservari."[55] The beguinage was a retreat, especially well adapted to
an urban society, where women living in common could pursue chastity without a vow ("ex voto vel sine voto") and earn a livelihood by
suitable work.[56] Obedience received a similar interpretation.[57] This
was a way of life which should therefore properly be termed semireligious, quasi-religious or extraregular—[58] outside the regular clergy, for
failure to endorse a monastic rule, but not altogether lay either. It
was that of other penitential groups. In turn there was a definite
tendency to equate beguine with religious not only by elastic interpretation of terms but by the conferring of similar privileges and
exemptions. The magistrates of Marsberg, by exempting the beguine
house from their jurisdiction, recognized its religious status.[59] The
life satisfied those lay folk who desired a religious retreat from the
world without absolute profession or complete severing of secular
ties or who were unable to meet the admission requirements of nunneries. The statutes often closely regulated daily life down to the
minutiae and prescribed on the basis of evangelical counsel[60] devotional exercises, the very completeness of which makes exclusively economic motivation difficult to defend. That ecclesiastical authorities
were anxious to reduce the undisciplined, independent beguines to a
minimum is demonstrated in the synodal statutes of Jean de Flandre
(February 16, 1288).[61] Admitting that beguines still live scattered
among the laity, the canon stipulates that enjoyment of beguine privileges is contingent on residence in the *curia beghinarum*.

Even after rehabilitation of the Belgian beguines under John

[54] "Greta becgina votum castitatis vovens ipsam in ecclesia nostra deo sacravimus
ut moris est religiosorum" (Asen, in *AHVN. CXI [1927]*, 89; cf. 90).
[55] *Westf. UB.* VIII, 569 (June 4, 1322).
[56] Béthune, *Cartulaire*, p. 74.
[57] 1323 statutes of Antwerp beguinage (Philippen, *Begijnhoven*, *p. 336:* "Oft
sy willen staen alsoe langhe als sy begyne syn sullen onder die gehoorsaamheyt
van haren parochiaen ende hare meesteressen ende leven na de ordinancie van
den hove..."; cf. p. 338); Robert de Thourote's recommendation, *ibid.*, pp. 308f;
Nimal, *Béguinages*, p. 49.
[58] Although not conveying exactly the same idea, see "extra religionem appro-
batam" (Council of Trèves, 1338, can. 51, Mansi, XXV, 262; Fredericq, *Corpus*, I,
188; Council of Trèves, 1310, can. 51, *ibid.*, I, 155; Council of Trèves, 1277, can.
8. *ibid.*, I, 142; *MDAC.* VII, 114; with respect to the Brothers and Sisters of the
Common Life, Fredericq, *Corpus*, II, 160ff).
[59] December 25, 1285, *Westf. UB.* IV, 858-859, no. 1860.
[60] E.g., Hoornaert, in *ASEB.* LXXII (1929), 1ff.
[61] *Statuts synodaux de Jean de Flandre, 16 fév. 1288* (ed. Schoolmeesters), p. 87,
no 19; Mansi, XXIV, 935, no. 29. This was but a continuation of Robert de Thourote's policy in 1246. However, in 1325 John XXII declared that certain beguines
were still living outside beguinages (Robert, *Les Béguines de Reims*, p. 6).

XXII and their unquestioned reconciliation with ecclesiastical authorities, the papal curia still persisted in handling them strictly as
quasi-religious or extraregulars: "Per hoc tamen statum beghinarum
et observancias huiusmodi, que sic esse permittimus, nisi de ipsis per
sedem apostolicum aliter ordinatum extiterit, nullatenus ex premissis
intendimus approbare."[62] This qualification, we have seen, was reiterated by Benedict XII,[63] Boniface IX,[64] and Clement VI, the last issuing
his decision on behalf of the beguines of St. Trond with a significant
addition to the formula: "Per hoc autem statum vestrum alias approbare nequaquam intendimus, nec etiam reprobare."[65] Adolph de la
Marck, bishop of Liége, in his commendation of orthodox beguines in
his diocese (October 24, 1324) includes an extension of this idea: Because of their righteous living, devotion, and obedience "status abolicionis
reprobarum non respicit mulieres hujusmodi *velut probas,* auctoritate
tam ordinaria quam apostolica declarando decernimus ... quod mulieres ipse ... sint in eo statu et esse pacifice permittantur absque molesta-
cione quacunque, in quo ante prohibicionem et abolicionem predictas
esse solebant ..."[66] To follow the *Codex Juris Canonici,* ecclesiastical
approbation merely signifies recommendation. That is the meaning of
the word *"probare"* in official texts. "Properly speaking, approbation is a
juridical act whereby the ecclesiastical superior (Holy See or local ordi-
naries) authorizes or officially recognizes the existence and organization of a pious association, founded by him, by the faithful, or by a
religious order."[67] We are considering here an example of how canonical legislation, coping with the religious yearnings of the laity, developed especially from the thirteenth century on as bishops and popes
approved the erection or establishment of pious associations which fall
into three categories: confraternities, third orders, and pious groups..
(*piae uniones*).[68] Beguines may be numbered among these associations
which, although not constituting an order, endeavor without public
vows but with the sanction of competent ecclesiastical authority to
promote among the members a more perfect Christian life, to perform
works of piety and charity, or to increase public worship (can. 685).
But they were more closely identified with the tertiaries "who strive
in the world and under the tempering of a religious order and in
conformity with the spirit of that order to attain Christian perfection

[62] *Racio recta non patitur* (August 13, 1318), Fredericq, *Corpus,* II, 74.

[63] E.g., bull of January 19, 1336, *ibid.,* II, 93.

[64] *Ex iniuncto* (January 7, 1394), *ibid.,* I, 254-256, no. 239.

[65] *Personas vacantes* (January 21, 1343), *ibid.,* II, 96; Straven, *Notice historique
sur le béguinage,* p. 118.

[66] Fredericq, *Corpus,* II, 87.

[67] Creusen, in *DDC.* I (1935), 1271.

[68] *Codex Juris Canonici,* II, *De personis,* tit. xviii-xix, *De fidelium association
ibus, can. 684-725;* Creusen, "Associations pieuses," *DDC.* I (1935), 1270-1285.

in a manner appropriate to secular life by practice of a rule approved
for them by the Holy See."[69]

During the discussion of the status of the Brethren of the Common
Life towards the close of the fourteenth century Everard Foec, dean
of St. Salvator church at Utrecht, agreed that without canonical prejudice men and women, belonging to free brotherhoods or sisterhoods
outside orders, might live and possess property in common, depending
on handwork for a livelihood,[70] choose superiors, confess to them, read
books of the Bible in the vernacular, and discipline one another. To
support his contention he fell back on the favorable papal decisions
relating to beguines: Clement V's *Cum de quibusdam*, John XXII's
Sancta Romana, Benedict XII's *Recta racio*, and above all Boniface
IX's *Ex iniuncto*. In conclusion the dean reminded these confraternities that although exempt from the inquisition they must secure
diocesan approbation.[71] This would meet the requirement most
recently imposed by *Ex iniuncto*.

No approbation is by itself required to create a pious association.
But it remains lay, outside the ecclesiastical framework, as long as it
has not obtained positive approval which is more than simple recommendation to which Can. 684 alludes.[72] If one takes vows either perpetually or temporarily in a religious order he cannot belong at the
same time to a third order even though he was previously enrolled in
it.[73] Approbation is an act of a competent authority, acknowledging
the existence of an association of faithful, guaranteeing moral and
spiritual values, and conferring on it certain rights. The group hereby
becomes a canonical association which renders it, although not a moral
person, capable of acquiring spiritual favors, especially indulgences
(can. 108). Yet simple approbation does not confer juridical personality in canonical circles (can. 687). This is not necessary for members
to govern themselves collectively and to acquire in the same way temporal goods. Nevertheless the association cannot appear as such in law
and its possessions are not church property.

[69] Can. 702, § 1; cf. Reinmann, *The Third Order Secular of St. Francis.*
[70] The question, "utrum sine offensa juris aliquibus extra religionem de suis
bonis temporalibus, si qua habent, ac de laboribus manuum suarum viventibus
cohabitare liceat et vivere in communi," is answered in the affirmative.
[71] Fredericq, *Corpus*, II, 160-166, no. 109; cf. nos. 110-113.
[72] Can. 686, § 1, echoing Can. 13 of the Fourth Lateran Council draws a careful
distinction between "erection" and "approval" of associations: "Nulla in Ecclesia
recognoscitur associatio quae a legitima auctoritate ecclesiastica erecta vel saltem
approbata non fuerit." Cf. can. 698, § 1: Erection is the act whereby a legitimate
superior formally decrees the constitution of a pious association into an ecclesiastical
moral person (can. 687, 100); Creusen, in *DDC.* I, 1274-1276; H. Durand, in *DDC.*
IV, 157-161.
[73] Can. 704, § 1: "Qui vota nuncupavit vel in perpetuum vel ad tempus in aliqua religione, nequit simul ad ullum tertium Ordinem pertinere, etsi eidem antea
fuerit adscriptus"; cf. § 2.

Statutes were prepared for the several beguinages, generally some time after foundation, under episcopal auspices, or through comital, ducal, or echevinal offices. The earliest rule is the one drawn up by Robert de Thourote about 1246 for the diocese of Liége, but it is really in the fourteenth century, in the period of institutionalization and justification, that they became more common. Although these statutes originally resembled the rules of the brothers and sisters who served hospitals and leper-houses, their local character must be emphasized, for never was a uniform, papal-approved rule promulgated. The above-mentioned rule was imitated within the diocese; but from diocese to diocese, and even from house to house, differences could be expected. They were only a codification of traditional customs and usages of the sisterhood for which they were granted, usually with the explicit purpose of tightening discipline and forestalling criticism. In general lines they reveal similarity, but in details discrepancies must be expected owing to the absence of congregational organization or visitatorial provision.

Representative statutes prior to 1530 include the following: Tirlemont,[74] Brussels (1271),[75] with subsequent legislation for Ter Kisten,[76] Aix-la-Chapelle (February 25, 1261),[77] Bruges (end of thirteenth century),[78] Valenciennes (1262),[79] St. Trond (fourteenth century?),[80] Courtrai (June 8, 1526),[81] Herenthals (1461–89),[82] Paris (1341),[83] Ypres (1270),[84] St. Elizabeth at Ghent,[85] Antwerp (1323),[86] Anderlecht,[87] the

[74] *Arch. f. Kulturgesch.*, XIV (1919), 280-284.

[75] May 17, 1271, original in AGR., arch. eccl., Carton 13402, no. 2; Flemish and Latin copies of XVIII C. in AAPB., Carton H. 262; ed. MF., II, 1006; Ryckel, pp. 179-182. Confirmed by Nicholas de Fontaines, bishop of Cambrai, July 13, 1272 (AGR., arch. eccl., Carton 13402, no. 3). On February 24, 1324, the day following acknowledgment of the orthodoxy of the beguines, Bishop Pierre de Levis-Mirepoix issued a vidimus for the statutes (Ryckel, pp. 179-182).

[76] June 11, 1308, orig. in AAPB., Carton B. 1452 (1); XIV C. copy, *ibid.*, B. 1460, f. 62r-62v, no. 160.

[77] Lacomblet, II, 288, no. 512.

[78] Hoornaert, "La plus ancienne règle du béguinage de Bruges," *ASEB.*, LXXII (1929), 17-79

[79] May, 1262, Figeac, *Documents historiques*, IV (Paris, 1848), 303-305; cf. Ryckel, pp. 529-531.

[80] Philippen, *Begijnhoven*, pp. 308-314; statutes of 1589, Straven, *Notice historique*, p. 163.

[81] Granted by Charles V, Van Rossum, "Documents concernant le béguinage de Courtrai," *AHEB.*, XIV (1877), 86-95, 95-98.

[82] *BG.*, 1949, pp. 200ff.

[83] Le Grand, *Les Béguines de Paris*, pp. 52-59. For the rule of the Bonnes Femmes Sainte-Avoye (1548) whom Le Grand carefully distinguishes from beguines (*ibid.*, pp. 45-49), see *ibid.*, pp. 64-67.

[84] MF. IV, 253-254.

[85] XIII C., Béthune, *Cartulaire*, pp. 17-22, no. 23.

[86] Philippen, *Begijnhoven*, pp. 336-338, Bijl. IV. For subsequent statutes see Bijl. VI, pp. 344-354 (1664); Bijl. VII, pp. 355-364 (1664, of the mistresses); Bijl. VIII, pp. 365-369 (July 27, 1689, of the *rentmeester*); Bijl. IX, pp. 370-371 (XVII C.); Bijl. XI, pp. 380 (1482, of the sacristan); Bijl. XIV, pp. 397-402 (of the Holy Ghost

Fins Amans in Picardy,[88] Cantimpré at Mons,[89] three convents in
Strasbourg: Turm,[90] Innenheim,[91] and Offenburg,[92] Lierre (1401),[93]
Diest,[94] Tongres,[95] Tournai,[96] Wesel,[97] Gerrits Lams beguinage at
Leiden (1403),[98] Amsterdam (1393),[99] the *puelle parve domus* at
Bocholt (June 4, 1322),[100] Gouda (February 22, 1396),[101] St. Christo-
pher at Liege,[102] and Worms (December 22, 1288).[103]

The statutes delegated supervision of the community to a *magistra*
or *grootmeesteres* who was elected by the sisters either freely or with
the cooperation of the pastor assigned to them by the magistrates or
the cleric, usually a Dominican or Franciscan, under whose direction
they stood. The statutes for the Bocholt community were drawn up,
in acknowledgment of the saving clause of the bull *Cum de mulieribus*
(December 31, 1320), by the ten beguines and sealed by the local

Table, XVI C.); Bijl. XIII, pp. 391-396 (of the beguine school, early XIX C.);
Bijl. XV, pp. 403-406 (of the mistress of the infirmary of the beguinage, 1590); Bijl.
XVI, pp. 407-410 (of the *kinderen* of the beguine infirmary, XVII C.); Bijl. XVIII,
pp. 414-416 (of the convent Sion, XVI C.); Bijl. XIX, pp. 417-421 (of the convent
New Jerusalem, 1590); Bijl. XX, pp. 422-424 (St. Barbara foundation, XVII C.).

[87] There is a paucity of documents for the early history of the Anderlecht beguinage dating from a foundation by the dean of the chapter of St. Pierre in
June, 1252 (MF. II, 998). The "ouden regulen van den Begynen tot Anderlecht"
were approved by the chapter of canons on June 23 and July 9, 1611 (AGR., arch.
eccl., no. 268; cf. J. Lavalleye, "Le béguinage d'Anderlecht," *Folklore Brabançon*,
X [1930], 33-35)

[88] Christ, *La Règle des Fins Amans*, pp. 173-213.

[89] Devillers, *Description*, II, 175-176; id., *Annales*, VI, 253-254. For a supplementary rule, presumably of the XIV C., see Devillers, *Description*, II, 211-217, no. 51;
id., *Annales*, VI, 289-295.

[90] April 12, 1276, *UB. Strasb.*, III, 27-28, no. 78.

[91] April 14, 1276, *ibid.*, III, 29, no. 79.

[92] May 4, 1276, *ibid.*, III, 30, no. 81.

[93] Philippen, *Begijnhoven*, pp. 339-343, Bijl. V.

[94] Latin statutes of St. Catherine "ten Velde" at Diest, April 1, 1361, Philippen,
in *BG.*, IV (1905), 327-335; for a Flemish rule, undated, but of the XV C., *ibid.*,
335-339. Cf. Statutes of the noviciate, 1627, id., *Begijnhoven*, pp. 382-390, Bijl. XII.

[95] Thijs, in *BSSLL.*, XV (1881), 439-444, no. 11 (May 3, 1353; approved by
Engelbert on May 10); October 7, 1453, *ibid.*, 451-470, no. 15.

[96] Delannoy, *Notice historique des divers hospices de Tournai* (Tournai. 1880),
p. 139.

[97] Analysis by Heidemann, in *Zeitschrift des bergischen Geschichtsvereins*, IV
(1867), 91-92 (December 11, 1326); 94 (July 11, 1309) for Convent auf dem Sande
(*super arenam*); text and summary of statutes for Mariengarten beguinage,*ibid.*,
103-109.

[98] *Kerkelijken Historie en Outheden der zeven vereenigde Provinciën*, III
(Leiden, 1726), 855.

[99] *Ibid.*, IV (1726), 200.

[100] *Westf. UB.*, VIII, 569-570, no. 1566.

[101] Van Mieris, *Groot Charterboek*, III, 638-639.

[102] 1246, Nimal, *Béguinages*, pp. 43-56; Philippen, *Begijnhoven*, pp. 303-308;
undated rule (belongs to reign of Jean de Hornes, 1484-1505), *AHEB.*, XXIII (1892),
82-88; cf. *Statuta Beghinarum Parochiae S. Christophori prope Leodium*, 1325
(Coens, *Disquisitio historica*, pp. 12-13; cited by Philippen, *Begijnhoven*, p. 199,
note 1).

[103] *UB. Worms*, I, 286-291, no. 438.

Dominican prior and echevins. Although none of the women named is designated *magistra,* it provided that rules for the houses must be established by the *maior pars et senior.*[104] At Tirlemont each house with two or more beguines was to have a mistress. As means to achieve the desired perfection and harmony, the statutes prescribed chastity, obedience to the house rules and to the superior, simplicity of life, abstention from dancing and dissolute songs, penalties for recalcitrance, curbs on incursions into the outside world, avoidance of the opposite sex—ordinarily any male over ten, but seven might also be critical—reading of the hours of the Virgin, daily attendance of mass, recitation of a certain number of Paternosters, and attendance at chapter or public confession.[105] The parish church (soon equated with the beguinage) was the meeting place of the members who, like other parishioners, remained subject to the local pastor. "De mulieribus que begine vocantur statuimus, ut plebano in cujus morantur parochia obedientiam faciant et ei in omnibus obediant sicut coeteri parochiales."[106] The primitive rule of the Bruges community even stipulated that care of the sick in the city depended on permission of the grand mistress, with further restriction to relatives and certain friends, and then only in cases of public necessity.[107]

Far from forming a well-defined, well-organized intercommunal movement, the beguinages were each completely self-contained; in the absence of a motherhouse and a single rule, each community regulated its own order of existence.[108] Some beguines lived at home with their families; others worked for their livelihood; some enjoyed substantial income, reflecting patrician origins, while others lived unattached lives, begging for subsistence. Just as all forms of female occupation and all classes of society were represented among the beguines, spiritual interests and affiliations appear to have been equally diverse. Piety found expression in rites conducted by the secular clergy, in special dependence on the mendicant orders, in religious devotion to voluntary poverty, and even in adherence to heterodox doctrine.[109] In spite of diversity, however, a semblance of uniformity among Flemish beguines may be found in a more or less common

[104] *Westf. UB.,* VIII, 569; cf. Tirlemont rule, in *Arch. f. Kulturgesch., XIV* (1919), 281.

[105] Cf. Philippen, *Begijnhoven,* pp. 78-83, 131.

[106] Synod of archbishop of Magdeburg, 1266, Hartzheim, III, 800.

[107] "Sonder der groter meestrigghen orlof so ne salmen gheen kind ... sieken te dienne in die port, ende dat sal syn vleescheliken maghen jof sonderlinghen vrienden. Ende dat sal syn nomen mynet mach ende in zeker stat ende omme openbare sake" (Hoornaert, in *ASEB.,* 1929, pp. 19-20).

[108] For an example of legislation for a whole archdiocese see the statutes promulgated by the archbishop of Malines in 1588 (Philippen, *Begijnhoven,* pp. 315-328, Bijl. II).

[109] Phillips, *Beguines in Medieval Strasburg,* p. 213.

purpose, dictated in part by similar economic and social conditions, but more particularly in a common Christian heritage whose ideals do not appear to have been as frequently subject to perversion as in the Rhineland. Such loose organization and inadequate leadership or visitatorial system nevertheless made it easy to confuse extraregular associations, despite favors and protection extended by princes and bishops, with the wide-spread, but ill-defined Rhenish sectaries known as the Brothers and Sisters of the Free Spirit.[110]

Wills of the thirteenth and fourteenth centuries frequently stipulate legacies contingent on the embracing or maintaining of beguinal status, thus underlining at once its temporary nature and socioeconomic importance. The beguine Aleydis, daughter of Gobelin Bolant von Nettesheim, provided in her testament of February 8, 1298, that if her sister Gertrude survived her and remained a *becgina sive virgo* the Cistercian abbey of Altenberg should pay her a pension. But as soon as Gertrude married or lost her virginity, the monastery was no longer obligated to her.[111] Here is a good example of how beguine was equated with chastity. The beguine, Mella de Scarmure, in March, 1272, left 35 *virgae* of land at Henis to the Holy Ghost Table at Tongres on condition that it pay annually to her niece Oda de Henis, if she became a beguine, one hogshead of rye of the measure of Tongres. When she willed another 18 *virgae* at Berg to the same Table, she reserved their usufruct to one of the daughters of her uncle Lambert de Henis, if she became a beguine, with the further stipulation that half a hogshead should be paid annually to the daughter of Ghisel de Huselt if the latter became and remained a beguine.[112] Finally Mella willed to the poor beguines 15 more *virgae* at Recstrothe, charged with a rent in behalf of the court of Coninxhem, and 10 *virgae* near Berg, similarly obligated in behalf of Walter, knight of Betuis, on condition that Otilia de Henis and her sisters receive annually half a hogshead of rye, Perone and Elizabeth, daughters of the late Ar., knight of Betuis, and Silla, daughter of Agnes of Berg, half a hogshead each, and Margaret de Gudegoven two, provided they remained beguines.[113] In like fashion the priory of Oignies granted for life to Emma d'Aiseau the beguine house that had belonged successively to Hawide de Charnoit and Hawide le Gehotte unless she married, received suspected persons, or had a prolonged absence from the beguinage ("vel a beginagio de Oignies causa morandi recesserit").[114] In a will dated March 30, 1288, Clementia de Sancto Spiritu, beguine of Tongres, abandoned

---

[110] Moll, *Kerkgeschiedenis*, II, 3, 59-73; Haupt, in *ZKG.*, VII (1885), 503ff.
[111] *UB. Altenberg*, p. 341.
[112] Thijs, in *BSSLL.*, XV (1881), 290.
[113] *Ibid.*, 291.
[114] October, 1283, *ASAN.*, XXXI (1912), 237, no. 235.

the room alongside her own to her servant Metta with the understanding that she become a beguine.[115] On May 31, 1298, Catherine of
St. John, beguine of Tongres, left one half of 13 *virgae* to Notre-Dame
at Tongres, and the other half to the Holy Ghost Table, setting aside
for the priest Jean Joye the usufruct of half a hogshead of rye to be
paid by the Table; after his death this usufruct was to be enjoyed
by her daughter Catharina if she became a beguine.[116]

Even as those who lived outside the beguinage were expected to
wear a habit different from that of the inmates, so a beguine who left
the community or was expelled was forbidden to wear the approved
habit (*habitum beghinalem*).[117] Although never achieving recognition
as an order in the eyes of canon law, this extraregular status did entail
privileges and exemptions ordinarily conferred on religious bodies.
Moreover, to engage in business yielding more than ten marks meant
exclusion from beguine privilege at Liége and liability to customary
exactions.[118] At the same time the Diest statutes of 1361 forbade the
inmates of St. Catherine beguinage from claiming pre-emptive power
over its goods or offering her own property for usury.[119]

Full footing in the community depended on the successful completion of a period of probation, the duration of which differed from time
to time and from place to place, but which from the seventeenth century was fixed at two years.[120] This novitiate must be spent in one of
the convents or under the eye of a senior member. While the statutes of
Leiden (1403) refer only to a one-year probation, the Amsterdam
communities (1393) demanded one or one and a half years.[121] According to the thirteenth-century rules of St. Elizabeth at Ghent, novices
donned the habit after one year with profession following a year
later.[122] At first profession, which opened up the privileges of the
society, seems to have included here only obedience to the statutes.
Observance of chastity was understood, but the vow to continence,
although sometimes recommended with a vengeance that resembled
Catharist austerity, was taken privately at the hands of the confessor
or superior. This promise was executed by embracing beguinal exist-

---

[115] Thijs, in *BSSLL.*, XV (1881), 296.
[116] *Ibid.*, 311-312.
[117] Diest (April 1, 1361), *BG.*, IV (1905), 333.
[118] Mansi, XXIV, 935, no. 29: "Praeterea omnes beghinas negotiatrices vel
mercatrices manifestas amplius quam marchatum in negotiationibus habentes, a
privilegiis beghinarum excludimus, nec eas a solutione cotorum seu exactionum
volumus esse liberas. Alias autem in curiis commorantes declaramus ad praemissa
non teneri."
[119] Diest (1361), *BG.*, IV (1905), 329: "Item quod nulla ipsarum faciat aliquas de
aliquibus bonis preemptiones nec bona sua ad usuram exponat vel det que vulgariter dicitur te dachghoede..."
[120] Philippen, *Begijnhoven*, pp. 169-172.
[121] *Ibid.*, pp. 169-170.
[122] Béthune, *Cartulaire*, pp. 18-19.

ence. The triple obligation is well defined by the oldest statutes of St. Elizabeth at Ghent[123] as: (1) obedience to the grand mistress and conventual superiors;[124] (2) continence during affiliation with the community; and (3) a state of righteousness as a prerequisite for the enjoyment of temporal goods. In the beginning profession was very simple, but in the period of minute regulations and close discipline an elaborate ceremony developed.[125]

The essence of semireligious or extraregular life was thus provided by the informal character of profession. Yet a distinct tendency toward monastic prescription can often be detected, whether to safeguard morals or to strengthen the well-being of the house. If a beguine severed connections for marriage or without her superior's knowledge, she lost her right to claim what she had paid either as dowry or for lodging.[126] The beguinage was particularly anxious to retain full title to houses built within the enclosure.[127] When the Lübeck beguine Greteke Berghes left the Kranen convent in 1434, she renounced before her superiors her prebend, lodging, and the amount that had been paid at the time of her entrance pro prebenda."[128] In the beguine convents at Strasbourg each member was expected to possess sufficient independent means. Those under fourteen serving the year's probation were allowed to depart freely and to reclaim their property, but they were expected to pay their expenses at the rate of 40 d. for each month spent in the house. Older ones who left after agreeing to obey must relinquish all goods except clothes and bedding. On the other hand, if one left with the intention of entering a nunnery (claustrum), she was entitled to five pounds from the property she had brought with her. If a sister suffered a lapse of the flesh, was convicted of familiarity with a man, failed to avoid a suspected companion although admonished three or four times, disobeyed her mistress, or proved quarrelsome, she was expelled without taking anything except the clothes she was wearing. If the community dissolved, the common property was to be divided equitably.[129] A few years later (October 5, 1285) beguines who fell into poverty were allowed to sell their houses.[130]

The nature of the testament and the conditions under which it was

---

[123] Ibid., p. 19; cf. statute of Lierre (1401), Philippen, Begijnhoven, pp. 340-341, Bijl. V.
[124] Ibid., p. 305; cf. Christ, Règle des Fins Amans, p. 200, line 265; pp. 202-203, lines 333-379.
[125] E.g., Philippen, Begijnhoven, pp. 174-178.
[126] Cf. Rücklin, Religiöses Volksleben, p. 139.
[127] De Ridder, in Bull. cercle arch ... Malines, XLII (1937), 27 (June 3, 1278); cf. statutes of Lierre, Philippen, Begijnhoven, p. 340.
[128] Hartwig, in Hansische Geschichtsblätter, XIV (1908), 83.
[129] Strasb. UB., III, 27.
[130] Ibid., III, 61, no. 189.

to be prepared are fully described in the statutes of Herenthals (cap. 30).[131] Each beguine who is eligible to do so should make her will before relatives and witnesses within six weeks after admission for the disposal of all her goods. They reserved the right to recall, increase, diminish, and change after their wishes. Those who are unable to do this at the time they are received are obliged to comply within six weeks after eligibility. The beguines must provide in their wills before they die for the church which is very poor, for their lodging, light, wine etc., and for the Holy Ghost according to their condition. They must also remember the infirmary as is the "good old custom." Each beguine who receives alms from the proceeds of the Holy Ghost Table shall leave to it all her remaining goods as is done at Malines and elsewhere. Those who receive half their income from it should reimburse the Table with an equal amount. If something is willed to the church without specification of its use, the church will receive two-thirds for maintenance while the sacristan will get one-third for light, wine, bread, etc.

In conclusion, the statutes stipulated that admission to a beguinage was contingent on irreproachable conduct. The parents of the novice agreed to pay an entrance fee, furnish the room or house assigned to their daughter, and ensure a sufficient income to provide for the needs of the new beguine. Should she, in spite of such precautions, lose her property or be prevented by age or illness from earning a livelihood, the association granted relief and received her in the infirmary. The institution thus tended to resemble a retreat for independent widows or superfluous daughters of well-to-do burghers or a refuge for the dispossessed.

Although strict claustration is not often associated with the beguinage, the statutes make it clear that the inhabitants were not to absent themselves without permission from the superiors: they must abide by well-defined regulations governing the days and hours of departure and return, the companions on these sorties, and association with men and boys. Any claim that visitation and care of the sick, distribution of aid to the poor, manual work suitable to their sex, and instruction to children were all individual acts and not a duty imposed by their status, rests on insufficient analysis of beguine rules.

---

131 *BG.*, 1949, pp. 219-220; cf. statutes of Beguinage of Ypres (MF., IV, 254).

IV

Apostolic Poverty

The concept *vita apostolica*,[1] rendered particularly pregnant from the age of Gregorian Reform onwards, embraced three basic principles: imitation of the primitive church, poor, simple, and humble *(secundum formam primitivae ecclesiae)*, a passionate love for souls at home and far afield *(zelus et salus animarum)*, and finally, evangelical poverty and the common life, frequently mitigated, however, by the work of one's own hands *(labor manuum suarum)*.[2] It was a compelling program instinct with the fervor and spontaneity of the New Testament. Although it was equated in the time of Peter Damian and afterwards with the *vita canonica*, its appeal eventually was to be largely lay. It is significant that devotion to the apostolic life coincided with the communal movement and the more lively participation of townsmen in matters of faith.

The numerous new canonical congregations abiding by the Augustinian rule, on the one hand, and the often poorly organized but vigorous penitential and semireligious confraternities and associations, on the other, subscribed to these principles with varying degrees of emphasis and by divers methods The response could be orthodox, exacting submission to the hierarchy and the sacraments of the

---

[1] Mandonnet, *Saint Dominique*, II, 167-192; Philippen, *Het Ontstaan der Begijnhoven*, pp. 23-33; Mens, *Oorsprong*, pp. 16-95; Dickinson, *Origins of the Austin Canons*, pp. 7-90; Grundmann, *Religiöse Bewegungen, passim;* consult Van Rooijen, *Theodorus van Celles* for a case study.

[2] Jacques de Vitry signalized such work as characteristic of several forms of regular and extraregular life: Cistercians *(Hist. Occid.,* p. 300); Benedictine nuns *(Sermo XXVII, Ad moniales nigras,* in Pitra, *Anal. Nov.,* II, 375); Val-des-Choux *(Hist. Occid.,* p. 308); Humiliati *(ibid.,* p. 335; Ep. I [October 1216], *ZKG.,* XIV, 102; cf. Zanoni, *Gli Umiliati,* pp. 58-63, 109f); Friars Minor ("qui ad opus aliorum propriis manibus laborant, vel fidelium eleemosynas deportant," *Sermo XXXV, Ad Fratres Minores,* in Pitra, *Anal. Nov.,* II, 400; but compare the picture in *Hist. Occid.,* pp. 349-354); early Franciscan women (Ep. I, *ZKG.,* XIV, 104); *mulieres sanctae,* the prototype of the beguines *(VMO.,* 547 F); consult the *exemplum* of the poor layman "qui, propriis manibus laborando, victum tenuem omni die sibi acquirebat, nec ei plusquam cenaret quicquam remanebat" (Pitra, *Anal. Nov.,* II, 389; Crane, *Exempla,* p. 27); John of Wambaix, a "devotus et religiosus laycus" (Greven, *Exempla,* p. 5) for agricultural workers, *Sermo LX* (Pitra, II, 435).

Church, or heterodox, premised on the conviction that even if that
hierarchy were able to cleanse itself and assume effective leadership
its prerogatives and functions could still be challenged. Laymen, seeking to implement the program—the term is used here advisedly—therefore usurped the office which the hierarchy claimed as its prerogative,
namely preaching and teaching.

No matter what form the religious excitement of the medieval
reformation took as it tackled spiritual matters or socioeconomic
grievances, the *vita apostolica* was a way of life, sometimes defying
close definition, but nonetheless essentially religious in character.
Whoever its spokesmen might be, the gospels remained the fountainhead from which it derived its vitality. Some unity of purpose might
be found, first, in the will to enrich and freshen by evangelical counsel
spirituality and liturgy, already endangered by formalism, and secondly, as the secular clergy became more hopelessly enmeshed in temporal
affairs and monachism decayed, in reform of the ecclesiastical order.
Even if objectives were at first much the same, the paths to achieve
them led in widely different directions. In an effort to commune
directly with God, liturgy and hierarchy might be repudiated. To
implement the *vita apostolica* a premium was put on vernacular
preaching and biblical translation.

But one of the thorniest questions was the scope of voluntary
poverty. It touched too many vested interests and was basically romantic. Total renunciation of personal and corporate property, in imitation of Christ, was the solution most cogently proposed by St. Francis of Assisi. Jacques de Vitry observed with more than casual delight
how effectively the Poverello's immediate disciples emulated the poverty and humility of the primitive church, seeking to reproduce
the *vita apostolica* through self-denial, and how faithfully they followed, in their nakedness, the naked Christ.[3] Property entails subser-
vience to secular interests and compromise with original intent. The
officium praedicationis is incompatible with wealth. But Francis'
answer to the world's ills, premised on the spiritual recreation of man
through total renunciation, was impractical, doomed to failure from
the outset.[4] Nevertheless the *vita apostolica* did at once enjoin a
thorough reform of institutional religion and a reorientation of clerical functions, predicated on the dispensability of temporal possessions,
and recommend on the personal plane a daily livelihood derived from
individual labor.

[3] Jacques de Vitry, *Hist. Occid.*, p. 350. He ordinarily associates the primitive
church with the Franciscans (*ibid.*, p. 349; Ep. I, *ZKG.*, XIV, 104; Ep. VI, *ibid.*, XVI
83); cf. *Sermo XXXVIII, Ad fratres ordinis militaris* (Pitra, *Anal. Nov.*, II, 414);
Thomas of Cantimpré, *BUA.*, I, 2, 1 (p. 10); I, 13, 1 (p. 50).

[4] Cf. Ray C. Petry, *Francis of Assisi, Apostle of Poverty* (Duke University Press,
Durham, N.C., 1941).

The claims of evangelical poverty could be met either by mendicancy or observance of the Pauline injunction of *labor manuum*.[5] Beguines and beghards took both paths. Apart from deviations of piety a common charge hurled by opponents was mendicancy. As a peculiarity of this ascesis, it was considered a symptom of moral turpitude. The first error of "bechardorum et begutarum de voluntaria paupertate," runs one indictment,[6] is their belief in the excellence of begging after the example of Christ and the Apostles. Their experiment in communism rested on a simple formula before which all objections and grievances must dissolve. The mendicant orders too shared abuse on similar grounds from champions of hierarchical solidarity and the status quo. "Periculum est in mendicando," was Guillaume de Saint-Amour's verdict.[7] Mendicancy, in short, is the solvent of moral integrity and social values alike. But the Paris master's demand that begging should be countenanced only among the needy was officially rejected in 1256. Religious idealism suffices to justify its practice. Thomas Aquinas agreed that one who appeals to sentiment in order to humble himself or to set a good example for others does nothing extraordinary.[8] "Non modo religiosis, sed omnibus ad humilitatis assumptionem et exemplum mendicare licet."[9]

Manual work, on the contrary, was an essential ingredient of Christian asceticism; *opus manuum, opus Dei,* and *lectio divina* constituted the triple monastic occupation. From the apostolic age labor had been incorporated into religious life to discipline the body, to stir it out of lethargy, and to destroy the appetites and urges which find in it their origin and nourishment. Manual work, accordingly, is a form of mortification; it permits a dedication of physical powers to divine service. As a prerequisite for daily livelihood it serves as an equalizer by instilling a sense of humility.[10] For semireligious associations the injunction to work was equally essential in the pursuit of penitential life.

[5] I. Thes. II, 7-11; I Cor. IV, 12; cf. Acts, XVIII, 1-4; XX, 34; Eph. IV, 28.

[6] Haupt, in *ZKG.*, XII (1891), 88f.

[7] Denzinger, *Ench. Symb.*, p. 200; see below, p. 458.

[8] Thomas Aquinas, *Contra Impugnantes Dei Cultum et Religionem*, Cap. V: *An religious teneatur manibus laborare (Op. omn.*, XV, Parma, 1864, pp. 23-29, esp. 25); cf. Schröder, in *NAK.*, XVIII (1925), 129f; Thomas of Cantimpré, *BUA.*, II, 10, 7 (pp. 160-163).

[9] Cf. Thomas Aquinas, *ST.*, III, qu. 40, 3; II, 2, q. 19. 12.

[10] Delatte, *Commentaire*, pp. 346-354, esp. 347; Benedict, *Reg.*, cap. 48, *PL.*, LXVI, 703f; Pachomius, *Regula*, 5, 7, *PL.*, XXIII, 65f; Basil, *Regulae brevius tractatae, interrog.* 69, *PG.*, XXXI, 1131; *Regulae fusius tractatae, interrog.* 37, 41, *ibid.*, 1009, 1021; John Chrysostom, *In Matth. homil. VIII, PG.*, LVII, 87; *De sacerd., PG.*, XLVIII, 682; Jerome, *Ep. CXXV, ad Rusticum monach.*, no. 11, *PL.*, XXII, 1078f; *Ep. CXXX, ad Demetriadem*, no. 15, *ibid.*, 1119; Augustine of Hippo, *De Opere monachorum*, cap. 29, *PL.*, XL., 576; Thomas of Cantimpré, *BUA.*, I, 15, 1-2 (pp. 55f); II, 6, 2-3 (pp. 146f); II, 8, 1 (pp. 152f); I, 9, 1-2 (pp. 154f); II, 10, 2 (pp. 156f); cf. E. Dublanchy, "Ascétisme," *DTC.*, I, 2055-2077.

Since idleness is hostile to the soul and the chief cause and promoter of sin, and since hand work, when carried on industriously and devoutly, is, alongside the word of the prophet, useful for avoiding sin, all brothers, priests and laymen, by eschewing pernicious idleness outside divine office, will devote themselves at the behest of the minister to sacred duties as well as ordinary functions in the cell or in other work-rooms of the convent for the common good. Except during meals, each and all brothers will try to fulfil faithfully the task imposed on them by the love of him who renders to each his own according to his work. The minister will carefully denounce lukewarm and negligent work and will impose for such labor appropriate penance in chapter until they make amends. The brothers will take care to avoid in the workroom and other rooms in the convent, at times when they are allowed to speak, all harmful or infamous words which might upset or disgrace anyone . . . Those who are unable to work ought to be supported by the charity of all. But beware that they be received easily in convents and the order.

This recommendation for *labor manuum* in the 1487 statutes of the Zepperen brethren of the third order of St. Francis[11] is echoed, at least in spirit, in many a beguine rule. Not only does one obtain a liveli-hood by work, claim the primitive statutes of Bruges, but by it he may do penance as well as avoid temptation and foibles which lead the soul astray.[12] Beguines were held in high esteem by Bishop Grosseteste of Lincoln because they lived, not like mendicants on alms, but from the fruits of their own labor—thus they represented nothing short of the highest degree of Christian perfection.[13] That poverty and *labor manuum* were not mutually exclusive is admirably brought by Jacques de Vitry when, in his preface to the *Vita Mariae Oigniacensis,* he addresses the bishop of Toulouse on the *mulieres sanctae* of the diocese of Liege.

For you have seen, and rejoiced, in the lily gardens of the Lord many bands of holy virgins in different places who, spurning carnal pleasures for the sake of Christ and contemning the riches of the world for desire of the kingdom of heaven, cleave to the heavenly Bridegroom in poverty and humility and seek their slender fare by the work of their hands, although their parents have abundance, Yet, forgetting relatives and home, they prefer to bear hardships and poverty than to loll in ill-gotten riches or to remain in danger among the proud and pompous of the world. You have seen with exultation holy matrons serving God,—the great zeal with which they guard the modesty of maidens and instruct them with wholesome warnings in order that they may desire only the heavenly Spouse. Widows, too, through fasts and prayers, in vigils and hand work, in tears and supplication, serve the Lord; just as earlier

[11] Cap. XIX, Daris, *Notices,* XIII, 104. Cf. 1361 Diest statutes, *BG.,* IV (1905), 329f; Institutes of the Sisters of St. Sixtus at Rome, cap. 20: *De labore (labores manuum tuarum)* (Simon, p. 152); Fredericq, *Corpus,* II, 16off.

[12] Hoornaert, in *ASEB.,* LXXII (1929), 75.

[13] Thomas of Eccleston, *Liber de Adventu Fratrum Minorum in Angliam, MGH. SS.,* XXVIII, 568: "Begine sunt perfectissime et sanctissime religionis, quia vivunt propriis laboribus et non onerant exaccionibus mundum." Cf. Matthew Paris, *ibid.,* 449.

they tried to please their husbands in the flesh, so now they strive to please the heavenly Bridegroom in the spirit. They often recall the words of the Apostle: The widow who lives in pleasure is dead, but holy widows who answer the needs of the saints, wash the feet of the poor, grant hospitality, and stress deeds of mercy, well deserve the sixtieth fruit.[14]

Here emphasis is put on the two cardinal objectives of beguine life: chastity or continence and renunciation of worldly goods offset by hand work. The former has been considered elsewhere.

It is an incontrovertible fact that in the days of spontaneity and joyousness[15] the Belgian beguines, like Cistercian nuns and *conversae* and lay affiliates of the mendicant orders, generally came from families of substance and affluence and not from the lower classes. The Clarisses and friars of Umbria must have reminded Jacques de Vitry during his journey to the papal curia in 1216 of Mary of Oignies and her coterie.[16] This renunciation of wealth was found not only among the disinherited but among the very classes that enjoyed economic well-being. From an Old French fragment which contains a paraphrase of Tobit it is clear that some beguins and beguines thought of themselves as the fathers and mothers of the poor.[17] Theirs is the way of life that a certain maiden of Nivelles pursued when she entered a nunnery of that province and there "supported herself with the work of her hands, and spent all her spare time in prayer and fasting."[18] Embedded in Mary's biography is a brief but highly significant description of her at work: while she applied her hand deftly as her fingers clutched the spindle, she kept the psalter propped up in front of her and softly recited psalms.[19] The formula, *labore manuum,* is more closely defined by Gautier de Coincy who about 1220 wrote that the despised beguines

> Vilain mestier et ort aprenent,
> Quant il la laissent et lui prenent,
> Il font assez de putes oevres.[20]

Since discreet and devout maidens do not find it suitable to remain in their parents' homes among secular-minded and shameless persons with-

[14] *VMO.,* prol., 547 (3).
[15] Although it is pre-eminently the first-generation Franciscans whose aims and spirit under the guidance of the Testament deserve to be described "ut simul in Domino gaudeant et epulentur" (Jacques de Vitry's Ep. I, *ZKG.,* XIV., 104), nevertheless this semireligious movement in the north, particularly the feminine branch, betrays the same traits.
[16] *Ibid.,* 103-104; *AFH.,* XIX, 546; cf. Greven, *Anfänge,* pp. 64f.
[17] Hilka, in *Zeitschrift f. rom. Philologie,* XLVII (1927), 160.
[18] CHD., IV, 84 (ed. Strange, I, 251).
[19] *VMO.,* 553 A (26); Clarissa Leonard, too, lived with the mistress of the Malines beguines "ubi didicit legere psalterium et sartire linea vestimenta" (Gielemans, *Anec.,* p. 436). Cf. *V. Elizabeth, filiae regis Hungariae et dominae Thuringiae* (CCHB. I, 1, 407).
[20] Barbazan and Méon, *Fabliaux et Contes,* I, 310, vss. 1227ff.

out grave danger, they take refuge nowadays in monasteries ... But those
who are unable to find monasteries which will receive them live together
in a single house ... Under the discipline of one who excels the others
in integrity and foresight, they are instructed in manners and letters,
in vigils and prayers, in fasts and various torments, in manual work and
poverty, in self-effacement and humility. For we see many who, scorning
the riches of their parents and rejecting the noble and wealthy husbands
offered them, live in profound poverty, having naught else but what
they can acquire by spinning and working with their hands, content
with shabby clothes and modest food.[21]

This pregnant passage from the pen of Jacques de Vitry contains the
kernel of the nascent beguine movement.

It was therefore characteristic of the beguinage from the outset to
combine the *vita contemplativa* and appropriate devotional exercises
with a practical solution of daily problems. The beguine customarily
engaged in weaving, spinning, carding, charitable activity, sewing, and
the education of children. Before the fourteenth century, however, the
religious character of *labor manuum* was yielding to the harsh fact
of economic necessity.[22] The 1328 memorandum for the Ghent beguinage, by clearly recognizing the socioeconomic motives back of beguinal life, even at the outset, admitted the poverty of its inmates.
Instead of becoming a burden to others, they worked every day under
a *magistra operum* with their hands, particularly in weaving and the
washing sent to them from the city.[23] In 1463 the sisters at Lübeck
were also expected to earn their livelihood by handwork: "Quod ... in
communi viventes de operibus manuum vestrarum vitam ducatis."[24]
About 1452 beguines in Herenthals were wont to come to the home of
Mary of Lille, a beguine from Diest, to sew and spin for the poor.[25]
The *Miracles de Saint Louis* describes beguines who offset poverty
through the carding of wool.[26] In many German foundation documents mendicancy was expressly forbidden; certain houses might admit women who had begged in order to protect them from continuing the practice.[27] When Reinbold von Achenheim, who had sat on
the Strasbourg council, and his wife converted their house on July 18,
1332, into a dwelling for twelve poor women, they were cautioned not
to beg or to engage in noisy work. The founders also reserved for
themselves the appointment of sisters until their death, at which time
this right would devolve on the guardian of the Friars Minor.[28]

21 Greven, in *HJ.*, XXXV (1914), 46f.
22 E.g., statutes of Tirlemont beguinage: "...Ne forte bona pauperum dicte
curie propter multitudinem beghinarum receptarum et depauperatarum ad susten-
tacionem non sufficiant earundem" (*Arch. f. Kulturgesch.*, XIV, 1919, 284).
23 Béthune, *Cartulaire*, p. 74; Fredericq, *Corpus*, I, 176.
24 Hartwig, in *Hansische Geschichtsblätter*, XIV (1908), 87f.
25 Gielemans, *Anec.*, p. 419.
26 Bouquet, XX, 168f.
27 Cf. Schmidt, in *Alsatia*, 1858-1860, p. 153.
28 *UB. Strass.*, VII, 2, no. 4.

Margaret, widow of William Cassart, donated 1 bonnier of allodial land at Carevelt to the chaplain of the beguines of La Vigne at Brussels and their infirmary. The infirmary, after receiving 5 s. annually from the fruits of this property in compensation for its labor, was to distribute the rest of the income to thirty poorer inmates at the discretion of the rector.[29] Shortly after, the infirmary was described as holding ½ bonnier of land from the hospital of Terbank at Louvain as a "beghinarum pauperum conservatrix."[30] While the statutes of March 17, 1271, put a premium on the financial independence of those beguines who were able to build houses with their own means, they also took cognizance of the "poor beguines" who must rely on assistance. The dual purpose of the beguinage—to provide a spiritual retreat for the economically independent and a refuge for the dispossessed—is therefore further emphasized here by the contrast of proprietorship with *communia bona* or *bona infirmarie*.[31] Since the inmates were early described as leading a common life,[32] it is not surprising that Duchess Jeanne of Brabant in her privilege to the infirmary (December 8, 1372) acknowledged that "cum a longis temporibus in infirmaria curtis beghinarum de Vinea Bruxellensis mulieres devote pauperes et debiles que de suis propriis facultatibus sustentari nequeunt recepte fuerunt hospitate."[33] The chartrier and cartulary of the infirmary frequently make specific mention of "pauperibus beghinis,"[34]

[29] June, 1258 (orig., AAPB. H. 270 [1], Molenbeek-Carevelt; XIV C. copy, AGR. 13403, f. 85v, no. 163).

[30] January, 1263/4 (XIV C. copy, AAPB. B. 1460, f. 1v, no. 1).

[31] May 17, 1271 (orig., AGR. 13402, no. 2; MF., II, 1006); see below, p. 483.

[32] Hugh of St. Cher's protection letter, July 10, 1254 (Ryckel, pp. 178f); November 6, 1254 (orig., AAPB. H. 262; vidimus after November 6, *idem*); cf. vidimus issued by Henry, dean of Christianity at Brussels, on December 2, 1295 (orig., *idem*). The clause "locum sub quo sub communi vita degunt" was occasionally modified to read "locum sub quo sub continenti vita degunt" (February 21, dominica secunda quadragesimo), 1254/5, orig., *idem;* August 25, 1254 (orig., AGR., 13402, no. 1; for this document see below. p. 000).

[33] Orig., AAPB. H. 262; vidimus, October 17, 1471 (AGR., 13403, f. 379r-379v, no. 1076). Communal life was underscored again on November 6, 1427, when it was declared by Gerard Aelbrechs, curé of the beguinage, and the four grand mistresses that "die erfgoeden ende erfrenten die selen oec bliven int gemeyne, omme gemein custinge met te houden." Elizabeth and her companions are further described as "metten gemeynen goed ende gelt dat si int gemeyn gewonnen hebben" (orig., AAPB. H. 263).

[34] E.g., "congregatio pauperum beghinarum," April, 1251 (orig., AAPB. H. 263; AGR., 13403, f. 41r, no. 2); May, 1255 (orig., AAPB. H. 270 [3], Wesembeek; AGR., 13403, f. 157r, no. 411); August 1 (in sollempnitate beati Petri ad vincula), 1257 (orig., AAPB. B. 1453 [3]; *ibid.*, B. 1460, f. 49r, no. 133); will of Amelric Pipenpoy, dean of St. Gudule (February 23, 1257/8) (ed. Lefèvre in *BG.*, XIX [1928], 420f); "pauperibus beghinis per totam Vineam ubique commorantibus" (January, 1263/4, AAPB., B. 1460, f. 1v, no. 1); May, 1265 (*ibid.*, f. 49v-50r, no. 136); March 1265/6 (*ibid.*, f. 50r, no. 137); May, 1267 (AAPB., H. 269 [2], Machelen); March, 1270 (AAPB., B. 1452 [1], (Brusseghem-Molhem); February 12 (sabbato post octavam Purificationis beate Marie Virginis) (AAPB., H. 269 [2], Laeken); February 1272/3

"pauperibus beghinis domesticis in curia commorantibus,"[35] "pauperioribus beghinis magis indigentibus et in Vinea commorantibus,"[36] or "ad opus debiliorum pauperum."[37] Ter Kisten or the Holy Ghost Table in the 1270's was, as its qualifications indicate, primarily intended for the indigent.[38] Moreover, both the infirmary and Ter Kisten were frequent recipients of "pure alms" as a pious work.[39] The infirmary of Terarken (*domus Dei de Archa*), although designed by the founder Gautier Clutinc for beguines, did not actually develop into a second Brussels beguinage. But after the crisis of 1311 it was transformed into a hospital for aged and sick women.[40]

At all times the labors of the beguines were leavened by ordinary religious exercises. But let the memorial speak of this fusion of work with devotion at Ghent:

> In those houses many are so poor that they have nothing but their bed and chest of clothes, but they are burdensome to no one; by working with their hands ... they earn so much daily that they not only derive a modest livelihood but they obey the law of the Church and from that little they give alms. In the convent one is called the mistress of work whose business it is to superintend labor and workers so that all is done faithfully according to divine will. In working they have a certain rule that rising early they meet at church, each in her own place, so that the absence of anyone can be detected. When they have heard mass and each has said her prayers, they return to their own houses and work in silence all day so that they never cease from prayer; or they repeat the Miserere or other Psalms which they know. Late in the evening after vespers, when they have leisure for prayer and meditation, they go again to church and then retire. They frequently fast on bread and water, they use no linen next to their skin and sleep on beds laid on the floor. And with all this they are so circumspect in their manners and so learned in

(orig., H. 268; AGR., 13403, f. 146v, no. 363); May, 1273 (AAPB., B. 1460, f. 50v, no. 138); June, 1276 (*ibid.*, f. 2r, no. 4); etc.

[35] January, 1259/60 (orig., AAPB. H. 270 [1] Molenbeek); June, 1274 (orig., AAPB., H. 267 [2]; *ibid.*, B. 1460, f. 50v-51r, no. 140); June, 1274 (orig., AAPB., H. 267 [2]; June, 1274 (orig., AAPB., B. 1454, Schaerbeek); November, 1275 (AAPB., B. 203, f. 5v, no. 43); May, 1276 (orig., AAPB., B. 1453 [5], Laeken; *ibid.*, B. 1460, f. 2r, no. 3); August, 1280 (orig., AAPB., B. 1453 [3]; B. 1460, f. 51r, no. 141), etc.

[36] August, 1287 (orig., AAPB., B. 1455 [Vilvorde]; B. 1460, f. 51r-51v, no. 142).

[37] December, 1274 (AAPB., H. 1553, f. 3v, no. 24).

[38] "Cysta pauperum," March 9 (feria quinta ante festum beati Gregorii), 1272/3 (orig., AGR., 13402, no. 4); June, 1276 (AAPB., B. 1460, f. 2r, no. 4); "ad sistam pauperum beginarum" (will of Heela de Lombeek, January 13, in die Sancti Remigij, 1280/1, (orig., AAPB., B. 1452, [1]; July, 1284 (orig., AAPB., B. 149a; B. 203, f. 12v-13r, no. 101); "ad sistam pauperum beginarum Vinee Bruxellensis", April, 1288 (orig., AAPB., B. 1455, Vilvorde); "ad mensam sancti Spiritus pauperum beghinarum de Vinea" (March 18 [feria quarta ante Ramos Palmarum], 1288/9, AAPB., B. 1460, f. 42r-43v, no. 119); will of Heilwigis Rimmakers, ca. November 1, 1296 (orig., AAPB., B. 1452, 1).

[39] E.g., August 11 (sabbato ante assumptionem beate Virginis), 1257 (orig., AAPB., H. 270 [3]; AGR., 13403, f. 213v-214r, no. 588); October 8 (in vigilia Sancti Dyonisii), 1260 (orig., AAPB., H. 269 Lennick; AGR., 13403, 255v-256r, no. 704); etc., see below, p. 484.

[40] Bonenfant, *Une fondation patricienne pour béguines*, pp. 96-104.

household matters, that great and honorable people send their daughters to them to be brought up, hoping that to whatever state of life they are afterwards called, whether of religion or of marriage, they will be found better prepared than others... Their habit is gray, simple in form with nothing remarkable in any of its details.[41]

To understand the true significance of beguinal status it is just as essential to grasp the practical solution of socioeconomic problems which created the medieval *Frauenfrage* as the manner in which the Benedictine tradition dominated monastic asceticism, condensing, tempering, and adapting in the Latin and Germanic world the teachings of Eastern monachism.[42] Absolute poverty, undiminished in intensity and unmitigated by toil, served both as a goal and a technique whereby the world might be refashioned. But its exponents are pictured most favorably in hagiographical records. While charters, wills, and other documents testify abundantly that many a beguine continued to dispose of and acquire property like any lay person, the beguinage was also the creature of charity. Uhlhorn was right when he said: "Gebettelt haben rechte Beginen nie; wo bettelnde Beginen vorkommen, sind es ausgetretene, solche, die sich einem unordentlichen Leben ergeben hatten, wie ja auch ausgetretene Mönche und Nonnen vorkommen. Oft untersagen die Ordnungen des Hauses das Betteln ausdrücklich. Wohl aber flossen ihnen vielfach freie Gaben zu."[43]

Mary of Oignies, the daughter of a substantial family, was long tempted to epouse a mendicant life, but relatives persuaded her to abandon the plan.[44] Nevertheless she was drawn irresistibly to voluntary personal poverty and brought her husband with her into a state of debasement and humiliation; after distributing their goods among the needy, they began, in a brother-sister relationship, to serve the outcasts of the leper colony at Willambroux near Nivelles.[45] At first, at least as long as she and her husband devoted themselves to the care of the sick, she kept some property to aid her charges. But later, after spending nights in church and establishing herself as a beguine—or more properly, at this time, a *mulier sancta*—at Oignies,[46] she chose complete poverty and earned her livelihood by the work of her hands. Thus she truly became a *paupercula Christi*. But let her biographer and patron describe this stage of her spiritual growth:

[41] Béthune, *Cartulaire*, pp. 74f; Fredericq, *Corpus*, I, 176f.

[42]. Berlière, *L'ascèse bénédictine, des origines à la fin du XIIe siècle* (Maredsous, 1921).

[43] Uhlhorn, *Liebesthätigkeit*, II, 382.

[44] *VMO.*, 556 (45).

[45] *Ibid.*, 550 E (14); Baldwin of Ninove, *Chronicon, MGH. SS.*, XXV, 540. On the Willambroux leper house consult Tarlier and Wauters, *Géog. et hist. des communes belges. Ville de Nivelles*, p. 158.

[46] *VMO.*, 551 (17-18).

So great... was her love for poverty that she scarcely wanted the essentials. For this reason she was once determined to flee in order that, unknown and despised, she might beg from door to door among strangers and, naked, follow the naked Christ, after having left the cloak of all temporal things with Joseph, the urn with the Samaritan, and the sindon with John. She frequently contemplated and meditated the poverty of Christ who at birth had no place in the inn, no place to lay his head, no money to pay the tax,—who wanted to be fed by alms and to be received in the stranger's house. Sometimes she was so inflamed by this desire for poverty that she took a little purse to collect alms and a small cup to drink water or to hold the meal that would be given her as she begged. Clad in old clothes, she could hardly be restrained by the many tears of her friends. When however this *paupercula Christi* had bade them farewell and was about to set out in this garb with her purse and cup, there was such grief and weeping among her friends who chose her in Christ that she, as if overflowing with the deepest compassion, could not bear it. Thus urged by two, she, although desiring to flee and beg with Christ, elected to remain for the sake of her brothers and sisters to whom her absence seemed intolerable. But she did what she could. Her love for poverty continued so strong that sometimes she divided the napkin or linen on which they were eating their bread, keeping one part for herself and offering the other to the poor.[47]

Such emphasis on voluntary poverty and renunciation is a common characteristic of thirteenth-century ascesis as opposed to greed for riches not only in the lay world but among simoniac clergy.[48] Noble women, in the days of early enthusiasm, are reported to have been so impressed by this *devotio nova* that they donned the vilest garb of the poor to follow with greater freedom the steps of the Preachers as they went far and wide, from town to town, themselves like beggars.[49] Such stress on vagrancy, however, is more applicable to German beguines than to the Flemish women. But here too generalization must yield to caution. A direct outgrowth of the eleventh-century reform movement, the cult of poverty with its new orientation is often presented only in its south European form, above all through the example of the Poverello. Yet the biography of Mary of Oignies demonstrates conclusively that, in method as well as in aim, Liége and Brabant offered simultaneously a similar fervor independent of its Umbrian counterpart.

The twelfth-century witnessed the growth of devotion to the humanity of Christ—the child in the crèche[50] and the patient sufferer on the cross-with which the school of Bernard, Francis, Mary of Oignies, and Gertrude is instinct. This became the cardinal feature of medieval

---

[47] *Ibid.*, 557 (45).
[48] J. de Guibert, "Ascèse, ascétisme," in *Dictionnaire de spiritualité*, I, 979.
[49] Stephen of Bourbon, *Anec. hist.*, p. 75; cf. pp. 216, 229; Lecoy de la Marche, pp. 214-218.
[50] According to Van Rooijen (*Theodorus van Celles*, pp. 146f), the *VMO.* offers the earliest example of this particular motif.

piety, informing art, molding liturgy, and inspiring poetry. From it flows an ascesis that has as its end conformity to the mysteries of the earthly career of Christ. Without ceasing to be a means of expiating sins and suppressing unruly passions, penitential practices were more and more inspired and illuminated by the idea of *conformatio* or *configuratio* with the suffering leader of mankind, with the crucified Christ. With literal following of His acts and words as the basis of everyday life, these *mulieres sanctae* desired not merely to conform but actually to relive the passion, in all its excruciating horror. The culmination, it was believed, was stigmatization. "Principium conversionis ejus ad te," is Jacques de Vitry's summary of Mary's career, "primitiae dilectionis, Crux tua, passio tua fuit."[51] To answer the request of Foulques of Toulouse and others interested in such phenomena, he then offered, as a master of the *exempla* technique himself, a case history of this dedication to cross and poverty: "Non solum enim aliena abnegaverat, nihil alienum cupiendo: non solum sua, omnibus renuntiando; non tantum corpus, affligendo; sed semetipsam propriae voluntati penitus abrenuntiando."[52] Franciscan asceticism, which was inspired by obedience to a "gospel without glosses"—to poverty, humility, and the cross—was therefore not unique. It was a contagion, infectious in Belgium and the Rhineland as well as in Umbria and Tuscany; this corpus of Belgian *vitae* gives a detailed, faithful account of it.

As in the face of the corruption of Greco-Roman paganism and the subsequent compromise of the Church with the world the rigorous asceticism of the first monks and their frightful acts of austerity were a protest, so in the face of simony, of ecclesiastical wealth, and materialism of the bourgeois society emerged evangelical poverty, assuming its most appealing and constructive form in the mendicant orders. The *vita apostolica* served a dual purpose: to make its devotees really the *pauperes Christi* in the quest of spiritual perfection, and by stripping away externals and unessentials, to endow them with a driving power to reclaim and conquer souls.

Mary of Oignies' example of renunciation can be easily multiplied. Although of a prosperous family, Ida of Louvain worked at night to satisfy her own needs and those of the poor who resorted to her, for her patrimony provided naught but the room in which she lived.[53] When a pauper whom she had been prepared to aid *in cellae suae receptaculo* suddenly disappeared, leaving in a marvellous vision, a wound on the heart of his benefactress, she ran through the streets and squares in miserable attire which she had donned in a *recluso-*

[51] *VMO.*, 550 F (16); cf. 551 F (21); 552 (23).
[52] *Ibid.*, 551 F (21).
[53] *V. Id. Lov.*, 161 (10).

rium.[54] Ivetta of Huy had such compassion for the poor that if she had nothing of her own she would hand over to them the household effects. Her father, fearing that her sons would be dispossessed by their mother's liberality, took them from her for a time.[55] Beatrice, a novice at Florival, had to borrow a tunic from one of her companions to present herself decently.[56] Alice of Schaerbeek, "from infancy," renounced all that was not strictly necessary.[57] In these *vitae* the merchant and his commercial domain are constantly suspect. One of these *mulieres sanctae* donated to her abbey a part of her inheritance which she thought tainted by usury.[58] Another, considering her father's wealth as "poisoned things, germs of death," abstained as much as possible from employing it.[59] Nor did the Malines beguine Clarissa Leonard exhibit any aptitude for her grandparents' business.[60] Thomas of Cantimpré was informed by John of Nivelles who in turn had learned from the mouth of Mary of Oignies that her mother had engaged in unjust trade and usury.[61]

But the world of the hagiographer is an idealized one, premised on the pre-eminence of spiritual values. Ever the moralist, he presents only what he wishes to be believed and what is in need of reform. True, the Cologne beguines took a *professio paupertatis* in 1247,[62] while the rule of the Fins Amans recognized poverty as one of the pillars of the beguinage: "Povrétes fait droit jugement de vraie amour."[63] But voluntary poverty is the product of the early spirit of renunciation. Actually, these communities were not so much interested in poverty: any beguine who did not possess sufficient private capital must earn her livelihood. The obligation to work offered a means to implement the *vita apostolica*. At Ghent the new recruits agreed in the thirteenth-century to abide by chastity and obedience as well as "te vrede sullen sijn metten tijdelicken goede dat God hemlieden verleent heeft oft naermaels verleenen sal, bij tijdelicker winninghe, ghijften oft versteerften. Niemende tsijne te ontvremdene heymelic oft openbaer, huut noede noch anders, bij gheenen middele."[64] With frequent reference to "poor beguines" relying on the Holy Ghost Table, for example,[65] the provision in the statutes of the St. Trond beguinage,

---

54 *Ibid.*, 163 (18).
55 *V. Jut.*, 150 (25).
56 *V. Beat.*, ed. Henriquez, pp. 22f.
57 *V. Al. Scar.*, 472 (3).
58 *V. Id. Niv.*, ed. Henriquez, pp. 210f.
59 *V. Id. Lov.*, 159 (3).
60 Gielemans, *Anec.*, p. 436.
61 *BUA.*, II, 54, 18 (p. 529).
62 Ennen-Eckertz, *Quellen*, II, 270; cf. Haupt, in *ZKG.*, VII (1885), 541.
63 Christ, *La Règle des Fins Amans*, p. 198, lines 193-202.
64 Béthune, *Cartulaire*, p. 19.
65 E.g., Cuvelier, *Cartulaire de Val-Benoît*, p. 405; cf. will of Peter Conrad, March 21, 1274, *BG.*, XIX (1928), 125.

"Item noch ordineren wy op die pyne van verliesenis des hoefs dat eghene en wercke in die stat om hare penninghe te wennenen, te wetenen te scroedenen ocht te noppene," is more consonant with the facts.[66] Early documentation for St. Elizabeth at Ghent likewise indicates that here the cause of poverty was social rather than voluntary. While the inmates were referred to in December, 1236, simply as *religiosae mulieres pauperes*,[67] Countess Margaret at the outset of her reign (March 4, 1244) assigned 10 *l*. from her sister's will to aid the "aermer ende zieker vrouwen die gheheeten zijn beghinen."[68] Henry Damage and his wife Mary, citizens of Liége, left a will dated June 1–7, 1254, which exhibited wide interest in the beguine movement: to the *pauperibus beghinis* of St. Christopher in Liége 5 marks; to the *pauperibus beguines* of St. Adalbert 10 s., to those of St. Servais 10 s., and at St. Martin in Lille 20 s.[69]

---

[66] Philippen, *Begijnhoven*, p. 312.
[67] Béthune, *Cartulaire*, p. 2.
[68] *Ibid.*, p. 9.
[69] Cuvelier, *Cartulaire de Val-Benoît*, pp. 130f. Cf. testament of the widow Mary, February, 1261, which repeats several of the legacies, but singles out for special attention a number of recluses (*ibid.*, pp. 163f, 128).

V

Recognition by the Hierarchy

No person was devoted with greater constancy to the feminine religious movement in its early struggle against detractors or labored more strenuously by written word and personal solicitation to achieve early official recognition for the beguine way of life than Jacques de Vitry. For every manifestation of popular piety that could be fitted into the ecclesiastical pattern he showed the keenest interest. With the diocese of Liége acting as the anchor of much of his activity and his association with Mary of Oignies and the community of canons regular of St. Nicholas becoming the decisive event of his life, it is no accident that he betrayed a special fondness for Cistercian and beguinal spirituality.

In 1214 Jacques de Vitry was elected bishop by the canons of St. John of Acre[1] to fill the vacancy created by the promotion of Bishop Walter to the patriarchate of Jerusalem.[2] Primarily to receive consecration from Innocent III and to be appointed *defensor crucesignatorum* in France, he set out in June[3] on the journey to Rome which he has so vividly described for his Belgian friends[4] in his first letter, dated October, 1216. From Milan, the *fovea haereticorum*, where his sermons had been attended with little success, the bishop-elect journeyed south and on July 17 reached Perugia, which was then serving as the curial residence.[5] Here he learned that Innocent had died the day before. Looking at the almost naked body of the great pontiff, which during the night had been despoiled of its vestment as it lay in the church of San Lorenzo, Jacques could only reflect how brief and empty is the deceitful glory of this world.[6] Elected by the cardinals to the Holy See on July 18, the cardinal-priest, Cencio Savelli, took

[1] *VMO. Suppl.*, 580; *V. Lutg.*, 244 C; cf. Greven, *Anfänge*, p. 132, note 3.

[2] Walter seems to have been bishop of Acre on April 12, 1212 (Greven, in *HJ.*, XLIII [1923], 35, note 68); Gams (p. 434) offers no precise dating; cf. Funk, *Jakob von Vitry*, pp. 38f.

[3] For the date consult Greven, in *HJ.*, XLIII, 36, note 72.

[4] Cf. Greven, *Anfänge*, pp. 138f.

[5] Cf. Crane, *Exempla*, p. xxviii.

[6] Ep. I, *ZKG.*, XIV (1894), 102.

the name of Honorius III. In the words of the canon of Oignies, the new pope was simple and kind, ready to aid the poor in whatever way possible.[7] Although Jacques de Vitry does not say that Honorius consecrated him as bishop, he was installed in his new office on the succeeding Sunday (July 31).[8] He then adds in the description of his relations with the papal curia that, having entrance almost at will,[9] he obtained "letters with protectors and executors" as well as permission to preach "wherever he wished" in the East and the West. However, when he was thwarted by interested prelates from achieving one of his immediate objectives, namely, becoming defender of crusaders, he abandoned his plan to travel to France. Instead he made preparations for a departure for Acre, where the newly arrived crusaders and the population of his bishopric needed his admonition and exhortation.[10]

It was probably early in August, three years after Mary's death, that Jacques de Vitry seized the opportunity to regulate the affairs of the *mulieres religiosae* and to secure official recognition of their small communities in which they could perfect themselves in virtue by mutual assistance. Faced by strains on hierarchical authority and the inroads of heterodox thought, the Fourth Lateran Council had taken steps in canon 13 to curb novelties in monastic organization and the multiplication of orders, regular or extraregular, by insisting on the adoption of an approved rule: "Ne nimia religionum diversitas gravem in ecclesiam Dei confusionem inducat, firmiter prohibemus, ne quis de caetero novam religionem inveniat, sed quicumque ad religionem converti voluerit unam de approbatis assumat."[11] For the sake of economic or charitable activity, Belgian *mulieres religiosae* had been settling in the vicinity of a hospital or a church, but also on a piece of ground that would enable them to earn a livelihood. Having abandoned the paternal roof and worldly pleasures as much as possible, wrote Robert de Thourote in the preface to his statutes of 1246,[12] these women had gathered together in the environs of Liége and beyond, in the other towns and villages within his jurisdiction, in order to pursue more freely divine works. Although the beguinage at Diest was established on the banks of the Beverbeek in a district well adapted for the weaving of cloth,[13] the community nevertheless at the same time had a further objective "ut sese invicem mutuis exhorta-

[7] "Elegerunt cardinales Honorium, bonum et religiosum, simplicem valde et benignum, qui fere omnia, quae habere poterat, pauperibus erogaverat" (*ibid.*, 102f).
[8] Referring to Honorius' own consecration on Sunday, July 24, Jacques de Vitry adds: "Proxima sequente dominica episcopalem suscepi consecrationem."
[9] "Ita quod fere, quotienscumque volui, ad eum ingressum habui" (*ibid.*, 103).
[10] *Idem.*
[11] Hefele-Leclercq, V, 2, 1344.
[12] Philippen, *Begijnhoven*, p. 304, Bijl. 1; Nimal *Béguinages*, p. 57.
[13] Raymaekers, *Kerkelijk Diest*, pp. 422f.

tionibus ad bonum invitent"—to leaven daily life by religious practices. This was acknowledged by Innocent IV when he removed from them the disabilities of interdict.[14] Thus if one wished to bring together *mulieres religiosae* or *beguinae* who did not follow one of the approved monastic rules, in order that they "might fortify one another in doing good," and if such a community was to conform to the demands of orthodoxy, then he must obtain the approval of the Roman curia, which steadily became more conscious of the need for spiritual as well as administrative centralization.

In the pregnant letter of October, 1216, Jacques de Vitry announced his success in securing permission for the *mulieres religiosae*, not only in the diocese of Liége but in the kingdom of France and the German empire, to live in common and to assist one another by mutual exhortation: "Inpetravi, ut liceret mulieribus religiosis non solum in episcopatu Leodiensi, sed tam in regno quam in imperio in eadem domo simul manere et sese invicem mutuis exhortationibus ad bonum invitare."[15] From the life of Lutgard by Thomas of Cantimpré, a man who knew whereof he spoke, it is evident that the future cardinal of Tusculum was not alone in his sponsorship of the Belgian semireligious. Not long before his mission to the Roman curia John de Liro had started out for the south with the same purpose. But he perished in the Alps with no further indication of the nature of his plan.[16] Preparatory to the founding of Fontenelles, Robert de Courçon, then cardinal-legate in Cambrai, was also approached in behalf of "Christi discipulae."[17] The passage cited is all we have concerning the request for official recognition within the prescriptions of the Fourth Lateran Council. So far as is known, oral approval for these incipient *curtes beghinarum* was not accompanied by written confirmation or further directives. Although this confirmation failed to establish a precedent that would be cited later, it nevertheless marks the transition from "beghinae singulariter in saeculo manentes" or those scattered about the city to "congregationes beghinarum disciplinatarum."[18]

Jacques de Vitry describes in his *Sermo II ad Virgines* how, after the Roman curia had countenanced this experiment in lay piety, the first communities appeared with asceticism as their *raison d'être*. "Discreet and devout maidens cannot remain under the parental roof in the midst of worldly and shameless persons, without grave danger . . . But the wise men of Egypt (i.e., immoral prelates and dissolute laymen) try to divert them from their good intensions, saying: 'These women want to be beguines.'" When these *mulieres religiosae* fled

---

14 Bull of July 26, 1246, *ibid.*, p. 423, note 2 (text).
15 *ZKG.*, XIV (1894), 103.
16 *V. Lutg.*, 197f (II, 8).
17 See above, pp. 110.
18 Philippen, *Begijnhoven*, p. 80.

to the monasteries they were often unable to find retreats with open
doors in spite of the astounding multiplication of convents in the
early decades of the thirteenth century. Thus, coming together in one
house, they offered obedience to the one who excelled in virtue and
prudence. They were trained by both manners and letters in vigils,
prayers, fasts, and other penitential exercises, engaged in manual work,
and espoused voluntary poverty. Anticipating a sentence which became
a formula during the rehabilitation proceedings a hundred years later,
the bishop then added that these women attended religious services
in the parish church, read the psalter, received the sacraments regularly, confessed, and submitted to the precepts of the priests.[19]

Outside the *Vita Mariae Oigniacensis* the earliest evidence of beguines
in Belgium comes in August, 1232, when the priest René of Louvain
allowed the construction of a chapel for *mulieres religiosae* "de Hovis"
and approved the appointment of a priest for this chapel by William
of Brussels, abbot of Villers (1221-1237).[20] Although the word *beguina*
itself does not occur in the document, there is no doubt that these
extraregulars are meant here.

On May 30, 1233, in the bull *Gloriam virginalem*, Pope Gregory
IX assured recognition to the *mulieres religiosae* by taking the "dilectae in Christo filiae virgines continentes perpetuam Deo voventes
castitatem per Teutoniam constitutas" under his protection.[21] Outside
the oral approbation which Jacques de Vitry obtained from the papal
curia, this document appears to be the earliest recognition by Rome
of the feminine religious movement in the north. That it is a question
here only of beguines and not tertiaries seems evident.[22] Protection
privileges which prepared the way for exemption date from the ninth
century. Because of the weakness of Carolingian kingship and consequent political unrest,[23] monasteries sought to guarantee their posse-
sions by papal intervention. Since the original aim was to defend
monastic property, the usual protection document in the beginning
described monastic property only in general terms. Later it became
more specific, assuring to the protected abbey, by careful enumeration of temporal goods, not only greater security, but also acting in
difficulties as proof of ownership.[24] Protection grants which covered
only the property of a monastery—since temporal goods were the
principal source of dispute between abbot and bishop—were however

[19] Greven, in *HJ.*, XXXV (1914), 46

[20] Molanus, II, 1191; Wauters, *TC.*, IV, 152; De Moreau, *L'abbaye de Villers*,
pp. 60, 113f.

[21] *BF.*, I, 108, no. 108; Auvray, *Registres de Grégoire IX*, I (1896), 762, no. 1361;
P. 9212.

[22] Bihl, in *AFH.*, XIV, 139 and note 2; Greven, *Anfänge*, pp. 38f; Grundmann,
in *Arch. f. Kulturgesch.*, XXI (1931), 304f.

[23] Scheuermann, *Exemtion*, pp. 46-48 (on royal protection); 45f (episcopal protection).

soon to be loaded with other clauses, designed not only to defend but to safeguard the monks themselves against episcopal encroachment. These clauses could even constitute an attack on the authority of the bishop. Nevertheless it was not the original purpose of protection to obstruct the episcopal arm as exemption did,[25] but merely to prevent abuse.

The indult under question contains the classic formula "personas et bona vestra sub beati Petri et nostra speciali protectione suscipimus, et praesentis scripti patrocinio communimus"[26] in which the real idea of protection was expressed. In the fully developed document this clause was generally followed by curial sanction of the order on confirmation of the house, the naming of the rule, permission to possess and acquire property accompanied with a complete enumeration of possessions, houses, fields, vineyards, and *jura patronatus*; partial exemption from the tithe was often granted at the same time.[27] Certainly during the thirteenth century, the age of papal centralization, the right of direct appeal to Rome was implicit.[28] Next came the right to receive members, which was more commonly expressed in papal protection documents from the period of Innocent II and Eugenius III. Sometimes only a specific privilege was extended, e.g., the *clerici* could be admitted only with episcopal approval, or other monks might be accepted despite opposition from the superior.[29] Enjoyment of the perquisites of the house was contingent on residence. Again, it might be stipulated that monks, once professed, must not leave without the consent of the prior unless they embraced a stricter order, and even then they were not supposed to be received without letters of recommendation of the prior. Such was the full-blown protection letter of which the privileges granted to the beguines and beghards remain rudimentary examples. These provisions were premised on the claim of the Holy See to overlordship over protected monasteries.

The bull *Gloriam virginalem* was reissued by the papal curia a few

---

[24] *Ibid.*, pp. 44f, 48-50, 63-65; Blumenstok, *Päpstliche Schutz*, pp. 33-39; Schreiber, *Kurie und Kloster*, I, 6f. For protection and the Brethren of the Cross, see Ramaekers, *Privileges*, pp. 24-28.

[25] Scheuermann, *(Exemtion*, pp. 44f, 49-51) draws a close distinction between protection and exemption: "Der Schutz hat zum Hauptziel die materiellrechtlich Sicherung, nicht eine Sonderstellung gegenüber dem bischoflichen Ordinarius, wie sie die Exemtion bezweckt" (*ibid.*, p. 49).

[26] Ryckel, p. 627; cf. Innocent IV's protection of the Diest beguines (March 5, 1246) (Raymaekers, *Kerklijk Diest*, p. 422, note 1); in place of *patrocinio*, however, *privilegio* is often employed (cf. Hermans, Annales, II, 64 where the Huy house of the Ordo S. Crucis receives protection).

[27] E.g., Innocent III's bull for Oignies, July 17, 1207 (*ASAN.*, XXXI, 5f, no. 4; the bull of Honorius III, March 27, 1219, *ibid.*, 31f, no. 33).

[28] O. Lerche, "Die Priviligierung der deutschen Kirche durch Papsturkunden bis auf Gregor VII," *Archiv für Urkundenforschung*, III (1911), 163f.

[29] Schreiber, *Kurie und Kloster*, II, 335-337.

days later (June 4) with special reference to the "virginibus continentibus, perpetuam Deo voventibus castitatem per civitatem et diocesim Cameracensis constitutis."[30] Such early expressions of approbation from the hierarchy corroborate the evidence of the biographer of Mary of Oignies that contemporaries were most impressed by the cult of chastity observed by these *mulieres religiosae:* "Gloriam virginalem et castimoniae decus, sine qua nemo ad visionem Dei poterit pervenire." In December, 1235 Countess Jeanne of Flanders founded a chaplaincy for "religiosae mulieres pauperes" in Ghent[31] who were not called "beguines" until October, 1236.[32]

In January, 1236, Godfrey de Fontaines, bishop of Cambrai (1220-1237) signified his intention of recognizing these papal utterances as official confirmation of the "modum et honestatem vivendi sanctarum virginum et continentium in Begginarum habitu."[33] He too was persuaded to approve their way of life because they were commended and promoted by "multos bonos et religiosos ac doctores theologos."[34] Thus the young community had found patrons among the burghers and defenders among the clergy. In the same letter the bishop, appalled at their need, projected the construction of a hospital for sick beguines near the church of St. Sauveur in Cambrai. Because of the great number of *mulieres religiosae* living together in inadequate quarters, their bedrooms were so close to one another that if only one of the inmates took sick, the others perforce either became ill too or, what is inhuman, were deprived of rest and sleep.[35] Therefore, to meet these inconveniences they requested that a hospital be built for the specific use of the very poor and ailing inhabitants, without association with men. Their care should be entrusted to those capable of working.[36] This document, as Greven has pointed out,[37] offers convincing proof that by 1236 beguine life was fully developed in the city of Cambrai.

Such early evidence of papal recognition can, however, be justly

[30] Ryckel, pp. 626f; MF., III, 398; P. 9218; cf. *AFH.*, XIV, 139.
[31] Béthune, *Cartulaire*, pp. 1f, no. 2.
[32] *Ibid.*, pp. 2f, no. 3.
[33] Ryckel, pp. 627f; MF., III, 397.
[34] Ryckel, p. 627.
[35] "Attenderunt autem dictae personae, quod prae numerosa multitudine mulierum, simul in domunculis ibidem habitantium, tanta contiguitate constructa sunt earum cubicula, quod aliqua earum in infirmitate jacente, aliae vel de necessitate infirmantur, vel, quod inhumanum est, requie sive sopore privantur" (*ibid.*, p. 628).
[36] "Ad usum specialem religiosarum pauperrimarum et languentium vel aegrotantium inter eas, quae dicuntur Begginae, manentium, omni hominum excluso consortio, provisione loci penes mulieres industria de mandato episcopi remanente" (*idem*). Ryckel (p. 629) claimed without proof that Godfrey's successor, Guy of Laon, confirmed these concession by various letters and added new ones. In a subsequent indult (1236) (*ibid.*, pp. 628f) Godfrey confirmed the construction of this hospital and other buildings inside the enclosure.
[37] Greven, *Anfänge*, p. 38.

understood only in the light of the research of Asen and especially
Grundmann into the first beguines in the archdiocese of Cologne[38]
and the Osnabrück documents. While their presence may detected in
town records from 1223 onwards,[39] within a few years they had achieved enough prominence to secure special privileges from papal legates.
Cardinal Otto "in Carcere Tulliano" (1228–1231) allowed the Cologne
beguines to have communion outside their parish except on the three
high feasts.[40] Indeed, this privilege antedates considerably previously
known concessions from the curia. On November 21, 1235, Gregory IX
communicated to the canons of Osnabrück and the canon John, then a
crusade preacher, a protection brief on behalf of the beguines at
Osnabrück and Paderborn.[41] Yet this John was more than a protector.
The bull reveals that he had fostered and propagandized the movement, by kindling enthusiasm for extraregular life.[42] Was this a complement to his crusade sermons? A girding of the home front by
marshalling fervor in the vita. apostolica? It is quite possible, considering the interpretation already offered by Jacques de Vitry and the
twofold spirit of Cistercian vitae. Moreover, back of John's activity
may have been papal legates.

Two years later (October 27) the pope sent an identical bull to the
Cologne scholasticus Magister A. on behalf of the "dilecte in Christo
filie ...magistra et sorores converse que begine vulgariter appellantur"
in that city.[43] This document was in turn forwarded by the scholasticus on May 3, 1238, to John, now dean, in Osnabrück, who was to
execute its recommendations in that diocese.[44] According to the basic
text of these instructions it had been reported to the pope that the
beguines, whose aim was to serve God in poverty and chastity,[45] were
being misguided by corrupt priests and laymen to commit acts contrary to the demands of continence. Thus he ordered the scholasticus
to protect and promote them, to admonish evil-doers and those beguines who were subject to temptation, and to submit them to canonical
discipline. Thus it was a question of immoral conduct and errors on
the part of beguines, and not merely through the malevolence of

[38] Grundmann, "Zur Geschichte der Beginen im 13. Jahrhundert," Archiv f.
Kulturgeschichte, XXI (1931), 296-320.
[39] Asen, in AHVN., CXI (1927), 85ff; cf. Grundmann, op. cit., pp. 304f. Since 1223
beguines had been mentioned in Cologne documents; the foundation of a beguine
house can first be detected about 1230 (cf. Greven, Anfänge, pp. 35f).
[40] Osnabrücker UB., II, 266; Grundmann, op. cit., pp. 304, 311.
[41] Osnabrücker UB., IV (1902), 431f, no. 674.
[42] Cf. Grundmann, in Arch. f. Kulturgesch., XXI, 308, 310.
[43] Osnabrücker UB., II (1896), 287, no. 366; cf. 308, no. 393 (1240).
[44] Ibid., II, 296f, no. 378.
[45] "... Nichil pulchrius et utilius arbitrantes quam quod spretis carnis et mundi
fallaciis sub paupertatis habitu et castitatis observantia virtutum domino famulen-
tur" (cf. 1246 bull).

priests, as was understood from the letter of the legate Peter.[46] Apparently the complaint was lodged at Rome by the beguines themselves. In 1246 Pope Innocent IV repeated[47] the same order to the bishops of Osnabrück and Münster,[48] again entrusting its execution to the dean of Osnabrück. At the same time[49] the pope renewed by reiteration of *Gloriam virginalem* his predecessor's recommendations.

On November 10, 1250, the cardinal legate Peter of Albano[50] at Liége put under the protection of the provost Henry of Holy Apostles in Cologne local *mulieres religiosae, que begine appellantur* because they were being troubled by the clergy and laity who were supposed to be defending them. He expressly cancelled the earlier papal order which had charged the Cologne scholasticus with protection of these beguines.[51] When the cardinal legate Hugh of St. Cher stopped at Cologne in the fall of 1251, the beguines petitioned for confirmation of this protection letter as well as the other privileges previously extended.[52]

The legate Conrad of Urach, bishop of Porto (1224–1226) and a former abbot of Villers in Brabant, had during his sojourn in Germany labored to arouse crusade fervor.[53] To execute his reform program he commissioned with the approval of Archbishop Siegfried II of Eppenstein to preach in the archdiocese of Mainz Rudolf, canon of St. Maurice at Hildesheim, who proceeded to organize one branch of the feminine religious movement. As an apostolic preacher he brought together in many cities fallen girls to lead in common a pious life, in the foundation bull under the Benedictine rule, later after Augustinian prescriptions and the Institutes of St. Sixtus at Rome. He then obtained papal recognition for these communities, thereby bringing into existence an order which became widely spread in Germany not only for "penitents" but for women of gentle birth as well.[54] These "Sorores Poenitentes Beatae Mariae Magdalenae in Allemannia" or Penitential Sisters of St. Mary Magdalene who were eventually affiliated with the Dominican order elicited the same approbation from

---

[46] Asen, in *AHVN.*, CXI, 104; Grundmann, in *Arch. f. Kulturgesch.*, XXI, 303.

[47] June 19, *Osnabrücker UB.*, IV, 434f, no. 678. This is the oldest document for the Münster community.

[48] A second convent of beguines was founded in Münster in 1248 (*Westf. UB.*, III, no. 493). By 1332 there were seven communities. As for the rest of the diocese, Coesfeld did not have one until 1288; in Paderborn beguines were first mentioned in 1298, at Marsberg in 1259, and at Herford in 1288 (Grundmann, in *Arch. f. Kulturgesch.*, XXI, 306).

[49] June 18, 1246, *Osnabrücker UB.*, IV, 434, no. 677. The text is identical with Gregory IX's bull of 1233.

[50] Böhmer-Ficker, *Regesta Imperii*, V, 2, 1555.

[51] Ennen-Eckertz, *Quellen*, II, 298, no. 295.

[52] October 5, *ibid.*, II, 306, no. 301; privilege for Coblenz beguines (November 29, 1252), *RQ.*, XXXIII (1925), 160.

[53] Clement, in *RB.*, XXII (1905), 232ff; XXIII (1906), 62ff; 373ff; Hauck, V, 1,136f.

[54] *Res. Als.*, *MGH. SS.*, XVII, 234f; Simon, pp. 10ff.

the curia.[55] As additional evidence of papal satisfaction with extra-regular societies observing chastity as their reason for existence, Gregory IX sent to Rainer of Osimo instructions on March 15, 1233, that if the brethren called *Continentes* were compelled to return to the world they should not be obliged to accept public offices or to submit to new exactions or other civil obligations.[56] These *Continentes* should probably be identified with *Fratres de Poenitentia* or tertiaries of St. Francis.[57]

In accordance with the papal program the episcopal curia at Liége—whether under Robert de Thourote, Henry of Guelders, Jean d'Engh-ien, Hugh of Châlons, or Adolph de la Marck—by an unqualified endorsement of beguine life became its protector, encouraged its adoption, and safeguarded its integrity. Adolph acknowledged in the midst of persecution and doubt (April 30, 1324)[58] the privileges which Pope Boniface VIII had granted to St. Catherine beguinage at Tongres in 1299 in pursuance of ordinary papal policy.[59]

In determining the status of the beguines and their official accep-tance in the diocese, one can do no better than examine in conjunction with the 1246 statutes the celebrated letter which Henry of Guelders sent to Renier on August 1, 1266.[60] In the first place, the bishop, by delegating to his ailing scholasticus of Tongres visitatorial competence over both beguine and beghard communities as well as the *reclusoria*, hospitals, and leper-houses, was attempting a closer definition of extra-regular status in the church organism. On the other hand, the letter assigns antiquity to the Liége beguines: "Hec sancta religiosarum puellarum et matronarum, que beguine vocantur, plantatio... jam dudum in civitate Leodiensi et diocesi prima pullulavit..." The bishop further regarded them as the prototype of a "world-wide" movement.[61] Although this clause might be said to be a rhetorical flourish, it should be placed alongside the otherwise none too reliable *Vita Odiliae*, composed after 1241, which refers to the "Leodii novella plantatio religionis."

Renier was entrusted with spiritual supervision lest vices lurk

<hr/>

[55] June 10, 1228 (Boehmer, *UB. Frankfurt*, I, 51f); July 15, 1231 (*ibid.*, 55); April 22, 1232 (Simon, p. 29); July 8-15, 1232 (*UB. Frankfurt*, I, 56; P. 8969); Octo-ber 6, 1232 (*BF.*, I, 83, no. 74; P. 9009); August 2, 1235 (P. 9980); August 3, 1235 (*UB. Frankfurt*, I, 62; P. 9981); October 4, 1242 (*UB. Frankfurt*, I, 71f); July 26, 1248 (*ibid.*, 80f); 1247 (P. 12436); cf. Uhlhorn, *Liebesthätigkeit*, II, 299; Ennen, *Geschichte der Stadt Köln*, III, 830.
[56] P. 9124.
[57] De Kok, *Bijdragen tot de Geschiedenis*, pp. 164ff. for further exemptions and privileges under Alexander IV.
[58] Thijs, in *BSSLL.*, XV (1881), 33.
[59] *Ibid.*, 429, P.J. viii.
[60] *AHEB.*, XX (1886), 125-128; Paquay, in *BSSLL.*, XXIV (1906), 263-265, no. 104.
[61] "Et palmites suos longe lateque producens, pene per totum orbem flores pro-tulit et suavissimos profudit odores."

under the appearance of virtue. Women who wear the habit of beguines but, after leaving the *curtes* and congregations of the beguines,
live separately in the world,[62] must be subject to ecclesiastical censure
enforced, if necessary, by the secular arm. The deputy was also instructed to hold chapters among them for the sake of discipline. But
it is not clear whether these "capitula" were intended to impose
some sort of broad organization or whether they were prescribed only
for single houses. Of considerable interest is the sentence which
recommended that the statutes or "libellum" which Urban IV "is
said" to have drawn up twenty years earlier, while as Jacques de
Troyes he was archdeacon, and submitted for the approval of Robert
de Thourote, should be read often and closely observed in the several
congregations. This rule, which was published under episcopal auspices, must be regarded as the oldest of this kind and as a prototype
for many later ones.[63] However, the document lay long unknown
until Nimal who discovered it in the Archives de l'Etat at
Hasselt published a facsimile of the Flemish text accompanied with a
French translation.[64] If the rule issued by Bishop Robert was, as it
appears, fundamental for the beguinage St. Agnes at St. Trond, it is
understandable that the chronicle from the Benedictine abbey there[65]
reports that the beguine movement had its beginnings in the time of
this bishop.

Jacques Pantaléon continued his support of these communities
during his pontificate. In 1262, as Urban IV, he took the beguines and
recluses of the diocese and city of Liége under his protection, instructing the dean of Liége to preserve them from despoilers.[66] His
successor, Clement IV, at the request of Walter, rector of the church
at Peuthy, approved the exchange of lands which this priest had made
with the beguines of Vilvorde with the consent of the bishop of Cambrai and his chapter.[67]

This chapter may fittingly be brought to a close by summarizing a

[62] "...Mandamus quod beguinas, que habitum beguinarum deferentes, relictis
curtibus et congregationibus beguinarum disciplinatarum, singulariter in seculo
manent et conversantur in suarum detrimentum animarum et scandalum aliarum."
[63] The rule was recalled by Bishop Jean de Heinsberg on January 1, 1420:
"Cum plures et nonnulli reverendi in Christo patres et inter ceteros dominus Rober-
tus, simili divina gratia episcopi Leodienses nostri predecessores, ut ex ipsorum
colligimus scripturis noctes deduxerunt insomnes in condendis et faciendis certis
statutis regulis, privilegiis et ordinationibus pro beghinabus omnibus nostre Leodiensis diocesis" (Straven, *Notice historique*, p. 134). The opening words are similar
to those used by Engelbert de la Marck when he gave a rule for the beguines at
Tongres in 1353 (Thijs, in *BSSLL.*, XV [1881], 439).
[64] Nimal, *Béguinages*, pp. 43-56; 57-71 (French translation); Philippen, *Begijnhoven*, pp. 303-308.
[65] *MGH. SS.*, X, 395.
[66] July 7, 1262, MF., I, 429; P. 18376; July 11, 1262, MF., I, 430; P. 18380; Wauters, *TC.*, V, 273; cf. 322 (October 2, 1264).
[67] July 4, 1265, Hallmann, *Geschichte des Ursprungs*, p. 78; Wauters, *TC.*, V, 341.

document dated February 25, 1262 n.s., which has not heretofore attracted much attention. In it Bishop Henry of Liége undertook to unite the beguines at Aachen in communities under enclosure.[68] He had heard that in this town " a great multitude of religious girls and women, popularly known as beguines, live in different parishes and houses among the people, and are known to frequent churches among laymen to safeguard their souls." "To preserve the status of all beguines of our diocese unimpaired," the bishop had resolved at the advice of worthy men to gather these scattered beguines into a single fold under the direction of one pastor and in the interests of peace to segregate them from the lay world.[69] They had acquired an area outside the walls of Aachen, to which they proposed to transfer their houses and to establish a single *collegium*. Encouraged by pontifical authority, the bishop heartily agreed that all Aachen beguines, of whatever age or condition, should move to this location. Moreover, refusal to affiliate oneself with the community would entail deprivation of beguinal privileges. They would have a "collegium ... sub una clausura," with their own chapel and cemetery, under the direction of a pastor whom the four senior mistresses, appointed by "good" men, would select and present to the priest of Aachen. The latter was expected to invest the pastor who then had charge of the souls of the beguines, celebrated for them the diurnal and nocturnal offices in the chapel, administered the sacraments, heard their confessions, and buried the dead. In short, the culmination of beguine development was reached through the creation of a beguine parish under episcopal auspices.

[68] Lacomblet, II, 288, no. 512
[69] "... Decrevimus de consilio bonorum predictas becginas dispersas colligere et ad unum ovile ac sub uno pastore pariter congregare, et ut eo quietius et pacatius divine speculationi valeant intendere, a secularium consortiis segregare."

❧ VI ❧

Master Renier of Tongres

Renier, master of theology, canon-scholasticus of the collegiate chapter of Tongres, guardian and provisor of the beguinages of the Council of Tongres under Robert of Thourote (1240–1246), appointed by the cardinal legate, Hugh of St. Cher, apostolic visitor of the city and diocese of Liége, promoted, soon after, by Henry of Guelders, bishop-elect of Liége, to the role of spiritual administrator of the diocese or vicar-general ("vices gerens episcopi Leodiensis in spiritualibus"), and finally named diocesan visitor of the beguines and beghards, is one of the most eminent churchmen in the diocese during the middle decades of the thirteenth century.[1] Paquay brought together an impressive number of documents in which Renier appears as deputy, judge, and arbiter,[2] thus testifying amply to the confidence placed in his ability by his superiors in civil and ecclesiastical matters alike. Moreover the functions of apostolic visitor of the city and diocese of Liége were rendered more important and delicate by the relaxation of discipline that occurred under Henry of Guelders. The bishop-elect, although unlettered and dissolute,[3] put in charge of his government learned and able men, chief among whom, in addition to Renier, was Master Godfrey of Maestricht, archdeacon of Liége.[4] The abbots of St. Trond, Vlierbeek, Tongres, Villers, and the chapters

---

[1] Paquay, "Regesta de Renier écolâtre de Tongres, vicaire général de Henri de Gueldre," BIAL., XXXV (1905), 1-74; id., "Supplément au catalogue des actes de Renier de Tongres, vicaire-général de Henri de Gueldre (1253-1267)," BSSLL., XXV (1907), 399-409; id., "Cartulaire de l'ancienne église collégiale et archidiaconale de Notre-Dame à Tongres," ibid., XXIV (1906), 72-351 (especially 163-275 for Renier); id., "Regesta de Marcuald de Modène, archidiacre de Hesbaye, prévôt de Tongres, 1237-1274," ibid., XXIII (1905), 201-282; cf. table of Marcuald's acts in Leodium, III (1904), 118-124; Thijs, "Mémoire sur les écolâtres du chapitre de Tongres," Bulletin de la section littéraire de la société des Mélophiles de Hasselt, XX (1885), 37-111; Sassen, Hugo von St. Cher, pp. 90-94; Paquay, in BNB., XIX (1907), 118-119.

[2] Paquay, Regesta de Renier, pp. 13-74.

[3] This is the evidence that Hocsem offers (Gesta Pontificum, lib. V, t. II, p. 299); cf. Gesta Abb. Trud., cont. 3 a, pars 2, MGH. SS., X, 397.

[4] Sassen, op. cit., pp. 94-95; cf. Berlière, in Studien und Mittheilungen aus den Benedictiner- und Cisters. Orden, XVI (1895), 590-598.

of the collegiate churches all resorted to Renier as an intermediary in the difficulties which they encountered.[5]

Renier held his offices in the following order: he was priest-provisor of St. Jacques' hospital at Tongres from 1236 to 1241.[6] As canon of Notre-Dame in that town from 1238 on, he, together with the dean Daniel, was commissioned by Jean d'Eppes, bishop of Liége, to make a canonical visitation of the church at Cortessem and to erect a chapter there.[7] In recognition of his ability in this assignment Robert de Thourote appointed him in 1243 "conservator et custos begginarum in decanatu concilii Tongrensis commorantium." It was in this capacity that he drafted the document whereby Ida and Oda of Lude in the presence of two Dominicans of Liége donated, under certain conditions, their house, located near St. Jacques' hospital outside the Porte de la Croix at Tongres, to poor beguines ("in elemosinam pauperibus begginabus").[8] Whereas the priest Lambert succeeded Renier to the post of "provisor hospitalis Tongrensis," the latter, by becoming the first provisor of this beguinage, demonstrated an abiding but discriminating interest in the extraregular problem. From 1253 until 1266, the year before his death, Renier exercised the dual functions of apostolic visitor of the city and diocese of Liége, conferred on him by the apostolic legate, Hugh of St. Cher, and spiritual administrator appointed by the bishop.[9] Faced with the independence of the chapter of St. Lambert which had secured papal recognition[10] and with

[5] E.g., Paquay, *Regesta de Renier*, pp. 18-19, no. 13 (February 8, 1244); *CESL.*, I, 461, no. 8.

[6] On October 31, 1249 Henry of Guelders ordered Renier with others to examine and reform this hospital (*Leodium*, I, 78; *BSSLL.*, XXIV [1906], 222, no. 72). On December 13 Renier issued a rule (Paquay, *Regesta de Renier*, pp. 56-64, no. 1; cf. *BSSLL.*, XXIV [1906], 222, no. 73).

[7] Paquay, *Regesta de Renier*, pp. 16, no. 8 (July 21, 1238); Daris, "Notice sur la paroisse de Cortessen," *Notices*, X (1882), 173-179; cf. 91-95.

[8] The act is dated May 21 (Thijs, in *BSSLL.*, XV, 417-419; cf. 420-421; Paquay, *Regesta de Renier*, p. 18, no. 12; Wauters, *TC.*, VII, 754). With Theobald, priest and canon of St. Denis at Liége consenting, this agreement met the approval of Robert de Thourote, Johannes Theutonicus, Jean de Rumigny, dean of St. Lambert, and Marcuald (*BSSLL.*, XXIII [1905], 250-253, no. 6; cf. 210-211, no. 8; XXIV [1906], 192-193, no. 60); cf. *BSAHL.*, XV, 119-122; *BSSLL.*, XXIV (1906), 194, no. 61; XXIII (1905), 212-213. For further approval by Marcuald, October 16, 1246, see *BSSLL.*, XXIII, 253, no. 7; XXIV, 196, no. 63; 213, no. 9. Henry of Guelders confirmed the settlement on July 30, 1253 (*BSSLL.*, XXIV, 228, no. 80; XXIII, 260).

[9] Master Godfrey, dean of St. Servais at Maestricht, archdeacon of Famenne, and Master Renier received the appointment from Hugh on June 23, 1253 (Daris, in *Notices*, X, 181; Paquay, *Regesta de Renier*, pp. 23-24, no. 25). Earlier that year (January 27) a "Magister Renerus" appeared as witness in an act in which Ida, recluse of Othée, gave to the abbey of Val Benoît the rights she possessed over her property at Fallais (Cuvelier, *Inv. des archives de Val-Benoît*, 1902, p. 85).

[10] March 30, 1230 (*CESL.*, I, 264, no. 201). A year earlier (before April 12, 1229) Hugh had been obliged not only to allow the chapter to excommunicate malefactors and impose interdict on their lands, but also to relinquish appellate jurisdiction (*ibid.*, I, 252-253, no. 191; Poncelet, *Hugues de Pierrepont*, p. 257, no. 276).

the restlessness of the collegiate churches,[11] the episcopal and legatine authorities chose jointly "provisores in spiritualibus, in spiritualibus procuratores, vices agens in spiritualibus"[12] to conduct canonical visitation and chapter reform.

Renier's name figures in many jurisdictional disputes and business transactions affecting the feminine religious movement in the diocese during its formative period. When Thomas, abbot of St. Trond, authorized the beguines at Diest in September, 1247, to build on land in the parish of Webbecom, belonging to the monastery, he was approving a settlement, to which Renier had been party, between the pastor of Webbecom and the abbot on the one hand, and the beguines on the other, concerning the erection of a chapel and the appointment of a chaplain.[13] Almost twenty years later (May 16, 1265) Master Renier announced that their chapel and all appurtenances in the parish of Webbecom were separate from that of Diest.[14] He was designated as "vices gerens Henrici electi Leodiensis circa provisionem et procurationem beginarum" in the charter of the beguinage of Bilsen (October 24, 1256).[15] The bishop-elect authorized him to transfer the beguinage of Tongres inside the walls of the town (August 5, 1257).[16] On October 19 (in crastino Luce evangeliste) Master Marcuald sanctioned the transfer[17] while the bishop in 1264 allowed the beguines "crescente multitudine numerosa ad dictum locum confluentium" to annex neighboring meadows in return for an annual rent.[18] In May, 1258, Renier appeared as a witness for the construction of the beguinage at St. Trond.[19] In another parochial dispute Master Godfrey, dean of St. Servais at Maestricht, and Master Renier, acting in the name of the bishop-elect, exempted the beguinage at Tirlemont from the jurisdiction of the chapter of St.

[11] By 1259 persistent obstinacy bore fruit in the formation of a confraternitas, including the collegiate church of Tongres, whose defense of the several privileges was to be implemented by suspension of divine offices. This aggressiveness remained the rule for the remainder of the century (CESL., II, 348-352, no. 734, September 18, 1282; 355-356, no. 738, March 9, 1283).

[12] Paquay, Regesta de Renier, p. 4.

[13] Raymaekers, Kerkelijk Diest, p. 423, note 3; Piot, Cartulaire de St. Trond, I, 232-233, no. 195; Paquay, Regesta de Renier, pp. 19-20, no. 16.

[14] Raymaekers, Kerkelijk Diest, p. 428; Paquay, Regesta de Renier, p. 40, no. 62; Wauters, TC., V, 336. This document was confirmed by Henry of Guelders on June 25, 1265 (Raymaekers, Kerkelijk Diest, p. 428; id., in Messager des sciences historiques, 1862, p. 18; Paquay, Regesta de Renier, pp. 40f, no. 63).

[15] Leodium, I (1902), 47-56; 79, no. 8; Paquay, Regesta de Renier, pp. 27-28, no. 32.

[16] Thijs, in BSSLL., XV (1881), 423f; Paquay, Regesta de Renier, pp. 28f, no. 34; Leodium, I (1902), 79, no. 9.

[17] Thijs, in BSSLL., XV (1881), 424f; Paquay, in BSSLL., XXIII (1905), 265-266, no. 18.

[18] Thijs, in BSSLL., XV (1881), 426-427; Paquay, in BSSLL., XXIII (1905), 268-269, no. 20.

[19] Piot, Cartulaire de Saint-Trond, I, 321; Paquay, Regesta de Renier, p. 29, no. 35.

Germain and the local priests.[20] In January, 1259, the bishop-elect confirmed an agreement concerning the beguinage at Grathem which had been reached by the abbot of Villers and the priests of Looz and Hendrieken largely through the mediation of Renier, who had been appointed with the approval of Master Marcuald, archdeacon of Hesbaye, and Arnold, count of Looz.[21] When Urban IV's four letters of July 1262 on behalf of the beguines and recluses in the diocese of Liége[22] were promulgated simultaneously six months later (December 29), it was Renier who was entrusted with their publication.[23]

In a communication of August 1, 1266, Henry of Guelders notified Renier[24] that at his insistent request and in view of his failing health he had been relieved[25] of his duties as spiritual administrator of the diocese or vicar-general "gerens curam provisionis spiritualium nostrorum." In recognition of his keen interest in the semireligious, the bishop then proceeded to confer on him full visitatorial power over beguines, beghards, and recluses as well as other religious persons living in hospitals and leper-houses throughout the diocese.[26]

At least twice he appeared as executor of wills of Tongres citizens: on February 17, 1263, Gerard Poitevin left a considerable legacy to the beguinage in that town;[27] the following year Renier drew up the will of Mettula de Niel, beguine.[28] As the crowning act of his consistent defense and patronage of the beguines for a quarter of a century, he was to provide for the several communities in the diocese in his will which he dictated "decumbens in lecto egritudinis."[29] He died three months later on October 29. The document is a veritable summary of the extent of the movement in the diocese: half a mark to the "poor beguines" of St. Christopher at Liége; a similar amount to the beguine hospital at the same place; one mark to the beguines in Maestricht; 5 s. to the beguines at Eyck; one mark to those at Hocht; 5 s. each to those at Bilsen and Hasselt; 10 s. to the beguines

---

[20] 1250, Paquay, in *BSSLL.,* XXV (1907), 409.

[21] Daris, *Notices,* XII, 167-170; Paquay, *Regesta de Renier,* p. 30, no. 38.

[22] See above p. 163, note 66.

[23] De Louvet, *L'Origine nivelloise,* p. 59, P.J. 3.

[24] This important document has been edited many times: Thijs, in *Bullet. soc. Mélophiles de Hasselt,* XX (1883), 105; *AHEB.,* XX (1886), 125-128; Paquay, in *BSSLL.,* XXIV (1906), 263-265, no. 104; *Leodium,* II (1903), 61-62; Paquay, *Regesta de Renier,* pp. 43-44, no. 69; Wauters, *TC.,* V, 365.

[25] By the word *nuper* is meant after January 13, 1266 (cf. Paquay, *Regesta de Renier,* p. 42, no. 66).

[26] "Ac regimen earumdem committimus beginarum et beggardorum, nec non et aliarum religiosarum personarum, infirmarum et sanarum, in reclusoriis, hospitalibus ac leprosorum domibus degentium, in civitate et diocesi Leodiensi constitutorum."

[27] Thijs, in *BSSLL.,* XV (1881), 289; Paquay, *Regesta de Renier,* pp. 37-38, no. 55.

[28] Paquay, in *BSSLL.,* XXV (1907), 406-407, no. 11; Thijs, in *BSSLL.,* XV (1881), 289.

[29] Paquay, *Regesta de Renier,* pp. 70-74; cf. pp. 45-46, no. 71.

at Diest; one mark to the beguinage of St. Agnes at St. Trond; 10 s. to
the beguines at Léau; one mark to those at Tirlemont; 10 s. to Ten
Hove at Louvain; 10 s. to the beguinage at Looz (Grathem lez-Looz);
one mark to the beguines at Nivelles; 10 s. to those at Nerehayn
(Noirhat between Court-Saint-Etienne and Bousval); 5 s. to the community at Thorembais; 6 s. to those at Malèves[30] (canton of Perwez),
one bonnier each for the use of the beguines at St. Catherine in
Tongres and for the poor in their hospital. A life pension was also
provided for Lutgard de Coninxheim, beguine, in return for 5 marks
of Liége which she had given to him for the purchase of land. In
conclusion, it should be pointed out that Renier's benevolence was
not exclusive: Dominicans, Franciscans, Cistercians, and the Boni
Pueri (Bon-Enfants) at Liége were also remembered.[31]

---

[30] For the identification see Nimal, *Béguinages*, p. 29, note 2; cf. Daris (*Notices*,
XI, 14f) who read Malonia.
[31] Similar catholic interest in the beguines of Flanders was exhibited by the
canon of Tournai, Arnold de Maldenghem, in his will dated January 24, 1275
(*ASEB.*, 2nd ser., VII [1849], 360, 362). To the beguinages of Ardenburg, Lille,
Tournai, Ghent (St. Elizabeth), and Bruges he left 100 s.; to those in Audenarde
and Ten Hoeye at Ghent, 50 s.; to the beguine infirmary at Bruges and the beguinage at Courtrai, 40 s. each; to the communities at Ysendike (Janssen in *Bijdragen tot de Oudheidkunde en Geschiedenis*, I, Middelburg, 1856, 333, merely
says that there was one here before 1331), Oostburgh, Damme, Ghistelles, Turnhout,
and Deynse, 20 s.

VII

Beguine Parochial Organization
Under Cistercian Auspices

So intimate were these religious and economic bonds between the *mulieres religiosae* and Cistercian abbots, monks, and conversi that one eminent student of the beguinage developed as his major thesis the proposition that the movement was an offshoot of Citeaux.[1] Hereby he gave a new direction to the studies of the Belgian feminine religious movement, cutting his way through tradition and legend, on the one hand, and exaggerated economic interpretation, on the other, to arrive at a fresh perspective and fruitful results. More recently it has been cogently argued that there was not, properly speaking an order of Cistercian nuns, but rather a feminine branch of the Cistercian order.[2] Beguinal life was not at first an institution deriving directly from Citeaux; but, considering the frequent and intimate relations between Cistercians and beguines, it appears as an extension of the apostolate of the white monks. Greven's failure to consider the legislation of the general chapters restricting the *cura monialium* did not really invalidate his conclusions. After all, the chapters, while attempting to curb this function, at the same time were displaying tolerance by recommending the incorporation of nunneries into the order. Despite Walter's reluctance to assume new burdens, Villers and, even more so, its daughter-house on the Scheldt took a lively interest in the *mulieres religiosae quae beghinae dicuntur,* guiding and supervising spiritual concerns and temporal affairs, helping to organize beguine parishes, and in turn having their own outlook molded by association with them.

To the knotty jurisdictional questions which semireligious communities raised the abbots of Villers attempted a solution. The Great Beguinage at Louvain was authorized in August, 1232, to have its own chapel.[3] In this document, which significantly referred to the inhab-

[1] Greven, *Anfänge*, pp. 119-131, 139-158; id., in *HJ.*, XXXV (1914), 26.
[2] Roisin, *L'efflorescence cistercienne*, pp. 342-378.
[3] Molanus, II, 1191-1192, no. 26; Van Even, *Louvain*, p. 536. A tradition that goes

itants merely as *religiosae de Hovis*, the priest of Louvain, Renier, following approval by Duke Henry, Godfrey, the provost, and John, chaplain of St. Quentin Ten Hove, consented to presentation by the abbot of Villers, with nomination and installation being reserved to the canons of St. Pierre. Thus a beguinage would seem to have taken shape as early as 1230 at Ten Hove,[4] not far from the church in the parish of St. Quentin on the Dyle, where the manor which Ryckel[5] called the Old Castle or Alteburg was originally located. Nevertheless the beguine church was not declared independent of St. Quentin until 1250,[6] as the result of an agreement made in the *charta curiae* between G., the deacon, and the chapter of St. Pierre and the administrators of the beguine house. It was stipulated that the beguines could henceforth have their own priests provided they maintained and paid the pastor of St. Quentin, since he still enjoyed his rights for the four great feast-days, an annual sum of 2 *d.* per person. In the burial of the beguines the pastor of St. Quentin was to receive 2 *d.* of the offering, the rest going to the pastor of the beguinage. "In order that discipline might not be brought into contempt by worthless ministers," the abbot of Villars had the right to present the priest who officiated in the beguinage. This last cleric, known as *primarius capellanus,* was to conduct every Sunday high mass and canonical hours as well as to preach.[7] Later the same year the bishop of Liége issued a vidimus, confirming the action of the dean and chapter of St. Pierre, and thus recognized formal foundation of the Great Beguinage.[8] On May 30, 1297, Jean de Diepenbeek, pastor of St. Quentin, and the priests of the beguinage, Guillaume

---

back at least to the sixteenth century claimed that the beguinage had its origins at Meldert, not far from Tirlemont (Boonen, *Geschiedenis van Leuven,* ed. Van Even, II, 467-468). This probably started, however, from the fact that the beguinage owned much property in this village (Bourguignon, *Inv. de Louvain,* p. xli). Servranckx (*Mémoire historique,* p. 109) admits the year 1234, adding however that it was then that a chapel was built at the entrance of the infirmary (according to Boonen, *l.c.*); the pastor of the beguinage, G. J. Enoch, gave the dates of 1234 for the beguinage and 1305 for the church.

[4] Molanus (I, 348) put the beginning of the community in 1205. Ryckel (p. 236) restated the Meldert hypothesis of Boonen.

[5] Ryckel, p. 237. The superiors of the beguinage preserved in their archives four brief documents on parchment, treating business transactions and property donations for the period, 1245-1247, because they established the antiquity of the *curia de Hovis* (AGR., Assistance publique de Louvain, nos. 2650; original is no. 141 of 2nd ser. of chartrier, with a poor copy of the XVIII C., made by the pastor Enoch); 2651 (no. 142 of 2nd ser. of chartrier); 2652 (March 14, 1247 n.s., no. 143 of 2nd ser. of chartrier); 2653 (April 21, 1247, no. 144 of 2nd ser. of chartrier).

[6] AGR., archives de l'Assistance publique de Louvain, no. 2654 (three copies on paper, of which two belong to the XVI C. and the third to the XVIII C.); Molanus (I, 349-350) published the original which resides in the Archives de la ville de Louvain (cf. Cuvelier, *Inv. des archives de Louvain,* III, no. 4623 *bis*).

[7] Molanus, I, 349-350.

[8] AGR., archives de l'Assistance publique de Louvain, no. 2654; Molanus, I, 350.

Hugo and Jean of Aerschot, settled other technical points which the 1250 charter had left untouched.[9] From then on the community enjoyed autonomy in spiritual affairs.[10] Yet the abbot of Villers kept the right of visitation which was recognized by the bishop of Liége on September 29, 1296.[11]

On January 1, 1270,[12] Abbot Arnold of Ghistelles published instructions to the pastors and administrators of the beguinage, indicating that he had just urged Godfrey *de Banco,* dean of the chapter of St. Pierre, as well as the mambours to require henceforth observance of the statutes, namely, beguines who had had a house (*domus*) or a room (*camera*) constructed in the enclosure (*super aeram curie*) or who had obtained either through purchase, must not sell it again. They were to derive no further advantage from the dwelling than as a residence for life. Nor could they without authorization abandon their dwellings for the purpose of living outside the community. The mambours must not sell houses to beguines unless they agreed to occupy them for life; they could not allow a beguine to re-enter the community once she left her dwelling or who after invitation had not returned within a year and a day. Finally, they must refuse residence in the establishment to beguines who failed to conduct themselves properly; they were authorized to sell the dwelling of the recalcitrant member just as they were accustomed to do following death, and to use the proceeds to restore other houses in the community. As one small example of material well-being, the beguinage bought from Walter de Jodoigne, abbot of Villers, on March 20, 1253, eight bonniers of arable land, located at Binszervyk.[13] The first pastoral benefice of the beguinage church was erected into an independent cure by Bishop Adolph of Liége on March 21, 1313, with confirmation on March 28, 1317.[14] The pastor, or as he was then called, the *primarius,* was invested with complete authority over his subordinates, the two chaplains, designated as *secundarius* and *tertiarius.* He alone had the right to administer the sacraments and to collect the fees of certain offices.[15]

The oldest statutes came from the visitor, the abbot of Villers, who,

9 AGR., Assistance publique de Louvain, no. 2667 (original on parchment, no. 146 of 2nd ser. of chartrier).

10 Bourguignon, *Inv. de Louvain,* p. xlii.

11 AGR., Assistance publique de Louvain, no. 2681 (copy on paper, no. 157 of 2nd ser. of chartrier).

12 January, 1271 (Molanus, II, 1210-1212); for the date in 1270, see Van Even, *Louvain,* p. 536.

13 *Ibid.,* p. 537. For the properties of the infirmary, see Bourguignon, *Inv. de Louvain,* pp. liv-lv.

14 AGR., Assistance publique de Louvain, no. 2668 (copy on paper, no. 148, 2nd ser. of chartrier).

15 A decision of the provost of St. Gertrude of Louvain, February 21, 1313, mentioned the existence of a third chaplain. One of them, Gautier, held the title of *primarius,* enjoying pre-eminence over his colleagues (*ibid.,* no. 2710).

according to Servranckx,[16] received from John II, duke of Brabant, the right of proprietorship over the beguinage. No text confirms this, while several contradict it by indicating that the abbot enjoyed only the right of visitation and presentation of chaplains.[17] It was by virtue of this visitatorial power that he formulated the first statutes in March, 1271. The following January (1272) Abbot Arnold completed these statutes;[18] they were augmented or amended in 1339, 1429, and 1466.[19] Subsequently, the archbishop of Malines promulgated on March 22, 1588, a general rule for the beguinages of his diocese. This rule was published at Louvain the following July 23.[20]

The extent to which Villers interested itself in supervising beguine parishes is admirably illustrated by the beguinage of Grathem near Looz. The rule approved in 1497 indicated without precise dating that, founded and endowed by the counts of Looz, the community had been from the beginning under the direction and protection of the abbot of the Brabançon monastery.[21] It was towards the middle of the thirteenth century that *mulieres religiosae* settled near the hospital, probably founded by Louis I, count of Looz (1145–1171),[22] attended the chapel, and were entrusted to the rector.[23] A conflict quickly arose between the abbot of Villers, who named the rector and chapter of Looz, and

---

[16] Servranckx, *Mémoire historique*, p. 109.

[17] Bourguignon, *Inv. de Louvain*, p. xlv.

[18] Cuvelier, *Inv. des archives de Louvain*, no. 4624 *bis*.

[19] AGR., Assistance publique de Louvain, nos. 2656, 2658, 2659.

[20] *Ibid.*, no. 2659. The year before (August 13, 1587) the archbishop transformed the benefices of the Great Beguinage into simple offices, with the consent of the chapter of St. Pierre and the abbot of Villers (*ibid.*, no. 2671, no. 151 in 2nd ser. of chartrier); for the act whereby the Villers prelate authorized on June 27, 1587, the transformation of these benefices into *nuda officia* (*ibid.*, no. 2670; no. 150 of 2nd ser. of chartrier).

[21] Daris, *Histoire de Looz*, I, 144. His handling of the beguinage in this work was rendered somewhat out-of-date by the subsequent consideration of the 1259 document (Daris, *Notices*, XII, 1885, 165-166; id., *Histoire du diocèse de Liége pendant le XIIIe et le XIVe siècle*, pp. 208-209).

[22] Daris, *Notices*, XII, 162-164. Louis' widow, Agnes, endowed the hospital with her holding at Hex. Its income was also used to pay 25 d. weekly to canons of Looz who sang a Requiem mass each Friday in the hospital chapel for her husband (*ibid.*, 163). In 1174 she turned it over to Villers provided the abbot installed in it monks of his own order(Daris, *Histoire de Looz*, II, 2-3, P.J. iii). For the arrangement in 1175 when the countess transferred the Cistercians from the hospital to the Munckhoff farm, see *ibid.*, II, 3-4, P.J. iv; *Notices*, XII, 163. In 1230 Count Arnold IV fixed the charges of Villers with respect to the chapel and hospital of Grathem: the abbey must pay the Looz canons 10 s for the anniversary of Count Louis and 10 s. for his wife's, the rector of the chapel 30 s., 6 hogsheads of rye, 1 hogshead of wheat, and 2 hogsheads of barley for his beer; the provisor of the hospital 10 s., 5 hogsheads of rye, and 2 hogsheads of rye and 2 of barley after St. John the Baptist for the purchase of firewood. These *rentes* were all secured on the Munckhoff farm at Hex (Daris, *Histoire de Looz*, II, 11-12, P.J. x). The provisor of the hospital, established by the abbot, was called the *gasthuismeester*: he collected funds to lodge pilgrims and the poor.

[23] Henry of Guelder's brief, January, 1259 n.s., Daris, *Notices*, XII, 167.

the priests of Looz and Hendrieken; the two priests wisbed to preserve
inviolate their competence over all parishioners including the beguines. Renier, *scholasticus* of Tongres, was chosen by both sides with
the consent of Marcuald, archdeacon of Hesbaye, and Arnold, count
of Looz, to settle the dispute.[24] "In order to safeguard the souls from
danger,"[25] he determined that the beguines should have the chapel
and the hospital with its area; a piece of ground of 22 *virgae* adjacent
to the hospital and which belonged to the sacristan of the chapel;
another piece of 14 ½ *virgae* located at Grevenberg, an allod of the
monastery; a *curtis* beside the chapel cemetery from which the dean of
the chapter derived an annual rent of 12 *d.* and 2 capons and the
chapter itself two capons; a house with its enclosure alongside the
hospital towards St. Trond, which yielded to Villers an annual rent
of 12 *d.* in Liége money and 2 capons. Here the beguines were allowed
to erect their houses to form an enclosure which would be entered
by a gate; the abbot of Villers retained his customary right to appoint
the rector of the chapel but he must then receive from the archdeacon
canonical investment and cure of the souls of the inhabitants of the
hospital enclosure ("cura animarum infra clausuram hospitalis praedicti habitantium"). The chaplain was to celebrate divine offices; as
parish priest of the *curtis*, he was also expected to administer the
sacraments and give burial in the chapel cemetery. The rector of the
chapel was to pay annually to the abbot of Villers one gold denier
with a value of 12 d. of Liége in recognition of his authority; at the
same time the beguines must pay him annually one hogshead of barley
for the piece of ground of 13 ½ (sic) *virgae* and for half of the land
on which the hospital was built. The sacristan of the chapel was to
receive each year two hogsheads of rye for the other tract of 22
virgae; the beguines must also pay annually at Christmas to Villers 2
s. of Liége and 6 capons in rent for the two above-mentioned *curtes.*
Since the pieces of ground and hospital land on which the beguines
had built their houses lay partly in the parish of Looz and partly in
that of Hendrieken, the beguines living on Looz territory must pay the
respective priest 12 *d.* annually, while those residing on Hendriken
territory must give theirs 4 *s.* for parish rights. The two priests could
demand no more: in all other respects the beguines, their sacristan,
and provisors were exempt from their jurisdiction. This agreement
was approved in January, 1259, by Bishop Henry of Guelders who
entrusted the beguinage to the monastery, by the archdeacon Marcuald, Arnold, count of Looz, the abbot of Villers, John, priest of
Looz, and Louis, priest of Hendrieken.[26] The abbot continued to confer

24 See above, p. 68.
25 Daris, *Notices*, XII, 167; *Leodium*, I (1902), 79, no. 10.
26 The text of the document is published by Daris, *Notices*, XII, 167-170; cf.
Paquier, in *BIAL.*, XXXV (1905), 30, no. 38.

the nine prebends, the cure of the beguinage, and the two benefices founded in the chapel, one in honor of the Virgin, the other in honor of St. Catherine, until 1582 when the community passed to the cathedral chapter of Liége. The monastery exchanged with the cathedral the Munckhoff farm for the properties it held at Mont-Saint-André.[27]

It was only natural that Villers should control the beguinage at Thorembais-les-Beguines, for the Brabançon monastery was really the principal landowner in that area.[28] About 1232 Duke Henry I exempted from taxes the property and tenants of Villers at Thorembais and Cocquiamont, adding that the mills of the monastery were not subject to his jurisdiction.[29] On July 23, 1479, a representative of Villers and the mambours of the beguinage agreed that the beguines should pay a fee for admission and that their movable goods should become the property of the house.[30]

Beguines settled in Tirlemont near the "new bridge" (Nieuwbrug)[31]

[27] Daris, *Histoire de Looz*, I, 183. When the abbot of Villers conferred on Robert Ghilsen before 1462 the cure of the beguinage at Grathem, the prince-bishop of Liege soon after added a co-canonicate in the collegiate church at Looz. Although the chapter called to Ghilsen's attention that the statutes and customs of the collegiate church forbade canons and co-canons from holding a second benefice outside the church, it allowed him to keep the appointment on condition that he discharge faithfully his pastoral duties in the beguine house. His neglect of these duties, however, obliged the chapter in 1482 (February 16) to demand his removal from the Grathem church. The order was not carried out, for it had to be renewed in 1487 (April 10) (Daris, *Histoire de Looz*, II, 1). In his will of April 1, 1490 (text published, *ibid.*, II, 2-4), Robert Ghilsen called himself (*ibid.*, II, 2) "presbyter licet indignus Leodiensis diocesis, concanonicus venerabilis ecclesiae sive capellae Beatae Mariae Magdalenae conventus beguinarum de Grathem prope Loscastrum." He then elected burial in the choir of the beguine church.

[28] Tarlier and Wauters, *Géog. et hist. des communes belges. Province de Brabant. Arrondissement de Nivelles. Canton de Perwez* (1865), 144; De Moreau, *L'abbaye de Villers*, p. 177; Daris, *Histoire du diocèse de Liége pendant le XIIIe et le XIVe siècle*, p. 215.

[29] Tarlier and Wauters, *op. cit.*, p. 143.

[30] *Ibid.*, p. 146.

[31] "Curiam in loco dicto prope novum pontem in Thenis" (document of 1250; P. V. Bets, *Histoire de Tirlemont*, II, 223). Ryckel published (p. 591) and Foppens reproduced in the *Opera diplomatica* of Miraeus (IV, 529) an echevinal letter from Tirlemont, dated November 15, 1202 (*feria VI post Martini hyemalis*), in which Gerard de Porta or Vander Poorten donated to the beguines in the town their dwelling in the rue des Beguines. Bets (*op. cit.*, II, 146) accepted the date without question. Yet the very fact that the word *beguine* occurs twice in the document ("curtem sitam apud Thenas in platea Begginarum Thenensium ... ad opus curiae begginarum"), thus implying existence during the twelfth century, makes it historically impossible. Granted that the word could have been employed this year, its deprecatory significance made it unsuitable for official use, without further qualification, until the middle of the thirteenth century (for the problem, see below, p. 000). Therefore Tarlier and Wauters (*Géog. et hist. des communes belges. Arrondissement de Louvain. Canton de Tirlemont*, 1882, p. 154) would read either 1252 or 1302. Vinc. Dillen ("Een woord over het begijnhof van Tienen," in *Hagelands Gedenkschriften*, I [1907], 159) preferred the latter, emphasizing that the family De Porta, Poetere, Poitere does not appear before the end of the fourteenth century. Cf. Philippen, *Begijnhoven*, p. 112 and note 6.

during the first half of the thirteenth century. One part of the beguinage was contained in the parish of Hakendover,[32] whose priest,
Guillaume, approved in 1250 its acquisition of a house that belonged
to Oliver and Henry de Castel and allowed them to buy a bonnier of
land next to this dwelling. As this place was too far from his church to
allow administration of the sacraments to the beguines, he authorized
them to have an independent chaplain, provided they paid him and his
successors 5 d. of Louvain, and an equal amount each time they
bought a new house there. Henry of Guelders sanctioned this change
in jurisdiction later the same year.[33] At the same time Magister G.,
deacon of Maestricht, and Renier, canon of Tongres,[34] undertook to
establish an independent beguine parish in Tirlemont. The two
priests of St. Germain, to whom belonged the right of naming the
chaplain, relinquished this right to the abbot of Villers.[35] To aid the
construction of a church the bishop granted indulgences to the faithful who contributed.[36] Again, in February, 1288–89, John, pastor
of Hakendover, allowed the beguines living in his parish to receive
the sacraments from the hands of the chaplain of the beguinage at
Tirlemont.[37] Although in 1399 Boniface IX granted the community
the right of naming its own priest[38] or preferably delegating this
function to superiors,[39] the abbot of Villers continued long to enjoy
supervision over the beguinage. The pastor named by the *rectrices*
was presented by him to the bishop for confirmation. This practice
lasted until 1782 when the abbot abandoned it, after claiming the
right to name as well as to present the candidate.[40]

In accordance with the common pattern, official recognition was
extended to the Brussels beguines after they had long lived scattered
in the city and used for common worship the chapel of La Vigne

[32] For the parish consult Bets, *Geschiedenis der gemeente Hakendover*, p. 41.
[33] MF. IV, 529.
[34] That Magister G., *decanus trajectensis*, whom Philippen (*Begijnhoven*, p. 112)
failed to identify more closely, was Godfrey, dean of St. Servais at Maestricht and
archdeacon of Liége from December 20, 1252, to November 6, 1261, may be concluded from a number of documents which they promulgated jointly when Renier
was apostolic visitor to the city and diocese of Liége and vicar general of Henry of
Guelders (Paquay, in *BIAL.*, XXXV 1905, 23-25, nos. 25-27). The series begins,
however, three years (June 23, 1253) after the 1250 document in question which
Paqua did not list in the Renier register.
[35] Bets, *Histoire de Tirlemont*, II, 223f, P.J. II.
[36] Dillen, in *Hagelands Gedenkschriften*, I, 162.
[37] *AHEB.*, IX (1872), 377f, no. 2. This resolution was approved by a letter from
the archdeacon of Liege, December 9, 1300 (*ibid.*, 378).
[38] Ryckel, p. 552.
[39] This prerogative was confirmed on April 13, 1432, by Eugenius IV (*ibid.*,
p. 552). Although the document was issued in the second year of the pontificate
(Eugenius was elected on March 3, 1432, and consecrated on the 11th, Eubel, *HC.*,
II, 7), Bets (*Histoire de Tirlemont*, II, 147) dated it 1434.
[40] *Ibid.*, II, 147, 150; Tarlier and Wauters, *Géog. et hist. des communes belges.
Arrond. de Louvain, Canton de Tirlemont*, p. 155.

where a priest, Renier de Breeteyck, conducted services for them. From the first statutes (May 17, 1271), approved by Duke John I of Brabant, it is evident that he was regarded by his contemporaries as the founder.[41] Yet they emerged from obscurity on December 1, 1246, when Boniface of Lausanne dedicated a cemetery there, but evidently not for the exclusive use of the beguines.[42] The following year (June 21) Innocent IV authorized them to attend religious services during interdict with customary restrictions.[43] That the provisors and mistresses of the beguinage assured their pastor in August, 1251, an income of 30 l. "de reddibus nostre infirmarie" yearly in case of interdict[44] indicates that the community had been accumulating property. Three documents from 1248 treating donations and purchases, two from Master Renier, the provisor, and one from Siger Habosch, a knight, confirm this.[45] On March 6, 1251, the women were recognized as an independent community when the bishop gave their provisor permission to establish a *curtis* where the beguines Beatrice, Catherine, Helewide, and Ade, four daughters of Michael Le Chien de Goyck, as well as their niece Catherine, were to live together.[46] As evidence that the hierarchy as a whole encouraged and fostered beguinages, hoping thereby to supervise the feminine religious movement and withdraw them from the threat of heresy, the chapter of St. Gudule and the pastor of Molenbeek, intent on eliminating possible future litigation, authorized the beguines in April, 1252, to settle on favorably located ground, to have their own priests, to collect offerings made in their chapel, and to bury members of their community in their own cemetery. Outsiders could elect burial there only with permission of the dean and chapter of St. Gudule. In turn each beguine must remit annually 2 d., one-half at Easter and the remainder at Christmas. Two-thirds of the total was earmarked for the chapter of St. Gudule and the rest for the priest of Molenbeek.[47] This agreement, which erected

[41] Orig. in AGR., Carton 13402; two eighteenth-century copies in Flemish and one of the same period in Latin in AAPB., H. 262. Cf. Van der Rest, *aperçu historique*, p. 82; Henne-Wauters, *Hist. de Bruxelles*, III, 530.

[42] *Ibid.*, III, 529. The source is not cited.

[43] See below, p. 244.

[44] Orig. in AAPB., Carton H. 262.

[45] Two are dated April: the first, orig. in AAPB., Carton H. 270 (1); AGR., 13403, f. 102v-103r, no. 229; the second, orig. in AAPB., Carton H. 268 (Evere); AGR., 13403, 146r, no. 361; the third lacks the month (AAPB., H. 269, 2, Merchten; AGR., 13403, f. 178r-178v, no. 490).

[46] MF. IV, 720. In the two documents of April, 1248, it is clear that sick beguines already inhabited the infirmary: "debilium in infirmitorio degentium"; "ad indigentias debilium bechinarum in infirmitorio decumbentium."

[47] *AHEB.*, II (1863), 172; Wauters, *TC.*, V, 28; cf. *Beschryvinghe van het Begijnhoffe van Brussel*, Bibl. roy. de Belg., cod. 16566-74, f. 2v; Lefevre, *L'organisation ecclésiastique*, p. 112. Interest of St. Gudule in the infirmary first appears in the *fonds* when the dean in February, 1250-51, granted 3 journaux of land on the

178   THE BEGUINES AND BEGHARDS

the beguinage of La Vigne into an independent parish, was given
episcopal approval in October (1252)[48] and papal sanction by Urban
IV (January 12, 1263).[49] Demonstrating how the Belgian extraregulars
were able to conciliate ecclesiastical officials and at the same time
maintain their autonomy, the Brussels beguinage secured its first protection letter from the Roman curia in 1253. The cardinal-legate,
Hugh of St. Cher, at the request of the beguines—"vestris devotis
postulationibus grato concurrentes assensu"—took them and their

corner near the infirmary for an annual pension of 1 hogshead of rye (orig. in
AAPB., Carton H. 264, 1).

[48] *AHEB.*, II, 172; Henne and Wauters, *Histoire de Bruxelles,* III, 530. In addition to purely beguinal problems, the 1252 document raises the question of the
original parish of Brussels and relations between St. Gudule and Molenbeek. It adds
an argument in favor of the thesis of Lefèvre who, relying on the bull of Alexander
III "Le problème de la paroisse primitive de Bruxelles," *Annales de la société royale
d'archéologique de Bruxelles,* XXXVIII (1934, 106-116), held that the primitive
parish of Brussels was St. Gudule, limited at the Senne, and that it had in its
dependency the parish church of Molenbeek (*ibid.,* p. 108). The church of St. Gudule, he contends, claimed the rights of sepulture in the daughter church, of tithe
and patronage (*ibid.,* p. 114). In the 1252 document it is the chapter of St. Gudule
that grants permission for burial of outsiders in the beguine parish; to it also went
not the whole tithe, but two-thirds, the third part being the pastoral share, almost
always reserved for the priest; again, it is the chapter that has the right to name
the pastor of the beguinage. Without doubt the beguinage was in the parish of
Molenbeek, any possible boundary of the parish of St. Gudule beyond the Senne
being out of the question. Furthermore, it is clearly stated that the beguines settled
in the parish of Molenbeek; "Universitas... congregavit in unum in curia que
Vinea dicitur extra muros oppidi Bruxellensis in parrochia de Molenbeke" (April,
1251, orig., AAPB., Carton H. 263; AGR., 13403, f. 41r, no. 2). In November, 1275
(AGR., Carton 13402, no. 4; ed. MF. III, 611) it was stipulated that one-third of the
annual sum paid by the beguines must be given by the chapter of St. Gudule to the
pastor of Molenbeek "quia dictus jam locus de Vinea situs est in parochia de
Molembeka". All evidence, Jacqueline Bardiaux points out in her unpublished
dissertation (*Le béguinage de Bruxelles au moyen-âge,* p. 52), supports the thesis
that makes Molenbeek a daughter parish of St. Gudule. Documents into the
fourteenth century ordinarily describe the beguines as living next to or near Brussels: e.g., "universitati begginarum de Vinea iuxta Bruxellam," (July 10, 1254,
Ryckel, pp. 178f; August 25, 1254, orig., AAPB., Carton H. 262, etc.); "infirmaria
beghinarum de Vinea iuxta Bruxellam" (July, 1255, orig., AAPB., H. 269 [1],
Merchtem; AGR., 13403, f. 179v, no. 494); "degentium in hospitali beghinarum de
Vinea juxta Bruxellam" (November 18, 1294, orig., AAPB., Carton H. 262, vidimus
of letter of November 20, 1254); "ad opus infirmarie beghinarum de Vinea prope
Bruxellam" (October, 1263, orig., AAPB., Carton H. 270 [1], Ossele; AGR., 13403,
f. 193v, no. 524; August, 1268, ibid., 268r-268v, no. 748; Statutes of May 17, 1271);
„magistre beghinarum in Vinea infra opidum Bruxellense" (May, 1281, orig., AAPB.,
Carton 270 [3], Vilvorde; AGR., 13403, f. 172r, no. 467); "siste sancti spiritus in
Vinea iuxta Bruxellam" (March 4, 1288-89, orig., AAPB., Carton B. 1453 [6], Lennick; *ibid.*, B. 1460, f. 9, no. 22). Infrequent variants include: "ad sistam in Vinea
de Bruxella" (*ibid.,* f. 4v, no 12, August 15, 1279); "ad sistam pauperum beginarum
Vinee Bruxellensis" (April, 1288, orig., AAPB., Carton B. 1455, Vilvorde); "quatuor
presbiteris in Vinea beginarum Bruccellensium celebrantibus" (January 13 [in die
Sancti Remigij], 1280-81, orig., AAPB., Carton B. 1452 [1]); "pauperibus beghinis
in Vinea ubique commorantibus" (May, 1265, AAPB., B. 1460, f. 49v-50r, no. 136);
"infirmarie seu hospitali beghinarum de Vinea in Bruxella" (June 20 [feria tercia
ante nativitatem sancti Johannis Baptiste], 1290, orig., AAPB., Carton H. 264).

[49] Lefevre, *L'organisation ecclésiastique,* p. 112, note 2.

goods ("terras, possessiones, reditus et alia bona mobilia et immo-
bilia, sicut ea omnia juste et pacifice possidetis") under the protection
of the Holy See.[50] This act was supplemented in 1254 by others issued
by the legate Peter Capoccius, cardinal deacon of St. George *ad velum
aureum* (September 27, 1244-April 30, 1259). On August 25, 1254, he
placed the beguinage and its property once again under the protection
of the Apostolic See.[51] In November 1275, the *jus patronatus* of the beguinage of La Vigne was transferred at ducal recommendation from the
chapter of St. Gudule to the abbot of Villers. He in turn, working
with the guardian of the local Friars Minor, handed the prerogative
over to the abbot of St. Bernard on the Scheldt who was to have the
cooperation of the four mistresses. Disagreement between the beguines
and the abbot of St. Bernard would be settled by the Villers abbot.
Similarly, failure of the pastor to appoint chaplains with the approval
of the mistresses warranted further abbatial intervention.[52] The next
month (December 15) the pastor "at the behest of John I" accepted
the decision.[53] A week later (December 22) the bishop of Cambrai
voiced his approval.[54] It was the abbot of Lieu Saint Bernard who
announced in May, 1282, that Basilia and Elizabeth of Léau, beguines

[50] July 10, 1253, Ryckel, pp. 178f; MF. II, 998.

[51] AGR., Carton 13402, no. 1, This document is peculiar in having had its date,
VIII⁰ kalendas Septembris, anno Domini M⁰ CC⁰ LIIII⁰, falsified by the skillful
scratching out of one of the C's. The hole at the bottom of the document leaves
no doubt that the seal was also torn off. This presumably was the work of beguines
or sympathizers who in the seventeenth century were feverishly seeking documents
prior to 1200 in order to prove that St. Begga was the founder as well as the
patroness of the beguinages. It was with this purpose in mind that Puteanus, in
answer to Coens' close reasoning (*Disquisitio historica de origine Beghinarum et
Beghinagiorum Belgii*, Liege, 1629), brought forward in 1630 the three Vilvorde
documents, all bearing dates that are historically impossible. The document in
question may have been mutilated at the same time. At least this is the conclusion
of H. Nelis ("Document falsifié relatif à l'origine des béguines [1154]," *Revue belge
de philologie et d'histoire*, III [1924], 120-124). Unknown to him, however, are five
documents in the AAPB. which emanated directly from Peter Capoccius or were
preserved in subsequent confirmations. Whereas the AGR. document is addressed
to beguines themselves, he issued for the abbot of the Premonstratensian house of
Grimberghen on the same day an identical letter (Carton H. 262) which is in good
condition and still provided with the better part of an oval seal of brown wax,
charged with St. George and the dragon, and suspended by a double cord. For the
acknowledgment in which the abbot called himself "conservator universitatis
beghinarum de Vinea juxta Bruxellam," see the document dated February 21,
1254/55 (*idem*). Again, on November 6, 1254 (*idem*) the cardinal despatched the
letter to the dean of Christianity at Brussels. Its seal is in even better condition. The
same carton contains an undated vidimus of the latter document and bearing the
seal of Amelricus, canon of St. Gudule. Finally Peter Capoccius allowed the provisor
of the beguinage to seize goods lacking a legitimate owner as well as ill-gotten
property up to 40 *l*. of usual money. This privilege is contained in the vidimus of
Guillaume d'Avesnes, bishop of Cambrai on November 18, 1294.

[52] Orig. in AGR., Carton 13402, no. 4; MF. III, 611f.

[53] Orig. in AGR., Carton 13402, no. 6.

[54] *Ibid.*, no. 4; MF. III, 612.

at La Vigne, affirmed that a piece of land between the bakery and the house of Heilwige de Foro belonged entirely to the infirmary.[55]

To implement the program outlined by the Roman curia in the bull *Cum de mulieribus* (December 30, 1320)[56] to relieve the Belgian beguines from the burdens of Clementine legislation, a commission was appointed, presumably in 1323, by Pierre de Lévis-Mirepoix, bishop of Cambrai, to examine the status of the Brussels community and to dispel the suspicion of heresy as a preliminary to rehabilitation. The favorable summary which the abbot of St. Bernard, the dean of St. Gudule, and John of Alost, priest of Morseele, reported on December 8, 1323,[57] compelled episcopal approval on February 23, 1324. Since the beguines attend church faithfully and refrain from preaching or from being involved in disputes over the Trinity and divine essence— to use a clause which becomes a formula in all rehabilitation proceedings—they merit the hearty endorsement of the hierarchy and the protection of civil officials. St. Bernard on the Scheldt continued to exercise this function until 1649, when the separation of the bishopric of Antwerp and the abbey which had been annexed to it took place.[58]

By supervising the semireligious communities at Breda, Malines, Lierre, and Vilvorde, in addition to Brussels, St. Bernard established itself as a worthy rival to Villers in this work. At Breda the beguines originally lived scattered in the town and assembled at fixed times in some church. As their number steadily grew were given use by some benefactor of a piece of ground outside the walls where different houses quickly were built.[59] On March 2, 1267, Henry, lord of Breda, recognized full ownership by the beguinage of this ground with the houses. This donation may properly be regarded as the foundation of the *curtis* at Breda. Not only did Henry give land with buildings in full ownership but he declared the inhabitants free from all obligations and even promised to erect a chapel on the spot and lay out a cemetery.[60] On November 27, 1270, Henry, bishop of Liége, took the beguinage

[55] AGR., 13403, f. 103r, no. 230.
[56] See below, pp. 540 f.
[57] AAPB., Carton H. 262; Fredericq, *Corpus*, II, 81-83, no. 50.
[58] Henne and Wauters, *Histoire de Bruxelles*, III, 531, note 1.
[59] According to an old chronicle, Godfrey IV of Breda and his wife Matilda of Diest made the donation in 1240 (Van Goor, p. 92). Juten (*Cartularium*, p. vi) put no stock in it. Cf. his article, "De oudste heren van Breda," *Taxandria*, XII (1905), 228f. For further evidence of Godfrey's activity, see MF., IV, 713 (1241), 857 (1243). In 1246 he gave the „begginae clausae" at Antwerp 20 *s.* of Louvain (Ryckel, p. 623). When in 1487 the old briefs were rewritten at the request of the chapter of Breda, the beguines brought forward as the oldest document the one dated 1267 (Juten, *Cartularium*, pp. 118-119, P.J., no. 151; cf. p. vi, note 3; *Taxandria*, XII, 236-237, Bijl. II). This is the vidimus issued by the deacon and chapter of Breda on March 15, 1487, for the document of March 2, 1267.
[60] Juten, *Cartularium*, p. 1, no. 1 (Latin text); p. 2, no. 1 B (Flemish text); Van Goor, p. 420. Since this land lay outside the walls of the city, the document dated June 17, 1296, mentions "in curte Beghinarum sita apud Breda" (Juten, *Cartula-*

under his protection, promising that they should have their church and cemetery.[61] Twenty years later (1291) the documents speak of a chapel in honor of St. Catherine.[62] Shortly thereafter (June 17, 1296) Jacob, abbot of St. Bernard, assumed spiritual guidance of the beguines.[63]

The beguines who inhabited Malines were authorized by the papal bull of March 27, 1248, to attend during interdict mass which was read by their chaplain in the church where they assembled.[64] Soon afterward they undertook to create for themselves an area in which most of them, still living scattered about the city, could settle. Although beguine convents had been formed in different parts of the city, common religious services nevertheless were held for the beguines in the chapel that was attached to the foundation where the superannuated priests of Malines were housed. Probably a part of these women submitted to their direction.[65] On July 23, 1259, Nicholas de Fontaines, bishop of Cambrai, issued a document in which he answered the request of the "dilectae in Christo filiae universae beghinae in Machlinia commorantes" to transfer their chapel to the "enclosed" community.[66] At the same time he granted them the possessions of the old priests' home with the exception of the income of its chapel, with the understanding that they should care for the priests who still resided there. The new location of the *beghinae clausae* was outside St. Catherine gate, on the banks of the Dyle.[67] At first they had as spiritual directors monks from the abbey of St. Bernard.[68] In 1260 H. de Surs acted as chaplain of the Malines beguines.[69] In 1276 the church of the beguinage was dedicated by order of the bishop of Cambrai, but the beguines still had no pastor.[70] Ten years later (1286) the deacon of the Malines chapter allowed the beguinage to receive the offering of its church provided it paid the deacon annually 11 *l.* of Louvain, the first half at Christmas, the second on St. John's day. After the death

rium, p. 9); but with new enclosure by Jan van Polanen in 1350 it was brought into the town (*ibid.*, p. vii).

[61] *Ibid.*, p. 4, no. 3 A (Latin text); pp. 4-5, no. 3 B (Flemish text). A truncated version will be found in MF., I, 773.

[62] December 24, 1291, *ibid.*, pp. 5-6, no. 4.

[63] *Ibid.*, pp. 9-10, no. 7.

[64] *AHEB.*, XII (1875), 22, no. 1.

[65] Philippen, *Begijnhoven*, p. 117.

[66] *AHEB.*, XII (1875), 23-24, no. 2.

[67] Philippen, *Begijnhoven*, p. 118.

[68] Philippen(*l.c.*, p. 118, note 1) cited "De H. Romuldus en het opkomend christendom in Mechelen. Door een priester van het Aartsbisdom Mechelen," Malines, s.d., p. 44.

[69] Hermans, *Inv. des archives de Malines*, p. 291: it is a document witnessed by W., priest of Saint-Rombaut, H. de Surs, chaplain of the beguines of Malines, Wauthier de Stadeyken, echevin, and the provisors of the beguinage whereby the last named recognized a life pension of 20 *d.* of Louvain due Jacques Crudenare and his wife (August 24, 1260, "feria quarta ante decollationem Beati Johannis Baptiste").

[70] Ryckel, p. 639.

of their officiating chaplain the beguines were to be permitted to choose a successor who should assume pastoral duties. But the appointment was still reserved to the chapter. Thomas, the officiating chaplain, might serve in this capacity himself since a satisfactory benefice could be assured.[71] To implement the agreement the bishop of Cambrai approved the independence of the beguine parish.[72]

The beguines who inhabited the city of Lierre must have long attended mass and completed their other religious duties in the parish church of the town dedicated to John the Baptist.[73] At the request of the chapter and priest of the city that there be no more *vagatio beghinarum*—i.e., the running of beguines from the parish church to their residence—the bishop of Cambrai in April, 1258, granted that they should have a chapel in their *curtis sancte Margarete* where services were to be conducted by their own pastor or another priest. He was to administer the sacraments but might not hear confession except with special permission; at the same time the bishop agreed to establish an independent cemetery.[74] The following year (February, 1259) William, deacon of Lierre, who was so well disposed to the beguines that he later became their provisor, and the priest of the city decided to give them not only their own chapel but recognize their residence as a separate parish. The beguinage was henceforth to be *penitus absolute* from the parish of Lierre in which the pastor might handle burials as well as church services. For these advantages the beguines must each pay annually 2 *d.*, one during Easter octave, the other during Christmas octave. The beguinage pastor must likewise relinquish one-half of the wax and burial offering to the pastor of the parish church. The offering on the four great feast-days—Christmas, Easter, Pentecost, and All Saints, as well as the days of the Virgin belonged to the parish church of Lierre. The beguines were not to ring mornings until prime had been finished in the main church. Appointment of the pastor of the beguinage was given to the abbot of St. Bernard who must present the candidate to the deacon and chapter of St. Gummar.[75] The autonomy of the parish was confirmed by Nicholas, bishop of Cambrai, on August 1, 1264.[76] Nevertheless failure to provide a prebend for the pastor obliged the beguinage to be satisfied with its chaplain for a few years. Some be-

---

[71] MF., IV, 573.

[72] Ryckel (p. 642) lists the early benefactors in 1276, 1298, 1293.

[73] Van Lom, *Beschryving der Stad Lier*, p. 348. Van Lom (p. 346) puts its origins in 1200 as one of the three oldest beguinages in Brabant. This opinion was accepted uncritically by Anton Bergmann (*Geschiedenis der Stad Lier*, p. 48).

[74] Philippen, *Begijnhoven*, p. 119, note 1. According to Van Lom (*op cit.*, p. 347) the first church owed its origins to a donation of Duchess Aleidis, wife of Henry III.

[75] Goetschalckx, "Het Begijnhof van Lier," *BG.*, III (1904), 42-44, no. 1 (text); cf. *ibid.*, 37-38; for endowment of the pastor (March, 1272), *ibid.*, 44-46.

[76] *Ibid.*, 44, no. 2.

guines as well as the beguinage were acting as security for a sum of 60 *l.* of Louvain when the mistress and community in an act of March, 1263,[77] n.s. assured, on the strength of new gifts, their future pastor income of 10 *l.*

The beguinage of Vilvorde[78] occupies a peculiar position because, on the basis of three documents bearing the spurious dates of 1065, 1129, and 1209, Erycius Puteanus in 1630 attempted to prove that St. Begga was the founder and patron of the institution. Established in the territory of the commune of Peuthy at Steenwart (hence *Begginae de Steenvort juxta Vilvort*) rather than in the town itself, the beguinage experienced the normal development of all similar communities. First the beguines settled in the vicinity of a chapel or a building devoted to charity. Next they acquired an infirmary and their own church which eventually served as a nucleus for an independent parish. What drew the *mulieres religiosae* of Vilvorde to Steenvort was probably a chapel called *Solatium Mariae Virginis*, a name that was already current before 1239.[79] By the end of that year Bishop Guy of Cambrai had given his permission for the erection of a hospital for the exclusive use of the *consortio*.[80] Within the next few years the community was repeatedly taken under papal protection.[81] When the growth of the community dictated ten years later construction of a new church, Peter Capoccius, cardinal-deacon, granted on October 7, 1254, an indulgence to the faithful.[82] Under Pope Clement IV (1265–1268) the area on which the dwellings and the church of the beguines stood was separated from the parish to which it had belonged and erected into an indepedent parish with its own pastor.[83] It was Honorius IV (1285–1289) who assigned the *jus patronatus* to the abbot of St. Bernard, while on November 11, 1294, Bishop Guillaume of Cambrai put him in charge of the superior of the beguinage.[84]

Closer to Antwerp itself, fragmentary evidence makes the role of St. Bernard in the affairs of the beguinage appear more tenuous. Among the witnesses of a donation of 100 *l.* to the Antwerp beguinage from

[77] While the original document in the archives of Antwerp is dated *1262, mense martii* (Philippen, *Begijnhoven*, p. 120, note 2), another copy bearing the date of 1272 was inserted by Elout in the "Liber Secretorum" and published by Goetschalckx in *BG.*, III (1904), 44-46, no. 3.

[78] The legends that surrounded the origins of the Vilvorde beguinage were completely demolished by Philippen (*Begijnhoven*, pp. 425-432); Hallmann, *Geschichte des Ursprungs*, pp. 65ff; cf. Wauters, *Histoire des environs de Bruxelles*, II, 499-508.

[79]. Hallmann, *op. cit.*, p. 64.

[80] *Ibid.*, p. 65.

[81] Jacques of Preneste, apostolic legate, February 5, 1240 (*ibid.*, p. 66); Innocent IV (February 10, 1244, *ibid.*, p. 67; Urban IV, May 23, 1262, *ibid.*, p. 77).

[82] *Ibid.*, p. 77; two years before (June 1, 1252) Hugh of St. Cher had granted a similar privilege (*ibid.*, p. 76).

[83] *Ibid.*, p. 79.

[84] *Idem.*

"Beda de Antwerpia, clericus" on December 1, 1257, for the founding
of a chaplaincy were two brothers of the monastery, Friar William
(de Eeke?) of the Dominican order, and Gerungus, the provisor of the
beguinage.[85] In July, 1281, the monastery admitted the beguines to
monastic prayers.[86] Again, the father of Margaret Bovinne, a beguine, who was cantor of Notre-Dame at Antwerp, had entrusted to St.
Bernard the necessary capital to provide an annual pension of 4 *l.*
of Louvain for his daughter.[87] In the presence of two echevins on
October 31, 1288, she got her principal back,[88] perhaps an indication
that she left the community.

At Hasselt it was the abbesses of the Cistercian abbey of Herckenrode who completely supervised the beguinage.[89] Whereas the habit of
these beguines was the same as that worn by the *conversae*, the "grand
mistress" dressed like the nuns of Herckenrode.[90]

Although other orders betrayed some interest in the organization
of beguine parishes, the Cistercians met no real competition in this
work save from the friars who steadily absorbed many of these extraregulars into the tertiary ranks or at least offered them spiritual
guidance. Nevertheless the Augustinian prior and canons of St.
Gertrude at Louvain were instrumental in establishing an independent parish for the Aerschot beguines. On March 17, 1258, the *provost*
and the convent, under Prior Arnold, regulated at the instance of
Duke Henry of Brabant and his wife the relations between the parish
of Aerschot and the local beguines whose appearance had previously
met the approval of interested parties. The extraregulars were to have
priests in their own church; but on the four main feasts each must
give 2*d.* to the pastor of the conventual church, payable partly in the
Easter octave, partly at Christmas. Of the offerings at the burial of
beguines, whether one or several masses were celebrated the pastor
should receive one-half of the contributions, the rest being earmarked
for the priests of the beguines. They were also allowed to bury their
members and others who elected sepulture with them, in accordance
with parochial prescriptions.[91] In January, 1259, a new settlement
over these questions was reached with the beguines.[92] The following
month the bishop of Liége[93] and shortly after (March) the echevins[94]
confirmed with the usual exemptions this agreement. Surviving in a

[85] Prims, in *BG.*, XIX (1928), 60.
[86] *Ibid.*, 61.
[87] *Ibid.*, 200.
[88] *Ibid.*, 301 (text).
[89] Lambrechts, *Het oud Begijnhof van Hasselt*, p. 87.
[90] *Ibid.*, p. 103.
[91] *BG.*, XXIX (1928), 137-139, no. 2.
[92] *Ibid.*, 139-142, no. 3.
[93] *Ibid.*, 142-143, no. 4.
[94] *Ibid.*, 143-144, no. 5.

vidimus of Godefridus Roy de Slusa, Arnold Venoit, and Arnold Faber, echevins of Aerschot, is Henry III's approval of the new community,[95] supplemented by confirmation of the duchess.[96] On May 3, 1259, the archdeacon of Liége instructed the prior of the Dominicans at Louvain to name the priest.[97]

We have already examined the lively interest taken by the Benedictine monastery of St. Trond under Guillaume de Ryckel in the local beguines. It now remains to survey briefly its transactions with St. Catherine beguinage at Diest. As early as March 5, 1245, these women under a mistress received from Innocent IV at their own petition customary papal protection of person and property.[98] A piece of land in the parish of Webbecom, which belonged to the abbey of St. Trond and was held in fee by Scbastian of Nedermolen, was now ceded to the beguines for an annual rent of 13 d. of Louvain. When they decided to erect a beguinage on it,[99] the prior of the scholars at Léau, Renier, scholasticus of Tongres, and the pastor of Jescheren reached an agreement with the pastor of Webbecom,[100] whereby the latter was to accept an annual indemnity of 17 s. of Louvain for any compromise of parochial rights. After Sebastian abandoned his title to the property, the abbey granted the *allod* to the beguines. In September, 1247 Abbot Thomas authorized them to erect houses and a chapel and to appoint a chaplain to conduct services.[101] Each beguine who was subject to the new chapel, whether resident or not, must pay the abbey annually on the day before the feast of St. Trond one denier of Louvain. As soon as episcopal approval for construction had been secured, the mistresses and mambours of the community were to choose a secular priest for their chaplain. The abbot would then present the nominee to the archdeacon of Liége for confirmation. Since Thomas died on October 29, 1248, before the plan could be carried out, its fulfilment was entrusted to his successor Guillaume. Meanwhile Arnold IV, lord of Diest, had determined to extend the territory of his town to the south. He opened negotiations with the new abbot and exchanged one of his holdings which lay outside the city for the tract where the beguines intended to settle. On March 5, 1251, he interfered directly in affairs of the community.[102] Following the advice of

[95] *AHEB.*, XII (1875), 27-28 (July, 1259).
[96] *Ibid.*, 29 (July, 1259).
[97] *Ibid.*, 27.
[98] Raymaekers, *Kerkelijk Diest,* p. 422, note 1 (text). For a history of the beguinage, see *ibid.*, pp. 421-501; Philippen, "Het Begijnhof van Sint-Catharina 'ten Velde,' te Diest," *BG.,* III (1904), 501-518; id., *Begijnhoven,* pp. 109-112.
[99] Raymaekers, *Kerkelijk Diest,* p. 424.
[100] *Ibid.*, p. 424, note; *BCRH.*, 3rd ser., II, 455-457, no. 11; Paquay, in *BIAL.,* XXXV (1905), 19-20, no. 16.
[101] Piot, *Cartulaire de Saint-Trond,* I, 232-233, no. 195.
[102] Raymaekers, *Kerkelijk Diest,* p. 425, note 1 (text) (Feria sexta post dominicam qua cantatur Oculi).

substantial burghers, he determined that those beguines who lived on the *Campum* and the others residing in Diest were obliged, on pain of expulsion, to obey the magister or procurator appointed by the bishop of Liége, to lay aside the beguine habit and to lose all other privileges. This document thus makes it clear that not only did they have their own habit but discipline was enforced to get rid of recalcitrants and others who compromised the reputation of the community. Following Arnold's agreement with Guillaume de Ryckel, Gerard, canon of Notre-Dame at Namur, and the priest of Webbecom over the exchange of property (May 31, 1253)[103] and the duke's extension to this property on June 28, 1253,[104] of the same exemptions as other city land enjoyed, the lord of Diest subsequently (April, 1254)[105] allowed the beguines to occupy the site and to build a church. However the lords of Diest reserved for themselves patronage of it. Arnold moreover granted the chaplain the 17 s. which the beguines previously had been required to pay each year to the pastor of Webbecom and which, after the transaction, had fallen to the lord of Diest. In January, 1255,[106] Arnold not only authorized the beguines to have their own chaplain and priests, but he created an independent parish out of their territory. Significantly, St. Trond was not mentioned. A few months later (June 19) the bishop-elect of Liége sanctioned the erection of the parish which was dedicated to St. Catherine and authorized the inhabitants of the *Campum* to move to the new site. At the same time he regulated the appointment of the pastor of the new parish.[107] On December 16, 1261, the abbot of St. Trond sold to the mistresses of St. Catherine for 60 *l*. of Louvain 4 bonniers of land at Hunshem, near Donck, since they were too far to be cultivated.[108] About 1265 difficulties arose over the boundaries of the new parish. Under episcopal auspices Master Renier, scholasticus of Tongres, together with Guillaume de Ryckel, Louis, dean of St. Servais at Maestricht, Master Walter de Becke, canon of the same church, the friars, Prior Philip and Rixo of the Order of Preachers at Louvain, and William, pastor of Setrhut, set the limits of the parish (May 16, 1265).[109] The settlement was confirmed by Bishop Henry on June 25.[110]

103 *Ibid.*, p. 426.
104 *Ibid.*, p. 201; cf. Philippen, in *BG.*, III (1904), 506-507; id., *Begijnhoven*, p. 111.
105 Raymaekers, *Kerkelijk Diest*, p. 425.
106 *Ibid.*, p. 426.
107 Philippen, in *BG.*, III (1904), 510-511.
108 Piot, *Cartulaire de Saint-Trond*, I, 299-300, no. 252.
109 Raymaekers, *Kerkelijk Diest*, p. 428; Wauters, *TC.*, V, 336; Paquay, in *BIAL.*, XXXV (1905), 40, no. 62; *BCRH.*, 4th ser., III (1876), 185.
110 Raymaekers, *Kerkelijk Diest*, p. 428, note 1; Wauters, *TC.*, V, 340; Paquay, in *BIAL.*, XXXV (1905), 40, no. 62; Delescluse and Brouwers, *Catalogue des actes de Henri de Gueldre*, p. 91.

VIII

"Muro Inexpugnabili Bellatorum"

From the first clearly defined Dominican constitution of 1228,[1] though firmly rooted in the legislation of the founder's lifetime, it is evident that the *cura monialium* was considered a distraction to the primitive aims of the Order of Preachers. The *raison d'être* of the congregation was twofold: the ferreting out and the destruction of "heretical pravity" and, as a means to the defense and extension of the church,[2] a vigorous and unrelenting attack on ignorance and correction of intellectual error through the capture and promotion of higher education and entrusting the preaching of the faith and systematic missionary activity to well-trained minds.[3] The inward-searching, self-sufficient world of monachism, nourished on daily devotional exercises, now yielded before the driving impulse to subdue the external world. However heavily indebted the Dominican constitutions might be to the experience of Prémontré, an entirely fresh spirit permeated the work of the friars; in place of helping canons to become holy men, heretics must be converted.[4] Great as was their contribution in ordinary preaching, in the office of the inquisition, by political and diplomatic missions for the Holy See, and by their apostolate to the infidels, dedication to learning was something entirely new. A comparison of Dominican *Acta* of general chapters and constitutions with older monastic legislation and customs immediately reveals the change in emphasis and perspective. "Sint fortes, parati, litterati vel in logica

---

[1] Denifle, "Die Constitutionen des Prediger-Ordens vom Jahre 1228," *ALKM.*, I, 165-227. The text appears on pp. 193-227. For the passage in question see p. 222: "...Prohibemus, ne aliquis fratrum nostrorum decetero laboret vel procuret, ut cura vel custodia monialium vel quarumlibet aliarum mulierum nostris, fratribus committatur. Et si quis contraire presumpserit, pene gravioris culpe debite subiaceat."

[2] E.g., general chapter of Bologna (1242) (*MOPH.*, III, 24); cf. chapter of 1244 (*MOPH.*, III, 29).

[3] *ALKM.*, I, 194, prol to Dist. 1: "...Cum ordo noster specialiter ob predicationem et animarum salutem ab initio noscatur institutus fuisse, et studium nostrum ad hoc principaliter ardenterque summo opere debeat intendere, ut proximorum animabus possimus utiles esse."

[4] Galbraith, *Constitution of the Dominican Order*, pp. 175ff; Knowles, *Religious Orders in England*, pp. 146ff.

vel in jure competenter," was the advice that the provincial wrote to
the students at Bologna on the reception of novices.[5] Imperfect knowledge of the Latin tongue and a few liturgical formulas, conducted
under customary auspices, provided small hope for the spreading of
the divine word.

In short, their eyes were focussed with singlemindedness on the
enlightened salvation of souls which were in danger of defection from
or threatened the integrity of the ecclesiastical organism.[6] To this
single objective all other interests must submit, and to this task the
preacher must bring unbounded enthusiasm.[7] The sermon was a
calling, to exhort and edify.[8] But first of all, theirs was an order of
apostles—men who knew the doctrine they taught, who grasped its
meaning, and who could face all its opponents. Manual work, once
enjoined by Benedict of Nursia as a means of thwarting idleness and
adding to the support of the community, was considered not only aimless but actually a hindrance.[9] From now on it must be "scientia, cui
tamquam turri fortitudinis nititur ordo noster."[10]

The chapter, the priors general, priors provincial, priors conventual,
and *diffinitores* all looked upon study as the foremost obligation,[11] and
their continual concern for painstaking preparation is reflected abundantly in the General Chapter Acts throughout the century. Every
convent was a school, the foundation of a well-organized scholastic
pyramid conducting through the *studia particularia* or *solemnia* to
the *studia generalia,* and the presence of a doctor of theology was a
reason for its establishment.[12] In 1229 (April 11) the bishop of Liege
notified Jordan, provincial of Germany, and the general chapter that
he had authorized the establishment of a Dominican house in the
city so that they might teach theology there and, throughout the diocese, preach, hear confessions, and absolve penitents.[13] Before Dominic's death in May, 1221, Conrad Scharfeneck, bishop of Metz, expressed in a letter pleasure at the presence of the friars in his see

[5] Finke, p. 71, no. 33.
[6] *ALKM.,* I, 222, dist. II, cap. 27; see especially Innocent IV's bull of September 26, 1252 (*BOP.,* I, 217; P. 14720) which will be discussed below. Cf. Denifle,
ALKM., II, 641ff, particularly p. 642, note 3.
[7] So speaks Hugh of St. Cher: "Talis potest alios inflammare qui prius fuerit
inflammatus, quia qui non ardet non incendit" (quoted by Bennett *The Early
Dominicans,* p. 80).
[8] Scheeben, *Der heilige Dominikus,* p. 141.
[9] *ALKM.,* I, 224, dist. II, cap. 31; cf. Denifle, *l.c.,* I, 181, 191.
[10] Finke, p. 94, no. 67 (ca. 1215).
[11] Douais, *Organisation,* pp. 1-13; cf. Mortier, *Histoire des maîtres généraux,* I,
222-252; 544-566.
[12] *ALKM.,* I, 221, dist. II, cap. 23: "Conventus... sine priore et doctore non
mittatur." Cf. *Acta,* 1246 (*MOPH.,* III, 35-36); 1259 (*MOPH.,* III, 99).
[13] Poncelet, *Hugues de Pierrepont,* p. 250, no. 267.

because their sermons were good for the laity and their theological discourses for the clergy.[14]

Students, assigned to the *studia,* must not be turned aside from their studies by outside associations and distractions or useless labors.[15] Every kind of dispensation was granted to prevent interference with study;[16] liturgical prayer was sharply curtailed; the soliciting of alms was considered an obstacle to preaching.[17] Hours must be said briefly and succinctly in church so that the brethren might not lose devotion and study would not suffer.[18] It was precisely this passion for learning with its practical application that set the Dominican apart from the older forms of monachism and canonical life.[19] Similarly, Dominic's whole conception of the order and its objectives—communal poverty and apostolic sermon—had more in common with Waldensian experience than the Benedictine-Cluniac or Cistercian bodies which had built on corporate holdings. Dominic's aim was simply to found a society of preachers who, in place of and yet subject to diocesan authority, would take over by word and example religious instruction informed with apostolic simplicity. Like Peter Waldo he desired to reform the cure of souls, not monasticism.[20]

To implement this clearly conceived program chapter legislation repeatedly defined and circumscribed the friar's relationship with nuns and extraregulars.[21] Not only did they, no less than other monastic congregations, fear contamination from the proximity of and association with the opposite sex,[22] but the chapter of Milan in 1255 looked askance at efforts to commit the *cura monialium* to the order.[23] Such disapproval echoed the double prohibition recommended by the general chapter at Paris in 1228: (*1*) cure and guardianship of nuns or

---

[14] *GC.,* XIII, instrum. 43, col. 410.

[15] General chapter of Vienna, 1282: "Item, studentes studiis deputati studio diligenter intendant, et a familiaritatibus, et discursibus, et occupationibus superfluis arceantur" (*MOPH.,* III, 216, 218); cf. Finke, pp. 106-107, ep. 84 (ca. 1278).

[16] *ALKM.,* I, 223, dist. II, cap. 29: "Circa eos qui student taliter dispensetur a prelato, ne propter officium vel aliud de facili a studio retrahantur vel impediantur." Cf. *ibid.,* I, 194, prol. to dist. I.

[17] Bennett, *op. cit.,* pp. 80-81.

[18] *ALKM.,* I, 197, dist. I, cap. 4: "Hore omnes in ecclesia breviter et succincte taliter dicantur, ne fratres devotionem amittant et eorum studium minime impediatur." Cf. *ibid.,* I, 196, dist. I, cap. 1; 223, dist. II, cap. 29.

[19] Humbert de Romans, *Expositio Regule Beati Augustini:* "Notandum est vero quod, licet omnibus religiosis expediat libenter legere, tamen Fratribus predicatoribus magis incumbit; et hoc propter utilitatem multiplicem, quam assecutus est Ordo eorum, et assequitur ex studio" (Douais, *Organisation,* p. 159, App. II).

[20] Scheeben, *Der heilige Dominikus,* pp. 142-143.

[21] Besides the chapter of Bologna (1242) mentioned above, see chapter (1240) which allowed the friars to administer only penance to *mulieres religiosae* (*MOPH.,* III, 17); the chapter at Cologne (1245) forbade ministration of extreme unction (*MOPH.,* III, 32); cf. chapters of Montpellier (1247), *ibid.,* III, 40; London (1250), *ibid.,* III, 53; Valencia (1259); *ibid.,* III, 98; Bologna (1262), *ibid.,* III, 116.

[22] Chapters of Oxford (1280), *ibid.,* 209; Paris (1286), *ibid.,* 231.

[23] *Ibid.,* 85; cf. chapter of London (1250), *ibid.,* 53; Paris (1256), *ibid.,* 79.

other devout women and (2) admission of women to tonsure, habit or profession.[24] Whether this particular legislation was more than coincidental with Cistercian reluctance is immaterial: in either case, while hostility to pastoral activity among women was being registered in official circles, sentiment for incorporation and extension of the cure of nuns continued to grow.[25] In 1290, after the pastoral obligation had been clearly acknowledged by the Dominican order, the brethren, and especially the younger ones, were warned not to enter the *clausura* of nuns "nisi pro necessitate evidenti"; nor were others given this permission "nisi ex causa rationabili et urgenti."[26] Eight years later an attempt was made to regulate the friars who, residing in convents of sisters, formed a college under the supervision of a special prior, as at Prouille and St. Sisto.[27] After the turn of the century Dominicans were anxious that students in *studia generalia* should refrain from fraternization with beguines, then suspect of immorality and subversive ideas.[28] In the already cited *Exemplum* LXXX of Crane's collection, Jacques de Vitry had earlier reported, with beguines in mind, that when the Preachers.

> came to those regions (i.e., the Rhineland) in which religion flourished before other places, especially among nuns and other virgins living together in various communities (*collegiis*), they began to preach and to hear confessions. Some of these women revealed their weaknesses and temptations and the lapse of their fragile character in confessing to them, as to religious men, so that they might be aided more particularly by their prayers. The Preachers not only rashly suspected that other women were like these but preached in various congregations of clerics as well as laymen, who detract from the aforesaid religion by their habits, that such congregations of holy virgins are brothels rather than religious convents, and attributing the faults of a few women to all, so far as defaming the order approved by God and God-fearing persons, they shocked many.[29]

Sensitive to Clementine recommendations at the Council of Vienne,[30] the general chapters cautioned young friars, absorbed in study, against frequent and indiscreet visitation in towns of "mulierum religiosarum et beghinarum necnon et aliarum levium et suspectarum feminarum" who have provoked shocking scandals "in different provinces."[31]

---

[24] *ALKM.*, I, 222.

[25] For early evidence of hostility under Jordan of Saxony with regard to Diana and St. Agnes convent in Bologna, see Decker, pp. 59-65.

[26] Chapter of Ferrara (1290), *MOPH.*, III, 256; cf. chapter of Strasbourg (1307), *ibid.*, IV, 24.

[27] Chapter of Metz (1298), *ibid.*, III, 290. In addition to Decker consult Mortier, I, 534ff.

[28] Chapter of Bologna (1302), *MOPH.*, III, 315.

[29] Crane, *Exampla*, p. 36; cf. above, pp. 36-37.

[30] Cf. Chapter of Lyons (1318), *MOPH.*, IV, 107.

[31] Chapter of Bologna (1315), *ibid.*, 78, 80; see reiteration of act by Chapter of Montpellier (1316) with only "suspect women" being mentioned (*ibid.*, 93).

Similarly, the Provincial of Germany Ulrich (Engelbert von Strasbourg) (1272-1277) had advised his charges to avoid *conventicles* of
beguines, not to tarry there longer than necessary, and not to be
generous to such poor persons.[32]

After 1230 hostile decisions concerning the *cura monialium* became
increasingly numerous.[33] To forestall any departure from basic objectives through additional time-consuming engagements, sufficient pressure was exerted by the opposing wing—led by the ministers-general
Raymond of Penafort (1238—1240) and Johannes Theutonicus (1241—
1252), an astute canonist, respectively—on Gregory IX[34] and Innocent
IV[35] to obtain for the friars deliverance from the cure of nuns. A
former bishop and legate, Johannes, in particular, exhibited throughout his generalate a fierce and consistent antagonism to this problem
as well as to the *cura temporalium* from the burden of which he was
determined to relieve the order. After 1243 the nunneries lodged
strong protests at the curia. The pope therefore agreed that the
Dominican general and the provincial at Rome ought to teach the
sisters of St. Sisto, provide friars for their direction, establish a resident
prior, and correct their errors as "Dominic, Jordan, and Raymond had
done."[36] Johannes' efforts to discountenance these recommendations[37]
were promptly overridden by Innocent.[38] Other convents followed the
example of the Roman house: from May 14, 1244, through 1246 many
monasteries were incorporated under papal auspices.[39] On April 4,

[32] Finke, p. 83, no. 52: Friars "vitent quoque begginarum conventicula et ibi,
ultra quod decuerit, non morentur nec sint talibus honerosi paupericulis, quibus
labor manuum est pro censu." For Ulrich see Denifle, in *ALKM.*, II, 240 and note 1.

[33] Decker, pp. 65-69, 79-84. From papal letters of 1236 to Jordan urging acceptance of the *cura monialium* at Prouille and Madrid it appears that the general
chapter had forbidden the friars to carry on pastoral work among women (March 31,
P. 10133; March 24, *BOP.*, I, 86, no. 149; P. 10127; for Madrid, March 27, *BOP.*, I,
87, no. 151; P. 10132; April 7, *BOP.*, I, 87, no. 153; P. 10137).

[34] Bull, *Inspirationis divinae*, of October 25, 1239 (*BOP.*, I, 107): "Recipere curam
monialium, seu religiosarum quarumlibet, nulli fratrum vestrorum de cetero per
litteras apostolicas teneantur, nisi expresse de hac indulgentia fecerint mentionem."
Renewal, November 18 (*BOP.*, VII 16). For Raymond's pressure see Decker, pp. 85f;
Mortier, I, 348; cf. Axters, in *OGE.*, XIII (1939), 168.

[35] September 3, 1243 (renewal of 1239 bull), *BOP.*, I, 120; P. 11122. cf. Decker,
pp. 86-89.

[36] The sisters of St. Sisto at Rome succeeded in persuading the pope to keep
them under Dominican surveillance: bull, *Cum vos incluse*, February 3, 1244 (*BOP.*,
I, 130, no. 43; P. 11241); January 1 (*BOP.*, VII, 17) and March 1, 1244 (*BOP.*, I, 134,
no. 51; P. 11272).

[37] Mortier, I, 352f.

[38] May 14, 1244, *BOP.*, I, 143, no. 73; P. 11384.

[39] The most notable case was Amicia de Joigny (near Auxerre), daughter of
Simon de Montfort, who founded Montargis for fifty sisters, richly endowed, and
entrusted by papal letter to the general (April 8, 1245, *BOP.*, I, 148, no. 84; P. 11624).
This devoted friend of the Order of Preachers is reported to have gone several
times to the Roman curia before obtaining the necessary letters to found the convent (*Chronicon*, *MOPH.*, I, 322). Through the mediation of Amicia and her son,
who capitalized on the close ties of the Montforts with Alsace, several houses in this

1246, the pope, angered at the general's lukewarm cooperation, informed him "that in spite of previous privileges the Order of Preachers must accept the charge of any monastery it pleases the Holy See to force upon it."[40] Dissatisfaction over property provisions caused the nuns of St. Agnes in Strasbourg to urge Amicia to intercede again on their behalf. In consequence Innocent IV, by his bull of October 12, 1247,[41] reversed the decision of April 4, 1246, and obliged the general to assume their cure within the scope of the bull of May 7, 1245. But failure to give this bull universality indicates that the papal curia did not pursue a uniform policy.[42]

The pendulum soon swung in the other direction. Johannes Theutonicus' stubbornness brought desired results shortly before his death (November 4, 1252).[43] In the bull *Evangelice predicationis officium* (September 26) Innocent IV made obligatory only the guidance of the two oldest nunneries: the house at Prouille not far from Toulouse, and St. Sisto in Rome.[44] The former had been founded by Dominic and his superior, Bishop Diego of Osma, in 1206[45] on the one hand to answer the needs of noble women whose parents, reduced to economic straits, entrusted them to the schools of heretics,[46] and at the same time to direct this informal lay society, imbued with evangelical fervor, towards missionary work and the education of the young.[47] Since the Roman convent had been designed by Innocent III

area were incorporated: St. Agnes at Strasbourg, May 7, 1245 (*BOP.*, I, 148, no. 85; P. 11658); St. Mark (March 13, 1246, *BOP.*, I, 158, no. 123; P. 12024) and St. Margaret (April 20, 1246, Berger, 1827, 1828), both in the same city; Offenburg in Alsace (July 11, 1246, *BOP.*, I, 166, no. 156; P. 12214, 12215); Husern at Basel (July 11, 1246, *BOP.*, 167, nos. 158, 159; P. 12216, 12217; *UB. Basel*, I, 133, no. 190). Blanket incorporation for the Strasbourg nunneries was enjoined on July 4, 1245 (*BOP.*, I, 150, no. 89; P. 11706; *BOP.*, I, 150f, nos. 90-94, P. 11707); cf. *BOP.*, I, 149, no. 86; P. 11659; July 14, 1245, *BOP.*, I, 151, no. 95; P. 11726; September 9, 1245, *BOP.*, I, 153, no. 98; P. 11862; March 19, 1246, *BOP.*, I, 158, no. 127; P. 12029. For the significance of incorporation consult Decker, pp. 88-92, 95; for a list of houses incorporated in Germany, *ibid.*, pp. 94-95.

40 Bull, *Licet olim, BOP.*, I, 160, no. 132; P. 12055; cf. Decker, p. 92. From 1247 to 1252 incorporation of nunneries was far less frequent (*ibid.*, p. 96).

41 *BOP.*, I, 178, no. 186; P. 12721.

42 Decker, pp. 96ff.

43 *Ibid.*, pp. 97-99.

44 *BOP.*, I, 217, no. 269; P. 14720.

45 Bernard Gui, *Historia Fundationum Conventuum Ordinis Praedicatorum Tolosanae et Provinciae Provinciarum* (*MDAC.*, VI, 437-439); *BOP.*, I, 1; cf. Decker, pp. 33-46; the three stages of development in Scheeben, *Der Heilige Dominikus*, pp. 66-91; cf. pp. 243ff.

46 "Ad susceptionem quarumdam nobilium feminarum, quas parentes earum ratione paupertatis egestate compulsi tradebant haereticis, qui illo in tempore in eisdem partibus et locis circumvicinis plurimi habitabant, erudiendas et nutriendas ab eis, imo et revera erroribus potius deludendas et in anima perimendas" (Bernard Gui, in *MDAC.*, VI, 437; Jordan of Saxony, in *AA. SS.*, XXV (August 4, i), 544 D, no. 21; cf. Theodoric de Appoldia, *ibid.*, 565-566, no. 32; Humbert de Romans, in *Bibl. Max. Vet. Pat.*, XXV, 480 G.

47 Decker, p. 35; Scheeben, *Der Heilige Dominikus*, p. 74.

for the reform of decadent nunneries in that city, it too deserved special attention. It had been affiliated by Honorius III (December 17, 1219),[48] with the Dominicans following the failure of the Gilbertines to carry out his predecessor's original project. In his proclamation Innocent IV specified the reasons for removing the cura monialium. Before the sermon intended for the containment of heresy other wholesome soul work must be neglected.[49]

St. Agnes at Bologna and the Madrid house, as well as the more recent foundations, were thus abandoned, episcopal authority assuming responsibility for appointment of chaplains and confessors.[50] Although the sisters adopted the rule and habit of the order and shared its privileges and indulgences, the friars no longer exercised over them spiritual or temporal control. If the women were not long in lodging complaints with the new minister-general Humbert de Romans (1254–1263), who was less adamant than his predecessor, they found in Cardinal Hugh of St. Cher, who had just returned from Germany, a patron whose interest in nuns and beguines was an abiding one.[51] At the general chapter (Milan) in 1255, only a year after his election, Humbert, probably not without Hugh's intercession, proposed a middle course. While the primitive constitution forbidding the friars to affiliate nuns remained untouched, the chapter reserved the right to consider requests from women for possible incorporation.[52] Such incorporation, however, must be predicated on favorable decisions of three consecutive chapters, the same as for the constitution.[53] Furthermore the chapter of 1256[54] forbade friars to encourage recognition of the cura monialium by the order. In the meantime Amicia, prioress of Montargis, petitioned Alexander IV for incorporation of her convent. Permission was contained in the bull of January 23, 1257.[55] Three months later St. Agnes at Bologna, with the assistance of Hugh of St. Cher, obtained a similar concession.[56]

[48] MOPH., XV, 124f, no. 104; 158; cf. Scheeben, Der Heilige Dominikus, pp. 290ff, 322, 328ff; Decker, pp. 48-50.

[49] Cf. bull of July 15, 1252 (BOP., VII, 30): "Quia ... minus libere propter hoc (curam monialium) potestis praedicationis officium exercere."

[50] Bull, Exigentibus devotionis, February 26, 1253, BOP., I, 226, no. 292; P. 14898. For the Madrid nunnery see Decker, pp. 46-48; Scheeben, Der Heilige Dominikus, pp. 259ff; for the St. Agnes convent at Bologna, see Decker, pp. 51-59.

[51] E.g., Hugh's concern for the Penitents of Mary Magdalene at Louvain (Wauters, TC., V, 38, August 5, 1252); cf. the cardinal's authorization on December 2, ibid., 46); for solicitude for Dominican nuns see Decker, pp. 98, 102-109; Sassen, Hugo von St. Cher, pp. 154ff; for concern over beguines see above, p. 161.

[52] Mortier, I, 535.

[53] MOPH., III, 75. This provision was approved at Paris in 1256 (ibid., 79) and at Florence in 1257 (ibid., 84), thus giving it force of law.

[54] Ibid., 83.

[55] BOP., I, 328, no. 138; P. 16692.

[56] April 22, ibid., I, 335, no. 153; P. 16827. Already on March 13, 1254 (BOP., VII, 33) the nunnery had received a favorable decision through Hugh's intercession.

He had already (February 10) put all German nuns who had been admitted to the order by a master or general chapter under the direction of the general or the provincial of Teutonia with the obligation of original *cura*.[57]

But such recognition did not go unchallenged by the friars in assembly. The chapter at Florence (1257) which the cardinal attended required all provincials to send to the next chapter an exact description of the nunneries in each province: the number, population of each monastery, resources and revenues, and especially by what authority these houses were subject to their jurisdiction.[58] Before the results were known Humbert solicited a renewal of privileges granted by Innocent IV, exempting the order from all jurisdiction over the sisters.[59] Such official hostility nevertheless was being offset by the sympathetic response of other Dominicans. Concessions were again conferred on those houses which traced their paternity back to Dominic.[60] Under Humbert's direction the chapter of 1259 (Valenciennes) discouraged the brethren from considering women sisters unless they had been committed to the order by a general, a chapter, or a pope. This was intended to thwart overzealous friars. Provincial priors must conduct an investigation and report to the master in the next assembly how many and what nuns they had.[61]

It was not until the generalate of John of Vercelli that the nuns formally triumphed. Clement IV's bull of February 6, 1267, abrogated the privileges granted by Innocent IV and renewed and confirmed by Alexander IV. Henceforth the Preachers were entrusted with nunneries. To the friars, charged with this ministry by their superiors, belonged the right of visitation, correction, and reform. They reserved for themselves the right to install and depose prioresses, although free election was generally observed, subject to confirmation. The friars enjoyed full power to confess and administer the sacraments.[62] For monasteries where friars were not in residence, chaplains must be appointed. To the section of the constitution *De domibus concedendis* which provided for approbation by three chapters was not added significantly the clause "vel nisi per dominum papam ordini committatur."[63]

Thus after much confusion and reluctance a formula was found

---

[57] Decker, p. 105.
[58] *MOPH.*, III, 88.
[59] Bull, *Inspirationis divinae*, November 16, 1257, *BOP.*, I, 354.
[60] E.g., Madrid, bull, *Devotionis augmentum*, June 13, 1258, *BOP.*, I, 365. Cf. Mortier, I, 537; Denifle, in *ALKM.*, II, 641ff; Finke, pp. 52-53, no. 4 (April 19, 1257).
[61] *MOPH.*, III, 98.
[62] Bull, *Affectu sincero sic, BOP.*, I, 481, no. 59; P. 19936. For supervision of nuns and *beguinae clausae* during this period, see Wilms in *QF.*, XXIV, 64, 70-71, 84; Decker, pp. 89-92.
[63] *ALKM.*, V, 549.

whereby the friars were to exercise spiritual control over the sisters without being absorbed by this new ministry. As the Dominican order expanded, the number of beguines, penitential sisters, and nuns who submitted to administrative supervision[64] and spiritual guidance of the brethren by embracing the rule of St. Augustine and the customs of St. Sisto steadily grew.

Germany, it has been said,[65] was the real home of the Dominican nuns. When they first arrived in Germany, writes a contemporary chronicler, they found *mulierculas inclusas* near chapels whom they multiplied and organized into *mulierum claustra*. They cared for *pauperes sorores,* that is, women who wore some religious habit. Nor were wealthy widows and gentle maidens neglected.[66] In Latin lands convents were not numerous, for by 1277 there were but twelve nunneries in Spain, France, and Italy.[67] On the other hand, in no province was the following of women greater, or more devoted, than in the Provincia Teutoniae which as far as the Low Countries were concerned, included Bruges and Ghent until 1259[68] and afterwards only Brabant and Holland.[69] How successful Friar Henry of Cologne, for example, was in conducting early the *cura monialium* is attested by Jordan of Saxony.[70] The general's letter to the Provincial of Lombardy Stephen[71] reflects his lively interest which the friars in Germany were exhibiting in beguines and *mulieres sanctae* and which the 1228 prohibition was expected to arrest. But the influx to nunneries continued so strong that limitations had to be put on the number of professed and novices[72] while an entrance fee was exacted to ensure main-

[64] Wilms, in *QF.,* XXIV, 25; Axters, in *OGE.,* XIII, 168f.
[65] Sassen, *Hugo von St. Cher,* p. 154.
[66] *Res. Alsat., MGH. SS.,* XVII, 234.
[67] Decker, p. 70.
[68] *MOPH.,* III, 96.
[69] The German Dominican province, owing to its size, was divided into "nationes" (Von Loë in *QF.,* I, 5ff, Löhr, in *QF.,* XIX 156f) in accordance with the 1275 chapter of Bologna (*MOPH.,* III, 177). Each was entrusted to a vicar (*vicarius nationis*) who was wholly dependent on the provincial (Reichert, in *RQ.,* XV [1901], 124). Teutonia, after the creation of the new province of Saxony (Chapter of Cologne [1301], *MOPH.,* III, 304; Bologna [1302], *ibid.,* 313-314; Besançon [1303], *ibid.,* 319; cf. Von Loë, *Statistisches über die Ordensprovinz Saxonia, QF.,* IV), consisted of four nations: Alsatia (Alsace, Baden, Switzerland), Suevia (Württemberg, Swabia, Franconia), Bavaria (Bavaria, Austria), and Brabantia (Brabant and the Rhineland) (König, in *Freib. Diöz-Arch.,* XIII [1880], 207f). Saxonia comprised eight nations in 1308: Saxony, Thuringia, Meissen, Westphalia, Brandenburg, Holland, Slavenland, Friesland.
[70] "Fr. Henricus ... missus autem pro Priore Coloniam, quam copiosum ibidem et uberem manipulum animarum in virginibus, in viduis, et vere poenitentibus per assiduam praedicationem lucrifaceret Christo" (*AA. SS.,* XXXV (August 4, i), 549 E, no. 58); cf. Decker, p. 73; *QF.,* XX, 49ff.
[71] *QF.,* XX, 49-51, no. 49.
[72] When Hermann von Minden, as prior in Strasbourg, established rules on February 3, 1284 for St. Agnes nunnery in Freiburg, he fixed the congregation of professed and novices at forty (*RQ.,* XXXIII, 1925, 166-167, no. 3; cf. 161, for the house see Wilms, in *QF.,* XXIV, 48-49; *Freib. Diöz-Arch.,* XIII, 208ff).

tenance and clothing.[73] To each convent a definite district (*termini predicacionis*) was assigned within which only its members might preach and collect alms. The jurisdiction of each prior therefore extended beyond the walls of the cloister. To these *termini* also belonged the nunneries for whose spiritual well-being the convent was responsible.[74]

Although Cologne witnessed the comparatively early appearance of beguine houses and penitential bands, it was not until 1263 that the first real Dominican nunnery was established in the city.[75] Anna von Munzingen in her chronicle admits that when the group of beguine-like women from which Adelhausen developed first appeared there was not yet a Dominican house in Freiburg, but Countess Kunigunde von Sulz, sister of Rudolf of Hapsburg, in 1236, fifteen years after St. Dominic's death, entrusted the women to Preachers from Strasbourg.[76] According to Bernard Gui two-thirds of the Dominican nunneries in 1277 belonged to Teutonia, while the province possessed fifty-three men's houses in addition to forty nunneries.[77] By 1287 the provincial of Germany, Hermann von Minden, had under his charge no less than seventy nunneries [78]—a number that surpassed that of houses for men[79]—whereas the other seventeen provinces com-

[73] Löhr, in *RQ*., XXXIII (1925), 161.

[74] Löhr, in *QF*., XIX, 157; for description attributed to Hermann von Minden of the powers of vicars over sisters and their confessors, *RQ*., XXXIII (1925), 161-164, no. 1. A closer description of convents with the nunneries in their *termini* is given by Johannes Meyer in his *Ämterbuch* published by König in *Freib. Diöz-Arch.*, XIII, 207-209 (nationes Alsatiae et Sueviae) and Reichert in *RQ*, XV (1901), 126-127 (nationes Bavariae et Brabantiae), on the basis of the MS. Ämterbuch of the St. Agnes nunnery in Freiburg (1481). In the *terminus* of the Trèves convent were two nunneries in the city: St. Barbara (Wilms, *QF*., XXIV, 61-62) and St. Catherine (*ibid.*, 62-63); in the *terminus* of the Cologne convent was St. Gertrude (*ibid.*, 64-65); Val-Duchesse at Auderghem depended on the Louvain house (*ibid.*, 65-66). The Ämterbuch then adds that many convents in the *nacio Brabantiae* have no nunneries in their *termini*: Mainz, Frankfurt, Aachen, Coblenz (but see Wiems, *QF*., XXIV, 63-64), Antwerp, Bois-le-Duc and Maestricht.

[75] Decker, p. 73.

[76] *Freib. Diöz-Arch.*, XIII (1880), 153; cf. 132. It soon claimed the attention of the well-to-do ("biderbe lute") (see König's identification, *ibid.*, 133). Bishop Henry of Constance allowed Dominicans to settle in Freiburg in 1235 (*Freib. UB.*, I, 43-44, no. 56). The following year (December 13) the local priest admitted them to his parish (*ibid.*, 44-45, no. 58) while the city appealed for friars (December 14) (*ibid.*, 45-46, no. 59). But when the bishop took Adelhausen under his protection on October 12, 1234 he referred to "quasdam pauperculas et religiosas sorores . . . que sub habitu religionis imitando regulam beati Augustini de ordine Predicatorum" and "secundum consuetudinem Sancti Marci in Argentina" (*ibid.*, 42-43, no. 55).

[77] Cf. *Historia Fundationum Conventuum Ordinis Praedicatorum Tolosanae et Provinciae Provinciarum*, MDAC. VI, 437-540.

[78] Finke, p. 46; cf. *Numerus monasteriorum monialium Ordinis Fratrum Praedicatorum*, MDAC., VI, 539-548; ALKM., II, 643. Decker (p. 111) lists seventy-four convents of women in Germany and only sixty-seven in the other sixteen provinces. According to Grundmann (*Religiöse Bewegungen*, pp. 312-318) there were 58 Dominican nunneries in 1277; 70 in 1287; 141 in 1303 whereas Franciscan nunneries numbered 285.

[79] Denifle, in *ALKM.*, II, 643. In other provinces the ratio was reversed, not to mention two provinces which had no nunneries.

bined (including the *provincia Saxoniae* with its nine women's convents) possessed perhaps ninety. At the separation of Teutonia and Saxonia in 1301 the *Codex Cracoviensis* mentions for these two provinces together seventy-seven nunneries, with eleven being forgotten, and forty-six men's houses.[80] Among the German cities in which semireligious as well as regular life found abundant and multifarious expression, Strasbourg must be singled out for special comment. Feminine piety which appears to have been particularly active here must have come under the influence of the Friars Preachers shortly after their first appearance in the Rhenish city,[81] for Bernard Gui noted the existence of no less than seven Dominican nunneries,[82] all dating before 1250. Even as Henry of Cologne was well disposed towards the *cura monialium*, so in Strasbourg it was the prior and lector Walter, known as the "fundator diversorum cenobiorum sororum ordinis," who contributed to the founding of the convents of Unterlinden[83] at Colmar and Adelhausen at Freiburg.[84] St. Mark's in Strasbourg[85] played within a narrower orbit than St. Sisto a significant role in extending Dominican paternity and establishing internal organization of numerous nunneries in southwest Germany.

The additional burden which the feminine religious movement put upon the shoulders of the provincial for Germany was fully appreciated by Hermann von Minden (1286—1290),[86] for he pointed out to his subordinate priors in a memorandum that "the sisters might encounter some harm, unless you look after them."[87] Finke included in his collection of Dominican letters a number of Hermann's which reveal "a vast knowledge of practical monastic life, its requirements and difficulties, and a born organizer and prelate."[88] In his *Admoni-*

---

[80] Axters, in *OGE.*, XIII, 166; Wilms, in *QF.*, XXIV, 21-74, 88-98.
[81] 1224, according to Ellenhard, *Argentinensis Annales, MGH. SS.*, XVII, 101; cf. *Ann. Colmar., ibid.*, 169, an. 1226. That asceticism made an ever stronger appeal among women after 1100 is eloquently demonstrated by the multiplication of convents and foundations: in 900 there were but seventy in Germany; the number had increased to about 150 in 1100, but by the middle of the thirteenth century there were more than five hundred (Hauck, IV, 416).
[82] *MDAC.*, VI, 546-547. See Hermann von Minden's memorandum to the subpriors of the houses (St. Mark, St. Agnes, St. Elizabeth, St. Nicholas, St. John, St. Catherine, St. Margaret), *ALKM.*, II, 651-652. For these houses consult Wilms, in *QF.*, XXIV, 52-58.
[83] *Ibid.*, 49-50.
[84] Decker, p. 74; cf. König, "Zur Geschichte der Freiburger Klöster," *Freib. Diöz.-Arch.*, XII (1878), 291-303.
[85] Wilms, in *QF.*, XXIV, 54f; Decker, p. 74. The *modus vivendi* of the convent conformed to the rule of St. Augustine and the customs of St. Sisto.
[86] For Hermann's life and work see Finke, pp. 22-43; Löhr, in *RQ.*, XXXIII (1925), 159-167.
[87] *ALKM.*, II, 649: "... Sorores possent aliquod, nisi respicerentur a vobis, incurrere detrimentum."
[88] Löhr, in *RQ.*, XXXIII, 160. See documents edited by Von Loë where Hermann "waz gar ser fast geflissen an dem ampt" (*QF.*, I, 27; cf. 45).

tiones drawn up in 1286—1287 the provincial enjoined the friars to
lend support to the claustration of nuns and to instill reverence for
discipline.[89] The *Liber Officium* of Humbert de Romans (1259), a
manual for Dominicans, was put into German a century and a half

[89] *ALKM.*, II 649f; cf. *Res Alsat.*, *MGH. SS.*, XVII, 234. In 1289 Hermann entrusted the prior of Esslingen with the removal of evils, especially in claustration, in St. Mary's convent at Steinheim a. d. Muhr (dioc. Speyer) and at Gmünd (dioc. Augsburg), both in Württemberg (Finke, pp. 133f, no. 113; Wilms, pp. 41, 44). The preceding year he had recommended frequent visitation of St. Bartholomew's at Neuburg m. Neckar (dioc. Worms) (Finke, pp. 118f, no 95 and note; Wilms, p. 76) and regulated Himmelskron convent at Hochheim near Worms (Finke, p. 119 note; Wilms, p. 58; cf. 83). At the same time he instructed the priors of Regensburg and Nürnberg to prevent violation of nunneries committed to their care (Finke, pp. 118f, no. 95). The Provincial also exercised jurisdiction in the Himmelswonne convent at Löwental near Friedrichshafen (dioc. Constance) (*ibid.*, pp. 137f, no. 119; Wilms, p. 36). Whereas the legate John Boccamazzi on October 29, 1287, withdrew from the Strasbourg nunneries under the jurisdiction of the Order of Preachers permission to hold service once a week in one of their cloisters (*Strasb. UB.*, II, 89, no. 128; cf. Finke, p. 133 note to 112) Hermann formulated two years later rules for these houses during interdict (*ibid.*, 128-131, no. 108; Wilms, pp. 52-53; cf. 55-56). In 1289 he entrusted St. Bartholomew's (before 1274 St. Mary's) at Pettendorf in Bavaria (dioc. Regensburg) to the prior of Regensburg with reference to a second incorporation following the conflagration of 1274 (Finke, pp. 135f, no. 116; Wilms, p. 28). The sisters of St. Lambert in Bavaria (dioc. Speyer) who had petitioned *stulte* were forbidden by Hermann while still a mere friar (1277-81) to eat in public (Finke, pp. 105f, no. 83; Wilms, p. 68). As provincial he addressed his Admonitions to Val-Duchesse at Auderghem (dioc. Cambrai) (Finke, p. 108, no. 86; Wilms, p. 65), founded in 1262 by Aleida, widow of Duke Henry III of Brabant. St. Mark's in Würzburg and St. Mary's in Rothenburg ob der Tauber were specifically mentioned as Dominican nunneries (Finke, pp. 135f, no. 116; Wilms, pp. 66, 70). In the same year (1289) he delegated the subprioress and the sisters Agnes von Hohenstein and Gertrude von Königshofen of St. Mark's to investigate two sisters (Finke, p. 132, a women's convent in Plauen and promised to send "suitable persons" (1289 *ibid.*, no. 136, no. 117). Again, he reprimanded the inmates of St. Margaret (Strasbourg) for admitting Franciscans (*ibid.*, p. 133, no. 112). He allowed the establishment of a women's convent in Plauen and promised to sent "suitable persons" (1289 *ibid.*, pp. 156f, no. 144; Wilms, p. 93). To the convent at Brunnadern near Berne (dioc. Lausanne), founded in 1286 by Mechtild von Seedorf, the provincial sent four sisters from Ötenbach to instruct it in the customs of the order (Von Loë, in *QF.*, I, 27; Wilms, p. 78; cf. Hermann's letter of 1289 to the prior and subprior in Zurich with reference to a beguine, Finke, p. 123, no. 102). It was presumably Hermann who wrote to the prioress and sisters of Unterlinden in Colmar (*RQ.*, XXXIII [1925], 166f, no. 3; cf. Wilms, pp. 38, 84ff). In 1289 the provincial ordered the prior at Colmar to punish a brother who had entered St. Agnes convent at Strasbourg and another who by deceiving simple women arrogated to himself authority to hear confessions (Funke, pp. 132f, no. 111). In the same year Hermann, after permitting Countess von Regenstein to choose sisters from the convent of Wedderstedt (Wiederstedt) to establish the St. Nicholas house in Halberstadt (*ibid.*, pp. 145f, no. 128), fixed the obligation of Wedderstedt for the new foundation (*ibid.*, pp. 157f, no. 146). St. Nicholas was recognized by the city on May 13, 1289, and confirmed later that year (November 14) by Pope Nicholas IV (Wilms, p. 90). For St. Mary's at Wedderstedt (dioc. Halberstadt) see *ibid.*, pp. 90f). The countess herself was to remain with the sisters in the habit of a widow or a beguine (Finke, p. 145). Cf. *ibid.*, pp. 152f, no. 139. The provincial restored to Friar Arnold of Lübeck, although permanently disqualified from full status by a crime, his place in the choir provided that he preach in less conspicuous places and not hear confessions, above all from women (1289, *ibid.*, p. 143, no. 124). See his decision with respect to a hospital for a reference to "beguines or nuns," *ibid.*, p. 152, no. 138; cf. p. 143, no. 125; pp. 154f, no. 142.

later (1454) by Johannes Meyer with suitable modification for the comfort and instruction of the sisters.[90] Abuses had appeared under
Hermann's predecessor. In a letter to the prior of Chur (1289) the
provincial forbade traffic with strangers in the convent.[91] A worse
evil was the habit of Swabian nuns of leaving the cloister to visit
relatives and friends. Whoever persisted in this practice was banned
and suspected of apostasy.[92] Besides regulations in which the friars
were instructed in the proper method of handling the *Ordo Sororum
Poenitentium Beatae Mariae Magdalenae* which John Boccamazzi,
bishop of Tusculum, had confided during his legation in Germany
(1286—88) to the provincial,[93] Hermann carefully drew up, with full
cognizance of the new obligations, detailed recommendations for those
members on whom the *cura monialium* devolved. It was primarily
the learned friars—masters of arts and lecturers in theology—who were
designated to deliver the sermons in women's convents.[94] Elsewhere
the prior is urged to provide sermons at time of communion for the
sisters; these sermons were to given on vigils rather than saints' days
in order that the people should not be attracted from parish churches
to the friars.[95] Although preaching and pastoral care were thereby
extended to the nunneries, the sisters were nevertheless warned not
to summon friars save in cases of necessity, for the men were expected
to devote themselves to schools, choir, study, confessions, and other
observances proper to the order.[96] Such a policy had long before been
anticipated in recognition of the importance of beguine needs: "Prio-
res in domibus nostris ubique confessores beginarum instituant certos
maturos et paucos".[97] To the Strasbourg nuns who protested their
spiritual needs General Munio explained in May, 1289, that their
chaplains, whether in the habit of the order or in other suitable clerical

[90] Published in part by König, in *Freib. Diöz.-Arch.*, XIII (1880), 196-206.
[91] Finke, pp. 134f, no. 114; cf. p. 46.
[92] May, 1289, *ibid.*, pp. 138f, no. 120.
[93] *Res Alsat., MGH. SS.*, XVII, 234; *Ann. Colm. Mai., ibid.*, 213: "Commisse sunt
sorores que dicuntur Penitentes fratribus Predicatoribus ad regendum." On November 20, 1286, the legate put under the provincial of Germany all the convents of
St. Mary Magdalene in that region, charging him with their administration within
the scope of the rule of St. Augustine and the Institutes of St. Sixtus. This was not
incorporation but rather, as the Colmar chronicler indicates, a simple commission
involving new supervision without disturbing previous status (Simon, pp. 86f; for
John Boccamazzi, see *ibid.*, pp. 85-94). Cf. Wilms, pp. 21, 67f, 74, 84, 86.
[94] "Providete, ne refectione careant verbi dei, sed, sicut erudicioni ipsarum con-
venit, per fratres doctos sepius predicetur" (*ALKM.*, II, 650).
[95] "Temporibus communionis provideat prior, quod sermones fiant eis (srori-
bus) ... pocius fiant in vigiliis quam in festis" (*ibid.*, II, 645).
[96] "Moneo insuper sorores, quod vocent fratres sicut possunt rarius utilitate vel
necessitate legitima non existente, cum ipsi scolis, choro, studio, confessionibus et
aliis observanciis proprii ordinis debeant intendere" (*idem*).
[97] Chapter of Paris (1243), *MOPH.*, III, 26; *MDT.*, IV, 1684.

attire, should all have equal power in the several houses in administering the sacraments and hearing confessions.[98]

The official hostility which we traced above had as little adverse
effect on pastoral and administrative work among·local beguines by
Dominican friars as the chapter legislation of Citeaux had had. If
the monks lost interest, it was in some measure due to competition
from the friars. In Belgium the Dominicans from their earliest appearance identified themselves with the *Frauenfrage*.[99] They occur in
innumerable documents as witnesses of testaments, leases, and other
business transactions, recipients of donations, sometimes in return for
anniversary masses, administrators of *temporalia*, confessors, and
pastors.[100] The *Acta* of Christine of Stommeln, we shall see, is a detailed study of the interpenetration of the Friar Preacher and the feminine religious movement. But Thomas of Cantimpré had already reflected in his own career a generous acquaintance with these fresh
spiritual currents and the folklore with which they were enmeshed.
His life of Lutgarde introduced into hagiographical fabric the late
Jordan of Saxony as a sort of bridge with the Cistercian world.[101]
Another Dominican "confided in the saint above all other women, so
much so that he thought of her as mother and fosterer of the whole
Order of Preachers. We have also seen her devoted and diligent above
all other orders to the friars; wherefore and in their behalf she daily
exhibited zealous complaisance to God."[102] "Trustworthy" friars were
ready to corroborate Thomas' account of a Brabançon girl who had
been favored with the stigmata.[103] The hatred of Guillaume de Saint-

[98] Finke, pp. 138f, no. 120. The provincial Hermann subsequently changed a provision of this letter with respect to communion through the window (*ibid.*, p. 140,
no. 121).

[99] Philippen, *Begijnhoven*, pp. 93-95, 112ff; Ollivier, *Le grand béguinage de
Gand*, pp. 82-96; Axters, in *OGE.*, XIII (1939), 149-184; Chapotin, *Histoire des Dominicains*, pp. 511ff.

[100] E.g., Boehmer, *UB. Frankfurt*, I, 343, 347 (November 12, 1302), 405f; cf. 391f;
Phillips, *Beguines in Medieval Strasburg*, pp. 219-225. The *Res Alsaticae* even
records that beguines as well as *conversi* and serfs were used by both Franciscans
and Dominicans in the fields and vineyards (*MGH. SS.*, XVII, 234, 235); see above
p. 125 n. 24.

[101] *V. Lutg.*, 204f (III, 2-3).

[102] *Ibid.*, 205 B (III, 3); cf. 205 F (III, 7). The Dominican friar Bernard visited
Aywières two years before Lutgard's death for which she was daily preparing (*ibid.*,
206, III, 9); for Bernard, 205 (III, 5, 7).

[103] Thomas of Cantimpré, *BUA.*, I, 25, 7 (p. 105). Besides the intimate details
contained in his other hagiographic writings: the lives of Christine Mirabilis (cf.
ibid., II, 53, 23, pp. 505f) and the Dominican Margaret of Ypres as well as the
Supplementum to *VMO.* (cf. *ibid.*, II, 54, 18, pp. 529f), the *BUA.*, too, faithfully
reflects Thomas' avidity as friend, eyewitness, and mere listener for accounts in
Belgium of the ecstasies, temptations, and pious works of Cistercian nuns, recluses,
beguines, or any woman interested in such matters: I, 11, 3; 23, 2; 25, 7; II, 10, 8;
25, 8-9; 29, 16; 29, 20; 29, 30; 29, 39-40; 30, 31; 54, 10; 57, 14; 57, 15; 57, 53; 55,
25; 57, 66-67. Stephen of Bourbon (d. ca. 1261), on the contrary, was so indebted to
secondary sources, above all to Jacques de Vitry and plain hearsay, that seldom does

Amour and Rutebeuf for the beguines is explainable by their dislike for the Friars Preachers, so close were their relations with the feminine religious movement. In towns where a Dominican convent existed, the beguines and penitents were often put under its direction. Indeed, Richer's oft-cited judgment, "que videns plurimas mulieres sub doctrina dictorum Predictorum specie religionis florere, que beguine appellantur,"[104] implies that the diffusion of beguines was conditioned by that of Dominicans.

They were especially active in this work in Flanders and Hainault where they acted as spiritual advisers of the two countesses to whom many a beguinage owed its well-being. In October, 1236, Walter, provisor of the Ghent beguines, was appointed their chaplain. He was to enjoy the income of the post as long as he filled the office of provisor, subject to approval of the abbess of La Biloke and the Dominican prior. Acknowledging that comital sponsorship of St. Elizabeth was no longer adequate, Count Guy on July 17, 1282, entrusted its affairs to the prior of the Dominicans and Pierre Uten Hove.[105] On October 15, 1312, Count Robert of Flanders informed the prior that he would have full jurisdiction over the beguinage: he could appoint the mistress, install and depose chaplains.[106] Margaret, in giving statutes to the Ypres beguinage and its infirmary in 1270, entrusted its direction to a *souveraine maitresse* who was expected to follow the counsels of the local Dominican prior.[107] The Dominican convent founded by the countess in the parish of St. André at Lille lay close to the beguinage.[108] It is possible that the Dominicans of Ghent gave impetus to the foundation of the beguinage of Alost in 1261 by Walter de Ghier and his wife. Two friars appear with the clergy of St. Martin's as witnesses of the donation act.[109]

The same relationship is revealed in the dioceses of Cambrai and Liége. On May 3, 1259, the archdeacon of Liége approved the establishment of a beguine parish at Aerschot, charging the prior of the Louvain Dominicans to appoint the priest.[110] In 1246 the same prior had been involved in the disposal of property by John of Zanthove in behalf on the beguines of Antwerp. The transaction was made in

he betray personal acquaintance with the feminine religious movement (for exceptions, see *Anec. hist.*, nos. 78, 210; cf 19, 21, 77, 78, 88, 110, 134, 135, 154, 206, 237, 248, 362, 371, 380). Belonging in the main to a masculine world, his examples reflect the ardent crusade preacher (nos. 163, 227, 310, 343) and inquisitor (nos. 18, 170, 366, 370, etc.) but not the zealous sponsor of the *cura monialium*.

[104] Richer, *Gesta Eccl. Senon., MGH. SS.*, XXV, 308.
[105] See below p. 410
[106] See above p. 96.
[107] MF., IV, 253f; Wauters, *TC.*, V, 445; see below p. 213.
[108] Wauters, *TC.*, V, 533.
[109] Soens, *Cartularium*, pp. 8f.
[110] De Ridder, in *Hagelands Gedenkschriften*, VI (1913), 22.

the Dominican convent in that city.[111] In 1270 the Antwerp prior and Friar Leonius were responsible for erecting and administering the beguine parish of Herenthals.[112] At Léau the prior of the Louvain convent to appoint the confessor of the beguines.[113] At Diest, Philip, prior of the Louvain house, and Friar Rixo helped in 1265 to fix the boundaries of the beguine parish.[114] As for the St. Christopher beguinage, which remained the only feminine society in Liege until the fifteenth century,[115] the prior acted as judge extraordinary whenever special difficulties arose in the community.[116] A collection of documents cited by Wilmotte in *Romania*[117] and taken from the Dominican archives in Liége, demonstrates how continuous these relations could be. The donation that made the foundation of the Tongres beguinage possible in 1243 was witnessed by Renier and two Dominicans, Michael and Godeschalk, both of Liége.[118]

At Bois-le-Duc the Dominican nuns of Val-Duchesse played a role in the founding of the beguinage. Probably at their request Friar Franco, prior of the Dominicans in Louvain, in agreement with the deacon of Cuyck and the pastor of St. Peter's at Vucht, ordained in 1274 the erection of an independent parish. On July 6, 1274, the beguines accordingly were allowed to have their own church, cemetery, and pastor to administer the sacraments and conduct burial. The prioress of the Dominicans became patron of the beguine church, presenting the priest to the archdeacon for appointment. The pastor must be satisfied with the *oblationes* and *obventiones* coming from the beguines and must promise not to encroach on the prioress.[119]

The Dominicans were equally concerned with the extraregular in other countries. When Bishop Arnold of Amiens founded the beguinage where in 1264 Elizabeth the Elder, an admirer of the Friars Preachers, was superior, he entrusted its administration to Dominicans.[120] The Paris beguines attracted their attention, with Geoffrey of Beaulieu dedicating himself to their spiritual well-being.[121] They were supervised by the friars until the fifteenth century; the grand mistresses had the right to be buried in the Dominican church. Even

[111] March 26, 1245/46, Prims, in *BG.*, XVIII (1927), 228.

[112] Philippen, *Begijnhoven*, pp. 94, 120f.

[113] Tarlier and Wauters, *Géog. et hist. des communes belges, Prov. de Brab. Canton de Léau*, p. 69.

[114] Raymaekers, *Kerkelijk Diest*, p. 428.

[115] Kurth, *La Cité de Liége*, II, 255.

[116] *AHEB.*, XXXII (1906), 273.

[117] *Romania*, XVII (1888), 588-589: "March, 1290, testament of "Sibile beghine de waremme" on behalf of the Friars Preachers of Liége et al; testament of "Vde de sain Servais beguine" (October, 1297); document of 1293.

[118] Thijs, in *BSSLL.*, XV, 417.

[119] MF., III, 128; cf. Philippen, *Begijnhoven*, p. 125.

[120] Ollivier, *op. cit.*, p. 28.

[121] See below pp. 225, 341f.

in Budapest two *curtes beguinarum* were supervised by the Preachers. An altercation between the grand mistresses Albatha and Christine in 1308 over possession of a vineyard and house was resolved in the Dominican convent.[122]

But it was above all the German Friars Preachers who organized various groups of religious women into convents affiliated with their order. Wilms lists several Dominican nunneries which developed from beguine houses, or *Samenunge* of devout, poor women and maidens who lived like beguines, into hearths of mysticism in the thirteenth centuries.[123] Before 1276, in Strasbourg, Turm and Offenburg were

[122] Ollivier, *op cit.*, p. 35.

[123] The White Cloister (*das weise Klösterle*) in Coblenz (dioc. Trèves, nation Brabant) was founded in 1276 by Gertrude, who donated with the advice of a Dominican prior a stone house for the use of six "poor beguines" who might live in chastity and charity. The prior had the right to substitute new beguines at his discretion. Documents of the beguine convent extend only to 1346 (Wilms, p. 63). St. Lawrence house at Vienna (dioc. Passau) started as a beguine community at an unknown date; in 1301 the sisters were obliged by Bernhard of Passau to embrace an approved rule. Thereupon they chose the Dominican constitution, joined the nuns of Tulln, and came under the supervision of the prior at Vienna (Wilms, pp. 24f). Originally a beguine house, the Katharinental convent was founded in Diessenhofen (dioc. Constance), then moved in 1242 to its permanent location where the nuns followed the rule of St. Mark's in Strasbourg (*ibid.*, p. 36; Hauck, IV, 991). Innocent IV incorporated this center of mysticism in the Order of Preachers in 1245 (*Freib. Diöz.-Arch.*, XI, 20). St. Mary's at Weil in Württemberg (dioc. Constance) was founded on July 11, 1230, when Bishop Conrad approved an agreement between the deacon Henry of Nellingen and some beguines of Esslingen for a settlement there (Wilms, pp. 40f; Hauck, IV, 990; incorporated on September 9, 1245, *BOP.*, I, 153, no. 98; P. 11862). For Adelhausen, which started before 1232 as a beguine community and was incorporated on June 12, 1245, and May 18, 1249 (*Freib. Diöz.-Arch.*, XII [1878], 295, 301; König, in *ibid.*, XIII, 132-135, 154, 195), see above note 75. The book *Von der genaden vberlast* describes a similar society in Nürnberg: "Ez waz ein cleinew samenunge von begin in der stat" (ed. K. Schröder, Stuttgarter liter. Verein, CVIII [1871], p. 1; cited by König, in *Freib. Diö-Arch.*, XIII, 153, note 11; *Deutsches Nonnenleben*, p. 264). The *inclusorium* at Weissenburg in Alsace, located near the Dominican convent, was mentioned in 1305 (*Strasb. UB.*, III, 175, no. 561). After following the Augustinian rule, the beguines were united on December 8, 1425, by the bishop of Speier with the Dominican nunnery known as Merenbrunnen (Wilms, p. 84). Engelthal (dioc. Eichstätt) was founded about 1240 by Adelheid who headed some beguines in Nürnberg. In 1243 the sisters removed to the farm at Schweinach, called Engelthal, which Ulrich von Königstein had given to them. Their acceptance of the Augustinian rule and the constitution of the Order of Preachers was confirmed by Innocent IV on October 10, 1248 (*ibid.*, pp. 70-71). St. Gertrude's at Cologne, founded by Hetwigis of Strasbourg (Löhr, in *AHVN.*, CX [1927], 158) owed its origins to the removal of beguines about 1257 to the New Market (*ibid.*, 65; Ennen-Eckertz, *Quellen*, II, 183, no. 183; Wilms [p. 64, note 2] corrects the date of this document from 1238 to 1338). While Alexander IV on November 13, 1257, took these Augustinian *inclusae* under papal protection and confirmed their possessions, his successor on September 17, 1263, instructed Archbishop Engelbert II to allow the sisters to follow the Dominican version of the Augustinian rule if their resources permitted common life (*ibid.*, p. 64; incorporated by General Munio de Zamora in 1285, Löhr, in *QF.*, XVI, 43, no. 79) and confirmed by the legate John Boccamazzi two years later (December 8) (Wilms, p. 64). The beguine convents at Cologne were entrusted by Archbishop Conrad of Hochstaden to the local Dominican prior (Ennen-Eckertz, *Quellen*, II, 445-6, no. 428; Greving, in *AHVN.*, LXXIII [1902], 63f).

located alongside the Dominican convent, and Innenheim a short distance away. In 1276, to ensure the maintenance of common property,[124] their inhabitants, in the presence of their father and relatives who presumably sponsored these communities, agreed upon statutes which were identical for each house. Their Dominican confessor, Frederick von Erstheim, probably supervised this step, which was directed to eventual transformation of these houses into convents.[125] In the same year a beguine convent rose at Coblenz from a donation of a stone house by one Gertrude in behalf of six poor beguines living "in chastity and charity" and at the advice of the local Dominican prior. Other foundations followed until a fully developed women's convent emerged. Documents of the beguine house go back only to 1346. But what passes for a Dominican nunnery may be merely a continuation of this early establishment.[126] At Cologne the beguine Bertha vom Walde converted her house into a dwelling for twelve poor beguines who were put under the care of the Dominican prior (October 9, 1287).[127]

[124] Phillips, *Beguines in Medieval Strasburg*, pp. 165, 166.
[125] *Strasb. UB.*, III, 78, 79, 81.
[126] Wilms, p. 63.
[127] Ennen-Eckertz, *Quellen*, III, 260,261, no. 289. On October 29, 1295 Mathilda, a beguine and daughter of Hermann of Lagge, made available one half of her house for seven beguines who were entrusted to the Dominicans (*ibid.*, III, 404-405, no. 421; cf. June 18, 1305 *ibid.*, III, 506-507, no. 531).

❧ IX ❧

Comital Patronage in Flanders

Under comital auspices the beguinages, like other forms of religious and extraregular life, waxed as strong in Flanders and Hainault as in the diocese of Liége and the duchy of Brabant.[1] Baillis and echevins were instructed repeatedly to implement the willingness of the prince to defend inmates from despoilers. Such a general order was despatched by Jeanne when she acknowledged in 1241 that women consorted with beguines, intending to live with them "piously and devoutly."[2]

The term *mulieres religiosae* appears to have been employed for the first time in Flanders, and specifically in Ghent, in a document dated June, 1233. Abbess Elizabeth of the Cistercian nunnery Port-Saint Marie or Biloke, at the request of Jeanne of Flanders and Hainault put at the disposal of "mulieres religiosae caste et sub disciplina vivere volentes" a piece of land "extra portam Gandavi versus Heckerghem," near the Biloke, for the purpose of erecting buildings which, at the advice of *probi viri*, would be made available to these women. The document makes it clear that the beguines merely enjoyed the usufruct of this land subject to residence on it. To them was also assigned a chaplaincy which had been founded at la Biloke when its members resided beside St. Michael's in the former Wittox hospital, then belonging to the Dominicans. Although some *mulieres religiosae* were still living dispersed in the city, others were beginning to lead a common life under mistresses, for the document speaks of "mulieres alique in magisterio ibidem constituto." Furthermore, *viri probi*, as advisers to these beguines, promulgated ordinances which served as the nucleus of a rule.[3]

---

[1] Jacques de Guise, *Ann. Han., MGH. SS.,* XXX, 1, 276; Luykx, "Gravin Johanna van Constantinopel en de godsdienstige vrouwenbeweging in Vlaanderen gedurende de eerste helft der XIIIe eeuw," *OGE.,* XVII (1943), 1-30; id., *Johanna van Constantinopel,* pp. 345-359, 412-420.

[2] MF., III, 592.

[3] Béthune, *Cartulaire,* pp. 302-303, no. 1 *bis.* When Ryckel (p. 563) published and Miraeus-Foppens (IV, 541-542) reprinted the document whereby John son of Alexander, or Sersanders, donated a ditch to the beguines of St. Elizabeth in return for celebrating an anniversary for his late wife, Elizabeth Rijms, and himself, they

After Ferrand's death (1233) the countess became more solicitous for their well-being. In December, 1235, she assigned to the abbess of la Biloke "for the salvation of his soul and ours" an annual income of 15 l. 5 d. from new land in the parish of Assenede with the understanding that this sum should be applied to the *religiosae mulieres pauperes* until they had a chaplain and chapel of their own.[4]

In October 1236, Master Walter, provisor of the beguines, was installed as their first chaplain with the approval of the abbess of la Biloke and was to receive the above-mentioned 15 *l.* as long as he filled the office of provisor with the consent of the abbess and the prior of the Dominicans.[5] The women, who were given the name *beguine* in this document for the first time, nevertheless remained bound to the abbey, since its church was used by their chaplain for their chaplain for their services.[6] The steady growth of the movement encouraged Jeanne to provide it with additional land in 1242. The countess, who had been negotiating since 1233 with the abbess of la Biloke for the establishment and endowment of a refuge for these *religiosae mulieres pauperes*, was finally obliged, in view of her demands,[7] to resort to the generosity of the echevins and castellan in Ghent to organize a *curtis*. On May 14 Jeanne called on the Ghent echevins to make available to the beguines the area called the "Broeck" for the construction of a house.[8] The echevinage promptly acceded to the request.[9] During the same year the countess issued a document which not only expressed concern for ample quarters for the Dominicans in the city but also assigned to the *mulieres religiosae* the property next to the hospital of Wittox which had been acquired from the echevins, with the specific recommendation that it should be used as a hospital, dedicated to St. Elizabeth, for sick beguines. Should

erroneously dated it July, 1227 (cf. Wauters, *TC.*, IV, 41). Béthune (*Cartulaire*, p. 1, no. 1) analyzes it under this date but prints it under the correct year 1277 (*ibid.*, pp. 30-31, no. 37; cf. p. v). Internal evidence alone — the use of the term *beghinae* — argues against the earlier date.

[4] Béthume, *Cartulaire*, pp. 1-2, no. 2.

[5] *Ibid.*, pp. 2-3, no. 3. This document, like the preceding one for December, 1235, received a vidimus from Countess Margaret and her son Guy on July 19, 1263 (*ibid.*, pp. 15-16, no. 20), another on May 12, 1300 (*ibid.*, 50, no. 69), and finally one from Walter, abbot of St. Bavon, at Ghent on November 23, 1301 (*ibid.*, p. 52, no. 72).

[6] According to Moulaert (*Het groot Beggijnhof*, p. viii), Margaret founded a second chaplaincy in 1254, but Béthune (*Cartulaire*, p. 8, note 1) was unable to locate confirmation of a third chaplaincy which Moulaert attributed to a certain Henry and was approved by Walter, bishop of Tournai, in 1258. At the same time Béthune (*ibid.*, p. 8, no. 10) hesitated to accept Van Lokeren's (*Analyse succincte des chartes et documents de l'abbaye de Saint-Bavon*, p. 27) analysis of a document of 1242 whereby the provisors of St. Elizabeth presented Robert van Schelden as a candidate for the second chaplaincy. The date is too early.

[7] Béthune, *Cartulaire*, pp. 302-303.

[8] *Ibid.*, p. 3, no. 4; Wauters, *TC.*, IV, 369; cf. Fris, *Histoire de Gand*, p. 31.

[9] May, 1242, Béthune, *Cartulaire*, p. 4, no. 5; Wauters, *TC.*, IV, 370.

they cease to occupy it, it must not be assigned to laymen unless it reverted to the ownership and jurisdiction of the town. To this hospital was now transferred the chaplaincy which had belonged to the hospital next to St. Michael's before it was consigned to the Friars Preachers. The abbess of La Biloke, at the advice of the Dominican prior, must contribute each year 15 *l.* to maintain the chaplain who ministered to the *mulieres religiosae* and the hospital of St. Elizabeth. Jeanne in turn had assigned the abbess 15 *l.* of rent next to her convent between Haghe and Trist. The countess also promised 300 *l.* for the construction of St. Elizabeth. St. Bavon and the parish priests were to enjoy the same rights in the new hospital and its chapel which they previously had in the hospital of St. Michael when the latter was transferred to the Dominicans.[10] The abbot of the Benedictine monastery within whose jurisdiction the piece of ground donated by Jeanne lay agreed in July, 1242, to the building of the church and the laying out of a cemetery for the exclusive use of the sisters. The abbot claimed the right of appointing the chaplain. At least once a year the beguines must confess to the priest (*proprio sacerdoti*) in whose parish the community was located. As a token of dependence on St. Bavon they were expected to pay the abbot one gold piece, worth 5 *s.*, each year. At the same time the bishop of Tournai had the right to install the provisors.[11] This arrangement met the approval of the countess the following month.[12] In November of the same year Hugh, castellan of Ghent and lord of Hosdaing, relinquished, at the request of Thomas and Jeanne, all claims to the land of the beguinage outside Ghent, between Borcstrate and Overbroch.[13] On October 21, 1243, Jeanne raised the annual income of these beguines by 10 *l.* to be paid each Christmas for the chaplain, who, however, had not yet been appointed ("ad opus capellani qui ibidem deserviet"), by Master Henry of Badelinghem, canon of Tournai, from the proceeds of waste lands.[14]

So great was the expansion of the beguines in Ghent that a second beguinage had grown up in the meantime in a section called "Ten

[10] Béthune, *Cartulaire*, pp. 4-5, no. 6. The document received a vidimus in 1300 from the prior of the Friars Preachers and from Walter, abbot of St. Bavon, in 1301 (*ibid.*, p. 5, note).

[11] *Ibid.*, pp. 6-7, no. 7; Wauters, *TC.*, IV, 375. On February 16, 1378, Philip, bishop of Tournai, acknowledged the patronage of the abbot of St. Bavon over the chaplaincies of the beguinage in accordance with the agreement of July 14, 1259 (this document is not published by Béthune) and recalled Jeanne's foundation (Béthune, *Cartulaire*, pp. 116-117, no. 164). On August 19, 1418, an understanding was reached between the abbot and the superiors of the beguinages of St. Elizabeth and Ten Hoeye on the subject of lands at Eckerghem, (*ibid.*, pp. 138-140, no. 199).

[12] *Ibid.*, p. 7, no. 8; Wauters, *TC.*, IV, 377.

[13] Béthune, *Cartulaire*, p. 8, no. 9; Wauters, *TC.*, IV, 382.

[14] Béthune, *Cartulaire*, p. 9, no. 11. This document was reproduced in a vidimus of the Friars Preachers in 1300 and the following year by Walter, abbot of St. Bavon.

Hoeye" in St. John's parish. Already in 1240 the community had been established with church approval but without satisfactory settlement of parochial rights claimed by the priests of St. John.[15] The sources, however, make no reference to Jeanne's role in its organization.[16]

The beguines at Bruges were organized into a large parish in 1245, a year after Jeanne's death. But these *mulieres religiosae* must have been living for some time, scattered about the town, without chaplain or chapel. They first emerge from obscurity in 1242 when Jeanne took them under protection[17] and, according to Jacques de Guise, established their first chaplaincy.[18] At Ypres the beguines had been organized in 1240. Lambert, the provost, and the chapter of St. Martin's church declared in June that at the request of the count of Flanders they were making available to "pauperes mulieres, que Beghine vocantur," a piece of land at Briel at a rent of 60 s.[19] To her reign also has been attributed the first appearance at Valenciennes of "fratres beghini et sorores beghinae," in addition to a mixed hospital, with the approval of the bishop of Cambrai and the prior of St. Sauveur.[20] Margaret afterwards enlarged this beguinage. At Courtrai the beguinage, dedicated to St. Catherine, was founded in 1241 at the instigation of Jeanne who donated a house bought from Dignard of Halle.[21] From the beginning she apparently had shown special fondness for this city where her father Baldwin IX had projected Notre-Dame. The countess made frequent visits there, particularly during Ferrand's imprisonment at Paris.[22] Actually, the presence of beguines may be detected in this town as early as 1238;[23] presumably they were there much earlier.

Jeanne indicated in her will, dated December 4, 1244, that of the 200 *l.* of annual income which her sister Margaret had given to her to be disposed freely she was allotting 40 *l.* to Jean de Monsteruel, 10 *l.* to Marie de Castello, 100 *s.* to the beguinage at Douai, 100 *s.* each to the Friars Preachers at Valenciennes and those at Berges. The remaining 135 *livres* were to be distributed as the two Dominicans saw fit.[24]

15 Ryckel, p. 316; MF., III, 685-686; for a summary of its history, see Philippen, *Begijnhoven*, pp. 102-103. On January 13, 1330, Jan de Goutsmet willed not only to the infirmary of the beguinage 10 esc., but remembered the beguine house Ten Hoeye among other religious establishments (Béthune, *Cartulaire*, pp. 78-79, no. 108).
16 Luykx, in *OGE.*, XVII (1943), 23; id., *Johanna van Constantinopel*, p. 419.
17 Callewaert, in *ASEB.*, LVI (1906), 466-467; cf. De Jonghe, *Belgium Dominicanum*, p. 193.
18 *Ann. Han., MGH. SS.*, XXX, 1, 274.
19 Feys and Nelis, *Cartulaires de St. Martin*, II, 102-103, no. 153.
20 Jacques de Guise, *Ann. Han., MGH. SS.*, XXX, 1, 275 (XX, 48); cf. MF., II, 155; Wauters, *TC.*, IV, 317, 319.
21 MF., III, 108.
22 Luykx, in *OGE.*, XVII (1943), 24; id., *Johanna*, p. 419.
23 De Potter, *Gesch. der Stad Kortrijk*, III, 419.
24 *Inv. Lille*, p. 331, no. 808.

On March 4, 1245, Countess Margaret, with the encouragement of the Dominicans Henry van der Eeke and Michael, proceeded to execute that part of Jeanne's will which provided for the annual distribution of 200 *l.* in alms; the Ghent beguines—the "aermer ende zieker vrouwen die gheheeten zijn beghinen"—were to receive 10 *l.* of Flanders.[25] Like her sister, Margaret continued to bestow gifts on the beguinage,[26] to increase their domain through the sale of property,[27] to issue letters of protection recommending them to her officials and granting immunities,[28] and to show interest in its internal life, whether it be the statutes[29] or business transactions.[30]

Among the beguinages which owed much, from inception on, to comital patronage, Cantimpré or Cantimpret at Mons in Hainault must be singled out for special consideration. In February, 1245, the chapter of St. Germain, at the advice of the bishop of Cambrai and at the request of Margaret, transferred to the beguines of Pré-Notre-Dame near Mons (Cantimpret) full title to the property, comprising 6 bonniers of meadow outside the old walls in the parish of Cuesmes, where their hospital could be built.[31] The following June 5 Bishop

[25] Béthune, *Cartulaire*, pp. 9-10, no. 12; cf. *Inv. Lille*, p. 337, no. 824.

[26] In September, 1245, Margaret transferred as alms to the beguinage six bonniers between Assenede and Haghe to be held at the rate of 2 d. annually per bonnier (Béthune. *Cartulaire*, pp. 10-11, no. 13). This donation was confirmed by her son, Guy, in August, 1275 (*ibid.*, pp. 27-28, no. 32). In March, 1263, the countess granted to the infirmary the goods which Catherine Bruusch, a citizen of Ghent, had entrusted to her, through the *bailli* Walter Wilde, to be used for some charitable purpose. The hospital was expected to pay Catherine at Christmas 39 *l.* of Flanders as long as she remained alive "in quocumque habitu fuerit sive statu"; besides, she retained a right to dispose of the fruits of this property. Should the hospital cease to exist, the prior of the Dominicans would apply them to other pious ends (*ibid.*, pp. 14-15, no. 19). The Friars Preachers confirmed the donation on September 16, 1299 (*ibid.*, pp. 49-50, no. 66). Cf. *ibid.*, 15-16, no. 20; 22, no. 24.

[27] After Margaret, grand mistress of the beguinage, purchased in January, 1257, on behalf of the infirmary some tracts of land in Overbroeck (*ibid.*, pp. 12-13, no. 16), the countess sold the community three more bonniers of waste land at Overbroeck the following April (*ibid.*, pp. 13-14, no. 17). This act was ratified by Count Guy on October 9, 1279 (*ibid.*, p. 33, no. 40). Cf. *ibid.*, p. 22, no. 24 (March 1270); cf. Wauters, *TC.*, V, 447.

[28] In April, 1247, Margaret granted protection letters to the beguines with specific instructions to her baillis to prevent molestation (Béthune, *Cartulaire*, p. 11, no. 14). On March 12, 1249, the countess recommended them to the bailli of Ghent for safekeeping against molesters and troublemakers (*ibid.*, pp. 11-12, no. 15). Margaret issued another protection letter in 1260 (*ibid.*, p. 14, no. 18) and again on February 5, 1275 (*ibid.*, p. 27, no. 31).

[29] On May 21, 1269, Margaret prescribed (*ibid.*, pp. 17, no. 22) close observance of the statutes (for the rule, *ibid.*, pp. 17-22, no. 23).

[30] On July 18, 1277, Margaret and Guy sold to the beguinage ½ bonnier and 33 verges of marsh at Assenede (*ibid.*, p. 30, no. 36). In June, 1277, Margaret reviewed the donation made to the infirmary by the five daughters of Walter, son of Thomas de Bassevelde, of the land which they inherited from their parents, on condition that the mistress pay the daughters each year 20 *l.* of Flanders to be divided equally among them as long as they lived (*ibid.*, p. 29, no. 35).

[31] Devillers, *Description*, II, 139-140, no. 1; id., *Annales*, VI, 217-218; Wauters,

Guy of Cambrai approved the cession made by the chapter of St. Waudru at Mons for the sum of 120 *l. parisis* and with reservation of *jus
patronatus* and justice, of the place called Cantimpré for the use of
local poor beguines.[32] Papal recognition was secured when Innocent
IV on May 23, 1246, instructed the bishop of Cambrai to allow the
magistra et sorores to build a hospital[33] "as povres béghines et as
malades."[34] The bishop, at the request of the countess and with the
approval of the chapter of St. Waudru, then proceeded in July, 1243,
to establish the cure of the Cantimpré convent into a separate parish.
The priest of Cuesmes was to be indemnified by the chapter and the
priest of the new parish.[35] Thus the church and cemetery of the beguinage were founded under certain conditions with the approval of
the provost, dean, and the whole chapter on Margaret's recommendation. The chapter which enjoyed the collation of the cure must
maintain the buildings and religious objects. In January, 1249, the
countess, with the consent of her son John of Avesnes, assigned to this
hospital an annual income of 30 *l. de blancs* which several mentioned
persons were paying to Margaret for the area between the Epinlieu
road and the stream of Trouille, at the rate of 10 s. per bonnier.[36]
Later (April, 1250) Master Jean de la Place, priest of St. Germain,
handed over to the hospital with the consent of the chapter his
parochial rights over the garden of Aloudus Cambier, a citizen of
Mons, and the adjoining meadow in return for 4 *s. de blancs* payable
each year at the Nativity of John the Baptist.[37] On September 5,
1250, the cardinal-legate, Peter of Albano, approved the above-mentioned donation of 30. *l.* made by Margaret and John d'Avesnes.[38]

TC., IV, 441. For a brief history of Cantimpré, see Devillers, *Description*, II, 122-
138; id., *Annales*, VI, 200-217.

[32] Devillers, *Description*, II, 140-141, no. 2; id., *Annales*, VI, 218-219; Wauters
TC., IV, 447. Bishop Nicholas of Cambrai confirmed this grant on January 19, 1270
(Devillers, *Description*, II, 160-161, no. 17; id. *Annales*, VI, 238-239).

[33] Devillers, *Description*, II, 141, no. 3; id. *Annales*, VI, 219; Wauters, *TC.*, IV,
471-472.

[34] Devillers, *Description*, II, 175; id., *Annales*, VI, 253.

[35] Devillers, *Description*, II, 142-144, no. 4; id., *Annales*, VI, 220-222; Wauters,
TC., IV, 531. Margaret agreed in August, 1253, that the community should henceforth depend on St. Waudru (Devillers, *Description*, II, 155-156, no. 12; id., *Annales*,
VI, 233-234; Wauters, *TC.*, V, 65). Cf. the chapter's acceptance of the direction of
the hospital on February 21, 1274 (Devillers, *Description*, II, 169, no. 22; id., *Annales*, VI, 247; Wauters, *TC.*, V, 535).

[36] Devillers, *Description*, II, 144-146, no. 5; id., *Annales*, VI, 222-224; Wauters,
TC., IV, 552. The grant was consummated in July (Devillers, *Description*, II, 146-
148, no. 6; id., *Annales*, VI, 224-226; Wauters, *TC.*, IV, 567).

[37] Devillers, *Description*, II, 148-149, no. 7; id., *Annales*, VI, 226-227; Wauters,
TC., IV, 586. Cf. the similar act issued by the provost, dean, and canons of St. Germain (Wauters, *TC.*, IV, 587). On May 12, 1250, the bishop of Cambrai approved
the cession by St. Germain (Devillers, *Description*, II, 149-150, no. 8; id. *Annales*,
VI, 227-228; Wauters, *TC.*, IV, 588).

[38] Devillers, *Description*, II, 152-154, no. 10; id., *Annales*, VI, 230-232; Wauters,
TC., IV, 598.

The following day the cardinal further informed the countess that at her recommendation he had confirmed the gift of 1200 *l.* made by her sister to various religious establishments, especially the beguinage at Mons.[39] During the same month Margaret declared that at her suggestion the mayor and echevins had exempted the beguines of Cantimpré from the obligation of paying the *kachage* or right of passage of commodities which they were forwarding or having shipped for their own use.[40] But a beguine acting as a merchant was subject to the same dues as laymen.[41]

On May 2, 1260, Margaret authorized Jean le Hieru to sell to the beguinage at 2 *d.* each two bonniers of meadow which he held of her in this town.[42] On February 27, 1266, Guillaume, provost of the church at Mons, relieved the beguinage of the payment of 2 *s.* which it owed for the burial of members dying there.[43] The following January Bishop Nicholas of Cambrai transferred to Master Nicholas l'Orfèvre, canon of St. Waudru, for the advantage of the beguinage, two houses located near the bridge of Cantimpré and which Saincte de Mons and the beguine Marie de Lens had abandoned on behalf of the community.[44] On January 24, 1270, the bishop confirmed the letters whereby his predecessor had sanctioned the cession of Cantimpré to the beguines.[45] Master Bernard, canon of Soignies, was delegated by Margaret to examine rights[46] which Master John, pastor of Cantimpré, claimed his altar had on an annual income of 45 *s.* coming from a gift

[39] Devillers, *Description*, II, 154-155, no. 11; id., *Annales*, VI, 232-233; Wauters, *TC.*, IV, 599.

[40] Devillers, *Description*, II, 151-152, no. 9; id., *Annales*, VI, 229-230; Wauters, *TC.*, IV, 601.

[41] "Et s'il avient ke il i ait aucune béguine marcande, aperte et manifeste, bien volons et consentons ke de lor besongnes on prende chou k'èles doient" (Devillers, *Description*, II, 151; id., *Annales*, VI, 229).

[42] Devillers, *Description*, II, 156-157, no. 13; id., *Annales*, VI, 234-235; Wauters, *TC.*, V, 223. For Jean le Hieru, see Devillers, *Description*, II, 167-168, no. 21; id., *Annales*, VI, 245-246.

[43] Devillers, *Description*, II, 157-158, no. 14; id., *Annales*, VI, 235-236; Wauters, *TC.*, V, 354.

[44] Devillers, *Description*, II, 158, no. 15; id., *Annales*, VI, 236; Wauters, *TC.*, V, 377. In February, 1271, Nicholas founded a chaplaincy in the beguine church (Devillers, *Description*, II, 163-165, no. 19; id., *Annales*, VI, 241-243). Subsequently this was sanctioned by the chapter of Saint Waudru (May, 1278) (Devillers, *Description*, II, 173, no. 2; Wauters, *TC.*, V, 635). For the will of Nicholas l'Orfèvre, see Devillers, *Description*, II, 177-178, no. 28; id., *Annales*, VI, 255-256.

[45] Devillers, *Description*, II, 160-161, no. 17; id., *Annales*, VI, 238-239; Wauters, *TC.*, V, 445. In June of the same year the provost and chapter of Saint Waudru donated to the beguinage 8 bonniers of meadows and arable land, located at Sourhon, and assigned to this property an annual rent of 100 *s.* for the distribution of herring to the beguines during Lent (Devillers, *Description*, II, 165-167, no. 20; id., *Annales*, VI, 243-245; Wauters, *TC.*, V, 457). This donation met with the approval of the bishop of Cambrai (June 11, 1271, Devillers, *Description*, II, 165-167, no. 20; Wauters, *TC.*, V, 479).

[46] Devillers, *Description*, II, 170, no. 23; id., *Annales*, VI, 248; Wauters, *TC.*, V, 573 (November 17, 1275).

from Heluise de Landrecies, a *povre encluse*, in 1270 for the main-tenance of a chaplain.[47] The canon concluded that this sum belonged to the hospital. Shortly before her death (August 29, 1279) Margaret prescribed a rule for Cantimpré.[48]

The collection of documents published by Devillers casts no light on the history of this beguinage during the persecution of the four-teenth century. That it continued to receive favors from civil author-ities may nevertheless be concluded from the decision of Margaret of Hainault, Empress of the Romans, to allow the community to have its grain ground at will.[49]

When Count John II of Avesnes decided to incorporate the beguinage in the new walls of Mons, it formed a separate locality called the Court de Cantimpret, which had a parish church, a hospital, and a cemetery. The count undertook in 1295[50] to acquire it as well as the possessions of the castellan and the sire de Bailloeul within municipal limits.

Since the Flemish counts reserved for themselves jurisdiction of the Bruges beguinage, and legal cases were judged exclusively by the court of the *burg*, the community was called the *Princelick hof*. The bailli was designated from the beginning to defend its rights; he examined its accounts in the name of the count.[51] On July 24, 1244, Walter de Marvis, bishop of Tournai, suggested to Margaret, who was then proposing to shift to La Vigne the chaplaincy of the castellan of Bruges, that she transfer at the same time the chapel itself and erect the beguinage into a separate parish.[52] The following May (1245) the beguinage of La Vigne, on the Reie, near St. John's hospital (*Vinea supra Roiam juxta domum sancti Johannis*) was constituted with its *multitudo beghinarum* into an independent parish in spite of protests of the priests of Notre-Dame, Saint-Sauveur, and St. Michael to whom the priest of the beguinage must pay an annual rent.[53] In January, 1245, Margaret transferred the chaplaincy of the castellan of Bruges from the castle where it was located to La Vigne where services would be held for the "religiosae mulieres que Beghine vocantur." The countess also regulated the conditions of nomination to the chaplaincy.[54] At the same time (May, 1245) she assured to the infir-

[47] Devillers, *Description*, II, 161-163, no. 18; id., *Annales*, VI, 239-241. This do-nation was confirmed by the chapter on November 18, 1363 (Devillers, *Description*, II, 163 note 2).

[48] Devillers, *Description*, II, 175-176, no. 27; id., *Annales*, VI, 253-254; Wauters, *TC.*, V, 658; MF (III, 732) misdates it as 1248.

[49] Devillers, *Description*, II, 200-201, no. 45; id., *Annales*, VI, 278-279.

[50] Devillers, *Description*, II, 124, note 7 (text).

[51] Delepiere, in *ASEB.*, 1840, 171; Callewaert, in *ibid.*, LVI (1906), 466f.

[52] Callewaert, in *ibid.*, 5e ser., t. 17 (1904), 283-284, no. 18; the mutilated text is found in Ryckel (p. 658) and MF (I, 717); cf. Wauters, *TC.*, IV, 422.

[53] Callewaert, in *ASEB.*, 1904, 286-288, no. 21.

[54] *Ibid.*, 284-285. On April 18, 1245, Walter de Marvis sanctioned the transfer of the chaplaincy from the castle to the beguinage of La Vigne (*ibid.*, 285-286, no. 20;

mary the annual income of 10 *l.* which her sister had willed to it.[55] A few months later (November 23)[56] and again in 1265 (July 10)[57] she enjoined her baillis, subbaillis, and echevins to protect from molestation the recruits for the beguinage. In February, 1265 Margaret, with the approval of her son Guy, sold to the beguinage for 200 *l.* of Flanders land near its *curtis* which Baldwin de Arsebruer, a vassal, had surrendered in order to obtain her pardon; she also assigned to the mistress the 20 *l.* above which the land was worth.[58]

To assure to the beguines spiritual direction and to the Order of Preachers moral patronage Margaret prescribed that the Dominican prior at Ypres should appoint and depose, if need be, the grand mistress of the beguinage.[59] She in turn was bound on his counsel for the appointment of the superiors of the convents and for the contracting of debts and furnishing of securities. The countess also promulgated for the Ypres community statutes in French which were to be enforced by *souveraine mestresse* in cooperation with the Dominican prior. The same considerations dictated comital policy with respect to the Bruges community. The prior shared with the grand mistress the appointment to the parochial cure and the two chapellancies established by the countess in July, 1272.[60] Previously (January, 1271) Jean d'Enghien, bishop of Tournai, had approved her foundation of a second benefice whose presentation belonged to the counts, whereas collation of the chapel in St. Sauveur remained in episcopal hands.[61] On the prior, together with the dean of St. Donatian, was soon after conferred the right of visitation.[62]

In elaboration of this policy, Louis de Male on March 10, 1329, added to the Dominican prior the guardian of the Franciscans and the bailli for the purpose of examining the accounts of the Bruges beguinages.[63]

As in the case of the Ghent and Bruges beguinage, Jeanne's will was the starting point of Margaret's beguinal policy for St. Elizabeth beguine house at Lille in the parish of St. Andrew.[64] In May, 1245, she

the text is incomplete in MF (I, 717) and Ryckel (pp. 658-659); Wauters, *TC.*, IV, 444.
[55] Callewaert, in *ASEB.*, 1904, 288-289, no. 22; Delepierre, *Précis analytique*, I (1840), p. xliii; *Inv. Lille*, p. 339, no. 831. The act was confirmed by her son Guy in May, 1281.
[56] Callewaert, in *ASEB.*, 1904, pp. 289-290, no. 23.
[57] MF., III, 592; Wauters, *TC.*, V, 341.
[58] MF., III, 123-124; Wauters, *TC.*, V, 329; *Inv. Lille*, p. 551, no. 1395.
[59] Iweins, *Monographie*, pp. 14-15; Chapotin, *Histoire des Dominicains*, p. 515.
[60] MF., III, 592; Wauters, *TC.*, V, 502; Delepierre, in *ASEB.*, 1840, p. 173 (text).
[61] MF., II, 1005; Wauters, *TC.*, V, 469; *Inv. Lille*, pp. 663-664, no. 1721; cf. no. 1722.
[62] *Inv. Lille*, pp. 663-664, no. 1721 (January, 1271); cf. *ibid.*, p. 664, no. 1722; MF., II, 1005.
[63] Delepierre, in *ASEB.*, 1840, p. 172 (text).
[64] *Inv. Lille*, p. 337, nos. 825, 825*bis*. Guy confirmed this on June 11, 1296 (*ibid.*, nos. 3810-3811).

donated to the hospital outside the gate of St. Pierre its site up to the moat of La Barre and 3 bonniers of land between the moat and the street which ran to the Countess Hospital (*Hospitalis Dominae Comitissae*). This land the countess had bought from Alard de Berkehem who held it from her in fee. Should this hospital cease to exist the land would revert to the master of the Countess Hospital.[65] Shortly before, in March, Walter de Marvis, bishop of Tournai, declared that in the presence of Simon, archdeacon of Tournai, Alard de Berchem and Margaret, his wife, had sold to Jean Crokevilain, for the beguines at Lille, these bonniers in the parish of the Apostles near the beguine hospital. Failure to comply with this transaction merited excommunication.[66] In July the countess carefully determined the income and obligations of the chaplain Baldwin at the hospital of the Lille beguines in St. Andrew parish.[67] On September 8, 1247, she further instructed the master, brethren, and sisters of the Countess Hospital to pay 8 *l.* every year on November 11 to the beguinage at Lille.[68] When old age and infirmity hampered Baldwin's exercise of his office, Margaret acknowledging in May, 1260, his "long" service, took steps to ensure to him a pension.[69] Towards the end of her life (October, 1277) she increased the donation made by Jeanne for the foundation of a chaplaincy in this hospital, adding that the chaplain should celebrate divine offices in the beguinage.[70]

In February, 1245, Margaret allotted for the dwellings of the *mulieres religiosae* 60 *s.* to be collected every year on the income from the meadow attached to her house beyond the Lys. This was subtracted from the 200 *l.* which Jeanne had set aside in her will, with the advice of Dominican friars.[71]

The Courtrai beguinage received the same attention from Jeanne's successor. In February, 1245, Margaret complied with her sister's

[65] *Ibid.*, pp. 340-341, no. 835; confirmed by Waeter, bishop of Tournai, July, 1245 (*ibid.*, p. 341, nos. 836-838); cf. further episcopal confirmation in the same month (*ibid.*, p. 345, no. 846). For additional grants by Margaret, see *ibid.*, p. 659, no. 1708 (October 4, 1270); pp. 659-660, no. 1709.

[66] *Ibid.*, p. 338, no. 826.

[67] Hautcoeur, *Cartulaire*, I, 294, no. 345. At the same time Gilles, master of the Countess Hospital, promised to pay Baldwin 20 *l.* of Artois, one half at Christmas, the rest at Ascension, in accordance with the above agreement.

[68] *Inv. Lille*, p. 367, no. 900; MF., III, 594; Wauters, *TC.*, IV, 505.

[69] Hautcoeur, *Cartulaire*, I, 388, no. 545. In July Gobert, master of the hospital, announced acceptance of the expense (*ibid.*, I, 388, no. 546).

[70] MF., III, 419; Wauters, *TC.*, V, 623.

[71] *Inv. Lille*, p. 335, no. 818; no. 818 *bis* (MF., III, 593). In February, 1271, Margaret made it known that Baude Li Boirgne, knight, and his wife Maroie renounced to her their claims to the inheritance of the late Henry Mauchin, Maghain de Santes, and Alix Langloise, held in fee of Alard de Berchem, at the walls of the beguines outside Lille. Baude and his wife also renounced in behalf of the beguine hospital a steady income of 8 *s.*, 6 capons, and 6 *d.* of Flanders in exchange for 1 1/2 ferton of fine silver which this hospital collected every year on the house of Aubert Patin, burgher at Lille (*Inv. Lille*, p. 664, no. 1723; cf. no. 1724).

wishes by assigning to the community an income of 60 s. annually
from marshes on the Leie around the castle. In event of suppression
or decay the sum would be transferred to the abbey of Marcke.[72] In
1278 she granted an income of 20 l. while Heila of Lille, wife of
Daniel Taillefin, founded and endowed the chaplaincy in 1284.[73]

In September, 1254, Margaret ordered the lord of Wervi, receiver
of the espier at Ypres, to pay annually to the beguine hospital at Ypres
10 livres of Artois.[74] In 1260 since the beguines in the infirmary were
prevented from attending divine offices in the parish of Bruel, the
provost Baldwin and the convent of St. Martin at Ypres agreed, at the
countess' recommendation, to allow a separate chapel for their use but
still subject to local authorities.[75] As further evidence of comital
concern for the well-being of the community, Margaret authorized
a rule for it and the infirmary.[76]

It is possible that the beguinage at Braine was founded about 1250
from gifts from the countess and Jean d'Avesnes.[77] Although the
origins of the Damme beguinage remain equally obscure, it has been
suggested that it too must be attributed to Margaret.[78] But there is no
proof. It was in existence in 1275, for the canon Arnold of Maldeghem
remembered it in his will bearing that date.[79]

In November, 1277, Count Guy exempted from tailles and tonlieux
the beguines living in the community in St. Andrew parish at Lille.[80]
Mahaut of Béthune, first wife of Count Guy, was also generous to the
semireligious in Flanders, making donations on March 27, 1259, to
the beguinages at Lille (10 l.), Douai (10 l.),Ypres (100 s.), Berghes
(40 s.), Ghent (100 s.) Valenciennes 100 s.), Cantimpré at Cambrai
(10 l.), Aunoit (60 s.), le Quesnoy (60 s.), and Cantimpré at Mons
(100 s.). She likewise remembered the communities in the diocese of
Liege with 20 l. in return for prayers after her death.[81]

In July 1267, Hugh II, castellan of Ghent, confirmed his father's
donation of 1242 but not without reclaiming three bonniers of mea-

---

[72] MF., III, 593f; De Potter, Gesch. d. Stad Kortrijk, III, 420. Cf. Margaret's brief
of December, 1251 (Mussely, Inv. des archives de Courtrai, I, 79, no. 6).

[73] De Potter, Gesch. d. Stad Kortrijk, III, 421. As a result of the battle in 1302
the beguinage was burned; gifts made possible its reconstruction (Charterboek des
Begijnhofs, p. 51, cited by De Potter, l.c., 421-422, note 1).

[74] Inv. Lille, p. 446, no. 1098.

[75] Feys and Nelis, Cartulaires de S. Martin, II, 143, no. 213.

[76] Inv. Lille, pp. 633-634, no. 1627 (January, 1270); MF., IV, 253.

[77] Joseph Croquet, "Notice historique sur l'église paroissiale et sur les institutions
religieuses de Braine-le-Comte," Annales du cercle archéologique d'Enghien, III
(1887), 433-437.

[78] J. Opdedrinck, "Het oude begijnhof van Damme en de Cistercienser Vrouwenabdij van Bethlehem uit Schouwen," ASEB., LXIII (1913), 28-30; Tanghe, Parochieboek van Damme, p. 85.

[79] Testament of Arnold de Maldeghem, in ASEB., 2nd ser., VII, 345.

[80] Wauters, TC., V, 624.

[81] Hautcoeur, Cartulaire, I, 127; Inv. Lille, p. 485, no. 1202.

dow facing Wondelghem which he maintained had never been included in the original grant. Evidently the beguines appealed to the
countess, for Hugh admitted that he had re-examined the matter at her
request and agreed that the beguinage was entitled to the property
in question.[82] Seven years later (October, 1274) the countess, with her
son's approval, confirmed this donation which the castellan had been
persuaded to make in answer to the beguines' plan to "enlarge their
position."[83]

We have seen how Count Guy identified himself with his mother's
beguine policy from 1263 on.[84] Conscious that administration and
surveillance of St. Elizabeth at Ghent belonged to the counts, he
displayed the same lively concern for its well-being through protection and donations. But acknowledging that the pressure of business
had made it impossible to discharge this obligation, he handed over
on July 17, 1282, supervision of the community to the prior of the
Friars Preachers and to Pierre de la Court (uten Hove), a local
burgher.[85] On January 23, 1273, Guy approved the acquisition of 24
bonniers of allodial land in the parishes of Vlierzele and Zonnegem.[86]
In April, 1280, he sold through Eustache, a monk of Cambron, to
Gilbert de la Court property at Selzate.[87] Béthune surmises that such
transactions, although without reference to the beguinage, later contributed to the extension of its domain.[88] In addition to frequent
confirmation of previous donations,[89] the count took keen interest
in the business transactions of the beguinage.[90] About 1284 the beguines complained to him that the bailli of Ghent had entered their
convent and asked them to render account of their goods.[91] Attached to
this undated document is another, issued on October 10, 1284, which
is evidently Guy's answer to the petition. The count allowed the inmates to elect their *souveraine maistresse* according to the customs

[82] Béthune, *Cartulaire* pp. 16-17, no. 21; Wauters, *TC.*, V, 390.
[83] Béthune, *Cartulaire,* pp. 26-27, no. 30; Wauters, *TC.*, V, 550.
[84] Béthune, *Cartulaire,* pp. 15-16, no. 20.
[85] *Ibid.,* p. 38, no. 47.
[86] *Ibid.,* p. 24, no. 27.
[87] *Ibid.,* pp. 34-35, no. 42; cf. *ibid.,* p. 35, no. 43 (April, 1280).
[88] *Ibid.,* p. 35 note.
[89] February 21, 1274 (*ibid.,* p. 26, no. 29), a confirmation of the 1262 act (*ibid.,*
pp. 14-15, no. 19), later (September 16, 1299) given a vidimus by the Friars Preachers
(*ibid.,* pp. 49-50, no. 66); August, 1275 (*ibid.,* pp. 27-28, no. 32); October 9, 1279
(*ibid.,* p. 33, no. 40); ratification of Margaret's sale of April, 1257 (*ibid.,* pp. 13-14,
no. 17).
[90] April 30, 1284 (amortization of 17 bonniers of land, *ibid.,* p. 39, no. 49); on
December 22, 1287, Guy approved the purchase of lands at Sleydinge and Loven-
deghem (*ibid.,* pp. 42-43, no. 56); on January 30, 1289, the count sold to the infirmary 2 1/2 bonniers and 35 *virgae* of marsh (*ibid.,* p. 43, no. 57) at Selzate; in the
same place he made another sale on December 11, 1290 (*ibid.,* p. 44. no. 59);
cf. sales at Selzate on July 11, 1293 (*ibid.,* p. 45, no. 61) and May 7, 1295 (*ibid.,*
p. 46, no. 62).
[91] *Ibid.,* pp. 39-40, no. 50.

in practice since Margaret. This new head was to render account to a comital agent each year.[92]

Elsewhere we shall have occasion to examine how Guy's successor, Robert de Béthune (1305-September 17, 1322), handled the community during the persecution.[93] Shortly after assuming the title to Flanders he promulgated the usual protection letter.[94] Of much greater importance is his protest against the encroachment of Guy, bishop of Tournai, on the beguinage, for it affords a valuable insight into comital understanding of extraregular status. Arguing from the secular rather than religious nature of beguinal life, the count claimed "from ancient custom" full temporal jurisdiction as well as the ability to install and depose the mistress, who in turn was obliged to render account of the property to the count. Furthermore he has been accustomed to have mass celebrated by suitable priests in a chapel in the beguinage itself, "ordained and established by papal authority." From him likewise comes the necessary income for this purpose, since there are no special vicars or chaplains. Such had been the case for sixty years or more.[95] The bishop of Tournai had already allowed (October 3, 1270) the chaplains of the beguinage to administer in daytime the sacraments of eucharist and extreme unction without the priest of St. Michael. At night they could do likewise for sick beguines notwithstanding the prohibition of parochial authorities. These chaplains might also recite vigils for dead beguines.[96] On June 23, 1311, the supervisors of the beguinage—Friar John, prior of the Dominicans at Ghent, the subbailli, and the grand mistress, as well as John Palster, procurator of the count—approved this action.[97] The following year (October 15, 1312) Robert reiterated the document of July 17, 1282, by entrusting the administration of the beguinage to the prior of the Friars Preachers; again, he acknowledged that this function had been assigned to Ivo de Vaernewijck, a knight, but since the latter was burdened with comital affairs, full control of the grand mistress and chaplains must henceforth be adjudged within the competence of the Dominican.[98]

[92] *Ibid.*, p. 40, no. 51. Cf. vidimus of dean of St. Pharaïlde at Ghent (September 27, 1353), *ibid.*, p. 89, no. 129
[93] See below, p. 543.
[94] December 9, 1305 (Béthune, *Cartulaire*, p. 56, no. 79).
[95] June 20, 1311 (*ibid.*, pp. 60-62, no. 88).
[96] *Ibid.*, p. 23, no. 25.
[97] *Ibid.*, pp. 62-63, no. 69.
[98] *Ibid.*, p. 66, no. 92.

X

Relations with lay Authorities in Brabant and Holland

Through donations and protection letters which were frequently renewed and confirmed, the dukes of Brabant consistently supported the beguines as well as the beghards. Never reluctant to supervise extraregular communities within their competence, John I intervened to approve the statutes for La Vigne at Brussels.[1]

The first ducal recognition of the beguinage is found in Henry III's (February 1, 1248-February 28, 1261) approval of a donation of one and a half *bonniers* of land made by the dean and chapter of St. Gudule in April, 1251.[2] In November, 1252, the duke acknowledged that a parcel of land between the house of Wellin and the Porte de Laeken had been made available to Renier, rector of the beguines, for a rent of 2 *s.* of Louvain.[3] Notwithstanding this approbation of landholding, the earliest known protection brief dates only from August, 1270, when John I (1261-1294) took the infirmary, i.e. the whole beguinage since the *communia bona* were the goods of the infirmary, under his jurisdiction, instructing his *baillis* and mayors to lend their support whenever needed.[4] Such a privilege was renewed periodically during the next half century.[5]

At the request of John I the chapter of St. Gudule relinquished to the abbey of St. Bernard its *jus patronatus* over the Brussels beguines. He then granted the chapter free election to two prebends.[6]

---

[1] See above p. 177.

[2] AAPB., Carton H. 263; AGR., arch. eccl., 13403, f. 41ʳ, no. 1. AAPB. possesses the original of the donation document as well as the vidimus of Nicholas de Fontaines in July, 1251 (AAPB., Carton H. 263; AGR., arch. eccl., 13403, f. 41ᵛ, no. 3).

[3] AAPB., Carton H. 263. Arnold, treasurer of St. Gudule, issued a vidimus on February 21, 1295 (AAPB., Carton H. 263).

[4] AAPB., Carton H. 262.

[5] April 23, 1293 (AAPB., Carton H. 262); January 25, 1295 (AAPB., Carton H. 262); May 5, 1306 (AAPB., Carton H. 262).

[6] November, 1275, AGR., arch. eccl., Carton 13402, no. 4; see below, p. 000; cf. confirmation by Godeschalk, beguine pastor, on December 15, 1275 (AGR., arch. eccl., Carton 13402, no. 6).

The bishop of Cambrai announced on December 22, 1275, that an agreement had been reached between the dean and chapter of St. Gudule on the one hand and the beguines of La Vigne on the other, with the consent of John I; this settlement was made through the abbot of Villers and the guardian of the Friars Minor.[7]

In addition to parochial problems the duke showed concern for the material well-being of the community. In 1271 (June 13) he granted the beguines, in return for an annual rent of 12 *d.* of Louvain, a piece of land below their walls in order to build a mill exclusively for their own use.[8] Other donations or limited grants were made until the beginning of the next century, either through the duke[9] or the receiver of Brabant.[10] In 1304 La Vigne received the ordinary exemptions from gabelles, tailles, and other exactions extended to religious communities.[11]

This privilege ended the first series of concessions, the next one not appearing for sixty years. Unless documents have been lost for the intervening period, which hardly seems probable since so many property titles and business transactions have been preserved, an explanation may possibly be found in connection with the inquisitorial proceedings. On September 7, 1369, Duchess Jeanne resumed ducal intervention by instructing her officials to enforce the discharge of

[7] AGR., arch. eccl., Carton 13402, no. 4; ed. MF., III, 612.

[8] AAPB., Carton H. 263.

[9] May 10, 1304 (AAPB., Carton H. 270, 1, Ruysbroeck; AGR., arch. eccl., 13403, f. 237v, no. 651); October, 1309 (AAPB., Carton B, 149 A, no. 160; AAPB., B. 203, f. 21r-21v, no. 160); May 6, 1299 (AAPB., Carton H. 262); cf. September, 1281 (AAPB., Carton H. 269, 2, Laeken) when Henry Parochiaen granted, on behalf of the duke, to Elizabeth of Asche, beguine in La Vigne, a piece of land to be held for 1 d.; January 17, 1297 n.s. (AAPB., H. 266, Steenwech; AGR., arch. eccl., 13403, f. 90r, no. 183); May 11, 1297 (AAPB., H. 266, Steenwech; AGR., arch. eccl., 13403, f. 90r, no. 184); March, 1297 (AGR., arch. eccl., 13403, f. 90r-90v, no. 185); June 4, 1298, Carton H. 270, 2, St. Gilles; AGR., 13403, f. 80v, no. 145.

[10] On June 20, 1290, Hugh of Coudenbergh gave a meadow to the beguinage for a rent of 4 d. of Brussels (AAPB., Carton H. 264; ed. Martens, *Actes*, pp. 57-58, no. 23); Mathias de Beerte, receiver of Brussels, August 10, 1321 (AAPB., Carton H. 264, 1); Thierry Loeze, receiver of Brabant, rented a tract of uncleared land, December 14, 1301 (AAPB., Carton H. 264; ed. Martens, *Actes*, pp. 52-53, no. 20).

[11] February 8 or 15, 1304 (*satersdaechs vore grote vastellavont*, variant according to Giry or Grotefend): "Dat wi, om de verlichtenesse onser sielen ende der sielen dar wi af comen sijn, hebben ghenomen ende onfaen in onse bescermenesse sunderlinghe alle de beghinen die nu wonen ende namaels wonen selen int hof van den beghinen dat men heet den wiengart neven Brusele, ende haer ghoet ende gheloven hen vore ons ende vore onse hoir dat wi noch onse hoir noch onse nacomelinge en selen van hen noch van heren ghoede wart gelegen es onder ons niet nemen, noch doen nemen noch ghedoeghen te nemene engeen ongelt dat men heet bede noch taille noch dies ghelike nu noch nummermeer maer dat wise selen houden ende doen houden na onse macht alse here cummermeerboef in goeden paise ende bescermen van onrechte; ende hir ombe soe ghebiede wi alle den ghenen die onder ons sijn ende selen sijn dat si op de voreseide beghinen noch op hare ghoet nu noch nemmermeer engeen onghelt ensciten noch daer af en nemen noch bede noch tonllje . . . ." (AAPB., Carton H. 262); besides this original there is a Latin translation, ed. Ryckel, p. 178; MF., II, 1011; cf. Wauters, *TC.*, VIII, 103.

debts in corn, money, rents, or capons, to the infirmary or Ter Kis-ten.[12] Three years later (December 8) she allowed the infirmary to claim all movable and immovable goods of beguines who died there without legitimate issue.[13] Subsequently Duke John issued a vidimus for the acts of 1293 and 1306.[14]

Ducal privilege for the Brussels community found before and after Vienne their counterpart in episcopal favor and regulation, culmi-nating in the bull of Calixtus III (April 20, 1455).[15] At the request of the beguines they were authorized by the bishop of Cambrai, Guy de Collemedio, to expel at the end of a day and night those male-factors who had taken refuge in the church of the beguinage, but also to lead them to a safe place so that no harm would be done to them.[16] Ghiselbert Mutsaert, dean of St. Pierre at Turnhout, confirmed on September 28, 1425, by virtue of Martin V's bull (July 4, 1425) the mistresses of the beguinage in their rights regarding the choice and presentation of their pastor.[17] Not long after (January 16, 1428) the bishop of Cambrai, Jean Lytdekirche, forbade the inmates, on pain of excommunication, to confess in the beguinage to any priest other than the pastor or his chaplain, or someone designated by him.[18] In 1379 (February 28) the bishop reiterated the privilege granted by the papacy in 1252 concerning service during interdict.[19]

The same privileges inspired at Brussels were enjoyed by the be-guinage at Tirlemont. Philip the Good on February 2, 1432,[20] con-firmed previous concessions by the ducal house of Brabant in their behalf. John II in 1303 had freed them "ab omni servicio talliarum, assisiarum, precariarum, exactionum."[21] Just as the duke in 1310 approved the long-standing right to choose their own administrators for temporal affairs, so his successor during 1327, in the wake of the persecution and rehabilitation proceedings, sought to regulate their life.[22] Recalcitrance or violation of the statutes justified expulsion. Ducal officials in the town were to see to that. At the same time any citizen who invaded the sacred precincts after curfew laid himself open to prosecution. His wife Margaret took the community under her pro-

[12] AAPB., Carton H. 262.
[13] AAPB., Carton H. 262; vidimus on October 17, 1471, AGR., arch. eccl., 13403, f. 379r-379v, no. 1076.
[14] December 10, 1422, AAPB., Carton H. 262.
[15] AAPB., Carton H. 262.
[16] October 3, 1303, AAPB., Carton H. 262.
[17] AAPB., Carton H. 262.
[18] AGR., arch. eccl., Carton 13402, no. 13.
[19] AAPB., Carton H. 262.
[20] Bets, *Histoire de Tirlemont*, II, 235-244, P.J. 17.
[21] *Ibid.*, 236-237; again in 1303 (*ibid.*, 237), 1308 (ibid., 237-238), and 1310 (*ibid.*, 238).
[22] *Ibid.*, 238-239.

tection the following year, renewing exemptions from taxes.[23] Jeanne in 1367[24] and Antoine in 1409,[25] as well as Philip himself, took similar action. In the presence of the mayor, vassals of the duke, and the echevinage Gerard of Gingelom had donated back in 1259 to the beguines of Tirlemont property between Neer-Winden and Raetshoven.[26] In 1399 Boniface IX, with subsequent confirmation by Eugenius IV (1434), permitted the beguines to name their pastor or to delegate the right to their superiors.[27]

Not only did the duke together with his wife intercede on behalf of the beguinage at Aerschot in the dispute with St. Gertrude at Louvain (1258–1259)[28] leading to the establishment of parochial rights,[29] but he had confirmed its holdings while the local echevinage freed them from taxes and other exactions.[30] Furthermore Duke Henry III, in consonance with the wishes of his aunt, Empress Marie, donated to the community a chaplaincy at Miskom (January, 1261)[31] to which Arnold, lord of Wezemael, renounced his rights.[32] These last two acts received a vidimus from Master Renier, scholasticus of Tongres (January, 23),[33] and from the bishop of Liege the following March.[34]

In August, 1270 John I, at the request of the beguines themselves, entrusted the same community to the echevins to ensure peaceful possession of Paridaens *beempt*.[35] Similarly, the Lierre beguines in 1274 were promised protection by ducal officials.[36]

The counts of Holland exhibited the same willingness to aid the semireligious as Jeanne and Margaret. Matilda, mother of William of the Romans, donated property to the hospital and beguines at Gravenzande (September 21, 1255) "so that they might later have

---

[23] *Ibid.*, 239-240.

[24] *Ibid.*, 240-241.

[25] *Ibid.*, 241-242.

[26] Ryckel, p. 595; MF., IV, 530; Wauters, *TC.*, V, 217.

[27] Bets, *Histoire de Tirlemont*, II, 147.

[28] *BG.*, XXIX (1938), 137, 139.

[29] March 17, 1258, *ibid.*, 137-139, no. 2; cf. *AHEB.*, XII (1875), 27-28, no. 4a. Duchess Aleidis subsequently sealed (July, 1259) the privilege with the grant of 20 *l.* of Louvain annually (*ibid.*, 29, no. 4b). These vidimuses are contained in a document issued by Godefridus Roy de Slusa, Arnoldus Venoet, and Arnoldus Faber, echevins of Aerschot.

[30] March 1259-60, *BG.*, XXIX (1938), 143-144, no. 5; vidimus by the pastor and three other priests of Aerschot on May 1, 1341 (*ibid.*, 154, no. 13). The preceding February the bishop-elect of Liége had confirmed this settlement (*ibid.*, 142-143, no. 4).

[31] *Ibid.*, 145, no. 6; cf. *AHEB.*, XII (1875), 30-31.

[32] *BG.*, XXIX (1938), 146, no. 7; *AHEB.*, XII (1875), 31-32.

[33] *BG.*, XXIX (1938), 146-147, no. 8.

[34] *Ibid.*, 147-148, no. 9; *AHEB.*, XII (1875), 30-32; nos. 6, 7, 9 in *BG.*, XXIX (1938), received a vidimus from the pastor and two other priests of Aerschot on June 18, 1330 (*ibid.*, 153-154, no. 12).

[35] Wauters, *TC.*, V, 459; cf. *AHEB.*, XII (1875), 29-30, no. 4 c.

[36] Ryckel, p. 302; Wauters, *TC.*, V, 553.

beer to drink in their refectory."[37] In 1266 (October 14) she added, "in view of the indulgence of our predecessors," the whole area that they had surrounded with ditches and trees at their own expense and labor because of the growth of the congregation.[38] In May, 1255, John of Diest, former chaplain of Count William II, granted a forty-day indulgence to those who contributed to the building of the beguinage.[39] The count himself made available at the same time (May 17) alms amounting to 20 s.[40] Previously (February 7, 1254) he had exempted from all obligations and tailles the property of the beguines at Middelburg.[41] Not only were nuns, mendicant orders, the Saccati, and the beghards at Middelburg remembered in the will of Aleida, wife of John d'Avesnes (October 18, 1271), but she left sums of money to several beguine communities: at Haarlem 5 l., at Delft 5 l., in Rivo 15 l., at Ziericksee 10 l., at Liliendale 10 l., at Middelburg 10 l., at Dordrecht 5 l., and to the infirmary at Gravenzande 10 l.[42] Two years later (October 3) she provided the priest of the Haarlem beguines with income from her mill at Gravenzande.[43]

In September, 1266, Bishop Henry of Utrecht authorized the abbot at Middelburg to confer on one or two of his charges the cure of the beguinage.[44] Afterwards John of Nassau, bishop-elect, confirmed on June 2, 1271, the privileges of these beguines made by his predecessor, Otto of Holland (1235–1249), recognizing for them "living in one enclosure and under one obedience" their own chapel and cemetery.[45] On February 17, 1272, Arnold, priest of Haarlem, willed to the local beguinages his house and land.[46] Henry, lord of Breda, gave as allod on March 22, 1267, to the beguines in that town, then in the diocese of Liége, the land on which they resided, subject to a rent; they were not allowed to erect a chapel or lay out a cemetery.[47] Theoderic (Dirk) of Zassenem left to the beguines in Utrecht 1 l. and to those of Haarlem 1 l.[48] The burgomaster, echevins, and jurés of Middel-

[37] Van den Bergh, Oorkondenboek, I, 327, no. 617. Cf. Matilda's second donation on December 13, 1263 (ibid., Suppl., 95-96, no. 145; De Fremery, in Fruin, Bijdragen, 3rd ser., VIII [1894], 329-330, no. 5).
[38] Van den Bergh, Oorkondenboek, II, 66, no. 145; Wauters, TC., V, 370.
[39] Van den Bergh, Oorkondenboek, I, 325, no. 612; cf. ibid., I, 325, no. 610; II, 64, no. 140. De Fremery in Suppl., pp. 82-83, no. 127 (May 17-23, 1255) published an identical brief designed to aid the Gravenzande beguines in the construction of their beguinage; cf. also in Fruin's Bijdragen, 3rd ser., VIII (1894), 327-328, no. 3.
[40] Van den Bergh, Oorkondenboek, I, 324-325, no. 610.
[41] Van Mieris, Charterboek, I, 280; Wauters, TC., V, 76.
[42] Van den Bergh, Oorkondenboek, Suppl., by De Fremery, 1901, pp. 111-113, no. 163.
[43] Ibid., p. 121, no. 171.
[44] Van den Bergh, Oorkondenboek, II, 66; Wauters, TC., V, 370.
[45] Van den Bergh, Oorkondenboek, II, 93; no. 213; Wauters, TC., V, 478.
[46] Van den Bergh, Oorkondenboek, II, 99, no. 225.
[47] So dated by Wauters (TC., V, 380); in Ryckel (p. 624) and MF., I, 773 the date is given as 1265; cf. Henry of Liége's act of 1270 (Wauters, TC., V, 465; MF., I, 773).
[48] April 13, 1282, Van den Bergh, Oorkondenboek, II, 199, no. 449.

burg on August 4, 1273, appointed Wisse, son of Peter (Pieterzoon) to take the place of the late Arnold, son of John (Janszoon), in pastoral work in the beguine church.[49] The beguinage at Dordrecht, too, must have sprung up under comital auspices, for in 1326 William acknowledges the patronage of his forefathers when he took it under his protection.[50]

---

[49] *Ibid.*, II, 112, no. 255; Wauters, *TC.*, V, 525.
[50] Van Mieris, *Charterboek*, II, 392. Van Heussen put its foundation in 1303.

XI

Royal Patronage in France

However much Louis IX was interested in every manifestation of religious and extraregular life, even showing good will to congregations which failed to meet the approval of the second council of Lyons (1274) a scant four years after his death,[1] the feminine religious movement[2] and the mendicant orders appear to have received consistently preferential treatment. As "father and consoler of the poor,"[3] the king founded the well-known beguine house in Paris near the gate Barbeel[4] in the parish of St. Paul. According to the investigation conducted on behalf of the Ghent beguines in the spring of 1328 St. Louis had visited them; expressing pleasure over their earnestness and fervor, he secured from the bishop of Tournai a church for the community and obtained for their benefit privileges and immunities. It was in imitation of this institution that the king then proceeded to establish and endow the Paris community as well as "several others in different places."[5] The patronage which the knight Philip de Montmirail extended before 1262 to extraregulars and Cistercians in France, Burgundy, and Provence[6] could therefore have expected hearty royal approval.

Although it is impossible to determine exactly the date of the Paris foundation, it was erected before November, 1264, for in that year Abbot Stephen of the Benedictine monastery of Tiron, in whose

[1] Joinville, *Vie de St. Louis,* in Bouquet, XX (1840), 299 A.

[2] *Ibid.,* 298 A, C.

[3] Geoffrey of Beaulieu, *V. S. Lud. Regis,* in Bouquet, XX, 12 A; *AA. SS.,* XXXIX (August 25, v), 548-549, no. 31.

[4] *Vie de Saint Louis* by the confessor of Queen Margaret in Bouquet, XX, 76 E: "De rechief il fonda la meson des Beguines de Paris, delez la porte de Barbeel"; *Vita II S. Ludov. Reg., AA. SS.,* XXXIX (August 25, v), 584 A (Latin version); cf. *Comm. praev., ibid.,* 502, no. 1050; Statutes of 1341, Le Grand, *Les béguines de Paris,* p. 52. For the Paris beguines, consult in addition to Le Grand, Ollivier, *Le grand béguinage de Gand,* pp. 29-33; Felibien, *Histoire de la ville de Paris,* I, 380, no. 19; Chapotin, *Histoire des Dominicains,* pp. 511-512, 520-521.

[5] Béthune, *Cartulaire,* p. 76; Fredericq, *Corpus,* I, 177-178; cf. *E Chronico Normanniae,* in Bouquet, XXIII (1876), 215: "Beginasque in regno suo fere ubique seminavit."

[6] See above, p. 52.

224

jurisdiction the beguinage lay, relinquished the land that the king had bought for the beguines "in the street. running from the gate of the said beguines to the false postern of St. Paul."[7] This cession was made for the sum of 100 *l.* of Tours, which presupposes the acquisition of a rather sizable piece of ground.[8] From the two documents at the beginning of the fourteenth century it is evident that the *hostel des beguines* had lent its name to the gate.[9] According to contemporary account a large site was needed to lodge the multitude[10] of "honestarum mulierum, quae beguinae communiter appellantur"[11] to whom the king offered refuge. Geoffrey of Beaulieu, confessor of Louis IX, estimated their number at about four hundred in his *Vita.*[12] Not only did court connections assure the Dominican information on royal patronage of regular and extra-regular communities but he was himself vitally concerned with pastoral care by frequently delivering sermons in the beguinage.[13] His preaching was supplemented by numerous other Friars Preachers.[14] Unlike many beguinages in modern Belgium which had their inception under Cistercian auspices and partook of Bernardine piety, this sisterhood in Paris was thus directed from the beginning by the friars. The mistresses had the right to be buried in the Dominican church.[15] To them likewise they looked for a leavening of their spirituality.[16]

Many of the beguines, the confessor pointed out further, belonged to noble families, but were poor; thus Louis had to provide for their upkeep[17]—which he did with his usual generosity.[18] In the *Miracles*

[7] Le Grand, *Les béguines de Paris,* pp. 13-14 and note 1; cf. Le Nain de Tillemont, *Vie de Saint Louis,* V, 312f.

[8] Le Grand, *Les béguines de Paris,* p. 14, note 2.

[9] See the two foundation charters of the new Carmelite convent near the Place Maubert, April, 1309 (Felibien, *Histoire de la ville de Paris,* III, 217-218: "extra portam Beguinarum"); November, 1317 (*ibid.,* III, 218-219).

[10] Thomas of Cantimpré, BUA., II, 29, 40: "Rex devotissimus Ludovicus, in tantum amplectitur virgineae dignitatis pudicitiam consectantes, ut Parisijs collegerit Beghinarum maximam multitudinem, ut se in humilitatis obsequiis exerceat et salute." Cf. Guillaume de Saint-Amour: "in regno Franciae multitudo infinito" (Mosheim, p. 26).

[11] *Beati Ludovici Vita,* in Bouquet, XXIII, 171.

[12] *V. S. Ludov.,* Bouquet, XX, 12 A; *AA. SS.,* XXXIX (August 25, v), 548 F, no. 30: "Domum insuper Paris. honestarum mulierum, quae vocantur Beguinae, de suo adquisivit, et eisdem assignavit, in qua religiose et honeste conversantur circiter quadringentae."

[13] Quétif-Echard, I, 267 b, no. ix; 270 a-b; see below, p. 341. For Geoffrey consult *HLF.,* XIX (1838), 234-237.

[14] Quétif-Echard, I, 266 a-268 b; Lecoy de la Marche, pp. 119ff; 467ff; see below, pp. 341-343.

[15] Chapotin, *Histoire des Dominicains,* pp. 520f.

[16] *Ibid.,* pp. 519-520

[17] *V. S. Ludov.,* Bouquet, XX, 12 A; *AA. SS.,* XXXIX (August 25, v), 548 F, no. 30: "... pluribus exceptis, maxime pauperibus nobilibus, quamdiu viverent, de sustentatione quotidiana providit." Cf. *Comm. praev., ibid.,* 502, no. 1050; Mosheim, p. 44.

de Saint Louis, under the years 1269–1275, they were described as
particularly active in the carding of wool. One Aales Malachine who
lived in the beguinage was independent until sickness reduced her to
poverty.[19] As a result of royal patronage, the community put lively
faith in his miracles.[20] Not content with helping them during his own
lifetime, the king provided for them in his will by leaving 100 *l.* of
Paris to maintain the buildings of the beguinage and 20 *l.* to aid the
poorest inhabitants. To other indigent beguines in France he left 100
l. and to those in Cantimpré near Cambrai 40 *l*;[21] he then recommended to his heir to continue the pensions which he had established
for the beguines in the kingdom.[22] The request was heeded, for we see
that from the time of his successor sixteen beguines in Paris received
14 *l.* 8 *s.* on the list of royal alms;[23] these gifts were continued during
Philip IV's reign.[24] Philip III, imitating his father, bequeathed in
1285 to the beguinage of Paris a considerable sum for the age, namely
600 *l.,* not counting the 100 *l.* which the executors of the will were to
allot to the other beguines of the realm.[25] The princes of the royal
house were equally interested in this convent; thus from 1265 Alphonse of Poitiers contributed alms of 50 *s.,*[26] while Pierre d'Alençon
left it in 1282 100 *s.* with masses and prayers as the condition.[27]

The favor that the Paris beguines enjoyed among the immediate
successors of St. Louis in memory of their founder continued into
the next century; in 1340 Philip VI granted to them again 8 *l.* in
pension, "pour l'affection et dévotion que nous avons aus prières de
noz amées la matresse et la communauté des béguines du béguinaige

[18] *Beati Ludov. Vita,* Bouquet, XXIII, 171 D: ". . . et eisdem magna largitate
providit."
[19] Bouquet, XX, 168-169.
[20] Guillaume of Chartres (*De vita et miraculis Sancti Ludovici,* in Bouquet, XX,
40 B-D) relates that in 1271 Agnes la Maque, "manens Parisius prope domum
beguinarum" (B-C), and Michael Hamiage, "commorans Parisius prope domum de
Barbeel in parochia S. Pauli" (D), came to Louis' tomb to be healed.
[21] Duchesne, *Historiae Francorum Scriptores,* V, 439; Mosheim, p. 44: "Item
legamus ad aedificandum et ampliandum locum Beguinarum parisiensium c libras,
et ad sustentationem pauperiorum ex ipsis xx libras. Item legamus pauperibus
mulieribus beguinis in regno Franciae constitutis c libras. Item pauperibus Beguinis
de Cantiprato iuxta Cameracum xxxx. libras." Cf. MF., II, 298-299.
[22] Duchesne, *Historiae Francorum Scriptores,* V, 439; Mosheim, pp. 44-45.
[23] *Ceratae Petri de Condeto tabulae,* Bouquet, XXII (1865), 470 H: "Beguinae
parisienses xvi, ad elemosinas: xiiii l. viii s." (March 7, 1284). Cf. *Tabula Roberti
Mignon anno circiter 1325 confecta,* Bouquet, XXI, 528.
[24] Bouquet, XXII, 488 M (December 11, 1285): "Beguinae parisienses ad elemosinas, XII l. XVI s."; *Compotus ballivorum Franciae* (1285), *ibid.,* 665 K: "Pro bur-
sis beguinarum, XXIX l. VIII s. Pro censu domus earum, pro duobus terminis,
iiii l. vi. s. viii d."
[25] "As povres béguines de Paris, six cens livres tournois; as autres povres béguines
en nostre domaine, c livres tournois a départir par nos exécuteurs" (Mosheim, p. 47).
[26] Boutaric, *Saint Louis et Alfonse de Poitiers,* p. 461.
[27] "Aus Beguines de Paris cent sous, et requerons messes et oroisons pour nous"
(Mosheim, p. 47).

de Paris, lequel monseigneur saint Loys fonda, et pour ce que nous, nostre très chère compaigne la Royne et touz noz enfans soions participans a leurs-dites prières et bienffaiz."[28] The pope, like the crown, lent a favorable ear to the demands of the beguines: on August, 8, 1286, Honorius IV issued a privilege exempting them from judicial proceedings outside Paris.[29] In 1289 (October 7) Nicholas IV granted an indulgence of 100 days to attract the faithful to their church on the feast and during the octave of St. Catherine to whom it was dedicated.[30] Since the parish in which the beguinage rose was that of St. Paul, it appears that the crown undertook from the beginning to indemnify the parochial authorities for whatever prejudice the erection of the new chapel might cause.[31] In 1290 it brought about accord between the priest and the beguines whereby the former, among other obligations, was to celebrate mass in the beguinage once a year as long as there were semireligious.[32]

As a safeguard against heretical currents and delinquency, the administration of the community was entrusted to a mistress, appointed by the almoner of the king who had full control over religious establishments of royal foundation.[33] At the same time the mistress was immediately dependent on the prior of the Friars Preachers in Paris to whose custody the king had delivered the house.[34] She was expected to follow his advice in all important matters,[35] to render account of her financial activity,[36] and finally receive from him a council of three or four of the older inmates who would assist her in administration.[37]

[28] Le Grand, Les béguines de Paris, p. 16. Philip VI also gave a pension of wheat to a beguine named Mary the Scot: "Maria Scota beguina pro denariis sibi debitis inter debita Reginaldi Bouton, receptoris nuper vicecomitatus Parisiensis, de termino Candelose CCCXLVII, pro vi sextariis bladi per compotum granorum" (ibid., p. 16, note 1). It is possible that beguines were included among the "pauperibus hospitalibus pauperum mulierum viduarum" at Paris whom Jeanne Malaunay remembered in her testament (January 8, 1311 n.s.) alongside recluses in St. Germain des Prés and in St. Denis (Bulletin de la société de l'histoire de Paris et de l'Ile-de-France, XIX [1892], 167-170, especially 168).

[29] Prou, Registres d'Honorius IV, col. 416, no. 599; not in Potthast. The same bull was also addressed to "dilectis in Christo filiabus religiosis mulieribus Parisiensibus, filiabus Dei vulgariter nuncupatis", i.e. Filles-Dieu (idem).

[30] Chapotin, Histoire des Dominicains, p. 520, note 1. Another indult for the feasts of the Virgin was issued on March 15, 1290 (ibid., p. 521 note).

[31] Compotus ballivorum Franciae (1285), Bouquet, XXII, 624 H: "Capellanus Sancti Pauli, pro capella beguinarum, pro medietate, 7 l. 10 s."

[32] Le Grand, Les béguines de Paris, p. 16, note 4.

[33] Ibid., p. 33.

[34] Statutes of 1341, art. 16 (ibid., p. 55): "Item, que ladite matresse ne reçoive nulle fame en l'ostel pour demourer sanz le conseil des anciennes béguines, trois ou quatre, qui seront ordenees et esleues par le conseil du prieur des Frères prescheurs de Paris à estre du conseil de ladite matresse ou du souprieur en l'absence dudit prieur, lesquelz nozdiz devanciers ont establi, et nous aussi les establissons gardes et gouverneurs de ladite maison."

[35] Statutes, art. 19 (ibid., pp. 56-57) and 21 (p. 57).

[36] Statutes, art. 19 in fine (ibid., p. 57).

[37] Statutes, art. 16 (ibid., pp. 55-56); cf. art. 3 (p. 53), 9 (p. 54), 15 (p. 55), 21 (p. 57).

To supplement the beguinage at the gate Barbeel, Constance de Saint-Jacques and Alix des Pavillons established about 1283 a new beguinage in Paris, known as St. Avoye, for forty widows at least fifty years old.[38] The dean of St. Merry reserved direction of this house while the inhabitants of St. Catherine submitted to the Order of Preachers in whose church their mistresses enjoyed by royal privilege the right of burial.[39] But the *Bonnes femmes* of St. Avoye never achieved much prominence.[40] St. Catherine, on the contrary, flourished throughout the fourteenth century but in the succeeding period suffered from the difficulties that beset the Dominicans. In 1480, when Louis XI allowed the beguines to embrace the third rule of St. Francis, the university and Preachers forced his retraction of the measure by their protests. The tertiaries then offered a counterproposal that was accepted; they called to replace them the Franciscan sisters who had settled in a convent rebuilt by Charlotte of Savoy in 1471 and whose new church had been dedicated twenty-four years earlier by Denys du Moulin, bishop of Paris and counsellor of Charles VII.[41]

The patronage extended by Louis IX and his successors to the Paris beguines was by no means exceptional. Beguine houses sprang up in many parts of the kingdom, but especially in those provinces oriented to Belgium—thus, not quite as ubiquitously as Guillaume de Saint-Amour or the *Norman Chronicle* suggests—and were remembered in royal alms and legacies.[42] Joinville singles out as the cardinal virtue of a beguinage preservation of chastity, an attribute which recommended the institution to the king[43] as well as to Jacques de Vitry or Foulques de Toulouse. The impatience and disapproval of

---

[38] Felibien, *Histoire de la ville de Paris,* I, 380, no. 19; Ollivier, *Le grand béguinage de Gand,* pp. 30-31; Le Grand, *Les béguines de Paris,* pp. 45, 48-50.

[39] At the church of the convent of St. Jacques the French Revolution uncovered three of their tombs: Domicella Agnes de Orchio (d. 1284), Jehanne la Bricharde (March, 1312), and Jehanne la Romaine (June 11, 1335) (Chapotin, *Histoire des Dominicains,* p. 519). The statutes of 1341 (art. 16) provided that the prior should be "garde et gouverneur de la maison" (Le Grand, *Les béguines de Paris,* p. 55).

[40] Le Grand (pp. 45-49) stresses the difference between these Bonnes femmes and beguines. He publishes the rule of the Bonnes femmes Sainte-Avoy (1548) on pp. 64-67.

[41] Ollivier, *Le grand béguinage de Gand,* p. 33. Helyot (*Histoire des ordres monastiques,* VIII, 4) held that these beguines were really Franciscan tertiaries. In 1485 Innocent VIII issued to the inhabitants of this convent a bull allowing them to go over the order of St. Clara (Wadding, *Ann. Min.,* XIV, 593; cf. *AA. SS.,* XXXIX [August 25, v], 502 E).

[42] Guillaume de Nangis is more restrained: "Similiter in pluribus regni sui civitatibus et castris domos Beguines mulieribus ad habitandum providit, et eis in victu de suis sumptibus ministravit" (*Gesta S. Ludovici,* in Bouquet, XX, 406 D-E).

[43] Joinville, *Histoire de S. Louis,* Bouquet, XX, 298 C: "... Et fist en pluseurs liex de son royaume mesons de beguines, et leur donna rentes pour elles vivre, et dommanda len que en y receust celles qui vourroient fere contenance a vivre chastement." Cf. *Vita S. Ludov., ibid.,* XX, 12 A.

Louis' family and household at these lavish gifts he disarmed simply by his unworldliness in such matters.[44] Nor is it without significance that Thomas of Cantimpré introduced the reference to the Paris beguinage already cited with a brief account of the King's sister who, as the wife of Conrad of Germany, preferred virginity and the contemplative life.[45] All religious of whatever order, providing they secured the approval of the Holy See, could expect wholehearted royal support.[46] Although not constituted as an independent order, the beguines, who regularly received privileges of various kinds and protection briefs, were clearly numbered among legitimate communities countenanced by the papal curia.

St. Louis is credited by another chronicler with the foundation of the beguine house at Rouen.[47] In Picardy the convent at Amiens, established by Bishop Arnold (1236–1247) at la Hotoie, had for its superior in 1264 Elizabeth the Elder; thereafter it was under the direction of the Order of Preachers.[48] The beguinage at Abbeville was founded in 1266 by Ida de Boubers, the mother of Bernard, bishop of Amiens and Arnold's successor.[49] At Corbie a community flourished which offered for one year at the close of the fourteenth century shelter to Colette (January 13, 1381 n.s.–March 6, 1447 n.s.)[50] who cultivated there further her precocious religious interests[51] by visiting churches and shrines and hearing mass and divine offices daily.[52] She attracted the attention of local burghers, in particular Domicella Guillerma Gamelina, widow of the late John le Seneschal, once provost of Corbie, who had a small dwelling put up to serve as a reclusorium. Here

---

[44] Joinville, in Bouquet, XX, 298 C; Guillaume de Nangis, Gesta S. Ludov., ibid., XX, 406 E.

[45] Thomas of Cantimpré, BUA., II, 29, 40 (pp. 318f).

[46] Geoffrey of Beaulieu, Vita S. Ludov. Reg., in Bouquet, XX, 12; AA. SS., XXXIX (August 25, v), 548-549, no. 31.

[47] Extrait d'une chronique de Rouen continuée jusqu'en 1492, in Bouquet, XXIII, 353 (an. 1227).

[48] Ollivier, Le grand béguinage de Gand, p. 28; Christ, La règle des Fins Amans, p. 185.

[49] Ollivier, Le grand béguinage de Gand, p. 28. The beguines at Abbeville were replaced by Franciscans in 1436 (Corblet, Hag. du diocèse d'Amiens, IV, 175).

[50] Vita B. Coleta by Pierre de Meaux, 538-590 and Miracula post obitum, 590-626; cf. Emile Varenbergh's article in BNB., IV (1873), 276-281.

[51] V. Col., 539-540, nos. 4-8; 541 B-C, no. 10.

[52] Comm. praev., de B. Col., 535 A, no. 15. While the beguines are specifically mentioned in a notarial document of March 6, 1471 (ibid., 534-535, nos. 14-17), the vita fails to employ the term. Nevertheless it relates how her father, ever sympathetic to his daughter's predilections (ibid., 541 B-C, no. 10), made one of his houses available to "pauperculas mulieres dissolutas et deviatas a via puritatis et honestatis" (ibid., 541 B, no. 10). Again, mention is made of "virgines et viduae, quae relictis omnibus habitis et habendis, seipsas mancipaverunt divino servitio per ingressum sacrae Religiones: aliae vero jam ligatae matrimonio, vitam suam dexterae Excelsi mutatione reparantes, stratum suum fideliter et salutifere servaverunt" (ibid., 541 C, no. 11). This sounds much like a profession of beguinal life.

Colette spent three years[53] under the spiritual guidance of Jacob Guiot and his brother John, pastor of St. Martin, who acted as her confessor.[54] Afterwards she turned to the austerity of the Benedictine hospital where she prepared herself for the reform of the Franciscan order by founding the Colettine Poor Claras. According to the rules of 1307 the beguinage des Grènetiers was an asylum for old women rather than an ordinary beguinage.[55] The Orléans beguinage appears to have owed its origins to Flemish cloth merchants who frequented the Easter fairs with their wives and daughters. This is confirmed by the fact that beguines first settled in a loft of the Tanners' hall. In 1256 Louis bought for them a modest dwelling[56] and the following year he donated 100 l. to furnish it and support its nine inhabitants; in 1285 the income allotted to them was raised from the original nine ecus to twelve.[57] Again, 1256, the king donated 10 l. in alms to the mistress of the beguinage at Cambrai,[58] 40 l. (September 13) through Geoffrey of Beaulieu to a beguine at Senlis for the purchase of a house,[59] and 20 l. to the beguines and mistresses at Tours and Orleans.[60] While St. Omer had in the days of Countess Mahaut a beguine community—"un grant couvent et XV autres petis couvens de beguines"—[61] which afterwards was subject to echevinal surveillance,[62] Gervais Deleville in 1245 gave his house in Douai to lodge "de pauvres femmes appelées vulgairement beguines."[63]

To the northeast, Rheims witnessed the rise of two beguinages: the first, founded in 1249 in the parish of Saint-Denis, was eventually known as the Grand Cantipré.[64] On July 24[65] Prior Eudes and Friar Jean de Longeville, both of the Dominican convent, sold two houses to Alis Corgnie and Dude Lelarge of Rheims for 250 l. of Provins. The following month the two women abandoned their acquisition to the

[53] Ibid., 535 A, no. 15.

[54] Ibid., 535 B, no. 16.

[55] Le Grand, Les béguines de Paris, p. 11.

[56] Ollivier, Le grand béguinage de Gand, p. 28.

[57] Le Grand, Les béguines de Paris, pp. 13-14; Le Nain de Tillemont, Vie de Saint Louis, V, 312-313.

[58] Tabulae Ceratae Johannis Sarraceni, in Bouquet, XXI, 356; "Item magistra beguinarum de Cambrey, quando rediit, Parisius, per Petrum Marcel, x. l."

[59] Ibid., XXI, 356: "Beguinae Silvactenses, pro domo empta, per fratrem G. de Bello Loco, xl. l."

[60] Ibid., XXI, 356: "Rich. de Bec, pro beguinis et mètresses menare Turones et Aurelianum et reducere a Roan, a Coan, Verneuil, xx. l." Cf. ibid., XXI, 372.

[61] Richard, Mahaut, p. 90.

[62] On March 17, 1418, the mayor and echevins of Saint-Omer applied to "le maison et hostel des béguines sur le rivière d'Erbostade" the rule of the great convent (Giry, in Mémoires de la société des antiquaires de la Morinie, IV [1876], 150, no. 201). On July 6, 1428, the echevins confirmed the customs and rule of the great beguinage (ibid., 161, no. 224).

[63] Le Grand, Les béguines de Paris, p. 11.

[64] Robert, Les béguines de Reims, p. 13.

[65] Ibid., P.J. I.

abbot of St. Denis and the prior of the Friars Preachers to establish
beguines in the house of the late Gontier de Rethel.[66] It is evident
that the Dominicans were responsible for its organization, for under
their supervision the founders assumed direction of the community.
The second house, in the parish of St. Timothy, was of obscure origin,
but is mentioned in 1275 in the will of Perrecard de Villedommange, a
local burgher, who owned a part of the seigniories of Aussonce and
La Neuville-en-Tourne-a-Fuy.[67] The historian of the Rheims communities produced no evidence to indicate royal patronage; instead, it
was the cathedral officials as well as Dominicans who promoted their
well-being. In 1285 Hugh de Large, dean of the cathedral chapter,
willed 20 s. parisis to the poor beguines in the parish of St. Timothy
and 10 l. to the larger beguinage.[68] In 1296 Herbert aux Braies, canon
in the same chapter, left 20 s. to each community.[69] Whereas Archbishop Robert de Courtenay assigned 40 s. to them on April 20, 1314,
Garin Goujon, canon of St. Symphorien and St. Timothy, the following month left 40 s. to each beguinage.[70]

The above-mentioned beguinage of Cantimpré near Cambrai,[71]
singled out by Gregory IX in 1238 for special concessions, although
couched in the form of the ordinary protection bull,[72] received
numerous acquisitions under its superior, Isabelle de Flecquières (d.
December 19, 1264)[73] who, on Ryckel's authority,[74] was recognized by
the community as its founder or benefactor. These possessions Louis
confirmed to the hospital in February, 1256.[75] Exactly ten years before
(February, 1246) Bishop Guy of Cambrai had officially recognized
Isabelle as the superior of the beguinage, giving her full power to
receive, remove and transfer inmates, as well as supervision of the
hospital with all its appurtenances. Whatever changes she should
make in the future merited episcopal blessing.[76]

Pierre d'Alençon shared his alms in 1282 with the poor at Auxerre,
Cambrai, Nivelles, Douai, and Liége by granting them 60 livres in

[66] Ibid., pp. 24-26, P.J. II. Stephen of Bourbon (d. 1261) refers in his Anecdotes,
compiled shortly before his death (ed. Lecoy de la Marche, p. xx), to a "beguina,
noviter conversa" at Rheims (pp. 335f, no. 380).

[67] Robert, op. cit., p. 4.

[68] Ibid., pp. 4-5.

[69] Ibid., p. 5.

[70] Idem.

[71] Ryckel (p. 626) notes that Cantimpré was founded "juxta portam et intra
paroeciam suburbii Cantipratensi"; Bishop Godfrey of Cambrai in 1236 (p. 629)
and Innocent IV in 1246 (ibid., p. 630) speak of it as "apud sanctum Salvatorem
juxta Cantipratum" and "juxta civitatem Cameracensem" respectively.

[72] Ibid., pp. 629-630.

[73] This is the date given by Ryckel (p. 631) who followed an epitaph visible in
his day in the chapel of the beguinage.

[74] Ibid., p. 631.

[75] MF., III, 398; Ryckel, p. 632; Wauters, TC., V, 123.

[76] Ryckel, p. 632; Wauters, TC., IV, 464.

return for masses and prayers.[77] Royal gifts continued during the reign of Philip IV. In 1308 the beguines of Senlis received a sum for the purchase of tunics and wood.[78] Not only were nine beguines at Orléans remembered,[79] but aid was extended to Aelipdis, a beguine at St. Quentin,[80] and another bearing the same name at Amiens.[81] The nuns of Gaud and the beguines of Caen equally received 8 l.; the Filles-Dieu and the beguines of Rouen a similar amount for the purchase of wood; the latter, moreover, were given an additional 64 s. for tunics.[82] The account books also note small alms for the beguines at Chartres,[83] Crespy,[84] Mantes,[85] Melun,[86] and Sens.[87]

Just as the French communities owed their stimulus and organization in large measure to Flemish pattern, so with the political penetration of the crown northward patronage tended to shift from comital to royal auspices. Bruges is a case in point. In 1299 the beguinage received from Philip IV a charter of exemption whereby the king of France reserved for royal officials jurisdiction over all cases and suits that arose from the lands of La Vigne.[88] Henceforth it was a royal beguinage, no longer dependent on the local *bailli,* but only on the tribunal of the king. St. Elizabeth in Ghent, on the other hand, continued to receive protection from comital officials and the echevinage.[89]

Political changes of the fourteenth and fifteenth centuries continued to have repercussions on the external history of the Flemish beguinages. On August 26, 1386, Philip the Bold, in answer to the beguines' request for relief, remitted two-thirds of 20 l. of Paris which St. Elizabeth at Ghent still owed him. Financial inability was attributed to the losses and damage sustained by the late wars in the county.[90] On June

---

[77] Mosheim, p. 47.

[78] *Tabulae ceratae,* Bouquet, XXII, 559. According to the *Compotus baillivorum Franciae (ibid.,* 630) six beguines in the same town received: "vii s. vi d. per septimanam, vii l. x. s."

[79] *Ibid.,* XXII, 637: xii s. 4 d. each per week, with a total of 12 l. 6 s. 8 d.

[80] *Compotus baillivorum Franciae, ibid.,* 625.

[81] *Ibid.,* XXII, 634; *Fragmenta computorum,* Bouquet, XXII, 751, 762 (1295).

[82] November 27, 1308, *Tabulae ceratae,* Bouquet, XXII, 560 L.

[83] February 13, 1307, *ibid.,* XXII, 551: "Carnotense hospitale Sancti Lifardi et beguinae Carnotenses."

[84] *Itinera, dona et Hernesia,* Bouquet, XXII, 602 (1239): "Pro beguinis Crespiaci, per consergiam, 40 s."

[85] *Tabulae ceratae* (an. 1308), Bouquet, XXII, 558.

[86] *Ibid.,* 560.

[87] *Compotus Ballivorum Franciae,* Bouquet, XXII, 656.

[88] Hoornaert, in *ASEB.,* 1929, p. 14.

[89] November 3, 1336 (Béthune, *Cartulaire,* p. 84, no. 121); March 31, 1359 (*ibid.,* pp. 94-95, no. 134); cf. April 1, 1311 (*ibid.,* p. 60, no. 87).

[90] *Ibid.,* p. 121, no. 172; cf. October 18, 1395 (*ibid.,* pp. 128-129, no. 185). On October 2, 1387 the echevins of Ghent authorized the grand mistress of the beguinage to take possession of the inheritance of Mergriete Bertoens (*ibid.,* p. 122, no. 174).

8, 1405, John, duke of Burgundy, urged the maintenance of the former limits of the beguinage.[91]

Adolphe Hocquet[92] refuted the tradition that Bishop Walter de Marvis founded the beguinage in the parish of La Madeleine at Tournai.[93] In May, 1241, the town magistrates sold to Jacques le Tendeur, an echevin from 1233 to 1245, the land near the Porte Sainte-Fontaine. He acquired this property *aoés les béguines*[94] for the construction of a beguinage. Although reluctant to have either an abbey or conventual house erected here, the commune agreed to the sale provided it retained full temporal jurisdiction over it. A few days after the transaction, or perhaps the same day, the bishop persuaded the archdeacons of Tournai and Flanders who were charged with the supervision and visitation of hospitals, leperhouses, and monasteries to recognize the validity of the sale. That appears to have been the extent of episcopal contribution to the foundation of the Tournai beguinage.[95]

[91] *Ibid.*, p. 135, no. 194.
[92] Hocquet, "Le béguinage, son véritable fondateur," *Annales de la société historique et archéologique de Tournai*, N.S. VII (1902), 75-80.
[93] Cf. *GC.*, III, 219 where the epitaph recalling Walter's patronage, but without specific designation, is published:

> Ipse bonos pueros, moniales, ac seniores
> Fundat presbyteros, Beguinas atque Minores,
> Et Comminenses ad se vocat ac Aenenses.

Cf. inscription found in 1680 in the choir of the cathedral (*l.c.*) where the beguines are omitted in an otherwise similar passage.
[94] Hocquet, *op. cit.*, p. 78, P.J. 1.
[95] *Ibid.*, pp. 79-80, P.J. 2.

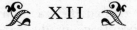

XII

The Beguinage and Indulgences

The practice of granting indulgences, rooted in the dogma of the communion of Saints, grew out of the crusades. Worthy contrition ensured the removal of the *culpa* which sin entailed. But there still remained the temporal penalty (*poena*) for which substantial satisfaction was demanded by the church. Although for centuries it had been customary for ecclesiastical authorities to impose heavy canonical penalties, the indulgence never involved remission of sin.[1] Since it was often impossible to conform to the harsh prescriptions, it became increasingly common from the seventh century on to allow the mitigation of arduous penance through vicarious experience. From this elasticity of the penitential system, originally countenanced by the confessor only in special cases, slowly developed indulgences the very essence of which was commutation or reduction of penalty.[2]

If there was but one way to obtain plenary indulgence, of which the promise tendered in Pope Urban II's summons to a crusade at Clermont (1095)[3] is the most celebrated example, the methods of granting partial indulgence were numerous. Popes, cardinals, and bishops ordinarily granted remission of fractions of penance, for example, one-fourth, one-third, one-half, generally measured from an early period in terms of days and years. Thus the faithful were given indulgences of seven, ten, twenty, or forty days, and occasionally of one, two, three,

---

[1] *Codex Juris Canonici,* can. 911: "...Remissionem coram Deo poenae temporalis debitac pro peccatis, ad culpam quod attinet jam deletis, quam ecclesiastica auctoritas ex thesauro Ecclesiae concedit pro vivi's per modum absolutionis, pro defunctis per modum suffragii." Protestants, like medieval chroniclers and even early popes, fail to distinguish between temporal penalty and remission of sin theologians came to demand (cf. Gottlob, *Kreuzablass und Almosenablass,* p. 3). The most authoritative treatment of indulgences is Nikolaus Paulus, *Geschichte des Ablasses im Mittelalter* (3 vols., Paderborn, 1922-1923); cf. Delehaye, "Les lettres d'indulgence collectives," *AB.,* XLIV (1926), 342-379; XLV (1927), 97-123; 323-344 Et. Magnin, "Indulgences," *DTC.,* VII, 2 (1923), 1594-1636.

[2] Paulus, *Geschichte des Ablasses,* I, 13-38.

[3] Can. 2: "Quicumque pro sola devotione, non pro honoris vel pecuniae adeptione, ad liberandam ecclesiam Dei Jerusalem profectus fuerit, iter illud pro omni poenitentia reputetur" (Mansi, XX, 816).

or more years.[4] In the eleventh century it became common for episcopal authority, above all in southern France and northern Spain, to
grant indulgences for the giving of alms to churches, monasteries, and
hospitals, for construction or maintenance or for visitation of certain
churches—a practice that acquired currency in northern Europe in the
following century.[5] For the most part these indulgences amounted to
forty days, occasionally a year, and after 1200 sometimes longer,
perhaps a year and forty days. Greater indulgences for alms and visitation, however, were rare.[6] Needless to say, such an institution was of
considerable importance for the monastery in the founding of daughter-
houses or for the erection of new churches.[7]

In spite of appearances and suppositions, indulgences for contributions and church visitation, whether in written or oral form, were
not too profuse before 1215.[8] The Fourth Lateran Council registered
lively concern at the liberal distribution of indulgences and determined that at dedication ceremonies, whether performed by a single
bishop or several, the indulgence should not exceed a year while
forty days must be the limit for anniversaries.[9] However, when the
council complained at the "indiscretas et superfluas indulgentias, quas
quidam ecclesiarum praelati facere non verentur et claves ecclesiae
contemnuntur et paenitentialis satisfactio enervatur,"[10] it was addressing itself primarily to the reprehensible conduct of "some" prelates.[11]
It called attention to the fact that moderation was customarily observed by the popes even though they enjoyed plenitude of power.[12]

The Lateran text speaks of two categories of indulgences: those
granted at the dedication of churches and those on all other occasions
("pro quibuslibet causis").[13] Although the *mulieres religiosae* at Oig-

[4] Paulus, *Geschichte des Ablasses*, I, 193; Delehaye, in *AB.*, XLIV (1926), 345-346,
348; XLV (1927), 97-109.
[5] For the whole problem, see Paulus, *Geschichte des Ablasses*, I, 132-194; cf. Lallemand, *Histoire de la charité*, III, 99; Jan Boendale, *Jan Teesteye*, vss. 479-489 (ed.
Snellaert, *Nederlandsche Gedichten*, p. 153).
[6] Paulus, *Geschichte des Ablasses*, II, 1-24. For indulgences granted to the
Brethren of the Cross, see Ramaekers, *Privileges*, pp. 56-64.
[7] By 1284 the little hospital of the Holy Ghost at Halberstadt had already received fourteen letters granting forty-day indulgence and others of lesser amount
(Uhlhorn, *Liebesthätigkeit*, II, 244).
[8] Paulus (*Geschichte des Ablasses*, I, 192) subscribes to Lea's comment (*History
of Auricular Confession*, III [1896], 163, note 4) on the canon of the Fourth Lateran
Council: "I have not been able to find any authentic cases of undue profuseness
prior to the Lateran council."
[9] Can. 62, Mansi, XXII, 1050; Hefele-Leclerq, V, 2, 1382f; c. 14, *de poenitentiis*,
V, 38.
[10] Cf. Paulus, *Geschichte des Ablasses*, I, 176-177.
[11] Mansi, XXII, 1051; Hefele-Leclercq, V, 2, 1383: „Cum Romanus pontifex, qui
plenitudinem obtinet potestatis, hoc in talibus moderamen consueverit observare";
cf. Delehaye, in *AB.*, XLV (1927), 98-99.
[12] Cf. Lea, *History of Auricular Confession*, III, 163, note 4: "I am inclined to
think that the slur thus cast upon the bishops was undeserved."
[13] Delehaye, in *AB.*, XLV (1927), 102-109.

nies derived at least indirect benefit from the indulgence declared by Jacques de Vitry in 1227 for the church made famous by his mentor,[14] the pontificate of Gregory IX and the legation of Bishop Jacques of Preneste offer the earliest examples of such indulgences being dispensed to those who aided in the founding or contributed to the building of beguine churches. Hallmann published an indult which the cardinal issued in 1240 (February 5) to the faithful of the province of Rheims offering them an indulgence of thirty days for alms given to the beguinage known as *Solatium Beatae Mariae* at Vilvorde.[15] The number of *mulieres religiosae* or beguines who, residing in the neighborhood of the hospital of St. Christopher at Liége, attended the services in its chapel, had grown so large by 1241 that Jacques was again persuaded to grant an indulgence to those who contributed to the construction of a new church where the beguines could gather.[16]

But it was above all during the pontificate of Innocent IV (1243–1254) that the Roman curia showed increasing interest, both negative and positive, in the feminine religious movement. In September, 1247, Thomas, abbot of St. Trond, allowed the beguines of Diest to construct houses, erect a chapel, and appoint a chaplain,[17] a privilege that was renewed in April, 1253,[18] and January, 1254,[19] by Arnold IV, lord of Diest. From the ordinary indulgence brief issued by Cardinal Hugh of St. Cher on June 20, 1253, "to all the faithful in the kingdom of Germany" with the qualification, "quas mitti per questuarios districtius inhibemus,"[20] it is evident that construction of the chapel had already begun. On the other hand, Edmund, bishop of *Turonensis*,[21] granted a new indulgence on May 6, 1273, indicating that the structure was not yet finished. A forty-day indulgence was granted not only for the building of the church but also for assistance to "poor beguines living in the infirmary."[22] The beguinage of St. Catherine in the Field

[14] *Comm. praev., VMO.*, 542 (1).

[15] Hallmann, *Geschichte des Ursprungs*, p. 66. This bull was accompanied by a brief of Bishop Guy of Cambrai which contained a copy of it. In this copy the date "nonis Februarii" is changed to "VI Idus Febr." (i.e., February 8) (*ibid.*, p. 67).

[16] Ryckel, p. 573; in September the archbishop of Cologne made a similar grant (*idem;* Wauters, *T.C.*, IV, 358). On the recommendation of Hugh of St. Cher, cardinal-legate, on February 22, 1253, the abbot of Saint-Laurent at Liége allowed the rector of the beguinage to administer extreme unction to the inmates (Schoolmeesters, in *Leodium*, VI [1907], 156).

[17] Raymaekers, *Kerkelijk Diest,* p. 423. note 3 (text).

[18] *Ibid.*, p. 425, note 2 (text); Wauters, *TC.*, V, 57.

[19] *Ibid.*, p. 426, note 1 (text).

[20] *Ibid.*, p. 456, note 2 (text); cf. *ibid.*, pp. 427-428; Wauters, *TC.*, V, 61; Böhmer-Ficker, no. 10406; Schoolmeesters, in *Leodium*, VI (1907), 157.

[21] Eubel (HC., I, 503), following Gams (p. 640), lists no Edmund for Tours. The bishop for this date was Jean de Montsoreau (January 16, 1271-d. January 26, 1285). Nor is there one with this name for Tournai (Eubel, HC., I, 489; cf. Gams, 251); Jean d'Enghien, who was bishop from 1267 until his translation to Liége, was succeeded by Philip Meusius (1274-d. ca. 1282). No Edmund appears in either list.

[22] Raymaekers, *Kerkelijk Diest,* p. 457, note 1 (text); Wauters, *TC.*, V, 517

at Diest continued to receive similar indulgences in the following century.[23]

In 1248 the master, brothers, and sisters of St. Jaques' hospital in Tongres petitioned the papacy to allow them to follow the rule of St. Augustine, to extend curial protection to their community, and to have the dean of St. Paul at Liége appoint a guardian for their property and rights. Furthermore, since their small chapel could no longer accommodate the "multitude of beguines who had settled around it, enjoying parochial rights" conferred by Robert de Thourote and receiving the sacraments, they joined the beguines in making a request for an indulgence of twenty days to enable the reconstruction and enlargement of the chapel.[24]

Hugh of St. Cher exhibited continuous interest in the feminine religious movement whether by promulgating protection briefs or granting indulgences. On June 1, 1252, he offered "the faithful in the German kingdom" ("fidelibus per regnum Alamaniae") an indulgence of forty days on behalf of Vilvorde.[25] The same community obtained a similar concession on October 7, 1254, from Peter Capoccius of St. George *ad velum aureum,* then in Antwerp.[26] Again, on November 12, 1251, Hugh of St. Cher, while in Cologne, used the same device to encourage the faithful to assist the beguines at Aerschot in the construction of the beguinage.[27] The Antwerp community merited an indult the following year.[28] To make effective rehabilitation in the wake of the Clementine legislation Adolph de la Marck, bishop of Liége, in 1326 (April 9) approved an indulgence granted by several bishops to the chapel of the Aerschot beguine house.[29]

Papebroch reports that in 1295 several bishops took steps to aid the

[23] The Bibliothèque royale de Belgique in Brussels (Cod. II, 2807) possesses the original of the indulgence letter of fifteen bishops for the Diest beguinage in 1333 (April 23) (on parchment, om.51 x om.718). A large miniature represents St. Catherine and an angel with a nun in prayer before her. The text has been published by Delehaye in *AB.,* XLIV (1926), 369-371, no. 15. The Cabinet des Manuscrits also possesses copies in Flemish of indulgences granted to the Diest beguinage in the sixteenth century (cod. II, 2795, f. 4r-6r): "Desen naeghescreven aflaet heeft ghegheven ende ghelaten mondelijcken onse eerwerdighe ende heer Georgius van Oostenrijck bisscop tot Luyck allen beghijnen vanden beghijnhoff van Diest int jaer ons heeren dysent CCCCC LVIJ den v dach van april ende den selven aflaet heeft noch eene ghegeven mondelijcken den selven beghijnhoff die eerwerdighe heere Gregorius Sibius suffragaen van Luyck int selve voerschreven iaer op sinte Vrselen dach" (f. 4r). *Ibid.,* f. 6-8v: "Dit is den aflaet ende remissie verleent van neghentien bisscoppen der kercken ende godshuijs van sinte catherijnen int beghijnhoff inder stat van diest geleghen inden navolgender manieren" (f. 6r). These indulgences were unknown to Raymaeker.
[24] Thijs, in *BSSLL.,* XV (1881), 422-423.
[25] Hallmann, *Geschichte des Ursprungs,* p. 76; Schoolmeesters, in *Leodium,* VI (1907), 153.
[26] Hallmann, *Geschichte des Ursprungs,* p. 77.
[27] Evers, in *BG.,* XXIX (1938), 136-137, P.J. 1.
[28] Ryckel, p. 175; Schoolmeesters, in *Leodium,* VI (1907), 153.
[29] De Ridder, in *Hagelands Gedenkschriften,* VI (1912), 33.

beguines at Ghent.[30] To encourage visitation of their chapel, dedicated to St. Elizabeth, and the altar to St. Alexis founded in the infirmary of their convent, a forty-day indulgence was granted in 1353 (May 22) to all penitents who came on Christmas, Circumcision, Epiphany, Good Friday, Easter, Ascension, Pentecost, Trinity, Corpus Christi, Invention and Exaltation of the Cross, all the feasts of the Virgin, St. Michael the archangel, the nativity and beheading of John the Baptist, the feast of the apostles Peter and Paul, of the other apostles, evangelists, and the four doctors of the church, and the feast of All Saints'; for the dedication of the chapel and altar of St. Alexis, on the feasts of Stephen, Lawrence, Denis, Blaise, Nicholas, Mary Magdalene, Katherine, Agatha, Margaret, and through the octaves of all feasts having octaves, and Sundays and sabbaths during the year.[31]

On July 6, 1295, the bishop-elect of Liége granted an indulgence of forty days to those who visited the beguine church at Breda on almost the same feasts.[32] The following year (May 15) Bonaventura of Parma, archbishop of Ragusa in Dalmatia (1281–1292), together with eleven bishops, mostly Italian, offered forty days of indulgence to those who visited the chapel of St. Catherine of the beguines at Breda.[33] On May 9, 1326, Adolph de la Marck, bishop of Liége, approved this last concession, adding two other indulgences: thirty days for visitation of the chapel and "extending the hands" and ten for praying "for us."[34] In like fashion John of Diest, bishop of Lübeck and former chaplain of Count William II, granted on May 9-16, 1255, an indulgence of forty days to the beguines at Gravenzande to aid in the construction of their convent.[35] In 1300 the chapel of St. Catherine at Alost, in the diocese of Cambrai, received a similar privilege.[36] On July 2, 1290, eight bishops granted an indulgence to the church of the Herenthals beguines who had recommended themselves by their

[30] Papebroch, *Annales Antverpienses*, I, 75.

[31] Béthune, *Cartulaire*, pp. 88-89, no. 128. In 1475 Ferricus de Clugny, bishop of Tournai (1473-1483), approved the indulgence pronouncement. This document is however unreadable (*ibid.*, p. 175, no. 266; cf. Moulaert, *Het groot Beggynhof van Gent*, p. 13 note; Moulaert also renders a Flemish translation of the 1353 document, *ibid.*, pp. 11ff note).

[32] Juten, *Cartularium*, pp. 6-7, no. 5.

[33] *Ibid.*, pp. 8-9, no. 6; a vidimus was issued by the dean and chapter of Breda on September 15, 1334 (*ibid.*, p. 9 note).

[34] *Ibid.*, pp. 12-13, no. 11: "... Confessis ad dictam capellam venientibus manumque porrigentibus adjutricem triginta" (for the formula see Tangl, *Die päpstlichen Kanzlei-Ordnungen*, pp. 331-332, no. 137) "et pro nobis jugiter orantibus decem dies indulgentiarum."

[35] Van den Bergh, *Oorkondenboek van Holland en Zeeland*, I, 325, no. 612; Wauters, *TC.*, V, 105; J. de Fremery (in *Oorkb. Suppl.*, pp. 82-83, no. 127) published an identical letter, dated May 17, 23, 1255, to aid the beguines of Gravenzande in their construction of a *curtis*. Cf. also de Fremery, in Fruin, *Bijdragen voor vaderl. Gesch. en Oudheidkunde*, 3rd ser., VIII, 327-328, no. 3.

[36] Soens, *Cartularium*, p. 25.

election of chastity.[37] Similar assistance was extended to the beguines at Mons for the dedication of their altar of St. John the Baptist[38] and to those at Tirlemont for the construction of a church.[39] We have already examined the privileges enjoyed by La Royauté in Nivelles.[40]

In the middle of the fourteenth century Falcon de Lampage, of Pistoia, master-general of ducal moneys, founded on a tract of property on the north side of Antwerp, known as Valkenbroek, a hospital and chapel (sacellum) for tertiary women who, although not bound by religious vows, "desired to live together in continence and obedience, serving God under a humble habit."[41] In 1346 their patron obtained from sixteen bishops for the chapel, dedicated to the Eleven Thousand Virgins, a forty-day indulgence for those who visited the chapel on specified occasions or favored it with donations. This indulgence was subsequently approved by the bishop of Cambrai and his suffragans in two acts annexed to this brief.[42] In 1352 Falcon granted to the chapel of the sisters of Valkenbroek, this time through seventeen bishops, indulgences for the faithful who visited it on certain days or contributed to its construction. This privilege too was ratified by the bishop of Cambrai following an act attached to the brief.[43]

Although the evidence gathered here is admittedly spotty and rests exclusively on written indults, it does demonstrate that suspicion and persecution in the fourteenth century did not seriously curtail privileges for Belgian extraregulars. In 1351 (April 12) the beguine church at Léau, in the diocese of Liége, obtained such a grant,[44] while several archbishops and bishops granted indulgences on behalf of the church of the Aerschot beguinage in 1324 (October 16).[45] Nicholas IV had conferred on the beguines at Paris the same benefits.[46] The Amsterdam beguinage too received indulgence-letters repeatedly.[47]

Indulgence briefs for the beghards are not so plentiful. On June 12, 1317, Herman, episcopus Enensis or Henensis or Hennensis, suffragan bishop of Liége (1315-1332),[48] having dedicated the chapel of the beghards in Malines in honor of the cross, the Virgin, and St. Bartholomew, granted indulgences to the faithful who visited or assisted it.

[37] Delehaye, in AB., XLIV (1926), 356, no. 4. The date, July 7, 1296, is a misreading; Delehaye corrects himself in ibid., XLV (1927), 109, note 2; 115.
[38] Devillers, Description, II, 182-183, no. 32.
[39] Dillen, in Hagelands Gedenkschriften, I, 162.
[40] See above pp. 66-67.
[41] Papebroch, Annales Antverpienses, I, 135-136; Vannérus, Anvers, 546-547.
[42] 1346-1352, Vannérus, Anvers, p. 569, no. 3.
[43] Ibid., pp. 469-470.
[44] BG., VI (1907), 242.
[45] Ibid., XXIX (1938), 148-150.
[46] Chapotin, Histoire des Dominicains, p. 520, note 1. The register of the same pope contains under March 15, 1290, a new indult for the feasts of the Virgin.
[47] 1397, July 5, 1426, 1516, Eeghen, Vrouwenkloosters en Begijnhof, pp. 320f.
[48] Berlière, "Les évêques auxiliaires de Cambrai aux XIIIe et XIVe siècles," RB., XX (1903), 23-25.

An indulgence of one year and forty days was offered for visitation of the chapel on the Sunday preceding Pentecost, which Sunday marks the dedication of the church, and through its octave. A forty-day indulgence was granted for the feasts of the cross, Mary, and Bartholomew, patrons of the church.[49] On February 10, 1379, Bishop John of Cambrai extended a like privilege to those who visited the beghard chapel at Antwerp on certain feasts or contributed to its lights and ornaments.[50]

[49] Vannérus, *Malines*, pp. 245-246, no. 6.
[50] Vannérus, *Anvers*, pp. 605-606, no. 18.

XIII

The Beguinages and the Interdict

Interdict is basically an ecclesiastical censure, rather than a penalty, of indefinite duration whereby celebration of and participation in divine offices, administration and reception of sacraments, and ecclesiastical burial are suspended or curtailed. Unlike excommunication, which falls immediately on the guilty, interdict indirectly affects the innocent without cutting them off from the fold. Distinction was made in personal, geographical, or mixed interdict according to whether persons, places, or both were affected. Both personal and geographical interdict can be private or general. Under private interdict an individual or several persons, a single church or specific area were punished, while under general interdict the penalty extended either over a community of persons, or over towns or dioceses, church provinces and even entire countries.[1] The sentence which the papal legate, Peter of Capua, imposed on France in 1198 may be taken as a useful summary of the disciplinary measure. Churches were closed to the faithful, admittance being allowed only for the baptism of children. One mass might be celebrated each week—on Friday—with one cleric assisting the priest. Although mass was forbidden on Sunday, a sermon could be delivered in front of the church, and canonical hours recited outside, with no laymen listening. While mass was forbidden in holy week, priests could hold it on Easter in private with one assistant. Communion was extended only to the

---

[1] F. Kober, "Das Interdict," *Archiv für katholisches Kirchenrecht mit besonderer Rücksicht auf Oesterreich und Deutschland*, XXI (N.S. XV) (Mainz, 1869), 3-45; 291-341; XXII (N.S. XVI) (1869), 3-53; Edward Benjamin Krehbiel, *The Interdict, its History and its Operation with Especial Attention to the Time of Pope Innocent III, 1198-1216* (American Historical Association, Washington, D.C., 1909); James Goldschmidt, "Die charakteristischen Unterscheidungsmerkmale des allgemeinen und besonderen örtlichen Interdicts (eine Interpretation der Stelle cap. 17 X de Verborum Significationibus V. 40)," *Archiv für katholisches Kirchenrecht*, LXXVI (N.S. LXX) (1896), 3-24 (this is Innocent III's bull to the bishop of Coimbra and other bishops of Portugal on February 7, 1199, Friedberg, II, 916-917; Lib. I, Ep. 604, PL., CCXIV, 506-507); Hinschius, *System*, IV, 802ff; V, 13-16, 516-541; J. B. Haring, in *Lexikon für Theologie und Kirche*, V (1933), 435-436; L. Godefroy, in *DTC.*, VII, 2 (1923), 2280-2290.

dying. At Easter parishioners might be summoned in front of the church to be informed of the end of Lent. The faithful were allowed to confess on the steps of the church, or at best on the threshold. Extreme unction for the sick and burial in consecrated ground were prohibited.[2]

For the beguines and beghards the general-geographical interdict, whereby an entire city or area is deprived of religious services, is of importance. All inhabitants, including regulars and extraregulars alike, were thus affected.[3] During the twelfth and thirteenth centuries interdict as an ecclesiastical penalty had been imposed with increasing frequency because of the sharpening of church-state relations. But it was Innocent III (1198–1216) who forged the penalty into an effective weapon for his lofty theocratic designs. An interdict on cities was by no means exceptional, for entire lands were punished in this way, as in 1198 in France, and the kingdom of Leon,[4] and in 1209 in England.[5] Since the penalty was attended with a cessation of religious life, a long interdict inevitably resulted in a retrogression of spiritual experience and knowledge of dogma as well as decay of morals. This in turn laid the way open for an advance of heterodox thought. Stephen, bishop of Tournai (1193-d. 1203), for example, addressed an urgent appeal to the archbishop of Rheims for counsel and aid because Flanders, scarcely freed from one interdict, was already being threatened by another. It was all the more necessary that the new danger be diverted from the unfortunate, for the earlier wounds had not yet healed—the wounded had not yet regained their breath; should a second blow fall, spiritual reath must follow. Heretics who were then just appearing would find renewed strength.[6] The bishop and chapter of Bergamo were equally dubious about the effectiveness of the weapon in a communication to Innocent III: "Propter divinorum subtractionem quidam indevotiores effecti amplius duruerunt et sectatores haereticae pravitatis falsa sui erroris dogmata liberiori fronte proponunt." When this pope substituted for the interdict on France the excommunication of the king alone, holding that it is better that one man should suffer than that the whole people be destroyed,[7] he must have had in mind these dangers and disadvantages which undermined morale of the people during interdict.[8]

Faced with these practical considerations, the popes of the thir-

2 MDT., IV, 147-148.
3 Cf. the interdict and the Brethren of the Cross, Ramaekers, in *Clairlieu*, I (1943), 37-44.
4 Lib. I, Ep. 92, *PL.*, CCXIV, 79-80; Lib. II, Ep. 75, *ibid.*, CCXIV, 610-611; Lib VII, Ep. 67, *ibid.*, CCXV, 345; Lib. VII, Ep. 94, *ibid.*, 376.
5 For other examples see Kober, *Das Interdict*, XXI (1869), 20.
6 Ep. CCXII, *Bibl. max. vet. pat.*, XXV (1677), 47.
7 Roger de Hoveden, *Annales*, ad ann. 1200 (Bouquet, XVII [1878], 603).
8 Cf. Council of Ravenna (1314), can. 19, Mansi, XXV, 549-550.

teenth century were obliged to introduce an alleviation both through canon law and by the granting of concessions. But it was with Boniface VIII (1294–1303) that signs of relaxation became pronounced.[9] Even though general interdict had been imposed, it was permissible to baptize and educate not only children, as previously provided,[10] but even adults;[11] consecration of the chrism on Maundy Thursday was allowed; the dying might receive the sacraments of confession and extreme unction; but under Boniface penance was extended to the strong too;[12] priests and monks who had supported the interdict might be buried in consecrated ground, but without the ringing of bells or other elements of a burial service.[13] In conventual churches canonical hours could be read but not sung, and mass could be celebrated "as before," not for the whole community but by twos and threes, with subdued voices and closed doors, so that the outside world would not hear.[14] On the four great feasts—Christmas, Easter, Pentecost, and Assumption—the doors could be opened, the bell rung, and services held publicly with only the excommunicated forbidden to attend.[15] Exceptions that had been made since Innocent III for foreigners (peregrini) and crusaders, as well as bishops,[16] were now extended to all.

[9] Innocent III was not much interested in softening the decrees of his legates. Although he admitted that a sentence of interdict pronounced by bishop or archbishop could not, except with specific instructions from the Holy See, affect a convent (PL., CCXIV, 122-123, Lib. I, Ep. 137,[1198], he nevertheless delegated to the episcopal arm power to subject all diocesans, even the religious, to the penalty (Lib. I, Ep. 132 [1198], PL., CCXIV, 120; Ep. 265 [June 11, 1198], ibid., 222). The bishop of Pampeluna was allowed to celebrate mass daily in spite of general interdict on the kingdom of Leon, but with the provision: "clausis januis, exclusis excommunicatis et interdictis, non pulsatis campanis, suppressa voce" (Lib. I, Ep. 287 [July 15, 1198], ibid., 244-245). Again, the prohibition was not levelled at bishops who were innocent of the interdict; they could hold mass secretly (c. 24, de privil. et excess. privil., V, 33; Friedberg, II, 866-867; cf. c. 25, de privil. et excess. privil., V, 33, ibid., 867), On March 21, 1203, Innocent III allowed the monks of St. Germain-l'Auxerrois "to ring one bell upon the death of a member" during interdict, "and even on the day of burial, provided the ringing was continuous and not prolonged" (Lib. VI, Ep. 23, PL., CCXV, 27). When the city of Ferrara was put under the interdict in 1208 with suspension of all sacraments except baptism of children and penance for the dying, the pope approved confirmation (Lib. XI, Ep. 267, ibid., 1582-1583; Decretal. Gregor. IX, c. 43, De sentent excom., V, 39; Friedberg, II, 907).
[10] Cf. c. 11 (Alexander III), de spons. et matrim., IV, 1; Friedberg, II, 665; Hinschius, V, 528.
[11] Sexti Decretal., c. 19, de sent. excomm., V, 11; Friedberg, II, 1104.
[12] Sexti Decretal., c. 24, de sent. excomm., V, 11; Friedberg, II, 1106.
[13] Cf. Sexti Decret., c. 20, de sent. excomm., V, 11; Friedberg, II, 1104-1105.
[14] Sexti Decretal., c. 24, de sent. excomm., V, 11; Friedberg, II, 1106-1107. Mitigation of this canon refers not to the special but the general geographical interdict (Hinschius, V, 524, note 6). Whereas only one service had been allowed heretofore, now all the priests might say mass even when several services were being conducted simultaneously in the same church (Kober, Das Interdict, 308; cf. 306-307).
[15] Sexti Decretal., c. 24, de sent excomm., V, 11; Friedberg, II, 1106.
[16] Decretal. Greg., c. 11 (Innocent III), de poenit., V, 38; Friedberg, II, 887; Decretal. Greg., c. 25 (Innocent III), de privil. et excess. privil., V, 33; Friedberg, II, 867.

Notwithstanding these concessions, the imposition of interdict remained for the semireligious as well as the regulars a severe test, since religious life could be rendered almost impossible. The beguines of La Vigne in Brussels, for example, secured in 1247 from Innocent IV the privilege to celebrate divine services during interdict: "Devocionis vestre precibus fuerit interdictum, liceat vobis, clausis januis, excommunicatis nominatim et interdictis exclusis, non pulsatis campanis, suppressa voce, divina officia celebrare, dummodo causam non dederitis interdicto, nec id vobis contingat specialiter interdici."[17] This sentence which became a formula before the middle of the thirteenth century[18] deserves close analysis. By the phrase "divina officia celebrare" the pope meant celebration of mass, the holding of canonical hours, and administration of the sacraments. They might be allowed only under certain conditions: the doors must be closed so that no outsider would have the opportunity of attending the services. No one was permitted to enter unless he belonged to the congregation or order, all others including *conversi* or service personnel of a monastery as well as lay people remained as *interdicti* excluded. The bells must not be rung since no one from the outside might be admitted to these services; the service must be conducted in a subdued voice, especially without song so that nothing would be heard outside the door.

Similarly, the beguines might invoke the privilege only when they were innocent of the interdict.[19] Since mention is made here merely of *divina officia*, the community remained subject to the other consequences of the interdict: the administration and reception of sacraments and ecclesiastical burial. At all times a strict distinction was drawn between *divina officia, sacramenta,* and *sepultura.*[20] Since the sermon did not belong to the *officia divina*, it might be delivered

[17] Copy of XVI or XVII on paper in AAPB., Chartrier de Ter Kisten, Carton B. 1452 (1). An almost identical bull was issued from Lyons, July 26, 1246 (vii kal. Augusti, pontificatus nostri anno quarto) by Innocent IV in behalf of the beguines of Diest (Raymaekers, *Kerkelijk Diest*, p. 423, note 2, text); Stallaert, in *BCRH.*, 1876, 175-176.
[18] For the wording, see Innocent III's letter, February 7, 1199, Lib. I, Ep. 604, *PL.*, CCXIV, 506-507; reproduced in Decretal. Greg., c. 17, *de verb. signif.*, V, 40 (Friedberg, II, 916-917). Cf. the formula in the *privilegium commune* of the Augustinian order (Tangl, *Die päpstlichen Kanzlei-Ordnungen*, p. 233, no. 9; cf. 310, no. 110). Cf. *Privilegium Cartusiense, ibid.*, pp. 239-240, no. 12; *privilegium Cisterciense, ibid.*, p. 232, no. 20.
[19] For an interpretation of the formula, see Hinschius, V, 524 with notes 7-9, 525 with notes 1, 12; Kober, *Das Interdict*, pp. 308-310; for exclusion of the *familiares* and *domestici*, Sexti decretal., c. 11, *de privil. et excess. priv.*, V, 7 (Friedberg, II, 1089). The phrase *voce suppressa* is interpreted by Innocent III in Decret. Greg., c. 11, *de poenit. et remiss.*, V, 38 (Friedberg, II, 887): "Voce ita dimissa quod *exterius* audiri non possint."
[20] Sexti Decretal., c. 8 (Boniface VIII), *de priv.*, V, 7; Friedberg, II, 1087-1088; Decretal. Greg., c. 8, *de haeret.*, V, 7 (Friedberg, II, 779-780). Hinschius, V, 524, 528, 531; Kober, *Das Interdict*, 338-339.

during a general interdict.[21] In the formula the condition is added to the usual stipulations: "Dummodo causam non dederitis interdicto, nec it vobis contingat specialiter interdici." This confirmation, however, did not bring new elements, for it is only at the close of the century that the general right of interdict, as we have seen, had undergone various changes.

In August, 1251, the provisors, mistresses, and superior of the infirmary of the Brussels beguinage assured their pastor who had taken steps "ne lupi rapaces oves suas invadant," and to endow the community with definite resources, of an annual income of 30 *l.* in case of interdict. Should the penalty be imposed for less than one year, the stipend would be apportioned accordingly.[22]

That the "pauperes virgines religiose viventes," residing near a hospital at Nivelles,[23] were beguines is clear from the document of July 11, 1272, in which Gregory X permitted the beguins, beguines, and recluses of the parishes of Gouthal or Goutalle, Saint Sépulchre, Saint Jacques, Willambroux, and Saint Syr to hear mass with closed doors during interdict.[24] The beguines of St. Trond, rehabilitated by Clement VI (January 21, 1343), received the usual privileges.[25]

Earlier, on March 27, 1245, Innocent IV had allowed the beguines of Malines to have mass celebrated in time of interdict.[26] This occurred several years before Nicholas de Fontaines, bishop of Cambrai, authorized them to form a community (July 22, 1259).[27] This concession nevertheless suggests once again that before the creation of beguine parishes the semireligious, although still living scattered about the town, were being treated as a privileged group whose common interests and aims met the satisfaction of ecclesiastical authorities.

[21] Decretal. Greg., c. 43 (Innocent III to bishop of Ferrara), *de sent. excomm.,* V, 39; Friedberg, II, 907; Kober, *Das Interdict,* pp. 305, 320; Hinschius, V, 528.
[22] Original in AAPB., Carton H. 262.
[23] See above pp. 62-66.
[24] Tarlier and Wauters, *Géog. et hist. des communes belges, I, Arrondissement de Nivelles,* part I (1873), 150, De Louvet, *L'Origine nivelloise,* p. 59f, P.J. 4.
[25] Fredericq, *Corpus,* II, 96. For the beguines in the city and diocese of Cologne (1247) see Ennen, *Quellen,* II, 270, no. 270.
[26] *AHEB.,* XII, 22, no. 1.
[27] *Ibid.,* 23-24, no. 2.

XIV

The Beghards

Similar to the beguines in interests, aims, and spirit were the confraternities of devout, hardworking craftsmen of extra-regular status, variously known in the late Middle Ages as *beguin* in southern France, beghards in Germanic lands[1] and, as at Bruges, Louvain, Diest, and elsewhere, through corruption, Bogards,[2] or generally by poplar usage, *goede kinder die men heet Beggarde*,[3] Lollaerts,[4] Conversi,[5] *boni pueri*,[6] and *Boni Valeti* in France in the reign of

[1] Van Mierlo, in *VMKVA.*, 1930, 284-285. Beghardus occurs in many variants and corruptions (*bigardi, beggardi, begehardi, begihardi, beginhardi, bogardi, bogaard*). In the Rhenish provinces these extraregulars were labelled "vulgo Beghardi seu Lolhardi et Swestriones, a se ipsis vero pauperes Fraticelli, sive pauperes pueruli" (Döllinger, *Beiträge*, II, 381ff, 407). Ducange (*Glossarium, s.v. beghardi*) on the basis of Conrad of Megenberg (*De erroribus begehardorum, Bibl. Max. Vet. Pat.*, XXV, 310; Mosheim, p. 313) equates the word with *beguine*: "Qui vulgariter Begehardi, quoad viros, et Beginae, quoad foeminas, nominantur." The mendicant life of beghard "floaters" has suggested to some historians and philologists a connection with the Saxon word *beggen*. Cf. Mosheim, pp. 166-195; Callaey, in *Neerlandia Franciscana*, I (1914), 10; Logeman, in *Leuvensche Bijdragen*, XX (1928), 115-117; Gilliodts-van Severen, III, 6; Lea, *History of the Inquisition*, II, 350.

[2] Gilliodts-van Severen, I, 6; Mosheim, pp. 166-167; for Louvain, see Molanus, II, 1218, nos. 72-73.

[3] *Reghele der goeder kinder die men heet Beggarde*, September 21, 1291 (Gilliodts-van Severen, II, 26).

[4] See below, pp. 266-67.

[5] Mosheim, pp. 62ff. From *Ann. Colmar.*, an. 1302 (*MGH. SS.*, XVII) it appears that the term was also affixed to lay brethren (*Fratres Conversi*) of the mendicant orders.

[6] Document of the bishop of Tournai, Michael of Warenghien, March 29, 1291: "boni pueri qui Beghardi vocantur... unus de dictis bonis pueris seu Beghardis" (Gilliodts-van Severen, II, 22, no. 13; cf. brief of April 25, 1291, *ibid.*, II, 24: "boni pueri Brugenses, Beghardi vulgariter nuncupati"). The term was elastic, however, for Innocent IV granted poor scholars at Paris, called *boni pueri* ("pauperum scolarium Parisiensium, qui dicuntur Boni pueri"), whose custody belonged to the chancellor of Paris, the right to have their own chapel (November 24, 1248, *CUP.*, I, 214, no. 184; DuBoulay, *Hist. Univ. Paris.*, III, 217; Potthast, 13083). Louis IX had such students in mind in his will (Duchesne, *Historiae Francorum Scriptores*, V, 439 B; cf. Geoffrey of Beaulieu, *V. Ludov.*, Bouquet, XX, 14 A; *Compotus Balliv. Fr.*, in *ibid.*, XXII, 624 H). Under Philip III assistance was given to the "Bons-Enfants de Paris" (Boutaric, *Saint Louis*, p. 461) and the "Bonshommes de Vincennes," (*ibid.*, p. 460). Such students Renier of Tongres remembered in his legacy to *boni pueri* in Liége in 1267 (Paquay, *Regesta de Renier*, 73; cf. the will of Jean de

Louis IX,[7] "apostolic men" *(apostolici)* or simply "poor men."[8] So closely intertwined is the history of these brotherhoods with that of the feminine religious movement that it is difficult to dissociate one from the other, especially in Germany during the post-Clementine persecution. On the other hand, the beghards have never received the same careful or devoted monographic treatment which abundant sources on the *mulieres sanctae* have warranted.[9] It is significant, moreover, that except for southern France and Italy the masculine form *beguinus* was seldom employed, the term being reserved, after its introduction in the north towards the middle of the thirteenth century, almost exclusively for adherents of the feminine movement. Beghard houses occur less frequently in the imperial provinces than beguine societies; since the former were only in exceptional cases founded by patrons or officials, information pertaining to their origins and development is meager.[10]

Although beghards, like beguines, are one more manifestation of the religious excitement, the will to reform outwardly and inwardly, the ascesis, and lay piety instinct in the Gregorian program, they never achieved the same measure of permanence or spread as widely in the north as did the feminine religious movement.[11] They were not organized in beguinages; nor did they form parishes. "Begardism," wrote Van Mierlo, "was not a definite institution with its own forms, way

Huldertingen, canon of Tongres, December 1, 1274, Daris, *Notices*, XI, 16). Cf. Daris, *ibid.*, 14 note, 16, note 1.For the Bons-Enfants of Brussels, see Lefèvre, *L'organisation*, pp. 45, 220f, 255; Henne and Wauters, *Histoire de Bruxelles*, I, 179; III, 284, 580.

[7] Mosheim, pp. 36-41, 167, 178.

[8] Not only could the beguins of the south be confounded with Waldensians and Spiritual Franciscans but also, as in the case of Marsiglio of Padua with the bands of *Fratres Gaudentes* (*Defensor Pacis*, ed. C. W. Previté-Orton, Cambridge University Press, 1928, dictio ii, cap. viii, p. 185: "Neque hiis adhuc clausi limitibus, laicos quodam, quos in Italia Fratres gaudentes, alibi vero Beginos appellant"). Cf. Dante, *Inferno*, XXIII.

[9] Major contributions on the beghards include: Mosheim, pp. 166-195; Gilliodts-van Severen, I, 1-56; Fredericq, *Gesch. d. Inquis.*, II, 11-39, 135-149 and *passim*; Lea, *History of the Inquisition*, II, 350ff; Van Mierlo, "Het Begardisme. Een synthetische studie," *VMKVA.*, 1930, 277-305; Callaey, "De Nederlandsche Beggarden in St. Franciscus' Derde Orde en de weefnijverheid tijdens de Middeleeuwen," *Neerlandia Franciscana*, I (1914), 7-32; id., "Les beggards aux Pays-Bas," *Annuaire de l'Université catholique de Louvain*, LXXV (1911), 438-445 (as reported by Robert Gits); Raymaekers, *Kerkelijk Diest*, pp. 298-307; Asen, "Die Begarden und die Sackbrüder in Köln," *AHVN.*, CXV (1929), 167-179; Vannérus, "Documents concernant les Bogards de Malines (1284-1558), *BCRH.*, LXXX (1911), 215-286; id., "Documents concernant le Tiers-Ordre à Anvers et ses rapports avec l'industrie drapière (1296-1572)," *BCRH.*, LXXIX (1910), 471-672; Mens, *Oorsprong, passim*; Des Marez, "Les Bogards dans l'industrie drapière à Bruxelles," in *Mélanges P. Fredericq*, pp. 278-287; Jones *Studies in Mystical Religion*, pp. 197ff; Hauck, V, 1, 427ff; Olivier, *Le grand béguinage de Gand*, pp. 39-49; Deansley, *The Lollard Bible*, pp. 58-60, 69-71, 81-84, 89, 101.

[10] Cf. Hauck, V, 1, 427.

[11] Grundmann, *Religiöse Bewegungen*, pp. 351ff.

of life, and doctrine. It was a general name for the popular religious movement, above all in Germany. It was not a religious congregation; it not only embraced regulars, both men and women, who lived in common or under obedience to spiritual leaders, but perhaps an even greater number of men and women who strove in the world, in their own way, towards their ideal of spirituality."[12] Absence of ecclesiastical discipline and guidance laid them open to heterodoxy. Without official permission or education some, imbibing Free Spirit doctrine or clinging to apocalyptic faith, arrogated to themselves the office of preaching, offering false premises to simple folk. Beghard convents were always less numerous and contained fewer inhabitants. While Cologne had over one hundred beguine houses and Strasbourg about sixty, neither city ever possessed more than two beghard houses.[13]

Judging from conciliar legislation of the thirteenth and fourteenth centuries, it appears that unorganized, itinerant beghards posed a perennial problem; in Germany they drew recruits principally from the floating population and absorbed disgruntled clergymen as well as women into their ranks. Alvarus Pelagius (Alvaro Pelayo) (ca. 1275–1352), a Franciscan and penitentiary of John XXII and bishop of Coron and Silves, offers in his *De Planctu Ecclesiae*, written with papal knowledge between 1330 and 1332 at Avignon and revised in 1340 at St. James of Compostella, a partisan picture of beghards. According to this implacable foe of "sectarians," they found ready welcome among the lower classes—laborers, coal-men, blacksmiths, swineherds—by offering them a more attractive life. They persuaded these people to leave their hard work and to espouse with the beghards a life of wandering and mendicancy. In the upper classes they made an appeal under the cloak of religion. They introduced themselves in the capacity of directors of conscience to well-to-do burghers and widows, accepted hospitality which was extended to them in the name of charity, and seized every opportunity to spread their teachings. To women devoted to the religious life they presented a mien of simple piety, delivered edifying discourses, and sought to insinuate themselves gradually into their familiarity.[14] Yet persecution was not altogether indiscriminate, even in the Rhineland. In 1308 Archbishop Henry of Cologne instructed the priest of Holy Apostles church in the city, in whose parish a beghard convent lay, to acquit excommunicated beghards.[15] Even in the face of growing hostility they continued to receive donations and clerical patronage.[16]

[12] Van Mierlo, in *VMKVA.*, 1930, 289.

[13] Cologne had two convents: zum Olvunde (1299) and zur Lunge (ca. 1306) (Asen, in *AHVN.*, CXIV (1929), 167).

[14] Jundt, *Histoire du panthéisme*, p. 100; for Alvarez, see G. Delorme in *DHGE.*, II (1914), coll. 857-861.

[15] *AHVN.*, L, 80, no. 164.

[16] From the will of Adolf von Revele (1317) the "pauperes becgardi mendicantes

As for disciplined beghards, little is known about the organization of their conventicles before the Council of Vienne. They were probably similar to beguine communities. According to Matthew Paris, their members were bound by no perpetual vows: they merely promised chastity for the duration of their residence in the community together with obedience to local rules and to their superior or spiritual leader.

> Eisdemque temporibus (i.e., 1243) quidam, in Alemannia, precipue, se asserentes religiosos, in utroque sexu, set maxime in muliebri, habitum religionis, sed levem, susceperunt, continentiam et vite simplicitatem privato voto profitentes, sub nullius tamen sancti regula coartate, nec adhuc claustro contenti. Earumque numerus in brevi adeo multiplicabatur, ut in civitate Colonie et partibus adiacentibus duo milia invenirentur.[17]

These brotherhoods, like the beguinages, sprang up spontaneously in response to socioeconomic and religious needs created by urban culture of the Low Countries and adjacent regions. Grundmann concludes that the beghard communities derived their raison d'être not primarily from economic causation but from religious factors.[18] He then falls back on the fact, often slighted by historians of the sociodogical school, that the first beguini included members of the nobility and upper bourgeoisie, although in smaller numbers than among the early beguines.[19] Gilliodts-van Severen, on the other hand, offered the generalization that whereas the beguines answered social needs and religious yearnings, the beghards owed their origin rather to the demands of the economic order.[20] Throwing his support to socioeconomic causation, Des Marez observed that the true point of departure for the bogard community at Brussels was to be sought in the cloth industry. It was at the outset only an association of weavers, united in the aim to lead a common life of work and piety. It was not a religious order properly speaking, but merely a free brotherhood, similar to the other extraregular groups taking shape in Belgium at the end of the twelfth century.[21] Whereas the majority of German

in Colonia" received 60 marks (Ennen-Eckertz, Quellen, IV, 35). The next year the subdeacon Hermann von Rennenberg bequeathed to them 13 s. (Asen, in AHVN., CXIV [1929], 168).

[17] Matthew Paris, Cronica maiora, MGH. SS., XXVIII, 234.
[18] Grundmann, Religiöse Bewegungen, p. 353: "Dass auch die Begardengemeinschaften nicht in erster Linie aus wirtschaftlichen Gründen entstanden sind, sondern das religiöse Motive auch hier bestimmend waren für den Zusammenschluss und für Beschäftigung mit gemeinschaftlicher Handarbeit, vor allem der Weberei." Vander Straeten (Recherches, II, 95) assigned to the beghards, following Mosheim (p. 178: "Hoc quidem facile crediderim, eos [Bogardos] primum Fratres textores appellatos esse"), origins that are at once economic and religious.
[19] See above, pp. 81-82.
[20] Gilliodts-van Severen, I, 9; Fredericq, Gesch. d. Inquis., II, 13; Hauck, V, 1, 428.
[21] Des Marez, in Mélanges Paul Fredericq, p. 28.

brethren came from the lower classes and were consequently more guilty of doctrinal deviation and moral aberration, the Belgian beghards generally adapted themselves readily as skilled and unskilled labor in the cloth guilds[22] and thus, no more than the beguines, did they constitute a segment of the floating population.

Decrees and statutes promulgated by German lay and ecclesiastical authorities as early as 1259[23] indicate, on the contrary, that begging in extraregular associations was much more common in imperial lands. On June 9, 1369, Emperor Charles IV urged his officials to extirpate with the aid of the papal inquisitor, Walter Kerling, the "sectam Beghardorum et Beghinarum seu Swestronum conventualium, quae vulgo *Wilge Armen* vel *Conventschwestern* dicuntur, vel quae simul mendicando dicunt Brod durch Gott...[24] Nor was this familiar cry, "For God's sake, bread!" echoed repeatedly by diocesan legislation as the primary characteristic of heretical beghards, confined to Rhenish cities alone during the fourteenth century. On November 17, 1331, Jakèmes (Jacques) Foukiers of St. Omer in the diocese of Terouanne is reported to have donated a house and garden to a group of impoverished beghards or Lollards who were accustomed to beg.[25]

From the statutes of the Antwerp bogards who had adopted the third rule of the Franciscans,[26] it is clear that legacies[27] and income from work allowed the members of the convent to increase their personal fortune. Not only was one not expected to renounce his earthly goods but nobody was received in the community unless he could provide a certain endowment. In his will of May 10, 1356, Henry de Santhoven thus left to the convent land and *income* to assist, by gifts and loans, men who desired to join but could not furnish the necessary security.[28] The statutes cast light on the *jus possidendi* enjoyed by each member: they provided for the expulsion of a brother who appropriated the property of another.[29] Each of the two religious designated annually by the community to distribute *rentes* and alms

---

[22] Hauck, V, 1, 428f.

[23] Mansi, XXIII, 997; see below, p. 509.

[24] Fredericq, *Corpus*, I, 208-210, no. 210; see below, pp. 561-62.

[25] Fredericq, *Gesch. d. Inquis.*, II, 13: "Le maison des povres freres Noolars (i.e. Lollards) de ceste ville, prians leur pain pour Dieu . . . ; par telle condicion que ly povre de volenté, que on dist Broot omme Gode, qui a présent sont en le ville de Saint Omer et cil qui apres y seront, warder et avoir le dessusdit héritage si comme il est édefiés."

[26] The statutes of July 20, 1361 are published by Vannérus, *Anvers,* pp. 588-592.

[27] On June 14, 1401, for example, Arnold Moens, son of Arnold, a burgher of Antwerp, left to Brother John Willem's son, "Bogardus Antwerpiensis," 20 *sols de gros de Flandre* (ibid., p. 509).

[28] *Ibid.*, pp. 583-585, no. 10. The 1361 statutes (*ibid.*, p. 590, no. 20) stipulated that recipients should pay for the "pitance": . . .So soude hi nochtan den vorseiden broederen ende den convente pitanche moeten gheven, gheliic dat men te doene plucht als men die broeders ierstwerf ontfaet in onse vorseide convent.

[29] *Ibid.*, p. 590, no. 18.

to the poor was to receive for the day that was spent in making this distribution in the city two *gros tournois,* equivalent to his pay in the convent.[30] The religious were also forbidden to traffic in money or to lend unless it was necessary for the handling of their inheritance or income.[31] Whoever engaged in such traffic was to be expelled for one year and must on his return contribute to the "pitance" of the convent a fine of five *scellinge* per *livre.* An accessory to these forbidden practices was to be excluded for half a year.[32] Thus every bogard retained full control over his own private fortune, which he could increase by manual work. It is not surprising that the sixteenth-century copyist annotated on the back of his copy of the 1361 statutes the point that struck him most forcibly in the two-hundred-year rule: "De proprio labore vivebat quisque pro se."[33] Similarly, the rule of March 24, 1377, for the Bruges bogards declares that each member weaver works for himself, assuming all risks and perils.[34] As in the case of the beguines, documents are legion which show the members administering their fortune and, like laymen, disposing of it by will and sale.[35]

If in way of life and outlook the *boni homines, boni pueri,* and *boni christiani* may regarded as the masculine counterpart of the *mulieres religiosae* and *virgines continentes,* in the history of terminology, too, there is a remarkable parallel. Just as the word *beguine* was originally a term of deprecation, not losing its pejorative connotation until the middle of the thirteenth century, so *boni homines, beguini,* and beghards usually, but not exclusively, designated heretics or at least those who were considered to be on the periphery of orthodoxy. Christian poverty in emulation of the primitive church and the apostolic life of the itinerant preacher remained the essence of heresy in northern Europe as well as in the south, even after the church had made a halfhearted attempt to utilize the program in papal-directed reform through the friars. The heretics (*Publicani*) who went from Flanders to England in 1160 and were given a hearing at a synod in Oxford explained that "Christianos se esse et doctrinam apostolicam venerari."[36] In the inquisitorial proceedings against the Albigensians at Carcassonne, 1308–1309, one hears that "recepti in sectam bonorum hominum dicebant, quod ipsi tenebant viam et vitam dei et apostolorum."[37] At the same time the

[30] *Ibid.,* pp. 590-591, no. 21.
[31] *Ibid.,* p. 591, no. 22: "Item so en mach en gheen van onsen vorseiden broederen comanscap doen met ghelde in gheenrehande manieren, noch lenen te halver winningen, maer allene t'sier nootdorfte om erve oft om liiftocht."
[32] *Ibid.,* p. 591, no. 25.
[33] *Ibid.,* p. 510.
[34] Gilliodts-van Severen, II, 46: "So wat broedere van den wullin wevers dat hi sal moeten weven up hem selven, heift bate of scade dat hise hebben sal."
[35] For examples see Vannérus, *Anvers,* pp. 510ff.
[36] William of Newbridge (d. 1208), *De rebus Anglicis* (Fredericq, *Corpus,* II, 8).
[37] Döllinger, *Beiträge,* II, 22.

celebrated Dominican inquisitor, Bernard Gui, was offering a similar interpretation with greater elaboration.[38] Examples of the "secta bonorum christianorum"[39] or the "secta bonorum hominum"[40] are frequent from the latter half of the twelfth century well into the fourteenth century.[41]

That these brotherhoods were receiving by the middle of the thirteenth century the same privileges as orthodox beguines from civil and ecclesiastical authorities may be demonstrated even better by Flemish experience. Here *beghardus* appeared later than *beguinus*. Whereas the latter was already receiving currency at the end of the twelfth century in the form of *beguina* and *beguinus,* there are no examples of *beghardus* before the second half of the thirteenth century.[42] The term *beghard* presumably appears for the first time in

[38] Bernard Gui, *Practica*, ed. Mollat, I, 22-24: "Ipsi sunt boni christiani, qui non jurant nec mentiuntur (cf. objections raised by Vidal in *Revue des questions historiques*, LXXXVI [1909], 11-12) nec maledicunt alicui; nec occidunt nec hominem nec animal nec aliquid quod habeat vitam respirantem et quod tenent fidem Domini Jhesu Christi et evangelium ejus, sicut docuit Christus et apostoli ejus; et quod ipsi tenent locum apostolorum et quod propter predicta illi de ecclesia Romana, videlicet prelati, clerici et religiosi, persecuntur eos, et precipue inquisitores hereticorum, et vocant eos hereticos, cum tamen ipsi sint boni homines et boni christiani . . ." Cf. Döllinger, *Beiträge*, II, 27 (inquisitorial acts against the Albigensians at Carcassonne, 1308-1309).
[39] *Ibid.*, II, 154; for further examples of *boni christiani, ibid.*, II, 4, 5, 17, 25, 31, 39, 109, 170, 195, 207, 217, 251.
[40] *Ibid.*, II, 27; for further examples of *boni homines, ibid.*, II, 22, 37, 136, 165, 195, 208, 212, 214, 225, 250, 369, 392, 394. It is significant that the term had an exact feminine parallel (*ibid.*, II, 165: "ita sunt bonae mulieres, sicut et boni homines"). This occurs in the confession of Raymond Valsiera of Aix on Manichaean errors.
[41] The council of Lombez (1165) condemned "eos, qui faciunt se nuncupari boni homines" (Mansi, XXII, 159); Abbot Benedict (*Vita Henrici Angliae Regis*, in Bouquet, XIII [Paris, 1869], 173) describes for 1178 a "gens perfida, que se bonos homines appellari fecerant, in terra Tolosana congregata erat, et quod ipsi Christianae fidei contraria praedicabant . . ." Pierre de Vaux-Cernay, *Historia Albigensis,* ed. Luchaire, cap. 4, p. 19: "Heretici enim a fautoribus suis boni homines vocabantur, etc." *Ibid.*, cap. 2, p. 8: "quidam inter hereticos dicebantur 'perfecti' sive 'boni homines,' alii 'credentes hereticorum'; Schönbach, in *Sitz-ber. d. phil.-hist. Classe d. Wiener Akad. d. Wissensch.*, CXLVII, Abt. V (1904), 45; the formulary for the inquisition against Cathari (Charles Molinier, in *Archives des missions scientifiques et littéraires*, 3rd ser., vol. XIV, Paris, 1888, 163): "Queratur primo a quolibet et occulte, si vidit unquam hereticos aut bonos homines"; Stephen of Bourbon (ed. Lecoy de la Marche, p. 35): The women whom Dominic converted in Provence referred to the heretics: "Illos homines, contra quos predicas, usque modo credidimus et vocavimus bonos homines." At the beginning of the fourteenth century the brethren of the Free Spirit are sometimes called "boni homines" (Döllinger, *Beiträge,* II, 392-393: "Quod boni homines non doleant si incidant in peccata qualiacunque, quia Dominus sic praeordinavit, nec talis praeordinatio debebat impediri"; cf. *ibid.*, II, 394, nos. 23, 17, 22, 25, 27).
[42] Not a single example of the word *beghardus* occurs during the first half of the thirteenth century (for the dating of the 1277 synod of Treves, see below, p. 000). Cf. Van Mierlo, in *VMKVA.*, 1930, 283-284. The evidence that there were beghards at Louvain in 1220 and at Antwerp in 1228 rests on a statement of Gramaye that beghards had already appeared at Louvain in 1120. Mosheim, in citing him, supposes that either Gramaye was mistaken or it was a typographical error for 1220. In like fashion Ryckel, relying on a late fifteenth-century document, held that

Countess Margaret's charter of 1252 (December 22), exempting the brethren from the weavers' tax and other exactions just like the beguines *in Vinea*.[43] A protection document issued by her earlier in the same year (March 16) reveals that they had been known as the "beghini apud Brugas commorantes."[44]

Beghards are first mentioned in Cologne documents in 1258.[45] From scattered sources one can detect such brethren in Germanic lands at an earlier date. Writing between 1234 and 1237 the Frisian Premonstratensian abbot, Emo von Wittewierum, mentioned in his chronicle "quidam simplices, qui dicuntur Beggini."[46] Again he considers the mendicant orders, Humiliati, beggini, and religious women living in common as a peculiar phenomenon of the age of Gregory IX.[47] On the authority of Matthew Paris Yvo, a priest of Narbonne who had fled France about 1215 because of charges of heresy, reports in a letter to Archbishop Gerald of Bordeaux in 1243 that on a journey through Italy over the Alps into Carinthia and Austria he had been lodged at Neustadt by some *novi religiosi* called *beguini*.[48] We have noted above that Matthew Paris acknowledged the existence of men alongside the extraregular women at Cologne in 1243. Elsewhere he speaks of *beguini sive beguinae*.[49]

Beghards first appeared in the Low Countries about 1220—1250, although the term itself was evidently not employed before the middle of the century.[50] While Margaret ordered the magistrates of Bruges to

beghards existed in Antwerp in 1128; again, Mosheim concludes that this must read rather 1228 (pp. 177ff; Gramaye, *Antiquitates Belgicae, in Lovanio,* pp. 17-18; Ryckel, p. 15; cf. *GC.,* V, 125). Gramaye and Ryckel both believed that the word *beguine* and *beghard* were derivatives of St. Begga; consequently, this supposed remote origin governed the dating of the communities even as Puteanus sought to implement his arguments with the Vilvorde documents.

[43] Gilliodts-van Severen, II, 2, no. 2: "Vobis mandamus et volumus quatinus Begardos in tali libertate teneatis et immunes ab omni exactione sicut Beghinas in Vinea commorantes." Cf. Margaret's document of May 15, 1275, for the same sentence (*ibid.,* II, 3-4, no. 5).

[44] *Ibid.,* II, 1-2, no. 1. For this document, as well as eleven others, the abbots, William of Doys, Peter of St. Andrew near Bruges, and Walter of St. Bartholomew of Echout in Bruges, issued a vidimus on December 20, 1302 (*ibid.,* II, 32, no. 20).

[45] Asen, in *AHVN.,* CXI (1927), 87f; CXV (1929), 167, 171.

[46] *MGH. SS.,* XXIII, 517.

[47] *Idem:* "Multe sequidem novitates in diebus domni Gregorii noni pululdarunt. Prima est religio Predicatorum, qui ut nubes volant; item Humiliatorum seu Nodosorum vel Nudipedum (i.e., Friars Minor); item quorundam simplicium, qui dicuntur Beggini; item collegia communium feminarum."

[48] Matthew Paris, *Chron. major., MGH. SS.,* XXVIII, 231; for the letter, 230-233; cf. Mosheim, p. 170.

[49] *Hist. Angl., MGH. SS.,* XXVIII, 417. Elsewhere in the *Chronica majora* (ad an. 1250, *ibid.,* XXVIII, 320, 430) he speaks only of women; nor are men considered in the *Abbreviatio Chronicorum Angliae* (ad an. 1243, *ibid.,* XXVIII, 449), taken from his writings.

[50] According to Gramaye, the oldest beghard convent was the one in Louvain, founded in 1220 (*Antiquitates Brabantiae,* I [Brussels, 1606], 175); Hoffmann von Fallersleben, *Horae Belgicae,* IV (Hanover, 1854, 231). Scribani (*Origines Ant-*

protect the local *beguini* early in 1252, the following year Guillaume de Ryckel, abbot of St. Trond, mentions in his account book a "Hermannus, becgardus de Sancto-Gengulpho"[51] and a "Petrus de Sancto-Petro, becgardus, vir pauper et religiosus,"[52] to whom he granted alms regularly each week. But it was not until about 1270 that the St. Trond beghards formed a community in the founding of which Guillaume, who had already in 1265 established the beguinage of St. Agnes, probably had a hand.[53] About 1250 they settled at Diest and these are the earliest that Vannérus[54] found in Brabant. According to the testimony of the mayor and echevins of the duke of Brabant and the knight, Jean de Meerbeek at Becquevoort in September, 1257, the *fratres obedientes dicti Beggardi de Dist*, leased perpetually, under certain conditions, to Arnold de Joechalede eight bonniers of land, with house and barn, which they held in fee of the said knight. Their share of the harvests was to be carried in Arnold's cart to the part of the barn which they reserved for themselves.[55] Thus this brotherhood was primarily engaged in agriculture. Beghards made their appearance in Brussels before 1277[56] and were perhaps also in Tirlemont.[57] Shortly after this date they can be detected in documents in Louvain,[58]

---

werpiensium [Antwerp, 1610], 103) held that beghards first appeared in Antwerp in 1228. Cf. Diercxsens, *Antverpia*, I, 200. There is, however, no proof for these statements.

[51] Pirenne, *Le livre de Guillaume de Ryckel*, p. 363.

[52] *Ibid.*, p. 364.

[53] Simenon, "Les Bégards de Saint-Trond," *Leodium*, VI (1907), 123. Their convent, dedicated to St. Matthew, was located in the rue de Diest, then called Steenstrate, and belonged to the parish of St. Gangulphe.

[54] Vannerus, *Anvers*, p. 476.

[55] Raymaekers, *Kerkelijk Diest*, p. 304, note 2; cf. p. 299; Stallaert, in *BCRH.*, 4th ser., III (1876), 183; Wauters, *TC.*, V, 165. On July 3, 1268, the echevins arbitrated a dispute that arose between the "congregatio sive societas Begardorum de Dist" and Louis, son of Louis, knight of Pont, over their respective holdings (Raymaekers, *Chronicon Diestense*, *BCRH.*, 3rd ser., II [1860], 468-469), id., *Kerkelijk Diest*, p. 299.

[56] Des Marez, *Les Bogards*, p. 279; Vannerus, *Anvers*, p. 472; Henne-Wauters, *Histoire de Bruxelles*, III, 478; Lefèvre, *L'organisation*, pp. 113-114; Peene, I, 30, 48f.

[57] In 1276 Duke John I took the community under his protection; the following year Edmond, suffragan of the bishop of Liége, dedicated the altar of their chapel (Bets, *Histoire de Tirlemont*, II, 135; Tarlier and Wauters, *Geog. et hist. des communes belges. Arrondissement de Louvain. Ville de Tirlemont* (1874), 150-151). Bets (*op. cit.*, I, 51) originally had placed the foundation in 1266. In the same volume (p. 259) he indicates that these beghards were engaged in trade in 1291.

[58] The earliest document is dated August 16, 1280, when John I took the beghard under his protection (Molanus, II, 1212-1213, no. 66; cf. I, 294). Elsewhere, however, Molanus (I, 294) says that until the time of Margaret "fratres Bogardi conventus Lovaniensis fuerunt laici et textores usque ad tempora dominae Margaritae. Neque a Romanis Pontificibus unquam vocantur Bogardi." According to Laenen (*Kerkelijk Brabant*, II, 79), this was Margaret of York (ca. 1450-1503), widow of Charles the Rash (cf. A. Beeckman, in *BNB.*, XIII [1894-1895], 669-672). However, if Molanus' chronology means anything, this must be Margaret of Flanders, duchess of Brabant (d. 1285) who became the second wife of John I (1273) (cf. Wauters, in *BNB.*, XIII, 631). Cf. Daris, *Hist. du dioc. au XIIIe et XIVe siècle*, p. 218.

Aerschot,[59] Léau,[60] Nivelles,[61] Malines,[62] and Tournai.[63] In the early part of the next century they were found at Saint-Omer,[64] Middelburg,[65] Bois-le-Duc,[66] Maestricht,[67] Antwerp,[68] and still later at Ophem-lez-Wezembeek[69] and Hoegaarden. (Hougarde).[70]

The earliest documents that indicate their presence represent the beghards as being united in an association at once religious and socio-economic.[71] It is a question of obedient brethren living in common under the same roof, in congregation, society, or convent, while engaging in ordinary religious routine, agriculture, commerce, or the textile industry. The bogards of Brussels, Diest, Tirlemont, Louvain, Aerschot, and Léau were at first only laymen, obliged to seek a livelihood by manual work and trade while performing charitable duties. When Countess Margaret extended to the "beghini apud Brugas commorantes" protection and privileges in 1252, they evidently were not yet residing inside the city but still limited themselves to its second wall. Nevertheless they lived within the scope of the echevi-

[59] Van Gestel, *Hist. Mechl.*, I, 243: "In hoc oppido est virilis sexus coenobium Bogardorum qui laici olim erant, textrinis operam dantes, institutum anno 1283, cura publica et privatorum eleemosynis, tertiam regulam S. Francisci assumpserunt anno 1323 1. Maii."

[60] A charter granted at Léau by Duke John I in 1291 indicates the presence in this town of a beghard community, also called *Fratres tertii ordinis de Lewes*. (Tarlier and Wauters, *Géog. et hist. des communes belges contin. Arrondissement de Louvain, Canton de Léau*, p. 68).

[61] The first indication of beguins or beghards in Nivelles occurs in Gregory X's bull of July 11, 1272 (De Louvet, *L'Origine nivelloise*, pp. 59f, P.J. 4; cf. pp. 32, 75, Ann. 23.

[62] The oldest document for the Malines community is dated December 17, 1284 (published by Vannérus, *Malines*, pp. 236-237, no. 1); two years later (July 24, 1286) Bishop Guillaume of Hainault confirmed its existence (*ibid.*, 237-238, no. 2). Cf. Laenen, *Gesch. van Mechelen*, pp. 354ff.

[63] In 1298 the beghards of Tournai concluded peace with the magistrates of the town (Fredericq, *Gesch. d. Inquis.*, II, 13, note 2).

[64] Early fourteenth century (Giry, in *Mémoires de la société des antiquaires de la Morinne*, IV (1876), 88-89.)

[65] 1331, Van Mieris, *Charterboek*, II, 523.

[66] The beghards adopted the Franciscan third rule (Daris, *Hist. du dioc. au XIIIe et XIVe siècle*, pp. 512-513).

[67] Although founded about the middle of the thirteenth century and conforming to the third rule of Francis, the beghards in Maestricht did not possess their own chapel until 1308 (*ibid.*, pp. 217-218). It was on February 22 of that year that the chapel of Notre-Dame authorized them to have a chapel for recitation of canonical hours and to establish a cemetery. Cf. Franquinet, *Beredeneerde Inventaris*, I, 82, note 1; 89-92, no. 50.

[68] The earliest document mentioning the begards of Antwerp is dated July 20, 1296 whereby the duke of Brabant, John II, took the "fratres Beggardos manentes in conventu eorum apud Antwerpiam" under protection (Vannerus, *Anvers*, pp. 567-568, no. 1; cf. *ibid.*, 488). Diercxsens reported them in the city before 1250. Cf. Prims, *Gesch. van Antwerpen*. III. *Onder Hertog Jan den Tweede*, pp. 226-227.

[69] According to Van Gestel (*Hist. Mechl.*, II, 108) the Ophem convent which subscribed to the Franciscan third rule was not founded until 1474 by Jan Wautier de Heetvelde.

[70] First mentioned in 1411, Laenen, *Kerkelijk Brabant*, II, 79.

[71] Cf. Des Marez, *L'organisation du travail*, pp. 425ff.

nage, for they were subject to magisterial jurisdiction. In July, 1266, Guy de Dampierre required the *bailli* of Bruges to take them under protection with the significant provision that this should include those affiliated with the Friars Minor as well as the Dominicans.[72] This last document suggests the existence of two beghard associations, a fact which finds confirmation in the agreement of the clergy of Notre-Dame at Bruges over the erection of a chapel for the inhabitants of the "larger convent."[73] The arbitration decision of the echevins of Bruges over the quarrels between the wool weavers and the beghards on February 29, 1268, indicates that the latter were then living in a convent beyond Notre-Dame bridge and that Lambine vanden Porchine was their superior or master.[74] Margaret's pronouncement on May 15, 1275,[75] confirms that beghards were already established in a convent beyond this bridge which formed the limit of echevinal authority of Bruges. The ground on which it was built really belonged to the seigniory of Sysseele. At this time, however, the commune was compelled by expansion to extend its boundaries. To the south the town had just annexed the whole area up to the Zuutleye. The countess, in approving the document of December 22, 1254, which granted to the beghards financial immunities and equal status with the beguinage, declared that incorporation of Sysseele by the town did not alter the rights of the brotherhood.[76]

An echevinal act of 1268 refers to the Diest beghards as a "congregatio seu societas Begardorum"; later (August 19, 1281) they are spoken of as "fratres Beggardi manentes in conventu eorum prope Diest"[77] when John I took them and their property under ducal protection. John I's charter, exempting the Louvain beghards from tailles, exactions, and obligations of a military character, called them "fratres Bogardos manentes in conventu eorum apud Lovanium" (August 16, 1280).[78] Just as a similar document, issued by John II in 1296 on behalf of the Antwerp beghards, indicates that they formed

---

[72] Gilliodts-van Severen, II, 2, no. 3; also contained in the vidimus of December 20, 1302.

[73] December 20, 1290, *ibid.*, II, 19, no. 12; published without date in MF., III, 145.

[74] Gilliodts-van Severen, II, 3, no. 4; also in vidimus of December 20, 1302.

[75] *Ibid.*, II, 3-4, no. 5.

[76] *Ibid.*, II, 4: "Et si quod pro cora aliqua exactum est ab eis, hoc eisdem restitui faciatis, non obstante quod officium de Zisielle officio Brugensi est adiunctum." Cf. *ibid.*, I, 15-16.

[77] Raymaekers, *Kerkelijk Diest*, p. 300, note 1; id., in *CRHB.*, ser. 4, III, 191 (with date August 18).

[78] "Quod nos fratres Bogardos manentes in conventu eorum apud Lovanium atque res eorum usquequaque sub nostra recipimus protectione, et absolvimus eos ab omni servitio talliarum precariarum, exactionum et expeditionum nobis aut nostris faciendo" (Molanus, II, 1212; cf. I, 294). Cf. Van Even, *Louvain*, p. 478; Van der Linden, *Gesch. der stad Leuven*, p. 112.

a convent,[79] so cohabitation was the rule at Tournai, Brussels, St. Omer, Middelburg, and Bois-le-Duc.

Their exemptions were the same as those conferred by John I on the Brussels community on April 25, 1277.[80] Despite the inquisitorial process Antwerp beghards, for example, continued to secure privileges from Duke John IV as well as Popes Clement V, John XXII, and Urban V. Prims reports "on the master and the brethren of St. Mary's beghard house at Antwerp" in 1308.[81] In 1317 the father of an Antwerp beghard, Matthew Bosschere, the earliest known master of St. Julian's hospital,[82] rode to the papal court at Avignon and obtained an indulgence letter. Following ducal example, the magistrates and the guild of cloth-workers at Louvain granted to local bogards that protection and exemptions not accorded to weavers provided they did not accept in their convent outsiders and those exercising a trade or business, the latter not being exempt from communal taxes.[83] This indicates at least partial recognition of religious status. On the other hand, in a privilege granted the citizens of Léau by John I on September 21, 1290, it was stipulated that the bogards and beguines residing in the town must pay for fifteen years the same *accise* as the townsmen.[84]

Therefore the secular clergy did not at first exercise direct control over these semireligious communities. The masters of the beghards treated directly with princes, magistrates, and deans of the weavers' guild, without mediation of spiritual authority. The latter became interested in their affairs only after the brotherhoods had matured. In short, they owed their origins first to their own efforts and secondly to the protection of the prince, magistrates, and the guild.[85]

Each beghard house, like the beguinage, had its own rule to which the inmates were subject. It specified the time for religious practices, labor, and charitable activity. To obtain a fiat for their orthodoxy and to avoid inquisitorial processes, above all after the Council of Vienne, the beghards adopted the third rule of St. Francis. This did not mean deviation in work or aims, for the Poverello of Assisi had founded the lay brotherhood for those who wished to leaven everyday life with religious practices while remaining in the world. It must be emphasized that tertiaries, far from being closely organized, merely wished to abide by certain fundamentals of conduct.[86]

[79] Diercxsens, *Antverpia*, 1, 347.

[80] Henne and Wauters, *Histoire de Bruxelles*, III, 478; cf. Wauters, *Duc Jean I*, p. 378.

[81] Prims, *Gesch. van Antwerpen*, II, 23.

[82] Laenen, *Kerkelijk Brabant*, II, 78.

[83] Municipal document, May 24, 1293, and guild document, April 4, 1294, Molanus, II, 1218, nos. 72-73.

[84] Vannerus, *Anvers*, pp. 482f.

[85] Callaey, in *Neerlandia Franciscana*, I (1914), 14f.

[86] K. Müller, *Anfänge*, pp. 117ff; id., in *ZKG.*, XXIII, 496ff; Mandonnet, *Les*

By founding penitential brotherhoods the mendicants were both extending the old practice of associating *conversi* or oblates with monastic orders and injecting new elements into the organization. They thereby unconsciously created a useful instrument for defining through obedience to the hierarchy and sacramental system the ecclesiastical status of the extraregular. Desiring to found an order that would cultivate the apostolic life in accordance with evangelical precepts, Francis found himself obliged to form both the second and third orders to cope with the unprecedented demand. Although Sabatier contended that the penitential order was an essential part of the original apostolic mission of Francis,[87] the beginnings are quite obscure. Members of these brotherhoods not only participated in special charitable work, but their entire life and *Weltanschauung* were conditioned by definite religious principles. Strict simplicity in daily life, complete renunciation of worldly pleasures, frequent fasting, and finally reliance on devotional exercises—such constituted the essence of the penitential life. The bull *Supra Montem* (August 17, 1289)[88] which served as the norm for most beghard communities in the Low Countries, regulated details of habit of tertiary brothers and sisters, as well as fasts and abstinence, divine offices and works of piety to be practiced by them: thus each member must confess and commune three times a year, at Christmas, Easter, and Pentecost. Ministers who acted as spiritual directors must be chosen preferably from the Friars Minor. Visitors were expected to supervise their respective congregations annually, to expel incorrigibles, to punish other recalcitrants, in short to suppress all abuses which were denounced to them.

The papacy considered third orders essentially religious, not subject to secular jurisdiction. This religious character, in spite of imperfect separation from the world, conferred an autonomous juridical status, based on the canonical principle of exemption. As a religious body, it depended on ecclesiastical authority only. Members were to engage in no judicial decision before the secular bench and if harm were done to them, they must seek redress through an ecclesiastical court. The first papal privilege, specifically for the penitents under the bishop of Rimini (December 16, 1221),[89] aimed to create such an autonomy. On March 30, 1228, Gregory IX extended this privilege to all penitents in Italy: they could take oaths only in the interest of peace and the faith, to clear themselves of calumny, to bear witness in court, or to sustain a

origines de l'Ordo de Penitentia (Freiburg, 1898); Phillips, *Beguines in Medieval Strasburg*, pp. 165ff, 183, 219ff; Van den Borne, *Anfänge*, pp. 67f.

[87] Sabatier, *Life of St. Francis*, pp. 155, 265. See Goetz on Jacques de Vitry's knowledge of tertiaries among the Humiliati, but not among the Franciscans (in *Hist. Vierteljahrschrift*, VI [1903], 29-30).

[88] *BF.*, IV, 94, no. 150; *Bullar. Rom.*, IV, 90, no. 4; Gilliodts-van Severen, II, 8-17; P. 23044.

[89] *BF.*, I, 8, no. 8; P. 6736; *DCC.*, IV, 575f.

"contractum emptionis, venditionis, et donationis."[90] Military exemption was contained in other privileges.[91] Strict pacificism was nevertheless conditioned by Nicholas IV's provision that brethren might bear arms only in defense of the Church, the faith, and their lands, and then only with the permission of their ministers ("pro defensione Romanae ecclesiae, Christianae fidei, vel etiam terrae ipsorum aut de suorum licentia ministrorum").[92] Gregory IX also relieved tertiaries of public offices which municipal authorities and local lords were trying to impose on them.[93] In addition to exemption in military, civil, and judicial matters, they enjoyed, like religious orders, such ecclesiastical privileges as immunity from interdict.[94] Legitimate taxes must be paid unless they became unjust.

Official recognition notwithstanding, the tertiaries were almost as much of an embarrassment as a consolation to ecclesiastical authorities; bishops and ministers-general bandied the order back and forth, like the *cura monialium,* being more concerned to avoid responsibility for its care than to draw support from its alliance. Nowhere are the problems more squarely faced than by Bonaventura in his *Libellus Apologeticus.*[95] When the charge of neglect was hurled at the Friars Minor because of their unwillingness to support the Penitents, the general offered the following answer:

> The reason why we labor among others, that they may be converted and go forward in righteousness, is because we thus get fruit and keep out liberty, avoiding all inexpedient entanglements in their affairs. But these Penitents, if they multiplied, would hinder us and diminish our help to others; for they would then demand of us, as a right, that we should stand by them in all their concerns. Otherwise they would revile us for having brought them into the Order when we would not accept their care ... If any of them were taken prisoner, or molested by his master or by any other man, he would desire the Friars to take up his cause and to run hither and thither for his liberation, even as the widow came to Elisha for liberation from the vexation of her creditor. If any were destitute of other bodily help, he and others would expect us to provide for

90 *BF.,* I, 39f, no. 20; *BOP.,* I, 27, no. 25; P. 8159.
91 Cf. Frédégand, in *Et. franc.,* XXXII (1921), 470f.
92 Cf. Nicholas IV's bull, *Unigenitus Dei filius* (August 8, 1290), *BF.,* IV, 167, no. 296; P. 23355; bull *Ad audientiam* (September 20, 1291), *BF.,* IV, 293, no. 551; P. 23823.
93 *Nimis patenter* (May 26, 1227), *BF.,* I, 30f, no. 7 (Sbaralea dates it June 25); P. 7919; *Cum dilecti filii,* June 4, 1230 (*BF.,* I, 65f, no. 53; P. 8565); *Nimis patenter* (April 5, 1231), *BF.,* I, 71, no. 59; P. 8697b; *Ne is qui bonus* (March 15, 1233), *BF.,* I, 99, no. 94; P. 9124; cf. Alexander IV's renewal, *Pia desideria,* April 27, 1255 (*BF.,* II, 42, no. 50; P. 15827); cf. Frédégand, *l.c.,* p. 472. For Celestine V's privileges on this score: *Dignum esse,* September 2, 1294 (*BF.,* IV, 330, no. 2; P. 23954).
94 March 29, 1222, *BF.,* I, 9, no. 10; P. 6808; April 5, 1231, *BF.,* I, 71, no. 58; P. 8697a. Cf. Frédégand, *l.c.,* p. 475.
95 Bonaventura, *Opera omnia* (ed. A. C. Peltier, Paris, 1868), XIV, 534-536; the translation is drawn by courtesy of the Cambridge University Press from Coulton, *Five Centuries of Religion,* II, 150; cf. Reinmann, p. 37; Wyngaert, in *AFH.,* XIII (1920), 74, note 5.

him as his spiritual brethren; and it may be that many would join the Order in the hope of such assistance, especially the women, or Beguines. If any of these women became ill-famed of fornication or adultery, those who perchance love us not would forthwith publish this abroad to our dishonor, saying: "Lo! how these barefoot sisters bring them forth barefoot sucklings; of whom should they conceive them, but of those who are busy with them all day long" And wanton clergy or laymen would be the more unjust to these sisters in hatred to us, striving either to corrupt them or to destroy their good name, since their dishonor would fall more specially upon us If ever a quarrel arose among them, we should need to busy ourselves with making peace, lest others should be scandalized . . . . [Our enemies], not being able to grieve us in our own persons, would seek by all means to trouble them. Moreover, they would sully our good name when we held secret Chapters with these Penitents, as though we were celebrating heretical conventicles in dark places, saying that the church authorities ought rather to correct and punish their offences according to church law. For even their masters, who are called Provincials, being laymen and sometimes married men, bear a certain resemblance to the leaders of the heretics; and, even though there be no purpose here, yet in fact they have lay rulers whom they call Masters or Teachers, even as the heretics name their own rulers in contempt of the clergy. And seeing that we Friars, who live after a single Rule and under an elaborate constitution, can scarce keep our Order in its vigor, how could we long keep that Order sound, wherein each goeth to his own home, and doeth his own business, having the care of house and wife and children, and mingling in worldly affairs and subject to manifold temptations of the world and the flesh? . . . It was different with St. Francis; for then there were many different conditions of land and of time in relation to the Order and to other men; moreover, the worldwide sanctity of our holy father Francis and the first brethren made many things work then for good which would turn out differently in these days and in other lands.

While submitting to the basic third rule, certain beghard communities elaborated other ordinances specifically adapted to their way of life. The rule of the beghards at Middelburg (October 23, 1331)[96] prescribed that every brother should preserve chastity, confess and commune at least seven times a year. A master and submaster were superiors of the convent, and each brother owed them obedience unless undesirable orders were exacted. No member was to divulge the secrets of the community or leave the convent during the night. Before starting to work, one must recite prayers. At the last sound of the bell, he was to attend common exercises which took place in the chapel and refectory. Whenever a brother died, the rest must say for the salvation of his soul a psalm or seven hundred Paternosters and Aves, or recite one hundred fifty times the psalm *Miserere mei Deus*. Drawn up when Jan Hubrecht and Matheus Hoeft, echevins of Bruges, were masters of the great beghard convent in that city,[97] the

[96] Van Mieris, *Charterboek*, II, 523.
[97] Gilliodts-van Severen, II, 30.

Flemish rule of the "goeder kinder die men heet Beggarde"[98] (September 21, 1291) offers in its forty-five articles a good example of the close surveillance of private and public life and the regulation of religious, economic, and social activity down to minutiae which one associates with the age of the guild. The rule underlines at once the effort to create a religious atmosphere in which the brethren might pursue their daily work and to ensure mutual assistance as a step to achieve social security.

A member may not leave the convent (1), much less the town (4) without the master's permission (9, 10) and without a companion being assigned to him (1). While breakfasting and supping in the town were discouraged, dining was permissible provided a companion was present (19). Sunset was the critical hour governing return to the convent except under extenuating circumstances (21). Recalcitrance (26) or absence from the convent for three days without leave called for discipline in chapter, the penalty in the latter instance being fifteen meals to be eaten on the floor (8). Guests were not to be invited without the superior's approval (5); as in the case of all monastic rules and legislation, special concern, in the interests of maintaining moral standards (32),was registered over female companions whose presence in or near the convent must be carefully scrutinized (6, 40). Each brother is instructed to sleep with his shirt on (22). Like other extra-regular associations and heretical communities, the convent sought to prevent the divulging of secrets that emanated from its chapter; infraction of this article entailed discipline in chapter and the usual eating on the ground (7).Revealing important secrets brought expulsion (cf. 25). Whoever severed connections with the community must of course relinquish his belongings (17). Lending what was owned in common was subject to punishment (18).

The brothers were to recite the same office as the lay-brethren of the Friars Minor (23).[99] It is possible that because of the similarity of the pious practices imposed on beghards and the laymen associated with the Franciscans and Dominicans that these conversi were sometimes called begihardi.[100] Chapter was to be held each fortnight; each member must confess there (24). Similarly, each brother was expected to attend chapel (13) and to hear mass three times a week (15). Matins and primes should precede work (14). He must recite seven canonical hours daily (16); with evening bell, all members adjourned to the chapel to pray in common and observed silence thereafter (13). The lord's supper must be received at least seven times a year (33), on the major feast days (34). At the death of a member, each brother was to

[98] Ibid., II, 26-30, no. 17.
[99] "Elc broedre segghe telken ghetide sdaghes als 1 leec broedre vanden grawen ordine" (ibid., 28).
[100] Cf. Ducange, Glossarium, I, 637.

read one Psalm or seven paternosters and as many Ave Marias. The same procedure must be observed for the deceased master *(44)*. At the sound of the bell, all the brethren were to repair to the refectory, maintain silence during the meal, and recite the Benedicte before and grace after it; they could leave the table only with permission *(II)*.

Duly assigned tasks took precedence over all other work except with the master's dispensation *(2)*. This article was further defined by No. 3: in order to implement the primitive conception of equality, inherent in early guild organization, which demanded that each should earn his livelihood with the work of his own hands, members were forbidden to practice two trades or to have apprentices. Craft jumping was likewise frowned upon *(20)*. Under certain conditions the use of apprentices was countenanced. The brother who became ill or left town for legitimate reasons could with the master's consent be replaced by an apprentice; he would moreover profit from all that the latter earned beyond his salary *(30)*. Again, the beghard who was no longer fit to work could secure with the approval of the master and community a substitute who would maintain him *(31)*. On the other hand, if a member's work justified the engaging of an apprentice, whatever the latter earned beyond his salary was to go to convent *(29)*.[101] As evidence that the convent's existence was in part premised on demand for mutual assistance, the rule provided that the member incapacitated by sickness should receive from the treasury forty *solidi*; when he recovered, he must restore them *(37)*. To aid the sick beghard it was provided that he should receive from the treasury twenty-eight deniers a week; besides, each brother was to give him one denier a week *(38)*. Each new member must pay an entrance fee of three pounds, fifty *solidi* of which were assigned to the treasury and ten *solidi* to the infirmary *(41)*.[102]

Insistence on the obligation of self-support identified the beghard with the *vita apostolica* which put a premium on *labor manuum*. The remainder of the income derived from manual labor was to be distributed to the poor. On April 21, 1312, Ida de Wyneghem (or Ida van der List), widow of Gilbert l'Amman, making known the rule that she, together with the canon Jean Tuclant (d. 1312), had adopted for St. Julian's hospital in Antwerp seven years before, stipulated that the master of this hospital must be a faithful and prudent man, chosen by the *mambours* from the bogard convent in this city. In

---

[101] "So welc van den broedren omme noet des werkes enighen knape bi orlove mach houden, so wat die knape wint buuten sire besproken huren dat comt al ter ghemeente van den covente" (Gilliodts-van Severen, II, 28).

[102] "So wat nieuwe broedre die word ontfaen hi moet gheven iij lb. dit es te verstane L s. ter husinghe ende x s. ter fermerie" (*ibid.*, 29).

any case, he must earn his livelihood by the work of his hands.[103]

Such regulations gave these penitential associations an intermediate position between the world and the cloister: "Quia multi sunt, qui dicunt quod non possunt in saeculo poenitentiam agere nec religiones volunt intrare ... providentia divina ordinavit, ut esset in medio quidam modus faciendi poenitentiam."[104] Bernard of Besse, Bonaventura's secretary, offered his definition in De Laudibus (ca. 1280). "The Third Order is that of the Brethren and Sisters of Penitence, which is common to clergy and laity, maidens and widows and married folk, who have resolved to live honestly in their own homes, to devote themselves to pious works, and to flee from the pomp of this world."[105]

Steps were taken early to circumvent the weaknesses inherent in autonomous convents. Not only did a visitor, usually a Franciscan or a Dominican, come annually to each beghard house to weed out abuses and restore discipline, but several convents united to help one another.[106] Similarly, Franciscan tertiaries in the diocese of Liege petitioned Nicholas V for a habit which would distinguish them from those who continued to live in their own homes or ran about in riotous fashion. The pope thereupon recommended the habit worn in Holland and Zeeland as well as in the diocese of Terouanne.[107]

On September 29, 1346, delegates assembled from seventeen beghard houses—Cologne, Aachen, Maestricht, St. Trond, Léau (Zoutleeuw), Tirlemont, Louvain, Malines, Antwerp, Bois-le-Duc, Aerschot, Diest, Ghent, Middelburg, Zierikzee, Roermond, and St. Omer—to compose differences, to lend assistance to brethren who desired to embrace the third rule, to assist poor convents, and to hold annual meetings at which each house should be represented by two of its inmates. On June 26, 1367, the beghard masters at Brussels, Malines, Antwerp, Louvain, Aerschot, Diest, St. Trond, Léau, and Tirlemont assembled in the last named city to appoint brothers to handle financial matters in the several houses to the advantage of the whole order.

In 1425 the priest Jean de Coloma and the brothers Jean de Dorsten and Gilles de Saint-Trond asked the bishop of Liege to unite in a religious body the beghards professing the third rule and to allow

---

[103] Diercxsens, Antverpia, II, 31-34; cf. Statuta tertii ordinis S. Francisci, Bibl. roy. de Belg., 4909-10, f. 25.

[104] Humbert de Romans, De erudit. praed., II, 39 (Bibl. Max. Vet. Pat., XXV, 474).

[105] Cited by Coulton, Five Centuries of Religion, II, 149.

[106] Daris, Notices, XIII (1887), 102-105; Van den Gheyn, Catalogue des manuscrits de la Bibl. roy. de Bruxelles, VI, 211ff; H. Nelis, "Le manuscrit no. 757c des archives générales du Royaume," in Revue des bibliothèques et des archives de la Belgique, II (Brussels, 1904), 364; A. Hansay in ibid., IV (1906), 86-93; Van den Gheyn, in ibid., p. 176; cf. Archives belges, 1906, nos. 195, 225; Callaey, in Neerlandia Franciscana, I (1914), 20.

[107] Molanus, I, 294.

them to build a convent on 3½ bonniers which Jean Gorren had donated for this purpose. On February 15, 1425, Bishop Jean de Heinsberg complied with their request, authorizing them to form a community like Franciscan tertiaries. As many as twenty companions or novices might be admitted.[108] Pope Nicholas V afterwards wanted them to hold a general chapter each year at Zepperen with legislative competence. Whatever was recommended by the diffinitors and the minister general was to be observed in the first year, examined in the second, and approved in the third.[109]

To the guardian of the Friars Minor at Tirlemont were confided visitatorial duties. The brethren must attend the parish church regularly and receive the sacraments like other parishioners. The bishop approved the brotherhood again on June 22, 1435, and granted several privileges. They could erect a public oratory, have their own cemetery, and wear the habit of the bogards in the diocese of Utrecht. They might take the triple vows and choose for visitor a prelate of an approved order until their convent was incorporated in the general chapter of bogards in the diocese of Utrecht. The visitor was to allow them to adopt the habit and receive novices for profession. He also appointed their confessor and friar-minister who could administer the sacrament of extreme unction and perform burial rites. Yet it is uncertain whether incorporation in the general chapter of the bogards in the diocese of Utrecht took place.[110] In 1443 the bishop of Liege organized the convents of the diocese into a congregation with the motherhouse at Zepperen; in each convent of the congregation a priest was to be chosen as superior; the assembled convents would elect a provincial superior and a provincial visitor taken from another order.

This rule was approved by Pope Eugenius IV (1431—1447). The document of 1446 makes it clear that the minister general of the bogards in the diocese, Barthelemy Opstegen, lived at Zepperen. The cardinal legate, Nicholas of Cusa, being at Liége in October, 1451, approved the establishment of the bogard convent at Zepperen as a mother house and granted indulgences of 100 days to those who would make an offering to the church of the convent. The bogards in the diocese held a general chapter each year.[111] In the one convoked on July 31, 1485, at Hougarde, it was agreed that full ownership of movable and immovable goods should be granted the congregation in order to prevent deflection from their purpose. Usufruct was to remain with

---

[108] Daris, *Notices,* XIII, 402.

[109] Molanus, I, 294.

[110] Daris, *Notices,* XIII, 103.

[111] Bibl. roy. de Belgique, cod. 4909-10, ff. 23r-24v. This MS. includes on f. 12v "die statute der bruederen vander derde orden Sinte Francisci"; on ff. 31v-46; "Ordo ad induendum fratres III ordinis S. Francisci" (cf. Van den Gheyn, *Catalogue,* VI, 211-221).

each house. The inmates of the Zepperen convent executed this decision on October 16, 1486. At the time the brotherhood consisted of six priests and sixteen lay brothers. The bogards wanted the privileges granted by the bishop on June 22, 1435, to be approved by the chapter of Saint-Servais and the priest of Zepperen. On June 20, 1445, Jean de Novo Lapide, dean of Saint-Servais, and Bernard Roemervat, priest of Zepperen, approved these privileges but provided that the religious ought to pay them an annual sum of 6 setiers of rye in compensation for rights they had relinquished. Many foundations of masses and anniversaries were made in the Zepperen convent during its whole existence. On April 1, 1445, Jacques Hustyn de Merchwezet founded in the convent a daily mass for himself and his relatives. On days when this mass could not be said because of some legitimate obstacle, the brethren, joined in church, would recite seven psalms of penitence with litanies and collects. Brethren who could not read would say 20 Paternosters with the *de profundis*. If mass was missed more than five or six times a year, the delinquent must pay for each omission ½ setier of rye to be distributed to the poor.[112]

[112] For the statutes of the brothers of the Third Order of St. Francis, coming from the general chapter of Zepperen as they were adopted in 1487 and renewed in 1533 see further Daris, *Notices*, XIII, 102-105; Nélis, in *Revue des bibliothèques et archives de Belgique*, II (1904), 364-370; Hansay, in *ibid.*, IV (1906), 86-93; Van den Gheyn, in *ibid.*, 176-177; text published by Vannérus (*Anvers*, pp. 506-507).

✖ XV ✖

The Cellites

In the wake of chronic plagues and the devastation of armies in the late Middle Ages there sprang up without leadership in all parts of Christendom innumerable lay brotherhoods and sisterhoods which dedicated themselves to the care of the sick and to burial of the dead.[1] In the Low Countries the Black Death gave impetus to the amorphous movement known as the Cellites (*Cellebroeders*), a term derived from the Latin *cella*, which at first meant a cellar, an underground storehouse for wine and oil; later it came to signify a small room, the dwelling place of a monk, and might even denote the monastery itself.[2] It has been translated, wrongly perhaps, *grave*, but this connotation would explain the adoption of this name by those who specialized in burying the dead.[3] Originally, however, the pious laymen who composed these semireligious communities were merely called beghards (*fratres voluntariae paupertatis*) or Lollaerts[4] because they were wont to babble or mutter their prayers (*lollen*), or as *Mate-Mannen* and *Mate-Wiven* because they were poor and belonged to the commoners,[5] or else Alexians from the patron Saint Alexius (d. July

---

[1] Liese, *Geschichte der Caritas*, II, 39. The beguines at Leiden and Amsterdam, for example, were wont not only to nurse the sick but also to prepare the corpses for burial (Philippen, *Begijnhoven*, p. 194). For a bibliography, see Liese, *op. cit.*, II, 39-43; Laenen, *Kerkelijk Brabant*, II, 81-88, 101; id., *Geschiedkundige Aanteekeningen;* Ennen, *Geschichte der Stadt Köln*, III, 831f; Raymaekers, *Kerkelijk Diest*, pp. 308-314; Marx, *Development of Charity in Medieval Louvain*, pp. 67ff.

[2] Du Cange, *Glossarium, s.v. cella.*

[3] Marx, *op. cit.*, pp. 67-69: "... Before 1350 the terms Lollards or Matemans were used to denote the Cellites. This would indicate that before the Black Death they were simply pious communities of laymen scarcely distinguishable from the Beghards. It was the Black Death which gave them their special mark of distinction...." (*ibid.*, p. 69). Cf. Moll, *Kerkgeschiedenis*, II, 2, 159-163.

[4] Practically all writers mentioning Cellites indicate that they were also called Lollaerts (e.g., charter establishing Cellites at Diest, February 13, 1375: "Den Celbruderen die men gemeinlic den Lollaerden," Raymaekers, *Kerkelijk Diest,* p. 309).

[5] Boendale, *Jans Teesteye* (ed. Snellaert), vss. 1996-2001:

> "In sie nieman edel op ertrike,
> Hine si mechtich ende rike;
> Hoe, hebben si dedelheyt allene,
> Ende dat matevolc en heeft enghene?

17, 417).[6] There is no single point of origin for these lay brotherhoods: they are a spontaneous development out of the religious and social conditions of the towns of the Low Countries and Germany.[7] The fact that the brethren were commonly called Lollaerts or Matemans seems to indicate that the Cellites were closely related to the beguines and beghards except that they emphasized more the care of the sick and the burial of the dead.[8] It is probable that after the Black Death they began to come together in cloisters, living in cells like those used by the monks, but not adopting a monastic rule. Nevertheless they were often brought closer into line with the ecclesiastical program by embracing the Franciscan third rule.

Cellites are said to have been at Liége in the thirteenth century;[9] they have been detected at Malines in 1305[10] and shortly afterwards at Louvain.[11] At Antwerp (1342) they appeared under the name of Matemans,[12] at Tirlemont (1340) under the name of Lollard,[13] at Diest (1375) as Celbruders or Lollards;[14] at about the same time they may be seen at St. Trond,[15] Brussels (1368),[16] and Hasselt[17] while

> Selke liede segghen also:
> Si quame vander rijcheyt toe."

Laenen holds that the Mate-Mannen and Mate-Wiven were originally much like the beguines and beghards except they emphasized more the care of sick and burial of the dead (*AAAB.*, LIV, 1902, pp. 6ff; also *Gesch. van Mechelen*, pp. 357-358). For his claims of German origin he seeks confirmation in the name "swesteren" or swestriones given to them (*Kerkelijk Brabant*, II, 82).

[6] *Vita Alexii Confessoris, AA. SS.*, XXXI (July 17, iv), 251-261; cf. 246f (31-32).

[7] The cell sisters of Amsterdam not only nursed but also sustained themselves either by alms or, in the manner of beguines, by income derived from spinning and sewing (Moll, *Kerkgesch.*, II, 2, 163). Meyerus (*Annales Flandriae*, f. 154v-155, cited by Fredericq, *Corpus*, I, 198-199, no. 201) equates with the flagellants of 1349-1350 from upper Germany ("ex Germania superiore") Flemish Lollards, Cellites, and beghards who associated with them: "Coepit se illis iungere ex omni fere ordine et aetate magna hominum multitudo. In Flandria se illis sociabant sectae quaedam novae, quae Lollardi, Cellani et Beggardi vocabantur . . . ."

[8] Laenen, *Gesch. van Mechelen*, pp. 357-358.

[9] *BIAL.*, XI, 233; Alberdingk Thijm, *Wohlthätigkeitsanstalten*, p. 196; id., *Liefdadigheid*, pp. 339-342.

[10] Van Gestel, *Hist. arch. Mech.*, I (1725), 77; Laenen (*Geschied. v. Mechelen*, p. 358) does not assign such an early date.

[11] There is no agreement on the first appearance: Servranckx (*Mémoire*, p. 82) gives 1328; Boonen (*Geschiedenis*, pp. 462-463); 1342; Van Even (*Louvain*, p. 481); cf. Bourguignon, *Invent.*, p. xcvii.

[12] Henne and Wauters, *Histoire de Bruxelles*, III, 470. An Antwerp chronicle reads: "Anno 1342, begonst t'Antwerpen de vergaderinge van twee devote mannen, die de arme soeken te bedde liggende; zy wierden genoempt Matemans en Lollaerts" (cited, *ibid.*, III, 470, note 1). A dispute with the Antwerp magistrates on account of their hesitation to bury pestilence victims is reported to have broken out in 1399 (Mertens and Torfs, II, 210; IV, 572, 209ff).

[13] Bets, *Histoire de Tirlemont*, II, 178. "inter domos Lollardorum et Franconis"; Tarlier and Wauters, *Géog. et hist. des communes belges. Arrond. de Louvain. Cantons de Tirlemont, Ville de Tirlemont*, p. 170. According to a request they presented to the magistrates on July 8, 1660, their community was founded about 1300 by two brothers from Brussels.

[14] Raymaekers, *Kerkelijk Diest*, pp. 308-314.

[15] *BIAL.*, XI, 14, 274f; Piot, *Cartulaire de Saint Trond*, II, 366.

Ghent, Bruges, and other Flemish cities had them by the middle of the fifteenth century.[18]

The bull of December 2, 1377,[19] whereby Gregory XI declared to the episcopate in Germany, Brabant, and Flanders his intention to protect, without closer definition however, "nonnulli pauperes utriusque sexus, qui humiliter et honeste in fidei puritate et honestis vestibus aut habitibus in paupertate et castitate vivunt et ecclesias devote frequentant," was renewed by Eugenius IV on May 12, 1431.[20] On this occasion protection was extended specifically to Cellites and the Voluntary Poor ("dilectos filios de cellis seu voluntariae paupertatis pauperes communiter nuncupatos")[21] in the wake of an investigation in the dioceses of Cologne and Worms, which had established their obedience to ecclesiastical prescriptions.

Like the other Belgian extraregulars, the Cellites in the fifteenth century generally embraced the Augustinian rule. When several brethren left the Liége house in 1496 without the knowledge of their superior they were soon replaced by Bishop Erard de la Marck.[22] The Brussels Cellites illustrate how warmly they might be received by lay authority. Here the magistrates, attracted by the willingness of *fratres de cella* to earn their livelihood solely by burial, without social distinctions, above all in the wake of pestilence, promised them aid on April 30, 1423. On June 23, 1432, Philip the Good instructed Louis Salaert, his master of *corvées*, to assist them in drawing their wood out of the forest of Soignes.[23] They were twelve in number when on October 14, 1462, they abandoned the third rule of St. Francis for the regulations of St. Augustine.[24] Early in the following century (1524) they were permitted by the abbot of St. Sepulcre, the provost of la Chapelle and the pastor of this church to build a chapel, install bells, and to bury their dead.[25]

The courage of the Diest Cellites during the plague of 1349 persuaded one Gerard van Blanklaar in the presence of lay and church officials to donate a dwelling. This property was steadily increased, with Gregory XI, Eugenius IV, and Nicholas V confirming to the brethren their goods. While the last named allowed them to erect their own chapel, Bishop Louis de Bourbon gave a rule. An agreement was

[16] Henne and Wauters, *Histoire de Bruxelles*, III, 470.
[17] Alberdingk Thijm, *Wohlthätigkeitsanstalten*, p. 197.
[18] *Idem.*
[19] Fredericq, *Corpus*, I, 238; Mosheim, pp. 401-402. Cf. Boniface IX's bull of January 31, 1396, against heretical beghards, Lollards, and Swestriones (Fredericq, *Corpus*, I, 257; Mosheim, pp. 409-410).
[20] Fredericq, *Corpus*, I, 319-322; Mosheim, pp. 668-673.
[21] Fredericq, *Corpus*, I, 320.
[22] Alberdingk Thijm, *Wohlthätigkeitsanstalten*, p. 197.
[23] Henne-Wauters, *Histoire de Bruxelles*, III, 470.
[24] *Ibid.*, 470-471; cf. Mertens-Torfs, II, 216f.
[25] Henne-Wauters, *Histoire de Bruxelles*, III, 471.

reached with St. Sulpicius church whereby the Cellites could collect all offerings except those which were customarily earmarked for the priest on the four great feasts.[26] The bishop conferred additional religious privileges and the town authorities granted tax exemptions together with other favors, especially when the community took over the municipal hospital in 1470. Brothers were not to be admitted to the congregation before their twentieth year, sisters not before their eighteenth. They must be hale and unmarried. Out of respect for the prerogatives of the parish church the inmates attended it four times a year for communion.

[26] Raymaekers, *Kerkelijk Diest*, p. 311.

XVI

The Extraregular in Industry

However broad and consistent the patronage which counts, dukes, and echevins generally extended to Belgian religious and charitable houses, it was by no means unconditional. When centralization of secular power through elimination of competing authorities and vested interests was being matched by an aggressive ecclesiastical policy, increasingly narrow in defense of contested time-worn prerogatives, the prospect of alienation of wealth through acquisition by regular and extraregular was not welcomed. The cost of bureaucratic government and the drain of war translated argument into fact. But other forces were at work dissolving monastic self-sufficiency: crusade-tithes, declining revenue, a money economy. St. Michael at Antwerp was discouraged in March, 1282, from receiving guests as long as its financial condition deteriorated, for it was burdened with life-pensions and impoverished by disastrous inundations.[1]

While demanding subsidies from monasteries in return for exemption grants, John I of Brabant forbade any church in his duchy to inherit property without his consent. This explains why the three brothers of Braine who wished to endow the local nunnery with the seigniory of Wauthier-Braine made a pretense of ceding it to Simon Tondeurlent.[2] Later, after making fresh demands for money, the duke confirmed in 1292 the property and privileges of almost all monasteries provided they sought his approval or that of his successors before acquiring land. Henceforth they could own but one house in each of the seven chief towns of Brabant (Louvain, Brussels, Antwerp, Bois-le-Duc, Tirlemont, Léau, Lierre); the rest must be sold or leased.[3] He had also taken steps for certain convents, notably St. Michael's in Antwerp[4]

---

[1] Willems, *Rymkroniek van Jan van Heelu, cod. dipl.*, 573, no. 215; cf. Wauters, *Duc Jean I*, pp. 364ff, especially his citation from the *Chronicon Bonae Spei* on pp. 364-365.

[2] January 11, 1281, Tarlier and Wauters, *Géog. et hist. des communes belges. Prov. de Brabant. Canton de Nivelles* (1859), p. 116.

[3] Document granted at Afflighem, April, 1292 (*Cartulaire de l'abbaye d'Afflighem*; cited by Wauters, *Histoire des environs de Bruxelles*, I, 487).

[4] Prims, in *BG.*, XIX (1928), 209-215.

and St. Jacques de Coudenberg, which entailed the alienation of goods through sale or lease and exemption charters in return for forced loans. Moreover he attempted to arrest their accumulation of property. In April, 1288, the duke authorized them to acquire allods or rents up to 30 *l.* of Louvain for St. Michael and 100 *l.* for the other.[5] A municipal ordinance in Antwerp in 1390 prohibited the clergy or religious institutions from inheriting additional property or income except houses which they would occupy themselves. Abandonment of a house meant its return to lay hands.[6]

Similar restrictions were imposed on the Brussels beguines at the beginning of the fourteenth century. In 1303 (September 10) John II limited the ability of the *pauperes beghinae* of Ter Kisten to acquire income on their property in excess of 10 *l.*[7] Singling out the Holy Ghost Table again on September 11, 1305, he re-established its ability to collect revenue of 10 *l.* on his lands.[8] Such action nevertheless did not curb the flow of property even in the era of suspicion, so numerous were the donations even though often negligible in value.

The magistrates of Tirlemont, too, subjected the beguines to public law. An article in the 1291 constitution stipulated that the sales tax must be paid by each inhabitant, whether monk, prelate, knight or of any other class. Another article prohibited within fifteen years the assigning of property to a religious community unless it remained subject to municipal tailles and *accises.*[9] In 1303 the beguines were required to bear local burdens with other townsmen for the next ten years. Engaging in business entailed payment of the tax. Three years later each inhabitant was forbidden to bequeath anything to a monastery or to monks.[10]

We have seen that beguines lacking independent means were generally expected to earn their own livelihood, a premium being put upon *labor manuum.* It was an emphasis well suited to middle class "respectability." While some plied the crafts of washing, sewing, knitting, brewing, others entered the textile industry, spinning, weaving, bleaching, and carding. But competition with guild organization, complicated by beguinal privileges, provoked a new set of problems to replace those previously posed by actual or alleged heterodoxy and immorality.[11] A common vocation was nursing. Although the early settlements of beguines were made in the vicinity of a hos-

[5] Henne and Wauters, *Histoire de Bruxelles*, III, 353.
[6] Prims, *Geschiedenis van Antwerpen*, V, 2, 168-174.
[7] AAPB., Carton B. 1452, 1.
[8] AAPB., Carton B, 1452, 1.
[9] Bets, *Histoire de Tirlemont*, I, 64-65.
[10] *Ibid.*, I, 65.
[11] Ennen, *Geschichte der Stadt Köln*, III, 826-828; Schmidt, in *Alsatia*, 1858-1860, pp. 154, 173, 178, 237; Stein, II, 691, 693, 694; Philippen, *Begijnhoven*, pp. 194-196, 281-301; Nimal, *Béguinages*, pp. 98ff.

pital, they were less concerned with care of the sick in Belgium than in Holland and Germany.[12] Yet even in the last-named country it is wrong to look upon this activity as an obligation imposed at the foundation.[13] It was a duty assumed in Cologne, for example, at the behest of the council.[14] On June 20, 1500, that body recommended that the provisors of the Holy Ghost house should henceforth allow only those beguines to accept alms "who went out daily and looked after the sick."

Still another valuable social contribution were the schools which the beguines kept, presumably in the main for girls, since the statutes uniformly frowned upon the presence of even young boys within the precincts.[15] One may assume that only elementary subject matter was handled together with substantial religious instruction. It was to their school in Léau that Beatrice of Nazareth was entrusted by her father for initiation to the liberal arts.[16] At Antwerp an anniversary was founded on September 3, 1293, by the burgher family from the Kipdorp, Baldwin and Iota, in behalf of the infirmary of the beguinage. They gave their goods at Nispen (Brueckacker), assigning annually 3 sextaria of corn and 22 s. In return two anniversaries were to be held each year, with the priest getting 3 d. and the domicellabus ibidem scholam exercentibus 12 d.[17] On December 9 or 16, 1294, the archdeacon Betto resolved a dispute between the scolares curtis beghinarum at Antwerp on the one hand, and the mistress of the infirmary on the other.[18] Foundation acts for houses in Brussels indicate further that while most beguines earned their livelihood from the cloth industry, some raised children.[19]

Many of the early Belgian statutes took cognizance of hostility which accompanied privileges. The Liége synod of 1287[20] explained that privilegia beguinalia going back almost half a century[21] were

[12] Philippen, Begijnhoven, p. 194.
[13] For a criticism of Ennen's conclusion (Geschichte der Stadt Köln, III, 827) that the beguine convents in Cologne were obliged by the founder to tend to the sick, see Greving, in AHVN., LXXIII (1902), 28.
[14] Stein, II, 691, 693.
[15] Statutes of St. Trond (XIV C.),Philippen, Begijnhoven, p. 309; Diest (April 1, 1361), id., in BG., IV (1905), 332; cf. 333; Liége statutes of 1246, Nimal, Béguinages, p. 49; Rule of St. Christopher (1484-1505), AHEB., XXIII (1892), 85.
[16] See below p. 386.
[17] Prims, in BG., XIX (1928), 201, cf. 174.
[18] Ibid., 305-306, no. 7.
[19] Bouchout house, April 21, 1369: "... Dat men er af nemmermeer en make werkende convent ... noch joncfrouwen daer in wonen soelen die ute soelen gaen werken als noppen, scroeden, verlesen, oft lakenmaken, die kinderbedden gaen achterwaren ...." (AAPB., H. 262); house vanden Steenwege, November 6, 1427: "... inden voirs. huse nimmermeer wonen en selen beginen die kynderbedden gaen achterwaren ....," (AAPB., H. 263).
[20] See above, p. 138; below p. 477.
[21] See document of November 5, 1258, whereby Alexander IV confirmed the im-

not intended for women who carried on business in excess of ten marks. The statutes of the Diest beguinage (1361) forbade beguines to weave more than five whole pieces of cloth or to have them made in their name. The excess must be handed over to the *infirmarie pauperum beghinarum*.[22] Nor were the sisters allowed to employ a hand shuttle on pain of confiscation of the loom. On the other hand, a fine of 20 *s.*, to be distributed to poor beguines, was imposed for fulling cloth after the first sound of the curfew or before first mass.[23] Steps were also taken to prevent beguines from carding or weaving outside the beguinage.

The Cologne council was at first sympathetic to the beguines and frequently defended them against their persecutors. Although in 1375 it sided with the extraregular in the attack from the Dominican inquisitors,[24] the magistrates nevertheless regarded these convents as late as the fifteenth century as secular institutions, even though such an interpretation no longer corresponded with the facts. A change in policy took place when certain communities embraced a rule which conferred immunity on property and withdrew them from civic obligations. By an edict of October 2, 1385, the council determined to put curbs on the acquisition of property.[25] Nor were the Cologne beguines looked upon with favor by the textile industry. In 1469, 1470, and 1480 the guild of silk spinners registered its disapproval by demanding expulsion from the guild for giving work to beguines and other religious. In the last year the penalty was commuted to a fine of ten marks.[26] This prohibition was dictated by the fact that many silk manufacturers, in order to enlarge their business and at the same time to utilize cheap labor, farmed out silk work to the beguines. Gerhard von Wesel in his report[27] denounced such a practice which created hardship for the wage-earner.

The disputes growing out of such competition from beguine convents had already engaged the attention of the town council repeatedly before 1469. In 1456 the silk spinner complained to the magistracy that nunneries and beguine convents were poaching on their preserves, whereupon the council prohibited silk spinning in religious houses. But when the beguines objected that they would lose their livelihood, this ruling was modified by the ordinance of December 1, 1456.[28]

munity granted by Henry of Guelders to the Liége beguines (*AHEB.*, XXXII [1906], 268). Cf. Ennen-Eckertz, *Quellen,* II, 270, no. 270 (an. 1247).

[22] Philippen, in *BG.,* IV (1905), 330.

[23] *Ibid.,* 331-332.

[24] See below pp. 568-69.

[25] Stein, I, 130-133; cf. II, 383, no. 8.

[26] Behaghel, *Die gewerbliche Stellung der Frau,* pp. 42ff; Koch, *Geschichte des Seidengewerbs in Köln vom 13.-18. Jahrhundert* (Cologne, 1907), pp. 58f.

[27] Behaghel, *op. cit.,* p. 43.

[28] Lösch, II, 419-420, no. 651; Koch, *op cit.,* p. 58.

Eight convents which are listed by name, but only these, were allowed
to engaged in the work for ten years, with certain restrictions. Violation of this ordinance involved the loss of the right to manufacture.
The act seems to have remained a dead letter, however, for the guild
soon after was again forbidding work to be given out to religious
persons. In 1470 this prohibition was recalled by another ordinance[29]
which established a commission to enforce its provisions.[30] This
prohibition, however, was no more effectively observed than the
earlier inquisition proceedings. Another town ordinance in 1504
provided that no more silk was to be farmed out to convents.[31] Two
years later the prohibition was renewed, but again without success.[32]
Besides, the beguines were involved in the manufacture of inferior
silk, thus leading in 1654 to the threatening of the convent with a
penalty.[33]

Not only the silk guild but other textile craftsmen like the linen and
wool weavers collided with the beguines. From 1421 to 1452 friction
was persistent between the linen workers on the one hand and the
beguines of Schelenconvent in St. Gereonsstrasse on the other.[34] In
1421 (November 4) the guild allowed the extraregulars to have six
stools for weaving linen, but no serge on pain of 10 gulden and the
loss of the stools. All work was subject to the supervision of the guild.
A beguine who left the convent must, if she wished to resume work,
submit to the usual apprenticeship.[35] The following year the guild
announced its intention of protecting the convent in its possession
of these six stools.[36] In 1434 (November 29) the guild decided what
the beguines should weave on these stools to be granted to them and
the other five which had already been granted. On the first they could
weave linen and what belonged to the linen guild as well as kerchiefs
from cotton. On the latter they could weave chasubles and veils and
whatever was made out of silk and raw thread. Violation of this ordinance brought intervention from the masters. In 1437 (November 22)
the council, at the request of the linen guild, cut the number of stools
in the convent from six to three. Since the council, especially after
the middle of the fifteenth century, was anxious to curtail the number
of beguines and to impose on their work restrictions which would
render their competition with the crafts less acute, they had to depend
more than ever on charity.[37] In 1486 masons and carpenters were for-

[29] Lösch, II, 420, no. 653a.
[30] Ibid., II, 420, no. 653b.
[31] Koch, op. cit., p. 59.
[32] Idem; Behaghel, op. cit., p. 44.
[33] Koch, op cit., p. 59.
[34] Lösch, II, 324-327, no. 555; Behaghel, op. cit., pp. 64-65.
[35] Lösch, II, 555; I, 324.
[36] Ibid., II, 324, no. 555.
[37] Stein, II, 624f; 687-694.

bidden to undertake new construction in beguine and beghard convents or to erect wooden or stone altars.[38]

By the end of the thirteenth century most Belgian towns had associations of unmarried weavers who conceived of work and subsistence
in common, tempered by a spirit of practical piety, especially counting
on mutual aid during illness and old age. The little houses constructed
by the brotherhoods comprised a single convent with a common building for weaving (*textorium*) and a *camhuys*. The beghards of Ghent
like those of Bruges and Audenarde, were devoted to wool manufacture.[39] This is evident not only from a passage in the town accounts
mentioning the difficulties they had in 1314 with the weavers of
Bruges but also by the presence in their convent of a *weefhuys* and a
camhuys which were still there in the sixteenth century.[40] Each
beghard-weaver had in the workroom his own loom where he worked
at his own expense and risk. Two brothers assigned to the same piece
shared expenses. A novice was also an apprentice who must help a
beghard for at least two years. He then demonstrated his proficiency
in anticipation of full footing. The beghard had a fixed sum to pay
for the purchase of raw material. The master was required to provide
each member with work. For each piece of cloth the beghard made
in the convent he was to pay a fee to the master. Washing and com-
bing of cloth was done at the expense of the convent under the master's supervision. Infractions of work rules carried a fine, one half
of which went to the convent treasury, the other half to the weavers'
guild. Old and sick beghards were assigned to the serge looms, since
the manufacture of coarse cloth usually produced less profit. What
apprentices earned beyond their pay went to the convent and not to
the brethren who had taught them the trade. Without the master's
permission combs could not be lent outside the convent. However the
weaver's guild often rented or bought combs made by the brethren.

The master in charge of the weaving room must render account of
his administration twice a year, at the Nativity of St. John and at
Christmas. His responsibility was twofold: he depended in part on the
jurés of the guild to whom he owed the fines. As soon as a brother
incurred a penalty, the master was to notify the guild. He also assigned
work to the brethren. In many cities—Bruges, Antwerp, Brussels,
Louvain—the magistrates established two *mambours* or protectors for
the convent who represented the beghards in the town and supervised
their conduct.[41]

[38] Lösch, II, 450, no. 692; Stein, II, 594.
[39] Espinas and Pirenne, *Recueil*, II, 372; I, 264, 557.
[40] By then the community no longer existed. It had been dissolved at the end of
the fourteenth century and its property given to the weavers' guild.
[41] See rule of Antwerp beghard (July 20, 1361), Vannérus, *Anvers*, p. 120; Bruges
(March 24, 1377), Gilliodts-van Severen, II, 45, no. 33. At Brussels the beghards had

As long as there was no fear of competition with local weavers, magistrates and deans of guilds were kindly disposed to them. They were even exempt from exactions ordinarily imposed on the weavers.[42] But as the beghard industry grew, rules became stricter. In 1276 the jurés of the Bruges guild made it known that they would favor only the beghard convent beyond Notre-Dame bridge which was subject to the spiritual supervision of the Friars Minor. They disregarded the privileges of the second beghard house which was dependent on the Dominicans.[43] In 1309 the Louvain magistrates wrung from local beghards the promise not to allow further meetings of weavers in their convent, to operate no more than fourteen wool and four linen looms, and not to enlarge their house.[44]

The beghards in Brussels retained a basic industrial character until 1359 and even contributed to the development of the cloth industry.[45] The brotherhood recruited its members from the weavers and permitted the convent to be used as a meeting-place for wool artisans. In 1359 (October 31), however, the magistrates allowed the weavers to adopt the third rule of St. Francis and thereby to assume a strictly religious character. Such a reform which intensified hostility between weaver and beghard was dictated by the lack of discipline which attended extraregular status. Recognizing that these new tertiaries were identical with the *fratres laici et textores*, the echevins stipulated that they were bound by the same obligations to town and guild as before. Nevertheless the consequences of the transformation of a free lay brotherhood into a recognized religious order were too profound, and by 1366 the defection of the tertiaries from the cloth industry was evident when they successfully protested against the heavy expenses by the annual banquet which they accustomed to give for the masters and jurés. This obligation aside, however, the bogards fulfilled industrial duties for most of the fifteenth century. After 1470 there was a constantly growing demand for a revision of the two obligations that bound the religious to the guild: first, every newly admitt-

---

been under the supervision of two *mambours* since 1366 (Desmarez, *Les Bogards*, p. 287). For Louvain, see Van Even, *Louvain*, p. 478. On May 12, 1364, the magistrates of Audenarde chose one of the echevins as protector of the beghards (Vanderstraeten, II, 99, note 3).

[42] On Sunday in Trinity (May 24), 1293, the Louvain magistrates confirmed to local beghards the exemptions previously conferred by Duke John I, with the exception that if anyone undertook to buy or sell in public he must be subject to the same obligations as other citizens (Molanus, II, 1218, no. 72). In 1294 (Dominica qua cantatur Judica) the cloth guild agreed to this exemption from "omnibus exactionibus, expeditionibus et aliis subjectionibus" which were borne by other weavers (*ibid.*, 1218, no. 73.)

[43] Gilliodts-van Severen, II, 15-16.

[44] *Tabulae publicae Lovaniensium*, ed. F. C. de Nelis, p. 61; cf. provision of June 26, 1457 (Van Even, *Louvain*, p. 478).

[45] See Desmarez' article.

ed brother had to pay the entrance fees to the guild of wool weavers; and secondly, the religious community had to supervise the manufacture and repair of the combs indispensable for weaving. By an agreement reached on September 2, 1470, the brethren were henceforth exempt from affiliation with the weavers' guild and from payment of entrance fees in return for a fixed annual sum and a prestation of wood. The weavers, for their part, would have for their disposal a section of the *camhuys*, transformed at the expense of the convent into a guild assembly hall.

Other beghard communities experienced similar restrictions. In 1444 the deans of the guild of linen weavers at Antwerp determined how many outsiders the beghards might employ at their looms; a year later they specified the material that they were allowed to handle.[46] In 1470 the beghards of Bois-le-Duc promised the echevins to maintain no more than eight looms and to pay annually 3 *l.* to the local linen guild.[47] On April 24, 1474, the Antwerp beghards fixed their working hours in agreement with the deans of the guild of wool weavers.[48]

---

[46] Vannérus, *Anvers*, pp. 145-148.
[47] Callaey, in *Neerlandia Franciscana*, I (1914), 24.
[48] Vannérus, *Anvers*, pp. 188-193.

Part Three

SPIRITUAL CURRENTS IN BELGIUM
AND RHINELAND

I

Hildegarde of Bingen and Belgian Mysticism

The Cistercian monks of Villers-in-Brabant between Nivelles and Gembloux, continuing St. Bernard's passion for souls, were to exhibit in the thirteenth century an unmistakable fondness for the mysticism of the *mulieres religiosae,* just as in the preceding generation a lively correspondence had flourished between some of its monks and the masterful Benedictine abbess, Hildegarde of Bingen (d. September 17, 1179).[1] The fame of this prophetess and her talent for visions, which had already begun to appear at Disibodenberg (Disenberg) and fully matured at Rupertsberg, spread rapidly in many parts of Europe, but principally in the Low Countries, France, and Germany,[2] penetrating alike political and religious circles, then beset by crusade woes and the first blows between the Hohenstaufen and the papal curia. "Many, touched by the fragrance of her perfume," Guibert wrote to Rudolph of Villers, "just as the human mind always greedy for unusual things, hastened to her from fields and villages as well as cities. Some out of devotion, others because of curiosity, solicited the approval of her exhortation and prayers. Still others desired to know whether a prophetess had appeared in Israel and whether they might hear something of the future. Nevertheless when all returned they could astonish their listeners with the novelty of her utterances."[3] A master of theology at Paris, for example, describes how great her reputation was in that city and proceeds to pose to her a subtle and difficult question raised by Gilbert de la Porrée.[4] The time was ripe for prophetic literature. Her lively concern over contemporary issues was shared by Elizabeth of Schönau; in 1158 when their popularity

---

[1] *AA. SS., XLV* (September 17, v), 676-677, nos. 203-205; *AB.,* I (1882), 598. For her life see *Vita Hildegardis Virginis,* begun by the monk Godfrey and continued by the monk Thierry (*PL.,* CXCVII, 91-130; *AA. SS.,* XLV [September 17, v], 679-697); *Acta Miraculorum, ibid.,* 697-700; life of Guibert of Gembloux in Pitra, *Analecta Sanctae Hildegardis Opera Spicilegio Solesmensi Parata. Analecta Sacra,* VIII (Monte Cassino, 1882), 407-414.

[2] *PL.,* CXCVII, 67, no. 172.

[3] Pitra, *Anal. Sacra,* VIII, 576 (II); cf. 579 (XV), 575-576.

[4] Ep. 127, *PL.,* CXCVII, 351-352.

was at full tide the annalist wrote: "In these days God made manifest his power through the frail sex, in the two handmaidens . . ., whom he filled with a prophetic spirit, making many kinds of visions apparent to them through his messages, which are to be seen in writing."[5]

In her three principal writings, *Scivias, Liber Divinorum Operum Simplicis Hominis,* and the *Liber Epistolarum,*[6] not only did she anticipate events which were later associated with the Protestant Revolt but her appeal to free the church from corruption and worldliness and thereby to regenerate society assumed the form of a mission.[7] Capitalizing on the crisis created by Frederick Barbarossa, her voluminous, nondiscriminatory correspondence was largely responsible for sustaining her European-wide reputation.[8]

It is significant that Hildegarde achieved recognition in no small measure through the offices of Citeaux. During the preaching of the second crusade she sent St. Bernard a letter in which, in addition to a testimonial of admiration, she explained her visions and the uncertainty enveloping them.[9] The abbot of Clairvaux, distressed by the ubiquitous eagerness for learning, had hesitated to pass judgment on her capacity for supernatural phenomena—her "interior eruditio"—and therefore limited himself, evidently while papal pronouncement was pending, to recommending prudence and humility.[10] At the same time he seems to have recognized in her a new ally for his efforts to rejuvenate spiritual life. Towards the end of 1147 or the beginning of the following year Eugenius III presided over a synod at Treves at which Henry, archbishop of Mainz, who about this time countenanced the removal to Rupertsberg,[11] and St. Bernard presented a report on the abbess and her revelations.[12] The pope, astonished at their information, without delay sent Bishop Adalbert of Verdun, with other deputies, to obtain details from Hildegarde herself.[13] She framed a careful reply and handed over to the papal emissaries the books containing her revelations. The pope had them read before the council and even perused a considerable portion of the writings himself. From

---

[5] *Annales Palidenses, MGH. SS.,* XVI, 90.

[6] *Annales Stadenses, MGH. SS.,* XVI, 330. *Scivias* (i.e., *Sci vias Domini) sive Visionum ac Revelationum Libri Tres* (1141), *PL.,* CXCVII, 383-738 (for an explanation of the title see the fragment in *AB.,* I [1882], 599; for the circumstances of composition see the preface, *PL.,* CXCVII, 383-386); *Liber Divinorum Operum Simplicis Hominis, PL.,* CXCVII, 739-1038; *Liber Epistolarum, PL.,* CXCVII, 146-382.

[7] *Annal. Stad., MGH. SS.,* XVI, 300; cf. Alberic de Trois-Fontaines, *Chronica, MGH. SS.,* XXIII, 853, an. 1170.

[8] *Annal. Stad., MGH. SS.,* XVI, 300.

[9] Ep. 29 *responsum, PL.,* CXCVII, 189-190.

[10] Ep. 366, *PL.,* CLXXXII, 572; Ep. 29, *PL.,* CXCVII, 189; *Annal. Stad., MGH. SS.,* XVI, 330; for St. Bernard's role consult Vacandard, *Vie de S. Bernard,* II, 318-319, 322, 324.

[11] *PL.,* CXCVII, 21.

[12] Mansi, XXI, 737f; Hefele-Leclercq, V, 1, 821.

[13] *V. Hild., PL.,* CXCVII, 94-95; Mansi, XXI, 737.

this examination sprang unanimous conviction in the holiness of her life and the purity of her teaching. St. Bernard, in particular, urged Eugenius not to leave such a bright light under a bushel basket and to make an official pronouncement that these prophecies had really been divinely inspired.[14] Thereupon the pope wrote to Hildegarde a brief but laudatory letter in which he congratulated her on her powers but at the same time cautioned her to remain humble.[15] By telling her that she might repeat with suitable propriety what the Holy Spirit communicated to her,[16] Eugenius, on the authority of the two biographers, put the curial stamp of approval on the earlier writings together with their revelations—"quaecunque per Spiritum Sanctum cognovisset."[17] Anastasius IV soon after confirmed this papal policy.[18] This official recognition established her reputation as a prophetic voice within the church; her renown spread throughout the Rhineland and beyond, making Bingen a mecca for pilgrims. At the same time (1153)—the initiative was taken on this occasion by Citeaux—the abbots assembled in the general chapter had recourse to Hildegarde's intuition to learn by her revelations whether anything in their order might incur divine displeasure.[19]

Hildegarde carried on a lively correspondence with the clergy and laymen in the Low Countries, with Utrecht and Liége as the two focal points.[20] Bishops and abbots, canons and monks, nuns and women pilgrims, crusaders and nobles, travelled the roads between the Meuse and the Rhine while many were wont to carry letters for friends. Nor was it unusual to find Belgians from Brabant and Flanders on a pilgrimage to Rupertsberg eager to present to the abbess personal problems as well as political and theological questions. There are two letters extant which Bishop Godfrey of Utrecht (1156—1178) received

[14] "Monebatur summus pontifex, ne tam insignem lucernam silentio tegi pateretur, sed gratiam tantam, quam tempore ipsius Dominus manifestare vellet, sua auctoritate confirmaret" (*PL.*, CXCVII, 95).

[15] Ep. 1, *PL.*, CXCVII, 145; Mansi, XXI, 737f.

[16] Cf. St. Bernard's letter (Ep. 29), *PL.*, CXCVII, 189; *Annal. Stad., MGH. SS.*, XVI, 330.

[17] *V. Hild., PL.*, CXCVII, 95.

[18] Ep. 2, *PL.*, CXCVII, 150-151; cf. Adrian IV's interest, *V. Hild., PL.*, CXCVII, 101, no. 14; *ibid.*, 32, nos. 51-52.

[19] Alberic de Trois-Fontaines, *Chronica*, an. 1153, *MGH. SS.*, XXIII, 842. Hildegarde's reply is reproduced in entirety by Canivez (*Statuta*, I, 53-56). Cf. Ep. 144 and *responsum, PL.*, CXCVII, 380-381.

[20] Sejourné, "Les Correspondants de Sainte Hildegarde à Utrecht," *NAK.*, XVI (1922), 144-162; Herwegen, "Les Collaborateurs de Sainte Hildegarde," *RB.*, XXI (1904), 192-203, 302-315, 381-403; id., "Guibert von Gembloux und die heilige Hildegard von Bingen," *Belfried*, I (1917), 118-124; Lindeman, "S. Hildegarde en hare nederlandsche Vrienden," *OGE.*, II (1928), 128-160; Roth, "Studien zur Lebensbeschreibung der heiligen Hildegard," *Studien und Mitteilungen zur Geschichte des Benediktinerordens und seiner Zweige*, XXX (Salzburg, 1918), 68-118; Roisin, in *RHE.*, XXXIX (1943), 346-349.

from her;[21] the first, which treats of the schism, belongs to the period 1160—1165,[22] whereas the second is assigned by Stilting to the latter part of Hildegarde's life.[23] On April 18, 1163, the bishop was also in Mainz where he signed, perhaps in the presence of the abbess, a document confirming the property and privileges of her monastery at Rupertsberg. It has been suggested that she even travelled to Utrecht between 1152 and 1162, but journeys to the Low Countries, while quite probable, cannot be proved.[24] Among others from this region who communicated with her were Master Henry of Utrecht,[25] the H. Traiectensis canonicus of Ep. 134 with its answer[26]—possibly the canon Henry Troibant of St. Peter[27]—the provost Baldwin of St. Mary's at Utrecht, son of Count Dirk VI of Holland, who succeeded Godfrey as bishop (1178—1196),[28] and Sophia, abbess of the Benedictine nunnery of Oudewijck in a suburb of Utrecht, who during the first half of the century advice on the projected completion of claustration.[29] The Bollandist Stilting[30] also surmised that since Eberbutde or Eberbusde was a corruption of Averbode its abbot must have exchanged letters with the saint.[31]

[21] Ep. 20, PL., CXCVII, 176-177; cf. col. 60; Pitra, Anal. sacra, VIII, 565-566, no. 139. Cf. Sejourné, op. cit., p. 144; Lindeman, in OGE., II (1928), 131-132.

[22] Ibid., p. 132.

[23] PL., CXCVII, 60.

[24] Although Sejourné found this conclusion well grounded (op. cit., p. 145), see Lindeman's reservations (OGE., II, 130; cf. Pitra, Anal. Sacra, VIII, pp. ix-x).

[25] Ep. 123, PL., CXCVII, 346-347; cf. ibid., col. 42, no. 81; Sejourné, op. cit., pp. 151-154. Lindeman (OGE., II [1928], 132-133) identifies Master Henry with "Henricus Traiectensis ecclesie scolasticus et regie curie capellanus et notarius" whose name occurs frequently in Utrecht documents.

[26] PL., CXCVII, 361-362.

[27] Lindeman hesitates to identify Master Henry of Utrecht with this H. (in OGE., II (1928), 133f).

[28] Sejourné, op. cit., pp. 154ff; Lindeman, in OGE., II (1928), 134f. Hildegarde's answer to Baldwin, a pious man caught in the meshes of temporal affairs, is contained in the Vienna Codex 88: Baldwino Canonico de Traiecto Hildegardis (Pitra, Analecta Sacra, VIII, 526, 606; PL., CXCVII, 346). The answer to Baldwin was also forwarded to H(artmann) de Domo in Maguntia praepositus (1152-1158) (Ep. 91, PL., 311-312). Another letter is addressed in Pitra (Anal. Sacra, VIII, 574) to the priest Reginbert and in Migne to the abbot of Elten (Ep. 99, PL., CXCVII, 320-321). Another which in Migne bears the address ad abbatem de Eberbach (Ep. 31, PL., CXCVII, 194-195) was according to codex 253 of the Württembergische Landesbibliothek intended for the abbot of Neresheim (Lindemann in OGE., II (1928), 134-135). Thus Hildegarde sometimes sent duplicate letters to lesser correspondents.

[29] Ep. 100, PL., CXCVII, 321-322; cf. Sejourné, op. cit., pp. 158-162; Lindeman, in OGE., II (1928), 131, 135f.

[30] PL., CXCVII, 53, no. 128; AA. SS., XLV (September 17, v), 658 E, no. 128.

[31] Pitra, Analecta Sacra, VIII, 535, 558; Th. Heijman, "Norbertijner Vroomheid in de Nederlanden," OGE., IV (1930), 300f. Pitra discovered in a Vienna MS. (MS. theol. 147) a letter from Hildegarde to the abbas de Eberbusde and a little farther on another from the seeress to Andreas prepositus de Eberbutde. The first is primarily an expresssion of sympathy for the abbas de Eberbusde who had voiced in an earlier letter his gratitude to God for the favors bestowed on Hildegarde; the seeress also commends herself to his prayers. The letter to Andreas prepositus de Eberbutde, on the contrary, was addressed in Migne (PL., CXCVII, 300, ep. 78) to the

That Rudolph of Zähringen, bishop of Liége (1167—1191), who was often scourged by his contemporaries for dereliction of duty, incompetence, and even simony,[32] was conscious of his shortcomings may be assumed from an undated letter he wrote to Hildegarde. He admits that he is "a victim of a great fluctuation of body and soul and is in need of divine mercy because of the innumerable sins by which he has offended and irritated God." In deep humility he then asks for her intercession.[33] Yet these are the qualms which, under the circumstances, could have been penned just as well by the most saintly. Nor does Hildegarde's reply, couched in her usual difficult mystical language, give point or precision to Rudolph's confession.[34] That he was well disposed to the abbess may be concluded from two visits he made to her in one year.[35] The sibyl of the Rhine also corresponded with Philip (d. 1165), second abbot of the Parc (Parcus Dominorum), a Premonstratensian house founded about 1129[36] near Louvain,[37] and hermits like Gerlach (d. 1177) in Limburg.[38] Under Philip's direction many books, including the *Scivias,* were copied there.[39] Antoine, who had been associated with Norbert of Xanten at Nivelles[40] as one of the original Premonstratensians, became *prévôt*

abbas de Vescera; Lindeman (in *OGE.,* II [1928], 155) supposes that Hildegarde must have sent the same letter to two different persons, first to Andreas prepositus de Eberbutde and again to the abbot of the Saxon abbey of Vessra. Pitra did not consider the problem. Axters (*De Vroomheid,* I, 278) thinks that Lindeman's solution to the problem is not impossible. The identity of Andreas of Eberbusde or Eberbutde raises difficulties. The Bollandist thought that it was Andreas of Averbode(*AA. SS.,* XLV [September 17, v], 658 E, no. 128; Heijman, in *OGE.,* IV, 1930), 301 accepted this identification. When the seventeenth century authors of *GC.* (V, 106) treat Averbode, they use Everbeur, while in an act of 1139 in which Innocent II (d. 1143) recognized the foundation of the abbey, the two names Averbodium and Erebodium are used indiscriminately (MF., I, 100-101, no. 91). Thus inhabitants near the Brabançon house must still have spoken of Everbeur for Averbode; at the same time numerous documents indicate that it was under a certain abbot Andreas from 1139 or thereabouts to 1164.

[32] See below, pp. 572-573.
[33] Ep. 19 and *respons., PL.,* CXCVII, 175-176; *AA. SS.,* XLV (September 17, v), 663; cf. *PL.,* CXCVII, 59, no. 148.
[34] *PL.,* CXCVII, 175-176.
[35] Pitra, *Analecta Sacra,* VIII, 579.
[36] Raymaekers, *Geschiedkundige Navorschingen,* p. 29; Hauck, IV, 1005.
[37] Hildegarde sent three letters to Philip: Ep. 56, *PL.,* CXCVII, 275-276; *AA. SS.,* XLV (September 17, v), 662, no. 141; Ep. 58, *PL.,* CXCVII, 277-278; *AA. SS.,* XLV, 662, nos. 143-144; Ep. 59, *PL.,* CXCVII, 278; *AA. SS.,* XLV, 662-663, no. 145. The abbot sent one to her, Ep. 57, *PL.,* CXCVII, 276-277; *AA. SS.,* XLV, 662, no. 142. These letters were written from 1142-1165, during Philip's abbacy. For his identity see *Acta S. Hildegardis, PL.,* CXCVII, 58, nos. 140-145; cf. Pitra, *Analecta Sacra,* VIII, 578 (X); Raymaekers, *op. cit.,* pp. 12-13.
[38] The author of the *Vita S. Gerlaci Eremitae* (I, 8) (*AA. SS.,* I [January 5, i], 309) called Hildegarde "famosissima illa prophetissa Novi Testamenti, cum qua familiariter locutus est Deus, et ostendit ei secreta coelestia." Cf. Lindeman, in *OGE.,* II (1928), 157-158; *Acta, PL.,* CXCVII, 59, nos. 146-147.
[39] Cf. *PL.,* CXCVII, 58, nos. 140-145. The copy of the *Scivias* now rests in the Bibliothèque royale at Brussels (no. 11568, f. 174r Liber fratrum de Parcho).
[40] Madelaine, *Histoire de Saint Norbert,* I, 133.

of Ilbenstadt and corresponded with Hildegarde.[41] Philip of Alsace, count of Flanders,[42] venerated her as an oracle on the strength of her reputation, prided himself in being one of her faithful and desired to receive from her a letter or an interview concerning his impending crusade (1177—1178), preparations for which were then engaging his whole attention. Specifically he wanted to learn whether he ought to remain in the Holy Land or to return.

However it was Guibert (b. ca. 1124-d. after 1212),[43] afterwards abbot of Florennes (1188) and Gembloux (1194), who deserves credit for establishing contact between Villers and this mysticism of the Rhineland. From the small collection of sixteen letters that passed between him and the abbess we get a good idea how Hildegarde's visions and prophecies became a part of the spiritual heritage of Belgium.[44] For one student this friendship was a symbol of the coupling of Romanic form with German spirit in the high middle ages.[45] Of more immediate consequence, she helped to kindle, and certainly stimulated among the Cistercians interest in the *mulieres sanctae*. But it was the greatness of Hildegarde's towering soul that really carried the friendship. Recognizing Guibert's harmless naïveté, she valued his zeal and especially his deep awe before her supernatural gifts. His petty weaknesses she could overlook. In a highly informative letter to Rudolph, a monk at Villers,[46] written in 1180, Guibert meticulously traces his relations with the seer—relations which had eventually made him, following Volmar's death,[47] her spiritual adviser, the confidant of her revelations and the witness of her mystical experiences during the last two years of her life.[48] When Hildegarde left her daughters at Bingen without support on earth, Guibert continued to be their minister for almost a year[49] before undertaking a pilgrimage to St. Martin's grave at Tours in 1180.[50]

[41] De Moreau, *Histoire de l'église en Belgique*, III, 445.

[42] Ep. 28 and *respons.*, *PL.*, CXCVII, 187-188; cf. *AA. SS.*, XLV (September 17, v), 661ff; *PL.*, CXCVII, 60-61, no. 153; Lindeman, in *OGE.*, II (1928), 156-157.

[43] Delehaye, "Guibert, abbé de Florennes et de Gembloux (XIIe et XIIIe siècles," *Revue des questions historiques*, XLVI, 1889), 5-90 (based on correspondence scattered in three codices of Bibl. roy. de Belg., 5387-96, 5527-34, 5535-37; cf. *CCHB.*, I, 1, 484-506, 529-577); A. Bottandier, "Sainte Hildegarde, sa vie et ses oeuvres," *Revue des questions historiques*, XXXIII (1883), 395-425; Herwegen, "Les Collaborateurs de Sainte Hildegarde. IV. Guibert de Gembloux," *RB.*, XXI (1904), 381-403; Roth, *op. cit.*, pp. 107-116; Lindeman, in *OGE.*, II (1928), 137-150; Wauters, in *BNB.*, VIII (1884-1885), 406-416.

[44] For Hildegarde's impact on Villers, for example, see De Moreau, *L'abbaye de Villers*, pp. 107-109.

[45] Herwegen, in *Belfried*, I (1917), 124.

[46] Pitra, *Analecta Sacra*, VIII, 575-581, no. 164. For Rudolph, see *HLF.*, XVII (1832), 391f.

[47] Herwegen, in *RB.*, XXI (1904), 197-203.

[48] Delehaye, *op. cit.*, pp. 24, 35-46.

[49] *MDAC.*, I, 916ff.

[50] Delehaye, *op. cit.*, pp. 46ff.

But Guibert was cautious and did not easily believe everything he heard. To confirm the rumors that he had received about her visions and supernatural talent, he therefore first wrote her a letter containing a number of questions which he entrusted to a woman named Ida,[51] a "poenitens mulier charissima, nota tibi (i.e., Hildegarde) familiariter."[52] But she returned to Gembloux without bringing the desired answer. Hildegarde, before attempting a solution of his problems, wished to be informed by divine light.[53] Since she expected to satisfy the request after Assumption, Guibert should send another message after August 15. It was, however, the knight Siger de Wavre, "a man of considerable family,"[54] who used his influence as a frequent visitor at Bingen to obtain a detailed reply from the abbes, entitled *Hildegardis de modo visitationis suae*,[55] to Guibert's second letter, written August 14.[56] Siger later became a monk at Villers at Hildegarde's advice.[57] In this way she implemented her praise for the Cistercian order.[58] In the fall of 1175[59] Guibert travelled to Rupertsberg after a canon of St. Lambert at Liége had signified his intention of visiting Hildegarde and invited Guibert to accompany him.[60] Having received permission from his abbot, John, Guibert spent four days at Bingen. Hildegarde received the travellers with humility and took pleasure that she was so highly esteemed by her guests.[61] Guibert examined, in so far as time allowed, the life and work of the prophetess and came to the conclusion that there was no hypocrisy or deceit or fabrication that could detract from her humility and sincerity.[62] Before returning to Gembloux on his way back from Germany he stopped at Villers to acquaint the monks with Hildegarde's answer to his earlier letters and the details of his experiences "in too brief a time" at Rupertsberg.[63] He emphasized that she had given him deeper insight into her interior life than was contained in her books concerning her illumination.[64] This communication so inflamed the

---

[51] Pitra, *Analecta Sacra*, VIII, 328-330 (ep. 1); cf. Herwegen, in *RB.*, XXI (1904), 381; Lindeman, in *OGE.*, II (1928), 139.

[52] Pitra, *Analecta Sacra*, VIII, 575.

[53] *Ibid.*, 378-379.

[54] *Ibid.*, 381ff, no. 16.

[55] *Ibid.*, 331-334; cf. supplement in *AB.*, I (1882), 599-600.

[56] Pitra, *Analecta Sacra*, VIII, 378-379; cf. *ibid.*, 382, 576-577 (V); Roth, *op. cit.*, p. 109. For the date Delehaye (*op. cit.*, pp. 27 note 4, 29)/ offered August 14, 1177, which is much too late. See Lindeman, in *OGE.*, II (1928), 139.

[57] On the question whether Frater Sigerus is the same as Dominus Sigerus see Lindeman, in *OGE.*, II (1928), 143, note 70.

[58] Ep. 51, *PL.*, CXCVII, 260-268; Pitra, *Analecta sacra*, VIII, 334-336, no. 3.

[59] "Autumnali tempore a beatitudine tua regressus" (Pitra, *Analecta sacra*, VIII, 388; cf. Delehaye, *op. cit.*, pp. 29, 31).

[60] *Ibid.*, VIII, 577 (VI).

[61] *Ibid.*, 577 (VII-VIII).

[62] *Ibid.*, 577 (VIII).

[63] *Ibid.*, 388 (ep. 17).

[64] *Ibid.*, 577 (VI).

monks that, according to the inspiration of each, they were moved to forward to her through Guibert the famous thirty-eight questions on literary and theological difficulties.[65] From this letter it is clear that the Villers monks had not yet established relations with the prophetess. Infirmity and another work[66] were, however, to prevent her, at least for the present, from offering a full solution of these problems. The questions on obscure biblical passages and such matters as the elevation of Paul to the third heaven (24), the divine processions (23), the sort of bodies the angels had who appeared before Abraham (Gen. 18) (8), the realness of the fire that appeared to Moses in the bush without consuming it, or which lit up Mount Sinai (Ex. 19), or which on Pentecost fell on the disciples as cloven tongues (Act. 2), or which appeared over Martin's head as he administered the sacraments (11) give some idea of the speculative and mystical interests of the abbey. The works composed in the monastery and the books in its library, as well as open hostility to scholastic philosophy, demonstrate conclusively that Villers was a center of piety but not of learning.[67]

Guibert was reluctant to forward the monk's letter. When he returned to Villers after February 2, 1176, they asked whether he had sent their questions to Hildegarde.[68] Guibert excused himself by pleading absence of a reliable messenger. The monks then reproached him and grew angry because of the long delay. Judging from frequent reference to these problems in the correspondence, the monks must have kept steady pressure on Guibert. When he was at Villers on another occasion the priest Peter of Münster had just got back from a journey to Jerusalem. He had visited Rupertsberg and brought with him a letter from Hildegarde for the novices, Siger and Anselm,[69] which contained news of the death of Volmar, who was not only charged with the spiritual and temporal affairs of the abbey but also acted as Hildegarde's secretary. When Guibert arrived at Gembloux he found Abbot John preparing for a journey to St. Quirinus (at Neuss?)[70] *causa orationis* and intending to visit the seeress on his way back. Guibert addressed the letters of the Villers monks together with

---

[65] *PL.*, CXCVII, 1038-1054; Pitra, *Analecta sacra*, VIII, 402-404; cf. Roth, *op. cit.*, p. 110; Delehaye, *op. cit.*, pp. 31, 34.

[66] Pitra, *Analecta sacra*, VIII, 400, ep. 24.

[67] Arbois de Jubainville, *Etude sur l'état intérieur*, pp. 57-74; for studies at Villers see De Moreau, *L'abbaye de Villers*, pp. 115-125; Roisin, "Refléxions sur la culture intellectuelle en nos abbayes cisterciennes médiévales," *Miscel. hist. Leonis Van der Essen*, I, 245-256; Schuermans, "La bibliothèque de l'abbaye de Villers," *Annales de la société archéologique de l'arrondissement de Nivelles*, VI (1898), 193-236. See, for example, the prohibition of the general chapter (1199), Canivez, *Statuta*, I, 232, no. 1.

[68] Pitra, *Analecta sacra*, VIII, 390.

[69] *Idem.*

[70] Roth, *op. cit.*, p. 111. Lindeman (*OGE.*, II, 143, note 72) concludes that it was more probably the Benedictine abbey of Tegernsee in Bavaria.

his own to be sent to Bingen through the abbot's companion. That companion was to be Guibert himself. These details are inserted by him between the letter of the Villers monks and their questions.[71] The trip was made in the spring of 1176. But when the abbot reached Cologne the journey to Hildegarde was cancelled. Guibert thereupon sent the Villers communication, together with two of his own letters, to the abbess through a certain Baldwin and asked for an answer to the questions.[72] Since she was then unable to offer a solution to more than fourteen of them[73] she sent the monks her *Liber Vitae Meritorum*;[74] about the same time another of her books, the *Liber Divinorum Operum,* was also being read in the monastery.[75] The bearer of the letter, a novice named Siger, who is not to be confused with the converted knight, was expected to bring back the answers to the questions.[76] Rudolph of Villers drew up a second list of thirty-four questions for Hildegarde[77] but received from Guibert, then her secretary, the reply that he would do better to send them to some doctor at Paris.[78]

Thus the abbess appears to have numbered among her spiritual sons several Cistercian monks in Brabant: Anselm, John, Rudolph, and Siger. Another monk, Eustache, without having seen her, held her in high esteem.[79]

Rumors spread that Hildegarde had died. In January, 1177, the nun Matilda brought back Guibert's letter to Gembloux or Villers and denied these reports.[80] Later in the year Hildegarde called Guibert to take Volmar's place.[81] Having obtained permission from Abbot Philip of the Parc to travel to Rupertsberg, he set out in the company of the *custos* Walcher of St. Amand at Tournai "who was burning to see her." She received them kindly and asked Guibert to remain until she found another assistant.[82] It was on this occasion that he met Hildegarde's brother, a canon of St. Stephen at Mainz, who was acting as the representative of the provost of Rupertsberg, as well as another monk who was charged with the care of souls in the nun-

---

[71] Pitra, *Analecta sacra*, VIII, 389-392, no. xviii: ep. 5.

[72] *Ibid.,* 393 (ep. 19).

[73] *Ibid.,* 400 (ep. 24); cf. 380-381, ep. 15.

[74] *Ibid.,* 394 (ep. 20); cf. 397.

[75] *Ibid.,* 397; cf. Roisin, in *RHE.,* XXXIX (1943), 348.

[76] Pitra, *Analecta sacra*, VIII, 395 (ep. 21).

[77] *Ibid.,* 400-404 (ep. 25).

[78] *Epistola Guiberti ad Radulphum Monachum Villariensem,* in *CCHB.,* I, 1, 497.

[79] Roisin in *RHE.,* XXXIX (1943), 349. For the correspondence between the monks of Villers and Hildegarde, see Delehaye, *op. cit.,* pp. 33-34; cf. *PL.,* CXCVII, 49.

[80] Pitra, *Analecta sacra,* VIII, 397 (ep. 23). Guibert had written his seventh letter (*ibid.,* 396, no. 22) to the nuns to seek confirmation.

[81] *Ibid.,* 578: "Communicato cum amicis consilio ut meo illius (i.e. Volmar) loco fruer etur solatio."

[82] *Ibid.,* 578 (X).

nery.[83] It is not certain whether Cantor Hugh in St. Martin's at Mainz was Hildegarde's brother.[84] In any case he was not the canon to whom letters XCI[85] and CXXIX[86] in Migne's collection were addressed. With these two Guibert shared the direction of the community, although he admits difficulty owing to an ignorance of German.[87] He had spent scarcely two months at Rupertsberg when Walcher of St. Amand returned.[88] Shortly after Hildegarde's brother died of fever, and the monk entrusted with the pastoral care soon followed, thus leaving Guibert in full charge of the monastery and its pastoral duties.[89]

The following month John of Gembloux, at the insistence of the monks, called Guibert home and came himself to Rupertsberg. The nuns beseeched the abbot to allow Guibert to remain for daily ministry until a replacement could be found. The abbot yielded and returned to Belgium.[90] Guibert fondly dwells on the consternation which his possible departure caused among the sisters. At the same time it was not an assignment that gave him unqualified pleasure.[91] The next year (1178) Rudolph of Zähringen, who in his youth had been educated in the cathedral school at Mainz by Hildegarde's brother Hugh when he was cantor there, arrived at Bingen. The bishop "was so devoted to this pious mother that he was ready to obey her in all things." Hildegarde and her nuns requested Rudolph to allow Guibert to remain for life or at least until the death of the abbess.[92] The prelate must have given his approval as superior of Gembloux.[93] Guibert stayed at Rupertsberg until the year after Hildegarde's death, since the abbot of Disibodenberg, directives from the archbishop of Mainz notwithstanding, refused to assume charge of pastoral care lest his monastery be weakened.[94] Guibert maintained his ties with Gembloux and Villers. Rudolph of the latter abbey wrote him, without giving his name, that complaints at his long absence at Bingen were circulating among those who did not know the circumstances.

[83] *Idem.*
[84] *Ibid.*, 578, note 2.
[85] *PL.*, CXCVII, 311-312.
[86] *Ibid.*, 355-356. This letter was sent by N., deacon of St. Martin's.
[87] Pitra, *Analecta sacra*, VIII, 578 (X). A little later in this letter to Rudolph (*ibid.*, 580, xvii) Guibert writes: "Nam et ego, utpote novus adhuc theutonicae incola terrae, et disparis homo linguae, ad plenarium illi ministerium exhibendum in plurimis deficio."
[88] *Ibid.*, 578 (XI).
[89] *Ibid.*, 578 (XII).
[90] *Ibid.*, 578-579 (XII).
[91] *Ibid.*, 579: "Ego enim nusquam nisi in concilio et congregatione, non feminarum, sed virorum (et utinam justorum!) vitam, Deo juvante, terminare disposui."
[92] *Ibid.*, 579 (XIII).
[93] *Ibid.*, 579 (XIV).
[94] *Ibid.*, 580.

"We who know do not blame; we bear it with difficulty."[95] At the same time Guibert was faced by opponents who cast aspersions on his residence at Rupertsberg and his motives for visiting Hildegarde in the first place.[96]

Hildegarde's correspondence contains a passage that at once offers insight to her conception of her work and the role that Guibert, as secretary, should play. He was sensitive to style and the choice of words; she, not having had much formal training, emphasized substance. Was it to be the finely chiselled phrase of the savant that tickles the ear or the plain speech of the seeress who relied on inspiration alone?[97]

> In the correction of these and other things you have been diligent and generous with my defects, but you to take care not to add or subtract or change anything unless it departs from the rules and course of correct Latin; or if you prefer, because I have offered in this letter more than customarily—a whole series of visions—you shall not neglect to couch them in more seemly language. Just as food, useful in itself, is not eaten unless stored elsewhere, so these writings, although full of wholesome warnings, are disdained by ears accustomed to polished style unless they are presented in well-chosen language ... Even as you are wont to say with other things in mind, that what pleases the eye and ear flatters while disagreeable and harsh things offend, so also what is written directly and ably stirs and stimulates the mind of the reader, while what is awkward and prolix deadens and repels ... For to your way of thinking, the works of the prophets and apostles which were originally written art in Greek and Hebrew were later clothed by editors and translators in sparkling Latin dress ... Jerome, you will admit, offers the best kind of translation since he rendered scripture, not word for word, but according to the sense; likewise in the editing of whatever of my writings, I do not wish to urge you to remold step by step, but at least not to depart from my footsteps. My beloved Volmar who assisted me assiduously before you in making these corrections asked for no such freedom. He was content with the simplicity with which I was able to present what was inspired or revealed to me, not with polished words, but according to the rules of grammar. Be not therefore dismayed by the Latin of my earlier works, for the ability to use good Latin is not given to me to record what is revealed to me or which I am divinely ordained to make manifest. The intimate confidant of God, lacking ready speech and showing only awkwardness accepted as spokesman his brother Aaron to make up his deficiency and explain what he himself was unable to do; and Jeremiah attests that he could not speak. This celebrated preacher lacked skill, certainly not in wisdom, but only in eloquence.

The westerly radiation of Hildegarde's wisdom represents a step in the transition from the few isolated, but towering, Rhenish mystics in the age of Bernard to the full tide of articulate mysticism, first Cistercian, then Dominican and Franciscan, of the succeeding century in the

---

[95] Ep. 25, *ibid.*, 400-404; especially pp. 400-401.
[96] *Ibid.*, 579 (XV).
[97] *Ibid.*, 431-433.

Low Countries. The moral-didactic school of Flemish poetry, created by Jacob van Maerlant (ca. 1235—1300), seized upon Hildegarde's prophecies to lend weight to their strictures on current church corruption. Hadewijch had already shown deference to *Hildegaert die alle die Visione sach* in the list of the Perfect.[98] Yet it is doubtful that she knew the German mystic as more than a name. It was above all Lodewijch van Velthem who, in Book VII of his continuation of the *Spieghel Historiael*,[99] made use of a series of her prophecies,[100] with special attention to those which seemed to foreshadow the mendicant orders. For him the friars were merely another symptom of decay;[101] through flattery, avarice, hypocrisy, and deceit[102] they preyed on unsuspecting laymen and usurped the prerogatives of the hierarchy. It must be noted, however, that instead of translating directly Hildegarde's revelations Van Velthem followed rather a compilation prepared early in the thirteenth century (ca. 1220) by Gebeno, prior of the Cistercian abbey of Eberbach (Baden),[103] under the title of *Speculum Futurorum Temporum or Pentachronon Sanctae Virginis Hildegardis*,[104] for Magister Raymond Scholasticus and Magister Reiner, canon of St. Stephen in Mainz.[105] De Vries[106] explains that *Die Spiegel van comende tide*,[107] mentioned by Van Velthem but not among Hildegarde's writing, was the work of Gebeno. The entire fourteenth chapter in the Flemish adaptation, for example, is a literal translation from this

---

[98] Marie Helene Van der Zeyde, *Hadewijch. Eene Studie over de Mens en de Schrijfster* (Groningen-The Hague, 1934), p. 160; for Hadewijch and Hildegarde, see also Van Mierlo, in *Dietsche Warande en Belfort*, 1921, p. 456.

[99] Lodewijk Van Velthem, *Voortzetting van den Spiegel Historiael*, vol. III (ed. Herman Vander Linden, Paul De Keyser, Adolf Van Loey, Commission royale d'histoire, 1938).

[100] Van Velthem starts his treatment of Hadewijch with vs. 983 (*ibid.*, p. 278) and continues it through chapter 33 (vs. 2407, *ibid.*, p. 337). For the use made of *Scivias, Werke des Heren (Divina opera)* and *Epistelboec (Epistolae)*, see M. De Vries and E. Verwijs, *Inleiding tot de Spiegel Historiael* (3 vols., Leiden, 1863), I, pp. lxxxiii-lxxxix; J. Verdam, "Velthem's Episoden uit Hildegardis," *Tijdschrift voor nederlandsche Taal- en Letterkunde*, I (Leiden, 1881), 281-297. This article is narrowly philological in scope.

[101] De Vries and Verwijs, Inl. to *Sp. Hist.*, I, p. lxxxvii. Besides Chapters 19 and 20 which will be discussed below, Van Velthem's *Sp. Hist.* (V 7, 13, 95 (vs. 997) concludes a brief introductory recital of the evils of the age with the line, "Ende biddende orden word onwerd." Cf. Matthew Paris, *MGH. SS*, XXVIII, 234.

[102] *Sp. Hist.*, V 7, 19, 28-33 (vss. 1514-1519); this passage is a direct translation from the spurious *Prophetia Hildegardis contra monachos mendicantes* published by Fabricius, *Bibl. lat. med. et infim. aetatis*, III-IV (Florence, 1858), 243.

[103] After being populated by canons regular in 1116 and Benedictines in 1131, Eberbach became a daughter of Clairvaux in 1135 (Cottineau, I, col. 1017).

[104] *Acta S. Hildegardis*, PL., CXCVII, 8off, no. 195; *AA. SS.*, XLV (September 17, v) 675, nos. 195-196; for the date, see Potthast, *Wegweiser durch die Geschichtswerke*, I, 492.

[105] Cf. *Sp. Hist.*, V 7, 14, 1-7 (vss. 1105-1111).

[106] De Vries, Inl. to *Sp. Hist.*, I, p. lxxxvii; cf. *Voortzetting van den Sp. Hist.*, III, 286 note.

[107] *Sp. Hist.*, V 7, 14, 65 (vs. 1169) and note.

late compendium. It also appears that Gebeno included in his compilation the spurious *Prophetia Hildegardis contra monachos mendicantes*[108] from which the Flemish poet drew immediately Chapters 19 (*Wat Huldegard propheteert vander biddender orden*) and 20.[109]

The fifth part of the *Spieghel Historiael* leaves no doubt as to the date of composition. Book VI, he says, was finished *op onser Vrouwen avont* (i.e., August 14) in 1316[110] and at least a part of the seventh book was written during the same year.[111] The rest must have been composed shortly thereafter; Van Velthem hastened to finish it since *in die Sinxendag* of 1316 "sickness and other matters had snatched time from him."[112] The pestilence of 1315–1316 that followed in the wake of a famine[113] was regarded as having been announced by a comet. The sickness left him blind, his eyes causing him so much pain "dat hem dochte oft men met cniven daerin stake."[114]

As Van Velthem begins to recount Hildegarde's prophecies, he points out "that the clergy have heretofore been covered," but that there is no use in concealing "those things that must happen." He "will thus write boldly and acquaint the laity with the revelations."[115] At the same time he hopes "that some lord will reward him" for uncovering these hidden things "since it has been so difficult to put such matters in Flemish".[116] He was already being "slandered by those who thought he was after them."[117] especially for the two chapters criticizing the friars. The entire chapter 15 is both a statement of purpose and a petition for patronage. The continuation of Maerlant's chronicle was undertaken at the instance of Jan Visier, vassal of the nobleman Gerard, lord of Voorne, who would reward him with a benefice.[118]

The statement of purpose is a commentary both on the type of scholarship that prevailed in Maerlant's circle and on the persistent compulsion of authorities in Latin. Instead of castigating the clergy

[108] Fabricius, *op. cit.*, III-IV, 243-244.

[109] De Vries and Verwijs, Inl. to *Sp. Hist.*, I, p. lxxxvii. The editors of Maerlant's chronicle present a table listing the parallel passages between Hildegarde's three works and Van Velthem. Drawn directly from the seeress were Chapter 21, "Ene prophecie vanden leken, hoe si die papen selen dwingen," (vss. 2-62 after Hildegarde's *Lib. Div. Op.*, P. III, Visio x, c. 16, in *PL.*, CXCVII, 1017 D-1018 B) and 22, "Hoe die leke die ordenen selen berechten" (vss. 1-72, *ibid.*, 1018 B-D).

[110] *Sp. Hist.*, V 6, 31, 30-36. Cf. Te Winkel, *Ontwikkelingsgang* (2nd ed.), I, 495 note 7.

[111] *Sp. Hist.*, V 7, 13, 32-38.

[112] *Sp. Hist.*, V 8, 35, 14-19.

[113] Cf. Boendale, *Brab. Yeesten* (ed. Willems, Brussels, 1839), V, 845-850.

[114] *Sp. Hist.*, V 8, 33, 27-30.

[115] *Sp. Hist.*, V 7, 15, 31-44 (vss. 1201-1214).

[116] *Sp. Hist.*, V 7, 15, 31-49.

[117] *Sp. Hist.*, V 7, 18, 86-93 (vss. 1472-1479).

[118] "Om dat ic hope noch ... dat ic sijn pape sal wesen hierna" (*Sp. Hist.*, V. 7, 15, 64-65 (vss. 1234f). For the dedication, see vss. 6off (1230ff); cf. Te Winkel, *Ontwikkelingsgang* (2nd ed.), I, 491f.

of his day or passing judgment on their delinquency himself, Van Velthem painstakingly translated what the Bingen prophetess had written or what was supposed to be hers. He employed this method partly to anticipate the attacks that would come from his enemies; after all, how could they refute the words of a seeress whose prophecies bore the stamp of papal approval?[119] By thus adapting twelfth century Latin text to the contemporary scene, he is not a plagiarist for he readily acknowledges his sources; it is an attempt to document his protests against current evils and to disarm his opponents. When he finished Book VII with the explanation that Joachim of Flora (d. 1202) had given for the prophecies of Jeremiah,[120] he again explicitly disclaims all intention of adding anything of his own; he merely "wishes to produce a book as it stood in Latin."[121] Nevertheless he does admit that he has given the material a more polished and succinct treatment.[122] Once more, in the opening lines of Book VIII, Van Velthem explains, while calling on divine protection against his foes, that he presents nothing from himself but solely what he has found in Latin.[123]

According to Caesarius of Heisterbach as he underlines Hildegarde's renown, when the Friars Preachers arrived in Cologne about 1220 and the Friars Minor two years later[124] during the episcopate of Engelbert von Berg (1216—1225), they were spurned by the local clergy and castigated in the presence of the archbishop. They loomed as those "pseudoprophets"—men in humble attire, without money or worldly possessions—who, as Hildegarde had predicted by word of mouth and letter, would afflict the hierarchy and imperil the state.[125] Engelbert, who was well disposed to the friars, thwarted these attacks by maintaining that divine prophecy must be fulfilled and divine ven-

[119] Twice Van Velthem points out that his Latin authority had been approved by Eugenius III at the council of Treves (1145) (*Sp. Hist.*, V 7, 34, 72-75 (vss. 2479-2482); cf. V 7, 15, 23-30 (vss. 1193-1200).

[120] According to De Vries (*Sp. Hist.*, vol. III, 463), the Flemish poet used for *Sp. Hist.*, V 7, 34, 4-47 (vss. 2412-2454) Joachim's *Interpretatio in Jeremiam prophetam.*

[121] *Sp. Hist.*, V 7, 34, 59-66 (vss. 2466-2471).

[122] "Dat ict in vele steden in scine/ hovescher ende corter heb geseit,/ dan daer in gescreven steit" (*ibid.*, V 7, 34, 56-58, vss. 2463-2465).

[123] *Ibid.*, V 8, 1, 1-19. However common place Maerlant's own strictures on clerical delinquency, corruption, and privilege may be, they nevertheless become sharper as he sought to shield himself from attacks on the *Rijmbijbel* (*Sp. Hist.*, III 1, 43, 39-46; cf. *Der kerken Claghe, Eene Disputacie van onser Vrouwen*, vss. 290-295); Boendale, *Jans Teesteye*, ed. Snellaert, vss. 3138-3345; 3502-3829.

[124] Wiesehoff, *Die Stellung der Bettelorden*, pp. 7ff; *AA. SS.*, LXVII (November 7, iii), 650 note 2.

[125] Caesarius of Heisterbach, *Vita Engelberti* (I, 7) (Hilka, *Wundergeschichten*, III, 245f; *AA. SS.*, LXVII [November 7, iii], 650). Hildegarde's Ep. 48, *PL.*, CXCVII, 244-253; cf. Caesarius of Heisterbach, *Sontagshomilien* (Hilka, *Wundergeschichten*, I, 147ff, no. 208). In describing the fruition of Hildegarde's prophecies, Richer (*Gesta Senon. Eccl., MGH. SS.*, XXV, 306, lib. IV, cap. 15) dwells on their corporate

geance ought not to be obstructed. Here Caesarius sums up the characteristics which had been prophesied for the future *populus errans* who
capitalized on defective pastoral care and the menace of heresy.

We have seen how heavily indebted the monks of Villers as well
as other Belgian and Dutch prelates and laymen were to the prophecies of Hildegarde of Bingen. Linguistic barriers notwithstanding,
physical proximity of Cologne and the Rhineland to Belgium was
implemented by close trade relations, overlapping feudal jurisdictions,
and an interlacing ecclesiastical organization.[126] It could therefore be
expected that spiritual and intellectual interests, too, should not only
conform to the same pattern but actually react on one another in the
process of development. At the gates of Cologne, with Cistercian nuns,
lived the widow of the duke of Louvain, a fervent admirer and
disciple of Mary of Oignies, whom she had once seen at Willambroux. Hearing of Mary's approaching death, she hastened to be at her
side. "Thus came from different parts," adds the biographer, "Mary's
friends and notables to visit her."[127] Nor can Matthew Paris' description of the semireligious in Cologne, with emphasis on the feminine
religious movement, be divorced from Jacques de Vitry's lively account
of the *mulieres religiosae* in Belgium. Even as trade relations were
responsible for the spread of beguinages in northern France, so it was
Lübeck merchants in Flanders who seem to have introduced beguine
life to their city, leading to the establishment of five beguine convents.[128]

Just as the traditions and cult of the Liége saint Lambert, fixed by
the end of the thirteenth century, passed into the Rhineland by way
of Maestricht so that about thirty churches in the archdiocese of
Cologne and more than eighty in Germany as a whole were dedicated
to the saint,[129] so Belgium fell heir to the spiritual heritage of
Cologne. When Juliana of Cornillon, to whom the next chapter is
devoted, was struggling to overcome opposition to the projected
feast of the body and blood of Christ, she journeyed to Cologne to
pray to St. Peter, St. Andrew, and the other Apostles. She also visited
the church of St. Ursula to seek the intercession of that saint and the
eleven thousand virgins.[130] From this city she then proceeded to

as well as personal poverty together with preaching which "in the beginning" en-
deared them to the public. But he is silent about friction with the secular clergy.
Cf. *Acta, PL.*, CXCVII, 74, no. 185; Ennen, *Geschichte der Stadt Köln*, I, 697; Wiesehoff, *op. cit.*, p. 19; Hauck, IV, 410f.

[126] Demarteau, *Liége et les principautés ecclésiastiques*, pp. 124f, 212f.

[127] *VMO.*, 571 (106).

[128] Brehmer, in *Zschr. d. Vereins f. Lübeckische Geschichte*, IV (1884), 83-89.

[129] Demarteau, *Liége*, pp. 2ff, 148ff; these problems have been discussed in his
essay, "Tradition du culte de S. Lambert—Les anciens évêchés saxons," in *Liége*,
pp. 1-107; *BIAL.*, XXVII (1898), 309-415.

[130] *V. Jul. Cornel.*, 460 (11).

Notre-Dame in Tongres and to Saint-Servais, the first bishop of the diocese whose body rested in Maestricht.[131] Since the beginning of the twelfth century the Ursuline legend, to which the Bollandist[132] and the seventeenth-century Jesuit, Herman Crombach (1598—1680),[133] lent their ponderous scholarship, had claimed more and more attention in the regions west of the Rhine. Juliana may be regarded as but one of the long line of purveyors of the cult. Hildegarde's contemporary, Elisabeth of Schönau (1129—1164), had played a significant role in the growth and diffusion of the legend within the Rhineland itself.[134] To answer inquiries that came from all sides, she resorted to "visions," and these revelations whereby she shed light on obscure points of an increasingly complicated history were collected into the *Liber Revelationum Elizabeth de Sacro Exercitu Virginum Coloniensium*.[135]

By sharing fully the enthusiasm for these relics, Cistercian monasteries in Belgium, France, and Germany[136] broke the monopoly of the Cologne relics which the Benedictine order had heretofore enjoyed. In 1255 Archbishop Conrad of Hochstaden advanced the cult in Germany by securing from the general chapter of Citeaux permission to celebrate the feast in the abbeys of his province with special participation of the abbots of Heisterbach and Marienstatt.[137] With similar concessions being granted in the next few years[138] the way was well prepared for blanket permission to German monasteries in 1259.[139] Identical steps were being taken simultaneously in France, only here the king acted as patron. In response to Louis IX's request for an office with twelve lections and mass in the monasteries, the abbots of Camp and Val Saint Lambert in the diocese of Liége were delegated in 1260 to prepare the office and present it to the next general chapter.[140] Within two years the feast was extended to the whole order.[141]

---

[131] *Ibid.*, 461 (12).

[132] *AA. SS.*, LVII (October 21, ix), 73-303.

[133] Besides his *V. Urs.*, see Crombach's *AuctuariumUrsulae vindicatae* (Cologne, 1669). For him consult Ennen in *Deutsche Biog.*, IV (1876), 605f.

[134] Ph. Schmitz, "'Visions' inédites de Sainte Elisabeth de Schoenau," *RB.*, XLVII (1935), 181-183; *Comm. praev.*, *AA. SS.*, LVII (October 21, ix), 81-85, nos. 27-43; Crombach, *V. Urs.*, II, 495-496; 661-662.

[135] Ed. F. W. E. Roth, *Die Visionen ... der hl. Elisabeth* (Brünn, 1884, 1886), pp. 123-135; Crombach, *V. Urs.*, II, 718-743; cf. *Bibliotheca hagiographica latina antiquae et mediae aetatis* (2 vols., Brussels, 1898-1901), nos. 8431-8432.

[136] Cf. Hautcoeur, *Histoire de Flines*, pp. 68f; Crombach, *V. Urs.*, II, 663-668; CHD., VIII, 85 (ed. Strange, II, 151-153); 86-88 (II, 154-156). Cf. Schmitz, in *RB*, XLVII (1935), 183.

[137] Canivez, *Statuta*, II, 420, no. 49.

[138] Doberan, near Rostock, (dioc. Schwerin), *ibid.*, II, 430, no. 27, an 1257; its mother-house, Amelunxborn (dioc. Hildesheim) (*idem*); Lukana (or Wongrowitz, dioc. Gnezen) (*ibid.*), II, 444, no. 33, an. 1258).

[139] *Ibid.*, II, 454, no. 30.

[140] *Ibid.*, II, 464, no. 14; cf. *ibid.*, 443, no. 24, an. 1258.

[141] *Ibid.*, III, 3, no. 14; cf. III, 218, no. 5, an. 1282.

Again, the *Gesta Villariensis Monasterii* reveals how completely the cult had been appropriated by the Brabançon house. For Henry of Brussels the Cologne virgins performed an intermediary role.[142] For Theodard and Godfrey they loomed large in eschatalogical conceptions.[143]

Imène, abbess of Salzinnes, who offered refuge to Juliana and her companions, solicited in 1256, some months before the upheaval in her convent, from the abbess of St. Maccabees at Cologne relics of St. Ursula and the virgins. Owing to the intervention of her brother, Conrad of Hochstaden, her request for permission to excavate was answered on July 17, 1256.[144] The following month she was in the city procuring the body of one of Ursula's companions for her church.[145] Juliana had predicted, after praising the merits of the legend, that Imène and her uterine sister Aleida, abbess of St. Walburge in the diocese of Strasbourg,[146] would one day make a substantial contribution in extending reverence for these martyrs.[147] This prophecy was fulfilled during the interval between Juliana's death (April 5, 1258) and that of Conrad (September 28, 1261).[148] Of the five hundred bodies exhumed[149] the abbess of St. Walburge and Imène received a goodly number. Although the sisters of Flines would have liked to keep the entire collection, Countess Margaret advised the distribution to the principal Flemish churches. Hence the abbeys of St. Martin at Tournai, Marchiennes near Douai, Anchin, St. Gertrude and Le Parc near Louvain, Orval, the nuns of Val-des-Roses, Andennes, Mareuil near Arras, and the collegiate churches of St. Pierre and St. Arné at Douai each received at least one relic.[150] About 1271 St. Trond obtained ninety heads and innumerable bones, while in 1280 Les Dunes, during the abbacy of John of Oestburg, secured two bodies.[151] Master John de Wardo, because of his renown in Cologne, was able to secure relics for the last-mentioned monastery.[152]

---

[142] Bibl. roy de Belg., Cod. 7776-7781, f. 94r; MDT., III, 1366f.

[143] Crombach, *V. Urs.*, II, 882. Cf. Thomas of Cantimpré's reference to the Brussels woman (*BUA.*, II, 53, 7, p. 494).

[144] *AA. SS.*, LVII (October 21, ix), 250, no. 121; Crombach, *V. Urs.*, II, 675f.

[145] Hautcoeur, *Histoire de Flines*, p. 70.

[146] Cottineau, I, 376.

[147] *V. Jul. Cornel.*, 469 (34).

[148] *AA. SS.*, LVII (October 21, ix), 249f, no. 120. Berlière (*MB.*, I, 105) agreed with Hautcoeur (*op. cit.*, p. 71) that the translation took place in 1260.

[149] *AA. SS.*, LVII (October 21, ix), 140; cf. *V. Jul. Cornel.*, 469 (34); Alberic de Trois-Fontaines, *Chron.*, *MGH. SS.*, XXIII, 925 (an. 1229).

[150] See Margaret's letter of 1267 (*AA. SS.*, LVII [October 21, ix], 250, no. 121); Crombach. *V. Urs.*, II, 680f, 678.

[151] *AA. SS.*, LVII (October 21, ix), 250, no. 124; *Epistola* of Adrian de But (*Cronica de cartularium monasterii de Dunis* [Bruges, 1862], p. 51). For the Brethren of the Cross consult Hermans, *Annales*, II, 88-94; cf. *AA. SS.*, LVII (October 21, ix), 250, no. 122.

[152] De But, *Cronica* (*l.c.*, p. 11).

Beguines too entered into the spirit of the cult. From the sister of the priest of Stommeln, who was "in conduct and habit a beguine," Peter of Dacia received a relic from Cologne which he carried with him to Lübeck.[153]

However credulous he might be, Caesarius of Heisterbach, it must be remembered, was not deceived by the fake bones that were being turned up.[154]

[153] *Acta Chr. Stumb.*, 279 B (III, 14); cf. 278 B (III, 8).
[154] CHD., VIII, 88 (ed. Strange, II, 156).

✵ II ✵

Juliana of Cornillon: Devotion to the Eucharist

Juliana, born at Retinne, a suburb of Liége, in 1193, taking the habit at Cornillon in 1207 and becoming its prioress in 1222, is one of the best known representatives of a rich mystical tradition which, deeply rooted in Belgian soil, merited the approval of the Brabançon abbey of Villers and the Cistercian order in general.[1] Although never actually a Premonstratensian or Cistercian despite appearances and intimate association,[2] she preferred the interior life pursued in simplicity and tranquillity. To her task, whether of reform or the promotion of liturgy, the biographer adds, she brought

[1] In addition to the *V. Jul. Cornel.*, see Simenon, *Julienne de Cornillon*; Denis, *Sainte Julienne et Cornillon*; Coenen, *Juliana van Cornillon*; Bertholet, *Histoire de l'institution de la Fête-Dieu*, pp. 39ff. Bertholet (1688—1755) (Alphonse Le Roy, in *BNB.*, II, 1868, coll. 306-313) produced on the five hundredth anniversary of the feast (1746), in the midst of the multiple complaints provoked by his *Histoire ecclésiastique et civile du duché de Luxembourg et comté de Chiny* (8 vols., Luxembourg, 1741—1748), his ponderous treatise on the eucharist which partakes fully of the confidence of the Catholic reform and of the Jesuit offensive in particular. The outgrowth of a sermon delivered in St. Martin-du-Mont at Liege, this uncritical study which offered an opportunity to attack denials of the real presence (pp. 18-39 and *passim*), is couched in the eloquence of the seventeenth century, embodies the heroics and emotionalism of the baroque, and is instinct with naive faith in ubiquitous providence.

[2] Simenon, *Julienne de Cornillon*, pp. 19-20; Schuermans, in *ASAN.*, VII (1903), 30-31 and in *AAAB.*, 1900, p. 384. Denis explored the problem thoroughly in two chapters (for the Norbertine issue, *op. cit.*, pp. 88-97; Bertholet. *op. cit.*, pp. 46-48; for Citeaux, Denis, *op. cit.*, pp. 98-105; Bertholet, *op. cit.*, p. 46). The Jesuits were most insistent that she was never a Cistercian. Those who did support this contention relied principally on her predilection for burial at Villers. Actually another motive may be detected. On December 29, 1253, Cardinal Hugh of St. Cher had proclaimed at Liége the feast of the sacrament and had a few months earlier, on April 26, granted indulgences to those who would celbrate the event in the church of Villers. For the text of the indult see Schuermans, in *ASAN.*, VII (1903), 62-63, app. D; cf. *AAAB.*, 1900, p. 384. Villers therefore was the first place where the feast was proclaimed by an act of the Roman curia, represented by the papal legate. It is not difficult to understand why Juliana desired to be buried in the abbey, or conversely, why the monks were anxious to treasure her relics. They long continued to exercise strong appeal at Villers (Monchamp, *Les reliques de S. Julienne*). For a brief note on the problem of Juliana's monastic affiliation, see Laenen, *Kerkelijk en godsdienstig Brabant*, II, 30.

an extraordinary modesty.[3] Yet hers was a religious career that was constantly interrupted by foes outside the walls and inside the cloister itself.

Not only was she devoted to the writings of St. Augustine, to which she applied herself with enthusiasm, but she was also particularly well schooled in the works of St. Bernard of Clairvaux of whose sermons on the *Cantica Canticorum* she was reported to have known more than twenty from memory.[4] For him she showed preference because he seemed to be more deeply imbued with divine charity. Through visions, special gifts, and relics[5] she herself left a heavy imprint on Belgian religious life, both popular and official. With equal significance she succeeded, through a life-long preoccupation with the eucharist, in enriching the liturgical year by fashioning and promoting the feast of Corpus Christi. It is noteworthy that although steeped in Bernardine spirituality and seeking refuge in four Cistercian nunneries and finally burial in a daughter-house of Clairvaux, she derived support for this feast largely from the Order of Preachers. In this respect her biography offers a glimpse into the transition from a predominantly Cistercian world to the age of the friars.

At the same time Juliana desired that a special veneration of the Virgin might spread in the convents of nuns and among beguines.[6] Herein is suggested another role which is not the least important for this hectic career: she was above all one of those *mulieres sanctae* who bridged the gap between Citeaux and the extraregular world of beguines and recluses. She employed her peculiar talent to relieve the physical pain and mental anguish of nuns[7] and beguines,[8] one of whom she "instructed diligently and with motherly affection in the true religion."[9] Having heard of the renown of another beguine, Isabella of Huy, "who among all religious persons who knew her was held in highest esteem," Juliana was instrumental in having her admitted as a sister at Mont Cornillon.[10] But her closest confidant was the recluse, Eve of St. Martin,[11] who finished her friend's work by securing recognition of the feast from Urban IV.

So completely did Juliana disregard, deliberately or by force of

---

[3] "Erat quippe corpore juvencula, sed animo cana: amabat autem habitare secum, simplex plurimum et quieta, et ultra quam credi potest verecunda" (*V. Jul. Cornel.*, 443 E, no. 3).

[4] *Ibid.*, 444 D, (6); cf. *ibid.*, 451, (26).

[5] Lambert, in *Le Folklore brabançon*, XVI (1936), 100-114.

[6] *V., Jul. Cornel.*, 448 (17): "praecipue in conventibus monialium et begginarum."

[7] E.g., *ibid.*, 452-453 (31); 454 (37).

[8] *Ibid.*, 453-454 (36); 454 (38); 454-455 (41).

[9] *Ibid.*, 455 A.

[10] *Ibid.*, 458 E. (8).

[11] The sole source for Eve's life is the *V. Jul. Cornel.* Cf. Demarteau, *Eve de Saint-Martin.*

circumstances, social and monastic lines and so deeply did she penetrate the semireligious world that it is advisable to review briefly
her career. For this purpose the historian possesses a precious document, the details as well as general lines of which are on the whole
confirmed by cartularies. Whereas the *vitae* are sometimes little
more than editorials on eternity or else overloaded with supernatural
experiences, this biography, its hagiographic cadre and faulty chronology notwithstanding, describes consciously and vividly monachism at
once colliding with lay pressure groups of the city and being consumed
by internal decay.

THE SEARCH FOR SECURITY

After the death of Sapience (ca. 1230)—and now, adds the biographer
playfully, wisdom was greatly reduced[12]—who had supervised the
métairie of Cornillon in the valley of the Meuse noted as a dairy
farm,[13] the older sisters, probably at the behest of the prior of the hospital, Godfrey, elected Juliana prioress of her community.[14] As a five
year-old orphan, she, together with her older sister Agnes, had been
entrusted to these Augustinian nuns who served the hospital. When
she began forthright to use her office for the eradication of abuses
inherent in a double convent,[15] she provoked a revolt among the
younger and less zealous inhabitants who proceeded to slander the
prioress in anticipation of sympathy from the brethren. As long as
Godfrey lived (d. 1237), however, she could depend on his unstinted
support.[16] But his successor,[17] who obtained the post by simony[18]—one
of his partisans in the forthcoming episcopal investigation affirmed
that he had cost the house his weight in silver[19]—together with the
conflict between the town magistrates, incensed by the prior's accusa-

---

[12] *V. Jul. Cornel.*, 455 (2). Bertholet (*op. cit.*, p. 93) placed Sapience's death in
1222 when Juliana was twenty-nine; consult note in which Bertholet disputes the
date 1230 assigned by the Bollandist.

[13] For this dependancy of Cornillon, see Denis, *Sainte Julienne*, pp. 38-39. This
religious community must be distinguished from that of the Premonstratensians
who had maintained since 1120 a house on the summit of the hill of Cornillon.
This establishment was transferred in 1288 to the center of the city, on the
banks of the Meuse (abbey of Beaurepart) (cf. Henschenius, *Comm. praev. V. Jul.
Cornel.*, 438-440). The hospital at the foot of the hill was a double house administered by a prior and a prioress. Cf. Jacques de Vitry. *Hist. Occid.*, cap. 29,
pp. 337-341.

[14] For the founding and administration of this leper-house, see *V. Jul. Cornel.*,
455 (1).

[15] *Ibid.*, 456 (3).

[16] *Ibid.*, 456-457 (4); 464 D.

[17] *Ibid.*, 457 (5); 464 C-F (21). Simenon (in *Revue eccl. de Liége*, XIII [1922],
348) calls him Roger of Huy; cf. Denis, *op. cit.*, p. 57. Out of sheer speculation
Coenen (*Juliana*, pp. 68ff) labelled him "John the Bad."

[18] *V. Jul. Cornel.*, 464 E; 465 C (23).

[19] *Ibid.*, 465 C (23).

tions of Juliana,[20] and the prince-bishop over the direction of the leper-house[21] conspired to force her departure. Profiting from the disorders of the interregnum,[22] the prior, in anticipation of controlling the wealth of the leper-house which had been considerably increased by Juliana's fortune,[23] tried to seize the title-deeds and accountbooks after forcing the gates. Her flight to St. Martin's ended[24] when Robert de Thourote, recently elevated to the bishopric of Liége (August 3, 1240) vacant for almost two years, ordered, on the basis of an investigation into the temporal and spiritual affairs of the house, that the prior should be deposed, Juliana and her companions reinstated, and the administration of the house regularized by imposing close observance of the triple vows under Augustinian regulations.[25] The reform was specifically intended to withdraw the convent from echevinal jurisdiction and to prevent laymen from turning to their advantage internal discord. The right to appoint the prior and prioress remained the prerogative of the brethren and sisters without lay influence.[26] Poverty, in particular, was enjoined: "Quod si proprietas apud quempiam inventa fuerit post mortem, ipsa cum eo in signum suae perditionis extra atrium subterretur." The statutes further prescribed a semiannual accounting of the property by a council composed of the prior and twelve members of the community. It may be said advisedly that in the 1242 statutes Robert de Thourote officially introduced the Augustinian rule, recognition of which was now demanded in the profession of loyalty required from each inmate.[27]

[20] Juliana's enemies claimed that she had given money to Bishop Robert for the purpose of establishing a new feast (ibid., 464 E, 21).

[21] Simenon, Julienne de Cornillon, pp. 66-67; cf. p. 18. Henry, bishop-elect of Liege, asserted on November 14, 1247, that the leper-house of Mont Cornillon, having been established by the city, must accept lay administrators (CESL., I, 530-531, no. 436; Wauters, TC., VII, 806); cf. Kurth, La Cité de Liége, I (1909), 148.

[22] For the disputed episcopal election in consequence of Frederick II's demands, see Schoolmeesters, "Une élection épiscopale à Liége au XIIIe siècle," Leodium, I (1902), 6-8.

[23] V. Jul. Cornel., 468 E. See Denis (op. cit., p. 49) for an estimation of the size of the Retinne holdings (205 bonniers of land), coming for the most part from Juliana's dowry; cf. Simenon, Julienne, p. 20.

[24] Darsonville (in BSAHL., 1902, p. 349) believed that this flight occurred as late as 1242, since the bishop came to see her in person at St. Martin's (V. Jul. Cornel., 465 B, 23).

[25] The full text is contained in CESL., I, 434-436, no. 352; Henschenius published a fragment in the Comm. praev. V. Jul. Cornel., 438-439 (12).

[26] "Firmiter inhibemus ut nemo penitus vestrum proclamationes et querimonias unde domus vestra turbetur vel diffametur ad secularem audientiam deferre audeat" (CESL., I, 435).

[27] Ibid., I, 434; cf. Denis, op. cit., pp. 32-34. No mention had been made of the rule in previous documents (the archdeacon, Albert, in 1185, Denis, op. cit., app. pp. 151-152, no. 4; on November 4, 1186, Urban III addressed the lepers simply "sub communi vita manentibus ad radicem montis Cornillii leodien." ibid., p. 153, no. 5; cf. Bishop Rudolph of Zähringen in 1188 (Schoolmeesters, Regesta de Rudolphe de Zähringen, p. 72 and in BSAHL., I, 196); on January 21, 1238, Gregory IX, in exhorting the faithful to contribute alms to the leper-house, made no men-

However, such a bad odor had the internal discord of the abbey stirred up in the wake of episcopal vacancy that only the youthful and inexperienced John, who was later to compose a preliminary office for Corpus Christi, could be persuaded to accept the post.[28] Moreover the lay opposition was held only temporarily in abeyance, for with the bishop's death in 1246 a new period of sharper conflict was ushered in.

With the election of Henry of Guelders Juliana's troubles began again. The insistence of municipal authorities on controlling the leper-house, the bishop's restoration of temporal supervision of the institution on November 14, 1247 to the echevinage,[29] growing opposition to the feast on the part of St. Lambert, and internal discord provoked by the reinstatement of the deposed prior obliged Juliana, together with her companions, Isabella, Agnes, and Ozilia, to flee once more, first to the neighboring Cistercian nunnery of Robermont, then to Val-Benoît in a suburb of Liége, and finally to Val-Notre-Dame at Antheit near Huy.[30] The prior of Cornillon created successively in these monasteries difficulties which made permanent refuge impossible. At last they made their way to Namur which, the biographer points out, was accustomed to receive exiles.[31] So wretched were the women that they were compelled to beg from door to door. Nor were they successful in obtaining a lodging until poor beguines in the town took them in. With these extraregulars "they remained for some time in desperate straits."[32]

The plight of the Liégeois exiles aroused the sympathy of the

tion of a religious rule (Denis, op. cit., 164-165, no. 25). On the other hand the first extant document after 1242 is a brief from Innocent IV, dated Lyons, November 23, 1246, to the "priori et fratribus domus leprosorum Montis Cornelii ordinis sancti Augustini" (ibid., pp. 166-167, no. 28). Juliana was then still prioress and John, the author of the office, was superior. Thus Denis concluded that when Juliana arrived as a child the house was far from being a monastery. After repeatedly offering papal protection to Cornillon property (bulls of April 6, 1259, Denis, op. cit., p. 174, no. 40; June 9, 1260, ibid., p. 175, no. 43), Alexander IV, on June 27, 1260 (ibid., pp. 175-178, no. 46), confirmed the earlier bulls and added that the Augustinian rule must be observed; once profession was made, no one might leave the community with permission of the superior, unless it was for a more severe religious status ("nisi arctioris religionis obtentu" (ibid., p. 176). Also in this document the pope listed the taille rights: the farm called Boverie and all dependencies; the farms of Retinne, Juprelle, Once, Lantin and their dependencies; the mills of Jupille, Longdoz, Ans, and their waterways; finally all income in the city.
28 V. Jul. Cornel., 465 E.
29 CESL., I, 530-531, no. 436; Wauters, TC., VII, 806; Delescluse et Brouwers, Henri de Gueldre, no. 6. On December 20, 1247, Mont Cornillon recognized the right of the magistrates to appoint the priors subject to approval by chapter and bishop (Denis, op. cit., App. 168-169, no. 31; cf. p. 81; Jean d'Outremeuse published the document, but under the year 1258, ed. Borgnet, V, 348-349).
30 V. Jul. Cornel., 467 F (31).
31 Ibid., 468 A.
32 Ibid., 468 B-C (32).

abbess of Salzinnes, Imène,[33] whose uterine brother was Conrad von
Hochstaden, archbishop of Cologne (1238—1261). She informed Jean
d'Ais, canon of Saint-Aubain and archdeacon of Liége,[34] on which
Namur then depended,[35] that there were in the town *religiosae sorores*
who had been unjustly driven from one convent to another and were
in need of permanent residence.[36] The archdeacon who was accustomed to give aid to these beguines in Namur now came to the assistance
of Juliana and her companions. He made available one of his houses
hard by the church of St. Aubain. The relics of the Cross and Christ's
blood which the church possessed were a source of perpetual delight
to them.[37] Furthermore, the archdeacon, having later built near St.
Symphorien a hospital for indigent and infirm beguines, received
between it and the church land which he now ceded to Juliana.[38] A
house was put up for the refugees with the alms of the faithful. Although the guardians of her and her older sister Agnes had heavily
endowed hard-pressed Cornillon with their rich patrimony at Retin-
nes,[39] they continued to live in straitened circumstances, entirely
dependent upon alms. The abbess of Salzinnes, considering this
treatment unwarranted, intervened, with the help of other persons,
probably John of Lausanne and Eve, in order to secure from the
Liége house a life pension for the exiles. The administrators of Mont
Cornillon acquiesced on this score, expecting thereby to rid themselves permanently of the former prioress. The abbess, with the
approval of Guy or Guiard of Laon, bishop of Cambrai (1238—1247),
then suggested that Juliana submit to the obedience of the superior
of Salzinnes in order that she and her companions might live under
regular dependence,[40] enjoying the protection of the order. Although
the bonds between the abbess and Juliana were close, the latter
hesitated to accept the invitation "tribulationem et dolorem, quae
super venturae erant dictae domui, pertimescens."[41]

After the death of Agnes—evidently not to be confused with her

[33] *Ibid.*, 468 D (32); cf. *AA. SS.*, LVII (October 21, ix), 249. For the life of
Imène (Hymana,), see Hautcoeur, *Histoire de Flines*, pp. 61-73; Berlière, *MB.*, I,
104-105; Galliot, *Histoire de Namur*, IV, 304-306; Coenen, *op. cit.*, pp. 85-90.

[34] The *Vita* (468 D, no. 32) calls him "Joannes Leodiensis archidiaconus". In
Schoolmeesters' list (*Leodium*, II, 5) a John of Namur appears as archdeacon of
the Ardennes (1246-1252) and a John of Ardennes in 1254, probably the same
person.

[35] Simenon, *op. cit.*, p. 77; the archdeacon John died before 1265 (*AHEB.*, VI,
192).

[36] *V. Jul. Cornel.*, 468 D.

[37] *Ibid.*, 468 D.

[38] *Ibid.*, 468 E (32).

[39] *Ibid.*, 468 E (33).

[40] "Ne absque superiore, sed solo propriae voluntatis arbitrio, vivere dicerent-
ur" (*V. Jul. Cornel.*, 468 E, no. 33).

[41] *Ibid.*, 468 F.

sister[42]—and Ozilia and their burial at Salzinnes, Isabella alone remained with Juliana. She too suggested that in view of their infirmity they move to the nunnery. When Juliana finally yielded, she was loathe to accept sumptuous accommodations which she considered inconsistent with humility.[43] Following Isabella's death, Juliana had another inhabitant of Cornillon, Ermentrude, come to join her.[44] John, the real prior of the leper-house, although supplanted by a us- surper, visited her.[45]

Salzinnes, however, was itself to become the victim of violence in 1256. A mob rose in Namur against Empress Marie who had come to take over the government of the country, threatened by the ambition of John d'Avesnes, in the absence of her husband Count Baldwin of Courtenay. The protection which she extended to the nunnery to deliver it from the baneful effects of a nearby house of debauchery,[46] kept by a cleric who was related to a powerful Namur citizen, un- leashed the fury of the townsmen. They expelled the nuns and forced them to disperse.[47] Imène took Juliana to Fosses where she secured for her from the cantor a reclusorium[48] near the collegiate church of St. Feuillen.[49] She was present when her friend died here on April 5, 1258.[50] During the last years Juliana also relied on the monks of Villers for assistance and guidance. Moral support could be ex- pected particularly from her friend Gobert d'Aspremont,[51] who was eventually to arrange for the removal of her body to the Brabançon monastery.

INSTITUTION OF THE FEAST

From her earliest years Juliana had demonstrated a peculiar fond- ness for the eucharist, but humility, explains the biographer, was to prevent her for twenty years from agreeing to sponsor additional ritual.[52] Her desire to deepen and elaborate this sacrament was inten- sified about 1208 by a vision of the church under the appearance of a full moon having one dark spot. This signified the absence in the

---

[42] Cf. the Bollandist's conclusion, ibid., 469, note f.

[43] Ibid., 468-469.

[44] Ibid., 470 F (42).

[45] Ibid., 470 F-471 A.

[46] Ibid., 469 C (35).

[47] Ibid., 469 (35-36); 471 (43); cf. Gaillot, op. cit., I, 292f.

[48] V. Jul. Cornel., 470 D.

[49] Ibid., 471 (44).

[50] Ibid., 473 D-F.

[51] Ibid., 474 A.

[52] Ibid., 457-458 (7). Juliana wished to show deference to "magnis clericis, luminis scientiae fulgentibus, qui sciant et possint promovere tantum negotium." Cf. Simenon, "Les origines de la Fête-Dieu," Revue eccl. de Liége, XIII (1922), 345-358.

liturgical calendar of the feast with which her name is most intimately linked.[53] After taking the recluse Eve[54] and Isabella[55] into her confidence on this matter, she disclosed the vision to John of Lausanne, canon of St. Martin and her confessor, and requested him, "since he knew many great clerics and other religious persons who came to him for the sake of prayers," to call their attention to it.[56] Among them were Dominicans who had been recently admitted to Liége by Hugh de Pierrepont on the eve of his death (April 12, 1229) and established in the city by his nephew and successor, Jean d'Eppes.[57] Having been apprised of the project no later than 1240, Hugh, prior provincial of the Order of Preachers and later cardinal-legate,[58] Bishop Guy of Cambrai,[59] the chancellor of Paris, Philip de Grèves,[60] and Friars Gilles, John, and Gerard,[61] lectors of the Dominicans who had opened a house of studies at Liége in 1234, all registered their approval of the feast.[62] The matter was eventually laid before the archdeacon, Jacques Pantaleon of Troyes, who later became in succession bishop of Verdun (1254), patriarch of Jerusalem in the capacity of legate in Syria (1255), and finally pope as Urban IV.[63] Whatever his office, his interest in the religious excitement of Liége remained undiminished.

Under the compulsion of the revelations of Juliana and Eve,[64] as well as the persuasive powers of John of Lausanne and probably Boniface, former bishop of Lausanne who, a native of Brussels, had

[53] V. Jul. Cornel., 457 (6); 458-459 (8); 463-464.
[54] The V. Jul. (458 A) affirms that Juliana first disclosed her aims to John of Lausanne ("primum cuncta per ordinem patefecit viro vitae venerabilis domino Johanni de Lausenna"); yet she later assured Eve that this had never been revealed to anyone before ("nec unquam alicui demonstravi"). See Darsonville (in BSAHL., 1902, p. 346) on the problem. He concludes that John was made acquainted with the plan about 1230 (ibid., p. 350).
[55] V. Jul. Cornel., 458-459.
[56] Ibid., 458 A-B.
[57] Chapotin, Histoire des Dominicains, p. 129 and note.
[58] E. Mangenot, "Hugues de Saint-Cher," DTC., VII, 1, 223. Hugh was provincial for France for the first time in 1227 (ibid., 222). Cf. Quetif-Echard, I, 195; Sassen, Hugo von S. Cher.
[59] V. Jul. Cornel., 466 A. Guy was in Liége for the dedication of the Dominican church on August 13, 1242 and presumably was then made aware of the plan (Darsonville, l.c., 351 note 1).
[60] 1218-36; for identification see Glorieux, I, 282ff; Haskins, Studies, 43 n.
[61] The name is Gerard, not Renard, as the Bollandist made it read (cf. Axters, in OGE., XIII [1939], 152). Was this Gerard the lector of the Liége house who is mentioned by Henry of Ghent (De Scriptoribus ecclesiasticis, in Miraeus, Bibliog. eccl., I, 172-173, cap. 53) and who composed a tract for the religious on a text from Kings?
[62] V. Jul. Cornel., 458 C-D. The vita notes that their approval was unanimous.
[63] Ibid., 458 B-C For Urban IV see Darsonville, "Urbain IV et la Fête-Dieu à Laon avec une introduction et des notes par Mgr. Monchamps," BSAHL., 1902, 297-403; also published separately (Liege, 1902); Wilhelm Sievert, "Das Vorleben des Papstes Urban IV," RQ., X (1896), 451-505; XII (1898), 127-161. For the chronology consult Monchamps' notes to Darsonville (p. 61).
[64] Demarteau, Eve de Saint Martin, pp. 49ff; cf. V. Cornel., 450, nos. 22-23.

retired to the abbey of La Cambre about 1238 and who on several occasions filled in the diocese and city of Liége the functions of auxiliary bishop,[65] the bishop of Liége, Robert of Thourote, finally decided in 1246 to establish the feast of the Holy Sacrament[66] and to have it promulgated at an early synod,[67] in spite of certain opposition from the cathedral chapter. He wished to have the feast celebrated every year on the Thursday following the octave of Trinity Sunday, with the obligation to hear mass, to abstain from servile work, and to fast on the eve. But his sudden death at Fosses on October 16 prevented the fulfillment of this plan.[68] Nevertheless Robert caused the office to be drawn up by a "young and unlettered brother" John,[69] had twenty copies of it distributed, and ordered it to be read to him in his last moments.[70] Juliana remained its moving spirit throughout its composition. Unable to locate suitable learned men (*viros litteratos*), she had approached this young inmate of Cornillon. As he collated the text, he also composed the music; in both tasks— *in cantu et in littera*—Juliana sustained him with words of encouragement and suggested corrections.[71] Upon completion it was laid before notable theologians whose approbation was given without hesitation, for "nihil invenire potuerunt insipidum, incompositum, vel incultum."[72] The feast, celebrated for the first time by the canons of St. Martin at Liége, was built on this office, replete with antiphons, responses, lections, collects, and hymns, which continued in use in the churches of the diocese even after 1264.[73]

In 1251, after Frederick II's death, Innocent IV despatched to Germany a delegation led by the former provincial of the Friars Preachers, Hugh of St. Cher, cardinal priest with the title of St. Sa-

[65] *V. Bon.*, 155-162; Berlière, *Les évêques auxiliaires de Liége*, p. 21; Daris, *Hist. du dioc. de Liége pendant le XIIIe et le XIVe siècle*, p. 141.

[66] Cf. Robert's conversation with Juliana, *V. Jul. Cornel.*, 451, no. 26.

[67] Binterim, *Denkwürdigkeiten der Christ-Katholischen Kirche*, V, 1 (Mainz, 1838), 276. His letter to the clergy is published, *ibid.*, 276-279 note; Bertholet, *Histoire de l'institution de la Fête-Dieu*, P. J., pp. xxiii-xxv.

[68] *V. Jul. Cornel.*, 461 (13).

[69] *Ibid.*, 459 B (9): "Quemdam fratrem domus suae, Joannem nomine, juvenem quidem, sed plurimum innocentem ... licet in litterarum scientia nosceret imperitem .... Ille, licet ingenii et scientiae suae mensuram excedere non ambigaret onus tantum (modicae quippe litteraturae erat) ...."

[70] *Ibid.*, 461 (13); cf. De Moreau, *Histoire de l'église en Belgique*, III, 147, 541, 581-583, 608; Simenon, *Julienne*, pp. 51-63; id., "Les origines de la Fête-Dieu," *Revue ecclésiastique de Liége*, XIII (1922), 345-358; Lenaerts, "Het eerste officie van het Corpus Christi-Feest," *Studia euch.*, pp. 37-46; Monchamp, "L'office primitif de la fête du Saint-Sacrement," *Leodium*, I (1902), 31-32.

[71] *V. Jul. Cornel.*, 459 D (9); cf. Lenaerts, *op. cit.*, p. 41.

[72] *V. Jul. Cornel.*, 459 (9).

[73] Fisen (*Origo prima festi Corporis Christi*, Liege, 1629, p. 221) noted that whereas the canons of St. Martin kept a notable part of the office the work of Thomas Aquinas was universally accepted after 1264; cf Monchamp, in *Leodium*, 1902, p. 31.

bina, to gain recognition for William of Holland as king of the Germans. New life was put into the feast upon his arrival in Liége in the autumn of 1251,[74] for he seized the opportunity to authorize the feast as well as the office,[75] and then proceeded to celebrate it himself at St. Martin's as well as to preach a sermon there before "an outpouring of Liége citizens," both clergy and laymen.[76] The following year (April 26, 1252), passing by way of Villers, the legate signed a second decree granting a forty-day indulgence to the faithful for each hour of the office attended in the abbey church.[77] During another visit to Liége on December 29, 1252, he made the feast compulsory throughout the territory of his legation,[78] embracing Germany, Dacia, Bohemia, Poland, and Moravia, and circulated letters prescribing its celebration each year on the Thursday following the octave of Trinity Sunday. An indulgence for one hundred days was also granted the faithful who visited the church where the feast was being celebrated, either on the day itself or during the octave.[79] Peter Capoccius of St. George *ad velum aureum,* cardinal deacon, confirmed Hugh's concessions on November 30, 1254.[80]

The recluse Eve[81] near St. Martin's exhibited from the outset an interest that was not one wit less than Juliana's in a feast in honor of the body and blood of Christ; consequently she urged Henry III of Guelders to request the pope to extend the celebration.[82] Indeed, it would not be doing Juliana an injustice to call St. Martin's the cradle of the feast.[83] But it was not until August 11, 1264, that the former archdeacon of Liége issued the bull *Transiturus*[84] establishing the feast of Corpus Christi for the whole church and granting a limited

---

[74] Schoolmeesters, "Les actes du cardinal-légat Hugues de Saint-Cher en Belgique, durant les années de sa légation, 1251-1253," *Leodium,* VI (1907), 150-166; suppl., 172-176; id., "Le Cardinal Hugues de Saint-Cher en Belgique," *ibid.,* XI (1912), 60-63.

[75] Monchamp, "La Fête-Dieu à Liége en 1251," *Leodium,* I 1902), 3-6; Simenon, in *Revue ecclésiastique de Liége,* XIII, 352-353 and note 1.

[76] *V. Jul. Cornel.,* 461 C-D (14); "Et de sublimitate et gratia solennitatis et gratia solennitas praesentis sermonem fecit ad clericos et laicos elegantem." For approval of Hugh's action by the dean W. and the chapter of St. Martin's in November, 1251, see Bertholet, *op. cit.,* P. J., pp. xxix-xxx. Cf. Schoolmeesters, in *Leodium,* 1907, p. 152.

[77] Henriquez, *Lilia Cistercii,* p. 122; Darsonville, *Urbain IV et la Fête-Dieu,* introd. by Monchamp, p. xii; cf. Schoolmeesters, in *Leodium,* 1907, p. 152.

[78] *CESL.,* II, 32-34, no. 511; Bertholet, op. cit., P. J., pp xxv-xxvi; Wauters *TC.,* V, 47. Cf. act of January 1, 1253 (Schoolmeesters, in *Leodium,* XI, 1912), 61.

[79] Cf. Schoonbroodt, *Inv. des chartes de S. Martin,* p. 16, no. 55.

[80] Bertholet, *op. cit.,* P. J., pp. xxvi-xxvii; Böhmer-Ficker, 10475.

[81] Demarteau, *op. cit.,* p. 21 puts the date of her birth in 1210.

[82] This is the interpretation of Jean Hocsem who wrote before 1348 his history of the bishops of Liege (1247-1348); cf. Simenon, *Julienne,* pp. 112-113.

[83] *Ibid.,* p. 108.

[84] Mansi, XXIII, 1077-1080; P., 18998 (cf. 18999); Guiraud, *Registres d'Urbain IV, II, Registre ordinaire,* I, 423-425, no. 874; *Bullar, diplomat. et privil. s. Roman. pontif.* (Aug. Taurin., 1857-1860), III, 707.

indulgence to its devotees. Thomas Aquinas, then lector at the curia, was charged with the duty of drawing up a uniform office to replace John's.[85] In the bull *Transiturus* Urban IV was merely proclaiming what had long been a deep conviction, founded on the revelations of Isabella of Huy and Juliana, which would one day be established for the universal church.[86] The following month (September 7) he announced the news to Eve in a letter which credits her with the promotion of the feast after Juliana's death.[87] It is therefore possible that the papal instructions to the bishop of Liége the day before, urging the promulgation of the bull and active support of the feast within his competence, stemmed from Eve's intercession.[88] Papal interest notwithstanding, the feast was ignored in most countries, including Rome, until confirmation by Clement V at the Council of Vienne.[89] Its spread in the diocese of Liége was assured by episcopal intervention;[90] in the diocese of Passau in Austria it found a patron in Duchess Elizabeth from 1288 on.[91] By the fourteenth century it was making headway in French churches and abbeys, especially in the Midi, under unknown auspices.[92] Henceforth it began to spread under the title of "Officium novae sollemnitatis Corporis Christi." Within a few years the orders had extended official recognition to the feast.[93]

[85] For the authenticity of Thomas' office, see C. Lamblot, "L'office de la Fête-Dieu. Aperçus nouveaux sur ses origines." *RB.*, LIV (1942), 62-66; for its relationship to Strahov's office, see *ibid.*, 88ff.

[86] "Intelleximus autem olim,.dum minori essemus officio constituti quod fuerat quibusdam catholicis divinitus revelatum, festum huiusmodi generaliter in ecclesia celebrandum." This sentence was not reproduced in the bull addressed to the patriarch of Jerusalem (Guiraud, *Registres d'Urbain IV*, t. *II, Registre ordinaire*, I, 422-425). However it is to be found in *Bullarium dipl. Taur.*, III (Turin, 1858), 707, no. 1; The entire bull is reproduced on pp. 705-708; cf. Bertholet, *op. cit.*, P. J., pp. xxx-xxxiii.

[87] Mansi, XXIII, 1076-1077; P., 19016; *V. Jul. Cornel.*, 475 (55-56); Bertholet, *op. cit.*, P.J., p. xxxix; Demarteau, *op. cit.*, pp. 54-55.

[88] See document, *RB.*, LIV, 94, note 1; cf. Simenon, *Julienne*, p. 112.

[89] Binterim, *Denkwürdigkeiten*, V 1, 279; Brouwe, *op. cit.*, p. 108 and note 3; but see the opinion expressed by Hefele-Leclercq, VI 2, 717.

[90] See Jean of Flanders' statutes (1288) (ed. Schoolmeesters, p. 44):" ...quinta feria eiusdem hebomadae fiat sollempniter festum Eucharistiae, prout hactenus a nostris antecessoribus sunt statuta."

[91] Brouwe, *op. cit.*, pp. 108-109.

[92] Lamblot, in *RB.*, LIV, 61.

[93] The general chapter of Citeaux (1313) granted the request of the duke of Austria for the celebration of the feast in his territory (Canivez, *Statuta*, III, 327, no. 4). A few years later (1318) the feast received the approval of the order (*ibid.*, III, 338, no. 1). In like fashion the Acts of the general chapters of the Order of Preachers from 1318 to 1323 were concerned with the introduction of Corpus Christi. The chapters of Lyons (1318) *MOPH.*, IV [1899], 109) here the whole order was enjoined to observe the feast as stipulated in the canons of Vienne), Rouen (1320) (*ibid.*, IV, 120), Florence (1321) (*ibid.*, IV, 128-129), and Barcelona (1323) (*ibid.*, IV, 144) entrusted to the minister-general the duty of providing an office. Significantly enough, he was allowed to chose from the existing one (for an interpretation of this legislation in the light of Thomas' alleged role, see Lamblot, in *RB.*, LIV, 62). The acts of the Rouen and Florence chapters were

Although accepted in a few churches from 1312 to 1317, it was not until the latter, after the publication of the Clementine decrees, that the feast really gained in Romanic lands, England, and Scandinavia.[94]

ROOTS OF THE CULT

Far from being without qualification an innovator of eucharist practice, Juliana was simply tapping a source of native orthodox piety which, under the direction of Bernardine spirituality,[95] must already have been exeedingly strong among the *mulieres religiosae* and recluses as well as the Cistercian nuns in the diocese of Liége. The establishment of the Corpus Christi feast was the culmination of a movement that had been growing in the twelfth century.[96] But this fresh emphasis on the real presence and the incarnation did not go unchallenged. Hildegarde of Bingen characterized the Rhenish heretics of her day with the remark: "Homines ... sanctissimam humanitatem Filii Dei, et sanctitatem corporis et sanguinis sui, quae in oblationem panis et vini est, negant."[97] Thus they turned their backs on a teaching which received official approval and dogmatic precision at the Fourth Lateran Council. Sharing Gnostic-Manichaean hostility to this new conception of Christ as child, man, and the crucified one as well as the doctrine of the Trinity, Tanchelm anticipated at Antwerp a defection which had become widespread in the days of Jacques de Vitry.[98] Caesarius of Heisterbach, mindful of the aberra-

---

approved by the Vienne chapter in 1322 (*MOPH.*, IV, 139) in accordance with the requirement of passage by three successive chapters in order to make a law effective. Yet the Roman office attributed to Thomas Aquinas was not mentioned until the Barcelona chapter (1323) (*ibid.*, IV, 144-145; cf. the Bordeaux session [1324], *ibid.*, IV, 152).

[94] Brouwe, *op. cit.*, p. 143.

[95] Hontoir, "La dévotion au saint sacrement chez les premiers cisterciens (XIIe-XIIIe siècles)," in *Stud. Euch.*, pp. 132-156; Pourrat, *La spiritualité chrétienne*, II, 29-116; Mens, "De Vereering van de H. Eucharistie bij onze vroegste Begijnen," in *Stud. Euch.*, pp. 157-186.

[96] Hontoir, in *Stud. Euch.*, p. 152.

[97] Ep. xlvii *Ad Praelatos Moguntinenses*, *PL.*, CXCVII, 232.

[98] Madelaine, *Histoire de Saint Norbert*, I, 234ff; Döllinger, *Beiträge*, I, 74, 94-104; Vacandard, in *Revue des questions historiques*, LV (1894), 50-83; id., *Vie de Saint Bernard*, II, 207-242; Grundmann, *Religiöse Bewegungen*, pp. 13-38; Bodet, *DHGE.*, III (1924), 1037-1038; Vernet, in *Dict. de spiritualité asc. et mystique, I* (1937), 797-799. Thus Norbert in his antagonism to Tanchelm was regarded throughout the century as a champion of the real presence in the sacrament (Mens, in *Stud. Euch.*, p. 159). Cf. *CHD.* (V. 19), ed. Strange, I, 298-299; (V. 21), I, 300-303; (IX, 12), II, 175-176; (IX, 52), II, 207. Cf. Philippen, "De Heilige Norbertus ende Strijd tegen het Tanchelmisme te Antwerpen," *BG.*, XXV (1934), 251-288; Pirenne, "Tanchelin et le projet de démembrement du diocèse d'Utrecht vers 1100," *BARB.*, 5th ser., XIII (1927), 112-119; L. Van der Essen, "De Ketterij van Tanchelm in de XIIIe eeuw," *Ons Geloof, Apologetisch Tijlschrift*, II (1912), 354-361; M.H.Q. Janssen, "Tanchelijn," *AAAB.*, XXIII (1867), 374-450; A. Poncelet," Saint Norbert et Tanchelin," *AB.*, XII (1893), 441-446; Fredericq, *Corpus*, I, 22-29; II, 3-6; id., *Gesch. d. Ing.*, I, 10ff

tions of scholars as well as popular heresy concerning the sacrament, approached Book IX of the *Dialogue on Miracles*, replete with sixty-seven anecdotes on eucharistic wonders (*De Corpore Christi*), "with fear and trembling," for "where faith alone is operative and reason is altogether excluded, discussion cannot be held without danger."[99] This series he regarded as the culmination of the preceding books on contrition, confession, satisfaction, and singleness of mind.[100]

Ardent love for the humanity and passion of Christ explains this intense devotion.[101] The *vitae* and chronicles which came from Cistercian circles, especially the community of Villers, are instinct with this cult.[102] Nor were the Franciscans[103] and Order of Preachers hesitant to appropriate and sponsor it. One need only turn to that penetrating probing of beguine-Dominican spirituality, the *Acts* of Christine of Stommeln who experienced the stigmata.[104] Her whole biography was little more than a chain of visions and raptures which sprang from a passionate veneration of the "humanitas Christi." Participation in the eucharist was but the perpetual commemoration of her marriage to the heavenly Bridegroom.[105]

Eucharistic devotion from the last quarter of the twelfth century was marked by eagerness to see the host at the moment of consecration and thus to allow communicants this more sensuous contact with the humanity of Christ. Accordingly, elevation of the host was introduced.[106] The practice appears to have existed in the Cistercian order a little before 1210, for in that year the general chapter prescribed practices that must accompany the rite: everyone was expected to prostrate himself and remain in this position until the moment, after the consecration of the blood, the priest raised his hands again.[107] The same recommendation was reiterated in 1215.[108] At the same time the history of eucharistic piety reveals devotion to the sacrament apart from mass and communion. When the Cistercian *vitae* describe

---

[99] *CHD.*, (IX, prol), ed. Strange, II, 164; adapted after Scott-Bland, II, 103; cf. (IX, 1), ed. Strange, II, 166. Book IX is edited by Strange, II, 164-217.

[100] *Ibid.*, 165.

[101] Roisin, *Hag. cist.*, pp. 108-114; Korth, in *AHVN.*, XLVI (1887), 55; Raby, *Christian-Latin Poetry.* pp. 417ff; Axters, *Geschiedenis van de Vroomheid*, I, 207-223, 318-329; Mâle, *L'art religieux du XIIIe siècle en France*, *passim*.

[102] *Cron. Villar. mon.*, *MGH. SS.*, XXV, 199, 203, 205.

[103] See above, p. 150.

[104] *Acta Chr. Stumb.*, 244 F (I, 35), 245 A (I, 36), 254 F (I, 75), 256 A (I, 81), 269 D (II, 48); *V. Chr. Stumb.*, 368 D (5), 369 F (11), 373 E (31), 374 A (33), 376 A-B (43), 382 C (82).

[105] For ecstasy from communion, see for example *Acta*, 254 F (I, 75), 262 A (II, 19).

[106] Hontoir, in *Stud. euch.*, p. 150.

[107] Canivez, *Statuta*, I, 369, no. 5: "In elevatione Corporis Dominici omnes petant veniam et tamdiu sic maneant donec post consecrationem sanguinis sacerdos elevet manus suas." A thirteenth-century copy of this statute adds that at the sound of a little bell in the tower all who heard it knelt and uttered a prayer (*ibid.*, I, 369, note).

[108] *Ibid.*, I, 434 (1).

the intimate prayers before the host, it is reasonable to assume that this practice had its origins in Cistercian circles.[109] Since gazing on the sacrament ministered to a craving for the miraculous, the cult contributed heavily to folklore.[110]

The seventeenth-century Bollandist Daniel Papebroch did not hesitate to see in the prophetic announcement *de cantu novae solemnitatis* in the *VMO*.[111] an allusion to the new feast[112] for the preparation of which Juliana was as early as 1208 being favored with visions. Whether Jacques de Vitry was directly acquainted with her cannot be proven.[113] Yet no passage describes more faithfully the ground from which the feast sprang and the fervor which compelled Francis' admiration than the preface to the *VMO*, written in 1215–1216, before author's arrival in Perugia. When Foulques of Toulouse, expelled from his see by the Albigensians, travelled northward through France seeking assistance against his enemies, he arrived in the diocese of Liége, "drawn, as it were, by the fragrance and renown of those defending God in true humility. Nor did he cease to admire the faith and devotion, especially of the holy women, whose veneration for the church of Christ and its sacraments was most zealous."[114] Predilection for the eucharist among these *mulieres sanctae* was to remain a characteristic of the fully developed beguine movement in Belgium a century later. That they submitted to church-approved doctrine on the matter was recognized by all investigations in the wake of the Clementine legislation. When, for example, Bishop Pierre of Cambrai, on the basis of the examination by his commissioners into the faith of the beguines in La Vigne at Brussels, absolved them in 1324 from all suspicion of heterodoxy,[115] he was merely rendering a verdict at which all similar inquests arrived.[116]

[109] Brouwe, *Die Verehrung der Eucharistie im Mittelalter*, p. 20.

[110] Brouwe, "Die Eucharistie als Zaubermittel im Mittelalter," *Archiv f. Kulturgeschichte*, XX (1930), 134-154. Cf. Welter, pp. 91-2.

[111] *VMO.*, 571 (106): "Quaedam autem alicui nostrum secreto dixit quae post mortem eius debebant accidere ... quae quia sicut praedixit evenerunt, reliqua certissime exspectamus ventura. Scilicet de cantu novae solemnitatis, propter voces angelorum auditas sibi a Domino promisso."

[112] *Ibid.*, 572 note c.

[113] For the whole problem, see Callebaut, "Autour de la rencontre à Florence de S. François et du Cardinal Hugolin (en été 1217)," *AFH.*, XIX (1926), 530-558; Hildebrand van Hooglede, "Hoe Franciscus op reis ging naar het land van S. Lutgardis," *D. War. Belf.*, XXVIII (1928), 371-377; Mens *Oorsprong*, pp. 242-251; id., in *Stud. euch.*, pp. 178-185; id., in *Misc. hist... Alb. de Meyer*, I, 561-562; Coenen, *Juliana*, p. 25.

[114] *VMO.*, 547 D (2). For an interpretation of this extract with respect to Francis, see Callebaut, in *AFH.*, XIX, 553ff.

[115] The beguines "honeste et laudabiliter vixerunt atque vivunt, devote frequentant ecclesias, prelatis suis reverenter obediunt, et quod se disputacionibus et predicacionibus de summa trinitate et divina essencia non involuerunt nec involuunt nec hactenus presumpserunt..." (AAPB., carton H. 262; Fredericq, *Corpus*, II, 84).

[116] This problem is fully explored below, pp. 539-546.

Not only did Belgium experience the same exaltation that is associated with St. Francis in Umbria, but devotion to the eucharist which fired his imagination was really peculiar to Belgian piety. It was therefore no accident that the feast of Corpus Christi had its origins in the diocese of Liége. If this sacrament held forth the promise of spiritual refreshment for the recipient, rejection of it set off more sharply the unbeliever.[117] As custodial administrator in the Rhineland from 1223 on and consequently in a position to become acquainted with Bishop Hugh de Pierrepont, Thomas of Celano must have been conversant with the local spiritual forces.[118] We have it on his authority that the Poverello preferred "France" because of the emphasis put on the sacrament: "Saepe communicabat et tam devote ut alios devotos efficeret. Reverendum enim illud omni reverentia prosequens, membrorum omnium sacrificium offerebat, et agnum immolatum recipiens, illo igne qui in altari cordis semper ardebat spiritum immolabat. Diligebat propterea Franciam ut amicam Corporis Domini, atque in ea mori propter sacrorum reverentiam cupiebat."[119] The *Speculum* is even more explicit: "Eligo provinciam Francie, in qua est catholica gens, maxime quia inter alios catholicos sancte Ecclesie reverentiam magnam exhibent Corpori Christi: quod mihi plurimum gratum est. Propter quod libentius cum illis conversabor."[120] It appears certain that Francis had decided at the chapter of Pentecost, 1217, to journey to *Francia*. He set out, and reached Florence where he met Cardinal Ugolino[121] who persuaded him to remain in Italy. In employing the term *Francia*, Thomas of Celano had in mind the "Provincia Franciae" of the order to which Belgium belonged.[122]

At Perugia Jacques de Vitry may have met the founder of the Friars Minor,[123] for here he established communication with Cardinal Ugo-

[117] See below, p. 505.
[118] Callebaut, in *AFH.*, XIX, 554.
[119] II Cel. n. 201. Cf. Hilarin, in *Etudes franc.*, XXXIV (1922), 520.
[120] *Speculum Perf.* (ed. Sabatier), ca. 65, pp. 118ff; *Lég. de Pérouse, AFH.*, XV (1922), 313.
[121] I Cel., nos. 73-74; *AA. SS.*, L (October 4, ii) 703-4.
[122] Such was the understanding of Wadding in the seventeenth century (*Ann. min.*, I, 1731, 247 (ad. an. 1216, no. 2) and the Bollandist Suyskens (*AA. SS.*, L [October 4, ii], 835, no. 104). Cf. Hildebrand, in *D. War Belf.*, 1928, pp. 376-377.
[123] Jacques de Vitry came into contact with the Friars Minor first either in Perugia itself or "in partibus illis" (Ep. I, *ZKG.*, XIV, 102, 104). Francis had gone to the curia there to share in the decisions concerning his brotherhood (Callebaut, in *AFH.*, XIX, 550-551); cf. Grundmann (*Religiöse Bewegungen*, p. 172): "Jakob von Vitry hat wahrscheinlich auch Franziskus selbst gesehen und mit ihm gesprochen". Mens suggests (in *Stud. euch.*, pp. 182-183, note 5) that already before 1213, the date of Mary's death, or before 1215-1216, the preparation of the *vita*, the priest and biographer of the beguines of Oignies had heard reports of the new mendicant orders. "Dixit etiam ... quod Spiritus sanctus in proximo Ecclesiam suam visitaret, et copiosius solito per universam Ecclesiam operatores sanctos ad fructum animarum mitteret et mundum ex maxima parte illuminaret" (*VMO.*, 570, no. 100). Papebroch (*idem*, in note) concluded, "Scilicet ex ordinibus SS. Dominici et Francisci tunc nasci incipientibus."

lino, the protector of the new order. When Thomas of Cantimpré wrote with respect to Ugolino, "multa de ista (Maria)... admiranda percepi,"[124] he may have been referring to what the cardinal had already heard from Jacques at Perugia in 1216.[125] It is reasonable to conclude that during that summer Jacques de Vitry himself or his biography of Mary of Oignies, and perhaps both made the diocese of Liége known in Umbria.[126] Francis, by expressing a desire to journey northward, was merely following the example of Jacques and Foulques of Toulouse.

What adds weight to Callebaut's thesis—as Hildebrand has pointed out—that it was not a question of parallel development between the Franciscan movement in the south and the extraregulars in Belgium, but rather of actual and intimate interpenetration of ideas with Jacques de Vitry as the intermediary, is the copious evidence embedded in thirteenth-century Cistercian and Dominican hagiography, even though some of this literature is admittedly late. Many an example of eucharist life is contained in the life of Odilia (d. 1220), widow and beguine at Liége.[127] The biography of Ida of Louvain (d. ca. 1300) is likewise informed with this all-consuming fondness for the sacrament[128] which even led to a reward of the stigmata.[129] "Having despised the vanities of the world, she began to aspire to the heights of a more perfect life and is said to have conceived in her heart the most compelling desire to receive the life-giving sacrament of the Lord's body."[130] Agnes Blannbekin (d. 1315), a beguine at Vienna, might not herself experience stigmatization, but the five wounds possessed symbolical significance for her.[131]

Mary of Oignies languished for the sacrament;[132] the pyx excited visions of Christ.[133]

[124] VMO., Suppl., 578.

[125] Mens (in Stud. euch., p. 183, note 1) disagrees with Callebaut (in AFH., XIX, 550) when he says that in the same year "Jacques... finit par lui proposer (viz. Ugolino) la lecture de sa Vie de Marie, dont il lui céda même la relique qu'il portait." Mens holds that this episode in the Suppl. occurred some years later. Cf. Grundmann, Religiöse Bewegungen, p. 173, note 173.

[126] Callebaut, in AFH., XIX, 553; cf. 551.

[127] V. Od., 227, 232, 237, 238, 241, 267, 268, 269, 272, 273, 276, 280, 281, 283, 285, etc.

[128] V. Id. Lov., 160 F (8); 164-165 (20-24); 170 (45); 172 (5-7); 174 (12); 178-180 (27-33). On the pivotal role of the passion, see ibid., 161 A-C (9); 162 D-E (13).

[129] Ibid., 162-163.

[130] Ibid., 164 B (20). Cf. Thomas of Cantimpré, BUA., I, 25, 7 (p. 105).

[131] Chmel, p. 50 (cap. 6); cf. pp. 50 (cap. 5), 53 (cap. 19), 79 (cap. 168), 80 (cap. 170), 100 (cap. 233).

[132] VMO., 548 (8); 568 (92); 571 (105). Mary was sometimes so overwhelmed in looking at the Crucified One that she was obliged to turn aside for a time ("Unde... relicta humanitate, ad Christi divinitatem et majestatem animum attolleret"; ibid., 551, 16); cf. no. 17; 567 (88); 569 (99); V. Juet., 159 (7). The lives of the three Idas, Beatrice of Nazareth, and Lutgard are all impregnated with this "humanitas Christi."

[133] VMO., 567 (91); cf. 568 (92); 571 (105); V. Chr. Stumb., 367 F (2).

The eucharist soothed the unrest and yearning of her heart. Her sorrows were softened, her spirit strengthened. Through this highest and incomparable sacrament she bore patiently all the troubles of this pilgrimage, she conquered all the trials of this desert, and refreshed with this food, she reduced the evils of this misery. The holy bread braced her heart; the holy wine, gladdening her mind, intoxicated her: the holy body nourished; the life-giving blood, by its cleansing power, purified. She could not long without this comfort.[134]

Life and communion were one and the same to her. Lutgard, too, rejoiced in the perpetual sacrifice of Christ for sinners.[135] Spiritual marriage, the culmination of this current of mysticism, frequently led to ecstatic utterances.[136] During the celebration of the sacrifice some obtained the greatest favors: supernatural revelations, renewed strength in the struggle against nature, victory in temptations, and overflowing spiritual joy.[137] Lutgard was described as attending communion between two angels and even between the Virgin Mary and John the Baptist.[138] So great was her pleasure in the sacrament that it sorely grieved her to be deprived of it.[139] Since the eucharist was often accompanied by ecstatic experiences, the chapter of Cîteaux had to forbid communion to those who could not retain their senses during the ceremony.[140] Albertus Magnus, after acknowledging the popularity of the cult among women, argued that too frequent repetition, probably dictated by their "levity," undermines its effectiveness.[141] The appeal of the cult also may be partly measured by *exempla* which embody much folklore and faithfully register popular beliefs.[142]

Fearing that jealousy and ill-will might prevent her from receiving the sacrament, Ida of Louvain besought her "spiritual friends" to

[134] *VMO.*, 568 A (92).
[135] *V. Lutg.*, 198 (9); cf. Hildebrand, in *D. War. Belf.*, 1928, p. 373.
[136] *V. Id. Lov.*, 184 (8); *V. Lutg.*, 191 (I, 1).
[137] *V. Id. Lov.*, 179 (32); 180 (34); 182 (40); 188 (27); 172. *V. Id. Niv.*, ed. Henriquez, pp. 208f; *V. Beat.*, ed. Henriquez, pp. 45-47 (cap. 13); 47-52 (cap. 14); 104-106 (cap. 33); 126-128 (cap. 39).
[138] *V. Lutg.*, 203 (II, 39).
[139] *Ibid.*, 200 (II, 19).
[140] *V. Id. Lew.*, 113 (19-20). Although Roisin (*Hag. cist.*, p. 112, note 5) found no trace of this prohibition in the *Statuta*, it seems to be suggested by a 1261 canon (Canivez, *Statuta*, II, 477, no. 9): "Cum ex perceptione sanguinis Domini, quem post sanctam communionem in calice solent accipere personae Ordinis pericula gravia iam evenerunt, et possent evenire in posterum graviora, ordinat Capitulum generale quod monachi, conversi et moniales, exceptis ministris altaris, ad calicem more solito non accedant".
[141] Albertus Magnus, *De Eucharistia*, dist. VI, tract. II, cap. 3 (*Opera*, ed. P. Jammy, XXI, Lugduni, 1651, p. 139): "De his autem, qui mulieres omni die communicant, videtur mihi, quod acriter reprehendendi sunt, quia nimio usu vilescere faciunt sacramentum vel potius ex levitate mulierum putatur esse desiderium quam ex devotione causatum." Cf. Martin Grabmann, *Mittelalterliches Geistesleben, Abhandlungen zur Geschichte der Scholastik und Mystik*, II (Munich, 1936), 372f.
[142] See Caesarius of Heisterbach's above-mentioned Book IX of *Dial. mirac.*; De Vooys, *Middelnederlandse Legenden en Exempelen*, pp. 230-240; Van der Vet, *Het Biënboec van Thomas van Cantimpré*, pp. 231-239.

treat with the curia.[143] Yet the *vitae* present unusual examples. While
theologians were almost unanimous in their praise of frequent or daily
Communion, but only for those whose hearts are pure and charitable,
the faithful showed increasing evidence of lukewarmness in their reception of the sacrament.[144] The Fourth Lateran Council prescribed a
minimum of one communion a year, at least at Easter.[145] Weekly communion was thus considered frequent, and daily mass was underlined
as a fact worthy of admiration, if not of open rebuke. It was for Lutgard
an unheard of penitence when she was compelled to omit frequent
communion out of obedience to the abbess.[146] Lukarde (d. 1304), a
Cistercian of Oberweimar, communed at first every Sunday and
holy-day, then in addition every Friday and during Lent daily.[147]
Agnes Blannbekin, the Viennese beguine who lived within the Franciscan orbit,[148] had burned for the body of the Lord when she was but
eleven; she was anxious to become a beguine "so that she could
commune more often."[149] Again, she was wont to commune weekly,[150]
despite the fear that it was excessive.[151] The Roman curia answered
the petition of Ida of Louvain by authorizing her to commune as often
as she desired.[152] Without resorting to such measures, the desire for
union with the Bridegroom through the eucharist nevertheless revealed itself intensely with all *mulieres religiosae*: stratagems to achieve
it, careful preparation, frequent and ecstatic communion, and advice

[143] *V. Id. Lov.*, 180 (33). It is possible that these friends were Dominicans.
[144] The archbishop of Tarragona prescribed in 1239 public reception of the body
of Christ by all canons (several of whom were not priests) on three feasts a year:
"Item praecipimus et mandamus quod omnes canonici teneantur confiteri singulis
annis proprio confessori, et in tribus anni sollemnitatibus publice recipiant Corpus
Christi" (*Comm. praev. de S. Bernardo Calvonio, Conf. Pont. vici in Catalaunia
Hispanica, AA. SS.*, LX, [October 26, xii], 67 no. 120; such a recommendation was
not reflected in conciliar legislation that year according to Mansi (XXIII, 513-518).
The canons regular in Como (1217) received similar instructions (*Com. praev. de
B. Guillielmo Episcopo Comensi, AA. SS.*, LVII [October 21, ix], 418 D [13]: "Com-
municaturi vero ter in anno, scilicet in Pasca, Pentecosten et in Nativitate Domini..."). Cf. Hildegarde's letter to the prelates of Mainz (1179): "Et a participatione
Domini corporis, quoniam per singulos fere menses ex consuetudine frequentavimus,
abstinuimus" (Ep. 47, *PL.* CXCVII, 219). Urban IV's recommendation for Clarisses
in 1263 (*V. Paulae de Montaldo, AA. SS.*, LXI [October 29, xiii], 218, 9). "Confession and reception of the Sacrament thrice a year" were prescribed by Francis for
tertiaries (Wadding, *Ann. Min.*, II, 11; cf. 79). Bonaventura, *De Profectura Religiosorum*, II, 77 (*Op. omn.*, ed. Peltier, XII, 438); *Breviloguium*, VI, 9 (*ibid.*, VII, 323);
cf. E. Dublanchy on the frequency of eucharistic communion in *DTC.* III, I (1911),
515-551, esp. 528-30. It is clear that weekly communion was in Bonaventura's time
the usual practice of Franciscan novices (*Regula Novitiorum*, c. 4, *Op. omn.*, XII,
317f).
[145] Can. 21, Hefele-Leclercq, V, 2, 1350.
[146] *V. Lutg.*, 198f (II, 14).
[147] *AB.*, XVIII (1899), 317.
[148] Chmel, p. 53 (cap. 18); cf. p. 47.
[149] *Ibid.*, p. 58 (cap. 39).
[150] *Ibid.*, pp. 58f (cap. 41); 65 (caps. 90-91).
[151] *Ibid.*, p. 96 (cap. 219).
[152] *V. Id., Lov.*, 180 (33).

to commune given to afflicted and tempted persons.[153] Ida of Louvain, as a novice, secretly slipped into the ranks of the professed.[154] Alice of Schaerbeek dedicated for her preparation the entire eve of the day when she intended to commune.[155]

On the other hand, eucharistic devotion occupies a considerably smaller place in the biographies of Cistercian monks. But it is there, for mention is made of the "daily" celebration of mass. Similarly, the desire for frequent communion obliged the abbot of Villers to restrict in to only Sundays.[156] Such testimony notwithstanding, the passionate, the ecstatic element does not loom as great as for the women.

Beguine statutes, on the contrary, do not reflect the same fervor. They belong to a period of institutionalization which is marked by a decline in spontaneity and close definition of minutiae. The beguines were expected to observe daily a number of religious practices of which attendance at mass and the reading of canonical hours were the most important.[157] Like confession the eucharist is met with variation in divers statutes. The earliest rule for the Bruges beguinage provided that the inmates should commune at Easter, Pentecost, Christmas, and Candlemas, unless allowed by their confessor to refrain. Without specific permission they could commune seven times a year: Easter, Pentecost, Assumption, All Saints', Christmas, Candlemas, and Annunciation.[158] Unlike Agnes Blannbekin, Ida of Nivelles was induced in part to leave the beguine community near her home town to join the Cistercian order by the very frequency at which the nuns of Citeaux took communion.[159] At Lierre the be-

[153] Cf. Roisin, *Hag. cist.*, p. 113.

[154] *V. Id., Lov.*, 182f (2).

[155] *V. Al. Scar.*, 474 (13); *V. Id. Lew.*, 112 (16); 116 (28); 120 (40). Hadewijch, too, was much devoted to the sacrament: her feast days were those of communion. She depicted Christ as giving himself to eat and drink as often as one wishes (Van Mierlo, in *Revue d'ascétique et de mystique*, V. [1924], 400).

[156] *Gesta*, MDT., III, 1355; *V. God. Sacr., ibid.*, 1342; CHD., I, 35 (ed. Strange, I, 43). In the last passage Godfrey receives the gift of tears. Cf. *V. God. Pach.*, 266; *V. Arn.*, Villar., 559 (5); *V. Gob.*, 382 (27); 394 (88). For the reaction in other congregations see, for example, the account by Friar Otto of the Franciscans in Vienna of his reception of Christ's body at Easter when he was eighteen (Chmel, p. 58, cap. 39). Endowed with the gift of tears, John Bonus wept profusely especially while praying and partaking of the sacrament. This was noted, above all, at Easter, 1233 when he was eating with Friars Preachers (*Comm. praev. de B. Joanne Bono Erem. Ord. S. Aug.*, AA. SS., LVII, October 22, ix), 720, no. 100; cf. *Comm. praev. de B. Paula de Montaldo*, AA. SS., LXI (October 29, xiii), 220, note b.

[157] Béthune, *Cartulaire*, p. 20; Antwerp, 1323, Philippen, *Begijnhoven*, p. 336, Bijl. IV; St. Trond (XIV C.), *ibid.*, pp. 310, 312, 313.

[158] Hoornaert, in *ASEB.*, LXXII (1929), 32f.

[159] "Ut etiam frequenter a sacerdote in missa sanctam acciperet Eucharistiam, sicut monialibus in ordine consuetudo est" (*V. Id. Niv.*, ed. Henriquez, p. 206, cf. 274). This usually means Sunday: *ibid.*, p. 209; *V. Id. Lew.*, 113 (18); *V. Lutg.*, 199 (II, 14); 203 (II, 39); Chmel, pp. 58-59 (cap. 41). During novitiate the prescribed or general practice was to allow communion three times a year and no more (*V. Id. Lov.*, ed. *Henriquez*, p. 410; cf. *V. Id. Niv.*, p. 209). The second reason why Ida

guines were to receive the sacrament four times a year,[160] while at Ghent attendance was required on all the principal holy-days and on the feasts of the Virgin.[161] Frederick II of Sierck, bishop of Utrecht, recommended in 1318 (October 6) that Franciscan tertiaries, with whom the beguines and beghards are often confused, should confess and receive the sacrament thrice a year—at Christmas, Easter, and Pentecost. Furthermore, in line with Boniface VIII's policy, they were to receive the eucharist from Friars Minor except at Easter, when deference must be shown to parochial authority.[162] As one approaches modern times the number of prescribed communions diminishes. Whereas at Diest, in the statutes of the fifteenth century, it is stipulated that the sacrament be celebrated every fortnight or every Sunday or even more often, later the passage was altered to read eighteen times a year, on the eighteen principal feasts.[163]

Similarly, the cult of the Heart of Jesus,[164] promoted by St. Bernard and the Cistercians, found its most ardent devotees in German and Belgian nunneries of the twelfth and thirteenth centuries. It was particularly Gertrude of Helfta (1256–1334) who was responsible for its popularity. In the Low Countries Lutgard of Aywières was peculiarly attracted to this cult, by revealing the bleeding wound on her side, dispensation of divine favors, and the exchange of hearts.[165] Alice of Schaerbeek, plagued by leprosy, took refuge in the wounds and heart of Christ.[166]

In conclusion, this entire motif could assume no more striking form than stigmatization, a phenomenon that has loomed large for students of St. Francis. Yet Mary of Oignies, after intensive contemplation of the Passion, had already undergone an identical experience about twelve years earlier.[167] According to her biographer, she had

embraced the Cistercian order grows out of the ideals of poverty and evangelism, in short, the *vita apostolica*: "Ut scilicet omnibus expedita curis nihil omnino proprium haberet."

[160] 1401, Philippen, *Begijnhoven*, p. 341; cf. p. 188.

[161] Béthune, *Cartulaire*, p. 20.

[162] Fredericq, *Corpus*, II, 76f.

[163] Philippen, in *BG.*, IV (1905), 336f; statutes of Herenthals beguinage (1461-1489), cap. 29. ibid., ser. III, vol. 1 (1949), 219. For subsequent developments see Antwerp statutes of 1664, Philippen, *Begijnhoven*, pp. 346f; cf. pp. 188-189.

[164] Berlière, *La dévotion au Sacré-Coeur dans l'ordre de Saint Benoît* (Maredsous, 1923); K. Richstätter, *Die Herz-Jesu-Verehrung des deutschen Mittelalters* (2nd ed., Munich, 1924); Jeanne Ancelet-Hustache, *Mechtilde de Magdebourg (1207-1282). Etude de psychologie religieuse* (Paris, 1926), pp. 344ff. Cf. Christ, *La Règle des Fins Amans*, p. 306, note to line 10.

[165] *V. Lutg.*, 192 (I, 2); 193f (I, 12-14); cf. Roisin, *Hag. cist.*, p. 110 and note 7.

[166] *V. Al. Scar.*, 474 (10); cf. 476 (30); cf. *V. Id. Lov.*, 173f (11); 167 (32), 177 (22); *V. Beat.*, ed. Henriquez, pp. 177, 153; *V. Od.*, 215; for the role of Villers see Roisin, *Hag. cist.*, pp. 110f, note 7.

[167] E. Amann, "Stigmatisation," *DTC.*, XIV, 2 (Paris, 1941), col. 2617: "Il paraît bien qu'il faut mettre avant lui (i.e., Francis) la béguine Marie d'Oignie...;" *VMO.*, 547f; cf. H. Cowan, "Stigmata," *Encyclopedia of Religion and Ethics*, XI (1925), 857-860.

made wounds on her body representing those of Christ during an
ecstasy when she saw at her side a seraph; when her body was washed
following her death, these wounds were disclosed.[168] If the fact is
authentic—both date of composition and authority vouch for priority—
her experience must have been independent of what was reported
concerning Francis two years before his death.[169] Whereas this transformation of oneself into a living crucifix cannot be detected prior
to the thirteenth century, it became increasingly common, especially
among women, from the time of Mary of Oignies on, evidently
making a spontaneous appearance in different places before the Franciscan account established a pattern.[170] In any case, the Oignies example testifies further to the vigor and independence of Belgian spirituality. After describing unwarranted translation and erroneous interpretation of Scripture by beguines in their conventicles, the author of
the *Collectio de Scandalis Ecclesiae* relates in the 1270's that one of
them was already enjoying wide fame because she was marked with the
stigmata. "If this is true," he adds, not untouched by contemporary
suspicion of feminine religiosity,[171] "let her not foster deceit but may
this be move openly known; if it is not true, let hyporisy and simu-
lation be confounded".[172]

[168] *VMO.*, 552 (22).
[169] I Cel., *AA. SS.*, L (October 4, ii), 708f, nos. 93-96; *Leg. Trib. Soc., ibid.*, 741,
no. 69; Bonaventura, *Vita, ibid.*, 778, nos. 195, 199-201.
[170] Amann, in *DTC.*, XIV, 2, col. 2617.
[171] See below, pp. 439-440.
[172] Döllinger, *Beiträge zur politischen, kirchlichen und Cultur-geschichte*,
III, 199.

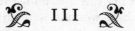

III

Citeaux and Beguine Spirituality

From the chronicle, *Gesta* and *vitae,* as well as the Polyptique, we possess for Villers-en-Brabant a goodly supply of material the like of which, in diversity and scope, is extant for no other Cistercian abbey in the Low Countries. Aulne must also have played a decisive role in directing the feminine religious movement, but in the absence of a coherent chronicle and ample spiritual biographies it is impossible to do more than offer a fragmentary picture based on scanty material in the brief lives of Wéry and Simon or elusive evidence contained in the cartulary. However wide was the jurisdiction of St. Bernard on the Scheldt, there is no concrete proof of close spiritual ties supplementing external relationship. The lively interest exhibited by the monks of Villers in the prophecies, visions, and ecstatic experiences of Hildegarde, though comprehended but imperfectly and through unreliable messengers, was undiminished during the next century as they established immediate contact with nuns and extraregulars on the periphery of monastic life. Having once made acquaintance with this fresh exuberant mysticism of the Rhineland, their taste for more of the supernatural and extraordinary was merely whetted. They were now able to converse daily with scores of these mystics, for the most part of local significance and minor stature. Yet taken as a whole they provide an exciting, fruitful chapter in the multifarious religious currents of the high middle ages.

Beguine spirituality was vigorous and diversified, springing from the Belgian soil itself. From a European-wide perspective it is one facet of a profound reform program, lay in appeal and abiding by the ascesis of the primitive church, which was set in motion throughout the west as early as the tenth century. The feminine religious movement had attained, before the arrival of the Burgundian monks, an importance sufficient to elicit the attention of Prémontré. More specifically, it represents above all in Liége, a peculiar devotion to the eucharist and the humanity of Christ, sometimes, to be sure, with

[1] For Villers hagiographical literature consult Roisin, *Hag. cist.,* pp. 23-73; Balau, *Sources,* pp. 475-486.

the accompaniment of marvellous phenomena and supernatural favors. While beguine life generally put a premium on chastity and evangelical poverty, it also was a response to socioeconomic demands of urban centers. The Belgian branch served consistently as a leaven against corruption within the fold and a counterpoise to external attacks.

The interaction between Cistercian and beguine was about equal. For the *mulieres religiosae* protection and guidance within the prescriptions of the rule and customs of Citeaux provided a safeguard against the infection of heresy. Such surveillance served at once as a defense against detractors and enemies and a means to assure, in the early stages, an acceptable place in ecclesiastical polity. Were the sermons of the abbot of Villers, Jacques de Bomal, extant they would undoubtedly illustrate this interaction and at the same time reveal the elements of mysticism as it was practiced at Nivelles.[2] On the other hand, however vast and complex these spiritual currents were in Belgium, the center always remained the piety of the beguines. Similarities with Bernardine piety are often less borrowings than points of contact in the emergence of the extraregular. On Cistercian nuns themselves it appears that beguine mentality left a deeper imprint than that of the order which had adopted them.[3] Conversely, to explain the subsequent divorce of Citeaux and the *mulieres religiosae* one may be led astray by the hostile legislation of the general chapters, for Villers and Aulne, as hagiographical sources clearly demonstrate, long continued to maintain close relations with these women, individually and collectively. A much more satisfactory explanation of the relaxing of these ties lies in the unquestioned ascendancy of the friars who completely eclipsed the older forms of monachism in spiritual effectiveness, administrative proficiency, and an awareness of lay yearnings.[4] Yet they too passed through substantially the same phases, from lukewarm, even hostile reaction to open espousal and supervision of the *cura monialium*.

Good reports concerning these *mulieres religiosae, quae beghinae dicuntur*, induced the knight Gobert d'Aspremont (ca. 1189–1263), after extensive pilgrimages to many abbeys, to journey to Nivelles. Although determined to don the Cistercian habit, he was still undecided as to a choice of monastery. Among the buiguines with whom he now associated was Emmeloth[5] to whom he opened his heart,

---

[2] *Cron. Villar. mon., Contin. II, MGH. SS.*, XXV, 211-212.

[3] In addition to De Moreau's contribution (*L'abbaye de Villers*, pp. xxvii-xlvi, 96-104) and Roisin's article in *RHE.*, XXXIX (1943) one must mention the latter's exhaustive study of Cistercian hagiography (*Hag. cist*) which sheds penetrating light on the several facets of this problem.

[4] Cf. Axters, "Dominikaansch Zielzorg in de Nederlanden der dertiende Eeuw," *OGE.*, XIII (1939), 149-184; id., *Geschiedenis van de Vroomheid*, II, 48-88.

[5] *V. Gob.*, 384, no. 37; *MGH. SS.*, XXV, 227; *MDT.*, III, 1320-1321. Cf. Roisin,

making known his search for a suitable house in which he might be "converted." She advised him to go to Villers where a "very perfect" monk, Abond by name, would tell him what course to pursue.[6] Through the latter's counsel Gobert chose Villers for his conversion.[7] A native of Huy, Abond (b. 1189)[8] had been designated by his family to learn letters in order that he might keep the accounts of his father, a man "wise in temporal affairs" but not sympathetic to religion.[9] When he displayed a precocity in religious matters, his sister Wiburge, who seems to have led a sort of beguine existence under the parental roof,[10] suggested that he adopt the monastic life. To define more closely his career Abond went to the recluse Yvette, but the attraction of Villers to which he was admitted at the age of seventeen for his noviciate[11] was stronger than that of Orval or Trois-Fontaines recommended by the widow.[12] She was probably the recluse of Huy whose older son entered the Cistercian abbey of Orval[13] and whose other son, after a dissolute life, was "converted" at her advice in Trois-Fontaines.[14] Indeed, her father, a burgher of some substance, had been persuaded by his daughter's example to identify himself with the religious life, first at Neufmoustier,[15] then at Villers.[16] Abond of Villers also arranged to have his sister, Mary, admitted to the nunnery of La Ramée. Engaged and close to marriage, the girl had given no thought to embracing the religious state, but her brother was able, so runs the hagiographical account, to persuade her immediately to give up her secular plans.[17] While another sister, Gela, entered the abbey of Val-Notre-Dame,[18] his two brothers, James and John, adopted the Cistercian

Hag. cist., pp. 38-41; Van Drival, in Annal. du cercle arch. d'Enghien, II (1883), 313 where the form Grimelothe is employed.

[6] V. Gob., 384, no. 38; 385, no. 41; MGH. SS., XXV, 227; MDT., III, 1353. This conversion took place between 1234 and 1238, most likely in 1237 (Roisin, Hag. cist., pp. 35, 39).

[7] V. Gob., 385, no. 41; MGH. SS., XXV, 227.

[8] The Vita Fratris Abundi Monachi Villariensis is preserved in codex 19525 of the Bibliothèque royale de Belgique, but its last folios have been truncated. The preface and table of contents have been edited by Fr. de Reiffenberg in Annuaire de la Bibliothèque royale de Belgique, VII (1846), 96-101. Fragments of the vita are also to be found in the Gesta, MDT., III, 1349-1354; MGH. SS., XXV, 232. For the MSS. problems consult Roisin, Hag. cist., pp. 34-35; for the authorship, ibid., pp. 35-38. Cf. De Moreau, L'abbaye de Villers, pp. 98-102.

[9] V. Ab., f. 2v; MDT., III, 1350.

[10] V. Ab., f. 3r.

[11] Ibid., f. 4v-5r; MDT., III, 1350; cf. De Moreau, L'abbaye de Villers, p. 99

[12] V. Ab., f. 5r. For the biography of the recluse, see Vita B. Juetta sive Jutta Vidua Reclusa, AA. SS., II (January 13, ii), 145-169.

[13] Ibid., 153, no. 42.

[14] Ibid., 157, no. 59.

[15] Ibid., 153, no. 40.

[16] Ibid., 153, no. 41.

[17] V. Ab., f. 14r-15r.

[18] Ibid., f. 2v.

habit at Val St. Lambert in spite of their father's remonstrance.[19] That Villers also had communication with *mulieres sanctae* at Namur appears from the report that Caesarius of Heisterbach gives of an *inclusa* or recluse Ida, who by prophetic light saw a flame on the head of a monk of the monastery while he was offering mass at Namur.[20] Similarly, Simon of Aulne entrusted to a Cistercian community one of his spiritual daughters.[21]

Among the monks whom the *Gesta* mention as having grown dissatisfied with other forms of monachism was Godfrey Pachomius from St. Gertrude, a house of canons regular of St. Augustine in Louvain,[22] recently founded by Henry I of Brabant[23] exclusively for nobles. Godfrey had been much disturbed about the state of his soul in a community which resounded with the noise' of the world and which women could penetrate even to the dormitory.[24] He drew along with him his two brothers, an older one Renier, who was then studying at Paris, and the younger Thomas,[25] who afterwards wrote his biography for their sister Aleide, a Cistercian nun at Parc-les-Dames.[26] Following his wife's death the father Renier, who had frequented the court of the duke of Brabant, also asked to be admitted as a *conversus*.[27] The mother herself " had had a holy and monastic life in so far as marriage allowed." She was wont to impose on herself vigils, prayers, discipline, and fasts, and to carry gifts to the needy and infirm who might live some distance away.[28]

The Cistercian order undertook to aid the poor[29] by granting life pensions to those in moderate or reduced circumstances[30] and by establishing inns and hospitals for the sick and infirm. However parsimonious certain abbots might be in the conduct of their own

[19] *Ibid.*, f. 2v.

[20] CHD. (IX, 31), (ed. Strange), 188; cf. Wilmet, in *ASAN.*, VI (1859-1860), 58.

[21] *V. Simonis*, f. 217r.

[22] *Gesta*, MDT., III, 1347; *AB.*, XIV (1895), 264.

[23] 1206, MF., I, 114; Wauters, *TC.*, III, 265.

[24] *AB.*, XIV, 265.

[25] *Idem; Gesta*, MDT., III, 1347; on Renier, see *ibid.*, 1348f; cf. Sanderus, *Chorogr. sac. Brab.*, I, 451.

[26] *AB.* XIV, 263. For her religious precocity and early admission to the nunnery, see *ibid.*, 265, cap. 3.

[27] *Ibid.*, 264; Sanderus, *Chorogr. sac. Brab.*, I, 450; cf. De Moreau, *L'abbaye de Villers*, p. 94. They made their profession in 1216 (*AB.*, XIV, 265-266). The father lived for eight more years (*ibid.*, 264); his oldest son died after six years of religious life (*ibid.*, 266). Godfrey died in 1262 (*ibid.*, 267-268).

[28] *Ibid.*, 264-265.

[29] Cf. H. d'Arbois de Jubainville, *Etude des abbayes cisterciennes*, pp. 202-205, 219-224. For Villers, see De Moreau, *L'abbaye de Villers*, pp. 261-266; *Cron. Villar. contin. II a, MGH. SS.*, XXV, 214. For Aulne, see the analysis of several donations in favor of the poor at the gate in Devillers, in *Annales du cercle arch, de Mons*, IV (1863), 272, no. 148 (an. 1224), and note 2; 276, no. 168 (an. 1232), and note 4; id., "Notice sur le chartrier de l'abbaye d'Alne," *ibid.*, IX (1869), 231.

[30] De Moreau, *L'abbaye de Villers*, pp. 153-160.

affairs, they were in the main generous to the poor.[31] The "gates" where the needy of the countryside could be assisted were entrusted to the *portarius,* in addition to his ordinary duties,[32] as Caesarius of Heisterbach illustrated on several occasions in his *Dialogue on Miracles.*[33] From the days of William of Brussels (1221—1236) the gate at Villers was provided with special funds.[34] Alms consisted of food, clothing, and shoes. The general chapters prescribed that although guests were to be better fed than the monks, they were not to receive meat.[35]

The *vitae* describe amply the charity of monks and lay brethren in episodes which closely resemble experiences of the Poverello of Umbria. Gobert d'Aspremont is a case in point. Finding an indigent beguine before the gates of Villers, he hastened to give her a pair of shoes.[36] When he was unable, on another occasion, to relieve a half-naked beggar in the bitter cold, he divested himself as evidence of his compassion.[37] The funds with which Gobert was entrusted he distributed to the poor so freely that a maximum amount which he must not exceed had to be set by his superior.[38] This is but one example of the concern shown by the Brabançon monastery in the poor problem.[39] At the outset of a journey the monks were accustomed to ask the abbot to provide them with money for the poor whom they might encounter on the way.[40] Godfrey Pachomius shared his meals with the poor. He visited the sick in the hospital of the monastery and, anxious about their souls,[41] held mass for them.[42] For several years he collected in the orchards fallen fruit which he distributed to the needy.[43] Nor did the elements hamper these efforts.[44] His brother Renier gleaned the fields after the harvest for the same purpose.[45] The *conversus* John of Witterzee, master of the grange Chenoit, was

[31] *Cron. Villar. mon., MGH. SS.,* XXV, 200-202, nos. 11, 16.
[32] *Usus Ordinis Cisterciensis,* cap. 87 (J. Paris, *Nomasticon Cisterciense,* pp. 192-193); cap. 119 (*ibid.,* p. 241); cap. 120 (*ibid.,* pp. 241-243). Cf. *Reg. Bened.,* cap. 53.
[33] *Dial. mirac.,* (IV, 31), ed. Strange, I, 202; (IV, 65), I, 233-234; (IV, 67), I, 235.
[34] *Cron. Villar. mon., MGH. SS.,* XXV, 200.
[35] Canivez, *Statuta,* I, 63, no. 33 (an. 1157); cf. *ibid.,* IV, 166, no. 23 (an. 1412).
[36] *V. Gob.,* 390, nos. 68-69.
[37] *Ibid.,* 390, no. 71.
[38] *Ibid.,* 389, no. 65; for another example of his charity, see *ibid.,* 392-393, no. 81.
[39] Roisin, *Hag. cist.,* pp. 127ff; De Moreau, *L'abbaye de Villers,* pp. 261-266. Caesarius of Heisterbach in *Dial. mirac.* (IV, 40, ed. Strange, I, 226-227) gives an illustration of scarcity restricting charity.
[40] *V. God. Pach.,* cap. xi, *AB.,* XIV, 266. For the account of a visit to the Parc-les-Dames in Louvain and dispensing alms to the poor, see *ibid.,* cap. xii, p. 266; cf. *Cron. Villar. mon., MGH. SS.,* XXV, 200.
[41] *AB.,* XIV, 267, cap. xvi.
[42] *Ibid.,* XIV, 266, cap. xii.
[43] *Ibid.,* XIV, 266, caps. xii-xiii.
[44] *Idem.* For an anecdote which is reminiscent of Francis of Assisi, see *V. Arn. Villar.* (II, 1, 4), 566. Cf. *AB.,* XIV, 267, cap. xiv.
[45] *Gesta,* MDT., III, 1349.

returning one day to the abbey with carts laden with wheat. Learning that the beguines of Nivelles were in dire need, he promptly rerouted the convoy to their "convents."[46] Arnulf's biographer relates how he took pigs to indigent families and distributed additional supplies of bread to the beggars at the "gate."[47] The chronicle, in praising the charity of William of Brussels, makes special mention of these *pauperes virgines*.[48]

Although details are not so plentiful for Aulne, this monastery appears to have exhibited the same interest in charity. Prior Wéry of Aulne, *magister conversorum laicorum* (d. 1217),[49] who had been converted by Bernard of Clairvaux from a canon of St. Lambert at Liége to the Cistercian habit, employed every possible means to relieve the wretched: soliciting funds from his brethren,[50] a lecture to the *conversi* in charge of them,[51] permission to keep money, gifts of his own clothing and shoes,[52] secret distribution of bags of flour in times of want,[53] and the throwing of pieces of money to the poor who followed him when the community went out to work in the fields.[54]

Thomas of Cantimpré comments in his *Bonum Universale de Apibus* on the number of Cistercian monks and others in the cloister who abided by long fasts, severe discipline for lengthy periods, almost continuous silence, coarse habit, and night vigils. In all these things they enjoyed meager fare and scarcely any rest, nor had they received letters of indulgence for their sins.[55] Nevertheless as a part of the program against *gyrovagi* and other vagabond clerks and monks the council convoked by Robert de Courçon in Paris in 1212 or 1213 had stipulated that when a monk or canon regular undertook a journey with his superior's permission, he was to be provided with horses and other necessities in order not to dishonor his position.[56] The Cistercian order took similar steps at the same time (1211) by delegating the abbot of Morimond to check on the monks of Monthéron in the diocese of Lausanne who, it was said, were begging from door to door. The measure was intended to prevent scandal to the order and injury

---

46 *Ibid.*, III, 1365 C.
47 *V. Arn. Villar.*, 566-567, nos. 4-5.
48 *Cron. Villar. mon.*, MGH. SS., XXV, 200. For the *conversus*, Herman, see *Gesta, MDT.*, III, 1362f; cf. *V. Id. Lov.*, 167, no. 35.
49 *Vita Werrici*, in CCHB., I, 445-463; De Theux, *Le chapitre de Saint Lambert*, I, 154-155.
50 CCHB., I, 447.
51 *Ibid.*, 449.
52 *Ibid.*, 451-453, 458.
53 *Ibid.*, 459-460.
54 *Ibid.*, 461.
55 *Bon. Univ. de Apibus*, II, 3, 12.
56 II, can. 11, Mansi, XXII, 828; cf. synod of Château-Gontier (1231), can. 28, Mansi, XXIII, 239.

to individual souls.[57] As relaxation of such austerity was officially
countenanced for older monachism, the original goals set by the mendicant orders acquired added significance. The Friars Preachers, ema-
ciated by continuous studies and vigils, were without money in their
belt. Without horses and carriages they travelled about preaching on
foot and with tired limbs. But what of the Friars Minor? They were
girt with a harsh cord and, without cowl or hood, they wore only a
tunic. They walked barefooted in the snow "as if it were wool,"
begging their bread daily like the poor.[58]

One member of Villers who counted several spiritual sisters among
the *mulieres religiosae* was Arnulf of Brussels, one of the most famous
novices Charles admitted. As a *conversus,* he spent his life either at
the abbey or in granges dependent on it, notably at Sart-Risbart,
Chenoit, and Neuve-Cour,[59] during the abbacy of Charles and his
first three successors, Conrad of Urach (1209–1214), Walter of Utrecht
(1214–1221), and William of Brussels. His biography, better than most
hagiographical accounts of this school, reveals in a series of episodes
how intimately the Cistercian monks were acquainted with the local
feminine religious movement. For these women Arnulf himself did
rigorous penance.[60] One of the recluses near the abbey called him her
"father";[61] another "had with him only one heart and one soul."[62]
He helped a poor girl, Gertrude by name, to fulfil her desire to become
a recluse by having a cell built for her with the alms which he himself
had solicited from wealthy persons.[63] Nor did he fail to visit his
spiritual daughters still in the world[64] or who had withdrawn to a
reclusorium.[65] The biographer moreover reports that he possessed a
miraculous knowledge of mystical gifts granted to these women.[66] As
further evidence of interpenetration we may cite from the same *vita*
the case of a woman named Alice, living next to Neuve-Cour, whose
daughter Clementia was plagued by evil spirits at night. For relief the
mother took her to the grange, then under Master Gumbert[67] who had
received in La Cambre confessions of nuns and offered them religious
instruction.[68] Theophania, the mistress of a hospital beside Notre-
Dame in Paris, having heard of Arnulf, desired to converse with him.
Since distance prevented this, she asked a cleric from Brabant who

---

[57] Canivez, *Statuta,* I, 385, no. 32.
[58] Thomas of Cantimpré, *BUA.,* II, 3, 12.
[59] *V. Arn. Villar.,* 568, no. 11; 572, no. 62; 567, no. 4.
[60] *Ibid.,* 565, no. 34.
[61] *Ibid.,* 572, no 33.
[62] *Ibid.,* 575, no. 47.
[63] *Ibid.,* 577, no. 58; cf. *ibid.,* 566-567, nos. 3-5.
[64] *Ibid.,* 577, no. 57.
[65] *Ibid.,* 572, no. 34.
[66] *Ibid.,* 575, nos. 47-48.
[67] *Ibid.,* 576, nos. 52-53.
[68] Sanderus, *Chorogr. sac. Brab.,* I, 445.

was studying there to convey her greetings and blessing to him.[69] She soon experienced rapture due to his intercession. A priest, fearing that he was hypocritical in his labors, was advised by a *mulier religiosa* to consult Arnulf.[70]

Other hagiographical writings also provide an insight into the interior life of the recluses and beguines of the Nivelles area. The two letters from the cantor Thomas, brother and biographer of Godfrey Pachomius, to his sister Aleide offer a specimen of the ascetic, scriptural, and mystical subjects developed by the two monks on a lofty vein when they made a visit to her.[71] The biography of Ida of Nivelles describes an ecstatic colloquy between the nun and an abbot of her order.[72] Ulrich, a cleric from Cologne who had become a monk at Villers, was acquainted with a recluse Oda who was reputed to offer divine revelations.[73] From the incident of a Cistercian monk who was sent by his abbot, "a friend of Mary of Oignies," to be cured of his illness, we have evidence of the interest this unnamed monastery took in her.[74] Although the Bollandist concluded that this abbey was either Aulne or Cambron,[75] it may well be that this is a reference to Villers. Abbot Walter took delight in relating how a monk was sent to a Cistercian nunnery to seek from a nun the gift of tears three times a week.[76] Mary in turn had had her own early religious impressions molded by the monks and *conversi* of the Cistercian order, presumably from Villers. Adopting the role characteristic of the beguines who occupied a position midway between the lay and regular world, she was wont, says her biographer, to admire the habit of the Cistercian monks who occasionally wandered past the parental home in Nivelles. A precocious interest in the monastic status induced her to abandon the pursuits of children and to follow in the footsteps of these monks.[77] As further proof of the hold of Citeaux on Mary, Jacques de Vitry relates that St. Bernard appeared to her in a vision.[78] That she was informed with Bernardine spirituality is beyond conjecture.[79]

[69] *V. Arn. Villar.*, 574-575, nos. 45-46.

[70] *Ibid.*, 573, no. 38.

[71] The *V. God. Pach.* makes allusion to a visit of the two brothers to Parc-les-Dames (*AB.*, XIV, 266, cap. XI). Cf. Roisin in *RHE.*, XXXIX, 372 and note 3.

[72] *V. Id. Niv.*, ed. Henriquez, pp. 256-268.

[73] *Gesta, MDT.*, III, 1355; *CHD.* (IX, 31), ed. Strange, II, 188; cf. (III, 33), I, 150ff. For the revelation that another recluse at Nivelles had concerning Renier, see Sanderus, *Chorogr. sac. Brab.*, I, 450.

[74] *VMO.*, 561, nos. 62-63.

[75] *Ibid.*, 561, note g. But for the abbot of Aulne as visitor of Aywières see *V. Lutg.*, 209 A-B (III, 20).

[76] *CHD.* (II, 19), ed. Strange, I, 88-89.

[77] *VMO.*, 550 B; cf. Greven, *Anfänge*, pp. 89-90.

[78] *VMO.*, 567 D, no. 90.

[79] For other examples of Mary's relations with the Cistercian order, see *ibid.*, 553-554, nos. 31-32.

Thomas of Cantimpré consciously traces the spiritual career of Lutgard in three books corresponding to the rungs of the mystical ladder: [80] (*1*) a novitiate in the Benedictine house of St. Catherine at St. Trond; (2) espousal of the Cistercian rule at Aywières in 1206 at the recommendation of John de Liro and Christine of St. Trond, better known as Christine Mirabilis; (*3*) her trials from blindness as she achieved perfection during the last eleven years of her life. The life is replete with incidents, factual or imagined, which cut across the regular and extraregular world alike. Among those for whom she interceded were a nun of Parc-les-Dames whose brother had been an apostate from the Friars Minor for twelve years;[81] Duchess Mary of Brabant, daughter of the "late" Philip Augustus; and Godfrey, castellan of Brussels.[82] To Abbot John and a lay brother William, both of Afflighem,[83] she offered encouragement during their visits, for she was especially fond of the brethren of this Benedictine monastery because of the fervor of their religion.[84] Just as Jacques de Vitry was in considerable measure molded by Mary of Oignies, so Thomas of Cantimpré attributed to Lutgard *sicut ad specialissimam mihi matrem* peace of mind and freedom from temptation. Self-assurance, he adds, had been gained sixteen years before when, as a youth approaching priesthood but not yet a Dominican, he had sought from her solace from the fear and tortured doubts which beset him in the confessional.[85]

A few days before his death in 1262, Godfrey Pachomius requested permission to visit the *sanctae animae* at Nivelles whose "conversation" he knew was more of heaven than earth. His biographer evidently intended to recount an episode in this circle, but the text ends abruptly with the words: "Est autem ibi quaedam beata anima semper languens..."[86] "There was at Nivelles," reports the chronicler of Villers on the authority of Caesarius of Heisterbach,[87] "a virgin named Tiedala who enjoyed grace and a glory no less by holiness of her life than by the celebrity of her name." On Christmas night the

---

[80] *V. Lutg.*, prol., 189 D.

[81] *Ibid.*, 202 B-C (II, 34).

[82] *Ibid.*, 202 D-E (II, 36).

[83] *Ibid.*, 201 E (II, 27); 207 F (III, 16).

[84] *Ibid.*, 207 F (III, 16); 201 B (II, 24): Afflighem "omnium illius ordinis ordinatissimo coenobio." Here Thomas imputes to Lutgard praise for this Benedictine house which he bestowed on it twice in *BUA*. It was "apud Affligeniense monasterium Brabantiae, in regulari observatione strictissimum" that Bishop Guy of Cambrai died (I, 5, 4); again, it was qualified as *religione probatissimum* and *in charitate praecipuum* (II, 13, 4). Cf. Sanderus, I, 39.

[85] *V. Lutg.*, 202-203 (II, 38).

[86] *V. God. Pach.*, 267, cap. 26.

[87] *Cron. Villar. mon.*, *MGH. SS.*, XXV, 205-206. The passage occurs in *Libri VIII Miraculorum* (I, 5) (Hilka, *Wundergeschichten*, III, 24-25; Kaufmann, *Caesarius von Heisterbach*, pp. 175-176).

CITEAUX AND BEGUINE SPIRITUALITY

child Jesus appeared to her and came to rest in her arms. But she cried out: "I shall not be able to taste fully this sweet vision if you do not permit my friend, a monk at Villers, to enjoy you in the same way." She was soon transported to the abbey and presented the child to the monk who was celebrating mass. The latter, wishing to know the cause of this apparition, came to visit her some days later. On his arrival the beguine said to him: "I know why you have come," and proceeded to describe in detail the favor of which they had both been recipients.

In the *Libri VIII Miraculorum,* written in 1225 or 1226,[88] the Cistercian devotes four chapters of Book I to brief case studies in order to arrive at a judgment of the feminine religious movement as a whole in the diocese of Liége. Beside the full-sized portrait of a Mary of Oignies or Lutgard of St. Trond, the sketch of Tiedala is of course a miniature, but nonetheless illuminating. Another *mulier sancta* who lived in Brabant also had a spiritual friendship with another monk of Villers.[89] The other two women in this galaxy were Heilwigis[90] and Ida,[91] both residing in Brussels. Furthermore it is possible that the *mulier religiosa* mentioned by Caesarius in *Homiliae II*[92] was none other than Mary, the report being derived from the *VMO.*[93] There is no doubt, therefore, that Nivelles was regarded by the Cistercian as well as by Jacques de Vitry and Thomas of Cantimpré as the fountainhead of this socio-mystical current. The *Dialogue on Miracles* no less than the *Libri VIII Miraculorum* is instinct with the naive faith and self-effacement of these nuns, recluses, and the *animae sanctae* in general.[94] Just as these *mulieres religiosae* felt the leaven of Bernardine piety, so the austerity which the Belgian extraregulars illustrated in their lives was well adapted in the beginning to the *arctior religio* of Citeaux.[95] To make his observations more impressionable Caesarius relates to a novice a number of events that have happened in Cistercian houses in the north in their own day.[96]

---

[88] Greven, in *H.J.*, XXXV (1914), 50; Hilka, *Wundergeschichten*, III, 13f. Cf. Poncelet. "Note sur les Libri VIII Miraculorum de Césaire d'Heisterbach," *AB.*, XXI (1902), 45-52.

[89] I, 4 (Hilka, *Wundergeschichten*, III, 22-24; Kaufmann, *op. cit.*, pp. 173-174).

[90] I, 6 (Hilka, *Wundergeschichten*, III, 25; Kaufmann, *op. cit.*, pp. 176-177).

[91] I, 7 (Hilka, *Wundergeschichten*, III, 26-27; Kaufmann, *op. cit.*, pp. 177-178).

[92] Hilka, *Wundergeschichten*, I, 128-129.

[93] Greven (*HJ.*, XXXV, 51-53) maintained that Caesarius of Heisterbach knew Jacques de Vitry's *VMO.* when he wrote the *Homiliae* before the *Libri VIII Miraculorum*. Thus he used it when he wrote the latter. Cf. Hilka, *Wundergeschichten*, III, 26, note 3; Schroeder, in *AHVN.*, LXXV (1903), 3.

[94] *CHD.*, (III, 6), ed. Strange, I, 116-120; (III, 47), I, 166; (IV, 84), I, 251; (V, 46), I, 331; (V, 47), I, 322f; (V, 50), I, 334-335; (VI, 34), I, 386.

[95] Cf. Schönbach, *Sitz.-ber. d. k. Akad. d. Wissenschaften in Wien, Phil.-Hist. Kl.,* CLIX, Abh. 4 (1908), 31.

[96] "Aliqua ex his quae in ordini nostro nostris temporibus miraculose gesta sunt" (*CHD.*, Prol., ed. Strange, I, 1).

In addressing Foulques of Toulouse Jacques de Vitry summarizes the spiritual experiences of these *mulieres sanctae* who, out of love for the heavenly Spouse, spurned carnal pleasures and despised the riches of the world. This was an age of renunciation and ecstasy. It was being described by a man whose realism and practical nature was offset by a peculiar fondness for visions and supernatural graces. It was an intense life, marked by raptures, excited by the mystery of the eucharist, and carried aloft by prayers, which is but rarely glimpsed in prosaic statutes. Such experiences, of course ,touched only rare members of medieval society.

You saw some of these women dissolved with such a particular and marvellous love toward God that they languished with desire, and for years had rarely been able to rise from their cots. They had no other infirmity, save that their souls were melted with desire of Him, and, sweetly resting with the Lord, as they were comforted in spirit they were weakened in body. They cried in their hearts, though from modesty their lips dissimulated: "Fulcite me floribus, stipate me malis, quia amore langueo" (*Cant*. II. 5). The cheeks of one were seen to waste away, while her soul was melted with the greatness of her love. Many had the taste of honey on their tongues when their hearts experienced the sweetness of meditation... Another's flow of tears had made visible furrows down her face... Others were drawn with such intoxication of spirit that in sacred silence they would remain quiet a whole day, 'while the King was on His couch' (i.e. at meat), with no sense of feeling for things without them, so that they could not be roused by clamor or feel a blow. I saw another whom for thirty years her Spouse had so zealously guarded in her cell, that she could not leave it herself, nor could the hands of others drag her out. I saw another who sometimes was seized with ecstasy five-and-twenty times a day, in which state she was motionless, and on returning to herself was so enraptured that she could not keep from displaying her inner joy with movements of the body, like David leaping before the Ark. Some in receiving the bread of Him who came down from heaven, obtained not only refreshment in their hearts, but a sensation in their mouths sweeter than honey and the honey-comb... So eagerly did they hasten after the fragrance of the sacrament that they were unable to go without it long: they found neither consolation nor rest, but languished unless their souls were frequently refreshed by the sweetness of this food. Let the infidel heretics blush who do not partake of this food. I knew one of these holy women who craved to be refreshed by the flesh of the Lamb; a real Lamb no longer able to bear to see her languish, offered itself to her and thus she recovered. And I saw still another who after she had lain for some time dead, before burial was permitted by the Lord to return to the flesh, that she might on earth do purgatorial penance; and long was she thus afflicted of the Lord, sometimes rolling herself in the fire, and in the winter standing in frozen water.[97]

Evidence of the renown of the spirituality of the Nivelles beguines needs to be supplemented by the episode which Guillaume de Nangis

---

[97] *VMO.*, 548 D-549 A; adapted in part after Taylor, *Medieval Mind*, I, 461-462, with courtesy of the Harvard University Press.

relates for the reign of Philip III, king of France (1270–1285), in his *Gesta Philippi Tertii Francorum Regis* and in a French translation.[98] The account at once illustrates the appeal the Belgian beguines sometimes enjoyed even at the French court and points out how much Philip was victimized by court intrigue.[99] Elsewhere we shall examine this evidence for contemporary opinion concerning *mulieres religiosae*. When Mary of Brabant, sister of Duke John I of Brabant and second wife of the French king, was accused through the machinations of the royal favorite, Pierre de la Broce, the chamberlain,[100] of poisoning Louis (d. 1276), oldest son of her husband by a previous marriage with Isabella of Aragon, and conspiring with enemies of state, Philip III, who hesitated to believe her guilty resorted to a vidame of Laon, a "very bad" Sarabite, and a beguine at Nivelles, all three with a reputation for supernatural gifts but "not approved by any religion." The Latin text further labels all three *pseudoprophetae*. The French translation, on the contrary, presents a more subtle appraisal, regarding the beguine, for example, as *une devine* conducting herself *comme sainte fame et de bonne vie*. Another version had it that the king was being slandered by a canon of Laon who claimed that two *mulieres sanctae* in the diocese of Liége, Aalis the leper, and Isabella of Sparbeek, had suggested that Philip had sinned against nature.[101] According to Guillaume de Nangis, others suspected that these *pseudoprophetae* had been bribed by Pierre de la Broce to speak out against the queen and the Brabançons. The king, subjected to such intrigue despatched Matthew, abbot of St. Denis, in whom he placed complete confidence, and Pierre de Benais, bishop of Bayeux and kinsman of Pierre de la Broce, to visit the beguine and learn the truth concerning his son's death. The bishop, having preceded the abbot to the beguine, obtained a reply but refused to divulge it on the grounds that it was a confessional secret. When the abbot reached her she claimed to have already communicated with his companion and refused to speak further on the matter. Discontented with the reports, the king next charged the bishop of Dol and Arnold of Wesemael, who was then a Knight Templar, with the duty of interrogating the beguine. This time, probably due to Arnold's presence—for he was a man not to be trifled with—it was reported that the queen was innocent. Following her exoneration she founded out of gratitude about 1280 in the parish of St. Syr a hospital

---

[98] Bouquet, XX (1840), 502 (Latin text), 503 (French text); cited below, pp. 450f.

[99] Lavisse, *Histoire de France*, III, 2 (Paris, 1901), 103-106; Tarlier and Wauters, *Géog. et hist. des communes belges. Prov. de Brab. Ville de Nivelles* (1862), p. 33; id., *Duc Jean I*, pp. 55-58.

[100] Lavisse, *Histoire de France*, III, 2, 104.

[101] *Ibid.*, 105.

for the poor beguines, supposedly the beguinage of La Royauté at Nivelles.[102]

To these *dilectae in Christo filiae, mulieres religiosae quae Begginae vulgariter appelantur* and *virgines continentes* clerics, religious, and laymen appealed with full confidence in the efficacy of their intercession to obtain cure of body and soul,[103] to be preserved from danger,[104] to receive supernatural favors,[105] to seek advice concerning a vocation,[106] expiation of sin,[107] or the foundation of a monastery. An Augustinian abbot having died, his sister, a nun in the same order, fearing for his salvation, begged Alice of Schaerbeek through mutual friends to tell the state of her brother's soul: she learned that it had been released from purgatory.[108] A friend of St. Nicholas found among his relics a bone of an unidentified saint without letters. He brought them to Mary of Oignies to be certified. She readily perceived the value and authenticity *in spiritu,* but did not know the meaning of the inscription A.I.O.L. without consulting a priest.[109] Eve, the recluse of St. Martin, hesitated to embrace this austere life until Juliana promised to visit her and give her solace.[110] We have seen how Abond determined Gobert to choose Villers for conversion. Arnulf was responsible for the building of Argensolles in Champagne and Val-des-Roses on the land of the Berthouts of Malines.[111] Barthelemy of Tirlemont did not undertake the foundation of Nazareth without first having recourse to the revelation of his daughter Beatrice.[112] Outsiders found in the spiritual conversations, even though, says Thomas of Cantimpré, they could not understand them, the heights to which their mystical contemplation brought them.[113] They exploited in particular their extraordinary gifts;[114] they tried to see them in ecstasy; with the

---

[102] See above pp. 66-67

[103] *V. Arn. Villar.*, 566, no. 2; 571, no. 28; 574, nos. 40-41; 576, nos. 52-53; in addition to examples cited above, *V. Lutg.*, 193 (I, 12); 200-201 (II, 20, 22, 25, 28); 202-204 (II, 34-43); 205 (III, 5). For a similar case, though rarer in the Dominican world, *Ann. Colm. Mai.*, *MGH. SS.*, XVII, 203.

[104] *VMO.*, 578 (20); Ep. I, *ZKG.*, XIV, 102.

[105] *V. Arn. Villar.*, 571 (29); 574-575 (45-46); *V. Ab.*, in *MDT.*, III, 1351f; *V. Lutg.*, 202 (34); *Gesta*, MDT., III, 1358; for Juliana of Cornillon, see Simenon, *op. cit.*, pp. 37-49.

[106] *VMO.*, 564 (77-78); *Suppl.*, 579 (22); Juliana (*V. Jul. Cornel.*, 466, 26) predicts that a bishop of Liége will never obtain the archbishopric of Rheims, presumably a reference to Hugh of Pierrepont.

[107] *Gesta*, MDT., III, 1364; *V. Arn. Villar.*, 577 (55); 575-576 (49).

[108] *V. Al. Scar.*, 476 (29).

[109] *VMO.*, 567-568 (91). The Bollandist (*ibid.*, 568, note g) identifies Aiolis with St. Aigulphus, or Aiulfus, archbishop of Bourges (811-835) (*Vita S. Aygulfis episcopi Bituricensis, AA. SS.*, XVIII [May 22, v], 177-180; cf. Adolphe Regnier, in *DHGE.*, I, 1142-1143; *GC.*, II, 21-22).

[110] See above, pp. 300, 306.

[111] See above, p. 113.

[112] *V. Beat.* 146.

[113] *V. Lutg.*, 194 (I, 15); 201 (II, 27).

[114] *V. Arn. Villar.*, 577 (56-57).

passion or the eucharist acting as the stimulus;[115] they verified ecstatic phenomena;[116] and their visions and revelations were revered.[117]
Hadewig, a recluse of St. Remacle near Liége, was accustomed to
relate how many things Juliana had predicted to her through the
spirit of prophecy.[118]

Nor were Villers abbots content with assisting the *mulieres religiosae* through their monks. Jacques de Bomal, the twentieth abbot
from 1276 until his abdication in 1283, often went to Nivelles to
preach.[119] Without doubt the greater part of his audience, the most
likely to be inflamed, as the chronicler puts it, "with love for the
heavenly land," was made up of the beguines of this town. Abbot
Arnulf of Louvain continued to live in the monastery after his
abdication. Whenever he went out with a companion, it was to
mingle with the recluses and holy souls in the neighborhood.[120] The
notice on Abbot Charles makes allusion to a *matrona* who could find
no consolation after his death. She was presumably one of his personal charges.[121] Conrad of Urach is reported to have visited diligently Mary of Oignies' tomb whenever he was in Brabant.[122] It is also
correct to surmise that he was the unnamed bishop, mentioned in her
biography,[123] who journeyed north from Italy to pay homage to
her memory. When a monk died, one of these mystics, it was claimed,
went into ecstasy.[124]

The seven bodies transferred *retro cancellum maioris altaris*—that
is, behind the high altar—in 1269[125] were those of four monks of
Villers: Abond of Huy,[126] the *conversus* Arnulf, also known as Arnold

---

[115] *V. Id. Lew.*, 117 (32).
[116] *V. Lutg.* 200-201 (I, 23).
[117] *V. God. Pach*, caps, xviii-xxi, *AB.*, XIV, 267; *V. Arn. Villar.*, 578 (61); 566
(2): knights who lived in the vicinity of his grange came to see Arnulf and
commend themselves to his prayers; he then predicted to them what would
happen; *V. Jul. Cornel.*, 450 (21); *V. Lutg.*, 193-194 (I, 11, 17); 199-200 (I. 18);
V. Id. Lov., 162 (13) (where Ida received the stigmata); *V. Al. Scar.*, 477 (33-34);
V. Gert. ab. Oosten, 352 (22, 25-28). For Juliana's revelation of the feast of Corpus
Christi, see *l.c.*, 453 (34).
[118] *V. Jul. Cornel.*, 453 (34).
[119] *Cron. Villar, mon., Contin. II, MGH. SS.*, XXV, 211-212.
[120] *Ibid.*, 208.
[121] *Gesta, MGH. SS.*, XXV, 225-226.
[122] *Cron. Villar. mon., ibid.*, 199; Thomas of Cantimpré, *BUA.*, I, 9, 2 (p. 37).
[123] *VMO. Suppl.*, 578 F.
[124] *Cron. Villar. mon., MGH. SS.*, XXV, 202.
[125] *Ibid., Contin.* I, 209. For the translation consult Schuermans, "Châsse des
XXXVI Saints à Anvers. Julienne de Cornillon," *AAAB.*, LII, ser. 5, II (1900),
381-448; id., "Les reliques de la B. Julienne de Cornillon à l'abbaye de Villers,"
Annales soc. arch. arrond. Nivelles, VII (Nivelles, 1903), 1-68; especially p. 60,
App. A.
[126] *Cron. Villar. mon. Contin. I, MGH. SS.*, XXV, 210 offers the epitaph (cf.
Schuermans, in *Annales soc. arch. Nivelles*, VII, 60-61, App. B) in which the monks,
together with the three women, are mentioned by name. For variants in the
spelling of this epitaph, see Van Mierlo, in *D. War. Belf.*, XXIV (1924), 108-109;

Cornebout of Brussels,[127] Boniface, former monk at Clairvaux and then at Villers,[128] and Godfrey the Sacristan.[129] In addition were three women of great virtue who exemplify the ecstatic feminine movement: Juliana of Cornillon,[130] Helwide, a recluse of the parish St. Syr in Nivelles,[131] and Marquine (Markine), another recluse of Willambroux (*et domine Markine incluse de Ewillenbruch juxta Nivellam*) near the the same town.[132] Two years later (1271) the mausoleum was opened and three more bodies were added.[133] These included two monks, Henricus de Geest[134] and William of Dongelbert,[135] and a beguine of Nivelles, Marie de Grez (de Gravio).[136] She may have been the sister of a relative of Elizabeth de Gravio to whom Thomas of Cantimpré makes reference.[137]

The veneration of Juliana deserves closer examination since it indicates so clearly the interest that the Brabançon monastery took in the feminine religious movement. She died at Fosses on April 5, 1258, and her cult followed immediately.[138] She had communicated

---

cf. id., *l.c.*, XXI (1921), 631. For further details on Abond's burial and epitaph, see *Gesta, MGH. SS.*, XXV, 232.

[127] The name Arnulf of Brussels occurs in *Gesta, MGH. SS.*, XXV, 234; for Arnold Cornebout, the first mention of the cognomen is in the translation of the body (*AHEB.*, XVII, 1898, 112, and is found in *Cron. Villar. mon., Contin. I, MGH. SS.*, XXV, 209); cf. Sanderus, *Chorogr. sac. Brab.*, I, 440f. Roisin, *Hag. Cist.*, pp. 32-34; De Moreau, in *DHGE.*, IV (1930), 603.

[128] *Cron. Villar. mon., MGH. SS.*, XXV, 196; Sanderus, *Chorogr. sac. Brab.*, I, 441; Manrique, *Annal. Cist.*, II, 502.

[129] The *Cron. Villar. mon.* notes that during the abbacies of Ulric (1160-1184) and William (1191-1197) respectively the remains of Boniface and Godfrey were put behind the high altar. Cf. Schuermans, in *Annales soc. arch. Nivelles*, VII (1903), 6-7.

[130] *V. Jul. Cornel.*, 474.

[131] Cf. Van Mierlo, in *D. War. en Belf.*, XXI (1921), 632-633. The view presented here that Helwide may be identified with the *magistra begginarum* at Nivelles mentioned by Thomas of Cantimpré remains only a hypothesis. Cf. his opinion, *ibid.*, XXV (March, 1925), 30f.

[132] *AB.*, XIV, 267. For her identity, see *AHEB.*, XXVII (1898), 112; De Louvet, *op. cit.*, p. 36.

[133] Laenen, in *AHEB.*, XXVII (1898), 112, note 27; Van Mierlo, in *D. War. Belf.*, XXI (1921), 631.

[134] *Cron. Villar. mon., MGH. SS.*, XXV, 209, 210 note.

[135] *Gesta, MDT.*, III, 1359; *MGH. SS.*, XXV, 209, 210 note, 235; Sanderus, *Chorogr. sac. Brab.*, I, 445. This William is not to be confused with William of Brussels (De Moreau, *L'abbaye de Villers, pp. 57f*; Schuermans, in *Annales soc. arch Nivelles*, VII [1903], 61, note 2).

[136] See above p. 64.

[137] *Ibid.*, XXIV (1924), 107.

[138] According to Henriquez (*Lilia Cistercii*, p. 142; the passage is also published by Schuermans, in *AAAB.*, 1900, 432, Ann. A), Hugh of St. Cher, one of the first promoters of the feast, showed his affection for its author by going to Villers to pray before the tomb. After venerating the relics, he was seized, so runs the account, by such compunction and moved by such fervor ("tantos interioris religionis et dulcedinis affectus sentiebat") that he did not wish to leave Villers without granting indulgences to those who would celebrate the feast. But this document is dated April 26, 1252, six years before her death (for the entire problem, see Schuermans, *AAAB.*, 1900, 383-384).

reference for burial at Villers to the former crusading knight, Gobert d'Aspremont, now a simple monk in the abbey and uncle of another Gobert d'Aspremont, the companion of Joinville on Louis IX's crusade.[139] It was he who hastened to have the body translated there directly after her death. The veneration, claims Schuermans,[140] began not before Juliana's death, but before the interment. The coffin had been set aside; imagination was already at work. Some priest, from an unknown place, appeared and pronounced a sermon on the feast of the Sacrament, then disappeared as quickly as he had come, without leaving a trace.[141] The monks of Villers whose credulity was struck by such circumstances decided that Juliana must not be subject to the custom of interment. The body, received on the sixth at the abbey, was therefore the next day, with unanimous consent, not buried but by exception immediately placed in the tomb reserved for bodies of the saints of the monastery, i.e., behind the high altar of the church.[142] The first translation of Juliana's relics thus occurred, as the fifteenth-century Florarium MS. asserts,[143] on April 7, 1258.[144]

When Urban IV, former archdeacon of the Liége church, proclaimed the feast in 1264 as valid for the whole church, special attention was henceforth attracted to the relics of the monastery, particularly those of Juliana. Thus a translation, the second for her, was made on June 14, 1269, by the abbots of Clairvaux and Igny.[145] The mausoleum back of the altar was reopened to receive the other bodies. The biography of Juliana, which we have examined elsewhere, was written by one of her contemporaries. A parchment copy was preserved at Villers where mention is made of it in the catalogue of the library drawn up in 1309.[146]

But officials of the several orders and the hierarchy rightfully feared that fraternization with *mulieres sanctae* would consume too much of the monk's time. Pope Gregory X in 1275 instructed the bishop of Liége to put an end to a scandal. Claiming the right of visitation which the abbot of St. Laurent had over the beguinage of St. Christopher, his monks were frequenting this house far too much.[147] Almost

[139] Bouquet, XX, 208 B; for the relationship, see Schuermans, in *Annales soc. arch. Nivelles*, VII (1903), 5.

[140] *AAAB.*, 1900, 384-385.

[141] *V. Jul. Cornel.*, 474 B (50).

[142] Fisen, *Hist. leod. eccl.*, II, 14: "Tantam porro virtutis suae famam sparserat virgo sanctissima ut non aliter quam inter sanctiora sui coenobii pignora sepeliendum existimaverunt."

[143] "VII Aprilis. Apud Villarium Brabantiae translatio Julianae virginis, santimonialis de Cornelino" (Schuermans, *Annales soc. arch. Nivelles*, VII (1903), 4 and note 1; *AAAB.*, 1900, 385).

[144] Schuermans, *Annales soc. arch. Nivelles*, VII (1903), 3-6.

[145] Laenen, in *AHEB.*, XXVII (1898), 112.

[146] Schuermans, *Annales soc. arch. Nivelles*, VI (1898), 197, 219, 225; *AB.*, XIV, 60. Other copies were to be found at Averbode and Rouge-Cloître.

[147] *CESL.*, VI, 259.

a century earlier Renier, monk of St. Laurent, wrote a short tract, *De Profectu Mortis*, which he addressed to a *scholasticus* Guillaume whom he had known well in Liége. In earlier discussions of the sin of the first parents they had lamented Eve's wickedness. But this is more than just another piece of antiwoman literature so common in the Middle Ages. The author recalls tales of holy recluses who have suffered a regrettable fall because they have been surrounded with women or have had spiritual relations with them. To associate with the opposite sex is to invite evil. Secular as well as sacred history proves that.[148]

To lend substance to these foregoing warm, spiritualized accounts of the enthusiastic and usually uncritical hagiographer one needs only to turn to the cold facts of the *Liber census,* which was prepared about 1274—1275 and published as the Polyptique of Villers. The partial interlacing of the two registers is suggested by the case of the beguine, Ida de Lathruy, who was to receive from the abbot and convent from 1259 on a life pension of half a hogshead of wheat.[149] Pensions paid to other nuns, recluses, and beguines, together with their own obligations, appear frequently in these lists.[150]

The Benedictine monastery of St. Trond under the masterful abbot Guillaume de Ryckel (1249—1272)[151] exhibited the same interest in the well-being of the extraregular. Not only did he gather together in June, 1265, at the advice of *multorum proborum,* in one place (*sub una clausura*), the beguines who then lived scattered "danger-ously" in the parishes of Ghovelingen, Rokendale, Saint-Sepulchre, and St. Gengulphe as well as in the suburb of Schuerhoven,[152] but he

---

[148] *PL.,* CCIV, 181-196.

[149] De Moreau, *Polyptique,* p. 368; cf. *AHEB.,* XXXIII, 126. The editor (*Polyptique,* pp. 368-369) compares the two documents with reference both to date and content.

[150] A life pension "ad hospitale a le Gouttail beginarum," a part of which was to be divided between the two beguines, Sibilia de Perevez and Aleidis (*AHEB.,* XXXIII, 125); the *portarius* of Risbart (Rasa Barba) owed half a hogshead "ad opus pauperum beghinarum ex parte Iuthe, recluse de Malevia" (Malèves at Nivelles) (*ibid.,* XXXIII, 126, 401); the pension to Iuthe de Molenbiscul was transferred, after her death, to one of her sisters if she was a beguine (*ibid.,* XXXIII, 127); the pension designed for Baudechon de Latuit was to be paid to his mother, Haluwidis, if she survived him and became a beguine (*ibid.,* XXXIII, 127-128); pension to Margaret, a beguine at Hasselt (*ibid.,* XXXIII, 159-160); the *curtis* of Diepenbeek owed an income for life to Heluwidis, a beguine at St. Trond (*ibid.,* XXXIII, 351);Stoisy (lez Nivelles) had a similar obligation to Iuthe, a beguine of Scarchines (*ibid.,* XXXIII, 354); a pension for Agnes, the prioress of Roateit, i.e., the mistress of La Royauté beguinage at Nivelles (*idem*); a pension to Arnold, the priest of Ten Hove (Hovis) at Louvain (*ibid.,* XXXIII, 140; cf. 361); cf. *ibid.,* XXXIII, 126, 150, 155-156. For obligations of beguines: at Thorembais-les Beguines the beguine de la Hayse and the beguines *que post morantur,* must pay *pro orta et terra* (*ibid.,* XXXII, 434); William and Agnes, a beguine, pay rent (*ibid.,* XXXII, 445); Clara, a beguine, owed *pro domo et orto* (*ibid.,* XXXIII, 130).

[151] Pirenne, *Le livre de l'Abbé Guillaume de Ryckel,* pp. vff.

[152] Piot, *Cartulaire de l'abbaye de Saint-Trond,* I, 321-325, no. 264; *Gesta Abb. Trud., Cont. Tertia, Pars II, MGH. SS.,* X, 400-401.

built near the monastery a church dedicated to St. Agnes in which he collected the relics of 132 saints.[153] Eight bonniers of land were made available with episcopal approval to the *universitas* which could now cut itself off more effectively from the outside. From this land the beguines or their procurators or mambours must pay the abbey five marks of Liége on the vigil of the Nativity of John the Baptist (June 23) and another five on Christmas Eve. In addition to these ten marks the procurators of the community were to pay the abbot on each feast of St. Trond (November 23) in acknowledgment of his jurisdiction and domination one gold denier worth three *solidi sterling*. The abbey also claimed on the four great feasts one-half of the alms of the faithful or other contributions solicited by the priests. The portion assigned to the infirmary or to the priests themselves was to be left untouched. At the same time Guillaume reserved for the abbots installation of the priest.[154] The beguines must also grind their grain in the mills at Merwele (Melveren), Gorssum, or Meysbruc, all near St. Trond.[155]

The continuer of the *Gesta Abbatum Trudonensium* then describes the charitable obligations of the abbey under Guillaume's direction. Twenty prebends were provided for *devotis pauperibus beginabus* and "a few men"; each week one denier of Liége was distributed for two white loaves of bread.[156] Eleven more loaves were handed out at the *curia* of the beguines.[157] In addition to these prebends the abbot established in 1253 a similar prebend in honor of saints Trond, Eucherius, Quentin, Remigius, and Libertus which was called the prebend of St. Trond.[158] Among the recipients of it were, besides Petrus de Sancto Petro, a beghard, the beguines or *puelle religiose*: the sisters Aleyde and Christine,[159] Ida de Vlidermale, Margaret de Gota, Margaret de Nuenhusen, and Margaret, daughter of Jordan, monk of Villers.[160]

To make more precise and concrete the information presented in the chronicle we need only to turn further to the Polyptique prepared by Guillaume de Ryckel and edited by Henri Pirenne. Herein are listed numerous beguine prebendaries and pensioners: Beatrice, daughter of Mechtild de Gelmen, who had been given in 1262 a prebend of 9 bonniers and 13 *virgae* of arable land, was to receive

[153] *Ibid.*, 400.

[154] Piot, *Cartulaire de Saint-Trond*, I, 323.

[155] *Idem* (for Melveren, *ibid.*, I, 50, note 12. The beguines were allowed to draw water from the stream through ditches so long as the mill at Merwele was not endangered (*ibid.*, I, 322).

[156] *Gesta Abb. Trud., Cont. Tertia, Pars II, MGH. SS.*, X, 401.

[157] *Ibid.*, 402.

[158] *Ibid.*, 401-402; Pirenne, *Le livre de l'abbé Guillaume de Ryckel*, p. 364.

[159] *Ibid.*, p. 364; cf. pp. 363, 365.

[160] *Ibid.*, p. 364.

after her mother's death 4 hogsheads of wheat from this land.[161] Beatrice de Borloo, daughter of Henry de Ophem, enjoyed 10 hogsheads of wheat.[162] In October, 1265, Ida de Korpt gave to St. Trond 1 bonnier of land at Milen; in return the abbey promised her 2 hogsheads of wheat annually and after her death 1 hogshead to Ida, her brother's daughter, for life.[163] In 1262 Adam de Borloo and Engelswendis, his wife, and Odina, their daughter and a beguine, were to receive for life at Borloo 1½ bonniers of land, 30 d. and 1 obol of Liége, 4 d. of St. Trond and 10½ capons.[164] The beguine Mary of Diest received a pension of 2 hogsheads of wheat[165] while Mella of Diest merited a like pension.[166] From July, 1261,[167] Lisa, Greta,[168] and Frideswide, sisters and beguines, received a pension of 5 hogsheads of wheat; following the death of the first two, 1 hogshead was to be deducted for each by the abbey, while the death of the third ended the obligation. If Ida, a beguine of Diest (d. July 24, 1261) and daughter of Lambert de Halle, was granted 3 hogsheads of wheat at Webbecom,[169] Ida de Rosen received a pension of 2 hogsheads.[170] In 1253 Machtild de Los was given a prebend worth 2 loaves and 1 d. of Liége weekly, on December 6 (in die beati Nicholai).[171] To these must be added many other beguine beneficiaries[172] as well as recluses.[173]

The beguine Lutgard (d. June 25, 1257)[174] had been paid 1 mark on September 30, 1253, for the mill of Serkingen.[175] To the beguine Ysenbela the abbey sold in October, 1265, 1 hogshead of wheat annually for life for 3½ marks of Liége.[176] In 1265 St. Trond sold to the

---

[161] *Ibid.*, p. 62. In 1270 Machtilde and her two daughters, Beatrice and Ida (for the latter, see *ibid.*, p. 64) held 11½ bonniers of land (*ibid.*, p. 66). Cf. *ibid.*, p. 280 (1257).

[162] *Ibid.*, pp. 57, 68, 369. Again (*ibid.*, p. 368), she held at Borloo 9 bonniers and 35 *virgae*, ½ hogshead of wheat, 12 d and 2 capons. On May 8, 1257, Marguerite, abbess of the monastery of Oeteren, and her convent approved the disposal of land and rent at Borloo in behalf of the abbey of St. Trond, "salvo tamen usufructu dictorum bonorum Beatrici becghine, quondam filie filie Henrici de Ophem" (Piot, *Cartulaire de St. Trond*, I, 278-279, no. 235).

[163] Pirenne, *Le livre de l'abbé Guillaume de Ryckel*, p. 64.

[164] *Ibid.*, p. 62; cf. pp. 65, 286.

[165] October 8, 1261, *ibid.*, p. 55; cf. pp. 58, 69, 367 (3 hogsheads).

[166] *Ibid.*, p. 58; cf. 367 (3 hogsheads).

[167] *Ibid.*, p. 61.

[168] Cf. *ibid.*, p. 69. This is possibly the Greta, beguine of Utrecht who in 1253 had 1 mark and 16 s. of Liége (*ibid.*, p. 12).

[169] *Ibid.*, p. 69; cf. pp. 58, 361.

[170] October 8, 1261, *ibid.*, p. 55; cf. pp. 58 (1265), 69, 361.

[171] *Ibid.*, p. 363.

[172] Mary, beguine of Huy, and her sister, *ibid.*, pp. 246, 367; Jutta de Camera, *ibid.*, p. 363; Lutgard, *ibid.*, p. 371; Bergtha, *ibid.*, p. 363; Christine de Volne, *ibid.*, Greta van der Leyen, *ibid.*, p. 364.

[173] *Ibid.*, pp. 363, 365.

[174] *Ibid.*, pp. 363, 365.

[175] *Ibid.*, p. 361; cf. 365.

[176] *Ibid.*, p. 64; cf. 68.

beguine Christine and her sisters Heylewidis and Marie 1 hogshead of wheat for 5 marks of Liége to build a lodging.[177]

As further evidence of the interpenetration of Cistercian with beguine life we may cite the example of Val-Benoit whose nuns had come from Robermont in 1231 [178] following consent by Abbot Gautier of Citeaux.[179] The monks moved on to Val-Notre-Dame in Gravioule which took the name of Val-des-Ecoliers.[180] On 28, 1241, John, chaplain of the church of Saint-Gilles near St. Lambert at Liége, handed over his house near La Madeleine to Val-Benoit. The abbess was expected to provide hospitality for twenty-four beguines *honeste conversationis et bone fame* each year. Mary, a beguine, who had occupied two rooms in the house, was to receive an annual pension until death.[181] Helwide Blandine, another beguine, willed to this Cistercian nunnery 3 bonniers and 1 journal of land under certain conditions.[182] In 1313 (January 13) Jean, pastor of Vyle, willed to *pauperibus beguinabus* of St. Christopher at Liége 3 *l*.[183] In 1352 (February 29) Magin, the daughter of Hanar de St. Barthelemy, executor of the will of Catherine de Vaux, a beguine who lived in the parish of St. Adalbert, collected 10 setiers of spelt on land in front of the nunnery and which Catherine had willed to it.[184] A hundred years earlier (January 27, 1253) Ida, recluse of Othée, yielded to Val-Benoit her rights over land at Fallais as well as all other property following her death.[185]

Similar cases can be cited for Germany. While Drutlindis, a beguine at Frankfurt, received from the Cistercian monastery of Arnsburg a pension from property which she had made over to it,[186] Adelheid von Vechenheim donated her Frankfurt house and goods on condition of life usufruct.[187] The *Urkundenbuch* of Altenberg likewise contains much information on the temporal affairs of beguines.[188]

[177] *Ibid.*, p. 64.
[178] Cuvelier, *Cartulaire de l'abbaye du Val-Benoit*, pp. 61-62, no. 50 (May, 1231); cf. *ibid.*, 97-101, no. 83 (April 12-30, 1243); 101-103, no. 84 (January 5, 1244); 103-105, no. 85 (between April 12, 1243 and April 3, 1244); 106-107, no. 86 (between January 5 and April 3, 1244). Cf. Berlière, *MB.*, II, 194ff.
[179] 1230, Cuvelier, *Cartulaire*, p. 61, no. 49.
[180] Berlière, *MB.*, II, 194.
[181] Cuvelier, *Cartulaire*, pp. 93-94, no. 80.
[182] February 4, 1259, *ibid.*, p. 151, no. 119.
[183] *Ibid.*, pp. 346-348, no. 267.
[184] *Ibid.*, pp. 463-464, no. 352.
[185] *Ibid.*, pp. 128-129, no. 101.
[186] August 12, 1300, Boehmer, *UB. Frankfurt*, I, 334-335. For Arnsburg in diocese of Mainz, near Giessen, see G. Allemang, *DGHE.*, IV (1930), 631-633.
[187] June 5, 1301, Boehmer, *UB. Frankfurt*, I, 339-340. See controversy between the beguine Paza von Scheuren and Heisterbach over property which she had given to the Cistercian monastery (April 8, 1309, *UB. Heisterbach*, pp. 291f, no. 215).
[188] Donations and legacies: The beguine Eufemia von Butzheim assigned on April 27, 1258, all her property to Butzheim and Nettesheim with provision therefrom for a life income for Altenberg (p. 156f, nos. 215-216). On April 2, 1299,

Christine von Königswinter, beguine, gave her property *ob salutem et in reme-dium animae suae* under conditions (pp. 351f, no. 463). In 1260 the beguine Elizabeth Krich and the beghard Wolbero assigned to Altenberg two-thirds of two lodgings under one roof opposite the vineyard of St. Ursula as well as two-thirds of the neighboring house (pp. 165f, no. 231). On June 22, 1313, the Coblenz beguine Hadewig von Kesselheim made available to relatives properties on condi-tion that they go to Altenberg after their death (p. 449, no. 573; cf. pp. 450-452, no. 574). The beguine Aleydis, daughter of Gobelin Bolant von Nettesheim, willed to the abbey 13 ½ journaux of land (February 8, 1298, pp. 340-342, no. 450; her memory was celebrated on September 5, p. 342, note 1); 1277, p. 249, no. 342; p. 289, no. 392 (December 1, 1284, June, 1292); June 23, 1264, p. 176, no. 251; cf. p. 331, no. 441 (1295); May 14, 1302, p. 379, no. 486; June 15, 1303, p. 395, no. 500; February 12, 1308, p. 435, no. 548; January 26, 1316, p. 466, no. 596; May 13, 1329, p. 506, no. 660; July 5, 1344, pp. 548f, no. 727; 1345, p. 569; 1357, p. 629, no. 809. The be-guine Elizabeth de Luzheim bought from the abbey a house and ground (February, 1271/2, p. 211, no. 302). In 1286 Bruno left with the approval of his abbot and brethren in Altenberg the life usufruct of his half of a property to his sister, the beguine Ida, after whose death it was to go to the monastery (p. 297, no. 401). Together with representatives of the abbey, among others, Talia, a beguine, witnessed a donation of a Cologne burgher (January 13, 1284, pp. 286f). A beguine Elizabeth, together with Cologne burghers, sold to Altenberg a house in Cologne February 18, 1274, pp. 228f, no. 322). On March 20, 1308, Abbot John and the monastery of Heisterbach sold with the approval of their visitor, the abbot of Himmerode, to Altenberg the right of ownership of property of the beguine Odilia von Winter (pp. 436f, no. 549). In 1298 Altenberg leased the properties which fell to it following the death of Ludwig von Kesselheim through his son, Herman, a monk in the abbey, to the latter's sister Margaret as well as to Mabilia and Hade-wig von Kesselheim, beguines at Coblenz, for life at 18 s. annually (pp. 347f, no. 459). For other transactions see: 1292 (p. 322, no. 427); 1295 (p. 330, no. 440); 1305 (p. 415, no. 524, involves a monk of Altenberg who assigns to his sister, a beguine, a property for life); February 25, 1307 (p. 428, no. 537); February 23, 1310 (p. 440, no. 556); 1311 (p. 446, no. 566); August 30, 1313 (p. 454, no. 578); January 17, 1315 (p. 462, no. 589); February 28, 1339 (pp. 529f, no. 702); July 17, 1340 (p. 535, no. 709); 1345 (p. 583).

IV

The Preachers and Beguine Spirituality

THE PULPIT

The general chapter at Trèves in 1249 forbade nuns and other women to write psalters or other books.[1] Combining such negative evidence with materials summarized in the next section, we may conclude that certain women who associated with the Order of Preachers knew how to write and possessed some knowledge of Latin. One sister might be active as a teacher of the language, while the writing or copying of books was for certain inmates their chief occupation in the convent. When the resistance of the Dominicans to the incorporation of nunneries in the order was broken under Pope Clement IV, these conditions were stabilized again, convents also had women who read at the table or in private but who were obliged to employ vernacular materials for want of sufficient Latin instruction.[2]

Besides ordinary offices which were recited in the chapel of beguinage or nunnery, sermons too must be attended. The rule for the Paris beguines prescribed that they should frequently listen to an explanation of the divine word;[3] hence the principal preachers of repute mounted the pulpit of the community. Geoffrey of Beaulieu, confessor and biographer of Louis IX, led the list of Dominicans who preached to the beguines of Paris about 1272–1273.[4] Among other friars whose activity is remembered by only two or three sermons, or

[1] *MOPH.*, III, 47: "Fratres non faciant sibi scribi psalteria vel alia scripta per moniales vel alias mulieres."

[2] For the same reason the rules of the order had to be read to sisters in German: see the Admonitions of Hermann von Minden in *ALKM.*, II (1886), 644: "Constitutiones secundum ordinationem ... magistra ordinis correctas habeant, que frequenter legantur et aliquotiens exponantur in vulgari." The *Engelthaler Nonnenbuch* (ed. Schröder, p. 2) relates that before the foundation of the nunnery, when the women still lived in Nürnberg as beguines, the mistress was wont to recite *in teutsche ze tisch* (Grundmann, *Religiöse Bewegungen*, p. 464, note 53).

[3] Le Grand, *Béguines de Paris*, pp. 57-58, no. 24. The 1323 statutes of the Antwerp beguinage prescribed in addition to daily mass sermons and hours on Sunday and saints' days (Philippen, *Begijnhoven*, p. 336); cf. Lierre (1401, *ibid.*, p. 341).

[4] Quétif-Echard, I, 267b (one sermon, no. 25, delivered on November 27, 1272 (Dom. I adv. ad Beguinas in mane; Lecoy de la Marche, *La chaire française*, p. 466, Table bibl.). Cf. Daunou, in *HLF.*, XIX (1838), 234-237.

just a single one, in a collection of Pierre de Limoges were the following: Gilles of Liége or Gilles de Orpio,[5] Evrard of St. Quentin,[6] Jean d'Orléans, chancellor of Paris,[7] Pierre de Tonnerre (or Tornaro),[8] Pierre de Verdun,[9] Guillaume d'Auxerre,[10] Jean de Liége,[11] Pierre de Lemet,[12] Nicholas de Corrant,[13] Nicholas de le Mans,[14] Fr. Episcopus Parisiensis Praedicatorum,[15] and Gilles of Orléans.[16] Thomas of Cantimpré alludes to a sermon which John Polinus, a canon regular in the monastery of Essoines before transferring to the Order of Preachers—"in which the divine word is not bound"—delivered in the "very religious" house of Cantimpré at Cambrai on the feast of the Apostles Philip and James (May 1) with many beguines in the congregation.[17] Thus *mulieres sanctae* received sermons from their own priests or occasional visitors who addressed themselves primarily to the women and their spiritual needs. We have seen how Hermann of

[5] Quétif and Echard distinguished two Dominicans with the name Gilles de Liége (I, 266a-266b) and Gilles *de Orpio* (I, 266b) who are really one and the same, as the title of sermon no. 141 indicates: "Sermo fratris Aegidii de Legio vel Orpio, ad S. Gervasium" (Lecoy de la Marche, pp. 467-468). Of seven sermons attributed by Quétif and Echard to Gilles de Liége two were delivered to beguines; no. 53, "In epiphania ad Beguinas in mane," and no. 65, "In festo S. Vincentii Beguinas in mane." One is assigned to Gilles *de Orpio*: no. 197, "Dominica infra octavas B. Dionysii ad Beguinas."

[6] Quétif-Echard (I, 267a) lists one for beguines in the six sermons *de tempore* delivered by Evrard; cf. Lecoy de la Marche, p. 465.

[7] Jean d'Orléans, also called Jean des Alleux (de Allodiis) had eight of his homilies preserved by Pierre de Limoges, including those for the beguines (Quétif-Echard, I, 268; Lecoy de la Marche, pp. 119f).

[8] Quétif-Echard, I, 268b; Lecoy de la Marche, p. 484. It is sermon 171: "Dom. infra octav. nativitatis B. V. ad Beguinas" (i.e. September 10, 1273).

[9] Quétif-Echard, I, 268b; Lecoy de la Marche, p. 484. Two of the three sermons were given to beguines: no. 38 (December 21, 1272, "in festo S. Thomae apost. ad Beguinas in mane"); no. 173 (August 27, 1273, "dom. xiii post pent. ad Beguinas mane").

[10] Quétif-Echard, I, 267b; Lecoy de la Marche, p. 470. Sermon 59, "dom. ii post epiph. ad Beguinas in mane" (January 15, 1273).

[11] Quétif-Echard, I, 268a; Lecoy de la Marche, p. 476. Of two sermons listed one (no. 169) was delivered to the beguines on August 20, 1273 ("Dom. infra octavas assumpt. B. Mar.").

[12] Quétif-Echard, I, 268b; Lecoy de la Marche, p. 483. Sermon 43 (December 26, 1272).

[13] Quétif-Echard, I, 268b; Lecoy de la Marche, pp. 481f, Nicholas de Gorran or du Mans (d. 1295). Sermon no. 211: "Dom. infra octavas S. Martini."

[14] Quétif-Echard, I, 268b. Two sermons are listed: no. 131, "In festo apostolorum Philippique Jacobi ad Beguinas" (May 1); no. 179, "Dom. 15 post pentec. ad Beguinas" (year not indicated).

[15] Quétif-Echard, I, 267a-b: no. 81 "Sermo Fratris Episcopi Parisiensis Praedicatorum ad Beguinas in mane Dom. in quinquag."

[16] *Ibid.*, I, 265b-266a. Of the twenty-three sermons which Gilles delivered in different churches at Paris from October 28, 1272 ("a festo SS. Simonis et Judae") to November 11-18 of the following year ("ad octavas S. Martini"), three were intended for the beguines: no. 11, "Sermo . . . in festo S. Martini mane"; no. 34, "dom. 3 adventus in mane"; no. 103, "dom. in Passione mane." Cf. Daunou, in *HLF.*, XIX (1838), 232-234; cf. XVI (1826), 165; Lecoy de la Marche, p. 468.

[17] Thomas of Cantimpré, *BUA.*, II, 49, 2 (p. 442); *RR.* vss. 12057f.

Minden provided that trained friars should preach more often to the sisters, as befitted their education.

Stephen of Bourbon heard from Jacques de Vitry that a certain woman was reduced to poverty from running after sermons from town to town. The Dominican himself had seen noble women so eager for the divine word that, having donned the meanest attire of the poor, they went on foot from city to city like beggars to be able to follow and take refuge in preaching.[18]

In the thirteenth century even abbesses, nuns, and mistresses of beguinages occasionally undertook to preach, although ecclesiastical authorities had consistently frowned upon such a practice since the council of Carthage in 398.[19] Certain educated women were permitted to instruct female catechumens only. Bernard of Fontcaude included in his indictment of the Waldensian program not only misguidance of women but, contrary to patristic and canonical tradition, extension of the preaching prerogative to them.[20] In 1210 (December 11) Innocent III expressed astonishment in a letter to the bishops of Palencia and Burgos, which was incorporated into canon law, that abbesses in their dioceses were presumptuous enough to bless their own nuns, hear confessions and, after reading from the gospels, dare to preach in public. No precedent can be found for such conduct, not even in the Virgin than whom no apostle is more worthy.[21] Humbert de Romans summarized to his own satisfaction and without doubt for the Dominican world as a whole four reasons for excluding women from the pulpit: "First, they do not have broad enough knowledge; secondly, an inferior role has been assigned to them; thirdly, if they preach they will provoke luxury; and fourthly, because of the folly of the first woman who, according to Bernard, upset the whole world by teaching."[22] Mary of Oignies refrained from preaching, but for reasons which her biographer does not make clear. Thus she was content to depend on Jacques de Vitry for pastoral care. From faithful attendance at sermons she in turn acquired instruction in Scripture.[23]

The collection of Pierre de Limoges contains fragments of two homilies which he gathered from the mouth of the mistress of the beguinage in Paris. Delivered inside the convent, they appear to have

[18] *Anec. hist.*, pp. 74-75, nos. 77-78; cf. p. 74, no. 75.

[19] Labbe-Mansi, III, 1207: "Mulier, quamvis docta et sancta, viros in conventu docere non praesumant."

[20] *Liber contra Waldenses*, PL., CCIV, 821-828, caps. 7-8.

[21] XIII, 187, PL., CCXVI, 356; Decret. Greg., c. 10, *de poenit.*, V, 38 (Friedberg, II, 886f).

[22] Humbert de Romans, *De eruditione praedicatorum* (I, 11), Bibl. Max. Vet. Pat., XXV, 435.

[23] *VMO.*, 562-563, nos. 68-69; see above, p. 23.

been transcribed *de auditu*.[24] Furthermore, the superior of the Cambrai beguines did not hesitate to raise objections to the arguments of the preachers. "When one of them formulated this proposition that the man whose charity goes straight cannot but act in a way above reproach, the mistress of the beguines asked him: 'Where in holy scripture, master, have you seen that charity is lame? If it limps and no longer follows a straight course, it is no longer charity.' The speaker was confused."[25]

Even as lay preaching in the vernacular was discountenanced as something heretical, so oral instruction laid women open to suspicion that they were skirting the fringe of orthodoxy. That beguines continued to violate the prohibition is suggested in the Clementine decree *Cum de quibusdam mulieribus* of 1311. "Some, as if induced by insanity, discuss and *preach* on the Trinity and divine essence and introduce concerning articles of faith and the sacraments opinions which contradict Catholicism."[26]

From the cure of German and Belgian nuns and beguines and under the leaven of their ascesis developed many a Dominican sermon. The broad wave of fourteenth-century mysticism gathered strength from the impact of scholastic philosophy on educated women in nunneries. Just as *mulieres sanctae* motivated the pastoral labors of the friars, so the latter encouraged women to press on in quest of spiritual perfection. The beguine Mechtild of Magdeburg not only listened to these sermons but she had a Dominican as her confessor. A reading public had been created, eager for sermons, tractates, and anecdotes, in the vernacular. The preparation for Meister Eckhart was long, with the mysticism he represents resulting from a lively interplay of spiritual forces in the Rhineland and the diocese of Liége since the days of Hildegarde and Elizabeth of Schönau.

"VIRGO DEVOTA ORDINIS PRAEDICATORUM"

Christine of Stommeln or Stumbelen (1242–1312), a village directly northwest of Cologne, has been eclipsed in modern research by the Belgian women mystics of the Nivelles-Liége area or her own gifted German contemporary, the beguine of Magdeburg. Most recently J. Gallén, in an admirable study[27] on the Order of Preachers in the

---

[24] Lecoy de la Marche, p. 33.
[25] *Ibid.*, p. 218.
[26] Fredericq, *Corpus*, I, 167. For usurpation of the confessional, *ibid.*, II, 154.
[27] Gallén, *La Province de Dacie* ... (Helsingfors, 1946), pp. 225-244; *passim*. From Hauck (V, 1, 382f), Preger (*Geschichte*, I, 47-52), and Michael (*Geschichte des deutschen Volkes*, III, 165-167) Christine received scant attention. Ernest Renan ("La bienheureuse Christine de Stommeln, béguine," *HLF.*, XXVIII [1881], 1-26) offered a substantial summary of her spiritual career, but without genuine appreciation for the feminine religious movement. Cf. G. G. Coulton, *Life in the Middle Ages*, I (Cambridge University Press, 1928), 132-149; neither Theodor Wollersheim (*Das Leben

province of Dacia, has accorded to her biography, with a Swedish perspective, the attention which it deserves as a source for external history. On the other hand, he neglects it as an invaluable case study of the impact of the mysticism of the feminine religious movement on student and preaching friars. Christine's *vita* and *acta*, as preserved in large measure by Friar Peter of Gothland or Dacia, who eventually became lector at the convent of Skenninge, then prior at Västeras and Wisby, offer a detailed and practical demonstration of Dominican pastoral care, together with its problems and diversions, among beguines and recluses.

The biography contains no evidence that Christine had ever been brought into close association with the Franciscans.[28] On the contrary, it is apparent that some hostility existed in the Cologne area between the two mendicant orders,[29] for the Friars Minor are reported to have cast aspersions on her little society to which they were not admitted. Their bitterness for the "deceptress" knew no bounds, not even halting at slander.[30] Again, devils, in the shape of an abbot and monks, declare amidst their curses: "This is the seductress of Stommeln who cannot be corrected by the religious, especially by Friars Minor."[31] On another occasion the demons condemned her whole life and behavior as misguided and perverse, making this declaration from the testimony of certain religious, especially Franciscans, who did not live that way.[32] At the end of Chapter II of Master John's *vita* the devil appears before Christine in the guise of a beghard, crying: "All your counsellors are deceivers, and these foolish shaven men lie whenever they speak." He singled out particularly the Preachers "who always clung to her."[33] The passage contains a twofold implication: first, beghards were viewed here with sufficient favor to warrant this role, and secondly, assuming, with full plausibility, that the beghard was a

der ekstatischen und stigmatischen Jungfrau Christina von Stommeln, Cologne, 1859) nor A. Steffens (*Die selige Christina von Stommeln*, Fulda, 1912) has been available to me. As a correction of the Bollandist edition see Johannes Paulson, *Intertiam partem Libri Juliacensis annotationes* (Göteborgs högskolas Ars-krift, II, 1896; *Jülicher-handskriften till Petrus de Dacia*, Göteborg, 1894; cf. *AB.*, XVI [1897], 532-534).

[28] Cf. *V. Chr. Stumb.*, 370 D (15).

[29] The appearance of four Dominicans and two Franciscans in the Stommeln church provoked the observation "quod raro contingere solet" (*Acta Chr. Stumb.*, 305, IV, 42).

[30] *Ibid.*, 318 E (IV, 93): "Imo ipsa est illa infelix et maledicta receptrix, de cujus perversitate saepe a Minoribus et ceteris Religiosis tot enormia audivimus." Cf. 318 B (IV, 91).

[31] *V. Chr.*, 381 F (79).

[32] *Acta Chr.*, 308 D (IV, 55). Embedded in an endless recital of torments from devils is another taunt hurled at Christine: "Nonne haec est illa sancta begina, de qua tanta miracula dicta sunt? numquid non modo omnia vera apponent, quae olim de ea Fratres Minores praedixerunt" (*ibid* 302 B, IV, 28).

[33] *V. Chr.*, 371 C (19); cf. *Acta Chr.*, 259 A (II, 9).

Franciscan tertiary, this incident too reflects antagonism of the Friars Minor and their protégés to the Dominicans.

Without actually belonging to the Order of St. Dominic, Christine was nonetheless closely affiliated with it by pastoral care and letters of confraternity.[34] From the order she drew her confessors, confidants, and scribes for her correspondence with Peter. However many friars from foreign lands visited her,[35] they were unable to fill the emptiness created by her friend's absence,[36] first at Paris and later in Gothland. To him she sent little gifts of money, trinkets,[37] or a book[38] or else she promised relics.[39] After announcing the satisfactory work of Christine's brother in a Swedish convent, Peter reminded her and Master John that they had promised some years before to forward to him certain writings on miracles. Since they had failed to do so, he protested: "Wherefore I ask that you correct this negligence."[40] In their letters Peter and the beguine discussed divine matters[41] and personal problems, not altogether without passion.[42] For the Cologne convent she became the *virgo devota ordinis Praedicatorum,* while for Peter she was his *filia spiritualis et amica singularis, a seculo relictae.*[43] Gladly would he cross the breadth of many lands and endure the dangers of the seas to see his spiritual daughter once more.[44] Christine in turn avowed that "of all religious orders I have embraced that of the Preachers with genuine preference and special devotion," for which reason she was afterwards anxious to have her brother Sigwin admitted to their company.[45] Until misfortune overwhelmed them[46] she lived with her parents, making an occasional trip to the city to

[34] For a table of the letters see Gallén, pp. 240-244. For references to Christine as a beguine see *V.,* 370 A (12): "Ubi moratur quaedam religiosa beghinae persona nomine Christina." Cf. *Acta,* 242 A (I, 24). The word *reclusorium* is employed (257 F, II, 4) almost as a beguine habitation (cf. Ducange, *Glossarium,* V, 620). One recluse in the Stommeln *reclusorium* (259, II, 10) was called a beguine (262 B, II, 19); in 1282 it was inhabited by a recluse (305, IV, 42) who is elsewhere called John) 313, IV, 72); *V. Chr.,* 369 E (11). For the recluse-beguine problem see Mens. *Oorsprong,* pp. 354ff; *consult Hanon de Louvet (L'origine nivelloise,* pp. 5ff) for a criticism of this equation with reference to the Mary of Oignies circle (see above, p. 7).

[35] *Acta,* 272 A (II, 56); 258 B (II, 5).

[36] *Ibid.,* 272 B (II, 56).

[37] *Ibid.,* 268 B (II, 43); cf. 259 C (II, 10).

[38] *Ibid.,* 268 E (II, 44); cf. 268f (II, 45). For Hilla de Monte's token of a veil see *ibid.,* 259 C (II, 10).

[39] *Ibid.,* 362 (V, 51); elsewhere Peter thanked Christine and Master John for the relics *(ibid.,* 360 E, V, 46).

[40] *Ibid.,* 360 (V, 44).

[41] Ep. XIV, 268 B (II, 43).

[42] *Ibid.,* 274 B (II, 64); 276f (III, 1, 3); cf. 259 (II, 10).

[43] *Ibid.,* 360 F (V, 47).

[44] *Ibid.,* 361 (V, 50).

[45] *Ibid.,* 293 D (III, 66).

[46] *Ibid.,* 276f (III, 1-3).

procure indulgences and to visit her friend[47] or in the company of Sigwin on business.[48]

Attracted from earliest childhood by the lives and manners of the saints, Peter was consumed by the desire that God "should show me one of His servants that in the conversation of His saints I might learn more accurately and clearly not only by words but by deeds and examples." For more than twenty years he had sought some revelation of divine grace with which to unite and associate by the bond of charity, to inform him with a way of life, to inflame him with devotion, to exalt him out of the sloth which had oppressed him from childhood, to illuminate him with conversation, to give solace through friendship and to compose by example all his doubts, particularly in what pertained to the behavior of saints. Eager meditation of the Passion, the sorrows of the Virgin, and the suffering of the martyrs kept him in a state of perpetual melancholy. His was an insatiable desire to converse with holy persons "because I found," he admits "in no one what I was seeking, and consequently my passion was never satisfied."[49] When Peter learned in 1279 of Christine's tribulations from her letters he approached the prior provincial Augustinus of Dacia to obtain permission to go to Cologne. The purpose of the journey was admittedly threefold: a) to be cured of a weak heart which had long afflicted him to the point of despairing for his life; b) to visit the patron saints, martyrs, and virgins lying in Cologne and to procure relics from them to take back home because for them he had conceived a peculiar devotion while he was studying there; c) to comfort Christine and at the same time to be illuminated by her.[50]

Eleven years did not diminished the memory of his first sight of Christine on December 21, 1267, for that event determined the course of his life until his death twenty years later.[51] The lady Alfrade, eminent for her illustrious marriage with a husband of noble family, fell sick and sent for Friar Walter, her old confessor. With Peter as his companion he went to her on St. Thomas' Eve. While Walter was hearing the lady's confession, Peter was approached by a beguine named Alice, who advised him of marvels which were being wrought in a girl in the village. The next evening the two friars lodged in the house of the parish priest where Christine was staying because of her "tribulation"; the visit was routine for Walter who had been her confessor almost from childhood. A willing subject for strange pheno-

[47] *Ibid.*, 245 E (I, 40). Christine once lost her senses in the Dominican church in Cologne which lasted for three days and three nights, leading the beguines to conclude that she was insane (*V. Chr.*, 368 E, 5).
[48] *Acta*, 291 F (III, 59); Paulson, p. 63.
[49] *Ibid.*, 239 (I, 15-16).
[50] *Ibid.*, 277 C-D (III, 4).
[51] *Ibid.*, 240-241 (I, 17-23).

mena, Peter exclaimed after beholding this state of ecstasy: "O happy night, O blessed night! thou wert to me the beginning of divine illuminations which know no difference of night or day. O sweet and delightful night! in which it was first granted to me to learn how kind is the Lord. This was the night in which I first deserved to see the spouse of my Lord."[52] Awful visions, assaults and temptations from demons, the alternation of celestial joy and terrestial sadness, cataleptic fits,[53] periods of ecstasy accompanied by suspended consciousness, prolonged and frequent fasts—such experiences which abound in the *Acta* attracted the attention of friars, not because of idle curiosity, Peter hastens to explain during his seventh visit in the company of Friar Albrandini on the feast of Mary Magdalene (July 22, 1268), but out of devotion. Prior Herman regarded these marvels as a part of the friars' education, all the more valuable for young men from remote places. It pleased him to see how excited his charges became over these events for "in old age," he told them, "you will be able to narrate them for the edification of others."[54]

Back in Sweden (February 6, 1271), where he was named lector at Skenninge (diocese of Linköpfing),[55] Peter found new *mulieres sanctae*,[56] some wearing the habit of his order, others in secular dress, while still others had donned the beguine habit. One of these women, a septuagenarian, submitted herself to extreme ascetic practices. Another "daughter" enjoyed divine favor and revelations; she abstained from meat, very seldom drank beer, rarely ate dairy produce, and clad herself in a hair-shirt. Every Saturday she fell into rapture from which she did not recover until the following vespers. Sometimes she had the stigmata, bearing on her body several signs of Christ's passion. Yet lengthy prayer and contemplation were balanced by an eagerness for almsgiving and service to the poor.[57] But such

---

[52] *Ibid.*, 241 C-D (I, 22).

[53] See Gerard von Greifen's testimony of fevers (*ibid.*, 257, II, 4). Friar Maurice described in a letter to Peter, then in Paris, Christine's seizure on the first Sunday in Advent (December 1, 1269) which distressed her parents and the friars, for in her raving she inflicted wounds on the prior of Brauweiler as well as on a Jew and his wife (*ibid.*, 261 E, II, 17).

[54] "Venimus, non curiositatis causa, sed devotionis" (*ibid.*, 247 A, I, 46); 250 B (I, 58).

[55] *Ibid.*, 272 A (II, 56, 59); 273 F (II 63).

[56] *Ibid.*, 275f (II, 67ff). The Dominican friar Herman of Wisby, *penitentiarius capellanus et nuntius*, put under protection of the Church the nun Agnes, daughter of the late Eric, king of the Danes, and two beguines Tybica and Elizabeth together with their *curia* and its appurtenances (March 15, 1263, *Dipl. Danicum*, I, 277, no. 367; cf. declaration of Roskild citizens, December 13, 1264, *ibid.*, I, 347, no. 448). On May 17, 1263, Margaret, widow of Johannes Gunnesen, willed to two beguines, Tore and Thruen, at Roskild 1 mark of deniers (*ibid.*, I, 292; cf. 290-292, no. 381).

[57] *Acta*, 352 (V, 13-15); cf. 351 A (V, 9). For problems of identifying the second personage see Gallén, pp. 126f.

THE PREACHERS AND BEGUINE SPIRITUALITY

spiritual daughters did not take the place of Stommeln. Lost in a "wild country," Peter was lonely.

John Elovsson, knight of the Teutonic order, after hearing about Christine from Peter, extended an invitation to her to come to Sweden. With King Magnus Ladulås giving his consent, Bishop Henrik of Linköping expressing willingness, and the Provincial Augustinus sending sisters, he pointed out that a suitable place had been made available at Skenninge to Dominican nuns for a convent. It was endowed from the patrimony of John and his brother Andrew as well as from the income from their sisters' property. John now desired that Christine should come with Sigwin to take the place of his recently deceased sister Christine. Not only had he inherited from his parents a special fondness for the Order of Preachers, but his two sisters were among the first in the kingdom to adopt its habit, which they "alone of their sex wore for more than ten years."[58] It was thus the other sister Ingrid who was most closely identified with this nunnery which developed into a primary center of Dominican spirituality.[59] Peter tried to implement John's invitation by adding in his own letter to Christine that "there are many who are anxious to see you in our country."[60] Two beguines of Gothland, Helborgis and N., corresponded for the same purpose. "Since your father and mother are dead." they wrote, "and you are without body comforts, the Lord has granted us from the paternal estate a small yard (curia) and modest houses in which no man lives except us two. We invite you to them as our beloved sister." Although they led a life of poverty, they received consolation from the Dominicans in the town.[61] In this way friar and beguine influenced one another.

Extraordinary spiritual tests, accompanied by excruciating physical pain, were not in the main characteristic of the beguinage. Moderation is underlined in statutes. Common sense marked the initial reaction of the Cologne beguines to the zeal of the young girl who had left home to join them.[62] Their advice to return to the parental roof she flatly refused, electing instead to remain with them. But "always sitting alone in prayer she cut herself off from all friendly intercourse." She fasted on bread and water on Sundays and vigils of saints' days. In place of linen she used a knotted girdle which bruised her sides. Every Friday she formed a cross as she recited the hours. She slept apart on wood and stone in order to waken more quickly to pray; before retiring she genuflected two hundred

---

[58] *Acta*, 357-358 (V, 33-34).
[59] Gallén, pp. 117f, 124-129.
[60] *Acta*, 358 (V, 35).
[61] *Ibid.*, 358 C (V, 36).
[62] See above, p. 445. For further evidence of intimacy with beguines see *Acta*, 303f (IV, 35).

times.[63] Freed from ecstatic seizures, she could be an attractive girl, naive and candid.[64] Peter was then so overwhelmed that he was inspired to compose verse. Social work—the *raison d'être* of many a beguinage—was slighted.

Among the cares which weighed on Christine was her brother Sigwin, or Gerard,[65] whom she had always preferred among all her "brothers and sisters of the flesh from childhood."[66] Since Prior Ingeld would not see her "for what negligence I know not" or speak to her about her brother,[67] she implored Peter to wrest Sigwin "from the stormy seas of this world" for the religious life.[68] After receiving her request at the provincial chapter at Skenninge, Peter consulted with Berthold, prior of Västerås (1281—1282),[69] how they might console Christine. The prior, moved by her predicament, sent 12s. to relieve her poverty and then took steps to secure Sigwin's admission to the order. Since Friar Maurice was accompanying the diffinitor to the general chapter at Vienna (1282), Peter and Berthold asked him to bring Sigwin with him to Sweden. Whereupon he arrived on St. Lawrence's Eve at Wisby where the provincial chapter was being held.[70] Maurice also carried a letter in which Christine urged Peter to welcome her brother and "to heap on him the benefits of charity more than on me were I there in person." She begged her friend to find a place for Sigwin in his own convent where he would be instructed in the religious life. If Peter, "in whom I confide more than any other mortal," was unable to do this, let Berthold and the other brethren take care of him. Sigwin's waywardness demanded fresh exhortation to do good.[71] Peter afterwards confessed that he had not been too hopeful, considering the great deliberation with which lay brothers were received in the order.[72] But Sigwin donned the habit on the feast of St. Bernard (August 20, 1282) at Västerås.[73] However Christine had not yet learned of his acceptance on All Saints' Day.[74] The adjustment seems to have been easy. Sigwin became cellarer, a post which he filled wisely. Peter also vouches for his devotion and strict observance of the statutes of the order.[75] Chris-

---

[63] *Ibid.*, 237 B (I, 8); cf. *V. Chr.*, 368 C (4).

[64] "Decenter affabilem et religiose jucundam" (*Acta*, 242 A, I, 24).

[65] The Swedish friars called him Gerard since the name Sigwin was not employed in their country (*ibid.*, 359f, V, 43).

[66] *Ibid.*, 293 C (III, 65).

[67] *Ibid.*, 292 F (III, 63).

[68] *Ibid.*, 292 (III, 62).

[69] Cf. Quetif-Echard, I, 410a.

[70] *Acta*, 293 (III, 64); cf. letter of Laurentius Dacus to Christine (359f, V, 42, 46).

[71] *Ibid.*, 293 (III, 65-66).

[72] *Ibid.*, 360 A (V, 43).

[73] *Ibid.*, 293 E (III, 66); cf. 359 F.

[74] *Ibid.*, 316 B (IV, 83); cf. 329 F (IV, 128).

[75] *Ibid.*, 360 A (V, 43); 361 F (V, 50).

tine's brother in turn was evidently happy in the convent.[76]

The Dominican convent at Cologne was in 1268 under the direction of Prior Herman of Havelbrecht.[77] In the *studium generale* established two decades before by Albertus Magnus were a number of students from Sweden who, after spending one or two years in Cologne, would be sent on by their superiors to Paris to complete their theological studies.[78] On their way back to Skenninge or Wisby the friars would perhaps stop again in the city for a short time.[79] Among the brethren from the northern province mentioned in the life were, besides Peter of Dacia, Charles who was returning in the spring of 1268 from Paris to Dacia by way of Cologne and whose appetite for manifestations of ecstasy was so much whetted by Peter that he went as his companion on the third visit to Christine;[80] John Hespe;[81] Helinricus who afterwards became a diffinitor, reporting the acts of the general chapter at Milan in 1278;[82] Andreas Aosiensis (Aciensis or Daciensem) who was on his way to Paris;[83] Laurentius Dacus;[84] and Laurentius Sweus, a student at Cologne in the winter of 1278—1279, who related the death of the parish priest John in a letter carried to Peter by Friar Nicholas of Westraaros.[85] Friar Folquin, who went as Peter's companion to Stommeln, wrote "rarely" to Christine. Yet it was he who on the day after the Nativity of the Virgin (September 9, 1289) notified Christine of Peter's death during Lent.[86] Maurice of Reval (de Revalia) some-

---

[76] *Ibid.*, 361 F (V, 50).

[77] *Ibid.*, 250 A (I, 58); 252 C (I, 67); 254 E (I, 75).

[78] *Ibid.*, 258 B (II, 5); 272 A (II, 56); cf. Thomas of Cantimpré, *BUA.*, II, 1, 8, (p. 115); II, 40, 3 (p. 401).

[79] To mitigate travel hardships Pope Innocent IV urged Queen Blanche of France to curb the levying of tolls on the horses and goods of Swedish prelates heading for the Apostolic See, clerics journeying to the schools, agents and pilgrims (March 18, 1251, *CUP.*, I, 221f, no. 195; Berger, no. 5163). In 1275 a doctor from Dacia seems to have provided a lodging-house at Paris for students from the north (*CUP.*, I, 536, no. 464; this doctor has been identified with Erland who was elected on April 15, 1274 archbishop of Lund and who died in August, 1276, *ibid.*, I, 536, note 1).

[80] *Acta*, 243 (I, 29-30); cf. Gallén, p. 260; Quétif-Echard, I, 410a.

[81] Johannes Dacus, dictus Hespe, who accompanied Peter on the eleventh visit studied at Cologne from 1269 to September 30, 1270 (*Acta*, 254, I, 74); 268 E (II, 44); *V. Chr.*, 375 (41); cf. Gallén, p. 258; Quétif-Echard, I, 410b.

[82] Helinricus was a student at Cologne on September 30, 1270 (*Acta*, 268 E, II, 44; Gallén, pp. 223, 231f, 257; Quétif-Echard, I, 410a). For his activity in 1278 see *MOPH.*, III, 194, note 1.

[83] *Acta*, 268 B (II, 43); Gallén, p. 253; Quétif-Echard, I, 410a.

[84] *Acta*, 359 F (V, 42).

[85] For Nicholas see *Acta*, 276-277 (III, 1-2); 268 F (II, 44) where he gave Christine his Paternoster which he had carried for four years; Gallén, p. 262; Quétif-Echard, I, 411a; for other friars named Nicholas see *Acta*, 244 (I, 36); 268 A; Gallén, p. 262. For Lawrence see *ibid.*, p. 260.

[86] *Acta*, 362 (V, 54). Folquin asked Christine to pray for his blood brothers, Friar Werner who died in Flanders about 1289, Friar John, lector, who died before 1289 in Reval, and Friar Albert, lector at Wisby, who was still alive. Cf. *ibid.*, 361 F (V, 50); Gallén, p. 267; Quétif-Echard, I, 410a.

times acted as Christine's scribe as well as accompanying Peter on visits to Stommeln.[87] As a student he helped to bruit her fame in Paris: "Ever mindful of you," he once wrote to her, "I have always recommended you not only in private prayers but in all discussions with worthy friars and outsiders. I hope and desire that you do the same for me as you promised."[88] Writing a year or so after the death of the prior of Brauweiler, hence in 1272–1273, Maurice admitted knowledge of Christine's multiple afflictions and sorrows arising from injury to her parents as well as bereavement and "aggravated by attacks from enemies."[89]

In addition to the Swedish element the circle claimed among its members Albrandini from the province of Tuscany, an "educated man and a good Preacher,"[90] who steadily became more excited over these hallucinations and demonological visitations;[91] Wipert Boemus from the province of Poland who accompanied Peter on his ninth visit;[92] Friar Baldwin from Flanders;[93] and a Friar Solomon Hungarus.[94] Several German friars were numbered in the company: John of Mussendorp (Muffindorp),[95] Walter of Cologne, Jacob of Andernach,[96] Godfrey Werde, William Bonentant (Bonefant),[97] and Henry of Beitbur (Bethbure).[98] Friar Gerard von Greifen not only acted as *magister studentium* but, as Christine's confessor and scribe, enjoyed until his transference to Coblenz as prior a relationship with the mystic whose intimacy was matched by few others. He accompanied Peter on four visits.[99]

In the background are Godfrey, prior of the Benedictine house at

---

[87] Maurice accompanied Peter to Paris and returned to Cologne in the spring, 1269; he was transferred to Paris to study in September, 1270, and was in the city again on February 13, 1272 (Gallén, p. 261; Quétif-Echard, I, 410b). The references are numerous: *Acta*, 245 (I, 40); 254 (I, 75); 250 (I, 59); 258 (II, 5); 247 (I, 48); 268 (II, 43); 270 (II, 52); 293 (III, 64); *V. Chr.*, 375 F (41).

[88] *Acta*, 351 B (V, 10).

[89] *Ibid.*, 351 (V, 12).

[90] *Ibid.*, 246 F (I, 46); 254 E (I, 75); *V. Chr.*, 374 (34-36).

[91] Cf. Albrandini's letter to Christine, *ibid.*, 349-350 (V, 5).

[92] *Ibid.*, 250 B (I, 59); 251 (I, 62-65); 252 B (I, 66); 256 C (I, 81); *V. Chr.* 374 (36-37); 376 B (43).

[93] *Acta*, 254 (I, 75).

[94] *Ibid.*, 256 C (I, 81); *V. Chr.*, 376 B (43).

[95] Also Musseltorp, *Acta*, 358 B (V, 35). After Peter's departure for Sweden Christine confessed to John, *ibid.*, 273 A (II, 59); cf. 244 F (I, 36); 254 E (I, 75); 252 C (I, 67); 278 A (III, 8); *V. Chr.*, 375 B (38).

[96] *Acta*, 269 A (II, 46); *V. Chr.*, 372 A (23).

[97] *Acta*, 258 E (II, 7).

[98] *Ibid.*, 245 F (I, 41).

[99] *Ibid.*, 241 F (I, 24); 269 (II, 46); 274 A (II, 63); 278 D (III, 11, 8); *V. Chr.*, 372 A (23). Ep. IV describes Gerard, who was "very faithful" to Christine, ill to the point of dying (*Acta*, 259 D [II, 10]. Once when plagued by two demons in the shape of Dominicans she recognized in them Peter and Gerard "sibi carissimorum atque fideliss morum necnon et secretorum ejus magis consciorum" (*ibid.*, 284 E [III, 31]. Cf. Gallén, pp. 228 note 8, 268).

Brauweiler, who was attended by Christine in his last illness,[100] and his companion, the cellarer, both of whom Peter admired;[101] a priest Henry and his sister,[102] the cleric Henry de Sincere who had once supervised the schools in the city;[103] Herman, prior of Cologne, and Arnold, prior of Strasbourg, who as diffinitor passed with his companions through Stommeln on the way to a general chapter.[104] Much sharper in focus is the parish priest and rector of the beguines, John of Stommeln (d. 1277),[105] who was frequently charged with Christine's correspondence.[106] Another secretary and confidant was the oft-mentioned Master John, her chaplain.[107] With him Peter corresponded often, expressing gratitude for his kindness to Christine[108] and concern for the beguines of Stommeln.[109]

Among the women who were drawn to this Christine-centered circle were John of Stommeln's two sisters, Gertrude,[110] who sang hymns with a pleasing voice,[111] and Hadewigis.[112] There were many unnamed *mulieres sanctae* and even recluses wearing the beguine habit[113] to whom salutations were often contained in the correspondence from Sweden.[114] Christine solicited prayers from Peter for recluses who had befriended her.[115] The highly respected Geva, abbess of St. Cecilia in Cologne, which had a *curtis*[116] at Stommeln, is pictured as being surrounded by noble young demoiselles[117] whom she was educating. So close was her association with the Dominicans that she was "like the mother of the friars." For the sake of pious conversation Christine once accompanied Master John and other *religious puellas* to a

---

[100] *Acta,* 273 F (II, 63); for Brauweiler, see GC., III, 758-765; P. Volk, in DHGE., (1938), 457f.

[101] *Ibid.,* 250 (I, 59-60); cf. 303 F (IV, 35).

[102] *Ibid.,* 361 F (V, 50).

[103] *Ibid.,* 313 A (IV, 72).

[104] *Ibid.,* 256 (I, 82).

[105] *V. Chr.,* 369 E (11); cf. 371 note c.

[106] *Acta,* 274 E (II, 66): "Scripserat Dominus Joanne Plebanus de Stumbele manu sua, quia ille erat Christinae familiarissimus, et benefactor praedipuus simul et confessor."

[107] *Ibid.,* 286 E (III, 38) ("capellanus"); cf. 305 (IV, 41); 361-362 (V, 49-51); 293 A (III, 63).

[108] *Ibid.,* 354 C (V, 21).

[109] *Ibid.,* 355 (V, 24).

[110] *Ibid.,* 245 C (I, 38); 251 A (I, 61); 252 B (I, 66); 253 D (I, 71); 268 E (II, 44); cf. *V. Chr.,* 369 E (VI, 11).

[111] *Acta,* 349 F (V, 5).

[112] *Ibid.,* 269 A (II, 46); 350 A (V, 5). Gertrude and Hadewigis are mentioned together (269 A); *V. Chr.,* 372 B (23).

[113] *Acta,* 259 D (II, 10); 361 F (V, 50). One girl is described as "voto castitatis ex corde voluntario in saeculari habitu obligata" (245 C, I, 38).

[114] E. g., *ibid.,* 361 F (V, 50); 362 F.

[115] *Ibid.,* 259 (II, 10).

[116] *Ibid.,* 249 note a; 256 note d.

[117] *Ibid.,* 247 C (I, 48); cf. 256 (I, 82). Friar Hiddo who had been prior provincial in Theutonia for nine years was Geva's confessor and special adviser (*ibid.,* 268A, II, 42).

hermit dwelling in a neighboring wood.[118] To the beguine community must also be added Christine's own sisters Gertrude and Hilla;[119] Hilla von Kingidorp (Ingendorp);[120] Engelrade, the advocate's daughter.[121] The old and infirm beguine Alice who, it was believed, had lost her sight by weeping, was pictured as a paragon of patience.[122] Hilla von Berg (de Monte),[123] Christine's kinswoman and the inseparable compassion of her tribulations, merited Peter's praise for cheerfulness and equanimity.[124]

If Christine remained the center of attention, it was primarily Peter who brought her out of isolation. Without doubt he was justified in claiming the name he had acquired among the villagers.[125] Just as the saint questioned him about priestly duties, the other women liked to hear him discuss matters of theology, annotate religious songs, and explain by Ptolemaic circles the hymn that was sung in the office of the virgins: *Post te canentes cursitant*.[126] The friar has left a delightful description of one of these meetings which occurred on the seventh visit. Geva went out into the field with her *puellis* and *domicellabus*, followed by four friars. From her own order were six well-lettered maidens whom Peter called *dominae* because of profession, but *domicellae* in deference to their nobility and youth.[127] Following the walk, the abbess took her seat on a hill with the friars and women gathered about. The priest suggested to her: "Here there are in your presence four students of the Friars Preachers from different provinces. Ask them to discuss some theological question." She accordingly turned to Peter "not because of his learning" but because she knew him best. He asked her to act as moderator, for he feared "that as usual an uproar would break out among the disputants." But since this was her first experience with a disputation

---

[118] *Ibid.*, 300 B (IV, 20).

[119] *Ibid.*, 258 E (II, 7); 252 (I, 66); 273 C (II, 61); 259 C (II, 10). Only one sister is mentioned with her brother (293 A, III, 63). Hilla appears alone (359 F, V, 42); 361-362 (V, 49-50); 362 F (V, 54).

[120] *Ibid.*, 252 B (I, 66); 259 C (II, 10); 273 C (II, 61); 277 B (III, 3); 361 (V, 49-50). Hilla is mentioned with recluses, 262 B (II, 19). For Hilla, Christine's niece, 259 C (II, 10).

[121] *Ibid.*, 362 F (V, 54).

[122] *Ibid.*, 245 C (I, 38); 245 D (I, 39); 352 F (V, 15); 361 (V, 49-50); *V. Chr.*, 371 B (19); 372 A (23).

[123] *Ibid.*, 245 B (I, 38); 251 A (I, 61); 252 B (I, 66); 253 D (I, 71); 255 E (I, 79); 293 A (III, 63); 286 C (III, 37); 288 C (III, 44); 295 (IV, 4); 361 (V, 49-50); 362 B (V, 51, 54); *V. Chr.*, 374 B (34). For "Hillas omnes" (*Acta*, 351-352, V, 9, 15).

[124] *Ibid.*, 245 (I, 38). For Peter's first letter to her, *ibid.*, 354-355 (V, 23).

[125] *Ibid.*, 247 A (I, 46).

[126] *Ibid.*, 246-246 (I, 41). During the fifteenth visit all the beguines of Stommeln assembled and prepared a meal for Peter, the priest, Folquin, the advocate's son Gerard, and Master John. Afterwards Peter gave a talk on spiritual joy (278 E, III, 12).

[127] *Ibid.*, 247 (I, 48): "Quas Dominas nominaverim pro professione, sed Domicellas pro nobilitate et quorumdam juniorem aetate."

she was curious to see the outcome. She thus propounded, at the instance of the pastor, the question whether it was more important that Christ committed the Church to St. Peter or his Mother, the Virgin, to St. John. Albrandini, being the oldest and a native of the Patrimony of St. Peter, defended St. Peter's dignity while Peter of Dacia defended St. John's purity and affableness. The debate was interrupted by a shout that Christine had fallen—Peter says the devil threw her—into a cistern. In the untold filth they could only make out her head being held up by Hilla de Monte. Peter needed the help of the pastor and Albrandini to pull her out. Upon recovering consciousness, she was horrified to learn that she had been handled by men.[128]

It is possible that Peter revisited Christine for a last time in 1287, on his way back from the general chapter at Bordeaux.[129] But with his death the following year the letters ceased. The contemporary *vita* offers a few more particulars, but the author adds significantly: "After the battle of Woeringen (June 5, 1288) all persecution of the Devil ceased altogether."[130]

Christine's biography gains its significance by carefully tracing the process whereby certain Dominican friars, a generation before Meister Eckhart, were developing a lively interest in the mystical currents, surging within semireligious associations or appealing to individual *mulieres sanctae*.

ECKHART'S PASTORAL CARE

If his German sermons and tractates alone are consulted, Meister Eckhart appears only as a mystic who had little in common with the schoolmen.[131] Partly for want of thoroughly authenticated works, in Latin and the vernacular,[132] and partly because of his own methods and views, veiled as they are in obscure language and subtleties as well as often being transmitted in imperfect form, the connection of the Dominican preacher with popular heresy has frequently been distorted and magnified. Ambiguity bewildered his own contemporaries. While Tauler and Suso regarded their master as a great theologian and a saintly man and whereas Elsbeth Stagel and Elsbeth von Begenhofen in the Swiss nunneries of Töss and Ötenbach respec-

---

[128] *Ibid.*, 247 F (I, 50); cf. 268 C (II, 43); V. Chr., 374 (34).
[129] *Acta*, 362 (V, 52).
[130] *V. Chr.*, 387 A (108), cf. Bollandists, 363 (V, 55).
[131] Pfeiffer, *Meister Eckhart* (Göttingen, 1857); for an appraisal of Pfeiffer's contribution see Beuken in *OGE.*, VIII (1934), 310-313.
[132] For a discussion of these works see Funke, *Meister Eckehart*, pp. 31-41; Vernet, in *DTC.*, IV (Paris, 1911), coll. 2060-2062; Axters' bibliography (in *OGE.*, VI, 1932, 113-125; pp. 124-125 summarizes the literature on Eckhart but makes no mention of the literature on the trial); P. Glorieux, *Répertoire*, I, 180-185.

tively admired his ideas, other Dominicans tried to soften what was reprehensible in his teaching.[133] Middle Dutch-Flemish translations of his writings demonstrate that Eckhart was widely considered an authority on the spiritual life.[134] He undertook to instruct the laity and extraregular communities—beghards and beguines as well as the *Gottesfreunde*—no less than the religious of his order, and for this purpose it was necessary to employ the vulgar tongue.[135] The Dominican nunneries at Strasbourg, which were developing into hearths of mysticism, heard him often. He also may have been a lector in the local convent. So closely, indeed, was Eckhart's name associated with this city that this may account for the tradition that he was a native of the city.

Successful as he was in expounding abstruse tenets of scholastic philosophy in an undeveloped language which he had to supply with words and fashion to his needs, yet it was in Latin that his ideas achieved greater precision.[136] He was accused of preaching to the people in their own tongue—which was not so bad in itself. But he offered instruction in matters which were construed as heretical. On March 27, 1329, Pope John XXII issued the bull *In Agro Dominico*[137] in which he condemned twenty-eight propositions, drawn from Eckhart's Latin and German writings, seventeen (1-15, 27, 28) as heretical, the rest as "ill sounding, rash, and suspect, although by means of many expositions and additions these can be interpreted in a Catholic sense."[138] "He has wished to know more than he should," was the papal verdict. Then followed the prohibition to defend or approve the condemned articles; the bull concludes by stating that Eckhart before his death unequivocally retracted any word, spoken or written, that was found to contain heresy or was capable of heterodox interpretation. On April 15 the pope instructed the archbishop of Cologne

---

[133] Raynaldus, ad an. 1337, n. 14; Quétif-Echard, I, 507. Raynaldus (ad an. 1329, nos. 50, 72) regarded him as a heresiarch and blasphemer. In any case Eckhart is treated casually with emphasis being put only on the propositions condemned by John XXII.

[134] J. H. A. Beuken, "Rondom een middelnederlandsche Eckehart-Tekst," *OGE.*, VIII (1934), 310-337; C. G. N. de Vooys, "Meister Eckart en de Nederlandse mystiek," *NAK.*, N.S., III (1905), 50-92, 176-194, 265-290; Langenberg, *Quellen und Forschungen zur Geschichte der deutschen Mystik*, pp. 183ff; D. de Man, in *NAK.*, N.S., XX (1927), 38-39; 285; idem, "Meister Eckehart in Weesper Handschriften," *ibid.*, XX (1927), 281-288; for the criticism of John of Léau or Afflighem (d. 1377), see *Een boexken van Meester Eckaerts leere daer hi in doelde*, Bibl. roy. de Belg., cod. 888-90; De Vooys, *l.c.*, Axters, *Jan van Leeuwen*, pp. xi-lxiii; Maria Alberta Lücker, *Meister Eckhart und die Devotio Moderna (Studien und Texte zur Geistesgeschichte des Mittealters*, I, Leiden, 1950).

[135] Denifle, in *ALKM.*, II, 527-528; Funke, *Meister Eckehart*, p. 38.

[136] Denifle, in *ALKM.*, II, 423: "Eckhart spricht eben in seinen lateinischen Schriften magistraliter; er lehrt als Scholastiker und schreibt für Scholastiker."

[137] Denifle, in *ALKM.*, II, 636-640, no. 4; Preger, *Geschichte*, I, 479-482, App. v.

[138] "Male sonantes, temerarii et suspectos de haeresi, licet cum multis expositionibus et suppletionibus sensum catholicum formare valeant vel habere."

to publish it so that the hearts of the simple, especially of those before whom the Dominican had preached, might remain free from the errors of his teaching.[139] Before Eckhart was reproached in the inquisitorial process of 1327, shortly before his death, and in papal pronouncement that he "dogmatizavit multa fidem veram in cordibus multorum obnubilantia, que docuit quammaxime in suis predicationibus coram vulgo simplici,"[140] he had probably encountered the complaint that he profaned high scholastic tradition by appealing directly to the uneducated. At the general chapter in Venice in 1325 it was pointed out that certain German friars, when preaching to the illiterate, were presenting objectionable and dangerous teachings in their sermons which could easily lead their listeners astray.[141] Three years later at Toulouse the chapter reprimanded those preachers who were trying to gain popular approval by subtleties which not only did not improve conduct but led directly to error. Lectors too were cautioned not to teach or embellish in their questions and lections such harmful things or what they might know imperfectly.[142] Whether Eckhart was the target of the first rebuke and whether the archbishop bore partial responsibility for the charge brought against him is not at all certain.[143] The Master's own answer was contained in his *Buch der göttlichen Tröstung* which was dedicated to Queen Agnes of Hungary: "If we are not to teach the untutored, no one will ever be taught. For we instruct the uneducated that they may become the educated. If there were nothing new, there would be nothing old."[144]

It was formerly maintained[145] on the strength of a letter written by Herveus, general of the Dominican order, to the priors of Worms and Mainz that Eckhart was transferred to Frankfurt after 1317 and that here suspicion was cast upon his orthodoxy because of alleged flirting with extraregular groups. Not only is the assumption false but the phrase *suspecta familiaritas* is used in the sense of improper

---

[139] Kisky, *Regesten*, IV, 438, no. 1818; Denifle in *Zeitschrift für deutsches Altertum*, XXIX, N.F. XVII (1885), 266, no. 3.

[140] *ALKM.*, II, 636.

[141] *MOPH.*, IV, 160-161.

[142] *Ibid.*, 180.

[143] Assuming that the complaints of 1325 are too general, Denifle (*ALKM.*, II, 623f) believed that they had reference to the interdict in which the conflict between the pope and Louis of Bavaria involved Germany, especially since the minutes of the Chapter joined this protest to that which accused certain German friars of gross negligence in the publication of the papal process against the Emperor. Cf. Funke, *Meister Eckehart*, p. 21. But granting that the affair was more concerned with errors of faith than political issues (S. Deutsch, "Meister Eckehart," *Realencyclopedie f. protestantische Theologie und Kirche,* V [1898], 144), nothing certain is known of the matter, not even the result of the investigation of the vicar Gervasius of Angers from the province of France (*MOPH.*, IV, 161).

[144] Cited by Quint in *Zschr. f. deutschen Kulturgeschichte*, V (1939), 215.

[145] E.g., Preger, *Geschichte*, I, 352; Jundt, *Essai*, p. 72.

familiarity with women and never of association with heretics.[146] This compromised position really rests upon confusion with frater Ekardus, prior of Frankfurt.[147] Had the suspicion been well grounded, it is improbable that some time previous to 1326 the provincial would have despatched Eckhart to Cologne to become professor of theology at the Dominican *studium generale*. On the other hand, a Strasbourg devotional writer named Rulman Merswin[148] relates that a devout priest called on Meister Eckhart to give him a friendly warning about his sermons and to urge him to give up preaching of matters that very few people could understand. Although Merswin was not a very reliable witness, the account seems to reflect the views of certain quarters at the time.[149] Eckhart did not in the main have personal relations with the beghards or the bishop of Strasbourg[150] and was not charged with heresy, nor did he provoke overt opposition, before he was brought to trial by the archiepiscopal court in 1326.[151] His own statement before the Inquisition the following January would appear to have been uttered in good faith. His order, he declared, had been at no time since its foundation dishonored by the heresy of any friar in the province of Germany.[152] Sensing that through the trial both he and the order were being disgraced before the public, Eckhart, after delivering the sermon in the Dominican church on February 13, 1327, begged Conrad of Halberstadt to read in public a declaration in Latin which he had previously drawn up. In this prepared statement he took pains to point out article by article that from the outset he had carefully avoided every error of faith and every lapse in morals. He then expressed his willingness to retract whatever heretical ideas he might have written or preached.[153]

The beghards of Strasbourg had been condemned by John of

---

[146] Denifle, in *ALKM.*, II, 618-624; Clark, *Great German Mystics*, p. 10 (the entire chapter on Eckhart, pp. 7-35, is illuminating).

[147] Denifle denies the identification (*ALKM.*, II, 631); cf. Funke, *Meister Eckehart*, pp. 19-20.

[148] Jundt, *Essai*, pp. 215-227; for Rulman see Clark, *op. cit.*, pp. 75-97.

[149] *Ibid.*, pp. 11f.

[150] Denifle, in *ALKM.*, II, 617; Funke, *Meister Eckehart*, p. 23.

[151] *ALKM.*, II, 616, 624; Delacroix, *Mysticisme speculatif en Allemagne*, p. 220; Funke, *Meister Eckehart*, pp. 22f.

[152] "Numquam a tempore sue fundationis nec in aliquo magistro sacre scripture vel in aliquo simplici fratre in provincia Theutonie fuit de heresi infamatus" (*ALKM.*, II, 628). And yet he had been summoned "cum semper fuerim bone fame iudicio bonorum hominum et communium" (*ibid.*, 629; cf. 617). Out of hostility to the rival order, the Franciscans must bear much responsibility for the proceedings at Cologne. Four friars in particular—Henry of Thalheim, Francesco d'Ascoli, William of Ockham, and Bonagratia of Bergamo—angrily reproached John XXII for favoring the Dominican Eckhart and neglecting the extirpation of heresy (Preger, *Geschichte*, I, 483-484, App. vi).

[153] *ALKM.*, II, 630-633, no. 2; Preger, *Geschichte*, I, 475-476, App. iii. For opinions on the sincerity of this statement see Funke, *Meister Eckehart*, pp. 27f; cf. Delacroix, *op. cit.*, pp. 227-229.

Dürbheim who called to the attention of his clergy seven errors of the beguines and beghards in his diocese and forbade all communication with them, including bestowal of alms.[154] Whether or not these errors were drawn from Eckhart's writings, he continued his preaching at Strasbourg until after 1322 without molestation on account of morals or conduct. There is no proof that he was ever harassed by the bishop of Strasbourg.

In a study of the beguines Eckhart's activity in Strasbourg as a professor of sacred theology and ordinary preacher has capital importance. The Latin sermons he addressed to the religious brethren either in monasteries or at chapters of the Order. But to the several convents of nuns and beguinages placed under his spiritual direction, as well as to the people, he preached in the vernacular. He was best known for sermons which completed within Dominican circles that bridge between mysticism and scholasticism for regulars and extra-regulars alike already presaged by Peter of Dacia a generation earlier. He won acceptance in the churches of Dominican nuns as much by his personality as by his preaching. Yet the ground had long been prepared for such activity, even as his prose had been anticipated by a vigorous Flemish tradition. That Dietrich von Freiburg, "one of the greatest medieval preachers of spirituality,"[155] is completely overshadowed by the Master is in no small measure due to the paucity of documentary evidence and the total absence of his sermons. Only an unnamed nun offers a clue to the content of sermons in a poem which praises the merits of three preachers.[156] The first, "the precious lector," is not named, as he is known to all.[157] The second is Master Dietrich, the "high master" who speaks exclusively of the beginning and wishes to "reveal to us the eagle's flight and to plunge our soul into the depths without depth."[158] The third is the "wise Meister Eckhart who speaks of Nothingness; whoever does not understand it, in him divine illumination has never shone."[159]

The origins of Eckhart's thought were two-fold. From scholasticism he took its dogmas, its phraseology, and its methods. Truly, he represented a continuation of Thomist tradition. On the other hand, inspired by the metaphysics, grounded on the hierarchy of emanations

[154] For John of Dürbheim's policy see below pp. 528-29, 531-34.

[155] Hauck, V, 1, 261-270; Krebs, *Meister Dietrich*.

[156] The text is published by Krebs, *op. cit.*, p. 148 and Funke, *Meister Eckehart*, p. 37, note 22.

[157] "Der werde lesemeister,/ Der wil ir einer sin,/Er wil dy sele reizzen/ Mit der minnen furbit./Siner minnen sticke/ Dvt er ir also heiz,/ Daz sy von recher minnen/ Nuderniden enweiz./ Scheden abe."

[158] "Der hohe meister Diderich/ Der wil vns machen froh,/ Er sprachet Ivter-lichen/ Al in principio./ Des adelares fluke/ Wil er vns machen kunt,/ In den grunt ane grunt/ Scheidet abe."

[159] "Der wise meister hechart/ Wil vns von niche san,/ Der dez nid enverstat,/ Der mag ez gode clan./ In den hat nit gelvchet/ Des gvdeliche schin./ Scheiden."

from the Absolute, of Neo-Platonism, he sometimes suggested the immanence of God, His full manifestation in human conscience, and the possibility of being absorbed in the divine. This was at once the source of his mysticism and of that doctrine which pose for modern scholarship as well as for his contemporaries profound difficulties. Although he himself condemned the immoral consequences that beghards and Free Spirits were able to deduce from quietistic principles, certain points in his own teaching nevertheless approximated theirs and could easily be appropriated by them.[160] He was accused, for example, of obliterating the division between the being of God and that of man. His best known doctrine was that of the Seelenfünklein, or spark of the soul. The fact that he believed in the creation and indestructibility of that spark as well as in divine grace negates the pantheism with which his name has been so closely identified.[161]

Eckhart's unique contribution lay in probing the depths of the soul, in exploring and charting the inner pathway to God, and in quickening others to desire the all-absorbing experience of God. To this end his extraordinary ability as a preacher in the vernacular aided immeasurably in capturing the lay audience; in the cure of nuns he was able to make articulate and give direction to the mystical yearnings prevalent in women's convents.[162] His immense reputation testifies to a wide-spread hunger for the deepening of spiritual life.[163] The sixth treatise, "Daz ist swester Katrei, meister Ekeharts tohter von Strâsburg," originated most probably among the beghards or the Brothers of Free Spirit who wished to shield themselves behind the name of Eckhart.[164] For the first time German Dominican nuns heard in their language scholastic speculations. But the nature of these subjects and his methods caused him to be often misunderstood, not only by the common people but even by the more learned who either heard or read his treatises. On one occasion when the complaint was voiced that nobody understood his sermons, Eckhart replied: "Whoever wishes to comprehend my sermons must have five things. He ought to be victorious in all conflicts, to strive unceasingly after the highest good, to perform all things that God asks of him, to be a beginner

[160] Delacroix, Mysticisme speculatif en Allemagne, pp. 100-101; for Eckhart and Neo-Platonism see ibid., pp. 239-261.
[161] Clark, Great German Mystics, pp. 19f.
[162] Rufus M. Jones, The Flowering of Mysticism (New York, 1939), pp. 70ff; cf. ALKM., II, 484ff; 518.
[163] Opponents too agreed on the acceptance of Eckhart's eloquence in Germany and diverse other regions: see Michael of Cesena's protest of September 18, 1328 (BF., V, 409): "Quod magnam multitudinem populi in provincia Theutonica et in aliis diversis partibus ad ipsas haereses credendas et divulgandas secum traxit."
[164] Ed. Birlinger, in Alemannia, III (1875), 15ff; less reliably by Pfeiffer, Deutsche Mystiker, II, 448-475; transl. C. de B. Evans, London, 1924, I, 312-334. For doubts concerning Eckhart's authorship see Grundmann, Joachim von Floris, p. 178; Hauck, V, 1, 411 and note 4; cf. Funke, Meister Eckehart, p. 34.

with beginners, and to annihilate the self, and become such a master of himself as to be incapable of anger."[165] He realized the difficulties: "There are many who do not understand this, and it does not surprise me, for to grasp the meaning one must be in great detachment and exalted above all these things."[166] "Whosoever is unable to follow this discourse, let him not worry. As long as he is not like this truth he shall not see my argument, for it is the naked truth straight from the heart of God."[167]

[165] Pfeiffer, II, 2.
[166] Pred. 66, Pfeiffer, II, 209.
[167] Pred. 87, Pfeiffer, II, 284.

Part Four

POPULAR DEVOTIONAL LITERATURE

❧ I ❧

Literacy in Cistercian and Beguine Circles

As the immediate connection between the pious circles formed under Lambert le Bègue's supervision in Liége and the tremendous surge of the feminine religious movement at the turn of the century remains an unanswered question, so are also wanting the links between Lambert's first contributions to a popular literature for these lay societies and the sizable religious works of the middle of the thirteenth century. It is possible, as Van Mierlo has suggested, that in the Belgian sisterhoods a whole body of mystical literature, hagiographical and devotional, already existed in the first half of the thirteenth century but, like Lambert's, was lost. It is difficult to conceive how such works as Hadewijch's *Visions* and lyrics or the *Seven Maniren van Heiligher Minnen* of Beatrice of Nazareth, the oldest piece of prose in Middle Flemish known at present,[1] could spring up almost simultaneously without some preparation for their language and intellectual climate through a vernacular moral-didactic literature. What makes them even more important is the fact that they appeared two generations before Eckhart's activity and anticipated Ruysbroeck and the *devotio moderna* which must be considered the culmination of medieval Belgian spirituality.[2]

In dealing with popular devotional writings in the beguinages and Cistercian nunneries other questions arise: Did the beghards and beguines themselves produce writings for their own edification and to satisfy the spiritual yearnings of the lay public? Did the beguine houses possess libraries and, if so, what were the contents? In what degree were the inhabitants literate? Unfortunately neither testaments, chronicle notices and charters, nor the relatively numerous statutes throw much light on these problems, since they are largely concerned with the external history of the movement or its *modus vivendi*. Occasionally spiritual biographies offer a clue. It is true that ordinary devotional practices are prescribed in the statutes and even sermons

---

[1] Van Mierlo, in *DHGE.*, VII (1934), 562.
[2] Van Mierlo, "Over het ontstaan der Germaansche mystiek," *OGE.*, I (1927), 11-37; id., "Hadewijch en Wilhelm van St. Thierry," *ibid.*, III (1929), 45-59.

365

were delivered by certain beguine superiors,[3] while admirers and opponents alike refer to the religious atmosphere, sincere or feigned as the author's predilection may be, which prevailed in the beguinage. But of a specific devotional literature, in vernacular prose or verse, that aimed to trace the progress of the spirit and to guide its yearnings for the mystical Bridegroom little is known, especially for the period of spontaneous development and full bloom.

All too frequently those beguines and beghards who were interested in quietistic mysticism and pantheism, and were consequently confounded by their opponents with the Brethren of the Free Spirit, were the most articulate. From the testimony of Conrad of Megenberg (d. 1374) one would conclude that the Free Spirits, for the most part coarse and energetic men, but quite unlettered and spurning manual work,[4] sought in their wanderings the hospitality of the beguines by offering them their teachings under the cloak of mystery or allegory (coloratis verbis), as if they were "the angel of the divine word." The beguines, he continues, assembled in the greatest secrecy to hear from strangers a discussion of the attributes of God and the nature of divine goodness; then, gradually coming down from these heights, they taught that man is created in the image of God and that by means of religious exercises he can attain a degree of perfection equal to that possessed by Christ on earth.[5] The Clementine decree, Cum de quibusdam mulieribus, found particularly reprehensible the willingness of beguines to dispute the Trinity and divine essence and in respect to the articles of faith and the sacraments to spread opinions that undermined the Church.[6] Far from revealing the true consequences of their doctrine, it was their practice to win appeal by employing symbolical language and allegorical interpretation of scripture. Earlier the Collectio de Scandalis Ecclesiae, a contribution of Gilbert of Tournai to the reform program of the second council of Lyons (1274), looked askance at translations and commentaries of the Scriptures in beguine meetings. "There are among us," he wrote, "women called beguines some of whom blossom forth in subtleties and rejoice in novelties. They have interpreted in ordinary French idiom the mysteries of Scripture which are scarcely accessible to experts in divine writing. They read them in common, irreverently, boldly, in conventicles, convents, and on squares. I have seen, read, and possessed the French bible a copy of which has been displayed by the booksellers at Paris to record the heresies and errors, doubts and untoward interpretations

[3] Lecoy de la Marche, pp. 32f; see above, p. 343.
[4] De erroribus Begehardorum ex codice manuscripto Conradi de Monte Puellarum Canonici Ratisbonensis contra Beghardos et Beginas, Max. Bibl. Vet. Pat., XXV, 310; Mosheim, p. 314.
[5] Max. Bibl. Vet. Pat., XXV, 310; Mosheim, pp. 314-315.
[6] Fredericq, Corpus, I, 167; see below, pp. 524,527.

contained therein."[77] On the other hand, Alphonso a Castro, the Franciscan who was confessor to Charles V, summed up in 1539 the longstanding complaint that from perverse understanding of Scripture came the Waldensians and the beghards, "all men untaught and quite ignorant of letters."[8] Following the lead of their "Martha," the Swestriones in the Utrecht and Rhenen congregations (1393—94) recited prayers and lections in the vernacular. Many, it was alleged, were well-educated (*boni literati*) but did not have the taste of Scripture.[9] Books in the vernacular continued the initiation of the best educated laymen while songs served better to impress their principles upon the popular mind. Opponents never cease to underline the passion of heretics for learning.[10] This heterodox literature appears to have been abundant although it is known only by references of antagonists or in fragments.[11]

Margaret Porete is a case in point.[12] She incurred episcopal hostility by circulating a book which contained views which the inquisitors considered erroneous. The fact that her teachings spread among simple folk leads to the conclusion that they must have been couched in the vulgar tongue. To lend weight to this supposition is evidence that she prepared a translation of Scripture[13] in which she committed errors in articles of faith. Nevertheless Margaret no longer belonged to the church-schooled, orthodox beguines of Belgium and northern France from whom she could very well have come as a native of Hainault. She must have been an unattached beguine, with no fixed residence, regarding mendicancy as a means of livelihood, pursuing a life of moral laxity, and refusing to submit to authority. For the fourteenth century she was a sectarian, far removed from the *beginae clausae* who dominated the extraregular scene in Belgium.

In like fashion Mary of Valenciennes (c. 1400) is known only through the eyes of her opponents. John Gerson was alarmed by the "incredible subtlety" of her book on divine love ("de dilectione Dei . . .

---

[7] Döllinger, *Beiträge zur politischen Kirchlichen und Cultur-Geschichte*, III, 199.
[8] Deanesley, *Lollard Bible*, pp. 51-52.
[9] Fredericq, *Corpus*, II, 153, cf. 154, 160, 163f.
[10] *Anon. Pass., Bibl. Max. Vet. Pat.*, XXV, 265 F, 273; Stephen of Bourbon,*Anec. hist.*, p. 308.
[11] Cf. Gerson, *De Mystica Theologia Speculativa* (Opp. omn., III, 369): "Propterea necesse est pro argutione, aut directione talium (i.e., beghards) esse viros studiosos in libris eorum, qui devotionem habuerunt secundum scientiam." In 1373 books and clothing of the Paris Turlupins were burned outside the gate of St. Honoré (Ray naldus, XXVI, 241, no. 21, an. 1373).
[12] For her life, ideas, and trial, see below pp. 490-492.
[13] Fredericq, *Corpus*, II, 65, *Axters* (*Gesch. van de vroomheid*, II, 162f, 170-178) attributes to Margaret the *Mirouer des simples ames* in which the author is greeted by the Trinity as a daughter and sister. The treatise enjoyed some currency in Italy.

libellum incredibile pene subtilitate compositum") which seemed all
the more dangerous to the chancellor of the University of Paris because it gave proof of the extraordinary sharpness and depth of her
spirit. If this able (*composita*) woman can confuse scholars, what must
she not accomplish with the simple and unlettered? This *begarda*,
as Gerson calls her,[14] used the vernacular to spread to a wider audience
her teachings on libertinism. Expressing views that link her to the
Amalrician and Ortlibian tradition, she applied what is set forth
about the divine fruition to the passions seething in her own soul,
and she argued that he who reaches the perfection of divine love is
released from the observance of all precepts.[15]

Finally, Bloemardinne of Brussels (d. 1336), long identified with
the poetess-mystic, Hadewijch,[16] was credited with a "considerable
literature on the spirit of freedom and the most abominable venereal
love which she called seraphic." Revered by her "many" followers as
the founder of a new doctrine, she was wont to sit, while teaching and
writing, on a silver seat which was presented after her death to the
duchess of Brabant who admired her ideas.[17] The more disciples she
had, even in the upper classes from which she herself possibly sprang,
the more significant was Ruysbroeck's exposure of her writings.

The Brothers of the Free Spirit and, by the same token, the beghards
and beguines presumably assimilated a number of Eckhart's propositions without following him to the heights of moral idealism to
which he would have lifted the spiritual life of the people. In this
palpably considerable body of heretical literature must be included
the writings of Walter the Hollander, burned at Cologne in 1322.
This Lollard or beghard, although deficient in Latin and ignorant
of French, was nevertheless skilled in disputation and was credited
with several little books (*plures libellos*) in Dutch (*sermone Theutonico*).[18] One Gerard published a treatise on the spiritual exercises
necessary to restore man from the fall, while a Frankfurt beghard
(*eynen Lolhartbruder*), Bosehans by name, was apprehended by the

---

[14] Gerson, *Tractatus de distinctione verarum visionum a falsis, Quintum signum Op. omn.*, I, 55). Cf. Lea, *History of the Inquestion*, II, 127, 405; Mosheim,
p. 308.

[15] Gerson, in *Op. omn.*, I, 55: "Et enim, si predicta Maria, non de viatoribus
utique ligatis ad preceptorum divinorum impletionem, sed de statu beatorum dilec-
tionem quam scribebat applicasset, vix altius quicquam de divina fruitione quo ad
aliqua dici potuerat. Sic fallebat eam sua tumiditas animi tante passioni dilectionis
immixta. Putabat igitur se frui Deo, dum vigebat hec passio fortis circa Deum in
eius animo quantumcumque a divinis preceptis longe esset."

[16] See below, pp. 494-495.

[17] Henry Pomerius, *Vita B. Joannis Rusbrochii, AB.*, IV (1885), 286, cap. 5.

[18] Mosheim, p. 273; Fredericq, *Corpus*, I, 172f; cf. Moll, *Kerkgeschiedenis*, II 3,
64-65. Nicholas Schatenius claimed that Walter was responsible for "sparsisque in
vulgus libellis Germanico idiomate scriptis" (Mosheim, p. 274). For Walter's career
see *ibid.*, pp. 270-277.

archbishop of Mainz in 1457 for a heretical tract.[19] In France the sect possessed several writings, some of which were burned in 1372, but of them Gerson could still see copies.[20]

The beghards were thus interested in providing a body of devotional literature in the vernacular for their conventicles. Some even thought that they could replace the Gospels, should they be destroyed, with sounder books.[21] It is therefore reasonable to assume that the inquisitorial processes of the fourteenth century wiped out much religious literature in the vernacular. Not only did John of Dürbheim enjoin his suffragans to prohibit "writings, hymns, and teachings,"[22] but Charles IV, in his third directive in June, 1369, called attention to the sermons, treatises, pamphlets, leaves, and bound books in the vulgar tongue which were being disseminated in lay and semi-religious circles—*personas laycas vel pene laycas*—and were causing widespread defection from orthodox piety.[23] Walter Kerling and Louis de Caliga were therefore urged to confiscate all such writings regardless of the rank of the author. The inquisitors would then be enforcing canon law which forbids lay people of either sex to read German scriptures.[24] The phrase *secundum canonicas sanctiones* would appear, however, to have been employed more loosely than papal response to translation justifies;[25] the emperor was concerned only with the pernicious writings of Jews, bad Christians, or heathen.

John Nider, a Swabian reformer belonging to the Dominican convent of Basel (d. 1438), described certain beghards in his *Formicarius* at the time of the council of Basel who

> use subtle, sublime, spiritual and metaphysical words, such as the German tongue can hardly express, so that scarcely any man, even an educated man, can fully understand them; and in these they wrap up lofty sentences about spirit, abstraction, various lights, divine persons, and the grades of contemplation. ... And certain German books full of their subtle sermons, plainly do good service to their evil intention, and use such expressions; and some of the books were written foolishly and rashly, or were allowed to be copied,—unless I much mistake; and there are some at least which are obviously falsely ascribed to certain honest and ancient doctors of religion by certain beghards or heretics. For they hide the poison of their depravity beneath the cloak of such words, and express the venom of their malignant heresy by means of them.[26]

---

[19] *Tractatus de spirituali exercitatione reparationis lapsus*, Mosheim, p. 376; Kriegk, I, 129.

[20] *Collectorium super Magnificat* (1427), *Op. omn.*, IV, 622.

[21] John of Dürbheim's letter of 1317 (Mosheim, p. 258): "Item dicunt, aliquos ex eis posse meliores libros reparare omnibus libris catholicae fidei, si fuerint destructi."

[22] Mosheim, p. 259.

[23] Fredericq, *Corpus*, I, 216.

[24] "Praesertim cum laycis utriusque sexus secundum canonicas sanctiones etiam libris vulgaribus quibuscumque de sacra scriptura uti non liceat" (*ibid.*, I, 216).

[25] Jostes, in *HJ.*, XI (1890), 12.

[26] Cited from Deanesly, *Lollard Bible*, pp. 82-83, with permission of the Cambridge University Press.

Against such collections of subtle sermons and the translations undertaken by laymen a sweeping measure of prohibition was enacted by the emperor. Charles IV, always a staunch defender of the Church, was himself interested in devotional literature, especially saints' lives. But in 1369 his interview with Urban V at Rome decided him to launch a campaign against German religious writings. We shall trace elsewhere the course of this persecution.

As itinerant bands of penitents, renowned for mortification of the flesh and fanatical zeal,[27] passed through the streets of a town in pairs about the time of the Black Death, they sang in their native tongues, the Flemings in Flemish, the men of Brabant in Brabançon, and the French in theirs,[28] hymns to God, the Virgin Mary, and the passion of Christ.[29]

> In Dietsche hadden si enen sanc,
> Wel ghemaect, redelijc lanc,
> Die op Gode riep met ernste groot,
> Dat Hise hoede vander gadoot.[30]

That singing in the vernacular was an effective means to create a spirit of brotherhood among the flagellants is clearly emphasized by the songs which are extant. Once in the market-place where they divested themselves, they "would sing, while doing penance, very piteous songs of the nativity of our Lord and His passion."[31] These French or Flemish songs, to which those members of the band who did not scourge themselves responded in chorus, were attuned to the rhythm of the arm which brandished the rod and inflicted the strokes. Phrases in the songs seemed to indicate the successive moments of the

---

[27] "Ordo flagellantium que dicebatur penitentia laycorum" was Salimbene's definition (Chron., MGH. SS., XXXII, 464f) of demonstrations in Italian communes about 1260; cf. ibid., 254; Continuatio Praedicatorum Vindobonensium, an. 1261, ibid., IX, 728. Consult Fredericq, De Secten der Geeselaars en der Dansers in de Nederlanden tijdens de XIVe eeuw (Brussels, 1897); reprinted in Gesch. d. Inquis., II, 61-102; id., Corpus, I, 190-201, nos. 194-202; II, 96-141, nos. 61-89; III, 13-39, nos. 15-28; K. Lechner, "Die grosse Geisselfahrt des Jahres 1349," HJ., V (1884), 437-462; Coville, "Ecrits contemporains sur la peste de 1348 à 1350—Documents sur les Flagellants," HLF., XXXVII (1938), 325-411; G. Bareille, in DTC., VI (1915), 12-18.

[28] "Cantando secundum suum ydioma, Flamingi in flamingo, illi de Brabantia in theutonico, et Gallici in gallico" (Gilles li Muisis, Chronicon, in Fredericq, Corpus, II, 108). For examples, Fredericq, Corpus, III, 23-27; Hoffmann von Fallersleben, Geschichte des deutschen Kirchenliedes, pp. 130-149.

[29] "Chantant haultement chanchons de Dieu et de Notre Dame, rimées et dictées" (Jehan le Bel, Les Vrayes Chroniques, in Fredericq, Corpus, II, 122); Gesta Abb. Trud., MGH. SS., X, 432; Het Boec vander Wraken, III, vss. 1995ff; 2027ff (ed. Snellaert, Ndl. Gedichten, pp. 470f); Jean d'Outremeuse, Ly Myreur des Histors (ed. Bormans), VI, 386f: Flagellants "aloient par les rues deux et deux, chantant haultement chanchons de Dieu et de Nostre-Damme faites en rymes, en thyese." For examples of French prayers and songs see Fredericq, Corpus, II, 137-140; III, 23-27; Colville, in HLF., XXXVII, 399-401.

[30] Het Boec vander Wraken, III, vss. 1995-1998.

[31] Froissart, Chroniques, in Fredericq, Corpus, II, 130f; Jehan le Bel, Les Vrayes Chroniques, in ibid., II, 122f; Gilles li Muisis, Chronicon, in ibid., II, 108.

flagellation: "batons nos charoingnes bien fort... batons noz pis... alons à genoulx par penance... vos bras estandez... chéons jus en croix à tous lez... tous a genoulx sans respit, rechéons en croix... relevons... et devers le ciel regardons... rebatons nostre char villainne... batons noz piz, batons no face, tendons noz de grant vouloir."[32] The first *cruusbroeders* to arrive in Liége from Germany quickly put their songs into French as they gathered followers.[33] When Pulkawa, who wrote his chronicle from old reports at the request of Charles IV, speaks of different tongues in which they sang ("secundum distinctiones linguarum cantantes"), he had in mind Slavic and German.[34]

Within this multifarious movement, as well as in other contemporary manifestations of semireligious life, can be discerned, a strong anticlerical and even antisocial element that grew up alongside and eventually replaced more orthodox tendencies.[35] Although usually assuming an intensely religious complexion, based on emotion and, under the strain of imponderables, in search of release from divine wrath, it often became an irrational lay protest, and sometimes a morbid one, against ecclesiastical organization and accepted social forms. The devotees considered their services and songs more efficacious than the sacraments and prescribed liturgy. Prayers rendered more intense by self-scourging were more potent for pardon. When the Benedictine monk of St. Amand, Jean du Fayt, then a young doctor of theology on the Paris faculty (d. February 7, 1395), delivered on October 5, 1349, his lengthy sermon on the flagellants before Clement VI and the sacred college at Avignon,[36] he regarded them as a "new

---

[32] *Ibid.*, III, 24-26.

[33] Jehan le Bel, *Les Vrayes Chroniques*, in Fredericq, *Corpus*, II, 123; cf. 122.

[34] Hoffmann von Fallersleben, *Geschichte des deutschen Kirchenliedes*, pp. 132f and note 4.

[35] According to Salimbene (*MGH. SS.*, XXXII, 465) the flagellants were so anxious to confess their sins that priests scarcely had time to eat. Penitence appealed to rich as well as poor (*La Chronique liégeoise de 1402*, ed Bacha; Fredericq, *Corpus*, III, 20, no. 22); even sons of dukes and princes were mentioned as members (*Breve chron. Flandriae*, cited by Fredericq, *Gesch. d. Inquis.*, II, 64, note 2). Again, "men and women, noble and ignoble, who did not know the Scriptures," approved the sect (Li Muisis in Fredericq, *Corpus*, II, 105). On the other hand, the hostile Jean du Fayt claimed in the sermon cited below that the sect could attract no literate men and the fewest possible substantial laymen; it was for him a predominantly popular movement, even though some priests and monks—the *vagati* and *gyrovagi* of conciliar legislation—followed these mendicants. By and large the majority came from the lower classes and consequently were untutored, ignorant, and coarse ("Nulli viri litterati et etiam paucissimi de laicis maioribus vigentibus intellectu huic secte adherent, sed quasi sunt omnes homines populares. Unde, licet aliqui sacerdotes vel religiosi istos mendicantes sequantur vel obsequantur eisdem, coram eis celebrando per viam, isti tamen non sunt viri litterati, sed asini coronati, legem Domini ignorantes.... Exceptis ergo huiusmodi sacerdotibus et religiosis mendicantibus, quasi omnes alii sunt homines populares et per consequens indocti, ignari et rudes," *ibid.*, III, 32; *BARB.*, 1903, 698f).

[36] Fredericq, "Deux sermons inédits de Jean du Fayt sur les Flagellants (5 octobre 1349) et sur le Grand Schisme d'Occident (1378)," *BARB.*, 1903, 688-693 (intro-

sect, or rather a superstition, observing new laws and ceremonies and adopting strange practices with respect to divine worship."[37] That the penitents who became exhausted by rigorous exercises met enormous success in indicated by Jehan le Bel: "So great an impression did they make in Liége that money was given to them and one was ashamed not to provide lodging. It seemed to all that they were holy people and that God had sent them to serve as an example to the masses to do penance and thus obtain remission of sins."[38] Nor was it long before other Liégeois took up their songs and imitated their way of life by wandering through the diocese into Brabant, Hainault, and Flanders, with even the clergy joining their ranks.[39]

Before considering the literature that might have been found in the orthodox beguinage, it will be useful to determine, within the limits of the fragmentary evidence, the extent of literacy among Belgian nuns, recluses, and beguines.[40] From the age of the missionary in Bel-

duction); 694-718 (texts); Fredericq also published the sermon in *Corpus*, III, 29-37, no. 26; cf. Coville's analysis, *l.c.*, 401-406; Fredericq, *Gesch. d. Inquis.*, II, 87. Consult Berlière, "Jean Bernier de Fayt, abbé de Saint-Bavon de Gand, d'après des documents vaticans," *ASEB.*, LVI (1906), 359-381; LVII (1907), 5-43; J. de Saint Genois, in *BNB.*, X (1888-1889), 414-415.

[37] Fredericq, *Corpus*, III, 31; cf. 34; *BARB.*, 1903, 696.

[38] Fredericq, *Corpus*, II, 123. Municipal archives, too, reflect the official stamp of approval on these processions, at least in the initial stage. The first *cruusbroeders* to reach Louvain received sums of money while straw was laid down in the market place for the repose of the wandering bands. Wine was offered the clergy and the beguines five times after the procession (before August 17 and later, in 1349, *ibid.*, II, 114; Molanus, II, 811, 882). The flagellants of Tirlemont and Lierre also were given wine, for the Louvain devotees had previously been so favored by the magistrates of those two cities (Fredericq, *Corpus*, II, 114). At Cologne, Malines, and Ghent (*ibid.*, 115, nos. 66-67) they received similar consideration Moreover royal and papal persecution is reported to have roused in the people of Tournai a *murmur magnum* (Gilles li Muisis, in *ibid.*, 110). The public exercise of penance, authorized by the vicar general of the bishop of Terouanne, met the hearty approval of Louis de Male, count of Flanders, in a letter dated from Courtrai, August 24, 1349. The good men of Ypres who were "meus en déuocion de faire aucunes pénitences corporeles" were recommended to the echevins; they were urged to welcome the flagellants and to grant them safe conduct (*ibid.*, III, 16, no. 17, Flemish text; 17, no. 18, French text). Since civil and religious authorities at Ypres were generally sympathetic to this expression of popular piety, Alard de Denterghem, provost of St. Martin's, defended these bands from suspicions that were being bruited by the dean of Courtrai (Berlière, in *RB.*, XXV [1908], 346).

[39] Clement VI's bull of October 20, 1349 (Sauerland, III, 314, no. 798; reported by Trithemius, *Annal. Hirsaug.*, Fredericq, *Corpus*, I, 201). The bands presumably first appeared in Austria and Hungary (Gilles li Muisis, Fredericq, *Corpus*, I, 190; II, 100; cf. *ibid.*, II, 120; Jan Boendale, *Brab. Yeesten*, ed. Willems, I, 588, vss. 4955ff, Fredericq, *Corpus*, I, 194; Jean du Fayt refers to Bohemia, *ibid.*, III, 33, 34; for further evidence see Fredericq, *Gesch. d. Inquis.*, II, 62, note 2), from whence they spread in 1348-1349 into the valleys of the Rhine, the Scheldt, and the Meuse (Fredericq, *Corpus*, I, 191; II, 101, 102, 106; *Contin. altera Chronici Guillelmi de Nangis, ibid.*, II, 125; cf. *ibid.*, III, 33). They were detected in Flemish-speaking regions of Flanders, Brabant, and Hainault in June, 1349 (*Memorieboek der stad Ghent, ibid.*, II, 136; cf. Gilles li Muisis, *ibid.*, II, 106; I, 193); cf. *ibid.*, II, 118f, no. 70; III, 20f.

[40] *AA. SS.*, LXI (October 29, xiii), 125ff; Baker, *Saints' Lives*, pp. 119-156; Ecken-

gium, women had received at least the rudiments of learning in convents. In the seventh century St. Gertrude, sister of Grimoald, mayor of the palace under Sigibert, king of Austrasia,[41] and St. Gudule of Brussels,[42] also from a distinguished family, were both educated in the Nivelles convent. Among Anglo-Saxon nuns active on the continent was Lioba, otherwise Leobgith, who had been educated at Wimbourne in Dorset and who sent St. Boniface in Germany verses she had composed in Latin and begged him to correct the rusticity of her style. This "divine art" Eadburg, abbess of the monastery in Thanet and herself a correspondent of the missionary,[43] had taught her. Lioba then concluded her letter with four lines of verse addressed to God as an example of what she could do.[44] Lioba and Eadburg are but two examples of nuns who carried on a correspondence with the apostle of Germany.[45]

Thus begins a long Latin tradition that persists, but not with complete uniformity, throughout the Middle Ages. Hrothswitha, the nun of Gandersheim, is the exception rather than the rule.[46] The Norman period brought a decline of literary activity—illumination, versification, copying—which had blossomed in the Anglo-Saxon age. English monastic authoresses were responsible, however, for the Life of St. Catherine in Norman French by Clemence, a nun of Barking near London in the late twelfth century.[47] Literature for English nuns included the *Luve Ron* of the Franciscan Thomas of Hales,[48] the remarkable *Ancren Riwle,* a rule for recluses in prose, by an anonymous author,[49] and the Latin letter from Ailred of Rievaulx to

stein, *Woman under Monasticism*, pp. 305-328; Power, *Medieval English Nunneries*, pp. 237-284.

[41] *Vita Gertrudis abbatissae Nivellensis, AA. SS.*, VIII (March 17, ii), 592f; cf. Delanne, *Histoire de Nivelles*, p. 183.

[42] *Vita S. Gudilae Virginis, AA. SS.*, I (January 8, i), 513-530. St. Gudule was trained by Gertrude (*ibid.*, 515) in divine letters. Cf. the literary activity of Herlinde and Renilde in Valenciennes in the eighth century (*De sanctis virginibus Herlinde et Reinule seu Renilde abbatissis Masaci in Belgio, AA. SS.*, IX [March 22, iii], 385 F, 386 D).

[43] Boniface's letters to Eadburg, Ep. 16-20, *PL.*, LXXXIX, 710-720.

[44] Ep. 21, *ibid.*, 720f (ad an. 725); for her life, see Rudolf of Fulda, *Vita de S. Lioba seu Leobgytha alias Truthgeba Virgine abbatissa Bischoffsheimensi in Germania, AA. SS.*, XLVII (September 28, vii), 709-717; cf. *Comm. praev., ibid.*, 698-709; Eckenstein, *op. cit.*, pp. 134-138; Boniface's letter to Lioba, Ep. 23, *PL.*, LXXXIX, 722.

[45] E.g., Ep. 22, *ibid.*, 721f. An anonymous Anglo-Saxon nun of Heidenheim wrote the lives of Willibald (*Vita S. Willibaldi episcopi, auctore virgine consanguinea sanctimoniali Heidenheimensi, AA. SS.*, XXIX (July 7, ii, 501-519) and Wunebald (*Vita S. Wynnebaldi, abbatis Heidenheimensis, fratris S. Willibaldi, MGH. SS.*, XV, 106-117; cf. Eckenstein, *op cit.*, pp. 139-142.

[46] Raby, *Secular Latin Poetry*, I, 277f.

[47] G. Paris, "La vie de Sainte Catherine de Soeur Clémence de Barking," *Romania*, XIII (1884), 400-403.

[48] Eckenstein, *op. cit.*, pp. 309-311.

[49] *Ibid.*, pp. 311-328; T. W. Coleman, *English Mystics of the Fourteenth Century* (London, 1938), pp. 48-63.

his sister from 1131 to 1161, offering advice for recluses analogous to that contained in the *Ancren Riwle*.[50] On the other hand if the Cistercian convent of Helfta near Eisleben in Saxony acquired renown through the successive literary efforts of the beguine Mechtild of Magdeburg, and the nuns Mechtild von Hackeborn and Gertrud the Great (d. 1311),[51] the Cistercian houses of Nazareth near Lierre and La Ramée, eminent as a school of calligraphy and illumination under Ida of Nivelles,[52] warrant a similar commentary even though their intellectual activity was less well known. Although Dominican nunneries in Germany subscribed to the exalted conception of learning which motivated the friars,[53] the transfer of a Benedictine nun occasionally stimulated studies in Dominican convents.[54]

As glimpsed in Cistercian and Dominican *vitae,* evidence of women Latinists is at best fragmentary. Among literate nuns at Aywières was Sybille de Gages whose epitaph for her friend and companion, Lutgard (d. 1246), suggests some familiarity with the Latin language.[55] Juliana of Mont-Cornillon was taught by nuns, especially Sapience,[56] at the Boverie and is described by her biographer as having been able "in a short time" not only to read the Psalter but to recite it from memory.[57] "Although she had learned to read easily all Latin and French Scripture, she read with much eagerness the books of St. Augustine."[58] Likewise she was reported to have committed more than twenty of St. Bernard's sermons to memory.[59] When the young John, who drew up the first office of the eucharist feast, submitted it to Juliana "si quid sit in cantu vel littera corrigendum,"[60] he undoubtedly was seeking as much approval of inspiration as confirmation of form. But Juliana's proficiency was extraordinary.

It is evident that that remarkable Franciscan-inspired beguine of Marseilles, St. Douceline, could read and write.[61] Not only did she possess sufficient knowledge of Latin to follow the Psalter, the formu-

---

[50] Eckenstein, *op cit.,* pp. 313f.

[51] *Ibid.,* pp. 328-353.

[52] Canivez, *L'ordre de Cîteaux,* pp. 187-193; Roisin, *Hag. cist.,* pp. 54-61.

[53] Margaret Finkin and Anna von Klingnau who used every free moment to learn to write Latin; a certain Elizabeth at Kirchberg was noted for her learning (Wilms, in *QF.,* XI, 28).

[54] *Ibid.,* 29.

[55] *V. Lutg.,* 209 B (III, 20). Cf. *ibid.,* 205 E (III, 6): "Prophetiae ergo spiritu tacta intrinsecus dixit Dominae Sybillae de Gagis cui in omnibus uit litteratiore moniali commissa fuerat procuranda." The section devoted to Sybilla (*AA. SS.,* LII [October 9, iv], 567-570) throws no light on the problem. Cf. L. Mahy in *Annales du cercle archéologique d'Ath et de la région,* I (1912), 113-184.

[56] *V. Jul. Cornel.,* 443 D.

[57] *Ibid.,* 443 F. For the *Cantica Canticorum, ibid.,* 444 D.

[58] *Ibid.,* 444 D.

[59] *Ibid.,* 444 D, no. 6; cf. *ibid.,* 451, no. 26.

[60] *Ibid.,* 459 D, no. 9.

[61] Albanés, *La vie de Sainte Douceline,* p. xlii; p. 12 (I, 12); p. 8 (I, 8).

las, and saints' lives, but she appears to have carried on a correspondence with Charles I, king of Sicily, "to whom she made known by writing the most secret things."[62] She is also reported to have fallen into ecstasy when she read the life of St. Francis.[63] On the other hand, if the *Vida* admits elsewhere that she was a simple and unlettered woman[64] and that she had no skill in letters,[65] these passages need not be taken literally. They are rather references to the chasm that existed between initial formal instruction and the knowledge which contemplation and mystical insight brought her.[66] This interpretation is consistent with the explanation which one would expect to encounter in hagiographical writing: instructed by the divine spirit, she answered questions with such clarity and depth that the most skillful were astonished.[67] The *Vida* raises one other problem of pertinence. Albanès,[68] in seeking to determine which of the Marseilles beguines was responsible for its composition, was confronted with a number of women in Douceline's convent who belonged to the upper strata of Provençal society. Some of them must have received an education that would have enabled them to write such a life.

That French noblewomen of the time of St. Louis received an education is further emphasized by his sister Isabella who seems to have had an exact knowledge of Latin with a feeling for the proper word. Her biographer, Agnes d'Harcourt, relates that the princess herself corrected the Latin of the letters which her chaplains composed for her.[69] She was accustomed to pray in her chapel until noon; then she retired to her cubicle where she studied until nones sacred writings, to wit, Scripture, the Gospels, and saints' lives.[70] Since her conscience was "very sensitive and refined," she kept as "soothers" of it masters of theology to whom she was as obedient in confession "as if she had been a nun."[71] According to the confessor of Queen Margaret, poor widows of knights who had perished in the Holy Land

[62] *Ibid.*, p. 156 (XI, 7-8): "E li mandava motas cauzas secretas e rescostas,"
[63] *Ibid.*, pp. 98-100 (IX, 44).
[64] "Car jassiaisso qu'illi fos simpla femena, e ses letras" (*ibid.*, p. 72: IX, 3).
[65] "Jassiaisso que d'autramens ill non agues sotileza de letras" (*ibid.*, p. 152: XI, 1).
[66] *Ibid.*, p. 152 (XI, 1): "Que ja l'avia menada l'auteza de sa contemplacion a l'entendement de las escripturas."
[67] *Ibid.*, p. 152 (XI, 1).
[68] *Ibid.*, p. xxx.
[69] *V. Isab.*, 800 B, no. 9; *HLF.*, XX, 101. For the education of French noblewomen in this period see Thompson, *Literacy of the Laity*, pp. 146-147; for the Latinity of English nuns, consult Power, *Medieval English Nunneries*, pp. 245-248.
[70] *V. Isab.*, 800 A, no. 8; cf. 798 F, no. 3.
[71] *Ibid.*, 800 B, no. 9. These masters included by preference Friars Minor whose approval had been solicited for the rule of the new abbey (*ibid.*, 801 D-E, no. 13): Bonaventura, Guillaume de Miletonne (cf. Thomas de Cantimpré, *BUA.*, II, 1, 16), Odo de Roni who served as her confessor (*V. Isab.*, 802 A, no. 16; cf. 804 E, no. 27), Godefridus de Vierson, and Guillaume de Harcombour.

came seeking aid of the king; he asked each woman whether any of her daughters had a knowledge of letters, promising that he would have those who had been instructed in letters received at the abbey of Pontoise.[72] A sister at Longchamp, named Juliana, wrote a book out of piety, but it was mislaid throught negligence.[73] Thomas of Cantimpré informs us[74] that the daughter of a very poor man who was eager to learn the Psalter, but too poor to acquire one, appealed to the Virgin. Although her appearance in an unsatisfactory dream merely increased the girl's disappointment, the father was persuaded to send his daughter on Sundays and holy-days to the mistress who taught the Psalter to the daughters of rich folk. After demonstrating an ability to read through the Virgin's intercession the girl's wishes were answered. Thereupon the wealthy women of the parish bought her a psalter and in later days, moved by her devotion, established her in a cell next to the church, as a *reclusorium.*

These isolated examples notwithstanding, the nuns and beguines who were credited with teaching reading and writing were probably not too proficient. The penitents of Mary Magdalene in Germany were taught only reading and singing, no "grammaticalia." Nor were they obliged to learn the psalter after the age of twenty-four.[75] While the official business of convents, their annual accounts and certificates, and personal correspondence were done by professional clerks or chaplains,[76] the interests of the inmates were in the main narrowly circumscribed with moral instruction of paramount importance. Too frequently what passed for knowledge of Latin actually amounted to memorization and familiarity with well-coursed content. Even casual references to classical letters are conspicuous by their absence.

It is thus much more common for the pious hagiographer and uncritical chronicler to underline inspiration rather than learning, divine assistance in place of formal schooling, inner light instead of reason. Such a source of knowledge or information immediately assigns to writings, *dictante Spiritu sancto,*[77] an authority that defies criticism. For this reason the *vitae* are usually hostile to or at least vague about literacy, whereas they almost unanimously applaud evidence of revealed knowledge and divine illumination. "Non plane acquisita per suam industriam litterali scientia sed potius revelatione divina."[78] Gielemans assigns to Clarissa Leonard, a beguine at Malines, the two-

[72] Bouquet, XX, 94-95.
[73] *V. Isab.,* 805 B, no. 32.
[74] *BUA.,* I, 23, 3 (pp. 93-4).
[75] Uhlhorn, *Liebesthätigkeit,* II, 300.
[76] Power, *Medieval English Nunneries,* p. 246.
[77] Henry Pomerius, *V. Joan. Rusb.* (II, 14), *AB.,* IV (1885), 293.
[78] *Ibid.,* 273 (I, 10); cf. Wilms, in *QF.,* XI, 30.

fold duty under the eyes of the mistress: learn the Psalter and sew.[79] The sources consist of brief passages from or allusions to the Scriptures, church fathers, doctors, patriarchs of the respective monastic orders, and liturgy; in any case it is material with which the monk or nun could be expected to be familiar through daily devotional practices.

Hildegarde of Bingen, for example, "had learned nothing from man beyond simple psalmody." When about 1141 she began with much trepidation and in ill-health to commit the *Scivias* to writing she made use of a monk, Godfrey of St. Disibode, a double Benedictine house in the diocese of Mainz, who not only served as her chaplain and confessor but acted as her scribe and counselled her generally in the matter of composition.[80] Later she employed the services of Volmar, who appears to have been more effective for her purpose than Guibert.[81] Insisting that inspiration carried a greater premium than learning, she chided her last counsellor for his careful emendation of her text. It also appears that she consulted Bernard of Clairvaux.[82] A miniature in the illustrated codex of *Scivias* at Wiesbaden depicted the seeress surrounded with the flames of the Holy Spirit and her assistants at work.[83]

When Thomas of Cantimpré states that Lutgard received a divine injunction in Latin to "enlighten those who sit in darkness and the shadow of death," he hastens to explain that, being illiterate (*utpote laica*) she did not understand the words and thus was obliged to have them translated by a sister.[84] From the life of Catherine of Siena, put down by her confessor, Raymond of Padua (1330-1399), we learn that in like fashion this remarkable mystic, the daughter of a dyer, had received no formal instruction; unable to write, she had recourse to secretaries to transcribe her writings.[85]

[79] Gielemans, *Anecd.*, p. 436.
[80] *Scivias, I. Praefat. PL.*, CXCVII, 386; Trithemius, *Chronica Spanheimensi*, anno 1179 (*PL.*, CXCVII, 19). Trithemius adds that in addition to an ignorance of Latin she was plagued by "crebras infirmitates et humidum caput" (*ibid.*, 20). Cf. Vincent of Beauvais, *Spec. hist.* (lib. xxvii, cap. 83), *PL.*, CXCVII, 73: Hildegarde "cum laica et illiterata esset, mirabiliter tamen rapta frequentius in somnis diceret, non solum quod verbis effunderet, sed etiam quod scribendo Latine dictaret, ut dictando Catholicae doctrinae libros conficeret." Cf. Richer, *Gesta Senoniensis Ecclesiae* (cap. 15), *MGH. SS.*, XXV, 306.
[81] See above, pp. 290-291.
[82] There is a measure of caution about Bernard's reply: "Caeterum ubi interior eruditio est, et unctio docens de omnibus quid nos aut docere possumus, aut monere? Diceris enim coelestia secreta rimari, et ea quae supra homines sunt, Spiritu Sancto illustrante, dignoscere. Unde rogamus magis, et suppliciter postulamus, ut nostri memoriam habeas apud Deum, et eorum pariter qui nobis in spirituali societate juncti sunt" (Ep. 366, *PL.*, CLXXXII, 572).
[83] Herwegen, in *Belfried*, I (1917), 119.
[84] *V. Lutg.*, 198 (II, 10); 198 A (II, 8); cf. 200 C (II, 20). In the question, "Quid mihi idiotae et rusticae et laicae moniali Scripturae secreta cognoscere?" the word *laica* is used as the antonym of *litterata* rather than as a synonym for *soror conversa* (*ibid.*, 193 B-C, I, 12); cf. Ducange, *Glossarium*, IV, 15, *s.v. laicus*.
[85] *Vita S. Catherine Senensis, AA. SS.*, XII (April 30, iii), 868 E, 869 B.

John of Schönau, after making a similar point in his defense of Ruysbroeck that the great Flemish mystic did not record his ideas in Latin but in Flemish (*theutonico*), adds: "For although he was of competent training, he nevertheless was not of such eminent learning that he was able to put his teaching into well-composed and elegant Latin . . . But a certain brother in the monastery, a capable and literate man, later, on account of the growth of all nations, undertook himself to render into Latin certain of these books."[86] Ruysbroeck's biography illustrates as well as any the confusion and distortion created by ordinary hagiographical devices in the problem of learning or literacy. Pomerius characteristically obscures the issue by focusing attention on precocity in spiritual matters.[87] The mystic attended school for a brief time and acquired scarcely the rudiments of grammar.[88] In any case, what difference does it make? Did he not rise above the errors of logic, the vain labors of philosophers, and even the lofty exhibitions of theologians?[89] From this deprecation of learning rose a legend which was repeated without question by subsequent biographers, Dionysius of Chartreux, Trithemius,[90] Valerius Andreas and in modern scholarship.[91] To controvert this tradition the Bollandist[92] cites a Latin letter prefixed to Ruysbroeck's *Adornment of Spiritual Marriage*[93] in which the mystic declares that he put these books into Latin for those who did not understand Flemish. The amazing knowledge of philosophy and theology exhibited by Ruysbroeck as well as by other mystics who presumably were illiterate—*illiteratus et idiota,* to use the hackneyed phrase—poses a problem which the hagiographer generally disregards. The *Scivias* and the *Spiritual Marriage* presuppose wide preparation. Far from being a contradiction of learning, mysticism in worthy hands is an expression of high intellectualism. Gerson, the chancellor of the University of Paris, clearly perceived the falseness of hagiographical devices when he drew up his indictment against Ruysbroeck's pantheistic views contained in the third book of *The Spiritual Marriage*: "It has been said that the man who wrote this book was illiterate and uneducated, and consequently an attempt has been made to regard it as inspired by the Holy Spirit, but the book gives evidence rather of human scholarship than of

[86] *Libellus Fratris Joannis de Schoenhavia . . . contra magistrum Joannem de Gerson, Cancellarium Parisiensem* (Gerson, *Op. omn.*, I, 66-67).

[87] Pomerius, *V. Joan. Rusb.* (II, 2), *AB.*, IV, 284.

[88] *Ibid.*, 273 (I, 10).

[89] ". . . Non jam logicorum fallacias, non philosophorum vanas industrias, verum etiam theologorum transcenderet alta spectacula" (*idem*).

[90] *De Script. eccles.*, n. 672, ed. Fabricius, p. 156.

[91] For a summary of the problem, consult Wautier d'Aygalliers, *Ruysbroeck l'Admirable*, p. 165 and note 1.

[92] *AB.*, IV, 273, note 2.

[93] Bibl. roy. de Belgique, cod. 4935-43, f. 59r.

divine inspiration... and the style is somewhat labored. Besides, in order to deal with such a subject, it is not sufficient to be pious, one must be a scholar."[94] D'Aygalliers, accordingly, set out to demonstrate not only the originality of the Flemish mystic but also his indebtedness to the philosophical and theological currents of the Middle Ages.

The daughter of a well-to-do father, presumably a knight, the German beguine Mechtild of Magdeburg, who eventually was identified with the vigorous mysticism of Helfta, was given the training which befitted a girl of her station, but in formal learning, and particularly for theological concepts beyond those which the church was accustomed to impart by sermon and catechism, she was totally unprepared. Nor did she have a command of Latin.[95] Although formal instruction was denied to her, it was nevertheless "constant participation in religious life, to which she as a beguine was obligated, and a lively association with clerics and monks that gave her an abundance of theological and ecclesiastical ideas."[96] These she proceeded to embody in her reflections on the times, prayers, meditations, and spiritual visions, some in prose, some in verse, but all couched in German. These writings were afterwards collected by a Dominican who issued them under the title of *The Flowing Light of Divinity*, while another friar, during Mechtild's lifetime, translated the work into Latin.[97]

This statement applies equally well to Christine of Stommeln, who was from 1268 to 1279 and even later, the center of a group of ecstatic men and women, leavened by Dominican instruction, in the Cologne area. According to the biographer John she was reciting as early as her seventh or ninth year a song beginning "Viridaria plena rosis vel liliis vel speciebus undique delectabilia adeo ut meus fraterculus Jesus Christus, si amoris sui daretur frui,"[98] which, as the Bollandist suggests,[99] may have originally been put in German verse and then given a Latin adaptation by the biographer. At the age of nine, her friend Peter of Dacia informs us,[100] she learned two sequences:

> Veni sancte Spiritus,
> Et emitte caelitus
> lucis tuae radium,

attributed to Innocent III,[101] and

---

[94] *Epistola ... ad fratrem Bartholomaeum, Op. omn.*, I, 59.
[95] Hauck, V, 1, 385-386 and note; Eckenstein, *Woman under Monasticism*, pp. 330ff.
[96] Hauck, V, 1, 386.
[97] Eckenstein, *Woman under Monasticism*, p. 332; cf. Dante, *Purg.*, XXVIII, 34f; see above p. ooo.
[98] *V. Chr. Stumb.*, 368 A (2).
[99] *Ibid.*, 369, note a.
[100] *Acta Chr. Stumb.*, 291 C-D; *V. Chr. Stumb.*, 368 A (3).
[101] *Analecta Hymnica medii aevi*, ed. Clemens Blume, LIX (Leipzig, 1915), 234-235, no. 153.

Ave rosa
generosa,
salve, candens lilium.[102]

Two years later, her *magistra* testifies, Christine learned the Psalter "well" within seven weeks.[103] Here again, such an observation must be considered with regard to familiarity of subject matter and cathechetical method. That she was unable to write is proven by the extensive correspondence which passed between her and Peter.[104] It was her confessors—Friar Gerard von Greifen,[105] who eventually became prior of the Coblenz convent,[106] Master John,[107] the parish priest of Stommeln who died in 1277,[108] Friar Lawrence,[109] or other friars from Cologne—who were called upon to pen her letters. Besides, Friar Lawrence admits that she asked him to read Peter's letters to her.[110] The clauses, *haec omnia vobis scripsi*,[111] or *quae omnia non habui tempus vobis scribere*,[112] which her letters often contain ought not to be taken at face value. Ep. VII, for example, makes such a claim, but Peter, on receiving it, adds: "Hanc litteram scriptam manu confessoris sui."[113] Certainly here was a beguine whose formal training had been defective.

Thomas of Cantimpré would have us believe that Christine of St. Trond was well versed in Latin and "fully" grasped the meaning of Scripture even if "she had not really learned her letters in childhood."[114] She was called upon to disclose to spiritual friends the most obscure questions in it. This she did unwillingly and rarely, saying that it was more proper for the clergy to expound the Bible and that the function did not belong to her.[115] The many injuries which she suffered from the clergy, especially the priesthood—for she was wont to chide them privately but "with due respect" for their wayward-

---

[102] *Ibid.*, LIX, 330-331, no. 209. The editor claims that the sequence was native to Cologne. The Bollandist did not know it (*AA. SS.*, XXV, June 22, v, 369, note b).

[103] *Acta Chr. Stub.*, 236 F, (I, 4); *V. Chr. Stumb.*, 368 B (4).

[104] For an analysis of this correspondence and its chronology, see Gallén, *La Province de Dacie*, pp. 225-244.

[105] *Acta Chr. Stumb.*, 257 F.

[106] *Ibid.*, 274 A (II, 63).

[107] Letter, May 24, 1280, *ibid.*, 281 F (III, 22); 271 E (II, 55).

[108] *Ibid.*, 268 E (II, 44); 266 E (II, 37); 273 B (II, 60); 274 E (II, 66).

[109] After the priest's death (*ibid.*, 276 E, III, 1) Lawrence wrote for Christine two letters with which Book III begins (*ibid.*, 276ff; cf. 353 D-F, V, 18-19).

[110] "Mandans ei me habere litteras sibi missas, a me personaliter exponendas" (*ibid.*, 277 B, III, 3); cf. 272 (II, 56); 258 B (II, 5): "Litteras vestras cum audirem legere"; Bollandist, *ibid.*, 259, note d.

[111] *Ibid.*, 259 B (II, 10); cf. 262 D (II, 21), 263 A (II, 23), 264 D (II, 28).

[112] *Ibid.*, 262 F (II, 22).

[113] *Ibid.*, 263 C; cf. 272 C (II, 57).

[114] *V. Chr. Mir.*, 657 (40): "Intelligebat ipsa omnem latinitatem, et sensum in scriptura divina plenissime noverat, licet ipsa a nativitate litteras penitus ignoraret."

[115] *Ibid.*, 657 (40).

ness—did not diminish her veneration for their status.[116] After the others had departed and the doors were locked following evening services, Christine Mirabilis often remained alone in the church and began to sing hymns and canticles in Latin, *mirisque consonantium clausulis exornatus.*[117]

After the death of Clarissa Leonard, a beguine of Malines (fl. 1453), the mistresses of the convent entered her house "as was the custom" and, examining her belongings, found a box "well closed" and full of little books which she had written herself. Some treated her own deeds; these they did not hesitate to translate from the vernacular with the hope of edifying readers or hearers.[118]

Mary of Oignies, writes Jacques de Vitry quite uncritically, was sufficiently instructed in Scripture, for she frequently listened to sermons.[119] No mention of reading is made here; but she kept at her side a little book from which she recited prayers and songs to the Virgin Mary.[120] As she approached death she sang in a high, clear voice of the ineffable nature of God, the angels, the Virgin, the other saints, her friends, and divine scripture.[121] The spontaneous character of the song which was inspired "without any difficulty" is underlined by the biographer.

> The whole following day [Jacques de Vitry continues] she praised God. The prior and her servant remained with her in the church, the doors being closed and all others excluded. They could not understand much of the heavenly mysteries which she unfolded. Nevertheless they did comprehend certain things. But, alas! they remembered little. On a high note she commenced her antiphon with the Trinity, praising at length the Trinity in Oneness, and Oneness in the Trinity and inserting marvelous things in her song. She expounded in a new and wondrous fashion from Scripture—the Gospels, Psalms, the New and Old Testament—what she had never heard, giving many subtle explanations. From the Trinity she descended to the humanity of Christ, then to the Blessed Virgin, the holy Angels, the Apostles, and proclaimed much concerning the other saints. Then, as if in the last and a weak point, she spoke of her friends who are still alive; commending them one by one to the Lord, she poured out many prayers for them to the Lord: all these things she uttered in verse in the Romance tongue ("haec omnia rithmice et lingua romana protulit").[122]

Furthermore she sang of St. Stephen, the first martyr, whom she called the rose-garden of Paradise[123] and explained the *Magnificat* in the

---

[116] *Idem.*
[117] *Ibid.,* 657 (39).
[118] Gielemans, *Ex Novali sanctorum,* in *Anecdota,* pp 435-436.
[119] *VMO.,* 562 E-F (68).
[120] *Ibid.,* 570 E (102).
[121] *Ibid.,* 569 D (98).
[122] *Ibid.,* 569 F (99).
[123] *Ibid.,* 570 A (100).

vernacular.[124] When, as if at the end of her song, she arrived at the Canticle of Stephen, she warmly commended to the Lord her friends, both men and women, but especially the *mulieres religiosae* who still remained in the city of Liége after the disaster of 1212; imploring peace for them, she repeated the first verse of the several strophes of the canticle *Nunc dimittis,* just as when she prayed for the religious of Nivelles and for many others living in the diocese of Liége, she always recited this hymn.[125] In her versification in the Romance tongue it is not clear whether it was the text of another or some original poem that she had put down earlier. Probably it was an improvisation of well-known themes, with the Evangelical Canticles providing substance.

Again, in describing Mary's passionate desire to preach in apostolic tradition, the biographer does not indicate whether it was physical weakness or obedience to ecclesiastical practice that persuaded her to be content with vicarious experience by welcoming Jacques de Vitry as her instrument.[126] Fragmentary knowledge of thirteenth-century literature makes it impossible to say how closely the example of Mary of Oignies was imitated by the *mulieres religiosae* in the Low Countries. But in this prototype of the Belgian beguine we see, on the one hand, this desire to convert and instruct bearing fruit in Jacques de Vitry, John of Nivelles, and possibly Theodore of Celles, and on the other hand, the beginnings of devotional literature in the vernacular.

The anonymous life of Alice of Schaerbeek describes her as a seven-year old girl entering La Cambre where her education, not with children of her own age but with older ones, was propelled by divine light. Vitally concerned with the role it played, the biographer then makes a significant observation about her *memoria tenax* [127] which was much desired for the exclusively catechetical training that she must have received.[128]

Ida of Léau busied herself with the allegorical sense (*sensus exterius corporales*) of Scripture and diligently wrote "several" religious books, including the correction of a ferial containing lections for matins.[129] After receiving a supernatural favor she composed verses in Flemish

---

[124] *Ibid.,* 570 B (101): "Cantilenam beatae Virginis scilicet Magnificat rithmice, et lingua romana exponendo, frequentissime replicavit, multumque suavitatem et dulcedinem reperit."

[125] *Ibid.,* 570 B (101). Cf. Van Mierlo, in *D. War. Belf.,* XXV (1925), 367, and *VMKVA.,* 1926, 71.

[126] *VMO.,* 562 (69).

[127] *V. Al. Scar.,* 472 C (1).

[128] *Ibid.,* 472 D (2).

[129] *V. Id. Lew.,* 113 A (18). This "liber ferialis non minimus, in quo legunter in Matutinis lectiones" and which Ida corrected is not to be confused with the *feriale* which contains the births of martyrs and has the form of a calendar; it was the *feriale* containing the *officium feriarum* (*ibid.,* 113-114, note f).

(*Theutonica*).[130] Brought into close association with recluses as well as beguines[131] before adapting the Cistercian habit, she complied with her mother's wishes that she learn to write[132] by attending at the age of seven one of the *literalis scholae scientiae*[133] presumably maintained by beguines. Such learning, the biographer hastens to add, is not intended to enlarge knowledge of the world, but only of divine matters.[134]

Under the direction of the abbess Ivette, Herckenrode became by the middle of the thirteenth century a lively center of spirituality. One of its nuns who was the sister of Guntram, prior of the abbey of St. Trond, transcribed for him a breviary which had long resided in this Benedictine monastery.[135]

Thomas of Cantimpré introduces Book II of his biography of Lutgard with the statement that the renown of her virtue persuaded the new Cistercian nunneries which were springing up in French-speaking areas (*in Gallicis partibus*)[136] to press for her election as abbess, although she knew nothing of the language. It is altogether probable that Aywières was among these foundations. So small was her aptitude for languages that, after spending forty years in this convent, she did not learn enough French to ask properly for bread when she was hungry.[137] Although French dialects were then much closer to Latin than at present, a residence of twelve years in the Benedictine nunnery of St. Catherine at St. Trond[138] had evidently availed her nothing. Although she called herself an *idiotae et rustica, et laica monialis*,[139] her biographer quickly points out that she was endowed with an extraordinary gift to comprehend the hidden meaning—but not the literal sense—of Psalms. Furthermore, spiritual colloquy transcends the limitations imposed by ignorance of French or Flemish.[140] Fleeing honors and the growing insistence by the convent that she become its head, Lutgard prayed to the Virgin to make her unable to learn French and thus discourage her election. Her prayers were answered and she remained a simple nun. At the same time she feared the dangers to her soul which the office involved.

The Rule of St. Benedict (cap. 38) underscored the desirability of reading at each meal. Rather than just any member fulfilling this

[130] *Ibid.*, 113 D (20). For use of Flemish see *ibid.*, 114 F, no. 24; 115 B, no. 26.
[131] *Ibid.*, 110 C (11).
[132] *Ibid.*, 110 A (9). According to the Liége MS. it was her father.
[133] *Ibid.*, 109 F (8). Cf. Ducange, *Glossarium, s.v. literalis, literatoria*.
[134] *V. Id. Lew.*, 110 A, no. 9.
[135] *Gesta Abb. Trud.* (ad ann. 1250), *MGH. SS.*, X, 397; Daris, *Histoire du diocèse de Liége pendant le XIIIe et le XIVe siècle*, p. 234.
[136] *V. Lutg.*, 196 D (II, 1).
[137] *Ibid.*, 196 E; cf. Van Roy, *Lutgardis*, pp. 84-85.
[138] *V. Lutg.*, 195 C (I, 22).
[139] *Ibid.*, 193 C (I, 12); cf. 199 B (II, 16).
[140] *Ibid.*, 203 C-D (II, 40).

duty, a monk was designated on Sunday to read throughout the week. Nor were brothers chosen by turn: ability to edify was the sole criterion. At table the deepest silence must be observed so that only the voice of the reader might be heard. Questions on the material were not invited, for they opened the way to discussion. The superior, however, might add something instructive from time to time. It was further stipulated (cap. 42) that the monks ought to study at all times in silence, above all at night. They were to rise quickly from the table, sit together while one read collations, lives of the Fathers, or something else which edified the listeners. But not the Heptateuch or 'Kings, for it is of no avail for weak minds to hear these books at that hour: let them be read at another time. Among Cistercians Bernardine sermons were naturally preferred.[141]

Such a program was endorsed by Humbert de Romans, who insisted that at the table not only physical man should be fed but also spiritual man through divine word. By listening the sisters would be discouraged from overeating and overdrinking. Gossip too would be throttled. Reading began immediately after grace. Two or three verses of Scripture were first recited, followed by a short pause until the sisters were all seated and quiet. With resumption of the reading servants began to bring in the food.[142] St. Augustine, Humbert reminded his charges, demanded assiduous reading, for only thereby is mind enlightened and understanding broadened. It informs how to conduct oneself in prayer and work. These are the weapons whereby the sisters can ward off the devil. These are the tools necessary for salvation. Nor can lay sisters find excuse because they can observe paintings that depict saints' lives and divine creation.[143]

Johannes Meyer included in his *Ämterbuch* four chapters on table reading among nuns: two on the office of the reader herself and two on the *correctrix mensae*. The reader was expected to prepare herself by careful perusal and to refrain from reading either "too high or too low, too softly or too loud, or too fast." When a new book was started it should be announced. If a homily was read, the biblical text must preface it. Likewise, a book should be concluded with the word "explicit." The overseer·had to correct, instruct, and punish the reader if she read badly or faultily. Such a function belongs to "a capable, intelligent, well-trained sister." She must be sure that the reading material had been corrected and provided with punctuation and directions. Before the assembled convent the *constituciones* and *ordinationes* of the superior, besides selections from the *ordinarium* of the *ruberick oder nottel*, must be read often each year. The *Ämterbuch* too was to

---

[141] Cf. Van Roy, *Lutgardis*, pp. 86-87; Delatte, *Commentaire*, pp. 301-306, 319-324.
[142] Hauber in *Zentralblatt für Bibliothekswesen*, XXXI (1914), 347.
[143] *Ibid.*, 348.

be read once a year as well as lives of the Fathers, histories, and the dialogues of Gregory. At the first *ymbis* biblical books should be read in common, while on feast days the corresponding books: on Maundy Thursday the sermons of the Sacrament, on Good Friday the complaint of Jeremiah, etc.[144]

We may assume that Lutgard, like other regulars, acquired her scanty knowledge of Latin by picking up words through such reading and by frequent repetition in the offices. That similar reading was conducted in beguine houses is proved, according to Hauber,[145] by two MSS. in the library of the Benedictine monastery of Einsiedeln: 277 which contains the only extant MS. of the Revelations of Mechtild of Magdeburg and a considerable number of sermons, etc.; and 278 which also consists of sermons. Dedicated to the sisters of Albegg, the second bears a XIV C. notation: "Dis buoch höret in die vier hüser in dem walde." This refers to the four houses in the valley of Einsiedeln in Switzerland: Alpegg, vor deren Au, in der hinteren Au, and on the Hagenrüti. The first MS. belonged to Margaret, daughter of a Basel merchant Nicholas zum Goldenen Ring. She maintained through her confessor Heinrich von Rumerschein, canon of St. Peter in that city, close relations with the sisters of vorderen Au and Alpegg. She was also acquainted with Henry von Nördlingen. These MSS., which were to remain in each house for one month, reflect the ideas that circulated in these societies.

Late as the evidence is, Ryckel's recommendation of books suggests the type of reading done in a beguinage. It is a list admittedly narrow in scope, intended exclusively for moral instruction. Worthwhile books include the *Imitatio Christi* of Thomas à Kempis, writings of Tauler, Sermons of Bernard, tractates of Ambrose, and Jerome's letters.[146] He then adds the warning that beguines should become familiar with works on the Passion of Christ rather than tracts on divine attributes. He undoubtedly recalled the official charge of the fourteenth century that they were flirting with heterodoxy by probing the mysteries of the Trinity and the nature of God.[147]

While many beguines cared for the sick, aided the indigent, and in general alleviated through social work the suffering caused by frequent plagues and wars, others conducted schools and brought up orphans.[148] They imparted to their charges reading and writing as

[144] König, in *Freib. Diöz-Arch.*, XIII (1880), 205.
[145] Hauber, *op. cit.*, 350.
[146] Ryckel, pp. 724-728.
[147] *Ibid.*, p. 726: "Suadeo tamen ut libros prius familiares reddant sibi de passione Christi, quam de attributis Dei tractantes, velintque potius cum mellitissimo doctore repere, attrito plagis vermiculo condolendo, quam volare, mysteria profunda divinitatis admirando." For books and manuscripts in the Amsterdam beguinage consult Eeghem, *Vrouwenkloosters*, pp. 324f.
[148] Axters, in *OGE.*, XIII (1939), 162; Chapotin, *Histoire des Dominicains*, p. 521;

well as moral instruction. Among these pupils was Beatrice (ca. 1202-August 29, 1268), who lived successively as a Cistercian nun in the abbeys of Florival north of Wavre, Val-des-Vierges (Magdendael) at Oplinter, northeast of Tirlemont, and finally, from 1236 on, Notre-Dame-de-Nazareth at Lierre near Antwerp, with which she is most closely identified.[149] The *Vita Beatricis* relates how her father, Barthlemy surnamed De Vleeschouwer,[150] a substantial burgher[151] of Tirlemont and founder of these three nunneries, entrusted the education of his seven-year-old daughter to the beguines of Léau as soon as his wife Gertrude died.[152] The biography underlines the moral instruction rather than formal learning which she derived from them.[153] But the next year she was an oblate at Florival.[154] To this former Benedictine abbey, just now undergoing Cistercian reform (1218), she must have been admitted as a novice some seven or eight years later.[155] The *vita* presents difficulties at this point, for it adds that she had been handed over to *magistris liberalium artium.*[156] The term *magistris*, employed only in this form, does not reveal the sex of the teachers, but presumably they were female. Furthermore, the text, "illam devoto Beghinarum collegio sociavit... per idem quoque tempus a patre magistris liberalium artium est commissa, disciplinis scholasticis quibus iam a matre iniciate fuerat,"[157] seems to indicate an establishment apart from the beguinage. On the other hand, the *literalis scholae scientiae* at Léau, mentioned in the *Vita Idae Lewensis*,[158] would appear to have been kept by beguines.[159] After profession and at the advice of the abbess of Florival, Beatrice was sent to La Ramée to acquire perfection in calligraphy "so that she would later

Nimal, *Les béguinages*, pp. 101-102.

[149] *Vita Beatricis*, in Bibl. roy. de Belgique, cod. 4459-4470, ff. 66r-138v; published in large measure by Henriquez, in *Quinque prudentes virgines*, pp. 1-167. For an analysis of the problems raised by this biography, consult Roisin, *Hag. cist.*, pp. 61-65. Cf. Van Mierlo, "Beatrijs van Nazareth," *VMKVA.*, 1926, 51-72; id., *Gesch. van de Letterk. der Nederlanden*, I, 259-262; id., "Beatrix de Nazareth," *DHGE.*, VII (1934), 110-112; Reypens and Van Mierlo, "Een nieuwe mystieke schrijfster uit de eerste helft der XIIIe eeuw," *D. War. Belf.*, 1925, 352-367.

[150] See above p. 110 and note 73.

[151] The *V. Beat.* speaks of her parents as "parentibus mediocribus" and her father as "huius saeculi labili honestate mediocriter quidem inter suos enituit" (p. 1), but his foundations indicate wealth.

[152] *Ibid.*, p. 1.

[153] *Ibid.*, p. 10.

[154] *Ibid.*, pp. 12, 28-31.

[155] Roisin (*Hag. cist.*, p. 62) makes the girl fifteen while Van Mierlo (*DHGE.*, VII, 110) thinks that she was eighteen. It is possible that her profession took place at the time that Florival was brought under Cistercian reform and received aid from her father, i.e. 1218, when she was about sixteen.

[156] *V. Beat.*, p. 11; cf. Roisin, *Hag. cist.*, p. 62, note 1.

[157] *V. Beat.*, pp. 10-11.

[158] *V. Id. Lew.*, 109 F, no. 8.

[159] This is the conclusion of De Buck (*ibid.*, 110-111, note e).

be able to write books needed by her church."[160] Here she spent a
year and established a friendship with Ida of Nivelles (d. 1232), who
had mastered the interior life under the direction of Hadewigis of
Nivelles (d. 1214).[161] Through its *ars scriptoria*[162] La Ramée where
Ida of Léau, by surpassing her sisters in her application to writing
and correcting liturgical books,[163] is said "studiose libros ecclesiae
scripsisse,"[164] had gained sufficient renown to attract the inhabitants
of numerous Belgian monasteries.

---

[160] *V. Beat.*, p. 32.
[161] *V. Id. Niv.*, ed. Henriquez, p. 204.
[162] *V. Beat.*, p. 41.
[163] *V. Id. Lew.*, 109-110 (8); 113 (18-19).
[164] *Ibid.*, 129 E; cf. *ibid.*, 111, note f.

II

Letters and the Beguinage

LAMBERT LE BÈGUE

It was for the common man of Walloon Belgium that Lambert le Bègue made during his imprisonment in the castle of Rivogne,[1] his translations of devotional literature, and put his moral axioms in vernacular verse—for the *mulieres sanctae,* cast in the mold of the future beguines, an adaptation of the life and suffering of St. Agnes, and for all in common a version of the Acts of the Apostles[2] into which were inserted exhortations to call the readers back to the holy-days.[3] His own words furnish the only contemporary evidence we have of his activity in the feminine religious movement. Following the account of the author of the *Vita Odiliae,*[4] Gilles d'Orval, a Cistercian from Liège recorded in his *Gesta Episcoporum Leodiensium* (ca. 1250) that Lambert, "although but little instructed in the study of letters,"[5] translated for the weavers and fullers the lives of saints and the Acts of the Apostles into French verse[6] in imitation of a certain *magister* of Flanders who had rendered into the vernacular the book of Psalms with glosses and commentaries,[7] and for maidens, presu-

[1] Fredericq, *Corpus,* II, 30; Fayen, p. 352. The life of St. Agnes was much admired in Belgium for its praise of chastity (*V. Od.,* 283-284; *V. Lutg.,* 192 (I, 3); 200 (II, 21). Cf. Greven, *Anfänge,* pp. 177-178; Van Mierlo, in *VMKVA.,* 1926, 625-628.

[2] *V. Od.,* 208; for the castle see *ASAN.,* VII, 306.

[3] Fredericq, *Corpus,* II, 30; Fayen, p. 352: "Unde et ego, bonis eorum studiis co-operans, virginibus vitam et passionem beatae virginis et Christi martyris Agnetis, omnibus vero generaliter actus apostolorum rithmicis concrepantes modulis ad linguam sibi notiorem e Latina transfuderam, multis loco congruo insertis exhortationibus, ut videlicet haberent quo diebus festis, mundo in rebus pessimis exultante, a venenato ipsius melle sese revocare potuissent."

[4] "Litterarum studiis parum instructus, rusticus, indoctus" (*V. Od.,* 206).

[5] "Quamvis litterarum studiis parum instructus fuisset" (Gilles d'Orval, *Gesta Episc. Leod.,* MGH. SS., XXV, 112).

[6] *Ibid.,* 112; *V. Od.,* 208 (I, 4). Cf. Lambert's letter to Calixtus III (Fredericq, *Corpus,* II, 30; Fayen, p. 352): "Actus apostolorum rithmicis concrepantes modulis and linguam sibi notiorem..." (Alberic de Troisfontaines, *Chron.,* MGH. SS., XXIII, 855) confirms this predilection: "...Multos libros et maxime vitas sanctorum et actus apostolorum de latine vertit in romanum"; Berger, *La Bible française,* p. 49; Daris, *Notices,* V, 187ff.

[7] Fredericq, *Corpus,* II, 31; Fayen, p. 353: "Est preterea apud eos liber psalmo-

mably forerunners of the beguine movement, the life and passion of Mary.[8] On the other hand, this very literary output together with an obviously considerable knowledge of scripture which he cites abundantly proves that he had received some training.

Although Gilles does not explicitly mention a translation of St. Paul's epistles, yet what he says with respect to the special reverence which Lambert showed for the apostle[9] may be considered a confirmation of the words of a vernacular twelfth century psalter which claims that the priest put it "en nostre langage."[10] In addition to confirming Gilles' account of Lambert's literary efforts, Alberic de Trois-fontaines added two other works: the *Antigraphum Petri*[11] and the *Tabula* or perpetual calendar,[12] the latter, it has been maintained, being preserved in the manuscript of Lambert's psalter.[13] Although Meyer hesitated to attribute the prayers in the Liége psalter to the priest of St. Christopher, it is not outside the realm of possibility that

rum cum omnibus glosulis suis et auctoritatibus eas roborantibus in vulgarem linguam a quodam magistro Flandriensi translatus." The Psalms were the first book of the Bible to be translated into French. The followers of Waldo brought to the Third Lateran Council (1179) a glossed Psalter (Berger, *op. cit.*, p. 64). For speculations on the Flemish master see Mens, *Oorsprong*, p. 157, note 167.

[8] Fredericq, *Corpus*, II, 30; Fayen, p. 352.

[9] "Paulus apostolus, quem ipse intimo cordis affectu diligebat" (*MGH. SS.*, XXV, 112); cf. *V. Od.*, 208.

[10] P. Meyer, "Le psautier de Lambert le Bègue," *Romania*, XXIX (1900), 528-545; especially pp. 535f. Cf. Berger, *op. cit.*, pp. 49-50.

[11] *Chron., MGH. SS.*, XXIII, 855; cf. Lambert's own testimony, Ep. VI, Fredericq, *Corpus*, II, 31; Fayen, p. 354. The work was first edited by Daris, *Notices*, XVI (1897), 25-74; then on the basis of both mss. (Hunter Museum at Glasgow and Bibliothèque nationale at Paris) by Fayen, *L'Antigraphum Petri et les lettres concernant Lambert le Bègue conservées dans le ms. de Glasgow*, BCRH., LXVIII (1899), 266-322. For the authorship see Greven, *Anfänge*, p. 161, note 1. Nimal (*Les béguinages*, p. 20), in his effort to whitewash Lambert of all anticlerical intention, rejected this work. Cf. Balau, *Etude critique des sources*, pp. 330-331.

[12] Alberic de Troisfontaines, *Chronica, MGH. SS.*, XXIII, 855.

[13] Meyer, *op. cit.*, pp. 536ff. Meyer compared five mss., forming a group of liturgical works, made for the laity rather than the clergy. All were of Liége origin during the thirteenth century. At the head was a calendar, adorned with miniatures, representing the monthly occupations. The calendar is followed by a table, made up of nineteen vertical columns pertaining to the lunar cycle and twenty-eight horizontal lines corresponding to the solar cycle. The table was designed to furnish the Easter date from 1140. In the Br. Mus. ms. the pascal table is followed by an image of a person with a halo, with the inscriptions:
>   In the two upper corners: "Sires Lambers".
> On the banner that the figure carries:
>   "Ge suis ichis Lambers, nel tenez pas a fable
>   Ki funda sain Cristophle, ki enscri ceste table."
> In the upper margin:
>   "Cist prudom fist prumiers l'ordne de beginage
>   Les epistles sain Paul mist en nostre langage."
This suggests that the person was Lambert le Bègue and that the table was the *tabula Petri* mentioned by Alberic. It is followed by prayers or poetry in French which are in part the same in all mss. (some of the poems have been published in the Bibliothèque de l'Université de Liége, *Catalogue des manuscrits*, pp. 13f). In the wake of these first leaves begins the psalter, also in French.

they were his, especially considering that the psalter comes from Lambert. Notwithstanding the complete disappearance of the translations of the Acts of Apostles, the epistles of Paul, the saints' lives, and other French writings, it becomes increasingly clear that the he greatly aided the beginnings of vernacular religious poetry in the diocese of Liége from the last quarter of the twelfth century.

Because of these translations Lambert was accused of revealing Scripture to the unlettered. Writing in his own defense to Calixtus III, he took special pains to point out that the above-mentioned Flemish "magister" had not incurred hostility by his translation of the psalter. Perhaps, he adds, with a touch of sarcasm, it was because "nemo propheta acceptus est in patria sua. Ille vero magister de patria ejus non fuit."[14] His own enemies had also imputed to him heretical view that "it was less a crime to trample the body of Christ under foot than to fail to listen to the word of God."[15] He had already answered other evidence of antagonism in his *Querimonia*[16] as well as the little book entitled *Antigraphum Petri*, a copy of which had been submitted to the pope.[17]

Again it must be emphasized that Lambert's translations, although designed as edifying reading matter for pious societies, were not, like Waldo's, manuals or aid for preachers alone, but chiefly didactic material for laymen who assembled on Sundays after the service for discussion and the singing of Psalms and hymns.[18] Whether the French prayers to which Paul Meyer once directed attention came immediately from the pen of Lambert himself is not too important;[19] it is, on the other hand, an incontrovertible fact that the priest of St. Christopher helped much to answer the demand for a devotional literature in the vernacular.

Thus these Sunday circles at Liége exhibit the necessary conditions for the development of a religious literature: a lay community wishes to employ devotional writings but is not sufficiently instructed in Latin to avail itself of existing Latin materials, and subsequently its

[14] Fredericq, *Corpus*, II, 31; Fayen, 354.

[15] "Adjiciunt etiam me pronunciasse minoris esse reatus corpus Domini pedibus conculcare, quam verbum Dei negligenter audire" (Fredericq, *Corpus*, II, 31; Fayen, 353-354). See above, pp. 72-73.

[16] Ep. IV (Fredericq, *Corpus*, II, 19-23; Fayen, pp. 330-337), addressed to Calixtus III, bears the title: "Querimonia Lamberti presbiteri, cum de carcere evasisset." The brief that the author calls in Ep. VI (Fredericq, *Corpus*, II, 31; Fayen, 354) "querimonie mee scedula" was thus actually sent to the pope (cf. Greven, *Anfänge*, pp. 163-164).

[17] Fredericq, *Corpus*, II, 31; Fayen, 354.

[18] "...Residuum autem diei usque ad vespertine laudis tempus, sollempnibus dico diebus, in psalmis, in ymnis et canticis spiritualibus expendebant, audita queque in ecclesia runimantes et sese mutuo ad custodiendum cohortantes" (Fredericq, *Corpus*, II, 30; Fayen, 352).

[19] Meyer, in *Romania*, XXIX (1900), 540-543.

spiritual advisers provide the members with vernacular writings.[20] These were not permanent, well organized societies, but only loose associations meeting on occasion. Didactic poetry was preferred to popular prose literature for recitation. Nor were there yet any real literary creations of pious laymen.

FRENCH MATERIALS

Scattered Old French prose and poetry prove that from the second half of the thirteenth century visionary mysticism and Franciscan poverty marked a part of the lay religious movement. From MS. Gall. oct. 28 of the Preussische Staatsbibliothek in Berlin, a devotional book for the use of beguines, E. Bechmann published three *Dits de l'âme*.[21] The third *Dit* asks in the opening stanza what is beguinage and then proceeds to offer an explanation:

> "Savés que j'apiel Beghinage?
> Consciënche ne mie large,
> pieue et devote affection,
> oster son coer de tout herbage,
> car l'esperit fait grant damage,
> de dieu sentir en orison.
> Deus larmes de contricion
> et trois par grant compassion
> valent l'avoir qui par mer nage.
> Mais celi de devotion
> ne poroit esprisier nuls hom,
> souvent fait a dieu son manage ..."[22]

In a prose selection[23] a Paris master had a beguine enlighten him on the life and aims of her community in words strongly reminiscent of Robert de Sorbon's observation.[24] Since the explanation betrays nothing hostile or unsympathetic to the mode of existence followed by the beguines, it must have come from a member or a friend of a beguinage. The language of the poems puts their composition in Picardy or northern France at the end of the thirteenth or beginning of the fourteenth century.[25]

Several MSS. of similar content and the same period come from Metz which since the appearance of the Waldensians in 1199 had offered fertile ground for semi-religious associations which employed

[20] Grundmann, *Religiöse Bewegungen*, p. 453.

[21] E. Bechmann, "Drei Dits de l'âme aus der Handschrift MS. Gall. Oct. 28 der königlichen Bibliothek zu Berlin," *Zschr. f. rom. Philologie*, XIII (1889), 35-84; the text appears on pp. 56-80.

[22] *Ibid.*, 72.

[23] Christ (in *La Règle des Fins Amans*, pp. 179-180) discusses these.

[24] "Quant li maistres l'oij, si dist: dont savés vous plus de divinité que tout li maistres de Paris" (*ibid.*, 180). For Robert see above, pp. 418-420.

[25] Bechmann, *op. cit.*, 39-53.

the vernacular. Besides pious tracts and sermons the Metz MS. contains several religious poems stamped with Franciscan ideas which must have emanated from beguine circles.[26] To claim, as Christ does,[27] that they sprang from beguine circles in close contact with Spiritual Franciscans may represent an attempt to push northward the well-known beguin-Fraticelli nexus of the south. A poem on poverty (no. 35) in MS. 535 of the municipal library at Metz which Meyer describes in detail contains the passage opening with the line, "Qui vuet droit beguinage avoir."[28] A subsequent reference to St. Bernard of Clairvaux is quite possible.[29] Another poem exhorts the beguines to pursue divine love.[30]

MS. Lat. oct. 264 of the Preussische Staatsbibliothek contains *Le Livre du paumier (Palma contemplationis)*[31], also of beguine origin, as the presence of the rule published by Christ and the other contents testify. The palm tree allegory which, derived from *Cantica Canticorum* (VII, 8), presents the mystical ascent of the soul to God as the step by step growth of a palmtree with seven branches, was popular in Germany. This tract thus reflects the mystical yearning of beguine piety; that it was cherished by the extra-regulars is proved by its inclusion in the Metz MS (no. 1).[32] The second French piece, offering guidance to a devout hearing of mass, is in theological collections as well as in the Metz MS (no. 3).[33]

CREATION OF FLEMISH PROSE

The *Seven Manieren van Minne* stamps Beatrice both as a talented wielder of Flemish prose and as a notable mystic of the thirteenth century who, together with Hadewijch, deserves to be regarded as a precursor of the full tide of spirituality in the days of Ruysbroeck and Eckhart.[34] Beatrice is also known to have recorded, probably before 1235, in the vernacular her spiritual growth between 1220 and 1235,—

[26] Meyer, "Notices du MS. 535 de la bibliothèque municipale de Metz renfermant diverses compositions pieuses (prose et vers) en français," *Bulletin de la société des anciens textes français*, XII (1886), 41-76.

[27] Christ, *La Règle des Fins Amans*, p. 180.

[28] Meyer, in *Bull. SATF.*, XII, 61-62: "Qui vuet droit beguinage avoir/ Il at mestier par estevoir/ Qu'il ne despesse fuer que lui,/ Et ce soit larges pour autrui;/ Ce fasse joie d'autrui bien/ Tout autresi conme dou sien./ Beguins ce doit mout bien garder;/ Il ne doit mie trop parler./ Sovent avient qui trop parole/ Qu'il a tot dit parole fole;/ Le monde puet il bien despire,/ Mais il ne doit avoir point d'ire."

[29] *Ibid.*, p. 62.

[30] *Ibid.*, p. 73.

[31] Christ, *La Règle des Fins Amans*, p. 161; Meyer, in *Bull. SATF.*, XII, 43-45.

[32] Christ, *La Règle des Fins Amans*, p. 182.

[33] *Idem.*

[34] Van Mierlo, "Over het ontstaan der Germaansche mystiek," *OGE.*, I (1927), 11-37.

visions, prayers, penitence, supernatural favors, and sundry religious experiences,—together with a sketch of her external history. It consti- tutes a precious document for the mystical currents in the beguinal and Cistercian worlds in the generation after Mary of Oignies' death. The brief mystical treatise, contained in a collection of sermons at the beginning of the fourteenth century, known as the *Limburgsche Ser- moenen,* and also separately in the later manuscript, *Van Seven Ma- nienen van Minne,* corresponds to a chapter in the biography: „De charitate Dei et septem ejus gradus".[35] After her death this auto- biography, which is no longer extant, was translated into Latin by a contemporary of Maerlant who was long thought to be Guillaume de Malines, abbot of St. Trond, but better known as Guillaume of Afflighem (d. April 14, 1297) where he first lived.[36] In the preface the translator avows explicitly that the biography was not so much his as Beatrice's.[37] The first manuscript was prepared by John of St. Trond when he was confessor in Parc-des-Dames.[38] The pseudo-Henry of Ghent, by summarizing in his *De Viris illustribus usque ad annum 1280* the literary activity of Guillaume offers a brief insight into the work of the transmitters of these Cistercian and Dominican *vitae.*

"William, monk of Afflighem and for some time prior there, turned the life of Lutgard, written in Latin by Brother Thomas (of Cantimpré), into Flemish couplets. He also rendered nicely enough in Latin certain material from a nun of the Cistercian order who had written in Flemish the many marvels she had experienced."[39]

[35] Van Mierlo, in *DHGE.,* VII, 111; Reypens, in *D. War. Belf.,* XXV (1925), 354f; Van Veerdeghem, *Leven van Sinte Lutgart,* pp. 56-57.

[36] Bets, in *AHEB.,* VII (1870), 77-78. Bets edited (*ibid.,* 80-82) the preface to the *Vita Beatricis* which, together with certain important passages in the body of the text, was omitted by Henriquez. Cf. Roisin, *Hag. cist.,* p. 63. For Guillaume d'Af- flighem see V. Leclercq. "Guillaume de Malines, moine d'Afflighem, abbé de Saint- Trond," *HLF.,* XXI (1847), 56-67; Balau, *Sources,* pp. 492-496.

[37] "Me solum huius operis translatorem existere, non autorem, quippe qui de meo parum admodum addidi vel mutavi; hec, prout in cedula oblata suscepi illa vulgaria, latino in eloquio coloravi" (*AHEB.,* VII, 81).

[38] *Ibid.,* 78.

[39] "Wilhelmus, monachus Affligemiensis et ibidem aliquando prior, vitam domi- nae Lutgardis, a fratre Thoma Latine scriptam, convertit in Teutonicum rithme duobus sibi semper rithmis consonantibus. Dictavit etiam Latine quamdam mate- riam satis eleganter de quadam moniali Cisterciensis ordinis, quae Teutonice multa satis mirabilia scripserat de seipsa" (Henry of Ghent, *De scriptoribus ecclesiasticis,* cited by Miraeus, *Bibl. eccl.,* p. 173). To the Brussels MS. 4459-4470 which dates from the fourteenth century has been added: "Hanc vitam conscripsit dominus Willelmus de Mechlinia monacus Haffligemensis, quondam prior in Wavria, post abbas Sancti Trudonis." Codex Gandavensis 165 of the seventeenth century an- nounces that the "Vita Beatricis, Ordinis Cisterciensis, priorissae in Nazareth prope Liram ab ipsa flandrice vel gallice conscripta, interprete anonymo" (Roisin, *Hag. cist.,* p. 63). Roisin accepts the second passage. Van Mierlo (*Leuvense Studieen en Tekstuitgaven,* XII, 1926, pp. 24ff) doubts whether Guillaume composed the Latin *vita.* Yet the tradition was established early, for John Trithemius (*De scriptoribus ecclesiasticis,* ed. Fabricius, p. 128, no. 528) mentions among his writings the *Visio- nes cujusdam monialis.* Cf. F. Pelster ("Der Heinrich von Gent zugeschriebene *Catalogus virorum illustrium* und sein wirklicher Verfasser," *HJ.,* XXXIX (1918-

It is significant that while the advisers of these *mulieres sanctae*, Jacques de Vitry, Guy and John of Nivelles, John de Liro, and Thomas of Cantimpré produced for them no vernacular moral literature, they sometimes prepared Latin lives to serve as examples for other circles. That vernacular writings lay at the basis of some of this Latin literature is clearly demonstrated by Guillaume's activity.

Although the author of the *Vita Julianae* reveals neither name nor titles, the text shows that he was one of the learned members of the Liége clergy. He mentions but once, and then unfavorably, the chapter of St. Lambert.[40] The manner in which he speaks of St. Martin's persuaded Demarteau that he belonged to the chapter of this collegiate church. In the course of the biography he further points out that in his youth he could have entered directly into relations with Juliana through the offices of mutual friends.[41] Among them was probably the canon John of Lausanne who, on the one hand, acted as a most zealous protector of the nun of Mont Cornillon and, on the other, befriended the biographer. It was at his request that he put into Latin a work on Juliana, previously drawn up in French.[42] However, Demarteau[43] forces too much the texts by inferring the existence of a vernacular life which he attributes to Eve herself. He even calls her "the first Walloon author." The biographer does not go so far. He simply says that he has heard persons, who have known her, relate details of the life and virtues of Juliana and that in order to preserve these accounts, a devout woman has taken care to transcribe them into Latin, namely the language in which they had been related. Without doubt such

1919), 253-268) who attributed the *Catalogus* to a monk of Afflighem; Le Clerc, in *HLF.*, XXI (1847), 56-67; P. Lehman, "Quellen zur Feststellung und Geschichte mittelalterlicher Bibliotheken," *HJ.*, XL (1920), 77-82; Van Veerdeghem, *Leven van Sinte Lutgart*, pp. 54ff, p. xv-xvi. Roisin (*Hag. cist.*, pp. 64-65) concludes that the author was a contemporary of Beatrice, writing shortly after 1268 and learning from Christine, the sister of the mystic, some details on her death (*V. Beat.*, in Bibl. roy. de Belg., 4459-4470, f. 137r).

[40] *V. Jul. Cornel.*, 461, no. 14 (II, 3).

[41] *Ibid.*, 474, no. 51 (II, 8).

[42] *Ibid.*, 443 A-B (Preface). The critical text to which further reference will be made runs as follows: "Quae vero conscripta sunt, a venerabilibus et fide dignis personis cognita sunt et relata: quarum quaedam, etsi non omni, tamen multo tempore quo vixit, cum ipsa (i.e., Juliana) conversatae; quaedam autem specialem dilectionis ejus gratiam consecutae, de vita et virtutibus ejus plurima cognaverunt, et sine falsitatis fermento sciscitantibus nobis narraverunt. Quae quidem per diligentiam unius valde religiosae personae, veluti quaedam fragmenta ne perirent, in lingua Gallica litteris commendata; et per Dominum Joannem de Lausenna, canonicum ecclesiae Sancti Martini Leodiensis, admirandae sanctitatis virum, approbata sunt: cujus etiam vita et mors, quae jam intervenit, pretiosam non brevem commendationem, sed opus proprium desiderat, si fuerit qui assumat . . . ." Demarteau, *Eve de Saint-Martin*, pp. 4-5; Balau, *Sources*, pp. 441-442; Lambot, "Eve de Saint-Martin et les premiers historiens liégeois de la Fête-Dieu," *Stud. euch.*, pp. 10-36; id., "Un precieux manuscrit de la Vie de Sainte Julienne du Mont-Cornillon," *Misc. hist . . . . Alberti de Meyer*, I, 603-612; Simenon, *Julienne*, pp. 12-13; *AB.*, XVI (1897), 531-532; Mens, *Oorsprong*, pp. 194-195, note 263.

[43] Demarteau, *Eve de Saint-Martin*, p. 12; see Balau's objections (*Sources*, p. 442).

reminiscences could come best from Eve, her confidant. But it is probable that it was she who related them by word of mouth while another *religiosae persona* put the fragments in Latin.[44] These notes pleased John of Lausanne. But rather than do the task himself he engaged one of his friends—educated and devout, but unnamed—to arrange them in an acceptable literary form. It is clear that the latter was not obliged to make a mere translation of these fragments—*quaedam fragmenta*. While he parades his school training and discusses as a theologian the elements of prophecy, he apologizes for omitting details with which he was acquainted: "volens et in hoc fastidiosis lectoribus providere." Thus the biography was written in two books about 1262, four or five years after Juliana's death.[45] The first traces her progress in spiritual matters, with due emphasis on virtues, prophecies and miracles; the second departs from the interior life to describe her difficulties at the leper-house and afterwards at Cistercian convents, together with the calling to proclaim the new feast.[46]

Belgian Latin hagiography of the thirteenth century thus is indebted to vernacular materials. Not only is this quite clear for the lives of Beatrice and Juliana but the same supposition would seem to obtain for the *vitae* of Ida of Nivelles, Ida of Léau, Christine Mirabilis, and Lutgarde.[47]

In handling that literature perhaps known to beguines and certainly reflecting their aims mention must be made of the *Bonum Universale de Apibus* of Thomas of Cantimpré, ever a forceful spokesman of the *vita apostolica*. With this spirit the entire Supplement to the *VMO.* is instinct. Besides at least sixty MSS. of the Latin text of the *Bonum Universale de Apibus,* there are two Flemish translations of which about a dozen manuscripts exist.[48] While the *Vita Christinae Mirabilis* was put into Flemish verse by a Franciscan Gerard, the *Vita Lutgardis* received three translations. The oldest of these three was the versified translation attributed to the Benedictine monk William of Affligem; the first book of it is lacking. A second translation was that of Brother Gerard who also did an adaptation of the *V. Chr. Mir.* Like the last named, the *Vita Lutgardis* was put into Flemish verse, but the text of the first book of *Het leven van Sinte Lutgardis* has come down imperfectly in the only known manuscript, whereas 257 verses are missing in the second book. Besides these

[44] *V. Jul. Cornel,* 443 B.

[45] Demarteau, *Eve de Saint-Martin,* p. 4.

[46] See above, pp. 301 ff.

[47] Mens, *Oorsprong,* pp. 194-195, note 263; cf. Van Mierlo, in *D. War. Belf.,* XXV (1925), 367; id., in *VMKVA.,* 1926, p. 71; Grundmann, *Religiöse Bewegungen,* pp. 455-456.

[48] For MSS. see Van der Vet, *Het Biënboec,* pp. 408ff; Axters, *Gesch. van de Vroomheid,* I, 334.

two translations in verse, a fragment of a third, in prose, survives.[49]

A DIALOGUE WITH THE BRIDEGROOM

The convent of St. Barbara at Delft which was directed by the Brethren of the Common Life from foundation had in its library in the second half of the fifteenth century, in addition to writings of Rulman Merswin and Suso,[50] a copy of the *Vita Mariae Oignia-censis*[51] as well as "een boec van Sinte Franciscus leven."[52] These Franciscan tertiaries owed their origins to St. Agatha at Utrecht where Gerard Groot had himself been active. It is evident that the mother house had sisters who could read Latin and that translation into Dutch was being encouraged.

Fragmentary knowledge of the thirteenth and fourteenth centuries makes it impossible to say how closely the biography of Mary was imitated or used by Flemish-Dutch beguines. On the other hand, in view of the literary output of Hadewijch and Beatrice of Nazareth, we must assume that certain beguines wrote. The *Verbum Jesu Christi ad Beginam Tungerensem* of an anonymous beguine of Tongres is a case in point.[53] The corrupt text suggests that the one extant manuscript should not be regarded as the original of the *Verbum*. Brother John of St. Trond had this collection of pious works composed in 1320 when he was confessor to the nuns of Parc-les-Dames (Vrouwen-Parc) at Wezemael, in the time of Abbot Jacques, the expense being covered by alms.[54] These circumstances suggest that the *Verbum* belongs to the thirteenth century. At the same time the opening words of this tract of spiritual life, "In beginagio tungerensi factum est verbum Ihesu Christi ad quandam iuvenculam innocentem valde,"[55] make it clear that the original of the text could not have been composed before the founding of the Tongres beguinage in 1243.[56]

The extreme intensity that the love of Jesus and the passion could attain in the daily experiences of a Christine of Stommeln or Juliana

---

[49] *Ibid.*, pp. 334-335.

[50] Moll, in *Kerkhistorisch Archief*, IV (1866), 252-253, no. 77; 259-260, no. 35; cf. 225, nos. 22, 35.

[51] *Ibid.*, 275, no. 71. Moll was not well informed about its nature or authorship.

[52] *Ibid.*, 225, no. 31. It is possible that this was Maerlant's adaptation, even as *Van coninc Alexander* (*ibid.*, 272, no. 105) may have also been his.

[53] Bibl. roy. de Belgique, cod. 4459-70, ff. 252r-252v; Axters, "De anonieme Begijn van Tongeren en haar mystieke dialoog," *OGE.*, XV, 1, 1941, 88-97; cf. id., *Gesch. van de Vroomheid*, I, 332-333. For the MS. see also de Reiffenberg, in *Annuaire de la Bibl. roy, de Belg.*, III (1842), 127-136; J. Van Gheyn, *Catalogue des manuscrits de la Bibliothèque royale de Belgique*, V (Brussels, 1905), 115-118, no. 3161.

[54] Bibl. roy. de Belg., cod. 4459-70, f. 1v.

[55] *Ibid.*, f. 252r.

[56] Thijs, in *BSSLL.*, XV (1881), 417.

of Cornillon, is well represented in the late medieval poem in Low German, *Legende von dem Beginchen von Paris,* which may very well have served in German beguinehouses as a favorite devotional reading and as a model for exemplary conduct.[57] In order to reside comple- tely in the presence of the divine, to share with Jesus, her beloved, His passion and human sympathy and to approximate his love with similar sacrifice a wealthy Parisian girl renounces the pleasures of the world in spite of the protests of her mother and assumes the gray habit of the beguines. Convinced that external forms of piety made impossible immediate contact with the godhead, she awaited Jesus for seven years in her cell without food or drink, refusing to share the everyday tasks of the other beguines—sewing and spinning.[58] The absorption of her entire being in the deity brought fulfillment of otherworldly experience, the appearance of Christ with whom she held conversations, unrestrained by fear of imperfection. This edifying poem thus illustrates the culmination of a deeply pious life led by a beguine who, although an extra-regular, depended on spiritual resources sanctioned by the church.

BEGUINE SPIRITUALITY IN DELFT

From the full-sized hagiographical portrait of Gertrude Van Oosten we derive an intimate picture of the interior life of this extra-regular movement in Holland.[59] This anonymous biography is for Delft and the Netherlands what the *Vita Mariae Oigniacensis* is, on a more com- plete scale, for Nivelles and Belgium. If the latter expresses the mili- tant anti-heretical mood among the *mulieres religiosae* during the Albigensian crusade, the life of Gertrude is nonetheless an affirmation of beguine orthodoxy in the wake of Clementine and Johannine legislation. However susceptible she was to ecstatic experiences, however inured to unmitigated asceticism and capable of prophetic

---

[57] Schade, *Geistliche Gedichte,* pp. 335-356; Stammler, *Geschichte der niederdeut- schen Literatur,* p. 38; L. Wolff in W. Stammler's *Die deutsche Literatur des Mit- telalters. Verfasserlexicon* (Berlin-Leipzig, 1933ff), I, 183-184.

[58] Stanza, 48.

[59] *De Venerabili Virgine Gertrude ab Oosten Beghina Delphensi in Belgio,* 348- 353 (the Latin life is drawn from an Utrecht MS.); cf. Van Heussen, *Batavia sacra,* I, 183-184; Ryckel, pp. 357-361; De Ram, *Hag. nat.,* I, 64-67. Alberdingk Thijm's study (*Geertruide Van Oosten. Geschiedenis van een Delfsch begijntien uit de XIV eeuw,* Amsterdam, 1853) is worthless for the historian; on pp. 60-70 one finds a Dutch adaptation of the *vita.* With respect to vernacular treatments the Bol- landist (*Comm. praev., V. Gert.* 349, no. 2) cites from Miraeus' *Fasti Belgici* and Molanus' *Natales Sanctorum Belgii:* "De ea quaedam leguntur in vulgaribus Hol- landiae chronicis: sed multo plura Latino sermone extant manuscripta." A Flemish version of the *vita* was published at Louvain in 1589 and reproduced by Rosweydus (*Het leven der HH. Maegden,* pp. 39-47; cf. the augmented French translation by Gilles de S. Aldegonde, *Les vies des sainctes plus illustres...* (Tournai, 1641), 60-77). Axters, *Gesch. van de Vroomheid,* II, 167-169.

utterances, neither these nor stigmatization ever provoked the charge of heresy. Only out of fear of the charge of vanity, the danger of presumption, and because of the press of the curious did she ask to have the stigmata removed.[60] Composing this work as if specifically for reading in a beguinage, the author emphasizes that her exercises conformed to the offices of the church[61] and that when she was about to be united with the heavenly Bridegroom she was fortified with the sacraments.[62] Not only was her life marked by frequent confessions[63] during the "many years" spent among beguines in austerity and with fervor[64] but adoption of voluntary poverty[65] was intended to ensure spiritual self-sufficiency.

Born of humble parents[66] in Voorburg midway between The Hague and Delft at the beginning of the fourteenth century,[67] Gertrude lived during the struggle between the Hoeks and Kabiljauws.[68] Although having but slender worldly possessions, she went to Delft to minister to the sick in the fashion of other *mulieres sanctae*.[69] The biographer reveals that at this time there were in the town no monasteries of sisters and brethren but only two temples, to wit a parish church with three altars and a hospital for the poor with an altar for the needs of the infirm. Both men and women hastened to them on feast days, not for the sermon but to sing.[70] Gertrude was so devoted to her hospital work[71] and had achieved such self-sufficiency through cultivation of the inner life that she often felt in the midst of a crowd as great a sweetness of divine goodness as she frequently experienced later in the beguine house.[72] The name Van Oosten was the vulgar form of de Oriente found in the opening line of an old Flemish song that she was wont to sing:[73] "Ab Oriente dies nascitur" ("Het dag het in den Oosten").[74] "Sed cantando," adds the biographer, "fere-

[60] *V. Gert.*, 351, no. 19.
[61] *Ibid.*, 350, no. 12.
[62] *Ibid.*, 352, no. 29.
[63] *Ibid.*, 350, no. 7.
[64] *Ibid.*, 352, no. 29.
[65] *Ibid.*, 350, nos. 7-8.
[66] "Villanis parentibus" (*ibid.*, 349, no. 2). Ryckel (p. 357) characteristically describes her as "nobilior revelationibus quam genere."
[67] *V. Gert.*, 349, no. 2.
[68] *Ibid.*, 352, no. 22. For the feud, consult Pirenne, *Histoire de Belgique*, II (1903), 165ff; Blok, *Geschiedenis eener Hollandsche Stad*, pp. 73-92.
[69] *V. Gert.*, 349, no. 2.
[70] *Ibid.*, 349, no. 3.
[71] *Ibid.*, 349, nos. 3, 5.
[72] *Ibid.*, 349, no. 3.
[73] *Ibid.*, 349, no. 4.
[74] Willems published the text in *Oude Vlaemsche Liederen*, pp. 111-113, no. 48, together with a Low German version (113-115, from Uhland's *Deutsche Volkslieder*) and a High German text (115-116: "Es taget in Oesterriche...", from Mone's *Anzeiger*, 1835, col. 455). Willems refers to Gertrude as "eene nederduitsche dichteresse" (*l.c.*, p. 113). Cf. Alberdingk Thijm, *Geertruide*, pp. 56-59; Axters, *Gesch. van de Vroomheid*, II, 168f.

batur spiritu, referendo carmen ad dilectum suum Jesum Christum."[75]

Two women, Lielt[76] and Diewer, both poor like herself, often visited Gertrude and the three would sing this hymn on the bridges of the town or in "other advantageous places." They, like Gertrude, were also persuaded to abandon worldly things while Diewer even lived with her in the beguinage.[77] To seek in Gertrude's marriage with the heavenly Bridegroom and her adoption of the beguine way of life a logical explanation, it is necessary to consider that she had only recently been jilted by her fiancé who "despised" her. Determined to preserve her chastity she entered the beguinage.[78] At the outset of her "conversion" she was obliged to beg.[79] She died in 1358 after living among the beguines "for many years"[80] and acquiring considerable renown for frequent ecstasy, revelations and predictions,[81] cognizance of the devil,[82] fervent meditation of the passion, and reception of the stigmata.[83] She left behind her in the beguinage a number of other *mulieres sanctae* imbued with the same devotional zeal.[84] In fact, an interlacing of Cellites and beguines is suggested.[85] Nevertheless, the biographer concludes, she was buried outside the gate of the tower on the south side of the old church of Delft "because the beguines were still without their own church and cemetery."[86]

Thus Gertrude remained the center of a spirituality which is best summarized in her *Asceses seu Exercitia quaedam familiaria*[87] as well as in the *Praxis meditationis localis super Passione Domini*.[88] Gielemans[89] in the following century mentions a beguine, once of Herenthals, but now living in Delft, in a house dedicated to Mary Magdalene, with a "large congregation of sisters and devout persons." She recalled how an observant Franciscan in this town had praised warmly Mary of Lille, another beguine at Herenthals for forty-three years.

DOMINICAN LEADERSHIP

A sound basis for religious prose literature in the vernacular could be found only when regular and semi-religious women's communities

[75] *V. Gert.*, 349, no. 4.
[76] *Ibid.*, 351, no. 15; Ryckel, pp. 389-393.
[77] *V. Gert.*, 349, no. 4.
[78] *Ibid.*, 349-350, nos. 5-6.
[79] *Ibid.*, 350, no. 8.
[80] *Ibid.*, 352, no. 29.
[81] *Ibid.*, 352, nos. 22-25; cf. 350, no. 9.
[82] *Ibid.*, 350, no. 10.
[83] *Ibid.*, 349, no. 1; 351, nos. 15-19. Cf. Ryckel's observations (p. 359) and an engraving with inscription in Foppens MS. in Bibl. roy. de Belg., cod. 6125.
[84] *V. Gert.*, 353, no. 30.
[85] *Ibid.*, 353, no. 30.
[86] *Ibid.*, 353, no. 29.
[87] Ryckel, pp. 362-382.
[88] *Ibid.*, pp. 390-393; Axters, *Gesch. van de Vroomheid*, II, 157f, 167.
[89] Gielemans, *Ex Novali Sanctorum* (III, 22), in *Anecdota*, p. 418.

without Latin clerical education but with the need for devotional writings and theological instruction adopted a permanent and ordered form, thus opening up the possibility of appropriating Latin theological-mystical material. Nowhere were these conditions so fully met as in the groups affiliated with or incorporated by the mendicant orders, especially the Dominicans. For one eminent German student such a literature best achieved permanence and success in German Dominican nunneries.[90] But Grundmann, whose attention was primarily focused on the local scene, fails to appreciate properly a century-long preparation in the Low Countries, among the beguines themselves. The content of that literature was peculiarly homogeneous and admittedly narrow in scope, much more so than in men's con vents. Nunnery catalogues, infrequent as they are, lacked glosses on the separate biblical books, or the Vulgate, patristic writings, but possessed more sermons, devotional manuals, and a larger proportion of vernacular works.[91]

We must also assume that such a popular religious literature existed in southern France (Prouille) and Italy (Rome, Bologna) where the feminine religious movement sought direction from both Dominicans and Friars Minor. Yet little is known about this problem in the thirteenth century. In Provence the oldest piece of religious prose of any importance appears to be the life of Douceline, written by her successor Philippine of Porcellet about 1300 within a Franciscan atmosphere. But interests of southern beguin(e)s must be approached cautiously, without application to the northern movement.[92]

[90] Grundmann, *Religiöse Bewegungen,* p. 458.

[91] For a summary of the earliest known nunnery catalogue, for Dominicans in Nürnberg (1456-1469) see Deanesly, *Lollard Bible,* pp. 111-113, 115 note 1. Consult the catalogue of Delft Franciscan tertiaries (Moll, in *Kerkhistorisch Archief,* IV (1866,), 213-228; Deanesly, *op cit.,* pp. 113-114). Cf. *ibid.,* pp. 115-116. For books written by nuns see Hauber's useful article in *Zentralblatt für Bibliothekswesen,* XXXI (1914), 341-373.

[92] The Dominican inquisitor, Bernard Gui, who had no fault to find with the heretics' way of life except that the school of Satan imitated the school of Christ as simple laymen imitate like monkeys the pastors of the church and the preachers of the gospel (*Practica,* ed. Douais, p. 266), offers illuminating observations on Sunday devotions as conducted by the beguins of Provence and Narbonne. On Sundays and saints' days they assemble, read or listen to readings in the vernacular (*ibid.,* pp. 266, 274) from precepts and articles of faith, lives of saints, the *Summa de Virtutibus et Vitiis* of Perrault (d. 1275), which serves as a transition from the writings of theologians to sermons of medieval preachers, (*ibid.,* p. 266; cf. HLF., XIX, 307-316), a commentary on the Apocalypse (Gui, *Practica,* pp. 273, 280), short tracts on poverty, mendicancy, the seven wicked spirits, and dispensations (*ibid.,* pp. 265, 273) and above all the writings and teachings of the Spiritual Franciscan Peter John Olivi (*ibid.,* pp. 265, 272). Among their other vernacular works was a little treatise called the *Transitus Sancti Patris,* which was studied frequently in their conventicles (*ibid.,* p. 287; cf. Ehrle, in *ALKM.,* III, 411). The whole text of St. Paul and Brother Peter John alike must be kept unaltered by the church (*ibid.,* ed. Mollat, I, 138); the latter's writings, and especially his *Postilla in Apocalypsim,* were valued only second to those of the Apostles (for esteem in which Olivi was held, see Douie, *Heresy of the Fraticelli,* pp. 252-253).

During the first half of the fourteenth century the Dominican friar Venturino da Bergamo, a penitential preacher keenly alive to the demands of the feminine religious movement, recommended to a certain Margaret Provençal moral writings for reading.[93] In France the *vita* of Isabella, sister of Louis IX and founder of the Franciscan convent of Longchamp at St. Cl.ud in 1259,[94] was written at the request of Isabella's brother, Charles of Anjou,[95] by Agnes d'Harcourt, also of noble lineage[96] and third abbess of the abbey (February, 1274).[97] Although she drew up the eulogy in French, narrating only what she had seen, heard, or learned from eye-witnesses,[98] the Bollandists preserved it in Latin translation. In Italy no such mystical prose literature seems to have appeared for these sisterhoods before the close of thirteenth century. The oldest letters, twenty-two in number, are addressed about 1260 by a Fra Guidone of Arezzo to his fellow brethren and sisters of the order of *Gaudentes* or to other friends in Tuscany.[99] The eight religious writings in Italian of Paula de Montaldo (1443-August 18, 1514), a Clarissa at Mantua, offer late evidence.[100] Grundmann[101] was unable to discover whether the translations of the writings of Angelo da Clareno[102] and of the Franciscan legend were created for the feminine following of the Friars Minor. Ventu-

---

[93] Clementi, II, 107-108: "Multum etiam te adiuvabit ut habeas cor attentum in orationibus, si occupes tempus tuum ad legendum evangelium, passiones sanctorum, vel aliquos libros in romancio, vel vitas patrum."

[94] *V. Isab.*, 801 C, no. 12; *Comm. praev.*, 788 B, no. 5; Guillaume de Nangis, *Chronica*, in Bouquet, XX (1840), 557; Joinville, *Vie de Saint Louis, ibid.*, XX, 293; *AA. SS.*, XXXIX (August 24, v), 753 E, no. 250.

[95] *V. Isab.*, 798 E, no. 1.

[96] Agnes was daughter of Jean, first lord of Harcourt, lord of Elboeuf, Antwerp, etc., who followed St. Louis on his first expedition to the Holy Land, and of Blanche d'Avaugour (otherwise Avancourt), his third wife. She died on the feast of St. Catherine (November 25), 1289. Cf. Louis Calendini, in *DHGE.*, I (1912), 979; *HLF.*, XX (1842), 98-103; *Com. praev., AA. SS.*, XL (August 31, vi), 787, no. 1. The *vita* is published in *ibid.*, 798-808.

[97] Jeanne d'Harcourt, one of Agnes' sisters of the same marriage was also a nun at Longchamp and abbess; she died before Agnes.

[98] *V. Isab.*, 799 B-C, no. 4; 799 D-E, no. 6; 800 B, no. 8; 801 B, no. 11; 801 E, no. 14; 802 B, no. 17; 803 B, no. 19. For French prose literature and poetry for beguine circles or nunneries from the second half of the thirteenth century, see Bachmann, in *Zeitschrift für romanische Philologie*, XIII (1889), 35-84; Hilka, *ibid.*, XLVII (1927), 120ff.

[99] T. Casini in Gustav Gröber, *Grundriss der romanischen Philologie*, II (in 3 Abt.: I (1902), II (1897), III (1901), Strasbourg), II, 3, p. 41.

[100] The titles adequately suggest the contents (*V. Paulae de Montaldo*, LXI (October 29, xiii), 219 B, no. 14): "I. Dulcis est amor Jesu, II. Qui in ore habet Jesu nomen non potest perire. III. Semper Jesus, Jesus, Jesus. IV. Per signum crucis de inimicis nostris libera nos Deus noster. V. Jesu in ore meo, Jesu in anima mea, Jesu semper in mente mea. VI. Domine, non sum digna ut intres sub tectum meum, sed tantum dic verbo, et sanabitur anima mea. VII. Memento homo quia pulvis es et in pulverem reverteris. VIII. Memorare novissima tua, et in aeternum non peccabis."

[101] Grundmann, *Religiöse Bewegungen*, p. 458, note 44.

[102] Zeffirino Lazzeri, "Un nuovo codice italiano delle due prime tribolazioni di Fr. Angelo Clareno," *AFH.*, XI (1918), 47-65.

rino da Bergamo drew up in 1334 in a letter to the nuns at Unterlinden the plan for a model nunnery in Bologna in which not only
all readings, but even the liturgy, were to be in the vernacular.[103]

Even though the Order of Preachers assumed pastoral duties in nunneries with considerable reluctance, there is evidence that from the
beginning certain friars took the initiative for the production of such
literature. The first prior at Cologne, Henry, not only made a strong
appeal as a preacher among the *mulieres sanctae* but also wrote didactic letters to them.[104] Their contents were apparently the same as in
the Latin letters that his friend, the minister-general Jordan, sent to
Diana and the women of St. Agnes in Bologna. The Cologne prior
wrote in German.[105] Thus the first Dominican whom we meet in the
Empire opens that chain or moral-mystical correspondence in the
German tongue. The chance mention of Henry's letters by Jordan
indicates that from the earliest contact with the feminine religious
movement certain Dominicans were inclined to contribute to a
vernacular literature for their charges. While Ida of Léau's Flemish
verses and Mary of Oignies' French songs both suggest the beginnings
of devotional literature in the language of the people, friars and lay
poets were busy in the Rhineland composing for "bonis mulierculis ac
devotis." As Friar Henry, prior of the Dominican convent at Basel[106]
and the wandering Freidank made German verses,[107] Conrad of Würzburg (d. 1287) fashioned rimes on the Virgin.[108] Such isolated traces
of German literature for *mulieres sanctae* or Dominican nuns gain
significance in view of the decision of the general chapter of the
Order of Preachers in 1242 which forbade all friars to translate
sermons, collations or other writings of religious nature from Latin
into the vernacular. This prohibition, in turn, is closely related to the
warning to the friars not to administer extreme unction to women, or
to offer them guidance or to exercise visitatorial powers over them.[109]

---

[103] Clementi, II, 124: "Et est meae intentionis, quod non cantent illae sorores
Kirie Eleison, nec Alleluia, nec alia cantica, sed habebunt lectiones, et alia quaedam
cantica in vulgari, cum quibusdam modis excogitatis, per quos eorum mentes poterunt devotionis et non vanitatis pinquedine saginari, ac pennis contemplationis ad
caelestia sublevari." Cf. Altaner, *Venturino*, pp. 76f.

[104] Grundmann, *Religiöse Bewegungen,* pp. 220, 459, note 45.

[105] *Ibid.,* p. 459.

[106] *De rebus Alsaticis ineuntis saeculi XIII, MGH. SS.,* XVII, 233. Grundmann
(*Religiöse Bewegungen,* p. 460, note 48) surmises that he may have been the first
prior of the Dominican convent founded in Basel in 1233, Henry of Westhofen
(d. 1252) who for some years (1234-1238) also had charge of the sisters of Unterlinden (then in Ufmühlen).

[107] *De rebus Alsat., MGH. SS.,* XVII, 233.

[108] *Idem;* cf. *Annal Colmar. Maiores* (1287), *MGH. SS.,* XVII, 214.

[109] Bologna, *MOPH.,* III, 24: "Fratres, qui monialibus vel aliis religiosis mulieribus sacramentum extreme unctionis administraverunt vel prelatos earum insti-
tuerunt vel destituerunt vel officium visitacionis in earum domibus exercuerunt,
iniungimus vii dies in pane et aqua, vii psalmos et vii disciplinas et virtute
obediencie districte precipimus, quod a talibus abstineant et eas de cetero non com-

While Lamprecht von Regensburg's brief testimony of the flowering of mysticism in Bavaria found confirmation from David von Augsburg,[110] the Dominican nunneries of south and west Germany and Switzerland were experiencing similar spiritual exaltation and fervent piety which far exceeded the demands of the Rule or local customs. Their literary output rivalled and eeventually superseded that of Cistercian nuns, above all at Helfta near Eisleben whose spiritual direction was provided by the Dominicans of Halle.[111] The principal luminary was of course the beguine Mechtild of Magdeburg who possessed no mean facility in vernacular expression.[112] She heard sermons preached by the friars and had a Dominican as her confessor. Although this beguine, like the nuns, participated in the divine service, the hours, communion, veneration of the saints, especially Mary, and shared too the folklore and naivité of medieval piety, she betrayed the mark of the true mystic by recognizing the insufficiency of formalism and externals.

Unlike the Clarisses[113] the Dominican convents exhibited greater eagerness to record the biographies of sisters who had been favored with visions or ecstasy. The interior life of thirty-four sisters of Adelhausen was described by Anna von Munzingen, its prioress in 1327, in a German work which bears the unsatisfactory title of *Chronicle*.[114] It is rather a series of spiritual portraits, instinct with that strict discipline and atmosphere of meditation which prevailed in Dominican nunneries.[115] At about the same time the inner experiences of some thirty sisters of Töss, southwest of Winterthur (dioc. Constance),[116] was traced by the nun Elsbeth Stagel, Henry Suso's spiritual daughter and correspondent.[117] Among noteworthy sisters who flourished in this nunnery at the end of the thirteenth century was Jützi Schultess.[118] To the same type of literature belongs the work of a sister who recounted the lives of about fifty nuns in Katherinental at Diessenhofen (dioc. Constance).[119] Early in the fourteenth century the Domi-

municent .... Nec aliquis fratrum de cetero sermones vel collaciones vel alias sacras scripturas de latino transferat in vulgare."
[110] Weinhold's edition of *Tochter Syon*, p. 523, vs. 2838.
[111] Michael, III, 174 and note 5.
[112] *Ibid.*, 187-199; Hauck, V, 1, 385ff, 428-434.
[113] For Franciscan centers, *ibid.*, V, 1, 395f.
[114] Ed. König, *Freib. Diöz-Arch.*, XIII (1880), 153-193; for her life see *ibid.*, 148f. Meyer referred to "ein schönes bückli von dem vergangenen seligen leben ettlicher heiligen swesteren ires closters Adelhusen" (*idem;* cf. 149 note 1).
[115] *Chronik*, ed. König, pp. 187-189. For Michael (III, 169) Anna's information possessed "medical rather than mystical interest".
[116] Wilms, in *QF.*, XXIV, 38.
[117] Michael, III, 172; Clark, *Great German Mystics*, pp. 66-67; Schiller, *Das mystisches Leben zu Töss.*
[118] Michael, III, 172-173; Preger, *Geschichte*, II, 257-261.
[119] Michael, III, 173; Birlinger, "Die Nonnen von st. Katharinental bei Diessenhofen," *Alemannia*, XV (1887), 150ff; for the house, Wilms, pp. 36-37.

nican Katherina of Gebweiler, prioress of Unterlinden, put down, at advanced age and with impaired eyesight, about fifty biographical portraits of sisters who had flourished in her nunnery at Colmar mostly during the preceding century.[120] These sketches do not exhibit, any more than many a longer *vita,* concern for externals. Nor is their substance derived from theological discussion or speculation. They are rather the effusions of divine love of women and girls who, often coming from beguine circles and nourished within a Dominican atmosphere, dedicated their thought and action exclusively to contemplation of God. This preoccupation frequently took the form of visions and rapture.

The Dominican nunnery of Engeltal near Nürnberg was distinguished by two mystics of considerable stature, Christine Ebner (d. 1356) of good family who surpassed her sisters in earnest pursuit of the penitential life and renunciation,[121] and the younger Adelheid Langmann (d. 1375).[122] The former has been credited with the well known book entitled *Von der Genaden Überlast.*[123] The latter committed the revelations of 1330-1347 to a brief work.[124] At the nunnery of St. Mary at Medingen, half way between Nürnberg and Augsburg (dioc. Augsburg) Margaret Ebner (1291–1351) arrived early from nearby Donauwörth.[125] This mystic whose excessive introspection increased with ill health discovered from 1332 on a fresh source of inspiration in Heinrich von Nördlingen who translated Mechtild von Magdeburg's work *Das fliessende Licht der Gottheit* into High German.[126] To him Margaret was a prophetess and he encouraged her to write down her revelations and visions.[127] Moreover Heinrich served as an intermediary between Medingen, Engeltal, Unterlinden, and Klingenthal and the Friends of God. To Ötenbach near Zurich, another lively center of mysticism, the widow of a knight came with her three daughters, one of whom could write and illuminate, the second being able to paint and third being artistic.[128] Another Alsatian nunnery whose mystical life made a real contribution in practical asceticism late in the fifteenth century was Schönensteinbach.[129]

[120] Michael, III, 168; Wilms, p. 47.

[121] Hauck, V, 1, 392-393; Preger, *Geschichte,* II, 247, 269ff.

[122] Hauck, V, 1, 393-394, 434-435.

[123] Ed. K. Schröder in Bibliothek des literarischen Vereins, Bd. CXVIII (Stuttgart, 1871); for authorship see Hauck, V, 1, 394, note 2; *Deutsches Nonnenleben,* pp. 263ff.

[124] Ph. Strauch, *Die Offenbarungen der Adelheid Langmann* (Strasbourg, 1878).

[125] Strauch, *Margareta Ebner und Heinrich von Nördlingen* (Freiburg, 1882); Preger, *Geschichte,* II, 277ff; Hauck, V, 1, 394f.

[126] Clark, *op. cit.,* p. 96.

[127] For Heinrich consult Hauck, V, 1, 436-438; Preger, *Geschichte,* II, 279ff.

[128] Hauber, in *Zentralblatt f. Bibliothekswesen,* XXXI (1914), 352; for the nunnery see Hauck, V, 1, 384, 435; Michael, III, 174; Wilms, pp. 37f.

[129] After the middle of the fifteenth century this convent undertook to reform

Johannes Meyer's *Buch der Reformacio Predigerordens* offers several pertinent examples of literary activity, although somewhat late. In St. Catherine's nunnery at Colmar Magdalena Frankengrünerin, in addition to other duties, helped with the writing, "especially with the beautiful choir books in divine service."[130] Margaret Merin was quite skilled in painting, writing, and for whatever else she was needed.[131] The art of writing which appears to have been well advanced in Schönensteinbach was introduced or at least stimulated in the reformed houses. Meyer relates that a lay sister Katherine Holtzhusin, a native of Nürnberg, wrote "fine useful books with good material."[132] Sister Lukardis of Utrecht was not only stewardess but also author of missals, graduals, antiphonies, books of lections, and other choir books.[133] "Never idle, she busied herself with reading, prayer, nursing, or writing which she had truly mastered as we may see in the large, beautiful, useful choir books which she wrote and annotated for the convent and which has caused astonishment among many fathers and priests who have seen the missal she prepared, written in a neat, correct script. She was an artistic person in many kinds of handwork and she knew how to use grammar and Latin at the table."[134] Claranna von Hochenburg, first prioress of the nunnery (d. 1423), also achieved renown because she "understood Holy Scripture so remarkably well that she could bring the text from heavy Latin books to the common table."[135]

---

a number of nunneries: Medingen (1468, Wilms, p. 33), Obermedingen (1468, p. 34), Diessenhofen (1482, pp. 36f), Gebweiler (1466, p. 47); St. Agnes in Freiburg i. Br. (1482, p. 49), St. Nicolas in Strasbourg (1478, p. 53), St. Agnes in Strasbourg (1474, p. 56), St. Margaret in the same city (1482, pp. 57f), Pfirzheim (dioc. Speyer) (1483, p. 86), Reuthin (dioc. Constance) (1482, p. 87); cf. König, in *Freib. Diöz.-Arch.*, XIII (1880), 136, 225-228. For exceptions see Wilms, pp. 30, 38.

[130] *QF.*, III, 101 (V, 42).
[131] *QF.*, III, 114 (V, 50).
[132] *QF.*, II, 103 (III, 42). Katherine was imbued with the reform policy of Schönensteinbach then penetrating Unterlinden (*ibid.*, 102f).
[133] *QF.*, II, 38 (I, 11).
[134] *QF.*, II, 86 (III, 26).
[135] *QF.*, II, 63 (III, 5): "Sy verstund so mercklich die hailgen geschrifft, daz sy von sweren latynschen büchern den text zu ordenlichem tüsch bringen kond."

Part Five

THE EXTRAREGULAR IN LITERATURE
POSITIVE AND NEGATIVE EVIDENCE

> "Nonoque Gregorio sed et Cordelite Nudum Christum predicant ut Israhelite Veri nudis pedibus; omnes miserantur Et per Christi famulos pie provocantur. Prodit sapientia, scismata dampnantur. Per hos duos ordines Begine velantur. Et de evangelio vivunt et lucrantur. Desperatos plurimos evangelizantur."
> *Chronicon rhythmicum Austriacum, MGH. SS.* XXV, 357-358, vss. 378-386.

"Hortus Deliciarum"

THE CLOSED CIRCLE

During the golden age of the beguinage, which extended from the middle of the thirteenth century through the pontificate of Clement V and even beyond adverse Clementine legislation, the French and Flemish-Dutch beguines received praise and recommendations from local prelates and the Roman curia, donations and legacies from noblemen and burghers of both sexes, and comital, ducal, echevinal, and royal protection, patronage, privileges, and exemptions customarily accorded religious congregations. Special foundations provided for needy beguines: Holy Ghost tables, the infirmary, prebends, and pittances. Although willing to give its stamp of approval to the beguinages as a worthy work deserving of indulgences and protection and even countenancing the expansion of the movement, the hierarchy nevertheless was not in general directly responsible for establishing these houses. Nor did this feminine religious movement, in spite of papal recognition and the erection of beguine parishes under spiritual directors drawn at first from older monastic bodies and eventually from the friars, ever enjoy in the medieval period the status of an officially recognized religious order, regulated by the triple vows and uniform statutes. Distinctive habit and profession of chastity, while setting the beguines apart from the world,[1] were not sufficient to confer true religious status. Nor did they, like the mendicants, in the main voluntarily subscribe to undiminished and unmitigated *paupertas;* observance of the injunction to live *labore manuum* remained consistently a prerequisite for the *vita apostolica.*

The *Vita S. Beggae* (1631) of the hagiographer, J. G. a Ryckel (1581–1642)[2] remained for a century and a half, until the posthumous appearance of Mosheim's masterful *Commentarius de Beghardis et Beguinabus* (1790), the standard work on the beguinal way of life. Conceived in the grand manner recommended by seventeenth-

---

[1] Council of Mainz (1261), can. 23, Mansi, XXIII, 1089; cf. Van Espen, *Jus eccl.* I, 359f; Matthew Paris *(MGH. SS.,* XXVIII, 320, 430, 449, 468); see above, pp. 126ff.
[2] Cf. Hermann Vander Linden in *BNB.* XX (1908-1910), 632-634.

century eloquence and confident in the success of Catholic reform, Ryckel's study fails to abide by sound historical canons, for in it the external forces are dwarfed as much as in Cistercian and Dominican *vitae*. In substance it is a vast editorial on continence and the garden of virtue; in form, an ambitious panegyric on "the chosen daughters of God," the namesakes of St. Begga. Their placid interior life, as an expression of mysticism, fascinated him;[3] religious motivation alone warrants attention. Paying only the scantiest attention to the defects of the semireligious and the persecution which they seemed to justify,[4] the author was content merely to praise the moral perfection and spiritual self-sufficiency within ecclesiastical prescriptions which, it must be admitted, the Belgian beguinages cultivated with a large measure of consistency.

If the beguinages did not seek unity and discipline through congregational organization, whether monarchical or federative in principle, the beguine parish remained an effective answer to the dangers inherent in autonomy. Failure to identify oneself with the approved community involved exclusion from beguine association and the loss of special privileges. Within fifty years the beguinage at Bruges, for example, acquired a complete and independent personality. Countess Margaret's foundation of a parochial benefice and dual chapellancies (1272) as well as other previous concessions were approved and confirmed by her son Count Guy in 1281. By the documents of 1245, 1271, and 1281 the beguinage under comital auspices thus acquired with the title of parish and the benefices which were attached to it its ecclesiastical personality. When the community received from Philip IV in 1299 a charter of exemption whereby the king of France reserved for royal officials jurisdiction over all cases and suits that arose from the property of La Vigne,[5] it was endowed with a civil and juridical personality. Henceforth, as a royal beguinage, it was dependent not on the *bailli* of Bruges but only on the tribunal of the Crown.

It is significant that when the abbot of St. Bavon consented in July, 1242, to the establishment of a cemetery and the building of a chapel in the beguinage of Ghent he closely defined its obligations to parochial authority: At least once a year the inmates must confess to their own priest (*proprio sacerdoti*); their chaplain will explain to them the other prerogatives of the parochial arm so that they may not slip from its jurisdiction. "Et beghine cavere debebunt ne occulte, vel aperte, aliquid faciant quod sit presbyteris parrochialibus in prejudicium, sive detrimentum." If the beguines cultivate fields of wheat, rye, or oats on lands which they possess, they will be required to pay

---

[3] E.g., Ryckel, p. 285.

[4] *Ibid.*, pp. 355-357 (persecutions); pp. 442-445 (lapsed beguines); pp. 504-508 (beghards at the Council of Vienne).

[5] Hoornaert, in *ASEB.*, LXXII (1929), 14.

the usual tithes. But tithes are not attached to gardens or orchards which provide for their own use and are not offered for sale.[6]

To the initial donation, usually made by a layman, were often added, sometimes through purchase or gifts of the inmates themselves, neighboring plots of ground to furnish an income or to provide heat and light for the beguine house. That the beguinages or Gotteshäuser owed their existence in large measure to medieval charity cannot be denied. Yet it is significant that foundation charters and wills call into being or endow these houses as a good work to assure the salvation of the benefactor's soul or of his relatives. They carefully stipulate that the inhabitants remember the patron and his family with prayers, masses, anniversaries, and contributions on fixed occasions.[7] The thirteenth century witnessed a multiplication of masses for the deceased and anniversaries; each church and charitable foundation must have a *liber anniversariorum* which eventually came to be known as an *obituarium*.[8]

In the celebrated letter sent by Henry of Guelders to Renier of Tongres August 1, 1266, relieving him of current duties but delegating to him visitatorial powers over beguine and beghard communities in the diocese of Liége, the bishop uttered only warmest praise for the "sancta religiosarum puellarum et matronarum, que beguine vocantur, plantatio" which had already for some little time (*iam dudum*) flourished in the city and diocese. It is evident that he regarded the movement as the product of his territory from whence it then spread "throughout almost the whole world." On the other hand, Henry acknowledged the necessity for close supervision lest vices insinuate themselves under the appearance of virtues.[9]

Even after rehabilitation of the Belgian beguines under Pope John XXII and their unquestioned absorption into the ecclesiastical fabric, the papal curia still persisted in handling them merely as quasi-religious or extraregulars. Although willing to admit the legality of beguinal status and customs, the papacy nevertheless had no intention of recognizing the movement as an independent order. According to

[6] Béthune, *Cartulaire*, p. 6.

[7] Consult the *fonds* of the beguinage of Brussels, Ter Kisten (AAPB. Cartons B. 1452-1455; Cartulary, B. 1460) and the infirmary (AAPB. Cartons H. 262-270; AGR., arch. eccl., 13403); for published material see, for example, Thijs, "Histoire du béguinage de Tongres," *BSSLL*. XV (1881), 7-707.

[8] Several are extant for Antwerp institutions: Notre-Dame where the priest and chaplains vouched for the anniversaries, Notre-Dame hospital, the beguinage, and St. Michael's (Prims, in *BG*. XIX [1928], 173f; cf. 198-200). The one for the beguinage, begun in 1266, is in Flemish whereas the others are in Latin. On February 3 of the beguine obituary occurs the foundation of "meestere Jans Wolsiagers die cureit was in den hof van den beginen in Antwerpen." Besides 10 s. for his anniversary he left "10 s. des jaers den scolieren, dat men alle daghe sal gaen te meester Jans grafte, ewelike." This of course entailed prayers for the peace of his soul.

[9] *AHEB*. XX (1886), 125f; see above, pp. 162f, 168.

Geoffrey of Beaulieu, Louis IX welcomed all religious, regardless of congregation, provided they had been confirmed by the Holy See.[10] On the other hand, even though the beguines were not constituted as an order abiding by a rule approved by the Fourth Lateran Council or further defined by the Second Council of Lyons, official sanction was nevertheless implied in the numerous papal and episcopal indults and directives prescribing careful distinction between the orthodox and the heterodox, with full commendation for the former. Good works, chastity, austerity, emphasis on self-support, all certified the sisterhoods and thus assured to them undiminished patronage of the devout king. No matter how full was his cup of piety, he did not allow it to overflow. Unlike some of his contemporaries he discovered nothing reprehensible in this manner of community life to compromise his good-will.

Beguine life, properly speaking, dates from the Investiture Struggle and the popular reform movement that rose out of it in reaction to simony and clerical marriage. That reaction was partly orthodox, partly heterodox; yet both currents were predicated on emulation of the *vita apostolica.* To achieve this end a concrete program of proselytism, continence, evangelical poverty—in short, to recover the merits of the primitive church—must be pursued. Whereas the Belgian beguinage held aloof from the heterodox forces at work in the Rhineland, the German sisters, not so well claustrated, were sometimes led astray by usurping the office of preaching, by discussing the doctrine of the Trinity and divine essence, and by casting aspersion on the sacraments. In addition, moral aberration and mendicancy, encouraged by ineffective organization, were attributed to them.[11] Yet charges of heresy and immorality could act as subterfuges for the defense of vested interests when extraregular privilege threatened traditional parochial prerogative. As spokesman of the Dominicans, Humbert de Romans refused to believe that perverse imitators were detracting from the "very holy life" led by the beguines.[12] As the thirteenth-century waned this dichotomy became increasingly patent to the thoughtful observer. For subsequent history of the semireligious this disparity of aims and methods within beguine ranks was to be a

[10] See above, pp. 224ff.
[11] "Het Belgisch Begijnenwezen is ... de orthodoxe en bijna uitsluitend Vlaamsche vertakking van den stam van het begijnendom, waarvan al de overige vertakkingen door de besmetting der heterodoxie aangetast waren of werden" (Philippen, in *Tijdschrift voor Geschiedenis en Folklore,* VI [1943], 62). Philippen's conclusion elsewhere, "Les écrits du 13e siècle prouvent que le reproche principal qu'on faisait aux 'beguinae' n'était pas celui d'immoralité, mais celui d'hétérodoxie," (in *AAAB.* LXXIII, ser. 7, III [1926], 235) is quite valid although he saw in the thirteenth century too much unity (cf. criticism of Van Mierlo, in *VMKVA.,* 1931, p. 1000 note 1; Grundmann, *Religiöse Bewegungen,* p. 312, note 3).
[12] *De modo prompte cudendi Serm.,* II, 54: *Ad Beguinas (Bibl. Max. Vet. Pat.* XXV, 483).

source of considerable embarrassment. Since the common term *beguine* for two radically different branches, together with the absence of a distinctive organizational character, made the measures against unregulated, itinerant beguinés unworkable, the disciplined communities were involved in the prosecution. Only after long, painful crises would clarification of status and rehabilitation be achieved.

Beguinal existence, like other manifestations of semireligious activity, was not equivalent to monachism: it was an expression of the *vita apostolica* which had more in common with the *vita canonica* than the *vita monastica*. As monasticism relies on the irrevocable triple vows, so the beguinage rests on four pillars[13] *seur quoi toute religions est fundée*: purity or chastity (*netetés*), poverty, humility,[14] and love or charity. The rule of the Fins Amans then turns to vestment[15] with its symbolical meaning corresponding to these four pillars, to daily prayer, and devotional practices which are designed to conduct to the Godhead through ecstasy.[16] A Dutch tract, *De Deugden van ene goede Begijn*, in the University of Leiden library assigns to the letters in the word *begijn* the salient features of beguine spirituality. As the first letter indicates that a beguine is the bride of the Lord, so the others suggest simplicity (*eenvoud*), mercy (*goedertierenheid*), sincerity (*innigheid*) before God and the saints, and humility (*nederigheid*)[17]. The *mulieres religiosae* who emulated the life of the Apostles[18] outside monastic rules were thus the first real beguines.

THE WELL-TENDED VINEYARD

For Jacques de Vitry, Foulques of Toulouse, John of Nivelles, and Thomas of Cantimpré the *religieuses de leur signeur*,[19] the *mulieres sanctae* or *religiosae*, the *virgines continentes*, the *mulieres Deo devotae*, the *sorores conversae*, the *incluse*[20] of the Nivelles-Oignies-Liége area at once provided a hopeful sign of moral regeneration in the

[13] Christ, *La Règle des Fins Amans*, pp. 197-199, lines 161-232.
[14] "Cesti doit toute religione ensievir et especiaument les religieuses. Car humilités est propre en vierge."
[15] *Ibid.*, pp. 199ff.
[16] *Ibid.*, pp. 200f, lines 269ff.
[17] Axters, *Gesch. van de Vroomheid*, II, 166.
[18] See the primitive rule (ca. 1300) of the Bruges beguinage: "Die Beghinen van den Wyngarde ende die hare zeden willen volghen sullen houden die regle van den Apostelen: dat syn die ghebode van der Heligher Kerke, ende te minne God vor alle dinc ende haren wenkerstinen als hem selven; ende zuverhede te houdene van herten ende van lechamen, dat es van willen ende van daden ..." (Hoornaert, in *ASEB*. LXXII [1929], 17).
[19] Christ, *La Règle des Fins Amans*, p. 197, line 155.
[20] E.g., August 15, 1279 (AAPB. B. 1460, f. 4v, no. 12). Heldewidis (Helindis), an *inclusa* at Willambroux, was brought up by Mary of Oignies for almost twelve years; she also received comfort from a *mulier religiosa* named Beselc (*VMO.*, 565 B, 80).

north and offered a potential counter-balance to widespread defection from orthodoxy in the south. To implement this sympathetic approach episcopal administrators and papal officials such as Renier of Tongres, Peter of Albano, and Hugh of St. Cher offered material assistance. Just as the beguine movement was one embodiment of the *vita apostolica*, so Cistercian hagiography, one of the primary sources for the world of the early *mulieres religiosae,* is instinct with that crusade fervor which channels apostolic life to combat infidel and heretic.[21] Owing to similarity with the Cathari and other antisacerdotal associations through espousal of virginity, poverty, and aversion to oaths,[22] attempts were made to avoid a heretical complexion or danger by calling several beguinages the "Vineyard" of the Lord.[23] This symbol was employed by Innocent III to open that letter of April 19, 1213, to the clergy of the province of Vienne in which he voiced the necessity for reform of the Church through a general council.[24] Alarmed by the inroads of lay mysticism and asceticism guided by evangelical perfection alone, the pope saw that vineyard being ravaged by beasts.

Just as the *hortus conclusus* again designated the enclosure of the church to which admission is denied to its foes,[25] so the clause *ne vulpes effodiant vineam Domini*[26] and the less frequent allusion to wolves (*ne lupi rapaces oves suas invadant*)[27] clearly reflect the steps

---

[21] E.g., CHD. X, 37-40 (ed. Strange, II, 245f); the *Vita Goberti Asperimontis* is instinct with the spirit of chivalry and crusade, but with the complication of Frederick II, that "apostata nefandissimus" (380-382, 18-25). Cf. Axters, *Geschiedenis van de Vroomheid,* I, 181f, 184f, 220f.

[22] See below, pp. 436-438.

[23] E.g., Henry of Guelder's letter to Renier of Tongres, August 1, 1266 (*AHEB.,* XX, 1886, 125); the earliest document relating to the Brussels beguinage—a sixteenth-century copy of Innocent IV's privilege of March 20, 1247—was addressed to "magistre et sororibus beginis de Vinea sancte Marie in Bruxella" (AAPB. Carton B. 1452); the earliest originals are dated April, 1248 (see above, p. 177).

[24] *PL.* CCXVI, 823f: "Vineam Domini Sabaoth multiformes moliuntur bestiae demoliri, quarum incursus adeo invaluit contra ipsam, ut ex parte non modica pro vitibus spinae succreverint et—quod gementes referimus—ipsae vites proferant pro uva labruscam infectae multipliciter et corruptae."

[25] *Cant. Cant.* IV, 12. The symbol was utilized by St. Ambrose, *De Virginibus ad Marcellinam sororem suam libri tres,* lib. II (PL. XVI, 207-220) and St. Augustine, *De Baptismo contra Donatistos (PL.* XLIII, 150ff).

[26] See, for example, the statement of Walter of Marvis, bishop of Tournai, when he wrote to Countess Margaret on July 24, 1244, concerning the transfer of the chaplaincy from the castellans of Bruges to La Vigne: "Cum bone memorie sororis vestre (Jeanne) piam voluntatem devotione debita prosequentes, capellaniam quae fuit de castellania Brugensi ad locum in quo manent Beghinae Brugenses qui dicitur Vinea velitis deinceps deserviri" (Callewaert in *ASEB.,* 1904, pp. 283f). Cf. Ezech. XIII, 4.

[27] August, 1251, AAPB. Carton H. 262. In the N.T. where sheep represent the disciples of Christ, their enemies are symbolized by wolves, the false prophets: Matt. VII, 15; X, 16; Luc. X, 3; John, X, 12; Acts, XX, 29; for only the rapacity of wolves: Eccli. XIII, 21; Ezech. XXII, 27; Jer. VII, 6. Peace will be the consequence of redemption: Is. XI, 6; LXV, 25; cf. Ambros., *De Virg.,* II, 4 (PL. XVI, 215); H. Lesêtre, in *Dictionnaire de la Bible*, IV, 1 (Paris, 1912), 374f.

to free beguines from heterodox influences. To the fox are also compared clerks and priests who, feigning religion and peace, seduce
women.[28] Again, these seducers of souls are like the wolf licking the
yoke of oxen with the intention of killing them.[29] Thus the beguinage
could become a palladium of orthodoxy for its inmates. The foundation charter of the Lierre beguinage (1274) mentioned that it was
established in order that the foxes would not ravage the Vineyard.[30]
In this figure of speech, taken from the *Cantica Canticorum* (II. 13,
15),[31] the foxes denote heretics (cf. Ezek. XIII, 4 where reference is
made to the false prophets who threatened Israel). St. Augustine, in
his commentary to Ps. LXXX, applied this text to heretics of his own
day.[32] More recently the symbolism had been given currency by St.
Bernard of Clairvaux in his two sermons (65 and 66) on the *Cantica
Canticorum*[33] when he applied the text specifically to anticlerical forces which went under the name of Apostolici in his own day and probably afterwards the *Begini* in the Low Countries. Thus preference
for the term *vinea* was dictated not by location but by the desire of
protectors and founders to guard against harmful or heretical influences.[34] From the middle of the thirteenth century on, Belgian beguinages were frequently entrusted to the Friars Preachers than
whom there was no more adamant foe of the Cathari and Albigensians. These friars who had launched their vigorous campaign on
behalf of dogma by fashioning a community of Catholic noble women
at Prouille near Toulouse eventually shared with the Franciscans
their mission in the north by accepting direction of the beguines
whose simplicity occasionally made them victims of moral aberration
and doctrinal deviation.

The beguine movement, unfolding in Belgium as one chapter in the
offensive against heresy, emphasized the efficacy of the sacramental
system, with peculiar stress on the eucharist. Nowhere is the protest
against anticlericalism more heavily underlined than in the biography
of Mary of Oignies.[35] Driven northward by the Albigensians, Foulques

[28] Crane, *Exempla*, p. 7, no. 20 *bis*.
[29] *Ibid.*, p. 7, no. 21. Consult the wolf-sheep equation in Stephen of Bourbon
(*Anec. hist.*, p. 23, note 3).
[30] Ryckel, p. 302: "Ne vineam Domini Sabaoth congregationem Begginarum in
Lyere demoliantur vulpes." Cf. Antwerp charter, 1285 (Mertens-Torfs, *Gesch. v.
Antwerpen*, I, 589).
[31] *Cant. Cant.* II, 13: "Vineae florentes dederunt odorem suum"; II, 15: "Capite
nobis vulpes parvulas quae demoliuntur vineas, nam vinea nostra floruit." Cf. Matt.
XX, 4: "Ite vos in vineam meam . . ." where Jesus likens the Church to the vineyard;
John XV, 1ff. For the appeal of the *Cant. Cant.* to medieval mystics, see Michael,
III, 132f.
[32] *Enarratio in Ps. LXXX, PL.* XXXVII, 1040-41.
[33] Sermo 65 (*PL.* CLXXXIII, 1088-1093); Sermo 66 (*ibid.*, 1093-1102).
[34] Philippen, *Begijnhoven*, p. 99.
[35] Greven emphasizes this devotion: "Die antihäretische Grundstimmung zeigt
sich sogar bei Maria von Oignies selbst ausgeprägt"; with respect to the preface

of Toulouse "could not admire enough the faith and reverence of the *mulieres religiosae* in the diocese of Liége who exhibited profound respect for the Church and the sacraments quite in contrast to his own country where they were scorned and ignored by almost everybody." [36] Attracted by this devotional emphasis on the eucharist and the Passion, Jacques de Vitry could only reproach impatiently unbelievers "who either from conviction or hardened heart disdained the sweetness of this food." [37] The prototype of the beguine, Mary, impelled by the claims of the *vita apostolica,* entered the fray against the Albigensians. Three years before the crusade was launched against them (1209) she saw, records her biographer, a great quantity of crosses descending on mankind from heaven and this was for her a clear indication of the eventual investment of the south. [38] So keenly did she feel this defection that she would eagerly have set out for Provence and Languedoc to suffer, if necessary, martyrdom in the camp of the heretics. [39] As further evidence of her preoccupation with this problem Jacques de Vitry relates how she discussed with him the vision she had of the slaughter at Montjoie (Mons Gaudii) in which a large number of Belgian crusaders were cut to pieces by the count of Foix. [40] Confronted by the sad and wan countenance of the Virgin who grieved that her Son had been "crucified by heretics and wicked Christians," Lutgard was easily persuaded to begin a seven-year fast "to appease the wrath of Christ." [41] A week before Pentecost in 1250 (May 15) and shortly before her death (June 11) [42] Alice of Schaerbeek, wasting away from leprosy, lost the sight of her left eye. "The fruit of this penance," continues her anonymous biographer, [43] "she assigned to the king of France who had exposed himself at that time at Jerusalem to the enemies of the Cross of Christ." [44] After listing his virtues

with its preoccupation with the eucharist, he adds: "Eine gewisse antihäretische Grundstimmung lässt sich dennoch nicht verkennen" (*Anfänge,* p. 58; cf. pp. 56f, 102f).

[36] *VMO.* prol., 547 (2); for Foulques' hostility to heretics see further Stephen of Bourbon, *Anec. hist.,* pp. 23f, note 3.

[37] *VMO. prol.,* 548 (8).

[38] *Ibid.,* 565 E (82). Jacques de Vitry points out that this was the first mention of heretics "in partibus nostris." Mens (*Stud. Euch.,* p. 165, note 2) claims with regard to this passage that the author introduced it primarily to prove that those who derived *begina* from *Albigeois* were wrong.

[39] *VMO.,* 565 F (82); cf. no. 83 and reference to the crusade "contra adversarios Christi Albigenses haereticos" in *VMO. Suppl.,* 574 (4).

[40] This episode occurred in 1211 (Alberic de Trois-Fontaines, *Chron., MGH. SS.,* XXIII, 892); *VMO.,* 566, note a; cf. Funk, *Jakob von Vitry,* p. 33.

[41] *V. Lutg.,* 196 E (II, 2); for further fasts "for sinners," *ibid.,* 198 A (II, 9); 205 B (III, 4).

[42] *V. Al. Scar.,* 477 A (32).

[43] Cf.*Comm. praev., ibid.,* 471 (1). From 477 B (34) ("cuidam personae, adhuc in corpore degenti") it is evident that the author flourished in the middle of the thirteenth century. He may have been a Cistercian monk, possibly a confessor in the monastery.

[44] *Ibid.,* 476 C (27). Three years earlier when Count William of Holland was besieging Aix-la-Chapelle she lost her right eye (*ibid.,* 475 D, 23).

and proficiency in learning, the anonymous hagiographer adds concerning Boniface of Lausanne, who had crossed the path of Frederick II and afterwards sought refuge in La Cambre, that "he was strict in discipline, fierce against heretics and unbelievers, and firm in the Catholic faith."[45] Such hagiographical accounts thus illustrate how short was the step from the program of the *vita apostolica* with its passion for the salvation of souls to crusade fervor.

SHEEP OR WOLVES

A number of Old French poems have come down which, while attributing to the beguines praiseworthy qualities, were actually attacks on hypocrisy and false piety for which the beguine habit often was a cloak. One beguine expressed a desire "to be hanged on the gibbet of contemplation, drowned in a flood of tears of contrition, burned in a fire of charity, and buried in the grave of humility."[46] Another prided herself on not having given cause for reproach: "If she laughs, it is companionship; if she weeps, it is devotion; if she speaks, it is prophecy; if she is silent, it is religion; if she sleeps, she is in ecstasy; if she dreams, she has visions; if she eats, it is to live; if she fasts, it is penitence; if she drinks wine, it is for nourishment; if she does not drink, it is abstinence."[47] Alongside this appraisal should be put the twenty-eight characteristics of the good beguine as they were drawn up in the thirteenth century on a scriptural foundation:[48] look down and have lofty thoughts; pray often and travel little; keep a clear conscience, straight intention, patience; have raised hopes, a burning love, pure thoughts, an ordered life, and honeyed words; speak in one's heart (*parler en taisant*), walk with the spirit, cry for joy, be watchful while asleep, fast while eating; be rich in poverty, wise in foolishness, strong but weak, and be comforted when in despair.[49]

If the intention of these lists is suspicious, there is no question about

---

[45] *V. Bon.*, 155 E (4). The Bollandists publish two anonymous *vitae,* one from a MS. in La Cambre (155-158), the other by a canon regular (158-162).

[46] Hilka, in *Zeitschrift für rom. Philologie,* XLVII (1927), 159: "Quaedam beguina dixit quod vellet suspendi, submergi, incendi, humo infodi: perdue au gibet de contemplacion, noiee en un flum de larmes de contricion, arse en un feu de charite, enfoie en la fosse de humilite." Cf. *ibid.*, 162, no. 4.

[47] *Ibid.*, 159; cf. 162, no. 1.

[48] Cf. "Vechi les .XXXII. propriétés de beginage" in MS. Lat. 15972 of Bibl. nat. Paris (beginning of fourteenth century in the Artois dialect), *ibid.*, 156-158. Le Grand (*Les Béguines de Paris,* p. 19) concluded from its antithetical character that its attitude was basically hostile to the beguines; thus the work constitutes a satire. Christ (*La Règle des Fins Amans,* p. 181), on the contrary, regarded it as sympathetic to the extraregular. A list of twenty-six bad characteristics will be found in *Zeitschrift f. rom. Philologie,* XLVII (1927), 158f.

[49] *Ibid.*, 156-158.

the sincerity of the twelve signs whereby the *Fins Amans*, i.e., beguines in northern France, may be recognized,[50] or the twelve joys with which they are favored.[51] That they gladly submit to lengthy prayers and frequent sermons suggests "true and secure religion."[52]

Robert de Sorbon (d. 1274) saw in the beguine house an unfolding of the interior life which is the wiser because it is marked by frequent and honest confessions—for which reason, he adds, the inmates are known as *Papelardi*.[53] The importance of confession is underscored in the several statutes as well as in legislative formulas.[54] Although in this passage the term *papelardi* may not have a disparaging connotation, it was often, as in the case of Gautier de Coincy in an important excursus of the poem, *De Seinte Leodade, qui fu Dame de Tolete, et du Saint Arcevesque* (ca. 1220),[55] equated with *beguine*. It was applied above all to feminine religious circles in Artois and around Noyon whose piety and conduct were both new and questionable.[56] "No one

[50] Christ, *La Règle des Fins Amans*, p. 194, lines 51-57: (*1*) haïr ce que ses amis het: c'est pechiés (*2*) garder les commandemens son ami; (*3*) regehir et descouvrir souvent son cuer a son ami; (*4*) amer loiaument; (*5*) penser souvent et ententivement a son ami; (*6*) oïr volentiers la parole de son ami; (*7*) demander soingnesement noveles de son ami; (*8*) aler souvent et volentiers ou liu eu ses amis est; (*9*) envoier souvent joiaus et biaux dons a son ami; (*10*) recevoir devotement les joiaux que ses amis envoie, qui sont povretés, mesaises, maladies et tribulations; (*11*) estre apareilliés de faire de cuer et de cors et d'avoir quanque ses amis veut et commande; (*12*) sont tous jours en vraie amor et en fins amans.

[51] *Ibid.*, pp. 194f, lines 72-112.

[52] *Ibid.*, p. 200, lines 260-261: "Volentiers et longement doit estre en orisons et sovent en sermons. Ce norist ame en vraie et en seüre religion."

[53] *De Consciencia* (ed. Chambon, p. 24; cf. the defective edition under the unjustifiable title *Sermo de Consciencia ad theologos* by Marguerin de la Bigne in *Bibl. Max. Vet. Pat.*, XXV, 350 D; after the latter Mosheim, p. 22 and Du Boulay, *Hist. Univ. Paris.*, III, 232): "Ergo Beguini, sive sint in seculo, sive in religione, in libro isto, scilicet Consciencie, sunt sapienciores, quia frequencius et diligencius confitentur, sicut patet ad oculum; immo propter hoc dicuntur papelardi, quia frequentant confessiones." Cf. Le Nain de Tillemont, *Vie de Saint Louis*, V, 311; Gilles li Muisis, *Li maintiens des beghines (Poésies*, ed. Kervyn de Lettenhove, I, 237); "Li confiesers souvent oste bien les pointures/Quand on fait les peckiés, et là mettent leurs cures"; "As frères mendians boins clers vont confiesser,/Et pour elles oïr les vont moult apprieser" (*ibid.*, I, 241).

[54] Statute of Valenciennes (1262): "Et encore par conseil a on ordennet que elles se confiesseront une fie le quinzainne au mains" (Christ, *La Règle des Fins Amans*, p. 208; Ryckel, p. 529); local customs reveal differences in confession and communion: confession was expected every fortnight at Ghent (13 C., Béthune, *Cartulaire*, p. 20); in Picardy: "Il doit soufire a fame de confesser de .xv. jors a autres une foie, se ele n'a raissonnable ensoigne par quoi il la convieigne dedens confesser" (Christ, *La Règle des Fins Amans*, p. 200, lines 256-258); elsewhere confession was recommended once a month (St. Trond early 14 C., "Item sij sullen hen biechten eens ter moent", Philippen, *Begijnhoven*, p. 312) or eighteen times a year (Diest, 15 C., "Allen jare sult ghij achtienwerf biechten met corten woerden ende met innicheyt ende puricheyt uws herten thegen die priesters van uwen convente...," Philippen, in *BG.*, IV, 1905, 336; cf. *Begijnhoven*, p. 188).

[55] Barbazan and Méon, *Fabliaux et Contes*, I, 270-546; for the excursus on "Pappelaridïe et beginage" (vs. 1531), see *ibid.*, pp. 307ff.

[56] *Ibid.*, vss. 1535ff; 1485f. To religious who hid behind feigned piety Gautier attached the term *papelart, pepelarde* (vss. 1151-59; 1438-42; cf. Lommatzsch, pp.

can live without property and goods, and whoever pretends that he can do so and is doing it is a horrible hypocrite detested by God. May fire consume all Papelards!"[57]

As a corollary to the statement mentioned above, Robert adds an observation on the necessity for inner religious experience that is not without interest in this connection. "People know many things but do not know themselves. They seek God through external means and neglect the interior life. Of what profit is the learning of Priscian, Aristotle, Justinian, Gratian, Galen, Hippocrates, and of many others in sheep and goat skins if you do not expel from the book of your conscience the letter of death? Of what advantage are things written and perceived unless you yourself read and grasp them? For to read and not to know is to neglect."[58] Under the direction of the Domini-

26-31; for criticism of prelates, ibid., pp. 16-26; *De Seinte Leodade,* vss. 1445-58). With the wan, gaunt countenance of penitents they slowly draw nigh, humbly keeping their heads bowed (vss. 1190-93). As synonymns Gautier used *begars* (vss. 1525-27) and *begins* (vss. 1391ff) and once *truanz* (vs. 1349), a term which by extension of the original idea of vagabond (cf. CHD. I, 3, ed. Strange, I, 9): "clericus actu trutannus quales per diversas vagari solent provincias"; VIII, 59 (ed. Strange, II, 131) signified a sharpster (see below, p. 510). Jacques de Vitry in his *Sermo ad Virgines* (Greven, in *HJ.,* XXXV, 1914, p. 19; for the passage, see above, p. 000 note 00) agrees that the term *papelarda* was commonly employed for beguines in France. The word also occurs early in the chronicle of Melrose, a Cistercian monastery in Scotland. This contains a report of a council held in Paris in 1210 at which French archbishops, bishops, and prelates in conjunction with the masters of the university convicted those persons of heresy *quos laici Papelardos appellaverunt* and whom the judges referred to as Amalricians and *Godines* (*Chronica de Mailros,* ed. Stevenson, p. 110; Bouquet, XIX, 250). A count, describing a visit to St. Louis in Paris, summed up his unfavorable impression of the king with the exclamation: "Vidi illum miserum papellardum regem" (Thomas of Cantimpré, *BUA.,* II, 57, 63, p. 588). By then the word in the main signified a hypocrite (cf. Ph. Mouskes, *Chronique rimée,* vss. 30730-30736 where it is used with *beghin* in the account of the papal election of 1241: "Li millour, par dévosion,/ Noumèrent l'evesque del Liége./ Mais li béghin et papelart? Furent encontre d'autre part:/ Si vorrent i béghin avoir/ Pour les autres a decevoir"; vss. 30725f: "Et tout çou li fisent béghin/ Et papelart et Jacobin,"; ed. Reiffenberg, II, 673). The late thirteenth century Flemish translation of the *V. Lutg. (Leven van Sinte Lutgart,* ed. Van Veerdeghem, p. 12, Bk. II, vss. 721-731: "Nu comt hir voert, gi papelarde:/ Ghi metten grisen langen barde,/ Die al volmaket schinen willet/ Ende al benijdt, ende al beghillet,/ Ende al begrijpt met fellen moede/ Dat men dengenen doet te goede/ In karitaten, dies behoeven./ Hort harewert,/ghi loese boeven,/ Die ommegaet met begardiën,/ Wis plach dis Godes brut verliën") identifies *papelard* and *beghard.* The whole problem has been thoroughly explored by Grundmann, *Religiöse Bewegungen,* pp. 357, 359, 377-389; Mens, *Oorsprong,* pp. 35f, 279-284; cf. Du Cange, *Glossarium,* VI, 145; Greven, in *HJ.,* XXXV (1914), 44, note 5; Godefroy, *Dictionnaire,* V, 727; X, 268. For Rutebeuf's evidence, see below, pp. 472-473.

[57] *"De Seinte Leodade,* vss. 1147-1152 (pp. 307f).

[58] "Multi multa sciunt et seipsos nesciunt. Querunt Deum per exteriora et relinquunt interiora sua. Sed quid prosunt littere erudicionis Prisciani, Aristotelis, Justiniani, Gratiani, Galieni, Ypocratis, et sic de aliis, in pellibus ovinis et caprinis nisi deleas de libro Consciencie tue litteras mortis? Quid prosunt hec lecta et intellecta, nisi teipsum legas et intelligas? Legere enim et non intelligere, negligere est." (ed. Chambon, p. 24; cf. *Bibl. Max. Vet. Pat.,* XXV, 570 D; Du Boulay, *Hist. Univ. Paris.,* III, 232).

cans these semireligious blossomed into a kind of order—"sub doctrina Praedicatorum specie religionis florere." By attending church regularly for matins and mass and relying on the sacramental system, many had submitted to the claims of institutional religion.[59] At the same time the beguine way of life offered, in place of rigid and academic disciplinary measures, a fresh approach to penitence and poverty which admirers were not slow to recognize and which enemies hastened to deprecate as hypocrisy. On the day of judgment, Robert continues, a simple beguine may be able to show more assurance than learned theologians or magistrates.[60] But in another contemporary poem, full of contradictions, a certain beguine defended her status against the reproaches of a doctor of theology: "You pluck, we choose; you talk, we act; you bring, we take; you chew, we swallow; you sell, we buy; you glow, we take fire; you think, we know; you ask, we take; you seek, we find; you love, we languish; you languish, we die; you sow, we reap; you work, we rest; you grow thin, we grow fat; you make sounds, we sing; you sing, we dance; you dance, we jump; you blossom, we bear fruit; you taste, we eat."[61] Elsewhere Robert de Sorbon employed the word *beguine* as a synonym for a devout woman, in short, a person resembling a Pietist of a later day who thrives on inner experience.[62] Similarly, a doctor of the Franciscan order, finding himself in Marseilles, is reported to have asked the beguine Douceline de Digne questions on difficult matters of faith. When she replied in a way that seemed correct, "he understood and admitted that the intelligence of the saint was raised higher by contemplation than he with all his learning would ever possess."[63] These heights of contemplation which Douceline had scaled, it was pointed out, also sharpened her prophetic powers.[64] On the other hand, the life of St. Elisabeth reports that the advisers of Louis of Thuringia, hoping to

[59] Richer, *Gesta Senon. Eccl., MGH. SS.,* XXV, 308.

[60] Theologians, masters, and magistrates "obmutescent in die Judicii coram omnibus, ubi aliqua papelarda, vel beguina, vel aliquis simplex conversus, vel monachus, optime respondebit, qui totam suam intencionem ponit ad scrutandum et sciendum librum Consciencie sue" (ed. Chambon, p. 25; *Bibl. Max. Vet. Pat.,* XXV, 350 E-F; Du Boulay, *Hist. Univ. Paris.,* III, 232). Penitence was sometimes ridiculed as a sign of beguine life: "...Aliquis incipit agere poenitenciam, irridetur ab aliquo qui dicit: Iste est beguinus, et tunc iste dicet tibi aliquid, quia modo aliquo tibi injuriatur: ignosce ergo, et aliquid lucratus es ad viam tuam" (*De Tribus Dietis,* ed. Chambon, p. 58). In the prose sections of the Picard MS. containing the *Dits de l'âme* a Paris master expresses himself in a similar vein: "Quant li maistres l'oij, si dist: dont savés vous plus de divinité que tout li maistres de Paris" (Christ, *La Règle des Fins Amans,* pp. 179, 180 and note 1).

[61] Hilka, in *Zschr. f. rom. Philologie,* XLVII (1927), 160.

[62] Mosheim, pp. 24f.

[63] *La Vie de Sainte Douceline* (XI, 2), ed. Albanès, p. 152: "E adoncs, aquell grans homs connoc e dis, que l'entendementz de la Sancta puiava plus aut, per esperit de contemplacion, que non fazia li sieu, per razon de la sciencia ques avia."

[64] *Ibid.,* p. 154 (XI, 2).

dissuade him from marriage, told him that such a beguine was not intended for him.[65] Again, Robert likens to the changeable bat

> those men who, when they are with *papelardis viris et religiosis,* say "Pray for me," act like a cock in the rain[66], and pretend to be penitent (*contrafaciunt Magdalenam*). When they are with laymen they act like laymen or worse, deprecating and deriding *beguinos et religiosos viros* to gain the good-will of other laymen. I saw a man who in the presence of great beguines (or papelards) wore a big, round super-tunic with ample sleeves of cameline while in the presence of laymen he wore a super-tunic of burnet, cut in front and back, tight-fitting, without sleeves, and with various furs. Wherefore one ought not to remain silent when he sees such men, but should repel and constantly avoid them until they cleave to good men."[67]

AN OASIS IN EGYPT

In his *Carmen Satiricum,* written between 1281 and 1283,[68] the Erfurt poet Nicholas de Bibera depicted the life of "good" beguines as an especially commendable expression of spirituality, but chastised the waywardness of "bad" beguines. Whereas the former, by working day and night, spinning for the most part, lead an existence pious and above reproach, "just like *claustrales,*" attend church faithfully, hear mass, fast, keep vigils, and give alms,[69] the others "sub falsa religione ocia sectantur et per loca queque vagantur." The distaff yields to pleasure. In his description of their consorting with monks, clerics, and students, Nicholas employs all the resources of biting satire.[70] It is significant that he distinguishes sharply between the beguines who earn their livelihood in their own houses and cultivate spiritual friendship with the mendicant orders and those women whose vagrancy plunges them into bad repute. Some even pass as infantici- des. That this was a bifurcated movement had already been clearly perceived by Humbert de Romans. In 1274 the former Dominican minister-general had demanded stern measures against itinerant *mulieres religiosae pauperes;* at the same time he inserted in his collection of sermons arranged by classes one for beguines, the *felices Beguinae et omni laude dignissimae* who *in medio perversae nationis ducunt vitam sanctissimam.*[71]

Jacques de Vitry reports in one of his *Exempla* that a Cistercian

---

[65] Le Grand, *Les Béguines de Paris,* p. 18.

[66] Cf. Gautier de Coincy: "Moult fesoit le coc empleu/ Li papelars, li ypocri- tes" (Godefroy, *Dictionnaire,* III, 66).

[67] *De Consciencia,* ed. Chambon, pp. 15-16.

[68] Nicholas de Bibera, *Carmen satiricum* (ed. Theobald Fischer), 2441 vss. in four *distinctiones;* for the date of composition, pp. 14-16; for the poet, pp. 9-14.

[69] *Ibid.,* p. 92 (vss. 1605-1627).

[70] *Ibid.,* p. 93 (vss. 1628-1654).

[71] *De modo prompte cudendi sermones* (lib. II, n. 5), *Bibl. Max. Vet. Pat.,* XXV, 483.

monk, upon learning that many powerful men, ill-disposed toward
the feminine religious movement, hounded it without rest, asked God
to show him what sort of women these were who were called *beguinae
seculares.* Hearing that they had a firm and lively faith that bore
fruit in good works—*inveniuntur in fide stabiles et in opere efficaces*—
he henceforth lined himself up against their detractors.[72] After describing how the "wise men of Egypt—the wise men of this world, to wit,
secular prelates and other malicious men"—[73] persecuted these holy
women, Jacques de Vitry added in his second *Sermo ad Virgines:* "Sed
aliquando a veris sapientibus defenduntur."[74] It is not without significance that the cardinal emphasizes their orthodoxy at this point.
"Why do you annoy these women? What harm have they done? Don't
they gladly attend church and read their psalter often? Don't they revere the sacraments of the Church and make confession the whole day
long and submit to the instructions of their priests who are the judges
of injustice and speak what they know?"[75] It was these orthodox beguines whom Thomas of Cantimpré had in mind when he described
the devout women in Nivelles, called beguines, whose spirituality
had spread "throughout the world."[76] Some years had passed (1226)
since Mary's death but, as we have seen from Jacques de Vitry's Belgian experiences, her personality continued to be the molding force
in his life while her relics kept on attracting pilgrims to Oignies. It
was precisely on the strength of such evidence of voluntary submission
to church decree and custom that Pope John XXII and subordinates
acting under his instructions recommended a century later that the
bishops whose dioceses comprised portions of Belgium should take
steps to protect the persons and property of orthodox beguines.[77]

If one wishes to be worthy of the beguinage, so runs another poem
of the thirteenth century which extends praise to the brotherhoods
(here the masculine form is employed),[78] he must be generous to his
neighbor, practice self-effacement and seek tranquillity; he must
exhibit patience in adversity and moderation in food and clothing.[79]
Far better is it to work fast, mortify oneself, and mourn (vss. 24-26).
This alone is the path to God. The true beguin is expected to pray

---

[72] Crane, *Exempla*, pp. 116f, no. 279; cf. pp. 252f; Greven, *Exempla*, p. 32, no. 45.

[73] Greven, in *HJ.*, XXV (1914), 44.

[74] *Ibid.*, 45; cf. Kurth, *La Cité de Liége*, II, 256.

[75] Greven, in *HJ.*, XXXV (1914), 46.

[76] See above, p. 329.

[77] E.g., Fredericq, *Corpus*, II, 82, 84, 87; see below, pp. 539-546.

[78] Hilka publishes the text in *Zschr. f. rom. Philologie*, XLVII (1927), 145-153.

[79] Vss. 1-12: "Qui vuet droit beguinage avoir,/ Il at mestier par estevoir/ Qu'il
ne despesse fuer que lui/ Et ce soit larges pour autrui,/ Ce fasse joie d'autrui
bien,/ Tout autresi conme dou sien./ Beguins ce doit mout bien garder; Il ne doit
mie trop parler./Sovent avient qui trop parole/ Qu'il at tot dit parole fole;/ Le
monde puet il bien despire,/ Mais il ne doit avoir point d'ire."

and attend mass and the sermons (vss. 38-40); he must wash the feet
of the poor and visit the sick (vss. 35f, cf. 95ff). Worldly pleasures such
as hunting and hawking are alien to him (vss. 43-48). The beguin
should liken himself to the swallow that wings its way upward to
God, seeking its food there and not the worm on the ground.[80] Avarice is the cardinal sin (vss. 105ff). The penitential hair cloth is the
most appropriate attire for true beguins who strive for poverty: thus
they imitate, on the one hand, the Friars Minor (vss. 107-110) who des-
pise and humiliate themselves and, on the other, the Cistercians whose
champion, St. Bernard of Clairvaux, bequeathed to them the *haire*
(vss. 129ff). Since this does not befit one who covets worldly power
(vss. 137-138), prayer, ceaseless toil, fasts, vigils, and harsh discipline
are their lot:

> Car povreteis et beguinages
> Doit estre ensi con mariages,
> Car cil qui n'aimment povretei
> Sont par despit beguin clamei.[81]

Christ was poor in such a *haire* when mankind was released by Him
from original sin and brought to salvation by the angel's Ave Maria
(vss. 183-192). Contrast this simplicity with the great prelates who now
live on goods that rightfully belong to the poor (vss. 209-214). Poverty,
the poet continues (vss. 227-236), is cherished only by the Friars
Preachers, the Friars Minor, and the Cistercians—otherwise it has been
banished.

The obscurity enveloping the origin of the term "beguine" offered
to some an incentive either to derive the word from or at least to
equate it with benign—or better still, *quasi bono igne ignitae*[82]—a trait

[80] Vss. 49-56: "Drois beguins est en leu d'oisel,/ Qui fait voleir son arondrel,/ Son cuer, a Dieu et sa pensee:/ La doit estre s'amours donnee,/ Car l'alondrë en mout bon tens/ Volentiers est en l'air volans/ Et en volant prant sa pasture/ Et quiert en l'air, de ver n'a cure" (*ibid.*, p. 146).

[81] Vss. 179-182, *ibid.*, p. 148.

[82] Quales sunt mulieres beguinae, quae beguinae ideo appellantur, ut asserunt, quasi benignae, vel quasi bono igne ignitae" (Mosheim, pp. 30, 292; Le Nain de Tillemont, *Vie de Saint Louis*, V, 309); "beguine, chou est benigne, autretant be- guine comme bons feus" (Christ, *La Règle des Fins Amans*, p. 196, lines 117-118; cf. p. 190). The Latin passage is contained in a polemic belonging to the Univer- sity of Paris dispute, entitled *Collationes catholicae et canonicae scripturae* which was long attributed (e.g. Mosheim) to Guillaume de Saint-Amour. But see Denifle, *CUP.*, I, 459, note 1; Philippen, *Begijnhoven*, pp. 17f; Greven, *Anfänge*, p. 3, note 1. A burgher of Münster, John Blanke, endowed on February 1, 1279, with the consent of his sons Hartmann and Alexander the nunnery at St. Gilles with four *solidi* to be paid annually from a house located near the *domum Benignarum* in the parish of St. Gilles (*Westf. U.B.*, III, 1871, 568, no. 1089). Béthune (*Cartulaire*, pp. 12f, no. 16) published a document describing the purchase of lands at Aver- brouck by Margaret, grand mistress of St. Elizabeth at Ghent, in January, 1257. The form *beginarum, benignas*, which occurs repeatedly, may originally have been a misspelling. Cf. *begninas* in *V. Chr. Stumb.*, 379 B, (62); however the sister of the Stommeln priest was called Benigna, "habitu et actu begina" (*Acta Chr. Stumb.*, 279 B, III, 14).

with which the adherents were, it was believed, eminently endowed.
This was a derivation which opponents in particular liked to dwell on.

> Beguin, ce dïent, sont benigne:
> Beguin, ce dïent, sont si digne
> Qu'il ne pensent à nule widive.
> Beguin, ce dïent, ce derive
> Et vient à benignitate.[83]

Embedded in the *Bonum Universale de Apibus* is the *exemplum*
which relates how those beguines who were more devout and had
reached an understanding of truth had those parts of the body which
had sinned set afire by divine flame. When they were brought to the
church of St. Gertrude at Nivelles these members were healed. One
girl of secular life who was brought burned with the sacred fire cried
out that she was not a beguine. Therefore why should she burn?
Forthwith her hand, together with a part of the arm, was consumed
and fell like charcoal. St. Gertrude then answered: Since you are not a
beguine, it will not be done to you as to a beguine.[84]

Before examining the full tide of adverse criticism it is necessary
to consider in detail a fourteenth-century chronicler and poet who
also recognized the dual aspect of the beguinal world. However, Gilles
li Muisis' strictures on decay and perversion were not motivated primarily by the desire to reform or to extirpate. They sprang from the
poignancy of an old man at the passing of happier days. The beguines,
like all institutions and classes, had seen better times; if they had
become disreputable, so had every other segment of contemporary
society.

GILLES LI MUISIS

Gilles li Muisis (1272–1352), abbot of St. Martin in Tournai from
1331 until his death,[85] although speaking of the beguines from hearsay rather than personal experience,[86] offers observations on the semireligious communities remarkable for their sympathy. That his judgment on the whole was more evenly balanced than is generally the
case with dour pessimists and savage critics of the moral-didactic
tradition who review contemporary estates in scathing diatribes is
emphasized in his favorable handling of the friars. By the middle of

---

[83] Gautier de Coincy in Barbazan-Méon, *Fabliaux*, I, 320.

[84] Thomas of Cantimpré, *BUA.*, II, 51, 12 (pp. 478f).

[85] A sound survey of Gilles' life and detailed analysis of his writings are given
by Alfred Coville, in *HLF.*, XXXVII (1938), 250-324; Langlois,*La vie en France au
moyen âge d'après des moralistes du temps*, pp. 304-353; Pirenne, in *BNB.*, XI (1890-
91), 798-806; Berlière, in *RB.*, X (1893), 256; Kervyn de Lettenhove, *Poésies de
Gilles li Muisis*, I, pp. i-xxxiii; Lemaître, *Chronique et Annales*, pp. ii-xxiv.

[86] *Poésies*, I, 238: "Antées les ay pau"; 239: "J'ay parlet des béghines de vir et
d'oïr dire"; cf. 241.

the fourteenth century criticism of the mendicants tended to be excessive and bitterly hostile in northern Europe. Langland's denunciation and Boendale's grievance were not extraordinary. From the abbot of St. Martin's, on the contrary, they received generous praise for maintaining schools and for preaching against the waywardness of the age.[87] His is a rare example of mellowness that belongs to an old man anxious to make his peace with the world and not to be "assailed."

At the same time this is the critique of a cleric who has lost touch with his own age and as an septuagenarian, forced into retirement, lives on the memories of an idealized past. Whatever aspersions he casts on the feminine religious movement are relieved by a consciousness that the beguinage has entered a state of decay. But such was not always the case.

> Dieu pri que béghinage se puissent soustenir
> Et ès boines coustumes anchiènes bien tenir,
> Boines oèvres dedens et dehors maintenir,
> Qu'avoec elles puissons en paradis venir.[88]

The same belief in contemporary degeneration of the institution was held by Ruysbroeck when he penned his verses for *Van den XII Beghinen*.[89]

To avoid idleness imposed upon him by blindness—*ensi que prisenier*,[90] as he puts it, cut off from the full life that he had known, without even *le solas et de vir et de lire*[91]—Gilles li Muisis began at Easter, 1350,[92] to dictate in abundant Latin prose and French verse what he had himself observed or at least learned from witnesses concerning the contemporary scene. Since almost all his writings belong to this three-year period of infirmity, they possess homogeneity in language, style, and point of view. In his quatrains he voices the righteous indignation which finds its stronghold in clerical and bourgeois circles. Although this tradition fashioned his outlook more completely as he approached death and was chastened by physical affliction to himself and a pestilence-ridden society, there really was no break between the practical concerns of the experienced admini-

---

[87] *Ibid.*, 257, 279f.

[88] *Ibid.*, I, 242.

[89] Ruysbroeck, *Werken*, IV (Mechelen, 1934), 6-7:
> Siet, dits de(n) staet van goeden beghinen
> Die seere na die doghede pinen,
> Die langhe hier te voren waren,
> Ende die oec leven in desen jaren.
> Maer dese staet (es) sere vergaen,
> Dat hevet ontrouwe te male ghedaen.

[90] *Poésies*, II, 231.

[91] *Ibid.*, II, 10. He had no *matere de rire (ibid.*, I, 86) for he loved the life he saw around him (*ibid.*, II, 234).

[92] *Ibid.*, I, 1; II, 267

strator, never insensitive to the honors of the world,[93] and the retired
life of the invalid, resigned to his fate, but withal, still hardworking.
"In my childhood, youth, and maturity," he recorded in his chronicle,[94] "I have labored as I should in the vineyard of the Lord, but I
have devoted my life much more to temporal and fleeting affairs than
to study of Holy Scripture and the acquisition of precious stones of
knowledge." Now he must humble himself and accept his suffering
as divine punishment.[95] No longer able to partake of the world's
goods, he admonishes others "ch'est toute vanités des honneurs de ce
monde."[96] Nor do the writings of Gilles li Muisis reflect broad reading
or interest in philosophical speculation. His tastes ran rather to
moral-didactic poetry, especially the *Roman de la Rose* of Jean de
Meung[97] which could have helped to mold the ideas of his youth.[98]
He also praised highly *Li Romans de Carité* and the *Miserere* of
"Renclus de Moiliens" (end of twelfth century or beginning of the
thirteenth) whom he considered an excellent moralist, a master who
spoke of the estates of the world[99] and flayed "les défautes de dont
sagement réprouva."[100] The sermons and poetry of the Franciscan,
Jacques Bochet, a contemporary, likewise made a strong appeal to
him.[101] For history he was content to cite Vincent of Beauvais[102] and
a historical poem of Adam de la Halle, *Le Dit du roi de Sicile.*[103]

As abbot he was acquainted with the folly, vices, scandalous habits,
and relaxed discipline of an effete monasticism. As a blind old man
he meditated and analyzed in detail the decay within all degrees of
the social scale, from kings to valets and *meskines.* As a native of
Tournai, he singled out for special attention the middle class:

> Li plus seurs estas assés, c'est li moyens;
> Des rikes et des povres est ainsi qu'uns loyens.[104]

He speaks with such warmth about this estate, which is exploited by
rich and poor alike,[105] that it is probable that he himself belonged to
it.[106] The fact that in his youth he possessed little more money than

[93] *Ibid.,* I, 94f.
[94] De Smet, *Corpus chron. Flandriae,* II, 137.
[95] *Poésies,* I, 11, 15, 24, 94.
[96] *Ibid.,* II, 150.
[97] *Ibid.,* I, 86, 91. For an evaluation of Gilles' *Belesenheit,* see Coville, in *HLF.,*
XXXVII, 262, 281.
[98] *Ibid.,* 262, 281.
[99] *Poésies,* I, 86f, 91, 355, 356; II, 9, 114; Coville, *l.c.,* 262, 281f. For Renclus de
Moiliens, consult Van Hamel, *Li Romans de Carite et le Miserere* (Paris, 1885).
[100] *Poésies,* I, 356; II, 9.
[101] *Ibid.,* I, 87f; cf. Kervyn de Lettenhove, *ibid.,* p. xii.
[102] *Chronique,* ed. Lemaître, pp. 1-3; cf. Coville, *l.c.,* 262, 281.
[103] *Chronique,* ed. Lemaître, p. xix, 8, 3.
[104] *Poésies,* II, 2.
[105] *Idem:* "Pour rikes et pour povres li moyen souvent paient."
[106] *Ibid.,* I, 16; cf. Coville, *l.c.,* 252. Kervyn de Lettenhove assigned him to "une
famille honorable plutôt que riche" (*Poésies,* I, 1).

for bare necessities[107] lends weight to this conclusion. At the same time it is a static society that he envisages: "A voir dire trestout faisons un seul linage"[108] with the same duties of honor, *courtoisie,* and simple honesty for all.[109] With enthusiasm he recalls from the distance of half a century what he had seen in his youth and what now in old age became for the instructor a golden era.

> Parler vorrai de chou que je vie en jonèce,
> Car, quant m'en souvient, au coer m'en vient grant léèce;
> Se m'oste de courous et de toute tristrèce,
> Et plus légièrement en porte me viellèce.[110]

Even as Dante had rested his hopes on Henry of Luxembourg, grandson of Guy de Dampierre, so Gilles li Muisis, distressed by the decay of noble sentiments in the ruling class,[111] singled this prince out as being particularly worthy of respect[112] in an age marred by usurers, counterfeiters,[113] and a corrupt clergy.

Thus, in treating the beguines as well as other sections of contemporary society, the poet presents a flattering picture of the past and a constant criticism of the present. He is the preacher and teacher, inveighing and admonishing against luxury, pride, worldly pleasures, and neglect of religious duties. Delighting in the age when *menoit jadis sainte gent sainte vie,*[114] he constantly reminds his reader of the possibility of sudden and brutal death, eternal punishment, and divine anger at hardened sinners. It is essentially the same line of thought, but with a little different emphasis, that we find in the fanatical penitents of his own day whose self-scourging he described so vividly and minutely in his chronicle.[115] His are monorimed, uninspired quatrains; tiresome, awkward, and redundant as the doggerel becomes, it nevertheless offers at once an illuminating commentary by an outsider of the defects that the several extraregular statutes were intended to legislate out of existence and an exhortation to recover the vigor of the primitive institution.

There are in many places, Gilles li Muisis observes,[116] beguine houses and demoiselles, aged, religious, and wise, who come from all estates and many *lignages.* They are much desired for the training of children. They wear cloaks, neckpieces, and simple habit. Exhorting

[107] *Ibid.,* I, 16.
[108] *Ibid.,* II, 95.
[109] *Ibid.,* I, 123; II, 54, 131, 153.
[110] *Ibid.,* II, 9; cf. I, 99.
[111] *Ibid.,* II, 20, 81, 131; 71, etc.
[112] *Ibid.,* I, 314-320.
[113] *Ibid.,* I, 278.
[114] *Ibid.,* II, 107.
[115] See above, pp. 370-372.
[116] *Poésies,* I, 237-242.

one another to do good each day, just as Jacques de Vitry had pointed out to the Roman curia in 1216, they gather in convents and houses. Many have benefited from their good deeds. Having chosen a superior to punish them without distinction, they must all submit to her and may not leave the *curtis* without her permission. This whole "religion" can only mean well. They seek their livelihood by spinning and other handiwork. Sometimes they do severe penance; in these beguinages fine rules may be observed. Many persons of substance have found much pleasure in them. If a member of the community does wrong, she must be punished; culprits are never allowed to stay for they only make bad company for the rest. They are wont to listen to sermons and recite scripture whereby their minds are kept pure and clean. Confessors remove the pricks whenever sins are committed and provide their cures. Should the superior acquire a reputation for being dishonorable, she is promptly removed; the community suffers no one, no matter how well raised, who with general consent deserves to be expelled. Formerly less well provided for than at present, they used to live more devoutly and to stay enclosed in their houses. Prelates were wont to visit them often and to impart to them sound instruction. Then they would set about doing good: they were more anxious to remain peaceful and cloistered. Just as the elders were honored by the younger inhabitants, so youth was guided by senior members. In the convents all lived together, youth alongside age. If they did not have an occupation, they spent day and night in deep devotion, frequently listening to sermons from clerics who offered to them sound advice. Since Gilles li Muisis had haunted them little, he did not know how to relate their good life and works. Prelates should exercise lordship over these communities, otherwise they could not exist. So necessary were they to the age that their services were often recommended. They attended mass after the offering. The fire of the Holy Ghost excited their pious hearts. Wherever they went, they were praised. Since humble deeds could break proud hearts, the beguines elected good works. The senior inmates used to address the younger ones who, six, eight, or ten at a time, assembled to listen. Kind hearts never grew weary in doing good; by performing good works one reached heaven. Therefore whoever spoke ill of the beguines, did little service to himself... Many spoke in their favor, some against them; it is the latter whose words multiplied without reason. If one spoke well of another, he was ridiculed and contemned, but if he spoke ill he was tolerated and applauded. Thus it is well for all to praise, for vituperation is never in season. Anyway, the poet adds, one should refrain from both praise and censure, for he satisfies many by saying little. He has spoken of the beguines by experience and hearsay:

Or me die aucun que trop mal les remire.
Li siecles est cangiés et cescun jour empire:
En ches estas partout che n'est fors tire tire.[117]

Too willingly did they say their hours with a young squire or a fine clerk who would school them. But Gilles could not entirely agree with the information given to him. The latter part of this chapter contains a digression in which he reminisces about the pleasures—good spirits, not folly—of the Paris clerks which he knew in younger years. In conclusion, he traces the interaction of good and bad—the old and the new—which coexist in his own day: "We do indeed still find good ladies, wise religious sitting in their chambers; but we also find very many foolish women who have no care to sit in their chairs and spin. Whereas the ancients speak to them of the good old days and good schools, these hold all that for a trifle and let the ancients go as chatterers."[118]

Corroborating these complimentary observations, the earliest documentary material concerning the beguines at Cologne suggests that the term may not always have had a derogatory connotation, even in the first examples of its application. But this does not invalidate the conclusion, as we shall see below, that originally the word *beguine* connoted a heretic. At first this term, since it was considered injurious, was usually not applied to *mulieres sanctae* or *dilectae Deo filiae* by well-intentioned men. Jacques de Vitry hesitated to use it. Gosuin de Bossut, even as the first documents for St. Elisabeth at Ghent and Cantimpré at Cambrai, employed the phrase *mulieres religiosae,* or some similar descriptive phrase, in the *Vita Arnulfi,* written before 1236, and in the *Vita Abundi* and the *Vita Idae Nivellensis* which are to be attributed to him and which date from the same period. In 1241 the beguines who were to receive hospitality from Val-Benoit required qualification: "beginas honeste conversationis et bone fame."[119] The later sources—the *Vita Goberti Asperimontis* (last third of the thirteenth century), *Vita Idae Lewensis* and *Vita Christinae Stumbelensis* (last quarter of the thirteenth century), the *Vita Beatricis* (shortly after 1268), the *Vita Julianae Corneliensis* (ca. 1268), the *Vita Idae Lovaniensis* (early fourteenth century), the *Gesta* (end of thirteenth or beginning of fourteenth century), and Chronicle of Villers (beginning of fourteenth century) used the term without qualification.[120]

---

[117] *Ibid.,* I, 239.
[118] *Ibid.,* I, 242.
[119] Cuvelier, *Cartulaire du Val-Benoît,* p. 93.
[120] Roisin, in *RHE.,* XXXIX (1943), 371, note 3.

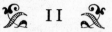

II

Etymology and Heresy

Contemporary opinion of the extraregular is reflected not merely in impressions and observations on conduct or competition with hierarchical prerogative, scattered through formal and popular literature, but even in the formation and use of the word *beguin, beguine*. The derivation and primitive meaning of these terms in their multiple variants or corruptions for the masculine and feminine forms[1] have long been the subject of much pedantic discussion among historians and philologists whose solutions frequently have been the outcome of personal interests or local patriotic considerations. To render the problem more difficult, the term often was unconsciously equated or even conveniently confused in the minds of adversaries with names applied to persons and associations already charged with heresy or at least suspected of being on the fringe of orthodoxy. Such confusion, deliberate or otherwise, was a natural consequence rapid expansion in the absence of uniform rule and monastic vow. Furthermore the movement would appear to have been originally tainted with heterodoxy. The similarity between the tenets of the Provençal beguins and those of the Zealots was so marked that it suggested the existence of some close bond between them and the Fraticelli.[2] The two terms are found together not only in the bull *Sancta romana atque universalis ecclesia,* issued by John XXII in 1317 against Angelo da Clareno and his followers,[3] as well as in a much earlier bull of Boniface VIII,[4] but also afterwards in Gerson.[5]

Legend and tradition, supported by the rivalries of the leading

---

[1] Ducange. *Glossarium, s.v. beguina,* Greven, *Anfänge,* p. 2, note 1; Philippen, *De Begijntjes,* pp. 5-16.

[2] Douie, *Heresy of the Fraticelli,* pp. 248ff. F. Vernet, "Fraticelles," *DTC.,* VI, (1915), 770-784.

[3] December 30, *BF.,* V, 297, p. 134; Mosheim, 623-626. This bull was reissued in 1322 and again in 1331 (*BF.,* V, 229, no. 474; 491, no. 896). In a letter from John XXII to Robert of Naples (May, 1325) the term *beguini* seems to be used for Fraticelli (*ALKM.,* IV, 65). Gerson, in *De susceptione humanitatis Christi (Op. omn.,* I, 455), equates *Fraticelli* and *Fraticellae* with *Begardi* and *Begardae*.

[4] Anagni, October 22, 1296. Cf. *ALKM.,* II, 156-158.

[5] *Op. omn.,* I, 455.

beguinages in the seventeenth century, contributed much to distort and becloud an understanding of the initial phases of the religious movement. St. Begga, daughter of Pepin of Landen and mother of Pepin of Heristal, was then traditionally considered by Zegerus van Hontsum, Elias of Saint Theresa, Erycius Puteanus, and J. G. a Ryckel, abbot of St. Gertrude at Louvain,[6] to be the founder and patron of the Belgian beguines or, better still, since she came too early, to have lent her name to the beguines. Yet it was not etymology alone which captured the imagination, for many a beguine, especially after the fifteenth century, must have regarded herself, but without a shred of evidence, as the direct heiress to the sister of St. Gertrude, patron of Nivelles, the sparkling spiritual and intellectual oasis founded by the Irish under the Merovingians.[7]

More serious and quite plausible, however, have been the efforts of those who, from the days of Miraeus' *Origo Beghinarum Virginum in Belgio* (1602) and Coens' two brief studies (1628, 1629),[8] desiring to discover a single founder as well as a source of origin, relied on Gilles d'Orval's comparatively late account (ca. 1250) of Lambert le Bègue by making the priest of St. Christopher in Liége responsible for the name as well as the new discipline.[9] The name *beguine* was attached to *mulieres religiosae* by adversaries or the people in general whether the term contains, according to Greven and later Van Mierlo[10] and.

---

[6] Zegerus van Hontsum, *Declaratio veridica quod Begginae nomen, institutum et originem habeant a S. Begga Brab. Ducis. ac. brevis simul refutatio historicae disputationis Petri Coens* (Antwerp, 1628); Elias of Saint Theresa, *Het Gheestelijck Palays der Beggijnhoven. In drij Boecken verdeylt. Waarvan den eersten bewijst S. Begga waerachtelijck der Beggijnen fondatersse te zijn*, etc. (Antwerp, 1628); Puteanus, *De Begginarum apud Belgas instituto ac nomine suffragium, quo controversia recens excitata sopitur* (Louvain, 1630); Ryckel, *Vita S. Beggae*. By the end of the fifteenth century in *Die Alder-excellentste Cronijcke van Brabant* (Antwerp, 1497) this theory was gaining currency. Cf. Philippen, *Begijnhoven*, pp. 3-4, 149-156; id., *Onze Begijntjes*, pp. 24-26; Greven, *Anfänge*, pp. 10-13.

[7] Delanne, *Histoire de Nivelles*, pp. 158ff, 173ff.

[8] Coens, *Disputatio historica et brevis disquisitio an Beghinae nomen, institutum et originem habeant a S. Begga, Brabantiae Ducissa* (Antwerp, 1628); id., *Disquisitio historica de origine Beghinarum et Beghinagiorum Belgii cum adjunctis notis quibus Declaratio veridica etc. illustratur* (Liége, 1629).

[9] *Gesta episcoporum Leodiensium, MGH. SS.*, XXV, 110-112.

[10] Van Mierlo, "De Bijnaam van Lambertus le Beges en de vroegste beteekenis van het woord begijn,"*VMKVA.*, 1925, 405-447; id., "Lambert le Beges in verband met den oorsprong der begijnen," *ibid.*, 1926, 612-660; id., "Les béguines et Lambert li Beges," *RHE.*, XXIII (1927), 785-801; id., "Ophelderingen bij de vroegste geschiedenis van het woord begijn," *VMKVA.*, 1931, 983-1006; cf.968-69 (an answer to Philippen, "Een vijftal oorkonden betreffende de Antwerpsche begijnen," *BG.*, IX [1931], 129-147); Van Mierlo, "Het vroegste optreden der Albigenzen,"*VMKVA.*, 1935, 931-947; id., "Slotwoord bij een debat over het ontstaan van 'begginus,'" *ibid.*, 1936, 621-625; id., "De wederwaardigheden van een etymologie, De vroegste geschiedenis van het woord 'begijn,'" *ibid.*, 1945, 31-51; id., "Béguinages," *DHGE.*, VII (Paris, 1934), 457-473; id., "Begardisme," *ibid.*, 426-441. Cf. H. Logeman, "The Etymology of the Name Beguine," *Leuvensche Bijdragen*, 1928, 110-137; J. Leenen, "Albigensis-Beghini," *ibid.*, XXI (1929), 21ff; J. Vercoullie, "De oorsprong van den

Philippen,[11] the accusation of heresy because Lambert le Bègue was a heretic, specifically one of the Apostolici,[12] for which reason *li beges* was applied to him, or, as Kurth maintained,[13] it was a sobriquet borrowed from the popular preacher. The Glasgow documents contain a letter in which Lambert describes his religious activity in the diocese. Although he put in verse, for the use of virgins, the life and passion of St. Agnes, there is no mention of a definite sisterhood. He admits a substantial following among clerics and laymen, but nowhere does he single out the element which afterwards would constitute the beguinage.

That the leading thirteenth century observers failed to agree on the origins makes it obvious that it is not possible to assign the beginnings of the beguinage to a single locality or to attribute the movement to the work or personality of one man. — Gilles d'Orval[14] capitalized on the tradition, perpetuated by the Liége beguines themselves and recently defined in the *Vita Odiliae Leodiensis* (ca. 1240),[15] which made the city the center of the movement and Lambert its founder, whereas Jacques de Vitry, together with Thomas of Cantimpré, threw their support to Nivelles priority. Although Matthew Paris localized the beguines with the vague designation of *Alemannia* and specifically described in round numbers ("mille vel plures", "plura milia", "ad milia milium") their multiplication in Cologne, he admitted the difficulty of etymology and origins.[16] The bishop of Acre himself acknowledged at the time of Mary of Oignies' death (1213)[17] her wide appeal, although this particular evidence cannot of course be employed to contradict the Lambert thesis. More decisive proof that

---

naam Begijnen," *Oost-Vlaamsche Zanten*, IV (Alost, 1929), 105ff; Prosper Poswick, "Lambert-le-Bègue et l'origine des Béguinages," BSAHL., XXXI (1946), 59-73 (with introductory note by Mad. Lavoye, "Le problème des béguinages," pp. 55-57); Fr. Callaye, "Lambert li Beges et les Béguines," *RHE.*, XXIII (1927), 245ff

[11] Philippen, "Het oudste zegel en de vroegste geschiedenis der Begijnen van Antwerpen," *BG.*, XXVI (1935), 81-97; id., "De vorming van het Woord Begginus," *ibid.*, XXVII (1936), 137-155; id., *Onze Begijntjes*, pp. 5-16.

[12] Mosheim, pp. 66-67.

[13] The word *beguine* "est en effet un sobriquet, et il est emprunté à la personne du fondateur, comme celui des chrétiens à celle du Christ" (Kurth, "De l'origine liégeoise des béguines," *BARB.*, 1912, 450; cf. Van Mierlo's answer in *VMKVA.*, 1926, 620-621).

[14] *Gesta Epis. Leod., MGH. SS.*, XXV, 110-112.

[15] *AB.*, XII (1894), 206-209.

[16] In 1243 "quedam mulieres in Alemannia, scilicet Beguine, esse inceperunt. Temporibus quoque sub eisdem quidam in Alemannia sub numerosa multitudine, mulieres precipue, habitum et mores religiosorum sibi assumentes, Beguinos sive Beguinas sese fecerunt appellari, ratione nominis incongnita, et auctore penitus ignoto" (*Hist. Angl., MGH. SS.*, XXVIII, 417; cf. 320, 468). Elsewhere he speaks of "in Alemannia precipue" (*Abbrev. Cron. Angl., ibid.*, 449; ed. Madden, III, 288). Under 1250 he refers in one place to the Church militant bringing forth in those regions (*in eisdem partibus*) holy women "nove (*Abbrev. Chron. Angl.*, ed. Madden, III, 318). religionis" (*ibid.*, 430) and again to France and Germany.

[17] *VMO.*, 547, no. 3.

the beguines were but one manifestation of lay yearnings on a Europeanwide scale is provided by the oft-cited passage from Jacques de Vitry's *Secundus Sermo ad Virgines:*[18] "Hec vult esse Beguina—sic enim nominantur in Flandria et Brabancia—vel Papelarda—sic enim appellantur in Francia—vel Humiliata—sicut dicitur in Lumbardia—vel Bizoke (i.e., Bizoche)—secundum quod dicitur in Ytalia—, vel Coquennune—ut dicitur in Theotonia." On the contrary, it would be more reasonable to consider that each of the beguinages which rose first as distinct and independent houses had in a sense a claim to seniority by virtue of the social and religious needs which everywhere produced the same manifestation of charity and asceticism. Important as may have been the voice of a zealous preacher in guiding and channelling this religious excitement, more often it was at the initiative of a prince or a substantial burgher that these yearnings were answered through the establishment of a semireligious community. Usually foundation is late; the spontaneous character of the early phase must be properly assessed.

Those communities to which the term *beguinus, beguina* was applied may be said, for the sake of convenience, to fall geographically into three areas: first, in southern France, with the chief centers at Narbonne, Toulouse, Provence, and extending as far south as Tarragona in Catalonia and even into Sicily and Calabria;[19] secondly, the imperial lands drained by the Rhine and the region to the east; and finally, Flanders, Hainault, Brabant, the diocese of Liége, and northern France. While the tenets and interests of the Provençal beguins resemble those of the various communities bearing the same name scattered throughout the Rhenish provinces and the Low Countries, it is difficult to establish that there was any steady intercourse between the movements in the north and south. True, while some Spiritual Franciscans or beguins—"nonnulli ... profane multitudinis viri, qui vulgariter Fratricelli, seu Fratres de paupere vita, aut bizochi, sive beghini, vel aliis nominibus nuncupantur"[20]—were being punished at Carcassonne at the beginning of the fourteenth century, others are reported to have fled to Germany seeking refuge at the court of Louis of Bavaria.[21] A century earlier Foulques of Toulouse, in making his memorable journey northward, was much fascinated by the feminine religious movement.[22] We have also seen that

[18] Greven, in *HJ.,* XXXV (1914), 44-45.
[19] Mosheim, p. 623; cf. 633, 638; Bernard Gui, *Practica,* ed. Mollat, I, 108, Vidal, *Bullaire,* p. 39, no. 16.
[20] *Extravagantes,* tit. VII, *de relig.* dom., c.l; Mosheim, p. 623.
[21] *Ibid.,* p. 499. Vernet (*DTC.,* VI, I, 771, 777) disputes the confusion of Michaelites with Fraticelli even though both adhered to a literal interpretation of the Franciscan rule and rejected John XXII's decision regarding religious poverty.
[21] *Ibid.,* p. 499.
[22] See above, p. 312.

Francis of Assisi must have been acquainted through reports, perhaps conveyed by Jacques de Vitry, with the eucharist cult in Liége and Brabant.[23] Metz where Waldensians in 1199 found rich soil for their semireligious movement, yielded manuscripts about 1300 containing spiritual poems the imprint of which is undeniably Franciscan.[24] They must have originated in beguine circles. Two beghard convents in Cologne appear to have sustained the impact of the propaganda of Peter John Olivi and the *beggardi voluntarie pauperes.*[25] The Clementine edicts charged the beguinages in the north with heresy on the matter of divine essence at the time that Olivi's views on this matter were being condemned at the same session of the Council of Vienne.[26] This similarity may have been coincidental, however, since such beliefs were current among the semireligious associations. One peculiarity of the Provençal beguins is their close connection with the Spiritual Franciscans, for the beguins, in order to deceive others, as John XXII emphasized in his bull *Sancta Romana atque universalis ecclesia,*[27] claimed to be members of the third order, often describing themselves as the poor brothers and sisters of penitence, and calling their houses the Homes of Poverty.[28] Their violent attitude towards the pope, for example, was highly colored by the fanatical-visionary millenarianism of the Cistercian monk of Calabria, Joachim of Fiore, adapted for Franciscan needs for the first time by the *Evangelium aeternum,* and leavened by the apocalyptic speculations contained in Olivi's *Postilla in Apocalypsim*[29] or the vernacular version of a little treatise called the *Transitus Sancti Patris.*[30] Yet the Belgian *mulieres sanctae* who first multiplied independently in the Nivelles-Liége-Aywières triangle under the form of regulars, *conversi,* or individual mystics were contemporaneous with and probably antedated the mission of Francis of Assisi.

Nor does an examination of the southern branches betray a homogeneity in aims or method which the term implies on the surface. Bernard Gui suggests that the beguins and Spirituals of southern France and the "Fratisselli" of Italy were not only separate but even hostile organizations, for the former had serious doubts as to the

[23] See above, pp. 312-314.

[24] Meyer, in *Bulletin de la SATF.,* XII (1886), 41.

[25] Asen, in *AHVN.,* CXV (1929), 172; cf. Ehrle, "Petrus Johannes Olivi," *ALKM.,* III, 409ff.

[26] Müller, *Das Konzil von Vienne,* pp. 248ff, 256ff, 266, 273ff, 293ff, 303, 305ff, 352ff, 357ff; cf. 236f, 240f, 243ff.

[27] Mosheim, p. 624.

[28] Bernard Gui, *Practica,* ed. Mollat, I, 108, 118; cf. Douie, *Heresy of the Fraticelli,* pp. 248-258.

[29] Bernard Gui, *Practica,* I, 112, 138, 140; Benz, *Ecclesia Spiritualis,* p. 349; see above, p. 400, note 92.

[30] Bernard Gui, *Practica,* I, 190; Ehrle, in *ALKM.,* II, 411.

ultimate salvation of the latter.[31] Certain beguines lived a community life, supporting themselves either by manual labor or by mendicancy,[32] while others dwelt in their own homes, differing from their neighbors only by a greater strictness of life and a more frequent attendance at church, where their exaggerated devotion caused them to be looked upon with suspicion.[33] Like the Franciscan Order, of which they claimed to be an off-shoot, they were firmly convinced that they were imitating Christ and his apostles by exacting both individual and collegiate poverty. Following the testimony of the famous Dominican inquisitor, St. Francis was for the beguins the greatest exponent of poverty after Christ and his mother,[34] and his rule was a renewal of the evangelical life and therefore possessed a sanctity that not even the pope could violate with a dispensation from the triple vow. Like the Spirituals, they regarded as the followers of Antichrist those clergymen, secular and regular, who lived delicately and luxuriously.[35] In Belgium, on the contrary, the beguines tended rather to seek guidance from ecclesiastical authority under Dominican auspices.

In the present century Van Mierlo, in numerous articles already cited, has established himself as the most ardent defender of the *al-bigen-sis* derivation, that is, the term originated in heterodox circles and was widely employed in corrupt forms by the masses. This actually is an extension of the old thesis of Balthasar Huydecoper[36] for whom *beguine* came from Albigeois as *fermerie* does from *infirmerie, spitael* from *hospital,* Sander from Alexander, and Dries from Andries. In answer to Kurth's contention that the term was the natural development of Lambert's sobriquet li Beges, Van Mierlo demonstrates that it is basically a corruption of Albigeois. But earlier, in 1913, Callaey[37] had already arrived at the same conclusion as Huydecoper on the strength of the references contained in two continuations (II, III) of *Chronica Regia Coloniensis* for the years 1209–1215.[38] The most important of the seven passages occurs in *Contin.*

---

[31] Bernard Gui, *Practica,* I, 146; cf. Douie, *Heresy of the Fraticelli,* p. 258.

[32] "Notandum quoque est quod inter eos sunt aliqui qui publice mendicant hostiatim quia, ut dicunt, noverunt evangelicam paupertatem. Sunt et alii qui non mendicant publice, set aliqua suis manibus operantur et lucrantur..." (Bernard Gui, *Practica,* I, 116).

[33] *Ibid.,* I, 118.

[34] *Ibid.,* I, 120.

[35] *Ibid.,* I, 134.

[36] Balthasar Huydecoper, *Rijmkronijk van Melis Stoke, met Historie-Oudheid en Taalkundige Aanmerkingen* (Leiden, 1772), III, 449; cited by Philippen, in *BG.,* XXVII (1936), 137.

[37] Callaey, "De Beggarden-wevers in de Nederlanden tijdens de Middeleeuwen," *Handelingen van het tweede Vlaamsch Philologencongres,* held at Ghent on September 20-22, 1918 (St. Amandsberg, s.d.), pp. 28-29; id., in *Neerlandia Franciscana,* I (1914), 7; id., in *RHE.,* XXII (1926), 184; XXIII (1927), 245.

[38] *Chronica regia Coloniensis,* in *SS. rer. germ.,* XVIII, 185, 187 (Cont. II); 229, 230, 231, 233, 234 (Cont. III).

III: "Eodem tempore (i.e., 1210) apud Hispaniam, que terra sancti Egidii nuncupatur, in civitate Tolosa *heresis quedam cuius cultores Beggini denominabantur,* emergens, ramos sue perversitatis in brevi longe lateque nimium propagando in tantum distenderat, ut non solum humiles atque meliores, verum etiam primores et principes totius Hispanie cum aliarum provinciarum capitaneis necnon innumerabili multitudine utriusque sexus huius perversi dogmatis error involveret."[39] The term was not used as a mere synonym for heretic or even Albigensian; from the italicized clause it is clear that *beggini* was the real name of the heretics of Albi. It was Beggini in Provence whom the Cistercians despatched by Innocent III were supposed to bring back to the faith.[40]

From a strictly etymological point of view it is difficult to subscribe to the *al-bigen-sis*-beguine thesis; but historical conditions indicate conclusively that the extraregular of the north must have been originally confounded with anticlerical sentiment and the Albigensians in particular. Just as the Gregorian reform movement became bifurcated in the days of Norbert and Tanchelm, so the beguinal life betrays similar dual tendencies: through pursuit of continence, veneration of the eucharist, and submission to church authorities, the Belgian *mulieres religiosae* were in the main fashioning an effective spiritual weapon to curb heresy; conversely, that very cult of virginity and voluntary poverty partook equally of the antihierarchical program sponsored by the Cathari and Waldensians respectively. We have seen how the orthodox, in order to forestall confusion with the heterodox, consciously adopted names—La Vigne, for example—implying a vineyard free of tares.

One could be a Catharist without suspecting that he would accordingly be considered a heretic. "Beguins and beguines were ... the Albigensians of the Low Countries and the Rhenish provinces; and the Albigensians were in their eyes but champions of chastity."[41] The very devotion to St. Catherine among the beguines in the thirteenth century had its origin in emulation of Catharist austerity.[42] Catherine, the pure one, was in legend the saint who best served as a model for the Cathari women who abided strictly by the demands of chastity. Not the legend alone but her very name made strong appeal to the feminine religious movement. Catherine was also the poor maiden who, equipped with a remarkable knowledge of Scripture, successfully disputed with learned men and who brilliantly applied herself to

[39] *Ibid.,* 185; MGH. SS., XXIV, 14.

[40] *Chron. reg. Colon., Contin. III, SS. rer. germ.,* p. 229; cf. Van Mierlo, in *VMKVA.,* 1931, 998-999.

[41] Van Mierlo, in *DHGE.,* VII, 459; cf. 428; id., in *VMKVA.,* 1930, 282; 1931, 1001.

[42] Van Mierlo, in *VMKVA.,* 1930, p. 282; 1931, p. 1004; Philippen, in *BG.,* XXVI (1935), 86-87.

preaching. She was the epitome of numerous ecstatic women, heterodox and orthodox, who in the age of Mary of Oignies took pleasure in reading scripture, saints' lives, patristic material in the vernacular and who did not hesitate to engage sometimes in preaching and the cure of souls. It is thus quite possible that this same special veneration for St. Catherine which Flemish beguines consistently exhibited was the result of some early association with the Cathari. The women called themselves *continentes,* even as orthodox beghards were known, like the Albigensians, as *boni pueri, boni homines, boni valeti,* and *fratres obedientiae.*[43] With the latter they shared an aversion to oaths, as some of the oldest statutes affirm.[44] Validity of profession depended on observance of Christian teachings rather than repetition of an oath.[45] Beguine organization and daily discipline presented many additional features which characterized Albigensian and other anticlerical associations: the one year noviciate; admission ceremonies; justification of lay preaching;[46] regular chapters with public chastisement; absolute secrecy for what transpired in them;[47] prohibition on sleeping without a shirt;[48] designation of the superiors of *beghinae clausae* as *magistrae* or *Marthae*;[49] substitution of seven paternosters

[43] Philippen, "Les béguines et l'hérésie Albigeoise," *AAAB.,* LXXIII (7th ser., III). 1926, 233-255; id., *Begijnhoven,* pp. 134-135, especially note 2. Berthold of Regensburg traces another development of the term *boni homines.* "Sunt heretici ... qui se vocaverunt primo 'pauperes', post 'waldenses', post 'scolares', nunc 'bonos homines', vel *wislôs* vel *weglôs,* toti stulti et rusticani, *unvolch* et idiote" (Schönbach, in *Sitzungsb. d. Acad. Wissenschaften in Wien, phil.-hist. klasse,* CXLVII, pt. III (1904), 45. For possible derivation from *schola* or *scholares vagi,* see *ibid.,* 101. Since the term *Bons hommes* was applied to Cathari and Humiliati alike, it, together with *patarins,* did not necessarily designate heretics but, in general, good men, poor men living a Christian life (Vernet, in *DTC.,* VII, I [1922], 317). Cf. Glaser, *Die franziskanische Bewegung,* pp. 32f; Zanoni, *Gli Umiliati,* pp. 271f.

[44] Rule of 1246: "Item ocht sij met ghesworenen eeden sonder noetsaecke yet sterct. Item ocht sij ghewoen is eeden ocht loeghenen" (Nimal, *Béguinages,* p. 45).

[45] "Item soe wanneer men daer eynighe nemen oft ontfaen sal, soe salse teerst gheloven by hare kerstelycker trouwen in stat van eede hare te stane der ordinantien des hoefs" (*ibid.,* p. 49;Philippen, *Begijnhoven,* p. 309).

[46] See above, pp. 366ff.

[47] Rule of Diest beguinage (1361): "Quod omnes beghine de dicta curia, dum capitulum per earum superiores exercetur in ipsas vel earum alteras saltem hee, que ad ipsum capitulum pertinent, ipso capitulo intersint, quavis earum excusatione non obstante, et secreta illius capituli custodiant eadem nullatenus revelando, et quecumque contrarium facientes penam incurrant decem solidorum turonensium..." (Philippen, in *BG.,* IV, 1905, 328f); Hoornaert, "L'ancienne règle du béguinage de Bruges," *ASEB.,* LXXII (1929), 31: "Niemen ne segghe die verholike dinghe van den huus self den gonen die int hof wonen het ne ware dat syt betren mochten." Cf. Döllinger, *Beiträge,* I, 412.

[48] Statute of 1246: "Item sij sullen sclaeppen in hare onderste habijt ende alleene te weten in haar himde" (Nimal, *Béguinages,* p. 56). Cf. Döllinger, *Beiträge,* I, 207.

[49] Nimal, *Béguinages,* pp. 48, 63; Philippen, *Begijnhoven,* pp. 135, note 2, 226, 239f; cf. Döllinger, *Beiträge,* II, 411, 407, 415; cf. Boniface IX's reference to John XXII's bull *Sancta Romana ecclesia:* "novam religionem seu conformem habitum assumere, congregationes et conventicula facere, in communi simul habitare, superiores, quos procuratores vel servos fratrum, aut Marthas sororum nuncupant" (*ibid.,* II, 381). For a detailed example of Marthas among Suestriones consult the

for canonical hours: the infirmary for sick or poor sisters; and recruiting from weavers. Many zealots, both men and women, deluded by
the absoluteness of austerity, therefore willingly adopted Catharist
customs and organization.

Van Mierlo demonstrates that until 1230, that is, the beginning of
institutional forms, the idea of heretical mysticism was attached to the
word *beghinus, beghina*. To support this view one may cite the episode which Caesarius of Heisterbach relates in the *Dialogus Miraculorum* concerning Walter of Villers, then a young monk, to whom
a woman addresses herself: "Quid vultis videre istas beguinas?" she asks
him as he travels to a Cistercian nunnery in Brabant in order to obtain
by the prayers of the nuns a greater measure of grace. "Vultis ego
ostendam vobis mulierem bonam quae quidquid vult obtinet a
Deo?"[50] Thus the word *beguine* is deliberately opposed to *mulier
bona*, a reliable devout woman. Although this incident was recorded
in 1222, it took place in 1199.[51] Furthermore, Cistercian nuns were
equally under consideration here, for so closely intertwined were
they with the beguine movement that they passed under the eyes of
the public as beguines.

list of complaints coming to the inquisitor Jacob of Soest (1393-94) (Fredericq, *Corpus*, II, 153f); with Submarthas among the Sisters of the Common Life (after 1398)
(*ibid.*, 182-184).
[50] CHD., ed. Strange, I, 88-90.
[51] Greven, *Anfänge*, p. 124, note 1.

The Crucible of Criticism

Wandering religious agitators in Swabia, to whom the names of Fraticelli, beghards, and beguines were applied indiscriminately in a derogatory sense, brought unrest in the ecclesiastical organization and awakened apprehension for the maintenance of orthodoxy; at the Council of Lyons (1245) the bishop of Olmütz reproached those fanatics for the vigor with which they attacked the accepted church structure: they held that one can much better serve God in freedom without being bound by rule or the discipline of an order. At the same time that such teaching prevailed in these Swabian communities, David of Augsburg was warning the religious circles—although recognizing sincere piety in the movement which was often unjustly contemned, ridiculed, and persecuted—against "deceptores et deceptos, qui spiritum suum vel alienum pro spiritu dei sequuntur et seducuntur, sed probandi sunt spiritus et sic judicandi."[1]

Similarly, Lamprecht of Regensburg soon after registered in the allegorical-didactic poem *Tochter von Syon* his surprise at the new religious *Kunst* among women in Brabant and Bavaria which through ecstasy brought within their reach divine wisdom.[2] On the other hand, he cautioned in the spirit of David of Augsburg against the excess and immoderateness of this feminine piety—the seeking for ecstatic experiences and visions together with the exaggeration of every small *Gnade* to fanatic exhilaration[3] Herein lay the principal source of

[1] Grundmann, *Religiöse Bewegungen*, pp. 400-401; cf. David's "formula novitiorum de reformatione interioris hominis," written before 1240, c. 33, cited by Preger, *Geschichte der deutschen Mystik*, I, 136, note.

[2] *Tochter von Syon* (ed. Karl Weinhold, Paderborn, 1880), vss. 2838-2843:

> diu kunst ist bî unsern tagen
> in Brâbant und in Baierlanden
> undern wîben ûf gestanden.
> herre got, waz kunst ist daz,
> daz sich ein alt wîp baz
> verstêt dan witzige man?

Lamprecht is the only authority for the spread of this mystical life in Bavaria (Preger, *op. cit.*, I, 53, 135).

[3] *Tochter Syon*, vss. 431ff, 2853ff, 2979ff.

danger for the popular religious movement: willingness to trust the individual as if he were imbued with divine spirit while giving unbridled expression to the emotions. When a woman eagerly turns to God, he continues, her gentle heart and untutored mind are kindled more quickly and she comprehends that wisdom which flows from heaven more easily than a strong man who is awkward in such things. Conversely, a man who shares this *Kunst* can conceal it much better from the public than a tenderhearted woman who

> von ungebaerd ir lîp
> ze der zît niht enthalten kan,
> sô diu gnâde sie bestêt.[4]

The man who shares similar experiences is thus more certain about such matters that the woman.[5]

> swenne in ein gnaedelîn
> tuot ein kleine fröude schîn,
> sô tuont sie reht alsam sie toben,
> daz selb ich an in niht wil loben.
> swer nie warmes enbeiz,
> den dunket dicke lâwez heiz
> und waent, kumt ez im in den munt,
> er sî gar von fiur enzunt.[6]

Woman lacks *mâze*. When her heart is inflamed with divine love humility leaps for joy, voluntary poverty grows rich, chastity burns with love, strength grows weak, and wisdom loses thought—even obedience is relaxed: each virtue oversteps its fixed limits unless tempered by moderation, the mother of all virtue.[7] Tranquil inner piety, a pure life ending in harmony with divine love, attainment of *wâren minne*—these are the goals towards which the soul of the true mystic strives. Lamprecht knew that this was attainable only through passionate impulse; in *Tochter von Syon* he describes the path which the soul must pursue for mystical union with God.

Lamprecht of Regensburg, after associating with the Franciscans of that city among whom were the *süsse Berchtolt*,[8] as well as the friars John, Henry, Herman, and "Reinhart der guote," faithfully rendered into German verse,[9] while still a layman (*werltliche knap-*

---

[4] *Ibid.*, vss. 2858ff.

[5] *Ibid.*, vss. 2845-2863.

[6] *Ibid.*, vss. 2981-2988; cf. vss. 2994-3040.

[7] *Ibid.*, vss. 2958-2975; cf. vss. 2977-2980.

[8] *Sanct Francisken Leben* (ed. Weinhold), vss. 3280ff; here Lamprecht praises as well Friar John of England who had been sent in 1229 to Germany as the first visitor of the Franciscan order; the following year he was elected provincial minister of the Rhenish province (Wadding, *Annal. Minor.*, I, 408; Eubel, *Geschichte der oberdeutschen [Strassburger] Minoriten-Provinz*, pp. 200f, note 42).

[9] *Francisk. Leben*, vss. 1750-1760 378ff.

THE CRUCIBLE OF CRITICISM

pe),[10] Thomas of Celano's life of St. Francis about 1240.[11] Hereby he hoped to make himself worthy of the order. In his youth, he acknow-ledges, the world had enslaved his whole mind; he had erred in earthly folly and had done everything a foolish young man of his rank might do.[12] However, association with distinguished Regensburg Franciscans conducted him to a life of renunciation—though he never became a sharp ascetic; after a close examination of their religious experiences and a burning personal struggle between flesh and spirit, accompanied with overwhelming conviction of the transience of earthly pleasures,[13] Lamprecht entered the order under the spiritual guidance of Friar Gerhard, provincial minister of the Franciscans in Upper Germany.[14] At his request he composed, about 1250, *Die Tochter von Syon* from the memory of information imparted by Gerhard, who drew from a Latin prose *Filia Syon*.[15] That Lamprecht did not have this Latin work in front of him, but knew it only from an oral version, presuma-bly from the provincial minister, is suggested not only by frank admission of indebtedness but by the passage in which he voices an objection to Gerhard over an expression in the *Filia Syon*.[16] The poem is an allegory depicting the conflict between transient secular goods and worldly pleasures in contrast to the stability of heavenly bliss on the one hand, and the union of the soul with God through the cultivation of the virtues in accordance with *mâze* on the other. Moderation, consistent with ecclesiastical demands, must remain the measure of effective mysticism.

Persecution of beghard-beguine communities was conditioned by a complexity of motives and external factors, all being reduced indis-criminately by the opposition to the ostensible purpose of preserving

[10] Lamprecht made the adaptation as a *knappe* (*ibid.*, vs. 376) and as a *weltlicher* (*ibid.*, vs. 3253). Twice in the *Tochter Syon* mention is made of early secular pur-suits—archery and bird hunting (vss. 3634-3770; 2480-2492).

[11] Weinhold, *Introduction*, p. 4.

[12] *Francisk. Leben*, vss. 311-320; 1756-1763;*Tochter Syon*, vss. 1354-1362. Con-version was gradual: in *Francisk. Leben*, vss. 1761f the poet admits uncertainty whether it has taken place.

[13] *Francisk. Leben*, vss. 1389-1417.

[14] "Provincialis minister der minnern brüeder Gêrhart" (*Tochter Syon*, vss. 50ff, 292, 3184, 4312ff). For want of definite information on this Gerhard, Konrad Eubel (*Geschichte der oberdeutschen [Strassburger] Minoriten-Provinz* [Würzburg, 1886], p. 158f) surmises that his dates must fall between 1246 and 1252. Lamprecht's inner struggle was far from being over after donning the religious habit (*Tochter Syon*, vss. 2280ff). Cf. Weinhold's introduction, pp. 8-9.

[15] For acknowledgment of Gerhard's authority see *Tochter Syon*, vss. 56-59 ("er ist der rede ein urhap./ von sinem munde er mir gap/ die materie und den sin,/ davon ich sin alrest began"), 292ff, 1413-1417, 3184ff; cf. Weinhold's introduction, pp. 282-283; Preger, *Geschichte der deutschen Mystik*, I, 284. Besides Lamprecht the monk of Heilsbonn at the beginning of the fourteenth century independently con-ceived of the soul striving for God as the daughter of Sion, i.e., the daughter of Jerusalem (Weinhold's introduction, p. 284; Preger, *Geschichte der deutschen Mystik*, I, 284).

[16] *Tochter Syon*, vss. 3184ff.

the integrity of the ecclesiastical fabric, both in doctrine and administration, and the accepted moral code, sanctioned by the state.
Submitting this objective to closer scrutiny, we see that the emergence
of extraregular produced or accentuated these sources of discord and
uneasiness: lay and clerical rivalry to the mendicant orders with which
these semireligious association came to be identified; the consequences entailed by evangelical poverty which endangered the material
possessions and temporal prerogatives of the hierarchy; renunciation
of the sacramental-hierarchical organization; the circulation of vague
communist ideas, cast in a primitive Christian mold; the theory of
autonomy which enunciated the right of the individual or the social
group to prescribe for himself or itself a way of life that was not necessarily sanctioned; and the perpetuation of a Tanchelmite tradition
or the adoption of speculative heresies, especially the Amalrician and
the deformed pantheism of John Scotus Erigena. Since many brotherhoods and sisterhoods lived under the protection and supervision of
the mendicant orders and shared their preserves and outlook, the
persecution waxed hot or was deferred, according as the diocesan clergy
and the papacy wished to restrict or accommodate the friars, particularly in the ticklish poverty problem posed by Spiritual Franciscans.
Such difficulties likewise conditioned the willingness of the mendicants
to accept responsibility for the semireligious movement.

Although many quarters were quick to respond sympathetically to
the *congregationes beghinarum disciplinatarum* as a weapon against
heresy, the multiplication of ecstatic laymen who renounced marriage
and formed self-contained conventicles did not meet the approval of
all ecclesiastical officials. The spread of Catharist doctrine had contributed too much to confuse heterodoxy with orthodoxy. Persecution was
the outgrowth of a complex of misunderstanding—of heretical teachings,
immorality, and folklore. Statutes even reflect the current belief that
sorcery engaged the attention of certain beguines.[17] There are shameless men, Jacques de Vitry wrote to Foulques of Toulouse, who, hostile
to all religion, maliciously spread evil reports about the piety of these
mulieres religiosae and "with the rage of dogs rant at customs quite
different from their own"; if they do not go further they nevertheless
invent new names to be used against them "just as the Jews called
Christ a Samaritan and Christians Galileans." But these women, their
eminent patron adds, bear this abuse and persecution with wonderful
patience, often recalling that passage: "If you were of the world, the
world would take what is its own."[18] The Humiliati—the *sancti homines*

---

[17] Statute of the Diest beguinage (1361, Philippen in *BG.*, IV, 1905), 332.
[18] *VMO.*, 548 A: "Vidisti etiam et admiratur es, imo valde detestatus, quosdam
impudicos et totius religionis inimicos homines. praedictarum mulierum religionem
malitiose infamantes, et canina rabie contra mores sibi contrarios oblatrantes: et
cum non haberent amplius quod facerent, nova nomina contra eos fingebant, sicut

and *religiosae mulieres*—whom he observed in Milan in the summer of 1216, were also called *patroni (i.e., paterini)* by "malicious, secular men" *(a maliciosis et secularibus hominibus)*.[19] The above-cited passage from the *Secundus Sermo ad Virgines* contains after the enumeration of new epithets the significant clause: "et ita deridendo eas et quasi infamando nituntur eas retrahere a sancto proposito."[20] To corroborate the bishop's observation, Robert de Sorbon remarked: "Aliquis incipit agere poenitentiam, irridetur ab aliquo, qui dicit: Iste est Beguinus, et tunc iste tibi dicet aliquid, quia modo aliquo tibi iniuriatur..."[21] Dominicans at Rheims enjoyed a story of three boys asleep in one bed. When thunder and lightning caused the one in the middle to sit up and pray, the others laughed and called him a beguin *(beguinum)*. Yet a flash of lightning left him untouched.[22] The rule of the Fins Amans reflects the same antagonism: "Those who are loved by God are hated by the world, for love of God and love of the world are contradictory."[23] The members are reminded that slander and hostility, to which beguines are exposed more than other religious associations, must be borne with sacrifice after the example of Christ.

Echoes of such antagonism, rooted in the preface to the *Vita Mariae Oigniacensis* and perpetuated by the *Chronicon monasterii Afflighemiensis*[24] and the chronicle of the Premonstratensian abbey of Grimberghen between Brussels and Malines,[25] may be found considerably later in the chronicle of Peter of Herenthals who died in 1390 as prior of Floreffe.[26] He too speaks of "multae mulieres tam senes quam juvenes" in 1207 who, although contemning the world with its distractions, are sorely beset by *tribulationes* and *contrarietates*.[27]

Judaei Christum Samaritanum et Christianos Galilaeos appellabant. Nec mirum: Aegyptii enim abominantur oves, et homines tenebrosi et malitiosi innocentium simplicitatem derident, inter potus et epulas, inter ebrietates et crapulas vitam abstinentium lacerantes." An echo of this hostility rings in the rule of the Fins Amans: "Quant les gens del monde... vos haront et reprendront, et descharniront, et diront tout le mal de vos qu'il poront pour moi, esjoïsiés vos et esleechiés vos, car vos loiers en est grans el ciel..." (Christ, *op. cit.*, p. 204, lines 385ff); "Je ne parole fors d'outraiges et de leus souspeçonneus et par persones escandelisiés *(ibid.*, p. 200, lines 252-253). Jacques' expression of sympathy was corroborated by Vincent of Beauvais who added *(Spec. Hist., MGH. SS.,* XXIV, 166) that in his life of Mary he "wrote many good things about the holy women who abounded in the region of Liege in his time and sharply rebuked their detractors." Cf. Greven, in *HJ.,* XXXV (1914), 47; id., *Anfänge*, pp. 70-74.

[19] Ep. I, ZKG., XIV, 102.
[20] Greven, in *HJ.,* XXXV (1914), 44f; cf. Mens, *Oorsprong*, p. 273, note 1.
[21] *Iter Paradisi, Bibl. Patrum Parisiensis,* V (Paris, 1589), 1492; cf. Mosheim, p. 24.
[22] Stephen of Bourbon, *Anec. hist.*, p. 62.
[23] "Car vraement, il convient que cil soient amé de dieu qui sont haï del monde. Car l'amour de dieu et l'amour del monde sont contraires" (Christ, *La règle des Fins Amans*, p. 204, lines 400-402; cf. entire passage, lines 380-424).
[24] Hallmann, *Geschichte des Ursprungs*, p. 40, note; Greven, *Anfänge*, p. 41.
[25] *Ibid.*, pp. 42f.
[26] Berlière, *MB.*, 1, 119; Greven, *Anfänge*, pp. 43f.
[27] *Ibid.*, p. 44; cf. 45; Nimal, *Béguinages*, p. 24.

Since the barking of dogs (Is. 56, 10) symbolized in medieval literature, as Jacques de Vitry abundantly testifies,[28] the office of preaching[29]
and the phrase, *canes muti non valentes latrare*, represents an indictment against the decay of this function,[30] it may be concluded from
the clause, *canina rabie contra mores sibi contrarios oblatrantes,* that
among the influential opponents of the *mulieres religiosae* were
church officials in the diocese of Liége who suspected the aims of the
new devotion and endeavored to stem it. The Papebroch text, con-
densed in the *Sermo secundus ad Virgines,* relates how a Cistercian
monk from Aulne, for example, suspects these women because of the
name given to them. But these thoughts are soon swept out of his
mind by the answer from above: "These women will be found stead-
fast in the faith and active in works."[31] The austere life of these
mulieres sanctae who, instead of withdrawing behind monastic walls,
continued to work among the people and usually adhered to orthodox
doctrine, acted on the luxurious and dissolute like an admonishing
conscience. But this was not accomplished without a full measure of
vituperation. They had to pay a price for their fervor and exemplary
conduct. The overzealous were regarded as fanatics; they brought ridicule on the movement as well as themselves. When Odilia died on
December 14, 1220, her son did not dare to bury the body in the
chapel of St. Gilles, for "the authority of those who had persecuted
the widow waxed too strong in the city." During the next seven
years "some of these men who had sought to ruin the widow died."[32]
Sometimes they were considered heretics; they left in their wake
disrepute and persecution. Those who claimed divine inspiration but
with a measure of moderation had to combat scepticism and derision.
In one of his sermons Caesarius of Heisterbach impugns the spirituality of both *begini* and *begine.*[33]

Granted that *le beges* can be equated in Liége with *begginus,* the
heretics who were first so designated may have been Apostolici. During
the second half of the twelfth century the meaning was enlarged to
include the "pious person who is unreliable in the field of orthodoxy;
piety with suspicion." Afterwards in the thirteenth century *begginus*
was used to designate more specifically the "unreliable pious person,"

[28] *Hist. Occid.,* (II, 5), pp. 271, 274; (II, 8), p. 283; (II, 9), 289; Crane, *Exempla,*
pp. 17f, no. 45; Greven, *Exempla,* pp. 8-10, no. 5; cf. Lecoy de la Marche, p. 37,
note 4.

[29] Greven, *Anfänge,* pp. 72f, note 2; id. in *HJ.,* XXXV, 37, note 2.

[30] Ep. I, *ZKG.,* XIV, 104; Innocent III's second sermon to the Fourth Lateran
Council, Mansi, XXII, 976; Lambert le Bègue had a similar conception in the
Antigraphum Petri (Fayen, 270, 276, 294); cf. *Speculum Exemplorum, sermo xxi*
(Pitra, *Anal. Nov.,* II, 446); Thomas of Cantimpré, *BUA.,* II, 16, 6 (p. 216).

[31] Prol. *VMO.,* 547; *Sermo II ad virgines,* ed. Greven, in *HJ.,* XXXV, 47f.

[32] *V. Od.,* 243-244.

[33] Schönbach, in *Sitz-ber. d. phil.-hist. kl. d. Wiener Akad.,* CLIX (1908),
Abt. IV, 27.

whereas the feminine form was applied more and more by the public to the *mulieres religiosae* who were sympathetic to claustration. After 1235, when parochial organization became the yardstick of official recognition, they were called with increasing frequency beguines without reproach, but still significantly enough, with the qualification of popular usage—"mulieres religiosae vulgariter dictae beginae" or, better still, "dilectae in Christo filiae, mulieres religiosae quae begginae vulgariter appellantur." By the middle decades the qualification had been dropped.[34]

Fanatical and extraordinary spiritual tests, interpreted as diabolical visitations and temptations and accompanied by excruciating physical pain together with periods of suspended consciousness, provide much of the substance of Cistercian and Dominican *vitae* but were not in the main characteristic of the beguinage. Evincing the precocity in religious growth that is emphasized in these biographies, Christine of Stommeln, faced with the prospect of marriage, deserted home and patrimony at the age of thirteen without her parents' knowledge in order to associate with the poor of Cologne and resort to alms for a livelihood.[35] So embittered were her parents that at first they refused to give her a loaf of bread.[36] Blows delivered to "property and person," however, soon made the father more conciliatory.[37] Yet his own insecurity found little relief in his daughter's fits.[38] After being reduced by inexperience to starvation, Christine was coolly received by the beguines with whom she hoped to live.[39] The claim that demons were plaguing her merely provoked smiles and drew forth from the extraregulars comments on mental derangement or charges of feigned holiness.[40] Whatever she implored in her prayers they deprecated.[41] At sixteen she received no encouragement from laity or clergy: "They would rather be prostitutes than live this way." "Thus in home and outside there was no one to console her."[42] Personal defects, too, provoked hostility. Recommendations in statutes for the punishment of irascible, quarrelsome beguines find a case in point in the *conversa* at Rheims who was wont to heap abuse on others.[43]

[34] E.g., document of 1245: "Innocentius... dilectis in Christo filiabus magistre et sororibus beghinarum oppidi de Dist" (Raymaekers, *Kerkelijk Diest*, p. 422).
[35] *V. Chr. Stumb.*, 368 C (4), 369 E; *Acta Chr.*, 236 F (I, 4).
[36] *V. Chr. Stum.*, 369 A (8); *Acta*, 237 F (I, 8).
[37] *Ibid.*, 249 F (I, 57).
[38] *Ibid.*, 261 E (II, 17).
[39] *Ibid.*, 237 B (I, 5); cf. 237 A (I, 4), 243 (I, 30).
[40] "Beghinae vero secum habitantes putabant ipsam insanire; atque caducum morbum habere, unde tamquam fatuam eam habebant" (*V. Chr. Stumb.*, 368 E [5]; 370 A [12], 371 B [19], 376 A [42]; cf. *Acta*, 237 F, I, 8).
[41] "Beghinae quoque deridebant opera ejus: quidquid enim de veniis et orationibus faciebat, totum vilipendebant" (*V. Chr. Stum.*, 369 A, 8); *Acta*, 237 F (I, 8); cf. John of Stommeln's suggestion, *V. Chr. Stumb.*, 369 E.
[42] *Ibid.*, 370 E (16); cf. 369 A (8).
[43] Stephen of Bourbon, *Anec. hist.*, pp. 335f; cf. Statutes of Diest (1361), *BG.*, IV

Through predilection for the beguinage at Malines, Clarissa Leonard likewise reaped in her tender years parental displeasure to the point of being reduced to poverty. Before reaching twelve she had submitted to the beguines to learn the psalter and sewing. After the mistress' death the girl returned home but refused to apply herself to the business affairs of her grandparents. Although at fourteen she was back in the beguinage, her mother obliged her the following year to leave. Within a year, however, she had returned to the community for the third time.[44]

Excessive eagerness for orthodox practices was regarded as a nuisance. Belief in divine favors often led to negligence of ordinary tasks, and thus deserved reprimands from superiors. One lay-brother in Himmerode was advised that there were fixed times for prayer, and fixed times for work.[45] Juliana was also, as a child, precocious in matters of the spirit, and accordingly proved troublesome to her companions and superiors. She continually derived her deepest satisfaction from the eucharist and, had her superior allowed it, would have attended mass daily. But this was not customary at the Boverie and Cornillon. Juliana could not be exempted from the regulations without displeasing the other sisters who were unable to attend church. Lest she attract attention to herself and appear too pious,[46] Sapience, feigning anger and desiring to frighten her, punished the girl for attempting, in spite of her youth, to participate in the fasts on her own initiative. Juliana's ready acceptance of the chastisement and prompt repentance are fondly treated by the sober biographer. He then hastens to add: let no one impute this fasting to the whim of a child; it was rather the prelude to the long fast that Juliana observed in the future.[47]

Ridicule, suspicion, and even active hostility were necessary concomitants of the saintly life. "When will the day come," cried the nine-old-daughter of a noble patrician, Christine Ebner, "when I may go out to beg for the sake of God?"As she abandoned her property, she answered the admonition of her relatives: "I am happy when I am poor."[48] The Benedictine nuns of St. Trond castigated Lutgard's stricter life which they themselves hesitated to imitate, and heaped torment by attributing to her a lack of perseverance.[49] Some ridiculed the excessive penitence of the *conversus* Arnulf and his

(1905), 331; Liége (1246), in Philippen, *Begijnhoven*, pp. 305ff; St. Trond, *ibid.*, p. 311; Lierre, *ibid.*, pp. 340f.
[44] Gielemans, *Ex Novali sanctorum* (III, 24), in *Anecdota*, pp. 436f.
[45] CHD., VIII, 95 (ed. Strange, II, 161).
[46] *V. Jul. Cornel.*, 445 F (11).
[47] *Ibid.*, 443f (4).
[48] Preger, *Geschichte der deutschen Mystik*, II, 269f.
[49] *V. Lutg.*, 192 (I, 8).

extraordinary ecstasy.[50] To words of derision and disparagement, as
well as to demonstrations of frivolity, Alice of Schaerbeek made no
reply.[51] Gilles of Oignies rejoiced over Mary's outburst of song
at the end of her life because on the next day laymen from different
parts assembled in the church as they were wont to do on Sunday.
Yet the prior's exultation was not undiminished. For if they heard her
sing constantly in such a sharp, high-pitched voice, might they not be
shocked and consider her foolish? "Sons of the world, sons of grief,
do not marvel if some one shouts out of distress or sorrow, as is the
case at childbirth; but they are astonished if anyone, exclaiming for
joy, is unable to remain silent because of the fullness of his heart."[52]
The transports which Franco experienced on his deathbed were
likewise regarded as foolish.[53] It is even reported in the life of Simon
of Aulne, charged, with levity,[54] that assassins armed themselves to
dispose of one to whom God had revealed their sins.[55] Unbelievers
scorned the mystical gifts of the contemplatives.[56] By the defiant they
were reproached for enacting a comedy through their ostentation.[57]
Ivan of Rèves, whose youthful interests, conversion under Mary of
Oignies' guidance, and renunciation of worldly goods fit perfectly the
pattern established by Francis of Assisi, had also to contend with the
same sort of ridicule and scorn from relatives and friends. Had his
conversion taken the usual form, with monastic status as the objective,
it would not have elicited resentment.[58] Mary's own austerity and introspection caused her parents to wonder what sort of a daughter they
had.[59] Parental indulgence such as Colette enjoyed is not too common
in hagiography.[60] Clerics distrusted them and suspected their intentions even to the point of injuring them.[61] Juliana was far from being
alone in encountering difficulties from monastic authorities.[62] When
Ida of Léau, who failed to share her sister's interest in worldly things,
was shunned by her, she merely desired to be edified and thus visited
both recluses and beguines.[63] Ida of Louvain experienced the same

[50] V. Arn. Villar., 564 (D-E (32); 566 (1); 567 (9); 570 (23).
[51] V. Al. Scar., 473 B-C (6).
[52] VMO., 569 D (98).
[53] V. Franconis, in MDT., III, 1337f.
[54] Bibl. roy. de Belg., cod., 8965-8966, f. 209r.
[55] Ibid., f. 213-214v.
[56] V. Lutg., 205 (III, 5).
[57] V. Id. Lov., 179f (32).
[58] VMO., 560 F (59).
[59] Ibid., 550 B (11).
[60] V. Col., 541 (10). Both parents allowed the girl to do "quidquid sibi coelitus
foret inspiratum" (cf. C).
[61] V. Id. Lov., 172 (5); 175f (17-19); 183 (5).
[62] The abbess of Aywières forbade Lutgarde to commune every Sunday (V. Lutg.,
198f, 14) while the head of Florival once opposed the admission of Beatrice of
Nazareth to the noviciate (V. Beat., ed. Henriquez, p. 30).
[63] V. Id. Lew., 110 (11).

lack of sympathy from her father.[64] Her ardor left the way open to reproach: even the charge of pregnancy was levelled against her. The daily visits of a Dominican tickled the imagination of her foes;[65] the biography carefully describes the tests to which she had to submit in order to prove her innocence.[66] But while the public might suspect her motives, the fact that fish caressed her hand[67] and roosters and hens heard mass with her[58] left no doubt that she had been vindicated. Abond of Huy experienced some trouble from his father when he pursued studies that seemed to interfere with his preparation for a commercial life.[69] Yet the merchant did not actually oppose his son's entrance to Villers, even though he threw obstacles in the path of his daughter Mary when she entered La Ramée at Abond's advice.[70] Another sister appears to have followed the beguinal life under the parental roof after obtaining reluctant permission.[71] Abond's two brothers, on the other hand, donned the Cistercian habit at Val-Saint-Lambert "against their father's wishes."[72]

A minute description of such precocity and the objections which it aroused was offered by the seventeenth-century hagiographer, Wiltheim, in his biography of a prioress of Marienthal in Luxembourg.[73] Early in the abbacy of Imene at Salzinnes[74] the imperious countess Margaret of Vianden (d. 1270), a relative, was accompanied on a visit to the Cistercian nunnery by her six-year-old daughter Yolanda, named after the maternal grandmother, wife of Pierre de Courtenay, emperor of Constantinople, and daughter of Baldwin IV, count of Flanders and Hainault.[75] Even at this tender age the girl (b. 1231),[76] notwithstanding parental disapproval,[77] exhibited a penchant for the religious life.[78] Once in the nunnery she seized the opportunity to urge

[64] *V. Id. Lov.*, 159 E-F (4).

[65] *Ibid.*, 175 (16-17).

[66] *Ibid.*, 175f (18).

[67] *Ibid.*, 166 (29).

[68] *Ibid.*, 166 C-D (30).

[69] *V. Ab.*, Bibl. roy. de Belg., cod. 19525, f. 15v.

[70] *Ibid.*, f. 15v.

[71] *Ibid.*, f. 3r.

[72] *Ibid.*, f. 2v.

[73] Alexander Wiltheim, *Vita Venerabilis Yolandae priorissae and Mariae Vallem in Ducatu Luciliburgensi* (Antwerp, 1674). Herman Vander Linden makes no mention of the forthcoming episodes in his article on Marguerite de Courtenay *(BNB.,* XIII, 629-631). The priory of Marienthal was founded shortly after 1231 by a lord of Mersch, Theoderic by name (*AHEB.*, XIX, 1883, p. 224).

[74] Berlière, *MB.*, I, 104; see above, p. 304.

[75] *V. Yol.*, p. 3.

[76] *Idem.*

[77] *Ibid.*, p. 4.

[78] *Ibid.*, p. 3. The biographer closely follows throughout ordinary hagiographical devices designed "ad aedificandum."

the novices to give her a monastic habit and to hide her.[79] Informed of these intentions, Imene reprimanded her.[80] Failing to get a favorable response from the abbess and confronted with marriage preparations,[81] Yolanda was eventually encouraged by the friar, Walter of Meysenburg, to enter the Dominican convent recently founded at Marienthal in the diocese of Trèves.[82] The abject poverty and total austerity of this house suited her tastes even better.[83] On the other hand, Yolanda was singled out by her contemporary, Thomas of Cantimpré, as a particularly noteworthy example of the "many daughters of counts and barons who spurned marriage and elected a life of chastity in monastery or congregation of virgins."[84] The girl turned a deaf ear to the protests and appeals of the priest, Francis,[85] her brother, Frederick,[86] as well as Imene and Aleida of St. Walburgis[87] who later were to seek a formula in Cistercian profession at Salzinnes.[88] Nor was the intercession of Imene's uterine brother, Archbishop Conrad of Cologne, of any avail.[89] However generous the countess herself was in endowing and fostering monastic establishments[90] in the midst of difficulties arising from her persistent claims to Namur, she refused to consider an impoverished house acceptable for Yolanda's conversion. The enraged mother[91] even attempted to set fire to Marienthal.[92] This failing, she returned to the convent with a party of retainers and vassals who, partly by force, partly by craft, dragged Yolanda back to Luxembourg where she was divested of the veil[93] and imprisoned. Further expostulations from her brother, Imene of Salzinnes, and Albertus Magnus remained unheeded.[94] Flight in the face of fresh preparations for marriage with Montjoy[95] again kindled her mother's wrath[96] in spite of the efforts of her brother Henry to effect a reconciliation.[97] Perhaps it was political adversity as well as the intercession of influential persons which contributed to

[79] *Ibid.*, p. 5.
[80] *Ibid.*, pp. 5f.
[81] *Ibid.*, p. 8.
[82] For its foundation, see Wiltheim's parenthetical remarks, *l.c.*, pp. 34f.
[83] *V. Yol.*, pp. 8-13, 21, 30-31, 34.
[84] Thomas of Cantimpré, *BUA.*, II, 29, 39 (pp. 317f.)
[85] *V. Yol.*, pp. 20-22.
[86] *Ibid.*, pp. 22f.
[87] *Ibid.*, pp. 27f.
[88] *Ibid.*, pp. 26-30.
[89] *Ibid.*, pp. 31f.
[90] Besides donations to Floreffe and Val-Saint-Georges near Namur, she founded the abbey of Grandpré (1231) (Vander Linden, in *BNB.*, XIII, 630).
[91] *V. Yol.*, pp. 39-46.
[92] *Ibid.*, pp. 46-48.
[93] *Ibid.*, pp. 48-58.
[94] *Ibid.*, pp. 59-75.
[95] *Ibid.*, pp. 76-83.
[96] *Ibid.*, pp. 83-88.
[97] *Ibid.*, pp. 89-95.

a softening of parental hostility and to eventual approval of Yolanda's conversion in the Dominican convent[98] but with pomp (1240).[99] With her affiliation and promotion, the house reaped a full measure of prestige and wealth, including an endowment from Blanche of Castille and other members of the French royal family.[100] After the death of her husband, and possibly exhausted by political difficulties, Margaret herself took profession in this once-cursed monastery,[101] dying there on July 17, 1270.[102]

We have noted elsewhere the esteem that the Nivelles beguines enjoyed at the French court because of their prophetic powers. The account of Philip III's recourse to one of them in an effort to ascertain the innocence of his second wife has come down in two versions: the Latin work of Guillaume de Nangis, *Gesta Philippi Tertii Francorum Regis*,[103] and an Old French translation.[104] A collation of these texts reveals a significant difference in spirit and interpretation concerning the extraregular. This discrepancy becomes the more interesting in seeking to describe contemporary opinion of the beguine way of life. The texts run as follows:

Erant tunc duo pseudoprophetae in Francia vicedominus Laudunensis ecclesiae, et quidam Sarabita pessimus; quaedam Beguina Nivellensis tertia pseudoprophetissa. Qui nulla religione approbati, Deo mentiti, per arctam vitam, quam deforis ostendebant, habere prophetiae spiritum dicebantur. Sed vere spiritus mendax in eorum ore factus multos decepit, et ad credendum eis quam plurimos provocavit. Suspectum enim fuit aliquibus, quod eos Petrus de Brocia promissionibus illexisset, ut de regina aliquid dicerent, per quod posset a regis amore vel gratia aliquantulum separari. Nam rex Philippus talibus motus ambagibus abbatem sancti Dionysii in Francia Mathaeum, quem prae ceteris fidelem consiliarium habebat, et episcopum Bajocensem Petrum uxoris Petri de Brocia consanguineum,

Si li fut dit et conté quil avoit a Nivelle une devine qui merveilles disoit des choses passees et a venir, et estoit en habit de Beguine et se contenoit comme sainte fame et de bonne vie; et si avoit a Laon un autre devin, qui estoit vidame de leglise de Laon, qui par art dingromante savoit moult de choses secrees; et plus avant vers Alemaigne estoit un convers qui avoit esté Sarrasin, qui grant maistre et sage se faisoit de tiex besoingnes, et moult disoit de choses qui sont a venir. "Par Dieu, dist le roy, aucun trouverra nen qui nous dira nouvelles de ce fait?" Si appela son clerc qui bien estoit privé et homme de secré, et li pria quil alast vers Laon et a Nivelle pour savoir lequel de ces prophetes estoit tenu au plus sage et qui miex et plus certainement diroit la verité de ce quel en li commanderoit. Le cler

---

[98] *Ibid.*, pp. 114-118.
[99] *Ibid.*, pp. 123-133.
[100] *Ibid.*, pp. 140-146; 146ff.
[101] *Ibid.*. p. 131.
[102] *Ibid.*, pp. 141-143.
[103] Bouquet, XX (1840), 502.
[104] *Ibid.*, 503.

misit ad Beguinam superius nomi-
natam, ut sciret de filio veritatem.
Sed episcopus, praevento abbate,
loquens cum muliere, quid sibi
dixerit vel responderit ignoratur.
Tamen abbas ad illam postea per-
veniens, illi mandatum regis pro
quo venerat aperuit, et ipsa nihil
aliud respondens dixit: "Episcopo
socio vestro locuta sum, et quod
a me petiit bene dixi." Abbas
autem, quia sine ipso locutus fuerat
cum illa episcopus, et responsionibus mulieris permotus, indignanter
recessit, cogitans ab ea aliquam pro-
ditionem esse factam. Redeuntes
igitur ad regem episcopus et abbas,
rex primo petiit ab abbate quid
apud mulierum illam invenerant
in responsionibus et mandatis. Abbas vero respondit, quod ipsum
praevenerat episcopus, nec ex quo
eidem locutus fuerat sibi quicquam
noluit mulier respondere. Rex
autem illico episcopum mandans,
et de praedictis ipsum interrogans,
respondit episcopus: "Domine rex,
mulier illa in confessione aliqua
mihi dixit, sed vobis nec alicui pos-
sum vel debes revelare . . ."

alla a Laon et a Nivelle et enquist
et demanda le plus sagement quil
pot lequel estoit tenu au plus sage
de tel besoigne. Si trouva que la
Beguine estoit la plus renommee
que les autres, et quelle estoit trop
miex creue que les autres de ce
quelle disoit. Au roy de France sen
retourna et conta tout ce quil avoit
trouvé. Le roy manda labbé de
saint Denis, qui avoit non Matyen,
car il se fioit moult en luy, et
Pierre evesque de Bayeux, qui estoit cousin de la Broce de par sa
femme, et leur commanda quil alas-
sent a celle Beguine et quil enqueis-
sent de ceste besoigne diligaument
de son fils. Au chemin se mistrent
et vindrent a Nivelle. Si comme il
furent descendus, levesque se parti
de la compaignie a labbé et fist
semblant quil vouloit dire son ser-
vise: si sen ala a celle Beguine et li
fist pluseurs demandes de lenfant le
roy qui avoit esté empoisonné, et li
pria quelle nen dist riens a labbé
de saint Denis en France qui avec
luy estoit envoyé . . .

In the Latin text the Nivelles beguine is numbered among the pseudoprophets who are approved by no religion, who deceive God, and
who are said to possess the spirit of prophecy through the austere life
of which they make an outward display. This beguiling spirit written
on their faces deceives many and compels conviction in their honesty.
Although underlining the prophetic talent of the beguine of Nivelles,
the French text, on the contrary, does not depict her exactly as a
pseudoprophetess. She is simply capable of telling things past and
future; in beguine habit she passes as a holy woman of good life. Similarly, the vidame at Laon and the *conversus* living closer to Germany
are presented as comparatively innocuous. The vidame is endowed
with the art of necromancy and the ability to probe secret matters.
The Sarabite of the Latin text—that third type of monk who, according to Benedict of Nursia, leads an eremitical existence without an
approved rule[105]—is presented as a *conversus* who had been a Sara-

[105] Benedict of Nursia, *Regula*, cap. 1 (PL., LXVI, 245-246): The third type of
monk is the Sarabaites "qui nulla regula approbati, experientia magistri, sicut
aurum fornacis; sed in plumbi natura molliti, adhuc operibus servantes saeculo
fidem, mentiri Deo per tonsuram noscuntur. Qui bini, aut terni, aut certe singuli,
sine pastore, non dominicis, sed suis inclusi ovilibus, pro lege eis est desideriorum

cen. He too has the power of prophecy. Later the beguine is described again as being more widely known than the others and as uttering words that instill greater confidence. This sentence, taken as a whole, indicates that although the author was far from giving unqualified support to the beguine movement, at the same time it serves as a complement to the clause that she acted "like a holy woman of good life." Thus we find that both texts have the net result of casting suspicion upon the prophetic powers of the beguines; yet it must be remembered that court intrigue, centering about Pierre de la Broce, itself lends to the whole proceedings an irregular appearance. Again, the Latin text more clearly identifies the Nivelles beguine with the pseudoprophets who deliberately try to deceive. In conclusion, however, she is vindicated, for it is her words which compose the king's doubts and lead to the exoneration of Mary of Brabant.

Too frequently, however, persecution breeds hypocrisy and deceit, particularly when unscrupulous beghards were ready to take advantage of the naïve beguines and their ill-defined organization. "The epicurians, clad in the tunic of Christ," wrote Gerson with reference to the Turlupins, "introduce themselves to women while feigning a profound devotion; they gradually gain their confidence and are not long in making them the plaything of their passions".[106] Elsewhere he claims that the beghards and Turlupins who take their own ideas as the criterion of truth attain to such a height of foolishness as to consider that man, once he has reached tranquillity of mind, is freed from all divine law.[107] If a woman wishes to pretend piety, another chronicler observes, there is no better way than to imitate the beguines who cultivate religious practices after the fashion of the Friars Preachers.[108] It was tempting for the opponents of mendicants and beguines alike to cast aspersions on their relationship.[109]

Richer recounts in characteristic anecdotal fashion in his chronicle on Sens, which extends to 1265, the career of Sibyl, a beguine of Marsal in the diocese of Metz, who for a time successfully exploited the simplicity of laity and clergy alike by feigning the life of the beguines. She attended church for matins and mass, as they were wont

---

voluptas...″; but the fourth type is the *gyrovagi* who are "per omnia deteriores sarabaitis". (*ibid.*, 246). Cf. Ivo, bishop of Chartres, ep. 192 (*PL.*, CLXII, 200 A): "Sarabaites, ut in privatis locis proprio jure vivant, et victum sibi de substantia pauperum per manum raptorum, et de foenore negotiatorum accipiant." John of Salisbury, *Policraticus* (lib. VII, cap. 23) (*PL.*, CXCIX, 700 C; ed. Webb, II, 700 C). For other examples consult Ducange, *Glossarium, s.v. Sarabaitae*, VI, 64-65.

[106] Gerson, *Opera omnia*, I (1726), 19: "Epicurei sub tunica Christi, qui mulierculis prima devotionem fingentes specie tenus, paulatim eis Fidem, tanquam lumen et oculos tollere quaerunt, quatenus eas licentius ad desideria sua maligna prostituant."

[107] *De triplici theologia,* consid. viii (*ibid.*, III, 369).

[108] Richer, *Gesta Senonensis Ecclesiae, MGH. SS.*, XXV, 308; Mosheim, p. 100.

[109] *Ibid.*, p. 29.

to do. This pretense of piety won over a certain woman and her husband in the town; they took her into their home and gave her a room where she could carry on her prayers and vigils. Encouraged by the early successes of her religious life, she began to claim that her spirit was transported to heaven. Lying on her bed as if asleep, neither eating nor drinking, she passed the day in the room to which no one was given admittance. The girl claimed that her spirit was suspended and that it was nourished with celestial feasts and that no earthly food was needed. However, a young priest was accustomed to bring secretly to her room each night food the aroma of which filled the room: "The odor, it was believed, must have been brought by the angels who came to her." The priest hid under the mattress of her bed what she could not eat—enough to last three of four days. The girl warned the landlady that she should not be frightened if she heard an unusual noise or anyone entering the room at night; it would only be the devil coming to disturb her. Her deceit met with complete success: Dominicans and Franciscans bruited widely her holiness and deeds. Counts and knights, prelates, monks, and common people—indeed, no less a person than Bishop Jacques of Metz (1239-1260)—came to marvel. But the girl was careful not to give audience to everyone, claiming that her spirit was in heaven and would not return for three days. So deeply did her experiences impress the medieval popular mind, writes the chronicler, that admirers came from many parts of Germany and surrounding regions. Even after the bishop had caused her to be transferred to another house in order that he might check on her veracity, she was able for a time to continue her deceit until one of the Dominicans, that he might better hear her conflict with the devil, peered through a crack in the wall and saw her who they all believed was rapt in ecstasy making her bed. "The beguines who had come to behold this virgin were unable to hear or see her. They covered their heads and weeping, because they wished to see no one for shame, they returned to their houses."[110] Although this account fails to add luster to the name of the beguines, it does illustrate the willingness of the friars to lend their support to the movement. The intimate association of the mendicants and the beguines is attested by the hostile Rutebeuf in his *Diz des Regles:*

> Je voi si l'un vers l'autre tendre
> Qu'en un chaperon a deus testes,
> Et il ne sont angles ne bestes . . .[111]

The Friends of God, a fellowship of preachers and laymen whose object was to explore the deficiencies of the visible church, to

[110] *MGH. SS.*, XXV, 310. In a French version of this tale it was a "beguinard" who discovered her (*ibid.*, p. 308 note 1).
[111] Vss. 168ff (Jubinal, I, 231). See below, pp. 471-473.

foster speculative mysticism and to live according to it themselves, were faced with the necessity of defending themselves against suspicion by distinguishing true spiritual freedom from the false liberty claimed by the sectarians. Without exception they pursued the outward ascetic life.[112] Tauler the "preacher" and Suso the Swabian "poet," both of whom are linked with Meister Eckhart to form the triumvirate of German Dominican mystics, as well as the Fleming Ruysbroeck and the anonymous author of the *Theologia Germanica* all protest against the false free men who were frequently numbered among the people who enthusiastically attended their sermons or consulted their writings. It is possible that Eckhart's experience before the episcopal inquisition sharpened their attacks on the sects. Yet the charges incurred by Tauler himself for attacks on clerical delinquency[113] were weighted with the suspicion of innovation which his emphasis on the interior life entailed. "But if one comes and warns them of the great danger in which they are living, and what a fearful death they are likely to die, they mock him and say scornfully (with reference to the beghards): 'This is the talk of a sectarian. Here come the New Spirits.' The unbelieving Jews or heathen do not contemn the Christians as much as do these false and dissembling Christians their sincere and charitable admonisher. 'See, we have here a New Spirit.' 'These are they of the lofty spirits.'"[114] In John of Dürbheim's indictment of 1317 against the beghards they are accused of holding that men should be more ready to believe the things that come from the heart than the gospels. The soul's inner voice (*instinctum interiorem*) is safer than the truths of the gospels which are being preached daily.[115] However harsh Ruysbroeck was on the beghards or Free Spirits in his *Adornment* of *Spiritual Marriage* (I, 76-77), he was himself not above suspicion. Gerson[116] believed that he belonged to the sect of beghards. Much as the Friends of God themselves valued the inner voice, Tauler constantly inveighs against the Free Spirits because they "strive after a false freedom, and on pretext of following the inward light, follow only the inclinations of their own nature.[117]" Suso may have designed his *Book of Truth* which distinguished between true and false freedom, as a polemic against the Free Spirits

---

[112] Anna Groh Seesholtz, *Friends of God. Practical Mystics of the Fourteenth Century* (Columbia University Press, 1934); Pourrat, *La Spiritualité chrétienne*, II, 319ff.

[113] Susanna Winkworth, *The History and Life of the Reverend Doctor John Tauler* (London, s.d.), pp. 146-147; cf. Seesholtz, *op. cit.*, p. 84.

[114] Second Sermon for the Third Sunday after Trinity (Tauler's *Predigten*, ed. Arndt and Spener, rev. Kuntze and Biesenthal, Berlin, 1841), p. 295. Cf. Seesholtz, *op. cit.*, p. 103.

[115] Mosheim, p. 258.

[116] *Epistola super tertia parte libri Ruysbroeck De ornatu spiritualium nuptiarum, Op. omn.*, I, 62.

and the beghards. It conceivably was a defense of Eckhart's teachings at the time of the master's death. We have seen that Eckhart's mysticism was not pantheistic, Nevertheless he had strayed in certain passages, Suso acknowledged. While he did not wish to be Eckhart's advocate as some had claimed or to free him from all charges of heterodoxy, he did set out to show that if the master erred in certain places, in others he followed orthodox doctrine and that if it was impossible to vindicate him in all points he certainly did not subscribe to the beghard position.[118] Yet Suso no less than Tauler was charged in a chapter meeting of Dominicans at Bruges with having "books in which were false teachings so that all the land was being smirched with heretical baseness."[119] Similarly, the author of the *Theologia Germanica* draws a distinction between a *vergotteter Mensch*, a deified person and "false light" or "a false free spirit."[120] In *The Book of two Men* Rulman Merswin regarded the doctrine of the sect as an obstacle to the growth of spiritual life.[121] Far from consorting with the Free Spirits the Friends of God were their bitter foes, never ceasing to denounce their aberrations.

[117] Quoted by Winkworth, *op. cit.*, p. 112.
[118] Vernet in *DTC.*, VI, I, 806.
[119] Seesholtz, *op. cit.*, p. 103.
[120] *Ibid.*, p. 158.
[121] Vernet, *l.c.*

🎐 IV 🎐

The Hierarchy Undiminished

No attack was delivered with greater virulence against the mendicant orders and their semireligious associates in the thirteenth century than the formal indictment that came from Guillaume de Saint-Amour[1] and the vernacular satire of his two confreres in spirit, Jean de Meung,[2] and above all the free-lance Rutebeuf.[3] The last named sprang to the master's defense after papal denunciation of his writings and at the same time voiced common resentment at Roman political pretensions. Ridicule from these poets was no less potent than academic polemical literature, for theirs was the quicker and wider appeal to townsmen.[4] Both poets derived their materials from the Paris master whether, as in the case of Rutebeuf, the information was obtained immediately by a contemporary from sermons, lectures, pamphlets, and personal contact with the university scene, or, as in the case of Jean de Meung, through the study of his writings.[5] As an earlier representative of this moral-didactic tradition we should mention, for the sake of completeness, Gautier de Coincy (1177-1236) who was once primarily remembered for his passionate veneration of the Virgin in the *Miracles de la Vierge*.[6] He was identified most closely with the abbey of St. Medard at Soissons where he began his monastic life at eighteen and eventually, in 1233, became its prior. But this is only one side of his character. The devotion to Mary was equalled by bitter thrusts at the delinquency and worldliness of the

[1] Perrod, *Maitre Guillaume de S. Amour;* Bierbaum, *Bettelorden,* pp. 241-272.
[2] *RR,* ed. Langlois, 5 vols., Paris, *SATF.,* 1914-1924.
[3] Rutebeuf, *Oeuvres complètes* (ed. A. Jubinal, 3 vols., Paris, 1874): *Li Diz du Maitre Guillaume de Saint-Amour. coument il fut escilliez* (1256 or 1257) (I, 84-92); *La Complainte Maitre Guillaume de Saint-Amour* (I, 93-102); *La Bataille des Vices contre les Vertus ou ci coumence Li Diz de la Mensonge* (II, 204-216); cf. Jubinal, II, 214-216, vss. 187-220; *Poèmes concernant l'Université de Paris,* ed. H. H. Lucas, University of Manchester-Paris, 1952. For Rutebeuf consult the works of Clédat, Feger, Dehm, and Kressner.
[4] Denkinger, *Bettelorden, in Franziskanische Studien,* II (1915), 63-109, 286-313; Hilka, in *Zsch. f. rom. Philologie,* XLVII (1927), 167ff.
[5] Denkinger, *op. cit.,* p. 311.
[6] *HLF.,* XIX (1838), 843-857.

456

estates.[7] The realism of his poem, *De Seinte Leodade*,[8] gives him a common berth with Rutebeuf and Jean de Meung. Unlike his contemporary, Jacques de Vitry, Gautier exhibits only impatience and indignation without understanding the significance of the new forms of lay spirituality. For him they were a cloak for subterfuge and hypocrisy.

Nowhere did the friars provoke such vigorous complaint as in the circles of French prelates who were growing increasingly conscious of the *iurisdictio* and *potestas* of their estate. So closely were their teaching functions bound up with pastoral duties and the conduct of ecclesiastical affairs that the secular theologians in the university guarded the more jealously their prerogatives.[9] Besides, they were being forced into unfavorable competition with an alien power that was supported by contributions from the outside[10] and whose popularity could not be stemmed. Guillaume de Saint-Amour became the outstanding exponent of the static hierarchical order, which had remained uncontested until the extraordinary preaching concessions during the post-Gregorian period, and the equally determined foe of any new form of religious life which seemed to threaten the stability of that traditional secular order. To his partisans the institution had become the palladium of the faith.[11]

Internal peace in the higher and lower ranks of the clergy depended on the *ius proprium,* the principle invoked to justify the status quo and the vested interests which it was designed to defend.[12] The principle meant not only the defense of prerogative in the sense of *suum cuique* but the exclusive exercise of spiritual jurisdiction which belonged within the diocese to the bishop and within the parish to the priest.[13] Although relegating monastic life to an inferior position, Saint-Amour heaped the full measure of his wrath on the mendicant orders and the extraregulars. To them without distinction was now applied what the Scriptures had said about seducers and hypocrites who were to harm the Church in the last days. The mendicant, even though sent by the Holy See and the bishop, cannot preach without

---

[7] Lommatsch, *Gautier de Coincy.*

[8] See above, p. 418.

[9] "Attendentes sacrarum eminentiam litterarum magis necessariam esse saecularibus clericis, qui ad curam animarum et ecclesiarum regimen frequentius evocantur, quam regularibus viris, qui ad ea rarius promoventur..." (*CUP.*, I, 254); cf. Seppelt, *Kampf der Bettelorden,* p. 85.

[10] Rashdall, *Universities,* I, 382. The secular clergy and especially the master of the University of Paris complained that the mendicants, in order to swell their membership, persuaded young boys to enter their orders against the wishes of the parents (Oliger, in *AFH.*, VIII, 389ff) and even pirated candidates from other orders (e.g., Hautcoeur, *Histoire de Flines,* pp. 62f).

[11] *RR.,* 12447.

[12] Schleyer, *Anfänge,* p. 158.

[13] *Ibid.,* pp. 78-80.

the invitation of parochial authority.[14] In defending his cause he exudes a confidence that comes from reliance on the written word—the Bible and canon law.[15]

Instead of attacking the friars directly, however, Saint-Amour was careful to conceal his protest in certain writings by launching it against the religious movement of voluntary poverty[16]—the men known vaguely as *Boni Valeti* and *pueri boni* as well as young women called beguines "who are scattered throughout the kingdom"—which, despite royal patronage, had only imperfectly been incorporated into the ecclesiastical structure. Since mendicancy conducts to flattery, deceit, and theft, it should be limited only to the needy: "Valido mendicanti facienda non est eleemosyna. Mendicans validus graviter delinquit."[17] But he failed to understand the true significance of apostolic poverty.[18] It was hazardous to assail the cult of poverty, for its logic had the support of evangelical precept while its aims and method fired the imagination. Once officially recognized, it defied frontal attack. But for his partisans the master "had upheld the truth and revealed hypocrisy, bald and bare."[19] Before an assembly of prelates belonging to the provinces of Sens and Rheims, Saint-Amour attempted on July 31, 1256, to defend himself from the blows of the Dominicans by employing such indefinite epithets as "false prophets"—the many dangers besetting the "ecclesia Gallicana per pseudo-predicatores et penetrantes domos"[20]—which could not be construed as libel against the friars.[21] This epithet was especially useful for usurpers of the confessional: these false preachers enter houses, that is, they invade the conscience which domain canon law has assigned to the *sacerdos proprius.*[22] Again, in the apologetic *Casus et articuli*, the master disclaimed any intention of detracting from the Dominicans and Franciscans.[23] But according to Matthew Paris the *De Periculis* had its desired effect in directing public opinion against the friars: People began to ridicule the mendicant orders; alms which had heretofore

[14] "Religiosi mendicantes, etsi a Summo Pontifice et ab episcopo missi sunt, praedicare non possunt, nisi a plebanis fuerint invitati" (Alexander IV, October 5, 1256, Denzinger, *Ench. Symb.*, p. 200; *CUP.*, I, 331).
[15] *De Periculis*, in Bierbaum, *Bettelorden*, p. 4.
[16] Crevier, I, 411; Mosheim, pp. 26f.
[17] Denzinger, *Ench. Symb.*, p. 200; Balthasar, *Geschichte*, pp. 51, 57f, 137.
[18] Schröder, in *NAK.*, XVIII (1925), 129-130.
[19] *RR.*, 12159ff.
[20] *CUP.*, I, 330.
[21] Du Boulay, *Hist. Univ. Paris.*, III, 326; *CUP.*, I, 329-330, no. 287; Rashdall, *Universities*, I, 387.
[22] "In hanc domum intrat per ostium rector animarum, qui curam habet ab ecclesia sibi commissam .... Hinc debet pastori ostium domus aperiri per confessionem .... Alienus autem qui curam non habet ... non intrat per ostium, sed aliunde ascendit et ideo dicitur penetrare domum tamquam fur et latro" (*De Periculis*, in Bierbaum, *Bettelorden*, p. 7-8; cf. p. 18).
[23] Du Boulay, *Hist. Univ. Paris.*, III, 317.

THE HIERARCHY UNDIMINISHED

been generously given were now refused; they were called hypocrites, successors of Antichrist, false preachers, flatterers and advisers of kings and princes, scorners and usurpers of priests; skillful intruders of royal apartments, prevaricators abusing the confessional; by travelling in countries where they are not recognized, they excite to sin with greater boldness.[24]

It was the *Tractatus brevis de periculis novissorum temporum*[25] — that "libellum pernitiosum et detestabilem"[26]—written in 1255 shortly after the bull *Etsi animarum,* which gave rise to voluminous, if often pedantic, pamphlet warfare[27] in so far as it concerned the religious-moral problem of Christian perfection rooted in poverty together with the canonical question of the commission of soul-cure to extrahierarchical agents. The attack on the highly popular[28] *Introductorius ad evangelium aeternum,* which was afterwards condemned by the curia for its *fatuitates*[29] rather than its heresies derived from Joachimite fantasies was for Guillaume only a means of combatting pseudoprophets.[30] His tract *De Periculis* was a call to the prelates to recognize, proclaim, and oppose the dangers which attended the rise of the friars,[31] particularly the Dominicans, for they "will give another law of living and organize the church otherwise."[32] He rightly discerned that the menace was twofold: evangelical poverty and a share in pastoral activity.[33] To this protest against usurpation of pastoral care the friars significantly retorted with an appeal to papal omnipotence.[34] The triple *potestatis plenitudo* of the curia offered to

[24] *Cronica Maiora, MGH. SS.,* XXVIII, 363.

[25] Extracts ed. by Bierbaum, *Bettelorden,* pp. 1-36.

[26] Alexander IV's judgment (*CUP.,* I, 362, 363).

[27] For the principal tracts, see Bierbaum, *Bettelorden,* pp. 262-265 and passim; Stroick, in *AFH.,* XXIII (1930), 20ff.

[28] *RR.,* vss. 11807ff.

[29] *ALKM.,* I, 63. Salimbene could write of his fellow friar: "Excogitavit fatuitatem componendo libellum et divulgavit stultitiam suam, propalando ipsum ignorantibus fratribus" (*Cron., MGH. SS.,* XXXIII, 237). The *Introductorius* contained "verba frivola et risu digna" (*ibid.,* 265), and "multas falsitates contra doctrinam abbatis Joachym, quas abbas non scripserat" (*ibid.,* 455). The first attention paid to the work came from Guillaume de Saint-Amour and his colleagues (*ALKM.,* I, 67-68 and note 1).

[30] Guillaume's *Liber de Antichristo* discusses Joachimism (Bierbaum, *Bettelorden,* p. 304; *CUP.,* I, 459, no. 412). Cf. MDAC., IX, 1273-1446 (text); Le Clerc, in *HLF.,* XXI, 470; *CUP.,* I, 296.

[31] See the heading of Chap. IX of *De Periculis:* "Quod praelaʲorum ecclesiae est praedicta pericula praevidere, praenuntiare et repellere" (Bierbaum, *Bettelorden,* p. 25).

[32] "Dabunt aliam legem vivendi et aliter disponent ecclesiam" (*ALKM.,* I, 86).

[33] "Duo enim sunt, quae ipsorum praedicationi fomentum praestant, videlicet, quia manibus otiosis vivere volunt de evangelio; et quod plerumque vivere volunt de curiositate, id est, de curando negotia aliena, quorum utrumque illicitum est eis" (Bierbaum, *Bettelorden,* p. 29).

[34] Thomas Aquinas, *Contra impugnantes Dei cultum et religionem* (*Op. omn.,* XXIX, 30-31).

Bonaventura a satisfactory answer,[35] in spite of the master's objection to papal right to confer at will unlimited preaching ability.[36]

When Everwinus of Helffenstein, the first prior of the Premonstratensian abbey of Steinfeld, had written as early as 1146 to St. Bernard of Clairvaux[37] asking aid and advice to cope with the Apostolici in the vicinity of Cologne, he announced that among these heretics "who set up their own pope" were "feminas (ut dicunt) continentes, viduas, virgines, uxores suas, quasdam inter electas, quasdam inter credentes."[38] In the sermon that contains his answer to this letter St. Bernard regrets that "not only lay princes, but some of the clergy, even of episcopal rank, who ought rather to be pursuing them, give them aid for the sake of gain, since they receive gifts from them."[39] Although the Cistercian monk had again warned the episcopate and priesthood of the dangers attending these alien preachers,[40] it was the university master, with his feet firmly planted on juristic and theological ground, who made, in the face of increasing competition, one of the most eloquent pleas for an uncontaminated and undiminished hierarchy. Even the pope was powerless to compromise or extend his prerogatives.

For Guillaume de Saint-Amour and, in the following century, the curialist, Petrus de Lutra,[41] those men, specially commissioned by the papal curia to supplement the work of the seculars without being integrated into the hierarchy, deserved to be called "pseudo." The Friars Preachers pre-eminently merited this label since they carried on pastoral work "for temporal gain, worldly honor, or the praise of men."[42] Underneath this more or less empty charge may be discerned anxiety, crystallizing into resentment and mingled with chagrin at publicized shortcomings, among the seculars over the successful encroachment of the mendicants on the vested interests of the hierarchy. So many "pseudopraedicatores et domos penetrantes," runs an early

[35] Bonaventura, *Quare Fratres Minores Praedicent* (*Op. omn.*, XIV, 543): "Triplex est autem hujus potestatis plenitudo, scilicet quod ipse Summus Pontifex solus habet totam plenitudinem auctoritatis, quam Christus Ecclesiae contulit, et quod ubique in omnibus Ecclesiis habet illam, sicut in sua speciali sede Romana, et quod ab ipso manat in omnes inferiores per universam Ecclesiam omnis auctoritas, prout singulis competit eam participari."
[36] "Non est verisimile, quod dominus papa infinitis vel pluribus licentiam concedat praedicandi plebibus alienis nisi a plebanis fuerint invitati..." (Bierbaum, *Bettelorden*, p. 11).
[37] Ep. 472, *PL.*, CLXXXII, 676-680; see above, p. 76.
[38] *Ibid.*, 679-680.
[39] *Sermo in Cantica*, 66, *PL.*, CLXXXIII, 1101-1102.
[40] Ep. 242, *PL.*, CLXXXII, 436f.
[41] See his *Liga fratrum* in Richard Scholz, *Unbekannte kirchenpolitische Streitschriften aus der Zeit Ludwigs des Bayern (1327-1354). Analysen und Texte* (2 vols., Rome, 1911), II, 42-63. For Peter's life see *ibid.*, I, 22-24.
[42] *De Periculis*, 61.

THE HIERARCHY UNDIMINISHED

indictment which sees in them the advent of Antichrist,[43] have entered
the Church and broken up into such a multitude of sects and divisions
that they can scarcely be numbered. So many appear to undermine
women, to scrutinize property, and to penetrate the secrets of conscience that they resist correction and truth. Disregarding all devout-
ness, they preach under the guise of piety.

The term *pseudo-praedicator*, being generic, was used indiscriminately for false preachers who invaded the "home" with evil design
or usurped other rights of the hierarchy. Whereas Guillaume de
Saint-Amour and Petrus de Lutra narrowed its meaning to the mendicant orders and their protégés, Jacques de Vitry[44] and before him
Maurice de Sully[45] had previously identified them with prelates who
neglected their duties. The term may therefore connote four different
classes of preachers, depending on the period and the predilection of
the author: (a) individuals and brotherhoods guilty of anticlerical
teaching; (b) delinquent or unqualified clergymen including collec-
tors of alms (*quaestores*);[46] (c) duly licensed and officially approved
preachers who were intended to supplement but actually usurped the
prerogatives of the seculars; and (d) as a further complication women,
abbesses, nuns, and beguines claimed the office of preaching despite
inveterate hostility from church authorities. Caesarius of Heisterbach
offered a pointed observation on the problem:

> In the first place the preacher ought to examine the text of divine
> scripture on which he intends to preach to see whether it is appropriate
> for the audience in time and place. Then he ought to explain the mystical
> meaning of the authorities in order that the congregation may be edified.
> But if he lacks knowledge for this purpose, let him read the commen-
> taries of others in order to have in the treasury of his heart that from
> which he may quote both old and new. In this way his mouth ought
> to open in preaching. Since today the illiterate preach in the church of
> God, not having any knowledge of scripture, they shock many and some-
> times preach errors, and what is more serious, heresies.[47]

Preaching and pastoral care, Guillaume declared, are reserved
to those divinely appointed; this is interpreted to mean only
the twelve disciples and their successors, the parish priests (Luke
10, 1ff; cf. Num. 11, 16) as well their representatives, the archdeacons

---

[43] *Liber de Antichristo*, MDAC., IX, 1297; cap. v. *ibid.*, IX, 1293ff.
[44] *Hist. Occid.*, cap. 9, pp. 290-294.
[45] Lecoy de la Marche, p. 31.
[46] *Collect. de Scandalis eccl.*, *AFH.*, XXIV (1931), 41; cf. Fourth Lateran Council,
can. 62, Hefele-Leclercq, V, 2, 1381-1383; Mansi, XXII, 1050-1051; *Corpus jur. can.*,
lib. III, tit. 45, *De Reliquiis*, cap. 2; lib. V, tit. 38, *De paenitentiis*, cap. 14; Council
of Narbonne (1227), can. 19, Hefele-Leclercq, V, 2, 1454; Mansi, XXIII, 26; Council
of Trèves (1227), can. 8, Hefele-Leclercq, V, 2, 1461.
[47] Schönbach, "Studien zur Erzählungsliteratur des Mittelalters. 7 Teil: Über
Caesarius von Heisterbach," *Sitz-ber. d. phil.-hist. Classe d. kaiserlichen Akademie
der Wissenschaften*, CXLIV (Vienna, 1908), 31.

and vicars.[48] No provision was made for any other agency, monastic or lay. It is beyond the capacity of any authority, the papacy not excluded, to delegate the office except to those expressly called for this unalterable order. Guillaume was here interpreting a concept of *ordo praedicantium* which that redoubtable ascetic and reformer Peter Damian had turned to advantage in his plea for the apostolic life during the investiture controversy.[49] Establishing as the principle, scorn of pecuniary gains, rejection of avarice, and absence of personal property, Damian identified the *ordo clericorum* with the *ordo canonicorum*, and that in turn with the *ordo praedicantium*. The bond or common denominator that brings unity to these diverse functions and inspires them can be only the *vita apostolica*, the *conversatio primitivae ecclesiae*. Every cleric who follows it, even a monk, is a minister. Imitation of the apostles confers the right to pastoral ministry and preaching.[50]

Guillaume, on the contrary, was a legalist, quite impervious to the reform program. The arguments of Chapter II of *De Periculis* turn on the *pseudopraedicatores* who include all, no matter how well educated or sincere, who preach without being "sent"; even though they perform miracles or are clairvoyant[51] they may not preach unless delegated to do so.[52] The Paris master sought proof for the exclusiveness of this function in the logic of apostolic succession. *Non sunt veri apostoli, nisi missi* is the formula. The corollary is: *Missi non sunt, nisi qui ab ecclesia recte eliguntur.*[53] But they are not delegated to perform these functions unless they are specifically chosen by the Church. This discrimination belongs only to the bishops, priests, and deacons, the

---

[48] Bierbaum, *Bettelorden*, pp. 9-10, 12. "Nullus ergo habet regimen animarum, nisi episcopi et parochiales presbyteri, aut eorum opitulatores eis opem ferentes, vel ab eis legitime instituti aut vocati" (*ibid.*, p. 10). Guillaume uses the number seventy-two. Cf. Damian who employs seventy (*PL.*, CXLV, 508).

[49] Op. XVIII, *PL.*, CXLV, 389 A-B; cf. 508-509. Cf. Mandonnet, *Saint Dominique*, II, 167ff.

[50] *Apol. monach. adv. clericos*, *PL.*, CXLV, 508-509, 511. Cf. the same comparison in the canons of an unknown eleventh-century author (Mansi, XIX, 704). Just as the Friars Preachers had twelve provincial priors, corresponding to the twelve apostles, so Elias wished to establish within his order seventy-two ministers, like the seventy-two disciples (Thomas of Eccleston, *Liber de Adventu Minorum in Angliam*, in *Monumenta Franciscana*, London, 1858 [ed. J. S. Brewer], collatio viii, p. 32). Salimbene (*Chron.*, *MGH. SS.*, XXXII, 290-291) collected all the traditional scriptural texts on this matter and demonstrated that the preachers of Gerald Segarelli did not deserved to be called "Apostolici," since they were not prefigured by the numbers 12 or 70. For polemics at the beginning of the twelfth century which demanded the same right of pastoral ministry and preaching for monks as for canons, see Rupert of Deutz, *Altercatio monachi et clerici, quod liceat monacho praedicare*, *PL.*, CLXV, 537ff (cf. J. J. Laminne, "La dispute de Rupert de Deutz avec Anselme de Laon et Guillaume de Champeaux," *Leodium*, XV, 1922, pp. 25-40); A. Cauchie, Rupert de Saint-Laurent or de Deutz, in *BNB.*, XX (1908-1910), 426-458; *De Vita vere apostolica*, *PL.*, CLXX, 611ff; Hugh of Rouen, *Dialogorum*, *PL.*, CXCII, 1219.

[51] Bierbaum, *Bettelorden*, p. 9.

[52] *Ibid.*, p. 10.

[53] *Ibid.*, p. 9.

three degrees of the perfect (*ordo perficientium*). The three degrees of the inferior order of those to be perfected (*ordo perficiendorum*) —monks, laity, and catuchumens—may not preach in public.[54]

While Gautier de Coincy, writing a decade after Amaury de Bène's condemnation, had treated the *papelardi* with distrust and disdain, Guillaume represented an entirely new orientation of the problem: a satirist turned publicist. Since the beguines did not constitute an order recognized by the Church, they were much more susceptible to attack than the friars. Thus, appealing to canon law, the theologian could maintain that unless they embraced a rule, it was a grievous sin, or so he was alleged to have said, for *mulieres sanctae,* living in the world, to change their habit or to cut their hair for the sake of religion.[55] Their sin is greater for the pride which is hidden under mean dress entails an added portion of insincerity. They should be excommunicated. On the other hand, Guillaume took pains to disavow this statement even while maintaining that no man or woman, lay or regular, can change from one habit to another after profession. To wear coarser habit in order to distinguish oneself from others and to be regarded as more pious, is hypocrisy.[56] These extraregulars are accused of idleness, for they aim to live on alms under the pretense of pursuing a life of prayer.[57] Whoever in monastic status, he asserts in the *Casus et Articuli,* is without income or property and, although able-bodied, prefers alms to manual work, is not in a state of grace and may not be excused by the office of preaching. "Some believe that if men pray, the earth will bear more fruit without cultivation."[58] It is false modesty alone that induces these women to don humble attire.[59] Guillaume cites St. Paul's words of caution (I Tim. II, 9-12) approvingly when he advises women to observe modesty, which can be done not through the habit or strange and beguiling words of beguines, but

---

[54] *Ibid.,* pp. 12-13: "Cum igitur in ecclesiastica hierarchia, quae ad instar coelestis hierarchiae ordinata est, ut ibidem dicitur (Dionysius the Areopagite, *Eccl. Hier.,* cap. 5, I. par. 3-7 and cap. 6. I. 3; *PG.,* III, 503ff, 531), non sint nisi duo ordines, scilicet 'episcopos, presbyteros et diaconos' sive ministros; 'et ordo perficiendorum,' qui est inferior, habens similiter tres gradus, 'viros,' scilicet 'regulares,' qui et ibi 'monachi' appellantur, et 'fideles laicos et catechumenos'; nulli autem spiritui angelico licitum sit operari, praeter quam ordinatum sit a Deo, ut dicit Dionysius in *Coelesti Hierarchia,* cap. 3, par. 2, *PG.,* III, 166); a Deo autem ordinatum sit, ut nullus inferior exerceat officium superioris nec influat super eum, sed contentus sit officio suo, ut dicitur in eodem capitulo. Relinquuntur, quod 'viri regulares,' qui a beato Dionysio 'monachi' appellantur, dum manent in ordine 'perficiendorum,' qui est ordo inferior, superiorum, id est, 'perficientium,' officium, quod est 'purgare, illuminare, et consummare,' ut dicitur in eodem cap., id.est. officium 'docendi, praedicandi et sacramenta ministrandi' nequaquam poterunt exercere."

[55] Du Boulay, *Hist. Univ. Paris.,* III, 319; Mosheim, p. 27.
[56] Du Boulay, *Hist. Univ. Paris.,* III, 320; Mosheim, pp. 27-28.
[57] Du Boulay, *Hist. Univ. Paris.,* III, 319; Mosheim, p. 27.
[58] Du Boulay, *Hist. Univ. Paris.,* III, 319.
[59] Mosheim, p. 27; cf. p. 34.

464 THE BEGUINES AND BEGHARDS

through good works alone.[60] Again and again, he hammers home the charge of hypocrisy, with the reproach that his victims dazzle by false affectation of holiness; they follow none of the austerities of the religious life.[61] "Although not regulars, they appear to others to be more pious and gain converts through the novelty of externals."[62] Such practices by the laity would deal a blow to the *ordo* of the Church and the sin should be made punishable by excommunication.

In summary, Guillaume's indictment against the extraregular resolves itself into three points: the beguines and beghards are young and capable of work, but prefer to depend on alms; because of their tender years chastity vows must be enforced by strict monastic discipline; and they enjoy too intimate association with the Dominicans who encroach on parochial rights. As the Friars Preachers spread, they often took these women under their protection. They heard their confessions, delivered sermons, conducted mass, conversed with them, exchanged letters, and provided them with alms.[63] However much Guillaume tried for his own protection to dissociate the friars from the extraregular, his antimendicant campaign was pointed and comprehensive to leave any doubts as to the position of the orders in his system. These pseudopreachers who prepare the dangers of these last times, will come in monastic habit and will pretend such great holiness that they will appear as the elect of the church.[64] He denies categorically to all regulars, even though long exercised in chastity and presumably firm in their vows, the right to visit *mulieres sanctae* for the purpose of instructing them in good conduct and consoling them. This function belongs to the secular clergy whose duty is to visit devout widows and girls and who will not enter their houses alone.[65]

---

[60] *Ibid.*, p. 34.

[61] *Ibid.*, p. 33; letter (1270-1271) to Nicholas of Lisieux (*Chart. Univ. Paris.*, I, 498, no. 440).

[62] "Faciunt beguini et beguinae hypocritae, qui licet non sint regulares proprie; tamen, ut sanctiores aliis videantur, et populum in se vitae novitate convertant, superstitiosas, tam in habitu, quam in aliis exterioribus, inveniunt novitates, et ad eos, quoscunque possunt, inducunt, cum tamen magis curandum esset, differre a peccatoribus conversatione et mentis puritate interiori, quam habitu vel cultu exteriori" (Mosheim, p. 33). Cf. Le Nain de Tillemont, *Vie de Saint Louis*, V, 314-315; VI, 179, 189.

[63] See above, pp. 341ff.

[64] Du Boulay, *Hist. Univ. Paris.*, III, 324.

[65] *Collectiones catholicae et canonicae scripturae ad defensionem ecclesiasticae hierarchiae* (*Opera*, p. 267; cited by Grundmann, *Religiöse Bewegungen*, p. 324, note 9).

❧ V ❧

The Protest of Rutebeuf

It is significant that whereas the mendicant orders and extra-regulars received at most the scantiest attention in thirteenth-century German and Dutch-Flemish moral-didactic literature,[1] bitter satire against religious orders in general was singularly abundant in the vernacular poetry of northern France, among the contemporaries of Freidank, Maerlant, and Hugo von Trimberg. Not until the following century, when the mendicant way of life had been well coursed and was being rotted by its foes, heresy and money, do we find Van Velt-hem[2] and Jan Boendale, clerk of the Antwerp echevinage,[3] singling

[1] Hugo von Trimberg and earlier, Freidank, the leading exponents of the moral-didactic tradition in thirteenth-century Germany, offer no pointed comment on the encroachment of the *Ordo* by the friars. (G. Ehrismann, *Der Renner von Hugo von Trimberg,* published by the Literarischer Verein in Stuttgart, Bde. 247, 248, 252, 256, Tübingen, 1908-1912; cf. Leo Behrendt, *The Ethical Teaching of Hugo of Trimberg* [Catholic University of America, Washington, D. C., 1926], pp. 32-36, 40-50). Before the rise of the mendicant orders Thomasin von Zirclaria (*Der Wälsche Gast,* ed. Heinrich Rückert, Quedlinburg-Leipzig, 1852, vss. 2471f, 2489, 12683ff; 11269ff; 17027ff; Hans Teske, *Thomasin von Zerclaere. Der Mann und sein Werk,* Heidelberg, 1933) and Freidank (*Bescheidenheit,* ed. H. E. Bezzenberger, Halle, 1872, vss. 13507ff, 17321ff, 13540, 17597ff, 22003ff) had voiced alarm at heresy (Sister Catherine Teresa Rapp, *Burgher and Peasant in the Works of Thomasin von Zirclaria, Freidank, and Hugo von Trimberg,* [Catholic University of America, Washington, D. C., 1936], pp. 106-113). Although painfully conscious of clerical delinquency Jacob van Maerlant makes but one veiled reference in his voluminous writings to these associations—the beghards (*Ene Disputacie van Onser Vrouwen ende van den Heilighen Cruce,* vss. 326-338). cited below p. 513). With Flanders unruffled by the not yet mature Spiritual-Conventual feud, Maerlant contented himself with his usual banal observations on clerical negligence when he put into Flemish verse (ca. 1272) St. Bonaventura's "official" life of Francis of Assisi (*Leven van Sint Franciscus,* ed. J. Tideman, Leiden, 1848). For his criticism of the clergy see above; cf. Te Winkel, *Maerlants Werken als Spiegel van de dertiende Eeuw* (2nd ed., The Hague, 1892), pp. 124-242; J. Van Mierlo, *Jacob van Maerlant, zijn Leven, zijn Werken, zijn Beteekenis* (Antwerp-Brussels-Ghent, 1946). During and after the waves of persecution of the beguines and beghards popular hostility to the extra-regulars as parasites and hypocrites can be detected in German literature. "Pfaffen, Mönche und Begheinen/ Sind nicht so heilig als sie scheinen," runs one proverb (Simrock, *Deutsche Spruchwörter* [1881], p. 420; Schmidt, in *Alsatia,* 1858-1860, p. 222).

[2] See above pp. 292-294. Cf. F. H. Lippens, "Les Frères Mineurs à Gand du XIIIe au XIVe siècle," *La France franciscaine,* XIII (1930); Leon Vanderkindere,

out from the mass of the religious the friars and their dependents
upon whom they could give vent to their animosity. By the time of
Langland, Chaucer, and Wyclif they had become the object of contempt in the eyes of thoughtful Englishmen.

On the other hand, it was unquestionably the acrimonious controversy at the University of Paris in the 1250's that was primarily responsible for the torrent of ridicule heaped on the new forms of religious and semireligious life in France. If the jurisdictional question
was superficial, the deeper issues were often obscured by imputing
to the intruder lack of sincerity and moral turpitude. Defense against
competition justified the outburst of righteous indignation which
an attack on vested interests always inspires. For those whose conser-
vatism was dependent on the preservation of a secular hierarchy inviolate, the lively interest exhibited by Louis IX in these new forms was
a cause of increasing alarm, for he planted at Paris not only Dominican and Franciscan convents, but in succession Carmelites (also known
as Frères Barrés),[4] Austin friars, Trinitarians, beguines, the short-
lived Brethren of the Sack,[5] Guillelmites, the "White Mantles,"[6] the
Filles-Dieu,[7] and Carthusians who had deserted their solitudes for
Paris.[8] "The king," wrote his biographer, "loved all people who set
themselves to serve God and put on themselves the religious habit;
nor did any come to him but he gave them what they needed for a
living."[9] Similarly, the mendicant friars and poor scholars at Paris
were remembered in his testament by special legacies.[10]

The most articulate of the opposition to voice resentment in the
vernacular was Rutebeuf who had distinguished himself as a partisan
of Guillaume de Saint-Amour in the campaign against Dominican
aggressiveness[11] and Franciscan aberrations. On June 26, 1259, the
pope condemned along with Guillaume's primary work "certain
other well-known little books which rivals of the friars have prepared in vernacular sermon and rime and song to detract from their

*Le siècle des Artevelde. Etudes sur la civilisation morale et politique de la Flandre
et du Brabant* (Brussels, 1907), pp. 235-288.

[3] Boendale, *Jans Teesteye,* ed. Snellaert, vss. 3314-3345.

[4] Rutebeuf *Les Ordres de Paris,* vss. 25-36. Unless otherwise noted, citations are
from the Jubinal edition. Cf. *RR.* 12135ff.

[5] Joinville in Bouquet, XX, 299 A; cf. Asen, "Die Begarden und die Sackbrüder
in Köln," *AHVN.,* CXV (1929), 167-179 (only p. 179 deals with the Saccati); Emery,
"The Friars of the Sack," *Speculum,* XVIII (1943), 323-334.

[6] Joinville, in Bouquet, XX, 299 A.

[7] *Ibid.,* 298-299; Rutebeuf passes them all in review in *Les Ordres de Paris*
(I, 187-201) and the *Chanson des Ordres* (I, 202-207).

[8] *Les Ordres de Paris,* vss. 145ff.

[9] Joinville, in Bouquet, XX, 297-298; cf. Geoffrey de Beaulieu, *V. Ludov.,* in
ibid., XX, 7 B-C, no. 12.

[10] *CUP.,* I, 484-485, no. 430 a; for Louis' esteem for the Order of Preachers consult Chapotin, *Histoire des Dominicains,* pp. 494-510.

[11] E.g., *Les Ordres de Paris,* vss. 37-48; cf. Clédat, *Rutebeuf,* pp. 70-86.

name."[12] That the "indecent" rimes which circulated in the master's behalf refer to Rutebeuf's poems is plausible.[13] The menacing growth and popularity of the mendicant orders, competition from other regular and extraregular communities, the consequent undermining of the established social and ecclesiastical fabric, the suspicions which greeted the *Evangelium Aeternum*,[14] the contest between university and friars rendered acute by royal grants and papal political pretensions,[15] the *cause célèbre* of Guillaume de Saint-Amour, church-state relations, a flagging crusade fervor, support of Charles of Anjou in the war of Pouille for the conquest of Sicily,[16] cognizance of an expanding money economy with the resultant changing moral standards, and the three wounds of the world: the laity, the churchmen, and chivalry,[17] such is the stuff from which the poet fashioned his acrid rimes.

While the drama *Le Miracle de Théophile*,[18] allegory,[19] saints' lives,[20] fabliaux,[21] and personal poems,[22] altogether some fifty in number and all composed in a vigorous style between 1250—1285, testify to Rutebeuf's versatility as a jongleur-trouvère, it was primarily contemporary issues and events, not conventional love themes or flights of imagination, that informed his lyric impulse. As adversity

---

[12] *CUP.*, I, 391: "Quosdam alios libellos famosos in infamiam et detractionem earundem fratrum ab eorum aemulis in literali et vulgari sermone necnon rythmis et cantilenis indecentibus de novo, ut dicebatur, editos... faceret publice coram omnibus igne cremari."

[13] Rutebeuf complains that he was unable to speak freely (cf. *Dit d'Hypocrisie*, vss. 47-53). Jubinal was inclined to identify Rutebeuf's verse with the proscribed poems (II, 220, note 1). Cf. Kressner, *op cit.*, p. 20; *HLF.*, XX, 719ff; Jean de Meung, *RR.*, ed. Langlois, III, 321; Clédat, *Rutebeuf*, p. 86.

[14] *Complainte de Constantinople*, vss. 44-45; *Ordres de Paris*, vs. 72; cf. *RR.*, 124443ff.

[15] Although Rutebeuf could lay his cudgel heavily on the secular clergy as well, he nevertheless expresses keen sympathy for clerics in minor orders—the students—who were studying at the university (*Dit de l'Université de Paris*, I, 183-186) as well as its secular masters (Lucas *Poémes concernant l'Université*, pp. 17f.

[16] *La Chanson de Pouille* (I, 174-177; Bastin and Faral, 44-46) was a contribution to the propaganda in behalf of the Sicilian crusade, the preaching of which was ordered by Urban IV on May 4, 1264 against Manfred and the Saracens. *Li Dit de Pouille* (I, 168-173; Bastin and Faral, 49-51), which contains an appeal to the count of Poitiers (vss. 45-52), was intended to solicit aid for Charles of Anjou on his Sicilian expedition (middle of 1265).

[17] *Plaies du Monde* (II, 24-29).

[18] II, 231-262.

[19] *Renart le Bestourné* (I, 233-242; cf. Leo, *Studien zu Rutebeuf*); *La Voie de Paradis ou La Voie d'Umilite* (II, 169-203).

[20] *Vie de Sainte Elysabel, fille du roi de Hongrie* (II, 310-389); *Vie de Sainte Marie l'Egypcienne* (II, 263-309).

[21] *Li Diz de Freire Denize le Cordelier* (II, 63-77); *Charlot le Juif, qui chia en la pel dou lièvre* (II, 98-104); *La Desputoison de Challot et du Barbier* (II, 8-14).

[22] Under personal poems Harry Lucas (*Les poésies personnelles de Rutebeuf, étude linguistique et littéraire*, Paris, 1938) includes *Le marriage Rutebeuf* (*ibid.*, 76-80; I, 5-12); *La complainte Rutebeuf* (Lucas, pp. 81-86; I, 13-21); *La priere Rutebeuf* (Lucas, pp. 87-88; I, 22-25); *La Griesche d'Yver* (Lucas, pp. 89-92; I, 26-31);*La Griesche d'Este* (Lucas, pp. 93-96; I, 33-36); *C'est de la povretei Rutebeuf* (Lucas, pp. 97-89; I, 1-4); *Ci coumence la repentance* (Lucas, pp. 99-101; I, 37-43).

sharpened his wits, hard-hitting realism supplanted allegory. His practical mind grew impatient with subtleties and polite conceits. His was a fiery polemical nature unable to accept anything uncritically. The moral earnestness that made him a satirist accounts for dismay at hypocrisy, now mistress of Paris.[23]

Acute personal problems—recurring poverty, the vicissitudes of fortune, an unhappy married life, the loss of one eye after a long illness, and timed with his first-born,[24] all hardened his judgment, increased moroseness, and clouded his vision.

> Cist mot me sont dur et diver,
> Dont mult me sont changie li ver
> Envers antan . . . .
> Li mal ne sevent seul venir.[25]

His talents were worth money and he did not hesitate to make his services available for a price. As a publicist, he knew how to capitalize on the rivalry of interests in the capital. Passion and prejudice often combined with an essentially conservative spirit to present a devastating indictment of his age. Thus dependence on patronage for a livelihood and support of "party" sentiment may open to suspicion his motives and sincerity of conviction. Yet Rutebeuf was no mere timeserver. His loyalty to Guillaume de Saint-Amour, even in exile, cannot be explained by hope of gain.[26] The frankness of his faith made him a confirmed supporter of crusades.[27] Since the friars with their *nueve remenance* and *granz fondemenz*[28] which a docile king maintained are presented in *La Complainte de Constantinople*, written about 1262, shortly after the capture of the city by Michael Paleologus, as responsible for the peril in the Holy Land, his dislike for St. Louis further increased as royal preference for these "hypocrites" dictated state policy on this vital matter, even in the face of disaster.[29] The king merited his praise only on the day he took the cross for the second time.[30] Nor does the poet seem to have been much happier

---

[23] *La Complainte de Constantinople*, vss. 47-48.
[24] *La Complainte de Rutebeuf*, vss. 23ff; 94ff.
[25] *Ibid.*, vss. 80-82, 107.
[26] See Rutebeuf's reproach to Guillaume's colleagues for forgetting their spokesman and friend (*La Complainte Maitre Guillaume de Saint-Amour*, vss. 66-114). Lucas, *Poèmes concernant l'Université*, pp. 82ff). Cf. *CUP.*, I, 401-402, no. 353; 402-403, no. 354.
[27] Consult the excellent introductions which Bastin and Faral publish for Rutebeuf's eleven crusade poems.
[28] *La Complainte de Constantinople*, vss. 43, 119; for analysis and criticism see Bastin and Faral, pp. 28-35. Cf. Guillaume de Nangis, in Bouquet, XX, 398-400; Guillaume de Chartres, *De Vita . . . S. Ludovici*, in *ibid.*, 36 B-C.
[29] *La Complainte de Constantinople*, vss. 41ff, 73-84.
[30] *La Voie de Tunes*, vss. 29-40; *La Complainte du Comte de Poitiers* (late 1271), vss. 25ff. The other princes received similar commendation: "Monseigneur" Philip, his brother Jean Tristan, count of Nevers, Count Robert of Artois, and the king of Navarre.

with other members of the royal family: but he offered his services to Charles of Anjou and Alphonse of Poitiers.[31] It is also evident that he obligated himself to Thibaut de Navarre, Eudes de Nevers, Geoffroi de Sergines, Erart de Valéri, and Guillaume de Beaujeu or else their group.

However Rutebeuf was no sycophant. Beneath his barbed attacks we can discern in this fruitful moral-didactic poet with a proclivity to satire a determination that anticipates the secularist and "anticlerical" character of modern Western culture. Gallicanism and lively hostility to the mendicant orders remained the one constant element in his thought; his was basically a political approach.[32]

On the other hand, however much he had in common with a lay world in which the bourgeoisie eventually contested successfully theological prescriptions and clerical prerogatives, Rutebeuf nevertheless was a child of the thirteenth century as much as Louis IX. Salvation was still the desired end of earthly existence. The crusade might implement French political expansion, but its ostensible value must be measured by a spiritual yardstick. Life is short; let young men therefore take the cross for the salvation of their souls.[33] If one aids the king of Sicily in an enterprise where he exposes his body to earn remission of canonical penalties,[34] he will be furthering his own salvation.[35] The appeal is then reinforced by the example of St. Andrew for whom paradise was worth martyrdom.[36] If clerics and knights are taken to task in the *Complainte d'Outre-Mer* (end of 1265-beginning of 1266)[37] it is done in the interests of religion—to awaken their somnolent faith.[38] Unlike the satirical *Complainte de Constantinople*, this poem resembles a sermon in tone and content. The arguments are those expected from the pulpit.[39] Heresy is the *cousine germaine* of hypocrisy "which in seizing the land" has destroyed many a man and woman.[40] Although anxiously exposing the ills at the papal curia and Rome[41] which, instead of acting as the foundation of the faith, is beset

[31] I, 55-64.

[32] E.g., *Vie du Monde*, vss. 42-45; cf. Leo's judgment (*Studien zu Rutebeuf*, p. 103); for the intellectual climate see Schleyer, *Anfänge des Gallikanismus*.

[33] *Chanson de Pouille*, vss. 9-32; *Dit de Pouille*, vss. 13-16; cf. *La Voie de Tunes*, vss. 69-136; *Complainte du Comte de Poitiers*, vss. 1-24. In *La Disputaison du Croisé et du Décroisé* (1266-67) the Decroisé offered arguments against crusading which were wide-spread by midcentury (vss. 185ff); cf. Throop, *Criticism of the Crusade*, pp. 153ff, 161, 165, 188f, 191, 241.

[34] *Chanson de Pouille*, vss. 1-8.

[35] *Dit de Pouille*, vss. 1-12.

[36] *Ibid.*, vss. 25-26.

[37] Cf. Bastin and Faral, pp. 52ff.

[38] Appeal to prelates, vss. 87-108; to prebended clerics, vss. 109-134; to "tournoyeurs," vss. 135-148; cf. Bastin and Faral, p. 65.

[39] Cf. vss. 51-56; *Voie de Tunes*, vss. 1-28.

[40] *Du Pharisian ou C'est d'Ypocrisie*, vss. 7-9.

[41] *Ibid.*, vss. 18ff.

by simony and avarice,[42] the poet cast no aspersions on the See of St. Peter itself. On the contrary, it remained for him the stronghold and preserver of dogma.[43] Nor was his confidence in the institution shaken by the realization that after Clement IV's death (1268) the court was haunted by "Vaine Glorie, Ypocrisie, Avarisce, et Covoitise."[44] Rutebeuf, far from adumbrating the ultimate dissolution of the ecclesiastical order, illustrates rather how concern over contemporary social and political evils informed that current of moral-didactic literature which remained substantially conservative. Zeal to preserve the old order of things led poet and preacher alike to overemphasize the good conditions of the past and to exaggerate the faults of their own times.[45] As traditional beliefs were challenged without respite and customary practices yielded before new forces, the moral indignation of the sober critic became more aroused and satire grew sharper in the hands of the disillusioned.[46]

Just as Rutebeuf's defense of the church is not invalidated by blanket[47] or specific indictment of the clergy, so he did not reject the principles of monasticism. After admitting in La Vie du Monde (vss. 106-109) that he would gladly seek a religious order to save his soul were not most of them congregations in habit and name only, Rutebeuf recognized the triple vow:

> Qui en relegion velt saintement venir,
> Trois coses li covient et voer et tenir:
> Casté, povreté, et de cuer obéir;
> Mais on voit trestouz la contraire avenir.[48]

Nevertheless, in the allegorical poem, La Voie de Paradis, the poet finds praise for a single order—the canons of St. Victor. "No one follows the path of charity save the monks of St. Victor. Never have such wise men been seen; they do not make God out of their paunches as the other monks do."[49] But over Christendom hangs a perpetual cloud; it is Rome and its demand for tribute that cause sorrow and anger. For many the poet's name has become synonymous with anticlericalism. Yet for all his satire on clerics and ridicule of the orders,

---

[42] Vie du Monde, vss. 1off, 30-31, 34-37; Dit d'Ypocrisie, vss. 159ff; cf. 122ff.

[43] Vie du Monde, vs. 30.

[44] Dit d'Ypocrisie, vss. 202f.

[45] Cf. Freidank, Bescheidenheit, ed. Bezzenberger:
Swa man lobet die alten site,
Da schiltet man die niuwen mite (52, 8f).

[46] W. Rehm, "Kulturverfall und spätmittelhochdeutsche Didaktik," Zeitschrift für deutsche Philologie, LII (1927), 304; Hans Delbrück, "Die gute alte Zeit," Preussische Jahrbücher, LXXI (1893), 1-28.

[47] Such charges (L'Estat du Monde, vss. 161-164), after all, are pointless.

[48] Vie du Monde, vss. 110-113; cf. 114ff.

[49] Vss. 726-732; cf. Vie du Monde, vss. 122-125. Compare these observations with those of Jacques de Vitry (see above p. 34). For a different conception of the canons regular see L'Estat du Monde, vss. 16ff.

he was unquestionably religious and even pious, offering conventional praise to the Virgin. It is not too much religion, but rather too little of the right kind, that produces the ills of the world.

> Sainte Eglise se plaint; ce n'est mie mervelle:
> Cascuns de guerroier contre li s'aparelle.
> Si fil sont endormi; n'est nul qui por li velle;
> Elle est en grant péril se Diex ne la conselle
> Puisque justice close, et drois pent et encline,
> Et verités cancelle, et loiautés décline,
> Et carités refroide, et fois faut et défine,
> Jou dit qu'il n'a ou monde fondement ne racine.[50]

As false commodities are peddled, usury is practiced, and chastity decays, each one thinking only of his body while forgetting the soul.[51] The cause for this declension from a once good world[52] is the loss of reverence which has been undermined by papal overlordship.[53]

It was particularly the Paris beguines who, together with the friars, bore the brunt of this satire. In *Les Ordres de Paris* Rutebeuf charges that the beguinage offers an easy life: in the absence of perpetual vows it is possible to take one's departure to secure a husband. On the other hand, whoever bows her head and wears a wide, full dress becomes a beguine without the cloister.[54] Nor can it be denied that they have tender skin. If for such feeble efforts God rewards them with eternal bliss in Paradise, then St. Lawrence must have paid too dearly for it.[55] To gain preferment or consideration one should be affiliated with some beguinage, for the beguine, and by that term Rutebeuf here alludes to the religious in general, dominates the world.[56] At the end of the twenty-line *Diz des Beguines,* which is one of his most sententious statements on the feminine religious movement—the more merciless because of its lively irony—the poet includes a forceful attack on the sympathy and patronage which Louis IX was wont to extend to it.[57] Elsewhere the king is held directly responsible for the growing influence of this movement.[58] His predilection for the friars did not fail to elicit expressions of contempt from many quarters. "You should be king of France!" cried Sarete de Faillouel as she contemplated the

---

[50] *Voie de Paradis,* vss. 10-17.
[51] Scarcely any class escapes Rutebeuf's denunciation: against merchants (*L'Estat du Monde,* vss. 121-134); against "genz menues (vss. 135-146); cf. *Vie du Monde.*
[52] *L'Estat du Monde.*
[53] Kressner, in *Franco-Gallia,* XI (1894), 20.
[54] En s'an ist bien por mari prandre;
 D'autre part qui baisse la chiere
 Et a robe large et pleniere,
 Si est Beguine sans li randre (vss. 39-42; cf. *Ordres de Paris,* vss. 61ff).
[55] *Ibid.,* vss. 43-48.
[56] *Li Dit des Beguines,* vss. 1ff.
[57] I, 221-223.
[58] *Ordres de Paris* (I, 194-197); *Complainte de Constantinople,* vss. 145ff; cf. Alexander IV's letter to Louis IX (August 11, 1257), CUP., I, 363, no. 315.

priest-ridden court. "Better for another to be king than you, for you are ruler only of the Friars Minor and Friars Preachers, of priests and clerics. It is a shame that you are king of France; it is a wonder that they do not chase you out."[59] Since Saint Louis had aided the Filles-Dieu in Rouen, Orléans, and Beauvais as well as Paris,[60] the poet raised his voice to complain about the profusion of women's communities:

> Li Roi a filles à plantei,
> Et s'en at si grant parentei
> Qu'il n'est n'uns qui l'osast atendre,
> France n'est pas en orfentei;
> Se Diex me doint boenne santei,
> Jâ ne li covient terre rendre
> Pour paour de l'autre deffendre:
> Car li Rois des filles engendre,
> Et ces filles refont auteil.[61]

Nor could he fully convince himself of the king's charitable intention,[62] above all when the Holy Land was in dire peril.

Whatever the beguine says, runs the *Diz des Beguines,* full of sarcasm at ecstatic women and deriving its vigor from a contradictory nature common to several poems of the period,[63] listen only to what is good. Whatever happens in her life is religious in character. Her word is prophecy. If she laughs, it is good manners; if she weeps, it is devotion; if she sleeps, she is in ecstasy; if she dreams, it is a vision; if she lies, think nothing of it. If the beguine marries, it is her sociableness. Her vows and profession are not for life. Last year she wept, this year she prays, next year she will take a husband. Now she is Martha, now Mary. Sometimes she watches herself, sometimes she marries. But don't speak ill of her, for the king will not tolerate it.[64]

Mere affiliation with a beguinage, continues Rutebeuf, is a stamp of "respectability." Each of the thirteen stanzas of the *Chanson des Ordres* ends with the refrain

> Papelart et Béguin
> Ont le siècle honi.

[59] Callebaut, in *AFH.,* X (1917), 318.
[60] *Chanson des Ordres,* vss. 55-60.
[61] *Ordres de Paris,* vss. 109-117.
[62] *Ibid.,* vss. 85-86.
[63] See above pp. 417, 420.
[64] I, 221-223: "En riens que Béguine die/ N'entendeiz tuit se bien non;/ Tot est de religion/ Quanque hon trueve en sa vie./ Sa parole est prophécie;/ S'ele rit, c'est compaignie;/ S'ele pleure, dévocion;/ S'ele dort, ele est ravie;/ S'el songe, c'est vision;/ S'ele ment, non créeiz mie./ Se Béguine se marie,/ S'est sa conversacions;/ Ces veulz, sa prophécions/ N'est pas à toute sa vie./ Cest an pleure et cest an prie,/ Et cest an panrra baron./ Or est Marthe, or est Marie;/ Or se garde, or se marie,/ Mais n'en dites se bien non:/ Li Rois no sofferroit mie."

suggesting that the two terms were synonymous with hypocrite.[65] Many
are the beguines who wear full dress: what they do under them it is
impossible to say.[66] Some are virtuous, the poet admits in *La Voie
de Paradis*, but the majority are far from exemplary, for "avoec les
sages sont les folles."[67] Again, the beguins and beguines may lead a
good life, but "one must not put a glutton with fine wine, a hen with a
cock, or a cat with the bacon."[68] Rutebeuf thus consistently exhibits
a special aversion for the beguines, reproaching them for too intimate
relations with members of different orders, particularly the Dominicans[69] and the Carmelites or the Barrés.[70] The latter maintain a
convent hard by the beguines. Twenty-nine of them are their neighbors; one need only pass the door. For by the divine authorities, examples, and teachings which the one brings to the other, there is no
detour. They lead a respectable life by fasts and discipline, the one
comforting the other.[71]

The principal charge hurled at beguin(e)s by Jean de Meung was
hypocrisy. Beneath their "long drawn bloodless faces" and miserable
gowns many a trick is concealed to delude the prince.[72] Again, false-
seeming allies itself with Abstinence which "appears as a demure
beguine, attired in robe of cameline, with fair white kerchief round
her head, the while with saintly look she read her psalter."[73] The
paternoster that hung at her waist had been given to her by a friar,
her spiritual guide and preacher who visited her often for sermon and
confession.[74] By preference he took an interest only in the well-born
and affluent, among whom were numbered beguines.[75]

[65] I, 202-207. Elsewhere the "papelars" are labelled hypocrites (*Frere Denise*, vss.
235ff). For Robert de Sorbon's use of the term see Mosheim, p. 22; see above p. 418.
[66] *Chanson des Ordres*, vss. 61-64.
[67] II, 228-230.
[68] *Vie du Monde*, vss. 154-157: "Molt mainnent bone vie Bégines et Bégin:/ Avec
eus me rendisse ennuit u le matin,/ Mais jà ne croira jà glouton delès bon vin,/ Ne
geline avec coc, ne chat avec fain."
[69] *Des Regles*, vss. 150ff.
[70] *Ordres de Paris*, vss. 25-36; *Chanson des Ordres*, vss. 43ff; *Requeste des
Meneurs*, vss. 131ff.
[71] *Ordres de Paris*, vss. 25ff.
[72] *RR.* vss. 11938-11948.
[73] *RR.* vss. 12044-12049 (*SATF*); adapted from F. S. Ellis' translation in Temple
Classics, vss. 12712-12727).
[74] *RR.* vss. 12050-12064.
[75] *RR.* vss. 11577-11586.

Part Six

THE EXTRAREGULAR
AND THE INQUISITION

"...Vestis nequaquam re-
ligionis differentiam fa-
ciat, sed in omni habitu
qui timet Deum et ope-
ratur iustitiam acceptus
est illi"
John of Salisbury, *Poli-
craticus, VII, 23, PL.*
CXCIX, 700.

I

"Institutum Beghinarum est Belgio Proprium"[1]

The haphazard and ineffective persecution of heresy by German episcopal officials prior to the Johannine legislation, which rested in large part on the Vienne decisions of 1311 and ultimately on the Lateran legislation of 1215, must in no small degree be explained in terms of external factors. The poverty of many Rhenish beguine and beghard communities would appear to have offered little inducement, at least in the thirteenth century, to those church authorities or the members of the secular arm who would be motivated by a desire to confiscate property. The inhabitants of Belgian and French beguinages, it is true, possessed a certain measure of wealth, derived either from donations or from personal resources, but they generally enjoyed influential patronage. Yet rehabilitation proceedings underlined the necessity of restoring property confiscated during the inquisitorial processes.[2] Above all, they were much more successful in holding themselves aloof from the heterodox movements, which compromised their German brothers and sisters, by becoming early interwoven with the fabric of the Church or at least having a working agreement with ecclesiastical authorities. In 1287 the synod of Liége deprived all who did not live in beguinages—and here the question specifically concerned the feminine branch—of the right to wear a peculiar habit and share the privileges of beguines. The prohibition also included those who engaged in business amounting to more than ten marks.[3]

It is difficult to estimate the assets of the sometimes almost infinitesimal German "convents."[4] But from the fact that the beguines were directed to earn their livelihood through work or begging[5] we may

[1] Report of Cardinal Thomas Philip of Alsace de Boussu, archbishop of Malines and primate of the Catholic Netherlands, to Pope Clement XII in 1730 (Greven, in *Der Belfried*, I, 1917, 355).

[2] E.g., Benedict XII's bull of May 28, 1335 on behalf of St. Elizabeth at Ghent (Béthune, *Cartulaire*, p. 83, no. 118).

[3] See above pp. 138, 272f.

[4] Greving, in *AHVN.*, LXXIII (1902), 27, 63; Asen, in *ibid.*, CXI (1927), 102; Woikowsky-Biedau. *Das Armenwesen des mittelalterlichen Köln*, p. 33; cf. Phillips, *Beguines in Medieval Strasburg*, pp. 16ff.

[5] Cf. Stein, *Akten*, II, 690, no. 19: "Item die 12 personen in der zellen in Smeir-

conclude that their income was negligible. The Goch house, for example, commanded little wealth, for real estate which often constituted the bulk of the wealth of religious communities is scarcely mentioned.[6] When voluntary poverty, religious in essence and aim, lost its appeal, in place of the women of substantial family who had willingly surrendered dowry and inheritance[7] came others in the fourteenth century who looked upon the convent as a refuge from misery and need. Here unattached widows and girls received lodging and sometimes money, bread, light, and fuel.[8] Although they were often remembered in wills, the legacies of land and rents were generally small. Their own bequests of insignificant parcels of land or personal belongings—bedding, clothes, and household utensils—[9] even in Belgium, usually testify in like fashion to moderate or meager means. Charitable persons often donated land or pensions to convents or foundations of the church provided the amount of the legacy was distributed to poor women who had attended mass on the anniversary of thefounder's death fur the peace of his soul.[10] By the same token, distribution of alms to certain beguines implies ownership and inequality among the beguines. At Rheims the superior and the four counsellors were to distribute alms after their conscience to the poor women according to need and ability to work.[11] The protocol for the Cologne houses published by Greving[12] offers a larger fund of specific data for the eighty-eight beguinages in that city. Twenty-four *non habent redditus,* fifteen others had income of different kinds, money or natural goods (wheat, rye, wine, wax), or in rights (in mills). The remaining forty-nine possessed income in the form of annual revenue. Of these, thirty-seven convents had upwards to 20 marks, six from 20-40 marks, three from 40-60 marks, and three from 60-80 marks. On the other hand, eleven convents had obligations amounting to six marks and one as much as 20 marks.[13]

Members of a beguine association lived either dispersed throughout

---

straissen zo blijven ind sijch in yrme getzale myet zo vermeirren, want dat synt arme ellendige sustergen ind bidden broit ind wardent der siechen." Cf. Asen, in *AHVN.,* CXI (1927), 96-97, 102.

[6] Schroeder, in *AHVN.,* LXXV (1903), 15.

[7] For social as opposed to religious motivation see above pp. 81-89.

[8] E.g. Ennen-Eckertz, *Quellen,* IV, 416 with regard to the convent of Poulheim at Cologne.

[9] E.g., Cuvelier, *Cartulaire de Val-Benoît,* 540-542 (May 18, 1366; inventory of objects willed by Agnes de Hanse, beguine, to Sybille, d'Oreye, beguine of St. Christopher at Liége); testament of Ida Oliviers de Maillart, beguine at Tirlemont (September 15, 1431), *AHEB.,* XIII (1876), 341-343; Thijs, in *BSSLL.,* XV (1881), 290ff; Albanès, pp. 259f, 264f, 270ff, 281ff.

[10] Greving, in *AHVN.,* LXXIII (1902), 28.

[11] Robert, *Les béguines de Reims,* p. 50, P.J. xii.

[12] Greving publishes the text in *AHVN.,* LXXIII, 41-60; for a description of it, see *ibid.,* pp. 35-40.

[13] *Ibid.,* 63.

towns and villages or else, and more commonly in Belgium, gathered together in sizable *curtes* which, generally built in the beginning just outside the city walls, constituted independent parishes. The beguinage, which has been represented as an attempt to harmonize the individual and the communal of the Middle Ages,[14] might actually be a town on a miniature scale, with the church as the hub. Physically, the institution ranged from the petty, impoverished beguinage at Anderlecht, founded in 1252 hard by the collegiate church of St. Pierre and St. Guido, to the attractive, comparatively sumptuous buildings that encircle the yard of St. Elizabeth at Bruges and give on the Minnewater to the east. The *curtis* resembled sometimes the enclosure of a humble nunnery, with only a well to enliven its drabness, sometimes the tree-studded square of a well-developed city. The community had its own administrative machinery subject, of course, to external controls; but these controls were in the main minimized by immunities and concessions granted by ducal, comital, or echevinal authority and sanctioned by ecclesiastical officials. Although not achieving the stature of an independent order with congregational unity or direction from a motherhouse, the Belgian extraregulars were nonetheless considered from the beginning an effective counterbalance to heresy. Despite their quasi-religious status, their peculiar habit endowed late medieval streets with a monastic character. The full-blown beguinage comprised a church, cemetery, hospital, public square, and streets and walks lined with convents for the younger sisters and pupils and individual houses for the older and well-to-do inhabitants. In the Great Beguinage at Ghent, with its walls and moats, there were at the beginning of the fourteenth century two churches, eighteen convents, over a hundred houses, a brewery, and an infirmary.[15] For the construction

[14] Ollivier (*Le grand Béguinage,* p. 79) characterizes the Great Beguinage at Ghent: "Ainsi, depuis l'an 1233, huit cents personnes librement reunies, continuent à faire, en toute liberté, un merveilleux essai de vie communale, avec son autonomie sans isolement—ses industries très personnelles bien qu'associées, son budget indépendant des economies privées—son autorité centrale fortement assise et agissante, mais tempérée par un conseil qui la rattache à la double autorité superieure de l'Eglise et de l'Etat . . . ." Cf. Francke, *Kulturwerte,* I, 170: ". . . Die Beginen suchen die Zucht und die Strenge des Klosters mit der Freiheit bürgerlichen Lebens zu vereinen." For a romantic description of the beguinage and its life, see Greven, in *Der Belfried,* I, 356. Gertrude Robinson in *The Dublin Review,* CLX 1917, 214, 227-228) considered these societies as an expression of the "democratic spirit."

[15] 1328, Béthune, *Cartulaire,* p. 73; Fredericq, *Corpus,* I, 176. The beguine house, founded outside Malines about 1249, gradually grew into a small walled town (cf. Ullmann, *Reformatoren vor der Reformation,* I, 24); De Potter, *Gesch. d. Stad Kortrijk,* III, 418. The *Obituarium* of St. Pierre's church at Anderlecht lists a numberu of beguines belonging to XIII-XVI C.: Elysabet de Pollaer , for whose anniversary 35 s. were assigned from a bonnier, of meadow in Wolfspute (January 4, ed. Stockmans, *B.G.,* III, 1904, 534); Gertrude, beguine *de Bigardis* (February 13, *ibid.,* 540); Alice, beguine of Bodeghem (February 21, ibid., 541); Lucia de Keleghem (April 7, *ibid.,* IV, 1905, 70); Heilewidis de Zone (June 28, *ibid.,* 80); Alissia de Yserghem (August 14, *ibid.,* 519); Ymme, beguine de Bodeghem (August 28, *ibid.,* 521); Heil-

of a mill Duke John I of Brabant in 1271 (June 13) granted the beguinage of La Vigne at Brussels the necessary land in return for a yearly rent of 12 deniers of Louvain.[16]

Such cohesiveness among the several houses was absent in German cities, save for a few places like Strasbourg where the beguines may be detected in larger units. Real beguinages did not exist in Germany. The beguine parish failed to develop. Only in Wesel, thus in the immediate vicinity of the center of the beguine movement, did a beguine house, called Mariengarten, take shape: it consisted of a large walled *curtis,* with buildings for lodging and work, a chapel, and a bleaching center.[17] Elsewhere the German beguines resided in numerous small houses in which as few as three or four or as many as fifteen to twenty lived together.

The increase in the number of dwellings depended primarily on the extent to which women of substance were admitted. To controvert the oft-cited but all too easy conclusion that the beguinage was a poorhouse, one need only note that the property qualification for admission appears in many of the oldest constitutions. "Item nulla ibidem vidua recipiatur," runs the statute of the Brussels community (1271), "nisi faciat domum inibi de sua propria sorte, vel suis bonis edificari, dum tamen eidem suppetant facultates: que scilicet domus, post mortem hujusmodi vidue, similiter remaneat ad honorem Dei, et de eadem disponatur."[18] Construction of a house was thus the *sine qua non* for admission. Of those houses which had been built from their own resources the beguines possessed no more than the usufruct; after their death these dwellings were earmarked for the poorer inhabitants who were unable to erect their own.[19] Emphasis is rightly put on the voluntary nature of beguinal status and the consequent nonmonastic competence to acquire and alienate property, subject to good conduct. However, this too may become an oversimplification. These statutes often contain clauses which should make the student alive to qualifications which must attend any definition of extraregular or quasireligious. As a case in point, the Brussels statutes stipulate that the

Vigis, beguine of Waienberghe (October 1, *ibid.,* V, 1706, 89); Heilvigis de Rome (November 13, *ibid.,* 95); Ida, beguine of Papsem (November 23, *ibid.,* 95; cf. November 26, *ibid.,* 96); for the *curtis beghinarum* (June 8, *ibid.,* IV, 78; cf. August 26, *ibid.,* 521).

[16] Original in AAPB., Chartier de l'infirmerie de Bruxelles, Carton H. 263.

[17] Heidemann, "Die beguinenhäuser Wesels," *Zeitschrift des bergischen Geschichtsvereins,* IV (1867), 85-114; Uhlhorn, *Liebesthätigkeit,* II, 378-379.

[18] May 17, 1271, original in AGR., arch. eccl., Carton 13402, no. 2.

[19] *Idem:* "Item ad illas domos, quas alique puelle de suis propriis bonis edificari faciunt ibidem, ipse edificatrices non magis optineant vel sibi proprietatis asscribant, quam usufructum, et post earum decessum, hujusmodi domus, ad honorem Dei remaneant, et sub titulo caritatis, ad opus scilicet aliarum pauperum begginarum, proprias sibi domos edificare non valentium, nec eas habentium, talibus prestande ad inhabitandum eas, prout magistratui ipsius curie videbitur expedire."

beguine did not enjoy an absolute property. A concept of corporate ownership imposed restrictions on the claims even of close relatives to inheritance. On the other hand, the householder might designate a lay relative or friend who had expressed a preference for beguinal life to the world.[20] The statutes for Tirlemont (1269 n.s.) underline this principle of usufruct in contrast to ownership: "Quicumque in dicta curia clausa nunc domos construerent, licet aliquantulam quique dederint vel dent aliqui pecuniam pro solo edificii ad communitatem et commoditatem pauperum sublevandum, non tamen hereditatem fundi vel domus proprietatem optinent, sed curia sive communitas curie fundi existentis infra clausuram beghinarum sive domorum hereditatem et proprietatem dinoscitur possidere et habere; inhabitantibus ibidem quamdiu sub magisterio curie obedientes esse voluerint retento quamdiu vixerint usufructu. Consuevit etiam curie magistratus bonis et obedientibus indulgere liberaliter et benigne ut, post mortem ipsarum, aliis beghinaliter vivere volentibus semel ad unam vitam vel duas conferre valeant usufructum, proprietate et dominio hereditatis semper penes communitatem curie residente et remanente."[21]

The Antwerp beguines likewise ordained that when any one who had built or otherwise acquired a house or room and afterwards left the beguinage for marriage, the mistress and rectors could freely dispose of the dwelling with the proceeds being applied to the community. Should the beguine return after her husband's death, she was in no position to reclaim the lodging. At the solicitation of the beguinage this clause received the wholehearted approval of the bishop of Cambrai.[22]

In the beginning the number of buildings that stood in the *curtis* was very small. In an effort to multiply them it was often stipulated that every widow who gained a footing in the community must build a house at her own expense. After death or separation the dwelling became the property of the beguinage. Whereas there were only a few houses in the *curtis* of Tongres in 1272,[23] by 1322 they numbered fifty,

[20] *Idem*: "Nec in hujusmodi domibus in fundo curie sic edificatis, aliquis consanguineus proximus, vel heres defunctarum quicquam proprietatis, proximitatis vel hereditatis asscribere sibi poterit, vel debet deinceps petere quocumque modo vel reclamare. Verum tamen rationi consonum esse videtur et pietati, ut si aliqua puella secularis consanguinea hujusmodi defuncte vel amica seculum relinquere, et ad societatem ipsius curie vel conventus se transferre voluerit, bene et laudabiter vivere, vel etiam se iam transtulerit, hujusmodi puelle fiat gratia de inhabitatione hujusmodi domorum; eo tamen condicto, quod hoc arbitrio et conscientie magistratus curie relinquatur."

[21] Dillen, in *Hagelands Gedenkschriften*, I (1908), 169; cf. Soens, *Cartularium*, pp. 18-20.

[22] November 11, 1294, published by Philippen, *Begijnhoven*, p. 129, note 1.

[23] In that year the beguine Mella de Scarmure willed to Oxilia a little room above the cellar, to Lone and her sisters a room beside the kitchen, to the daughters of Arnold de Betho, knight, a room adjacent to the one occupied by the donor and which was now given to the daughter of Libert de Heynis (Thijs, in *BSSLL.*, XV,

each bearing its own name, either that of the beguine who had caused it to be erected or that of the saint to whose protection it was entrusted. All were charged with rents to be paid for the advantage of the community.[24]

For the nature of property rights and the extent of holdings the beguinage at Brussels may be taken as a case study. We are particularly fortunate in possessing a vast corpus of original documents, dating from 1248. An abundance of titles, donations, wills, and rents is contained in the two *fonds* in the Archives de l'Assistance Publique in Brussels: the Chartrier de l'infirmerie du béguinage (H. 262-270) and the Chartrier de la fondation de Ter Kisten (B. 1452-1455). In addition to the originals which in the majority of cases are in good condition and authenticated with well-preserved ducal, echevinal, and clerical seals, the AAPB. has a cartulary (B. 1460) for Ter Kisten, containing in a fourteenth-century hand 165 entries with a few duplications while the Archives Générales du Royaume, also in Brussels, owns a voluminous cartulary (arch. eccl., 13403) for the infirmary, with more than one thousand acts running from the middle of the thirteenth century well into the fifteenth century. From these collections, as well as from other *fonds,* we can obtain an ample picture of internal growth, with special emphasis on economic-juridical questions, the fullness of which appears to be without parallel for other beguine convents.[25] Similarly, for external history the quality and amplitude of the material will compare favorably with the collection published by Béthune for the beguinage of St. Elisabeth at Ghent.

Numerous donations of real property were made to the beguinage by individuals for the good of their souls and their relatives. Sometimes the donors received the land back to enjoy its use during their life time. The community acquired either real estate outright or subject to a quitrent, or rents (*cens*) secured by immovable property, both inside and outside the *oppidum* of Brussels, and even in distant areas. These titles were given in *aelmoessenen, in pura elemosina,* with or without security. Cases where such parcels of land were donated as allods are rare. This real property included either land suitable for building, vineyards, meadows, woods, or lime-kilns, breweries, etc.

The beguinage comprised in addition to houses, convents, a church, and a cemetery—the physical ingredients of parochial organization—

290-291, no. 3). Similar provisions were contained in the wills of Elizabeth de Berge (1290) (*ibid.,* 299-300, no. 7) and Helwidis de Angulo (1291), (*ibid.,* 301-303, no. 9).
[24] *Ibid.,* 430-432, no. 9.
[25] From the analyses which Thijs gave of numerous wills and other documents in his *Histoire du Béguinage de Tongres* one may obtain a good picture of the property holdings of the Tongres community.

the infirmary and Holy Ghost Table or Ter Kisten.[26] We have just seen that the infirmary, being, as elsewhere, the earliest foundation of the Brussels beguinage, developed into the most richly endowed institution. As a retreat for the sick, it would appear to offer a *raison d'être* for the beguine movement: "Cum a longis temporibus in infirmaria curtis beghinarum de Vinea Bruxellensis mulieres devote pauperes et debiles que de suis propriis facultatibus sustentari nequent recepte fuerunt hospitate..."[27] This becomes more evident upon examination of the site of the original settlement. At Nivelles the beguines with whom Ida associated lived near the chapel of St. Sepulchre which in the beginning was the place of worship for the hospital that bore its name.[28] Multiplication of such an example is easy: at Liége it was St. Christopher, at Tongres, St. James' hospital; at Loon it was the hospital maintained by Villers.[29] While the beguinage at Ghent sprang up in the vicinity of the hospital of Biloke,[30] the Malines community was lodged near the refuge for superannuated and incapacitated priests.[31]

The infirmary was directed by a special mistress who herself depended on the grand mistress and who was in turn aided by assistants. Since the infirmary was regarded as an ordinary hospital, it was subject to surveillance of municipal authorities who installed two *mambours*.[32] In treating property the 1271 statutes of Brussels[33] distinguished the *bona curie* which were also called *bona infirmarie* or *communia bona*. From this property not only were the chaplains and debts of the infirmary paid, but it also provided for ordinary maintenance of the entire *curtis* whether it was the construction or repair of the enclosure or wall, moats, bridges, or roads that was intended. Again, it distributed alms to the poor. Alongside the *bona infirmarie* were the *bona ecclesie* which must keep up the church, its ornaments, altars, doors, offerings, utensils, lights, windows, and roof. This property came entirely from alms: rents, produce, land, meadows, etc. Its disposal rested with the pastor and four mistresses and

[26] For a summary of these institutions see Philippen, *Begijnhoven*, pp. 281-301.

[27] AAPB., Carton H. 262, December 8, 1372. See the inventory made on September 26 (*feria quinta ante festum beati Michaelis Archangeli*) 1308 by Catherine Marlemans, mistress of the infirmary of the beguinage, and Jotha de Strombeek, mistress of the Holy Ghost Table, of donations "ad o pus infirmarie ac mense sancti spiritus sive chiste elemosinarie... Vinee beghinarum" at Brussels (original) in AAPB, Carton H 270 [3]; two XIV C. copies: I) AAPB, B. 1460, Cartul. de Ter Kisten, ff. 59r-61r, no. 155; 2) AGR., arch. eccl., 13403, ff 43v-45r, no. 9).

[28] Tarlier and Wauters, *Géog. et hist. des communes belges, Canton de Nivelles*, I, 150; Greven, in *HJ.*, XXXV (1914), 57.

[29] Greven, in *Belfried*, I, 364.

[30] Béthune, *Cartulaire*, p. 302.

[31] *AHEB.*, XII (1875), 23.

[32] Philippen, *Begijnhoven*, pp. 286-287.

[33] AAPB., Carton H. 262 (two copies in Flemish and one in Latin of XVIII C.); original is in AGR., arch. eccl., Carton 13402, no. 2.

procurators. Just as this institution with its possessions was taken under the protection of the dukes of Brabant in 1270[34] and 1293,[35] so on February 8 or 15, 1304 John II, for the salvation of his soul, relieved the beguines from the gabelles and tailles on goods.[36] From 1372 on the infirmary enjoyed automatically, after the death of beguines who had lived and been buried there, the right to inherit all movable and immovable goods unless the inmates had at the time of their death legitimate children.[37] Malefactors who claimed to be their heirs had been appropriating the modest property of the deceased. Furthermore, the privilege of Duchess Jeanne of Brabant makes it clear that the infirmary was not only a hospital for the sick but also a charitable foundation for the indigent.[38] It was of vital importance that the charges of the infirmary should not alienate its property.

The donation acts often specify the destination for the rent or revenue granted, whether the distribution of wine or food on certain feast-days.

The Holy Ghost Table or Ter Kisten (*chista*) at Brussels was a foundation, modelled after the municipal charitable institutions, to aid through the distribution of food or money a certain number of sisters who were unable to support themselves. By the twelfth century the old charitable organization of the parish had broken down as a result of confiscation of its revenues by priests and nobles. But coinciding with the flowering of communal life in Belgium, new institutions rose to take its place.[39] Specific mention must be made of the agency known as the Tables of the Holy Ghost, Tables du Saint-Esprit, Tables des pauvres, Tafels van den Heiligen Geest, armendisch, mensae Sancti Spiritus, mensae pauperum.[40] It was an essentially

---

[34] John I (August, 1270), AAPB., Carton H. 262.

[35] April 23, 1293, AAPB., Carton H. 262.

[36] Original in Flemish, AAPB., Carton H. 262. Since the date is „saterdaechs vore grote vastellavont," it would be February 8 if one follows Grotefend or February 15 according to Giry. For a Latin edition see Ryckel, p. 178; MF., II, 1011; cf. Wauters, *TC.*, VIII, 103.

[37] "Proles de carne sua legitime procreatas" (Jeanne of Brabant's privilege of December 8, 1372, AAPB., Carton H. 262; a French translation of the 18th [?] century is contained therein). That heirs of the beguines continued to claim their inheritance is evident from the vidimus of October 17, 1471 (AGR., arch. eccl., 13403. Cartulaire de l'infirmerie, f. 379r-379v, no. 1076). Henne and Wauters. (*Histoire de Bruxelles.* III, 531) report, on the flimsy evidence of Sanderus, that in this year there were 1200 beguines in the community.

[38] Cf. statutes of May 17, 1271, AGR., arch. eccl., Carton 13402, no. 2.

[39] " 'Tafels van den Heiligen Geest,' of korter 'Heilig-Geesten' of 'Tafels der Armen,' heet men te onzent die weldadigheidsinstellingen, welke specifiek parochieel in hun werking, diep godsdienstig in hun geest, maar burgerlijk en gemeentelijk in hun oorsprong en in gansch hun wezen, het regelmatig ondersteunen ten doel hebben der noodlijdende leden van de parochie-familie, en zulks in al hun noodwendigheden" (Withof, in *Handelingen van den Mechelschen Kring*, XXXII, [1927], 85).

[40] *Ibid.*, 85-134; *ibid.*, XXXIII (1928), 35-89; Laenen, *Introduction*, pp. 196-211;

Flemish institution unknown in France and Germany.[41] Founded spontaneously by laymen, these tables more than filled the lacuna left by the disappearance of the former charitable organization of the parish, and in the middle ages became by far the most important centers for the distribution of poor relief in the towns of the Low Countries.[42] Like the beguinages themselves, they developed in each town without formal creation, entirely local in origin and administration. Whereas the Bruges[43] and Audenarde[44] tables appeared first, in the twelfth century, most of the other Flemish towns received theirs in the following century: Antwerp (1239)[45] Tongres,[46] Léau[47] and Lierre,[48] (1243), Tirlemont (1257),[49] Fosses (1234),[50] Malines (1220),[51] Louvain (1236),[52] Dinant,[53] and Bouvignes.[54]

The beginnings of Ter Kisten of the beguines in Brussels, also known as "la Caisse de la Vigne" and Table of the Holy Ghost in La Vigne ("die Heilige Ghest van den Wingaerde") in the summary of Ter Kisten property, drawn up in July, 1300, under Alice vander Coestraten,[55] are obscure, but certainly the foundation dates later than the infirmary. The statutes of 1271 make no reference to it with the other institutions of the beguinage. Since it is first mentioned in

id., *Geschiedenis van Mechelen*, pp. 373-375; Ligtenberg, pp. 158-207; Marx, *Development of Charity*, pp. 47-50; Leuridan, *Les Tables des pauvres à Roubaix*; Geudens, *Le compte moral*, pp. xii-xxiv; Laenen, in *La vie diocesaine*, VI (1912), 489-505; Alberdingk Thijm, *Wohlthätigkeitsanstalten*, pp. 47-50.

[41] Withof, p. 86; Laenen, *Introduction*, p. 199; Marx, *Development of Charity*, p. 49.

[42] These tables must not be confused, as Alberdingk-Thijm (*De Gestichten*, pp. 105-106; *Wohlthätigkeitsanstalten*, pp. 48-49) and Liese (II, 17-18) did, with the order of the Holy Ghost, founded by Guy of Montpellier (d. 1208) in the latter part of the twelfth century with the aim of establishing hospitals in Western Europe (Marx, *Development of Charity*, pp. 49-50; Withof, pp. 96f). Cf. Innocent III's bull of April 22, 1198, where he commends Guy as the "fundator hospitalis S. Spiritus apud Montem Pessulanum ac eius fratrum" (*PL.*, CCXIV, 83, no. 95; Potthast, no. 96; cf. Honorius III's bull of April 8, 1225, Potthast, no. 7394).

[43] De Schodt, *Meréaux*, p. 291; Van Hoorebeke, *Description*, p. 132.

[44] Vanderstraeten, *Recherches*, II, 139.

[45] Geudens, *Le compte moral*, pp. xiii-xiv; in parish of St. Walburge, 1262, see will of Catherine Wilmarsdochter, April 24 (*BG.*, VI [1907], 334).

[46] In his will of 1267 Renier de Tongres mentioned immediately after his legacy to the beguines of St. Catherine's and their hospital that he was leaving one bonnier of land "ad mensem sancti Spiritus" (Paquay, *Regesta de Renier*, p. 73); it is not clear whether this was the table in the beguinage or in the town. But since Renier followed this bequest with one for the church of Poperinghe and Villers it is probable that it was the municipal table.

[47] Bets, *Zout-Leeuw*, I, 222ff; Laenen, *Introduction*, p. 199.

[48] Stockmans, *Beknopte inventaris*, p. 9.

[49] Bets, *Histoire de Tirlemont*, II, 224-227, P.J. 12; cf. *ibid.*, pp. 163-165.

[50] "Tabula pauperum," *Cartul. de Fosse*, ed. J. Borgnet, p. 10, no. 5.

[51] Laenen, *Geschiedenis van Mechelen*, pp. 381-382; id., *Introduction*, p. 200.

[52] Van Even, *Louvain*, pp. 640-644; Marx, *Development of Charity*, pp. 55f.

[53] In 1283 Dinant had a hospital, a beguinage, and a *mensa s. Spiritus* (Alberdingk Thijm, *Wohlthätigkeitsanstalten*, p. 62).

[54] *Cartul. de Fosses*, ed. Borgnet, p. 11, no. 5.

[55] AAPB., Registre B. 1461, ff. 17, 38.

July, 1274,[56] it was probably founded between these two dates. However, donations to Ter Kisten do not become numerous until after 1290. Nor does the Holy Ghost Table in St. Elizabeth beguinage at Ghent emerge from obscurity, on the basis of Béthune's cartulary, until December, 1278, through a donation of Simon Braem. Margaret and Elisabeth of Alost, beguines and procurators of the Table, accepted 21 livres.[57] But its assets were built up above all during the fourteenth century. Alms from Ter Kisten and the infirmary must be used by the inmates for their own needs. When a beguine was maintained for life, her goods were divided between the two institutions. Maintenance by the infirmary and Ter Kisten at Lierre was contingent on residence in the *curtis* for at least three years.[58]

No energetic scramble for property such as motivated the northern French knights on the Albigensian crusade marked the anti-beguine action. At the same time, however, John XXII in his bull *Racio recta* (August 13, 1318) implied that confiscation of property accompanied the persecution of orthodox semi-religious.[59] In 1317 John of Strasbourg, in an exhortation to the clergy, ordered that houses and goods of heretical beguines should be handed over to the Church to aid the poor.[60] In the numerous special enactments in which John XXII took certain beguine communities under his protection, he demanded the inviolability of their property.[61] It is amply evident that, in the wake of the repressive steps that marked John's pontificate, beguine property was being seized.[62]

[56] AAPB., B. 1460, Cartul. de Ter Kisten, f. 1v, no. 2.
[57] Béthune, *Cartulaire*, pp. 31-32, no. 38.
[58] Statutes of 1401, Philippen, *Begijnhoven*, p. 340.
[59] "Si quid forsan ex hoc in bonis aut juribus suis quibuscumque contra eas attemptatum est hactenus" (Fredericq, *Corpus*, II, 73). Cf. Papebroch, *Annales Antverp.*, I, 74-75.
[60] Mosheim, p. 259.
[61] Letter to the Brussels beguines (May 23, 1319) in which he took under protection the Brabançon beguines and their "terras, domos, possessiones, prata, paschua et alia bona" (Fredericq, *Corpus*, II, 79; cf. *Beschrijvinge van het beggijn hof van Brussel* [Bibl. roy. de Belg., cod. 16566-74], f. 3v). For further examples, see below pp. 000-000.
[62] The pope ordered confiscated property to be returned to the beguinages at Termonde (January 13, 1317) (J. Broeckaert, *Cartularium van het begijnhof van Dendermonde,* Oudheidkundige Kring der stad Dendermonde buitengewone uitgaven, no. 10, Termonde, 1902), p. 19, no. 14; Fredericq, *Corpus*, III, 160-161, no. 139. Later in that year (September 7) he sent similar instructions to the cantor of Notre-Dame at Antwerp on behalf of the beguinage at Alost (*ibid.*, III, 161-162, no. 140: ". . . Easdem decimas, terras, domos, possessiones, castra, grangias, piscarias, prata, nemora, molendina, jura, jurisdictiones et quedam alia bona ipsius domus Dei," p. 161). On January 23, 1346 Clement VI, without specifying hostile acts, repeated the previous order to the cantor of St. Gudule at Brussels to return property to the infirmary of the beguinage of Termonde (Broeckaert, *Cartularium van het begijn hof van Dendermonde,* pp. 30-31, no. 24; Fredericq, *Corpus*, III, 165, no. 144). In a directive to the clergy in charge of the beguinages (October 24, 1324) the bishop of Liége, Adolph de la Marck, forbade molestation of person of property with regard to the beguines of St. Christopher in the Liége suburbs, Tongres, Maestricht,

Moreover concomitants of external well-being of these associations were internal decay and corruption of customs and doctrine, introduced by absorption of heterogeneous elements. As the beguines and beghards experienced an enormous expansion, they were less able to withstand the appeal of the heretical movements with which they came into contact, owing to the absence of centralized authority and a well-ordered life based on a rule. We have seen that in the period of spontaneous growth the Belgian beguines were not immune from local attack and demanded protection from such churchmen as Jacques de Vitry. As early as 1242 Jeanne of Flanders deemed it necessary to instruct her magistrates to defend them against their despoilers. Three years later (November 23, 1245) her sister Margaret reiterated the recommendation.[63] In 1261 Urban IV enjoined the dean of Louvain "to assist them against those who would rashly afflict them, and not to allow anyone to molest them by process either in person or property."[64]

Although it would be presumptuous to claim[65] that the decline of beguine-beghard communities began with Gregory X's renewal of the Fourth Lateran prohibition of new forms of religious life at the second council of Lyons (1274),[66] nevertheless it was increasingly apparent during the last quarter of the thirteenth century that to justify their *raison d'être* in the face of abundant charges of heresy and immorality these confraternities must seek recognition by adopting a third rule or Augustinian prescriptions.

St. Trond, Louvain, Tirlemont, Léau, Diest, Borchloon, Hasselt, and Aerschot (*ibid.*, II, 87). In 1335 (January 15) he again lodged protest, this time against the ducal officials who were disturbing the property of the Léau beguines (*ibid.*, II, 301-302). A similar directive had been sent by Adolph in 1325 (March 1) to the pastor of the new beguinage at Roermond (*ibid.*, II, 88-89, no. 54).

[63] Hoornaert publishes (*ASEB.*, 1904, 289-290, no. 23) Margaret's instructions. MF. (III, 592) contains a document "ex archivis Beguinagii" of Bruges which is identical with that of the countess, but comes from Jeanne and is dated April 5, 1242. Although there is no trace of the earlier one—not even a vidimus or confirmation from Guy de Dampierre and Louis de Nevers who generally approved privileges granted by their predecessors to the beguinage at Bruges—both texts are general and make no specific mention of the community (cf. Hoornaert, *op. cit.*, 289, note 1).

[64] Mosheim, pp. 140f.

[65] Jundt, *Histoire du panthéisme*, p. 46.

[66] Can. 23, Hefele-Leclercq, VI, 1, 201-202; Mansi, XXIV, 96-97.

II

Tares in the Vineyard

Just as personal acts and beliefs were adjudged treasonable in the sixteenth century if they were considered subversive of the social conventions and political institutions demanded by recently matured omnicompetent nation-states, so similar convictions and conduct that threatened to rend the fabric of the all-absorbing medieval Christian Commonwealth—the *Respublica Christiana*—fashioned, guided, and disciplined under papal auspices, were labelled heretical in the days of Innocent III and his successors.[1] What is said of one isolated movement that spread widely applies well to all: "So varied and manifold is it that it cannot be easily comprehended by a single term."[2] Discussions of popular heresy or sectarianism usually concentrate on well-known movements—the Albigensians, Cathari, Waldensians, and the Free Spirits—evangelical or—Gnostic-Manichaean or neo-Platonic in content, or else on certain heresiarchs, but often neglect the wide prevalence of heterodox notions and superstitions that flourished among the illiterate. These misconceptions and yearnings—half—submerged, and often ill-defined and confused—nevertheless could be potent if only a spokesman, with the aid of socioeconomic unrest, should rise to channel them into a coordinated and determined attack on existing civil and ecclesiastical institutions.

WILLIAM CORNELIUS

More than a century after Tanchelm, Antwerp witnessed another petty heresiarch, William Cornelius, who is known almost exclusively from Thomas of Cantimpré's testimony,[3] who was then coadjutor of Bishop Nicholas of Cambrai.[4] "In our time (i.e., ca. 1252)," writes the

[1] Letter of March 25, 1199, to the magistrates of Viterbo, Ep. II, 1, *PL.*, CCXIV, 537-539.

[2] Letter of Liége clergy to Lucius II, 1145, Fredericq, *Corpus*, I, 32; MDAC., I, 776-777.

[3] *BUA.*, II, 47, 3; Fredericq, *Corpus*, I, 120-121, no. 126; id., *Gesch. d. Inquis.*, I, 84; Prims, in *BG.*, XVIII (1927), 217-224.

[4] Fredericq, *Corpus*, I, 121, note.

Dominican, "there was at Antwerp one William Cornelius who attempted to rend the Lord's tunic of faith by an unreasonable heresy." Long given over to hypocrisy and dissimulation, he relinquished the fruits of his prebend under pretense of complete poverty, while yielding at the same time entirely to pleasure. He taught that just as rust is consumed by fire so sin is annihilated by poverty and destroyed before God's eyes. A poor prostitute is better than a chaste person who owns property; for this reason he condemned the entire clergy (*religiosi*). Thomas had heard "from the most reliable source" that in 1248 the heretic was buried with honor in the church of Our Lady, but that three days later his tomb was discovered open and empty. After examining, exposing, and condemning the heresy for four years the bishop had the body removed from the grave and burned. It has been assumed from *prebende beneficium* and church burial that William was a canon.[5]

What adds stature to William is the social implication of his teaching. Not only did indulgences, hell, excommunication, confession, and communion encourage Antwerp heretics to break with the Church, but they proclaimed the virtue of total poverty. This is most clearly brought out in a fragment bearing the title, "Hec sunt hereses, que fuerunt dampnate contra quosdam de Antwerpia,"[6] which is contained in MS. 15954 (f. 263ᵛ) of the *fonds latin* in the Bibliothèque nationale at Paris, dating earlier than 1300. It is a list of twenty-one propositions which Prims has conveniently grouped in three categories:

   I *Importance of poverty.*
     Alms can never become excessive. Since every rich person is avaricious, he cannot aspire to salvation. The poor are in a state of grace and cannot be condemned. "Simplex fornicatio" is not sinful for one living in poverty. Ownership of two garments of the same kind obstructs salvation. It is just to take from the rich to give to the poor. Invitation of a rich man to one's table entails mortal sin.

  II *Mortal sins are threefold:*
     envy, avarice, and "prodigalitas indiscreta et cognoscere uxorem suam impregnatam." There is no sin against nature.

 III *Indulgences from prelates are not efficacious.*
     A priest in mortal sin is unable to consecrate, absolve, or impose penance. On the other hand, any priest can absolve from sin as well as a bishop. The existence of hell is denied; no one can be excommunicated or excommunicate. It is better to receive the body of Christ once a year, even in a state of mortal sin, than not to receive it at all.

Bishop Guy of Cambrai set out for the city on the Scheldt to sup-

[5] E.g., Diercxsens, *Antverpia*, I, 237: "Inter canonicos erat Willelmus." Prims (*l.c.*, 221, cf. 219) concluded that William shared a chaplaincy with Nicholas Pride.
[6] Fredericq, *Corpus*, I, 119-120, no. 125.

press this heresy but he died on the way at the monastery of Afflighem in 1247.[7] It therefore remained for his successor to continue the prosecution. That episcopal pressure was put on the Antwerp heretics is suggested in a bull of Alexander IV (January 9, 1257) addressed to the abbot of St. Guilain and the provost of St. Géry. It called for a substantial assessment of church property in view of the heavy debts which the bishop had contracted, particularly in his prosecution of local heretics with the help of the secular arm.[8]

THE "BEGUINE CLERGERESSE"

Even though a certain area might be considered "loyal," the appearance of a few heresiarchs such as Margaret Porete of Hainault[9] or Bloemardinne of Brussels who went under the name of *beguine* had the immediate consequence not only of casting discredit upon the feminine movement but of sharpening the antagonism of ecclesiastical and secular authorities to extraregular associations generally. The trial and execution of Margaret[10] at Paris in 1310 could very well have been a case in point for the opposition to the semireligious voiced at the Council of Vienne.[11]

According to the continuer of the chronicle of Guillaume de Nangis, Margaret was a "beguine clergeresse"[12] who had first been active at Valenciennes. Later in Lorraine—and hence within the jurisdiction of the arch bishop of Rheims — she published a book, presumably in Latin, which, in the opinion of the theologians who examined it, contained many errors. This first prosecution would appear to have occurred at least fifteen years before her death in Paris. She taught, for example, that a "soul which annihilates itself in the love of its Creator can without regret accord to nature everything that it desires."[13] The report of an examination of Margaret's book by theologians of Paris,

[7] Thomas of Cantimpré, *BUA.*, I, 4, 4 (p. 21).

[8] Fredericq, *Corpus*, I, 128-129, no. 133; cf. id., *Gesch. de Inquis.*, I, 85.

[9] Fredericq, *Corpus*, I, 155-160, nos. 164-166; II, 63-65, nos. 37-39; id., *Gesch. d. Inquis.*, II, 16-19; Lea, *History of the Inquisition*, II, 123, 575-578 (App.); Langlois, "Marguerite Porète," *Revue historique*, LIV (1894), 295-299.

[10] For B. Hauréau (*HLF.*, XXVII, 1877, p. 70) and Ollivier (*op. cit.*, p. 41) Margaret was a forerunner of Molinos and Mme. Guyon, the quietists.

[11] Henne and Wauters, (*Histoire de Bruxelles*, I, 87) regarded Bloemardinne, active during this period in Brussels, as a cause for the antibeguine legislation at Vienne.

[12] *Les grandes chroniques de France*, June 1, 1310 (ed. Paulin Paris, 1837), V, 188; Fredericq, *Corpus*, II, 64, no. 38. Jean d'Outremeuse in his *Ly Myreur des Histors* (ed. Bormans), VI, 141 refers to Margaret as "une beghine en clergrie mult suffissant, en cheli lieu propre que ons nom Margarite-porte," Cf. Fredericq, *Corpus*, II, 64, no. 39; *Continuatio Chronici Guillelmi de Nangiaco*, Bouquet, XX (1840), 601; *Chronique de Saint-Denis depuis 1285 jusqu'en 1328*, Bouquet, XX (1840), 685-686.

[13] Guillaume de Nangis, in Fredericq, *Corpus*, I, 160: "Quod anima annihilata in amore conditoris sine reprehensione conscientiae vel remorsu potest et debet naturae quidquid appetit et desiderat concedere, quod manifeste sonat in haeresim."

including a canon John of Ghent, at the request of the inquisitor, William (April 11, 1310), discloses two articles in the book which were adjudged heretical.[14] This *anima annihilata,* far from acting as a law for virtues, actually marshals them to its service. Through this complete absorption of the soul in God all human obligations, all prescriptions and ethics, dissolve: they are "annihilated." Here is the kernel of a pantheistic doctrine whereby she could claim kinship with the Brethren of the Free Spirit or the heretics in Ries[15] and which may also link her with an enriched Tanchelmite tradition. It was further claimed that she had translated Scripture with the result of introducing errors.[16]

Bishop Guy II of Cambrai (1296-1306) had first spared Margaret in Hainault, while forbidding her on pain of execution from circulating her book or disseminating its ideas. At the same time he ordered the book to be burned publicly in her presence at Valenciennes. Yet when her persistence in distributing the work among the simple folk known as beghards,[17] and even the audacity of presenting the prohibited book to Bishop John of Châlons, brought her before Guy's successor, Philippe de Marigny and the inquisitor of Lorraine, she again escaped without suffering penalty. In 1308 she extended her propaganda to Paris where she fell into the hands of the Dominican inquisitor, Guillaume de Paris, chaplain of the pope and confessor of the king, before whom she obstinately refused to take the preliminary oath required for examination. Until the beguine reached the city she had crossed the path of the episcopate only; in Paris it was the papal inquisitor who supervised the process. Presumably too preoccupied with the Templar affair[18] to give Margaret prompt justice, the inquisitor kept her imprisoned for a year and a half. This would have sufficed for her conviction as an impenitent heretic, but her previous career made her a relapsed heretic. The inquisitor relates in the decision how he spent many months gathering evidence against the beguine, examining her life and acquainting himself with her relations with the bishops of Cambrai and Châlons.[19] Instead of calling an assembly of experts, as was customary in Languedoc, the inquisitor laid a written

[14] The first, "Quod anima adnichilata dat licentiam virtutibus nec est amplius in earum servitute, quia non habet eas quoad usum, sed virtutes obediunt ad nutum"; and the fifteenth, "Quod talis anima non curat de consolacionibus Dei nec de donis ejus, nec debet curare nec potest, quia tota intenta est circa Deum, et sic impediretur ejus intentio circa Deum." Lea, *History of the Inquisition,* II, 575-578; Fredericq, *Corpus,* II, 63-64; Langlois, in *Revue historique,* LIV (1894), 296-297.

[15] Grundmann, *Religiöse Bewegungen,* pp. 431-432.

[16] See above, pp. 367-368. For Margaret and the *Mirouer des simples ames* see Axters, *Gesch. van Vroomheid,* II, 169-178.

[17] "Pluribus aliis personas simplicibus, Begardis et aliis" (Fredericq, *Corpus,* I, 157).

[18] Cf. Fredericq, *Gesch. d. Inquis.,* II, 114-120.

[19] Fredericq, *Corpus,* I, 156-157; Lea, *History of the Inquisition,* II, 577-578.

statement of case before the professors of canon law at Paris—William called Frater, archdeacon of St. Andrew's in Scotland; Hugh of Besançon, canon of Paris; Jean de Tollenz, canon of St. Quentin in Vermandois; Henry of Béthune, canon of Furnes; and Peter de Vaux, pastor of St. Germain l'Auxerrois at Paris. They unanimously decided on May 30, 1310, that if the facts as stated were true she was a relapsed heretic and must be relaxed to the secular arm. The following day she was accordingly handed over, with the usual adjuration for mercy, to the *prévôt* of Paris who had her burned the next day in the Place de Grève. She conducted herself with such resignation and courage that she drew tears from the spectators.[20] One of her disciples, a clerk of the diocese of Beauvais named Guion de Cressonessart, attempted to save her; on being seized, he followed her example by refusing to take oath during eighteen months of imprisonment. He called himself the Angel of Philadelphia who had been despatched by God to comfort the followers of Christ. Finally he was degraded from orders and condemned to perpetual imprisonment.[21]

It would be presumptuous to claim that Margaret was a member of the ecclesiastically-minded, orthodox beguine movement with which she was identified in Hainault; nor can her affiliation with the beguines in the strict sense be proved by the use of the term *beguina*. As we have repeatedly seen, it was indiscriminately applied to the adherents of many an extraregular association or to lay affiliates of religious orders.[22] Margaret may very well have been one of the free beguines—and her wandering life points to it—who had no permanent residence, lived by begging, were guilty of moral laxity, hesitated to submit to ordained spiritual officials, and were receptive to heretical ideas. She was a sectarian, far removed in spirit and practice from the real beguine movement, the *beguinae clausae*, who in Belgium and northern France had long been bound to a well-ordered existence.[23] It is not without reason that she has been called the first French representative of the German sect of the Brothers and Sisters of the Free Spirit.[24]

BLOEMARDINNE OF BRUSSELS

The Poretist pantheistic doctrine, which perhaps ultimately derived from Tanchelm, was soon after to be revived by the shadowy personage known as Bloemardinne of Brussels.[25] She too taught that man

[20] Continuer of *Chronicon* of Guillaume de Nangis, in Fredericq, *Corpus*, I, 160.
[21] *Ibid.*, p. 159.
[22] Haupt, in ZKG., VII (1885), 532, 541.
[23] Philippen, *Begijnhoven*, p. 134; Christ, *La Règle des Fins Amans*, pp. 177f.
[24] Lea, *History of the Inquisition*, I, 136.
[25] For the old studies which confused Bloemardinne with Hadewijch see Frede-

could attain a state in which sin as well as moral development became impossible for him, and that in this state of complete passivity before God he might indulge with impunity his every passion, even the most shameful.

In the biography of Ruysbroeck which Henry de Pomerio or Henry vanden Bogaert (1382-1454), canon of Groenendael, inserted about 1440 in his *De Origine Monasterii Viridisvallis*[26] there is a brief chapter (II, 5) entitled "Quomodo occultam quamdam haeresim et ejus fautricem, dictam vulgariter Bloemardinne, in oppido Bruxellensi famosam, confutavit."[27] Although written about half a century after Ruysbroeck's death and almost one hundred years after the heresiarch, this fragment remains the primary source for both her career and teachings.[28] The text runs as follows:

At the same time that the servant of God (i.e., Ruysbroeck) was still a secular priest there lived in the town of Brussels a woman who clung to perverted doctrines and who was commonly called Bloemardinne. Such was popular esteem of her that it was imagined that whenever she appeared before the altar to receive the Holy Communion she walked between two rows of Seraphim. Since she had written much on the spirit of freedom and on the most abominable venereal love which she called seraphic, she was revered by many followers as the founder of a new doctrine. Indeed when teaching and writing she sat on a silver seat which, it is said, was offered after her death to the duches of Brabant

ricq, *Gesch. d. Inquis.*, II, 40-50; id. "De Geheimzinnige Ketterin Bloemardinne (Zuster Hadewijch) en de Secte der 'Nuwe' te Brussel in de 14e Eeuw," *VMKVA.*, 3rd ser., XII; also extract, Amsterdam, 1895; Edward van Even, „Bloemardinne: De Brusselse Ketterin, gestorven in 1335 en hare Volgelingen in de 15e eeuw," *VMKVA.*, VII (1894), 357-390. Van Mierlo has been most responsible in rehabilitating Hadewijch as an orthodox poet of the thirteenth century, not in any way to be identified with the heresiarch: "Hadewijch en Wilhelm van St. Thierry," *OGE.*, III (1929), 45-59; "Was Hadewych de Ketterin Blomardinne?" *D. War. Belf.*, 1908, 267-286; "Hadewijch, een Gelukzalige Bloemardinne?" *ibid.*, XXV (1925), 28-49; "Uit de Geschiedenis van onze middeleeuwsche Letterkunde: Wanneer heeft Hadewijch geleefd?" *ibid.*, XXI (1921), 135-153; "Beata Hadewigis de Antverpia," *ibid.*, XXVII (1927), 789-798, 833-843; "Was Hadewijch de Ketterin Blommardine?" *ibid.*, X (1908), 267-286; "Hadewijch en Eckart," *ibid.*, XXIII (1923), 1138-1155; "Hadewijchiana I-III," *VMKVA.*, 1927, 195-225, 425-442; "De poëzie van Hadewijch," *ibid.*, 1931, 285-439; "Hadewijch, une mystique flamande du treizième siècle," *Revue d'ascetique et de mystique*, V (1924), 269-289, 380-404; "Hadewijch en de Ketterin Blommardinne," *Tijdschrift voor nederlandsche Taal en Letterkunde*, XI (1921), 45-64; *Hadewijch* (Brussels-Amsterdam, 1926); "Encore Hadewijch et Bloemardinne," *Revue belge de philologie et d'histoire*, VII (1928), 582-595; "Adelwip," *VMKVA.*, 1933, 581-598; "De Bloemardinne-episode in het leven van den gelukz. Joh. van Ruusbroec," *OGE.*, VII (1933), 305-341; "Hadewijchiana," *OGE.*, XVII (1943), 179-184. Cf. Wautier d'Aygalliers, *Ruysbroeck l'Admirable*, pp. 76ff.

[26] *AB.*, IV (1885), 263-322; for Henry see A. Van Renterghem, *BNB.*, XVII (1903), coll. 925-927; *Messager*, 2nd ser., XXXIV (1866), 284; *BARB*, 1864, p. 679.

[27] *AB.*, IV (1885), 286.

[28] Henry drew from a biography written by an associate of Ruysbroeck at Groenendale for four years, namely Jean de Schoonhoven, Johannes de Schoenhovia, who became a monk in the monastery in 1377 and died in 1431 (Willem de Vreese, in *BNB.*, XXI (1911-13, 883-903). Cf. Henry Pomerius' introduction, *AB.*, XV (1885), 263-265.

because of her admiration of her ideas. The halt believed thaat by touching her dead body they could be made well again. This man (Ruysbroeck), filled with the spirit of piety, felt pity for this error and opposed the perverted teaching. However many disciples she may have had, she took up the shield of truth and rightfully exposed her fallacious and heretical writings which she was accustomed, as if inspired by God, to spread each year in order to undermine our faith. In this she displayed a determined spirit of wisdom and daring neither fearing the ambushes of her followers nor being deceived by the paint of her false doctrines which had the appearance of truth. I can affirm from my personal experience that these writings, though excessively baleful, have such an aspect of truth that no one can perceive in them any seed of heresy save with the grace and assistance of Him who teaches all truth."[29]

Identification of Bloemardinne with the poetess of the thirteenth century and contemporary of Beatrice of Nazareth can no longer be maintained. But it is possible that she is the "domicella Heilwigis dicte Blomards" mentioned in echevinal letters at the beginning of the fourteenth century.[30] This Heilwigis bought several houses in Brussels between 1305 and 1306 and was able to lend money to numerous ecclesiastics, including canons of Saint Gudule.[31] The wealth at her command agrees with the detail of Pomerius' description of the silver seat and her appeal to the ruling class. Near her house lived

[29] "Erat in oppido Bruxellensi eo tempore quo Dei famulus adhuc presbyter mansit in seculo, mulier quaedam perversi dogmatis, dicta vulgariter Bloemardinne, tantae famae et opinionis ut etiam tempore sacrae communionis, quando videlicet ad aram accederet, inter duos gradi seraphim crederetur. Haec multa scribens de spiritu libertatis et nefandissimo amore venereo, quem et seraphicum appellabat, tanquam inventrix novae doctrinae a multis suae opinionis discipulis venerabatur. Sedebat quippe docens et scribens in sede argentea: quae quidem sedes, ob suae opinionis redolentiam, post ejus obitum ducissae Brabantiae fuisse dicitur praesentata. Cujus etiam defuncti corporis attactu claudi se putabant posse consequi sanitatem. Huic igitur errori compatiens vir plenus spiritu pietatis, illico perversae se doctrinae opposuit; et quamvis multos haberet aemulos, scuto circumdatus veritatis, scripta fucata et haeretica quae tanquam divinitus inspirata illa quotannis in fidei nostrae derogationem disseruit, ipse veraciter denudavit. In quo profecto spiritum sapientiae et fortitudinis sibi ostendit satis imbibitum, non veritus insidias aemulantium, nec fuco deceptus falsorum dogmatum sub consonantia veritatis. Expertus enim de testimonium, quod scripta illa nefandissima taliter fuere prima facie veritatis specie supervestita, quod nemo possit erroris deprehendere seminarium, nisi per Illius gratiam et auxilium qui docet omnem veritatem" (*AB.*, IV, 286; Fredericq, *Corpus*, I, 186, no. 189).

[30] Van Mierlo (in *OGE.*, VI, 1932, 304-306) concludes that Bloemardinne was that Heilwijch Bloemarts who appears in Brussels documents as the daughter of Willem Blomaerts, an echevin in, the city (1281, Wauters, in *Annal. soc. arch. Bruxelles*, 1894, 427; in 1282, 1283, 1284, *ibid.*, 427; in 1285, 428). Cf. Peene, *Land- en Cijnsboek St. Janshospitaal*, III (Brussels, 1949), 489, no. 112.

[31] Bloemardinne lived near the present Rue des Paroissiens in 1305: "... Heilwigis dicta de Merbeke contulit domicelle Heilwigi dicte Bloemart et Machtildi dicte de Bigarden demidium domistadii, ab opposito Gerelini Heincart, et domum sitam in dicto domistadio, demidium domistadii, sitam in cono, ab opposito fratrum dictorum Cryenblike et demidium domistadii contigui, versus Hospitale sancte Gudule, ab opposito dictorum fratrum, etc." (echevinal act of 1305, Van Even, *op. cit.*, p. 15, note 1).

Jan Hinckaert, a canon of St. Gudule and son of Gerelm Hinckaert, an echevin of Brussels at the close of the century.[32] John Ruysbroeck belonged to the same neighborhood. Little more is known about the mystic except that she presumably died at Brussels about 1336.

Bloemardinne was a beguine, but probably did not live in a beguinage. Applied to a free agent, the word must be understood in a generic sense: a pious woman who dedicated herself to a more than ordinary life of Christian perfection. She belonged to those mystical currents of the thirteenth century which had received direction from Beatrice and Hadewijch. Her teaching must be regarded as an extension or perversion of the earlier mysticism from the school of Hadewijch.[33] She appears to have enjoyed wide appeal among the upper classes of Brussels and the duchy, for even the Duchess Maria of Evreux was numbered in her following. Thus she had strong protectors. Pomerius relates that the seat from which she was wont to teach was given after her death to the duchess, probably as a relic. Since the latter died in October, 1336, Bloemardinne's own death must have occurred shortly before.[34] That the beguine was honest in her convictions, not suspecting that she was falling into heresy, finds confirmation in the fact that Ruysbroeck did not attack her teaching until after her death. Pomerius underlines the subtlety of her doctrine, however: detection of error required special divine assistance. Among her disciples, even the clergy, she continued to be regarded as a *mulier religiosa*. She is also credited with the foundation of Trinity hospital. It is possible that the question of her orthodoxy discouraged the chapter of St. Gudule from recognizing the institution for fifty years.[35]

John van Meerhout, a monk at Diest, asserts that almost a century later, in 1410,[36] Pierre d'Ailly, bishop of Cambrai, appointed Henry

---

[32] *Idem.* For Gerelm, see AAPB., B. 1460, f. 19r, no. 51.

[33] Van Mierlo, in *OGE.*, VI (1932), 305.

[34] The Brussels acts in which Heilwijch Blomarts appears as a beguine suggest that she died shortly after July, 1336. The obituary of St. Gudule lists her anniversary under August 24. Thus Van Mierlo concludes "dat de Bloemardinne wel die Heilwijch Bloemarts der schepenakten is geweest, en dat zij den 24n Augustus, 1336, overleed" (*ibid.*, 305).

[35] For this foundation see Lefèvre, *L'organisation ecclésiastique*, p. 232; cf. p. 160. note 1. Lefèvre disagreed with Van Mierlo's conclusions in two articles: "Le séjour du mystique brabançon Jean de Ruusbroec à Bruxelles," *RHE.*, XXIX (1933), 387ff and "La valeur historique des écrits de Pomerius sur la vie de Ruusbroec et les origines de Groenendael," *Annal. soc. archéol. Brux.*, XL (1936), 148-165. Van Mierlo's answer in 1933 ("De Bloemardinne-episode in het leven van den Gelukzaligen Joh. van Ruusbroec," *OGE.*, VII, 305-340) was no more convincing for him. Cf. Dom Botte, in *Bulletin de théologie ancienne et médiévale*, II (1934), 237-238.

[36] J. Latomus and J. Hoybergius included in their *Corsendonca* in 1644 (pp. 84, 86-88) an excerpt from Henry Pomerius, but attributed the reference to John van Meerbout of Diest (middle of the fifteenth century) as coming from his work *Liber de mirabilibus eventibus*, c. 125. Cf. Fredericq, *Corpus*, I, 186-187; the document is published in *ibid.*, I, 266-267, no. 248.

Selle,[37] provost of the monastery of Corsendonck at Herenthals and Laurens Gerunts, prior of Groenendael, inquisitors to exterminate the remnants of Bloemardinne's heresy, known at the beginning of the fifteenth century as the Men of Intelligence. This commmission was faithfully executed against the heretics who, as Free Spirits, neither recognized divine precepts nor respected the sacramental system but rather asserted absolute individual freedom. To exhibit their hatred for Henry Selle, the heretics composed and sang in the streets of Brussels songs of contempt in Flemish. Besides, an attempt was made to ambush him as he was journeying from the city to Groenendael, but he was able to escape by flight.[38]

FREEDOM OF THE SPIRIT

The views of heretical beghards and beguines, instinct with Free Spirit doctrine, may be gleaned from the following representative sources which unfortunately come in the main from opponents or ex-beghards: the second Clementine decree *Ad nostrum, qui desideranter*,[39] promulgated at the Council of Vienne in 1311; the anonymous thirteenth-century list of 120 errors held by the Brethren of the Free Spirit;[40] the brief reference of Henry of Virnebourg in 1306;[41] the informative letter of John of Strasbourg (1317);[42] Eckhart who, after organizing the vague mystical aspirations of the untutored into a complete doctrine, was to have his own orthodoxy suspected;[43] the tract of John Wasmod of Homburg against beghards, Lollards, and *swestriones* (1395-1404);[44] John of Brünn's confession; John Hartmann's interrogation at Erfurt (1317) at the hands of Walter Kerling;[45] and the numerous writings of Ruysbroeck.[46]

[37] For Henry Seele see Sanderus, *Chorog. sac. Brab.*, II, 114; Henne and Wauters, *Histoire de Bruxelles*, I, 180.

[38] Fredericq, *Corpus*, I, 267.

[39] *Ibid.*, I, 168-169; Mansi, XXV, 410.

[40] Preger, *Geschichte der deutschen Mystik*, I, 461-471; cf. 172, 207; cf. "Articuli haereticorum Beghardorum" in Döllinger, *Beiträge*, II, 702.

[41] Fredericq, *Corpus*, I, 151-154, no. 161; Hartzheim, IV, 100-102, 106; Mosheim, pp. 210-218.

[42] *Ibid.*, pp. 255-261; cf. Jundt, *Histoire du panthéisme populaire*, pp. 51-54.

[43] For the trial see Aug. Daniels, "Eine lateinische Rechtfertigungsschrift des Meister Eckhart, mit einem Geleitwort von Cl. Baeumker," *Beiträge zur Geschichte der Philosophie des Mittelalters*, XXIII, 5, Münster i. w., 1923; G. Théry, "Contribution à histoire du procès d'Eckehart, 1926; first appeared in *Vie spirituelle, Etudes et Documents*, Jan. 1924 (93-119), March, 1924 (164-183), May, 1925 (149-187), Jan. 1926 (49-95), June, 1926 (45-65); new ed. of tract by Théry in *Archives d'histoire doctrinale et littéraire du moyen-âge*, I, 1926, 129-268; Otto Karrer and Herma Piesch, *Meister Eckharts Rechtfertigungsschrift vom Jahre 1326* (Erfurt, 1927); Van Mierlo, "Een geding over Eckehart's Rechtgeloovigheid," *OGE.*, I (1927), 225-254, 337-346; Clark, *The Great German Mystics*, pp. 7-35.

[44] Haupt, in *ZKG.*, VII (1885), 567-576.

[45] Döllinger, *Beiträge*, II, 384-389.

[46] D'Aygalliers, *Ruysbroeck l'Admirable, passim*.

For a concise statement of the libertine type of Free Spirit teaching it is instructive to turn to the list of eight errors attributed to these lay brotherhoods in the second Clementine decree. *I.* Man can attain in his present life such a degree of perfection that he will be rendered completely incapable of sinning and will no longer be able to make progress in divine grace. For they say, if a person can perfect himself indefinitely, he might in time become more perfect than Christ.[47] *II.* After attaining the highest degree of perfection, a person will have no more need of fasting or praying because the senses are now so completely subject to the control of the soul and reason that the body may be granted absolute liberty.[48] *III.* Those who have achieved this state of perfection and absolute freedom of spirit are no longer subject to obedience and law or obligated to follow ecclesiastical regulations, for where divine spirit rules, there is liberty.[49] *IV.* Man is able to achieve in the present life the same blessedness that he will

[47] "Quod homo in vita presenti tantum et talem perfectionis gradum potest acquirere quod reddetur penitus impeccabilis et amplius in gratia proficere non valebit; nam, ut dicitur, si quis semper posset perficere, posset aliquis Christo profectior inveniri." Cf. the thirteenth-century propositions (Preger, *Gesch. d. deutschen Mystik*, I, 461-471: In the person united with God he works all things [15] "Quod homo ad talem statum potest pervenire quod deus in ipso omnia operetur" and especially [14] "Homo possit fieri deus", and the person in such condition cannot sin [24] "Homo unitus deus peccare non possit tollere est liberum arbitrium ab homine"); he now possesses the power of doing what he wishes (no. 72) and no matter what his actions may be he cannot sin (94, 100: "Quod tantum uniri possit homo deo, quod de cetero quicquid faciat non peccat"). For him what is considered sin is not sin and thus is not harmful (nos. 55, 74, 94), for nothing is sin except as it exists in the mind (no. 61). As sin is no obstacle, so virtue is of no value (no. 85). The individual must completely submerge himself in the divine being and regard rest, body comfort, and absence of unpleasant and distracting experience as a condition for the reception of the Holy Spirit (no. 121: "Item quod libertas mala et quies et commodum corporale faciant locum et inhabitationem in homine spiritui sancto"). Van Mierlo, "Ruusbroec's bestrijding van de ketterij," *OGE.*, VI (1932), 330-332 considers these eight propositions of the Clementine decree in connection with Ruysbroeck's system.

[48] "Quod jejunare non oportet hominem nec orare, postquam gradum perfectionis hujusmodi fuerit assecutus, quia tunc sensualitas est ita perfecte spiritui et rationi subjecta, quod homo potest libere corpori concedere quicquid placet." On the question of the union of the soul, and especially the will, with God—the fundamental problem of mysticism—the orthodox mystics were obliged to fight on two fronts: first, against the rigoristic conception of the Fraticelli who greatly exaggerated renunciation of will, and secondly, against the libertine conceptions of certain beghards and the Brethren of the Free Spirit who allowed the individual, once fully united with God, to do whatever he desired because he was no longer separated from him. For the Brethren of the Free Spirit confession, prayer, fasts, and other disciplines hinder perfection (Preger, *Gesch. d. deutschen Mystik*, I 461ff, nos. 50, 79, 110: "Quod homines impediant et retardent perfectionem et bonitatem per ieiunia flagellationes disciplinas vigilias et alia similia"). Confession contradicts "veritatem evangelicam" (no 64).

[49] "Quod illi qui sunt in predicto gradu perfectionis et spiritu libertatis, non sunt humane subjecti obedientie nec ad aliqua precepta ecclessie obligantur, quia, ut asserunt, ubi spiritus Domini, ibi libertas"—a refutation of II Cor. 3, 17; Gal. 5, 18. Ruysbroeck branded this as false freedom (Van Mierlo, in *OGE.*, VI, 331).

possess in life eternal.[50] *V*. Every rational being is in himself by his very nature blessed. The soul therefore has no need of the divine light to behold God and to enjoy him in bliss.[51] *VI*. Virtuous acts are necessary only for the imperfect person; but the perfect soul no longer has need of virtues.[52] *VII*. Sexual intercourse is not a sin as long as nature demands it, especially if the person who indulges is strongly tempted, but when nature does not dictate it becomes a mortal sin.[53] The freedom demanded by certain beghards like Johann Hartmann von Aschmansteten in the Erfurt hearing (1367)[54] justified, from the social point of view, the severe condemnation by ecclesiastical authorities. *VIII*. It is not necessary to rise when the body of Jesus is presented in divine service or otherwise to show respect to the host, for it would be a sign of imperfection to come down from the heights of pure contemplation to dwell on thoughts of the eucharist or the passion of the Savior.[55]

JOHN OF BRÜNN

Among the several disclosures "de secta beghardorum et beginarum et (in) liberate spiritus vivencium," the confession made by John of Brünn[56] to the Dominican Gallus von Neuhaus, who had been appointed inquisitor for the kingdom of Bohemia (diocese of Prague)

---

[50] "Quod homo potest ita finalem beatitudinem secundum omnem gradum perfectionis in presenti assequi, sicut eam in vita obtinebit beata."

[51] "Quod quelibet intellectualis natura in se ipsa naturaliter est beata quodque anima non indiget lumine glorie ipsam elevante ad Deum videndum et eo beate fruendum."

[52] "Quod se in actibus exercere virtutum est hominis imperfecti et perfecta anima licentiat a se virtutes." The Brothers of the Free Spirit (Preger, *l.c.*) objected to the priesthood (no. 16), mass (65: "Non oportere inclinari coram corpore Christi eo quod homo deus sit . . ."), confession (41, 50, 9, 63, 79), and marriage (53: "Quod soluta concubendo cum soluto non plus peccat quam admittendo matrimonialiter coniunctum"). Baptism, confirmation, and extreme unction, although not specified, merit the same contempt.

[53] "Quod mulieris osculum, cum ad hoc natura non inclinet, est mortale peccatum; actus autem carnalis, cum ad hoc natura inclinet, peccatum non est, maxime cum tentatur exercens." The Free Spirits (Preger, *l.c.*) likewise subscribed to free intercourse (53, 81, 82), and whoever is completely united with God may without fear enjoy the pleasures of the flesh (106: "Quod unitus deo audaciter possit explere libidinem carnis per qualemcunque modum etiam religiosus in utroque sexu"; cf. 111, 112, 121). Cf. Dolcino's teaching, Muratori, *Scriptores*, IX, 457, nos. 14-15.

[54] "Impeccabilis talis homo potest agere quidquid vult et sibi placet, et si natura inclinaret eum ad actum venereum, potest licite ipsum perficere cum sorore sua carnali vel matre et in quocumque loco sint, etiam in altari" (cited by Müller, *Das Konzil von Vienne*, p. 585, note 75).

[55] "Quod in elevatione corporis Jesu Christi non debent assurgere nec eidem reverentiam exhibere, asserentes quod esset imperfectiones eisdem si a puritate et altitudine sue contemplationis tantum descenderent, quod circa ministerium seu sacrum eucharistie aut circa passionem humanitatis Christi aliquando cogitarent."

[56] Wattenbach, "Über die Sekte der Brüder vom freien Geiste," *Sitzungsberichte der kon. Akademie zu Berlin*, 1887, 526-529; John's account is published on pp. 529-537, with the confession appearing on pp. 535-537.

by Benedict XII in 1335, deserves special attention. After living in Brünn as a married man, John had asked a friend, Master Nicholas, how he could attain the perfect life.[57] He was advised to join the voluntary poor and to give his possessions to them. "The life of the beghards, living in poverty, is more perfect than any other status because they imitate more closely evangelical truth than do clerics, monks, or laymen."[58] John thereupon sold what he had, left one-half to his wife who was not in accord with his decision, sent her away,[59] and entered the community of voluntary poor at Cologne located at St. Stephen's in the new city (in novo civitate).[60] This was presumably the beghard house zur Lunge where a Nicholas de Mysene served as procurator from 1321 to 1326.[61] John was further dissuaded at the outset from seeking counsel from priests concerning his decision, so great was their hatred for this concept of perfection.[62] Novices were also discouraged from confessing fully. Far from embarking on an easy path, however, the novice had a probation which lasted twenty years. John then spent eight years as a member of the Brethren of the Free Spirit, following the precepts which allowed him full liberty. Since he had become one with divine essence, he could not sin; natural drives could be followed blindly. Inasmuch as the teachings described by him are of profligacy, the veracity of his statements need not be doubted. But if their lurid details might suggest an effort to discredit his past life, the arrogant, unequivocable tone which dominates the confession lays the sincerity of his conversion open to suspicion.[63]

More important than moral aberration, however, is the close imitation the apostolic life which better summarizes the beghard way of life. Upon admission John was briefed concerning the austerity of the order: "The true disciple of poverty shall have nothing of his own, but ought to be free from all temporal things even as Christ was on the cross." Naked and kneeling, he was received into the hands of the members. They provided him with a tunic of a hundred pieces reminiscent of what Christ had worn pro derisione et contemptu. At the same time, the beghards, mindful of recent conflicts over the poverty issue, were conscious of the heretical nature of a literal ob-

[57] Ibid., p. 529.
[58] Idem: "Quod vita beghardorum in paupertate viventium esset perfeccior omni statu in mundo existentium, quia perfeccius veritatem ewangelicam imitarentur, quam quicunque alii, sive sint clerici sive religiosi sive layci."
[59] One of the propositions which Henry of Virnebourg had hurled against the beghards in 1307 stated that one could put his wife away even against her will if this was for the good of his soul (Fredericq, Corpus, I, 151; cf. Bernard Gui, Manuale, ed. Mollat, I, 88).
[60] Wattenbach, in Sitz.-ber. d. k. Akad. zu Berlin, 1887, p. 527.
[61] Asen, in AHVN., CXV (1929), 169.
[62] Wattenbach, in Sitz-ber. d. k. Akad. zu Berlin, 1887, p. 529.
[63] Ibid., p. 528.

servance of the *vita apostolica*. If, in crossing the city, one should be called a heretic, or should be shoved or struck, or otherwise molested, he ought to bear the attack with patience. With his companion he was expected to go out to beg his bread, with eyes ever downcast.[64] The brother whose spirit is free can preach in public with much greater clarity than the priest because poverty strips away all obstructions before divine truth. To the query, "How does one know that truth when he is unable to read or to probe Scripture?" he can answer that it is better to see Scripture and truth than to read.[65]

THE TURLUPINS

Energetically suppressed after its first appearance in northern France under the direction of Margaret Porete, the popular heresy returned from the shadows about two generations later when the persecution, actively organized in Germany by the inquisitors from Rome, obliged a number of beghards and Free Spirits to seek refuge beyond the frontiers. Paris and the Ile-de-France were once again the seat of a pantheist sect, as they had been in the days of Amaury of Bena and David of Dinant. Gravely concerned over its preserves in the kingdom, Urban V in 1365 (September 3) addressed from Avignon a bull to the bishop of Paris, Stephen IV, in particular to denounce the presence in his diocese "of the children of Belial of both sexes, commonly called beghards or beguini," and to inform him of their way of life and errors, as well as the regions which they inhabited.[66] A few years later (1373) Gregory XI issued the same appeal to the princes, municipal officials, and nobles in France and Belgium.[67] These sectarians who, popularly known as Turlupins,[68] "rejoiced in being numbered in a society of the poor,"[69] had as their leaders Jeanne Dabenton and an unnamed male companion. The trial was directed by the inquisitor of the Ile-de France, Jacques de Morey. As a result, capital punishment was inflicted in 1372 on a large number of these heretics, including Jeanne Dabenton, whose body was burned with that of another leader of the movement who had just died in prison. The following year Charles V gave 50 francs to Jaques de Morey as compensation for missions and expenses entailed by the prosecution.[70] At the same time the king received from Pope Gregory XI high praise for the

[64] *Ibid.*, p. 528.
[65] *Ibid.*, p. 533.
[66] Mosheim, p. 412; Fredericq, *Corpus*, I, 206, no. 208; Raynaldus, VII, 118, ad an. 1365, no. 17.
[67] Fredericq, *Corpus*, I, 228, no. 219. Raynaldus, VII, 240-241, ad an. 1373.
[68] Gerson, *De Examinatione doctrinae* (*Op. omn.*, I, 19); Raynaldus, VII, 241, no. 19, ad an. 1373.
[69] Raynaldus, VII, 241, no 21, an. 1373.
[70] February 2, 1373, Vidal, *Bullaire*, p. 376, note 1; p. 394, note 1. A letter sent

firmness with he had uprooted "the sect of beghards, called Turlupins."[71]

Just as the Albigensians and Waldensians, together with several off-
shoots, had earlier given grave concern to the lay and church authorities in southern France,[72] so in the fourteenth and early fifteenth
centuries the episcopal authorities of Cambrai, Arras, Rheims,
and Tournai were occupied with petty heresiarchs and their
followers of the Free Spirit stamp who had spilled over from
Belgian and Rhenish centers. The heresy problem, as we have seen,
was further aggravated by Flagellants and Dancers. The persecution
of 1372 brought a blow from which the Turlupins did not recover.
Some of the adherents emigrated to Savoy where Count Amédée was
urged by the pope to prosecute them vigorously.[73] The rest remained
in France and continued to disseminate their teachings secretly. Owing
to the disorders caused by the schism and the war with the English,
they escaped the attention of their enemies and were no longer syste-
matically disturbed.

The parlement which eagerly absorbed inquisitorial functions[74]
handed down on June 30, 1403, an important decision concerning
differences that had developed between the bishop of Cambrai and the
Dominican Nicholas of Peronne, deputy of the inquisitor-general, on
the one hand, and the archbishop of Rheims and his officials on the
other over the disposition of one Marie Ducanech of Cambrai who had
been suspected and prosecuted as a heretic. When the first party
claimed that Marie did not have the right to appeal to the metropolitan, the Parlement decided against them.[75] By this adverse decision
the court asserted the supremacy of episcopal jurisdiction over that
of the Inquisition and at the same time strengthened its own encroachment on the spiritual arm.

About 1424 a woman was condemned at Lyons who claimed that she
was one of five women sent by God to redeem souls from hell; her
feigned piety succeeded in deceiving many simple women. No doubt
belonging to those who based their principle of spiritual liberty on
the theory of the three ages, she was imprisoned at Bourg in Bresse.[76]
Gerson admits that the sect still possessed representatives in central

by the curia to the inquisitor on February 1, 1373 indicates that some heretics
voluntarily sought reconcilation with the Church rather than await prosecution.
The inquisitor was authorized to absolve them, with the imposition of penance,
provided their repentance was sincere (ibid., pp. 393f, no. 274).

[71] March 27, 1373, ibid., pp. 396f, no. 276. In the same letter Charles was
reproached for lukewarmness in pursuing the Waldensians in Dauphiné and his
tolerance of officials who seemed to be in their service.

[72] Raynaldus, VII, 228-229, no. 34, ad an. 1372.

[73] Ibid., VII, 229, ad an. 1372; Jundt, op. cit., p. 110.

[74] Lea, History of the Inquisition, II, 131-132.

[75] Fredericq, Corpus, I, 261-264, no. 245.

[76] Gerson, De Examinatione doctrinae (Op. omn., I, 19-20).

France in his day; they would flee populous areas in order to hide in isolated and little known places. They continued to cling to tenets, common enough in Free Spirit literature, which proclaimed that man when he attains peace and tranquillity of spirit is freed from observance of divine laws.

Of much greater significance was the action taken in 1411 by Pierre d'Ailly, bishop of Cambrai, with the support of the prior of the Dominicans of St. Quentin, papal inquisitor for the diocese, against a segment of the Free Spirits in Brussels who went under the name of Men of Understanding.

HOMINES INTELLIGENTIAE

The metaphysics of the Men of Understanding who flourished in Brussels under Gilles Cantor, an unlettered layman, and the Carmelite William of Hildernisse during the first quarter of the fourteenth century was substantially that of the Brethren of the Free Spirit.[77] The age of Mosaic law, they claimed, was that of the Father, the age of the the age of Elias (Elijah) through allegorical interpretation[78] of the transfiguration of Christ.[79] Moses, Jesus, and Elias therefore are representatives of three stages in divine revelation. Even as the coming of Christ abolished what had been considered truth, so the Catholic Church will dissolve in the new era. The sermons and teaching of saints and doctors will yield before the new doctrine. Scriptural truths will be revealed more clearly than ever before; the Holy Spirit will illumine human intelligence more sharply than in any previous time, more so than even among the apostles, for theirs was merely the shell of truth. The three virtues, poverty, chastity, and obedience, will be replaced by freedom of the spirit.[80]

If man henceforth unites with God, Gilles Cantor will serve as the savior of mankind.[81] Direct enjoyment of divine splendor fills the soul

[77] *Errores sectae hominum intelligentiae et processus factus contra fratrem de Alliaco, episcopum Cameracensem, anno Christi MCCCCXI,* published by Baluze, *Miscellanea,* II (Paris, 1679), 277-297; Fredericq, *Corpus,* I, 269-279. For the sect, see C. Van der Elst, "Les mystagogues de Bruxelles, Egidius Cantoris, 1410," *Revue trimestrielle,* XXIX (Brussels, 1861), 101-123; Jundt, *Histoire du panthéisme populaire,* pp. 111-116; For Gilles de Leeuw or Aegidius Cantor, Cantoris, or de Cantere, see Emile Varenbergh in *BNB.,* VII (1880), 771-772; this article relies for the most part on Van der Elst, who regarded him as a member of the patrician Brussels family of De Leeuw or Leeuws one branch of which bore the name of De Cantere. From it came the name Cantersteen given to the building and then street between St. Gudule and the rue de la Madeleine (Van der Elst, *op cit.,* p. 114, note 5; cf. Henne and Wauters, *Histoire de Bruxelles,* I, 280). For William of Hildernisse, see Wauter in *BNB.,* VIII (1884-1885), 481-484.

[78] "Item sibi invicem idioma fabricantes" (Fredericq, *Corpus,* I, 272, no. 10).

[79] *Ibid.,* 272, no. 18; cf. 276f.

[80] *Ibid.,* 274 (10).

[81] *Ibid.,* 271 (1); cf. 275.

with elation of security by giving it a sense of eternity. Moreover, it opens up a clearer understanding of the Bible, so well indeed that, as William admits, he must preach in accordance with Scripture.[82] Whoever listens to the words of the preacher illumined by the Holy Spirit hears truth undefiled; by following the doctors of the Church he will sink deeper and deeper into error.

Of what does the new revelation consist? "God," they taught, "is everywhere, in stones, in the limbs of man, in hell as well as in eucharist bread. Every individual possesses God perfectly in himself taking communion."[83] So well can one identify himself with divine being that his conduct, whatever it may be, does not entail sin. God is henceforth the author of all human action; He not only permits man's will to produce such works as please him; His existence in him is efficacious will which produces these works whether they are good or bad. Consequently man no longer has merit or responsibility; his actions neither bring salvation nor draw him into damnation, for "Christ has acquired all merit on the cross, and by his Passion he has done satisfaction for all."[84]

Once, as Gilles was travelling on the road, the Holy Spirit revealed that he entered spiritual childhood and that in the future he must not fast during Lent. His followers, freed from canonical prescription, could flout with impunity penance and prayer; confession to unworthy priests was invalid. To avoid suspicion, their foes complained, these sectarians appear in church if only to confess venial sins while carefully concealing mortal sins which might lay them open to the charge of heresy.[85] Renunciation of external law before the sole authority of inner spirit led them to consider all conduct similar to theirs as being inspired by the Holy Spirit.[86] In their sermons they disparaged chastity and continence. "External man does not corrupt inner man; nor will inner man be damned."[87] Indeed, by censuring a sinner one commits a more grievous error.[88] All men will be saved: Christians, Jews, pagans, even demons, all will return to the Godhead and will merely form a singly flock under one shepherd.[89]

The brother of one of the administrators of the Table of the Poor at Malines, William of Hildernisse (b. ca. 1358), entered the Carmelite convent in that town, became a priest, and successively lector of the convent at Trèves, subprior at Mainz, lector at Malines, then at Brussels where he was also prior in 1392, 1393, and 1399-1400. At the

[82] *Ibid.*, 274 (12, 14); 278 (5).
[83] *Ibid.*, 274 (13).
[84] *Ibid.*, 273 (4-5).
[85] *Ibid.*, 271 (5-7).
[86] *Ibid.*, 272 (19).
[87] *Ibid.*, 273 (6-7).
[88] *Ibid.*, 273 (9).
[89] *Ibid.*, 273 (1, 9).

end of his life he was still lector: at Tirlemont in 1422 and at Brussels for the next three years, thus indicating that his orthodoxy was not beyond rehabilitation. Although both Gilles and William were closely associated in their work and had a similar approach, the latter, being more learned, presented his views under regular forms and invoked Scripture to combat official dogmas. His sermons attracted many, particularly women. The meetings were held in a tower outside Brussels which belonged to one of the echevins.[90] When the bishop of Cambrai, Pierre d'Ailly, after an inquest, summoned him before his court and had him read the opinions attributed to Gilles Cantor, he rejected them as being contrary to the faith and witnessed this denial with his signature.[91] William also disclaimed other errors which he was accused of propagating. Warned by the prelate that he would be understood in his defense, he protested his full submission to the Church and announced his firm intention of abjuring all heretical or scandalous propositions of which the bishop or his deputies would judge him guilty. Following the advice of several theologians including the prior of the Dominicans of St. Quentin, Pierre d'Ailly declared William suspect of sharing errors of Gilles Cantor. He was condemned to abjure them, first in the episcopal palace at Cambrai, then at St. Gudule at Brussels, and finally in the beguinage in that city. Admitting that he did not have full proof against the accused and that were but suspicion and rumors, the bishop ordered him to abjure eight articles. With this William complied. He was thereupon sentenced to a three-year imprisonment in the castle of Seilles near Cambrai, or longer in a convent of his order outside the diocese.[92]

---

[90] *Ibid.,* 272, 277.
[91] *Ibid.,* 271-273.
[92] *Ibid.,* 278.

III

Suspicion in Thirteenth-Century
Synodal Legislation

Germany and Belgium witnessed in the thirteenth century a recrudescence of popular heresy which was probably Waldensian in heritage with a strong admixture of Gnostic-Manichaean elements.[1] This infection provoked the rigorous repressive measures published by Frederick II in 1220[2] and renewed with the force of law at Ravenna in February and March, 1232.[3] The *Annales* of Worms[4] and the *Gesta Trevirensium Archiepiscoporum*[5] describe the spontaneous persecution that was directed against heretics in 1231 throughout Germany. In the city of Trèves alone, the *Gesta* relates, three schools of heretics were discovered.[6] On this occasion a certain Luckardis who passed as a very devout woman is reported to have been burned for refusing to accept the fall of Lucifer[7]—an idea which may have been borrowed under the influence of Henry Mimique (Mundikinus) whose case had been the cause of synodal action a decade earlier.[8] Many of these heretics had German translations of the Bible; some practiced rebaptism, several denied the eucharist,[9] others held that unworthy priests could not consecrate; still others insisted that consecration could take place anywhere in any vessel and by man or woman. Some rejected as useless confirmation and extreme unction, mediatory functions of the priesthood, papal prerogative, and prayers for the dead. From the

---

[1] Alberic de Trois-Fontaines, *Chronicon, MGH. SS.,* XXIII, 931, for heresy in Germany during this period see Hefele-Leclercq, V 2, 1534ff; for the Low Countries, Fredericq, *Geschiedenis der Inquisitie,* I, 35ff.

[2] November 22, 1220, *MGH. Legum,* II, 108, art. 6.

[3] February 22, 1232, *Constitutio contra Haereticos, MGH. Legum,* II, 194f; March, 1232, *Mandatum de haereticis teutonicis persequendis, ibid.,* II, 195-197. Cf. Henry's decree of June 2, 1231 (*ibid.,* II, 284).

[4] *MGH. SS.,* XVII, 38f; Böhmer, *Fontes rerum german.,* II, 175f.

[5] *Gestorum Treverorum Continuatio IV, MGH. SS.,* XXIV, 400-402.

[6] *Ibid.,* XXIV, 401; *MDAC.,* IV, 242; Mansi, XXIII, 241.

[7] *MGH. SS.,* XXIV, 401.

[8] Hefele-Leclercq, V 2, 1444ff.

[9] Mansi, XXIII, 241.

teachings of William Cornelus at Antwerp it is evident, moreover, that such anticlerical sentiment gathered strength from social unrest.[10]

The count of Sayn whom Conrad Marburg, Gregory IX's choice for papal inquisitor,[11] was threatening with confiscation of castles if he did not acknowledge his heresy, asked the archbishop of Mainz to convoke a council. This assembly was held in Mainz on July 25, 1233, in the presence of King Henry, Archbishop Siegfried, and several ecclesiastical and lay princes; Conrad of Marburg was present.[12] The principal objective was to cope with the "frightful" progress of heresy in imperial lands—"from what source we know not"—and to tighten discipline in the church. It is quite probable that forerunners of the beguines were under consideration in the statutes which Guy, bishop of Preneste and apostolic legate, promulgated for the canons of St. Lambert in 1203. Not only was suspicion voiced at the translation of Scripture—perhaps an echo of Lambert le Bègue's activity—but reclusion was to be sharply curbed: "Nullus vel nulla recludatur absque licentia episcopi."[13] Hereby a double blow was struck at lay spirituality at Liége

Not much later than in Lombardy the poor men of Lyons appeared in imperial land, first in the French-speaking parts. Repressive measures against the Waldensians in the Lorraine towns began in Toul where the bishop, Eudes de Vaudemont, ordered all the heretics called *Vaudois* to be brought in chains before the episcopal see.[14] The synod of Toul was obliged to take action against them as early as 1192.[15] Of greater significance was the Waldensian disturbance at Metz in 1199 in connection with which vernacular translations of portions of the Bible are mentioned.[16] In this diocese and especially in the city, so Innocent III was informed by the bishop, there were "a great number (*multitudo*) of lay people, men and women, who have made translations in French of the Gospels, Epistles of St. Paul, the psalter, the *Morals* on Job by Gregory the Great and many other books which they read together and expound resisting the priests who would restrain them."[17] It was not so much the desire for knowledge of

[10] See above, pp. 488-490.
[11] Fredericq, *Gesch. d. Inquis.*, I, 37.
[12] Hartzheim, III, 546-547, 548; *Annal. Col. max., MGH. SS.*, XVII, 843; Hefele-Leclercq, V 2, 1545ff.
[13] *CESL.*, I, 135; cf. Van Rooijen, *Theodorus van Celles*, p. 95.
[14] *MDT.*, IV, 1180.
[15] Hartzheim, III, 456, can. 9f; Mansi, XXII, 650, can. 9. For the Waldensians in Germany see Hauck, IV, 901.
[16] Alberic de Troisfontaines, *Chron., MGH. SS.*, XXIII, 878; cf. Berger, *Bible française au moyen âge*, pp. 38ff; Suchier in *Zeitschr. f. rom. Philologie*, VIII (1884), 418ff.
[17] Ep. 141, *PL.*, CCXIV, 695. When the archbishop wrote the pope in July, 1199, for confirmation of the repressive measures to be employed against the Waldensians, Innocent III answered with two letters, one to the faithful at Metz (*PL.*, CCXIV, 695-698), the other personally to the archbishop (*ibid.*, 698-699).

scripture that caused the pope to complain; what was objectionable to the curia was the practice of holding secret assemblies which tended to abrogate the right of preaching, to elude the simplicity of the priesthood, and to scorn the company of those who did not cling to these things.[18]

Mone discovered in a thirteenth-century manuscript at Reichenau the undated legislation of a Council of Mainz in fifty-one canons.[19] For want of space the copyist omitted the usual formulas in introduction and conclusion. But little doubt remains that this was the council that was held in 1233.[20] With respect to the feminine religious question the council sought to regulate the lives of women who took private vows of chastity without entering a convent or professing a rule; they must live in their houses from their own resources. If they were poor they should earn their livelihood by manual work or in service to others. Moreover these women were to submit to their parish priests and be governed by their counsel.[21] In this Mainz legislation the women were not called *beguines* but were referred to as "muliercule... voventes continentiam" and "virgines, deo virginitatem suam offerentes." In other words, this council qualified the devout women who followed the *modus vivendi* of the beguines with the very phrases which Gregory and the bishop of Cambrai were employing at this time.[22] To lend weight to this identification a synod held in Fritzlar in 1244 repeated this regulation and supplemented it with two sentences in which these women were called beguines and in which the reason for such measures was brought out more sharply.[23] Because

---

[18] *Ibid.*, 696.

[19] Mone, "Kirchenverordnungen der Bistümer Mainz und Strassburg aus dem 13. Jahrhundert," *Zschr. f. d. Gesch. d. Oberrh.*, III (1852), 129ff. Cf. Hefele-Leclercq, V 2, 1546ff.

[20] Although the date is omitted, canon 3, says Mone (*l.c.*, p. 135), pertains to papal and imperial legislation which prescribes the confiscation of the property of heretics. Since this action is recommended in the laws of Frederick II (February 22, 1232, art. 1-2, *MGH. Leges*, II, 194f) the council of Mainz may be regarded as the enactment of these imperial instructions and the supplementing of papal letters in 1231 (P. 8753, 8754; Raynaldus, *Annales*, ad ann. 1231, n. 14). For the council see Hartzheim, III, 542f, 544, 547; cf. Gregory IX's brief to King Henry (*MDT.*, I, 950; Hartzheim, III, 545-546). Furthermore, the first article mentions the papal and imperial regulations against heretics as "noviter promulgatae" (*Zschr. f. d. Gesch. d. Oberrheins*, III, 135).

[21] Can. 45, *ibid.*, III, 141: "Item sacro approbante concilio prohibemus statuendo, ne muliercule, que voventes continentiam habitum quodammodo mutaverunt, nec tamen professioni alicujus certe regule se astrinxerunt, per vicos a modo decurrant, sed in domibus suis vivant de proprio, si hoc habent, si vero sunt pauperes, victum et alia necessaria laboribus manuum suarum vel alii serviendo conquirant. Hoc idem de virginibus, deo virginitatem suam offerentibus, duximus statuendum. Subdite sint et hujusmodi femine suis plebanis, et eorum consilio regantur." Cf. Mainz (1261), Mansi, XXIII, 1089.

[22] See above pp. 157, 159.

[23] The statutes of this council are published in Mansi, XXIII, 1089 and Hartzheim, III, 603 under the legislation of the provincial council of Mainz of 1261. That

young beguines break their chastity vows too frequently this council decreed that henceforth only blameless women over forty could pursue the beguine life; for the same reason all clerics and monks were forbidden admission to the beguinages. Only in church and before witnesses were they allowed to speak to beguines. Simultaneously with the council of Mainz in 1261, the synod of Magdeburg, held under Archbishop Rupert, declared that "beguines ought, like other parishioners, to obey the priests of their parishes or suffer excommunication."[24]

Such prescriptions were deemed more necessary since the moral order among the beguines had not been strengthened by a firm rule demanding claustration and by strict discipline. Complaints often came from the beguines themselves. For the Belgian sisters who in the main constituted a front against heterodoxy danger lurked not in the peculiar conditions of their existence but in the clerics and laymen who took advantage of the unprotected status of semireligious. In answer to their appeals Pope Gregory IX thus advised the northern prelates in 1235 to safeguard them from molestation and seduction by clerics, monks, and laymen, and to punish wrong-doers. Nevertheless, in view of the frequent lapse of young beguines, the same minimum age was reaffirmed by the council of Mainz in 1310.[25] That the newly instituted inquisition was employed in the 1230's against certain Belgian beguines—or at least against heretics to whom this corruption of *Albigensian* was being attached for the sake of convenience and without definition—is suggested by Hadewijch's assertion: "Ene beghine die meester Robbaert doodde."[26] This is evidently a reference to the notorious papal inquisitor, the Dominican friar Robert le Petit, better known as Robert le Bougre,[27] who was active, as the chronicler put it, in "various cities and towns of France, Flanders, Champagne, Burgundy, and the other provinces."[28]

they belong to 1244 and refer to the synod of 1233 is proven by Finke *(Konzilienstudien*, pp. 22ff; cf. Grundmann, *Religiöse Bewegungen*, p. 326, note 15). After an almost literal repetition of the earlier measure comes the supplement: "Ad hoc, quia juvencularum Beginarum lapsus frequens et evidens statum religionis deformat et plurimos scandalizat, statuimus, ut nulla de cetero in earum numerum admittatur, nisi quadragesimum etatis sue annum excesserit et probate opinionis existat; sexagenarium numerum, quem prescripsit Apostolus talibus assumendis (I Tim. 5, 9), propter fragilitatem nostri temporis ad quadragenarium restringentes . . . ." Finke *(op. cit.*, p. 35) supposes that these sentences were already issued at an earlier Mainz synod, soon after 1233.

[24] Hefele-Leclercq, VI 1, 109.

[25] Mansi, XXV, 325.

[26] Van Mierlo, in *VMKVA.*, 1930, 289; also *Gesch. van de Letterk. d. Nederlanden*, I, 245.

[27] Haskins, "Robert le Bougre and the Beginnings of the Inquisition in Northern France," in *Studies in Mediaeval Culture*, pp. 193-244; Fredericq, *Gesch. d. Inquis.*, I, 42-59; Tanon, *Histoire des tribunaux*, pp. 113-117; Lea, *History of the Inquisition*, II, 113-117.

[28] *Annales Sancti Medardi Suessionensis, MGH. SS.*, XXVI, 522.

The Free Spirits who were often so closely intertwined with the other German semireligious associations formed isolated communities whose members were distinguished by a peculiar kind of life and habit. Theirs was the mendicant way of life, unmitigated by active social service and lacking "stability." Usually these brotherhoods were headed by a priest or a layman who, according to his own lights, spun out philosophic teachings accepted by the entire group. Hence arose many interpretations of the same pantheistic doctrine in application to matters of faith. Moreover, their secret mixed meetings at night, allegedly held in an underground location called a temple, offered ready fuel to those who eagerly seized every opportunity to charge them with moral aberration.[29]

We have already seen[30] that in France Guillaume de Saint-Amour bitterly reproached the beguines for living on alms and feigning extraordinary piety while wearing in public tattered attire. They were hypocrites incarnate. In Germany the synod of Fritzlar, presided over by Archbishop Gerhard of Mainz, had decreed as early as 1259 that beghards who run through the streets shouting that oft-repeated cry, "Bread, for God's sake, give us bread." (*Brod durch Gott*)[31] should be warned on three successive Sundays or feast days by their priests to abandon their peculiarities, to conform to the accepted Christian way of life and recognized habit, to refrain from preaching "underground or in other secret places," and not to consort with beguines or to imitate them. Failure to obey would entail expulsion from the parishes. The same provisions were applicable to dangerous beguines: "Idem etiam de beguinis pestiferis statuimus."[32] Even as happened at Fritzlar, so at the synod of Trèves, probably held in 1277,[33] the deacons and priests of the diocese were urged to prevent uneducated beghards or *conversi* from preaching outside the church, in the streets and squares,

[29] Cf. John of Victring, *Chronicon*, an. 1327, in Böhmer, *Fontes rerum German.*, I, 401; Mosheim, 270ff.

[30] See above, pp. 463f.

[31] Rutebeuf, *De l'estat du monde*, vs. 33: "Donez, por Dieu, du pain aus freres" (Jubinal, II, 17). Dominicans, Franciscans, Augustinian friars, Barrés, Bons-Enfants, Filles-Dieu all shouted for bread (Guillaume de la Villeneuve's *Crieries de Paris*, in Méon, *Nouveau Recueil des Fabliaux*, II, 280; cf. Jubinal, II, 17 note 1). Arnold Heymerick wrote in *Epistola doctrinalis de esurie et arte mendicandi ad pauperem scholarem* (1482) (ed F. Schröder, "Ars Mendicandi, Ein Beitrag zur Geschichte des mittelalterlichen Schülerbettels," *NAK.*, NS. XVIII, 1925, 136): "Vetustum hoc pauperum carmen utputa 'panem propter Deum' deificum magis est quam miserabile aut verecundum."

[32] Mansi, XXIII, 997; Hartzheim, IV, 577; Hefele, *Conciliengeschichte*, VI, 62; Hefele- Leclercq, VI, 1, 92.

[33] For the dating of this synod whose statutes bear the date 1227, see Franz Arens "Zur Datierung einer Trierischen Synode des 13. Jahrhunderts," *ZKG.*, XXXIII (1912), 84-105; Hauck, IV, 9, note 6; Grundmann, *Religiöse Bewegungen*, p. 389; Fredericq, *Corpus*, I, 142 note; Fredericq, *Geschiedenis der Inquisitie*, II, 14. But Hefele-Leclercq (V 2, 1454ff; VI 1, 237) were certain that this council was misdated by Mansi and that it belongs to the year 1227.

in competition with the duly ordained clergy and the recognized orders; priests were to admonish their parishioners not to heed these sowers of heresies and errors.[34] At the same time steps were taken to suppress *trutanni* and other wandering students (*vagi scholares*) or *goliardi* who were forbidden by the clergy to sing songs on the *Sanctus* or the *Agnus Dei* during mass and in divine offices. This practice disturbed the priest in canon and distracted the congregation.[35] In either case it was a question of itinerant bands which encroached on the domain of the parish priest: the *begardi* arrogated to themselves the function of preaching without proper training or ordination whereas the *trutanni* obstructed divine offices with their songs.[36] The council of Eichstätt (ca. 1280) forbade every cleric, on pain of a fine of 60 *d.*, to lodge wandering students who, by loose conduct and despicable habits, dishonor the ecclesiastical state.[37] The extreme of this form of apostasy is provided in Caesarius of Heisterbach's account of the Cistercian who, after joining a band of brigands (*quorum multitudo Rutta vocatur*), murdered, burned, and violated like one possessed.[38] Ida of Nivelles (d. 1231), while travelling with a Cistercian abbess, encountered on a return from Louvain to her convent at La Ramée a young Norbertine from Ninove who was plaguing the Brabant countryside as an armed adventurer.[39] From such fragmentary evidence one may conclude that the ranks of the *Brabanciones* were open to renegade priests and monks.[40]

Similarly, wandering or begging students, the *pauperes scolares, mendicantes scolares,* swelled a constant and unwieldy floating population.[41] In the fourteenth century they formed a specific class of the poor: they were youths who either had left school and struck the road in order to get bread or had finished school but could not yet earn a livelihood. The latter were sometimes numbered among the local poor and thus might receive a stipend from the chapter or the Holy Ghost

---

[34] Can. 94, Mansi. XXIV, 201; *MDAC.*, VII, 114-115, no. 66; Fredericq, *Corpus.* I, 142, no. 147; Hartzheim, III, 531; cf. Fredericq, *Gesch. d. Inquis.*, II, 14; Lea, *History of the Inquisition*, II, 354; Moll, *Kerkgeschiedenis*, II 3, 84-96.

[35] Can. 94, Mansi, XXIV, 201; Hartzheim, III, 532 (can. 9): "Item precipimus, ut omnes sacerdotes non permittant trutannos et alios vagos scolares aut goliardos cantare versus super Sanctus et Agnus dei aut alias in missis vel in divinis officiis, quia ex hoc sacerdos in canone quam plurimum impeditur et scandalizantur homines audientes." Cf. Hefele-Leclercq, V, 2, 1463. See also council of Mainz (1233), can. 46, Mone, *Zeitschrift für die Geschichte des Oberrheins*, III (1852), 141.

[36] For a full discussion of this problem, see Grundmann, *Religiöse Bewegungen*, pp. 390-393. See above p. 419 n.

[37] Can. 29, Hefele-Leclercq, VI 1, 291.

[38] *CHD.*, (II, 2), ed. Strange, I, 58-59.

[39] *V. Id. Niv.*, ed Henriquez, pp. 237-238.

[40] Mens, "De 'Brabanciones' of bloeddorstige en plunderzieke aventuriers (XIIe-XIIIe eeuw)," *Misc. hist .... Alb. de Meyer*, 1, 558-570.

[41] Mone, in *Zschr. f. d. Gesch. d. Oberrh.*, I (1850), 35f; Alberdingk Thijm, *Geschichte der Wohlthätigkeitsanstalten*, pp. 78-79, 119; Kriegk, *Deutsches Bürgerthum*, I, 170; Moll, *Kerkgeschiedenis*, II 2, 234, 281; II 3, 322.

Table. Since they were required to sing in the choir, they were described as *choro ligati, scolas et chorum frequentantes, choro et scolis deservientes.*[42] Craftsmen often attached themselves to these wandering students. They might also be identified with those vagabond clerics and monks against whom synods and civil authorities alike fulminated so persistently.[43] The synod of Salzburg (1310)[44] was merely reiterating a decree of Boniface VIII against vagabond clerics —*ioculatores, goliardi vel bufones*—which found its way into canon law.[45] The council of Trèves held in the same year, in forbidding monks to wander outside the convent in the city without abbatial consent,[46] attributed the evil to the alienation of monastic properties.[47] But the chronic disturbances of the Middle Ages—war, epidemics, famine—contributed more heavily to the poor problem.[48] An earlier synod at Salzburg (1274) had ordained that the abbot must not release from the vow of obedience a monk who wished to pass to a stricter order, for obedience was of the very essence of monachism ("... obedientia, quae monachorum ossibus inseparabiliter est affixa").[49] A few years later the council of Lambeth (1281) offered a variation on the principle by urging bishops to prevent fugitive monks (apostates) from seeking reinstatment or transfer to a more lenient rule.[50] Nevertheless such a position as the Salzburg assembly had adopted contradicted canon law which, in several texts, expressly declared that transfer to a to a stricter order is permissible regardless of the abbot's refusal.[51]

From the frequency of this conciliar legislation we must conclude that these *Eberhardini* and *vagi scolares* were particularly numerous in Germany during the second half of the thirteenth century.[52] The

---

[42] E.g. council of Mainz (1233), can. 46, Mone, in *Zeitschr. f. d. Gesch. Oberrheins*, III (1852), 141; Mone, *l.c.*, I (1850), 131.

[43] For vagabonds and beggars, see Alberdingk Thijm, *op. cit.*, pp. 78f; Lallemand, *Histoire de la charité*, III. *Le moyen âge*, 342-352.

[44] Can. 3, Mansi, XXV, 227.

[45] Sexti Decret., c. 1, *de vita et honest. cler.*, III, 1; Friedberg, II, 1019.

[46] Can. 28, Mansi, XXV, 257.

[47] Can. 27, Mansi, XXV, 256-257.

[48] Lallemand, *Histoire de la charité*, III, 343ff.

[49] Can. 2, Mansi, XXIV, 137; cf. council of Salzburg (1281), can. 6, Mansi, XXIV, 399.

[50] Can. 20, Mansi, XXIV, 417.

[51] Decret. Greg., c. 10 (Alexander III), *de regularibus et transeuntibus*, III, 31; Friedberg, II, 571; c. 18 (Innocent III, 1206), Friedberg, II, 575-576.

[52] Provincial synod of Rouen (1231), can. 8, Mansi, XXIII, 215 (can. 10 in *MDT.*, IV, 177); synod of Château-Gontier (1231), can. 21, Mansi, XXIII, 237 ("clerici ribaudi, maxime qui dicuntur de familia Goliae"); Mainz (1233), can. 46, Mone, *Zeitschr. f. d. Gesch. Oberrheins*, III (1852), 141: "... vagi scolares, qui vulgo Everhardini vocantur"; Fritzlar (1259), can. 3, Mansi, XXIII, 997; council of Mainz (1261), can. 17, Mansi, XXIII, 1086 (nomadic clerics, known popularly as *Eberhardins*, are not eligible for alms, cf. Hefele-Leclercq, VI 1, 101); the same statute was renewed by the council of Mainz in 1310 (Mansi, XXV, 311); synod of Magdeburg (1261), can. 20, Hefele-Leclercq, VI 1, 110; (here reference is made to *eberhardins*); council of Salzburg (1274), can. 2, Mansi, XXIV, 137; cans. 15-16, Mansi,

Franciscan preacher, Berthold of Regensburg (d. 1272), by listing in one of his Latin sermons the vagabonds hated by God and man in his day, illustrates the confusion of names applied to them: "Pikardi (false Begardi), Everhardini, lusores, armigeri, falsi mendici et huiusmodi pauperes, falsi religiosi . . . ."[53]

Far from devoting themselves primarily to charitable activity, the Belgian beghards for the most part spent the bulk of their time in manual work (*labor manuum*). As in the case of the beguines, self-sufficiency distinguished them from the Italian and German beghards who generally did not have fixed dwellings, led a vagabond life, depended on alms, and preached on unacceptable matters. These are the beghards of the poor life. Some of them evidently had appeared in Bruges and by 1285 were distressing Guy de Dampierre. The count, without censuring the way of life itself, proscribed the hypocrites who were concealing their parasitical existence under the beghard habit: They "mainent vie deshonnete, et veulent leur deshonnetete couvrir par labyt des Beggards; et par les fais de tels sunt li autre sans leur coupe souvent escandelisiet."[54] The following year (July 24, 1286) Guillaume d'Avesnes, bishop of Cambrai, decreed that *beggards* who had been expelled from the Malines convent or had taken an unauthorized departure, would lose all rights over buildings and possessions of the convent. The beghard habit was forbidden to natives and outsiders in Malines who lived outside the *curtis Beggardorum*. Exiles or refugees who intended to remain in the town must abandon the beghard habit within seven days.[55] The reasons given for such proscription are singularly vague: excesses, lightness of mind, or "any other reasonable cause".[56]

Contemporary Flemish literature is surprisingly silent on the

XXIV, 141f; council of Salzburg (1281), can. 6, Mansi, XXIV, 399; Würzburg (1282), can. 29, Hefele-Leclercq, VI 1, 291; synod at St. Hippolytus (1284), Mansi, XXIX, 511; Hartzheim, III, 677-678, no. 26 (omitted in Hefele-Leclercq); Salzburg (1291), can. 3, Mansi, XXIV, 1077-1078; cf. Fourth Lateran Council (1215), can. 18, Mansi, XXII, 1006-1007; Hefele-Leclercq, V 2, 1348; cf. Mens, in *Misc. hist . . . Alb. de Meyer*, I, 564, note 1; 569 note 3. After asserting that the *scholasticus* was expected to receive all students who desired to attend the schools of Tongres, the statutes of the collegiate church added: "De scolaribus autem mendicantibus et circumeuntibus per claustrum nichil debet exigere vel recipere nam eos tenetur gratis docere. Caveat tamen diligenter ne nimius sit numerus mendicantium sed restringat et temperet ad congruum moderamen secundum temporis exigentiam et capituli pacem" (Paquay, "Les plus anciens statuts de la collégiale de Tongres," *Bull. de la soc. archéol. et litt. de Tongres*, 1906, 344).

[53] Schönbach, in *Sitzungsb. d. Acad. d. Wissenschaften in Wien, phil.-hist. Klasse*, CXLVII, pt. V (1904), 81, 106-107. Mens (*Misc. hist . . . . Alb. de Meyer*, 567 n. 1) identifies the "armigeri" with "routiers". Such terms signified for Berthold *semi-heretici*, not *sectarii*.

[54] Gilliodts-van Severen, I, 7, no. 8.

[55] Vannérus, *Malines, 237-238*, no. 2.

[56] "Propter suos excessus vel ex alia causa quacumque racionabili ejectus fuerit vel amotus vel qui inde recesserit animi levitate" (*idem*).

problems raised by the extraregular. From the voluminous writings of Jacob van Maerlant (ca. 1235–1300) one can glean but a single allusion and that is far from being pointed. In his *Disputacie van Onser Vrouwen ende van den Heilighen Cruce,* presumably written about 1270,[57] he flays the hypocrisy of the "beggaert" who, while vowing to abandon worldly pleasures, actually yields to the fleshpots of Egypt and derives no satisfaction from the spiritual food of Jerusalem.[58] Another Flemish poet denounced the idleness of „swesters, baghinen, lollaerde."[59]

Again, at the diocesan synod celebrated at St. Pölten in Austria by Bishop Godfried of Passau (March 17, 1284), priests were enjoined in a blanket recommendation to caution their flocks not to listen, on pain of excommunication, to those laymen who in secret conventicles dare to preach in public and lead simple souls astray.[60] Similarly, the synod of Aschaffenburg, convoked by Gerhard, archbishop of Mainz, on September 15, 1292,[61] prohibited any cleric or lay person of either sex to preach publicly, teach secretly or maintain that a priest in mortal sin cannot receive the body of Christ or bind and loose his parishioners from sin.[62] Another diocesan assembly held at Eichstätt by Bishop Reimboto (1279–1297) in the 1280's[63] warned against unauthorized lay preachers who deliver sermons in clandestine meetings and lead the public into error.[64] The Dominican John Nider (d. 1438) sums up in the time of the council of Basel the standing complaint of almost two centuries against those beghards who "use subtle, sublime,

[57] Te Winkel, *Maerlant's Werken,* 2nd ed., 162.
[58] Strophe 26, vss. 326-338:

> Sulc es die ontcropen scheen
> Der werelt, ende liet haer leen
>   Ende leerde den beggaert maken;
> Die liet bedinghe ende ween,
> Up thout te slapene ende up steen
>   Ende dat langhe waken.
> Nu loopt hi ghelijc der reen
> Die werelt dore alineen,
>   Waer hi hare mach ghenaken.
> Egypten, daer hi teerst in green,
> Dinct hem so goet, dat hem engheen
>   Jherusalem dinct smaken:
>   Ic kenne al dese saken.

(ed. Verdam and Leendertz, *Jacob van Maerlant's Strophische Gedichten,* p. 101).
[59] *Altniederländische Schaubühne, Abele Spelen ende Sotternien,* ed. Hoffmann von Fallersleben (Breslau, 1838), p. 126.
[60] Hartzheim, III, 677; Hefele-Leclercq, VI, 1, 291f.
[61] Hefele-Leclercq, VI, 1, 341; cf. Mosheim, 202-203.
[62] Can. 1, Mansi, XXIV, 1081. The text as reproduced by Mansi, XXIV, 1081-1094 and Hartzheim, IV, 7-16 makes no reference in the twenty-six canons to "Beghardos et Beghuttas" as Mosheim (pp. 202, 235) suggests.
[63] Hefele-Leclercq, VI 1, 289. It is impossible to establish exactly the date of the council, but the year 1281 seems plausible. At least it reflects none of the legislation of the national council at Würzburg in March, 1287 (*ibid.,* VI 1, 307ff).
[64] Grundmann, *Religiöse Bewegungen,* p. 393 and note 85.

spiritual and metaphysical words, such as the German tongue can hardly express, so that scarcely any man, even an educated man, can fully understand them; and in these they wrap up lofty sentences about spirit, abstraction, various lights, divine persons, and the degrees of contemplation."[65]

What is equally important in the above-mentioned Eichstätt decision, it at once expressed for the first time what had not been considered at the Council of Lyons (1274) and anticipated the "saving clause" of the Vienne decree, *Cum de quibusdam mulieribus.* In the absence of unified direction and a well-knit organization, the beguine movement had developed such multifarious forms that blanket regulations for all beguines could not be established or enforced. The council therefore acknowledged the existence of some beguines whose integrity and probity have given to them an unimpaired and irreproachable renown. As for the rest who adopt a specious form of regular life in order to conceal an immoral life in all its enormity, they deserve to be visited with the severest penalties: they are to be brought to a public place called the "Schreiat" (i.e. pillory) and be whipped in the presence of the people. Should a beguine whose excesses have been detected move to another parish to avoid punishment, the local priest must inflict on her similar penalties.[66]

John Nider informs us in his *Formicarius,* written about 1435,[67] that Albertus Magnus observed in the manual he wrote with his own hand that a variety of heresy similar to that which had flourished in the Swabian Ries in the diocese of Augsburg was being entertained in Cologne in his own day.[68] But further evidence is lacking on these pantheistic and antinomian trends until the close of the century. It is probable that Albertus Magnus obtained his information either from Regensburg where he spent two years about 1240 as lector in the Dominican house and from 1260—1262 as bishop, or from his native town of Lauingen hard by the Ries.[69] At the provincial chapter of the Franciscans in Colmar in 1290 two beguines and two beghards were apprehended by the lector of the Friars Minor from Basel on the grounds of heresy; others were arrested in Basel.[70] A decade later bands of begging beghards appeared at provincial chapters of both mendicant orders[71] without establishing any definite relation with the orders.[72]

---

[65] *Formicarius* (lib. iii, c. 5), cited by Deanesly, *The Lollard Bible*, p. 82.
[66] Grundmann, *Religiöse Bewegungen*, p. 342 and note 41; Hefele-Leclercq, VI 1, 290-291, can. 26.
[67] Quétif-Echard, I, 792a-794a.
[68] *Formicarius* (III, 5), Mosheim, p. 198: "Reperi in libro manuali, quem pro se totum dominus Albertus manu conscripsit propria, eum annotasse, quod suo tempore Coloniae fuerit eadem heresis..." F. Vernet in *DTC.*, VI, I (1915), 800.
[69] Haupt, in *ZKG.*, VII (1885), 505.
[70] *Annales Colmar. Maiores* (1290), *MGH. SS.*, XVII, 217.
[71] The *Annal. Colmar.* (*ibid.*, 227) report on the provincial chapter of the Domi-

It is clear that by the end of the thirteenth century there was a sizable floating population in the Rhineland to which failure to obtain a stake in society in a period of marginal subsistence, coupled with a growing religiosity, made attractive those elements of popular piety then enjoying wide currency: penitence, flagellation, apostolic poverty, vernacular devotional literature, immediate communion with God, and even millenarianism. From this floating population no order or sect was formed that bore a common name or the imprint of a dominating personality which could give it organization as well as direction. However much this ill-defined movement might dissolve or distort the traditional conception of ecclesiastical order, in the parochial and monastic worlds alike, it could not be easily exterminated by uniform measures. The heresy of these extraregulars or semireligious was not definite but their orthodoxy was suspected. More and more, as the thirteenth century progressed, traces of pantheism and antinomianism, together with steadily sharper anticlerical implications, were detected among German beguines and beghards, thus encouraging their opponents to confuse them with the Free Spirits. Yet thirty years were to pass after the Ries heresy and the Council of Lyons before the church took a determined stand with respect to these sectarians. While the center of gravity for the Spiritual Franciscans must be sought in the lands bordering on the Mediterranean, a scene roughly analogous to their conflict with ecclesiastical authorities was being enacted in the valley of the Rhine.

nicans in Basel in September, 1302: "In hoc capitulo fuerant conversi seu begihardi seu fratres non habentes domicilia LXXX in una processione, mendicantes cibaria." When the chapter of the Friars Minor was held the following year in Colmar, "conversi seu Beghardi 300 bini et trini in processione per Columbariam transeuntes elymosinam mendicabant" (ibid., 228).

[72] Bihl, in AFH., XIV (1921), 169.

IV

Henry II of Virnebourg

More significant than these early experiments in suppression was the condemnation which the archbishop of Cologne, Henry II of Virnebourg (1306—1332),[1] pronounced on February 13, 1307,[2] against the beghards and Apostolici of both sexes, who are referred to as *idiotae* in recognition of lay-status, in his diocese and in the territories of his suffragans, Liége and Utrecht. Thereby was inaugurated in earnest systematic episcopal persecution which, guided by papal directives, would continue, even though sporadically and without real consistency, to the beginning of the following century and would end in the annihilation of the Free Spirit heresy. At the diocesan synods[3] held during his episcopate (1307, 1308,[4] 1321,[5] 1324,[6] 1326,[7] 1327,[8]

[1] G. Schwamborn, *Heinrich II, Erzbischof von Cöln (1306-1332)* (diss., Neuss Münster, 1904). It was Henry II and not Henry I, as Mosheim (p. 210) and Fredericq (*Corpus*, I 150-151) held.

[2] Kisky, *Regesten*, IV, 42-43, no. 229; Fredericq, *Corpus*, I, 150-154, no. 161; Hartzheim, IV, 100-101; Mosheim, pp. 210-218, 230ff; Schwamborn, *op. cit.*, pp. 65ff. Whereas Fredericq (*l.c.*; *Gesch. d. Inquis.*, II, 14) insisted on February 14, 1306, Hefele-Leclercq (VI 1, 599) and Binterim (*Deutsche Concilien*, VI, 117) dated it February 21. Cf. Asen, in *AHVN.*, CXV (1929), 167.

[3] Whereas Schwamborn (*op. cit.*, pp. 53-64) refers to seven diocesan synods, Binterim (*Deutsche Concilien*, VI, 117) considered eight. Besides, two provincial synods were held during the episcopate: the first, called by Clement V on March 9, 1310, was occasioned by the bull *Faciens misericordiam* (Hefele-Leclercq, VI, 1, 607f; Hartzheim, IV, 118-127; Kisky, *Regesten*, IV, 99-103, no. 498; cf. Binterim, VI, 124; see below, p. 000). The second was convoked on October 31, 1322, after the disastrous battle of Mühldorf (Mansi, XXV, 723f; Hartzheim, IV, 282; Kisky, *Regesten*, IV, 316-324, no. 1337; cf. *ibid.*, 324, nos. 1338-1339, October 31); Hauck, VI 1, 139-140 and note 1, Binterim, VI, 117, 128. For Mühldorf, see Boehmer, *Font. rer. germ.* I, 161-165.

[4] March 4, 1308, Kisky, *Regesten*, IV, 58-61, no. 304; Hartzheim, IV, 107-113; Binterim, VI, 118f.

[5] October 2, 1321, Kisky, *Regesten*, IV, 290-291, no. 1262; Binterim, VI, 126f; Hartzheim, IV, 278-280; Schwamborn, *op. cit.*, pp. 54ff.

[6] March 5, 1324, Kisky, *Regesten*, IV, 347-348, no. 1439; Mansi, XXV, 735; Hartzheim, IV, 289-291; Schwamborn, *op. cit.*, p. 57.

[7] October, 1326, Binterim, VI, 132. Although pressed by Louis, Henry called the synod to enjoin, among other things, strict claustration for nuns. Kisky does not mention this synod.

[8] March 2, 1327, Kisky, *Regesten*, IV, 400, no. 1645; Binterim, VI, 133; Hartzheim, IV, 293-296.

1330)[9] Henry brought out again and again the obligation that he felt his high office had imposed on him for improving the religious-moral conditions of the diocese.[10] He consistently combatted with energy the lack of discipline and immorality among clergy and laymen alike. In his first synod he outlined the program which he would henceforth promote mercilessly against the beghards who at the beginning of the fourteenth century had made Cologne the principal center of their agitation. "Since a new prohibition is necessary to make a deeper impression than an old decree, we impose excommunication and anathema on all heretics, together with their supporters and patrons, who teach and preach otherwise concerning matters of faith, sacraments, and marriage—in short, all who deviate in their teaching from belief in the Roman Church which is the mother and teacher of all the faithful."[11] In a later decree addressed to the authorities of Cologne (April 24, 1326), in which he demanded the arrest of certain heretics, the archbishop wrote that it was his earnest desire to extirpate the poison of heresy and that he would prevent the growth of heretical tares with all means at his disposal.[12]

In violation of canon xiii of the Fourth Lateran Council governing a *nova religio*, and incidentally canon xxiii, the beghards, so runs Henry's first indictment, had failed to court the favor of the older orders or to secure papal approval for their new kind of life and habit pursued under the pretext of voluntary poverty. With wan and sad countenance some men and women derive their livelihood by begging instead of by gainful employment, as they once did, to the disadvantage of the faith and the recognized mendicant orders.[13] Those lay men who thwart the efforts of the preaching orders by conducting their own sermons must therefore be strenuously prosecuted. Within a month they must remove the habit of their brotherhood and again live by the work of their hands, or face excommunication and punishment by the secular arm. At the same time, the beghards in Maestricht in the diocese of Liége (*magister totusque conventus Bagardorum Traiectensium Leodiensis diocesis*) do not appear to have offended the clergy for the chapter of Notre Dame, with the sanction of St. Lambert in Liége and the bishop himself, granted them the right

[9] February 26, 1330, *ibid.*, VI, 134; Kisky, *Regesten*, IV, 453-454, no. 1879; Schwamborn, *op. cit.*, pp. 56ff. Binterim (VI, 135-136) indicates that a second synod was held this year (October 2) in Bonn; cf. Kisky, *Regesten*, IV, 460, no. 1909; Hartzheim, IV, 308-310.

[10] Hartzheim, IV, 278f (Council of Cologne, 1321); *ibid.*, IV, 282-285 (Council of Cologne, 1322); *ibid.*, IV, 293-296 (statutes of 1327); *ibid.*, IV, 308ff (statutes of 1330).

[11] Fredericq, *Corpus*, I, 154; Hartzheim, IV, 102, can. 3.

[12] Ennen and Eckertz, *Quellen*, IV (1870), 115, no. 130.

[13] Fredericq, *Corpus*, I, 151-152; Mosheim, pp. 211-212; cf. Jundt, *Histoire du panthéisme populaire*, p. 49.

to have their own cemetery and a chapel in which mass might be read by their own chaplain.[14] It is important to note, accordingly, that Henry's prohibition was not levelled against the real beguines as the heading of the first chapter makes clear, for there mention is made specifically of "Beggardos" and "Beggardas" who pass under the name of Apostolici.[15] The Suestriones with whom episcopal legislation was later frequently expected to be concerned were popularly regarded as the female followers of the beghards. Thus they are understood to be the *beggardae* that Henry had in mind.[16] This argument gathers weight in the light of subsequent prosecution—in 1335, 1357, 1367, and 1396[17]—which was directed against the Suestriones as well as the beghards. How weak the term *Suestriones* really was can be concluded from a community of Black Sisters at Brussels who went under that name.[18]

One important facet of the 1307 crisis is the alleged part played by Duns Scotus. Much uncertainty envelops the motives governing the transfer of this eminent Franciscan scholastic philosopher and theologian from Paris to Cologne.[19] For some it has the appearance of an exile, self-imposed or otherwise, warranted by disfavor or jealousy which he had incurred in Paris.[20] Again, it has been suggested that he wished to establish a school that would successfully compete with the Dominican institution,[21] or merely to defend the mendicant way of life.[22] For Van Mierlo his arrival was intended to compose differences

[14] February 22, 1308, Fredericq, *Gesch. d. Inquis.*, II, 15, note 4.

[15] For the Apostoli see council of Würzburg (1287), Mosheim, p. 220; council of Trèves (1310), Fredericq, *Corpus*, I, 155, can. 50; Mosheim, p. 222.

[16] Asen, in *AHVN.*, CXI (1927), 87, 106.

[17] See below, pp. 538, 560, 562-63, 571.

[18] These Suestriones appeared during the second half of the fourteenth century in the quarter of St. Géry. In 1458 they adopted the rule of Augustine on orders from Pius II. Their convent which was increased in 1465 by the purchase of land from the chaplain of the collegiate church, Pierre Fabri (d. 1517), was put under the direction of the prior of the Carmelites of Malines. The Black Sisters cared for the sick in their homes (Lefèvre, *L'organisation*, p. 116; Henne and Wauters, *Histoire de Bruxelles*, III, 167). In the *Liber capellaniarum*, written in 1464-1474, Pierre a Thymo summarized their purpose: "Operi caritatis et misericordie diligenter intendunt sorores Suestriones, infra metas capelle sancti Gaugerici, sub directione prioris fratrum Carmelitarum Machliniensium simul degentes, que infirmes and quas vocantur fideliter ministrantes assistunt" (cited by Lefèvre, *op. cit.*, p. 116, note 2; cf. pp. 254f). A Cologne document (October 18, 1306) pertaining to a beguine Ida who built a house at her own expense distinguishes beguine from *swestere*: a house and lot "contingentes ex uno latere domum Blize vidue de Speculo beghine et ex alio latere pauperum que dicuntur swestere" (*UB. Altenberg*, p. 417).

[19] Lampen, in *Coll. Franc. Neerl.*, II, 291-305.

[20] Hauck, V, 1, 299-300; P. Raymond, in *DTC.*, IV, 2 (1920), 1866.

[21] C. R. S. Harris, *Duns Scotus* (2 vols., Oxford University Press, 1927), I, 11f. Harris makes no mention of the beghard problem. Cf. Ennen, *Geschichte der Stadt Köln*, III, 836 and note 1.

[22] Cf. Vernet, in *DTC.*, II, 1 (1910), 530; Scotus (*Opera omnia*, ed. Wadding, Lugduni, 1639, I, 12f) came to defend the Mendicants, a supposition which rests on Wadding's edition of the works.

between the two bodies of friars rather than to combat heresy.[23] Finally, Henry of Virnebourg himself has been held responsible for requesting the theologian's presence in the city in order to put teeth into the resistance that was being built up against the beghards. The archbishop was looking for some one who could explain to the faithful the dangers and untenability of the alien doctrines.[24] No one was better qualified to defend the cause of the friars whose aims and mendicant way of life the sectarians were either attacking or emulating. What makes these laymen especially obnoxious, Henry adds in his first indictment, is the zeal with which they, although unacquainted with letters, contradict publicly the Dominicans and Franciscans in their sermons.[25] Whatever may have been the explanation for the theologian's transfer, it was to bear little fruit, for Duns Scotus died in November, only a few months after his arrival.

Increasing agitation of the extraregulars in Cologne and Strasbourg in 1317 moved the archbishop once again to demand the dissolution of their conventicles or else their incorporation in approved orders. Eckhart is supposed to have been accused of excessive tenderness for those in the latter city at this time. Yet his denials in the trial a decade later possess a genuineness that undermines this insubstantial allegation.[26] About 1322 Walter of Holland was burned in Cologne for unacceptable teachings.[27] The condemnation of this petty heresiarch, brought out of obscurity by Mosheim, coincided with the council which followed Mühldorf. An explanation for the absence of statutes dealing with the episode was sought by Schatenius in the simple reenactment of previous legislation: "Multa in ea synodo salubriter statuta, ac pleraque renovata ex synodis Engelberti archiepiscopi."[28] What little we know of Walter's career adds up to this: He was a native of Holland who recognized in the Rhenish cities a more fertile ground for his propaganda. Although he "had too little knowledge" of Latin, and French was beyond his ability, he nevertheless appears to have answered his judges with persuasiveness, if also with obduracy, and was sufficiently tutored to expound his views in the vernacular. His many tracts ("plures... libellos") were presumably in Dutch.[29] Following a sojourn in Mainz, Walter arrived at Cologne where he was

[23] Van Mierlo, in *VMKVA.*, 1930, p. 290.
[24] Schwamborn, *op. cit.*, pp. 45, 67f. That Scotus came to Cologne at the request of the archbishop is, according to Lampen (*l.c.*, p. 297), not only unproven but improbable. Cf. Mosheim, pp. 232-234; Wadding, *Ann.*, VI (a. 1308), 108; Döllinger in Wetzer and Welte, *Kirchenlexicon*, X (2nd ed., Freiburg i. B., 1897), 2129-30.
[25] Fredericq, *Corpus*, I, 153.
[26] See above, pp. 358-59.
[27] Trithemius, *Annal. Hirsaug*, in Fredericq, *Corpus*, I, 172f, no. 177. Cf. Mosheim, pp. 270-277.
[28] Cited by Mosheim, p. 271.
[29] See above, p. 368.

apprehended by the archbishop. Confusion of names and inadequate comprehension of teachings led Trithemius to label him "Fraticellorum princeps et haeresiarcha pessimus" and then a few lines below "Lohareus" or Lollard. While it is too much to call him a founder of the Lollards or to consider him a Waldensian priest,[30] it is most probable that he was a beghard.[31]

In 1323 a priest was degraded and burned on the charge of heresy, without further definition.[32] Two years later (1325) a number of beghards, suspected of holding irregular noctural conventicles, are reported to have died in flames or in the waters of the Rhine.[33]

Henry's immediate successor to the archbishopric, Walram, merely restated this earlier legislation in his decree of 1335 (October 1). against the beghards and *Suestriones* together with their patrons. He hit especially hard at their practice of adopting a peculiar habit.[34] Impatient with the seemingly moderate treatment at the hands of the inquisitors and alarmed at the fruitless results, Walram ordered his entire clergy to ferret out the culprits. In the meantime (1334) several "brothers of the highest poverty" (*fratres de altissima paupertate*) were burned in Metz by the inquisitor Garin; with their emphasis on the imitation of Christ and repudiation of capital punishment and oaths, these beghards may have come under the influence of Waldensian ideas, once entrenched in the city[35].

[30] Cf. Mosheim, p. 272.
[31] *Ibid.*, p. 277.
[32] *Gesta Trev.*, MDAC., IV, 410.
[33] Mosheim, pp. 299ff; cf. Lea, *History of the Inquisition*, II, 373.
[34] Fredericq, *Corpus*, I, 184f, no. 188; Mosheim, pp. 296-298.
[35] Döllinger, *Beiträge*, II, 403-406; Hauck, V, 1, 410; Delacroix, *op. cit.*, pp. 114f.

V

The Clementine Decrees

Bishops and inquisitors had thus for more than half a century been endeavoring to curb in France and later, but with special emphasis, in Germany the baneful influence of semireligious societies, infected by the ill-defined body of Free Spirit doctrine and making a bid for recognition as champions of voluntary poverty. Although papal inquisitors were not at first active in the Low Countries, regulations of provincial councils and synodal statutes as well as decrees of lay officials indicate that suppression of heresy claimed wide attention.[1] But indecision marked every step of the way, whether under episcopal or papal auspices. If Guillaume d'Avesnes, recently elected bishop of Cambrai, adopted a strong stand with respect to the beghard convent at Malines in July, 1286,[2] four months later (November 28) Walter Berthout, lord of Malines, was taking the "fratres Beggardos manentes in conventu eorum in Machlinia" as well as their property under his protection; furthermore, he exempted them from all tailles, aides, and military obligations. On the other hand, their work must be suspended in time of war: "inhibentes eisdem ne tempore guerre sive expeditionis dummodo omnia officia infra Machliniam prohibeantur, operari presumant, donec dicta officia communiter resumantur."[3]

The growing concern exhibited by the papal curia over voluntary poverty and extraregular problems in general was matched at the beginning of the fourteenth century by the zeal of German bishops whose reform measures and tightening of discipline were attempted either under papal compulsion or in the hope of better centralizing their authority during fresh papal-imperial conflicts. Episcopal surveillance of suffragans in the prosecution of heresy was a prerogative not to be diminished by competition. "Ne aliquis se intromittat in casibus episcopalibus," was he decision of the council of Trèves in 1338.[4]

[1] Fredericq, *Gesch. d. Inquis.*, pp. 158-170.
[2] Vannérus, *Malines*, pp. 237-238, no. 2.
[3] *Ibid.*, p. 239, no. 3.
[4] Can. 92, Mansi, XXV, 271; Fredericq, *Corpus*, I, 188.

In the wake of Henry of Virnebourg's first synodal decisions the council of Trèves,[5] convoked by Baldwin in April, 1310, primarily to deal with the Templars[6] along the lines recommended in the bull, *Faciens misericordiam* (August 12, 1308),[7] for the most part, however, merely re-enacted, like the councils held almost simultaneously[8] in Salzburg,[9] Cologne (March 9, 1310),[10] and Mainz (May 13, 1310),[11] old legislation pertaining to clerical delinquency and those on the fringe of orthodoxy.[12] Once again the beghards who, aiming only at idleness, refuse to work but claim the right to hold conventicles and to explain Scripture to the simple are admonished to abandon their way of life or face excommunication. The archbishop refers to them as the *begardi laici* who have taken refuge as beggars under a specious order. They are clad in long robes and mantles with wide cowls.[13] Priests were to urge them to desist from their practices within fifteen days and to secure gainful employment. All assistance, alms or otherwise, must be withheld from *illi rustici* who are contemptuously labelled Apostolici.[14] The council of Würzburg (March, 1287) had already prescribed such laymen—the *rustici* and *illiterati*.[15]

By 1310 Guy d'Avesnes, bishop of Utrecht was seeking to implement the decisions of his metropolitan.[16] But not all suffragans of Henry of Virnebourg had been so prompt to execute the 1307 decree. Scarcely a year after this order *the Bagardi* at Maestricht, with the approval of the cathedral chapter of Liége and its prince-bishop Thibaut de Bar, received permission to possess a consecrated

---

[5] Mansi, XXV, 247-294; Hartzheim, IV, 127-165; Hefele-Leclercq, VI, 1, 611-623. These editions contain the long form, with 156, canons, whereas the short one, with 114 canons, will be found in Binterim (VI, 366-435). For beghard legislation, see Fredericq, *Corpus*, I, 154-155, no. 163; the canons were reiterated at the council held in April, 1338 (*ibid.*, I, 188, no. 191). Cf. Fredericq, *Corpus*, I, 639.

[6] Cf. Hefele-Leclercq, VI, 1, 607f, 611, 624.

[7] *Ibid.*, VI, 1, 549, 607.

[8] Robert, dean of St. Servais at Maestricht, was named by the bull of October 30, 1309, papal inquisitor general in Germany, Bohemia, Poland, Prussia, and Sweden. Since he was to be present in person at the provincial synods where final sentence was pronounced against the Templars, these councils were held within the space of a few weeks, starting at Cologne (Hefele-Leclercq, VI, 1, 607).

[9] *Ibid.*, VI, 1, 606-607.

[10] *Ibid.*, VI, 1, 608-610; Mansi, XXV, 230-248; Hartzheim, IV, 117-127.

[11] Mansi, XXV, 297-350; Hartzheim, IV, 174-225 (especially 200f); cf. Mosheim, pp. 202-203.

[12] Cf. Binterim, VI, 125; Hefele-Leclercq, VI, 1, 607-608, 611.

[13] Fredericq, *Corpus*, I, 155; Mansi, XXV, 261; cf. council of Treves in 1338 (Fredericq, *Corpus*, I, 188).

[14] *Ibid.*, I, 155; Mansi, XXV, 261. At the beginning of 1326 similar bands had appeared in the province of Sens under the names of *begardi* or *penitencie homines* (Le Grand, *Les Béguines de Paris*, p. 24, note 3).

[15] Mansi, XXIV, 86, can. 34.

[16] Fredericq, *Corpus*, I, 161, no. 167; cf. Moll, *Kerkgesch.*, II, 1, 356; II, 3, 109. Frederick concludes (*Gesch. d. Inquis.*, II, 159, note 2) that this decision must have been rendered on April 28, 1310 instead of February 8, 1311, the date given in *Corpus*, I, 161.

cemetery and a chapel where their own chaplain could say mass.[17]

In a letter written on April 1, 1311, to the bishop of Cremona, Rainer of Casale, Clement V expressed concern over "the sect of the Free Spirit" in that region. "In some parts of Italy," the pope writes, "in the province of Spoleta and neighboring areas, there are a number of men and women, religious and lay alike, who wish to introduce into the Church a kind of abominable life which they call freedom of the spirit, that is, license to do whatever pleases them."[18] Then follows bitter invective against this conception of liberty. It is doubtful, however, that this represents a trickle of heresy from the Rhineland across the Alps. It is rather an indigenous protest. John XXII's bulls a decade later illustrate how beguins and bizoches had fused with the Fraticelli and other native groups.[19] In any case, extraregulars who bear these names in Italy and southern France must be treated apart from the Belgian and German counterparts, even though the papal curia sometimes handled the problem without distinction.

It remained for the two Clementine decrees promulgated at the Council of Vienne in 1311, together with subsequent re-enactments of John XXII and his successors, to define—although actually much confusion was to ensue from their efforts—the beguine-beghard problem and to enlist papal support in the attempts of the German and French episcopate to crush these heretical confraternities.[20] Conceivably this legislation was dictated under pressure of sporadic outbursts from visionaries and petty heresiarchs of the Margaret Porete type or the *pseudo mulier* from Metz who flourished about the same time. The latter feigned piety under the habit of the beguines and lived in Flanders among them, claiming false and specious revelations. By her deceitful words, relates the chronicler, she often deluded the king and queen as well as the nobles, especially since the crown was then preparing an attack upon the Flemings.[21] The *Annales Colmarienses Maiores* had reported earlier (1282) the seizure of a priest who confessed he was a heretic and that he had learned his errors from an *inclusa*. The context strongly suggests identification with a beguine-like person.[22]

---

[17] Franquinet, *Beredeneerde inventaris*, I, 89-92.

[18] Mosheim, p. 242; Raynaldus, *Annal. eccl.*, ad ann. 1311, no. 66, XV, 90.

[19] For the beguins and bizoches in Italy and southern France, see Ehrle, "Die Fraticellen," *ALKM.*, IV (1888), 8-20; *CUP.*, II, 215ff; Bernard Gui, *Practica Inquis.*, ed. Douais, pp. 264ff; Douie, *Heresy of the Fraticelli*, pp. 248-258; on the beguins of Tarragona, MDAC., VII, 306; Raynald. ad an. 1247, no. 56; ad an. 1306, n. 18; 1312, nos. 17, 57; Delacroix, *Le mysticisme spéculatif en Allemagne*, pp. 77ff.

[20] Fredericq, *Corpus*, II, 67-70, no. 41; Mansi, XXV, 389-392; for a detailed study of the council see Ewald Müller, *Das Konzil von Vienne, 1311-1312* (Münster i.W., 1934).

[21] The continuer of the Chronicle of Gerard de Frachet, an. 1304, in Bouquet, XXI (1855), 23.

[22] *MGH. SS.*, XVII, 210.

In the first of these decrees, *Cum de quibusdam mulieribus*, the beguines were admonished to abandon, on pain of anathema, their pursuit of common life without vows or profession of approved rule. Theirs is not the religious form, for upon affiliating themselves with these communities they do not promise obedience or renounce their property. They usurp the right of wearing a peculiar habit and submit to the direction of whatsoever religious their disposition inclines them. Of such fundamental importance in this decree that it is feasible to cite the text in entirety:

> There are certain women, commonly called beguines who, although they promise no one obedience and neither renounce property nor live in accordance with an approved rule, and consequently can in no wise be considered regulars, nevertheless wear a so-called beguine habit, and cling to certain religious to whom they are drawn by special preference. It has been repeatedly and reliably reported to us that some of them, as if possessed with madness, dispute and preach about the Highest Trinity and divine essence and in respect to the articles of faith and the sacraments of the Church spread opinions that are contradictory to the Catholic faith. They deceive many simple persons in these things and lead them into various errors; they also do and commit under the veil of holiness much else which endangers their souls. Therefore, after hearing frequently from these and others about their perverted principles on account of which suspicion has rightfully fallen on them, we believe that we must, with the approval of the holy council, prohibit forever their status and abolish them completely from the church of God. We must forbid these and all other women, on pain of excommunication which we wish to impose forthwith on the recalcitrants, to retain in any way in future this status which they perhaps have long assumed or to be allowed to accept it again in any form. Moreover the aforesaid regulars who are said to promote these women in the status of the beguinage or induce them to assume this status are strictly forbidden, on pain of like excommunication which they shall immediately incur if they oppose prescribed rules, to admit any women who long ago adopted the status in question or perhaps wish to adopt it again, or to offer such sectarians any counsel, aid, or favor. Against the preceding regulations shall no privilege prevail.[23]

This apparently unequivocable and irreconcilable stand was, however. qualified by a concluding "saving clause" which left the door open for the continuation and foundation of worthy beguinages.

Such was substantially the position also taken by John of Dürbheim, bishop of Strasbourg (1306—1328),[24] in that highly significant

---

[23] *Constit. Clement.*, lib. III, tit. xi. *De religiosis domibus*, c. 1; Hefele-Leclercq, VI, 2, 681f; Mosheim, p. 245; Fredericq, *Corpus*, I , 167-168, no. 171.

[24] Rosenkränzer, *Johann I von Strassburgs genannt von Dürbheim* (diss., Treves, 1881). From Mosheim to Preger and Jundt John of Dürbheim was confused with John of Ochsenstein. The death of the bishop of Strasbourg, Friedrich von Lichtenberg, in 1306 created a disputed election in which four candidates made a bid for the office: John of Florchingen, Magister John of Ochsenstein, Hermann von Thierstein, and Johann von Erenberg, the first being provost, the other three archdeacons of the Strasbourg church. The provost died in the interim; his elec-

letter written to his clergy on August 13, 1317,[25] which nevertheless hearkened back not to the Clementine canons, but rather to the decisions of the council of Mainz[26] of which province he was a suffragan. John had served Albert I (1298—1308) as chancellor until the latter's death;[27] later he became adviser to Frederick of Hapsburg after Henry VII's death (1313).[28] But these political activities did not detract from his episcopal duties. Relying on data gathered by an inquisitorial commission throughout his diocese, the bishop exhorted his clergy to oppose the "ceremonies, conventicles, habit, and teachings" of men and women commonly called "beghards" and "begging sisters" or *Schwestrones*[29] who shout for alms in the squares and streets. Under the appearance of piety they referred to themselves as "the Sect of the Free Spirit" and "brothers and sisters of voluntary poverty."[30] Yet the fact that among these sectarians, who after all were widely scattered in the city and diocese, were numbered many clerks in holy orders, monks, and married people,[31] would lead to the conclusion that their opinions were perhaps entertained among those who were not necessarily wandering beggars. "True beguines never begged; where mendicant beguines appear, they are outcasts—those who had given themselves over to an irregular life, as renegade monks and nuns often did."[32] At the same time the Rhenish sects may have offered a *raison d'être* to these *gyrovagi* against whom medieval councils fulminated so insistently. Beghards are under the illusion, the bishop claims in a brief analysis of their seven fundamental errors,[33] that men, being divine by nature, can become one with God so that his will, power, and actions are identical with divine will, power, and actions. In consequence of this natural union (*per naturam*) with God such

tors then chose John of Arzilières, later bishop of Toul. Each candidate solicited unsuccessfully recognition from the pope and the chapter at Mainz. When Albert dispatched his chancellor John and Philip of Rathsamhausen to Clement V to press for the election of his cousin John of Ochsenstein, the pope gave the office to the bishop of Eichstätt and appointed the other envoy to the see of Eichstätt. See Rosenkränzer, *op. cit.*, pp. 15-16; Denifle, in *ALKM.*, II, 616, note 2.

[25] *Strassb. UB.*, II, 309-313, no. 358; Mosheim, pp. 253-261. On the question whether the ideas contained in the document were inspired by Eckhart, see Denifle in *ALKM.*, II, 616-617; Haupt, in *ZKG.*, VII (1885), 521-529; *AFH.*, XIV, 172-173.

[26] *Strassb. UB.*, II, 311; Mosheim, p. 258. On July 22, 1318, the bishop called to the attention of his clergy a number of decisions of the council of Vienne (*ibid.*, II, 325, note 1; see the document of August 5, 1318, *ibid.*, II, 324-326, no. 370).

[27] Rosenkränzer, *op. cit.*, pp. 18ff.

[28] *Ibid.*, pp. 43ff.

[29] Whereas the people called the men "beghardi," the women were labelled "Schwestrones," with the qualification *Brod durch Gott* (Mosheim, p. 262). For John of Strasbourg's relation to the beguine-beghard problem, see Rosenkränzer, *op. cit.*, pp. 76ff.

[30] Mosheim, pp. 256, 260; cf. Binterim, VI, 63-64.

[31] Mosheim, p. 256; *Strassb. UB.*, II, 310; cf. *AFH.*, XIV, 173.

[32] Uhlhorn, *Liebesthätigkeit*, II, 382; see above, p. 149.

[33] *Strassb. UB.*, II, 310-311.

men are no longer capable of sin, and even if they should indulge in a sinful act, for them it would not be so considered. They repudiate Christ, his passion and divinity; they deny the prerogatives of the secular and regular clergy; they affirm the ability of the layman to administer the sacraments; they challenge the belief in hell and purgatory, for neither Jew nor Saracen can be damned—his soul, too, will be reunited with the Godhead; since much of Scripture consists of poetry, it cannot compel conviction; and finally, their conception of absolute perfection undermines the veneration of saints —whether the Virgin or Paul—since their merits are rendered puny alongside theirs. Because of their devastating attack on the visible church and its penitential system, these heretics, the indictment continues, are to be driven from their abodes and the houses used for their meetingplaces should be confiscated for the benefit of the church and the poor. The books that contain their doctrines and hymns are to be turned over to the priests within fifteen days and burned. All who do not repent and abandon their peculiar habit within three days after publication of the episcopal edict shall be excommunicated, and those who give them charity shall be dealt with in like fashion. Nor was John content with mere threats. He made a visitation of his diocese in which he found many of the sectaries. He organized an inquisition of learned theologians by whom they were tried; those who recanted were on the first occasion required to do penance, whereas those who remained obdurate he handed over to the secular arm to be burned. On the other hand, this document, like the decree *Cum de quibusdam mulieribus,* contains a very significant qualifying clause: the bishop does not wish to create prejudice for those religious who belong to the third order of the Friars Minor (i.e., tertiaries of both sexes who lead a common life) or orthodox secular beguines (i.e., tertiaries residing in their own family) or any other affiliates of the approved friar orders who govern themselves by their counsel.[34]

In the second and more precise decree *Ad nostrum, qui desideranter* (November, 1311)[35] Clement V extended his condemnation of extraregular societies to the "sect" of "wicked men," the beghards, as well as to the "faithless women," the beguines, particularly in imperial lands (*in regno Alemanie*). The pronouncement of eight specific errors [36] which harmonize with Free Spirit doctrine had the practical result of associating the conduct and metaphysics of orthodox beghards and beguines, above all in Belgium, with those professing pantheism. These errors all resolve into the one cardinal doctrine: man can attain in this life complete perfection and in this state, which

[34] *Ibid.,* 312.
[35] *Constit. Clement.,* lib. V, tit. iii, *De haereticis,* c. 3; Fredericq, *Corpus,* I, 168-169, no. 172; Hefele-Leclercq, VI, 2, 682-684.
[36] See above, pp. 497-98.

renders him incapable of sin, he can dispense with fasts, prayers, good works, and all ecclesiastical prescriptions. Heterodoxy undoubtedly was characteristic of the disorganized mendicant beghards in Germany who ran through the streets individually or in loose bands shouting "Brot durch Gott!" Not only was this identification of beghard with Free Spirit constantly reiterated in fourteenth-century sydonal decisions, but is possible that the Flemish mystic Ruysbroeck unconsciously came under the influence of Scotus Erigena through these beghards and the Brothers of the Free Spirit.[37] Yet the unsettled life, the aimless wandering from place to place, which contemporary sources present as characteristic of the beghard movement in the Rhineland, has been considered rather as a consequence of the asceticism and voluntary poverty of orthodox beguines and beghards and perhaps inquisitorial action taken against them than a symptom of the restlessness and libertine doctrine of the Free Spirits.[38]

A comparison of the two Clementine decrees indicates that while in the decree Cum de quibusdam mulieribus the general dissolution of the beguine movement was solemnly proclaimed, the pope in the concluding clause expressly exempted from inquisitorial processes those women who, with or without a vow of chastity, remained firm in the faith and honestly desired to do penance in their convents.[39] Clement V was therefore obliged to recognize that this desire for an untrammeled religious life, the renunciation of the agitation and distractions of the world, and a retreat into the tranquillity of the beguinage were inspired by evangelical examples. This concession notwithstanding, the "saving clause" is not tantamount to admitting that the Christian is free to do penance in his own way provided it causes no unrest in Christendom and no injury to the church. For at all times ecclesiastical prescription is expected to mold and direct even the religious life of the extraregular. This was the principle that continued to inform papal policy during the fourteenth century. Although the popes were ever reluctant to confer on these semireligious communities the status of an order, a means for incorporation into the ecclesiastical fabric was provided through generally voluntary adoption of Augustinian regulations or a third rule. The terms mulieres religiosae, sorores, begine, or paupercule begine which had previously been

[37] To use the words of Gerson (Op. omn., I, 62): "The author was not a conscious heretic, but probably, unknown to himself, came under the influence of the doctrine of the beghards to whom he himself was opposed." Cf. d'Aygalliers, Ruysbroeck, p. 282; cf. 281.
[38] Haupt, in ZKG., VII, 533ff
[39] "Sane per predicta prohibere nequaquam intendimus quin si fuerint fideles alique mulieres que, promissa continentia vel etiam non promissa, honeste in suis conversantes hospitiis penitentiam agere voluerint et virtutum Domino in humilitatis spiritu deservire, hoc eisdem liceat prout Dominus ipsis inspirabit" (Fredericq, Corpus, I, 168; Mosheim, p. 247).

employed in foundation documents were now often replaced by the phrases "sorores de tertio ordine b. Francisci," "mulieres paupercule aut sorores ordinis predicatorum."[40] Since third orders were not closely knit associations but merely collections of individuals bound to similar conduct, profession of a penitent rule by the inhabitants of certain beguinages ought not to be confused with corporative or conventual organization within the house.[41]

It is significant that the bishop of Strasbourg in the above-mentioned letter to his subordinates exempted from punishment those beghards who accepted the third rule of the Friars Minor or who came under some order approved by the Church. He also added the colorless exception of beguines who lead a pure and pious life. Such persons were to be tolerated in certain provinces[42]—presumably a reference to Belgium. On the other hand, the decree *Ad nostrum qui desideranter,* which appears to have been more particularly designed to answer the complaints of German prelates, was primarily concerned with religious conditions in the Empire: it condemned indiscriminately the masculine branch—the beghards—against which the archbishops of Trèves and Cologne had taken stern measures earlier. Here none was represented as innocent or righteous. The problem was well-nigh insoluble. There was nothing more delicate than to distinguish between orthodox beghards, heretical beghards, and tertiaries. Habit, daily life, outward appearances were the same. But what is more important, it was so easy to feign the piety of the orthodox. The more menacing the persecution became, the more closely the heretics sought to resemble the orthodox and to emulate their devotion.

Although the Vienne decrees furnished the groundwork for subsequent legislation against semireligious associations, they did not receive full legal force by authoritative publication under Clement V. Following a revision which he had proposed, they were adopted by a consistory held on March 21, 1314, and copies were sent to some of the universities. But the pope's death on April 20th caused new delay. The continuer of the chronicle of Guillaume de Nangis[43] and Gerard de Frachet[44] inform us that the Clementine decretals were for a time suspended because they seemed much too severe. After John XXII had them revised again, they were finally published at Paris and

---

[40] Phillips, *Beguines in Medieval Strasburg,* p. 183.

[41] *Idem.*

[42] "Per hanc autem nostram sententiam et praescription damnationis nostrae processum, Religiosis, qui sunt de tertia Regula FF. Minorum, aut Beguinis honestis secularibus, vel etiam quibuslibet aliis familiaribus fratrum approbatorum ordinum, et secundum eorum consilium se regentibus, nullatenus volumus praeiudicium generari, sed eos iuxta modum servatum in aliis provinciis perdurare" (Mosheim, pp. 260f).

[43] Guilllelmus de Nangis *Continuatio Chronici,* an. 1317, Bouquet, XX, 618.

[44] Girard de Frachet *Continuatio Chronici,* an. 1317, *ibid.,* XXI, 48.

other "scholae solemnes"[45] on October 25, 1317, two months after John of Dürbheim's action.[46] The contradictory character of the provisions concerning beghards and beguines is perhaps attributable to these repeated revision.[47] Indecision and compromise notwithstanding, these decretals mark the real turning point in the development of the extraregular movement.

Contemporary chronicles uniformly suggest the difficulties that beset the beguines. "Beguinae," wrote the continuer of Gerard de Frachet,[48] "super hoc specialiter sunt turbatae, quaniam in eis sine omni discretione status beguinagii condempnatur." "There were many," the *Chronica Provinciae Argentinensis* records,[49] "who interpreted wrongly and failed to distinguish between good and bad; these brought down serious scandals and unwarranted hardships on the faithful and unfaithful alike. How many German prelates who interpret the decretal indiscreetly and prosecute unfairly have compelled devout and humble women to take off their simple, harsh habit, to don thin dresses and to resume colored lay clothes. They have persuaded continent women, bound by the vow of chastity, to marry and what is more detestable have cast *inclusae* out of their habitations and obliged them to live in the world. They even applied this decretal to members of the third order which St. Francis founded, and in this way tried to involve the Friars Minor as patrons of condemned persons in the sentence of excommunication." On this latter point John of St. Victor makes a significant observation:[50] the beguines henceforth were deprived of their beguinages and their "order" condemned; no longer did they sing or read in them. But thanks to the Dominicans and Franciscans it was declared that the beguines in Paris and several other "good" towns might remain in their status.

In view of continued confusion the pope issued the bull *Etsi apostolicae* (February 23, 1319)[51] forbidding the Vienne decretal to be extended to the "Tertium Ordinem Poenitentium seu Continentium S.

[45] *Idem*; Bouquet, XX, 618. For the date of publication see Müller, *Das Konzil von Vienne*, pp. 389-408.

[46] Ehrle, in *ALKM.*, I (1885), 541-542; John of St. Victor, *Vita Joannis XXII*, in S. Baluzius, *Vitae Paparum Avenionensium*, I (ed. G. Mollat, Paris, 1914), 120; *Chronicon provinciae Argentinensis*, AFH., IV (1811), 681-682; RQ., XIV (1900), 247-248; John of Winterthur, *Chronicon*, *Archiv für schweizerische Geschichte*, XI (1856), 66.

[47] Lea, *History of the Inquisition*, II, 369.

[48] Bouquet, XXI, 48; cf. continuer of the Guillaume de Nangis chronicle, *ibid.*, XX, 618.

[49] AFH., IV (1911), 682-683; RQ., XIV (1900), 248; cf. John of St. Victor, *Excerpta e memoriali historiarum*, Bouquet, XXI, 666.

[50] Bouquet, XXI, 666, note 13: "Dont lors les Beguines furent privées de beguinage et leur ordre dampns; ne n'i chantoit on, ne n'i lisoit on: mès Dieu merci et l'ordre de Saint Dominiien et l'ordre de saint François, il fu puis declaré que celles de Paris et de pluseurs autres bonnes villes demourroient en leur estat."

[51] BF., V, 163-164, no. 354; Mosheim, pp. 267f; Fredericq, *Corpus*, II, 77f.

Francisci." Even then, the chronicler adds,[52] clerics did not desist from persecuting the brethren, but "increasing in evil not only against them but also against their friends, to wit *personas saeculares,* they proclaimed the most wicked sentences... The pope, taking compassion on the brethren, accordingly gave them protectors and judges, to wit, the archbishop of Besançon, the bishops of Metz and Würzburg, so that the brethren might have refuge and receive more prompt redress." This was the intention of the bull *Dilectos filios,* issued the following April 26.[53]

Notwithstanding similarities in details and outlook with the foregoing chronicles, it will be useful to cite extensively from the Franciscan, John of Winterthur, who offers in his account, written between 1340 and 1347,[54] a vivid, albeit biased description of the consequences that attended the promulgation of the Clementine decretals.

> Such disgraceful perils, strife, and unrest produced in the people so much fear and bewilderment, at least in Germany, that no one can describe it. This was especially due to one decretal in Book VII beginning with the words, *Cum de quibusdam mulieribus.* When it was published and although poorly understood and yet stubbornly and deceitfully promulgated in the chanceries of Germany, innumerable hearts of the sisters of the third order of St. Francis and of many others were sorely wounded. For, having laid aside their religious habit, they had to don the secular. Many had been serving the Lord in chastity and the other virtues and by good works in their own or their parents' houses for forty years and more in gray, black, and white garments. Now they are obliged by their parishioners to wear reds, yellows, greens, and blues. Having laid the others aside, they were compelled to appear in church in these. If they did not conduct themselves like laymen, they gave little pleasure to the pastors and parishioners. How much ridicule, contempt, foolhardiness and rashness these modest and chaste sisters endured God alone knows! They were turned into a spectable and a proverb by all men. O how often have they suffered great humiliation when they were shamefully dragged and mauled in public. The confusion that was brought upon them under pretext of the Clementine decree was, sad to say, the cause of ruining many. For those who had long practiced celibacy for the Lord returned to the world, now that the vow of chastity had been broken, and either contracted marriage or what is worse committed all kinds of fornication. But those who clung to the vow of continence in the face of this tremendous fury of persecution, just like gold being tested in the furnace, prepared in their purity a dwelling worthy of God. How much labor and expense the Friars Minor used at the Holy See for the repair and reinstatement of their sisters no one one can easily estimate. For through the apostolic see the brothers and sisters of the third order of St. Francis, due to the intercession of the Friars Minor and their friends, were shortly restored to their original status. If any one should see or hear, as I have, sobs,

---

[52] *RQ.,* XIV (1900), 248.

[53] *BF.,* V, no. 365; Mollat, 9347.

[54] For the dating of the chronicle see Georg von Wyss, *Archiv für schweizerische Geschichte,* XI (1856), p. xxiii.

moaning, bitter lament, high pitched wailing, and tearful faces, accompanied with the most shrill shouts, I do not doubt that he would grieve from the innermost depths of his heart. They are coerced by parishioners, blinded by hatred, ignorant of scripture, unable to comprehend the words of this decretal,—or some of them know but carefully twist the meaning of the words out of jealousy and perverseness—under pretense of papal injunction and through fear, threats, and slander, through fulmination of excommunication and deprivation of sacraments, through frightening and shameful barking, horrible noises, in view of all men on Sundays in church . . .[55]

Following his defense of the third order, the chronicler points out that the decree was directed only against the beguines who owed obedience to no one, refused to renounce their property, and failed to profit from any approved rule. Then echoing the common charges, he adds that some of them, in their insanity, dispute the trinity and divine essence and by preaching introduce into matters of faith and the sacramental system opinions contrary to the church.

Since John of Strasbourg was very anxious to publish and spread among the clergy of his diocese the legislation of the councils of Mainz and Vienne, he held several synods to cope with the problem. Similarly, a number of regulations, ambiguous and contradictory as they often were, testify to his zeal to make the prelates more fully cognizant of their spiritual functions,[56] especially in view of the "multitude" of beguines.[57] But the episcopal persecution demanded on August 13, 1317, was only transitory and ineffective; far from settling the issue, John of Dürbheim's pronouncement had merely confounded beghards and the Brethren of the Free Spirit and labelled heretical their habit previously not considered objectionable. He was accordingly obliged to ask pope to define the criterion for distinguishing between heterodoxy and orthodoxy during the process[58] and to call upon specialists in civil and canon law to prosecute the extraregulars more vigorously.[59] Since some sectarians had fled to neighboring dioceses, Bishop John wrote the episcopal authorities concerned to take action against them. In a letter of June 26, 1318, he urged Bishop Heinrich of Worms, whom he calls "amicorum suorum praecipuum," to guard his diocese more closely.[60] In carrying out papal instruction he admits with the chroniclers, however, that much injustice had been

[55] *Ibid.*, 66-67.
[56] Rosenkränzer, *op. cit.*, pp. 73ff.
[57] For John XXII's repetition of the bishop's estimate see below, pp. 539ff.
[58] Haupt, in *ZKG.*, VII (1885), 521.
[59] Rosenkränzer, *op. cit.*, pp. 77-78.
[60] Mosheim, pp. 268-269, cf. 267; *Strassb. UB.*, II, 332, note 2. This is not the Emerich who helped John to settle the Essen affair in 1312 at the request of Clement V (Rosenkränzer, *op. cit.*, pp. 39f). For the tertiaries and beguines in Worms, see Bihl, "De tertio ordine S. Francisci in provincia Germaniae Superioris sive Argentinensi syntagma," *AFH.*, XIV (1921), 186-196.

visited on the orthodox beguines and recluses "to the irritation and concern of the faithful." The bishop thus appears to have been ready to inject fresh blood into the ecclesiastical body. Urged by the pope to extend to the Friars Minor his protection so that they might preach and hear confessions without restraint, he had encouraged not only them but the Dominicans as well to administer the sacrament of penance. In 1319 the bishop, apparently under pressure of the secular clergy, was obliged once again to issue letters, declaring that the Clementine decretals and the bull, *Sancta romana atque universalis ecclesia*,[61] had been enforced elsewhere, but not in the diocese of Strasbourg.[62]

Emphasizing that final clause in the pronouncement of August 13, 1317, did not specifically exempt tertiaries from prosecution, the prior of the Friars Preachers in Strasbourg called to the bishop's attention that in the spring of 1276 the three houses of beguines, popularly known as *reiche Samenungen,* to wit, "zum Turm," Innenheim, and Offenburg,[63] all near the convent of the Order of Preachers, had received from Friar Frederick of Erstein identical regulations. By thus submitting to the Dominicans the fifteen sisters listed "zum Turm," for example, hoped "materiam dissolutionis suspectae et nocivae diffugere et ad disciplinam conmendabilem coherceri."[64] Besides, it is possible that the seven convents of women at Strasbourg which the Dominicans had brought before 1281 under the rules of St. Augustine and their own constitution owed their origin to beguine circles.[65] The Friars Minor presumably adopted a similar course for their convents of women.[66]

That the secular clergy of Strasbourg was strongly incensed against the Order of Preachers and the Friars Minor is proven by the accusation that the cathedral and other collegiate chapters hurled on August 5, 1318, against both orders for ministerpreting Clement V's decrees.[67]

[61] See below, pp. 536-37.
[62] Haupt, in *ZKG.,* VII (1885), 522-523.
[63] See above, pp. 203-04.
[64] *Strassb. UB.,* III, 27.
[65] Bihl, in *AFH.,* XIV, 141-142, 164-165; Bernard Gui's evidence in MDAC., VI 546-547; Denifle, in *ALKM.,* II, 651-652.
[66] Schmidt, *Strassburger Beginenhäuser,* p. 212. Whereas the Order of Preachers supervised seven convents, the Friars Minor had been controlling since 1244 a convent of Clarisses located "auf dem Rossmarkt" (*ibid.,* p. 159; for evidence of February 18, 1254 (*Strassb. UB.,* I, 289, no. 381; 15243; *BF.,* I, 704, no. 519) and February 4, 1255 (*Strassb. UB.,* I, 291, no. 385; *BF.,* II, 15, no. 19; 15671) and Cardinal Hugh's concession of December 24, 1254 (*Strassb. UB.,* I, 291, no. 384; *BF.,* II, 8, no. 9; P. 15640). In 1299 they acquired another Clara house "outside the walls auf *dem Werde*" (Wörth) (Schmidt, *Strassburger Beginenhäuser.* p. 160). It is possible that there were not yet in 1287 many houses of Franciscan tertiaries leading a common life except the "domum Episcopi" founded in 1286 by the bishop of Toul for twenty-six poor beguines and entrusted to the abbess of the St. Clara convent "auf dem Rossmarkt" (*ibid.,* p. 164).
[67] *Strassb. UB.,* II, 324-326.

There is reason to believe that reference was being made specifically to the patronage which the mendicants enjoyed over their penitents. Thus John of Strasbourg, accommodating himself to the demands of his local clergy, recommended in his ordinance of January 18, 1319,[68] that the beguines abandon their *statum beginagii* and religious habit within a fortnight under pain of excommunication and return to their parish churches. He points out further that whereas neighboring bishops believed that the status of the beguines had been condemned without exception by the new decretal[69] and thus have long enforced that injunction in areas within their competence, he has not been able to decide "ex quibusdam probabilibus et specialibus motives" on implementing this policy lest unrest and danger be stirred up among the people. This "new constitution" appears to have been Clement V's decretal *Cum de quibusdam* which John XXII had added to the Clementines on October 25, 1317. Only through disagreeable and dangerous circumstances, above all the stubborn agitation of the parish priests, had he been persuaded to abolish the *statum beginarum*. Thus he was opposing the papal bull which explicitly allowed the beguines to retain their habit.

Only four weeks were to pass before Bishop John found himself obliged by ensuing confusion to elaborate this order by exhaustive instructions. In his third decree of February 17[70] he maintained that the dissolution of the beguine communities pronounced in the earlier edict was justified and specifically forbade the sisters to use gray outer garments or cloaks. Other colors were permissible so long as the beguines—even the orthodox *beguinae clausae*—did not adopt a uniform one. Another concession was granted when those beguines whose poverty made it impossible to obtain new clothes were allowed to continue to wear their former attire. He likewise released the recluses ("reclusas in suis reclusoriis perseverantes") from the obligation of changing their habit. There is little doubt that this injunction was directed against the habit of the Penitents of the Third Order. The ambiguous word *beguine* was becoming more dangerous to the cause of the Penitents in the eyes of the clergy who were hostile to them and the mendicant orders.

However, a new element was introduced at this stage when the Franciscan friar, Vitalis de Furno, cardinal-priest of St. Martin's (1312—1327),[71] issued two briefs in behalf of the tertiaries. The first letter, dated at Avignon on January 14, 1319,[72] was principally con-

---

[68] *Ibid.*, II, 331-333, no. 376; Haupt, in *ZKG.*, VII (1885), 560-651.
[69] "Statum beginarum virtute constitucionis nove indifferenter esse reprobatum."
[70] *Strassb. UB.*, II, 333-334, no. 377; Haupt, in *ZKG.*, VII (1885), 561-562; Bihl, in *AFH.*, XIV, 175-176, no. 15.
[71] Eubel, *HC.*, I 2, 15; cf. *AFH.*, II, 634.
[72] Bihl, in *AFH.*, XIV (1921), 176, no. 16; cf. *ibid.*, p. 174.

cerned with the German priests who were unjustly compelling Franciscan tertiaries or Penitents to abandon their status, habit, and rites
as if this had been stipulated in *Cum de quibusdam.* The second
brief,[73] which was addressed a little later in the year to John of Strasbourg, not only attacked the episcopal decrees of January 18 and
February 17 but also made reference to the bull *Etsi apostolicae.* The
cardinal reprimanded the bishop for extending, contrary to the intention of the recent bull and the privileges bestowed by the curia, the
Vienne decretal to affiliates of the third order of St. Francis—hence
they and the friars had been denied the sacraments. Moreover he had
presumed to implement the Clementine legislation by prohibiting the
tertiaries to use the *pannum humilem grisei coloris,*[74]—a measure
which the clergy of Strasbourg had zealously enforced to the disadvantage of the papal bulls. Thus the bishop was admonished to revoke his
orders and to inform the cardinal promptly through the messenger
who delivered the letter unless he wished to suffer papal discipline.[75]

John of Dürbheim's reply to Cardinal Vitalis is not extant.[76] But
further correspondence between him and the pope indicates that he
was changing his attitude towards the beguines. Making a distinction
between the orthodox and heretical, he had already motified John
XXII that heterodoxy did exist, but "preter prescriptam prophanam
sectam esse mulieres alias laudabilis status in partibus prelibatis in
excessiva copia quasi ducentorum milium numerum excedentes a
primis omnino diversas." [77] Yet prelates were compelling them to
return to the world. On rare occasions even recluses who had spent
fifty years in their cells were obliged to abandon their way of life.[78]

By October 8, 1319, the change in John of Strasbourg's policy
towards the Penitents can be detected at the papal court. For on that
day Fr. John of the Order of Knights Hospitallers of St. John, the
suffragan of Constance, complained bitterly at Avignon [79] of a certain
forger who had brought false letters of Fr. John himself into Germany
which contained disparaging remarks about the bishop and religious
persons (perhaps tertiaries) as well as fabricated letters of Berengar,
cardinal of Tusculum: John XXII had renewed the Clementine decree
by abolishing "all beguines indiscriminately." The suffragan of Constance then proceeded to warn all not to believe these letters and at

---

[73] *Ibid.,* 176-178, no. 17; cf. Al. Schulte, "Ein Formelbuch der Minoriten von
Schaffhausen," *Zeitschrift für Geschichte des Oberrheins,* XL (N.F. I) (1886), 213-
214.

[74] Bihl, in *AFH.,* XIV (1921), 175, no. 15.

[75] *Ibid.,* 176, no. 16.

[76] *Ibid.,* 178.

[77] *Strassb. UB.,* II, 332, note 2.

[78] *Idem.*

[79] Bihl, in *AFH.,* XIV, 179-180, no. 18; Schulte, in *Zschr. f. Gesch. d. Oberrheins,*
XL (N.F. I) (1886), 214-215.

the same time praised the zeal of the bishop in behalf of the beguines and tertiaries.

We have already noted that unwillingness to confuse heresy and orthodoxy in the application of the conciliar decrees in full rigor was amply exhibited by John XXII and his entourage in a number of pronouncements.[80] Expressing regrets for errors that had been committed, the pope had admonished the bishop of Strasbourg in an undated letter[81] to protect women who lead a life above reproach. In marked contrast to the German *beghinae singulariter in saeculo manentes*[82] who tended to deviate from traditional piety, the majority of Belgian and Dutch beguines and beghards continued to rely on the sacramental system and cling to customary devotional practices; nor do contemporary sources mention them as begging in the same measure as the German extraregulars are depicted. "The condemnation notwithstanding," wrote the continuer of Guillaume de Nangis' chronicle, "their condition improved with the passage of time; . . . for among them were many good and religious persons who performed deeds of practical charity."[83] In John XXII the beguines of the Low Countries found an ardent champion who issued a number of decretals to implement the saving clause of *Cum de quibusdam mulieribus*. While he exhibited increasingly active concern over the status of these semireligious associations in the north, it was the Spiritual Franciscans with their cult of extreme poverty who received primary attention.[84] Throughout 1317 and early 1318 he wrote repeatedly to Frederick of Sicily,[85] demanding the expulsion of the Tuscan zealots who had fled southward under the leadership of Henry de

[80] Cf. letter from Cardinal Nicholas of Ostia to John of Dürbheim: "Ne novellae constitutionis rigor nimius, interpretatio falsa, crudelis et indiscreta executio fas nefasque confunderet, religionem cum superstitione deleret et prudentes virgines cum fatuis coaequaret" (cited by Delacroix, *Le mysticisme spéculatif en Allemagne*, p. 97, note 2).

[81] Mosheim, pp. 630-632.

[82] Philippen, *Begijnhoven*, pp. 133-134.

[83] Continuer of Chronicle of Guillaume de Nangis, Bouquet, XX, 618 : "Quod tamen mandatum non sine consilio et adjutorio creditur esse factum. Nonnulli volunt asserere, quod ordines mendicantium non nisi aequivoce seu solo nomine mendicabat, quamdiu Beguinatii status in suo robore perdurabit."

[84] Douie, *Heresy of the Fraticelli*, pp. 15-16. The special sect in the south which went under the name of *beguin* harbored a deep-seated hatred for the papacy. But its views resembled those of the Spiritual Franciscans. An expression of anger at John XXII's sanction of the bulls, *Exiit qui seminat* (1279) (*BF.*, III, 404-416; cf. V. Maggiani, "De relatione scriptorum quorumdam S. Bonaventurae ad bullam "Exiit" Nicolai III [1279]," *AFH.*, V [1912], 3-21) and *Exivi de paradiso* (*BF.*, III, 80-86, no. 195) by the promulgation of the decretal *Quorundam exigit* (*BF.*, V, 128-130, no. 289), the protest of the strict champions of the Testament was simultaneous with the reissue of the Clementine decrees. Not only had John XXII lost all authority to bind and loose but he was commonly believed to be the mystica Antichrist who was to prepare the way for one greater and even more wicked than himself (Douie, *Heres; of the Fraticelli*, p. 251).

[85] March 15, 1317, *BF.*, V, 110-111, no. 256; *Gloriosam ecclesiam* (January 23,

Ceva[86] in order to escape that threat of excommunication launched against them by the archbishop of Genoa and the bishops of Bologna and Lucca.

At the close of 1317 (December 30) the pope issued the bull *Sancta romana atque universalis ecclesia*,[87] which was specifically directed in the spirit of canon 13 of the Fourth Lateran Council against the southern extraregulars variously known as *fraticelli, fratres de paupere vita, bizoti (bizochi)*, or *beghini*—in general all those leading an eremitical or semireligious existence under the third rule of St. Francis and who claimed for their congregations and conventicles the privileges granted by Celestine V. They were located principally in Italy, Sicily, Provence, Narbonne, and Toulouse.[88] Charges were lodged against them for electing their own superiors—who were called ministers and guardians,—receiving recruits into their sect, wearing a religious habit, erecting, buildings for common life, and openly begging "as if their sect were one of the orders approved by the Holy See." Similarly, the *beguini* in the dioceses of Maguelonne and Béziers received official attention.[89] More to the point, however, was John XXII's important qualification in his bull *Racio recta non patitur* (August 13, 1318) that "in many parts of the world" there are women who, under the name of beguines, live with relatives or in their own houses; they lead a life beyond reproach, attend church regularly, and submit to the local clergy.[90] Such persons, he explained in a special letter to the bishop of Strasbourg, should be allowed to keep their former vestments and pursue their way of life without diminution of property or rights. This bull was reissued by the successor to the apostolic see, Benedict XII, on January 19, 1336[91] and thus, alongside the Clementine decretals, remains fundamental to fourteenth century legislation concerning this problem.

In short, the ordinances of the bishop of Strasbourg in 1317, his letter of June 22, 1318, to the bishop of Worms, the two ordinances of 1318 together with John XXII's letter of the same year all make it possible to determine at least for one German diocese the course of

---

1318), *ibid.*, V, 137-142, no. 302. On February 4, 1325, the pope sent to Robert of Sicily a constitution directed against those called Spirituals but not against the Friars Minor (*ibid.*, V, 282, no. 565).

[86] *AFH.*, II, 158-160; Vidal,*Bullaire*, p. liii, note 3; p. 40, no. 16 *bis*.

[87] *BF.*, V, 134-135, no. 297; Mosheim, pp. 623-626; *AFH.*, II, 253ff, 505ff; Oliger, in *AFH.*, VI (1913), 721.

[88] *BF.*, V, 136; Mosheim, p. 623; cf. Boase, *Boniface the Eighth*, pp. 29-51; Vidal *Bullaire*, pp. 7off; 40, note 1; 106, note 4.

[89] September 18, 1318, *BF.*, V, 157-158, no. 340; Vidal, *Bullaire*, pp. 42f.

[90] *Extrav. commun.*, lib. III, tit. IX, Friedberg, II, 1279f. Fredericq, *Corpus*, II, 72-74, no. 44; Mosheim, pp. 627-629; Peter of Herenthals, *Vita Joannis XXII* (Baluzius, I, 179); Schmidt, in *Alsatia*, VII (1858), 213; cf. the bull *Lectae coram* (*AFH.*, II, 178, no. 2);Gerard Groote, *De Simonia*, ed. De Vreese, p. 3.

[91] Fredericq, *Corpus*, II, 92-94, no. 56.

persecution unleashed against the beguines and beghards in the second decade of the fourteenth century and the procedure employed against them. Significantly enough, John XXII, in spite of his concessions to orthodox beguines, refused consistently to recognize them as an independent order and continued to urge close episcopal surveillance.[92] In his examination of the papal decretals, *Sancta romana, Etsi apostolicae, Dilectos filios, Dudum dilectis (April 18, 1320),*[93] *Cum de mulieribus* (November 22 and December 31, 1320), and *Si ea quae* (February 26, 1322),[94] Oliger[95] mentions no less than twenty petitions written in favor of the Third Order against which the bull *Sancta romana* had served as an instrument of persecution.[96] The evidence suggests that a formidable campaign was waged in several countries against and secular tertiaries, especially the regular who were confused in the blanket condemnation of extraregular sects.

Even though the pope attempted to draw fundamental distinctions between the orthodox and heterodox, it would be too much to expect that the deputies, particularly the inquisitors, charged with the execution of the instructions, could satisfactorily cope with the fine distinctions in concrete cases or resist pressure groups and direct their attention only against the proscribed. The ordinance of January 18, 1319, makes it clear that for some time John of Strasbourg had been in dispute with other church officials over the interpretation of the *Sancta romana*. Whereas in the neighboring dioceses papal stipulations had been interpreted with the purpose of preserving the beguines, the bishop of Strasbourg was reluctant to define more closely his earlier order touching these *mulieres sanctae*.[97] It is significant that, far from being closed, the *Gotteshäuser* actually increased in number in Strasbourg from 1318 to 1340.[98] Such institutions for the poor met a need of the age. Although the Brethren of the

---

[92] See above, p. 000.

[93] *BF.,* V, 183-184, no. 396.

[94] *Ibid.,* V, 222-223, no. 462. In this bull the pope ordered the bishops of the south to examine the beliefs and claims of the tertiaries and to punish only the suspect (Vidal, *Bullaire,* pp. 68f, no. 37; see the letters with the same import to the archbishop of Rheims and the bishops of Noyon and Amiens [June 13, 1325], Mollat, nos. 22548, 22537, 22538). Owing to fresh violence in the Franciscan conflict (Vidal, *Bullaire,* pp. LIV-LV) John XXII found it necessary on August I (1322) to remind the episcopate and inquisitors of the penalties in *Sancta romana* (*ibid.,* pp. 70-2, no. 39).

[95] Oliger, "Documenta inedita ad historiam Fraticellorum spectantia," *AFH.,* VI (1913), 724, 728; cf. ibid., VIII (1915), 318.

[96] *Ibid.,* IV, (1911), 537-540.

[97] Haupt, in *ZKG.,* VII (1885), 523. Cf. the case of the priest Pierre de Tournemire, who having embraced as a youth the beguin life, died under persecution in Carcassonne (Vidal, *Bullaire,* pp. 293f, no. 189 [June 13, 1343]; cf. p. 142, note 4); the case of Adhémar de Mosset, *ibid,* pp. 195f, nos. 130 *bis* and *ter,* March 31, and April 18, 1333; pp. 197f, no. 132, September 13, 1333; p. 200, nos. 135-136, October 7; pp. 202f, no 139, January 13, 1334.

[98] Schmidt, in *Alsatia* (1858), 214; *AFH.,* XIV (1921), 181-182, 153-154.

Free Spirit were persecuted in Alsace intermittently, being condemned at the synod of Strasbourg in 1335 and thirty years later sought out and punished by Henry de Agro,[99] the orthodox beguines were left pretty much unmolested. Even subsequent persecution failed to suppress completely the extraregular. In 1412 the Halle convent got from the patrician Heinrich his house together with a rule governing its internal life. But by restricting admission to tertiaries only the statutes sought defense against heretical beguines.[100] In Rothenburg the beghards who followed the third rule of St. Francis in 1400 depended on alms for a part of their livelihood. The Dinkelsbühl convent was even more so a poor house. Furthermore, the bishop of Würzburg, far from remaining hostile, took the beghards under his protection in 1403.[101]

[99] Mosheim, pp. 332-333; see below pp. 560-561.
[100] Rücklin, pp. 138f.
[101] Ibid., p. 140 and note 255.

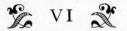

VI

Rehabilitation of Beguinages

BELGIUM

For the sake of precision with respect to the Belgian scene the bull *Racio recta* was supplemented on May 21, 1319, by another bull, *Sacrosancta romana*, putting the *beguinae clausae* of Brabant and their property under papal protection.[1] This brief, which was also addressed in another communication to the *dilecte in Domino filie beghine* of Brussels,[2] indicates that assistance had been solicited from the papal offices by the Brabançon sisters, as John XXII explains, "vestris iustis postulationibus grato concurrentes consensu." In consequence of this decretal, the beguines in Brabant who had hesitated to submit to a dissolution of their communities and had thus resisted the ecclesiastical ban were now reconciled to the Church. The brief that was issued a few months later (November 25, 1319) at Malines[3] by one John, bishop of Vaison (*Visionensis*)[4] and commissioner of the bishop of Cambrai in whose territory most of the Brabançon sisters resided, brought about a similar reconciliation for the beguines inhabiting the beguinage known as the *Solatium beatae Mariae*[5] at Vilvorde near

---

[1] Frederick, *Corpus*, II, 78-79, no. 47; cf. Hallmann, *Geschichte des Ursprungs*, p. 81.

[2] The unpublished post-Ryckel *Beschryvinghe van het Beggijnhoff van Brussel* (Bibl. roy. de Belgique, Brussels, cod. 16566-74, 3ᵛ-4ʳ) offers in connection with the 1323 proceedings the substance of this bull, "gegeven tot Avignon den 21 van mey in het derde jaer van ons Pausdom." It affirms that "de Roomsche h. kercke heeft altydt zeer bemindt de godvruchtige ende ootmoedige kinderen." Sanderus (*Chorog. sac. Brab.*, III, 228) published the Latin text of the bull which is identical with the one addressed to the Brabançon beguines save for the new addressee: "Dilectis in Christo filiabus magistrae et sororibus hospitalis pauperum juxta Bruxellam, Cameracensis dioecesis". However, Sanderus gives the date as May 23.

[3] Fredericq, *Corpus*, II, 79-80, no. 48.

[4] Although it is possible that *Visionensis* is an error for *Vasionensis* (Vaison in Orange), nevertheless the bishop at this time was Raymond de Beaumont (*ibid.*, II, 80, note 1; Eubel, *Hier. cath.*, I, 547). Cf. Wauters, *Histoire des environs de Bruxelles*, II, 499f.

[5] "Conventus Begginarum apud solatium beatae Mariae commorantium" (1240), cited by Hallmann, *Geschichte des Ursprungs*, p. 66; cf. Innocent IV's protection bull of February 10, 1244 (*ibid.*, p. 67). For the Vilvorde beguines about 1318, see Wauters, *Histoire des environs de Bruxelles*, II, 505; cf. 500.

Brussels. John acquainted the dean of Christianity in the city with the provisions of this agreement and recommended the imposing of the usual penance.

In order further to curb irregularities the pope, on the strength of "reliable reports" concerning virtuous and faithful beguines, instructed the bishops of Toulouse,[6] Tournai,[7] Cambrai,[8] and Paris[9] in the bull *Cum de mulieribus* to conduct an investigation in person, or through a commission, of the faith and morals of the *mulieres religiosae* in their respective dioceses with the purpose of defending the material and spiritual interests of the orthodox. A similar directive was passed along to Pierre de Chappes, bishop of Arras (1320–1326), on November 24, 1321,[10] and the bishop of Liége four years later (June 22, 1324).[11] Faced with interminable delays, the pope concluded the latter brief with the demand for prompt action.[12] As a summary of curial opinion on this matter, the bull *Cum de mulieribus* deserves partial quotation:

We have learned through reliable reports that in your city and diocese there are many of these women, called beguines, who run the gamut of virtue, live respectably, attend church frequently, obey their superiors, and care naught for disputes nor fall into error. They are not deceived, nor do they deceive others, by false opinions, opposed to evangelical truth. On the contrary, they live in wholesome simplicity: some reside in their own houses, others with relatives, some rent their dwellings, others live in common with a respectable family; finally, there are those who, driven by necessity and for closer observance of chastity, dwell together in the several beguinages. Heretofore they have lived and continue to live virtuously so that we have never been able and cannot now bring against them any complaint or reproach. For that reason it has been called to our attention how unjust it is to confound under the same penalty the innocent with the guilty. We have been informed that on this occasion there were in your city and diocese (i.e., Cambrai) dissensions and even dangers of war; we have been asked to intervene on their behalf by virtue of the providence of the Holy See. We therefore beseech you by this apostolic letter to conduct either yourself or through a deputy an inquiry into the life of these women. If you find that the information given to us is correct, see that they are not molested either in person or goods

[6] Bull *Cum de mulieribus*, December 20, 1320, Fredericq, *Corpus*, I, 171.

[7] December 20, 1320, Béthune, *Cartulaire*, pp. 69-70, no. 98; Fredericq, *Corpus*, I, 170-171, no. 175.

[8] Cf. *ibid.*, I, 173-175, no. 178 (the bull of December 30 is contained in the bull of February 23, 1323); ibid., 3-4, no. 5 (January 31, 1321); cf. Mollat, 12800. It is possible that the bull was also sent to the bishops of Liége and Utrecht (Fredericq, *Corpus*, I, 172). Cf. Haupt, in *ZKG.*, VII (1885), 516, 524.

[9] *BF.*, V, 195, no. 417: "Episcopis Cameracensis, Tornacensis, Parisiensis idem mandat de beghinis, quod paulo ante mandaverat episcopo Tolonensis" (the date given here is December 31, 1320).

[10] Fredericq, *Corpus*, II, 80-81, no. 49; Mollat, 14796; Riezler, *Vatikanische Akten*, pp. 140-141, no. 269.

[11] Fredericq, *Corpus*, II, 85, no. 52; Mollat, 19808.

[12] Fredericq, *Corpus*, II, 85: "De quibus necnon et vita et conversatione ipsarum frequenter inquirere solerti diligentia, super quo tuam oneramus conscienciam, non postponas."

until the Holy See makes another decision with respect to their status; if you discover someone who molests them, pursue them with ecclesiastical penalties. But in any event, warn these women not to engage in subtle questions contrary to the legislation of our predecessor...

This admonition, like the previous ones, appears to have fallen on deaf ears, for the Belgian bishops were in general remiss in their obedience to the papal order. Although John XXII had sent his letters to the bishops of Tournai and Cambrai at the end of December, 1320, the first did not take action until 1322 or 1323[13] while the second waited until 1328. The bishop of Cambrai, Pierre III de Lévis-Mirepoix, in whose diocese Margaret Porete had brought discredit before compromising them at Paris, was the French successor of Philippe de Marigny who himself had succeeded Guy de Collemèdio, the first judge of her errors. Pierre was sympathetic to John XXII who transferred him from Cambrai to Bayeux in 1324. The delay in the diocese of Cambrai may be attributed to popular uprisings.[14] The bishop of Arras did not open an investignation before 1323 and the bishop of Liége in 1324.[15] A letter couched in the same terms as the one sent to the bishops of Cambrai and Tournai was addressed to the bishops of Lombardy and Tuscany in 1326 (June 1).[16]

The several episcopal investigations all worked to the advantage of the Belgian and French beguines: at Valenciennes,[17] Brussels,[18] Antwerp,[19] Alost,[20] and Termonde[21] in the diocese of Cambrai; at Douai

[13] Mertens and Torfs, *Gesch. van Antwerpen*, I, 425-426.

[14] Papebroch, *Annal. Antw.*, I, 91.

[15] There is no evidence that the papal directive was forwarded to the bishop of Terouanne whose diocese extended in Flanders as far as Ypres and Furnes (Fredericq, *Gesch. d. Inquis.*, II, 32).

[16] The letter is reproduced in the second appendix of Mosheim, p. 638. He also published (p. 630) a similar communication to the bishop of Strasbourg in 1318. Cf. Haupt, in *ZKG.*, VII (1885), 517. On August 1, 1322, the inquisitors in Sicily, Italy, Narbonne, and France were instructed to requisition Friars Minor to reinforce the bull *Sancta Romana* which was aimed against the Fraticelli (*BF.*, V, 229-230, no. 474).

[17] August 5, 1322, Fredericq, *Corpus*, III, 4-5, no. 7. The investigation was conducted by Godfrey, abbot of Vicogne, throughout the diocese of the bishop of Cambrai—at Antwerp, Brussels, and other Flemish and Brabançon communities (*ibid.*, III, 6-7, no. 9, July, 1323).

[18] December 8, 1323, *ibid.*, II, 81-82, no. 50. The abbot of St. Bernard at Antwerp, the dean of St. Gudule at Brussels, and John of Alost, pastor of Morseele, all examined the beguines of the Vineyard (*curtis de Vinea*) at the order of Bishop Pierre III. Cf. *ibid.*, III, 6f. AAPB. Carton H. 262 contains a copy of this report (XV C?). On February 23, 1324 Pierre reported the results of the investigation (Fredericq, *Corpus*, II, 83-85, no. 51 published the document from the XV C. copy on paper which reposes in AAPB. Carton H. 262. The original, however, may be found in AGR., arch. eccl., 13402, no. 7). La Vigne was closed between 1317 and 1321; in spite of favorable decisions from above it was still closed on June 4, 1324, and in 1328. Sometime before March 19, 1333, after this prolonged delay, it was reopened, but Ter Arken had after 1311 been converted into a hospital for old women (Bonenfant, *Une fondation*, p. 103 and note 1).

[19] February 23, 1323, Fredericq, *Corpus*, I, 173-175, no. 178; MF., I, 215-216;

in the diocese of Arras;[22] at Bruges, Ardenbourg, Damme, Ghent,[23] and Audenarde[24] in the diocese of Tournai; at St. Christopher at Liége, Tongres,[25] Maestricht, St. Trond,[26] Louvain, Tirlemont, Léau, Diest, Borchloon, Hasselt,[27] Aerschot,[28] Roermond,[29] and Breda[30] in the diocese of Liége. After the decision restored all rights to the beguines of Cambrai, the Antwerp magistrates in 1325 returned to them the hospital of Clapdorp[31] which had been founded primarily for needy, sick beguines who lived not as *clausae begginae* but scattered, either in their parental home or their own houses.[32]

An earnest effort to render justice to those worthy beguines in the diocese of Liége whose proximity to the Rhenish sisters was a source of perpetual danger was again reflected in a communication of Adolph de la Marck (1313–1344) dated April 23, 1325.[33] There it was specifically a question of the *mulieres religiosae* in the parish of St. Christopher whose life had been above reproach "since they visit orphans and widows in their sorrow." He expressed the hope that under his auspices the community would flourish. Although his predecessors had shown interest in the well-being of the beguinage and had provided it with sound rules, these had proven inadequate. Adolph then proceeded to draw up a new ordinance governing obedience to the parish priest, attendance of sacraments and divine offices, residence in the beguinage,

cf. Diercxsens, *Antverpia*, II, 58-59; Mertens and Torfs, *Gesch. van Antwerpen*, I, 426; Papebroch, *Annal. Antwerp.*, I, 90.

[20] September 7, 1317, Fredericq, *Corpus*, III, 161-162, no. 140.

[21] On January 13, 1317 (*ibid.*, III, 160-161, no. 139) John instructed the cantor at Termonde to return to the beguinage all confiscated property. Cf. *ibid.*, III, 163-164, no. 142 (February 23, 1324).

[22] August 16, 1323, *ibid.*, III, 7-8, no. 10. The bishop of Arras re-established the beguines at Douai.

[23] May 17, 1328, *ibid.*, I, 178-181, no. 180; cf. *ibid.*, II, 391.

[24] Vanderstraeten, *Recherches sur les communautés religieuses*, II, 97-98.

[25] Thijs, in *BSSLL.*, XV (1881), 33: On April 30, 1324, Adolph de la Marck renewed the bull that Boniface VIII had granted the beguinage of Tongres in March, 1299 (for the bull, see *ibid.*, 429, P. J. viii; cf. *ibid.*, 26).

[26] In addition to the blanket injunction Bishop Adolph also renewed in 1328 (Straven, *Notice historique*, pp. 115-116, no. 6) for St. Agnes in St. Trond permission to receive the sacraments and to enjoy ecclesiastical sepulture during interdict granted in December, 1311 (*ibid.*, 110-111, no. 4). Again, on January 21, 1343, Pope Clement VI issued a bull to confirm exemptions allowed by the bishop of Liége (*ibid.*, 116-118, no. 7).

[27] Lambrechts, *Het oud Begijnhof van Hasselt*, pp. 170-174, no. 4.

[28] October 24, 1324, Fredericq, *Corpus*, II, 86-88, no. 53.

[29] Adolph de la Marck's instructions (March 1, 1325), *ibid.*, II, 88-89, no. 54; Sivré, in *Publication soc. hist. arch. dans le duché de Limbourg*, XI (1874), 188-190, P. J. iv; cf. *ibid.*, 169f.

[30] April 1, 1330, Juten, *Cartularium*, pp. 13-16, P. J. xii.

[31] Diercxsens, *Antverpia*, II, 62, cf. 55, 63-64; Prims, *Gesch. van Antwerpen*. IV. *Onder Hertog Jan den Derde (1312–1355)*, Bk. II (Antwerp, 1933), 130ff.

[32] Diercxsens, *Antverpia*, II, 62-64. A number of chaplaincies were founded in the beguinage at Antwerp from the XIII C. on (*BG.*, I, 1902, 312f, nos. 130-135, 141).

[33] *AHEB.*, XXIII (1892), 73-77.

and the interior life. Some sympathy for the extraregulars may also be seen in a brief of July 22, 1322, in which Engelbert Françoys, canon in Liége, appointed by the bishop to protect the beguines at Roermond, charged the pastor of the church to prevent Reynald of Guelders together with the bailiff and echevins of the town from interfering further with the liberties and customs which Adolph had granted the sisters.[34] In 1353 Engelbert de la Marck, bishop of Liége from 1345 to 1363, testified to the integrity of the Belgian beguines with special reference to those living in Diest by declaring that they had nothing in common with the German sisters.[35] He was persuaded to approve on April 1, 1361, statutes for the beguinage of St. Catherine *ten velde*. He pointed out in the preface that carefully defined regulations are necessary for the preservation of discipline. It is significant that no mention is made of the intrusion or appeal of heretical thought; immoral practices which attended semireligious life alone are aimed at.[36] Jurisdictional disputes continued to plague the Brussels beguinage. Ghiselbert Mutsaert, dean of St. Pierre at Turnhout, confirmed on September 28, 1425 by virtue of Pope Martin's V's bull of July 4 the right of the four mistresses of the beguinage to choose and present their pastor. The installing, we have seen, belonged to the abbot of St. Bernard "de antiqua et approbata ac hactenus pacifice observata consuendine." On January 16, 1427/8 Jean V de Gavre, bishop of Cambrai (1413-38), forbade the beguines, under penalty of excommunication, to confess in the beguinage to any priest other than the pastor or his chaplains, or someone designated by him.[37]

Just as the count of Namur exempted the beguines of Oignies from mortmain and *fourmorture* (October 14, 1327),[38] so on June 12, 1319, Count Robert of Flanders entrusted the defense and protection of the *mulieres religiosae* in St. Elizabeth at Ghent to Master Henry Braem, canon at Tournai.[39] The following February 28 the count took the beguinage under his protection.[40] Guillaume de Ventadour, bishop of Tournai (1326—1333), during his absence from the province, delegated in two documents dated March 24, 1328,[41] his authority to three deputies, the deacon F., Raymond de Pinoliis, a canon, and Jean Cordiele, the official of Tournai, as vicar-generals and empowered them to

[34] Sivré, *l.c.*, XI (1874), 187-188, no. 3.
[35] Raymaekers, in *Messager*, 1862, p. 88; id., *Kerkelijk Diest*, p. 439 (here the date is given as 1355).
[36] Philippen, in *BG.*, IV (1905), 327-328.
[37] AAPB., Carton H. 262; see above p. 176ff; for original of 1427/8 document see AGR., arch eccl., Carton 13402, no. 13.
[38] *ASAN.*, XXXII (1913), 53-54, no. 334.
[39] Béthune, *Cartulaire*, p. 67, no. 94. Earlier the count had entrusted the administration of the beguinage to the prior of the Friars Preachers (October 15, 1312), *ibid.*, p. 66, no. 92.
[40] *Ibid.*, p. 68, no. 96.
[41] *Ibid.*, p. 72, no. 104; p. 73, no. 105; Fredericq, *Corpus*, I, 178-180, no. 180.

examine the beguines in accordance with John XXII's bull of December 30, 1320. They went to Bruges, Ardenbourg, Damme, and Ghent to gather information. They listened to witnesses; at Ghent a lengthy memorandum, which is of capital importance for an understanding of the movement, was presented to them on May 14 to call for the protection of the Ghent sisters.[42]

After testifying to the purity of their faith—that they did not dispute or preach concerning the Trinity or divine essence or undermine and mislead the untutored—the memorandum recalled the kind of modest life led by the sisters in St. Elizabeth, poor to the point of misery. Even though many living in common were so impoverished that they had only their clothes and a bed, it stressed their diligence in manual work lest they become a burden to others. By sewing and washing clothes sent to them daily from the city they derived such profit that not only did they provide their meager fare, but they paid their tithes and were generous in their alms. The deputies commended them for their obedience to the superior in each convent, the *magistra operum* who supervised the work and workers. In offering a defense for the beguine status the investigation, however, described most minutely their orthodox religious practices and primarily on this basis found their *raison d'être*. Rising at the break of dawn they first gathered at the church for mass and prayers, each being assigned to her own place so that absence might be more easily checked. They then returned to their homes to spend the day working in silence; yet while so engaged they did not cease from prayer, for two beguines in each convent who were more capable read aloud the *Miserere* and the other psalms they knew, as well as the *Ave Maria*, one taking one verse, the other the next and the rest reading silently with them or paying close attention to what they recited. In the evening after vespers they attended church again for prayers and meditation. Sundays and holy-days were given over to mass, sermons, prayers, and meditation; on these days no one could leave the beguinage without permission of the superior. They were content to eat coarse bread and sauce and to quench their thirst with cold water or weak beer. Many were accustomed to fast on bread and water and to avoid the use of linen either for clothing or on their beds, employing rather straw mats. They were so well ordered in their manners and trained in domestic matters that the well-to-do and respectable (*magne et honeste*) were wont to entrust to them their daughters for rearing, for they hoped that to whatever condition the girls might be called in the future, whether religion or marriage, they

---

[42] The memorandum is published by Béthune, *Cartulaire*, pp. 73-76; Fredericq, *Corpus*, I, 175-178, no. 179. For the decision of the deputies on May 14th, see Béthune, *Cartulaire*, pp. 76-78, no. 107; Fredericq, *Corpus*, I, 178-180, no. 180. For motives contained in the report see above pp. 148f.

would be found better prepared. So much was their conversation informed with fear of God and the Virgin that never had anything extra-ordinary or suspect been heard from the congregation. If an inmate died the others in the convent attended the funeral with prayers and commendations. The gray color and simple, rough cut of their habit were uniform so that they could be compelled more strictly to avoid whatever was suspected by others. The beguinage was administered by a beguine appointed by the heads of the convents and known as the *magistra principalis curie* or the *magna magistra*. She was retained or removed from office, after the annual check on the accounts, according to the wishes of the convent heads. She in turn governed the superiors of the several convents with the consent and advice of the houses and the burghers (*proborum*). She was charged with the punishment of delinquents either through action within the beguinage or by transferring the culprit to another convent. Without her permission no one could leave the beguinage or spend the night in town. No one could leave the house at any hour without the consent of the conventual mistress. Even then she must not go out unless accompanied by one or more members of the convent. The memorandum concludes: "This place was visited with devotion by the illustrious confessor and very pious king, St. Louis. He took so much pleasure in their piety that he obtained the consecration of their church by the bishop of Tournai. He secured for the beguines many privileges and liberties to encourage their holy life; finally, on the pattern of this place, he founded and endowed a beguinage at Paris as well as several others in different places."

Papal intervention to assure restoration of confiscated property in response to pleas from St. Elisabeth's at Ghent remained constant among John XXII's successors, with the abbot of Eename (diocese of Cambrai),[43] the dean of St. Pharaïlde (diocese of Tournai),[44] and the abbot Grammont (diocese of Cambrai)[45] as the recipients of the injunctions. Alongside the church authorities the civil heads, too, continued to support the beguinage at Ghent without hesitancy. Count Louis de Crecy issued the usual type of protection letter on November 3, 1336.[46] In 1354 Louis de Male, count of Flanders, in supplementing the statutes of Countess Margaret, acknowledged in his preface the social problems with which the beguinal movement was grappling.[47] Learning that there were persons "in various towns" who were trying to compromise or abrogate the privileges and immunities which these beguines had

[43] Benedict XII's instructions of May 28, 1335 (Béthune, *Cartulaire*, p. 83, no. 118).
[44] Pope Clement VI on June 22, 1342 (*ibid.*, p. 85, no. 123).
[45] Gregory XI on February 11, 1371 (*ibid.*, p. 104, no. 154). The following May 14 the abbot published the bull for the mistress of the hospital (*ibid.*, p. 105, no. 155).
[46] *Ibid.*, p. 84, no. 121.
[47] *Ibid.*, pp. 89-92, no. 130.

enjoyed of old, he reaffirmed their rights on March 31, 1359.[48] Later in
the year (August 14, 1359) the count appointed two citizens of Ghent,
Simon the Amman and Simon van Vaernewijc, to assist in the supervision of the community.[49] Although the documents published by
Béthune do not reflect nearly the same lively preoccupation with
beguine affairs as the fonds in the Archives de l'Assistance Publique
de Bruxelles and the Archives Générales du Royaume do for the Brussels beguinage, the Ghent echevinage nevertheless occasionally offered
its services to St. Elizabeth[50] and individual officials appear from time
to time as witnesses to business transactions. The dukes of Burgundy
exhibited similar concern for the community. On August 26, 1386,
Philip the Bold answered a request of the beguines for relief by remit-
ting two-thirds of a rent of 20 *livres parisis* which they owed him.
Their financial dilemma was attributed to the losses and damage
caused by recent wars in Flanders.[51] Shortly after (October 18, 1395) he
undertook to assure the beguinage payment of certain back rents in
Ghent.[52] His successor John moreover ordained on June 8, 1405, that
the former limits of the beguinage should be maintained.[53]

Donations, anniversaries, legacies continued to increase the wealth
of St. Elizabeth's beguinage, the waves of persecution notwithstanding.
But the one significant conclusion that can be drawn from Béthune's
cartulary was the increasing attention paid in the fourteenth century
to the Holy Ghost Table which, from its earliest appearance in the
records in December, 1278,[54] now shared with the infirmary[55] a claim
to these gifts and foundations.[56]

FRANCE

However harsh the criticism, concrete evidence of the popularity
of the movement is the donations bestowed on the beguine hou-

[48] Béthune *Cartulaire*, pp. 94-95, no. 134:" ...IJ verstaen dat men hemlieden in
diversen steden van haren rechte vercranken wille ende moeijenesse doen, ende
speciallic dat men hemlieden pijnt te heesschene ende volghen wille van enighen
yssuen, taillen of exactien, die zij van ouden tiden niet sculdich zijn nog ghecos-
tumert hebben te gheldene, also zij segghen, ende zij ons hebben ghedaen supp-
lijeren dat wij hemlieden daerof in rechte houden wilden ende bescermen als onse
voorders ghedaen hebben" (*ibid.*, p. 95). A week later (April 6), a vidimus was
issued for this document by Friar John, prior of the Dominicans at Ghent and confessor of the count of Flanders (*ibid.*, p. 95, no. 135).
[49] *Ibid.*, p. 96, no. 137.
[50] E.g., May 8, 1425, *ibid.*, 147-148, no. 208; on January 27, 1438, they confirmed to the beguinage its fishing rights at the Waelpoorte (*ibid.*, p. 160, 232; cf.
ibid., pp. 163-164, no. 242, January 15, 1445).
[51] *Ibid.*, p. 121, no. 172; cf. October 18, 1395, *ibid.*, pp. 128-129, no. 185.
[52] *Ibid.*, pp. 128-129, no. 185.
[53] *Ibid.*, p. 135, no. 194.
[54] *Ibid.*, pp. 31-32, no. 38.
[55] Cf. inventory of income of the infirmary in 139...? (*ibid.*, pp. 124-126, no. 178).
[56] For the obligations of the infirmary to the Holy Ghost Table in 1367, see
ibid., p. 102, no. 150.

ses.[57] Being informed that the beguines of Rheims were conducting themselves in a manner above suspicion by refraining from theological discussion and by submitting to conventional church attendance, the pope in like fashion instructed the archbishop on June 13, 1325, not to disturb the persons or property of the *plurimae* beguines in the province, if an episcopal investigation warranted moderation.[58] The archbishop appears to have proceeded slowly, for it was not until seventeen years later (April 10, 1342) that Jean de Vienne agreed to maintain both Cantiprés.[59] The beguinage in Paris, protected by royal authority, did not suffer from these repressive measures, but by the latter half of the fifteenth century it had practically decayed out of existence.[60] Foucard de Rochechouart, bishop of Noyon, certified the orthodoxy and good conduct of the beguines in his diocese.[61] Jean de Soissons, canon of Sainte-Perine at Saint-Quentin, was instructed to have one of John XXII's bulls executed prescribing the maintenance of the beguines at Noyon according to episcopal recommendation.[62] The same recognition was extended by the papal curia on no less than three occasions to the beguines of Roubaud in Marseilles, founded by St. Douceline, in the heart of the Spiritual Franciscan country. In a bull of November 22, 1320,[63] John XXII informs the bishop of Toulouse that on the authority of Santia, queen of Sicily, he has learned that there are in the *castro de Areis* several women, known as the beguines of Roubaud who "running through the fragrance of the virtues," live respectably, attend church, obey their prelates, and do not become involved in disputations and errors; nor do they deceive with damnable presumption their own minds or those of other people. Nor do they depart from evangelical truth. Accustomed to simplicity, they remain in the same habitation in order to observe chastity more closely. Three years later (December 18, 1323)[64] this recommendation, couched in identical language, was addressed to the bishop of Marseilles.

Thanks to the support of the Dominicans and Franciscans and also owing to their own good renown the French beguines were able to resist the attacks of their foes and were consequently listed by the pope among those who deserved to be maintained, as Charles IV in-

---

[57] Kurth, *La Cité de Liége*, II, 256.

[58] Robert, *Les béguines de Reims*, pp. 41-43, P. J. ix.

[59] *Ibid.*, pp. 44-45, P. J. x.

[60] So far had it decayed that in 1471, when Louis XI transferred the beguinage to the Franciscan tertiaries, it numbered but two (Le Grand, *Les Béguines de Paris*, p. 44).

[61] *Ibid.*, p. 27, note 1.

[62] *Idem.*

[63] Albanés, *La vie de Sainte Douceline*, pp. 299-300, P. J. xiii *bis*.

[64] *Ibid.*, pp. 276-277. Cf. the letter to the provost of the church at Aix (February 16, 1325) with reference to the beguines of Roubaud (*ibid.*, pp. 277-280, P. J. XV.

dicated in the preamble of the rule he gave them in 1327.[65] He recalled with satisfaction that the Clementine decrees pertained only to
those beguines "outside our kingdom." Strong with the approval of
the Holy See, the beguines had solicited royal sanction for their organization. They submitted to the French king the statutes that they had
received from the prior of the Friars Preachers, to whose direction
Philip the Fair, Louis X and Philip V had previously entrusted them.[66]
After they had been revised by Friar Pierre de la Palu, a Dominican,
and Masters Richard des Champs and Jean Justice, with the collabo-
ration of the mistress and the elders of the beguines, the king had
these ordinances reviewed, *pour plus grand fermete d'ycelles*, by
Friar Wilbert, his confessor, and Master Michel de Mauduit and
other members of his council. He finally promulgated them in May.[67]
A few years later, in 1341, these rules were again confirmed and completed by Philip VI and thus constituted the final form of the charter
of the Paris beguinage.[68]

There is no evidence that the Rheims sisterhoods were disturbed
by the new prohibitions issued by Gregory XI in 1371.[69]

THE NETHERLANDS

During the pontificate of John XXII, who had given currency to the
Clementine legislation, repressive measures were however repeatedly
levelled against the German sisters—in Mainz, Cologne, Strasbourg,
and Constance[70]—while Bishop Emicho of Speier was reproved for
weak prosecution of the associations. In Friesland and Groningen,
where Franciscan tertiaries and sisters of the common life became
numerous, the beguinages failed to flourish. Whereas they were more
prominent in the provinces of Utrecht, North Brabant, Zeeland, and
Guelderland, it was above all in the county of Holland, where certain
cities like Dordrecht, Haarlem, Delft, Leiden, and Alkmaar had two
or three beguine houses each, that the movement attained sizable
proportions.[71] Under Count William III (1304—1337), who acted as
protector of monastic and quasi-monastic communities during the
proscription period,[72] the beguines were defended against the Cle-

[65] Le Grand, *Les béguines de Paris*, pp. 27-28, note 4. Le Grand concludes that
the document was issued in May.
[66] *Ibid.*, p. 52 (Philip VI's preface to the rule of 1341).
[67] *Ibid.*, p. 28 and note 1.
[68] *Ibid.*, p. 29. /
[69] Robert, *Les béguines de Reims*, p. 16.
[70] Hauck, V, 1, 408.
[71] Moll, *Kerkgeschiedenis*, II, 2, 153-154; Römer, I, 237-238, 631; for a bibliography on the several Dutch beguinages, see Philippen, *Begijnhoven*, pp.
457-463.
[72] Delprat, "De Geschiedenis van het S. Aagte-klooster te Delft," *Kerkhistorisch
Archief*, IV (1866), 23-77.

mentine decrees and their cause was actually promoted through donations and foundations.

The beguinage at Haarlem, established in 1262 by Arnold of Sassenheim, pastor of St. Bavo,[73] was the object of frequent endowment: by Dirk of Sassenheim in 1282, Cille Eggaerts in 1301, and Jan Persijn in 1353.[74] In 1382 (September 8) Count Albert I (1358—1404) allowed the beguines free choice of a confessor[75] and seven years later took the sisterhood under his protection, gave it a rule, and enjoined the magistrates to punish its offenders.[76] On November 29, 1401, the duke granted the beguines, at the request of his second wife Margaret of Cleves, the right to choose their own priest.[77] On the other hand, the beguine house that Margaret van Rozenburg founded at Rijnsburg in 1362[78] apparently languished.[79] The founder of the beguinage at Heusden[80] was the same knight, William of Kroonenburg, through whose offices the Cistercian monastery of Marienkroon (Corona B. Mariae)[81] was transferred from Heesbeen, where it had been founded in 1338 as a nunnery by Mechtild of Oud-Heusden, widow of the knight, Herbaren van Riede, to Heusden in 1382.[82] The house of Gorinchem presumably existed before the fifteenth century.[83] The beguinages at Eindhoven and Oudheusden[84] appear late, the former not being founded until November 21, 1571, by Bishop Metsius at the request of Joannes Constantius Gijskens.[85]

As early as 1346 a beguinage was established at Amsterdam when Coppe van der Lane donated before the echevins on July 31 a building to some women already residing in it (den ioncfrouwen den beghinen tot enen vrien eyghen).[86] This groote or ronde beguinage, located in

[73] Van Heussen, Batavia sacra, II, 290 (here the date of foundation is given as 1262); 369-370 (1269 is reported here.) Cf. ibid., II, 290 (Catalogus pastorum d. Bavonis Harlemi, an. 1273). Van Heussen, Historia episcopatuum foederati Belgii, II (Harlem, 46).

[74] Römer, I, 243; 633.

[75] Van Mieris, Charterboek, III, 390.

[76] Ibid., III, 544.

[77] Ibid., III, 748; cf. Römer, I, 633.

[78] Römer, I, 244.

[79] Ibid., I, 633.

[80] Ibid., I, 247, 641; Coppens, Nieuwe Beschrijving, III, 2, 51; Foppens, Hist. episc. Silvaducensis, p. 333.

[81] Coppens, Nieuwe Beschrijving, III, 2, 26, 48; Foppens, Hist. episc. Silvaeduc., p. 254; GC., V, 408; Van Heussen, Hist. epp. Belg. Ultraj., p. 253; Moll, Kerkgesch., II 2, 27.

[82] Römer, I, 137-138, 304-305; Coppens, Nieuwe Beschrijving, III, 2, 26, 48.

[83] Römer, I, 247.

[84] Coppens, Nieuwe Beschrijving, III 2, 60; Daris, Hist. du diocèse de Liége, p. 217.

[85] Coppens, Nieuwe Beschrijving, III 1, 78.

[86] Wagenaar, Amsterdam, II (1765), 365, no. 1; cf. ibid., 348. Between the preparation of volume I (1760) and volume II Wagenaar unearthed documents which compelled a considerable revision of his early judgment (I, 29). Cf. Eeghen, Vrouwenkloosters en Begijnhof, pp. 29-32, 319-351.

front of the sisters of St. Lucia, who followed the third rule of St. Francis,[87] has been called "one of the oldest religious foundations in the city."[88] In 1389 (April 25) the town council ordained on behalf of these *armer beghinen* that none of their property should be alienated or sold without the consent of the sisters.[89] Four years later (August 17) Albert granted a charter prescribing a rule for the house and offering ducal protection.[90] Not only did the community have its own chapel and special privileges conferred by local church authorities before the end of the fourteenth century,[91] but it continued to receive favorable attention from clergy and laity alike well into the sixteenth century.[92] The prince showed similar indulgence towards the beguine house at Rotterdam in 1378 (April 14).[93] Within two years (April 4, 1380) the city officials prescribed a rule for the first inhabitants.[94]

Leiden was the seat of three beguine communities. St. Agnes, also known as the Great Beguinage because it consisted of more than forty houses inhabited by the sisters,[95] was already in existence in 1316[96] and eventually was to abide by a rule drawn up in 1420 (January 18) by Count John of Bavaria,[97] after he invested the city.[98] The Pieter-Simons-beguinage, which was established before 1400 and presumably named after its founder, well known for his charitable activities,[99]

---

[87] *Wagenaar*, I, 29.

[88] *Ibid.*, II, 348; cf. Van Heussen, *Hist. episc.*, II, 112: "Coetus virginum Amstelodami, vulgo Beghinasium, pro urbis istius, modo amplissimae memoria, vetustus est, omnes fere monachorum aut monialium coetus aetate illic superans."

[89] Van Heussen, Hist. episc., II, 113; Wagenaar, *Amsterdam*, II, 365, no. 2; cf. 349; *Batavia sacra*, II, 395.

[90] For the document see *Batavia sacra, II, 394-395*; Le Long, *Beschryving*, pp. 236-237; Van Heussen, *Hist. episc.*, II, 112-113; Wagenaar, *Amsterdam*, II, 365-366; cf. II, 351.

[91] *Batavia sacra*, II, 395 (here a list of rectors is given); Römer, I, 639-640. The chapter of Notre Dame in The Hague issued a brief on August 18, 1419 (Wagenaar, *Amsterdam*, II, 367, no. 5) allowing the Amsterdam beguines to choose a secular priest for their chaplain. For confirmation by Frederick, bishop of Utrecht, see *ibid.*, II, 367f.

[92] Wagenaar, *Amsterdam*, II, 366-367, no. 4 (April 15, 1417); II, 368, no. 6 (January 26, 1475); for privileges and indults, see Van Heussen, *Hist. episc.*, II, 113-114.

[93] Van Mieris, *Charterboek*, III, 342; *Batavia sacra*, II, 193.

[94] Van Mieris, *Charterboek*, III, 372-373.

[95] Van Mieris and Van Alphen, *Beschrijving der stad Leiden*, I, 148-153; 11; cf. *ibid.*, 1057-1058; Blok, *Gesch. eener Hollandsche Stad*, pp. 57, 284.

[96] The will of Peter of Leiden, canon of St. Peter's at Utrecht and Middelburg, attested on November 10, 1316, among others, by the guardian of the Friars Minor at Middelburg and Friar Walter of Kaysnoet, lector of the friars at Valenciennes (Van Mieris, *Charterboek*, II. 175-176). The beguine house was mentioned again six years later in one of Count William's letters (*ibid.*, II, 297). Cf. Blok (*Gesch. eener Hollandsche Stad*, pp. 284) who gives the date 1293.

[97] Van Mieris and van Alphen, *Beschrijving der stad Leyden*, I, 148-149.

[98] *Ibid.*, I, 148; cf. Römer, I, 633-634; cf. 244.

[99] Van Mieris and Van Alphen, *Beschrijving der stad Leyden*, I, 28, 158; Römer, I, 244; for Pieter Symonsz. van den Oerde, consult Ligtenberg, *De Armezorg te Leiden*, pp. 237ff; cf. 162ff.

was obliged, when the clergy of St. Peter's took steps in 1400 to enlarge their cemetery,[100] to move to St. Joseph's square [101] and was henceforth known as Sion. The third beguinage was St. Pancras or, presumably after its founder, Gerrit Lams, beguinage,[102] with its seven inhabitants. The action that the Leiden officials took on December 13, 1403,[103] to prescribe a rule for the Pieter-Simons-beguinage received the count's stamp of approval two months later (February 16, 1404).[104] At the beginning of the fourteenth century Count John of Bavaria prescribed measures to prevent the spread of heresy and moral degeneration in these semireligious communities.[105] The inhabitants must lead a "godlic, eerlic, zedelic, vreedzaemlic ende gheestelic leven" and "Gode vlitelic dienen in gehoersaemheit der H. Kercken sonder enich bewint van waertlike saken." He defined the authority of the mistress of the beguinage who must consult the "outste ende vroetste" members on matters of discipline.

The beguinage at Schiedam is mentioned in the will of Cille Eggaerts.[106] Another sisterhood which, although not specifically called a beguinage, bore the characteristics of such an extraregular community, was established by the municipal authorities on September 17, 1405, to enable girls and widows "in een rein, ootmoedig leven zamen te wonen." [107] The beguinage at Dordrecht was founded by the count of Holland in 1303.[108] Tithe-exemption which William II had granted the beguinage at Gravenzande, one of the oldest in Holland,[109] was confirmed by Count Albert.[110] In the middle of the thirteenth century it had enjoyed the patronage of Matilda of Brabant, the wife of Floris IV (1222–1234),[111] and had later been remembered by Cille Eggaerts in his will in 1301.[112] Beguines had also settled in Utrecht [113] and Gouda.[114] Two houses were in existence in Delft during the four-

---

[100] Van Mieris and Van Alphen, *Beschrijving der stad Leyden*, I, 158. For St. Peter's, see *ibid.*, I, 29.

[101] *Batavia sacra*, II, 258.

[102] Van Mieris and Van Alphen, *Beschrijving der stad Leyden*, I, 153-154; for a list of the inhabitants at the beginning of the fifteenth century, see *Batavia sacra*, II, 258-259; Blok, *Gesch. eener Hollandsche Stad*, p. 286.

[103] Van Mieris and Van Alphen (*Beschrijving der stad Leyden*, I, 153-156) give the text of the rule.

[104] *Ibid.*, I, 156-157; cf. Delprat, *op. cit.*, pp. 32-33.

[105] Van Mieris and Van Alphen, *Beschrijving der stad Leyden*, I, 148.

[106] Römer, I, 245, 639; *Batavia sacra*, II, 203.

[107] Van Mieris, *Charterboek*, IV, 23.

[108] In 1326 (June 24) Count William III took under his protection the beguines at Dordrecht who had identified themselves with the order of penitence (*ibid.*, II, 392). For the date of foundation see Römer, I, 245; *Batavia sacra*, II, 168.

[109] Römer, I, 242; *Batavia sacra*, II, 258.

[110] Römer, I, 632.

[111] *Ibid.*, I, 242; cf. Van Mieris, *Charterboek*, I, 236.

[112] Römer, I, 243.

[113] *Batavia sacra*, II, 118; Ryckel, p. 354.

[114] Van Mieris, *Charterboek*, III, 638.

visited on the orthodox beguines and recluses "to the irritation and concern of the faithful." The bishop thus appears to have been ready to inject fresh blood into the ecclesiastical body. Urged by the pope to extend to the Friars Minor his protection so that they might preach and hear confessions without restraint, he had encouraged not only them but the Dominicans as well to administer the sacrament of penance. In 1319 the bishop, apparently under pressure of the secular clergy, was obliged once again to issue letters, declaring that the Clementine decretals and the bull, Sancta romana atque universalis ecclesia,[61] had been enforced elsewhere, but not in the diocese of Strasbourg.[62]

Emphasizing that final clause in the pronouncement of August 13, 1317, did not specifically exempt tertiaries from prosecution, the prior of the Friars Preachers in Strasbourg called to the bishop's attention that in the spring of 1276 the three houses of beguines, popularly known as reiche Samenungen, to wit, "zum Turm," Innenheim, and Offenburg,[63] all near the convent of the Order of Preachers, had received from Friar Frederick of Erstein identical regulations. By thus submitting to the Dominicans the fifteen sisters listed "zum Turm," for example, hoped "materiam dissolutionis suspectae et nocivae diffugere et ad disciplinam conmendabilem coherceri."[64] Besides, it is possible that the seven convents of women at Strasbourg which the Dominicans had brought before 1281 under the rules of St. Augustine and their own constitution owed their origin to beguine circles.[65] The Friars Minor presumably adopted a similar course for their convents of women.[66]

That the secular clergy of Strasbourg was strongly incensed against the Order of Preachers and the Friars Minor is proven by the accusation that the cathedral and other collegiate chapters hurled on August 5, 1318, against both orders for ministerpreting Clement V's decrees.[67]

[61] See below, pp. 536-37.
[62] Haupt, in ZKG., VII (1885), 522-523.
[63] See above, pp. 203-04.
[64] Strassb. UB., III, 27.
[65] Bihl, in AFH., XIV, 141-142, 164-165; Bernard Gui's evidence in MDAC., VI 546-547; Denifle, in ALKM., II, 651-652.
[66] Schmidt, Strassburger Beginenhäuser, p. 212. Whereas the Order of Preachers supervised seven convents, the Friars Minor had been controlling since 1244 a convent of Clarisses located "auf dem Rossmarkt" (ibid., p. 159; for evidence of February 18, 1254 (Strassb. UB., I, 289, no. 381; 15243; BF., I, 704, no. 519) and February 4, 1255 (Strassb. UB., I, 291, no. 385; BF., II, 15, no. 19; 15671) and Cardinal Hugh's concession of December 24, 1254 (Strassb. UB., I, 291, no. 384; BF., II, 8, no. 9; P. 15640). In 1299 they acquired another Clara house "outside the walls auf dem Werde" (Wörth) (Schmidt, Strassburger Beginenhäuser. p. 160). It is possible that there were not yet in 1287 many houses of Franciscan tertiaries leading a common life except the "domum Episcopi" founded in 1286 by the bishop of Toul for twenty-six poor beguines and entrusted to the abbess of the St. Clara convent "auf dem Rossmarkt" (ibid., p. 164).
[67] Strassb. UB., II, 324-326.

sealed at Middelburg,[127] the prince, with the approval of the local magistrates, ordered the restoration of the beguines to their former status. The abbot and echevins were to take the necessary measures to accomplish this. From a later document issued by the town magistrates it appears that Bishop John III of Diest, second successor of Frederick II of Sierck, assisted in the work of rehabilitation. On April 15, 1327,[128] the "scepenen, burghemeesters ende ghemeene raedt der poorte van Middelburch" took new measures to handle the problem. A decretal had arrived from the pope, so ran their statement, advising that the beguines should no longer exist because of the many grave errors of which they were guilty. But the beguines of Middelburg were and have been free of such crimes and have thus been wrongly afflicted by this edict. Since the bishop of Utrecht and the count of Holland understood the situation and the pope never intended that the innocent should be punished, the sisters should retain their freedom and protection as before. Nor would their property be diminished. Foreseeing that they might again be proscribed by the papacy,[129] the magistrates provided that the property should under such circumstances go to the town. Four commissioners were to be appointed, two by the count and two by the magistrates, to protect the beguines and to examine their annual account. Two other documents issued by Count William III concern the Middelburg beguinage: on September 20, 1329, he appointed the abbot of Middelburg to act as judge of the community;[130] seven years later (August 9, 1336) he had to charge an *oeverste meestersse* and other beguines to govern the house which had been upset *bi versumenesse van beleede*.[131] Approval was granted and rules were drawn up by Albert for the same community on April 11, 1368,[132] in a text that was almost identical with the document of April 4, 1390.[133]

On February 22, 1396, the magistrates of Gouda, with comital approval, prescribed a rule for the "poor beguines" or sisters of St. Margaret in that town.[134] Within three years (September 26, 1399) they appear to have adopted the rule of St. Francis; when Albert extended his protection to their persons and property and also allowed them to establish a chaplain, they were called sisters of Penitence of St. Francis.[135] Duke William subsequently approved

[127] Van Mieris, *Charterboek*, II, 352-353; cf. Römer, I, 248-249.
[128] Van Mieris, *Charterboek*, II, 423; cf. Fredericq, *Gesch. d. Inquis.*, II, 25-26.
[129] "Het en ware dat sake, dat zy hier naemaels by der heyliger Kercken met regte van der Beghynscip geset worden."
[130] Van Mieris, *Charterboek*, II, 487.
[131] *Ibid.*, II, 581.
[132] *Ibid.*, III, 223-224.
[133] *Ibid.*, III, 557.
[134] *Ibid.*, III, 638-639.
[135] *Ibid.*, III, 706-707.

their conversion into *een besloten klooster* (October 3, 1411).[136]

The beguinage at Zierikzee was similarly spared. On January 17, 1321, Count William III took the sisterhood under his protection with the provision that it should lend the count or countess while at Zierikzee twelve beds with bedding.[137] Some three years later (May 14, 1324) he recalled that he had given protection to the "respectable" beguines, whose convent had been founded by his forefathers, "na der tyd, dat die ghemene Beghinscippe ontset was van den Hove te Rome." He adopted this policy so that the "righteous women who live a good life may reside in peace." At the same time he charged the priest and guardians of the community to forestall any moral laxity and deviation from piety.[138] It is evident that by 1331[139] and certainly by the following year (August 9) the reform was not having the desired effects, because he must once again bind the beguines to their old customs.[140] At the beginning of the next century (June 28, 1405) Duke William took the beguines of this town under his protection and confirmed all earlier privileges.[141] The same measure was restated on May 2, 1416, after fire had destroyed the original document.[142] Civil authority thus was not merely content with protecting and founding religious houses but closely regulated their interior life by prescribing rules and governing the number of inmates.[143]

The beguine hospital at Alkmaar was established at least by 1341. The priest Werembald explained on April 25 that the foundation projected by Aloud van Oudeschie would cause no prejudice to the parish church. Hugo, abbot of Egmond, admitted on the following day that he had no grievance on the west side of the church. Henry of Mierlaer, provost and archdeacon of Utrecht, acting in the name of the vicar-general Nicholas, authorized the community on June 5 in a brief addressed to the abbot. Town ordinances in 1460 and 1465 stipulated that this St. Elizabeth hospital was not intended "as a retreat for healthy persons," but only for the poor and sick.[144]

Frederick II of Sierck, bishop of Utrecht (1317–1322), early tried to implement the papal decision against the *beghinae clausae* and their patrons.[145] Alongside this condemnation he admitted, however,

---

[136] *Ibid.*, IV, 181.

[137] *Ibid.*, II, 250.

[138] *Ibid.*, II, 341; cf. Römer, I, 250-251.

[139] *Ibid.*, I, 251.

[140] Van Mieris, *Charterboek*, II, 533.

[141] *Ibid.*, IV, 16, 367.

[142] *Ibid.*, IV, 367; *Bijdragen voor Geschiedenis van het Bisdom van Haarlem*, XXXI (1908), 357-358. Cf. confirmation on October 1, 1420.

[143] Cf. the provision of February 2, 1377, Van Mieris, *Charterboek*, III, 653.

[144] Bruinvis, "Het Middel-Begijnhof te Alkmaar," *Bijdragen voor de Geschiedenis van het Bisdom van Haarlem*, XXX (1906), 411-418.

[145] Decree of October 6, 1318, Fredericq, *Corpus*, II, 74-77, no. 45.

that much confusion had arisen in his diocese from the close resemblance *in statu et habitu* between the beguines and affiliates of the Franciscans whose orthodoxy merits episcopal favor. The brothers and sisters of this order were accordingly taken under his protection. But close examination of articles of faith and insistence upon obedience to ecclesiastical authority, together with a year of probation, were prerequisites for the adoption of the third rule. To the regulations governing vestment, food, feast-days, confessions, and devotional practices was added the further stipulation: married women might not enter without the consent of their husbands. This document makes it abundantly clear that adoption of the third rule served as one solution to the problem of the extraregulars whom ecclesiastical officialdom was loathe to recognize as an independent order. Accordingly, the *beghinae clausae* at Groningen,[146] Dordrecht,[147] Noordwijk,[148] and Delft[149] became tertiaries. The provision which William III, count of Hainault, Holland, Zeeland, and lord of Friesland, made on June 24, 1326, for the beguinage at Dordrecht which had joined the Order of Penitence is particularly illuminating and deserves quotation. "Since a number of young women of the beguinage at Dordrecht have taken an order called the Order of Penitence which, we understand, has been founded and confirmed by the Holy See which we praise and love, we take under our protection so long as they remain respectable *(eerlicke)* these maidens and all others who join them in the aforesaid order in Dordrecht and the other women who were beguines and still live in this *curtis*. We desire that they own and use their convent and property with all the rights to which they are accustomed, although they are beguines. For the beguinage was first founded and established by our ancestors, the counts of Holland." In conclusion he ordered his judges, echevins, and town council to protect the community.[150]

To conclude this chapter we may add a word on the beghards in Poland. Information on such extraregulars in eastern Europe is fragmentary. Yet Poland, like many other outlying parts, witnessed the appearance of such a "sect" bearing the name *beghard*. In a bull to the bishop of Posen and the scholasticus of Gnesen John XXII indicates on September 11, 1319, that Gerard, bishop of Vladislav (1301–1323), informed him that his predecessor Wyslaus had donated immovable property belonging to the episcopal table in the diocese of Culm

[146] Frederick, *Gesch. d. Inquis.*, II, 23-24.

[147] Van Mieris, *Charterboek*, II, 392; cf. Römer, I, 246, 639; Balen, *Beschrijvinge der stad Dordrecht*, I, 154-156; for 1326 brief in Dutch, *ibid.*, 155.

[148] Römer, I, 633; cf. Philippen, *Begijnhoven*, pp. 135-136.

[149] Cf. town ordinance of December 12, 1402 (Delprat in *Kerkhistorisch Archief*, IV [1866], 29).

[150] Van Mieris, *Charterboek*, II, 392.

to local beghards on condition that the goods be returned to the bishop should the "sect" ever be destroyed.[151] The Clementine decrees were to act as a lever, the more so, since two of them had been burned for heresy. The bishop thus petitioned the curia to compel the beghards to restore the property to the table after an investigation *sine strepitu*.[152]

[151] Theiner, I, 149-150, no. 230; Mollat, 10333.
[152] Theiner, I, 163-164, no. 253; Mollat, 12869. Riezler, p. 126, no. 234.

VII

Charles IV and the Second Crisis

Just as the flagellants of the fourteenth century scarcely differed in aims and practices from the earlier wave of enthusiasm which Salimbene described so eloquently, so it was easy in retrospect to identify them with Lollards, Cellites, and beghards.[1] Almost seventy years after Jean du Fayt's pronouncement before the papal curia, Gerson, expressing horror at the crudities of their exercises, emphasized before the Council of Constance (July 18, 1417) that these sectarians did not consider the sacraments of confession and penance efficacious. Entertaining the gravest apprehension for the security and integrity of the hierarchy, confronted with undisciplined and seditious competition, he then proceeded to expose the prejudice, superstition, unrest, and insubordination that attended this *pollutio sanguinis*.[2] To strengthen his argument, the chancellor of Paris cited the canonical prohibition of beghards and beguines. From these penitents, he adds, can come only heterodoxy, vilification of the priesthood, deprecation of the sacramental system, and extortion of money. Just as the *Annales Grussavienses* concluded that the flagellants of 1260-1261 were intent on destroying the Christian faith,[3] so Ruysbroeck seems to have had those of 1349 in mind when he referred to persons who undergo extraordinary penance to appear holy.[4] It was an age when dissent was tantamount to treason and conformity became a requisite of unity.

From testaments, business transactions, and municipal regulations which mention the beguines in the *Urkundenbücher,* it is obvious that suppression had been neither continuous nor determined and certainly not conclusive. By midcentury heterodoxy had made such progress from various quarters that it was deemed necessary to establish in Germany inquisitorial machinery especially geared to cope with it. Charles IV, a zealous but by no means unqualified partisan of

---

1. Meyerus, *Annal. Flandriae* (Fredericq, *Corpus,* I, 198).
2 *Tractatus contra Sectam Flagellantium (Op. omn.,* II, 660-662).
3 *Zschr. d. Vereins f. Geschichte von Altertum Schlesiens,* 1856, p. 203.
4 Van Mierlo, in *OGE.,* VI (1932), 329.

the papacy,[5] was to lend effective assistance. Under pressure of the tribunals established in the provinces of Magdeburg and Bremen, the beguines and beghards, against whom Urban V and later Gregory XI incited the emperor, fled into the Rhineland, to Brabant and Holland.[6] This inquisition, entrusted to Dominicans and rendered independent of episcopal jurisdiction, was to enjoy Charles' full support. However resolute the intentions, the processes still assumed in the face of legitimate grievances a pattern analogous to the previous course of persecution alternating with reconciliation under John XXII. Nor was the problem resolved with further satisfaction fifty years later under Gregory XI. Although these extraregular associations continued to threaten the integrity of the universal church, the provincial council of Cologne fulminated as late as 1452 against unauthorized brotherhoods and sisterhoods,[7] and the following year Nicholas V ordained that the beghards should live in accordance with the third rule of St. Francis.[8]

On May 1, 1348, Clement VI named the Dominican John of Schadelant, while lector in Strasbourg, inquisitor for Germany[9] and at the

[5] Hauck, V, 2, 665.
[6] Raynaldus, an. 1372, VII, 228, no. 34; Fredericq, Corpus, I, 225, no. 217; cf. Mosheim, pp. 269-270.
[7] Mansi, XXXII, 147.
[8] Binterim, VII, 315; Mosheim, pp. 183, 192f.
[9] Löhr, in QF., XV, 53. The inquisitor (born 1311 or 1312) was the son of Christine vanme Schadelande of Cologne. His name appears in several testamentary documents: On January 20, 1329, Christine bequeathed all her property after her death to Friar Otto de Schoninburch, prior of the Dominican convent in Frankfurt, and her son John, O.P. (QF., XVI-XVII, 130, no. 314). Otto had been present at Eckhart's trial in Cologne in 1327 and had possibly once been active as a preacher in that city where Christine came to know him (QF., XVI-XVII, 130, no. 314 note). Two years later (July 9, 1331) John donated to his monastery in Cologne the house of Petrissa de Luppe under certain conditions (QF., XVI-XVII, 135, no. 330; cf. QF., XV, 52-53); for Petrissa de Luppe's donation to Fr. Henricus dictus de Fossa, prior of the Dominican monastery in Aachen (July 30, 1325), see QF., XVI-XVII, 117, no. 280; cf. ibid., 137, no. 334 (September 25, 1331); 163-164, no. 415 (August 22, 1337); 164, no. 416 (August 22, 1337); 196, no. 522 (February 18, 1348); 196-197, no. 524 (March 31, 1348) produces the letter of the council of Cologne on the sale of Petrissa de Luppe's house. Following his inquisitorial assignments, John spent the last years of his life in several episcopal appointments: from December 16, 1359, to March 22, 1363, he was bishop of Culm; from March 22, 1363, until his translation to Worms, August 20, 1365, John was bishop of Hildesheim (Geschichtsquellen der Provinz Sachsen, XXII, 197, no. 716). He filled the see of Worms from 1365 until his translation to Augsburg, June 16, 1371 (Schannat, Hist. episc. Wormat., I, 399-401; cf. ibid., 401 for epitaph; Quétif-Echard, I, 672). He held the bishopric of Augsburg from 1371 until his resignation at the beginning of 1373; he died on April 1 in Coblenz. During his last appointment he administered the spiritual and temporal affairs of the diocese of Constance (from June 18, 1371, to March 31, 1372). While bishop of Hildesheim, John exhibited a love for books and study which to contemporaries seemed ill-suited to the prevailing tastes of German bishops (QF., XVI-XVII, 198, no. 526 a, note). After his appointment to the bishopric of Culm, he interceded with Innocent VI on behalf of those who had aided him in the inquisitorial duties: John of Mainz, his notary, Christian Stiggelink, his brother, Hermann Stilkin of Schadelant, and Werner de Brocha (Sauerland, IV, 234, no. 606, January

pope's request he was promoted to master.[10] On July 15, 1353, Innocent VI despatched him across the Alps with instructions as inquisitor to pursue and destroy those semireligious communities which were suspected of error. German authorities, lay and ecclesiastical, were exhorted to give aid to make available to him their prisons since the inquisition in that country did not yet possess its own houses of detention.[11] In a later communication (July 15, 1355)[12] the pope ordered the archbishops of Mainz, Cologne, Trèves, Salzburg, Magdeburg, and Bremen to provide John of Schadelant with 580 gold florins annually for his expenses.[13] That this amount may not have been paid in full or else proved inadequate is suggested by a subsequent inquiry sent by John to Innocent VI (November 9, 1357).[14]

The processes evidently were sporadic. The only victim of this persecution known to us is Berthold of Rohrbach[15] who, seized at Würzburg in 1356, retracted and succeeded in getting his release from prison; but taken a second time at Speier where he had begun again to preach his ideas, he submitted to the stake for refusal to agree to a new recantation. He was not charged with any practical error; he was condemned, like Constantin of Erfurt[16] and many another petty heresiarch, only for having professed heterodox doctrine. In him one finds the usual teachings of the Brethren of the Free Spirit mingled with certain subjective ideas, the product of an intelligence not well cultivated and prone to aberration. Christ, he held, was so certain of his abandonment by God during the Passion that He did not know whether his soul was saved or damned. On the cross He had cursed his mother, the Virgin Mary, and the ground that absorbed His blood. Berthold added at Speier that man could attain on earth such a degree of perfection that henceforth it was no longer necessary for him

7, 1360). In answer to this request Innocent VI advised the deacon of St. Gereon's in Cologne to reserve for Hermann a post *cum cura vel sine cura* at St. George's in that city (*ibid.,* IV, 235, no. 609, January 7, 1360). Cf. *ibid.,* V, 168, no. 446 (September 27, 1365).

[10] Denifle, in *ALKM.,* II, 224, no. 129; in Quétif-Echard, I, 672 he is not listed as *magister.*

[11] Fredericq, *Corpus,* I, 204-205, no. 206; Raynaldus, an. 1353, VI, 589, no. 26; *BOP.,* II, 243; Sauerland, IV, 27-28, no. 67 (extracts); cf. Mosheim, p. 324. See the second papal letter, bearing he same date, Sauerland, IV, 26-27, no. 66.

[12] Sauerland, IV, 102-103, no. 253; *Geschichtsquellen der Provinz Sachsen,* XXII, 27-28, no. 93; cf. Eubel, *H.C.,* I, 217, note 4.

[13] Of this sum the archbishop of Mainz was to provide 40 fl. and his suffragans, including the bishop of Bamberg, 210; the archbishop of Cologne, 50 and his suffragans, 100; the archbishop of Trèves, 20; the archbishop of Salzburg, 40 and his suffragans, 40; the archbishop of Magdeburg, 20 and the suffragans 20; and the archbishop of Bremen, 15 and the suffragans 25. Urban made further provision for maintenance on October 17, 1364 (Sauerland, V, 128, no. 328).

[14] *Ibid.,* IV, 170-171, no. 454 (November 9, 1357).

[15] Mosheim, pp. 325-329; the text in Raynaldus (VI, 589, no. 27, an. 1353) is fragmentary.

[16] Mosheim, pp. 298-300.

to pray or fast and thet nothing would be sin for him. From this premise confidence in the freedom of spirit was derived. Prayer aloud was not necessary for it did not promote salvation; it sufficed to pray inwardly without moving the lips. A layman, unlettered but illumined by intuition, was more capable of attaining perfection and causing others to advance in this direction by his teaching than that priest who was most learned and best versed in Scripture. One should put faith in the sermons and teaching of such a layman whom the spirit illuminates and obey him rather than cling to the prescriptions of the Gospel and the words of doctors. Everyone who had thus given himself to God could find in food and ordinary drink a grace equivalent to that conferred by the partaking of the body and blood of Christ.

The elevation of William of Gennep to the archbishopric of Cologne on February 25, 1357, provoked fresh persecution of the *Beggardi et Suestriones*—the *pestifera secta*—and their patrons.[17] He hearkened back to the policies of his predecessors, Henry of Virnebourg and Walram, which had entailed many terrible trials (*multiplices formidabilesque processus*). But episcopal suppression was inadequate, and the number of heretics of both sexes continued to grow.

At the same time the beguines and beghards had once more attained sufficient proportions in the towns and villages of France to engage the attention of Urban V. On September 3, 1365, therefore, he addressed a bull[18] to the episcopate and inquisitors of the kingdom with the usual admonition and exhortation. In order better to acquaint the prelates with the dwelling places, the way of life, and errors of this sect, the pope sent along with the bull to the bishop of Paris, Stephen IV, a memorandum of which the bishop was instructed to prepare copies for each of his suffragans.[19]

From a MS. sentence of June 6, 1366, printed by Mosheim,[20] we learn that the Dominican, Henry de Agro, was at that time commissioned as inquisitor of the province of Mainz and the dioceses of Bamberg and Basel, the latter belonging to the province of Besançon. He was conducting an inquisition in the diocese of Strasbourg whose bishop, John of Luxembourg, had gratified episcopal jealousy by not allowing him to perform his office independently, but had supplemented his work with a vicar, Tristram, who conducted himself in the matter not simply as a representative of the bishop in the sentence, but as co-inquisitor. According to the rules of the inquisition the judgment was rendered in an assembly of experts. The victim in this

[17] Fredericq, *Corpus*, I, 523-524, no. 207 bis; cf. *ibid.*, I, 205, no. 207; Mosheim, pp. 330-331; Hartzheim, IV, 482-483; cf. Binterim, *Conciliengeschichte*, VI, 146-147.
[18] *Ad audientiam nostram*, Fredericq, *Corpus*, I, 205-206, no. 208; Mosheim, pp. 411f; Raynaldus, VII, 118, no. 17 (an. 1365).
[19] This memorandum is not extant. See Fredericq. *Gesch. d. Inquis.*, II, 138.
[20] Mosheim, pp. 333-334.

case was a woman, Metza von Westhoven, a beguine, who had been tried and who had abjured in the prosecution under Bishop John of Zürich, nearly a half a century before. As a relapsed heretic there was no pardon for her, and she was duly relaxed.[21] Similarly, a beghard, John Hartmann, is reported to have been burned at Erfurt the following year (1367) and to such activity may well be attributed the temporary suppression of the sect. When John was interrogated in accordance with the directives of the Clementine decree *Ad nostram,* the usual free spirit doctrine was revealed: man is identical with God and consequently impeccable.[22]

Three years before, on October 11, 1364, Urban V had written to the bishops John of Strasbourg and John of Hildesheim with respect to the appointment of four Dominican inquisitors, Louis de Caliga, Henry de Agro, Walter Kerlinger, and John de Moneta for the dioceses of Mainz, Trèves, Cologne, Salzburg, Bremen, Magdeburg, Riga, Camin, Bamberg, and Basel, and ordered them to assign each to a definite territory.[23] About a week later (October 17) he again instructed the same two bishops to collect annually for these inquisitors sent to Germany 200 gold florins from the archbishops and bishops to whose dioceses they were despatched.[24] In another communication issued on the same day the pope notified the German episcopate and their suffragans of this step.[25] On October 22 he ordered the city of Magdeburg (and hence Erfurt and the archbishops of Mainz and Magdeburg) to support the inquisitor.[26]

Thus far Charles IV seems to have taken no part in the efforts of the papacy, and without the imperial exequatur the commissions issued to inquisitors had but a moderate chance of enjoying the respect and obedience of the prelates. It was not until April 15, 1368, perhaps in the wake of the Hartmann case, that Urban V returned to the task in Germany by recommissioning the two inquisitors, the friars Louis de Caliga and Walter Kerlinger, with power to appoint vicars.[27] Although

[21] Cf. Lea, *History of the Inquisition,* II, 387.

[22] Döllinger, *Beiträge,* II, 384ff. He may have been one of those mentioned in *Gesta Archiep. Magdeb., MGH., SS.,* XVI, 441. Greifswald MS. ff. 109-111 contains a notarial record of the interrogation before Kerlinger on December 26, 1367 (Wattenbach, in *Sitz.-ber. Berlin,* 1887, pp. 537-538; for text, *ibid.,* 538-543).

[23] *Geschichtsquellen der Provinz Sachsen,* XXII, 173-174, no. 632.

[24] *Ibid.,* 174, no. 634.

[25] *Ibid.,* 174, no. 635.

[26] *Ibid.,* 175, no. 637 (text), *Gesta Archiep. Magdeb., MGH. SS.,* XVI, 441. *UB. der Stadt Erfurt,* ed. Carl Beyer, II, in *Geschichtsquellen der Provinz Sachsen,* XXIV, 433, no. 574 (text); *UB. der Stadt Magdeburg,* ed. Gustav Hertel, I, in *ibid.,* XXVI, 298, no. 467.

[27] Fredericq, *Corpus,* I, 207, no. 209; Mosheim, pp. 336-337. Fredericq (*op. cit.,* I, 207-208 note; *Gesch. d. Inquis.,* II, 138) indicates that the date 1368 is more accurate than 1367 to which Mosheim (p. 335) and Lea (*History,* II, 387) subscribed. This document is in large measure merely a restatement of Innocent VI's bull of July 15, 1353. Walter Kerlinger is not mentioned in Urban V's bull, but on the

the beghards alone were singled out in this directive for persecution, the clause, *haereticos seu suspectos de haeresi utriusque sexus,* implies wider application. Prelates and magistrates were ordered to lend assistance and to put all prisons at the disposal of the Friars Preachers until the German inquisition should have such places of its own. This was the most comprehensive measure yet taken to organize the Holy Office in the empire and was entrusted to capable inquisitors.

Of Friar Louis little is known. The son by a first marriage of a father bearing the same name, he came from Cologne and was first mentioned in his father's testamentary disposition of March 24, 1332.[28] As inquisitor for the provinces of Cologne and Trèves in 1368 (December 3), he acknowledged the receipt of 125 gold gulden from Archbishop Kuno of Trèves, administrator of Cologne, for expenses incurred in the fulfillment of his duties.[29] The following year the emperor expressly referred to him as inquisitor in his third brief on the heresy problem.[30]

Yet it is not without significance that Walter Kerlinger looms in the imperial letters of 1369 as the primary inquisitor. He was a man of influence, the chaplain and favorite of the emperor,[31] who desired to magnify his office. In 1369 he became Dominican provincial of Saxony and continued to perform the duplicate functions until his death in 1373. As early as 1364 (October 25), on the occasion of the initial appointment as papal inquisitor, Urban V had asked John of Schadelant, then bishop of Hildesheim, to examine Walter's ability.[32] On March 15, 1372, Gregory XI entrusted the provost Herbord of St. Severi in Erfurt, Walter Kerlinger, professor of theology and inquisitor in Germany, and Rudolf of the order of Augustinian hermits to have Bishop Albrecht of Halberstadt retract his heretical teachings.[33] A little later in the same year (May 28) Walter was empowered by the curia, because of the absence of notaries in Germany, to give to suitable persons on oath the *officium tabellionatus.*[34] His death, prior to September 2, 1374, was to provoke one of those numerous controversies between the papal curia and city officials over

---

basis of the previous appointment and extensive subsequent activity he must have received instructions at this time. On the same day the pope addressed another bull *Imminente nobis cura* to German spiritual and temporal authorities who were enjoined to cooperate with the inquisitor, Henry de Agro, and his assistants (*Geschichtsquellen der Provinz Sachsen,* XXII, 224, no. 815 a).

[28] *QF.,* XVI-XVII, 143, no. 353; cf. *QF.,* XV, 53.

[29] Sauerland, V, 250, no. 637; cf. *QF.,* XVI-XVII, 233, no. 633.

[30] Fredericq, *Corpus,* I, 215-216; cf. 219.

[31] Charles IV called him repeatedly not only *capellanum nostrum* but also *commensalem, domesticum et familiarem suum dilectum et fidelem* (ibid., I, 209, 211, 215, 219).

[32] *Geschichtsquellen der Provinz Sachsen,* XXII, 175, no. 638.

[33] *Ibid.,* 276, no. 1003.

[34] *Ibid.,* 281-282, no. 1028.

control of church property. Gregory XI on that day charged the legate, Bishop Nicholas, to collect the goods of the deceased inquisitor in the provinces of Bremen and Magdeburg, since he owed the papal treasury 1500 gold florins.[35] After communicating on June 9, 1375, with the master of the Order of Preachers over the failure of the Erfurt council to disgorge Walter's money,[36] the pope charged the abbot of Hersfeld, the provost of St. Severi in Erfurt; and the cantor of Mainz to put pressure, at the request of the inquisitor, Hermann von Hellstedt, prior provincial of Saxony, on the town council to give up the money entrusted to it by Walter.[37] Hermann was soon after (August 5) instructed to hand over to Bishop Nicholas *Mayerien*. the correspondence of his predecessor who had deposited at Erfurt moneys of the *camera apostolica*.[38] At the same time Urban V renewed his appeal to the burgomaster and the council to release the deposit.[39] The outcome of the dispute is not indicated.

Complete accord between empire and papacy was to be assured on this problem of heresy by four imperial decrees promulgated at Lucca during the month of June, 1369, in less than ten days, with the purpose of strengthening the inquisition and destroying the extraregulars. In recognition of his embittered hostility to heresy, Charles IV was to be called by Gregory XI "pugil fidei praefatae magnificus ac promtus haereticorum persecutor."[40] The first edict, on June 9,[41] addressed to all spiritual and temporal authorities, expressed the desirability of furthering papal inquisition against the sect of beghards, beguines, and "Swestronum conventualium, quae vulgo *Wilge Armen* vel *Conventschwestern* dicuntur, vel quae simul mendicando dicunt *Brod durch Gott*."[42] The blanket provisions, prescribing excommunication for those abetting and aiding as well as actively participating in the semireligious communities, were designed to help Kerlinger in his work as inquisitor-general in Germany.

The following day (June 10) a second imperial decree was issued.[43] Charles IV recalled that Urban V had established Kerlinger and other Dominicans in Germany to combat the heretics. Wishing that these inquisitors might fulfil their duties without obstacle, he extended to them the broadest rights and privileges with specific instructions to

[35] Nicholas was the bishop of the indistinguishable *Mayerien*. (*ibid.*, 320, no. 1189).

[36] *Ibid.*, 332, no. 1232; *UB. der Stadt Erfurt*, II, in *ibid.*, XXIV, 553, note.

[37] July 7, 1375, *ibid.*, XXII, 333, no. 1236; cf. no. 1238 July 21, 1375).

[38] *Ibid.*, 334, no. 1244.

[39] August 5, *ibid.*, 335, no. 1245; *UB., der Stadt Erfurt*, II, in *ibid.*, XXIV, 553, no. 757.

[40] Fredericq, *Corpus*, I, 222; Mosheim, p. 364.

[41] Fredericq, *Corpus*, I, 208-210; Mosheim, pp. 350-355.

[42] Fredericq, *Corpus*, I, 209; Mosheim, p. 352.

[43] Fredericq, *Corpus*, I, 211-214, no. 211; Mosheim, pp. 343-350.

the dukes of Saxony and Brunswick, the counts of Schwarzenberg and Nassau, and the knights of Hanstein and Witzeleyeven who were to act as protectors. One-third of the movable property of the heretics must be handed over to the inquisition. Failure to comply with the imperial order would entail a ,fine of one hundred gold marks, one-half of which were payable to the imperial treasury, the other half to the injured party. Anyone who obstructed or molested the inquisitors or their agents would face possible confiscation of property for the benefit of the fisc and loss of all perquisites and immunities.

A week later, on June 17, the emperor broadened the scope of inquisitorial processes by issuing a third edict [44] to the papal inquisitors, Kerlinger, and Louis de Caliga, as well as to the two Dominicans who had been appointed by the former as assistants. This directive was primarily concerned with getting rid of the devotional literature that was reported to be circulating in the vernacular among the unsuspecting laymen. All such writings, tracts, sermons, sheets, and codices [45] must be handed over to the inquisition for examination, subject to destruction. As a consequence of this imperial decree, it was actually entrusted with a new weapon—censorship—ostensibly to curb the propaganda of Brethren of the Free Spirit ideas. [46] As one of several antiheretical pronouncements of January 5, 1372/3 Gregory XI was also to call upon the German inquisitors to examine, with the aid of theologians and canonists, books of sermons written in the vernacular. [47] On April 22, 1376 he again conferred papal approval to the policy of destroying and suppressing heretical writings that were being used to provide unlettered and simple laymen with unauthorized sermons and unguided reading. It became an offense punishable by the tribunals to copy, possess, buy, or sell books containing errors. At the same time unlicensed preaching was to be sharply curbed. [48]

Finally, on the same day (June 17), a fourth decree was issued by Charles IV to prescribe in greater detail methods for disposing of the confiscated property of German beguines and beghards. [49] After praising the inquisitors for their successful labors in the provinces of Magdeburg and Bremen and in Thuringia, Saxony, Hesse, and other parts of the empire, he declared that since the inquisition in Germany did not at that time possess houses, buildings, or towers to contain the suspected or relapsed heretics for short terms or life, all the *domus et conventicula* of the beguines must be delivered up to it. This property would then be sold. One-third of the proceeds would be used by the

[44] Fredericq, *Corpus*, I, 214-217, no. 212; Mosheim, pp. 368-375.
[45] See above, p. 369.
[46] Lea, *History of the Inquisition*, II, 391; III, 612.
[47] *Geschichtsquellen der Provinz Sachsen*, XXII, no. 1084.
[48] Fredericq, *Corpus*, I, 237, no. 224; Mosheim, pp. 378-379.
[49] Fredericq, *Corpus*, I, 218-221, no. 213; Mosheim, pp. 356-362.

inquisitor, with the assistance of a cleric and a layman, as alms to the poor, the church, penitent heretics, and those imprisoned who were wanting the means of livelihood. The second portion was designated for the inquisitor or his vicar to defray the expense of the processes. The last third was earmarked for repairing the walls, streets, and squares of the cities in which confiscated property was located. The sale of such property was to be completed within the month in which the edict was promulgated; three days' notice was considered adequate to effect the expulsion of the extraregulars. Whoever opposed the order should pay for each infraction one hundred gold marks to be allotted as recommended in the second decree. At Kerlinger's request, Gregory XI confirmed on June 9, 1372, Charles IV's ordinance concerning the disposal of beguine and beghard property.[50]

These June decrees mark an important advance made by the temporal power in the matter of the inquisition during the fourteenth century, for they amounted to the establishment of the tribunal in the empire. The spirit in which they were drafted was without question uncompromising. While they contained the denial that extra-regular ranks might be comprised of orthodox members, Kerlinger's zeal in forcing conformity or meting out punishment was attended by remarkable success. In the confiscation of beguine and beghard property and its transformation into badly needed prisons for the new tribunals, we may discern an attempt to solve by expediency an imme-diate problem by proscribing communities that were not fully incor-porated into the ecclesiastical fabric and thus suspected of heretical tendencies. Therefore the orthodox must be sacrificed, like a scape-goat, to the promotion of the inquisitorial machinery.

Presumably in the wake of this legislation Kerlinger ordered the burning of seven recalcitrant heretics out of more than forty men and women who had been seized in Nordhausen in Thuringia.[51] Although this sect is not named, it is probable that it is a question here of beghards. To support this contention Hermann Corner adds details to Kerlinger's persecution of the beghards, beguines, and Swestriones "everywhere in Germany." Two who remained obdurate were burned in Erfurt; others became penitent and abjured the sect.[52] One beghard was burned for attempting to violate a girl, but Kerlinger is not men-tioned here. The friar's ruthlessness may be demonstrated by his treatment of four of the beguinages—the "conventuales"—at Mühl-hausen. On February 16, 1370, they were delivered by him to the magistrates to be converted to "pious" uses.[53]

---

[50] *Geschichtsquellen der Provinz Sachsen*, XXII, 282, no. 1030.
[51] Mosheim, p. 341.
[52] *Ibid.*, p. 342; *Gesta Archiep. Magdeb., MGH. SS.*, XVI, 441.
[53] George Henry Martin's appendix to Mosheim, pp. 541-542.

Gregory XI on June 7, 1371,[54] sanctioned imperial provisions for the use of the confiscated property of the beghards and beguines following Kerlinger's examination. On January 5, 1372–1373, the pope urged Charles IV[55] and all spiritual and temporal authorities in Germany to support the inquisitor in his prosecution of the flagellants as well as the beguines and beghards and to make available to him their prisons.[56] It is probable that this papal intervention was dictated by jealousy of the bishops at the growing independence of the inquisition in their dioceses, with its own prisons and landed properties. On July 23, 1372, Gregory XI offered, on the other hand, additional instructions to the master and prior provincial of the Order of Preachers in Germany with regard to the appointment of five inquisitors in the dioceses of Mainz, Cologne, Utrecht, Salzburg, and Magdeburg-Bremen.[57] Although Kerlinger and Louis de Caliga were included in this assignment, the former now witnessed a division of his authority.[58]

This vigorous persecution was responsible for expelling from the central provinces not only beghards and beguines but members of other free associations. Raynaldus in his *Annales Ecclesiasticae* under the year 1372,[59] for example, links up beghards and Fraticelli in Magdeburg and Bremen who fled to the border areas along the Rhine, to Holland, Brabant, and even to the duchy of Stettin—a fact which gave the pope some cause for rejoicing[60]—with John Wyclif's followers. Their growing strength in the west obliged Gregory XI to call on the emperor and princes to come to the assistance of the inquisitors. The papal bull is not extant,[61] but we possess the sharply-worded injunction of Charles IV, sealed at Trèves on February 17, 1373,[62] in which he urged the archbishops of Trèves and Cologne and the bishop of Liége, the dukes of Luxembourg, Limburg, Brabant, and Julich, and lesser princes of Mons and Cleves, together with the counts of La Marck, Kirchberg, and Spanheim to welcome and protect the papal inquisitor, John Bólant, a Dominican and imperial chaplain, as being specially charged by the Holy See to eradicate the extraregular menace in the three dioceses. John Bolant was probably from Cologne. Before the notary Henry von Lintorp, alias de Prato, the Cologne lady, Richmodis

---

[54] Fredericq, *Corpus*, I, 221-222, no. 214; Mosheim, pp. 364-366; cf. assignment of July 8, 1371 (*Geschichtsquellen der Provinz Sachsen*, XXII, 260, no. 944).

[55] *Ibid.*, 295, no. 1083.

[56] *Ibid.*, 295, no. 1081.

[57] Fredericq, *Corpus*, I, 222-224, no. 215; Mosheim, pp. 380-383; cf. bull of July 27, 1372 (*Geschichtsquellen der Provinz Sachsen*, XXII, 286-287, no. 1044; 285-286, no. 1043; November 24, 1374, *ibid.*, 322, no. 1197).

[58] Lea, *History of the Inquisition*, II, 390-391.

[59] Fredericq, *Corpus*, I, 225, no. 216. Cf. Raynaldus, VII, 228, nos. 33-34, an. 1372.

[60] *Geschichtsquellen, der Provinz Sachsen*, XXII, 295, no. 1082 (January 5, 1372-1373).

[61] Fredericq, *Gesch. d. Inquis.*, II, 143.

[62] Fredericq, *Corpus*, I, 225-228, no. 218; Mosheim, pp. 388-392.

vanme Clocringe, explained on May 2, 1372, that she had earlier obtained from the Friars Preachers for cash the house *ad Rapam* opposite St. Andrew's gate which Hermann de Summo, scholasticus of St. Andrew's, owned. She now granted the usufruct of it to John Bolant, her relative.[63] On February 5, 1359, he had been prior in Trèves,[64] on December 9, 1370, he was serving in the same capacity in Cologne.[65] Since Gregory XI had appointed him as inquisitor for these regions, the ecclesiastical authorities were admonished to aid him and his co-workers in collecting the third part of confiscated movable and immovable property.

Although the Brethren of the Free Spirit were the chief target in this inquisitorial activity, other semireligious associations were not neglected. On the authority of Raynaldus, the pope applied the same harsh measures to the beguines and beghards, Turlupins and Lollards in France.[66] In Germany and the Low Countries there was, moreover, a recrudescence of the flagellant movement in 1372, asserting the efficacy of its penance as a substitute for the sacraments of the Church. In 1373 and 1374 it was to take the form of intense spiritual excitement, known at the Dancers—bands of both sexes, consisting for the most part of poor and simple folk, who poured into Flanders from the Rhineland.[67] Although not itself really heresy it could easily absorb erroneous teachings concerning the sacraments and thus put a strain on both the normal penitential channels and disciplinary powers of the church. An additional problem was raised by heretical and schismatic things contained in the *Speculum Saxonum* which was in use in parts of the empire and Bohemia. Innocent VI had already announced in a bull, dated October 15, 1356,[68] that he was forwarding to Charles IV letters in which he condemned these ideas. The almost identical bull was now despatched by Gregory XI to the emperor (October 15, 1374).[69] The archbishop of Mainz and his suffragans, too, had received the preceding spring (April 8, 1374) the bull *Ad perpetuam rei memoriam* in which the *Sachsenspiegel* was condemned.[70]

Armed with these papal and imperial weapons, Lambert von Burne, bishop of Strasbourg (1371—1374), launched on August 19, 1374, an

---

[63] Richmodes likewise donated the property *inter vivos* to the prior and convent of the Cologne Dominicans who, after John's death, could dispose of it freely. See Löhr, *QF.*, XVI-XVII, 235, no. 638. Cf. Löhr, *QF.*, XVI-XVII, 235, no. 638. Cf. Löhr, in *QF.*, XV, 53.

[64] *Ibid.*, XVI-XVII, 221-222, no. 599; XV, 53.

[65] *Ibid.*, XVI-XVII, 234, no. 636; XV, 53.

[66] Fredericq, *Corpus*, I, 228, no. 219.

[67] Fredericq, *Gesch., d. Inquis.*, II, 103-113.

[68] Sauerland, IV, 138-139, no. 360.

[69] *Geschichtsquellen der Provinz Sachsen*, XXII, 320-321, no. 1191.

[70] *Ibid.*, 316, no. 1176.

energetic offensive against the sectarians in his diocese.[71] Like John of Strasbourg almost sixty years before, he protested on the strength of reports borne to him that these women adopted a habit peculiar in cut and color—sufficient to warrant the charge of autonomy—,formed congregations and conventicles, and elected superiors known as mistresses. Some lived in common in a kind of college or convent while others, although able-bodied, begged in public. Especially on the sabbath did they confess to their superiors or among themselves, and usurping the power of the keys, received penance from these mistresses in the form of sermons and blows. This they termed discipline. They presumed to expel from their ranks; they refused categorically to observe the rites of the church and boldly had the eucharist administered by the religious in place of parish priests, without respect for canon law. Withal, they flouted the claims of excommunication. For the next three Sundays and feast-days the clergy was enjoined to drive home to these women the prerogatives of the hierarchy, to warn them to cease their practices within six days of publication and to abandon their previous way of life within a fortnight unless they wished to incur the wrath of the inquisition.

Confronted with this indiscriminate sharpening of papal, episcopal, and imperial legislation against suspected semireligious communities, the houses in the dioceses of Liége, Trèves, and Strasbourg determined to lodge a joint protest to the papal curia. Dietrich of Brussels, for the Liégeois, Henry of Coblenz, for the beguines of Trèves, and Otto of Neuweiler and Hugo of Zabern, for those of Strasbourg, journeyed to Avignon to present the list of grievances on behalf of the orthodox.[72] In like fashion, it was possibly the energetic suppression by John Bolant in the diocese of Cologne that provoked the petition of the town council. In February or March, 1375, the magistrates of Cologne complained to Gregory XI over the methods of an inquisitor of the Friars Preachers who had come into the city to employ his office against "poor men and women" who beg in conformity with scripture.[73] They embrace a life of voluntary poverty in accordance with orthodox faith and have demonstrated their piety in such a way that they are deemed true worshippers of Christ (*pro veris christocolis*). In order to ascertain whether they deserved the complaints that the inquisitor had lodged against them, the burghers called together the parish priests under whom these extraregulars lived like their own parishioners and inquired from them of what sort they considered these poor men and whether

[71] Haupt, in *ZKG.*, VII (1885), 562-564; P. J. 4; Döllinger, *Beiträge*, II, 378-380, no. 36; *AFH.*, XIV, 183-184 (here the date August 20 is assigned to a truncated version).

[72] Schmidt, in *Alsatia*, 1858-1860, p. 215; Fredericq, *Corpus*, I, 229-231; Mosheim, pp. 394-398.

[73] Ennen and Eckertz, *Quellen*, V, 88-90, no. 82.

there was any article of faith about which they seemed to err. These priests, so the complaint runs, averred without pressure or bribe that they were good Christians, poor men leading a contemptible, albeit Christian life for the sake of God [74] and observing orthodox practices by confessing and receiving the eucharist. Then with a sly argument the municipal authorities add: "Forsooth, most holy Father, this inquisitor propounds to these poor and unlettered laymen such difficult and unanswerable questions that a great theologian can scarcely offer a solution to them without much deliberation and consulting of books. Over these questions mere laymen ought not to be examined; it seems sufficient that they know the articles of faith as befits laymen."

In the wake of such testimony the orthodox extraregulars were to get in Avignon a new lease on life. To the archbishops of Cologne, Trèves, and Mainz, together with their suffragans and other prelates in Germany, Brabant, and Flanders, the pope addressed on April 7, 1374, a bull [75] in which he acknowledged that since the promulgation of earlier bulls reports had reached him, indicating that many men and women live in poverty, chastity, and righteousness, attend church regularly, and carefully eschew all deviations of piety. Since these *personae pauperes*—Gregory XI scrupulously avoids the terms beguines and beghards— have appealed to the curia to obtain permission to pursue their way of live without interruption, the pope ordered an investigation into the merits of the case. On December 31, 1374, this bull was submitted to the episcopal official in Strasbourg, Rainbold von Gemünd, [76] and to it as well as the concessions of the later bull of Boniface IX *Ad ea quae* [77] the Strasbourg beguines were to owe their freedom from further molestation in the closing decades of the fourteenth century.

Gregory XI's measures thus act as a complement for the bull *Cum de mulieribus* which had aimed to implement the Clementine decrees without doing injustice. But John XXII had only the beguines in mind and mentioned them by name in the first line of his bull. Gregory, on the other hand, was concerned about extraregulars in general when he employed the less precise phrase *personae pauperes utriusque sexus*.

For want of documents [78] it is impossible to describe accurately episcopal reaction to papal recommendation. However we may safely con-

[74] "Quod ipsi essent boni christiani, pauperes homines vitam despectivam christianam tamen ducentes propter deum" (*ibid.*, V, 89).

[75] Fredericq, *Corpus*, I, 228-231, no. 220; Mosheim, pp. 394-398; *Geschichtsquellen der Provinz Sachsen*, XXII, 316, no. 1175; Sauerland, V, 401, no. 1016 (here the date is given as April 6).

[76] Haupt, in *ZKG.*, VII (1885), 526.

[77] *Ibid.*, 565-567, P. J., v; Döllinger, *Beiträge*, II, 381-383.

[78] Fredericq, *Gesch., d. Inquis.*, II, 145.

clude that no thorough examination of the problem was conducted, for Gregory XI was obliged on December 3, 1377, to issue a second bull[79] to the same prelates in Germany, Brabant, and Flanders and couched in similar language. Yet it was no mere repetition of the first decree in an effort to push the investigation. It represented, on the contrary, papal intervention on behalf of the persecuted Brothers and Sisters. Once again he explained how reports had reached his ears that there were poor men and women in this region who were free of any taint of heresy. They had been unjustly persecuted by the bishops and inquisition under the pretext that they donned a clerical habit (occa-sione vestium) without permission. These proceedings were expressly forbidden and the pope extended protection to the extraregulars. If some had been cut off from the sacraments, the bishops were to restore them to their status.

The following year Archbishop Frederick III of Cologne entrusted John de Cervo with enforcement of this decree. Thus by October 20, 1383, he took under his protection the pauperes persone utriusque sexus of Cologne, especially the sisters in the convents zur Zelle, Keppler, zur Hand, Holzweiler, Grunewald, etc.[80] This new perse-cution was apparently directed against Suestriones, for in most of the convents cited Suestriones had been previously been mentioned.[81]

Although Gregory's bull appears to have ended the second crisis in favor of the ortholox semireligious, implementation of the papal program continued to be defective. Not twenty years later Boniface IX (1389–1404) was to hear fresh complaints and petitions,[82] thus indi-cating that the inquisitorial machinery had by no means scrupulously honored the instruction of the bull of 1377. Trithemius refers to the prosecution conducted in 1392 by Master Martin, inquisitor delegated by the Holy See to travel through Swabia to Würzburg. In the latter place he discovered a number of peasants and simple folk identified with a sect of flagellants and fraticelli. Their return to the Catholic fold he made contingent on joining a crusade then being preached against the Turks.[83] At Erfurt he found heretics—beghards and begut-tae; some were burned, others accepted penance for their errors, the

---

[79] Fredericq, Corpus, I, 237-238, no. 225; Mosheim, pp. 401-402; Geschichts-quellen der Provinz Sachsen, XXII, 354, no. 1303; Sauerland, V, 506-507, no. 1260 (here the date is given as December 2).

[80] Asen, in AHVN., CXI (1927), 107-108.

[81] The inmates of Grunewald were called in 1324 pauperes puelle, those of Mainz pauperes begine (1282); this expression is perhaps to be equated with Sues-triones, for in the will of Adolf von Revele of 1317 the benevole pauperes puelle were identified with swestir (Ennen and Eckertz, Quellen, IV, 32, no. 35). The in-mates of Zederwald were referred to in 1315 as pauperes beghinae, que swestere dicuntur (Asen, l.c., 108).

[82] Bull Ex iniuncto (January 7, 1394), Fredericq, Corpus, I, 254-256, no. 239; ibid., 253f, no. 238.

[83] Mosheim, p. 407.

rest fled.[84] About 1393 or 1394 the inquisitor Jacob of Soest received from "worthy persons" reports of congregations of sisters (Swestriones) at Utrecht and Rhenen. Under their respective Marthas they engaged in suspicious activity.[85]

In response to protests against the inquisition, Pope Boniface IX in the bull *Ex iniuncto* adopted a sympathetic policy with regard to "nonnullae personae pauperes utriusque sexus divisim, viri scilicet coniunctim in suis et mulieres etiam coniunctim in domibus suis absque mutua ipsorum conversatione commorantes, quae humiliter et honeste in paupertate et continentia sub humilitatis spiritu vivunt et ecclesias devote frequentant, Romanae ecclesiae earumque praelatis et curatis in omnibus reverenter obediunt, nullis erroribus se involvunt neque ritus neque modos reprobatos a iure seu aliter illicitos aut repugnantes salutaribus praeceptis observant..."[86] Shortly afterwards (December 1, 1395) the bishop of Rome reaffirmed Gregory XI's bull of July 23, 1372, concerning the reactivation of the inquisition in Mainz, Cologne, Utrecht, Salzburg, Magdeburg, and Bremen,[87] thereby foreshadowing the backward swing of the pendulum. On January 31, 1396, he committed to penalty again the "Beghardi seu Lullardi et Zwestriones, a se ipsis vero Pauperes pueruli nominati,"[88] recalling that for the past century these societies had been tainted with heresy. Scarcely a year had passed that some had not been burned in imperial lands.[89]

The same reproaches had been hurled by John Wasmod of Homburg, inquisitor at Heidelberg and afterwards, in 1399, professor of theology and rector at the university. He was commissioned in 1392 by Archbishop Conrad II of Mainz to introduce inquisitorial processes against the Waldensian sect in Mainz, against which action had already been taken in 1389. In the same year thirty-six Waldensians condemned by Wasmod at Bingen were executed; the investigation in 1393 and 1395 against the Mainz Waldensians must have been supervised by him.[90] He seems to have investigated beghards too, for he often relied on their confessions as evidence. Wasmod is also noted for his *Tractatus contra Hereticos Bekardos Lulhardos et Swestriones,*[91] which must have been written at the close of the century, since

[84] *Ibid.*, p. 408.
[85] Fredericq, *Corpus*, II, 153-156, no. 106.
[86] *Ibid.*, I, 255.
[87] *Ibid.*, I, 256, no. 240.
[88] *Ibid.*, I, 257, no. 241.
[89] "...Sub quorum etiam habitu et ritu vivendi ante centum annos usque in praesentiarum semper haereses et haeretici latitarent, et ob id in diversis civitatibus partium praedictarum fere singulis annis de hujusmodi sectis plures pertinaces judicialiter concremantur."
[90] Haupt, in *ZKG.*, VII (1885), 547ff
[91] *Ibid.*, 567-576, P. J. vi.

Boniface's bull *Sedis apostolicae* of January 31, 1396, is mentioned as "newly issued," whereas the bull *Ad ea quae* which belongs to the period 1400–1404 was not yet known.[92] Haupt pointed out that the errors which Wasmod attributed to the beghards actually embodied a number of Waldensian doctrines: the church is limited by the heretics to their own company of believers; they deny to the hierarchy the power of the keys because of unworthiness; opposition to indulgences; the inability of a priest in mortal sin to consecrate; usurpation of priestly functions without ordination. The Waldensians also contested the right of the secular arm to inflict capital punishment. Wasmod thus had in mind, adds Haupt, specifically the confessions of heretics condemned at Bingen in 1392 who claimed, for instance, the ability to grant absolution to anyone in a state of Christian perfection. Considering the heterogeneous orign of errors attributed to these sectarians, it is perfectly correct to see here the survival of Waldensian doctrine, but the Free Spirits and beghards had already subscribed, whether conscious of external influence or not, to many of these propositions.

Similarly, Johannes Buschius' (d. 1471) *Chronicon Windeshemense*[93] contains an illuminating passage on Gerard Groote's (d. 1384) defense of the Brothers and Sisters of the Common Life against the charge of heresy. The mendicant friars, fearing competition from devout priests and clerics living together in the house of Florentius Radewijns of Deventer and from sisters living in common without property in Gerard Groote's house, claimed that these brethren and *Gerardinae*[94] had been condemned by Clement V. But, the chronicler continues, Gerard Groote, a man well versed in law as well as in scripture, delivered public sermons in which he proved that their way of life corresponded to early Christianity and, unlike that of the condemned beguines and beghards, did not contradict canon law. Identification with the *Bachardi,* or Brethren of the Free Spirit, and the particularism of their eight articles in *Ad nostrum,* on the one hand, and the *Lullardi,* on the other, is categorically denied, for the exponents of the *devotio moderna* depended on manual labor rather than mendicancy. Citing the saving clause of *Cum de quibusdam* and John XXII's program for rehabilitation, the author concludes that Clementine legislation "does not prohibit priests, clerics, laymen, or even women not involved in error, from residing separately in apostolic fashion or from dwelling in a single house when nature is so inclined: for man is a social and political animal." Then he adds impatiently: "Would that these mendicants look back at their own order and declare to their brethren that all proprietors in their

[92] *Ibid.,* 547f.
[93] Fredericq, *Corpus,* II, 150-152, no. 105.
[94] *Ibid.,* II, 181. For the women who lived in Meester-Geertshuis see Hyma, *Christian Renaissance,* pp. 25, 32, 41-43, 45, 47f. Unlike beguines this society was not distinguished by a peculiar habit (*ibid.,* p. 42).

order are in a state of damnation instead of rising against the simple sheep of Christ living together, working with their hands, safeguarding mutually their chastity, abstaining from the snares of the world, obeying their prelates, spurning associations of religious in name and habit only, and fleeing from wayward and debauched brethren who do not keep the rule, cleave to the wishes of the Founder..." Resting his case on the papal decrees *Cum de quibusdam, Sancta Romana, Recta racio,* and *Ex iniuncto,* Everard Foec, dean of St. Salvator at Utrecht, agreed that confraternities, although not affiliated with orders, might cultivate the common life in apostolic fashion, delegate spiritual functions to their superiors, and employ scripture in the vernacular without incurring inquisitorial action.[95] In 1398 a number of canonists in the province of Cologne corroborated this favorable decision.[96] In spite of the rejection of this defense by the inquisitor in the Low Countries,[97] Frederick of Blankkenheim, bishop of Utrecht, deemed it advisable to support the position of the theologians and canon lawyers.[98]

Nevertheless the commission of the Council of Constance in charge of dogma was obliged to consider "begardos, beginas, phariseos et ypocritas in et extra terciam regulam fratrum Minorum existentes."[99] Again, depreciation and persecution of the Brethren of the Common Life were not to cease until the council in May, 1419, smiled kindly on the *devotio moderna.*[100] Even so, in 1421 Pope Martin V ordered Archbishop Dietrich II of Cologne to investigate the small convents of men and women who still lived under the appearance of religion but without espousing an approved rule.[101]

However, beguine convents had ceased to be primarily religious establishments; by the fifteenth century they had been reduced to poor houses whose inmates no longer busied themselves with theological questions. With full institutionalization Ryckel's summary observation gains strength: "Infirmariae in omnibus Begginagiis infirmis, senibus,

---

[95] Fredericq, *Corpus,* II, nos. 109-110; see above, p. 133; cf. Fredericq. *Corpus,* II, nos. 111-112.

[96] *Ibid.,* II, no. 113.

[97] *Ibid.,* II, no. 114.

[98] April 30, 1401, *ibid.,* II, no. 119. Cf. the affidavit (March 19, 1395) of five members of Windesheim vouching for the integrity and orthodoxy of the Brethren of the Common Life in the light of *Ex iniuncto* (*ibid.,* II, no. 109).

[99] *Acta Concilii Constanciencis, I. Akten zur Vorgeschichte des Konstanzer Konzils (1410-1414),* hrsg. v. Heinrich Finke, (Münster i. W., 1896), IV (1928), 676-680, no. 520.

[100] Fredericq, *Corpus,* II, 225, no. 136; cf. no. 132. The Dominican Matthew Grabow's protest to Pope Martin V (*ibid.,* no. 133; cf. nos. 139-140) was challenged by Pierre d'Ailly (no. 134), Jean Gerson (no. 135), and finally by the general council (no. 136; cf. nos. 137-138).

[101] Lacomblet, IV, 154, no. 130; cf. bull of January 6, 1420, relating to the Nicholas Serrurier case, Fredericq, *Corpus,* II, 237-242, no. 140.

indigentibus sunt refugio, solatio, subsidio."[102] Errors in doctrine and moral aberration were now replaced, as causes of persecution, by competition with guild organization and immunity from municipal ordinances and exactions. Criticism was increasingly focused on socio-economic problems with less reference to canonical prescription.

[102] Ryckel, p. 163.

Bibliography

UNPUBLISHED MATERIALS

I. Archives de l'Assistance Publique de Bruxelles (AAPB).
   B. 149 A   Chartrier des Pauvres de Sainte-Gudule
   B. 203   Cartulaire des Pauvres de Sainte-Gudule
   B. 1452-1455   Chartrier de la Fondation de Ter Kisten
   B. 1460   Cartulaire de la Fondation de Ter Kisten
   H. 262-270   Chartrier de l'Infirmerie du Béguinage de Bruxelles
   H. 1553   Cartulaire de Saint Jean

II. Archives Générales du Royaume à Bruxelles (AGR).
    Archives ecclésiastiques
    5338   Cartulaire de l'abbaye d'Aywières
    13402   Chartrier du Béguinage de Bruxelles
    13403   Cartulaire de l'Infirmerie du Béguinage de Bruxelles
    Assistance Publique de Louvain
    Nos. 2654-2710

III. Bibliothèque royale de Belgique à Bruxelles, Cabinet des Manuscrits.
     Gosuin de Bossut (?), *Vita Abundi*, cod. 19525.
     Vita Beatricis, cod. 4459-4470, ff. 66^r-138^v.
     Vita Fratris Simonis de Alna, cod. 8965-8966, ff. 209^r-224^r.
     Beschryvinge van het Begynhof van Brussel, cod. 16566-74.
     Sacra Dioecesis Namurcensis Chronologia, cod. 19668.
     Documents relatifs au comté de Namur, cod. 6594-6639.
     Rules of Third Order of St. Francis, cod. 4909-10.

UNPUBLISHED MANUSCRIPT

Bardiau, Jacqueline, *Le béguinage de Bruxelles au moyen-âge* (Mémoire manuscrit de la faculté de Philosophie et Lettres de l'Université de Bruxelles, 1941).

PRIMARY SOURCES

Acta Capitulorum Generalium Ordinis Praedicatorum, ed. Benedict Maria Reichert, in *MOPH.*, III-IV (Rome, 1898-1899).
Acta Christianae Stumbelensis, see *Vita Christianae Stumbelensis*.
Acta Sanctorum quotquot tote orbe coluntur, vel a Catholicis scriptoribus celebrantur .... new ed., J. Carnandet et al., Paris, 1863ff.
Agnes de Harcourt. *Vita B. Elisabethae seu Isabellae Virginis*, AA. SS., XL (August 31, vi), 798-808.
Albanès, J. H. *Li Vida de la Benaurada Sancta Douceline Mayre de las Donnas de Robaut* under title *La vie de Sainte Douceline, fondatrice des*

béguines de Marseille composée au treizième siècle en langue provençale. Marseilles, 1879.

Alberic de Trois-Fontaines. *Chronicon ab orbe condito (ad 1241),* ed. P. Scheffer-Boichorst, *MGH. SS.,* XXIII, 674-950.

Altaner, Berthold. *Die Briefe Jordans von Sachsen, des zweiten Dominikaner-generals (1222-37). Text und Untersuchungen, Zugleich ein Beitrag zur Geschichte der Frömmigkeit im 13. Jahrhundert (QF.,* XX), Leipzig, 1925.

Annales Colmarienses Maiores, ed. Ph. Jaffe, *MGH. SS.,* XVII, 202-232.

Anonymous of Passau (Pseudo-Rainier). *Liber contra Waldenses Hereticos,* in *Bibl. Max. Vet. Pat.,* XXV (Lyons, 1677), 262-277.

Axters, Stephanus, *Jan van Leeuwen, een Bloemlezing uit zijn werken.* Antwerp, 1943.

Bacha, Eugene. "Chartes de Val-Dieu (XIIIe et XIVe siècle), *CRHB.,* 5 ser., IV (1894), 123-164, 241-293.

Baluzius, Steph. *Miscellanea, hoc est collectio veterum monumentorum...,* 7 vols., Paris, 1678-1714; revised and enlarged by J. D. Mansi, 4 vols., Lucca, 1761-1764.

——. *Vitae Paparum Avenionensium; hoc est historia pontificum romanorum qui in Gallia sederunt ab anno Christi 1305 usque ad annum 1394,* ed. G. Mollat, 4 vols., Paris, 1914-1927.

Barbazan, Et. *Fabliaux et contes des poètes français des XIe, XIIe, XIII, XIVe et XVe siècles,* revised by D. M. Méon, 4 vols., Paris, 1808.

Baldwin of Ninove. *Chronicon,* ed. O. Holder-Egger, *MGH. SS.,* XXV, 515-546.

Bechmann, E. "Drei Dits de l'Ame aus der Handschrift Ms. Gall. Oct. 28 der königlichen Bibliothek zu Berlin," *Zeitschrift für romanische Philologie,* XIII (1889), 35-84.

Benedict of Nursia. *Regula cum Commentariis, PL.,* LXVI, 215-932.

Berger, Elie. *Les Registres d'Innocent IV,* Bibliothèque des Ecoles françaises d'Athène et de Rome. Paris, 1884ff.

Berlière, Ursmer. "Documents vaticans concernant l'abbaye de St. Bernard-sur-l'Escaut, XIVe-XVe s.," *BG.,* III (1904), 1-16, 57-69.

——. "Trois traités inédits sur les Flagellants de 1349," *RB.,* XXV (1908), 334-357.

Bernard of Clairvaux. *Epistolae, PL.,* CLXXXII, 67-662.

——. *Sermones in Cantica, PL.,* CLXXXIII, 785-1198.

Bernard de Fontcaude. *Liber adversus Waldensium Sectam,* in *PL.,* CCIV, 793-840.

Bernard Gui. *Historia Fundationum Conventuum Ordinis Praedicatorum Tolosanae et Provinciae Provinciarum,* in *MDAC.,* VI, 437-540.

——. *Practica Inquisitionis Heretice Pravitatis,* ed. C. Douais, Paris, 1886; also 1927. *Manuel de l'inquisiteur,* ed. and transl. G. Mollat, 2 vols., Paris, 1926-1927.

Berthold von Regensburg. *Deutsche Predigten,* ed. Franz Pfeiffer and Joseph Strobl, 2 vols., Vienna, 1862/80.

Béthune, Jean. *Cartulaire du béguinage de Sainte-Elisabeth à Gand.* Bruges, 1893.

Blommaert, Philipp. *Oudvlaemsche Gedichten der XIIe, XIIIe en XIVe Eeuwen.* 3 vols. in 1, Ghent, 1838-1851.

Boehmer, Johann Friedrich. *Fontes Rerum Germanicarum. Geschichtsquellen Deutschlands.* 4 vols., Stuttgart, 1843-1868.

Boonen, Willem. *Geschiedenis van Leuven geschreven in de Jaren 1593 en 1594.* ed. Ed. van Even, Louvain, 1880.

Borgnet, J., Bormans, S., and Brouwers, D. D. *Cartulaire de la commune de Namur*. 7 vols., Namur, 1876-1924.

Bouquet, Martin. *Recueil des historiens des Gaules et de la France*. Vols. 17-23, Paris, 1840-1865.

Bourguignon, Marcel. *Inventaire des archives de l'assistance publique de la ville de Louvain*. Tongres, 1933.

Bughetti, Benv. "Prima Regula Tertii Ordinis iuxta novum codicem," *AFH.*, XIV (1921), 109-121.

Caesarius of Heisterbach. *Dialogus Miraculorum*, ed. Joseph Strange, 2 vols., Cologne, 1851.

——. "Die Fragmente der Libri VIII Miraculorum des Caesarius von Heisterbach," *RQ.*, XIII (1901).

——. *Die Wundergeschichten*, ed. Alfons Hilka. 3 vols., Bonn, 1933-1937.

Canivez, J. M. *Statuta capitulorum generalium ordinis Cisterciensis ab a. 1116 ad a. 1787*, in Bibl. de la RHE., fasc. 9-14B, vol. I, *ab. a. 1116 ad a. 1220*, fasc. 9, Louvain, 1933; vol. II, *ab a. 1221 ad a. 1261*, fasc. 10, Louvain, 1934.

Cartulaire de l'église Saint-Lambert de Liége, ed. S. Bormans and E. Schoolmeesters, 6 vols., Brussels, 1893-1933.

Chmel. "Cyklus kleiner historischer Mittheilungen. III. (Pez, Das Leben und die Visionen der Agnes Blannbekin)," *Sitz.- ber. d. phil. -hist. Classe d. kaiserlichen Akademie der Wissenschaften*, II (Vienna, 1849), 46-102.

Choquet, H. *Sancti Belgii Ordinis Praedicatorum*. Douai, 1618.

Christ, Karl. "La Règle des Fins Amans. Eine Beginenregel aus dem Ende des XIII. Jahrhunderts," *Philologische Studien aus dem romanisch-germanischen Kulturkreise*, Festgabe Karl Voretzsch, hrsg. v. B. Schädel and W. Mulertt, Halle an der Saale, 1927, pp. 173-213.

Chronica regia Coloniensis (Continuationes), ed. G. Waitz (*Annales Colonienses Maximi*) in *MGH. SS.*, XVII, 823-847; XXIV, 1-20; *in Scriptores rerum Germanicarum in usum scholarum*, Hanover, 1880.

Chronica de Mailros, e codice nunc iterum in lucem, ed. Jos. Stevenson, Edinburgh, 1835.

Chronicon rhythmicum Austriacum, a. 1152-1268, W. Wattenbach, *MGH. SS.*, XXV, 349-368.

Chronicon universale anonymi Laudunensis, ed. G. Waitz, *MGH. SS.*, XXVI, 442-457.

Chronik der Strassburger Franziskaner-Provinz, ed. Leonhard Lemmens, in *RQ.*, XIV (1900), 233-255.

Codex Iuris Canonici Pii X Pontificis Maximi iussu digestus. Freiburg i. Br. Regensburg, 1919.

Corpus Iuris Canonici, ed. Emile Louis Richter and Emile Friedberg, Vol. II, *Decretalium Collectiones*, 2nd ed., Leipzig, 1881.

Cronica Villariensis Monasterii, with *Continuationes*, ed. G. Waitz, *MGH. SS.*, XXV, 192-219.

Crane, *Exempla*, see Jacques de Vitry.

Cuvelier, Joseph. *Inventaire des archives de l'abbaye du Val-Benoît lez-Liége de l'ordre de Cîteaux*. Liége, 1902.

——. *Cartulaire de l'abbaye du Val-Benoît*. Brussels, 1906.

——. *Les dénombrements de foyers en Brabant (XIVe-XVIe siècle)*, avec une *Table onomastique*, 2 vols., Brussels, 1912-1913.

David of Augsburg, "Tractatus de inquisitione hereticorum," ed. W. Preger, *Abhandl. d. histor. Classe der bayer. Akademie der Wissenschaften*, XIV, 2 (Munich, 1879), 181-235.

De Fremery, James, "Oorkonden tot aanvulling van het Oorkondenboek van

Holland en Zeeland," in Fruin, *Bijdragen voor vaderlandsche Geschiedenis en Oudheidkunde*, 3 rd ser., VIII (The Hague, 1894).

Denifle, Heinrich and Chatelain, E. *Chartularium Universitatis Parisiensis*, vols. I-II. Paris, 1889-1891.

Denzinger, H. and Bannwart. *Enchiridion symbolorum, definitionum*. Freiburg i. Br., 1921.

Deutsches Nonnenleben. Das Leben der Schwestern zu Töss und der Nonne von Engeltal, Büchlein von der Graden Überlast, ed. and transl. Margarete Weinhandl. Munich, 1921.

Devillers, Leopold. *Description analytique de cartulaires et de chartriers, accompagnée du texte de documents utiles à l'histoire du Hainaut*. 4 vols., Mons, 1865-1869.

——. *Chartes du chapitre de Sainte-Waudru de Mons*. Vol. I, Brussels, 1899.

——. "Cartulaire du béguinage de Cantimpret à Mons," *Ann. cercle arch. Mons*, VI (1865), 197-352.

——. "Mémoire sur un cartulaire et sur les archives de l'abbaye d'Alne," *ibid.*, IV (1863), 237-280; V (1864), 193-422.

d'Hoop, Alfred. *Inventaire général des archives ecclésiastiques du Brabant*. 5 vols., Brussels, 1905-1930.

Diplomatarium Danicum, [udgivet af det Danske sprog-og litteraturselskab med understøttelse af Carlsbergfondet.] Ser. 2. Vol. 1. (1250-1265), (ed. Franz Blatt and Gustav Hermansen), Copenhagen, 1938.

Ennen, Leonard and Eckertz, Gottfried. *Quellen zur Geschichte der Stadt Köln*. 6 vols., Cologne, 1860-1879.

Fabricius, Johann Albert. *Bibliotheca ecclesiastica in qua continentur de scriptoribus ecclesiasticis*. Hamburg, 1718.

Fayen, Arnold. "L'Antigraphum Petri et les lettres concernant Lambert le Bègue conservées dans le manuscrit de Glasgow," *BCRH.*, LXVIII (ser. V, vol. 9), (1899), 255-356.

Feys, E. and Nelis, A. *Les cartulaires de la prévôté de Saint-Martin à Ypres précédés d'une esquisse historique sur la prévôté*. 2 vols., Bruges, 1880-1881

Figeac, M. Champollion. *Documents historiques inédits tirés des collections manuscrites de la Bibliothèque nationale et des archives ou des archives ou des bibliothèques des departements*, IV (Paris, 1848).

Finke, Heinrich. *Ungedruckte Dominikanerbriefe des 13. Jahrhunderts*. Paderborn, 1891.

Franquinet, G. D. *Beredeneerde Inventaris der Oorkonden en Bescheiden van het Kapitel van O.L.' Vrouwekerk te Maastricht, berustende op het provinciaal Archief van Limburg*. 5 vols., Maastricht, 1870.

Frederick, Paul. "Deux sermons inédits de Jean de Fayt sur les Flagellants (5 octobre 1349) et sur le Grand Schisme d'Occident (1378)," *BARB.*, 1903, 688-718.

——. *Corpus documentorum Inquisitionis Haereticae pravitatis Neerlandicae*, vols. I-III, Ghent-The Hague, 1889-1906.

Frenken, *Exempla*. See Jacques de Vitry.

Gallia Christiana, in provincias ecclesiasticas distributa, 16 vols., Paris, 1716-1865.

Geoffrey of Beaulieu. *Vita Ludovici Noni*, in Bouquet, XX, 3-27.

Gerson, Jean. *Opera Omnia*, ed. L. E. Dupin, 2nd ed., 5 vols., The Hague, 1728.

Geschichtsquellen der Provinz Sachsen, I. *Erfurter Denkmäler*. Halle, 1870.

Gesta Abbatum Trudonensium, with *Continuationes, MGH. SS.*, X, 213-448.

Gesta Archiepiscoporum Magdeburgensium, ed. Guilelmus Schum, *MGH. SS.*, XVI, 374-486.

Gesta Episcoporum Mettensium, ed. G. Waitz, *MGH. SS.,* X, 531-551.

Gesta Sanctorum Villariensium (2nd ed.),ed. E. Martene, in MDT., III (Paris, 1717), 1309-1374; also *MGH. SS.,* XXV, 220-235.

Gesta Trevirorum, ed. Johannes Hugh Wyttenbach and Michael Franciscus Josephus Müller. 3 vols., Trèves, 1836-1839; *Gesta Trevirorum continuata, MGH, SS,* XXIV, 368-488.

Gilles li Muisis, *Poésies,* ed. Kervyn de Lettenhove, 2 vols., Louvain, 1882.

——. *Chronique et Annales,* ed. Henri Lemaître, Paris, 1906.

Gilliodts-van Severen, L. *Inventaire diplomatique des archives de l'ancienne école bogarde à Bruges, comprenant le texte ou l'analyse de tous les documents qui composent cette collection.* 3 vols., Bruges, 1899-1900.

Girard de Frachet. *Chronicon ab. O. C. usque ad a. 1266 aut 1268 cum anonyma eiusdem operis continuatione usque ad a. 1328,* in Bouquet, XXI, 3-70.

——. *Vitae fratrum Ordinis Praedicatorum,* ed. Benedictus Maria Reichert (*MOPH.,* I, Louvain, 1896).

Gielemans, John. *Anecdota ex codicibus hagiographicis Iohannis Gielemans canonici regularis in Rubea Valle prope Bruxellas,* ed. Bollandists. Brussels, 1895.

Gislebert de Mons. *La Chronique,* ed. Leon Vanderkindere, Brussels, s.d.

Coetschalckx, J. and Van Doninck, B. "Oorkondenboek der abdij van S. Bernaerts op de Schelde," *BG.,* IX (1910), 138-176, 473-525.

Gosuin de Bossut. *Vita Arnulfi Villariensis,* ed. D. Papebroch, *AA. SS.,* XXVII (June 29, vii), Paris, 1867, pp. 556-579.

——. (?). *Vita Abundi,* Prologue, ed. Fr. De Reiffenberg, in *Annuaire de la Bibl. roy. de Belg.,* VII (1846), 96-101.

Greven, *Exempla.* See Jacques de Vitry.

Guignard, Pierre Philippe. *Les monuments primitifs de la règle cistercienne publiés d'après les manuscrits de l'abbaye de Cîteaux.* Dijon, 1878.

Guillaume de Nangis. *Gesta Sancti Ludovici,* in Bouquet, XX, 310-465.

——. *Chronicon* with *Continuationes,* in Bouquet, XX, 544-646; *Chronique latine de 1113 à 1300 avec les continuations de cette chronique de 1300 à 1368,* ed. H. Géraud, *Société de l'histoire de France,* vols. 33, 35, Paris, 1843.

Hartzheim, Jos. *Concilia Germaniae,* 11 vols., Cologne, 1759-1790.

Haupt, Hermann. "Zwei Traktate gegen Beginen und Begharden," *ZKG.,* XII (1890), 85-90.

Hautcoeur, E. *Cartulaire de l'église collégiale de Saint-Pierre de Lille.* 2 vols., Lille-Paris, 1894.

——. *Cartulaire de l'abbaye de Flines.* Vol. I, Lille, 1873.

Henriquez, Chrysotom. *Quinque prudentes virgines, seu vitae B. Beatricis de Nazareth, B. Aleydis de Scharenbeca, B. Idae de Lovanio, B. Idae de Leewis.* Antwerp, 1630.

Herman of Tournai. *Liber de restauratione monasterii S. Martini Tornacensis,* ed. G. Waitz, in *MGH. SS.,* XIV, 274-327.

——. *De miraculis S. Mariae Laudunensis,* ed. R. Wilmans, *ibid., XII, 653-660;* also ed. Papebroch, *AA. SS.,* XX (June 6, i), 848-854.

Hildegarde of Bingen. *Opera Omnia,* PL., CXCVII, 145ff.

Hoornaert, R. "La plus ancienne règle du Béguinage de Bruges," *ASEB.,* LXXII (1929), 1-79.

Humbert de Romans. *De modo prompte cudendi sermones ad omne hominum et negotiatorum genus,* in *Bibl. Max. Vet. Pat.,* XXV, 456-567.

Hugues de Floreffe. *Vita S. Juettae Reclusae Huyi,* ed. G. Henschenius, in *AA. SS.,* II (January 13, ii), Brussels, 1863. pp. 145-169.

Inventaire analytique et chronologique des archives de la chambre des comptes à Lille. Paris-Lille, 1865.

Jacques de Guise. *Annales Historiae Illustrium Principum Hanoniae,* ed. E. Sackur, in *MGH. SS.,* XXX, 1, 44-334.

Jacques de Vitry (Jacobus de Vitriaco). *Libri duo, quorum prior Orientalis sive Hierosolimitanae, alter Occidentalis Historiae nomine inscribitur,* ed. Franciscus Moschus, Duaci, 1597.

——. *Epistolae:* Röhricht, R., "Briefe des Jacobus de Vitriaco," *ZKG.,* XIV (1894), 97-118; XV (1895), 568-587; XVI (1896), 72-114.

——. *Vita Mariae Oigniacensis,* ed. D. Papebroch, in *AA. SS.,* XXV (June 23, v), Paris, 1867, pp. 542-572.

——. *Exempla,* ed. F. F. Crane, *Folk Lore Society Publications,* XXVI (London, 1904).

——. *Die Exempla aus den Sermones feriales et communes,* ed. Joseph Greven *(Sammlung mittellateinischer Texte,* hrsg. Alfons Hilka, IX). Heidelberg, 1914.

——. *Die Exempla des Jacob von Vitry. Ein Beitrag zur Geschichte der Erzählungsliteratur des Mittelalters,* ed. Goswin Frenken, in *Quellen und Untersuchungen zur lateinischen Philologie des Mittelalters,* V (Munich, 1914).

——. *Selecta ex Sermonibus Vulgaribus,* ed. John Baptiste Pitra, *Analecta Novissima Spicilegii Solesmensis Altera Continuatio,* II, Tusculum, 1888, pp. 344-442.

Jean des Prez (d'Outremeuse). *Ly Myreur des histors, chronique de Jean des Preiz,* ed. Stanisl. Bormans *(Corps des chroniques liégeoises,* IV). Brussels, 1877.

Johannes Meyer, *Liber de Viris Illustribus Ordinis Praedicatorum,* ed. Paulus von Loë *(QF.,* XII, Leipzig, 1918).

——. *Buch der Reformacio Predigerordens,* ed. Reichert, I-III *(QF.,* II), IV-V *(QF,* III). Leipzig, 1909, 1908.

John of Winterthur (Vitoduranus). *Chronicon,* in *Archiv für schweizerische Geschichte,* XI (1856).

Joinville. *Histoire de Saint Louis,* in Bouquet, XX, 191-304.

Juten, G. C. A. *Cartularium van het Begijnhof te Breda,* Uitgave van het Provinciaal Genootschap van Kunsten en Wetenschappen in Noord-Brabant, *s.l., s.d.*

Kervyn de Lettenhove, J. B. M. C. *Codex Dunensis sive Diplomatum et Chartarum Medii Aevi Amplissima Collectio.* Brussels, 1875.

Kisky, Wilhelm, ed. *Die Regesten der Erzbischöfe von Köln im Mittelalter* (Publikationen der Gesellschaft für rheinische Geschichtskunde, XXI), 4 vols., Bonn, 1901-1915 (Vols. II-III, ed. Richard Knipping).

König, J., ed. "Die Chronik der Anna von Munzingen," *Freiburger Diözesan-Archiv,* XIII (1880), 129-236.

Kurth, Godefroid. "Documents historiques sur l'abbaye de Neufmoustier près de Huy," *BCRH.,* 5e. ser., II (1892), 39-67.

Lacomblet, Theodore Joseph. *Urkundenbuch für die Geschichte des Niederrheins oder des Erzstifts Cöln, der fürstenthümer Jülich und Berg, Geldern, Meurs, Cleve und Mark, und der Reichsstifte Elten, Essen und Werden.* 4 vols., Düsseldorf, 1840-1858.

Lahaye, Leon. *Cartulaire de la commune de Walcourt.* Namur, 1888.

Lamprecht of Regensburg. *Sanct Francisken Leben und Tochter Syon,* ed. Karl Weinhold, Paderborn, 1880.

Lefèvre, Plac. "Testaments bruxellois du XIII siècle," *BG.,* XIX (1928), 360-370, 417-445.

———. ed. *Les Statuts de Prémontré réformés sur les ordres de Grégoire IX et d'Innocent IV au XIIIe siècle* (Bibliothèque de la Revue d'histoire ecclésiastique, fasc. 23). Louvain, 1946.

Leven van Sinte Christina de Wonderbare, in Oud-Dietsche rijmen, naer een perkementen Hs. uit de XIVde eeuw ..., ed. J. H. Bormans, Ghent, 1850.

Leven van Sinte Lutgart, tweede en derde boek, naar een Kopenhaagsch Hs., ed. Fr. Van Veerdeghem. Leiden, 1899.

Loesch, Heinrich von. *Die Kölner Zunfturkunden nebst anderen Kölner Gewerbeurkunden bis zum Jahre 1500 (Publikationen der Geschellschaft für rheinische Geschichtskunde,* XXII, 2 pts.). Bonn, 1907.

Löhr, Gabriel. "Drei Briefe Hermanns von Minden O. P. über die Seelsorge und die Leitung der Dominikanerinnenkloster," *RQ.,* XXXIII (1925), 159-167.

———. "Das Necrologium des Dominikanerinnenklosters St. Gertrud in Köln," *AHVN.,* CX (1927), 60-179.

Maerlant, Jacob van. *Sinte Franciscus Leven* (Werken uitgegeven door de Vereeniging ter Bevordering der Oude nederlandsche Letterkunde, Jg, IV, Afl. III), Leyden, 1847.

———. *Spiegel Historiael,* ed. M. de Vries and E. Verwijs, 3 vols., Leiden, 1863.

———. *Strophische Gedichten,* nieuwe bewerking der uitgave van Franck en Verdam by J. Verdam and P. Leendertz (Bibliotheek van Middelnederlandsche Letterkunde). Leiden, 1918.

Mansi, J. D. *Sacrorum Conciliorum nova et amplissima collectio.* Florence and Venice, 1759ff.

Martène, Edmond. *De antiquis ecclesiasticis ritibus,* III (Venice, 1783; Antwerp, 1737).

———. and Durand, Urs. *Veterum scriptorum et monumentorum historicorum dogmaticorum, moralium, amplissima collectio.* 9 vols., Paris, 1724-1733.

———. and Durand. *Thesaurus novus anecdotorum.* 5 vols., Paris, 1717.

Martens, Mina. *Actes relatifs à l'administration des revenus domaniaux du duc de Brabant (1271-1408).* Brussels, 1943.

Matthaeus, Antonius. *Veteris aevi analecta, seu, vetera monumenta hactenus nondum visa.* 5 vols., The Hague, 1738.

Matthew Paris. *Chronica maior* and *Historia minor,* ed. F. Liebermann, *MGH. SS.,* XXVIII, 107-389, 390-434.

Miraeus, Aub. and Foppens, J. F. *Opera diplomatica et historica.* 4 vols., Louvain-Brussels, 1723-1748.

Mittarelli, Johannes Benedictus and Costadoni, Anselmus. *Annales Camaldulenses ordinis S. Benedicti.* 9 vols., Venice, 1755-1773.

Mouskès, Philippe. *Chronique rimée,* ed. F. A. F. Th. de Reiffenberg, 2 vols., Brussels, 1836; *Ex Historia Regum Francorum,* ed. Adolf Tobler, *MGH. SS.,* XXVI, 721-821.

Mussely, Ch. *Inventaire des archives de la ville de Courtrai.* 2 vols., Courtrai, 1854, 1858.

Nelis, Franciscus Cornelius, ed. *Tabulae publicae Lovaniensium, sive veteres chartae quibus concessa Lovaniensibus privilegia et alia plurima continentur ab anno 1233 ad annum usque 1368.* Louvain, 1767.

Nelis, H. "Les statuts du Tiers-Ordre de St. François édictés à Zepperen en 1487," *Franciscana,* IV (1921), 76-84, 193-204s.

Nicholas de Bibera. *Carmen satiricum,* ed. Theobald Fischer, *Geschichtsquellen der Provinz Sachsen,* I. *Erfurter Denkmäler.* Halle, 1870.

Oliger, Livarius. "Documenta inedita ad historiam Fraticellorum spectantia," *AFH.,* III-VI (1910-1913), *passim.*

Paquay, J. "Regesta de Marcuald de Modène, archidiacre de Hesbaye, prévôt de Tongres (1237-1274)," *BSSLL.*, XXIII (1905), 199-282.
——. "Regesta de Renier écolâtre de Tongres, vicaire général de Henri de Gueldre," *BIAL.*, XXXV (1905), 1-74.
——. "Cartulaire de l'ancienne église collégiale et archidiaconale de Notre-Dame à Tongres," *BSSLL.*, XXIV (1906), 73-351.
——. "Supplément au catalogue des actes de Renier de Tongres, vicaire-général de Henri de Gueldre (1253-1267), *BSSLL.*, XXV (1907), 399-409, 419-420.
Petrus de Vaux-Cernay. *Historia Albigensis,* ed. A. Luchaire, Bibliothèque de la faculté des lettres, Université de Paris, XXV, Cinquième mélanges d'histoire du moyen âge. Paris, 1908, pp. 1-75; also in Bouquet, XIX, 1-113.
Piot, Ch. *Cartulaire de l'abbaye de Saint-Trond.* 2 vols., Brussels, 1870-74.
Pirenne, Henri. *Le livre de l'abbé Guillaume de Ryckel (1249-1272), polyptiques et comptes de l'abbaye de Saint-Trond au milieu du XIIIe siècle.* Brussels, 1896.
Pitra, Joannes Baptista. *Analecta Sanctae Hildegardis, Opera Spicilegio Solesmensi Parate.* Monte Cassino, 1882, vol. VIII.
——. *Analecta Novissima Spicilegii Solesmensis altera Continuatio.* Vol. II, Tusculum, 1888.
Pomerius, Henry. "De origine monasterii Viridisvallis et de Gestis Patrum et Fratrum in primordiali fervore ibidem degentium," *AB., IV (1885),* 263-322.
Poncelet, Edouard. "Chartes du prieuré d'Oignies de l'Ordre de Saint-Augustin," *ASAN.*, XXXI (1912), 1-300; XXXII (1913), 1-168.
——. *Inventaire analytique des chartes de la collégiale de Sainte-Croix à Liége.* 2 vols., Brussels, 1911.
——. *Actes des princes-évêques de Liége. Hugues de Pierrepont, 1200-1229.* Commission royale d'histoire de Belgique, Brussels, 1941.
Philippen, L. J. M. "Een vijftal Oorkonden betreffende de Antwerpsche Begijnen," *BG.*, XXII (1931), 129-147.
——. "Het Begijnhof van Sint-Catharina 'ten Velde', te Diest," *ibid.*, III 1904), 501-518.
Philippe Mouskès. See Mouskès (Mousket).
Poswick, E. "Documents inédits sur la haute avouerie de Hesbaye," *BIAL.*, XI (1872), 189-200.
Potthast, A. *Regesta Pontificum Romanorum (1198-1304).* 2 vols., Berlin, 1874-75.
Preger, W. "Der Tractat des David von Augsburg über die Waldesier," *Abh. d. hist. Classe d. königlich bayerischen Akademie der Wissenschaften,* IV, 2. Abt., Munich, 1878, pp. 183-235.
Prou, Maurice. *Les Registres d'Honorius IV publiés d'après le manuscrit des archives du Vatican.* Paris, 1888.
Raymaekers F. J. "Chronicon Diestense," *BCRH.*, 3rd ser., II (1861), 393-521.
Reiner, monk of St. Jacques. *Annales S. Jacobi Leodiensis 1066-1230, MGH. SS.*, XVI, 651-680.
Res Alsaticae (De Rebus Alsat.) ineuntes saeculi XIII, ed. Ph. Jaffe, *MGH. SS.*, XVII, 232-237.
Richerus Senoniensis, *Gesta Ecclesiae Senoniensis (ad 1264),* ed. G. Waitz, *MGH. SS.*, XXV, 249-345.
Riezler, Sigmund, ed. *Vatikanische Akten zur deutschen Geschichte in der Zeit Kaiser Ludwigs des Bayern,* hrsg. Historische Commission bei der königlichen Akademie der Wissenchaften. Innsbruck, 1891.

Robert de Sorbon. *De Conscientia et de Tribus Dietis,* ed. Félix Chambon. Paris, 1903.

Ripoll, Thomas. *Bullarium Ordinis Fratrum Praedicatorum,* ed. Antonius Bremond. Rome, 1729ff.

Roman de la Rose, by Guillaume de Lorris and Jean de Meung, ed. E. Langlois, 5 vols., *SATF.,* Paris, 1914-24.

Rutebeuf. *Oeuvres complètes,* ed. Achille Jubinal, 3 vols., Paris, 1874.

——. *Onze poèmes de Rutebeuf concernant la croisade,* ed. Julia Bastin and Edmond Faral (Documents rélatifs à l'histoire des croisades publiés par l'Académie des Inscriptions et Belles- Lettres). Paris, 1946.

——. *Poèmes concernant l'Université de Paris,* ed. H. H. Lucas. Paris-University of Manchester, 1952.

Sabatier, Paul, ed. *Speculum Perfectionis.* Paris, 1898.

——. *Regula antiqua Fratrum et Sororum de Paenitentia seu Tertii Ordinis Sancti Francisci* (Opuscules de critique historique, fasc. 1). Paris, 1901.

Salimbene de Adam. *Cronica,* ed. Oswald Holder-Egger, *MGH. SS.,* XXXII.

Sauerland, Heinrich Volbert, ed. *Urkunden und Regesten zur Geschichte der Rheinlande aus dem Vatikanischen Archiv* (Publikationen der Gesellschaft für rheinische Geschichtskunde, XXIII). 7 vols., Bonn, 1902-1913.

Sbaralea, Joannes Hyacinthus. *Bullarium Franciscanum.* Rome, 1759ff Aug. by Conrad Eubel, Quaracchi, 1898ff.

Schade, Oskar. *Geistliche Gedichte des XIV. und XV. Jahrhunderts vom Niederrhein.* Hanover, 1854.

Scholz, Richard. *Unbekannte Kirchenpolitische Streitschriften aus der Zeit Ludwigs des Bayern (1327-1354), Analysen und Texte* (Deutsches historisches Institut in Rom. Bibliothek, Bd. 9-10). Rome, 1911.

Schoolmeesters, E. *Les statuts synodaux de Jean de Flandre, évêque de Liége (16 février 1288),* publ. and transl. by E. Schoolmeesters, Liége, 1908.

——. *Les actes du cardinal-légat Hugues de Saint-Cher en Belgique, durant les années de sa légation, 1251-1253," Leodium,* VI (1907), 150-166, 172-176.

——. "Les Regesta de Raoul de Zähringen, prince-évêque de Liége (1167-1191)," *BSAHL.,* I (1881), 129-203.

Schoonbroodt, J. G. *Inventaire analytique et chronologique des archives de l'abbaye du Val-St-Lambert, lez-Liége.* 2 vols., Liege, 1875-1880.

——. *Inventaire analytique et chronologique des chartes du chapitre de Saint-Martin à Liége.* Liége, 1871.

Schröder, F. "Ars Mendicandi, Ein Beitrag zur Geschichte des mittelalterlichen Schülerbettels," *NAK.,* N.S., XVIII (1925), 124-145.

Snellaert, F. A. *Nederlandsche Gedichten uit de veertiende eeuw van Jan Boendale, Hein van Aken en anderen naar het Oxfordsch Handschrift.* Brussels, 1869.

Soens, E. "Cartularium en Rentboek van het Begijnhof St. Katharina op den Zavel te Aalst," *Annalen van den oudheidkundigen kring van de stad en het voormalig land van Aalst,* VIII (1912).

Stein, Walter. *Akten zur Geschichte der Verfassung und Verwaltung der Stadt Köln* (Publikationen der Gesellschaft für rheinische Geschichtskunde, X, 1 and X, 2) 2 vols., Bonn, 1893.

Stephen of Bourbon. *Anecdotes historiques, légendes et apologues tirés du recueil inédit d'Etienne de Bourbon,* ed. A. Lecoy de la Marche, Paris, 1877.

Theiner, Augustinus. *Vetera Monumenta Poloniae et Lithuaniae, gentium-que finitimarum historiam illustrantium,* I (Rome, 1860).

Thomas of Cantimpré. *Bonum Universale de Apibus,* ed. Georgius Colve-nerius, 2nd ed., Douai, 1627.

——. *Vita Mariae Oigniacensis, Supplementum,* ed. D. Papebroeck, in *AA. SS.,* XXV (June 23, v), 572-581.

——. *Vita beatae Christinae Mirabilis Trudonopoli in Hasbania,* ed. J. Pinius, *AA. SS.,* XXXII (July 24, v), Paris, 1868, 637-660.

——. *Vita Lutgardis,* ed. G. Henschenius, in *AA. SS.,* XXIV (June 16, iv), Paris, 1867, 187-210.

——. *Vita Margaretae Yprensis,* ed. H. Choquet, in *Sancti Belgii Ord. Praed.,* pp. 140-200.

Thomas (cantor of Villers). *Vita Godefridi Pachomii* extracts, ed. A. Poncelet, *AB.,* XIV (1895), 263-268.

Tangl. Michael. *Die päpstlichen Kanzleiordnungen von 1200-1500.* Innsbruck, 1894.

Urkunden, Hessische, ed. Ludwig Baur. 5 vols., Darmstadt, 1860-1873.

Urkundenbuch der Abtei Altenberg, ed. Hans Mosler (*Urkundenbücher der geistlichen Stiftungen des Niederrheins*), vol. I (1138-1400), Bonn, 1912.

——. *der Abtei Heisterbach,* ed. Ferdinand Schmitz (*Urkundenbücher... des Niederrheins*). Bonn, 1908.

——. *der Reichsstadt Frankfurt,* ed. J. F. Boehmer. Vol. I (Frankfurt a. M., 1836).

——. *der Stadt Basel,* ed. R. Wackernagel and R. Thommen. Basel, 1890ff.

——. *der Stadt Erfurt,* ed. Carl Beyer, vol. II, *Geschichtsquellen der Provinz Sachsen,* XXIV (Halle, 1897).

——. *der Stadt Magdeburg,* ed. Gustav Hertel, vol. I, *Geschichtsquellen der Provinz Sachsen,* XXVI (Halle, 1892).

——. *der Stadt Strassburg,* ed. Wiegand and Schulte. Strasbourg, 1879ff.

——. *der Stadt Worms; Quellen zur Geschichte der Stadt Worms,* ed. Heinrich Boos. 3 vols., Worms, 1886, 1890, 1893.

——. *des Stiftes Kaiserswerth,* ed. Heinrich Kelleter (*Urkundenbücher... des Niederrheins*). Bonn, 1904.

——. *Freiburger,* ed. Friedrich Hefele. Vol. I, Freiburg i. Br., 1940.

——. *Osnabrücker,* ed. F. Philippi. Vols., II-IV, Osnabrück, 1896-1902.

——. *Westfälisches, Fortsetzung von Erhards Regesta Historiae Westfaliae,* ed. Vereine für Geschichte und Altertumskunde Westfalens. Münster, 1847ff.

Van Mieris, Frans. *Groot Charterboek der Graaven van Holland, van Zeeland en Heeren van Vriesland.* 4 vols., Leyden, 1753-1756.

Van Velthem, Lodewijk. *Voortzetting van den Spiegel Historiael (1248-1316),* opnieuw uitgegeven door Herman Vander Linden and Willem de Vreese. 3 vols., Brussels, 1906-1938.

Van Veerdeghem. See *Leven van Sinte Lutgart.*

Vidal, J. M. *Bullaire de l'inquisition française au XIVe siècle et jusqu'à la fin du grand schisme.* Paris, 1913.

Vita Aleydis Scarembecanae, ed. G. Henschenius, *AA. SS.,* XXII (June 11, ii), Paris, 1867, 471-477; also in Henriquez, *Quinque prudentes virgines,* pp. 168-198.

Vita Beatricis de Nazareth, ed. Henriquez, l.c., pp. 1-67.

——. *Prologue,* ed. P. V. Bets, in *AHEB.,* VI (1870), 78-82.

Vita B. Bonifacii Episcopi Lausanensis, AA. SS., VI (February 19, iii), 155-162.

Vita Caroli Abbatis, ed. G. Henschenius, *AA. SS.,* III (January 29, iii), Brussels, 1863, pp. 591-595; in *Gesta Sanctorum Villariensium,* ed. G. Waitz, in *MGH. SS.,* XXV, 220-226.

Vita Catharinae, ed. G. Henschenius, *AA. SS.,* XIV (May 4, i), Paris, 1866, pp. 537-539.

Vita B. Christinae Stumbelensis, ed. D. Papebroeck, *AA. SS.,* XXV (June 22, v), 367-387; *Acta, ibid.,* 236-367.

Vita B. Coletae reformatricis Ordinis S. Clarae (by Pierre de Meaux), *AA. SS.,* VII (March 6, i), 538-590; *Miracula post obitum, ibid.,* 590-626.

Vita Franconis, in 2nd ed., *Gesta sanctorum Villariensum,* ed. Martene in Martene-Durand, *Thes.,* III, 1333-1339.

Vita Venerabilis Virginis Gertrudis ab Oosten Beghinae Delphensis in Belgio, AA. SS., I (January, 6, i), 348-353.

Vita Goberti Asperimontis, ed. P. Dolmans, *AA. SS.,* XXXVIII (August 20, iv), Paris, 1867, pp. 370-395.

Vita Godefridi Pachomii, monachi Villariensis, AB., XIV (1895), 263-268.

Vita Godefridi Sacristae, ed. J. Bueus, *AA. SS.,* XLIX (October 2, i), Paris, 1866, pp. 531-537.

Vita B. Guilielmi Presbyteris Eremitae, fundatoris coenobii Olivae in Hannonia, ed. Henschenius, *AA. SS.,* V (February 10, ii), 495-500.

Vita Idae Lewensis, ed. R. De Buck, *AA. SS.,* LXI (October 29, xiii), Paris, 1883, pp. 100-135; also in Henriquez, pp. 440-458.

Vita Idae Lovaniensis, ed. D. Papebroeck, *AA. SS.,* XI (April 13, ii), Paris, 1866, pp. 156-189; also in Henriquez, pp. 298-439.

Vita Idae Nivellensis, ed. Henriquez, *Quinque Prudentes Virgines,* pp. 199-297; extracts in *CCHB.,* II (Brussels, 1889), 222-226.

Vita Julianae Corneliensis, ed. G. Henschenius, *AA. SS.,* X (April 5, i), Paris 1865, pp. 435-475.

Vita Odiliae Viduae, ed. Chr. Pfister, *AB.,* XIII (1894), 197-297.

Vita Simonis Alnensis, ed. Fr. Moschus, in *Beatorum Arnulphi Villariensis et Simonis Alnensis ... Vitae.* Arras, 1600.

Vita Werrici, in *CCHB.,* I (Brussels, 1886), 445-463.

Walters, J. *Geschiedenis der Zusters der Bijloke te Gent.* 3 vols., Ghent, 1899-1930.

Willems, J. F. *Oude Vlaemsche Liederen ten deele met de melodiën.* Ghent, 1848.

SECONDARY SOURCES

Acquoy, J. G. R. *Het klooster te Windesheim en zijn invloed.* 3 vols., Utrecht, 1875-1880.

——. "Het geestelijk lied in de Nederlanden vóór de Hervorming," *ANK.,* II (1887), 1ff.

Aegerter, Emmanuel. "L'affaire du De Periculis Novissimorum Temporum," *Revue de l'histoire des religions,* CXII (1935), 242-272.

Alberdingk-Thijm, J. A. *Geertruide van Oosten.* Amsterdam, 1853, transl. by l'Abbé de Carnel, *Gertrude d'Est: légende,* Paris, 1859.

Alberdingk-Thijm, P. P. M. *De Gestichten van Liefdadigheid in België van Karel den Groote tot aan de XVIe eeuw, in Mémoires couronnés et mémoires des savants étrangers* publiés par l'Académie Royale des sciences, des lettres et des beaux-arts de Belgique, XLV (Bruxelles, 1883).

——. *Geschichte der Wohlthätigkeitsanstalten in Belgien von Karl dem Grossen bis zum sechzehnten Jahrhundert.* Freiburg i. Br., 1887.

Alphandéry, P. *Les idées morales chez les hétérodoxes latins au début du XIIIe siècle* (Bibl. de l'Ecole des hautes études, Sciences relig., XVI, 1). Paris, 1903.

Altaner, Berthold. *Venturino von Bergamo 1304-1346: eine Biographie* (Kirchengesch. Abhandl., IX, 2). Breslau, 1911.

——. "Zur Beurteilung der Persönlichkeit und der Entwicklung der Ordensidee des hl. Dominikus," *ZKG.*, XLVI (1928), 396-407.

Altmeyer, J. J. *Les précurseurs de la réforme aux Pays-Bas.* The Hague, 1886, 2 vols.

Ancelet-Hustache, Jeanne. *Mechtilde de Magdebourg (1207-1282).* Paris, 1926.

Annaert, F. J. "Eene Heiliggeesttafel in de 16e eeuw," *Annales du Cercle archéologique du Pays de Waes,* XX (1900-1901), 149-250.

Ansieux, P. "Les Prieurs des Frères Prêcheurs en la Cité de Liège," *BSAHL.,* XXVII (1937), 93-158.

Arens, Franz. "Zur Datierung einer Trierischen Synode des 13. Jahrhunderts," *ZKG.,* XXXIII (1912), 84-105.

Asen, Johannes, "Die Beginen in Köln," *AHVN.,* CXI (1927), 81-180; CXII (1928), 71-148; CXIII (1928), 13-96.

——. "Die Klausen in Köln," *AHVN.,* CX (1927), 180-201.

——. "Die Begarden und die Sackbrüder in Köln," *AHVN.,* CXV (1929), 167-179.

Auger, A. *Etude sur les mystiques des Pays-Bas au moyen-âge* (Mémoires couronnés et autres mémoires de l'Academie royale de Belgique, XLVI). Brussels, 1892.

Axters, Stephanus. "De anonieme Begijn van Tongeren en haar mystieke dialoog," *OGE.,* XV (1941), 88-97.

——. *Geschiedenis van de vroomheid in de Nederlanden.* I. *De vroomheid tot rond het jaar 1300.* Antwerp, 1950; II. *De Eeuw van Ruusbroeck* (1953).

——. "Hadewijch en de Scholastiek," *Leuvensche Bijdragen. Tijdschrift voor moderne Philologie,* XXXIV (1942), 99ff.

——. "Dominikaansche zielzorg in de Nederlanden der dertiende eeuw," *OGE.,* XIII (1939), 149-184.

——"Bijdragen tot een bibliographie van de nederlandsche dominikaansche vroomheid," *OGE.,* VI (1932), 5-39; 113-156; VIII (1934), 39-104, 141-204.

Bach, Joseph. *Meister Eckhart der Vater der deutschen Speculation. Als Beitrag zu einer Geschichte der deutschen Theologie und Philosophie der mittleren Zeit.* Vienna, 1864.

Bachofen, Charles Augustine. *A Commentary on the New Code of Canon Law. Vol. III: Religious and Laymen (can. 487-725).* 5 th. ed., St. Louis, Mo., 1938.

Baker, A. T. "Saints' Lives Written in Anglo-French: Their Historical, Social and Literary Importance," *Essays by Divers Hands being the Transactions of the Royal Society of Literature of the United Kingdom,* N.S., IV (London, 1924), 119-156.

Balau, Sylv. "L'organisation paroissiale de la ville de Nivelles au XIIIe siècle," *BSAHL.,* XIII (1902), 59-88.

——. *Etude critique des sources de l'histoire du Pays de Liège au moyen-âge.* (Mémoires couronnés par l'Acad. roy. Belgique, LXI (Brussels, 1903).

Balen, M. *Beschrijvinge der Stad Dordrecht.* 2 vols., Dordrecht, 1677.

Balthasar, K. *Geschichte des Armutsstreites im Franziskanerorden bis z. Konzil von Vienne* (Vorreformationsgesch. Forsch., IX), Münster, 1911.

Barbier, J. "Obituaire de l'abbaye de Brogne ou de Saint-Gérard," *AHEB.,* XVIII, (1882), 289-370.

Barbier. "Nécrologe de l'abbaye de Floreffe, de l'ordre de Prémontré, au diocèse de Namur," *AHEB.,* XIII (1876), 5-70, 190-286.

Basedow, Arnim. *Die Inclusen in Deutschland, vornehmlich in der Gegend des Niederrheins um die Wende des 12. und 13. Jahrh. unter besonder Berücksichtigung des Dialogus Miraculorum des Cäsarius von Heisterbach.* Heidelberg, 1895.

Behaghel, Wilhelm. *Die gewerbliche Stellung der Frau im mittelalterlichen Köln.* Dissert., Berlin-Leipzig, 1910.

Bennett, R. F. *The Early Dominicans. Studies in Thirteenth-Century Dominican History.* Cambridge University Press, 1937.

Benz, E. *Ecclesia Spiritualis: Kirchenidee und Geschichtstheologie der Franziskanischen Reformation.* Stuttgart, 1934.

Berger, Elie. *Thomase Cantipratensis Bonum universale de Apibus quid illustrandis saeculi decimi tertii moribus conferat.* Paris, 1895.

Bergmann, Anton. *Geschiedenis der stad Lier.* Lierre-Brussels, 1873.

Berlière, Ursmer. "L'exercice du ministère paroissial par les moines du XII au XVIIIe siècle," *RB.,* XXXIX (1927), 340-364.

——. "A propos de Jacques de Vitry. Une lettre d'Oliver de Cologne," *RB.,* XXVII (1910), 521-524.

——. L'exercice du ministre paroissial par les moines dans la haut moyen-âge," *RB.,* XXXIX (1927), 227-250.

——. "Visitations-Recesse des Benediktinerklosters St. Trond aus dem Jahre 1252, und Statuten des Cardinals Hugo von St. Sabina," *Studien und Mittheilungen aus d. Benedictiner-und Cisters.- Orden,* XVI (1895), 590-598.

——. "Jean Bernier de Fayt, abbé de Saint-Bavon de Gand, d'après des documents vaticans," *ASEB.,* LVI (1906), 359-381; LXII (1907), 5-43.

——. La dévotion au Sacre-Coeur dans l'ordre de S. Benoît. Paris, 1923.

——. "Jacques de Vitry. Ses relations avec les abbayes d'Aywières et de Doorezeele," *RB.,* XXXV (1908), 185-193.

——. "Le nombre des moines dans les anciens monastères.," *RB.,* XLI (1929), 231-261; XLII (1930), 19-42.

——. "Le recrutement dans les monastères bénédictins aux XIII, et XIVe siècles, Mémoires de l'Acad. roy de Belgique, 2 nd ser., XVIII, fasc. 6. Brussels, 1924.

——. Les monastères doubles aux XIIe et XIIIe siècles, Mémoires de l'Acad. royale. de Belgique, 2nd ser., XVIII, fasc. 3. Brussels, 1923.

——. Monasticon belge. 2 vols., Maredsous, 1890-1929.

——. "La fondation de l'abbaye d'Epinlieu," *RB.,* IX (1892), 381-383.

——. "Les évêques auxiliaires de Liége," *RB.,* XXX (1913), 79-111.

——. "La chronique de Jean de Sivry, prieur de Bonne-Espérance," *Annal. cercle arch. Mons,* XXV (1895), 143-153.

——. 'Notice sur d'anciennes archives de l'abbaye d'Aywières," *BCRH.,* 5. ser., II (1892), 572-583.

——. "Le moine Baudouin d'Aulne," *Ann. soc. archéol. Mons,* XXII (1892), 487ff.

——. "Les origines de Cîteaux et l'ordre bénédictin au XIIe siècle," *RHE.,* I (1900), 442-471; II (1901), 253-290.

Bertholet, Jean. *Histoire de l'institution de la Fête-Dieu avec la vie des bienheureuses Julienne et Eve, toutes deux originaires de Liége.* Liége, 1746.

Bertin, Paul. "Le Béguinage d'Aire-sur-la-Lys," *Revue du Nord,* XXXI (1949), 92-104.

Bets, P. V. *Histoire de la ville et des institutions de Tirlemont.* 2 vols., Louvain, 1860-1861.

——. *Zout-Leeuw, beschrijving, geschiedenis, instellingen,* I, Tirlemont, 1887.

——. *Geschiedenis der gemeente Hakendover en van dezer miraculeuze kerk.* 5th ed., Zout-Leeuw, 1898.

——. "Notice sur la ladrérie de Ter Banck," *AHEB.*, VII (1870), 307-328; VIII (1871), 59-69.

Beuken, J. H. A. "Rondom een middelnederlandsche Eckehart-Tekst," *OGE.*, VIII (1934), 310-337.

Bierbaum, H. *Bettelorden und Weltgeistlichkeit an der Universität Paris. Texte und Untersuchungen zum literarischen Armuts- und Exemtions-streit des 13. Jahrhunderts (1255-1272).* Münster in Westf., 1920.

Bihl, Michael. "De Tertio Ordine S. Francisci in provincia Germaniae superioris sive Argentinensi Syntagma," *AFH.*, XIV (1921), 138-198, 442-460; XV (1922), 349-381; XVII (1924), 237-265; XVIII (1925), 63-89.

Bihlmeyer, Karl. "Mystisches Leben in dem Dominikanerinnenkloster Weiler bei Esslingen im 13. und 14. Jahrhundert," *Württembergische Vierteljahrshefte für Landesgeschichte*, N.F., XXV (1916), 61-93.

Binterim, Anton Joseph. *Die vorzüglichsten Denkwürdigkeiten der Christ-Katholischen Kirche*, V, 1 (Mainz, 1838).

——. *Pragmatische Geschichte der deutschen National-, provinzial- und vorzüglichsten Diöcesanconcilen vom vierten Jahrhundert bis auf das Concilium zu Trient*, VI (Mainz, 1845).

Birlinger, A. "Leben heiliger alemannischer Frauen," *Alemannia*, IX (1881), 275-292; X (1882), 81-119, 128-137; XI (1883), 1-20.

Blok, P. J. *Geschiedenis eener Hollandsche Stad. Eene hollandsche stad in de Middeleeuwen.* 2nd ed., The Hague, 1910.

Blumenstok, A. *Der päpstliche Schutz im Mittelalter.* Innsbruck, 1890.

Bonet-Maury, Gaston. *Les précurseurs de la réforme et de la liberté de conscience dans las pays latins du XIIe au XVe siècle.* Paris, 1904.

Bonnard, Fourier. *Histoire de l'abbaye royale et de l'ordre des chanoines réguliers de St. Victor de Paris.* 2 vols., Paris, 1907.

Bonenfant, Paul. "Une fondation patricienne pour béguines à Bruxelles au XIIIe siècle," *Mélanges Georges Smets* (Brussels, 1952), 91-104.

Bouman, A. C., "Johannes Ruusbroec en de duitsche mystiek," *Tijdschrift voor nederl. Taal-en-Letterkunde*, XLI (1922), 1ff.

——. "Die litterarische Stellung der dichterin Hadewijch," *Neo-philologus*, VIII (1923), 270-279.

Boutaric, Edgar. *Saint Louis et Alfonse de Poitiers. Etude sur la réunion des provinces du midi et de l'ouest à la couronne et sur les origines de la centralisation administrative.* Paris, 1870.

Boyd, Catherine E. *A Cistercian Nunnery in Medieval Italy. The Story of Rifreddo in Saluzzo, 1220-1300.* Harvard University Press, Cambridge, Mass., 1943.

Braun, Jos. "Die Paramente im Schatz der Schwestern U. L. Frau zu Namur," *Zeitschrift für christliche Kunst*, 1906, coll. 289-304.

Brehmer, W. "Beiträge zur Lübeckischen Geschichte: 1. Lübeckischen Beginenhäuser," *Zeitschrift des Vereins für Lübeckische Geschichte und Altertumskunde*, IV (1884), 83-89.

Brigué, L. "Ruysbroec," in *DTC.*, XIV, 1 (1939), 408-420.

Browe, P. "Die Ausbreitung des Fronleichnamsfestes," *Jahrbuch für Liturgiewissenschaft*, VIII (1928), 107-143.

——. "Die Eucharistie als Zaubermittel im MA.," *Archiv für Kulturgeschichte*, XX (1930), 134-154.

——. *Die Verehrung der Eucharistie im Mittelalter.* Munich, 1932.

Brouwers, D. D. *L'administration et les finances du comté de Namur du XIII au XVe siècle. Sources. I. Cens et rentes du comté de Namur au siècle.* 2 vols., Namur, I: 1910; II, I: 1926; II, 2: 1911.

Bruinvis, C. W. "Het Middel-Begijnhof te Alkmaar," *Bijdragen voor de Geschiedenis van het Bisdom van Haarlem*, XXX (1906), 411-418.

Bücher, Carl. *Die Frauenfrage im Mittelalter*. Tübingen, 1882.

——. *Die Bevölkerung von Frankfurt am Main im XIV. und XV. Jahrhundert. Socialstatische Studien*. Vol. I (Tübingen, 1886).

Bulaeus, see Du Boulay.

Callaey, Frédégand. "Lambert li Beges et les Béguines," *RHE.*, XIII (1927), 254-259.

——. "De nederlandsche Beggarden in St. Franciscus' Derde Orde en de weefnijverheid tijdens de Middeleeuwen," *Neerlandia Franciscana*, I (1914), 7-32.

——. "Les Béggards aux Pays-Bas," *Annuaire de l'Université catholique de Louvain séminaire historique*, 1911, 438-451.

Callebaut, André. "Autour de la rencontre à Florence de S. Francois et du Cardinal Hugolin (en été 1217)", *AFH.*, XIX (1926), 530-558.

Canivez, Joseph-Marie. *L'ordre de Citeaux en Belgique des origines (1132) au XXme siècle. Aperçu d'histoire monastique*. Forges-lez-Chimay, 1926.

Capelle, G. C. *Autour du décret 1210: III. Amaury de Bène, Etude sur son panthéisme formel* (Bibl. thom., Sect. hist., XIV), Paris, 1932.

Cauchie, A. "Nicole Serrurier, hérétique du XVe siècle," *AHEB.*, XXIV (18), 241-336.

Celis, G. "De Begijnhoven in Oost-Vlaanderen. Geschiedkundige studie," *Oostvlaamsche Zanten*, IV (1929), 88-94.

Ceyssens, J. "Au Val-Dieu. Un vieux manuscrit," *Léodium*, XIV (1921), 68-72.

——. "Ses scriptoria du Val-Dieu," *Leodium*, XV (1922), 50-52.

Chapotin, Marie-Dominique. *Histoire des Dominicains de la province de France. Le siècle des fondations*. Paris-Rouen, 1898.

Clark, James M. *The Great German Mystics, Eckhart, Tauler and Suso*. Oxford, 1949.

Clédat, Leon. *Rutebeuf*. Paris, 1891

Clément, Ambroise, "Conrad d'Urach, de l'ordre de Cîteaux, légat en France et en Allemagne," *RB.*, XXII (1905), 232-243; XXIII (1906), 62-81, 373-391.

Clementi, Giuseppe. *Il. B. Venturino da Bergamo dell'ordine de' Predicatori (1304-1346), Storia e documenti*. 2 vols., Rome, 1904.

Clerinx, P. *De Heilige Christina de Wonderbare*. Louvain, 1950.

Coenen, J. "Les neuf premiers monastères de la région hutoise," *Annales du cercle hutoise des sciences et beaux-arts*, XX (1926), 103-169.

——. *Juliana van Cornillon*, in coll. *Heiligen van onzen stam,,* Bruges-Brussels, 1946.

Coens, Petrus. *Disquisitio historica de origine Beghinarum et Beghinagiorum Belgii, cum adiunctis notis, quibus Declaratio veridica, quod Beghinae nomen, institutum et originem habeant a S. Begga Brab. duc., illustratur*. Liége 1629.

Colvin, H. M. *The White Canons in England*. Oxford, 1951.

Commelin, Caspar. *Beschryvinge van Amsterdam*. 2nd ed., 2 vols., Amsterdam, 1726.

Coppens, J. A. *Nieuwe Beschrijving van het Bisdom van 's Hertogenbosch*. 's Hertogenbosch, 1841ff.

Corblet, J. *Hagiographie du diocèse d'Amiens*. 5 vols., Amiens, 1868-1875.

Cottineau, L. H. *Repertoire topo-bibliographique des abbayes et prieurés*. 2 vols., Macon, 1935-1937.

Coville, A. "Ecrits contemporains sur la peste de 1348 à 1350," *HLF.*, XXXVII (1938), 325-411.

Crevier, Jean Baptiste Louis. *Histoire de l'Université de Paris, depuis son origine jusqu'en l'année 1600.* 7 vols., Paris, 1761.

Crombach, Hermannus. *Vita et martyrium S. Ursulae et sociarum undecim millium virginum etc. ex antiquis monumentis bona fide descriptum, notabilibus argumentis quibus historiae fides satis solide fundari posse videatur confirmatum.* 2 vols., Cologne, 1647.

Cruel, R. *Geschichte der deutschen Predigt im Mittelalter.* Dortmund, 1879.

Cuthbert, Father. *Life of St. Francis of Assisi.* London, 1912.

Daniels, Aug. "Eine lateinische Rechtfertigungsschrift des Meister Eckhart, mit einem Geleitwort von Cl. Baemker," *Beiträge zur Geschichte der Philosophie des Mittelalters,* XXIII, 5, Münster i.W., 1923.

D'Arbois de Jubainville, H. *Etudes sur l'état intérieur des abbayes cisterciennes et en particulier de Clairvaux au XIIe et XIIIe siècle.* Paris, 1858.

Daris, J. *Notices sur les églises du diocèse de Liége.* 17 vols., Liége, 1867-1899.

——. "Examen critique de la vie d'Odile et de Jean, son fils," *Notices,* IV (1871), 161-196; also in *BIAL.,* XI (1872), 153-188.

——. *Histoire du diocèse et de la principauté de Liége pendant le XIIIe et le XIVe siècle.* Liége, 1891

——. *Histoire de la bonne ville, de l'église et des comtes de Looz suivie de biographies lossaines.* 2 vols., Liege, 1864-1865.

——. Les Alexiens à Liége," *Notices,* III (1872), 75-84; also in *BIAL.,* XI (1872), 273-282.

Darsonville, l'Abbe. *Urbain IV et le Fête-Dieu à Laon avec une introduction et des notes par Mgr. Monchamps.* Liége, 1902. Also publ. in *BSAHL.,* 1902, 297-403.

Decker, Otmar. *Die Stellung des Predigerordens zu den Dominikanerinnen (1207-1267). QF.,* XXXI, Vechta-Leipzig, 1935.

Dehm, Christian. *Studien zu Rutebeuf.* Diss., Würzburg, 1935.

De Jonghe, Bernardus. *Belgium Dominicanum sive Historia provinciae Germaniae inferioris sacri ordinis FF. Praedicatorum.* Brussels, 1719.

De Kok, David. *Bijdragen tot de Geschiedenis der nederlandsche Klarissen en Tertiarissen voor de Hervorming.* Utrecht, 1927.

Delecroix, Henri Joachim. *Essai sur le mysticisme speculatif en Allemagne au quatorzième siècle,* Paris, 1900.

Delanne, Blanche. *Histoire de la ville de Nivelles des origines au XIIIe siècle. Nivelles,* 1946.

Delatte, Paul. *Commentaire sur la règle de Saint Benoît.* 2nd ed., Paris, 1948.

Delehaye, Hippolyte. "Les lettres d'indulgence collectives," *AB.,* XLIV (1926), 342-379; XLV (1927), 97-123; 323-344.

——. "Guibert, abbé de Florennes et de Gembloux (XIIe et XIIe siècles)," *Revue des questions historiques,* XLVI (1889), 5-90.

Delepierre, Oct. *Précis analytique des archives de la Flandre occidentale.* 4 vols., Bruges, 1840-1844.

——. "Notice historique sur quelques couvents, hospices et institutions pieuses de la ville de Bruges,"*Annales de la société d'émulation pour l'histoire et les antiquités de la Flandre Occidentale,* II (1840), 171-201.

Delescluse, Alph. and Brouwers, D. *Catalogue des actes de Henri de Gueldre prince-évêque de Liége* (Bibliothèque de la faculté de philosophie et lettres de l'université de Liége, fasc. V, Brussels, 1900).

Delprat, G. H. M. "De geschiedenis van het S. Aagte-klooster te Delft," *Kerkhistorisch Archief,* IV (1866), 23-77.

De Man, D. "Heinrich Suso en de moderne Devoten," *NAK.,* XIX (1926), 277-283.

——. "Een vermeend tractaat van Salome Sticken," *NAK.,* XX (1927), 275-280.

Demarteau, Joseph. *La première auteur wallonne, la bienheureuse Eve de Saint-Martin. Notes d'histoire.* Liége, 1896.

——. *Liége et les principautés ecclésiastiques de l'Allemagne occidentale. Etude d'histoire comparée.* Liége, 1900. Extract from *BIAL.,* XXVII (1898), 309-415; XXVIII (1899), 291-410.

De Moreau, Ed. *L'abbaye de Villers-en-Brabant aux XIIe et XIIIe siècles, Etude d'histoire religieuse et économique, suivie d'une notice archéologique par R. Maere.* Brussels, 1909.

——. *Histoire de l'église en Belgique. I. La formation de la Belgique chrétienne des origines au Xe siècle; II. La formation de l'église médiévale. Du milieu du Xe siècle aux débuts du XIIe siècle* (Brussels, 1940); III. *L'église féodale* (1122-1378) (Brussels, 1948).

Denifle, Heinrich. "Über die Anfänge der Predigtweise der deutschen Mystiker," *ALKM.,* II (1886), 641-652.

——. "Actenstücke zu Meister Eckharts Process," *Zeitschrift für deutsches Alterthum und deutsche Litteratur,* XXIX (1885), 259-266.

——. "Der Plagiator Nicolaus von Strassburg," *ALKM.,* IV (1888), 312-329.

——. "Das Evangelium Aeternum und die Commission zu Anagni," *ALKM.,* I (1885), 49-98.

——. "Die Constitutionen des Prediger-Ordens vom Jahre 1228," *ALKM.,* I (1885), 165-227 (text from 193ff).

——. "Meister Eckeharts lateinische Schriften und die Grundanschauung seiner Lehre," *ALKM.,* II (1886), 417-615.

Denis, Emile. *Sainte Julienne et Cornillon. Etude historique.* Liége. 1927.

Denker, T. "Die Bettelorden in der französischen didaktischen Literatur des 13. Jahrhunderts, besonders bei Rutebeuf und im Roman de la Rose," *Franziskanische Studien,* II (1915), 63-109, 286-313.

Denkinger, "Die Bettelorden in dem sogenannten Testament und Codicille des Jehan de Meun," *ibid.,* III (1916), 339-365.

Depaquier, W. "L'abbaye de Solières," *BSAHL.,* X (1896), 49ff.

De Pauw, Napoleon. "Middeleeuwsche Boekerijen in Vlaanderen van Priesters, Heeren en Poorters," *Nederlandsch Museum,* II (1879), 131-176.

De Potter, Frans. *Geschiedenis der stad Kortrijk.* 4 vols., Ghent, 1873-1876.

De Ram, P. F. X. *Hagiographie nationale. Vies des saints et des personnes d'une eminente piété qui ont vécu dans les anciennes provinces belges,* I (Louvain, 1864).

De Ridder, C. B. "Quelques mots sur l'origine des béguines," *AHEB.,* XII (1875), 5-32.

De Ridder, F. "De conventen van het oud Begijnhof te Mechelen," *Bulletin du cercle archéol., litt., et artistique de Malines (Handelingen van den Mechelschen Kring voor Oudheidkunde, Letteren en Kunst,* XLII (1937), 22-83.

——. "De Pastoors van het Oude Begijnhof te Mechelen," *ibid.,* XXXVIII (1933), 43-74.

——. "De geestelijkheid van het oude Mechelsche Begijnhof," *ibid.,* XLIV (1939), 17-48.

——. "Het archief der Kerk van Aarschot," *Hagelands Gedenkschriften,* VI (1912), 15-78.

De Louvet, R. Hanon. "L'Origine nivelloise de l'Institution béguinale 'La Royauté' fondation béguinale d'une Reine de France Marie de Brabant et la légende de la béguine de Nivelles," *Annales de la Société archéologique et folklorique de Nivelles et du Brabant Wallon,* XVII (1952).

Des Marez, G. "Les Bogards dans l'industrie drapière à Bruxelles," in *Mélanges P. Fredericq*, Brussels, 1904, pp. 278-287.

——. *L'organisation du travail à Bruxelles au XVe siècle* (Mémoires couronnés par l'Acad. roy. de Belgique, LXV, Brussels, 1904).

De Reiffenberg, Fr. "Un croisé belge, Francon d'Arquenne," *BARB.*, 1. ser., XII (1847), 262-267.

De Schodt, Alphonse. *Méréaux de bienfaisance ecclésiastiques et religieux de la ville de Bruges.* Brussels, 1873-1878.

De Seyn, Eugene. *Dictionnaire historique et géographique des communes belges.* 2 vols., 3rd ed., Turnhout, 1950.

De Theux, J. *Le chapitre de Saint Lambert à Liége.* Vol. I (Brussels, 1871).

De Vooys, C. G. N. *Middelnederlandse Legenden en Exemple. Bijdrage tot de kennis van de prozaliteratuur en het volksgeloof der middeleeuwen.* 2nd ed., Groningue, 1926.

Dickinson, J. C. *The Origins of the Austin Canons and their Introduction into England.* London, 1950.

Dickson, Ch. "Le cardinal Robert de Courson. Sa vie," *Archives d'histoire doctrinale et littéraire du moyen âge,* IX (1934), 53-142.

Diercxsens, Joannes Carolus. *Antverpia Christo nascens et crescens seu acta ecclesiam Antverpiensem.* 7 vols., Antwerp, 1773.

Dillen, Vinc. "Een woord over het begijnhof van Tienen," *Hagelands Gedenkschriften,* I (1907), 157-171.

Doerr, Otmar. *Das Institut der Inclusen in Süddeutschland (Beiträge zur Geschichte des alt. Mönchtums und des Benedictinerordens hrsg. v. Abt Ildef. Herwegen, t. XXVIII).* Münster i.W., 1934.

Dolberg, Ludw. "Die Liebesthätigkeit der Cistercienser im Beherbergen der Gäste und im Spenden von Almosen," *Studien und Mitteilungen aus dem Benedictiner-und dem Cistercienser-Orden mit besonderer Berücksichtigung der Ordensgeschichte und Statistik,* XVI (1895), 10-21; 243-250, 414-418.

——. "Die Satzungen der Cistercienser wider das Betreten ihrer Klöster und Kirchen durch Frauen," *ibid.,* XV (1894), 40-44, 244-249.

Dorresteyn, H. "De phasen van het mystieke leven volgens Jan van Leeuwen," *OGE.,* VIII (1934), 5-38.

Douais, C. *Essai sur l'organisation des études dans l'ordre des frères prêcheurs au treizième et au quatorzième siècle (1216-1342).* Paris-Toulouse, 1884.

DuBoulay (Bulaeus), Caes. Egass. *Historia Universitatis Parisiensis.* 6 vols., Paris, 1665-1673.

Duchesne, A. *Historiae Francorum Scriptores.* 5 vols., Paris, 1636-1649.

Ducange, Charles Dufresne. *Glossarium Mediae et Infimae Latinitatis,* rev. D. P. Carpenter and G. A. L. Henschel. 8 vols., Paris, 1840-1857.

Duhr, J. "La confrérie dans la vie de l'Eglise," *RHE.,* XXV (1939), 437-478.

Douie, Decima L. *The Nature and the Effect of the Heresy of the Fraticelli.* University of Manchester Press, 1932.

Duvivier, Charles. *Actes et documents anciens intéressant la Belgique, nouvelle série.* Brussels, 1903.

Ehrle, Franz. "Die Spiritualen, ihr Verhältniss zum Franziskanerorden und zu den Fraticellen," *ALKM.,* I (1885), 509-569; II (1886), 106-164; III (1887), 553-623; IV (1888), 1-190.

——. Beiträge zu den Biographen berühmter Scholastiker. I. Heinrich von Gent," *ALKM.,* I (1885), 365-401, 507-508.

Eikelenberg, Simon. *Alkmaar en zyne Geschiedenissen.* Alkmaar, 1739.

Emery, Richard W. "The Friars of the Sack," *Speculum,* XVIII (1943), 323-334.

——. *Heresy and Inquisition in Narbonne.* Columbia University Press, New York, 1941.

Emond, L. "De Mariakultus in de orde van het H. Kruis," *OGE.*, I (1927), 49-55.

Ennen, Leonard. *Geschichte der Stadt Köln.* Vol. 3, Cologne, 1869.

Erens, A. "Les soeurs de l'ordre de Prémontré," *Anal. Praem.*, V (1929), 5-26.

——. "Prémontrés," *DTC.*, XIII, 1 (1936), 1-31.

Ernst, M.S.P. *Tableau historique et chronologique des suffragans ou coévêques de Liége pour servir à l'histoire ecclésiastique de ce pays.* Liége, 1806.

Eubel, Konrad. *Geschichte der oberdeutsche (Strasburger) Minoriten-Provinz.* Würzburg, 1886.

——. *Hierarchia Catholica medii aevi sive summorum pontificum*, S. R. E. Cardinalium ecclesiarum antistitum series ab anno 1198 usque ad annum 1431 perducta, I (Münster, 1913).

Fabricius, Jo. Albertus. *Bibliotheca latina mediae et infimae aetatis cum supplemento Christiani Schoettgenii.* 6 vols., Florence, 1858.

Fallon, Henri, "La recluse de l'église Saint-Nicolas," *ASAN.*, XXIV (1900), 401-424.

Feger, Gerhard. *Rutebeufs Kritik an den Zuständen seiner Zeit.* Dissert. Freiburg in Baden, 1920.

Felder, Hilarin. *Geschichte der wissenschaftlichen Studien im Franziskanerorden bis um die Mitte des 13. Jahrhunderts.* Freiburg i. Br., 1904.

Felibien, Michel. *Histoire de la ville de Paris*, revised by Guy-Alexis Lobineau. 5 vols., Paris, 1725.

Finke, Heinrich. *Konzilienstudien zur Geschichte des 13. Jahrhunderts.* Münster, 1891.

——. *Die Frau im Mittelalter.* Kempten and Munich, 1913.

Fisen, Bartholomaeus. *Flores Ecclesiae Leodiensis sive vitae vel elogia Sanctorum et aliorum qui illustriori virtute hanc diocoesim exornarunt.* Lille, 1647.

Fleury, Claude. *Histoire ecclesiastique*, Vol. 16, Brussels, 1723.

Fliche, Augustin, Thouzellier, Christine, and Azais, Yvonne. *Histoire de l'Eglise depuis les origines jusqu'à nos jours. X. La Chrétienté romaine 1198-1274).* Paris, s.d.

Förster, H. "Der Heilige Bonifaz in Lausanne," *Hist. Jahrb.*, LVII (1937), 290-304.

Foppens, J. F. *Historia episcopatus Silvaducensis, continens episcoporum et vicariorum generalium seriem, et capitulorum abbatiarum et monasteriorum fundationes.* Brussels, 1721.

Foppens. *Bibliotheca belgica sive virorum in Belgio vita, scriptisque illustrium catalogus, librorumque nomenclatura continens scriptores a clariss. viris Valerio Andrea, Auberto Miraeo, Francisco Sweertio, aliisque recensitos usque ad annum M.D.C. LXXX.* 2 vols., Brussels, 1739.

Franz, Adolph. *Die Messe im deutschen Mittelalter. Beiträge zur Geschichte der Liturgie und des religiösen Volkslebens.* Freiburg i. Br., 1902.

Francke, Kuno. *Die Kulturwerte der deutschen Literatur des Mittelalters.* 2nd ed., Berlin, 1925.

Frédégand, P. "Le Tiers-Ordre de Saint François d'Assise," *Etudes franciscaines*, XXXII (1921), 360-382, 468-488; XXXIV (1922), 66-85, 195-210, 367-391, 538-561.

Frederichs, J. *Robert le Bougre, premier inquisiteur général en France* (University of Ghent public., VI, Liege, 1892).

Fredericq, Paul. *Geschiedenis der Inquisitie in de Nederlanden.* 2 vols., Ghent-The Hague, 1892-1897.

594   THE BEGUINES AND BEGHARDS

Funk, Philipp. *Jakob von Vitry, Leben und Werke (Beiträge zur Kulturgeschichte des Mittelalters und der Renaissance,* hrsg, v. Walter Goetz, Hft. 3, Leipzig-Berlin, 1909).

Funke, Mary Elizabeth (Sister Odilia). *Meister Eckehart.* Diss., Catholic University of America, Washington, D.C., 1916.

Gachet, Em. "Le couvent de l'Abbiette, à Lille. Sa fondation par la comtesse Marguerite et par Guy de Dampierre," *Messager,* 1852, 12-57.

Galbraith, G. R. *The Constitution of the Dominican Order 1216 to 1360.* Manchester University Press, 1925.

Gallen, J. *La province de Dacie de l'ordre des frères prêcheurs.* I. *Histoire générale FF. Praedicatorum Romae ad S. Sabinae,* Helsingfors, 1946.

Galliot, Charles François Joseph. *Histoire générale, ecclésiastique et civile de la ville et province de Namur.* 6 vols., Liége, 1788-1791.

Gams, Pius Bonifacius. *Series Episcoporum ecclesiae catholicae quotquot innotuerunt a Beato Petro Apostolo.* Regensburg, 1873.

Geubel. "Notice sur l'abbaye de St. Rémy," *ASAN.,* III (1853), 293-312.

Geudens, Ed. *L'Hôpital St. Julien et les asiles de nuit à Anvers depuis le XIVe siècle jusqu'à nos jours.* Antwerp, 1887.

——. *L'ancien béguinage d'Anvers. Essai de topographie.* Antwerp, 1906.

——. *Le compte moral de l'an XIII, des hôpitaux civils d'Anvers.* Antwerp, 1898.

Giard, Rene. "Le Tiers-Ordre à Reims en 1330, et les Frères de la Charité de Notre-Dame," *La France franciscaine,* I (1912), 206-212.

Ginsburger, M. "L'empoisonnement des puits et la peste noire," *Revue des études juives,* LXXXIX (1927).

Giry, A. "Analyse et extraits d'un registre des archives municipales de Saint-Omer," *Mémoires de la société des antiquaires de la Morinie,* IV (1876), 88ff.

Glaser, Friedrich. *Die franziskanische Bewegung. Ein Beitrag zur Geschichte sozialer Reformideen im Mittelalter* (Münchener Volkswirtschaftliche Studien, hrsg. v. Lujo Brentano and Walther Lotz, Hft. 59, Stuttgart-Berlin, 1903).

Glorieux, P. *Repertoire des maîtres en théologie de Paris au XIIIe siècle.* 2 vols., Paris, 1933.

Goetschalckx, P. J. "Het begijnhof van Lier," *Bijdragen tot de Geschiedenis,* III (1904), 36-51.

Goetz, W. "Die Regel des Tertiarierordens," *ZKG.,* XXIII (1902), 97-106.

——. "Die ursprünglichen Ideale des hl. Franz von Assisi," *Historische Vierteljahrschrift,* VI (1903), 19-50.

Goldberg, Martha. *Das Armen-und Krankenwesen des mittelalterlichen Strassburg.* Diss., Strasbourg, 1909.

Goldschmidt, James. "Die charakteristischen Unterscheidungsmerkmale des allgemeinen und besonderen örtlichen Interdicts (eine Interpretation d. Stelle cap. 17 x de verborum significationibus v. 40)," *Archiv für katholisches Kirchenrecht,* LXXVI (1896), 3-24.

Grabmann, Martin. *Mittelalterliches Geistesleben, Abhandlungen zur Geschichte der Scholastik und Mystik.* 2 vols., Munich, 1926-1936.

Grauert, H. "Konrads von Megenberg Chronik und sein Planctus ecclesiae in Germaniam," *Hist. Jahrb.,* XXII (1901), 631-687.

Greven, J. "Die Entstehung der Vita Engelberti des Cäsarius von Heisterbach," *AHVN.,* CII (1918), 9ff.

——. "Frankreich und der fünfte Kreuzzug," *Hist. Jahrb.,* XLIII (1923), 15-52.

——. "Belgische Beginenhöfe," *Belfried.* I (1917), 355-366.

——. *Die Anfänge der Beginen, Ein Beitrag zur Geschichte der Volksfrömmigkeit und des Ordenswesens im Hochmittelalter (Vorreformationsgeschichtl. Forschungen* hrsg. v. H. Finke, vol. VIII), Münster i. W., 1912.

——. "Der Ursprung des Beginenwesens, Eine Auseinandersetzung mit Godefroid Kurth," *HJ.*, XXXV (1914), 26-58, 291-318.

Greving, Joseph. "Protokoll über die Revision der Konvente der Beginen und Begarden zu Köln im Jahre 1452," *AHVN.*, LXXIII (1902), 25-77.

Grundmann, Herbert. *Religiöse Bewegungen im Mittelalter: Untersuchungen über die geschichtlichen Zusammenhänge zwischen der Ketzerei, den Bettelorden und der religiösen Frauenbewegung im 12. und 13. Jahrhundert und über die geschichtlichen Grundlagen der deutschen Mystik (Historische Studien,* Hft. 267), Berlin, 1935.

——. "Zur Geschichte der Beginen im 13. Jahrhundert," *Archiv für Kulturgesch.*, XXI (1931), 296-320.

——. *Studien über Joachim von Floris (Beiträge zur Kulturgeschichte des Mittelalters und der Renaissance,* Bd. 32). Leipzig-Berlin, 1927.

——. "Die geschichtlichen Grundlagen der deutschen Mystik," *Deutsche Vierteljahrsschrift für Literaturwissenschaft und Geistesgeschichte,* XII (1934), 400-429.

Guiraud, Jean. *Histoire de l'inquisition au moyen âge.* Paris, 1938.

Gutjahr, Franz Seraph. *Petrus Cantor Parisiensis, sein Leben und seine Schriften; ein Beitrag zur Literatur-und Gelehrtengeschichte des zwölften Jahrhunderts, auf Grund des Nachlasses von Otto Schmid.* Graz, 1899.

Gutsch, Milton R. "A Twelfth Century Preacher," in *The Crusades and Other Historical Essays Presented to Dana C. Munro,* ed. by Louis J. Paetow. New York, 1928.

Haass, J. B. *Die Convente in Köln und die Beghinen.* Cologne, 1860.

Haass, Rob. "Kreuzbrüder-Kreuzherren. Ein Beitrag zum Wechsel ihrer Bezeichnung und zu ihrer inneren Wandlung," *Rheinische Vierteljahrblätter,* III (1933), 124-129.

——. *Die Kreuzherren in den Rheinlanden (Rheinisches Archiv,* XXIII). Bonn, 1932.

Hachez, Felix. "Le béguinage de Mons," *Messager* 1849, 277-302.

——. "Les fondations charitables de Mons," *Ann. cercle arch. Mons,* I (1857).

Häpke, Rudolf. "Der deutsche Kaufmann in den Niederlanden," *Pfingstblätter des hansischen Geschichtsvereins,* Blatt VII, 1911, Leipzig.

——. *Brügges Entwicklung zum mittelalterlichen Weltmarkt (Abhandlungen zur Verkehrs-und Seegeschichte im Auftrage des Hansischen Geschichtsvereins,* hrsg. v. Dietrich Schäfer, vol. I). Berlin, 1908.

Hahn, Christoph Ulrich. *Geschichte der Ketzer im Mittelalter, besonders im 11, 12 und 13. Jahrhundert nach den Quellen bearbeitet.* 2 vols., Stuttgart, 1845, 1847.

Hallman, Ernst. *Die Geschichte des Ursprungs der belgischen Beghinen nebst einer authentischen Berichtigung der im 17. Jahrb. durch Verfäschung von Urkunden in derselben angestifteten Verwirrung.* Berlin, 1843.

Hansay, A. "Note sur un manuscrit de Hasselt concernant les Bogards ou Frères du Tiers Ordre de St. François à Zepperen," *Revue des bibliothèques et archives de Belgique,* IV (1906), 86-93.

——. *Etude sur la formation et l'organisation économique du domaine de l'abbaye de Saint-Trond, depuis les origines jusqu'à la fin du XIIIe siècle* (University of Ghent, Recueil de travaux publiés par la faculté de philosophie et lettres, XXII). Ghent, 1899.

Hanssens, Silvère. "De legatiereis van Robert van Courson in Vlaanderen en

Henegouwen," in *Miscellanea historica in honorem Alberti de Meyer*, I, 528-538.

Hartwig, Julius. "Die Frauenfrage im mittelalterlichen Lübeck," *Hansische Geschichtsblätter*, XIV (1908), 35-94.

Haskins, C. H. "Robert le Bougre and the Beginnings of the Inquisition in Northern France," in *Studies in Mediaeval Culture* (Oxford University Press, 1929).

Hauber, A. "Fragment einer Beginenordnung von Tirlemont," *Archiv für Kulturgeschichte*, XIV (1919), 279-292.

——. "Deutsche Handschriften in Frauenklöstern des späteren Mittelalters," *Zentralblatt für Bibliothekswesen*, XXXI (Leipzig, 1914), 341-373.

Hauck, Alb. *Kirchengeschichte Deutschlands*, IV (Leipzig, 1913); V (1911-1920).

Haupt, Herman. "Beginen und Begarden," *Realencyklopädie für protestantische Theologie und Kirche*, II (Leipzig, 1897), 516-526.

——. "Lambert le Bègue, prêtre liégeois du XIIe siècle et l'origine des béguinages," *Wallonia, Archives Wallonnes historiques, ethnographiques, littéraires et artistiques*, XI (1903), 5-10, 34-53.

——. "Beiträge zur Geschichte der Sekte von freiem Geiste und des Beghardentums," *ZKG.*, VII (1885), 503-576.

Hautcoeur, E. *Histoire de l'église collégiale et du chapitre de Saint-Pierre de Lille.* 3 vols., Lille-Paris, 1896-1897, 1899.

——. *Histoire de l'abbaye de Flines.* Paris-Brussels, 1874.

Hefele, Ch.-J. and Leclercq, H. *Histoire des conciles*, V-VI (Paris, 1912-1915).

Heidemann, J. "Die beguinenhäuser Wesels," *Zeitschrift des bergischen Geschichtsvereins*, IV (1867), 85-114.

Heimbucher, Max. *Die Orden und Kongregationen der katholischen Kirche.* 3rd ed., 2 vols., Paderborn, 1933-1934.

Helbig, Jules. *La sculpture et les arts plastiques au pays de Liége et sur les bords de la Meuse.* Bruges, 1890.

Hene, Benedict. "Einiges über die Cistercienserinnen," *Cistercienser-Chronik*, IX (1897), 48-57, 84-89, 110-118.

Henne, A. and Wauters, Alphonse. *Histoire de la ville de Bruxelles.* 3 vols., Brussels, 1845.

Henriquez, Chrysostom. *Menologium Cistertiense notationibus illustratum.* Antwerp, 1630.

——. *Fasciculus sanctorum ordinis Cisterciensis, complectens Cisterciensium ascetarum praeclarissima gesta, huius ordinis exordium,* 2 vols. in 1, Cologne, 1631.

Hermant, Paul. "Le Folklore dans l'oeuvre de Th. de Cantimpré," *Le Folklore Brabançon*, XVI (1937), 329-393.

Heijman, Th. "Norbertijner Vroomheid in de Nederlanden," *OGE.*, IV (1930), 298-315.

——. "De geschiedenis van het geestelijk leven in de Nederlanden in den tijd van de opkomst der Cisterciensers en Norberijnen," *OGE.*, VII (1933), 50-61.

Herwegen, Ildefons. "Guibert von Gembloux und die heilige Hildegard von Bingen", *Belfried*, I (1917), 118-124.

——. "Les collaborateurs de Sainte Hildegarde," *RB.*, XXI (1904), 192-203, 302-315, 381-403.

Hilarin. "S. François et l'Eucharistie," *Etudes franciscaines*, XXXIV (1922), 520-537.

Hooglede van Hildebrand. "Hoe Franciscus op reis ging naar het land van S. Lutgardis," *D. War. Belf.*, XXVIII (1928), 371-377.

Hilka, Alfons. "Altfranzösische Mystik und Beginentum," *Zeitschrift für romanische Philologie*, XLVII (1927), 121-170.

Hilpisch, Stephanus. *Die Doppelklöster; Entstehung und Organisation*, in *Beiträge zur Geschichte des alten Mönchtums und des Benediktinerordens*, Hft. 15, Münster in Westf., 1928.

Hinschius, Paul. *Das Kirchenrecht der Katholieken und Protestanten in Deutschland*. 5 vols. in 6, Berlin, 1869-1895.

Hocquet, Adolphe. "Le Béguinage, son veritable fondateur," *Annales de la société historique et archéologique de Tournai*, N.S. VII (1902), 75-80.

Hoffmann von Fallersleben. *Geschichte des deutschen Kirchenliedes bis auf Luthers Zeit*. 3rd ed., Hanover, 1861.

Hofmeister, P. "Die Verfassung des holländischen Kreuzherrenordens," in *Festschrift U. Stutz, Kirchenrechtliche Abhandlungen*, Hft. 117-118 Stuttgart, 1938), 189-223.

Hontoir, Camille. "La dévotion au saint sacrement chez les premiers cisterciens (XIIe-XIIIe siècles)," in *Stud. Euch.*, pp. 132-156.

Hoornaert, Hector, *Ce que c'est qu'un béguinage*. Lille-Paris-Brussels, 1921.

Hucq, Eugene. "Le sarcophage présumé de la bienheureuse Marie d'Oignies," *ASAN.*, XXXVIII (1927), 231-244.

Huefner, A. *Das Rechtsinstitut der klösterlichen Exemtion in der abendländischen Kirche*. Mainz, 1907.

Huemer, Blasius. "Verzeichnis der deutschen Cisterzienserinnenklöster," *Studien und Mitteilungen zur Geschichte des Benediktiner-Ordens und seiner Zweige*, XXXVII (1916), 1-47. Just a list.

Hugo, C. L. *Sacri et Canonici Ordinis Praemonstratensis Annales*, 2 vols., Nancy, 1734.

Huyben, J. "De verspreiding der Nederlandsche spiritualiteit in het buitenland in de XIVde en XVde eeuw," *OGE.*, IV (1930), 168-182.

Iweins, Henri Marie. *Monographie du couvent des Frères-Prêcheurs à Ypres (1278 à 1797)*. Ypres, 1864.

Janauschek, Leopoldus. *Originum Cisterciensium*. I (Vienna, 1877).

Jansen, J. E. *La Belgique norbertine*. Averbode, 1921.

Janssen, M. H. Q. "Tanchelijn," *AAAB.*, XXIII (1867), 274-450.

Jansen, M. "Bijdragen tot de Geschiedenis van Sittard. II. Het Begijnhof," *Publications de la société historique et archéologique dans le duché de Limbourg*, XIV (1877), 357-361.

Janssen, H. Q. "Het Begijnhof te Aardenburg, hervormd tot een klooster van de derde Orde van St. Franciscus," *Bijdragen tot de Oudheidkunde en Geschiedenis, inzonderheid van Zeeuwsch-Vlaanderen*, I (1856), 332-343.

Jones, Rufus M. *Studies in Mystical Religion*. London, 1909.

Jörres. "Beiträge zur Geschichte der Einführung des Frohnleichnamsfestes im Nordwesten des alten deutschen Reiches," *RQ.*, XVI (1902), 170-181.

Jostes, Franz, "Die Schriften des Gerhard Zerbold van Zutphen. 'De libris Teutonicalibus'," *Hist. Jahrb.*, XI (1890), 1-22, 709-717.

Jundt, Auguste. *Histoire du panthéisme populaire au moyen âge et au seizième siècle (suivie de pièces inédites concernant les Frères du Libre Esprit, Maître Eckhart, les Libertins Spirituels, etc.)*. Paris, 1875.

Juten, G. C. A. "De oudste heren van Breda," *Taxandria*, XII (1905).

Karrer, Otto. *Meister Eckhart, das System seiner religiösen Lehre und Lebensweisheit, Textbuch aus den gedruckten und unged. Quellen mit Einführung*. Munich, 1926.

——. and Piesch, Herma. *Meister Eckeharts Rechtfertigungsschrift vom Jahre 1326*. Erfurt, 1927.

Kaufmann, Alexander. *Thomas von Chantimpré*. Cologne, 1899.

——. *Caesarius von Heisterbach, Ein Beitrag zur Culturgeschichte . . ., zweite, mit einem Bruchstück aus des Caesarius "VIII Libri Miraculorum" vermehrte Auflage.* Cologne, 1862.

——. "Wunderbare und Denkwürdige Geschichten aus den Werken des Cäsarius von Heisterbach," *AHVN.,* LIII (1891).

Keins, Paul. "Rutebeufs Weltanschauung im Spiegel seiner Zeit," *Zeitschrift für rom. Philologie,* LIII (1933), 569-575.

Knowles, David. *The Religious Orders in England.* Cambridge University Press, 1950.

Kober, F. "Das Interdict," *Archiv für katholisches Kirchenrecht mit besonderer Rücksicht äuf Oesterreich und Deutschland,* XXI (1869), 3-45, 291-341; XXII (1869), 3-53.

Koch. *Geschichte des Seidengewerbes in Köln vom 13.-18 Jahrhundert.* 1907.

Korth, Leonard. "Köln im Mittelalter," *AHVN.,* L (1890), 1-91.

——. "Verhandlungen über die Hausweberei im Kloster der Tertiarier zu Köln," *AHVN.,* LVI (1893), 180-188.

——. "Der heilige Rock zu Köln," *AHVN.,* XLVI (1887), 48-59.

Kothe, W. *Kirchliche Zustände Strassburgs im 14. Jahrh. Ein Beitrag zur Stadt-und Kulturgeschichte des Mittelalters.* Diss., Freiburg i. Br., 1902.

Krehbiel, Edward Benjamin. *The Interdict, its History and its Operation with especial attention to the time of Pope Innocent III,* 1198-1216. American Historical Association, Washington, D. C., 1909.

Krebs, Engelbert Gustav Hans. *Meister Dietrich (Theodoricus Teutonicus de Vriberg). Sein Leben, seine Werke, seine Wissenschaft (Beiträge zur Geschichte der Philosophie des Mittelalters, Texte und Untersuchungen,* hrsg. v. Baeumker and C. von Hertling, Bd. 5, Hft., 5-6). München, 1906.

——. Die Mystik in Adelhausen, in *Festgabe für H. Finke,* Münster, i. W., 1904.

Kressner, Adolf. "Rustebuef als Satiren-Dichter," *Franco-Gallia,* XI (1894), 17-23.

——. "Rustebuef, ein Dichterleben im Mittelalter," *ibid.,* X (1893), 165-170.

Kriegk, G. L. *Deutsches Bürgerthum im Mittelalter nach urkundlich Forschungen und mit besonderen Beziehung auf Frankfurt a. M.* 2 vols., Frankfurt a. M., 1868-1871.

Krüger, Joannes Baptista. *Kerkelijke Geschiedenis van het bisdom van Breda; dat is van het Noord-Brabandsch deel van het voormalig Bisdom van Antwerpen,* 4 vols., Bergen-op-Zoom, s.d.

Kurth, Godefroid. "De l'origine liégeoise des béguines," *BARB.,* 1912, 437-462.

——. *La cité de Liége au moyen âge.* 3 vols., Brussels-Liége, 1909-1910.

——. "Encore l'origine liégeoise des béguines," *BARB.,* 1919, 133-168.

Kwanten, Edmond. "Le collège Saint-Bernard à Paris. Sa fondation et ses débuts," *RHE.,* XLIII (1948), 443-472.

Laenen, J. *Introduction à l'histoire paroissiale du diocèse de Malines, les institutions.* Brussels, 1924.

——. *Geschiedenis van Mechelen tot op het einde der middeleeuwen.* 2nd. ed., Malines, 1934.

——. "Notice sur les Mate-Wiven et Soeurs noirs d'Anvers," *AAAB.,* LIV (1902), 5-48.

——. "De Tafels van den Heiligen Geest," *La vie diocesaine, Bulletin du diocèse de Malines,* VI (1912), 489-505.

——. *Kerkelijk en Godsdienstig Brabant vanaf het begin der IVe tot in de XVIe eeuw of voorgeschiedenis van het Aartsbisdom Mechelen.* 2 vols., Antwerp, 1935-1936.

——. *Geschiedkundige Aanteekeningen rakende de instelling en het klooster des Zwartzusters van Antwerpen.* Antwerp, 1902.

Lallemand, Leon. *Histoire de la charité.* III. *Le moyen âge* (du Xe au XVIe siècle). Paris, 1906.

Lambert, G. "Sainte Julienne de Liége dans le Brabant. Considérations sur ses reliques," *Le Folklore brabançon,* XVI (1936), 100-114.

Lambot, C. "Un precieux manuscrit de la Vie de Sainte Julienne du Mont-Cornillon," *Misc. hist. . . . Alberti de Meyer,* I, 603-612.

——. "L'office de la Fête-Dieu. Aperçus nouveaux sur ses origines," *RB.,* LIV (1942), 61-123.

——. Eve de Saint-Martin et les premiers historiens liégeois de la Fête-Dieu," *Stud. euch.,* pp. 10-36.

Lambrechts, Juliaan. *Het oud Begijnhof of beknopte Geschiedenis van het Begijnhof van Hasselt.* Hasselt, 1886.

Lamotte, G. *Etude historique sur le comté de Rochefort.* Namur, 1893.

Lampen, Willibrord. "Joannes Duns Scotus, Lector Coloniensis," in *Collectanea Franciscana Neerlandica* (2 vols., s'Hertogenbosch, 1931), II, 291-305.

Lamy, Hugues. *L'abbaye de Tongerloo depuis sa fondation jusqu'en 1263* (Univ. de Louvain, Recueil de travaux, XLIV), Louvain, 1914.

Langenberg, Rudolf. *Quellen und Forschungen zur Geschichte der deutschen Mystik.* Bonn, 1902.

——. *Über das Verhältnis Meister Eckarts zur niederdeutschen Mystik.* Diss., Göttingen, 1895.

Langlois, Charles Victor. *La vie en France au moyen âge, de la fin du XIIe au milieu du XIVe siècle.* 4 vols., Paris, 1924-1928.

——. "Marguerite Porete," *Revue historique,* LIV (1894), 295-299.

Lea, Henry Charles. A. *History of the Inquisition of the Middle Ages.* 3 vols., New York, 1888.

——. *A History of Auricular Confession and Indulgences in the Latin Church.* 3 vols., Philadelphia, 1896.

Lechner, Karl. "Die grosse Geisselfahrt des Jahres 1349," *HJ.,* V (1884), 443-462.

Lecoy de la Marche, A. *La chaire française au moyen âge.* 2nd ed., Paris, 1886.

Lefèvre, Plac. "Le problème de la paroisse primitive de Bruxelles," *Annales de la société royale d'archéologie de Bruxelles,* XXXVIII (1934), 106-116.

——. *L'organisation ecclésiastique de la ville de Bruxelles au moyen âge.* Louvain, 1942.

——. "La valeur historique des écrits de Pomerius sur la vie de Ruusbroec et les origines de Groenendael," *Annales de la société d'archéologie de Bruxelles,* XL (1936), 148-165.

Le Grand, Léon. *Les béguines de Paris.* Paris, 1893; extract from *Mémoires de la société de l'histoire de Paris et de l'Ile-de-France,* XX (1893).

Lehman, P. "Quellen zur Feststellung und Geschichte mittelalterlichen Bibliotheken," *Hist. Jahrb.,* XL (1920), 77-82.

Lejeune, Theophile. *Monographies historiques et archéologiques de diverses localités du Hainaut,* VI (Louvain, 1888): *Recherches historiques sur le Roeulx, ses seigneurs, et les communes de l'ancien bailliage de cette ville.*

——. "L'ancienne abbaye de l'Olive, 1218-1796," *ibid.,* II (Mons, s.d.), 199-214.

Le Long, Isaak. *Historische Beschrijvinge van de Reformatie der Stadt Amsterdam.* Amsterdam, 1729.

Lemmens, Leonardus. "De Sancto Francisco Christum praedicante coram Sultano Aegypti," *AFH.,* XIX (1926), 559-578.

——. "Chronicon Provinciae Argentinensis O.F.M. circa an. 1310-27 a quo-dam fratre minore Basileae conscriptum (1206-1325)," *AFH.*, IV (1911), 671-687.

——. "Die Anfänge des Clarissenordens," *RQ.*, XVI (1902), 93-124.

Lempp, Eduard. "Die Anfänge des Klarissenordens," *ZKG.*, XIII (1892), 181-245.

Lenaerts, R. B. M. "Het eerste officie van het Corpus Christie-Feest," in *Stud. Euch.*, pp. 37-46.

Le Nain de Tillemont, Louis Sebastien. *Vie de Saint Louis, roi de France* (Soc. de l'hist. de France, vols., 47, 50, 53, 55, 57, 66), Paris, 1847-51.

Leuridan, Th. *Les Tables des Pauvres à Roubaix.* Roubaix, 1884.

Liebe, Georg. "Das Beginenwesen der sächsisch-thüringischen Lande in seiner sozialen Bedeutung," *Archiv für Kulturgeschichte*, I (1903), 35-49.

Liese, Wilhelm. *Geschichte der Caritas.* 2 vols., Freiburg, 1922.

Ligtenberg, Christina. *De Armezorg te Leiden tot het einde van de 16e eeuw.* The Hague, 1908.

Lindeman, H. "S. Hildegarde en hare nederlandsche vrienden," *OGE.*, II (1928), 128-160.

Linneborn, S. Joh. "Die westfälischen Klöster des Zisterzienser-Ordens," in *Festgabe für Heinrich Finke*, 1904, pp. 253-352.

Leo, Ulrich. *Studien zu Rutebeuf; Entwicklungsgeschichte und Form des Renart le Bestourné und der ethisch-politischen Dichtungen Rutebeufs.* Halle, 1922.

Lippens, F. H. "Les Frères Mineurs à Gand du XIIIe au XIVe siècle," *La France franciscaine*, XIII (1930).

Löhr, Gabriel M. *Die Teutonia im 15. Jahrhundert. Studien und Texte vornehmlich zur Geschichte ihrer Reform (QF., XIX, Leipzig, 1924).*

Logeman, H. "The Etymology of the Name Beguine," *Leuvensche Bijdragen*, 1928, 110-137.

Lommatzsch, Erhard. *Gautier de Coincy als Satiriker.* Halle, 1913.

Lucas, Harry. *Les poésies personnelles de Rutebeuf. Etude linquistique et littéraire.* Paris, 1938.

Lüers, Grete. *Die Sprache der deutschen Mystik des Mittelalters im Werke der Mechthild von Magdeburg.* Munich, 1926.

Luykx, Theo. "Gravin Johanna von Constantinopel en de godsdienstige Vrouwenbeweging in Vlaanderen gedurende de eerste helft der XIIIde Eeuw," *OGE.*, XVII (1943), 5-30.

——. *Johanna van Constantinopel, Gravin van Vlaanderen en Henegouwen, haar Leven (1199/1200-1244), haar Regeering (1205-1244), vooral in Vlaanderen.* Antwerp, 1946.

Madelaine Godefroid. *Histoire de Saint Norbert, fondateur de l'Ordre de Prémontré, archévêque de Magdebourg.* 3rd ed., 2 vols., Tongerloo 1928.

Mahn, Jean Berthold. *L'ordre cistercien et son gouvernement, des origines au milieu du XIIIe siècle. (1098-1265).* Paris, 1945.

Mahy, L. "Notice sur Sybille de Gages, plus connus sous le vocable de Sainte Sybille," *Annales du cercle archéologique d'Ath et de la région*, I (1912), 1-74.

de Maisières, Thibaut. "Le Béguinage de Bruxelles," *Revue de Saint Louis.* Brussels, (1930), 41-51.

Mâle, Emile. *L'art religieux du XIIIe siècle en France.* Paris, 1948.

Mandonnet, Pierre. *Saint, Dominique, l'idée, l'homme et l'oeuvre, étapes, perspectives.* Augmenté de notes et d'études critiques par. M. H. Vicaire and R. Ladner. 2 vols., Paris-Bruges, 1938.

——. "Les origines de l'Ordo de Poenitentia", *Compte rendu de IVe congrès scient. internat. des Catholiques tenu à Fribourg en 1897,* Freiburg, 1898.

Mann, J. *Die Kirchenpolitik der Stadt Strassburg am Ausgang des Mittelalters.* Diss., Strasbourg, 1914.

Manrique, Angelus. *Cisterciensium, seu verius eccleciasticorum, annalium.* 4 vols. in 2, Lyons, 1642-1659.

Mathis, B. *Die Privilegien des Franziskanerordens bis zum Konzil von Vienne* (1311). Paderborn, 1928.

Matrod, H. "Les Bégards, essai de synthèse historique," *Etudes Franciscaines,* XXXVII (1921), 5-20, 146-169.

Matthieue Ernest. *Histoire de la ville d'Enghien.* 2 vols., Mons, 1876-1878.

——. "Les recluseries de Cantimpré et de Saint-Nicholas à Mons," *Ann. cercle arch. Mons,* XXXVIII (1909), 257-263.

Matzner, Franciscus Leopoldus. *De Jacobi Vitriacensis, crucis praedicatoris, vita et rebus gestis.* Diss., Münster, 1863.

Mens, Alcantara. *Oorsprong en Betekenis van de nederlandse Begijnen- en Begardenbeweging, vergelijkende Studie: XIIde- XIIIde eeuw.* Antwerp, 1947.

——. "De vereering van de H. Eucharistie bij onze vroegste Begijnen," in *Stud. Euch.,* pp. 157-186.

——. "Innerlijke drijfveeren en herkomst der kettersche bewegingen in de middeleeuwen. Religieus ofwel sociaal oogmerk?" *Misc. hist ... Leonis van der Essen,* I, 299-313.

Mertens, F. H. and Torfs, K. L. *Geschiedenis van Antwerpen sedert de Stichting der stad tot onze tyden.* 8 vols., Antwerp, 1846-1854.

Meyer, Paul. "Notice du Ms. 535 de la bibliothèque municipale de Metz renfermant diverses compositions pieuses (prose et vers) en français," *Bullet. de SATF.,* XII (1886), 41-76.

——. "Le psautier de Lambert le Bègue," *Romania,* XXIX (1900), 528-545.

Michael, Emil. *Culturzustände des deutschen Volkes während des dreizehnten Jahrhunderts.* 5 vols., Freiburg i. Br., 1897-1915.

Miraeus, Aubertus. *Origo Beginarum virginum in Belgio hodieque frequentium.* Antwerp, 1602.

Miscellanea historica in honorem Alberti de Meyer (Université de Louvain, Recueil de travaux d'histoire et de philologie, 3rd ser., fasc. 22-23). 2 vols., Louvain-Brussels, 1946.

Molanus, Johannes. *Natales sanctorum Belgii et eorundem chronica recapitulatio.* Duaci, 1616.

Moll, W. *Kerkgeschiedenis van Nederland voor de Hervorming.* 4 vols., Arnhem, 1864-1869.

——. De Boekerij van het St. Barbara-klooster te Delft in de tweede helft der vijftiende eeuw, een bijdrage tot de geschiedenis der middeleeuwsche letterkunde in Nederland," *Kerkhistorisch Archief,* IV (1866).

Monchamp, Georges. "La Fête-Dieu à Liége en 1251," *Leodium,* I (1902), 3-6.

——. *Les reliques de S. Julienne de Cornillon à l'abbaye de Villers, contribution à l'histoire de son culte.* Liége, 1898.

Mone, F. J. Articles in *Zeitschrift für die Geschichte des Oberrheins,* 1849ff.

Mortier, R. P. *Histoire des maîtres généraux de l'Ordre des Frères Prêcheurs.* 6 vols., Paris, 1903-1913.

Moschus, Fr. *Coenobarchia Ogniacensis sive antistitum qui Ogniacensi ad Sabim monasterio hactenus praefuere numero undetriginta catalogus, cum eulogiis et anagrammatis.* Duaci, 1598.

Mosheim, J. L. *De Beghardis et Beguinabus commentarius, edidit et locuple-tavit* G. H. Martini. Leipzig, 1790.

Müller, Gregor "Das Beginenwesen, eine Abzweigung von den Cisterciense rinnen," *Cisterzinser Chronik,* XXVII (1915), 33-41.

Moulaert, B. C. B. *Het Groot Beggynhof van Gent.* Ghent, 1850.

Moulart, F. J. *De Sepultura et coemeteriis.* Diss., Louvain-Paris-Tournai, 1862.

Müller, Ewald. *Das Konzil von Vienne 1311-1312: seine Quelle und seine Geschichte (Vorreformationsgeschichtliche Forschungen,* hrsg. v. Heinrich Finke, XII). Münster i. W., 1934.

Müller, Johannes. *Die Bibel und der biblische Gedankenreis in Hugos von Trimberg "Renner".* Diss. Greifswald, 1924.

Müller, Karl. *Die Anfänge des Minoritenordens und der Bussbruderschaften.* Freiburg, 1885.

——. *Die Waldenser und ihre einzelnen Gruppen bis zum Anfang des 14. Jahrhunderts.* Gotha, 1886.

Nélis, H. "Le manuscrit no. 757c des archives générales du Royaume," in *Revue des bibliothèques et des archives de la Belgique,* II (1904), 364ff.

——. "Document falsifié relatif à l'origine des béguines (1154)," *Revue belge de philologie et d'histoire,* III (1924), 120-124.

Nimal, H. *Vie et oeuvres de quelques-uns de nos pieux écrivains dans les siècles passés.* Liége, 1898.

——. "Les Béguinages," *Annales de la société archéologique de l'arrondisse-ment de Nivelles,* IX (1908), 1-126.

Norrenberg, Peter. *Frauenarbeit und-Arbeiterinnen in deutscher Vorzeit.* Cologne, 1880.

Oliger, Livarius. "De Pueris oblatis in ordine Minorum (cum textu hucusque inedito Fr. Iohannis Pecham)," *AFH.,* VIII (1915), 389-447; X (1917), 271-288.

——. "De origine regularum ordinis S. Clarae," *AFH.,* V (1912), 181-209, 413-447.

——. *De secta spiritus libertatis in Umbria saeculo XIV, Disquisitio et docu-menta (Storia e letteratura, Raccolta di studi e testi* a cura di A. Schiaf-fini e G. de Luca, vol. III). Rome, 1943.

Ollivier, R. F. *Le grand Béguinage de Gand.* Paris, 1903.

Opdedrinck, J. "Het oude Begijnhof van Damme en de Cisterc. vrouwenabdij van Bethlehem uit Schouwen," *ASEB.,* LIV (1914), 28-56.

Owst, Gerald Robert. *Literature and Pulpit in Medieval England; a Neg-lected Chapter in the History of English Letters and of the English People.* Cambridge University Press, 1933.

Paquay, J. B. "La charte d'érection du béguinage de Bilsen par Henri de Gueldre, le 24 octobre 1256," *Leodium* I (1902), 45-48.

——. "Marcuald de Modène, archidiacre de Hesbaye, prévôt de Tongres," *ibid.,* III (1904), 118-124.

Paris, Julian. *Nomasticon Cisterciense seu antiquiores ordinis Cisterciensis Constitutiones.* Paris, 1670.

Paulus, C. *Welt-und Ordensklerus beim Ausgang des 13. Jahrhunderts im Kampfe um die Pfarr-rechte.* Diss., Göttingen, 1900.

Paulus, Nicolanus. *Geschichte des Ablasses im Mittelalter vom Ursprung bis zur Mitte des 14. Jahrhunderts.* 3 vols. in 2, Paderborn, 1922-1923.

Peene, Leo. *Land- en Cijnsboek St. Janshospitaal, Brussel. Excerpten uit Car-tularium 1307 en uit originelen van 1195 tot 1356. Onomastische Studien.* Vol. 3, Brussels, 1949.

Pelster, F. "Der Heinrich von Gent zugeschriebene Catalogus virorum illustrium und sein wirklicher Verfasser," *Hist. Jahrb.*, XXXIX (1918-1919), 253-268.

——. Thomas von York, O. F. M. als Verfasser des Traktates 'Manus quaecontra Omnipotentem tenditur'," *AFH.*, XV (1922), 3-22.

Perrod, Maurice. *Maître Guillaume de S. Amour: l'Université de Paris et les ordres mendiants au xiiie siècle* (Paris, 1895), revised as "Etude sur la vie et sur les oeuvres de Guillaume de Saint-Amour," in *Mémoires de la société d'émulation du Jura*, ser. 7, vol. 2 (Lens-le-Saunier, 1902), pp. 61-252.

Pfeiffer, Franz. *Deutsche Mystiker des 14. Jahrhunderts*. 2 vols., Leipzig, 1857.

Philippen, L. J. M. "Les Béguines et l'hérésie Albigeoise," *AAAB.*, LXXIII (7e ser., vol. III) (1926), 233-252.

——. "Het ontstaan der Begijnhoven. Antwerp, 1943.

——. "De beteekenis van het oprichten van het Begijnhof te Antwerpen en in de volkrijke Vlaamsche steden," *Tijdschrift voor Geschiedenis en Folklore,* VI (1943), 61-78.

——. Het begijnhof van S. Catharina 'ten Velde' te Diest," *BG.*, IV (1905), 327-339, 423-433, 532-548.

——. "De Heilige Norbertus en de strijd tegen het Tanchelmisme te Antwerpen," *ibid.*, XXV (1934), 251-288.

——. "Begijnhoven en spiritualiteit," *OGE.*, III (1929), 165-196.

——. *Onze Begijntjes-hun Naam-hun Leven*. Antwerp, 1944.

——. "Het oudste zegel en de vroegste geschiedenis der begijnen te Antwerpen," *BG.*, XXVI (1935), 81-97.

——. "De vorming van het woord 'begginus'," *ibid.*, XXVII (1936), 137-155.

——. *De Begijnhoven, Oorsprong, geschiedenis, inrichting*. Antwerp, 1918.

——. "De editio princeps van de 'Disquisitio historica de origine Beghinarum' van Petrus Coens," in *Lode Baekelmans ter eere 1945*, II (Antwerp, 1946), 60-70.

Petit, Francois. *L'ordre de Prémontré*. Paris, 1927.

Pfleger, Luzian. "Beiträge zur Geschichte der Predigt und des religiösen Volksunterrichts im Elsass während des Mittelalters," *HJ.*, XXXVIII (1917), 661-717.

Phillips, Dayton. *Beguines in Medieval Strasburg. A Study of the Social Aspect of Beguine Life*. Stanford University Press, Palo Alto, 1941.

Piot, Ch. "Notice historique sur la ville de Léau," *Revue d'histoire et d'archéologie*, I (1859), 13-48, 395-419; II (1860), 52-76.

Pirenne, Henri. "Tanchelin et le projet du démembrement du diocèse d'Utrecht vers 1100," *BARB.*, ser. V, vol. XIII (1927), 112-119.

——. *Histoire de Belgique, I: Des origines au commencement du XIVe siècle*. 5th ed., Brussels, 1929.

Pourrat, P. *La spiritualité chrétienne*. 4 vols., Paris, 1919-1928.

Pouzet, Ph. "Les origines lyonnaises de la secte des Vaudois," *Revue d'histoire de l'église de France*, XXII (1936), 5-37.

Preger, Wilhelm. *Geschichte der deutschen Mystik im Mittelalter*. 3 vols., Leipzig, 1874-1893.

Prims, Floris. "De godsdiensttoestanden in het Brabantsche in de XIIIde eeuw," in *Collect. Mechlin.*, XVI (1927), 745-765.

——. "Kerkelijk Antwerpen, van de visitatie van Bisschop Wiard tot het einde der XIIIde eeuw (1238-1296)," *BG.*, XVIII (1927), 197-241, 321-382; XIX (1928), 1-320.

——. *Geschiedenis van Antwerpen*, II. 3: *De geestelijke orde* (Brussels, 1929); IV. 2: *De Geestelijke orde* (Antwerp, 1933).

Quétif, Jacob and Echard, Jac. *Scriptores Ordinis Praedicatorum*. 2 vols., Paris, 1719-1721.

Quinaux, C. J. *Notice historique sur l'abbaye de Leffe avec de nombreuses pièces justificatives et un appendice sur la paroisse de Leffe*. Namur, 1884.

Quint, Josef. "Meister Eckehart. Ein Vortrag," *Zeitschrift für deutsche Kulturgeschichte*, V (1939), 209-231.

——. "Die Sprache Meister Eckeharts als Ausdruck seiner mystischen Geisteswelt," *Deutsche Vierteljahrsschrift für Literaturwissenschaft und Geistesgeschichte*, VI (1928), 671-701.

Raby, F. J. E. A. *Histoiry of Secular Latin Poetry in the Middle Ages*. 2 vols., Oxford Press, 1934.

Ramackers, Johannes. "Adlige Praemonstratenserstifte in Westfalen und am Niederhein," *Anal. Praem.*, V (1929), 200-238, 320-343, VI (1930), 281-332.

Ramaekers, A. *De Privileges der Kruisheerenorde vanaf haar Ontstaan tot aan het Concilie van Trente* (Universitas Catholica Lovaniensis, Sylloge excerptorum e dissertationibus ad gradum doctoris in sacra theologia vel in jure canonico, X, 5). Louvain, 1943; extract from *Clair-Lieu*, I (1943), 9-82.

——. "De Kruisherenaflaat," *Clair-Lieu*, VI (1948), 3-52.

Rashdall, Hastings. *The Universities of Europe in the Middle Ages*, revised by F. M. Powicke and A. B. Emden, 3 vols., Oxford University Press, 1936.

Raymaekers, F. J. *Geschiedkundige Navorschingen over de aloude Abdij van 't Park*, transl. J. E. Jansen, Antwerp, 1904.

——. *Het kerkelijk en liefdadig Diest. Geschiedenis der Kerken, Kapellen, Kloosters, liefdadige Gestichten, enz., welke in deze Stad vroeger Bestonden of thans nog bestaan*. Louvain, 1870.

——. "Coup-d'oeil historique sur l'ancienne industrie drapière à Diest," *Messager*, 1860, pp. 440ff.

——. "Notice historique sur le béguinage de Sainte-Catherine à Diest," *ibid.*, 1862, pp. 73-97, 121-156; also Ghent, 1862.

Rayssius, Arnold. *Hierogazophylacium Belgicum, sive Thesaurus Sacrarum Reliquiarum Belgii*. Duaci, 1628.

Reichert, B. M. "Zur Geschichte der deutschen Dominikaner am Ausgange des 14. Jahrhunderts," *RQ.*, XIV (1900), 79-101; XV (1901), 124-152.

Reicke, Siegfried. *Das deutsche Spital und sein Recht im Mittelalter (Kirchenrechtliche Abhandlungen*, hrsg. Ulrich Stutz and Johannes Heckel, Hft. 111-112). 2 vols., Stuttgart, 1932.

Reinmann, Gerald Joseph. *Third Order Secular of St. Francis*. (Canon Law Studies, no. 50). Catholic University of America, Washington, D. C., 1928.

Remans, Gilb. "Eenige onbekende Charters uit het Begijnhof van Tongeren," *OGE.*, XX (1946), 378-389.

Renan, Ernest. "La bienheureuse Christine de Stommeln, béguine," *HLF.*, XXVIII (1881), 1-26.

Reypens, Leonce. "Le sommet de la contemplation mystique chez le bienheureux Jean de Ruusbroeck" *Revue d'ascétique et de mystique*, III (1922), 250-272; IV (1924), 33-59.

——. "Markante Mystiek in het Gentsch Begijnhof, Claesinne van Nieuwland (ca. 1550-1611)," *OGE.*, XIII (1939), 291-360, 403-444.

——. "Sint Lutgarts mystieke Opgang," *OGE.*, XX (1946), 7-49.

——. "De zalige Beatrijs van Nazareth en haar zalige Vader," *OGE.*, X (1936), 19-47, 164-174, 278-322; XXI (1947), 74-78.

——. "Ruusbroec-studien," *OGE.*, V (1931), 143-185; VI (1932), 257-281; XII (1938), 158-186, 392-411; XVII, pt. 2 (1943), 9-17.

——. and van Mierlo, J. "Een nieuwe schrijfster uit de eerste helft der dertiende eeuw, de geluksalige Beatrijs van Nazareth (1200?-1268)," *D. War. Belf.*, XXV (1925), 352-368.

——. "Het toppunt der beschouwing voor Ruusbroec. I. De biograaf van Beatrijs van Nazareth," *OGE.*, V (1931), 429-434.

——. "Werden de zal. Beatrijs van Nazareth en zaar zal. vader ooit vereerd?" *OGE.*, X (1936), 164-174, 278-322.

Robert, Gaston. *Les béguines de Reims et la Maison de Sainte-Agnes.* Reims, 1923.

Robinson, Gertrude. "The Beguines; a Study in the Vocations of Uncloistered Women," *The Dublin Review*, CLX (1917), 214-233.

Röhricht, R. "Bibliographische Beiträge zur Geschichte der Geissler," *ZKG.*, I (1876), 313-321.

Römer, R. C. H. *Geschiedkundig overzigt van de kloosters en abdijen in de voormalige graafschappen van Holland en Zeeland.* 2 vols., Leiden, 1854.

Roisin, Simone. *L'Hagiographie cistercienne dans le diocèse de Liége au XIIIe siècle* (Université de Louvain, Recueil de travaux d'histoire et de philologie, 3e ser., fasc. 27). Louvain-Brussels, 1947.

——. "L'efflorescence cistercienne et le courant féminin de piété au XIIIe siècle," *RHE.*, XXXIX (1943), 342-378.

——. La méthode hagiographique de Thomas de Cantimpré," *Misc. hist....* Alb. de Meyer, I, 546-557.

Roland, C. "Les seigneurs et comtes de Rochefort," *ASAN.*, XX (1893), 63-144, 329-411.

Rops, Paul. "Une oeuvre inédite de Frère Hugo," *ASAN.*, XXIV (1900), 349-360.

Rosenkränzer, Nikolaus. *Johann I von Strassburgs genannt von Dürbheim.* Diss., Trier, 1881.

Rosseweide, Heribert. *Les vies des sainctes vierges plus illustres, qui depuis le temps de nostre Seigneur iusques à ce siecle ont vescu au monde dans le sainct et honnorable estat de la virginite.* Tournai, 1641. Trans. of *Het leven der HH. Maegden die van Christus tyden tot deze eeuwe in den salighen staet der suyverheydt in de wereld gheleeft hebben, met een cort tractaet van den maeghdelycken staet.* Antwerp, 1626.

Roth, F. W. E. "Studien zur Lebensbeschreibung der heiligen Hildegard," *Studien und Mitteilungen zur Geschichte des Benediktinerordens und seiner Zweige*, XXX (1918), 68-118.

Ryckel, Joseph Geldolph. *Vita S. Beggae, ducissae Brabantiae andetennensium, Begginarum, et Beggardorum fundatricis.* Louvain, 1631.

Rücklin, Gertrud. *Religiöses Volksleben des ausgehenden Mittelalters in den Reichsstädten Hall und Heilbronn (Historische Studien, 226).* Berlin, 1933.

Sanderus, Antonius. *Chorographia sacra Brabantiae sive celebrium aliquot in ea provincia abbatiarum, coenobiorum, monasteriorum, ecclesiarum, piarumque fundationum descriptio.* 3 vols., The Hague, 1726.

Sanderus, W. "Vader Theodorus van Celles," *De Zegepraal des Kruises*, XX (1941), 179-189.

——. "De oudste Constituties der Kruisherenorde," *Miscellanea historica in honorem Leonis van der Essen*, I (Brussels-Paris, 1947), 315-327.

Sassen, J. H. A. *Hugo von St. Cher, seine Tätigkeit als Kardinal 1244-1263.* Bonn, 1908.

Schannat, John Frederick. *Historia Episcopatus Wormatiensis, pontificum romanorum bullis, regum, etc.* 2 vols., Frankfurt, 1734.

Scheeben, Heribert Christian. *Der Heilige Dominikus.* Freiburg i. Br., 1927.

———. *Jordan der Sachse.* Vechta in Oldenburg, 1937.

Scheuermann, Audomar. *Die Exemtion nach geltenden kirchlichen Recht mit einem Überlick über die geschichtliche Entwicklung* (Görres-Gesellschaft, Veröffentlichungen der Sektion für Recht-und Staatswissenschaft, Hft. 77). Paderborn, 1.

Schiller, Ernst. *Das mystische Leben der Ordenschwestern zu Töss bei Winterthur.* Diss., Zürich, 1903.

Schleyer, Kurt. *Anfänge des Gallikanismus im 13. Jahrhundert; der Widerstand des französischen Klerus gegen die Privilegierung der Bettelorden (Historische Studien,* Hft. 314). Berlin, 1937.

Schmidt, Ch. "Die Strassburger Beginenhäuser im Mittelalter," *Alsatia, Jahrbuch für elsässische Geschichte,* VII (1858-1861), 149-248.

Schönbach, Anton E. "Studien zur Erzählungsliteratur des Mittelalters. Teil 4: Über Caesarius von Heisterbach," *Sitzungsberichte der philosophisch-historischen Classe der kaiserlichen Akademie der Wissenschaften,* CXLIV (Vienna, 1902); CLIX (1908).

———. "Das Wirken Bertholds von Regensburg gegen die Ketzer," *ibid.,* CXLVII (1904).

Scholten, Robert. *Zur Geschichte der Stadt Cleve.* Cleve, 1905.

Schoolmeesters, Emile. "Une élection épiscopale à Liége au XIIIe siècle," *Leodium,* I (1902), 6-8.

———. "Lambert li Bègue et l'origine des Béguines," *ibid.,* XI (1912), 125-132.

Schröder, F. "Ars Mendicandi, Eine Beitrag zur Geschichte des mittelalterlichen Schülerbettels," *NAK.,* XVIII (1925), 124-145.

———. "Die Beginen in Goch," *AHVN.,* LXXV (1903), 1-67.

Schuermans, H. "Les reliques de la B. Julienne de Cornillon à l'abbaye de Villers", *Annales de la société archéologique de l'arrondissement de Nivelles,* VII (1903), 1-68.

———. "La bibliothèque de l'abbaye de Villers," *ibid.,* VI (1898), 193-236.

———. "Châsse des XXXVI Saints à Anvers. Julienne de Cornillon," *AAAB.,* LII (5th ser. t. 2) (1900), 381-448.

Schwamborn, G. *Heinrich II, Erzbischof von Cöln* (1306-1332). Diss., Neuss, 1904.

Seibertz, J. S. "Beghinen und Begharden in Westfalen," *Anzeiger für Kunde der deutschen Vorzeit,* N. F., X (1863), 313-319.

Séjourné, Paul. "Les correspondants de sainte Hildegarde à Utrecht," *NAK.,* XVI (1922), 144-162.

Seppelt, Franz Xavier. *Der Kampf der Bettelorden an der Universität Paris in der Mitte des 13. Jahrhunderts.* Diss., Breslau, 1907.

Servranckx, G. J. *Mémoire historique et statistique sur les hospices civils et autres établissements de bienfaisance de la ville de Louvain.* Louvain, 1843.

Sievert, Wilhelm. "Das Vorleben des Papstes Urban IV." *RQ.,* X (1896), 451-505; XII (1898), 127-161.

Simenon, G. "Les origines de la Fête-Dieu," *Revue ecclésiastique de Liége,* XIII (1922), 345-358. (

———. "Les Bégards de Saint-Trond," *ibid.,* VI (1907), 123-126.

———. *Julienne de Cornillon.* Brussels, 1946.

Simon, André. *L'ordre des Pénitentes de Ste.-Marie-Madeleine en Allemagne au XIIIe siècle.* Fribourg, 1918.

Simrock, Karl. *Die deutschen Spruchwörter.* Frankfurt a.M., 1881.

Sivré, J. B. "Geschiedkundige Schets van het Oud Begijnhof te Roermond," *Publications de la sociéte historique et archéologique dans le duché de Limbourg*, XI (1874), 163-219.

Smit, J. P. W. A. "Het Begijnhof van Oisterwijk," *Bossche Bijdragen. Bouwstoffen voor de Geschiedenis van het Bisdom 's-Hertogenbosch*, III (1919), 40-55.

Snelten, Joh. "Hadewijch mystica," *Tijdschrift voor nederlandsche Taal- en Letterkunde*, XXXI (1912), 114-170.

Spaey, E. "Over middeleeuwsche heiligenliteratuur," *OGE.*, III (1929), 291-303, 409-425.

Stallaert, Ch. "Inventaire analytique des chartes concernant les seigneurs et la ville de Diest," *BCRH.*, 4th ser., III (1876).

Stengers, Jean. *Les Juifs dans les Pays-Bas au Moyen âge*. Mémoires de l'acad. roy. De Belgique, XLV, fasc. 2. Brussels, 1950.

Stöckerl, D. *Bruder David von Augsburg. Ein deutscher Mystiker aus dem Franziskanerorden*. Munich, 1914.

Stockmans, J. D. *Beknopte inventaris der oude archieven van het Bureel van Weldadigheid te Lier*. Lierre, s.d.

Strauch, Philip. *Die Offenbarungen der Adelheid Langman*. Strasbourg, 1878.

Straven, François. *Notice historique sur le béguinage dit de Sainte-Agnes à Saint-Trond*. St. Trond, 1876.

Stroick, Aubert. "Wer ist die Stigmatisierte in einer Reformschrift für das zweite Lyoner Konzil?" *HJ.*, L (1930), 342-349.

——. "Verfasser und Quellen der Collectio de Scandalis Ecclesiae (Reformschrift des Fr. Gilbert von Tournay, O. F. M., zum II. Konzil von Lyon, 1274)," *AFH.*, XXIII (1930), 3-41, 273-299, 433-466; new ed. of "Collectio", *ibid.*, XXIV (1931), 33-62.

Studia Eucharistica DCC anni a condito festo sanctissimi Corporis Christi, 1246-1946. Antwerp, 1946.

Tanghe, G. F. *Parochieboek van Damme, met een schetsje van Houcke en Meunikenreede*. Bruges, s.d.

Tanon, L. *Histoire des tribunaux de l'inquisition en France*. Paris, 1893.

Tarlier, Jules and Wauters, Alphonse. *La Belgique ancienne et moderne. Géographie et histoire des communes belges*. 3 vols., Brussels, 1859-1887.

Taylor, Henry Osborn. *The Mediaeval Mind. A History of the Development of Thought and Emotion in the Middle Ages*. 2 vols., Harvard University Press, 1951.

Te Winkel, Jan. *De Ontwikkelingsgang der nederlandsche Letterkunde. I. Geschiedenis der nederlandsche Letterkunde van Middeleeuwen en Rederijkerstijd*. 2nd ed., Haarlem, 1922.

——. *Maerlants Werken als Spiegel van de dertiende eeuw*. 2nd. ed., The Hague, 1892.

Ten Brink, Jan. *Geschiedenis der nederlandsche Letterkunde*. Amsterdam, 1897.

Thery, G. *Autour du decret de 1210: III. Amaury de Bène, Etude sur son panthéisme formel* (Bibliothèque Thomiste, XVI. Paris, 1932.

——. "Edition critique des pièces relatives au procès d'Eckhart contenues dans le manuscrit 33 b de la bibliothèque de Soest," *Archives d'histoire doctrinale et littéraire du moyen âge*, I (1926), 129-268.

——. "Contribution à l'histoire du procès d'Eckehart," in *Vie spirituelle, Etudes et Documents*, Jan. 1924 (93-119), March, 1924 (164-183), May, 1925 (149-187), Jan., 1926 (49-95), June, 1926 (45-65).

Thompson, James Westfall. *The Literacy of the Laity in the Middle Ages*. University of California, Berkeley, 1939.

Thouzellier, Christine. "La place du 'De Periculis' de Guillaume de Saint-Amour dans les polemiques universitaires du XIIIe siècle," *Revue historique*, CLVI (1927), 69-82.
Thijs, Ch. M. T. "Histoire du béguinage de Tongres," *BSSLL.*, XV (1881), 5-707.
Toussaint. Chanoine. *Histoire civile et religieuse de Walcourt*. Namur, 1887.
——. *Histoire du monastère d'Oignies de l'ordre des chanoines réguliers de Saint-Augustin*. Namur, 1880.
——. *L'abbaye de Floreffe de l'ordre de Prémontré. Histoire et description*. 4th ed., Namur, 1901.
Troeltsch, Ernst. *Grundlagen der christlichen Kirchen und Gruppen*. Tübingen, 1923.
Uhlhorn, Gerhard. *Die christliche Liebesthätigkeit im Mittelalter*, II (Stuttgart, 1884).
Ullmann, C. *Reformatoren vor der Reformation vornehmlich in Deutschland und den Niederlanden*. 2nd ed., Gotha, 1866.
Vacandard, Elie. *Vie de Saint Bernard, abbé de Clairvaux*. 4th ed., 2 vols., Paris, 1895.
Van Asseldonk, A. "Handschriften van Kruisheren uit de XVe en XVIe eeuw over het ontstaan der Orde van het H. Kruis," *Clairlieu*, I (1943), 83-102.
Van Cappel, E. "De Hongersnood in de Middeleeuwen tot de XIIIde eeuw," *ASEB.*, LVI (1906), 16-40, 143-164.
Van den Borne, Fidentius. *Die Anfänge des franziskanischen dritten Ordens. Vorgeschichte, Entwicklung der Regel: Ein Beitrag zur Geschichte des Ordens-und Bruderschaftswesens im Mittelalter*, in *Franciskanische Studien*, VIII, Münster i. W., 1925.
——. "Analecta de tertio ordine," *AFH.*, IX (1916), 118-133.
——. "Problemen der geschiedenis van het geestelijk leven tijdens de opkomst der bedelorden," *OGE.*, VII (1933), 188-212.
Van den Gheyn, J. "Encore les statuts des Bogards de Zepperen," *Revue des bibliothèques et archives de Belgique*, IV (1906), 176-177.
Van den Wyngaert, Anastasius. "De Sanctis et Beatis Tertii Ordinis iuxta codicum Fr. Mariani Florentini," *AFH.*, XIV (1921), 3-35.
Van der Elst, C. "Les mystagogues de Bruxelles, Egidius Cantoris, 1410," *Revue trimestrielle*, XXIX (1861), 101-123.
Van der Essen, Leon. *Etude critique et littéraire sur les vitae des saints mérovingiens de l'ancienne Belgique*. Louvain-Paris, 1907.
——. "De ketterijen van Tanchelm in de XIIde eeuw," *Ons Geloof*, II (1912), 354-362.
Van der Linden, Herman. *Geschiedenis der stad Leuven*. Louvain, 1899.
Van der Rest, J. F. *Aperçu historique sur les établissements de la ville de Bruxelles*, Brussels, 1860.
Vanderstraeten, Edmond. *Recherches sur les communautés religieuses et les institutions de bienfaisance établies à Audenarde, depuis le XIIe siècle jusqu'à la fin du XVIIIe*. 2 vols., Audenarde, 1858-1860.
Van der Vet, W. A. *Het Bienboec van Thomas van Cantimpré en zijn Exempelen*. The Hague, 1902.
Van der Zeyde, Marie Helene. *Hadewijch, eene studie over de Mens en de Schrijfster*. Groningen-The Hague, 1934.
——. "Hadewijch en Duitsland," *Tijdschrift voor nederlandsche Taal- en Letterkunde*, LV (1936), 35-40 .
Van Drival, E. "Le bienheureux Gobert d'Aspremont," *Annales du cercle archéol. d'Enghien*, II (1883), 301-323.
Van Espen, Zegerus Bernardus. *Jus ecclesiasticum universum*, I (Cologne 1777).

Van Even, Edward. *Louvain dans le passé et dans le présent.* Louvain, 1895.
——. "Bloemardinne: De Brusselsche Ketterin, gestorven in 1335, en hare volgelingen in die 15e eeuw," *VMKVA.,* VIII (1894), 357-390.
Van Gestel, Cornelius. *Historia sacra et profana archiepiscopatus Mechliniensis.* 2 vols., The Hague, 1725.
Van Goor, T. E. *Beschrijvinghe der stadt en lande van Breda.* The Hague, 1744.
Van Heussen en van Rijn. *Batavia sacra sive regestae apostolicorum virorum, qui fidem Bataviae primi intulerunt in duas partes divisa.* Brussels, 1714.
Van Hoorebeke, Minard, *Description de Méreaux.* Ghent, 1877.
Van Leuridan, M. *Les Tables des pauvres à Roubaix.* Roubaix, 1884.
Van Lom, Chr. *Beschryving der stad Lier in Brabant.* The Hague, 1740.
Van Mieris, Frans and van Alphen, D. *Beschryving der stad Leyden.* 3 vols., Leyden, 1762-1784.
Van Mierlo, J. "Hadewijch une mystique flamande du treizième siècle," *Revue d'ascétique et de mystique,* V (1924), 269-289, 380-404.
——. "Ophelderingen bij de vroegste geschiedenis van het woord begijn," *VMKVA.,* 1931, 983-1006.
——. "Op den drempel onzer dertiende eeuw," *ibid.,* 1925, 819-834.
——. "Het Begardisme, een synthetische studie," *ibid.,* 1930, 277-305.
——. "De Poëzie van Hadewijch," *ibid.,* 1931, 285-439.
——. "Lambert le Beges in verband met den oorsprong der begijnen," *ibid.,* 1926, 612-660.
——. "De bijnaam van Lambertus le Beges en de vroegste beteekenis van het woord begijn," *ibid.,* 1925, 405-447.
——. "De 10e Brief van Hadewijch en het 41ste der Limburgsche Sermoenen. Invloed van Hadewijch op de Limburgsche Sermoenen," *ibid.,* 1932, 373-387.
——. "Beatrijs van Nazareth," *ibid.,* 1926, 51-72.
——. "Willem van Afflighem en het Leven van Jesus en het Leven van Sinte Lutgart," *ibid.,* 1935, 775-915.
——. *Jacob van Maerlant, zijn Leven, zijn Werken, zijn Beteekenis.* Antwerp-Brussels, 1946.
——. "Over den Ouderdom van de Limburgsche Sermoenen," *VMKVA.,* 1935, 1081-1093.
——. "Hadewijchiana I-III," *ibid.,* 1927, 195-225, 425-442.
——. "Hadewijch en Eckart," *D. War. Belf.,* XXIII (1923), 1138-1155.
——. "Uit de Geschiedenis onzer middeleeuwsche Letterkunde. Wanneer heeft Hadewych geleefd?" *D. War. Belf.,* XXI (1921), 309-327, 441-465.
——. "Was Hadewijch de Ketterin Blommardine?" *ibid.,* X (1908), 267-286.
——. "Beata Hadewigis de Antverpia," *ibid.,* XXVII (1927), 789-798, 833-843.
——. "Een vergissing van Pomerius?" *ibid.,* 1925, 610-625.
——. "Hadewijch een gelukzalige Bloemardinne?" *ibid.,* 1925, 28-49.
——. "Een hopeloos pleit," *ibid.,* XXVI (1926), 468-480, 580-594.
——. "Uit de Geschiedenis onzer middeleeuwsche Letterkunde, Hadewijch," *ibid.,* 1921, 480-496, 622-635.
——. "Over het ontstaan der Germaansche mystiek," *OGE.,* I (1927), 11-37.
——. "Een Geding over Eckehart's rechtgeloovigheid," *OGE.,* I (1927), 225-254, 337-346.
——. "Hadewijch en Wilhelm van St. Thierry," *OGE.,* III (1929), 45-59.
——. "Naar aanleiding van de Bloemardine-episode in het leven van Ruusbroec," *OGE.,* VIII (1934), 224-225.
——. "De Bloemardine-episode in het leven van den Gelukzaligen Joh. van Ruusbroec," *OGE.,* VII (1933), 305ff

"Ruusbroec's bestrijding van de Ketterij," *OGE.*, VI (1932), 304-346.
——. "Begardisme," *DHGE.*, VII (1934), 426-441.
——. "Les béguines et Lambert li Beges," *RHE.*, XXIII (1927), 785-801.
——. "Hadewijch en de Ketterin Blommardine," *Tijdschrift voor neder-landsche Taal en Letterkunde*, XL (1921), 45-64.
——. *Hadewijch. Brussels-Amsterdam*, 1926.
——. *De Letterkunde van de Middeleeuwen* (vols. 1-2 of *Geschiedenis van de Letterkunde der Nederlanden*, 2nd ed., Antwerp, s.d.
——. "Het ontstaan der Middelnederlandsche letterkunde ," *D. War. Belf.*, XXVIII (1928), 582-595.
"Encore Hadewijch et Bloemardinne," *Revue belge de philol. et d'hist.*, VII (1928), 469-510, 867-869.
——. "Adelwip," *VMKVA.*, 1933, 581-598.
——. "Slotwoord bij een debat over het ontstaan van 'begginus'," *ibid.*, 1936, 621-625.
——. "Hadewijchiana," *OGE.*, XVII (1943), 179-184.
——. "De wederwaardigheden van een etymologie, de vroegste geschiedenis van het woord 'begijn'," *VMKVA.*, 1945, 31-51.
Vannérus, Jules. "Documents concernant le Tiers-Ordre à Anvers et ses rapports avec l'industrie drapière (1296-1572)," *BCRH.*, LXXIX (1910), 471-672.
——. "Documents concernant les Bogards de Malines (1284-1558)," *BCRH.*, LXXX (1911), 215-286.
Van Rooijen, Henri. *Theodorus van Celles, een Tijd- en Levensbeeld.* Cuyck, 1936.
Van Roy, Alb. *Lutgardis van Tongeren (Heiligen van onzen Stam*, Bruges-Brussels, 1946).
Van Wintershoven, Ed. "Notes et documents concernant l'ancien béguinage de St. Christophe à Liege," *AHEB.*, XXIII (1892), 61-115.
——. "Recluseries et ermitages dans l'ancien diocèse de Liége," *BSSLL.*, XXIII (1906), 96-158.
Verbeek, Beda. "De Komst der Minderbroeders in het Hertogdom Brabant en hun vestigung te 's Hertogenbosch (1228)," *Coll. Franc. Neerl.*, II, 61-131.
Vercoullie, J. "De Oorsprong van den naam Begynen," *Oostvlaamsche Zanten*, IV (1929), 105-108.
Verdam, J. "Velthem's Episoden uit Hildegardis," *Tijdschrift voor neder-landsche Taal- en Letterkunde*, I (1881), 281-297.
Vidal, J. M. "Doctrine et morale des derniers ministres albigeois," *Revue des questions historiques*, LXXVI (1909)., 357-409; LXXXVI (1909), 5-48.
Volpe, Gioacchimo. *Movimenti religiosi e sette ereticale nella societa medie vale italiana (secoli XI-XIV)* (Collane storica, VI), Florence, 1926.
Von Loë, Paulus. *Statistisches über die Ordensprovinz Teutonia (QF.,* I). Leipzig, 1907.
——. *Statistisches über die Ordensprovinz Saxonia (QF.,* IV). Leipzig, 1910.
Wadding, Luke. *Annales Minorum seu Historia Trium Ordinum a S. Francisco Institutorum.* 25 vols., new ed., Quaracchi, 1931-1935.
Wagenaar, Jan. *Amsterdam in zyne opkomst, aanwas, geschiedenissen, voor-regten, koophandel, gebouwen, kerkenstaat, schoolen, schutterye, gilden en regeeringen.* 3 vols., Amsterdam, 1760-1767.
Walter, Johannes von. *Die ersten Wanderprediger Frankreichs: I. Robert von Arbrissel; II. Vital von Mortain, Bernard von Tiron, Norbert.* Leipzig, 1903, 1908.
Wattenbach, D. "Über die Secte der Brüder vom freien Geiste. Mit Nach-

trägen über die Waldenser in der Mark und in Pommern," *Sitzungsberichte der königlich preussischen Akademie der Wissenschaften zu Berlin*, XXVIII, 1887, 517-544.

——. *Deutschlands Geschichtsquellen im Mittelalter bis zur Mitte des dreizehnten Jahrhunderts.* 2 vols., Berlin, 1894.

Wauters, Alphonse Jules. *Table chronologique des chartes et diplômes imprimés concernant l'histoire de la Belgique* (Acad. roy. de Belgique, 11 vols., Brussels, 1866-1912).

——. *Le duc Jean I et le Brabant sous le règne de ce prince (1267-1294).* Brussels-Liége, 1862.

——. *Histoire des environs de Bruxelles.* 3 vols., Brussels, 1855.

Wiesehoff, Josef. *Die Stellung der Bettelorden in den deutschen freien Reichstädten im Mittelalter.* Diss., Leipzig, 1905.

Williams, Watkin. *Monastic Studies.* Manchester University Press, 1938.

Wilmet, Ch. "Histoire des béguinages de Namur," *ASAN.*, VI (1859-1860), 43-90.

Wilmotte, Leon. "Notice historique sur le couvent des Croisiers de Huy," *Annales du cercle Hutois des sciences et beaux-arts*, XX (1926), 195-248.

Wilms, Hieronymus. *Das älteste Verzeichnis der deutschen Dominikanerinnenklöster (QF.*, Hft. 24). Leipzig, 1928.

——. *Das Beten der Mystikerinnen dargestellt nach den Chroniken der Dominikanerinnenklöster zu Adelhausen, Diessenhofen, Engeltal, Kirchberg, Oetenbach, Töss und Unterlinden* (QF., Hft. 11). Leipzig, 1916

Wigger, F. "Urkundliche Mittheilungen über die Beghinen und Beghardenhäuser zu Rostock," *Jahrbücher des Vereins für Meklenburgische Geschichte und Alterthumskunde*, XLVII (1882), 1-26.

Wilthemius, Alexander. *Vita venerabilis Yolandae Priorissae ad Mariae Vallemcum appendice de Margarita Henrici VII sorore.* Antwerp, 1674.

Winter, Franz. *Die Prämonstratenser des zwölften Jahrhunderts und ihre Bedeutung für das nordöstliche Deutschland. Ein Beitrag zur Geschichte der Christianisirung und Germanisirung des Wendenlandes.* Berlin, 1865.

——. *Die Cistercienser des nordöstlichen Deutschlands.* 2 vols., Gotha, 1868-1871.

Withof, J. "De Tafels van den Heiligen-Geest te Mechelen," *Handelingen van den Mechelschen Kring voor Oudheidkunde, Letteren en Kunst*, XXXII (1927), 85-134; XXXIII (1928), 35-89. Extract Malines, 1928.

Woikowsky-Biedau, V. *Das Armenwesen des mittelalterlichen Köln in seiner Beziehung zur wirtschaftlichen und politischen Geschichte der Stadt.* Diss., Breslau, 1891.

Zanoni, Luigi. *Gli Umiliati nei loro rapporte con l'eresia, industria della lana ed i communi nei secoli XIIe XIII (Bibliotheca Historica Italica*, ser. II, vol. 2). Milan, 1911.

Zarncke, Lily. *Der Anteil des Kardinals Ugolino an der Ausbildung der drei Orden des heil. Franz (Beiträge zur Kulturgeschichte des Mittelalters und der Renaissance*, XLII). Leipzig-Berlin, 1930.

Zoepf, Ludwig. *Die Mystikerin Margaretha Ebner.* Leipzig, 1914.

Zuhorn, Karl. "Die Beginen in Münster, Anfänge, Frühzeit und Ausgang des münsterischen Beginentums," *Westfälische Zeitschrift. Zeitschrift für vaterländische Geschichte und Altertumskunde*, XCI (1935), 1-149.

Zypaeus, Franciscus. *Iuris pontificii novi analytica enarratio.* Cologne, 1624.

Addenda

Delepierre, O., and Prieme, F., *Précis analytique des documents que renferme le dépôt des archives de la Flandre Occidentale.* 12 vols., Bruges, 1840-1852.

Döllinger, Johann Joseph Ignaz von. *Beiträge zur politischen, kirchlichen und Culturgeschichte der sechs letzten Jahrhunderte.* 3 vols., Regensburg, 1862-82.

——. *Beiträge zur Sektengeschichte des Mittelalters,* 2 vols., Munich, 1890.

Eeghen, Isabella Henriette van. *Vrouwenkloosters en Begijnhof in Amsterdam van de 14e tot het Eind der 16e Eeuw.* Amsterdam-Paris, 1941.

Groote, Geert. *De Simonia ad Beguttas. De middelnederlandsche Tekst,* ed. Willem de Vreese. The Hague, 1940

Hyma, Albert. *The Christian Renaissance: A History of the "Devotio Moderna".* Grand Rapids, Mich., 1924.

Löhr, Gabriel. "Die Mendikanten in den Kölner Schreinsbüchern," *AHVN.,* CXXXIV (1939), 1-33.

Lavisse, Ernest. *Histoire de France depuis les origines jusqu'à la revolution,* vol. III in 2 pts., Paris, 1901.

Nolet, W. and Boeren, P. C. *Kerkelijke Instellingen in de Middeleeuwen.* Amsterdam, 1951.

Schreiber, Georg. *Gemeinschaften des Mittelalters: Recht und Verfassung, Kult und Frömmigkeit.* Regensburg-Münster, 1948.

Stockmans, J. B. "Het Obituarium van Sint-Pieterskerk te Anderlecht," *BG.,* III (1904), 527-541; IV (1905), 66-80; 515-525; V (1906), 89-100.

Theunissen, L. "Lijst der Kapelrijen, bestaande ten Jare 1619 in de Kerk van O.-L.-V. te Antwerpen," *BG.,* I (1902), 297-315.

Throop, Palmer A. *Criticism of the Crusade: A Study of Public Opinion and Crusade Propaganda.* Amsterdam, 1940

Welter, J. Th. *L'Exemplum dans la littérature religieuse et didactique du moyen âge.* Paris-Toulouse, 1927.

Index

Abbreviations: ab., abbot; abb., abbess; archb., archbishop; archd., archdeacon; b., bishop; cardl., cardinal-legate; OC. Cistercian; OFM, Order of Friars Minor, Franciscans; OP, Order of Preachers, Dominicans; OPr., Premonstratensians; OSB., Benedictine. (N) designates a nunnery.

Aachen. See Aix-la-Chapelle
Aales Malachine, beguine, 226
Abbeville. *See* beguines
Abond of Huy, 322, 332, 333, 448
Acre, St. John of (Ptolemais), 108. *See also* Jacques de Vitry
Adam, ab. of Cîteaux, 108, 110
Adam de Borloo, 338
Adam de la Halle, 426
Ade, beguine at Brussels, 177
Adeheid, beguine at Nürnberg, 203 n
Adelhausen, OP (N), 196, 197, 203 n, 403
Adelheid, abb. of Lichtenthal, 93
Adelheid von Vechenheim, 339
Adhémar de Mosset, 537 n
Adolf von Revele, 248 n
Adolph de la Marck, b. of Liége (1313-1344), 66, 132, 162, 172, 237, 238, 486 n, 542-43
Aelipdis, beguine at Amiens, 232
Aelipdis, beguine at St. Quentin 232
Aerschot, 108 n, *See also* beghards, beguines
Afflighem, OSB, 103 n, 328, 490
Agnes, beguine, daughter of Hellin of Launoy, 109
Agnes, beguine, 336 n
Agnes, beguine of St. Syr, 67
Agnes, daughter of Eric, king of Denmark, 348 n
Agnes, prioress of La Royaute of Nivelles, 336 n
Agnes, sister of Juliana of Cornillon, 301, 304
Agnes, Juliana's companion, 303
Agnes, countess of Looz, 173 n
Agnes Blannbekin, beguine, 314, 316, 317
Agnes de Hanse, beguine, 478 n
Agnes d'Harcourt, 97 n, 375, 401
Agnes von Hohenstein, OP, St. Mark's, 198 n

Agnes of Hungary, 357
Agnes la Maque, 226 n
Agnes de Orchio, mistress of Paris beguines, 228 n
Agnes du Vivier, beguine of St. Syr, 66, 68
Aigulphus (Aiulfus), St., archb. Bourges (811-835), 332 n
Ailred of Rievaulx, 373
Aire, 34 n
Aiseau, seigniory of: 11, 14
Aix, 252 n, 547
Aix-la-Chapelle, 37, 558 n. *See also* beghards, beguines
Alard de Berchem, 214
Alard de Denterghem, provost of St. Martin's at Ypres, 372
Alberic of Laon (de Humbert), archb. Rheims (1207-18), 31
Alberic de Trois-Fontaines, 71 n, 73; cited, 388 n
Albert, Friar (OP), lector at Wisby, 351 n
Albert I of Bavaria, count of Hainault and Holland (1358-1404), 549, 550, 551, 553
Albert I of Austria, emperor of H.R.E. (1298-1308), 525
Albert de Cuyck, b. of Liége (1194-1200), 8 n, 11, 12
Albert of Moha, 111
Albertus Magnus, 449, 514; cited, 315
Albi, 436
Albigensians, 4, 28, 29, 54, 251, 252 n, 415, 435-37, 488, 501, 508; crusade against, 23, 32, 37, 55, 397, 415, 486
Albrandini, Friar, OP, 348, 352, 355
Albrecht III, b. of Halberstadt (1366-1390), 562
Aleida, wife of John d'Avesnes, 222
Aleida, widow of Henry III of Brabant, 198 n

Aleida, abb. of St. Walburge, 297, 449
Aleida, sister of Godfrey Pachomius, 323, 327
Aleida, beguine at St. Trond, 337
Aleidis, beguine at Nivelles, 336 n
Aleidis, beguine and daughter of Gobelin Bolant von Nettesheim, 137, 340 n
Alexander, ab. of Neufmoustier, 42
Alexander IV (1254-1261), 93, 193, 194, 203 n, 272 n, 458 n, 490
Alexander I de Juliers, b. of Liége (1128-1135), 103 n
Alexander II of Oeren, b. of Liége (1164-1167), 74
Alexians. See Cellites
Alexius, St. 266
Alfrade, 347
Alice, beguine, at Stommeln, 347, 354
Alice, beguine of Bodeghem, 479 n
Alice, near Neuve-Cour, 326
Alice de Boulaere (Boulers), 111
Alice of Schaerbeek, 152, 317, 318, 332, 382, 416, 447
Alis la · Baconnelle, beguine at Rheims, 99
Alis Corgnie of Rheims, 230
Alissia de Yserghem, beguine, 479 n
Alix Langloise, 214 n
Alix des Pavillons, 228
Alkmaar. See beguines
Alost. See beguines
Aloud van Oudeschie, 554
Aloudus Cambier, 210
Alpegg, 385
Alphonse of Poitiers, 226, 469
Alphonso a Castro, OFM, 367
Alsace, 404, 538
Altenberg, OC, dioc. Cologne: annuities to beguines, 137, 339-40
Amatildo, lord of Pons, 110
Amaury de Bène, 463, 500; doctrine, 368, 419 n
Ambrose, St., 385, 414 n
Amédée, count of Savoy, 501
Amelricus, canon of St. Gudule, 179 n
Amelunxborn, OC, dioc. Hildesheim, 296 n
Amicia de Joigny, prioress of Montargis, 191 n, 192, 193
Amiens, bishop of, 537 n. See also Arnold, beguines
Amsterdam: Cellites in, 267 n. See also beguines
Anastasius IV, Pope (1153-1154), 283
Anchin, OSB, 297
Andenne, 297; exclusivism of, 63, 70, 89
Anderlecht. See beguines
Andreas, frater conversus at Oignies, 10 n

Andreas Aosiensis (Aciensis or Daciensem), 351
Andreas, Valerius, 378
Andrew, 349
Andrew, St., 468
Anglo-Saxon nuns, 373
Annales Colmarienses Maiores, 523
Annales Grussavienses, 557
Anna von Munzingen, 196, 403
Anniversaries, 411
Anselm, 288, 289
Antheit near Huy, 303
Antioch, Cistercians in, 52 n
Antoine, OPr., 285
Antoine, duke of Brabant (1406-1415), 221
Antwerp, 180, 201-02, 237, 270, 271, 465, 485. See also beghards, beguines, Tanchelm, William Cornelius
Apostolici, 76, 247, 415, 432, 444, 460, 516
Ardenburg. See beguines
Argensolles, OC (N), 113, 332
Argenton, OC (N), 111, 112 n
Arlon, 111
Arnold, count of Looz, 174
Arnold, prior of St. Gertrude's at Louvain, 184
Arnold, priest of Haarlem, 222
Arnold, b. of Amiens (1236-1247), 229
Arnold, seignior of Diest, 128 n, 185, 186, 236
Arnold, priest of Ten Hove at Louvain, 336 n
Arnold Cornebout. See Arnulf of Brussels
Arnold de Corswarem, knight, 111
Arnold of Ghistelles, ab. of Villers (1270-1276), 172, 173
Arnold de Joechalede, 254
Arnold de Lowaige, knight, 42
Arnold of Lübeck, OP, 198 n
Arnold of Maldenghem, canon of Tournai, 169, 215
Arnold of Sassenheim, pastor of St. Bavo, 549
Arnold Venoit, Aerschot echevin, 185
Arnold of Wesemael, Knight Templar, 331
Arnsburg, OC, dioc. Mainz, 339
Arnulf of Louvain, ab. of Villers (1240-1248), 114, 333
Arnulf of Brussels (or Villers), 46 n, 113, 325, 326-27, 332, 333, 446-47
Arras, 501, 541, 542. See also Pierre de Chappes
Arrouaise, abbey, 34
Artois, 418
Aschaffenburg, synod of (1292), 513
Asen, J., 98, 160
Assenede, parish in Ghent, 206, 209 n

Ath, 112 n
Au, vor deren, 385
Audenarde, 112, 485. *See also* beghards, beguines
Auderghem, OP convent at Brussels, 196 n, 198 n, 552
Augsburg, 404, 514, 558 n
Augustine, St., 34, 77, 300, 374, 384, 414 n, 415
Augustinians, 36, 50, 75, 108 n, 114, 184, 301; rule of, 8, 9, 16, 41, 54, 56, 57, 86, 91, 101, 104, 113, 129, 141, 161, 195, 196 n, 203 n, 237, 268, 302, 303, 323, 332, 487, 518 n, 527, 532; "royal middle path", 10, 34; and beguines, 127, 184
Augustinus, Provincial, 349
Aulne, OC, 43, 320, 321, 323, 325, 327, 447; direction of nunneries, 107 n 109, 113 n, 114 n, 115
Aunoit, beguines of: 215
Austin friars, 466. *See also* Augustinians
Austria, 253, 309, 513
Auxerre: poor in, 231
Averbode, OPr., 111, 284
Avignon, 248, 257, 371, 500, 533, 534, 568, 569
Aygalliers, Wautier d': 379
Aywières, OC (N), 15, 20, 21, 22, 39, 42, 43, 45 n, 47, 51, 90, 91, 107, 108, 109, 115, 200 n, 327 n, 328, 383, 434, 447 n

Bailloeul, sire de, 212
Baisy, 43
Baldwin, chaplain of Lille beguines, 214
Baldwin, OP, 352
Baldwin II, b. of Utrecht (1178-1196), 284
Baldwin IV, count of Hainault (1120-1171), 448
Baldwin IX, count of Flanders and Hainault (1194-1202), 208
Baldwin d'Arsebruer, vassal, 213
Baldwin of Barbençon, prior of Oignies, 8 n, 15-16, 18, 38
Baldwin of Brugelette, 49 n
Baldwin II of Courtenay, count of Namur, 111, 305
Baldwin of Loupoigne, lord of Aiseau, 11, 12, 13
Baldwin I of Luxembourg, archb. of Trèves (1307-1354), 522
Baldwin de Merlemont, canon of Moustier-sur-Sambre, 14 n
Bamberg, bishop of, 559 n, 560, 561
Barbara of Beer, beguine, 552
Barcelona: OP chapter of 1323, 309 n

Barrés. *See* Carmelites
Barthélemy de Tirlemont (de Vleeschouwer), father of Beatrice of Nazareth, 110, 332, 386
Barthélemy de Jura, b. of Laon (1113-1151), 102, 106, 107
Basel, 369, 560, 561; council of, 513. *See also* beguines
Basilia, beguine of Brussels, 179
Baude li Boirgne, knight, 214 n
Baudechon de Latuit, 336 n
Bavaria, 90, 198 n; mysticism in, 403, 439-40
Bayeux, 331, 541
Beatrice, daughter of Mechtild de Gelmen, 337
Beatrice, beguine at Brussels, 177
Beatrice or Bertha, widow of Eustache, 49
Beatrice de Borloo, daughter of Henry de Ophem, 338
Beatrice of Courtrai, 111
Beatrice de Hémelette, beguine, 66
Beatrice de Lens, 108
Beatrice of Tirlemont (Nazareth), 152, 332, 395, 396, 447 n, 494, 495; relations with beguines, 28-29, 272, 386; parentage, 98; writings, 365, 392-93; education, 386-87
Beatrice of Vandreuil, beguine, 99
Béatris Oulhyette, 66
Beaufort, lords of, 111
Beaupré, OC (N), 111
Beaurepart, OPr, 301 n
Beauvais, 472, 492. *See also* Vincent
Beauvechain, 112
Begga, St., 63, 179 n, 410, 431
Begarda, 368
Beghards, bogards, 59, 165, 246, 247, 248, 249, 253, 410 n, 439, 512; relations with municipal authorities, 6, 256, 257; etymology, 246-47, 251-52; indulgences, 239-40; compared with beguines, 247-48, 252-53, 257; motives, 248-50, 255; and heresy, 248, 250, 251, 268 n, 256, 452, 454-55, 491, 496, 499, 500, 519, 557-73; compared with Lollards, 246, 266; and Franciscan third rule, 250, 254, 257, 345-46, 558; first appearance in Low Countries, 253-54; occupations, 254, 256, 257, 275-77; relations with clergy, 257; organization, 263-65; desire translation of scripture, 369; and preaching, 509, 510, 522, 564; and mendicancy, 143, 509, 512, 522, 525, 527; and inquisition, 514, 516-20, 557-73; and flagellants, 557; in Aachen, 263; Aerschot, 255, 263; Antwerp, 240, 250, 252 n; 253 n, 255, 256, 257, 262, 263, 277; Audenarde,

275; Basel, 514; Bois-le-Duc, 255, 257, 263, 277; Bruges, 251, 253, 255, 256, 275, 276, 512; rule, 260-62; Brussels, 249, 254, 257, 263, 275, 276; Cologne, 248, 253, 263, 368, 434, 499; Diest, 254, 256, 263; Dinkelsbühl, 538; Frankfurt, 368; Ghent, 263, 275; Hoegaarden (Hougarde), 255, 264; Léau, 255, 263; dioc. Liége, 411; Louvain, 252 n, 254, 256, 257, 263, 275, 276; Maestricht, 255, 263, 517, 522; Malines, 239, 255, 263, 512, 521; Middelburg, 222, 255, 257, 260, 263; Neustadt, 253; Nivelles, 255; Ophem-lez- Wezembeek, 255; in Poland, 555; Roermond, 263, Rothenburg ob der Tauber, 538; Saint-Omer, 250, 255, 257, 263; St. Trond, 254, 263; Strasbourg, 248, 358-60; Tirlemont, 254, 263; Tournai, 255, 257; Zeeland, 203; Zepperen, 144; Zierikzee, 263. See also beguins, conversi, Free Spirits, John Hartmann, Lollards, Turlupins.

Beguins, 44, 66, 208, 245, 246, 249, 253, 415, 422-24, 430-35, 443, 444, 472-73, 523, relations with Fraticelli, 246n, 433, 434, in Provence and Narbonne, 400 n, 430, 433, 434; judgment of, 422-23

Beguines: stages of development, 5-6, 162-63; socio-economic motives, 3, 81-86, 146, 155-56, 321, 573; religious motives, 86-88; threats of heresy, 3, 5, 6, 123, 127, 162-63, 180, 227, 344, 412, 414-17, 434, 442, 508; lack of formal organization, 4, 159, 120, 134-35; counterbalance to heresy, 4, 121, 312, 414-15, 436, 479; midway between religious and lay, 4, 85, 122-27; ridicule of beguines, 5, 50, 51, 156, 190, 200-201, 319, 439-53, 471-73, 513; ridiculed in Old French poems, 417-20; beguinae clausae, 6, 7, 181, 194 n, 195, 367, 492, 533, 539, 542, 554-55; hospitals, 6, 66, 67, 155, 573; impoverished beguines, 60 n, 62, 67-68, 69, 84, 88, 94, 99, 146-53, 166, 204, 206, 208, 209, 210, 225, 226, 245, 271, 273, 304, 337, 525, 550, 553, 568; economic independence, 60-61, 62, 69, 99, 136, 137-40, 145-53, 155, 226; social classes, 71, 81-82, 88, 97-99, 136-140, 225; well-to-do, 88, 96-97, 480; property qualifications, 480-82; privileges and immunities, 6, 61, 65, 127, 131, 156-64, 178, 180-81, 210-11, 215, 218-19, 227, 409-12; differ from canonesses, 63; numbers, 64 (Nivelles);

94; 225 (Paris); 432 (Germany); parish priest safeguarded, 67-68, 96, 178 n, 212, 227; supernatural gifts, 65, 67, 450-52; submission to parochial authority, 66, 205-208, 410-11; occupation, 83, 146, 270-77, 377, 385-86, 397, 428; and guilds (industry), 84-85, 145-46, 211, 226; religious precocity, 87-88, 446-48; Dominican interest in, 99, 121, 126, 128 n, 135, 184, 185, 195, 198 n, 201-204, 206-207, 213, 214, 216, 217, 225, 228, 230, 231, 341-361, 399-405, 415, 419-20, 435, 452-53, 532, 543, 546 n, 547-48, 552; relations with towns, 100, 131, 479; enlaced with Cistercians, 106, 321-340, 438; legal status, 120-40; 410-12, 479; canonists' view of, 123-24, 463; habit, 124, 128-29, 138, 184, 186, 427, 477, 479, 529, 533, 534, 568, 570, 572 n; and Augustinian canons, 127, 184-85; as an expression of lay piety, 132, 569; statutes, 134, 136-37, 140; and Franciscans, 132, 135, 184, 213, 374-75, 573; magistra, 135-36, 568; internal organization, 135-37; religious practices, 136, 146, 148-49, 157, 300; spirituality, 320-33; zeal for eucharist, 312, 316-18, 415-16; frequency of confession, 418 n; care of sick, 136, 149, 206, 266, 271-72, 385; testaments, 137-38; property rights, 137-40, 480-81; similarity to Cathari, 138, 414, 436-38; probation, 138; vows, 139, 152; appraisal by Grosseteste, 144; by Humbert de Romans, 412; by Gautier de Coincy, 145; by Gilles li Muisis, 424, 427-29; disapproved by Bonaventura, 260; and labor manuum, 144-153, 271; parochial organization under Cistercian auspices, 170-84; Benedictine interest in parochial organization, 185-86; rehabilitation, 180, 220, 539-46 (Belgium); 540, 546-48 (France); 548-55 (Holland); patronized by Flemish counts, 201, 205-17, 410; relations with lay authority in Brabant, 218-221; patronage in Holland, 221-23; patronage by French crown, 224-233; and indulgences, 234-40; and interdict, 244-45; restrictions on property rights, 270-71; etymology, 430-38; pejorative connotation, 251, 429; difference in north and south, 430; hostility of magistrates, 273-75; interpretation of scripture, 319, 344, 366-67, 524, 531; and preaching, 341-44, 382, 412, 461; learning and literary activity, 365, 376-77, 380, 388-405; excessive zeal, 442-453; criticized for association with Dominicans, 452-53; motives for persecution of, 441-42, 477-78, 565, 566; property in Rhineland, 477-78, in Belgium, 477, 478-87; age qualification, 508; inquisition in Germany, 514, 557-78, 560-74; confiscation of property, 564-66, 567; physical description of beguinage, 479-80, 482-83; in Abbeville, 229; Aerschot, 184-85, 201, 221, 237, 239, 487 n, 542; Aix-la-Chapelle, 134, 164; Alkmaar, 548, 554; Alost, 201, 238, 486 n, 541; Amiens, 202, 229, 232; Amsterdam, 135, 138, 239, 266 n, 549-50; Anderlecht, 129 n, 134, 479; Antwerp, 128, 131 n, 134, 183-84, 201, 237, 272, 341, 411, 481, 541-42; Ardenburg, 169 n, 542, 544; Audenarde, 169 n, 542; Aunoit, 215; Basel, 129 n, 514; Berghes, 215; Bilsen, 167, 168; Bocholt, 131, 135; Bois-le-Duc, 202, 552; Borchloon, 487 n, 542; Brabant, 539-40; Braine, 215; Breda, 180-81, 222, 238, 542; Bruges, 86, 134, 169 n, 208, 212-13, 232, 410, 413 n, 414 n, 479, 487 n, 542; Brussels, 128, 134, 147-48, 176-80, 218-220, 244-45; 271, 272, 312, 414 n, 480, 482, 486 n, 539, 541; Budapest, 203; Caen, 232; Cambrai, 159, 215, 226, 230, 231, 342, 344, 429; Chartres, 232; Coblenz, 161 n, 204, 203 n, 340 n; Coesfeld, 161 n; Cologne, 64 n, 82, 87-88, 98-99, 123, 129, 152, 160, 161, 196, 204, 203 n, 245 n, 248, 249, 272, 273-75, 340 n, 349, 429, 432, 445, 478, 548; Corbie, 229; Courtrai, 134, 169, 208, 214-15; Crespy, 232; Damme, 169 n, 215, 542; Delft, 222, 397-99, 548, 551-52, 555; Deynse, 169 n; Diest (St. Catherine in the Field), 128 n, 135, 138, 146, 155, 169, 185-86, 202, 236-37, 273, 318, 338, 437 n, 487 n, 542, 543; Dordrecht, 222, 223, 548, 551, 555; Douai, 208, 215, 230, 541-42; Eindhoven, 549; Esslingen, 203 n; Eyck, 168; Frankfurt, 339; Ghent (St. Elizabeth), 123, 125 n, 128 n, 134, 138, 139, 148-49, 152, 153, 159, 169 n, 201, 205-207, 209, 213, 215, 216, 217, 224, 232, 238, 318, 410-11, 418 n, 429, 477 n, 479-80, 482, 483, 486, 543, 544-45, 546; (Ten Hoeye), 169 n, 208, 207 n; Ghistelles, 169 n; Goch, 478; Gorinchem, 549; Gouda, 135, 551, 553; Grathem, 168, 173-75; Gravenzande, 221-22, 238 n, 551; Groningen, 555; Haarlem, 222, 548,

549; Halle, 538; Hasselt, 168, 184, 336 n, 487 n, 542; Herenthals, 134, 140, 146, 202, 238, 318 n, 399; Herford, 161 n; Heusden, 549; Hocht, 168; Léau, 28, 169, 202, 239, 272, 386, 487 n, 542; Leiden, 135, 138, 266 n, 548, 550-51; Lens-Saint-Remy, 129; Liége, 71-72, 134, 135, 153, 168, 202, 236, 314, 335, 339, 432, 478 n, 483, 486 n, 542; (diocese), 162-63, 411, 568; Lierre, 128, 135, 180, 182-83, 221, 317, 415, 486; Liliendale, 222; Lille, 169 n, 201, 213-14, 215; Loon, 483; Looz, 169; Louvain, 112, 128, 157, 169, 170-73, 487, 542; Lübeck, 81 n, 139, 146, 295; Maestricht, 168, 486 n, 542; Mainz, 570 n, Malève, 169; Malines, 128, 152, 180, 181-82, 245, 381, 446, 479 n, 483; Mantes, 232; Marsberg, 131, 161 n; Marseilles, 374-75, 547; Melun, 232; Middelburg, 222-23, 552-53; Mons, 127, 135, 209-12; 215, 239; Mühlhausen, 565; Münster, 161; Namur, 69-70, 303-304; Nerehayn (Noirhat), 169; Nivelles, 64-68; 169, 239, 245, 325, 327, 330-32, 334, 424, 450-52, 483; Noordwijk, 555; diocese of Noyon, 547; Nürnberg, 203 n, 341 n; Oignies, 16, 19, 59-62, 543; Oostburgh, 169 n; Orléans, 230, 232; Osnabrück, 160; Oudheusden, 549; Paderborn, 160; Paris, 134, 202, 224-229, 239, 340, 343, 466, 471, 529, 545, 547, 548; in Picardy (Fins Amans), 135, 152, 418 n; le Quesnoy, 215; Rheims, 230-31, 445, 478, 547, 548; Rijnsburg, 549; Roermond, 487 n, 542, 543; Rotterdam, 550; Rouen, 229, 232; St. Omer, 230; St. Quentin, 232; St. Trond, 130, 132, 134, 152-53, 163, 169, 185-86, 245, 336-37, 418 n, 487, 542; Schiedam, 551; Senlis, 230, 232; Sens, 232; Sittard, 552; Stommeln, 353; Strasbourg, 82, 135, 139, 203-204, 248, 480, 532, 568, 569; in Sweden, 348-49; Termonde, 486 n, 541, 542 n; Thorembais-les-Beguines, 169, 175, 336 n; Tirlemont, 134, 136, 146 n, 167, 169, 175-76, 220-21, 239, 271, 478 n, 481, 487 n, 542; Tongres, 135, 137-38, 162, 163 n, 165, 166, 168, 169, 396, 481-82, 483, 485 n, 486, 542; Tournai, 135, 169 n, 233; Tours, 230; Trèves, 568; Turnhout, 169 n; Utrecht, 222, 551; Valenciennes, 134, 208, 215, 418 n, 541; Vienna, 203 n, 314, 316; Vilvorde, 163, 180, 183, 236, 237, 539-40; Wesel, 135, 480; Worms, 135, 531 n; Ypres, 128 n, 134, 201,

208, 213, 215; Ysendike, 169 n; Zie-rickzee, 222, 554; Zurich, 198 n. *See also* chastity, *mulieres religiosae, mulieres sanctae,* Swestriones.

Beguttae, 570

Bellevaux, OC, dioc. Besançon, 93 n

Benedict XII (1334-1342), 124, 132, 499, 536

Benedict, St. of Nursia, 188, 383-84, 451 n; order of, 33-34, 89 n, 90, 91, 107 n, 149, 207, 230, 296; nuns, 28 n, 91, 113, 141 n; rule of, 42, 64, 105, 161, 383-84, 451 n

Benigna, beguine and sister of Stommeln priest, 129 n, 423 n

Berengar, cardinal of Tusculum, 534

Bergamo, bishop of, 242

Berghes (Bergues), 208, 215

Berlière, U., 64, 109

Bernard, OP, 200 n

Bernard, Master, canon of Soignies, 211

Bernard of Besse, cited, 263

Bernard, St. of Clairvaux, 52, 76, 281, 291, 300, 325, 327, 374, 385, 392, 415, 423, 460; cited, 91, 377 n; on humanity of Christ, 150-51, 311, 318; on Hildegarde of Bingen, 282-83

Bernard of Fontcaude, 343

Bernard Gui, OP, inquisitor, 196, 197, 400 n, 434-45; cited, 192, 252, 435 n

Bernardine spirituality, 3, 52, 150, 225, 300, 310, 311, 320-21, 327. *See also* St. Bernard

Bertha vom Walde, beguine of Cologne, 204

Berthold, prior of Västerås, 350

Berthold of Regensburg, OFM, 77, 437 n, 440, 512

Berthold of Rohrbach, 559

Bertholet, J., 299 n

Berthout, Gilles, seignior of Malines, 113, 332

Berthout, Walter, seignior of Malines, 521

Besançon, archb. of, 530, 560

Béthune, J. 206 n, 216

Betto, archdeacon, 272

Béziers, 536

Bia von Regenstein, countess, 127 n, 129 n, 198 n

Bible: translation of, 142, 367, 388-90, 505; interpretation of, 319, 366-67

Biloke, la (Port-Saint-Marie), OC (N), 92, 111, 201, 205--207, 483

Bilsen. *See* beguines

Binche, 13 n. *See also* beguines

Binderen, OC(N) 114

Bingen, 571, 572. *See also* Hildegarde

Binzervyk, 172

Birlinger, A., 88

Bizoches, 433, 523, 536

Black Death, 266, 267, 370

Black Nuns. *See* Benedictine nuns

Blanche, countess of Champagne, 113

Blanche d'Avaugour (Avancourt), 401 n

Blanche of Castille, queen of France, 67, 351 n, 450

Blanke, John, burgher of Münster, 423 n

Blasius Boerii, tailor, 82 n

Bloemardinne of Brussels, 368, 490, 492-96

Bloemarts, Heilwijch, 491 n, 495 n

Boccamazzi, John, b. of Tusculum (1285-1309), 198 n, 199, 203 n

Bochet, Jacques, 426

Bocholt. *See* beguines

Boendale, Jan, 425, 465; cited, 235 n, 266

Bogards. *See* beghards

Bohemia, 498, 522 n

Bois-le-Duc ('Hertogenbosch), 270. *See also* beghards, beguines

Bolant, John, 566, 567, 568

Bologna, 36, 188, 190 n, 400, 536

Bonagratia of Bergamo, 358 n

Bonaventura, St. 316 n, 375 n, 460, 465; judgment of beguines and tertiaries, 259-60

Bonaventura of Parma, archb. **Ragusa** (1281-92), 238

Bonentant (Bonefant), William, OP, 352

Boni christiani, 5, 252

Boni homines, 437

Boni Pueri (Bons Enfants), 169, 246, 437, 458, 509

Boni Valeti, 246-47, 437, 458

Boniface VIII (1294-1303), 125 n, 162, 243, 244 n, 318, 430, 511

Boniface IX (1389-1404), 12, 132, 133, 176, 221, 268, 437 n, 569, 570, 571

Boniface, St. 373

Boniface, b. of Lausanne, 113, 177, 306-307, 417

Boniface, monk of Clairvaux and Villers, 334

Bonn, 41

Bonne-Esperance, OPr., 49 n, 50

Bonnes Femmes of Sainte Avoye, Paris, 228 n

Bonoeil, OPr., 102, 104

Borchloon. *See* beguines

Bordeaux: Dominican general chapter (1287), 355

Borloo, 338

Bosehans, beghard of Frankfurt, 368

Bosschere, Matthew, Antwerp beghard, 257

Bourges, council of (1286), 95

Bouton, Reginald, receiver of Paris, 227 n

Bouvignes, 485

Brabant, duchess of, 368. *See also* Alei-

da, Margaret of Flanders, Jeanne
Brabant, duchy of: mysticism of women,
439-41. *See also* beghards, beguines;
Antoine, Henry I, Henry II, Henry
III, John I, John II, John IV
Braem, Henry, canon of Tournai, 96,
543
Braem, Simon, 486
Braine l'Alleu, 108, 271. *See also* be-
guines
Brant d'Aiseau, knight, 10 n
Brauweiler, OSB, prior of, 348 n 352,
353
Breda. *See* beguines
Brehmer: cited, 81 n
Bremen, 558, 559, 561, 563, 564
Brethren of the Cross, 53, 55-58, 158 n,
235 n, 242 n, 297 n
Brethren of the Common Life, 131 n,
133, 396, 572, 573
Brethren of the Holy Ghost, 35 n
Bruel, parish of Ypres, 215
Brugelette, 13, 49 n, 60 n
Bruges, 111 n, 195, 455, 485, 544. *See
also* beghards, beguines
Brunnadern, OP (N), near Berne, 198 n
Bruno, 340 n
Brunswick, dukes of, 564
Bruso, Henry, father of Christine of
Stommeln, 98-99
Brussels, 91, 110, 113, 270, 443, 495, 502-
504. *See also* beghards, beguines,
Bloemardinne, Cellites, Terkisten
Budapest. *See* beguines
Bücher, Carl, 83, 84
Bulls, papal: *Ad audientiam nostram*
(1365), 560; *Ad ea quae*, 569, 572;
Ad perpetuam rei memoriam (1374)
567; *Cum de mulieribus* (1320), 180,
537, 569; cited, 540-41; *Cum vos incluse* (1244), 191 n; *Dilectos filios*
(1319), 537; *Dudum dilectis* (1320),
537; *Etsi animarum* (1254), 459; *Etsi apostolicae* (1319), 529, 534, 537;
Evangelice predicationis officium
(1252), 192; *Ex iniuncto* (1394), 571,
573; *Faciens misericordiam* (1308),
522; *Gloriam virginalem* (1233), 6,
157-59, 161; *Imminente nobis cura*
(1368), 562 n; *In agro dominico*
(1329), 356; *Inspirationis divinae*
(1239), 191 n; *Licet olim (1246)*, 192;
Nimis patenter (1227), 259; *Racio
recta non patitur*, 128, 133, 486,
536, 539, 573; *Religiosam vitam eligentibus*, 57; *Sancta Romana atque
universalis ecclesia* (1319), 57, 434,
430, 437 n, 532, 536, 537, 539, 541 n,
573; *Sedis apostolicae* (1396), 572;
Si ea quae (1322), 537; *Supra montem* (1289), 258; *Transiturus* (1264),

308, 309; *Unigenitus Dei filius*
(1290), 259
Burchard of Mansfeld, count, 89
Burga, widow of Conrad Metzer von
Hagenau, 94
Burgos, bishop of, 343
Burgundy, 52, 127 n, 224, 508, 546. *See
also* John, Philip the Bold, Philip the
Good
Buschius, Johannes, 572

Caen. *See* beguines
Caesarius of Heisterbach, 74, 106, 116,
122, 294-95, 298, 323, 324, 329, 444,
510; beguine origins in Nivelles, 62,
65, 106; on eucharist, 310-11; cited,
87, 122, 438, 461
Calixtus III (1455-58), 72, 74, 75, 76,
220, 388 n, 390
Callaey, F., 72, 435
Callebaut, A., 314
Calvin, John, 77
Camaldulensians, 91
Cambrai, 12, 108, 158, 163, 209, 219, 220,
231, 239, 481, 491, 501, 504, 507, 539,
540, 541. *See also* beguines, Godfrey
de Fontaines, Guillaume d'Avesnes,
Guy de Laon, Guy II de Colle
Medio, Guy IV de Ventadour, Hen-
ry of Berghes, Ingelram de Créqui
John III de Béthune, Jean V de
Gavre, Nicholas de Fontaines,
Philippe de Marigny, Pierre III de
Lévis-Mirepoix, Pierre d'Ailly Cam-
bre, la, OC (N), Brussels, 91, 113,
115, 307, 326, 382, 417
Cambron, OC, Mons, 115, 327
Camin, diocese of, 561
Camp (Kemp, Altencamp), OC, 296
Canivez, J. M., 106
Canonici S. Salvatoris, 36
Canterbury, council of 1236, 95
Cantica Canticorum, 300, 392, 414 n, 415
Cantimpré, Cantimpret. *See* Cambrai,
Mons
Carcassonne, 251, 252 n, 433, 537 n
Carmelites, 91, 225 n, 466, 473, 502, 503,
509 n, 518 n
Carthage, council of, 398
Carthusians, 34 n, 466
Cassart, William, 147
Catalonia, 433
Cathari, 252 n, 415, 436, 437 n, 442, 488.
See also Albigensians
Catharina, beguine, 138
Catherine de Vaux, 339
Catherine, widow of Lambert Borkenon,
60 n
Catherine, abb. of L'Olive, 48
Catherine, beguine of Brussels, 177

Catherine, St., 436-37
Catherine Bruusch, burgher of Ghent, 209
Catherine of St. John, beguine of Tongres, 138
Catherine, St. of Siena, 87, 377
Cecilia, 46 n
Celles, 54
Cellites (Cellebroeders), 266-69, 399
Châlons, bishop of, 491
Champagne, 46, 332, 508
Chapelle, la in Brussels, 268
Charles, ab. of Villers (1197-1209), 113, 326, 333
Charles IV, king of France (1322-28), 547
Charles V, king of France (1364-80), 500
Charles VII (1422-61), 228
Charles IV, emperor (1346-78), 250, 369, 370, 557, 561, 563-67
Charles V, emperor (1519-56), 367
Charles of Anjou, king of Naples, 375, 401, 467, 469
Charles of Westraaros, OP, 351
Charlotte of Savoy, 228
Chartres. See beguines
Chastity, continence, 3, 43, 72, 83, 86, 95, 121, 122, 123 n, 130-34, 137, 138, 139, 157, 159, 160, 205, 228, 239, 321, 399, 409, 412, 436, 507, 529, 540, 569, 573
Chaucer, 466
Chenois, 11 n
Chenoit, grange of Villers, 324, 326
Chrétien of St. Trond, abbot, 37 n
Christ, K., 417 n, 418 n
Christine von Königswinter, beguine, 340 n
Christine of Stommeln, beguine, 27, 87, 98-99, 200, 311, 344-55, 379-80, 396, 445
Christine, beguine at St. Trond, 337
Christine, beguine at St. Trond, 339
Christine (Mirabilis) of St. Trond, 33 n, 47, 200 n, 328, 380-81, 395
Christine vanme Schadelande, 558 n
Chronica Provinciae Argentinensis: cited, 529
Chronica Regia Coloniensis, 435-36
Chronicon Monasterii Afflighemiensis, 443
Chur, OP, prior of, 199
Cistercians: attitude to cura monialium, 5, 20, 50, 87, 102, 105-106, 112-19, 170, 189, 190, 200; nunneries, 3, 40, 47, 49 n, 52, 65, 89, 94, 122, 145, 200, 281, 282, 291, 295, 296-97, 299, 365, 393, 403, 448, 449; their spread, 105-119; their origins, 106; promoted by John of Nivelles, 44-45; incorporation of nunneries, 113-17;

interest in beguines, 68, 170-84, 225, 339-40, 438; adoption of rule of, 63, 90, 91, 105, 107 n, 113, 114, 322-323, 325, 328, 383, 448, 449; arctior vita of, 105, 113, 329, 386; concern for poor, 323-25; devotion to eucharist, 310, 320; cult of St. Ursula, 296-97
Cîteaux, 52, 200, 282, 283, 339; general chapter of, 91, 93 (1251); 309 n, 310, 312 (1313); 315 n (1261); 296 (1255)
Clairefontaine, OC, 107, 111
Clairlieu, 55, 56
Clairvaux, OC, 50, 91, 92, 107, 110, 113, 115, 300, 334, 335
Clapdorp, hospital in Antwerp, 542
Clara, beguine, 336 n
Claranna von Hochenburg, 405
Clareno, Angelo da, 401, 430
Clarissa Leonard, beguine of Malines, 98, 152, 376-77, 381, 446
Clarisses, Franciscan nuns, 34, 90, 145, 230, 401, 403, 532 n
Clemence, nun of Barking, 373
Clement IV (1265-68), 12, 163, 183, 194, 341, 470
Clement V (1305-14), 124, 133, 257, 309, 516 n, 523, 525 n, 526, 527, 531 n, 532, 572. See also Clementine decrees
Clement VI (1342-52), 93, 132, 245, 371, 486, 542, 558
Clementia, 326
Clementia de Sancto Spiritu, beguine of Tongres, 137-38
Clementine decrees, 129, 180, 190, 237, 247, 310, 312, 344, 366, 397, 409, 434, 496, 521-38, 548-49, 556, 561, 569; Cum de quibusdam mulieribus, 124, 133, 135, 344, 366, 514, 523-27, 530, 533, 534, 535, 572, 573; saving clause of, 135, 524, 526-27, 525; Ad nostrum, qui desideranter, 496, 561 572, 573; cited, 497-98, 526-27
Clutinc, Gautier, 148
Coblenz, 380, 558 n. See also beguines
Cocquiamont, 175
Coens, 431
Coesfeld. See beguines
Colette of Corbie, 229-30, 447
Collectio de Scandalis Ecclesiae, 319, 366
Colmar, 197, 198 n, 404, 405, 514, 515 n
Cologne, city, 58 n, 85, 87, 93, 99, 237, 327, 344, 518, 519, 558; archbishop, 8 n, 12, 37, 41, 268, 295, 516-20, 528, 559, 560, 561, 569; Dominican studium generale, 351, 358; cult of St. Ursula, 295-98; council of 1310, 94, 522; Dominicans in, 196, 346, 351, 380; flagellants in, 372. See also beghards, beguines, Conrad von Hochstaden, Dietrich II, Engelbert

von Berg, Frederick III, Henry of Mulnarken, Henry of Virnebourg, Sifrid II von Westerburg, Walram von Jülich
Como, canons regular in, 316 n
Congregation: definition, 124 n, 126 n
Conrad of Germany, 229
Conrad of Halberstadt, 358
Conrad von Hochstaden, archb. Cologne (1238-61), 203 n, 236, 296, 297, 304, 449
Conrad Metzer von Hagenau, 94
Conrad von Scharfenberg, b. of Metz (1212-1224), 188
Conrad II von Weinsberg, archb. of Mainz (1391-96), 571
Conrad of Megenberg, 246 n, 366
Conrad of Urach, ab. of Villers (1209-14), then cardl., 44, 161, 333
Conrad of Würzburg, 402
Constance: diocese of, 92, 403, 548, 558; council of, 557, 573
Constance de Saint-Jacques, 228
Constantin of Erfurt, 559
Constantinople: Cistercians in, 52 n
Conversae: and Premonstratensians, 101; and Cistercians, 107, 116, 117, 145, 184; relations to beguines, 121, 125, 445
Conversi, 10, 100, 107, 113, 124-25, 170, 200, 244, 246, 258, 261, 323, 324, 327, 333, 434, 451, 509
Coppe van der Lane, 549
Coquennune, 433
Corbie. See beguines
Cordiele, Jean, 543
Cornelius, William, 488-90, 506
Corner, Hermann, 565
Cornoz, Antoine, 109
Coron, bishop of, 248
Corpus Christi, feast of, 299, 300, 302 n, 303, 309; institution, 305-10; roots in diocese of Liege, 310-19. See Juliana of Cornillon
Corsendonck at Herenthals, 496
Cortessem, 166
Court, Gilbert de la, 216
Court, Pierre de la (Utenhove), 216
Courtrai. See beguines
Couture-Saint-Germain, 107 n
Couturelle, 11
Coyroux (Coiroux), dioc. Limoges, 106
Crespin, church of, 110
Crespy, See beguines
Crete, 56
Crokevilain, Jean, 214
Crombach, H., 296
Crusade, fifth, 17, 21; fervor, 4, 55, 161
Cuesmes, parish of, 209, 210
Culm, diocese of, 555, 558 n
Cura monialium, 37 n, 115, 116, 120,

170, 187, 189, 191, 193, 195, 199, 321; Premonstratensian concern, 101-105; Cistercian interest, 105-119; Dominican concern, 189-204
Cyprus, 56

Dabenton, Jeanne, 500
Dacia, 308, 345. See also Peter
Damage, Henry, burgher of Liége, 153
Damietta, 17, 21, 25
Damme. See beguines
Dancers, 501, 567
Dante, 427
Dauphiné, 501 n
David von Augsburg, 403, 439
David of Dinant, 500
Deleville, Gervais, at Douai, 230
Delft. See beguines
Demarteau, 394
Denifle, H., 36
Denys du Moulin, b. of Paris (1439-47), 228
Denys de Vedrin, 70
Des Marez, G., 249
Deventer, 572
Devotio moderna, 73, 572
Deynse. See beguines
Diana, 190 n, 402
Diedala. See Tiedela
Diego, b. of Osma, 192
Diepenbeek, 112, 336 n
Diessenhofen, dioc. Constance, 203 n, 403, 404 n
Diest, 97, 167, 267. See also beguines
Dietrich II, archb. Cologne (1414-63), 573
Dietrich von Freiburg, 359
Diewer, 399
Dignard of Halle, 208
Dijon, 106
Dinant, 54, 485
Dionysius the Areopagite, 463
Dionysius of Chartreux, 378
Dirk VI, count of Holland (1122-57), 284
Dirk of Sassenheim, 549
Disibodenberg (Disenberg), 281, 290
Dithmar, Master, priest of Frankfurt, 96 n
Doberan, OC, near Rostock (dioc. Schwerin), 296 n
Dol, bishop of, 331
Dolcino, 498 n
Dominic, St., 55, 188, 189, 191, 192, 252 n
Dominicans, 7, 14, 16, 18, 34, 36, 88, 89, 90, 92, 161, 169, 200-02, 208, 291, 294, 423, 455, 466, 502, 504, 509 n; and exempla, 28; rule of, 57, 58, 187; hostility to women, 37 n, 116, 187, 189-92, 341-43; aims of, 187-88; and

learning, 187-89, 306, 374, 399-405, 518; in Liége, 38, 89, 169, 188, 306; incorporation of nunneries, 191-196; frequency of nunneries, 195-97; prevalence in Germany, 195-200, 203-204; interest in beghards, 256; and Ghent beguines, 201, 205, 216; preaching in beguinages, 225, 341-44; *conversi* and beguines, 125 n, 200 n; *conversi* and beghards, 261, 276, 515 n; opposition to Franciscans, 198 n, 345, 358 n; hostility to, 200-201, 472, 519; criticized by Guillaume de Saint-Amour, 458, 459, 460-61, 464; and beguine spirituality, 341-361, 400; interest in Corpus Christi, 300, 306-07, 309 n, 311; and Eckhart, 355-61; as inquisitors, 501, 558, 560-68. *See also* beguines
Donauwörth, 404
Doorezeele, OC(N), 109
Dordrecht. *See* beguines
Douai, 297. *See also* beguines
Douceline, St., de Digne, of Marseilles, 374-75, 400, 420, 547
Doumont, 13
Drulin, Gilles, bailli of Mons, 127 n
Drutlindis, beguine at Frankfurt, 339
Ducanech, Marie, 501
Dude Lelarge of Rheims, 230
Dunes, les, OC, 297
Duns Scotus, 518-19
Dupont, Nicholas, 70 n

Eadburg, abb., 373
Eaucourt (Aidicurte), 91
Eberbach, OC, 292
Eberhardini, 511, 512
Ebner, Christine, 404, 446
Ebner, Margaret, 404
Eckhart, Meister, 344, 355-61, 368, 392, 454, 519, 525; trial of, 356-59, 496, 558 n
Edmund, b. of *Turonensis:* identification, 236
Eename, abbot of, 545
Egeno von Stoffen, 92 n
Eggaerts, Cille, 549, 551
Egmond, abbey of, 554
Eichstätt, council of (1280), 510, 513, 514; bishop of, 525 n. *See also* Reimboto
Eindhoven. *See* beguines
Einsiedeln, OSB, 385
Eisleben, Saxony, 374, 403
Ekardus, OP prior in Frankfurt, 358
Elizabeth, beguine of Cologne, 340
Elizabeth, beguine, 348 n
Elizabeth, Duchess, 309

Elizabeth, abb. La Bilōke, 205
Elizabeth, countess of Schwarzburg, 89
Elizabeth, superior of Amiens beguinage, 202, 229
Elizabeth of Alost, beguine, 486
Elizabeth of Asche, beguine at Brussels, 219
Elizabeth de Bierbais, abb. of Nivelles, 67
Elizabeth de Berge, 482 n
Elizabeth de Gravio, 44 n, 64, 65, 334
Elizabeth of Léau, beguine of Brussels, 179
Elizabeth de Luzheim, beguine, 340 n
Elizabeth de Merbes, 13
Elizabeth Krich, beguine, 340 n
Elizabeth of Schönau, 281, 296, 344
Elizabeth of Spalbeek, 98
Elovsson, John, knight of Teutonic Order, 349
Elsbeth von Begenhofen, 355
Elysabet de Pollaer, beguine, 479 n
Emicho, bishop of Speier (1314-1328), 548
Emma d'Aiseau, beguine, 61 n, 137
Emmeloth (Grimelothe), beguine of Nivelles, 65, 321-22
Emo von Wittewierum, OPr., 253
Engelbert de la Marck, b. of Liége (1345-63), 13, 163 n, 543
Engelbert von Berg, archb. of Cologne (1216-1225), 294
Engelbert Desbois, b. of Namur, 18 n, 19 n
Engelbert, Françoys, canon of Liége, 543
Engelbert von Strasbourg, provincial OP of Germany, 191
Engelswendis, wife of Adam de Borloo, 338
Engelthal, OP (N), dioc. Eichstätt, 99, 203 n, 404
England, 90, 106, 251, 310
Epernay, 113
Epinlieu, OC (N), near Mons, 49 n, 108
Erald de Rammery, 113
Erard de la Marck, b. of Liége, 268
Erart de Valéri, 469
Erbault, 14
Erfurt, 421, 496, 498, 561, 562, 563
Ermentrude, founder of La Biloke, 32
Ermentrude, inmate of Cornillon, 305
Ermesinde, widow of Thibaud de Bar, 111
Esslingen. *See* beguines
Eudes, prior of OP at Rheims, 230
Eudes de Nevers, 469
Eudes de Vaudemont, b. of Toul (1192-97), 506
Eufemia von Butzheim, beguine, 339 n
Eugenius III (1145-53), 75, 158, 282-83, 294 n

Eugenius IV (1431-47), 176, 221, 264, 268
Eustache, monk, 289
Eustache, monk of Cambron, 216
Eustache III, lord of Le Roeulx (1190-1210), 49
Eustache IV (1210-21), 49, 50
Evangelium aeternum, 434, 459, 467
Eve, widow, 69
Eve, recluse of St. Martin's at Liége. 300, 304, 306, 308-09, 332
Everwinus of Helffenstein, prior of Steinfeld, 76, 460
Evrard of St. Quentin, OP, 342
Exempla, 28-29, 315
Extraregular, 120, 121-40; definition of, 121, 131-32
Eyck. *See* beguines

Faber, Arnold, echevin of Aerschot, 185
Fabri, Pierre, 518 n
Falcon de Lampage of Pistoia, 239
Falemby, 45 n
Feminine religious movement, 3, 44, 47, 48, 71-72, 109, 110, 197, 200, 201, 224, 236, 247, 320, 326, 329, 365, 400, 401, 409, 433
Ferrand, count of Flanders (1212-33), 111, 206, 208
Ferrara, 243 n, 245 n
Ferricus de Clugny, b. of Tournai (1473-83), 238 n
Filia Syon. See Lamprecht von Regensburg
Filles-Dieu, 26 n, 232, 466, 472, 509
Fins Amans in Picardy, 135, 152, 413, 418, 443
Flagellants, 77, 267 n, 370-72, 501, 557, 566, 567. *See also* Penitential brotherhoods
Flanders, 6, 52, 205-17, 242, 251, 295, 433, 508. *See also* Baldwin IX, Ferrand, Guy de Dampierre, Jeanne, Louis de Male, Louis de Nevers, Margaret, Philip of Alsace, Robert III de Béthune
Flines, OC (N), 112, 297
Floreffe, OPr, 15 n, 18 n, 38, 39 n, 43, 62, 64, 103 n, 443, 449 n
Florence: Dominican chapter of, 194 (1257), 309 n (1321)
Florennes, OSB, 286
Floris IV, count of Holland (1222-34), 551
Florival, OC (N), 108, 110, 112 n, 114, 152, 386, 447 n
Foec, Everard, dean of St. Salvator at Utrecht, 133, 573
Foigny, OC, 38
Foix, count of, 416

Folquin, Friar, 351
Fontenelles, OC (N), 50, 102, 109-10, 115, 156
Fontevrault, 101
Fosses, OPr, 8 n, 9, 11, 12, 305, 334, 485
Foucard de Rochechouart, b. of Noyon (1317-30), 547
Foukiers, Jakèmes (Jacques) of St. Omer, 250
Foulques of Ghent, 32
Foulques de Neuilly, 26-27, 31, 41
Foulques of Toulouse, 4, 21 n, 55, 144, 151, 228, 314, 330, 413, 415-16, 433, 443; admiration for Liége, 312, 415-16
Francesco d'Ascoli, OFM, 358 n
Francis, St. of Assisi, 20, 35, 51, 97, 120, 150, 257, 258, 318, 319, 324, 375, 396, 434, 435, 441, 447, 465 n, 529, 530, 553; and eucharist, 312-14
Franciscans, 7, 30, 31, 35, 36, 60 n, 70, 81, 88, 89, 116, 144, 151, 169, 196 n, 229 n, 250, 255 n, 256, 263-64, 267, 291, 294, 311, 316 n, 328, 423, 440-41, 466, 472, 509 n, 514, 548; and beguines, 121, 146, 179, 213, 219, 228, 318, 374-75, 400, 401, 415, 453, 526-28, 530-31, 532, 547, 553, 555; tertiaries, 162, 257-65, 276, 318, 526, 529-30; and beghards, 345-46, 514, 558; *conversi* and beghards, 261; *conversi* and beguines, 125 n, 200 n; aberrations of, 459, 466-67; hostility to Dominicans, 198 n, 345, 358 n; attacked by Guillaume de Saint-Amour, 458-60; imitation of primitive church, 30, 141 n, 142, 391; Spirituals, 82, 247 n, 392, 401 n, 433-35, 442, 433, 434, 515, 535, 547. *See also* Fraticelli
Francke, K., 479 n
Franco d'Archennes, 447
Franco, prior of OP in Louvain, 202
Frankengrünerin, Magdalena, 405
Frankfurt, 82, 84 n, 85, 88, 339, 357, 558 n
Fraticelli, 246 n, 392, 430, 433, 439, 497 n, 520, 523, 536, 541, 566, 567
Frauenfrage, 3, 20, 40, 101, 116, 149, 200; definition of, 83-84, 86
Frederick, OP, 532
Frederick, Yolanda's brother, 449
Frederick Barbarossa, 54, 282
Frederick II (1215-50), 37 n, 113, 307, 414 n, 417, 505, 507 n
Frederick III, archb. of Cologne (1372-1414), 570
Frederick III of Blankenheim, b. of Utrecht (1393-1423), 573
Frederick de Erstheim, 204
Frederick of Hapsburg, 525

Frederick I of Sicily (1296-1337), 535
Frederick II of Siereck, b. of Utrecht (1317-1322), 129 n, 318, 553, 554
Free Spirits, 137, 248, 252 n, 360, 366, 454, 488, 491, 492, 501, 502, 509, 515, 516, 521, 523, 525-27, 531, 537-38, 559, 564, 567, 572; literary activity, 368-70; tenets, 496-504. See also beghards, Swestriones, Turlupins
Freiburg, 196, 197
Freidank, 402, 465
Friars Minor, See Franciscans
Friars Preachers. See Dominicans
Frideswide, beguine, 338
Friedrich I von Lichtenberg, b. of Strasbourg (1299-1305), 524 n
Friedrichshafen, 198 n
Friends of God. See Gottesfreunde
Friesland: Franciscan tertiaries, 548
Fritzlar: synod of 1244, 507; of 1259, 509
Fundatio Pitantiarum Vini Religiosorum Oigniacensium, 15, 16, 17, 121 n
Funk, Ph., 9 n, 22, 36, 39
Furnes, 492, 541 n

Gallén, J., 344
Gallicanism, 469
Gallus von Neuhaus, OP, 498
Garin, inquisitor, 520
Garin Goujon, canon of St. Symphorien, 231
Gaud, 232
Gaudentes, 247 n, 401
Gautier, ab. of Cîteaux, 339
Gautier de Coincy, 145, 518-19, 456-57; 463; cited, 424
Gebeno, prior of Eberbach (Baden), 292-93
Gebweiler, 405 n
Gela, Abond's sister, 322
Gembloux, OSB, 281, 286, 287. See also Guibert
Gempe, 38
Genoa, 17, 36, 536
Geoffrey of Beaulieu, 202, 224, 225, 230, 341, 412
Geoffroi de Sergines, 469
Gerald de Malemort, archb. Bordeaux (1227-1259), 253
Gerard, beghard, 368
Gerard, OP, at Liége, 306
Gerard, OFM, 395
Gerard, canon of N-D. at Namur, 186
Gerard, b. Vladislav (1301-1323), 555
Gerard, count of Looz, 111
Gerard, lord of Voorne, 293
Gerard, priest of Nivelles, 46 n
Gerard Aelbrechts, curé of Brussels beguinage, 147 n

Gerard van Blanklaar, 268
Gerard de Frachet, 528-29; continuer cited, 529
Gerard of Gingelom, 221
Gerard von Greifen (de Griffon), 348 n, 352, 380
Gerard de Huldenberg, canon of Nivelles, 66
Gerard de Marbais, castellan of Brussels, 11 n
Gerard de Momalle, canon of St. Denis at Liége, 19 n
Gerard of Rheims, OP, 16, 18
Gerard Poitevin, 168
Gerard de Porta (vander Poorten), 175 n
Gerhard von Wesel, 273
Gerhard, Friar, 441
Gerhard I, archb. Mainz (1251-59), 509
Gerhard II von Eppenstein, archb. Mainz (1288-1305), 96 n, 124, 513
Gerlach, hermit, 285
Gerson, Jean, 367-68, 369, 378, 430, 454, 501, 557, 573 n; cited, 367 n, 368 n, 378-79, 452
Gertrude the Great, 374
Gertrude, founder of White Cloister in Coblenz, 203
Gertrude, friend of Arnulf of Brussels, 326
Gertrude, Christine's sister, 354
Gertrude, sister of John of Stommeln, 353
Gertrude, beguine, 137
Gertrude, Barthélemy's wife, 386
Gertrude, St. Grimoald's sister, 373, 424, 431
Gertrude, beguine of Anderlecht, 479 n
Gertrude, beguine of Nivelles, 65
Gertrude, wife of Thierry II of Walcourt, 45
Gertrude of Helfta, 318
Gertrude von Königshofen, 198 n
Gertrude de Marlemont, 11 n
Gertrude van Oosten, 397-99, 552
Gerungus, provisor of Antwerp beguinage, 184
Gerunts, Laurens, prior of Groenendael, 496
Gervasius of Angers, 357 n
Gervasius of Prémontré, abbot, 104
Gesta Abbatum Trudonensium. 124, 337
Gesta Monasterii Villariensis, 320, 323, 429
Gesta Trevirensium Archiepiscoporum, 505
Geva, abb. St. Cecilia of Cologne, 353, 354
Ghent: memorandum of 1328, 83, 146, 544-45. See also beghards, beguines

Ghilsen, Robert, priest of Grathem be-
    guinage, 175 n
Ghisel de Huselt, beguine, 137
Ghistelles. *See* beguines
Ghovelingen, parish in St. Trond, 336
Gielemans, John, 34 n, 129, 376, 399
Gilbert of Mont Cornillon, 47
Gilbert de la Porrée, 281
Gilbert of Tournai, 122, 366-67
Gilbertines, 193
Gile of Emines, 69
Gilles, OP, at Liége, 306
Gilles Bofis, 19 n
Gilles Cantor, 502-04
Gilles of Liége, OP (Gilles de Orpio),
    342
Gilles li Muisis, ab. St. Martin's at
    Tournai, 77, 371 n 424-29
Gilles of Orléans, OP, 342
Gilles d'Orval, 71 n, 388-89, 431, 435
Gilles de Rochefort, 44, 45
Gilles de Saint-Trond, 263
Gilles de Tournai, canon, 61 n
Gilles of Walcourt, 8, 9 n, 12, 15, 24, 37,
    59, 61, 447
Gilliodts-van Severen, 249
Gisele of Brussels, 91, 113
Gislebert de Mons, 73, 75
Glons, 43
Gmünd, 198 n
Gnostic-Manichean criticism, 4, 252 n,
    310, 488, 505
Gobert d'Aspremont, knight, 321-22,
    324, 332, 335
Goch. *See* beguines
Godefridus Roy de Slusa, Aerschot
    echevin, 185
Godefridus de Vierson, 375 n
Godeschalk, OP at Liége, 202
Godeschalk, pastor of Brussels beguines
    218 n
Godfrey, 297
Godfrey IV of Breda, 180
Godfrey, ab. Vicogne, 541 n
Godfrey, castellan of Brussels, 328
Godfrey, dean of St. Servais of Maes-
    tricht, 166 n, 167, 176
Godfrey, patron of Oignies, 13
Godfrey, prior of Brauweiler, 352
Godfrey, prior of Mont Cornillon, 301
Godfrey the Sacristan, 334
Godfrey de Banco, dean of St. Pierre at
    Louvain, 172
Godfrey de Fontaines, b. Cambrai
    (1220-1237), 159, 231
Godfrey of Maestricht, archdeacon of
    Liége, 165
Godfrey of St. Disibode, 377
Godfrey, b. Utrecht (1156-78), 283-84
Godfrey Werde, OP, 352
Godfrey Pachomius, 65, 323, 327, 328

Godfried, b. Passau (1283-85), 513
Goede kinder, 246, 261. *See* beghards
Götz von Hohenloch, knight, 94
Goliardi, 510, 511
Gontier de Rethel, 231
Goreaux, 42
Gorinchem. *See* beguines
Gorren, Jean, 264
Gorze, 103 n
Gossuin de Bossut, 63, 113, 429
Gossuin of Liége, OP, 16, 18
Gottesfreunde, 356, 404, 453-55; attitude
    to beghards, 454-55
Gotteshäuser, 411, 537
Gottfried of Neuburg, abbot, 93
Gouda. *See* beguines
Gouthal (Goutalle), Nivelles parish, 66
Grabow, Matthew, OP, 573 n
Grammont, Augustinian abbey, 34, 545
Grandpré, OC, 114 n, 449 n
Grathem. *See* beguines
Gravenzande. *See* beguines
Greece, 52
Gregorian reform, 120, 141, 247, 436
Gregory the Great, 506
Gregory IX (1227-41), 12, 14, 22, 25, 30 n,
    34 n, 38, 55, 56, 57, 104 n, 162, 191,
    231, 236, 253; and beguines, 6, 157-
    59, 160-61, 507, 508; friend of Jac-
    ques de Vitry, 21, 25, 37, 313-14;
    and Franciscans, 258-59, 313-14
Gregory X (1271-76), 12, 65-66, 245, 335,
    487
Gregory XI (1370-78), 268, 500, 501, 548
    558, 562, 563, 564, 565-67, 568, 569,
    570, 571
Greta, beguine of Utrecht, 338
Greteke Berghes, Lübeck beguine, 139
Greven, J., 7, 22 n, 40 n, 83, 120, 159,
    170, 431
Greving, J., 478
Grimberghen, OPr, 179 n, 443
Grimelothe. *See* Emmeloth
Grimoald, 373
Groenendael, 493, 496
Groeninghe-lez-Courtrai, OC, 111
Groningen, 548. *See also* beguines
Groote, Gerard, 34 n, 73, 396, 572; cited,
    126
Grosseteste, Robert, b. Lincoln, 144
Grundmann, H., 81, 88, 160, 249, 313 n,
    400, 401, 402 n
Gudule, St., collegiate church in Brus-
    sels, 373
Guelderland, 548
Guibert, ab. Florennes and Gembloux,
    281, 286-91, 377
Guido, cantor at Cambrai, 46
Guido, Master, 11, 46, 66
Guillaume. *See also* William
Guillaume, priest of Hakendover, 176

Guillaume, provost of church of Mons, 211
Guillaume of Afflighem (of Malines), ab. St. Trond, 328, 393, 394
Guillaume d'Auxerre, OP, 342
Guillaume d'Avesnes, b. Cambrai (1286-96), 9 n, 11, 179 n, 183, 255 n, 512, 521
Guillaume de Beaujeu, 469
Guillaume de Champagne, archb. Rheims (1176-1202), 242
Guillaume de Harcombour, 375 n
Guillaume de Harenton, 111
Guillaume Hugo, priest of Louvain beguinage, 171-72
Guillaume de Joinville, 37 n
Guillaume de Miletonne, 375 n
Guillaume de Nangis and continuer, 228 n, 330, 331, 450-51, 490, 528, 535
Guillaume de Paris, OP, inquisitor, 491
Guillaume de Puy-Laurens, 21 n, 28 n
Guillaume de Ryckel, ab. St. Trond, 90 n, 185, 186, 254, 336-37
Guillaume de Saint-Amour, 123, 200-201, 225, 228, 423 n, 456-64, 466, 467, 468
Guillaume of St. Hubert, 43
Guillaume de Valloires, 115 n
Guillaume de Ventadour, b. Tournai (1326-33), 543
Guillelmites, 466
Guillerma Gamelina, 229
Guion de Cressonessart, 492
Guiot, Jacob, 230
Gumbert, Master, 326
Gunnesen, Johannes, 348 n
Guntram, prior of St. Trond, 383
Guy d'Avesnes, b. Utrecht (1301-17), 522
Guy de Boulogne, b. Tournai (1300-24), 217
Guy II de Collemedio (Colmieu), b. Cambrai (1296-1306), 220, 491, 541
Guy de Dampierre, count of Flanders (1278-1305), 201, 206 n, 209 n, 213, 215, 216, 217, 256, 410, 427, 487 n, 512
Guy (Guiard) de Laon, b. Cambrai (1238-47), 31 n, 183, 209-10, 231, 304, 306, 328, 489
Guy of Montpellier, 485 n
Guy of Preneste, cardl., 54, 74, 112 n, 506
Gyrovagi, 325, 525
Gijskens, Joannes Constantius, 549

H. de Surs, chaplain of Malines beguines, 181
H. Traiectensis canonicus, 284
Haarlem. See beguines

Hadewig, recluse of St. Remacle, 333
Hadewig von Kesselheim, beguine, 340 n
Hadewigis, sister of John of Stommeln. 353
Hadewigis of Nivelles, 387
Hadewijch, 64, 292, 317 n, 365, 368, 392, 396, 492 n, 495, 508
Hagenrüti, 385
Haghe, 209 n
Hagiography, 395; Cistercian, 314, 324, 374, 393, 410, 414, 445; antiheretical flavor, 4, 54, 160, 311, 416-17; Dominican 374, 393, 410, 445
Hakendover, parish, 176
Halberstadt, 198 n, 235 n. See also Albrecht III
Halle, 403. See also beguines
Hallman, E., 236
Haluwidis, mother of Baudechon de Latuit, 336 n
Hamiage, Michael, 226 n
Hanar de St. Barthélemy, 339
Harding, Stephen, 106
Hartmann, John, beghard, 496, 498, 561
Hartwig, J., 81 n
Hasius, Herman, 53 n
Hasselt in Limburg, 65 n, 267. See also beguines
Hauck, A., 81 n, 86
Hawide de Charnoit, 61 n, 137
Hawide le Gehotte, 61 n, 137
Hawidis, abb. Fontenelles, 110
Hawidis, beguine in Nivelles, 64
Heesbeen, 549
Heila of Lille, wife of Daniel Taillefin, 215
Heilewidis de Zone, beguine 479 n
Heilwige de Foro, 180
Heilwigis, 329
Heinrich III von Daun, b. Worms (1318-19), 531
Heinrich von Nördlingen, 385, 404
Heinrich von Rumerschein, canon of St. Peter's, 385
Heisterbach, OC, 296, 339 n, 340 n
Helborgis, beguine of Gothland, 349
Heldewidis (Helingis) at Willambroux, 413 n
Helewide, beguine of Brussels, 177
Helfta, OC (N), 89, 318, 374, 379, 403
Hellin of Launoy (de Alneto), 109, 110
Helmont, OC, 114, 115
Helrinricus, OP, 351
Heluise de Landrecies, 212
Heluwidis, beguine of St. Trond, 336 n
Helwide, recluse of St. Syr in Nivelles, 334
Helwide, recluse, 66
Helwide Blandine, beguine, 339

Helwide, recluse, 46
Helwidis de Angulo, 482 n
Hendricken, priests of, 174
Henricus dictus de Fossa, OP, 558 n
Henricus de Geest, monk of Villers, 334
Henrik, b. Linköping, 349
Henry, archdeacon of Liége, 115
Henry, priest, 353
Henry I, duke of Brabant (1190-1235),
    9 n, 11 n, 13, 38 n, 43, 108, 112, 171,
    175, 323
Henry II, duke of Brabant (1235-1248),
    111, 114
Henry III, duke of Brabant (1248-1261),
    184, 185, 198 n, 218, 221
Henry, king of Germany, 37, 506
Henry VII of Luxemburg, emperor, 427,
    525
Henry I, archb. Mainz (1142-53), 282
Henry I von Tanne, b. Constance
    (1233-48), 196 n
Henry, provost of Fosses, 11
Henry, dean of Christianity of Brussels,
    147 n
Henry, lord of Breda, 180, 222
Henry, Friar (OP) of Cologne, 195, 197
Henry, pastor of St. Symphorien, 69
Henry, prior of OP convent at Basel, 402
Henry, prior of OP convent at Cologne,
    402
Henry, provost of Holy Apostles at
    Cologne, 161
Henry de Agro, 538, 560, 561, 562 n
Henry of Albano, cardl., 73
Henry of Badelinghem, Master, canon
    of Tournai, 207
Henry of Beaumont, archdeacon of
    Liége, 14 n, 15 n
Henry of Berghes, b. Cambrai
    (1480-1502), 127
Henry of Beitbur (Bethbure). OP, 352
Henry of Béthune, canon of Furnes,
    492
Henry of Brussels, 297
Henry de Ceva, 535-36
Henry of Coblenz, 568
Henry de Dreux, 37 n
Henry of Ghent, 393
Henry III of Guelders, b. Liége (1247-
    74), 57, 58, 65 n, 70 n, 162, 164, 165,
    166 n, 167-68, 171, 174, 176, 180,
    184, 186, 273 n, 302 n, 303, 308, 411,
    414 n
Henry de Ham, 11 n
Henry de Jauche, provost and archdea-
    con of Liége, 76
Henry II of Leyen, b. of Liége
    (1145-64), 73, 74
Henry of Mierlaer, archdeacon of
    Utrecht, 554
Henry Mimique (Mundikinus), 505

Henry of Mulnarken, archb. Cologne
    (1225-37), 37
Henry of Nellingen, deacon, 203 n
Henry de Ophem, 338
Henry de Santhoven, 250
Henry de Sincere, 353
Henry of Thalheim, OFM, 358 n
Henry of Utrecht, Master, 284
Henry de Vianden, b. of Utrecht
    (1250-67), 222
Henry of Virnebourg, archb. Cologne
    (1306-32), 94, 248, 356-57, 496, 516-
    20, 522, 560
Henry of Westhoven, 402 n
Henry van der Eeke, OP, 209
Herbaren van Riede, 549
Herbert aux Braies, canon of Rheims,
    231
Herckenrode, OC (N), 106 n, 107 n, 111,
    184, 383
Herenthals. See beguines
Herford. See beguines
Herlaimont, church at, 75 n
Herman, abbot of Floreffe, 75
Herman, deacon of Bonn, 41
Herman, episcopus Enensis (Henensis),
    239
Herman of Havelbrecht OP prior at
    Cologne, 348, 351, 353
Herman von Kesselheim, 340 n
Herman of Tournai, 101-102, 107, 116
Herman of Wisby, 348 n
Hermannus, becgardus de Sancto
    Gengulpho, 254
Hermann de Cervo, 98
Hermann von Hellstedt, 563
Hermann von Minden, OP provincial,
    92, 127 n, 129 n, 195 n, 196-99, 200 n,
    341 n, 342-43
Hermann von Rennenberg, subdeacon,
    249 n
Hermann de Summo, 567
Hertogendael. See Val-Duc
Herveus, OP, 357
Hespe, John, OP, 351
Hesse, 564
Hetwigis of Strasbourg, 203 n
Heusden, 549. See also beguines
Heverlin de Fooz, ab. St. Lawrence, 75
Heylewidis, 339
Hiddo, Friar (OP), 353 n
Hildegarde of Bingen, 102 n, 281-295,
    310, 311 n, 320, 344, 377
Hildesheim, 161; bishop of, 558 n, 561
Hilla, sister of Christine of Stommeln,
    354
Hilla von Berg (de Monte), 354, 355
Hilla von Kingidorp (Ingendorp), 354
Himmelskron, 92 n, 198 n
Himmelswonne, OP convent at Löwen-
    thal, 198 n

Himmerode, OC, 340 n, 446
Hinckaert, Gerelm, echevin, 495
Hinckaert, Jan, canon of St. Gudule, 495
Hocht, OC (N), 107 n. See also beguines
Hoeft, Matheus, echevin of Bruges, 260
Hoegaarden (Hoegaerde). See beghards
Holland, 195, 548-55; beguine spirituality in, 397-99; beghards in, 263. See also Albert I, Dirk VI, Floris IV, John I, John II, John of Bavaria, William II, William III d'Avesnes
Holtzhusin, Katherine, 405
Holy Ghost, order of, 485 n
Holy Ghost Table, 134 n, 137-38, 140, 148, 152, 271, 409, 484-86, 503, 510-11, 546. See also Terkisten
Homines Intelligentiae, 496, 502-504
Honorius III (1216-27), 12, 30, 38, 41, 56, 94, 112 155
Honorius IV (1285-87), 64 n, 89, 183, 193, 227
Hontsum, Zegerus van, 431
Hoornaert, H., 86
Hrothswitha, nun of Gandersheim, 373
Hubrecht, Jan, echevin of Bruges, 260
Hugh cantor of St. Martin's at Mainz, 290
Hugh, castellan of Ghent, 207
Hugh II, castellan of Ghent, 215, 216
Hugh of Besançon, canon of Paris, 492
Hugh de Celles, scholasticus of St. Paul's in Liége, 15 n
Hugh III of Châlons, b. Liége 1295-1301), 104, 162, 172, 238
Hugh of Fosses, 103
Hugh de Large, dean of cathedral at Rheims, 231
Hugh of Oignies, artist, 9, 11
Hugh of Pierrepont, b. of Liége (1200-1229), 3, 12, 13 n, 14 n, 37, 38-39, 42, 55, 188, 306, 313
Hugh of St. Cher, cardl., 147 n, 161, 165, 166, 178, 183 n, 188, 193-94, 334, 414; grants indulgences, 236-37; and Corpus Christi, 229 n, 306-08
Hugh of St. Victor, 34
Hugo, ab. of Egmond, 554
Hugo of Trimberg, 465
Hugo of Zabern, 568
Humbert de Romans, OP General (1254-63), 92, 193, 194, 198-99, 384; cited, 189, 263, 343; on beguines, 412, 421
Humiliati, 35, 81, 82, 88, 129, 141 n, 253, 433, 437 n, 442
Huy, 38, 39, 57, 58, 61 n, 70, 108 n, 111, 158
Huydecoper, Balthasar, 435

Ida, beguine of Diest, 338
Ida, beguine of Papsem, 480 n

Ida, friend of Hildegarde, 287
Ida, recluse, 323
Ida, recluse of Othée, 166 n, 339
Ida, sister of Bruno, 340 n
Ida de Boubers, founder of Abbeville beguinage, 229
Ida of Brussels, 329
Ida de Korpt, 338
Ida de Lathruy, 336
Ida of Léau, 98, 382-83, 387, 395, 402, 447-48
Ida of Louvain, 97, 151, 314, 315, 316, 317, 448
Ida of Nivelles, 63, 66, 98, 317, 327, 374, 387, 395, 483, 510
Ida de Rosen, 338
Ida de Wyneghem (van der List), 262
Ida Oliviers de Maillart, beguine of Tirlemont, 478 n
Igny, 335
Ilbenstadt, 286
Ile-de-France, 500
Ile-Duc at Gempe, OPr., 38
Imène, abb. Salzinnes, 297, 304, 305, 448
Imitatio Christi, 385
Indulgences, 12, 24, 68, 222, 227, 234-40, 299 n, 308
Ingeld, Prior (OP), 350
Ingelram II de Créqui, b. of Cambrai (1274-86), 181, 219
Innenheim, Strasbourg, 135, 204
Innocent II (1130-43), 158
Innocent III (1198-1216), 12, 35, 38, 41, 55, 57, 103-04, 154, 242, 243, 244 n 245 n, 343, 379, 414, 435, 485 n, 488, 506
Innocent IV (1243-54), 12, 50, 57, 58 n, 92, 94, 104 n, 114, 156, 161, 177, 183 n, 185, 191, 192, 193, 194, 203, 210, 231, 236, 244, 246 n, 303 n, 307, 351 n, 414 n, 445, 539 n
Innocent VI (1352-62), 558 n, 559
Innocent VIII (1484-92), 127
Interdict, 58 n, 65 n, 66, 156, 177, 181, 198 n, 220, 241-45
Isabella, Louis IX's sister, 97 n, 375-76, 401
Isabella of Aragon, 331
Isabella of Huy, beguine, 300, 303, 305, 306, 308
Isabella de Flecquières, founder of Cantimpré at Cambrai, 231
Isaberon, beguine of Rheims, 99
Iuthe, recluse at Malèves, 336 n
Iuthe de Molenbiscul, beguine, 336 n
Ivan, priest, 15 n
Ivan de Rèves, knight, 51-52, 108, 447
Ivette, abb. Herckenrode, 383
Ivette, recluse of Huy, 152, 322
Ivo, bishop of Chartres, 452 n

Ivo de Vaernewijck, knight, 217

Jacob, ab. of St. Bernard, 181
Jacob of Andernach, OP, 352
Jacob of Soest, inquisitor, 438 n, 571
Jacques de Bomal, ab. of Villers
(1276-83), 321, 333
Jacques de Guise, 109-110, 208
Jacques (von Lothringen), b. of Metz
(1239-60), 453
Jacques de Morey, inquisitor, 500
Jacques de Vitry, 20-39; as bishop of
Acre, 5, 21, 23, 28, 38, 155-56, 432;
solicitation at papal court, 5-6, 20,
30, 47, 59, 145, 154-57, 428; zeal for
Oignies, 11, 12, 13, 16-18, 21, 24, 27,
33, 37-38, 236; and Cistercians, 20,
33, 52, 105, 106, 107-09, 112, 119;
interest in Belgium, 20-25, 27, 37-
39, 98; bridge between Franciscans
and beguines, 20, 34-35, 97, 145,
150, 312-14, 416, 434; birth and na-
tionality, 21, 27 n; fear of heterodoxy, 20, 25, 30, 54; auxiliary bishop of Liége, 20, 21, 37; and fifth
crusade, 20-21, 25, 154-55; evaluation as preacher, 21, 28-29, 98; and
Paris, 21, 22, 26, 27, 33; attitude
to learning, 21, 25, 33; friend of
Gregory IX, 21, 25, 56; and exempla, 21, 22, 28-29; evaluation of religious orders, 21, 33-36, 90, 119,
130 n, 301 n; and vita apostolica, 21,
30, 42, 56, 121, 141, 142, 144-45,
416; interest in Aywieres, 22, 39,
108-09; friend of Lutgard, 24, 33 n;
on efficacy of relics, 24-25, 32, 38;
as a moralist, 25, 29, 30, 32, 52;
suspects excessive zeal, 26, 30, 49 n;
on clerical delinquency, 30-31, 461;
concern for mulieres religiosae, 32,
35-36, 97, 98, 154-57, 228, 295, 329,
416; compared with Thomas of Cantimpré, 32; praises Franciscan nuns,
34-35, 97; praises Humiliati, 35; on
Dominicans, 36, 190; friend of Hugh
of Pierrepont, 37-39; esteems John
of Nivelles, 42, 43, 45; friend of
Theodore of Celles, 56; deplores
restrictions on canonesses, 63, 96-
97; description of Premonstratensian sisters, 102-03, 104; election as
bishop, 154-155; VMO., 22, 24, 25,
29, 33, 41, 46, 52, 97, 120, 157, 312,
314, 329, 396, 397, 415, 443; cited,
144, 150-51
Jacques Pantaleon. See Urban IV
Jacques of Preneste, cardl., 183 n, 236
James, Abond's brother, 322
Jan de Goutsmet, 208 n

Jan van Polanen, 181 n
Jan Wautier de Heetvelde, 255 n
Jardinet, OC (N), 9 n, 45, 114, 115
Jauchelette, 107 n
Jean, Odilo's son, 72
Jean, pastor of Vyle, 339
Jean, ab. of Cîteaux, 68
Jean of Aerschot, priest of Louvain be-
guinage, 172
Jean d'Ais, canon of St. Aubain, 304
Jean V d'Arkel, b. of Liége (1364-78), 14
Jean de Coloma, priest, 263
Jean de Diepenbeek, pastor of St.
Quentin, 171
Jean de Dorsten, 263
Jean d'Enghien: bishop of Tournai
(1267-74), 213, 217; as bishop of
Liége (1274-81), 67, 162, 236 n, 335
Jean II d'Eppes, b. of Liége (1229-38),
14 n, 15 n, 38, 39, 111 n, 166, 306
Jean du Fayt, 371, 557
Jean IV de Flandre, b. of Liége
(1282-91), 68, 131, 309 n
Jean V de Gavre (Lytdekirche), b. of
Cambrai (1413-38), 220, 543
Jean de Gossignées, chaplain of N.D. in
Namur, 70
Jean VIII de Heinsberg, b. of Liége
(1419-55), 70, 163 n, 263-64
Jean de Hévillers, prior of Oignies, 10
Jean le Hieru, 211
Jean de Huy, ab. of Floreffe, 15 n
Jean de Longeville, friar (OP) at
Rheims, 230
Jean de Liége, OP, 342
Jean de Meerbeek, knight, 254
Jean de Meung, 99, 426, 456, 457, 473
Jean de Monsteruel, 208
Jean de Novo Lapide, dean of St. Ser-
vais, 265
Jean d'Orléans, OP, 342
Jean d'Orval, 115 n
Jean d'Outremeuse, 42 n, 370 n, 490 n
Jean de la Place, Master, 210
Jean de Montsoreau, b. of Tours
(1271-1285), 236 n
Jean IV 'T Serclaes, b. of Cambrai
(1378-88), 240
Jean de Soissons, canon of St. Pierre's
at St. Quentin, 547
Jean de Tollenz, canon of St. Quentin,
492
Jean de Vienne, 547
Jean Hauchin, archb. Malines, 173
Jean Joye, priest of Tongres, 138
Jean Wiart, 70
Jean Willame de Selh, canon of N-D. in
Namur, 70 n
Jeanne, beguine, 109
Jeanne d'Harcourt, 401 n
Jeanne, of Constantinople, countess of

Flanders (1202-44), 13 n, 48 n, 92;
patronage of beguines, 83, 159, 205-
09, 214, 221, 487; patronage of Cis-
tercians, 108, 111; patronage of Do-
minicans, 201; testament, 208-09,
213
Jeanne, duchess of Brabant, 147, 219-20,
221, 484
Jehan le Bel, 370 n, 371 n, 373
Jehan le Petit of Glabais, 68
Jehan le Sermonneur, 64
Jehanne la Bricharde, 228 n
Jehanne la Romaine, 228 n
Jehans li Beguins. See John of Nivelles
Jerome, St., 291, 385
Jerusalem, patriarch of, 309
Jescheren, pastor of, 185
Joachim of Flora, 294, 434, 459
Johannes de Schoenhovia, 493 n
Johannes Theutonicus, OP General
(1241-52), 166 n, 191, 192
John, Master, 345, 346, 353
John, ab. Gembloux, 287, 288
John, Master, pastor of Cantimpré, 211
John, prior of Cornillon, 305
John: office for Corpus Christi, 303 n,
307, 309, 374
John, pastor of Hakendover, 176
John, husband of Mary of Oignies, 11,
46
John, Gilles' brother, 8
John, Gilles' father, 9 n
John, Master, pastor of Stommeln, 380
John le Seneschal, provost of Corbie,
229
John, pastor of St. Martin's in Corbie,
230
John, prior (OP) at Ghent, 217
John, canon of Osnabrück, 160-61
John I, duke of Lotharingia, Brabant,
and Limburg (1261-94), 66, 68, 177,
270, 331; patron of beguines, 218-
19, 221, 480; patron of beghards,
254 n, 255 n, 256, 257, 276
John II, duke of Lotharingia, Brabant,
and Limburg (1294-1312), 68, 173,
255 n; patron of beguines, 220, 271,
484
John IV, duke of Brabant (1415-27), 220,
257, 546
John V of Bavaria, b. of Liége
(1390-1417), 18 n
John XXII (1316-34), 53, 123 n, 124, 128,
131, 248, 257, 397, 422, 430, 433 n,
434, 437 n, 477, 523, 533-37, 545, 548,
555, 558, 572; rehabilitation proceedings, 131-32, 411, 422, 486, 539-
41, 544, 569, 572; condemns
Eckhart, 356
John, Abond's brother, 322
John, ab. Afflighem, 328

John, ab. Heisterbach, 340 n
John, chaplain of St. Quentin Ten
Hove, 171
John, chaplain of St. Gilles' at Liége,
339
John, b. of Zürich, 561
John, b. of Vaison, 539
John, OP at Liége, 306
John, priest of Looz, 174
John, duke of Burgundy, 233
John of Alost, priest of Morseele, 180,
541 n
John II of Arzilières, b. of Toul
(1310-20), 525 n
John, count of Hainault (after 1299 also
count of Holland and Zeeland), d.
1304, 13 n, 210, 212, 305
John of Bavaria, count of Holland
(1418-25), 550
John of Béthune, b. Cambrai (1200-19),
41, 48 n, 49
John Bonus, 317 n
John of Brünn, 496, 498-500
John de Cervo, 570
John of Châlons, 491
John of Diest, chaplain of Count Wil-
liam II, 222
John II of Diest, b. of Lübeck
(1254-59), 238
John III of Diest, b. of Utrecht
(1322-41), 553
John of Dinant, 11 n, 45, 120
John of Dürbheim, b. of Strasbourg
(1306-28), 359, 369, 454, 486, 496,
524 n, 528-29, 531-34, 535 n, 537,
568
John of England, friar, 440 n
John of Gembloux, 290
John of Ghent, canon, 491
John of Lausanne, canon of St. Martin's
at Liége, 304, 306, 394, 395
John of Léau or Afflighem, 356 n
John de Liro, 26, 31, 40, 42, 44, 46-47,
59, 90, 120, 328, 394; mission to
Rome, 47, 156
John van Meerhout, monk of Diest, 495
John of Mussendorp, OP, 352
John II von Lichtenberg, b. of Stras-
bourg (1353-65), 561
John of Lutzemburg, 552
John III of Luxembourg, b. of Stras-
bourg, (1365-71), 560
John de Moneta, 561
John of Nassau, b. of Utrecht
(1267-90), 222
John of Nivelles, 7, 15 n, 17, 20, 26, 31,
40-45, 46, 48, 72, 110, 120, 152, 382,
394, 413; identification with Jehans
li Beguins, 44
John of Oestburg, ab. Les Dunes, 297
John of Schönau, 378

John of St. Trond, confessor at Parc-les-Dames, 393, 396
John of St. Victor, 529
John of Schadelant, OP, b. of Culm (1359-63), of Hildesheim (1363-65), of Worms (1365-71), of Augsburg (1371-73), 558-59, 561, 562
John of Stommeln, priest of beguines, 353, 445 n
John of Strasbourg. See John of Dürbheim
John of Vercelli, OP general (1264-83), 194
John of Wambaix, 141 n
John de Wardo, Master, 297
John of Winterthur, OFM: cited, 530-31
John of Witterzee, conversus, 324-25
John of Xanten, 41
John of Zanthove, 201
John Polinus, canon regular of Essoines. 342
John Scotus Erigena, 442
John Sersanders, 205 n
John Wasmod of Homburg, inquisitor, 496, 571-72
Joinville, 228, 335, 466
Jordan of Saxony, OP provincial of Germany, general (1222-37), 188, 190 n, 191, 195, 200, 402
Jotha de Strombeek, 483 n
Juliana of Cornillon, 4, 98, 297, 299-309, 312, 332 n, 333, 334-35, 374, 394-95, 396-97, 446
Jully-les-Nonnains, 106
Justice, Jean, 548
Jutta, widow of Waleram of Montjoie, 552

Katherina of Gebweiler, 404
Katharinental, OP (N), dioc. Constance, 203 n, 403
Kerling, Walter, 250, 369, 496, 561, 562, 563, 564, 565, 566
Klingenthal, OP (N), 404
Knights Hospitallers, 33 n, 534
Knights Templars, 33 n, 491, 522
Kothe, W.: cited, 89 n
Kriegk, G. L., 88
Kunigunde von Sulz, 196
Kunigunde, widow of Götz von Hohenloch, 94
Kuno, archb. Trèves (1368-88), 562
Kurth, G. 432, 435

Labor manuum (manual work), 3, 34, 35, 97, 141, 143-56, 188, 262, 271, 409, 435, 507 n, 512; contrasted with mendicancy, 143, 146, 572
Lambert, cleric, 45

Lambert, provost of Ypres, 208
Lambert, St., 295
Lambert le Bègue, 7, 71-77, 120, 126; Liege priority for beguine origins, 40 n, 44, 71-72, 96, 431; alleged heterodoxy, 73, 432, 506; literary activity, 71-72, 75, 365, 388-91, 432
Lambert von Burne, b. of Strasbourg (1371-74), 567
Lambert de Halle, 338
Lambert de Henis, 137
Lambert le Petit, 74
Lambert de Tournai, burgher of Binche, 13 n
Lambeth: council of 1330, 95; of 1281, 511
Lambine vanden Porchine, master of beghards in Bruges, 256
Lamprecht von Regensburg, OFM, 403, 439-41; cited, 439, 440
Langland, 425, 466
Langmann, Adelheid, 404
Langton, Stephen, archb. Canterbury, 31
Languedoc, 416, 491
Laon, 48, 51; conversae (OPr), 102; nuns (OC), 106-07; vidame at, 331, 450, 451. See also Barthélemy de Jura
Lateran, Third Council (1179), 389 n
Lateran, Fourth Council (1215), 29, 37, 56, 235, 310, 316, 477; disapproval of religiones novae, 6, 123 n, 126 n, 133, 155, 156, 412, 487, 517, 536
Laurentius Dacus, 350 n, 351
Laurentius Sweus, 351
Lauingen, 514
Lausanne, diocese of, 325. See also Boniface
Lawrence, St., 471
Lawrence, friar (OP), 380
Lea, H. C., 235 n
Léau, 185, 270, 485. See also beghards, beguines
Legende von dem Beginchen von Paris, 397
Le Grand, L., 417 n
Leiden. See beguines
Lens-Saint-Remy, Brabant. See beguines
Leon, kingdom of, 242, 243 n
Leper-houses, 3, 13, 46, 112, 134. See also Willambroux
Lichtenthal, OC (N), 93
Liebert l'Ardenais, knight, 43
Liedekerke, church of, 37
Liége: religious excitement in diocese, 71-72, 73, 126, 144, 299-317, 365; clerical delinquency, 71, 73-74, 75, 76; plundering of city, 41, 130 n; synod of 1287, 138, 272, 477; Dominicans in, 38, 306; Flagellants in, 371, 372. See also Adolph de la Marck,

Albert II de Cuyck, Alexander de Juliers, Alexander II d'Oeren, beghards, beguines, Engelbert de la Marck, Erard de la Marck, Henry III of Guelders, Henry II of Leyen, Hugh III of Châlons, Hugh of Pierrepont, Jean V d'Arkel, Jean d'Enghien, Jean II d'Eppes, Jean IV de Flandre, Jean VIII de Heinsberg, John V of Bavaria, Robert de Thourote, Rudolph of Zähringen

Lielt, 399

Lierre, 47, 111, 270, 374, 385, 485; flagellants in, 372 n. *See also* beguines

Liliendale, 222

Lille, 32, 111, 201. *See also* beguines

Lillois, 51, 64, 107 n, 109 n

Limburg, 285

Limburgsche Sermoenen, 393

Linköping, 348, 349

Lioba (Leobgith), 373

Lisa, beguine, 338

Lithold of Noville, knight, 43

Lixhe, 40 n

Lixheim, 93 n

Löwenthal, 198 n

Loeze, Thierry, receiver of Brabant, 219 n

Lollards, Lollaerts, Lullardi, 246, 266-67, 368, 496, 513, 520, 557, 567, 572

Lombardy, 24, 35, 52, 82, 433, 506; bishops of, 541

Lombez, council of 1165, 252 n

Longchamp, St. Cloud, 401

Loos (Laus B. Mariae), OC, 115

Looz, counts of, 111, 168, 173. *See also* beguines, Louis I

Lorraine, 490, 491

Louis, dean of St. Servais at Maestricht, 186

Louis, priest of Hendriken, 174

Louis, son of Philip III, 331

Louis I, count of Looz (1145-71), 173

Louis IX (Saint Louis) (1226-70), 67, 224-226, 228, 230, 231, 246-47, 296, 335, 341, 375, 401, 412, 416, 419 n, 466, 468, 469, 471, 545

Louis X (1314-16), 548

Louis XI (1461-1483), 228, 547

Louis of Bavaria, emperor, 357 n, 433

Louis de Bourbon, 268

Louis de Caliga, 369, 561, 562, 566

Louis de Jemeppe, 62

Louis de Male, count of Flanders (1346-84), 213, 372 n, 545

Louis de Nevers or de Crécy, count of Flanders (1322-46), 487 n, 545

Louis of Thuringia, 420

Louvain, 108 n, 121, 147, 270, 295, 297, 323, 324, 372 n, 485, 510; Dominicans in, 186, 201, 202. *See also* beghards, beguines

Lucas of Mont Cornillon, 76

Lucca, 563

Lucia de Keleghem, beguine, 479 n

Ludwig von Kesselheim, 340 n

Lübeck, 295. *See also* beguines, John II of Diest

Lüzel, 93 n

Lukana (or Wongrowitz), dioc. Gnezen, 296

Lukarde of Oberweimar (OC), 316

Lukardis of Utrecht, 405

Lund, archbishop of, 351 n

Luppe, Petrissa, 558 n

Lutgard, beguine, 338

Lutgard de Coninxheim, beguine, 169

Lutgard, St., of St. Trond, abb. Aywières, 17, 20, 24, 33 n, 47, 91, 97, 108, 200, 315, 316, 318, 329, 374, 393, 395, 416; learning of, 47, 377, 383; ridiculed, 446; embraces OC, 47, 90

Lutzerath, 87

Luykx: cited, 205 n

Lyons: council of 1245, 57, 439; council of 1274, 91, 122, 126 n, 224, 366, 412, 487, 514, 515; heresy in, 71, 501, 506; Poor Men of, 506; Dominican chapter of 1318, 309 n

Mabilia, beguine of Coblenz, 340 n

Machtild de Los, 338

Madrid, OP convent of, 191 n, 193

Maerlant, Jacob van, 292-94, 465; cited, 30, 513

Maestricht, 186, 295, 296, 517, 522. *See also* beghards, beguines

Madeleine, la, parish of Tournai, 233

Magdeburg, 96, 508, 558, 559, 561, 564

Maghain de Santos, 214

Magin, beguine, 339

Magnus Ladulås, king of Sweden, 349

Maguelonne, 536

Mahaut of Béthune, wife of Count Guy, 215, 230

Maheau de Velaine, beguine, 61 n

Mainz, 26, 290, 357, 369, 377, 506, 531, 559, 560, 561, 566, 567; city of, 503, 519, 548; councils of, 507 (1233), 95, 508 (1261), 522, 525 (1310), *See also* Conrad II von Weinsberg, Gerhard I, Gerhard II von Eppenstein, Henry I, Peter Aspelt, Rupert von Querfurt, Siegfried II, Siegfried III

Malaunay, Jeanne, 227 n

Malderus, John, b. Antwerp; cited on beguine life,, 121-22

Malèves. *See* beguines

Malines: city of, 113, 332, 372 n, 443, 485, 503, 518 n, 539; diocese of, 7 n, 173, 477 n; Cellites in, 267. *See also* beghards, beguines

Manfred, 467 n

Manrique, Angelo, 106, 107

Mantes. *See* beguines

Mantua, 401

Marburg, Conrad, 506

Marchiennes, OSB, near Douai, 297

Marcke, OC (N), transferred from Marcke near Courtrai to Groeninghe, 215

Marcourt, church of, 44

Marcuald of Modena, Master, provost of Tongres, 166 n, 167, 168, 174

Mareuil near Arras, 297

Margaret, abb. Moustier, 14 n

Margaret, beguine, 486

Margaret, beguine of Hasselt, 336 n

Margaret, Queen, 375

Margaret, daughter of Nicholas zum Goldenen Ring, 385

Margaret, mistress of St. Elizabeth's in Ghent, 209, 423 n

Margaret, wife of Alard de Berchem, 214

Margaret, wife of Duke John II of Brabant, 220-21

Margaret, widow of Johannes Gunnesen, 348 n

Margaret, widow of William Cassart, 147

Margaret, countess of Flanders (1244-80), 112, 201, 297; patroness of beguines, 83, 153, 206 n, 208-17, 221, 253, 410, 414 n, 487, 545; and beghards, 253, 255, 256

Margaret Bovinne, beguine of Antwerp, 184

Margaret of Cleves, 549

Margaret de Glimes, 45

Margaret de Guines, 111

Margaret of Hainault (d. 1356), wife of Louis of Bavaria, 212

Margaret de Lens, 64

Margaret Porete of Hainault, 367, 490-92, 500, 523, 541

Margaret of Provence, 67

Margaret van Rozenburg, 549

Margaret of Vianden, 448-50

Margaret of Ypres, OP, 98, 200 n

Maria of Evreux, 495

Maria de Gravio, 65, 334

Maria Scota, 227 n

Marie, Empress, wife of Otto of Brunswick, 114, 221, 305

Marie Bernarde, beguine, 69

Marie de Castello, 208

Marie de Corroy, beguine, 61 n

Marie de Lens, beguine of Mons, 211

Marie d'Ohain dite Rocette, beguine, 61 n

Marie de Rèves, 51 n. 109 n

Marie of Walcourt, beguine of Huy, 61 n

Marienau, 93 n

Marienkroon (Corona B. Mariae), OC, 549

Marienstatt, OC, 296

Marienthal, OP, 448, 449

Marlemans, Catherine, 483 n

Maroie, daughter of Louis de Jemeppe, 62

Maroie de Velaine, beguine, 62

Marquine (Markine), recluse of Williambroux, 334

Marsberg. *See* beguines

Marseilles, 420. *See* beguines

Marsiglio of Padua, 247 n

Marthas, 367, 437, 571

Martin, Master, 570

Martin V (1417-31), 127, 220, 543, 573

Martin de Menonry, 61 n

Mary, Abond's sister, nun of La Ramée, 322, 448

Mary, beguine of Huy, 338 n

Mary, recluse of Williambroux, 63

Mary, beguine, 60 n

Mary Magdalena, Penitents of, 128 n, 161

Mary of Brabant, daughter of Philip Augustus and wife of Duke Henry I, 328

Mary of Brabant, sister of John I of Brabant and second wife of Philip III, 66-67, 68, 331, 452

Mary of Diest, 338

Mary of Fosses, 15 n

Mary of Lille, beguine of Herenthals, 399

Mary of Lille, beguine of Diest, 97, 146

Mary of Oignies, 4, 5, 7, 8 n, 10, 11, 14, 24, 38, 46, 86, 88, 109, 125, 318-19, 327, 329, 343, 402, 413 n; and Nivelles circle, 7, 45-46; aims of, 15, 23, 59, 145, 149, 382, 416; influence on Jacques de Vitry, 17, 21-25, 59 n, 328; and John of Nivelles, 40, 42, 44, 72; death of, 41, 51, 155, 313 n, 393, 422, 432; and Theodore of Celles, 53, 55, 56; and William of L'Olive, 47, 48, 50; influence on lay world, 50-52, 447; influenced by Cistercians, 87, 327; parentage, 97, 120, 149, 152; and voluntary poverty, 149-50, 151; as prototype of beguine, 121, 416; appeal of, 295, 333; and eucharist, 314-15; and learning, 381-82; spirituality, 120-21,150,332

Mary of Valenciences, 367-68

Maseyck, 63, 89

Mate-Mannen, 266, 267 n

Mathias de Beerte, receiver of Brussels, 219 n

Matilda, sister of Henry II of Brabant, wife of Count Floris IV of Holland, mother of William II, 221-22, 551
Matilda, wife of Wichard, 103 n
Matilda, nun, 289
Matthew, ab. St. Denis, 331
Matthew de Tamines, 15 n
Matthew Paris, 253, 295, 409 n 432, 458-59; cited, 35 n, 123, 249, 432 n
Maubeuge, canonesses of, 63
Mauchin, Henry, 214 n
Maurice of Reval, friar (OP), 349 n, 350, 351-52
Maurice of Sully, b. of Paris (1160-96), 26, 461
Mechtild of Oud-Heusden, 549
Mechtild von Hackeborn, 374
Mechtild of Magdeburg, 88, 97, 344, 374, 379, 385, 403, 404
Mechtild von Sayn, countess, 94
Mechtild von Seedorf, 198 n
Mechtild von Waldeck, 88 n
Medingen, 404, 405 n
Meer, 94
Mella of Diest, 338
Mella de Scarmure, beguine of Tongres, 137
Mellement, 112
Melrose, OC, 419 n
Melun. See beguines
Mendicancy, 143, 246, 250, 367, 509-11, 527
Mendicant orders, 222, 224, 258, 423; attacked by Guillaume de Saint-Amour, 456-64. See also Carmelites, Dominicans, Franciscans
Merchwezet, Jacques Hustyn de, 265
Merenbrunnen, OP (N), 203 n
Mergriete Bertoens, 232 n
Merin, Margaret, 405
Merswin, Rulman, 358, 396, 455
Merwele, mill at St. Trond, 337
Metsius, bishop, 549
Mettula de Niel, beguine, 168
Metz, 391, 392, 434, 452, 506, 520, 523, 530. See also Conrad von Scharfenberg
Metza von Westhoven, beguine, 561
Meuse, valley of, 40 n, 130 n, 301
Mévergnies, 13
Meyer, Johannes (d. 1485), 196 n, 199, 384-85, 403, 405
Meyer, Paul, 389, 390
Michael, OP, 209
Michael of Liége (OP), 202
Michael, priest of Walcourt, 60 n
Michael of Cesena, OFM, 360 n
Michael Paleologus, 468
Michael of Warenghien, b. of Tournai (1283-91), 246 n
Michel de Mauduit, 548

Middelburg, 550 n. See also beghards, beguines
Milan: center of heresy, 35, 154, 443; Dominican chapters, 189, 193 (1255); 351 (1278)
Milo of Beauvais, 37
Ministeriales, 89
Miraeus, 431
Miskom, 221
Moens, Arnold, of Antwerp, 250 n
Moignelée, church of, 11, 14 n
Molenbeek, 177, 178 n
Mone, F. J., 507
Mons: canonesses of, 63, 127. See also beguines
Monstreux, 43
Montargis, OP (N), 191 n, 193
Mont Cornillon, 75, 300, 301-02, 394, 446. See also Juliana
Mont-d'Or, OC, 111
Monthéron, OC, dioc. Lausanne, 325
Montjoie, 416
Montpellier, synod of 1215, 92
Montreuil-les-Dames, OC(N), 106
Moravia, 308
Morimond, OC, 325
Morlanwelz, 48, 50, 112 n
Moschus, 8 n, 10
Mosheim, 409, 560
Moulins, OC (N), 69, 111
Mouskes, Ph., 419 n
Moustier-sur-Sambre, 50, 63, 70, 89, 90
Mühldorf, battle of, 516 n, 519
Mühlhausen. See beguines
Mulieres religiosae, 3, 4, 32, 35, 41, 43, 46, 58, 92, 96, 97, 101, 121, 125, 153, 155, 156, 157, 159, 170, 173, 183, 189 n, 205, 206, 207, 208, 212, 214, 235, 236, 251, 281, 286, 295, 310, 316, 321, 327, 329, 326, 331, 332, 333, 382, 397, 413, 414, 416, 421, 429, 431, 443, 445, 495, 527, 540, 542, 543
Mulieres sanctae, 5, 7, 41, 71-72, 86, 96, 97, 105, 109, 141 n, 144, 149, 195, 247, 300, 312, 323, 329, 330, 335, 342, 344, 348, 353, 388, 394, 398, 402, 413, 429, 434, 464, 537
Munio de Zamora, OP general, 199, 203 n
Münster: bishop of, 161, 423 n. See also beguines
Mutsaert, Ghiselbert, dean of St. Pierre's of Turnhout, 220, 543
Muysen, OC(N), 112 n

N., beguine of Gothland, 349
Namur, 7, 10 n, 11 n, 13, 15 n, 17, 54, 61, 107-08, 111, 304, 323, 449, 543; canonesses of, 17, 63, 89. See also beguines

Nandrin, 42
Narbonne, 400 n, 433, 536
Nassau, counts of, 564
Nazareth near Lierre, OC (N), 111, 332, 374, 385
Neoplatonism, 360, 488
Nerehayn (Noirhat). *See* beguines
Nettesheim, Gobelin Bolant von, 340
Neuburg am Neckar, 198 n
Neufmoustier, 22 n, 38, 42, 322
Neuve-Cour, grange of Villers, 326
Nicholas, Master, 499
Nicholas IV (1288-92), 12, 198 n, 227, 239, 259
Nicholas V (1447-55), 263, 264, 268, 558
Nicholas de Bibera: appraisal of beguines, 421
Nicholas de Corrant, OP, 342
Nicholas of Cusa, cardl., 264
Nicholas II de Fontaines, b. of Cambrai (1249-73), 134 n, 181, 182, 210 n, 218 n, 245, 488
Nicholas zum Goldenen Ring, Basel merchant, 385
Nicholas de le Mans, OP, 342
Nicholas de Mysene, 499
Nicholas l'Orfèvre, Master, canon of St. Waudru, 211
Nicholas of Ostia, cardl., 535
Nicholas of Peronne, OP, 501
Nider, John, 513, 514; cited, 369
Nimal, H. 163
Ninove, OPr., 37, 510
Nivelles: religious excitement, 7, 11, 21, 44, 46, 57, 64, 120, 231, 281, 321, 344, 382, 397; possible seniority, 7, 40; abbey of, 15 n, 63, 64, 71, 89, 91, 373, 431; *mulieres religiosae*, 46, 321, 325, 328, 413, 422, 434; „circle" of, 45-47, 51; renown of beguines, 331-32; Franciscans in, 60 n
Noordwijk. *See* beguines
Norbert, St., of Xanten, 101, 102, 104, 105, 285; opposes Tancheln, 310 n, 436
Norbertine. *See* Premonstratensians
Nordhausen, 565
Nordheim, 93 n
Norrenberg, P., 84
Notre-Dame: in Courtrai, 208; parish in Bruges, 212; Namur, 70, 186; Paris, 326; Tongres, 296
Noyon, 418; bishop of, 537, 547. *See also* beguines
Nürnberg, 84 n, 198 n, 203 n, 400 n, 404, 405. *See also* beguines

Obermedingen, 405 n
Oberweimar, 315
Oberwesseling, 94

Oda, recluse, 327
Oda, wife of Baldwin of Loupaigne, 11
Oda of Looz, abb. Nivelles, 15 n
Oda de Henis, beguine, 137
Oda of Lude, 166
Odilia von Winter, beguine, 340 n
Odilo of Liége, 47, 314, 444
Odina, beguine, daughter of Adam de Borloo, 338
Odo de Châteauroux, b. of Tusculum, 28, 31 n, 42 n
Odo de Roni, 375 n
Ötenbach, OP (N), 92 n, 198 n, 355, 404
Offenburg, beguine convent in Strasbourg, 135, 203
Offus, Jaspar, prior of St. Nicholas, 19 n
Oignies, 7, 8, 10-11, 12, 13, 14-16, 17, 18-19, 45, 49 n, 51, 53, 56-57, 60, 62, 120, 137, 145-46, 149, 313 n, 413, 422; consecration of church, 24, 37-38, 235-36. *See also* beguines
Oliger, L., 537
Olive, L', OC (N), 42, 47, 50, 90, 112 n, 114, 115. *See also* William
Oliver, scholasticus of Cologne, 41
Olivi, Peter John, 400 n, 434
Ollivier, R. F., cited, 479 n
Olmütz, bishop of, 439
Oostburgh. *See* beguines
Oost-Eeckloo, OC (N), 112
Ophem-lez-Wezembeek. *See* beghards
Oplinter, 107 n, 112 n, 386
Opstegen, Barthélemy, 264
Ordo: definition of, 124 n, 462-63
Ordo Sororum Poenitentium Beatae Mariae Magdalenae, 199, 376. *See also* Mary Magdalena
Orienten, OC (N), 111
Orleans. *See* beguines
Orthen, 552
Ortlibian doctrine, 368
Orval, OC, 43, 297, 322
Osilia of Liége, 85 n
Osnabrück. *See* beguines
Otilia de Henis, 137
Otto, OFM, in Vienna, 317 n
Otto IV of Brunswick, 114
Otto „in Carcere Tulliano", cardl., 160
Otto III of Holland, b. of Utrecht (1235-49), 222
Otto of Neuweiler, 568
Otto de Schoninburch, OP, 558 n
Otto of St. Laurent, 37 n
Oude de Trazegnies, beguine, 60 n
Oudewijck, OSB, near Utrecht, 284
Oudheusden. *See* beguines
Overbroeck, 209 n
Oxford, synod of, 251
Ozilia, Juliana's companion, 303, 305

Paderborn. *See* beguines
Paix-Dieu, OC (N), at Liége, 111, 115
Palencia, bishop of, 343
Palster, John, 217
Pampeluna, bishop of, 243
Papebroch, 237, 312
Papelards, 418-19, 433; identification with beguin, 472-23
Parc, le, OPr, near Louvain, 38, 102 n, 103 n, 285, 297
Parc-les-Dames, OC (N), at Wesemael, Louvain, 107, 108 n, 112 n, 323, 324 n, 327 n, 328, 396
Paris, 21, 22, 26, 47, 87, 121, 143, 208, 225, 227, 246, 281, 323, 348 n, 352, 378, 419 n, 429, 468, 472, 490, 491, 492, 518, 540, 541, 560; university of, 26, 27, 33, 41, 342, 351, 368, 371, 457-60, 466, 467; council of 1212-13, 91, 94, 95, 325; Dominican chapters, 189-90 (1228), 199, (1243). *See also* Denys du Moulin, Maurice of Sully, Pierre de Nemours, Stephen IV
Parochiaen, Henry, 219 n
Passau, 309
Patarini, 437 n, 443
Patin, Aubert, burgher of Lille, 214 n
Paula de Montaldo, 401
Paza von Scheuren, beguine, 399 n
Pelagius, Alvarus (Alvaro Pelayo) (ca. 1275-1352), 248
Penitential bands, 131, 162, 196, 557; Franciscan tertiaries, 258-64, 529, 531, 533, 534, 553. *See also* flagellants, Penitents of Mary Magdalena
Pepin of Heristal, 431
Pepin of Landen, 431
Perrault, 400 n
Perrecard de Villedommange, Rheims burgher, 231
Persijn, Jan, 549
Perugia, 154, 312, 313
Peter, brother of Lambert le Bègue, 76
Peter Aspelt, archb. Mainz (1306-21), 93 n
Peter Cantor, 26, 27, 31 n, 41, 43 n
Peter Capoccius, card.-deacon of St. George, 58 n, 148, 179, 183, 237, 308
Peter Damian, 141, 462 n
Peter scholasticus, 42
Peter of Albano, cardl., 18, 60, 161, 210-11, 414
Peter of Capua, cardl., 241
Peter of Dacia, OP, 27, 298, 345-55, 359, 379, 380
Peter of Herenthals, 443
Peter the Hermit, 22 n
Peter of Münster, priest, 288
Peter de Vaux, pastor, 492
Peter the Venerable, 94

Peter of Walcourt, 56, 57
Petrus de Lutra, 460, 461
Petrus de Sancto Petro, beghard, 254, 337
Peuthy, 163, 183
Pfirzheim, 405 n
Philip, prior of Dominicans at Louvain, 186
Philip, ab. of le Parc, 102 n, 285, 289
Philip, marquis of Namur, 63 n
Philip Augustus, 242, 328
Philip III (1270-85), 226, 246; interest in Nivelles beguine, 65, 67, 331-32, 450-52
Philip IV (1285-1314), 226, 232, 410, 548
Philip V (1316-22), 548
Philip VI (1328-50), 226, 227 n, 548
Philip of Alsace, count of Flanders (1157-91), 286
Philip de Grève, 306
Philippe de Marigny, b. of Cambrai (1306-09), 491, 541
Philip de Montmirail, 52, 110, 224
Philip Meusius (de Meuse), b. of Tournai (1274-82), 236 n
Philip the Bold, duke of Burgundy, 232, 546
Philip the Good, duke of Burgundy (1419-57), 47 n, 220, 221, 268
Philippen, L. J. M., 5-6, 432
Philippine of Porcellet, 400
Phillips, D: cited, 84
Picardy, 102, 229; Fins Amans of, 135; French devotional poetry, 391-92
Pieret, son of Coulon de Menomy, 61 n
Pierre d'Ailly, b. of Cambrai (1396-1411), 495, 502, 504
Pierre d'Alençon, 226, 231-32
Pierre de Béneis, b. of Bayeux (1276-1306), 331
Pierre de la Broce, 331, 451, 452
Pierre de Chappes, b. of Arras (1320-26), 540
Pierre de Courtenay, emperor of Constantinople, 448
Pierre de Lemet, OP, 342
Pierre de Lévis-Mirepoix, b. of Cambrai (1309-24), 134 n, 180, 312, 541
Pierre de Limoges (d. 1306), 342, 343
Pierre de Nemours, b. of Paris (1208-19), 22
Pierre de la Palu, OP, 548
Pierre de Tonnerre, OP, 342
Pierre de Tournemire, 537 n
Pierre de Vaux-Cernay, 252 n
Pierre de Verdun, OP, 342
Pieter-Simons-beguinage, Leiden, 551
Pipenpoy, Amelric, dean of St. Gudule, 147 n
Pirenne, Henri, 337
Pius II (1458-64), 518 n

Plauen, 198 n
Poland, 308, 352, 522 n. *See also* beghards
Pomerius, Henry (vanden Bogaert), 378, 495; cited, 493-94
Poncelet, E., 8 n
Pont-Audemer: synod of 1279, 91
Pontoise, 376
Porziuncula, 59
Posen, bishop of, 555
Pouille, 467
Poverty, voluntary (*Wilge Armen*), 81 n, 91, 130, 142-43, 149, 152, 157, 160, 250, 268, 521, 525, 563, 568
Power, E., 83
Premonstratensians, 3, 38, 50, 91, 299, 301, 460, 510; and *cura monialium*, 101-105, 120, 320
Prémontré, 34, 62, 104, 187, 320
Pré-Notre-Dame, Mons, 209
Preuilly, 115 n
Primitive church, 5, 10, 17, 30, 35 n, 54, 56, 141, 251 462
Prims, F., 257, 489
Prouille, OP (N), Toulouse, 190, 191, 192, 400, 415
Provence, 52, 55, 224, 375, 400, 416, 433, 434, 436, 536
Provincia Teutonia, 194, 195, 196, 197
Prussia, 522 n
Pseudopreachers, 125, 458; defined, 460-61
Pseudoprophets, 294, 331, 414 n, 415, 450-52 458, 459
Publicani, 251
Pulkawa, 371
Puritanism, medieval, 76-77
Puteanus, E., 179 n, 183, 253 n, 431

Quakers, 82
Quesnoy, le, *See* beguines

Radewijns, Florentius, 572
Rainbold von Gemünd, 569
Rainer of Casale, b. of Cremona, 523
Rainer of Osimo, 162
Raissius, A., 64
Ramée, la, OC (N), 107, 114, 322, 374, 386, 387, 448, 510
Raymond de Beaumont, 539
Raymond of Padua, 377
Raymond of Pennafort, OP general (1238-40), 57, 191
Raymond de Pinoliis, canon, 543
Raymond Scholasticus, 292
Raymond of Usèz, 21 n
Raynaldus, 567
Reclusorium, 4, 66, 151-52, 229, 305, 326, 346 n, 376, 506

Recluses (*reclusus/a*), 60, 62, 65-66, 95, 102, 200 n, 227 n, 245, 300, 322, 323, 326, 327, 329, 332, 333, 334, 336, 338, 339, 353 373, 383, 532, 533; definition, 3, 4
Regensburg, 198 n, 514. *See also* Berthold
Reichenau, 507
Reimboto, b. of Eichstätt (1279-97), 513
Reinbold von Achenheim, 146
Reiner, canon of St. Stephen's at Mainz, 292
Religio: definition 73, 125-27
René, priest of Louvain, 157
René, prior of Neufmoustier, 42
Renier, brother of Godfrey Pachomius, 323, 324; father of Godfrey, 323
Renier, scholasticus of Tongres: patron of beguines, 65, 162-63, 165-69, 174, 176, 185, 186, 202, 411, 414, 485; and *boni pueri*, 246 n
Renier, monk of St. Laurent, 336
Renier, monk of St. Jacques, 37 n
Renier, Master, provisor of Brussels beguinage, 177
Renier, priest of Louvain, 171
Renier, rector of beguines of Brussels, 218
Renier de Breeteyck, priest of Brussels, 177
Retinne, 299, 302 n
Reuthin, dioc. Constance, 405 n
Rèves, 108
Reynald of Guelders, 543
Rheims, 12, 21, 37, 44, 236, 242, 443, 445, 458, 490, 501, 537 n; council of 1148, 75. *See also* beguines, Robert de Courtenay
Rhenen, 367, 571
Rhisnes, 13, 14 n, 15 n
Richard des Champs, 548
Richard of Manechan-Capella, 45
Richard of St. Victor, 34 n
Richer, 294 n, 452; cited 201
Richmodis vanme Clocringe, 566-67
Ries, heretics in, 491, 514, 515
Riga, 561
Rimini, bishop of, 258
Rivogne, castle of, 76
Rixo, friar (OP) at Louvain, 186, 202
Robermont, OC (N), 107, 108 n, 339
Robert, Gilles' brother, 8
Robert, count of Artois, 468 n
Robert, dean of St. Servais of Maestricht, 522 n
Robert, priest of Walcourt, 59
Robert III de Béthune, count of Flanders (1305-22), 96, 123, 125 n, 201, 217, 543
Robert le Bougre (also Robert le Petit), OP, 508

Robert de Courçon, 31 94, 110, 156, 325
Robert de Courtenay, archb. Rheims
  (1299-1324), 231
Robert de Cresch, 34 n
Robert of Lobbes, 37 n
Robert of Namur, ab. Villers
  (1647-52), 112 n
Robert of Sicily, 536 n
Robert de Sorbon, 391, 318-19, 420-21,
  443, 473 n
Robert de Thourote, b. of Liége
  (1240-46), 6, 7, 13 n, 16, 60, 127, 129,
  131 n, 134, 155, 162, 165, 166, 237,
  302, 307
Robert van Schelden, 206 n
Roemervat, Bernard, 265
Roermond, See beguines
Roger, canon of St. Croix at Liége, 43
Roisin, S., 393 n
Rokendale, parish of St. Trond, 336
Roman de la Rose, 426, 473
Rome, 30, 37, 39, 76, 89, 154, 158, 161,
  191, 192, 309, 400, 470, 500, 554
Rose la Picavette, beguine of Rheims,
  99
Roselies, 14
Rosières, OC (N), 102
Roskild, 348 n
Rothem, OC (N), 112 n
Rothenburg ob der Tauber, 198 n
Rotterdam. See beguines
Roubaud, Marseilles, 547
Rouen, 91, 92, 309 n, 472. See also be-
  guines
Rudolf, canon of St. Maurice's at
  Hildesheim, 26, 161
Rudolf of Hapsburg, emperor
  (1273-91), 196
Rudolph, monk of Vilers, 281, 289,
  290
Rudolph of Zähringen, b. of Liége
  (1167-91), 54, 73, 74, 76, 285, 290,
  302
Rummen, 111
Rupert of Deutz, 462 n
Rupert von Querfurt, archb. Magde-
  burg (1260-66), 508
Rupertsberg, 281, 282, 283, 284, 289, 290
Russelius, Henry, 53; cited, 55
Rutebeuf, 34 n, 116, 453, 456, 457, 466-
  73; dislikes beguines, 201, 471-73;
  cited, 468, 470, 471, 472
Ruysbroeck, 365, 392, 454, 493, 496,
  497 n, 527, 557; literacy of, 378-79;
  cited, 425 n
Ryckel, J. G. a, 44 n, 124, 171, 231, 252 n,
  385, 409-10, 431, 552; cited, 124 n,
  573
Rycwera, OPr. nun, 102
Rijms, Elizabeth, 205 n
Rijnsburg. See beguines

Saccati (Brethren of the Sack), 222, 466
St. Adalbert: beguines of, 153
St. Agatha's in Utrecht, 396
St. Agnes, OP (N), Strasbourg, 192, 198 n,
  405 n
St. Agnes, OP (N), Bologna, 190 n, 193,
  402
St. Agnes, OP (N), Freiburg i. Br., 92,
  195 n, 405 n
St. Agnes, Mainz, 93 n
St. Agnes' beguinage of St. Trond, 169
St. Arné, Douai, 297
St. Andrew's, Scotland, 492
St. Andrew, parish of Lille, 213, 214
St. Anthony, order of, 35 n
St. Aubain, beguinage of Namur, 15 n,
  69-70, 304
St. Aubert, Cambrai, 10
St. Avoye, Paris, 228. See also Bonnes
  Femmes
St. Barbara's, Delft, 396
St. Bavon, Ghent, 206 n, 207
St. Bavon's, Haarlem, 549
St. Bernard on the Scheldt (Lieu St.
  Bernard), OC, interest in cura
  mulierum, 114 n, 170, 179-84, 218,
  320, 541 n, 543
St. Calixtus' hospital, Namur, 69
St. Catherine's, OP (N), Colmar, 405
St. Catherine's, OSB (N), St. Trond, 47
St. Cecilia's, Cologne, 353
St. Christopher's, Liége, 41, 44, 71, 76,
  135, 153, 168, 212, 236, 335, 339, 389,
  431
St. Cloud, 401
St. Denis, Paris, 227 n
St. Denis, Liége, 166 n
St. Denis, parish of Rheims, 230, 231
St. Donatian's, dean of, 213
St. Feuillen's church, 12, 305
St. Gengulphe, parish of St. Trond, 336
St. Gerard of Brogne, abbey, 37
St. Gereon's, Cologne, 559
St. Germain-des-Prés, 227 n
St. Germain-l'Auxerrois, Paris, 243 n,
  492
St. Germain's, Mons, 209, 210
St. Gertrude's, OP (N), Cologne, 90,
  203 n
St. Gertrude's, Louvain, 38, 172 n,
  221, 297, 323, 431
St. Gertrude's, Nivelles, 63, 88, 424
St. Géry (Sanctus Gaucericus), Cambrai,
  provost of, 490
St. Gilles, Münster, 423 n
St. Gilles' church, Liége, 339
St. Gudule, collegiate church, Brussels,
  177, 178 n, 179, 180, 218-19, 486 n,
  494, 495, 502, 504, 541
St. Guilain, OSB., 490
St. Gummar, chapter of, 182

St. Hubert, OSB, 41 n, 44
St. Jakob's, Mainz, 93 n
St. Jacques' hospital, Tongres, 166, 237
St. Jacques, OSB abbey, Liége, 39, 43
St. Jacques de Coudenberg, 271
St. Jacques, parish of Nivelles, 66
St. James of Compostella, 248
St. Jean-des-Vignes, Soissons, 10
St. Jean's, Liége, 41, 42, 43
St. John's parish, Ghent, 208
St. John's hospital, Bruges, 212
St. Julian's hospital, Antwerp, 257, 262
St. Lambert, cathedral of Liége, 6, 39, 41, 74, 114 n, 166, 287, 325, 339, 394, 506, 517
St. Laurent, Liége, 41, 335, 336
St. Lawrence, Vienna, 203
St. Margaret's, OP (N), Strasbourg, 405 n
St. Maria in Reno, 36
St. Mark's, OP (N), Strasbourg, 196 n, 197, 203 n
St. Mark's, OP, Würzburg, 198 n
St. Martin's, Liége, 302, 306, 307, 308, 394
St. Martin's, Tournai, 103 n, 297, 424, 425
St. Martin-du-Mont, Liége, 299 n
St. Martin's Lille, 153
St. Martin's church, Ypres, 208
St. Martin's convent, Ypres, 215
St. Mary's, Medingen, 404
St. Mary's at Weil in Württemberg, 203 n
St. Mary's convent, Steinheim, 198 n
St. Mary's at Blois, 10
St. Maurice, Hildesheim, 161
St. Médard, O.S.B., Soissons, 456
St. Michael, parish in Bruges, 212
St. Michael's, Antwerp, 270
St. Michael's, Ghent, 32, 205, 207
St. Nicholas', OP, Strasbourg, 405 n
St. Nicholas, OP, Halberstadt, 198 n
St. Nicholas of Oignies, Augustinian priory, 5, 8-19, 59, 120
St. Omer, dioc. Térouanne. See beghards, beguines
St. Paul, parish of Paris, 227
St. Paul's, Liége, 15, 74, 237
Ste-Perine in St. Quentin, 547
St. Peter's, Vucht, 202
St. Pharaïlde, Ghent, 217 n, 545
St. Pierre's, Douai, 297
St. Pierre's, Lille, 32
St. Pierre's Louvain, 171, 172, 173 n
St. Pierre's church, Anderlecht, 479
St. Pierre's, Turnhout, 220
St. Pölten: synod of 1284, 513
St. Quentin, 492, 502, 547. See also beguines
St. Rémacle near Liége, 333
St. Remy, 44, 45

St. Sauveur, parish of Bruges, 212
St. Sauveur, Cambrai, 159, 208
St. Sepulchre, parish of St. Trond, 336
St. Sepulchre, parish of Nivelles, 66-68
St. Servais, Maestricht, 186, 296, 522
St. Severi, Erfurt, 562, 563
St. Sisto, OP (N), Rome, 190, 191, 192, 195, 197, 199 n
St. Sixtum, Nivelles, 46 n
St. Sixtus, Institutes of, 161
St. Stephen's at Mainz, 289
St. Severi, Erfurt, 562, 563
St. Symphorien, beguinage of Namur, 69-70, 304
St. Syr, beguinage of Nivelles, 64, 66, 67-68
St. Ursula, Cologne, 295
St. Theobald, chapel of, 55
St. Theresa, Elias of, 431
St. Timothy, parish of Rheims, 231
St. Trond, OSB., 47, 90, 165, 167, 185-86, 297, 328, 336-37, 383, 446. See also beguines
St. Victor's in Paris, 34, 470
St. Walburge, dioc. Strasbourg, 297, 449
St. Waudru, Mons, 127, 210, 211
Salaert, Louis, 268
Salimbene, OFM, 370, 371 n, 462 n, 557; cited 459
Salzburg, synod of 1310, 511, 522, 561, 566; of 1274, 511; archbishop of, 559
Salzinnes (Val-St.-George), OC (N), 70, 107, 108 n, 114, 448, 449
Sambre, 8, 60
San Damiano, 59
Santia, queen of Sicily, 547
Sapience, 301, 374, 446
Sarabite, 331, 451
Sarete de Faillouel, 471
Sart-Risbart, grange of Villers, 326, 336 n
Saulchoir, le, OC (N), 115 n
Savelli, Cencio. See Honorius III
Savoy, 501
Saxony, 564; OP province, 195 n, 197
Sayn, count of, 506
Scandinavia, 310
Scheldt, 112, 489
Schelenconvent, Cologne, 274
Schiedam. See beguines
Schmerlenback, 93 n
Scholares vagi, 437 n
Schönensteinbach, OP (N), 404, 405
Schuerhoven, 336
Schuermans, H., 335
Schultess, Jützi, 403
Scotland, 492
Sebastian of Nedermolen, 185
Sebilla de Donchery, beguine of Rheims, 99

Secta, 123, 250, 252, 267 n, 526, 555, 560
Sectarianism, 3, 35, 137, 488, 500, 519, 525, 526, 557, 568
Segarelli. Gerald, 462 n
Selle, Henry, provost of Corsendonck, 495-96
Senlis. *See* beguines
Sens, 458, 522 n. *See also* beguines
Serkingen, mill, 338
Servais, St. 296
Servranckx, G. J., 173
's Hertogenbosch. *See* Bois-le-Duc
Sibile, beguine of Waremme, 202 n
Sibille, beguine of St. Symphorien, 70
Sibilia de Perevez, beguine, 336 n
Sibyl, superior, 69
Sibylle d'Oreye, beguine of St. Christopher's, 478 n
Sibyl, beguine of Marsal, 452-53
Sicily, 433, 467, 469, 536, 547
Siegfried II von Eppenstein, archb. Mainz (1200-30), 161
Siegfried III von Eppenstein, archb. Mainz (1230-49), 506
Sifrid II von Westerburg, archb. Cologne (1274-97), 94
Siger, prior of St. Nicholas, 9 n, 13 n, 16
Siger Habosch, knight, 177
Siger de Wavre, knight, 287, 289
Sigibert, king of Austrasia, 373
Sigwin, brother of Christine of Stommeln, 346, 349, 350
Silla, daughter of Agnes of Berg, beguine, 137
Silves, bishop of, 248
Simon, archdeacon of Tournai, 214
Simon l'Amman, 546
Simon of Aulne, 320, 323, 447
Simon de Montfort, 191 n
Simon van Vaernewijc, 546
Sittard. *See* beguines
Skenninge, dioc. Linköpfing, 345, 351
Soest, hospital at, 129
Soignes, forest of, 268
Soignies, schools of, 46 n
Soleilmont, OC (N), 114, 115
Solières, OC (N), 111, 114
Solomon Hungarus, friar (OP), 352
Solre-sur-Sambre, 13
Sophia, abb. of Oudewijck, 284
Sophia, beguine of Cologne, 98
Sorores pauperes, 195
Spain, 106, 195
Spalbeek: seeress of, 65
Speier, 93, 559. *See also* Emicho
Spermaille (Spermalie), OC (N), Bruges, 111 n
Spoleta, 523
Spykers, Margaret, beguine, 552
Stagel, Elsbeth, 355, 403
Steinfeld. OPr, 76, 460

Steinheim a. d. Muhr, 198 n
Stephen, ab. of Tiron, OSB, 224
Stephen IV, b. of Paris (1363-68), 500, 560
Stephen, b. of Tournai (1193-1203), 242
Stephen, Dominican provincial of Lombardy, 195
Stephen, chaplain of Peter of Albano, 18
Stephen of Bourbon, OP, 252 n, 343; and Jacques de Vitry, 28, 200 n; on beguines, 52, 200 n, 231 n, 445
Stephen of Grammont, 10 n
Stephen of Obazini, 106
Steppes, battle of, 37
Stiggelink, Christian, 558 n
Stigmatized, the, 3, 39, 201, 311, 314, 318-19, 399
Stilkin, Hermann of Schadelant, 558 n
Stochemius, Johannes, 55 n
Stoisy-lez-Nivelles, grange of Villers, 67, 336 n
Stommeln (Stumbeln), 344. *See also* beguines, Christine
Strasbourg, 248, 358, 538, 548, 558, 560; Dominicans in, 90, 92, 192, 196-97, 203-04; and Eckhart, 358-59, 519. *See also* beghards, beguines, Friedrich I von Lichtenberg, John of Dürbheim, John II von Lichtenberg, John III of Luxembourg, Lambert von Burne
Suso, Heinrich, 355, 396, 403, 454-55
Suxy, convent of Brethren of the Cross near Chiny, 53 n
Swabia, 106, 199, 514
Sweden, 345, 349, 522 n
Swestriones (suestriones), 267 n, 367, 437 n, 496, 513, 518, 520, 525, 560, 564, 570
Switzerland, 385, 403
Sybille de Gages, 90, 374

Table of the Poor. See Holy Ghost Table
Taillefin, Daniël, 215
Talia, beguine, 340 n
Tanchelm, 310, 436, 488, 491, 492
Tarragona, 95, 316 n, 433
Tart, OC (N), 106
Tauler, Johannes, 355, 385, 454-55; cited, 454
Tegernsee, OSB., Bavaria, 288 n
Terarken, infirmary, 148, 541 n
Terbank, leperhouse, 112, 147
Terbeek, OC (N), 112 n, 114
Ter Doest, OC, 115 n
Ter-Hagen, OC (N), Ghent, 112
Ter Kisten, Brussels, 134, 148, 220, 271, 482-84, 485-86

Termonde. *See* beguines

Térouanne, dioc. of, 34 n, 263, 372 n, 541 n

Teutonic Knights, 33, 37, 349

Thenailles, OPr., 48

Theobald, canon of St. Denis at Liége 166 n

Theodard, 297

Theoderic (Dirk) of Zassenem, 222

Theodore of Celles, 53-56, 382

Theologia Germanica, 454, 455

Theophania, mistress of hospital at Paris, 326

Thibaud de Bar, 111

Thibaud de Navarre, 469

Thielt, 112

Thierry of Dinant, canon of Oignies, 15 n

Thierry II of Walcourt, 45

Thierry III of Walcourt, 9 n

Thierry of St. Hubert, 45

Thierry, ab. of St. Jacques, Liége, 39

Thiméon, 43

Thomas, brother of Godfrey Pachomius, 323, 327

Thomas, cantor of St. Aubain, 15 n

Thomas, ab. St. Trond, 167, 185, 236

Thomas à Kempis, 385

Thomas Aquinas, 143, 307 n, 309, 459 n

Thomas of Cantimpré, 16, 17, 24, 28, 32, 39, 40, 44 n, 46, 47, 54, 56, 59 n, 61-62, 116, 120, 121, 152, 200, 229, 297 n, 314, 325, 328, 332, 334, 342, 376, 377, 380, 383, 393, 394, 395, 413, 449, 488-89; and John of Nivelles, 40, 42, 156; on beguines of Oignies, 61-62; on seniority of Nivelles in beguine history, 62, 64, 65, 422; cited, 41 n, 46 n, 52 n, 61-62, 64 n, 97 n, 105 n, 225 n, 419 n, 424

Thomas of Celano, 313, 441

Thomas of Hales, OFM, 373

Thomas of Hemricourt, 44

Thomas of Savoy, 13 n, 207

Thomasin von Zirclaria, 465 n

The Hague, 398

Thorembais-les-Beguines. *See* beguines

Thruen, beguine of Roskild, 348 n

Thuringia, 564, 565

Tiedala, 65, 328-29

Tirlemont, 110, 171 n, 267, 372 n, 386, 485, 504. *See also* beguines

Tiron, OSB, 224

Tochter von Syon, 439-41

Töss, OP (N), 355, 403

Tondeurlant, Simon, 270

Tongerloo, 102 n, 103 n

Tongres, 237, 512 n; beguine author of, 396. *See also* beguines

Tore, beguine of Roskild, 348 n

Toul, 506, 532 n. *See also* Eudes de

Vaudemont, John II of Arzilières

Toulouse, 21 n, 192, 252 n, 415, 433, 436, 536, 540, 547

Tournai, 77, 83, 103 n, 123, 207, 224, 297, 426, 501, 540, 541, 542, 545. *See also* beghards, beguines, Guillaume de Ventadour, Guy de Boulogne, Jean d'Enghien, Michael of Warenghien, Philip Meusius (de Meuse), Stephen Walter de Marvis

Tours, 286. *See also* beguines, Jean de Montsoreau

Toussaint, 8 n

Tractatus brevis de periculis novissorum temporum, 459, 460, 462

Transitus Sancti Patris, 400 n, 434

Trèves, 12, 87, 196 n, 341, 449, 503, 505, 528, 559, 561, 562, 566; councils of, 294 n (1145), 282 (1147), 125 n, 252 n, 509 (1277), 126, 511, 522 (1310), 521 (1338). *See also* Trèves

Trinitarians, 466

Triple monastic vows, 5, 125 n, 130-31, 264, 409, 413, 470

Trithemius, John, 377 n, 378, 393 n, 520, 570; cited, 28 n

Troeltsch, E., 81 n

Trois-Fontaines, OC, 115 n, 322

Troyes, 76

Trutanni, 419 n, 510

Tuclant, Jean, canon, 262

Tulln, OP (N), 203

Turlupins, 367 n, 452, 500-502, 567

Turm, Strasbourg, 135

Turnhout, 220, 543. *See also* beguines

Tuscany, 20, 151, 541

Tusculum (Frascati), 28, 199

Tybica, beguine, 348 n

Ude, beguine of St. Servais, 202 n

Ugolino. *See* Gregory IX

Uhlhorn, G., 82 n, 149, 525

Ulm, 106

Ulrich, monk of Villers, 327

Ulrich von Königstein, 203 n

Umbria, 20, 97, 145, 150, 151, 313, 314, 324

Unterlinden, OP (N), Colmar, 197, 198 n, 402, 404

Urban II (1088-99), 234

Urban III (1185-87), 302 n

Urban IV (1261-64), 6, 65, 90, 163, 168, 178, 183 n, 300, 306, 316 n, 335, 467 n, 487

Urban V (1362-70), 257, 370, 558, 559 n, 560, 561, 562, 563

Ursula, St., 295, 296-98

Uten Hove, Pierre, 201

Utrecht, 133, 264, 283, 284, 367, 516, 552, 566, 571. *See also* beguines,

Frederick II of Siereck, Frederick III of Blankenheim, Godfrey of Utrecht, Guy d'Avesnes, Henry de Vianden, John of Nassau, Otto III of Holland

Val-Benoît, OC (N), 92, 108 n, 166 n, 303, 339, 429
Val-des-Ecoliers, 34, 43, 339
Val-des-Roses, OC (N), 112 n, 113, 297, 332
Val-des-Vierges (Maegdendael), OC (N), 110, 111 n, 115, 386
Val-Duc, OC (N), 111, 112 n, 114
Val-Duchesse, OP (N), 196, 198 n, 202
Valenciennes, 89, 109, 194, 208, 490, 491, 550 n. See also beguines
Valkenbroeck, 239
Val-Notre-Dame, OC (N), Huy, 107 n, 108, 111, 303, 322, 339
Val-Saint-Bernard, OC (N), Diest, 114
Val-Saint-Georges. See Salzinnes
Val-Saint-Lambert, OC, 39, 42, 114 n, 296, 323, 448
Valsiera, Raymond, of Aix, 252 n
Vander Coestraten, Alice, 485
Van Mierlo, J., 40 n, 44, 393 n, 495 n, 518-19; attitude toward Lambert, le Bègue, 71 n, 365, 431; definition of "begardism", 247-48; on etymology, 435-36, 438
Vannérus, J., 254
Van Rooijen, H., 150 n
Västeras, 345, 350
Vaucelles, 38
Val-les-Choux, 34, 141 n
Velthem, Lodewijch van, 292-94, 465
Venice: Dominican chapter (1325), 357
Venturino da Bergamo, OP, 401
Vermandois, 492
Vertus, dioc. Soissons, 113
Vervins, dioc. Laon, 48
Vichenet, 13, 61 n
Vienna, 203 n, 317 n. See also beguines
Vienne, 310, 414; council of 1311, 30, 190, 220, 249, 257, 309, 410 n, 434, 477, 490, 496, 514, 523, 529, 531
Villers-en-Brabant, OC, 11, 69, 161, 165, 297, 299, 308, 320, 322, 324, 332, 333-34, 429, 448; Polyptique of, 66-67, 320, 336; interest in beguines, 65, 67, 112, 168, 170-79, 219, 321, 326-27, 483; concern for cura monialium, 105-06, 112-19; and Hildegarde, 281, 286-90, 295, 320; and Juliana, 305, 311, 317, 334-35. See also Arnold of Ghistelles, Arnulf of Louvain, Charles, Conrad d'Urach Jacques de Bomal, Robert de Blocquerie, Robert de Namur, Walter

de Jodoigne, Walter of Utrecht, William of Brussels
Vilvorde. See beguines
Vincent of Beauvais, 426, 443 n; cited, 28 n
Virgines continentes, 3, 121, 251, 413
Visier, Jan, 293
Vita Abundi, 41, 429
Vita apostolica, 10, 17, 21, 24, 42, 45, 55, 56, 73, 86, 97, 121, 141-53, 160, 262, 321, 395, 409, 412, 413, 414, 416, 417, 500; and crusade fervor, 3, 4, 7, 53-56; definition, 141-42
Vita Julianae, 429; authorship of, 394-95
Vita Lutgardis, 393, 395
Vita Odiliae, 44, 71 n, 73, 162, 432
Vitalis de Furno, OFM, 533, 534
Viterbo, magistrates of, 488 n
Vlierbeek, OSB, 165
Vlierzele, parish of Ghent, 216
Vogenée, 13
Volmar, 286, 288, 289, 377

Wächterswinkel, 93 n
Walcher of St. Amand, 290
Walcourt, 45
Waldensians, 7, 81, 82 n, 189, 247 n, 343, 367, 391, 433, 436, 437 n, 488, 501, 505, 506, 520, 571, 572
Waldo, Peter, 71, 88, 189, 389 n, 390
Waleram of Montjoie, seignior of 552
Walram von Jülich, archb. Cologne (1332-49), 520, 560
Walter, friar (OP), 347
Walter, brother of Ivan de Rèves, 51, 108
Walter, ab. St. Bavon, Ghent, 206 n, 207 n
Walter, knight of Betuis, 137
Walter, provisor of Ghent beguines, 201, 206
Walter, seignior of Axel, 112
Walter, rector of church at Peuthy, 163
Walter, b. of Acre, 154
Walter of Cologne (OP), 352
Walter, prior (OP) in Strasbourg, 197
Walter de Becke, canon of St. Servais, Maestricht, 186
Walter de Ghier, 201
Walter of Holland, 368, 519
Walter de Jodoigne, ab. of Villers (1248 or 50-57/58), 114 n, 172
Walter of Kaysnoet, OFM, 550 n
Walter of London, 31
Walter Magnus (le Grand), 43
Walter de Marvis, b. of Tournai (1219-51), 86 n, 206 n, 212, 214, 233, 414 n

William of Brussels, ab. of Villers
(1221-37), ab. of Clairvaux (1238-42),
112, 113-14, 157, 324, 325, 326
414 n
Walter of Meysenburg, OP, 449
Walter d'Obaix, ab. Floreffe (1268-80),
104
Walter of St. Cyr, monk of Orval, 43
Walter of Utrecht, ab. of Villers
(1214-21), 20, 105-06, 114, 116, 170,
326, 327, 438
Wanfercée, 13, 14 n
Waudrez, 13 n
Wauters, A. J., 68
Wauthier-Braine, OC (N), 112 n, 114,
115; seigniory, 270
Wavre, 110 n, 112 n
Wazo, dean of St. Lambert's, b. of Liége
(1042-48), 54
Webbecom, parish, 167, 185, 186
Wedderstedt (Wiederstedt), OP, 198 n
Weert, Jan, of Ypres, 77
Weissenburg, Alsace, 203 n
Werembald, priest of Alkmaar, 554
Werric, priest of Nivelles, 45
Wéry of Aulne, 320, 325
Wéry III, seignior of Walcourt, 8
Wesel, 94. See also beguines
Wevelghem, 111
Wesemael, 396
Wicbert, Barthélemy's son, 110
Widle, beguine of Rheims, 99
Wigger, F., cited, 81 n
Wilbert, Friar, 548
Wilde, Walter, 209 n
Williambroux, leperhouse, 11, 46, 51,
63, 88, 120, 149, 295, 413 n
William called Frater, 492
William, inquisitor, 491
William, archdeacon of Paris, 21 n
William, OP, 184
William, deacon of Lierre, 182
William II, count of Holland (1234-56),
221, 238, 308, 416 n, 551
William III, count (1st in Hainault, 3d
in Holland and Zeeland) (1304-37),
223, 548, 551 n, 553, 554, 555
William of Afflighem. See Guillaume
William of Auvergne, Master, 26

William of Dongelbert, Villers monk,
334
William of Gennep, archb. Cologne
(1349-62), 560
William of Hildernisse, 502-04
William of Kroonenburg, 549
William of Ockham, OFM, 358 n
William de l'Olive, 26 n, 41, 42, 47-50,
110
Wilmotte, 202
Wilms, H., 203
Wimbourne, Dorset, 373
Winterthur, 403
Wipert Boemus, 352
Wisby, 345, 351
Wisse, Peter's son (Pieterzoon), 223
Withof, J.: cited, 484 n
Wittox hospital, Ghent, 205, 206
Woikowsky-Biedau, 84
Woeringen, battle of, 355
Wolbero, beghard, 340 n
Wolsiagers, Jans, 411 n
Wondelghem, 216
Worms, 198 n, 268, 357, 505, 536, 558 n.
See also beguines, Heinrich III von
Daun
Württemberg, 203 n
Würzburg, 198 n, 530, 538, 559; council
of 1287, 513 n, 522
Wyclif, John, 466, 566
Wyslaus, 555

Ymme, beguine of Bodeghem, 479 n
Yolanda, daughter of Margaret of Vian-
den, 448-50
Ypres, 372 n, 541 n. See also beguines
Ysenbela, beguine, 338
Ysendike. See beguines
Yvo, priest of Narbonne, 253

Zeeland. See beghards
Zepperen, 144, 264-65. See also beghards
Zierikzee. See beghards, beguines
Zonnegem, parish of Ghent, 216
Zuhorn, K., 86
Zurich. See beguines

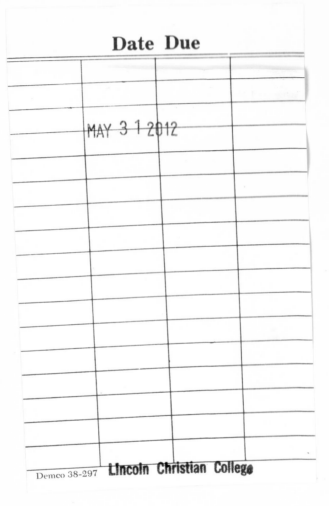